Contemporary
Literary Criticism

Guide to Gale Literary Criticism Series

When you need to review criticism of literary works, these are the Gale series to use:

If the author's death date is: **You should turn to:**

After Dec. 31, 1959
(or author is still living)

CONTEMPORARY LITERARY CRITICISM

for example: Jorge Luis Borges, Anthony Burgess,
Ernest Hemingway, Iris Murdoch

1900 through 1959

TWENTIETH-CENTURY LITERARY CRITICISM

for example: Willa Cather, F. Scott Fitzgerald,
Henry James, Mark Twain, Virginia Woolf

1800 through 1899

NINETEENTH-CENTURY LITERATURE CRITICISM

for example: Fedor Dostoevski, Nathaniel Hawthorne,
George Sand, William Wordsworth

1400 through 1799

LITERATURE CRITICISM FROM 1400 TO 1800
(excluding Shakespeare)

for example: Anne Bradstreet, Alexander Pope,
François Rabelais, Phillis Wheatley

SHAKESPEAREAN CRITICISM

Shakespeare's plays and poetry

Antiquity through 1399

CLASSICAL AND MEDIEVAL LITERATURE CRITICISM

for example: Dante, Homer, Plato, Sophocles, Vergil,
the Beowulf Poet

Gale also publishes related criticism series:

CHILDREN'S LITERATURE REVIEW

This series covers authors of all eras who have written for the preschool through high school audience.

SHORT STORY CRITICISM

This series covers the major short fiction writers of all nationalities and periods of literary history.

POETRY CRITICISM

This series covers poets of all nationalities, movements, and periods of literary history.

DRAMA CRITICISM

This series covers dramatists of all nationalities and periods of literary history.

BLACK LITERATURE CRITICISM

This three-volume set presents criticism of works by major black writers of the past two hundred years.

WORLD LITERATURE CRITICISM, 1500 TO THE PRESENT

This six-volume set provides excerpts from criticism on 225 authors from the Renaissance to the present.

ISSN 0091-3421

R

Volume 74

Contemporary Literary Criticism

Excerpts from Criticism of the
Works of Today's Novelists, Poets,
Playwrights, Short Story Writers, Scriptwriters,
and Other Creative Writers

Thomas Votteler
EDITOR

Laurie DiMauro
Elizabeth P. Henry
Jelena Krstović
Thomas Ligotti
Kyung-Sun Lim
Sean René Pollock
Joseph C. Tardiff
Bridget Travers
Janet Witalec
Robyn Young
ASSOCIATE EDITORS

 **Gale Research Inc.** • *DETROIT* • *WASHINGTON, D.C.* • *LONDON*

STAFF

Thomas Votteler, *Editor*

Laurie DiMauro, Elizabeth P. Henry, Jelena Krstović, Thomas Ligotti, Kyung-Sun Lim, Sean René Pollock,
Joseph C. Tardiff, Bridget Travers, Janet Witalec, Robyn Young, *Associate Editors*

Jennifer Brostrom, Paul James Buczkowski, Jeffery Chapman, Christopher Giroux, Ian A. Goodhall,
Dale R. Miller, Lynn M. Zott, *Assistant Editors*

Jeanne A. Gough, *Production & Permissions Manager*
Linda M. Pugliese, *Production Supervisor*
Paul Lewon, Maureen A. Puhl, Camille P. Robinson, Jennifer VanSickle, *Editorial Associates*
Donna Craft, Rosita D'Souza, Sheila Walencewicz, *Editorial Assistants*

Sandra C. Davis, *Permissions Supervisor (Text)*
Maria L. Franklin, Josephine M. Keene, Michele Lonoconus, Denise M. Singleton,
Kimberly F. Smilay, *Permissions Associates*
Brandy C. Merritt, Shalice Shah, *Permissions Assistants*

Margaret A. Chamberlain, *Permissions Supervisor (Pictures)*
Pamela A. Hayes, *Permissions Associate*
Karla Kulkis, Nancy Rattenbury, Keith Reed, *Permissions Assistants*

Victoria B. Cariappa, *Research Manager*
Maureen Richards, *Research Supervisor*
Robert S. Lazich, Mary Beth McElmeel, Tamara C. Nott, *Editorial Associates*
Andrea B. Ghorai, Daniel Jankowski, Julie Karmazin, Donna Melnychenko, *Editorial Assistants*

Mary Beth Trimper, *Production Director*
Shanna Heilveil, *Production Assistant*

Art Chartow, *Technical Design Services Manager*
Cynthia Baldwin, *Art Director*
Nick Jakubiak, C. J. Jonik, *Keyliners*

Library of Congress Catalog Card Number 76-38938
ISBN 0-8103-4978-7
ISSN 0091-3421

Printed in the United States of America

Published simultaneously in the United Kingdom
by Gale Research International Limited
(An affiliated company of Gale Research Inc.)

10 9 8 7 6 5 4 3 2 1

Contents

Preface vii

Acknowledgments ix

Preface

Named "one of the twenty-five most distinguished reference titles published during the past twenty-five years" by *Reference Quarterly,* the *Contemporary Literary Criticism (CLC)* series provides readers with critical commentary and general information on more than 2,000 authors now living or who died after December 31, 1959. Previous to the publication of the first volume of *CLC* in 1973, there was no ongoing digest monitoring scholarly and popular sources of critical opinion and explication of modern literature. *CLC,* therefore, has fulfilled an essential need, particularly since the complexity and variety of contemporary literature makes the function of criticism especially important to today's reader.

Scope of the Series

CLC presents significant passages from published criticism of works by creative writers. Since many of the authors covered by *CLC* inspire continual critical commentary, writers are often represented in more than one volume. There is, of course, no duplication of reprinted criticism.

Authors are selected for inclusion for a variety of reasons, among them the publication or dramatic production of a critically acclaimed new work, the reception of a major literary award, revival of interest in past writings, or the adaptation of a literary work to film or television.

Attention is also given to several other groups of writers—authors of considerable public interest—about whose work criticism is often difficult to locate. These include mystery and science fiction writers, literary and social critics, foreign writers, and authors who represent particular ethnic groups within the United States.

Format of the Book

Each *CLC* volume contains about 500 individual excerpts—with approximately seventeen excerpts per author—taken from hundreds of book review periodicals, general magazines, scholarly journals, monographs, and books. Entries include critical evaluations spanning from the beginning of an author's career to the most current commentary. Interviews, feature articles, and other published writings that offer insight into the author's works are also presented. Students, teachers, librarians, and researchers will find that the generous excerpts and supplementary material in *CLC* provide them with vital information needed to write a term paper, analyze a poem, or lead a book discussion group. In addition, complete bibliographical citations note the original source and all of the information necessary for a term paper footnote or bibliography.

Features

A *CLC* author entry consists of the following elements:

• The **author heading** cites the form under which the author has most commonly published, followed by birth date, and death date when applicable. Uncertainty as to a birth or death date is indicated by a question mark.

• A **portrait** of the author is included when available.

• A brief **biographical and critical introduction** to the author and his or her work precedes the excerpted criticism. The first line of the introduction provides the author's full name, pseudonyms (if applicable), nationality, and a listing of genres in which the author has written. Since *CLC* is not intended to be a definitive biographical source, cross-references have been included to direct readers to these useful sources published by Gale Research: *Short Story Criticism* and *Children's Literature Review, Contemporary Authors, Something about the Author, Dictionary of Literary Biography,* and *Contemporary Authors Autobiography Series* and *Something about the Author Autobiography Series.* Previous volumes of *CLC* in which the author has been featured are also listed in the introduction.

• A list of **principal works,** usually divided into genre categories, notes the most important works by the author.

• The **excerpted criticism** represents various kinds of critical writing, ranging in form from the brief review to the scholarly exegesis. Essays are selected by the editors to reflect the spectrum of opinion about a specific work or about an author's literary career in general. The excerpts are presented chronologically, adding a useful perspective to the entry. All titles by the author featured in the entry are printed in boldface type, which enables the reader to easily identify the works being discussed. Publication information (such as publisher names and book prices) and parenthetical numerical references (such as footnotes or page and line references to specific editions of a work) have been deleted at the editor's discretion to provide smoother reading of the text.

• A complete **bibliographical citation** designed to help the user find the original essay or book follows each excerpt.

• A concise **further reading** section appears at the end of entries on authors for whom a significant amount of criticism exists in addition to the pieces reprinted in *CLC*. In some cases, this annotated bibliography includes references to material for which the editors could not obtain reprint rights.

Other Features

• An **Acknowledgments** section lists the copyright holders who have granted permission to reprint material in this volume of *CLC*. It does not, however, list every book or periodical reprinted or consulted during the preparation of the volume.

• A **Cumulative Author Index** lists all the authors who have appeared in the various literary criticism series published by Gale Research, with cross-references to Gale's biographical and autobiographical series. A full listing of the series referenced there appears on the first page of the indexes of this volume. Readers will welcome this cumulated author index as a useful tool for locating an author within the various series. The index, which lists birth and death dates when available, will be particularly valuable for those authors who are identified with a certain period but whose death date causes them to be placed in another, or for those authors whose careers span two periods. For example, Ernest Hemingway is found in *CLC*, yet a writer often associated with him, F. Scott Fitzgerald, is found in *Twentieth-Century Literary Criticism*.

• A **Cumulative Nationality Index** alphabetically lists all authors featured in *CLC* by nationality, followed by numbers corresponding to the volumes in which they appear.

• In response to numerous suggestions from librarians, a **special paperbound edition** of the *CLC* title index accompanies *CLC-74*. Additional copies of the index are available upon request. Librarians and patrons will welcome this separate index: it saves shelf space, is easy to use, and is recyclable upon receipt of the following year's cumulation.

A Note to the Reader

When writing papers, students who quote directly from any volume in the Literary Criticism Series may use the following general forms to footnote reprinted criticism. The first example pertains to material drawn from periodicals, the second to material reprinted from books:

> [1]Anne Tyler, "Manic Monologue," *The New Republic* 200 (17 April 1989), 44-6; excerpted and reprinted in *Contemporary Literary Criticism*, Vol. 58, ed. Roger Matuz (Detroit: Gale Research Inc., 1990), p. 325.

> [2]Patrick Reilly, *The Literature of Guilt: From 'Gulliver' to Golding* (University of Iowa Press, 1988); excerpted and reprinted in *Contemporary Literary Criticism*, Vol. 58, ed. Roger Matuz (Detroit: Gale Research Inc., 1990), pp. 206-12.

Suggestions Are Welcome

The editors welcome the comments and suggestions of readers to expand the coverage and enhance the usefulness of the series.

Acknowledgments

The editors wish to thank the copyright holders of the excerpted criticism included in this volume, the permissions managers of many book and magazine publishing companies for assisting us in securing reprint rights, and Anthony Bogucki for assistance with copyright research. We are also grateful to the staffs of the Detroit Public Library, the Library of Congress, the University of Detroit Library, Wayne State University Purdy/Kresge Library Complex, and the University of Michigan Libraries for making their resources available to us. Following is a list of the copyright holders who have granted us permission to reprint material in this volume of *CLC*. Every effort has been made to trace copyright, but if omissions have been made, please let us know.

COPYRIGHTED EXCERPTS IN *CLC*, VOLUME 74, WERE REPRINTED FROM THE FOLLOWING PERIODICALS:

Agenda, v. 27, Spring, 1989 for "Living in and Living out: The Poet's Location for the Poetry" by John Bayley; v. 29, Winter, 1991 for "Two Irish Poets" by William Bedford. Both reprinted by permission of the respective authors.—*America,* v. 165, December 7, 1991 for "Vision and Revision: Seamus Heaney's New Poems" by John B. Breslin. © 1991. All rights reserved. Reprinted by permission of the author.—*American Film,* v. XV, June, 1990 for an interview with Bill Moyers by American Film. Copyright 1990 by *American Film.* Reprinted by permission of the author.—*American Heritage,* v. XL, November, 1989. Copyright 1989 by *American Heritage,* a division of Forbes, Inc. All rights reserved. Reprinted by permission of *American Heritage,* a division of Forbes, Inc.— *American Indian Quarterly,* v. 12, Winter, 1988. Copyright © Native American Studies Program, University of California, Berkeley. Reprinted by permission of the publisher.—*American Literature,* v. 57, May, 1985. Copyright © 1985 Duke University Press, Durham, NC. Reprinted with permission of the publisher.—*The American Scholar,* v. 38, Winter 1968-69. Copyright © 1969 by the United Chapters of the Phi Beta Kappa Society. Reprinted by permission of the publishers.—*The American Spectator,* v. 15, February, 1982; v. 16, July, 1983; v. 21, September, 1988. Copyright © *The American Spectator* 1982, 1983, 1988. All reprinted by permission of the publisher.—*The Antioch Review,* v. V, June, 1945 for "Richard Wright's Blues" by Ralph Ellison. Copyright 1945, renewed 1972 by Ralph Ellison. Reprinted by permission of the William Morris Agency, Inc., on behalf of the author.—*Arizona Quarterly,* v. 44, Spring, 1988 for "The Reader's Lessons in 'Ceremony' " by James Ruppert. Copyright © 1988 by Arizona Board of Regents. Reprinted by permission of the publisher and the author.—*Black American Literature Forum,* v. 24, Fall, 1990 for a review of "Ridin' the Moon in Texas" by Pinkie Gordon Lane. Copyright © 1990 Indiana State University. Reprinted by permission of the author./ v. 10, Winter, 1976 for " 'Black Boy': Richard Wright's 'Tragic Sense of Life' " by Claudia C. Tate; v. 17, Summer, 1983 for "Conflicting Impulses in the Plays of Ntozake Shange" by Sandra L. Richards. Copyright © 1976, 1983 Indiana State University. Both reprinted by permission of Indiana State University and the respective authors.—*The Bloomsbury Review,* v. 12, April-May, 1992 for "The Disharmonic Convergence" by M. Annette Jaimes. Copyright © by Owaissa Communications Company, Inc. 1992. Reprinted by permission of the author.—*Book World—The Washington Post,* April 25, 1971 for "I Hear America Talking" by Tom Wolfe. © 1971 Postrib Corp. Reprinted by courtesy of *The Washington Post* and the author./ August 8, 1976; November 1, 1981; October 12, 1986; December 9, 1990. © 1976, 1981, 1986, 1990, *The Washington Post.* All reprinted by permission of the publisher.—*Booklist,* v. 85, November 15, 1988. Copyright © 1988 by the American Library Association. Reprinted by permission of the publisher.—*Books in Canada,* v. 16, March, 1987 for a review of "Ha! Ha!" by Marc Côté. Reprinted by permission of the author.—*Canadian Review of American Studies,* v. 17, Fall, 1986. © *Canadian Review of American Studies* 1986. Reprinted by permission of the publisher.—*The Centennial Review,* v. XXXIII, Summer, 1989 for "Richard Selzer's Evolving Paradigms of Creativity" by Gayle Whittier. © 1989 by *The Centennial Review.* Reprinted by permission of the publisher and the author.—*Chicago Tribune—Books,* December 1, 1991 for "Dead Reckoning" by Alan Cheuse. © copyrighted 1991, Chicago Tribune Company. All rights reserved. Reprinted by permission of the author.—*CLA Journal,* v. XXVIII, June, 1985. Copyright, 1985 by The College Language Association. Used by permission of The College Language Association.—*Commentary,* v. 80, October, 1985 for " 'Our Genius': Norman Mailer & the Intellectuals" by Carol Iannone; v. 88, October, 1989 for "The Thinker as Everyman" by James Gardner. Copyright © 1985, 1989 by the American Jewish Committee. All rights reserved. Both reprinted by permission of the publisher and the respective authors.—*Commonweal,* v. CVIII, December 18, 1981. Copyright © 1981 Commonweal Publishing Co., Inc. Reprinted by permission of Commonweal Foundation./ v. CXVIII, February 22, 1991. Copyright © 1991 Commonweal Foundation. Reprinted by permission of Commonweal Foundation.—*Daedalus: Journal of the American Academy of Arts and Sciences, (In Praise of Books),* v. 105, Winter, 1976. Copyright © 1976 by the American Academy of Arts and Sciences. Reprinted by permission of *Daedalus: Journal of the American Academy of Arts and Sciences.*—*Encounter,* v. LX, February, 1983 for "In the Driver's Seat" by Mary Kenny; v. LXXX,

PHOTOGRAPHS AND ILLUSTRATIONS APPEARING IN *CLC*, VOLUME 74, WERE RECEIVED FROM THE FOLLOWING SOURCES:

Alan Ayckbourn

1939-

(Also wrote under the pseudonym Roland Allen) English playwright and lyricist.

The following entry provides criticism of Ayckbourn's works from 1983 to 1991. For further information on Ayckbourn's career, see *CLC*, Volumes 5, 8, 18, and 33.

INTRODUCTION

One of Great Britain's most popular and prolific playwrights, Ayckbourn is best known for his intricately plotted and inventively staged plays that explore daily middle-class life and marriage. In works that successfully balance tragic subject matter with comic events, Ayckbourn frequently centers on what he perceives as the monotony and emotional torment underlying his characters's lives and examines such themes as loneliness, unintentional cruelty, and self-interest.

Ayckbourn was born in London. His parents divorced in 1943, and his mother, a romance fiction writer, later remarried a bank manager. Ayckbourn was raised in a series of suburban towns in Sussex, which have served as settings for many of his plays. Influenced by his mother, Ayckbourn began writing at an early age. He attended Haileybury School in 1952, devoting most of his time to writing plays and acting. Upon the recommendation of a French instructor who had fostered his interest in the theater, Ayckbourn earned a position as assistant stage manager with Sir Donald Wolfit's company in the summer of 1956. The following year Ayckbourn toured with several repertory companies before beginning a fortuitous relationship with what was then called the Studio Theatre Company in the small resort town of Scarborough. There Ayckbourn gained experience in all aspects of theater under the tutelage of Stephen Joseph, an innovative stage manager who had introduced the concept of theater-in-the-round to England. Joseph encouraged Ayckbourn to write several plays, which were primarily light comedies that Ayckbourn admittedly had created as vehicles to advance his own acting career. During this time he met Harold Pinter and played Stanley in the Scarborough production of Pinter's *The Birthday Party.* Ayckbourn's first significant work, *Standing Room Only,* which concerns a London bus driver and his family who are caught in a twenty-year traffic jam, was produced in 1961 and is his only absurdist drama.

After receiving harsh reviews for *Xmas v. Mastermind* and *Mr. Whatnot,* Ayckbourn took a financially secure position at the BBC in 1965, producing radio dramas while concurrently writing plays for the theater. His first West End success came in 1967 when the farce *Relatively Speaking,* originally performed in Scarborough as *Meet*

My Father, opened in London to wide critical acclaim. Ayckbourn returned to Scarborough in 1970 as the company's artistic director and renamed it the Stephen Joseph Theatre-in-the-Round. His prolific output over the past two decades has prompted numerous critics to remark that his total number of plays now surpasses that of Shakespeare. In recent years Ayckbourn has written and directed works for the prestigious National Theatre and was appointed professor of contemporary theater at Oxford University during the 1991-92 academic year.

Many of Ayckbourn's plays present the foibles of middle-class married life within the structure of the "well-made" play. For example in such early plays as *Relatively Speaking*—which was modelled on Oscar Wilde's *The Importance of Being Earnest*—and *How the Other Half Loves,* Ayckbourn utilizes the conventions of mistaken identities and misunderstandings, complicated plots, and precisely timed exits and entrances to humorously explore marital infidelities. In *Bedroom Farce,* considered one of Ayckbourn's most uproarious plays, he focuses on the marriages of four couples. Staged in three bedrooms in three different homes, thus allowing for continuous, cross-cutting action, the play follows one couple, who in an attempt to reconcile their troubled marriage, disrupt the lives of the other three couples and force them to reevaluate their own discordant marriages. While adhering to many of the devices of the well-made play, Ayckbourn nevertheless eschews such conventions as the obligatory final scene in which all misunderstandings are resolved in a happy ending. Ayckbourn's plays characteristically conclude on an ambiguous note, as in *Relatively Speaking,* in which characters introduce new deceptions at the end of the play.

Time and Time Again and *Absurd Person Singular* mark the beginning of plays in which Ayckbourn has created more fully developed characters in the context of what he termed "the truly hilarious dark play." *Absurd Person Singular,* widely considered an early Ayckbourn masterpiece of dark comedy, concerns three unhappily married couples who take turns entertaining one another on three successive Christmas Eves. One of the wives, Mrs. Jackson, repeatedly attempts suicide by various ludicrous means in front of the other guests while they remain cruelly incognizant of her pain. Her character is frequently cited as an example of Ayckbourn's ability to portray the underlying tragedy beneath apparently comic episodes. In recent plays Ayckbourn has presented an increasingly dark portrait of middle-class life. *A Small Family Business,* which depicts the moral decline of an entire family through a series of humorous and complicated plot twists, is, nevertheless, noted for its unhappy conclusion: a drug-addicted daughter sits alone in her room shooting heroin while downstairs the family celebrates their entry into the drug trade. Continuing to emphasize the dark side of everyday existence, *Woman in Mind* charts the mental breakdown of Susan, the wife of a self-centered pastor. At first she fantasizes about an ideal family; however, her fantasy world eventually degenerates into uncontrollable hallucinations, and she is left utterly alone as her real family remains oblivious to her emotional needs.

Ayckbourn's staging techniques often allow his characters the ability to transcend space and time. In *How the Other Half Loves,* for example, two separate settings are superimposed onstage so that actions occurring in different places and at different times are seen simultaneously. Ayckbourn alters chronology and plot in what some critics have described as a jigsaw fashion. For instance, *The Norman Conquests,* a trilogy of three interlocking plays, achieves continuity by presenting offstage action in one play that becomes onstage action in another. In *Intimate Exchanges,* a play revolving around the random choices made by the characters and the outcomes of these choices, thirty-one scenes may be performed in sixteen different combinations within eight separate plays. *The Revenger's Comedies,* a two-part play, involves an intricate double plot structure in which the two main characters agree to enact revenge on the other's enemy.

Ayckbourn's reputation is based primarily on his ability to write entertaining comedies, yet most critics agree that his plays convey serious themes concerning the failures and tragedies of ordinary life as well as the moral and cultural decline of society. In particular, such plays as *A Small Family Business* and *Woman in Mind* not only de-

pict the foibles of individuals, but are noted for addressing such social issues as drug abuse, the shortcomings of organized religion, and the manipulative qualities of the media, which can be seen in *Man of the Moment* when a villainous character is made a hero by television journalists. Characterizing Ayckbourn's growing critical status, Michael Billington has denoted him "the best comic dramatist since Molière," while Peter Hall has asserted that "in 100 years' time, when he's forgiven for being successful, people will read his plays as an accurate reflection of English life in the 1960s, 70s and 80s. They represent a very important social document."

PRINCIPAL WORKS

The Square Cat [as Roland Allen] (drama) 1959
Standing Room Only [as Roland Allen] (drama) 1961
Xmas v. Mastermind (drama) 1962
Mr. Whatnot (drama) 1963
Meet My Father (drama) 1965; also performed as *Relatively Speaking,* 1967
The Sparrow (drama) 1967
How the Other Half Loves (drama) 1969
The Story So Far (drama) 1970; also performed as *Me Times Me Times Me* [revised edition], 1972 and *Family Circles* [revised edition], 1978
Time and Time Again (drama) 1971
Absurd Person Singular (drama) 1972
*The Norman Conquests (drama) 1973
Absent Friends (drama) 1974
†Confusions (drama) 1974
Bedroom Farce (drama) 1975
Just between Ourselves (drama) 1976
Ten Times Table (drama) 1977
Joking Apart (drama) 1978
Men on Women on Men [with Paul Todd] (revue) 1978
Sisterly Feelings (drama) 1979
Taking Steps (drama) 1979
Season's Greetings (drama) 1980
Suburban Strains [with Paul Todd] (musical) 1980
Way Upstream (drama) 1981
Intimate Exchanges (drama) 1982
It Could Be Any One of Us (drama) 1983
A Chorus of Disapproval (drama) 1984
Woman in Mind: December Bee (drama) 1985
Henceforward . . . (drama) 1987
A Small Family Business (drama) 1987
Man of the Moment (drama) 1988
Mr. A's Amazing Maze Plays (drama) 1988
The Inside Outside Slide Show (drama) 1989
Invisible Friends (drama) 1989
The Revengers' Comedies (drama) 1989
Body Language (drama) 1990
This Is Where We Came In (drama) 1990
Wildest Dreams (drama) 1991

*This work includes the plays *Table Manners, Living Together,* and *Round and Round the Garden.*

†This work includes the one-act plays *Mother Figure, Drinking Companion, Between Mouthfuls, Gosforth's Fête,* and *A Talk in the Park.*

CRITICISM

Elmer M. Blistein   (essay date March 1983)

[*Blistein is an American educator who specializes in drama studies. In the following excerpt, he analyzes Ayckbourn's treatment of setting, action, and time, focusing on ways in which the complicated structure of* The Norman Conquests *heightens the comedy of the play.*]

As *The Comedy of Errors* unties all its knots, as it finally reaches a moment of repose after a hectic and bewildering sequence of events, only two members of the dramatis personae are left on stage. They are identical twins, and they have just been reunited after thirty-three or twenty-five or twenty-three years. (Shakespeare is very precise about hours in this play, but he is cavalier in his treatment of years.) These identical twins, servants, have been crucial to the action, and they are the last to leave the stage. Twelve lines before *Exeunt*, Dromio of Syracuse says to his twin brother from Ephesus,

> There is a fat friend at your master's house,
> That kitchen'd me for you today at dinner.

Fine word, "kitchen'd," even though the *OED* suggests that used as a transitive verb it is obsolete, and so rare that it may even be a *hapax legomenon.*

Dromio is "kitchen'd" only once. The audience and readers of Alan Ayckbourn's *Absurd Person Singular* (1972) are kitchened for three acts of the three-act play on three successive Christmas Eves: first in "SIDNEY *and* JANE HOPCROFT'*s kitchen of their small suburban house. Last Christmas*"; then in "GEOFFREY *and* EVA JACKSON'*s kitchen in their fourth-floor flat. This Christmas*"; finally in "*The* BREWSTER-WRIGHTS' *kitchen. Next Christmas.*"

The "*Last,*" the "*This,*" and the "*Next*" may give us pause for a moment, but the joke—if, indeed, it exists—is a mild one and may safely be disregarded. The setting may not be disregarded. We have all experienced comedies set in drawing rooms, in forests, in fields, in marketplaces, on seacoasts, on beaches, on piers, in bedrooms, in dining rooms, on porches, in gardens, but it took an Alan Ayckbourn to exploit to its fullest the comic potential of the unromantic, practical, even banal kitchen.

We should not be surprised. Settings have always been important in Ayckbourn's plays. In *Standing Room Only* (1961), one of his earliest efforts, the setting is a bus caught in a traffic jam on Shaftesbury Avenue. The time is the early twenty-first century, and the bus has been in the traf-

fic jam so long that the driver's "two grown-up daughters have never known any other home, and indeed he has come to think that the bus's destination board announces his name, Hammersmith, with the letters BRDWY after it being his recommendation from London Transport: 'Best Ruddy Driver We've 'ad Yet'."

In *How the Other Half Loves* (1969), the setting and the manipulation of time are far more complex than either the characters or the dialogue. Ayckbourn's opening stage direction tells us "*The* CURTAIN *rises to reveal two living rooms, partially lit. Not a composite setting but with two rooms contained and overlapping in the same area.*" The overlap is so arranged that Fiona and Frank Foster and Teresa and Bob Phillips can entertain Mary and William Detweiler at separate dinner parties on the same stage at the same time. The audience, that is, watches the separate dinner parties taking place simultaneously. Actually, the Foster dinner is on Thursday evening and the Phillips dinner is on Friday evening. No, it is not all done with mirrors and fine wire, although we do expect some legerdemain when the program tells us that Act One, Scene 2 takes place on "Thursday AND Friday Night." The uppercase conjunction simply requires the Detweilers to have swivel chairs that enable them to turn from the Phillips table to the Foster table at will, the playwright's will, for their complicated performance in this scene.

In *Bedroom Farce* (1975), all of the action takes place in three bedrooms which belong to Ernest and Delia, Malcolm and Kate, and Nick and Jan. By means of cross-fades the audience's attention is drawn to one bedroom or another, but all are in view at all times. Just as another couple is needed to complicate the action in *How the Other Half Loves,* so another couple, Trevor and Susannah, Ernest and Delia's son and daughter-in-law, is required to complicate the action in *Bedroom Farce. . . .* Susannah and Trevor complicate matters by bringing their marital problems to all three bedrooms. At the conclusion they find themselves in Kate's and Malcolm's bed. Kate had urged Malcolm to take a bath to calm his nerves, after Trevor had arrived to say how sorry he and Susannah were that they had ruined Kate's and Malcolm's party. When Susannah joined Trevor in the bedroom and eventually in the bed, Kate prudently decided to find out how Malcolm was managing. When Trevor and Susannah are alone together, Susannah gives a strange but inevitable curtain speech that ends with her repeating for the third time in the play her incantation, her prayer, her mantra:

> Yes.
>
> [TREVOR *cuddles up to her*]
>
> [*She holds his head in her arms*]
>
> . . . I've been thinking. We must do something about our house. I think that's important. I want to start trying to make it more of a home. I—haven't been very good at that. I mean, somewhere nice . . . then you'll want to come home all the more, won't you? And I'll try and cook. I mean, really cook . . . and make sure you have some clean clothes in the morning and . . . well. You know what I mean, don't you? Trevor?

Trevor . . . ?

[TREVOR *is asleep*]
[*alone*] Oh . . . I am confident in myself. I
  have confidence in myself. I am not unattractive. I am attractive. People still find me
  attractive . . .

[*Lights fade slowly during this*]

CURTAIN

(pp. 26-8)

Ayckbourn's most popular and, perhaps, most interesting manipulations of setting and time occur in *The Norman Conquests* (1973). Ian Watson describes *The Norman Conquests* succinctly and accurately: "Three self-contained plays, featuring the same people at the same house over the same weekend. Each play stands as a complete entity and can be performed independently of the other two; although in practice, all three are usually played on consecutive nights, to be seen in any order" [*Conversations with Ayckbourn*]. I am not so sure about "any order." (p. 28)

The three plays [*Round and Round the Garden, Table Manners,* and *Living Together*] present six characters in search not of an author but of something less tangible. Annie, the spinster, seeks love and escape, but not necessarily in that order. Ruth, her myopic sister who refuses to wear glasses because of vanity, according to some, but because glasses irritate her sinuses, according to her, is looking for continuing success in her never-described career. Reg, their brother, really wants little out of life. He merely wants some people to play the board games he invents and an occasional person to laugh at his jokes as he is so willing to laugh at others'. Sarah, his shrewish, dominating wife, is the kind of person John Donne had in mind when he said, " . . . O, to some / Not to be martyrs is a martyrdom" ("The Litany,"). She seeks perfection in an imperfect world whose imperfections she has not only richly augmented, but also magnified. Tom, a bachelor and a veterinarian, is a kindly but dim soul who prefers animals to people, but who likes Annie and needs somebody to direct him into her arms. And finally, there is Norman, Ruth's errant husband, whose "Conquests" are ironically chronicled, and not merely in the title. In the social spectrum, Norman belongs at the infrared end; he is a social anarchist persuaded that social contracts are for other people, not him. Married to Ruth, he has already bedded—perhaps "rugged" would be a better term—Annie, the previous Christmas when Ruth was upstairs sick in bed. This weekend he manages to bed his wife, Ruth, on the same rug, and then replies in response to her "It's nice on the rug," "I told you it was. It can be our rug."(*Living*). Norman and Annie's rug, Norman and Ruth's rug, but not yet—and probably never—Norman and Sarah's rug, even though at one point in the hectic activities of the weekend, Sarah has just about agreed to go off with Norman for a couple of days to, perhaps, Bournemouth (*Living*).

And going away with Norman is what this involved action is all about. After the Christmas interlude on the furry rug, Norman and Annie had taken about six months to make arrangements by telephone and letter to spend a weekend together in Hastings. Discovering that Hastings was all booked, Norman made, or said he made, reservations in East Grinstead, and had purchased himself a new pair of pyjamas because, as Annie suggests, "just because you're unfaithful there's no need for your pyjamas to be as well" (*Garden*). Sarah had grudgingly agreed to come with Reg to take care of the offstage presence, Annie's, Ruth's, and Reg's mother, while Annie had a brief holiday. By her officious probing, Sarah discovered with whom Annie was going away, saw to it that the plan was canceled, called Ruth to inform her of her husband's and sister's attempted peccadillo and to insist that Ruth come at once to confront Norman. Norman, frustrated, gets blind drunk on homemade dandelion and parsnip wine—the thought of either makes a gourmand, let alone a gourmet, gag—and adds more confusion to the sixes and sevens that already exist.

But then there is that offstage presence. Annie, the spinster, needed somebody to spell her so she could go off for a weekend, for she is responsible for her bedridden mother. This mother never makes an appearance fortunately, if all we hear about her is true. She is described by Sarah, her daughter-in-law, as a tart. It seems clear from what her children, Reg, Ruth, and Annie, say about her that she may be charitably described as a woman who just seems to have liked men other than her husband. She is bedridden because, as Annie says to Ruth, and with some compassion: "She just has no desire to get up. No reason to. So she doesn't. Sad, really. Her whole life was centred round men, wasn't it? When they lost interest in her, she lost interest in herself " (*Living*).

Here, then, are three plays with twelve scenes, in three different settings, at eleven different times. Surely confusion should be worse confounded, but that does not happen. The story line is clear, for the integration of the three plays is skillfully done and highlighted by pertinent action, not merely movement. In the first scene of *Table,* Sarah, the whining shrew (that description is not an oxymoron in Sarah's case), throws a biscuit tin at Reg, her husband, and Annie appears with a dustpan. In the first scene of *Living,* Annie, Tom, and Norman hear the clatter; Annie leaves to discover the cause, reappears for a moment with a dustpan and brush as she goes to help clean up the mess; and Reg mentions the matter twice more in the second scene.

In the first scene of *Table,* Sarah sends Reg to check on Norman and Annie in the sitting room, because she does not trust them alone together. Reg enters just as Annie has *"impulsively"* kissed Norman on the cheek because he looks "so limp. Like an old tea towel." Reg picks up a wastepaper basket to justify his statement that he has "just come in for something," and exits (*Living*), Sarah then impels, and I choose the word advisedly, Tom to the sitting room (*Table*), and he joins Annie and Norman (*Living*).

Dialogue, too, integrates the plays. Norman, overcome by dandelion and parsnip wine (he may also have drunk some carrot wine, but that is not clear), becomes melancholy and weepy as he mournfully intones a half-dozen times: "Nobody loves me. . . . Nobody loves me at all," "(*to*

Sarah) Nobody loves me. (*To Annie*) Nobody loves me . . . " (**Garden**); "Nobody loves me. Nobody loves me any more" (**Living**). When he delivers these lines, both Annie and Sarah have a sympathetic yen for him, even though we should not call that yen love. Ruth is not yet on the scene, but she is married to him, and by the following scene she is snuggled in the sitting-room rug with him as she says, "It's nice on the rug" (**Living**). Both Tom and Reg have commented that he is a pleasant fellow, and will say so again, so Norman's "Nobody loves me" may safely be translated that Norman does not love himself.

Ruth's attitude toward Norman may be described as liberated, amused, occasionally bemused, but certainly not as sadly resigned. Consider a dialogue she has with Sarah:

> RUTH. Sarah dear, I've been married to Norman for five years. I have learnt through bitter experience that the last thing to do with Norman is to take him seriously. That's exactly what he wants. . . .
>
> SARAH. I'm amazed you've stayed with him. I really am.
>
> RUTH. Well, I don't really look at it that way. I rather think of him as staying with me. After all, I make all the payments on the house, most of the furniture is mine. It has crossed my mind, in moments of extreme provocation, to throw him out—but I don't know, I think I must be rather fond of him. It's a bit like owning an oversized unmanageable dog, being married to Norman. He's not very well house-trained, he needs continual exercising—mental and physical—and it's sensible to lock him up if you have visitors. Otherwise he mauls them. But I'd hate to get rid of him.
>
> SARAH. That's all very well if you keep him under proper control. When he goes upsetting other people's lives. Annie's, for example . . .
>
> RUTH. You really can't blame Norman entirely, you know. He only jumps up at people who encourage him. It's a general rule, if you don't want him licking your face, don't offer him little titbits. I don't mean just Annie either. (**Garden**)

A dog is, at least, animate. When Ruth has a conversation with Annie about Norman, she now compares him to something inanimate, a book. Norman is an assistant librarian, and I suspect the emphasis should be on the word assistant:

> ANNIE. I'm sorry. I never for a minute intended to take Norman away from you or anything.
>
> RUTH. Forget it. You couldn't possibly take Norman away from me. That assumes I own him in the first place. I've never done that. I always feel with Norman that I have him on loan from somewhere. Like one of his library books. I'll get a card one day informing me he's overdue and there's a fine to pay on him. (**Table**)

Norman would not, it seems, object to the comparison. He does not initiate, but freely uses the same comparison when speaking about Annie and himself in a conversation

with Sarah. She has accused him of stealing Annie away from Tom. He denies the possibility of theft:

> NORMAN. I wasn't stealing her, I was borrowing her. For the week-end.
>
> SARAH. Make her sound like one of your library books.
>
> NORMAN. She was borrowing me, too. It was mutual. It was a friendly loan. We never intended to upset anybody. We both agreed. That was the joy of it, don't you see? Nobody need ever to have known. (**Living**)

In this case Norman is talking to the wrong person. Sarah believes that all such information should be imparted to others, particularly if the information could possibly cause pain.

There is one line which Norman repeats so often, about a dozen times in the three plays, that it acts like a reprise. The line deals with Norman's desire to make people, particularly women, happy. Ruth has just kissed Norman at his request, and this dialogue ensues:

> NORMAN. Are you happy?
>
> RUTH. What?
>
> NORMAN. Do I make you happy at all?
>
> RUTH. Well . . .
>
> NORMAN. Say you're happy.
>
> RUTH. Why? Is it important?
>
> NORMAN. Yes. I want you to be happy. I want everyone to be happy. I want to make everyone happy. It's my mission in life . . .
>
> RUTH. Yes, all right, Norman. Well, let's not worry about other people too much, just concentrate on making me happy, will you? The other people will have to try to be happy without you, won't they?
>
> NORMAN. But you are happy?
>
> RUTH. Yes, I'm fairly happy. (**Living**)

The first we had heard about Norman's desire to make someone happy was at breakfast on the morning after Norman's drunkenness. Sarah, Annie, and Reg were doing their best to ignore Norman, so he indulged in a lengthy dialogue about his and other people's behavior. After Sarah and Annie left the room as a result of one of Norman's outrageous statements, only Reg was left to listen to Norman wallowing in his self-pity:

> I suppose you think I'm cruel, too, don't you? Well, I've damn good cause to be, haven't I? I mean, nobody's thought about my feelings, have they? It's all Annie—Annie—Annie—what about me? I was going to give her everything. Well, as much as I could. My whole being. I wanted to make her happy for a week-end, that's all. (**Table**)

The reprise is heard again toward the end of **Table,** when Norman, having suggested an assignation to Sarah, says:

"I'd like to make you happy, Sarah. . . . Is that wrong of me? To want to see you happy? . . . I'd very much like to make you happy." Two sides later, after a few entrances and exits, Sarah and Norman are alone for a moment and this considered dialogue occurs:

> SARAH. Reg gets home about half past six in the evening on weekdays.
>
> NORMAN. Busy man.
>
> SARAH. If you feel like giving me a ring, any time. I'm usually tied to the house. I don't get out much.
>
> NORMAN. I'd make you happy, Sarah.
>
> SARAH. Yes.
>
> NORMAN. 'Bye-bye.
> *Norman goes out to the house, eating the last of his toast.*
> *Sarah looks thoughtful. She gives a pleased grunt.*

The adjective "pleased" and the noun "grunt" tell us how Sarah reacts to Norman's proposition. How Norman reacts to her suggestion to call her is not difficult to ascertain, and his reaction is enhanced rather than vitiated by the speeches and action just before the final curtain some three sides later:

> *Annie flies at Norman and clings on to him*
>
> ANNIE. Oh, Norman. . . . (*muffled*) I want . . .
>
> NORMAN. Eh?
>
> ANNIE. I want . . .
>
> NORMAN. I can't hear you. What?
>
> ANNIE. (*in a wail*) I want to go to East Grinstead.
>
> NORMAN. (*soothing her*) All right. Fine. I'll take you. I'll take you.
>
> ANNIE. (*tearfully*) Will you?
>
> NORMAN. Just say the word. Come on now, don't cry. I'll make you happy. Don't worry. I'll make you happy.
> *Norman hugs her to him. Annie clings on. Norman looks towards the window, then out front, smiling happily*
>
> CURTAIN.

This passage certainly should be the coda, not another reprise. So far as the audience can figure out, Norman has been reconciled with his wife (*Living*), has an assignation pending with Sarah (*Table*), and a promised assignation with Annie (*Table*). The plays, after all, are called *The Norman Conquests.* Whatever the case for William the Norman, our Norman is a bastard in the colloquial if not in the literal sense. He cannot end up as a conqueror. He must get his comeuppance so that our bourgeois prejudices may be appeased. So, at the end of *Garden* Ayckbourn destroys our social anarchist. As departure time arrives, Norman's car will not start. Reg gets a rope in order to pull Norman's car to the top of an incline so that he can

get started. Reg warns Norman to give him sufficient time to get out of the way before Norman releases his hand brake.

What happens is obvious. Norman's car crashes into the back of Reg's. All must stay for another day. The myopic but insightful Ruth turns to Norman and this colloquy concludes the plays:

> RUTH. If I didn't know you better, I'd say you did all that deliberately.
>
> NORMAN. Me? Why should I want to do that?
>
> SARAH. Huh.
>
> NORMAN. Give me one good reason why I'd do a thing like that?
>
> RUTH. Offhand, I can think of three.
> *Pause*
>
> NORMAN. Ah. (*Brightening*) Well, since we're all here, we ought to make the most of it, eh? What do you say?
> *Norman smiles round at the women in turn*
> *Ruth gets up and without another word goes into the house*
> (*After her*) Ruth . . .
> *He turns to Annie but she too, rises and goes into the house*
> Annie . . .
> *He turns to Sarah. She, likewise, rises and follows the others*
> Sarah!
> *Norman is left alone, bewildered, then genuinely hurt and indignant*
> (*Shouting after them*) I only wanted to make you happy.
>
> CURTAIN.

Here is the coda, not another reprise. By outrageous behavior, by clever words, by dexterous hands, by eliciting sympathy when he is tipsy or drunk, Norman has managed to seduce—I do not think that is the wrong word; Norman manages to lead all three aside, at least temporarily, into the primrose path of dalliance—his wife, her sister, and her sister-in-law. If they all reject him at the end, if the moral indignation of all Pecksniffian audiences is assuaged, a cynic may well consider that united the women stand, divided they fall. When Norman is one-on-one with a woman, he is successful. Consider the last scenes of *Living* and *Table.*

Norman does want to make people, especially women, happy. If he knows only one, two, three, four ways to do that—behavior (outrageous), words (clever), hands and other body parts (dexterous), sympathy (elicited by tipsiness)—neither Reg nor Tom knows even one. But Norman's method is not rape, despite Annie's comment: "Norman doesn't bother with secret signals at all. It was just wham, thump and there we both were on the rug" (*Table*). Norman, and perhaps he does achieve conquests after all, makes three women happy occasionally; there is no evidence that either Tom or Reg ever makes any woman happy at any time. So, although Norman is merely the title character of *The Norman Conquests,* he is more important as an eponym than Cymbeline or King John.

Sarah may be "fifth Business," but Norman runs the show, and we are luckier and, yes, happier for it.

For what sets Ayckbourn apart from most contemporary writers of comedy is the fact, as Walter Kerr [in "Hail the Conquering Ayckbourn," *The New York Times,* 14 December 1975] and others have noted, that he can make us laugh without writing one-liners. His comedy depends upon the adroit juxtaposition of episodes, the clever manipulation of time, the dexterous use of props. In Ayckbourn's plays, a lawn chair, a biscuit tin, a rug, an easy-to-assemble-yourself dressing table, a wastepaper basket are more important than a clever line. He can write one-liners, but he seems to want to subordinate them to visual effects.

Ayckbourn's progress in the theater from actor to assistant stage manager to technical stage manager to director may have influenced the path his writing would take. But certainly over the last two decades he has given us comedies that test the traditional limits of time, place, and action. Events that normally happen offstage are brought onstage in *Absurd Person Singular.* In *The Norman Conquests,* although Ayckbourn requires three plays to accomplish the feat, every offstage action is brought onstage, and every onstage action has repercussions offstage. The solving of Rubik's Cube becomes child's play in comparison. But Ayckbourn has more than cleverness to offer. He writes comedies about people who genuinely concern us in situations that appear to be inevitable. What more can we ask? (pp. 28-34)

> *Elmer M. Blistein, "Alan Ayckbourn: Few Jokes, Much Comedy," in* Modern Drama, *Vol. XXVI, No. 1, March, 1983, pp. 26-35.*

Frank Rich   (review date 12 July 1985)

[*Rich is the drama critic for the* New York Times. *In the following excerpt from a review of* Season's Greetings, *he assesses Ayckbourn's strengths and weaknesses as a playwright.*]

Alan Ayckbourn is commonly labeled the English Neil Simon, and while that simple analogy does not tell the whole story, there's some truth to it. Mr. Ayckbourn is an incredibly prolific author of hit comedies about the middle class, and he has increasingly attempted to blend laughter and pathos in his work. Even so, there are real cultural differences separating the two writers—a fact that is most dramatically demonstrated by what happens when their plays cross the Atlantic. Mr. Simon has never been as popular in the West End as he is on Broadway, and such Ayckbourn London successes as *The Norman Conquests* and *Bedroom Farce* have failed to find equal favor in New York.

Season's Greetings . . . is unlikely to reverse that tide, but it is a modestly enjoyable evening that reveals its author's strengths and weaknesses in balanced measure.

Mr. Ayckbourn's characters are the antithesis of Mr. Simon's slick bourgeois New Yorkers. If they suffer from some of the same ailments—rocky marriages, calamitous dinner parties, obstreperous children and in-laws—they can't begin to cope. There's a Chekhovian inertia to Mr.

Ayckbourn's people—if not a comparable quality to his writing—and there's little hope that anyone will find redemption by the final curtain.

Although *Season's Greetings* does not offer one of its author's characteristic structural gimmicks, it is an otherwise representative effort. An extended family gathers for Christmas and Boxing Day festivities that are reduced to chaos by quarreling spouses, kitchen mishaps and an excess of alcoholic cheer. The principal catalyst for the disruptions is the one stranger in the celebrants' midst—Clive, a rising young novelist who has come to woo the family spinster but whose attention is soon diverted to his date's married sister, Belinda.

Clive, whose one novel is a comic treatment of marriage, condescends to his hosts, and his attitude is sometimes shared by Mr. Ayckbourn. We're constantly reminded that the characters are philistines addicted to television and boring hobbies; the husbands are sexual adolescents, the wives baby-bearing domestics. And, as the playwright sets up some of his gags mechanically, so he tends to bare the family's underlying despair as ham-fistedly as a child ripping open a Christmas present.

But thanks to one terrific scene . . . *Season's Greetings* also reminds us that Mr. Ayckbourn can rise above efficient craftsmanship to the full height of his artistic ambitions. The scene, which opens Act II, features the dry run of a puppet show that a childless uncle stages for the kids each year. The uncle is an incompetent doctor—a point brought home hilariously when he delivers a spectacularly wrong diagnosis at the play's climax—and he's scarcely more accomplished a puppeteer. For all the good intentions and complicated toy theatrical machinery he brings to his rendition of "The Three Pigs," it is riddled with glitches and guaranteed to bore children and parents alike.

The catastrophic puppet show rehearsal is uproarious, but it also uncovers the doctor's misery—without, for once, letting us see Mr. Ayckbourn pull his own characters' strings. Much as we laugh at the amateur puppeteer, we realize that his elaborate miniature theater is the sad repository of his dashed ambitions to be a father and a respected medical man.

> *Frank Rich, " 'Greetings', Ayckbourn Comedy," in* The New York Times, *July 12, 1985, p. C3.*

Martin Hoyle   (review date October 1985)

[*In the following excerpted review of* A Chorus of Disapproval, *Hoyle commends the complexity of Ayckbourn's characters.*]

Ayckbourn's play [*A Chorus of Disapproval*] chronicles the Candide-like bemusement of the well-meaning innocent, Guy, a newcomer to [a] particular corner of provincial life, who finds his dizzy career in the amateur operatic society (from walk-on to the lead) echoed by the sexual and financial intrigues of the locals. (p. 30)

[The] complexity of the characters hearteningly illustrates Ayckbourn's constantly ripening gifts. Guy may struggle to preserve his integrity (with the Ayckbourn irony, he ends up despised, vilified and mistrusted) but, no mere goody, he greedily grabs sexual gratification when available, no matter how unsuitable. Similarly, the downtrodden wife (a familiar Ayckbourn figure) is here a worm capable of turning and snatching ruthlessly at happiness, even if it means hurting others. And the archetypal Ayckbourn husband—crass, apparently unloving—is not simply the manipulating bully of *Absent Friends* or the blandly obtuse ignoramus of *Just Between Ourselves;* he is infuriatingly self-absorbed but vulnerable, vaguely aware of his own weaknesses and perhaps capable of a decency that Guy somehow misses. (pp. 30-1)

> Martin Hoyle, in a review of "A Chorus of Disapproval," in Plays & Players, No. 385, October, 1985, pp. 30-1.

Ayckbourn on morality:

There is definitely a dark side of human nature which I want to explore. I don't want everyone to leave the theatre all depressed with negative feelings, but recently I have wanted to show how power—political and private—often resides with the wrong person.

There used to be a Christian consensus in this country about how people should behave. Now there is none. There is no moral leadership.

My worry is we have so burned our boats with politicians from both sides that if we got a real nut, some "idealist", he could take the whole country with him.

> Alan Ayckbourn in "Making the Middle Class Squirm from a Seat by the Sea," in The Sunday Times, *18 June 1989.*

Bernard F. Dukore   (essay date Spring 1986)

[*Dukore is an American educator and critic who has written numerous studies on such twentieth-century dramatists as Bernard Shaw and Harold Pinter. He has also edited* Alan Ayckbourn: A Casebook *(1991). In the following excerpt, he examines the structure and characters of* Woman in Mind, *illustrating how Ayckbourn presents the tragedy of a woman's mental breakdown through a masterfully crafted comedy.*]

Although critics often undervalue writers of farcical comedy, the more discerning among them distinguish the artist from the hack whose formulas or gimmicks substitute for insight into psychology and society. Not only is such insight compatible with farcical comedy, but formulas and gimmicks are not confined to this type of play. Thus, King Louis XIV asked Boileau, one of the most prominent critics of the age, who in his professional judgment had been the best writer during his own reign; the discerning critic, unhesitatingly and very much to the king's surprise, named Molière.

To succeed in ridiculing human follies, Molière believed,

the comic writer must be faithful to life and portray human beings as they really are. His play *Improvisation at Versailles* makes comic capital of the notion that he did this so successfully, some people were upset because they imagined he modeled his characters on them. Nevertheless, critics frequently tend to regard the light treatment of serious subjects as a mark of triviality. Bernard Shaw has suffered charges that he is merely a mocker, therefore not to be taken seriously, or, in a more sophisticated variant, that his comedy defeats his moral, social, and political purposes since it distorts whatever realistic observations underlie them.

Furthermore, cleverly crafted comedies are now considered so old-fashioned that terms like well-made play are pejorative, not descriptive. No matter that Ben Jonson's major comedies have artfully intricate construction or that the plot of Oscar Wilde's *The Importance of Being Earnest* is that of a well-made play. Both writers are dead—or classics, which can be similar—and despite their admirers neither is fashionable.

His works translated into two dozen languages, Alan Ayckbourn, without forays into movies and television, is England's most successful playwright for the theater. Until recently, however, serious critical attention has eluded him. Even so, only one major academic journal has carried scholarly articles about his work, *Modern Drama,* whose March 1983 issue has two. Their titles, though accurate, may suggest what is necessary to persuade academic readers to pay attention to him: "Alan Ayckbourn: Few Jokes, Much Comedy" and "The Serious Side of Alan Ayckbourn." Only one book-length critical study is devoted solely to his plays, *Alan Ayckbourn,* by Michael Billington, theater critic of the *Guardian.* His appraisal pinpoints the disjunction between, to borrow terms from Wilde's subtitle of *The Importance of Being Earnest,* Ayckbourn's apparently trivial comedies and the concerns of earnest critics: "Alan Ayckbourn is popular. He is prolific. And he writes comedies. For all those reasons he is still, I believe, seriously underrated. He is constantly written about as if he were a boulevard lightweight whereas he shows an increasing capacity to handle the darker side of human nature while retaining his technical adventurousness." Published the same year as Billington's book is *Peter Hall's Diaries,* which, as if underscoring his judgment, contains an entry for 28 August 1973, after Sir Peter had seen a performance of Ayckbourn's *Absurd Person Singular:* "It is a hard, beautifully constructed play. But because it is commercial, it tends to be unregarded. I think Ayckbourn is much more likely to be in the repertoire of the National Theatre in fifty years' time than most of the current Royal Court dramatists."

Filled with photographs and as readable as a Sunday supplement, Ian Watson's *Conversations with Ayckbourn* (1981) technically qualifies as a coffee-table book, but the titular conversations are enormously valuable in documenting Ayckbourn's approach to his art. A practical man of the theater, he devotes much time to running the Stephen Joseph Theatre in the Round in Scarborough. As Director of Productions, he schedules his new plays for performance. Since his audience, residents of the seaside resort town and visitors on holiday, is not captive (as a former resident of a resort city, Honolulu, I can testify that the easiest thing for such an audience to do is not attend the theater), he must, together with whatever else he may wish to achieve, appeal to that audience in terms it can accept.

> I'm on a crusade to try and persuade people that theatre can be fun; but every time I start doing that, some hairy bugger from the left comes in and tells them it's instructive, and drives them all out again. If I want to be instructed, I go to night school. I may be instructed in the theatre, but I don't go in there predominantly for instruction. I go in there for entertainment, and of course all the best plays instruct me, or enlighten me—it's a better word than instruct. But if you put a label on a whisky bottle "For medicinal use only" on it, it rather puts you off the drink.

While Ayckbourn considers enlightenment, which includes what Billington calls the darker side, to be a by-product of entertainment, he does not ignore it: "In trying to write a rounded character, one obviously writes quite often the very unpleasant side of them. All my characters have flaws and are pock-marked, and I don't do a cosmetic job on them." A passage in Shaw's 1898 Preface to *Plays Pleasant* applies to Ayckbourn's comedies: "I have always cast my plays in the ordinary practical comedy form in use at all theatres; and far from taking an unsympathetic view of the popular preference for fun [. . .] I was more than willing to shew that the drama can humanize these things as easily as they, in the wrong hands, can dehumanize the drama."

On May 30, 1985, Ayckbourn's **Woman in Mind,** which he directed, opened in Scarborough. I saw it there on June 8th. If it follows the usual Ayckbourn path, it will open in London a year or two later and, still later, be published in a Samuel French Acting Edition. This essay, completed in 1986, will analyze the play first from the aspect of craft or dramatic technique, which necessarily involves interpreting its plot; then its depiction of character; and finally, tying them together, as comedy. Quotations and descriptions are from the typescript used at Scarborough, augmented by the production I saw.

The title is of course a pun. Particularly mindful of woman in today's world, **Woman in Mind** also deals with the mind of a particular woman. This comedy, about a woman who is suffering a mental breakdown, dramatizes the process, with remarkable technical dexterity, from her point of view. To focus on its structure, thereby clarifying what on stage and page is actually complex and subtle, I will divide its action into comprehensible phases.

Phase 1: We share Susan's view of reality. At the start, a woman is lying on the ground of her garden. Kneeling beside her is a man whose speech is not understandable. "Ah! Score ache." "Wo! Won't spider slit up pikelet." "Squeezy, cow, squeezy." "Climb octer bin sir. Mrs sure pardon choose 'un." However, we understand her. "What?" "Squeezy?" "I've no idea what you're saying." "Who are you, anyway?" Moments later, we hear him call her Susan and himself Bill Windsor, a doctor. It turns out

that Susan, who is in her forties, stepped on the end of a garden rake, which hit her on the head and knocked her unconscious. Only then do we understand that we have heard his words from her viewpoint, as gibberish, whereas her words were gibberish to him. What he said (as neither text nor performance explains) was "Ah! You're awake." "No! Don't try to sit up like that." "Easy, now, easy." "I'm Doctor Windsor. This is your garden, Susan." From Susan's viewpoint, we heard "Pea squeak jinglish," not "Please speak English."

Phase 2: Still sharing her view, we see her family. Understanding him is one step toward a cure, which involves adjustment to reality. When he leaves to check on an ambulance he ordered, she hears Andy's voice. As he speaks, the light brightens. Tall, athletic, charming, and like Bill a bit younger than her, her husband Andy fusses over her, professes his love, and is solicitous of her health, as are Lucy, her lovely daughter in her twenties, and Tony, her handsome younger brother, who also appear. "You really do spoil me, all of you," she tells them while they do so. Andy pets her, calls her intelligent and pretty, and adds that all of them would be lost without her, particularly he, who holds her more dearly and preciously than he can express.

Phase 3: The view we have shared becomes problematic. Just after Andy leaves to cancel the ambulance, Bill returns. When Susan tells him that her husband feels she should stay at home in bed, he is surprised, since he was unaware her husband had returned home. Her sister-in-law Muriel, he concludes, must have erred. But Susan denies having a sister-in-law, knowing a Muriel, or having been given a cup of tea by her—though Bill says he just passed her, returning from the garden with an empty tea cup. Susan insists the only woman she has seen all day has been her daughter, who was playing tennis with her brother. Bill recognizes something is amiss. Does she remember her son? She has none, she says. But Bill can see neither the tennis court, the swimming pool, nor the rose beds she declares are on the property. When he reports only a small, tidy garden, beyond which is a pond with a stone frog, we question the dramatized reality of the family we have seen. Her brother brought her champagne, she asserts, and we saw him do so; Bill points out that he left none behind. Although she dismisses him as doctor, he refuses to leave. When she consents to go to the hospital if her husband approves, he agrees and will wait for her husband's arrival. Upon the entry of a man and woman, it becomes evident that the family we saw existed only in Susan's mind and that the new, unattractive arrivals are her real family: a solemn husband, the Reverend Gerald Gannet, in his mid-forties, and a prim sister-in-law, Muriel. Susan faints.

Phase 4: No longer sharing her view, we observe her as part of objective reality. As at the start of the first scene, Susan awakens in the garden. We learn that her son Rick has arrived for lunch, that she not Gerald has difficulty sleeping at night, that both are unhappily married, that she still hallucinates, and that Muriel, a terrible cook, also hallucinates (about her late husband). For two years, Rick has been living with a religious sect which practices vegetarianism and maintains a vow of silence. According to Susan, he is afraid of women and he communicates by post with his father, not with her.

Phase 5: She retreats from reality into fantasy. Once the estrangement of mother and son is established, she hallucinates again. With Gerald present, her imaginary daughter appears, then her imaginary brother. When Bill arrives, he is encouraged to learn that Susan remembers she has a son. While he and Gerald, ignoring her, discuss the book Gerald is writing, a history of the parish since 1386. . . . Susan's mind leaves reality. Lucy brings champagne from Andy, who is preparing a gourmet lunch after which Lucy and Tony will tidy up so that Susan may convalesce for as long as she pleases—a contrast to Gerald having awakened her. In this hallucination, she is the family writer—"probably our most important living historical novelist," according to the *Observer*. Still ignoring her, Gerald and Bill enter the house. Unlike Susan's real son, her imaginary daughter confides in her, not the father. Although Lucy wants her father and uncle to like her fiancé, this matter seems to rest with the all-important Susan, who promises to make sure they do. After Lucy leaves, Bill announces he will stay for lunch, which to Susan's chagrin Muriel will cook.

Phase 6: Susan's fantasies invade reality. Imaginary world mixes with real world as Lucy returns with champagne and Susan addresses her, not Bill, about a chair each is adjusting. Although Susan recognizes what has happened, she denies she has had more hallucinatons. After she tells Bill what she does with her days and Gerald with his nights (writing), Gerald enters with a tray, glasses, and a dusty bottle of Marsala sherry, a far cry from the vintage Dom Perignon supplied by her imaginary family. Preparing Bill for what to expect at lunch, Susan despite Gerald's protests reveals their son does not speak to them. While the men drink Marsala, the distraught Susan, retreating into the world of her mind, drinks the glass of champagne left by Lucy. Muriel arrives to fetch them into the house for lunch. As Susan prepares to follow, Lucy invites her to lunch with the other family. Although she wavers, she chooses reality. Ayckbourn visualizes the moment: "LUCY *stands shattered.* SUSAN *turns to go, aware of the effect she has had upon her daughter. She nearly collides with* GERALD *returning.*" The shattered daughter mirrors the emotionally shattered mother, who is about to but does not yet collide with reality. Enter Muriel, who entreats Susan to come to table before the food burns. Gerald joins Muriel. Tony appears with a small garden table set for four. Torn between both worlds, Susan pleads with the imaginary family to let her enter the house. But they make her admit that those inside the house will hurt her as always, whereas they love her and do not want her hurt—that is, she tells this to herself through personifications.

Phase 7: Her fantasy people influence her behavior toward real people, but she cannot cope with unexpected reality. When reality returns, as the doctor calls her to lunch, her delusions dominate her. "Tell him to take a jump," urges Tony; "Mind his own business," prompts Lucy. "Drop dead," adds Tony, and Lucy repeats his advice. "Oh, Bill," says Susan, "do drop dead." As Bill leaves, the fami-

ly in Susan's mind, including Andy, cheerfully assures her she did well—that is, she tries to persuade herself she acted wisely. In the midst of their banter, enter Susan's real son, Rick, who contrary to expectations seems to be an ordinary young man. When he asks her to join everyone for lunch, she is dismayed and uncertain. Unable to distinguish between reality and hallucination, she sways unsteadily and asks, "I wonder if one of you would be so good as to hold on to me for a moment?" The only one who can possibly help her, Rick moves—in time to catch her as she faints.

Phase 8: When reality becomes unsettling, her fantasies dominate it. Like Act I, Act II opens with Susan emerging from a faint. Rick announces he has left the group and, newly married, lives in London. With this news, which Gerald has not yet heard, Susan conjures up her daughter (who unlike her son confided in her before marriage). Rick confesses that he will go with his wife Tess, a trained nurse, to Thailand, where she was offered a job. When Susan wishes she had a daughter, Lucy looks up. When Gerald intrudes, so does Tony, armed with a shotgun, ready to use on him (which Susan wishes a brother would do). After Rick departs, she tells Gerald of the marriage. However, her imaginary family, as before, voices her thoughts before she does until, not as before, she becomes so absorbed in the world of her mind that while she does not always have them cue her, she has them approve her words:

> SUSAN. You smug—
>
> LUCY. Self satisfied—
>
> SUSAN. Self satisfied—
>
> TONY. Conceited—
>
> SUSAN. Conceited . . . bastard!

When Muriel enters to support Gerald, Susan drives both away.

Phase 9: She attempts to keep a grip on reality. Heartbroken over what she did, she tries to banish her imaginary family, as she did her real one. To compensate, Lucy states that the *Sunday Times* called her the most brilliant female heart surgeon in the country. Susan tells her to shut up, since she is not a heart surgeon, and to go away. When Lucy tearfully does so, a remorseful Susan apologizes and asks her to return. But it is Gerald who returns, accepting her apology. Susan responds to his platitudes with sarcasm, provoking him to leave to work on his book. Although she pleads that his departure would destroy their relationship completely, he goes.

Phase 10: She loses control of her fantasies. As the light turns to a romantic sunset, her imaginary husband, offering warmth and comfort, replaces her real one. However, she recognizes that this family is different. Previously they came when she called them. Now they arrive, even enter her conversations with real people, as they please—that is, when she unconsciously calls them, a fact of which she remains unconscious. Though she tells Andy to leave, he stays. But when he suggests to her—that is, when she perceives through him—that he stays because she does not want him to go, she begins to defend her real husband and his book. Symptomatic of her increasing mental instability, her defense breaks down into garbled threats: "I might just pop upstairs and embarrass my son and discuss sexually transmitted diseases with him. Or help Muriel make a soap flake soup." Desperate, she recognizes that her imaginary family speaks her thoughts before she does. Her confusion accelerates. She adopts Andy's tone of voice, he hers; she adopts Tony's, then Lucy's; he adopts Tony's; in a single speech she adopts her own, Lucy's, and her own again; and so forth until she is utterly bewildered.

Phase 11: She may, we perceive, be adjusting to reality. As normal afternoon light replaces the romantic sunset, she is pleased with herself for having banished the people of her mind. While she commands them never to return, Bill unexpectedly returns. At first startled, she becomes happy, as she says, at the intrusion of calmness and sanity into her life. She confesses that her hallucinations have persisted. When Bill promises to arrange an appointment with a psychiatrist and to help her fight the problem, she is grateful. To her pleasant surprise, he confesses that he finds her attractive and has long admired her from afar.

Phase 12: Fantasy and reality appear to collide. As he is about to kiss her, Lucy appears. Is the family in her mind returning to separate her from reality? She tells Bill about Lucy. Although he cannot see her, he moves to where Susan says she is and pretends to talk to her. With her eyes fixed on Bill, Lucy joins her mother and, as he addresses what is now an empty space, questions her about this apparently insane stranger who chatters away to thin air. Tony enters, rifle at the ready, asking whether Susan needs protection. Andy enters, prepared to assist. Although he wishes to interrogate the intruder, Susan is confident Bill will not hear him.

Phase 13: What we perceived as reality, since we again adopted her view, we now see is a more complex fantasy, over which she has no control. The sky darkens. Andy asks Bill what he is doing. To Susan's alarm, Bill responds. In other words, his reassuring presence and declaration of love were a new form of Susan's delusions. Actually, we were warned of this possibility. Before leaving at the end of Phase 10, Andy exclaimed, "Nothing is who it is! No one is what he seems!"—a signal from a personified part of Susan's mind, forecasting a new phase of mental deterioration. Now, her imaginary husband threatens the supposedly real doctor, who is actually a Bill of her mind. As Tony prepares to chuck him into the lake, Andy begins to make love to her.

Phase 14: She rejects reality. Abruptly ending the scene is a blackout, followed immediately by a loud thunderclap, rain, and a flash of lightning. Alone, Susan sprawls on the grass, smiling, as rain pours on her. It is the middle of the night. An angry Gerald tries to make her return inside. Unaware of her actions, she has set fire to his study, destroying all but one page of his book, and has written a message to Muriel from her dead husband. "Why did you do it, Susan? Do you hate me that much?" asks Gerald. Although she denies having done anything, she admits hating him. Her brother Tony did it, she claims, and calls Bill to witness her whereabouts. But she has no brother,

says Gerald, and Bill helped to put her to bed much earlier (thereby, perhaps, prompting her delusions about him).

Phase 15: Victim of her delusions, she finds everyone in the real world turning imaginary and mixing with her fantasy figures. When Gerald leaves to phone for an ambulance, she screams at him until her imaginary family returns, bringing sunshine. Susan's delusions transform more figures from the real world into fantasy figures. Tess (offstage) becomes a dim-witted new maid, Bill a cheap bookie, Muriel a pregnant maid who brings everyone glasses of champagne with small frogs in each glass (echoing the stone frog in her pond), Gerald a jockey with a turned-around collar, and Rick a rickshaw driver (distorting his name and trip to Asia). In contrast to earlier hallucinations, everyone ignores Susan. When she shouts at them for attention, they rush forward to greet her—to her alarm. Suddenly, Muriel returns with more champagne, no longer pregnant but the mother of a child named Harry (her late husband's name).

Phase 16: Divorced from Susan's view, we perceive her total madness. Everyone warmly toasts Susan, who offers a speech to her friends and family, including "two wonderful children, Lucy and Rick." But her speech, begun in English, turns into the sort of gibberish spoken by Bill at the start of the play. Trying to say how deeply proud she is, she says "heaply cowed siam" (the last word also alluding to the country her son is going to). She becomes incomprehensible. One may recall that "December bee" is "Remember me" and interpret "Hang few" as "Thank you," but what remains, such as "Tinny beers a show," makes clear only that her mental breakdown is complete. Whereas we previously understood her, sharing her view, she no longer makes sense to us. With dazzling theatrical inventiveness, Ayckbourn has dramatized her mental deterioration.

"I think a big piece of us dies in a marriage," Watson records Ayckbourn as stating. Either we fail to adjust at all, or else "one personality, being stronger, will eclipse the other. Sometimes this happens by slow erosion—in the woman's case it's usually a long-term marathon: she'll just whittle away." In the man's it is a matter of shrinking: he diminishes. "One sees in Scarborough the man in the garden, smoking by the shed—I've seen that quite a lot—because his wife won't have tobacco smoke in the house.[. . .] And that's a case of one personality having just gently established a superiority." Although **Woman in Mind** emphasizes the woman, the play does not oversimplify life but portrays both cases.

The loving attention paid to Susan by her imaginary husband compensates for her real husband's inattentiveness. A doting brother replaces a grumbling sister-in-law. A daughter eager to confide replaces an uncommunicative son. Whereas Gerald would send her off in an ambulance, Andy wants to care for Susan himself. Her mind creates the affectionate family missing from her life. Early on, the doctor cautiously refuses to say that anything is wrong with her mind, but when she replies to his question, "You—don't recall whether you've got a son by any chance, do you?" with "A son? Certainly not," we suspect, since we take Bill to be the voice of reality, that something is amiss. "Please don't go on," she begs when he begins to describe her garden. Her appraisal of it as "some place I wouldn't choose to live in, even in my wildest nightmares" reveals that her life is a nightmare.

Susan's first scene with Gerald confirms our suspicions. Although it might seem reasonable to waken her since it is 11:30 a.m. and her son has arrived for lunch, Gerald's thinly veiled sarcasm suggests otherwise. "There is a school of thought that believes that sleep is for the night," he says. "You seem to be out to disprove them." To her plea that she finds it difficult to sleep at night, he retorts. "Hardly surprising. If you sleep all day." When she reminds him that the hospital discharged her only that morning, he replies, "Presumably they released you because they considered you fit and well." But Ayckbourn does not render this relationship simplistically. Soon she explains why she cannot sleep at night: "Perhaps it's because I'm not very happy, Gerald." "Well, who is?" he asks, and answers, "Very few." When she states that he seems among those few, his response indicates his torment: "Do I? Maybe I'm just better at hiding these things." As this exchange suggests, both members of an unhappy marriage suffer. Pompously, he tells her that if she worked harder during the day she might sleep at night. Angrily, she insists that she does work hard and begins a litany of such housekeeping drudgeries as cooking, washing up, laundry, and "the sheer boring slog of tidying up." But he has obviously heard "the catalogue" many times before. Just as his inability to understand her complaints annoys her, her reiteration of them annoys him. When both agree that something must be wrong, she articulates basic sources of her discontent:

> I don't know what my role is these days. I don't any longer know what I'm supposed to be doing. I used to be a wife. I used to be a mother. And I loved it. People said, Oh, don't you long to get out and do a proper job? And I'd say, No thanks, this is a proper job, thank you. Mind your own business. But now it isn't any more. The thrill has gone.

To this, Gerald tries to hide his sense of personal failure with the question, "Oh, we're back on that, are we?" and to change the subject by quoting John Keble's "The Christian Year": "The trivial round, the common task, / Should furnish all we ought to ask." Revealingly, Ayckbourn has him misquote the passage. "Will" replaces "Should," as Gerald tries to dominate her by certainties, and "need" replaces "ought," as he reasons not her need.

But the subject inevitably returns. *"Offhandedly,"* Susan tells him he must know she no longer loves him, nor for that matter does he love her. When he begins to protest, she interrupts him:

> SUSAN. We don't kiss—we hardly touch each other—we don't make love—we don't even share the same bed now.
> We sleep at different ends of the room—
>
> GERALD. That's just sex you're talking about. That's just the sexual side—
>
> SUSAN. Well, of course it is—

GERALD. There's more to it than that, surely?

SUSAN. Not at the moment there isn't.

Later, she blames his writing for their lack of sex: "That's tended to burn up most of his midnight oils." Small wonder, then, that she avenges herself by destroying his manuscript. Although she admits that sex has not been the only important aspect of their relationship, she perceives, "once that's gone—all *that*—it becomes important. Overimportant, really." When they shared sex, "everything else, the everyday bits, just ticked along nicely. But take that away, the really joyous part of us—and everything else rather loses its purpose." Sadly, Gerald does not understand. To him, her statements are only accusations that he has let her down, failed to deliver, and is at fault. But guilt underlies his anger. Whereas she made no charges, he clearly has accused himself. In doing so, he has unwittingly pronounced a verdict of guilty.

Partly because Susan is frustrated, she snipes at her sister-in-law, whose cooking, Gerald admits, is abominable. Sarcastically, the insecure Susan makes Muriel feel insecure. Although Muriel argues that she cooked for her mother during the old woman's last twelve years and for her husband during his last seven, all Susan says is, "I've no doubt you'll see us off as well, Muriel." Accurately, Gerald reprimands her, "That's a very unfeeling remark." Susan comically scores off Muriel, whom one tends to regard as she does, and Gerald is pompous, but Susan is not blameless.

While, given the perspective of the play, Susan is more sinned against than sinning, she inadvertently reveals her deficiencies in raising her son. "Sixteen years old and, until I told him, he thought his bed got damp in the night because the roof leaked. You did nothing for him, Gerald. Nothing. He could have died for all you cared. And now he's grown up he won't even speak to me." Apart from her preoccupation with herself, to which, as usual, she turns the subject, the baldness of her remarks suggests that she herself alienated Rick. His complaints to her in the second act show more of her failings as a mother. "I remember how you used to be with girls I used to bring home," he says. Although she recalls that they got on well together, he disabuses her of this fancy: "No, you didn't, Mum. I mean, frankly, you used to embarrass the hell out of them. [. . .] You used to get them into corners and start going on about—I don't know—contraception methods and multiple orgasms . . . I mean, I'd hardly even kissed them, you were asking them for their medical histories." She protests that these teenage girls needed sexual education and "I wasn't having a woman going out with a son of mine who didn't know what she was about. You'd have thanked me for it later . . . You? You didn't know a thing till I told you." "I did," says he, "We all did. It's just that we didn't necessarily want to sit down and talk to you about it." Her response to him parallels Gerald's to her. She regards Rick's statements as an accusation that she was a total failure as a mother. In vain, he denies having said that. She lashes out destructively: "I should have had a daughter. I could have coped with her. (*Rather waspishly*) Boys are all such delicate blossoms, aren't they." Naturally, he responds in kind: "God help any daughter who had you as a mother." He tries to appease her by pointing out his father's defects concerning his girlfriends: "Terrified they'd turn out to be the daughters of Beelzebub. Scarlet women after his son's body." However, none of this penetrates her mind. "It's no use," she replies. "You can be as loyal to your father as you like. I know which one of us was responsible for all this." Despite the sympathies Ayckbourn has generated for Susan, he is psychologically acute enough to show her flaws and to demonstrate that, with son as with sister-in-law, she attacks when hurt. But he also emphasizes her genuine pain.

Another aspect of Susan's character is low self-esteem. Told how she knocked herself out, she comments, "Typical of me." Not only does she watch too much television, "I watch such trash most of the time, I just sit there feeling guilty. Saying to myself, what on earth am I doing watching *this*? Why aren't I watching something useful? I mean," she explains, oxymoronically, "I do try sometimes to watch interesting programmes but I find them all so boring." A sense of worthlessness creates guilt, but unchanged behavior generates more guilt.

Although **Woman in Mind** does not portray the frightened, unassertive man smoking a cigarette by the garden shed, it shows that marriage has broken both husband and wife. Gerald's retreat from Susan into research parallels a retreat to the shed, and we see him flee to his study to avoid hearing her recriminations. Furthermore, when their son arrived, Gerald confesses, "I hid in the hall cupboard. Suddenly I lost my nerve and hid in the cupboard." Gerald's pompous self-assurance is a mask that fails to hide the suffering face beneath it.

As some quotations and paraphrases in this analysis of Ayckbourn's craft and characterization have suggested, **Woman in Mind** is essentially comic. Its humor is an integral part of these aspects. At the outset, when Susan and we cannot make sense of what Bill says, the play's mood, despite her fears, is not stark terror. Rather, we laugh at her reactions. "Oh God, I've died. That's what it is. I've died." Then, reducing death to tourism: "And—wherever it is I've gone—nobody speaks English." When Bill's "Choose 'un" turns to "Susan," she responds with comic incongruity: "Susan? Yes, that's me. (*pointing at herself, loudly, as to a foreigner*) Me Susan, yes." Laughter derives from the doctor's professional uncertainties, partly revealed in his mechanical catchphrases, partly in his repeated qualifications when he tries to reassure his patient. An ambulance will take her to the hospital, he says. "Better safe than sorry. Probably just an overnight stop, that's all. Be back home here tomorrow. Right as rain. Probably." Comic too is the contrast between his concern for his patient, who may have suffered a concussion, and his seemingly greater concern for his bag, which he cannot open because of a jammed lock, the incongruity underscored by her ironic awareness of it:

> BILL. [. . .] I mean I *can* get it open. In a real emergency. But it does entail a good deal of force in order to do so. And stuff tends to scatter. All over the place. So.
>
> SUSAN. Oh, well. Please don't bother on my account.

BILL. Thanks.

Much of the humor comes from character, notably as it functions in mutually destructive situations between husband and wife. When Gerald misquotes Keble about trivial daily tasks sufficing to fulfill one's expectations, Susan retorts with customary sarcasm: "Yes, it's usually about now that you come up with that invaluable piece of advice, Gerald," which she says is untrue. "Whoever wrote it was talking through his hat. Anyway, how can you possibly believe anybody who rhymes 'road' with 'God.' " His own retorts avenge such insults. To her question, "We've known each other rather a long time, haven't we?" he does not answer but instead denigrates her: "Said by anybody else, that could have been interpreted as an affectionate remark. Spoken by you, it sounds like an appalling accusation."

Passages concerning Muriel's ineptitude in the kitchen strikingly exemplify the creation of comedy from the interplay of characters. As Gerald tries to avoid wounding her, Muriel becomes defensive and Susan turns sarcastic:

> GERALD. This is an interesting cup of coffee, Muriel.
>
> MURIEL. Nice?
>
> GERALD. Very interesting. Yes.
>
> SUSAN. (*examining her cup for the first time*) What powder did you use?
>
> MURIEL. Here we go, the Spanish Inquisition—
>
> SUSAN. I was only curious—
>
> MURIEL. I used the coffee in the tin marked Coffee. All right?
>
> GERALD. That sounds logical to me.
>
> SUSAN. Yes, it is. Fairly. This is the ready ground coffee, Muriel, not the instant . . .
>
> MURIEL. I don't know what sort it is. If you don't want it, I'll take it back . . .
>
> GERALD. No, no, this is perfect, Muriel. First rate.
>
> MURIEL. (*muttering*) Can't do anything right, can I?
>
> SUSAN. Delicious, Muriel. You must give us the secret.

When Muriel prepares to make lunch, she asks Susan whether the herbs in a can near the teapot are thyme or sage. Answer: "That's Earl Grey Tea." Muriel's response hints that Susan's clarification has come too late: "(*worried*) Earl Grey Tea. Right. (*moving off*) I do wish you'd label things, Susan." After lunch, in conversation with Susan, Gerald confirms the hint: "You know that really was quite the most appalling meal I've ever tasted. I'd forgotten how bad she was. Burnt Earl Grey omelettes." Even following Susan's destruction of Gerald's book, Ayckbourn draws laughter from Muriel's culinary disabilities. Upon Rick's report that he asked her to make cups of cocoa for everyone, the clergyman comments in character, "All that and now compulsory cocoa. Locusts follow shortly."

A fertile source of comedy is skepticism as to Muriel's religious experiences, which include sensing her dead husband gazing at her and feeling his breath on her cheek—suggestive parallels to Susan's hallucinations. "God, in His Infinite Wisdom and with the entire cosmos to choose from," says Susan, "is unlikely to base the Kingdom of Heaven around Muriel's bedroom." When Gerald calls the remark blasphemous, she apologizes. When he tells her that it is not he to whom she should apologize, she says, "Sorry, God." When he explains that he meant Muriel, she retorts, "Oh, rather. Let's get our priorities right. Muriel, then God, then Gerald. I've got it. Sorry, Muriel." Upon what Muriel considers decisive evidence that her expectations are valid—her friend Enid, trying to will her late husband Desmond back, awoke one morning to discover, on the bedroom ceiling, words written in chalk: "LOVE . . . ENID . . . ETERNALLY"—both Gerald and Susan comment:

> GERALD. I recall, though, that they did establish it was Enid's handwriting, didn't they?
>
> MURIEL. Oh, yes. But then he worked through her hand, didn't he? Desmond made use of her hand . . .
>
> SUSAN. (*murmuring*) I hope he put it back when he'd finished with it . . .

Climaxing the sexually repressed Susan's dislike of her sexually repressed sister-in-law, Susan, before or after setting fire to Gerald's study, climbs on the chest of drawers in Muriel's room to write a message on the ceiling, supposedly from Muriel's late husband: "KNICKERS OFF, MURIEL."

Another fruitful source of comedy, as implied previously, is the series of misunderstandings revolving around the people in Susan's mind. Early in the play, she tells Lucy, concerning a bench, "Just put it there, darling, thank you." "Right," says Lucy. "Right you are," says Bill, who puts down a chair. Confused, Susan asks him whether she just said anything.

> BILL. Er—yes. You said—just put it there. Darling.
>
> SUSAN. I did?
>
> BILL. Did you—not know you'd said it?
>
> SUSAN. Yes, I knew I'd said it. I was just checking if you'd heard it. You had.
>
> BILL. Yes, I had. (*He smiles at her.*)
> *Pause.*
> No more hallucinations, I hope?

This exchange demonstrates Ayckbourn's complex weaving of comedy with craft and characterization. Funny—partly because of Susan's confusion, partly because of verbal repetitions, partly because of irony—the passage also foreshadows Susan's imagining Bill to declare his love for her and reveals, through her use of a term of endearment, her romantic interest in him.

When the family in her mind prompts her to tell Bill to drop dead, the sequence is extremely funny, as are those in which two sets of conversation—one by the imaginary family, the other by the real one—occur simultaneously, and the scene in which Susan and Andy speak in the manner of Lucy and Tony, and of each other. Predictably, Bill attempts to talk to Lucy, whom he cannot see; the result is predictably comic. Unpredictably, he turns out to be a Bill of Susan's mind and talks to her imaginary family; the unexpected turn of events is funnier. The further intrusion of figures from Susan's real life with those of her imaginary life—including Bill as bookie ("Honest Bill" is emblazoned on the bag he habitually carries), Muriel as a pregnant maid who serves champagne over frogs (kept in the can near the teapot), clergyman Gerald embracing Andy as "you old devil you" and calling the doctor "Billy Beelzebub himself" (recalling Rick's statement about how his father regarded his girlfriends), and so forth—are hilarious.

By this time, which is near the end of *Woman in Mind,* comedy diminishes more and more, for we perceive Susan's increasing desperation as her mind deteriorates. Before her hallucinatory intermingling of all members of both her families, she cries out to Gerald:

> I'm free of all of you now, you see. All of you. You with your prim little, frigid little, narrow-minded little meanness. And that priggish brat who's ashamed of me. Who'd faint at the sight of a pair of tits. As for her with her dead husband. No wonder he died. (*yelling*) What are you hoping for, Muriel? A phantom pregnancy? (*She laughs.*) Too late, dear. Too damn late. You and me both. Over the hill.

Such sentiments evoke compassion, not laughter. When, at the end of the play, Susan lapses into total gibberish, Ayckbourn leaves laughter behind. While only compassion remains, this feeling dominates because it had been present earlier, when it mixed with the comic. As Ayckbourn says, "All good comedy should make you cry." He echoes Shaw, who writes that "the finest sort draws a tear along with the laugh."

Woman in Mind validates the view of many comic theorists, from Trissino to Bergson and beyond, that, to use William Hazlitt's words, "as long as the disagreeableness of the consequences of a sudden disaster is kept out of sight by the immediate oddity of the circumstances, and the absurdity or unaccountableness of a foolish action is the most striking thing in it, the ludicrous prevails over the pathetic" ["On Wit and Humour," in *Dramatic Theory and Criticism,* edited by Bernard F. Dukore]. With superb craftsmanship and a sense of character, Ayckbourn sensitively balances the comically ludicrous and the sympathetically pathetic. In Billington's words, he treats "domestic pain and disaster from the wry standpoint of comedy and with the technical ingenuity of farce." In his "pained awareness of the unhappiness we inflict on ourselves and on each other," which he dramatizes with great virtuosity, he resembles "a laughing surgeon." His plays may well fulfill Peter Hall's prediction and become staples in the National Theatre's repertoire half a century from now. (pp. 23-39)

Bernard F. Dukore, "Craft, Character, Comedy: Ayckbourn's 'Woman in Mind'," in Twentieth Century Literature, *Vol. 32, No. 1, Spring, 1986, pp. 23-39.*

John Russell Taylor   (review date November 1986)

[*Taylor is an English film and drama critic. In the following excerpt, he reviews* Woman in Mind, *highlighting Ayckbourn's ability to balance tragedy and comedy.*]

Franz Werfel first labelled his version of *Jacobowsky and the Colonel*— not exactly the play recently revived at the [National Theatre]—'the comedy of a tragedy'. Alan Ayckbourn might say the same about nearly all his plays: he is constantly showing us that one man's tragedy is another man's uproarious farce, or that comedy and tragedy are just two faces of the same medal, showing or hiding themselves entirely according to how you hold the object up to the light. **Woman in Mind** . . . is perhaps the most precarious example yet of this tragicomic brinkmanship: even as we laugh, we know that a woman is going mad before our eyes, and that the experience, for her and for those around her, is agonizing.

And yet we do not stop laughing—or only very rarely. What is wrong with us? Or with Ayckbourn? Or with the play? It is certainly not an experience easy to fit in with our moral preconceptions. But then, the complexities of real life rarely are. The point is that Susan is often very funny about herself and her predicament, so that we are laughing with her much more than we are laughing at her. Her trouble is that in many respects she sees too clearly. She cannot ignore the boringness of her husband, with his constant preoccupation with a sixty-page history of the parish. She cannot overlook the awfulness of her only son, recently prey to a brainwashing sect that does not permit him even to speak to his parents. She is merciless to the shortcomings of her terminally incompetent sister-in-law, whose greatest triumph of mismanagement in the course of the play is to make *omlettes fines herbes* with Earl Grey tea, and burn them in the process. Her tongue on such subjects is sharp enough to amuse us, the safe onlookers the other side of the footlights, but to drive the objects of her (probably justified) scorn even further back into their own private worlds.

We just do not know too exactly what their private worlds are. We know rather too clearly about Susan's, since the play displays it corporeally for us. She takes refuge in a woman's-magazine dream-world where her beflannelled husband, brother and daughter, all wholly adoring, want constantly to know if there is anyone for tennis. At least, that is what they do as long as she can control them. But soon enough they too start to get out of hand, refuse to do what they are told, and torment her just as badly as her real family. This is where she starts to realise that she is going mad, though we have guessed it for some time. One of the troubles with the play is that we have to take an inordinate lot of novelettish whimsy first (and even after), which is not entirely compensated for by Ayckbourn's signalling that yes, he knows, and this is what he means us to be feeling. (Rather like an avant-garde playwright as-

serting loudly that he *meant* to be boring, boredom is deliberately built into the experience.)

However, the unpredictability of the play as a whole does almost make up for the fleeting discomforts. Ayckbourn is, as we should know by now, much more cunning than he appears, and while we seem to be seeing everything from Susan's point of view, sympathising with her against the rest of the awful people, he does tellingly let us see the other fellow's point of view. If they are awful, she is no doubt partly to blame for that. It is unlikely that her cleric husband would have taken refuge so completely in his piffling history project if he did not have a lot to take refuge from. And her son makes the point explicitly when he is countering Susan's view of her role as an unreasonably misunderstood mother by recounting some of the horrors attendant on bringing girls home to a weird woman who would launch straight into contraception instructions before he had managed a first kiss. (pp. 22-3)

John Russell Taylor, in a review of "Woman in Mind," in Plays & Players, *No. 398, November, 1986, pp. 22-3.*

Richard Hornby   (review date Winter 1987)

[*Hornby is an American educator specializing in drama. In the following excerpted review of* A Chorus of Disapproval, *he discusses humor, character, situation, and dramatic structure.*]

A good play that recently transferred to the West End from the National is Alan Ayckbourn's **Chorus of Disapproval**. Ayckbourn has received little serious critical attention, probably because he is so often compared to our Neil Simon. Like Simon, he writes comedies of contemporary life, and like Simon, he makes a lot of money at it, but otherwise the two are very dissimilar. Simon creates mostly eccentric characters, who are sometimes hilarious and sometimes all too predictable; Ayckbourn creates drab, ordinary characters who turn out to be oddly interesting and always funny. Simon's main source of humor is in verbal gags; Ayckbourn almost never uses them, relying instead on character and situation. Finally, Simon has little sense of dramatic structure (his main weakness), while Ayckbourn is obsessed with it; play after play involves some technical novelty, as in **The Norman Conquests,** a trilogy in which the same play is simply repeated three times in different parts of the same house; each play can be viewed independently, and differs in tone and viewpoint from the others, yet has the same six characters and follows the same events.

In **Chorus of Disapproval,** the key technical device is a play within the play; a provincial amateur drama group is performing John Gay's eighteenth-century satire, *The Beggar's Opera* (also the source for Brecht's *Threepenny Opera*). The characters, as usual with Ayckbourn, are ordinary middle class folk, who turn out to be involved in shady business deals, personal intrigue, and sexual aggression. A naive new member joins the troupe, who immediately project their fantasies on him; although he is just a decent, unassuming fellow with no talent, holding an unimportant job in a large corporation, they see him as a great lover, shrewd businessman, and lead performer. Seduced by two women, drawn into both sides of a dubious land scheme, he simultaneously moves up in the cast as it undergoes the attrition that is typical of amateur groups, until he is playing the lead—by which time he has lost his job, his fellow performers have developed total contempt for him, and the women have dropped him.

Ayckbourn plays off the inner versus the outer play with grace and humor; Gay's play is a send-up of the same middle class attitudes and values, particularly sexual prudery, venality, and hypocrisy, as are held by the characters playing them. Gay's song "I'm Bubbled," refers to the South Sea Bubble, the great land scheme of the time, which is reflected in the shady scheme in the outer play; Macheath's having two wives reflects his offstage problem of having two mistresses. Yet ironically there is no happy ending in the main, outer play as there is in *The Beggar's Opera*. Although his plays are very funny, Ayckbourn's vision is dark; sex is an ensnarement, while idealism and decency lead merely to loss. As with Chekhov, he combines an underlying sadness with great affection for his characters, yet is unsentimental about them. (pp. 642-43)

> *Richard Hornby, in a review of "A Chorus of Disapproval," in* The Hudson Review, *Vol. XXXIX, No. 4, Winter, 1987, pp. 635-43.*

Sheridan Morley   (review date August 1987)

[*Morley is an English arts and drama critic who contributes to such periodicals as* Tatler, Films and Filming, *and* Punch. *In the following excerpt, he reviews* A Small Family Business, *emphasizing Ayckbourn's incorporation of dark humor into farce.*]

Alan Ayckbourn is now to be found over the river, where on the Olivier stage of the National *A Small Family Business* is the first of his plays in many years not to have been written for and first seen at his own theatre in Scarborough. A bleak, dark and ultimately very black comedy about a family finally becoming the family in a Mafia sense of that word, this would appear at first sight to share many of the themes of relative values and filial betrayal which are at the heart of another current Ayckbourn National production, Arthur Miller's *A View From The Bridge*. . . .

[*A Small Family Business*] is not, of course, a play in anything like that classic or tragic league; but it does suggest that, having previously separated his scripts into the dark and the light, Ayckbourn is now ready within one admittedly faintly overlong evening to move from the total farce of the opening sequence, where a man comes home to take his wife to bed only to find ten of his closest relatives assembled in the dark for a surprise party, through to the final and chilling spotlit vision of a hopelessly drug-addicted daughter sitting alone in the bathroom while downstairs her parents and uncles and aunts are sorting out the disposal of an alien corpse.

What Mr Ayckbourn is telling us is that, like charity, corruption begins at home: his central figure [Jack] . . . comes back to take over an ailing family furniture factory which he intends to revive on the simple if unfashionable basis of total honesty. Once he discovers, however, that his daughter is shoplifting and his brother flogging off the firm's furniture at cut rates to Italian rivals, and what's more that every single relative is on some kind of fiddle at home or at work, he gradually gets himself caught up in a spiral of blackmail from which there is no escape but only surrender.

Across nearly three hours, things are apt to get a little repetitive especially as all the relatives live in the same onstage set, presumably because in a furniture business they would be likely to have identical homes. But when, in a final act of ritual submission to graft and evil, Jack actually dons a widely-pinstriped suit and delivers a speech about the family future which would not have disgraced the Godfather himself, we cannot be altogether shocked or even surprised. For all that, Ayckbourn remains the master writer of families in lives of gentle madness or total decay: here we have a husband so obsessed by cooking that his wife cannot get into the kitchen, another wife who has filled her bedroom with so many sexual aids that her husband sleeps elsewhere, not to mention a nephew with all the reasoning powers of a draft excluder and a private investigator with so many corruptions of his own flesh and soul that he barely has the time to profit from those of others. . . .

[In] this bravura hymn of hatred to English family life we are left with pieces of people being fitted into a jigsaw which, when complete, turns out to be a horror picture of Borgia proportions. (p. 17)

> *Sheridan Morley, in a review of "A Small Family Business," in* Plays & Players, *No. 407, August, 1987, pp. 16-17.*

Edward Pearce   (review date February 1988)

[*In the review excerpted below, Pearce addresses plot, theme, and characterization in* A Small Family Business.]

[Alan Ayckbourn] is interested *only* in the low. Somewhat disingenuously, posters for *A Small Family Business* depict a lady in high boots and net tights, carrying a whip. The part-time tarting of one member of the Ayres family, Anita, is the least of it. By depicting a family business moving in two-and-three-quarter hours from selling furniture to ancillary membership of the Mafia and wholesaling cocaine, Ayckbourn imposes a heavier and yet potentially more improbable plot than ever before.

I am not quite sure whether Mr Ayckbourn is embittered at the corruption of the human race or carried away by the mechanics of his own invention, but as an attack on yuppies *A Small Family Business* beats into a pulp that primitive piece of foul-mouthed fashionability, *Serious Money*, which has been the fey rage in London. Ayckbourn shows us the implosion of an honest man, Jack Mc-Cracken, into the bottomless corruption of his in-laws for whom larceny is a finger-end instinct. As plot it is heavily unlikely; as characters Ayckbourn's people are fearful. They have the marks of hatred on them. Obsessive, anorexic, dog-loving Harriet; greedy, food-connoisseuring Desmond; and possession-wise, fat, complaisantly cuckolded Cliff, a business executive with the ethics of a Maltese pimp—they are transcendentally horrible people.

Every previous excursion by the author into human fallibility looks like a trip round the bay compared to this voyage of disabuse. The irony is that Ayckbourn, who stresses his commonsense artisanship and refuses all the moral pretensions . . . has written a sort of moral pantomime with good and bad clearly defined, and bad as clearly triumphing. Honest Jack concludes the deal which will make him a cocaine baron by putting on a double-breasted striped suit jacket, kissing his brother on both cheeks *à la Siciliana,* and saying: "This business must be kept in the Family." All extremely funny in its way, except that in an upper room of the four-part set his daughter Sammy is sitting ashen-white and injecting herself. There is simply too much cargo for this sprightly little boat to carry. She doesn't sink, but the list is perceptible.

The sheer brilliance of Ayckbourn's craft, which carries the first half at a magnificent dazzling zip that has one calling for more, will keep the boat above water. But what really works are the characters. As long as they are unfolding and giving the piece the energy of their unwinding identity, we have enormous pace and fierce compulsion. However, the action of the plot demands a resolution too extravagant. Outside of overt thrillers, death on stage is usually a sign of desperation. Ayckbourn, more honest than many writers, tells us that sometimes he wants to be rid of a character and isn't sure how to do it. The disposal of Benedict Hough [a private detective] by banging his head against the bath may seem a touch extreme.

At about this time, plot (formal whale-boned figure-contorting old-style plot) takes over from character; and we all lose by it. Mr Ayckbourn will always look best in a liberty gown. Normally, relatively little happens in an Ayckbourn play: a quarrel certainly, a little fumbled adultery, much snubbing and point-scoring. But such is the delicacy of the participating characters, they get the main theme back out of its development and variations into the comfortable home key with a degree of finesse in which a thrown tea-tray is downright Wagnerian. By contrast, the characters of *A Small Family Business* are monsters, and accordingly create situations which are heavy metal for the sitting-room. Jack joins the Mafia at the end with the sort of resignation with which in earlier works he might have joined the Lions Club.

The play actually suffers from the author's skills. His little boast is that if a cup of tea has to be got from one side of the stage to the other, he can usually manage it. On this occasion he manages Samantha's tragedy of self-destruction, and makes it dreadfully real in circumstances where there is no room for it. To be bearable, these grotesques must be masques and humours. Intolerably and hurtfully, Samantha turns out real, with veins to take needles. (pp. 69-70)

Edward Pearce, "Death on Stage," in Encounter, *Vol. LXXX, No. 2, February, 1988, pp. 69-71.*

Clive Barnes   (review date 18 February 1988)

[*Barnes is an English-born American editor and the principal drama critic for the* New York Post. *In the following review of* Woman in Mind, *he assesses Ayckbourn's presentation of the relationship between reality and illusion.*]

Without question Alan Ayckbourn's ***Woman in Mind*** is a funny kind of tragedy.

Indeed even with question, this play of poignant fantasy that humorously relates the story of a dead marriage while also documenting a woman's journey into pathological schizophrenia, is uncommonly difficult to define.

It starts with a blow to the head. A woman is in her garden—an ordinary suburban garden. She has felled herself in that comic banana-skin fashion by stepping on a garden rake.

Now she is being assisted by a man who, as it turns out, is her doctor. But his conversation is strange . . . the words sound half-familiar, but foreign. He could be a man from Mars who had not quite picked up the local language on his Martian computer.

Soon we realize that we are perceiving the scene through the mind of the woman—she is called Susan, by the way—and Susan has just had a very nasty crack on the skull. She is also halfway to being schizophrenic, and that twilight language is apparently what some schizoid minds pick up.

Now the play and Susan—with us in dutiful tow—moves right along. Bill, the dull-boots doctor, buzzes off to fix an ambulance, and soon Susan is joined by her dazzling family—and they really are dazzling.

Susan may look like a squashed lettuce leaf but her husband, Andy, her daughter, Lucy, and her brother, Tony, fairly glow like fashion plates. They are ready for tennis in the grandest manner, and talk as if they are frozen in a rather silly play.

The physician comes back with news of the ambulance,

but Susan tells him that her husband has dismissed the idea of either an ambulance or a hospital. Bill persists—talks of her sister-in-law.

What sister-in-law? Susan doesn't have a sister-in-law. Susan is confused. So is Bill. So—when she arrives—is the sister-in-law, Muriel.

Things should be straightened out by the appearance of Susan's husband. But they are not. For the husband that now materializes is not the cheery, Noel-Cowardy Andy, but someone quite different. He is a tedious, pompous Anglican vicar, Gerald, whose idea of destiny is to write a history of his parish from the middle ages onwards.

Bingo! The play falls into place—Ayckbourn's purposes are clear. But are they? Well obviously Susan enjoys a rich fantasy existence to relieve the unadulterated tedium of a marital life dominated by the boorishly genteel Gerald and his whiningly incompetent sister. To say nothing of Rick, a difficult son who has just escaped from the clutches of a religious cult.

Yet this is more than just fantasy. There is an inner reality here—it is the subjective inner reality of alienation, that madman's truth of personal perception.

Moreover, Ayckbourn is inviting us to watch Susan right at the moment when fantasy is taking her over, to see her actually float out of one world and into the next.

Soon Susan, her illness and her playwright, are unaffectedly interleaving reality and illusion, rather as they might in a dream, and her two families can, to an extent which we as an audience are forced to define, inter-react.

Now the play is a comedy. That is basic. It is funny. It is meant to be funny—laugh lines are built in like the steel girders in a skyscraper.

Yet, as with most of Ayckbourn's recent work, the playwright is being funny about the darker side of the moon. He not only recognizes comedy's tragic face, he relishes and even sentimentalizes it.

But it is what he does with a text that is more important than the text itself—and, as a result, his plays virtually direct themselves. The map comes with the territory. Indeed the territory is—in the final count—nothing but a map.

This is not meant to be a put-down—or rather it is, but it is meant to be a put-down at the highest level of art. I enjoyed *Woman in Mind* as much as any play this season. I enjoyed it so much that I must note it doesn't go the final mile. It is, when the chips are down, still a work of contrivance rather than genius.

However with Susan . . . Ayckbourn has come his closest yet to a real character in real pain.

> Clive Barnes, "*Life on the Dark Side,*" in New York Post, *February 18, 1988.*

Robert Gore-Langton   (essay date 13 April 1989)

[In the following excerpt, Gore-Langton traces the development of Ayckbourn's career through Man of the Moment.*]*

For a man who has spent most of his professional life as a director, writing plays has turned out to be a noteworthy sideline for Alan Ayckbourn. *Man of the Moment,* the latest, was filed on his word processor as AA35. He has since keyed in a two-part show, *The Revenger's Comedies* (AA36 and 37). . . . At this rate, AA50 will be with us by the turn of the century.

If Ayckbourn is the most prolific, most produced, and one of the richest playwrights in English today, he is still somehow out on a limb—more in tune with his audience, whom he seems to know as instinctively as an Elizabethan dramatist, than with any Oxbridge theatre coterie. And now, his plays have become dignified—exalted, almost—by the same critics who once found him a suspect, lightweight boulevardier.

Educated at Haileybury public school, his father a leader of the London Symphony Orchestra and his mother a journalist, Ayckbourn's background is removed from the ordinariness of his chosen territory—the (alcoholic) fringes of the English suburban hinterland. In Ayckbourn's world, it is usually raining, Christmases and parties are always disastrous, broken appliances never get fixed. Everyday petty struggles spell defeat for characters unequal to the simplest tasks. But, rooted in heartache and misunderstanding, his theatre raises the comic stakes to dangerous, often thrilling levels, his comedy poised inches above a rising tide of human desperation.

Victims tend to be bullied women, their needs often misunderstood by myopic men. In *Absurd Person Singular* (1972), Ayckbourn's third West End play, Eva's suicide bid becomes farcically funny as someone offers to help clean the oven she's stuck her head in. In *Just Between Ourselves* (1976), the first of his 'winter plays', Vera is driven into a catatonic coma through loneliness and insecurity, quite unable to penetrate her husband's unremitting cheerfulness; her desperate plea, 'I need help, Dennis', he takes to mean as help around the house and invites her to make a list of things that want mending. In *Woman in Mind* (1985), Susan goes insane, unable to separate her Persil-fantasy family in the garden from the awful real one.

Says director Alan Strachan, who, among many other Ayckbourn productions, recently gave us a definitive period revival of *How the Other Half Loves:*

> Alan is a very old-fashioned writer. He still believes in virtues like clarity, narrative thrust and form. I always thought this "boulevardier" term a great misnomer: he is a mainstream writer who is deeply subversive.

> It all comes from a basic observation of what people do to each other. Throughout the corpus runs a fundamental theme of duplicity. And he *is* a deeply political writer, in that his plays are very much to do with class: all the stuff about him being purely a middle-class writer is just deceptive. In a great deal of the plays, the subtle nuances of the whole English class system [Strachan argues from the vantage point of the expatriate Scot] are very, very important. The theme

that engages him most is human exploitation—it is the one thing that seems to make him angry.

It is now a commonplace observation that Ayckbourn has become a darker playwright. The gnomes have become more menacing, the gardens more nightmarish. Ayckbourn is today less prone to the farce of collapsing DIY—more the critic of a society that itself is morally gimcrack. Even back in 1974, Michael Billington of the *Guardian* pronounced him (apropos of *Absent Friends*) 'a left-wing playwright using a right-wing form'. When *Way Upstream* appeared in 1982, it was called his SDP play, a submerged condemnation of all extremism.

Such pigeon-holing, though, has been resisted by the playwright himself. In his published conversations with Ian Watson, Ayckbourn says: 'I'm on a crusade to try and persuade people that theatre can be fun; every time I do that, some hairy bugger from the Left tells them it's instructive and drives them away . . . If I want to be instructed, I go to night school.'

[Rooted] in heartache and misunderstanding, [Ayckbourn's] theatre raises the comic stakes to dangerous, often thrilling levels, his comedy poised inches above a rising tide of human desperation.

—Robert Gore-Langton

The critic Martin Hoyle is a regular first-nighter at Scarborough, and was one of the first to write at length on the Ayckbourn phenomenon. 'Like all satirists, Ayckbourn is a moralist and, I suspect, a bit of a reactionary, too,' he says. 'But I've never seen him as a political writer at all—except in the very broad sense of sexual politics.'

Hoyle, citing both *Henceforward* (1987) and—in particular—*Man of the Moment,* argues that there is more of a moral, and almost spiritual, dimension to the later plays.

> It's true, I think, that there are fewer belly laughs, but Ayckbourn now usually pays dividends in other, more lasting ways. He remains as ingenious as ever; it's just that his view of human nature has darkened. The jester's grin has become, if you like, the *rictus sardonicus* of a death's head.

Whatever changes have taken place, Ayckbourn's method of composition—one month off, three weeks mooning about, a few days writing or dictation—is still geared to a specific audience and stage. For all his success, he remains attached, by a creative umbilical cord, to Scarborough. Scarborough remains his professional *raison d'être*.

The Ayckbourn career bridges two eras. His beginnings were at the emergence of writers' theatre in the late Fifties, while his early training with the great barnstormer Donald Wolfit goes back to a vanished era of West End potentates and the old star system. It was a system that touched

on his own work: Celia Johnson appeared in Ayckbourn's first London production, *Relatively Speaking,* in 1967, and Robert Morley made alterations to his part (then a star's prerogative) in *How the Other Half Loves*—effectively wrecking the play.

The old vices are now gone, but some of the old-fashioned virtues have been preserved at Scarborough—not least, the notion of theatre as entertainment, as a public service. It was an imperative that Ayckbourn inherited from his boss Stephen Joseph, who back in 1955 was writing in *Plays and Players* magazine of the virtues of arena staging and the need for theatre to 'win back' audiences. In the case of Ayckbourn, this philosophy has produced works that seem to suit the South Bank and the West End as well as they do East Yorks.

The Theatre in the Round at Scarborough remains Ayckbourn's Alma Mater. His ingenuity, the deftness of his manipulation of stage time and space, the bending of stage conventions are unflagging. His plays are unliterary, underivative (he has cited Priestley as an influence), but visually witty.

Says designer Roger Glossop, who has worked recently with Ayckbourn on *Woman in Mind, Tis Pity She's a Whore* and *Henceforward:*

> He writes to people's strengths. Alan knows I'm interested in videos; he asked me to design *Henceforward* and, lo and behold, the subplot is on video! He does this for certain actors, too. He knows what he wants: I receive plans for designs over the fax. He doesn't dictate, but he has a visual imagination that makes it very easy in the end.

(pp. 29-30)

Though Ayckbourn never has (and never will) write a state-of-England play, there is now a broadening of moral themes: *A Small Family Business* showed a nation's spirit degenerating, while society surrounding the artist in *Henceforward* was brutal and hostile. All this is a long way from the antics of *Bedroom Farce.* Currently in search of new outlets (a translation of a savage comedy by Henri Becque is looking for a production), there seems no sign of a let-up in creative energy.

As we read of a stash of explosives lately discovered in Scarborough, it's tempting to imagine Ayckbourn's mind elaborating—a housewife burying a case of Semtex in a moonlit copse, unwittingly digging herself into some terrorist plan, the plot spiralling into a vortex of orchestrated confusion . . . From Ayckbourn, our most complete man of the theatre, the surprises are always still to come. (p. 30)

Robert Gore-Langton, "Darkness on the Edge of Town," in The Listener, *Vol. 121, No. 3109, April 13, 1989, pp. 29-30.*

Michael Billington   (essay date 1990)

[Billington is an English drama critic who has been a writer for the Guardian *since 1971. In the following excerpt from his critical study* Alan Ayckbourn, *he sur-*

veys themes and techniques in Ayckbourn's plays from Intimate Exchanges *through* The Revengers' Comedies, *highlighting Ayckbourn's development of complex and darkly humorous dramas that increasingly address themes of social protest.*]

My conviction that Ayckbourn has the capacity for development of the true artist has been borne out by the events of the Eighties. At a time of life when other dramatists start to rest on their laurels, count their winnings or retire to Shropshire to pen disgruntled autobiographies, he has not only carried on writing but also broadened his canvas and refined his technique. The popular view is that he started as a boulevard lightweight and has since gone on to write increasingly dark and sombre plays. But there is more to it than that. I would say that he began as a ruthless and unsparing observer of sexual politics and middle-class manners. Now his subject is, more often than not, the state of the nation and the decline of our culture.

What is fascinating about Ayckbourn today is that he shows an ungovernable concern with the quality of British life: in particular, the prevailing moral, ethical and religious vacuum. The turning-point was obviously **Way Upstream** with its call to the shy, the sheepish and the non-committed to stand up to evil and to protect basic decencies. Since then Ayckbourn has written a number of plays just as much concerned with taking the moral temperature of the nation. **Woman in Mind** (1985) is not only about an emotionally neglected middle-aged woman's descent into madness but also about the failure of orthodox Christian morality to cope with individual unhappiness. **A Small Family Business** (1987) is as much a political play as Caryl Churchill's *Serious Money:* its very title invokes the entrepreneurial values we are all supposed to endorse and the action shows that those who make them their god end up endorsing theft, drug-trafficking and murder. In the futuristic **Henceforward** (1987) Ayckbourn posits a world where law and order have broken down and where people live in computerised bunkers enslaved by the very machines they have created. And in **Man of the Moment** (1988) he suggests we live in a world where the criminal is accorded heroic status, where his victim is regarded as a bit of a mug and where television offers daily distortions of reality.

Ayckbourn has become a much more pronounced moralist without sacrificing his capacity as an entertainer: his plays, with the exception of **A Small Family Business,** still get premiered in Scarborough where seaside audiences arrive looking for a good night out. As director of a theatre primarily devoted to new writing, he recently gave me a capsule definition of his whole philosophy: 'The brief I give writers is the one I was originally given by Stephen Joseph: by all means write what you want but for God's sake say it in a way that is going to appeal to people who come to the theatre. I think we encourage a healthy commercialism in the writer. In the end we say that if your message is an empty theatre it is useless. Let's see how clever we can be at saying unpalatable things in a palatable manner.' (pp. 164-65)

Ayckbourn has emerged in the late Eighties as our most complete man of the theatre: a writer, director and producer of boundless fertility. But in tracing his development during the decade one must begin with a work that both in its sheer scale and in its demands on its leading players has no exact precedent in the history of drama.

You leave a cinema but forget your raincoat. You go back and find in the next seat your future wife. Alan Ayckbourn once gave critic John Barber that example of the way our lives are governed by chance: the way a single moment may determine the whole pattern of our existence. It is an idea he pursues to its ultimate conclusion in **Intimate Exchanges:** a cycle of eight separate plays that present the characters with different choices leading to a totality of sixteen different versions comprising, in all, thirty-one scenes. Add to that the fact it is written for two actors and you have some idea of its complexity. (p. 167)

The question is: does **Intimate Exchanges** work? I would say 'Yes' and 'No'. The scheme is highly ambitious. The plays contain some of Ayckbourn's most brilliant writing. The practical problem is that you have to see or read all eight plays, with their multiple variations, to grasp the full complexity of what Ayckbourn is saying and in the real world that rarely happens. The plays were given with their original cast in Scarborough, Greenwich and for a season at the Ambassadors in London. They have since been seen in Toronto. But the tendency has been for regional companies to pick out the one play they prefer. The truth is you need to see all the plays to understand what Ayckbourn is driving at.

If he had taken up twenty hours of stage-time simply to prove that our lives are governed by chance, the work would be mechanical and repetitive. What Ayckbourn is actually saying is something much more complicated: that a momentary decision or a chance event may overturn our lives but that our destiny is also determined by character. In some plays the emphasis is on the fortuitous: in others people's lives remain obstinately untransformed because of who they are. *In toto,* the plays are about the contradictoriness of human existence and the casual way in which we often destroy those to whom we are closest.

But the whimsicality of chance and the mystery of human character are the twin ideas around which all the plays revolve. The operation of the former is seen at its most direct in the one that opens the cycle, **Affairs in a Tent.** Like all the others, it is set in and around Bilbury Lodge Preparatory School. Like all the others, it starts with Celia—the frustrated, menopausal wife of the school's headmaster Toby—deciding whether or not to have a cigarette (it may give smokers cause for cheer that in the four plays where she decides to have her first puff of the day she is a much nicer person than in the four where she disdains the weed). Like all the others, it spans a period of five years and ends in a churchyard.

As so often in Ayckbourn, the action springs from marital discontent and female frustration. Celia, who once worked for a firm that organised conferences, is trapped in a stale, pointless marriage to the alcoholic Toby who seethes with rage towards the world at large and who communicates with his wife largely through insult. So when Lionel Hepplewick, the school caretaker, comes to lay some crazy paving in Celia's garden and reveals himself to be a man of some sensitivity (who prefers Bruckner to Mahler) and ambition, it is not surprising that Celia responds to him both physically and intellectually. Here is a man of unrealised potential, like herself, who turns out to be a master baker ('A what?' Celia inquires, thinking she has misheard). Celia, in fit of slightly hysterical excitement, gets carried away by the idea of the two of them going into partnership and running their own bakery business.

At the end of the third scene a choice confronts Celia. Either she repents of her sudden rush of blood to the head, confesses all to her husband and tries to shake off the determined Lionel, or she tells Toby that she is going to leave him for a while to start up a new business venture. The latter choice leads into the central scene that gives the play its title. It is a piece of vintage Ayckbourn in that it starts as panic-stricken farce and ends with the total crack-up of the desperate heroine. The setting is a tea-tent during the School Sports Day where an overtaxed Celia is trying to cater for the VIPs with the help of nothing more than an iron-hard, monstrously inedible loaf baked by the ludicrously incompetent Lionel. It is a painful scene which climaxes in Celia presiding over an imaginary doll's tea-party and being wrapped up in a cloth by Miles, the Chairman of the Governors, and bundled under the table.

At this point we really do see how Ayckbourn's law of chance operates. In one scenario Toby, Celia's husband, enters to console his mummified wife and to promise to look after her always. That leads on to a final scene five years later in which Celia is a permanent invalid being looked after by a cossetting Toby while the hopeless Lionel has gone on to run a thriving fast-food joint known as Kwickieburgers. The other scenario has Lionel come in to rescue the trussed-up Celia who bites him in the leg for his pains and clings on to him for grim death. That leads to a final scene in which Celia is a high-powered executive with a luxury-food business, Lionel is her obeisant chauffeur and Toby is ekeing out his days in wretched solitude.

Clearly Ayckbourn is saying that chance is vital. If Toby discovers Celia during her tea-tent breakdown, she is doomed to a life of catatonic misery (one is reminded of Vera at the end of *Just Between Ourselves*). If Lionel discovers her, she eventually fulfils her potential but also sacrifices something of her humanity. Ayckbourn dramatises chance very skilfully. But in order to make his point he presents us with rather stark choices: Celia as pathetic wreck or Celia as bustling New Woman. And if Lionel is such a hopeless klutz who can't even bake a decent loaf or tend the school boiler without blowing it up, you rather wonder how he manages to turn into a successful entrepreneur. I am reminded, oddly enough, of *Romeo and Juliet* where Shakespeare undermines his own thesis that human affairs are governed by luck (or fate) by creating characters of such vividness that you feel they would transcend fortune. Although this play is very funny, Ayckbourn never quite solves this central problem; you feel that Celia and Lionel, particularly, are imagined in such depth that their lives would be determined by something more than the arbitrariness of chance.

But, as the plays go on, they become increasingly rich. The

characters acquire a novelistic density. The settings become ever more varied: one play revolves round a cricket match, another round a game of golf. What also happens is that Ayckbourn, like all good dramatists, starts to question and subvert his own thesis about the governing power of chance. By the time we get to the seventh play, *A One Man Protest,* Ayckbourn not only achieves a perfect synthesis between hilarity and despair but also leaves you feeling that we are all the victims of our own character. (pp. 169-72)

If there is any one message to be deduced from these multi-layered, seemingly contradictory, extraordinarily rich plays, it is that the pattern of our lives is determined by a multitude of things and that the illusion of chance is balanced by the imperatives of character. What is striking, however, is that the supposedly boulevard Ayckbourn is using the stage with the same kind of experimental freedom that writers like Robbe-Grillet and Sarraute brought to the *nouveau roman.* Ayckbourn may seem like an omniscient plotter mapping out the fate of his characters on the drawing-board but in the end this is less a thesis-drama than an extraordinarily open-ended exploration of human affairs, leaving us to decide whether chance or character has the upper-hand. (pp. 174-75)

[*A Chorus of Disapproval*] uses an amateur operatic society production of Gay's *The Beggar's Opera* as its springboard. It also has another unacknowledged source: Gogol's 1836 Russian comedy, *The Government Inspector.* In that, a humble St Petersburg clerk arrives in a small provincial town, is mistaken for the Inspector General and is enthusiastically fêted to prevent him exposing the bribery and corruption that is rampant in local government. You can see the hero as a calculating impostor. In fact, he is a happy-go-lucky nonentity who becomes whatever people wish him to be: in that sense, he resembles the lowly, blundering mafioso in David Mamet's film, *Things Change,* who remarks 'They always like you when you're someone else.'

Guy Jones, the hero of *A Chorus of Disapproval,* is very like Gogol's Khlestakov: a blank sheet upon whom the members of the community inscribe their own ruthlessness and ambition. When we first see him he has just enjoyed a modest triumph as Macheath in the Pendon Amateur Light Opera Society production of *The Beggar's Opera.* But the moment the curtain falls he is shunned by the rest of the cast and the play backtracks to explain why.

Guy has joined the Society as a lonely widower seeking to forge a new life after his wife's death. He is just a nice Guy who can't say No: a man whose moral conscience is no more than an echoing vacuum. The result is that he finds himself drawn into concurrent affaires with Hannah, the discontented wife of the production's shambling obsessive director, and with Fay Hubbard, a single-minded sexual swinger. Guy is also assumed to have insider knowledge of a proposed expansion by his firm which will greatly enhance the value of an adjacent piece of land which a number of people are hoping to buy cheap and sell dear. Partly because of his sexual availability and partly because he is thought to be acting on three different people's behalf over the land-sale, he finds himself rising within the company from the role of Crook-Fingered Jack to that of Filch and finally to the starring role itself. Guy's blank amorality promotes him within the company. The irony is that his personal rejection stems from his one act of altruism. He warns the land's owner of its rumoured purchase. This dishes Fay's husband, Ian, who has put both his wife and his role at Guy's disposal in the expectation of a return on his investment. In retaliation Ian tells the show's director, Dafydd, that he has been cuckolded by Guy. The hapless Guy winds up not only despised by lovers, friends and his director but also out of a job since his firm is contracting rather than expanding.

The social satire in the play works two ways. Obviously, Ayckbourn is exposing the greed, graft, corruption and the casual sexual promiscuity of these outwardly respectable Pendon burghers. But the play also exposes Guy as the innocent nonentity who wreaks havoc by his simple inability to say 'No'. In one sense, he harks back to Colin in **Absent Friends:** the well-meaning, also bereaved hero who destroys a whole network of human relationships with a cheerfully vacuous smile. In another sense, he anticipates Jack McCracken in **A Small Family Business:** as Ayckbourn remarked to Ian Watson, 'I was chasing the theme of inner corruption inside a society and how an honest man in a dishonest society looks like the biggest rogue of all.' Ayckbourn is, in fact, both using Guy as a means of uncovering the rottenness of this microcosmic society and at the same time warning us that it is the naïve nonentities in life who are often the most dangerous of people. Guy's weakness itself becomes culpable. And the point is clinched in a crucial scene where Guy turns up in the garden of Rebecca Huntley-Pike, the wife of the owner of the disputed piece of land, to return a bribe of £500 that has mysteriously arrived in the post. When Mrs Huntley-Pike suggests that Guy might do nothing to dispel the rumours about the impending sale, he reacts with a touch of maidenly horror. On the other hand, Guy is encouraged to keep the bribe. 'Guy', says the stage-directions, 'stares at the envelope undecided. He half moves away. He stops. After a second or so he returns to the money. He takes it up and pockets it.' Thus does Ayckbourn neatly spear the wibbly-wobbly moral vacillations of the Guys of this world.

It is no accident that Guy steps out of this scene straight into the costume of the highwayman Macheath; and part of the charm of this play is the way Ayckbourn uses Gay's opera to underscore the bubbling corruption of English life. Gay's popular ballad-opera showed eighteenth-century low-life to be a mirror-image of Sir Robert Walpole's bent political administration. With equal wit, Ayckbourn shows respectable pillars of the community jovially pretending to be thieves and robbers and then behaving with the same shark-like rapacity as the characters they are impersonating. (pp. 175-78)

Some people took the play to be a backstage farce on the lines of Michael Frayn's *Noises Off:* I see it as a Gogolian social comedy and proof of Ayckbourn's increasing interest in panoramic plays. He is now working with a wide-angled lens. But he also, in the characters of Hannah and Dafydd, pins down the pathos of a failed marriage with compassionate economy. Hannah (memorably incarnated at the National Theatre by Imelda Staunton as she crept apologetically into her own sitting-room) is a woman stunted by years of emotional neglect: Dafydd is an archetypal Welsh fanatic who has transferred his father's passion for Rugby football to the world of amateur theatre. You sense the aching loneliness of their marriage when Hannah reveals that the children have a Daddy-doll with whom they have tea, walks and supper ('I've stopped them taking it to bed with them now. I did think that was getting too much of a good thing'). But Ayckbourn also hints at a relationship haunted by some dark, unarticulated guilt. When Dafydd claims that Hannah is a woman of impenetrable frigidity who has virtually given up on sex ever since their wedding night, Guy cheerily points out that they still managed to have twins. To which Dafydd quickly replies 'Yes. Well we never talk about that. Never.' which leaves behind the unmistakable Strindbergian assumption that he may not be the actual father.

It is a sign of Ayckbourn's consummate maturity as a writer that he is able to weave so much sadness, pathos and bitterness into a play that is still a comedy. But then it is the very essence of late Ayckbourn that the dividing line between what is tragic and what is funny has become barely visible to the naked eye. One of the themes running through the play is that drama both feeds off life and excludes it: that the act of putting on a show, even *The Beggar's Opera* in Pendon, becomes all-consuming. Guy becomes methodically obsessive about his role as Crook-Fingered Jack even though it contains only one line. Dafydd graphically explains how getting the show on becomes paramount even when one's life and career are falling apart. And, in the best scene in the play, Ayckbourn demonstrates the devouring nature of theatre with heart-rending farce. While Dafydd uses Hannah and Guy to check the focus of his lighting, they are in the very middle of an agonising lovers' quarrel, in which Guy is trying to break off their relationship: thus the tromped, guileless, scruffy Dafydd, who has channelled whatever sexual urges he possessed into directing, potters about fixing lamps and perches, serenely oblivious to the fact that his wife and her lover are bitterly quarrelling as their relationship falls apart. You are caught between wind and water, laughter and tears as you so often are in Chekhov.

One argument used against Ayckbourn is that he despises his characters: that he presents us with what one critic called his 'familiar collection of frumps, nerds, creeps, would-be lovers and failed two-bit crooks from the suburbs.' But I sense neither loftiness nor derision in the writing. Steve Grant put it well in *Time Out* when he wrote that 'characters are observed in a gently objective way which reveals deficiency without moralising or rebuke.' Ayckbourn is certainly writing about crookedness, corruption, marital sadness and the mayhem caused by moral inertia. But he is writing a play, not reading us a lecture; and what he shows, with superb comic poignancy rather than sneery disdain, is how art consumes, shapes and organises life, leaving its participants infinitely sadder and wiser when it is over.

Women, it is commonly said, get a raw deal in our theatre. In many ways they do. (pp. 179-81)

Ayckbourn's play [**Woman in Mind**] . . . offers one of the most sympathetic, imaginative, compassionate accounts of womanhood written by any British dramatist since the war (Terence Rattigan's *The Deep Blue Sea* is its most serious rival). But the key word is 'imaginative'. Ayckbourn has written constantly about masculine insensitivity towards women and in **Just Between Ourselves** even wrote a particularly abrasive comedy about a woman driven into a state of catatonia by an uncomprehending husband. But Ayckbourn rather shudders at the label of 'feminist dramatist' and what is notable is that he never preaches at us about the way women are mistreated or abused by men. He makes his points through imaginative sympathy and through offering us ineradicable stage-pictures that lodge in our consciousness. 'Art' Shelley once wrote, 'ought not to go about doing good by direct moral precept but should content itself with invigorating people's imaginations and trust the invigorated imagination to do the moral good afterwards.' That is precisely how Ayckbourn goes to work.

What makes **Woman in Mind** unique in my experience is that it sees the action entirely from the protagonist's point-of-view: in that sense, it is the theatrical equivalent of the first-person novel. (pp. 181-82)

The woman is Susan. She is recovering from concussion by a garden-rake and in the opening minute of the play converses with a doctor, Bill Windsor, in a blurred nonsense-language that has faint echoes of the real thing. 'December bee?' she imagines the doctor saying. It is that phrase which snaps her back into a kind of sense, which gives the play its sub-title and its last line and which surely calls to mind Ayckbourn's prototype, *Hamlet,* in which the Ghost cries 'Remember me.' Like *Hamlet,* **Woman in Mind** is a play in which the protagonist is driven into a state of madness and is prey to visitation by equivocal phantoms (all right, singular in Shakespeare, plural here) who may be uttering important truths or who may be evil enchanters. 'The spirit that I have seen,' says Hamlet, 'may be a devil and the Devil hath power to assume a pleasing shape.' That is precisely Susan's predicament: as she sits in her garden, she conjures up an alternative, fantasy-family who may indeed be diabolical figures in pleasing form. I would not wish to push the comparison too far: other obvious differences aside, *Hamlet* is not a play in which the whole action takes place inside the hero's head. But I cannot believe that Ayckbourn did not have Shakespeare in mind and that he was not attracted by the idea of showing madness as a condition partly induced by a Hamlet-like alienation from one's surroundings.

Many plays, of course, deal with the supernatural. The unique thing about **Woman in Mind** is that Susan's real family and her fantasy-family start out as polar opposites existing in different dimensions but gradually merge in her imagination as the play proceeds. (pp. 182-83)

But if the play were simply contrasting reality and fantasy, it would offer a one-way ticket to nowhere: what it actually says is that the inability to distinguish between the two is a clinical symptom of madness. As Susan becomes more desperate, her two worlds start to merge; and what is fascinating is how Ayckbourn suggests, through purely theatrical means, that the Barbara Cartland-style fantasy-family may be demons. Not only do they start to put words into Susan's mouth and anticipate her every thought: they start to behave in a demonstrably cruel manner. Early on in the play Ayckbourn plants the idea of a neighbouring dog whose howls are inaudible to Susan. Later Gerald comes in to announce that Mrs Ogle next door is distressed over the loss of her dog. A minute later, as the sky ominously darkens, Susan's fantasy-brother enters with a blood-stained game-bag the contents of which he significantly refuses to disclose. This is typical both of Ayckbourn's thrift and of the way he offers strong visual, as well as verbal, hints of the malign tenacity of Susan's phantom-family.

Obviously Ayckbourn is writing primarily in **Woman in Mind** about the symptoms and causes of madness. He has acknowledged the influence of Oliver Sacks's *The Man Who Mistook His Wife For A Hat.* He has also revealingly remarked that he chose a woman as his protagonist because people would treat a man very differently in that situation and presumably step in earlier to take remedial action. But although this is a more private, less panoramic play than **A Chorus of Disapproval** it is, I believe, still dealing with an important public issue: the failure of religion in the modern world to cope with mental distress.

Consider. Susan is the wife of a clergyman and clearly has a Manichean notion of good and evil. Almost her first reaction on discovering that she is unstable is to ask 'Why have I gone to hell? Why me, I've tried so terribly hard too. Terribly hard . . . ' It is quite clear that Gerald has failed her on the most basic level as a husband. They sleep in separate beds, they don't kiss, they hardly even touch. And when Gerald asks if she is implying that sex is all that mattered in their relationship, she replies:

> All I'm saying is, that once that's gone—all
> *that*—it becomes important. Over-important
> really. I mean before when we—it was just some-
> thing else we did together. Like gardening. Only
> now I have to do that on my own as well.

But if Gerald is a lousy husband he is an even worse cleric. Even when Susan has come to believe that she is demonically possessed, she makes it clear that Gerald is the last person that she would consult on spiritual matters. With his batty book on the history of the Parish since 1386, Gerald represents the kind of clergyman who regards himself as a custodian of tradition and history rather than a man of incandescent faith. It is interesting that Alan Bennett in his TV series, *Talking Heads,* wrote a powerful and not dissimilar monologue about a vicar's wife driven into the arms of an Asian grocer in Leeds while her husband largely concerned himself with the flower arrangements in church. What both Ayckbourn and Bennett seem to be saying is that too many churchmen are indifferent to the suffering that takes place under their own noses.

Susan's sister-in-law, Muriel, is also a believer. But in her case faith takes the form of an eccentric spiritualism and the unsustainable belief that her late husband, Harry, is trying to get through to her by inscribing messages on the ceiling. Even Gerald, in his waffly way, tries to point out that although Harry may be *there* in general he is not *here* in particular: immanent but not imminent. And Susan tartly points out that 'It does seem to me that God, in his infinite wisdom and with the entire cosmos to choose from is unlikely to base the Kingdom of Heaven around Muriel's bedroom.' For Muriel, religion is simply a form of psychic self-delusion. As for Rick, who has retreated into a Trappist order in Hemel Hempstead from which he suddenly emerges to announce that he is married and about to make a new life in Thailand, he simply represents the declension of religion into a narcissistic sectarianism. I doubt that Ayckbourn sat down to write a tractarian work about the failure of religion to measure up to mental crisis. But what the play actually shows is Susan deserted, in her hour of crisis, by God's representative and Christian love. The consequence is that she falls into the arms of the Devil: quite literally, since she ends up being made love to by Satanic Andy (her onetime dream-husband) on her own back lawn in the middle of a thunderstorm at three in the morning. And any doubt that Andy and his accomplices are diabolical is dispelled when a fire breaks out in Gerald's study destroying all but one page of his precious book and a sign appears on his sister's bedroom ceiling with the immemorial injunction, apparently from her late husband, 'Knickers off Muriel.'

With this play the dated notion of Ayckbourn as a mild-mannered farceur is decisively laid to rest. He is writing about madness, menopausal female frustration and the failure of religion to do its proper work in the world. The miracle is that the play still manages to be hugely funny: the very factors that oppress Susan are made biliously comic and there are numerous little Ayckbourn curlicues, such as Bill Windsor's touching blindness to the fact that his wife is quite obviously having an affaire with his senior partner. (pp. 184-87)

Ayckbourn is not the first dramatist to see a solid English family as a symbol of conscienceless corruption. J. B. Priestley's *An Inspector Calls* (1946) takes apart the smug, safe, mahogany-and-leather world of the Birlings and shows how every member of the family shares responsibility for the suicide of a young girl: Father has sacked her from his factory, Daughter has had her discharged from a shop, Son has seduced her, Mother has had her barred from charity. Everyone shares in the moral guilt.

A Small Family Business . . . has certain affinities with Priestley's play: an inspector even calls though he is not remotely like Priestley's steely embodiment of conscience. But what makes Ayckbourn's play uniquely his is its brilliant combination of morality and farce. It is as political as Caryl Churchill's *Serious Money* in its devastating assault on the way we live now and on the way the entrepreneurial values we have been told to foster have become a mask for fraud, theft and wholesale self-deceit: by the end of a richly-plotted evening the words 'family' and 'business' have acquired sinister *mafioso* overtones. But the play, although it deals with bribery, blackmail, theft, industrial espionage, sado-masochism, drug-trafficking and homicide, is still biliously funny. In its use of a split-level suburban set to suggest the different houses of various

members of the same family, it also affords wonderful scope for fluidity of action. It reminds one yet again that Ayckbourn the playwright is as much a master-craftsman as a shipwright or a wheelwright.

It may be a morality play but it is anything but simpleminded: indeed it is compact with irony. On the surface, it shows honest, upright, undevious Jack McCracken taking over the family furniture firm, Ayres and Graces, and delivering a brisk moral homily on the importance of Faith and Trust. But Jack is forced to compromise his own principles when a slimy private detective, Hough, arrives to announce that Samantha, Jack's teenage daughter, has been caught shoplifting. After a good deal of huffing and puffing, Jack is eventually forced to buy off Hough with the promise of a security job at Ayres and Graces. To his horror, Jack also discovers that the family produce is being pirated and appearing on foreign markets under different labels. It transpires that it is a cunning family racket operated by Jack's brother-in-law, Desmond, who sells off the unlabelled furniture via the back door, and by Jack's brother, Cliff, and his wife Anita, who then buy the furniture 'legitimately' and resell it to an Italian firm called Rivetti. Since Hough has also discovered the racket, Jack is forced to act as bagman for the family, offering the private eye ever larger sums to procure his silence. When Hough asks for an unrealistically large amount, Jack emphatically draws the line at murder: somewhat needlessly since Hough has been inadvertently killed by Jack's wife and two daughters. The play ends, as it has begun, with a celebratory family party at which Jack accedes—after an initial show of reluctance—to the use of the furniture distribution network as an outlet for the Rivetti drug-ring.

Obviously Ayckbourn is writing about the slippery nature of moral compromise: the way a concession on a relatively small matter leads to a series of ever-greater concessions until an upright businessman ends up as a mafioso *capo*. He is also showing the Ten Commandments going down like ninepins. (pp. 187-89)

In *Way Upstream* Ayckbourn wrote a fable about evil. In *Woman in Mind* he showed the fallibility of religion. In this play he demonstrates what happens to a world devoid of God or even any basic moral precepts. But Ayckbourn is also a master ironist and depicts Jack McCracken not simply as a good man drawn insidiously into a network of corruption but as a man who in some ways is the architect of his own downfall. He makes a fine speech at the beginning about the importance of Effort and Trust. At the same time, Ayckbourn implies that his brand of inflexible morality makes no allowance for human weakness and that he is a negligent father whose indifference to Samantha (to whom he hardly speaks) has pushed her into the reclusive world of drugs. Jack's initial refusal to trade with Hough and allow his daughter to be prosecuted ('Where does it end, for one thing?' he prophetically enquires) may be morally correct. It is also unfeeling as his remark 'Look, to hell with Sammy, there's a principle at stake' graphically indicates. With considerable subtlety, Ayckbourn portrays Jack as a man whose honesty is theoretically admirable but whose indifference to his daughter is culpable; and this is clearly expressed through the drug issue which runs through the whole play. It is one of the play's numerous bitter ironies that it is Samantha who gives Hough the push into the tin-bath that kills him and that, as the stage-directions tell us, 'one gathers she was in a fairly dazed state when she started'. And, in a resonant final image, while Jack is agreeing to deals with the drug-trafficking Rivettis and the family is celebrating its solidarity, Samantha is alone upstairs in the bathroom mainlining.

That is the kind of effect it is very hard to convey in cold print. But one of the triumphs of the play is the way Ayckbourn uses the multiple rooms of his split-level set to suggest that people in one area are unaware of what is going in another. He uses this to hilarious effect at the beginning with the whole family crowded into Jack's sitting room for a party while Jack is stampeding through the hall and up the stairs divesting himself of his clothes and telling his wife that he is Erik the Hairy Viking with his big 'meaty axey'. Finally, Poppy retreats into the sitting-room where the trouserless Jack rampageously follows her only to discover a roomful of guests. This doesn't merely get the play off to a rousing start. It immediately establishes Jack as a sympathetic, red-blooded guy with whose physical predicament we can all identify; which is vital if we are to follow him in his labyrinthine moral predicament as the play progresses.

But Ayckbourn's most potent theatrical device is seen later on when Jack is busy rushing from one house to another trying to raise more loot to blackmail Hough while Hough himself is prowling through Jack's house trying to find a briefcase stuffed with notes. At one moment, we see Jack on ground level alone in Cliff's house while the creepy, reptilian, insidious Hough is tiptoeing into Jack's upper-storey bedroom where Poppy is hiding. A part of us wants to cry out a warning to Jack to go to his wife's rescue; except of course that Jack is in another house altogether. Ayckbourn plays with the properties of space much as Shakespeare does with the duality of time: both space and time have a double existence on the theatrical and the real level. Ayckbourn also plays skilfully on the audience's complex emotional and moral reactions to Hough's death. In practice I have noticed it is greeted with a mixture of horrified shock and yelping amusement; and the truth is that one side of us wants to see this perverted, rapacious monster, wrestling with the three women for possession of the briefcase, get his just deserts while another side of us withdraws in revulsion. To play on two emotions simultaneously is one of the highest dramatic skills. Ayckbourn does it here beautifully, not only by building up the suspense from moment to moment (we know something dreadful is going to happen but we half hope it won't) but also by having Jack inveighing against murder ('That's it. That's it. We have reached the pit. We have touched the sewage. We are back on all fours.') only seconds before it is about to be committed in his own house.

When Poppy finally confronts Jack with a corpse in the bloodstained bath all she can feebly say is 'I'm very sorry, Jack' (a line that gets a big laugh). But one of the points Ayckbourn is making in the play is that our moral sensibilities have become blunted because we constantly clothe things in euphemistic language. Jack says to his wife concerning the corpse 'We're going to get things cleared up and then we're going to put all this lot behind us' as if a dead body were simply a bit of unsavoury garbage. Earlier, Jack, clutching a suitcase containing five thousand pounds in notes, refers to it as 'Just paper. Bits of—bits of paper.' Anita, who is an S and M pro if ever there was one, conveniently describes herself as 'an amateur'. And people constantly talk of 'salting it away' when they are referring to money they have stolen. Until we use the right language, Ayckbourn suggests, we shall never be able to confront the consequences of our actions; and until we stop hero-worshipping the criminal (Jack's elder daughter, Tina, finds her respect for her wimpy husband has shot up ever since she discovered he was involved in the family racket) we shall sink further into a state of moral vacuity.

But again Ayckbourn's great gift is that he shows rather than tells. He doesn't harangue his audience about the evils of capitalism. He simply offers us a comic fable about a recognisably ordinary family whose materialistic hunger has allowed them to slither into crime. He also uses humour as the bait with which to hook his audience. I recall sitting at the Olivier behind a middle-aged couple who as the play started nudged each other with delight in the expectation of a harmless diversion. As the evening went on, they still laughed but without quite the same conspiratorial mutual glee as they showed at the beginning as if the argument of the play were penetrating their comfortable exteriors. I would guess that was precisely the effect Ayckbourn was after.

Ayckbourn is not a reassuring writer. His special talent is for stating uncompromising truths in a theatrically acceptable manner; and indeed all his recent work treads a delicate tightrope between comedy and despair (rightly so since as the heroine says in Peter Shaffer's *Lettice and Lovage,* 'Without danger there is no theatre'). But in **Henceforward** Ayckbourn has written his bleakest play yet: one that still manages to wring laughter out of desperation but also one that presents us, both in terms of its governing images and its prevailing ideas, with a pessimistic vision.

Three central, and closely related, themes thread their way through the play. One concerns the dilemma of the creative artist—in this case, a composer called Jerome—parasitically feeding off the lives, the emotions and needs of those closest to him. It is a problem that has guiltily obsessed writers down the ages and that Ibsen dealt with hauntingly in his last play, *When We Dead Awaken.* There, an aged sculptor, Rubek, is confronted by a former model, Irene, whose palpable human love he has sacrificed to the demands of his calling. 'Before all else,' he says, 'I was an artist. And I was sick—sick with a longing to create the one great work of my life. It was to be called "The Day of Resurrection".' In just such a manner Ayckbourn's Jerome, whose governing desire is 'to express the feeling of love in an abstract musical form', finally rejects proffered human love in order to capture what he sees as its essence on his digital keyboard.

Allied to the artist's specific dilemma is the universal theme of modern man's increasing subordination to technology (and the play is set in the not-too-distant future): as Charles Osborne wrote, 'we are all programmed, Ayckbourn seems to be telling us, no longer using but used by the technology we have created.' Thus Jerome lives in a computerised bunker surrounded by keyboards, synclaviers and video-screens flashing up messages of desperation from a beleaguered friend. Jerome is even serviced by an android, NAN 300F (which in the first act resembles his wife and in the second that of an idealised fiancée-companion) to which he relates more easily than people.

Closely allied to that is the notion of a society that is on the edge of breakdown: a Dystopian vision of hell in which outer London suburbs like Edgware are policed by mobs of vigilante feminists (the Daughters of Darkness) with purple stripes tattooed across their faces and in which even Kilburn is filled with regular armed patrols and masses of security cameras. Ayckbourn recounted to Ian Watson the story of an art historian in West Yorkshire who was frightened to walk to the shops because of the primitive tribes roaming around his house. Ayckbourn is projecting into the future the fear many people have today of walking the streets. But he is also suggesting that, even inside this *Clockwork Orange* society, lonely, isolated individuals still struggle to create art.

Ayckbourn's vision is dark, strong and clear. The problem he encounters is that, theatrically, it takes a good deal of time to establish both the precise nature of this nightmare universe and the racking, stunted solitude of Jerome himself: the result is that the first act plays a little slowly and that it is only in the second a genuine tension arises from the conflict between man and machine. In the second act—with the introduction of fresh characters—there is also a much stronger element of social comedy to alleviate the prevailing harshness. Oddly enough, the play gets funnier as it gets blacker and as it starts to exploit Henri Bergson's proposition that 'We laugh every time a person gives us the impression of being a thing': in this play, we laugh the more things start to behave like people.

In fact, the play starts with Jerome tinkering with NAN 300F—the prototype for an automatic child-minder that never went into full production—and Ayckbourn gets some good laughs both out of the sight of Jerome with his hand up her skirt and out of the android's split personality: she has both the brisk solicitude of a nanny and the reproving tones of a deceived wife. Jerome, it transpires, has been left by his wife Corinna and their daughter Geain (pronounced Jane) and in the four years since their departure has suffered a monumental creative block. He has even been forbidden to see his own daughter. And in an effort to convince the Department of Child Wellbeing and Corinna (both due to pay him a visit) that he is a fit father, he is auditoning a young actress, Zoe, to play the role of the perfect fiancée-companion and to help create an impression of domestic bliss. Zoe is touched by his story, goes to bed with him but is appalled the next morning to discover that every moment of their lovemaking has been recorded by Jerome. Since he cannot even understand her moral qualms about having their most intimate experiences recorded, reprocessed and used as raw artistic material, she sweeps out into vigilante-patrolled Edgware. Je-

rome decides the only solution is to reprogramme NAN in Zoe's image also using her vocal rhythms and inflexions.

Ayckbourn skilfully interweaves his three dominant themes in this act. Jerome is trying mechanically to achieve the sound of love but, in human terms, is incapable of understanding it. His life has also been taken over by blinking, flashing screens and machines that put a barrier between himself and reality; his musical friend, Lupus, keeps appearing on the video-screen with cries for help which Jerome easily ignores. And the menace of the streets is indicated by Zoe's arrival torn and bleeding after an encounter with the Daughters of Darkness who proceed to throw bricks at the barricaded shutters. But although the ideas lock securely into place it is, unusually for Ayckbourn, an act rather lacking in narrative momentum. We are exactly halfway through before we discover precisely why Jerome has hired Zoe and there is a faint air of doodling about the proceedings. Ayckbourn is so busy giving us the atmosphere—as in Jerome's remark that 'Since they fully automated the hypermarket, I don't think I've spoken to anyone for months'—that he almost forgets the obligation to keep the story driving onwards.

The second act is much richer both because it reminds us that Jerome's obsession with technology is universal and because it sharpens the conflict of man versus machine. It also *embodies* the central issue of the play in a chilling, funny horrendous image: the spectacle of NAN reprogrammed as Zoe dressed like an old-style Southern belle and reacting to every remark made to her by Corinna and Mervyn, the berk from Social Services, with a chirpy, robotical brightness. It is funny for sound, Bergsonian reasons: the way, for instance, NAN-Zoe greets everyone mechanically with a cry of 'Hallo. Hallo. Hallo. Welcome. Welcome. Welcome' like a demented parody of a TV chat-show host. It is chilling (in the way the first act isn't) because we already have seen the gauche, dippy, sexy, flesh-and-blood Zoe before she was turned into this Super-doll. And it is horrendous exactly because we see that Jerome is more at ease with the programmed android than he was with the unpredictable, unprogrammed Zoe. In the first act, Ayckbourn sometimes seems to be illustrating a thesis: in this act, he shows the consequences of his ideas in action.

But Ayckbourn also brings on new characters in this act and widens the social range. What is tragic in Jerome becomes comic in Mervyn, whose pocket-phones are always bleeping at inappropriate moments and whose Italian thermal singlet has to be unravelled at one point as if it were the intestines of a dead sheep. Jerome's daughter, Geain, also turns out not to be some idealised Goldilocks but a booted, belted, studded, vaguely threatening thug whom her father unkindly compares to a 'transvestite truck-driver' (another sign of his inability to cope with reality though in this case one can hardly blame him). And Corinna turns out to be not quite the rancorous, vindictive monster we had been led to expect but a surprisingly vulnerable, 40-year-old bank manager who sits crying in her office and who actually wants Jerome back.

These are not merely standard comic reversals. Ayckbourn is making the point that humankind is complex, contradictory, confused, messy and, above all, phenomenally *interesting* in a way that machines never can be. Jerome's whole tragedy is that he cannot see that; and it is symbolised by the moment where he defends the NAN 300F model even though production was aborted after one of them put a baby in a microwave over:

> MERVYN. I don't see how you can possibly take the side of a machine against a human being.
>
> JEROME. Against most human beings, very easily. If human beings behaved a bit less like human beings and a bit more like machines, we'd all be better off. . . .

That is Jerome's predicament in a nutshell; but the full tragedy of his position only becomes clear in the closing seconds. Corinna's reiterated cry of 'Love' in conversation has given him the vocal pattern he needs for his perfect sound; and at the end he rejects wife, daughter and life itself to play with the synthesised sound, oblivious to the fact that missiles are clanging against the shutters and the Daughters of Darkness have penetrated his inner sanctum. As the stage directions indicate: 'He sits all alone. And realizes how alone he is.' (pp. 190-99)

Ayckbourn never stands still. With each new play what he does, like any artist, is to elaborate on his obsessive themes and, at the same time, explore new ideas and experiment technically. He knows that each play has to appeal directly to his faithful Scarborough audience. At the same time, he is always trying to push the frontiers of drama outwards.

Man of the Moment (his 35th major, full-length play which had its Scarborough premiere in August, 1988) is a perfect demonstration of this and a brilliantly achieved piece of work. It continues the exploration of the nature of evil which really began with *Way Upstream* in 1981. It also shows Ayckbourn, as in *A Small Family Business,* wrestling with the problem of writing a comedy that includes a violent death. But he is doing much else in this play. He is dealing with a crucial reversal of moral values in our society that elevates villains to heroic status and that quickly throws true heroes on to the discard pile. . . . He is also tackling head-on the way television distorts and manipulates reality and often ignores the real truth about human beings. And, most daringly of all, he is writing a play in which much of the action is retrospective: not since Ibsen's *Rosmersholm* can I recall a play that depended so much for its effect on a recapitulation of past events and the way they continue to haunt the present.

The framework for the play is an attempt by a pushy, ambitious young TV presenter, Jill Rillington, to bring together an erstwhile bank robber, Vic Parks, and a one-time bank clerk, Douglas Beechey, who 'had a go' at him during a raid seventeen years previously. Vic, having served a nine-year sentence, is now a media star with two television series, a best-selling, sanitised autobiography and a huge popular following to his credit. He also lives part of the year, with his wife and family, in a Spanish Mediterranean villa where the TV programme, *Their Paths Crossed,* is to be shot. Douglas, who enjoyed a brief,

transitory fame as a popular hero seventeen years ago, is now a forgotten figure working for a firm of double-glazing consultants in his native Purley. It turns out that his act of heroism in tackling the bank-robbing Vic was prompted by his unrequited passion for a beautiful bank clerk, Nerys. In the ensuing mêlée, Nerys was shot in the face by Vic and scarred for life. Because Douglas was the one person who continued visiting her in hospital, they ended up getting married and are now contented with their lot, although they have forsworn sex for the last fifteen years and Nerys lives as a virtual recluse.

Jill Rillington's purpose in bringing Doug and Vic together again is to contrast the dowdy Purley existence of one with the glitzy celebrity lifestyle of the other and to depict Doug as a man envious of his former antagonist's success. But she is baffled at every turn by Doug's apparent dullness and admiration for Vic. History, however, repeats itself when Vic, an unreformed egotistical monster, is confronted by a wild onslaught from Doug. Vic, who throughout bullies and dominates the women around him, stands jeeringly by while the kid's nurse, Sharon, attempts to drown herself out of love for him. He wrestles with his wife, Trudy, who is outraged by his callousness. Vic is butted in the midriff by Doug, topples into the pool and is dragged under water by Sharon and subsequently dies. But, at the end, we see the poolside events reconstructed by actors for the benefit of the TV cameras and a studio audience. What, in effect, was murder is presented as a needless accident with Jill, who has missed the real story, solemnly telling the viewers 'That night marked not only the end of a life but the end of a living legend.'

As so often, Ayckbourn is dealing with good and evil and indicating that we live in a society that ignores the former and rewards the latter. Unlike Vince in *Way Upstream* who too nakedly embodies the Fascist spirit in action, Vic in this play is an instantly recognisable figure: the one-time criminal whose gift of the gab has turned him into a popular media star. But Ayckbourn's key point is that we sentimentalise such figures by turning them into adored celebrities. He makes it quite clear that Vic owes his public fame to the way he articulates a kind of late-Eighties populist aggression: Jill recalls at the end Vic's advice to a young viewer, 'Don't complain to me that people kick you when you're down. It's your own fault for lying there, isn't it.' That, in slightly exaggerated form, catches all too accurately the *sauve-qui-peut* philosophy of Britain today. Vic is presented as the people's champion; but we also see him, in private, as a bullying vulgarian who treats his wife, the children's nanny and the Spanish maid with a similar patronising contempt. In a line of stunning perceptiveness—one of the best in all Ayckbourn—Trudy remarks: 'He's like a lot of men I've met. They don't quite know what to do with a woman when they've got her so they shout at her.' And in a wickedly funny foretaste of the final drowning (and in an apt comment on TV values) Ayckbourn at the end of the first act shows Vic and the rest ignoring the fact that the Spanish gardener, Ruy, is struggling for his life in the pool and thereby interrupting a crucial establishing shot. The scene is played as farce and had the audience at Scarborough collapsing with laughter; but it nonetheless subliminally contributes to the atmosphere of evil and is part of the pattern of ironic repetition Ayckbourn uses throughout the play. (pp. 199-202)

The play's fundamental irony, however, is that Jill Rillington, the TV interviewer, knows in advance what she wants her programme to say, is disappointed and frustrated when reality turns out to be otherwise and then misses the real story when some of her initial suspicions are confirmed. She hauls Douglas out to Spain in the hope of catching his resentment towards and envy of the gold-plated shit, Vic. She then finds that Douglas is dismayingly happy as he is and has not the slightest desire to have a particle of the good life enjoyed by Vic: she even finds he has no desire to travel abroad, least of all to Sweden:

> DOUGLAS. Not attracted sorry. Despite their standard of living they always look a rather glum sort of people, don't you think? They certainly do on the television.
>
> JILL. Well, you can't always go by everything (she checks herself). Possibly.

But Ayckbourn delivers his final blow to the cathode-ray tube when he contrasts the messy, ugly, farcical circumstances of Vic's drowning with the clean, tidied-up, orderly version restaged by actors for the benefit of the TV audience. The fat and rather ungainly nanny is now delectably slim (though she has also become 'this simple, semiliterate version from Macclesfield'), the house-servants are more authentically Spanish and even the country and western music issuing from the house is now more romantic than it originally was. Everything is false, untrue, mythical; and we, by being treated as if we were the studio-audience, become conspirators in this fraudulent attempt to recreate reality.

This is Ayckbourn at the top of his bent: using comedy both to state fundamental truths about human nature and also to send us out of the theatre questioning the kind of topsy-turvy values of our society and the mendacity of our most popular form of communication. It is also a phenomenally daring play in that two-thirds of it consists of recapitulated action that explains precisely why people behave as they do in the present. But, with each new play, Ayckbourn seems to become a richer writer. He uses drama to say disquieting things while still taking his audience with him. He is a comic pessimist, a farcial Diogenes who takes an increasingly sombre view of the state of modern Britain while still giving audiences the tonic of laughter and a good night out. (pp. 204-05)

Revenge is clearly the theme [of the two-part play *The Revengers' Comedies*]. . . . And, lest we were in any doubt, the Scarborough programme was peppered with quotations that emphasised both the futility of revenge and, intriguingly, the fact that it is a particularly feminine weapon. Bacon's humanist condemnation ('A man that studieth revenge keeps his own wounds green, which otherwise would heal and do well') was balanced by quotations from Nietzsche ('In revenge and in love woman is more barbarous than man'), Molière ('A woman always has her revenge ready') and many others, implying a sexual distinction in the operation of revenge. Not the least fascinating feature of the play is seeing Ayckbourn, the instinctive

feminist, for the first time creating a female character of ruthless, implacable evil.

Ayckbourn is a matchless deviser of plots but, on this occasion, there is a clear and obvious source: the Patricia Highsmith novel, and subsequently Hitchcock film, *Strangers on a Train,* in which a totally innocent party gets caught up in a madman's obsessive desire for a double revenge-murder. But Ayckbourn begins, characteristically, on a note of brilliant comedy. Henry Bell, a sad little man who has been deserted by his wife and ousted from his job in a multi-national by the aggressively opportunist Bruce Tick, is about to throw himself off Albert Bridge. Just as he is about to kill himself he hears a cry for help from another would-be suicide, Karen Knightly. Self-slaughter turns to an act of Samaritanism as he rescues the impaled woman and together they repair to a motorway café to compare notes. Henry has been stung by the loss of his job. Karen is grieving over the loss of her lover, a married West Country farmer, who has apparently been lured away by his scheming and devious wife, Imogen Staxton-Billing. It is Karen who suggests that, instead of lamenting their fate, they each take care of each other's problem. Karen will, in some unspecified way, 'do for' the appalling Tick if Henry will wreak appropriate revenge on the Machiavellian Imogen. Shell-shocked by the Albert Bridge encounter, and lured into bed by the wily Karen at her 58-room family mansion, Henry dazedly agrees.

It is a blithe premise for a comedy in that it thrusts the twin protagonists into totally alien and unfamiliar worlds; and much of the fun lies in seeing how they either do or don't adjust. The criss-cross plotting is beautifully done with wealthy, beautiful Karen turning herself into a flat-heeled frump in order to get taken on as Bruce Tick's temporary secretary. Ayckbourn makes us relish her deviousness by depicting the dreaded Tick as an arrogant, opinionated, eructating boor and by showing Karen herself to be a woman of matchless ingenuity: as in *Les Liaisons Dangereuses* we are drawn into the conspiracy by a delight in tactics. Karen's method is to ruin Tick's home-life by sending breathy messages down the phone to his wife and sending sexy nighties through the post, suggesting that an affaire is in full swing. But Ayckbourn's most audacious stroke, as in **A Small Family Business** and **Man of the Moment,** is to make us virtual accomplices to murder. We long to see Tick get what's coming to him; and, in the superb scene where Karen (exuding a leggy glamour) interrupts a rendezvous between Tick and his estranged wife, we experience an horrific exhilaration as Tick slumps dead to the floor with a heart attack. This is top-flight Ayckbourn in that it manages to induce in the audience a macabre pleasure and a moral shock *both at the same time.*

But Ayckbourn gets double value out of his plot by contrasting Karen's smooth success in the world of office politics with Henry's visible discomfort with a life of rural grandeur. Kitted out in new togs by Karen, he is mistaken by the locals for her accountant. Left to his own devices in the vast, gloomy family mansion (also occupied by Karen's strangely laid-back brother) he finds himself at the mercy of a dragon-housekeeper and a nervously incompetent apprentice servant: Ayckbourn's gift for visual humour (reaching way back to *Mr Whatnot*) comes out superbly in the scene where the terrified, butter-fingered servant-girl finds even the dispatch of cornflakes to the plate too much for her. But Henry's greatest crisis comes when he discovers that his intended victim, Imogen Staxton-Billing, is not the diabolical siren he had been led to expect but a deceived and neglected wife with whom he falls instantly in love. (pp. 205-08)

This first play strikes me as a small masterpiece built around a series of deftly-woven contrasts: city versus country; female guile versus masculine helplessness; cold-hearted ruthlessness versus awakening tenderness. On the one hand, Ayckbourn gleefully enlists us in Karen's cause by making her victim a prize Tick (the kind of man who advertises his marital fidelity by announcing of his wife, 'I leave my balls back there with her in Sunningdale'). On the other hand, he makes us care about the growingly tender relationship between Henry and Imogen, who are thrown together after she has been severed from her horse in a riding accident. We want one part of the revenge-pact to succeed just as much as we want the other half to fail. But Ayckbourn also gets maximum value out of the contrast between the corporate warren of multi-national life and the enforced intimacy of the countryside where, as Karen says, 'You can't stop seeing people just because you've slept with them—otherwise you'd end up a hermit.'

The first half of *The Revengers' Comedies* is superb: the second half is less satisfying. Karen has accomplished her mission: Henry has no wish to fulfil his side of the bargain. So where does the plot have to go? In fact, Ayckbourn shows Karen worming her way to the top of the corporate heap by all kinds of devious tricks reminiscent of *How To Succeed In Business Without Really Trying*. It's all quite fun but you feel there is no reason for Karen to stay on in London once she has done what she set out to do. The rural scenes work far better since poor, blundering Henry gets the wrong end of the stick and spreads a rumour that Imogen's husband is having an improbable affaire with the Knightly's slightly dim-witted servant-girl. Henry has sullied the man's honour and broken the ethical code of country life and, in a scene of wonderfully dotty inventiveness, he is challenged to a duel which takes place under cover of a woodland shooting-party. The scene (arguably the first duel in modern drama since *Three Sisters*) is lunatically preposterous. At the same time, it neatly epitomises Ayckbourn's idea of the English countryside as a place full of dated concepts of male honour and hidden violence.

But, although the second play has some excellent scenes, Ayckbourn temporarily loses sight of his central concern: revenge. Instead, he becomes more interested in the opposition of good and evil. Henry, redeemed and given new purpose by his love for Imogen, clearly represents good while Karen, an increasingly dark and sinister figure who has apparently burned her parents alive in a summer-house blaze, is the embodiment of unmitigated evil. In a *Sunday Times* profile Ayckbourn remarked that, 'There used to be a Christian consensus in this country about how people should behave. Now there is none. There is no moral leadership.' Ever since *Way Upstream* his plays have increasingly reflected what he sees as a spiritual crisis

and, in particular, the way the moral vacuum in British life is being filled by those who enjoy the naked use of power: characters like Vince in *Way Upstream,* Vic in *Man of the Moment* and now Karen, whose upper-crust charm conceals a diabolical destructiveness.

Root-and-branch daemonism is a difficult concept to handle, and, although Karen is a fascinating character, we never quite find out what makes her tick. Is she the victim of class, environment, upbringing? Or is Ayckbourn simply saying that certain people are born with inherently warped and destructive natures? We are never quite sure; and my feeling is that Ayckbourn is far more secure with a character like Jack McCracken in *A Small Family Business*—who stumbles into moral chaos more by accident than by design—than he is with a figure of abnormal nastiness like Karen. In all his plays Ayckbourn is superb at showing how we destroy ourselves and others through small daily acts of indifference and casual cruelty. When he creates a walking monster, a female Iago, like Karen we crave more information about the circumstances that shape her.

But although *The Revengers' Comedies* is not exactly flawless, it does say something important about the vain, empty, boomerang nature of revenge. It also, in its final symmetrical scene on Albert Bridge where Henry is forced to choose between the harsh imperatives of Karen and the instinctive warmth of Imogen, shows life triumphing over death, love over hate and the continuity of existence over neurotic frenzy. It is, in the end, one of Ayckbourn's most optimistic works. It also shows him at 50 still experimenting, still pushing the frontiers outwards, still seeking that mysterious, elusive property: the perfect play. The public has always appreciated him. The signs are that critics and fellow-artists (who recently elected him, in an *Observer* poll, the Playwrights' Playwright) are beginning to realise that he is the best comic dramatist since Molière. (pp. 208-11)

Michael Billington, in his Alan Ayckbourn, *second edition, Macmillan Education Ltd., 1990, 225 p.*

Kate Muir   (essay date 24 May 1991)

[*In the following excerpt, Muir discusses* Wildest Dreams *and comments on Ayckbourn's status as a popular playwright.*]

As the most regularly performed playwright in Britain (Shakespeare comes a poor second at the moment), Mr Ayckbourn's talents have at last been recognised by the academic establishment, and he will follow Stephen Sondheim and Sir Ian McKellen in the year-long Oxford post. There is a frisson of sniffiness about the appointment of such a populist, the creator of such titles as *Bedroom Farce* and *How the Other Half Loves,* as though Jeffrey Archer had been asked to lecture in English literature.

But Mr Ayckbourn is endearingly direct. He admits he would not know a seminar if he met it in his soup. "I'm a complete fraud. I never even went to university, so I think the course will be intensely practical, not theoretical." He will teach what he is good at, writing and directing, bringing whole plays and casts down to Oxford to be dissected, front and backstage.

The 300-seat Stephen Joseph theatre is one of the few British repertory companies with a toehold in the black. As its (unpaid) artistic director, Mr Ayckbourn stages his new play each year, and directs a couple of others which are usually less lucrative. London's critics are forced to schlep up to Scarborough for the yearly Ayckbourn premiere, which tends to make them a little irritated and patronising. The latest production, **Wildest Dreams,** opened earlier this month to good reviews, although Irving Wardle in the *Independent on Sunday* said: "Why bother to write ambitious pieces if London is going to ignore them, when he can produce less taxing material to entertain his seaside customers?"

Mr Ayckbourn is at pains to point out he considers comedy to be the highest of art forms, and not the lowest. His work is occasionally described as "sitcom", much to his disgust, because he writes about middle classes in livingrooms. "Hmph. But so do they all."

As Mr. Ayckbourn gets older, his interest in insides grows. When he wrote his first play, **The Square Cat,** as a 20-year-old jobbing actor, he merely wanted to create a large part for himself and get the girl. Now, confidence in the basics of structuring a play means he can spend more time on character, and less on the surface situation. "If you scratch people, they get darker."

His comedy has gone from tasteful beige to completely black over the years. **Wildest Dreams** is a romp featuring a former abused child, an insane wife who regresses to babyhood, a stroke, and a couple of lesbians. It is the I-didn't-know-whether-to-laugh-or-cry school of comedy, and it has Scarborough's Saga-trippers twitching in their seats. "They do intake their breath when the women kiss, I must say," gloats Mr Ayckbourn from a flowered armchair in the middle of the round stage set, surrounded by seats. " 'Ooh,' they go, 'heavens'. But it is pretty harmless. It's a fact of life. They've had nudity, poor loves, full frontal male and female, and now they've got women kissing each other. Heaven knows what's next."

Although the content of the next play may be variable, the time it takes to write will be, as usual, one week. The playwright hates writing plays. He used to be a deadline junkie, unable to put hand to word processor until just a few days before rehearsals were about to start. The theatre would advertise the title and print the playbills four weeks beforehand to encourage the author to get down to it. Meanwhile Mr Ayckbourn would be at home, doing jigsaws and playing patience and waiting for ideas. Then suddenly, he would write non-stop and arrive one morning with an almost perfect manuscript.

Working for the National Theatre for the past four years has ended such slacking, since it requires notice of plays months ahead. Mr Ayckbourn was forced to imagine he had a deadline in October for the play produced the next year.

He considers directing to be the reward for the slog of writing, which he can cope with only for short periods.

> To hold eight people in your mind, with distinctive characters and voices, for more than a week is very hard. It begins to send you slightly barmy. I don't put down that a man has a neurotic mother, but I've got it in my head, and I'm holding on to all these characters with some crazy sense of splitting my personality quite radically.

The Ayckbourn personality must have a lot of female in it, since his women characters are very well observed. He was brought up mainly by his mother, a writer of romantic fiction for magazines, who was obviously important to him. She used to drag him along to work, and leave him sitting in the foyer of *Woman's Own* "watching these enormously tall women going past. They all seemed to be massive." His stepfather, a bank manager, was of little interest to him in real life, but has been well utilised in his plays.

Mr Ayckbourn went to a boarding school originally set up by the East India Company at Haileybury, Hertfordshire, where he got very interested in women. "They were off the syllabus for so many years one got incredibly curious about them." He pauses to giggle. "I married the second one I met just to find out what they were like." His marriage resulted in two children, separation, but not acrimony. For the last 20 years he has lived with the actress Heather Storey, writing about claustrophobia in others' marriages, while avoiding the institution himself.

His major obsession has been politics of the sexual rather than party kind, often seen from the female point of view. "The women must be part of me, dressed in convenient hand-me-down bodies. If you're writing from the heart it can only come out of you, not from observing others." He leans forward, half serious, from his seat in the middle row of the empty theatre. "Besides, I have the sum of all human faults in my character, so it is very easy to find material."

> *Kate Muir, "A Chorus of Approval for the Last Resort," in* The Times, *London, May 24, 1991, p. 12.*

Susan Rusinko   (essay date 1991)

[*Rusinko is an American educator and critic who has contributed frequently to such journals as* Shaw Review *and* Modern Drama. *In the following excerpt, she examines Ayckbourn's departure from the conventions of traditional English comedies.*]

When Alan Ayckbourn's first popular London success, **Relatively Speaking,** opened on 29 March 1967, at the Duke of York's Theatre, the second wave of the avant-garde dramatists (John Osborne's *Look Back in Anger* having initiated the first wave in 1956) was emerging. One of its most eloquent spokesmen that year was Tom Stoppard, whose *Rosencrantz and Guildenstern Are Dead* opened at the National Theatre at the Old Vic on 11 April 1967. Ayckbourn was labeled a traditional dramatist writing boulevard comedy, out of touch with the innovative trends sweeping both English and continental stages.

On the continent, Samuel Beckett and Eugene Ionesco, innovators in the post-World War II era, wrote tragicomedies. In London, Harold Pinter's comedy of menace, Joe Orton's black comedy, and N. F. Simpson's absurdist farces rendered traditional, well-made comedies old-fashioned. Stoppard's linguistically dazzling farces and new plays by David Hare, Howard Brenton, Peter Barnes, etc., continued the innovations of the first wave. The new dramatists were nurtured at theatres such as the Royal Court and the many fringe theatres that had sprung into existence. Ayckbourn and other traditional dramatists whose plays were produced in the West End were considered commercial. It was the fate of *Relatively Speaking* to be labeled a mindless farce and Alan Ayckbourn the English Neil Simon. In his own defense, Ayckbourn has written that he "did not set out consciously to write a 'well-made play.'" No playwright, he continues, can "shatter theatrical convention or break golden rules until he is reasonably sure what they are and how they are arrived at."

However, in a gradual reversal over the next twenty years, as the headiness of the new drama wore off, Ayckbourn enjoyed a growing reputation, one that included his association with the prestigious, non-commercial National Theatre, as both writer and director. Beginning in 1977, one comedy followed another at the National: *Bedroom Farce, Sisterly Feelings, Way Upstream, A Chorus of Disapproval,* and *A Small Family Business.* Ayckbourn was now an integral part of both the commercial and non-commercial London stage scene.

Basic to his London success, however, are his roots in the Library Theatre (later the Stephen Joseph Theatre) in Scarborough, where his first comedy, *The Square Cat,* was produced in 1959. Five comedies followed there before his first play appeared in London. Since then, Ayckbourn has managed with inexhaustible versatility to write (direct and produce, as well) at least one play a year.

In reviewing *Henceforward*. . ., Michael Billington characterized Ayckbourn as getting "more daring with each new play." A leading champion of avant-garde drama, Billington described the play as "brilliant," "biliously funny," "keeping an astonishing balance between comedy and horror." He attributes Ayckbourn's comic success to his use of the Bergsonian theory of humor—"that we laugh whenever the essential spontaneity of life is reduced to a series of automatic movements" ["Nan and Superman," *The Guardian,* 22 November 1988]. Automatic movements, as basis for comedy, date back to Plautus and Molière and to the Restoration comedy of manners of William Congreve, the eighteenth-century farce of Richard Brinsley Sheridan, and the nineteenth- and twentieth-century comedies of Oscar Wilde, George Bernard Shaw, J. B. Priestley, Noël Coward, and Terence Rattigan, the last of whom was also dismissed as out of touch with the new drama which swept the English stage. Rattigan's *Separate Tables,* in its second year of a successful run in the West End, seemed an anachronism in 1956, the *"annus mirabilis"* of the angry young man. Indeed, Rattigan com-

mented that in the future the success of a dramatist would depend on how unlike Terence Rattigan he was. Defensively, he created a mythical, middle-class figure, Aunt Edna, whom he held up as the voice of the theatre audience of the time. She is a middle-class, middle-brow lady from Kensington who enjoys laughter, tears, and excitement and who "hates a lot of philosophical talk on the stage with nothing happening at all."

In the 1950s, as tradition was challenged by experimentation, Ayckbourn was writing traditional plays, earning a reputation as a slick, well-made dramatist of entertainment, catering to the same popular audience as Rattigan's. Adhering to the conventions of that tradition, he wrote plays to entertain seaside vacationers in Scarborough on a rainy day. His version of Rattigan's Aunt Edna includes [according to Susan Ferraro in "A Writer's Resort," *New York Times* 14 October 1990] the "local merchants, landladies, Yorkshire retirees, and city folk on vacation" whose demands for "diversion and accessibility" he knows he must meet. His early plays, including his first success, *Relatively Speaking,* illustrate his developing mastery of the nuts-and-bolts of plot construction, the basis of traditional English comedy. The conventions of the well-made play, however, soon would be given his unique stamp, particularly with regard to plot structure, comic hero, and the metamorphosis of the satiric comedy of manners into the darker comedy, sometimes Ortonesque, of his later plays.

Four early plays illustrate Ayckbourn's witty use of the techniques of the traditional play: *Relatively Speaking, How the Other Half Loves, Time and Time Again,* and *Absurd Person Singular.* The usual subject matter, in the context of a satiric treatment of middle-class manners and mores, is an entertaining story about real or suspected marital infidelities, mixed with a dash of materialistic greed. The techniques of traditional comedy include (1) much physical action; (2) an intricate, fast-paced plot that progresses by split-second timing of convenient entrances and exits; (3) the importance of plot over serious characterization; (4) the use of mistaken identities and misunderstandings to create the plot complications, often referred to as quid pro quo actions and dialogue; (5) a crucial dependence on ordinary objects to help develop the plot (in *Relatively Speaking,* a cigarette packet and a pair of slippers); (6) initial lies or cover-ups that breed more deceptions; (7) flat (as opposed to fully developed) characters, who fall into one of two categories: the deceivers and the deceived (or gulls); (8) an obligatory scene, known also as the *scène à faire* or the big scene, in which all deceptions and misunderstandings are cleared up (the most famous, Sheridan's screen scene in *The School for Scandal*); and, finally, (9) a happy ending. As standard comic ingredients, these developed over time into the mechanical, frequently sentimental, Scribean formulaic well-made play, spurned by the new dramatists and critics.

In Ayckbourn's early plays, mistaken identities and misunderstandings are paramount, all other elements existing in order to progress the plot to its highest point of complication, the climax, and then to unravel that plot in the dénouement or falling action. Two plays especially, *Relatively Speaking* and *How the Other Half Loves,* illustrate his mastery of the mechanics of traditional comic construction.

Some details and techniques of *Relatively Speaking,* a four-character play, seem to come directly from the most famous of English comedies, Oscar Wilde's *The Importance of Being Earnest.* Ginny, in a relationship with a new lover, Greg, plans to visit her employer, Philip, an older man, at his home in Lower Pendon in order to end her affair with him and to retrieve her letters from him. Like the cigarette case in Wilde's play, a cigarette packet is an object on which Ayckbourn builds his improbable plot. From an address he notices on Ginny's cigarette pack, Greg plans his own investigation of suspicions he has developed as a result of the flowers and chocolates cluttering Ginny's flat. Like Jack/Earnest and Algernon in the Wilde play, Ginny and Greg, unbeknownst to each other, travel by different trains from London to the country where Philip resides with his wife Sheila. Lying to Greg about a visit to her "parents," Ginny then compounds that lie with another: that he may not accompany her, as her "mother" panics when visitors arrive unexpectedly. Their "bunburying" (Wilde's term) is thus underway.

Meantime, in Lower Pendon, Philip, expecting that his wife will attend church so that in her absence he can entertain Ginny, is devising his own deceptions, one of which is to take Ginny on a European trip, with business as the pretext. He is surprised that Sheila has decided not to go to church, and the two, when we meet them, bicker about letters Philip accuses her of receiving. He associates her not going to church with a letter, possibly from a lover. Into this situation come first Greg and, on a later train, Ginny.

By exploiting English characteristics of politeness and self-control, Ayckbourn realistically develops a day-long series of mistaken identities and misunderstandings. He has referred to reticence as an English national affliction. Sheila shows no surprise at the arrival of a complete stranger, Greg, nor at the arrival of a second, Ginny. Not only are the visitors greeted politely, but they are offered the same hospitality of polite conversation and luncheon which Sheila accords friends and relatives.

Quid pro quos grow at breakneck pace as Greg and Sheila, and to a lesser degree, Philip, misinterpret comments, some by Ginny and Philip intended to deceive and others by Greg and Sheila made out of ignorance. One of the funniest is Greg's interpretation of Sheila's truthful insistence that she is not Ginny's mother. He has mistakenly concluded that Sheila does not wish to admit to Ginny's illegitimate birth. Nowhere does Sheila or Ginny suggest illegitimacy, but Greg's suspicions feed on interrupted or unfinished comments in a fast-paced series of conversations, during which one or two characters are offstage.

The time-honored contrivance of exits and entrances used to complicate plots is deployed freely by Ayckbourn. For example, when a deception is in danger of being prematurely disclosed, someone must leave to find a garden hoe, to roll some dough, or to relieve choking on a sip of coffee. Not until the end of the play are all four on stage in any prolonged conversation. Thus, the absentees are suspensefully kept in the dark during those rare times when the audience discovers some information that remains hidden from some characters. This audience recognition is essential to the comic situation.

Laughter peaks when the games played by Philip and Ginny cross into real life, as Philip, attempting to assuage Greg's concern about Ginny's treatment by her former lover, suggests it was the woman (Ginny) who seduced the lover (himself). The suggestion gives the play a rare serious turn as Philip fantasizes on her "mincing round the office in a skirt that was far too tight and a damn sight shorter than anyone else was wearing—sort of coy and forward at the same time. . . . You can tell when a girl's looking for something like she was. Well—she got it. I expect." For a moment it seems that Ayckbourn is moving out of traditional comedy into the kind of fantasy world Pinter's characters inhabit, but he restores the comic mode as Sheila, rising to the occasion, reprimands her husband: "I've never heard anything quite so rude in my life."

There is one convention which Ayckbourn avoids, even in early plays—the complete exposure of deceptions by the play's end. The obligatory *scène à faire* in which all misunderstandings are cleared up, all secrets revealed, and all endings happily contrived does not occur. A number of matters are left unresolved. As Ginny and Greg depart happily, Greg is unaware that the European vacation just discussed as his and Ginny's was, in fact, Philip's plan for himself and Ginny. Ginny fails in her attempt to retrieve her letters from Philip. Indeed, Sheila even adds to Ginny's and Philip's deceptions one of her own—on her own terms—when she allows Philip's suspicions about her "lover" to remain. Thus, Ayckbourn deviates from the traditional artifice of an ending in a "big scene" in which all loose ends are tied together, as in the screen scene of *The School for Scandal,* or Miss Prism's clearing away the last of many misunderstandings in *The Importance of Being Earnest.* Instead, like the uncertain destinies of the students (and Diana as well) at the conclusion of Rattigan's *French Without Tears,* Philip remains unenlightened regarding Ginny's relationship to Sheila and Philip.

Ayckbourn on farces:

I love doing [farces], but they're bloody hard work. They're much the hardest thing to write, and you can't do more than one every five years, simply because the technique involved is phenomenal. It's like playing a very difficult Liszt sonata: you need to have so much muscle and ingenuity. And you have to use up a stockpile: I won't have that much ingenuity again for another five years. I've got gentle ingenuity for things like *Just Between Ourselves,* but not this massive construction job that has to go on, because the more unlikely the events you wish to portray, the more credible you have to make them, and that requires an enormous amount of artifice.

Alan Ayckbourn, in Ian Watson's
Conversations with Ayckbourn, *Macdonald,*
1981.

Despite changes in some traditional conventions, and despite snubs from "serious" critics as a boulevard comedy, Ayckbourn's first play was described by others as "deliciously heady," "a near miracle," and "a superbly constructed meringue" which gave its audience total and continuous delight, and established its young author as the "brightest new comic talent in the theatre." Successful as a traditional English comedy, its realistically comic ending is an early indication of a style that becomes a hallmark—and an increasingly assertive one—in Ayckbourn's work.

In *How the Other Half Loves,* Ayckbourn strikes out in a new direction through inventive use of stage space to reduce dependence on the obligatory doors and French windows through which characters in traditional comedies made contrived exits and entrances. In this play about three couples whose marriages are a bit shaky, he uses one stage space for two different dining rooms. Changing only a few amenities, such as pillows, to differentiate between the greater affluence of the Fosters and the Phillipses', he superimposes one dining room on another and even one table on another. The audience witnesses an eye-defying movement of comings and goings in which members of the two families use the same stage space at the same stage time. To avoid colliding with each other and to convince the audience that they are unaware of their many hairbreadth avoidances of collisions, the actors must move with split-second timing.

The suspense reaches its climax in the two dinner parties (staged as one) at which half the table is laid elegantly and the other half most inelegantly, with paper napkins and other downscale accessories. What the two dinners have in common, even though they occur on two different nights, are the guests, Mr and Mrs Featherstone. He is an innocent victim who is mistakenly hit by Teresa Phillips's soup (intended for her husband) in the same location at which the Fosters' upstairs toilet leaks on him. With both incidents converging on him, they accidentally expose the strain of the Featherstones' marital situation. Although all's well that ends well for the Fosters and Phillipses, who eventually reconcile, each to his/her own mate, the Featherstones seem to have been victimized. As in *Relatively Speaking,* the happy ending is a qualified one.

Whereas the plays just discussed demonstrate a masterful exploration of the techniques of traditional comic style, *Time and Time Again,* according to Ayckbourn in an interview, is interesting for its clear change in the direction his comedy takes. He described the change as "upsetting the balance." Normally, "the central character should be the driving force." However, Leonard, an ex-schoolteacher who is separated from wife and children and is living with his married sister Anna, and her husband Graham, has upset the balance. For Leonard is "a total vacuum . . . who took no decisions, did nothing, everything was done for him, and by simply taking no decisions, he affects the whole course of the play. Doing nothing he upsets about five lives. He comes through it in the most extraordinary way; everybody else ends up miserable . . . [H]e attracts people who have an irresistible impulse to push him in one direction, but he slides out of the push. Some people get angered by this type, others get concerned" [Alan Ayckbourn with Joan Buck, "The Joan Buck Interview," *Plays and Players,* September 1972]. Ayckbourn's comment may in part be an explanation of the occasional designation of his style as comedy of embarrassment.

In Tom Stoppard's farce *Travesties,* Lenin talks about two kinds of people, those who do things and those to whom things are done. Ayckbourn's Leonard, by doing nothing and by accepting what others do to him, indirectly succeeds in doing things to others. It is from a clash between expected behavior and his passive resistance to that behavior that laughter derives.

If Leonard, who by doing nothing sucks into his vaccum Anna and Graham, and their guests Joan and Peter, all four, in turn, agree to be sucked in. Anna dotes on Leonard. In his perverse way, Graham pushes Leonard, his long-standing hostilities fueled by his jealousy of Leonard's success with Joan. Peter, mistaking Graham for Joan's lover, engages him, rather than Leonard, in a fight over Joan. Finally, Joan, attracted to Leonard, actively joins him in his disruptive disregard of suburban rituals.

The character-derived humor in the play is further illustrated in Leonard's tale to Joan about his failed marriage. Having come home early from school one day, he found his wife at home with a male friend, sampling homemade wines. With no place to go, he spent that night in the local jail, entertaining the sergeant with his story. "Every time a fresh batch of coppers arrived for duty, he had me telling them all over again. It was like a one-man police concert." In the face of his wife's seeming infidelity, he falls into an indifferent gesture of least resistance. In keeping with Ayckbourn's developing emphasis on realistic rather than stereotypical characters and on realistic situations rather than contrived plots, as in *Relatively Speaking* and *How the Other Half Loves,* his main character is the catalyst for both plot and humor. The straight characters, foils to Leonard, illustrate the Bergsonian theory of habitual and therefore mechanical behavior from which Leonard recoils. Of these, Graham most clearly demonstrates obsessive actions and language habits which incrementally repeat his lack of wit. Ayckbourn gradually builds audience recognition from which laughter springs. For example, as Anna pours tea, Graham informs Peter, whose car has broken down, that he (Graham) always carries spare parts. The dialogue continues:

> PETER. Sorry to mess up your funeral, Mr Baker.
>
> GRAHAM. Wasn't my funeral. (*He laughs.*)
>
> ANNA. You couldn't help it, could you?
>
> GRAHAM. Did you hear what I said? I said it wasn't my funeral . . .

Soon:

> ANNA. You take milk, don't you?
>
> PETER. Thank you.
>
> GRAHAM. Spare fuses. They're useful things.

ANNA. Sugar?

PETER. Thank you Mrs Baker.

GRAHAM. Spare water, spare bulbs . . .

ANNA. Help yourself, then, Peter.

GRAHAM. And finally, a flashlight.

Another of Graham's linguistic habits is to top an anecdote just related by a guest with a catch phrase, "that happened to me once."

The character foils to Leonard make his passivity seem aggressive. To avoid being drawn into the banalities of tea-time conversation, he habitually quotes lines of poetry, explaining to Joan that he had "devised an infallible system to fool all headmasters and school inspectors" by learning "the first two lines of every poem in the Oxford Book of English Verse."

The ironic ending of the play finds Anna leading Graham upstairs for a consoling gargle (after he has been nearly choked to death by Peter), Joan flinging Leonard's book into the pond and leaving for good, and Leonard and Peter walking off to the playing field. With the exception of Joan's departure from the scene, normality has been restored, its conflict having surfaced in the final confrontation, not as traditional comedy would have it, between Leonard and Peter, but between Graham and Peter. With the increasing emphasis on realistic characterization, there is in *Time and Time Again* a diminishing reliance on the contrivances of mistaken identities, misunderstandings, and plot.

Among Ayckbourn's later heroes who follow Leonard as passive comic characters are Norman of *The Norman Conquests,* Simon of *Sisterly Feelings,* Guy Jones of *A Chorus of Disapproval,* Jerome of *Henceforward* . . ., and Douglas Beechey of *Man of the Moment.* All, like Leonard, upset the balance.

Still another distinctive technique of Ayckbourn's is his use of rooms other than the standard drawing room of his predecessors in English comedy. The dining room takes over in *How the Other Half Loves,* the kitchen in *Absurd Person Singular,* the bedroom in *Bedroom Farce.* These rooms serve as microscopes through which Ayckbourn observes in Zolaesque detail the manners and mores of the time. The accounts of kitchens, for example, indicating the relative affluence of middle-class couples, are entwined with the marital states of boredom, desperation, or metamorphosis of the human into an object (e.g., Mrs Jackson, whose pain is farcically ignored). In later plays, such as in *A Small Family Business* and *Henceforward* . . ., the farce changes to dark comedy.

In *Absurd Person Singular,* materialistic acquisitiveness becomes the context for his examination of suburbia with its marital rituals and relationships. The first couple aspires to the social status of its guests; a second couple has already achieved what the first couple is aspiring to; and the marriage of the third couple has long since been a situation of total non-understanding. The six meet on three successive Christmas Eves, the main action in each household, for various reasons, eventually moving into the respective kitchens. In all three households, the move is realistically dictated by emergencies, in one case by a hostile dog from which guests find refuge in the kitchen.

In the climactic scene, characterized by a hilarity that only makes more ironic the underlying tragedy, Mrs Jackson tries unsuccessfully, in a variety of ways, to commit suicide, even as the others, especially her husband and the other males, completely misunderstand what she is doing and thus ignore her real pain. All six crowd into the kitchen, hectically intent on chores, such as changing a light bulb. As in *How the Other Half Loves,* split-second timing to avoid collisions keeps laughter alive to the end of the play.

If place dominates Ayckbourn's suburban universe, time complements that place. But Ayckbourn adds a new dimension to the traditional domestic comedy in this particular excursion. His stage directions indicate Act I, last Christmas; Act II, this Christmas; Act III, next Christmas. His structure is a variation of Ben Travers's formula for a farce (the chronology is Travers's): "Act II—the sympathetic and guileless hero is landed into the thick of some grievous dilemma or adversity. Act I—he gets into it. Act III—he gets out of it" [Leslie Smity, *Modern British Farce*]. In Act I the Hopcrafts "get into it" as they manically maneuver their upwardly mobile strategies. In Act II, having realized some social upwardness, they land "into the thick" of the Jacksons' adversities. Their social aspirations are fully realized in Act III; yet Ayckbourn makes it clear that their success is only a reversion to the situations of the other two couples. They do and do not "get out of it." The Christmas eves past (Act I) and present (Act II) give Christmas eve future (Act III) the sense of a continuing suburban sterility. Ayckbourn described this play as his "first offstage action play" and made no apologies for the considerable darkening in its last scene.

In these four early comedies, Ayckbourn has clearly established a style whose frontiers he constantly expands. Adhering to most basic comic conventions, he has introduced some new twists, giving comedy his unique stamp. The realistic rather than artificial ending of *Relatively Speaking* characterizes all his plays. His experiment with inventive plotting in *How the Other Half Loves* takes even more ingenious turns in plays such as *Bedroom Farce, The Norman Conquests,* and *Sisterly Feelings.* The passive hero of *Time and Time Again* is imaginatively reinvented in later plays in which comedy takes on an increasingly ominous tone. And the change from upper-middle-class drawing rooms of traditional English comedy to the kitchens of the middle-middle class in *Absurd Person Singular* is appropriate for Ayckbourn's growing social commentary.

It is in his plays of the later 1980s that Ayckbourn breaks not only traditional comic molds, but his own as well. "You've got to keep surprising yourself. . . . You have to try to break the mold of what made you successful" [Benedict Nightingale, "It's Not Cricket, But the Score Is: Ayckbourn, 37; Shakespeare, 36," *New York Times* 3 August 1990]. When he reached his thirty-seventh play, *The Revengers' Comedies* in 1989 (making the score Ayckbourn 37, Shakespeare 36), he spoke of "inching like an iceberg" toward his aim, which is "to write a completely serious play that makes people laugh all the time." The shift is most noticeable in his expansion of the domestic concerns in earlier plays to societal problems such as corrupt real estate deals (*A Chorus of Disapproval*), involvement in the drug trade by a respectable furniture businessman (*A Small Family Business*), a neighborhood besieged by urban gangs *Henceforward* . . .),the world of multinational corporations (*The Revengers' Comedies*), and the shoddiness of the television industry *Man of the Moment*).

In *A Small Family Business,* Ayckbourn for the first time dramatizes the actual metamorphosis of a character. Jack and Poppy McCracken, a basically ordinary and decent English couple, are drawn into a spider's web of corrupt business dealings that involve members of their own family, a corrupt detective, and a Mafia-like family of Italian entrepreneurs. Once the momentum of greed and corruption begins with Jack's honest attempt to ferret out the traitor in the family business, that momentum, taking on a life of its own, overwhelms Jack. He and his wife eventually become accessories to a murder and ongoing victims of bribery. Ayckbourn balances the unpunished actions of greed with the outrageously farcical antics of one of the wives who goes through five Italian lovers, the brothers Rivetti: Lotario, Uberto, Orlando, Vincenzo, and Giorgio, all act-alikes. As Ayckbourn would have it, the laughter continues up to "ten seconds before the end of the play" [Nightingale, "A Woman of Two Minds, Both in Turmoil, *New York Times* 14 February, 1988]. But that last ten seconds is devastating in its focus on the young drug-addicted daughter of the family as she huddles in the bathroom while the festivities of a birthday party for the seventy-five-year-old family patriarch are going on downstairs.

Up to the ending, the progressive involvement of the entire family in the corrupt dealings is dramatized with comic-tragic brilliance in such characters as a wife who, in the middle of frantic activities involving thousands of pounds, worries only about not having her dog's sleep disturbed. There is also her husband who plans to invest his share of the money in a restaurant in the Balearic Islands where he will cook his Lancashire Hot Pot for English visitors. In one dizzyingly comic scene, the Hot Pot, dog, and Rivetti brothers come together in a sophisticated and hilarious variation of the plot confusion in the *How the Other Half Loves.*

As in the early plays, the failed human (mostly marital) relationships are still important, but they are intensified by additional failures in parental responsibilities and by wider societal issues, such as drugs. The hero, if the term applies, is collective: the McCracken family. With both serious comment and entertaining comedy deriving from the same characters and existing in nearly equal proportions, Ayckbourn almost succeeds in his precarious balancing act. However, the corruption of the two remaining decent family members and the final image of the drug-addicted teenager preclude that success. Still, the intricate plot complications are reminiscent of Ayckbourn's earlier comedies.

Man of the Moment returns to serious characterization as two characters, Douglas Beechey and Vic Parks, one sympathetic and the other repulsive, spark the plot not so much by what they do as by what they are. Character-generated action, rather than contrived plot, distinguishes this comedy. For most of the play, the very physical presence of Beechey, an ordinary former bank clerk (one of Ayckbourn's vacuums) is the main source of humor. At moments during which nothing is happening, Beechey merely walks on stage, stands motionless, or peers over a wall, and laughter erupts. John Peter describes his character . . . as "one of Ayckbourn's subtlest creations: a devastatingly boring man who is socially ham-fisted and morally unbearably noble" ["Requiem Scored for Screams and Laughter," *Sunday Times* 18 February 1988]. (pp. 41-52)

If Leonard in *Time and Time Again* is the first of Ayckbourn's passive comic heroes to upset the balance, Douglas Beechey is the pure embodiment of that character. A former bank clerk, he functions as a nearly anonymous, middle-middle-class character in Ayckbourn's middle-middle-class mythic universe. He lacks the upstanding, moral nature of Sheridan's Joseph Surface, the wit of language and ideas in the characters of Wilde and Shaw, the emotional affectiveness of characters in Pinero, Priestley, Coward, and Rattigan. He is essentially as ordinary as ordinary can be. Ayckbourn chooses not to invest him with any distinctive wit, philosophy, emotion, or morality, except for one brief moment when (like Herman Melville's Billy Budd) his passivity deserts him and he lunges at his antagonist.

Beechey's foil is Vic Parks, a dehumanized ex-convict, made affluent by talking about his crimes. He is as polished as Beechey is awkward. He is as abusive of his wife and servants as Beechey is vacuously sympathetic to them. If Beechey is elephantine in his un-self-conscious goodness, Parks is serpent-like in flaunting his un-self-conscious evil. In them Ayckbourn has created two morality play characters who are equally funny because both are equally strong: one as passively good, the other as actively evil.

Although the humor throughout the play grows out of the stark contrasts in character, there is one moment in which Beechey, unable to control himself in his indignation at Vic's abuse of women, hits Parks, inadvertently knocking him into the pool. Helpless in the situation, the obese maid who has been abused by Parks unintentionally steps on him, and he is pulled out, dead. The scene is pure farce, and like that in *A Small Family Business,* in which the detective is shoved into a tub and unintentionally killed by the women from whom he attempts to wrest a bagful of bribe money, is the means by which poetic justice and a dubious happy ending are realized. In one case the body is disposed of by the Mafia, and in the other a coverup explanation of the drowning is invented by the television medium.

With the filming for television of the meeting between Parks and Beechey (the latter an ironic beneficiary of Parks's defacement of an attractive woman), Ayckbourn continues his bleak vision of a cultural wasteland. In the framework of a tasteless but popular television program, the crew and the host—a woman—demonstrate their total impersonality, so that by comparison Beechey is made to seem heroic, and even Parks has a slight edge as a human. The glamorizing of crime and the financial enhancement of a criminal are squarely on the shoulders of a popular medium as television host and crew pander to the lowest mass tastes.

Ayckbourn's comment on a decade of Thatcherist economics and the cultural wasteland includes no cleansing of the body politic as in the tradition of tragedy. It offers no happy ending, either, as in traditional comedy. Instead, it makes a tragic situation entertaining by treating it with the traditional techniques of comedy. Thus, the traditional corrective purpose in both tragedy and comedy is not inherent in Ayckbourn's style or intent. In its place is the embarrassingly funny exposure of the foibles and failures of ordinary human beings, increasingly entangled in the nets of greed rampant in society, a twentieth-century version of Ben Jonson's *Volpone*. Ayckbourn admits to a certain unease about whether Britain has progressed or regressed under Prime Minister Thatcher. "It's no coincidence that you hardly ever see members of the present government in the theatre. . . . The arts and gentle, civilized living are being rapidly downgraded for the fast buck. It has a narrowing effect. It creates an uncaringness" [Nightingale, "It's Not Cricket"].

If the darkness of Ayckbourn's cultural tone has intensified, it has not stilled his comic voice, for the laughter in the audience still is there, only in the form of a "requiem scored for screams and laughter." This is essentially what constitutes his upsetting the balance in a wider sense than he perhaps intended when he used that phrase to describe Leonard in *Time and Time Again.* Although his comedies of the 1960s and 1970s continue the tradition of Sheridan, Shaw, Wilde, Coward, and Rattigan, those of the 1980s claim kinship to the seventeenth-century comedies of Jonson and Middleton, as the title of one of Ayckbourn's plays, *The Revengers' Comedies,* suggests. (pp. 53-4)

> Susan Rusinko, "Upsetting the Balance of the English Comic Tradition," in Alan Ayckbourn: A Casebook, edited by Bernard F. Dukore, Garland Publishing, Inc., 1991, pp. 41-55.

FURTHER READING

Bibliography

Page, Malcolm. *File on Ayckbourn.* London: Methuen Drama, 1989, 95 p.
> Contains a chronological listing of Ayckbourn's works through 1988, providing comprehensive performance and publication data, plot synopses, author commentary, and review excerpts. Also included are excerpts from numerous interviews with Ayckbourn and a selected primary and secondary bibliography.

Criticism

Ayckbourn, Alan. "Alan Ayckbourn." *Drama* 1, No. 167 (1988): 5-7.
> Discusses Ayckbourn's commercial plays, his development as a playwright and director, and his association with Stephen Joseph.

Beaufort, John. "Just Another Screwball Holiday with the Family." *The Christian Science Monitor* 77, No. 163 (16 July 1985): 25.
> Positive review of *Season's Greetings.*

Church, Michael. "Shakespeare of the South Bank." *The Sunday Times Books* (1 June 1986): 41-2.
> Traces Ayckbourn's development as a dramatist and discusses his position as the principal writer and director at the National Theatre.

Dukore, Bernard F. "Alan Ayckbourn's Liza Doolittle." *Modern Drama* XXXII, No. 3 (September 1989): 425-39.
> Examines the complicated structure of *Intimate Exchanges.* Dukore compares Ayckbourn's Sylvie and Toby to Bernard Shaw's Liza Doolittle and Henry Higgins in *Pygmalion,* analyzing ways in which "various situations and outcomes that result from different circumstances" within *Intimate Exchanges* address the unresolved issue of romance between a young female student and her middle-aged mentor.

——, ed. *Alan Ayckbourn: A Casebook.* New York: Garland Publishing, 1991, 206 p.
> Includes an interview conducted by Dukore; critical essays addressing Ayckbourn's themes and techniques and his stature as a significant dramatist; an interview and essays on production methods of his plays by such actors and directors as Peter Forbes, Mel Shapiro, and David Johnson; and a thorough primary and secondary bibliography.

Gussow, Mel. "Bard of the British Bourgeoisie." *The New York Times Magazine* (28 January 1990): 23-4, 26-7, 84.
> Biographical and critical overview that traces the development of thematic and technical elements in Ayckbourn's plays, highlights his work with the Stephen Joseph Theatre in Scarborough, and discusses the changing critical reception toward his plays.

Henry, William A., III. "From Laughter to Lamentation." *Time* 131, No. 9 (29 February 1988): 94.
> Praises Ayckbourn's complex depiction of insanity in *Woman in Mind.*

Hornby, Richard. "The London Theatre." *The Hudson Review* XL, No 4 (Winter 1988): 637-45.
> Survey of numerous contemporary plays in which Hornby commends *A Small Family Business* as superb tragicomedy and asserts that Ayckbourn is "a major playwright" who "combines literary sophistication with theatrical expertise."

——. "Ayckbourn in New York." *The Hudson Review* XLIV, No. 2 (Summer 1991): 285-91.
> Reviews *Taking Steps* and *Absent Friends,* praising Ayckbourn's innovative farcical devices, his presentation of "the theme of non-communication," and his ability "to write funny plays about dull people."

King, Robert L. Review of *A Small Family Business,* by Alan Ayckbourn. *The Massachusetts Review* XXIX, No. 1 (Spring 1988): 87-97.

Comments on numerous contemporary plays. King negatively assesses *A Small Family Business,* contending that the play exhibits more emphasis on theatrical technique than on meaning.

Lewis, Peter. "In at the Deep End Again." *The Sunday Times* No. 8634 (4 February 1990): E1, E3.
Biographical and critical survey occasioned by the opening of *Man of the Moment* that stresses Ayckbourn's move toward tragi-comedy.

Oliver, Edith. "Of Two Minds." *The New Yorker* LXIV, No. 2 (29 February 1988): 63.
Reviews *Woman in Mind,* faulting Ayckbourn's female characters as stereotyped.

Seibert, Gary. "In Their Places." *America* 158, No. 9 (5 March 1988): 242, 246.
Focuses on the tragic qualities of *Woman in Mind,* maintaining that Ayckbourn's "plays deal with people and situations that in lesser hands become soap operas and escapist boulevard; but a shadow always lurks menacingly in his comedies."

Simon, John. "A Christmas Corral." *New York* 18, No. 28 (22 July 1985): 57-8.
Favorable review of *Season's Greetings* in which the critic denotes Ayckbourn "the historian of insignificance."

———. "British Twilight, American Fog." *New York* 21, No. 9 (29 February 1988): 120, 122.
Praises the broad emotional range of *Woman in Mind.*

Walsh, John. "Funny Way to Get Serious." *The Sunday Times* No. 8719 (29 September 1991): Sec. 6, 4-5.
Stresses Ayckbourn's continued use of comedy in plays delineating increasingly dark themes.

White, Sidney Howard. *Alan Ayckbourn.* Boston: Twayne Publishers, 1984, 159 p.
Biographical and critical overview of Ayckbourn's career through *Way Upstream.* White includes a selected primary and secondary bibliography.

Additional coverage of Ayckbourn's life and career is contained in the following sources published by Gale Research: *Contemporary Authors,* Vols. 21-24, rev. ed.; *Contemporary Authors New Revision Series,* Vol. 31; *Contemporary Literary Criticism,* Vols. 5, 8, 18, 33; *Dictionary of Literary Biography,* Vol. 13; and *Major 20th-Century Writers.*

Gesualdo Bufalino

1920?-

Italian novelist, essayist, and poet.

The following entry provides an overview of Bufalino's career.

INTRODUCTION

Bufalino's novels have been greeted with critical acclaim in Italy, where he received the Campiello Prize in 1981 for *Diceria dell'untore* (*The Plague-Sower*) and the Premio Strega in 1988 for *Le menzogne della notte* (*Lies of the Night*). Like much of Bufalino's fiction, these novels are set in Sicily and feature protagonists whose circumstances force them to confront fundamental questions concerning the nature of human existence. Characteristic of Bufalino's prose style are numerous literary allusions drawn from a variety of sources, including Italian and French literature, puppet theater, and grand opera. The multitude of references in *The Plague-Sower* prompted Bufalino to provide a glossary to aid readers of the novel.

A teacher of literature in a provincial school in Sicily for most of his life, Bufalino did not publish his first novel until the age of sixty-one. The novel's publication can in part be attributed to the Sicilian novelist Leonardo Sciascia. Sciascia had been highly impressed with an introduction that Bufalino had written for a book about Comiso, Bufalino's native town, and subsequently arranged to meet him. During the course of their discussion, Sciascia persuaded Bufalino to publish *The Plague-Sower,* a fictional account of Bufalino's experiences as a soldier during World War II and as a patient in a Sicilian tuberculosis sanatorium immediately following the war. Prior to his meeting with Sciascia, Bufalino had been reluctant to publish *The Plague-Sower,* a novel on which he had worked intermittently since 1950, due to his extreme modesty and demand for artistic perfection. Following *The Plague-Sower*'s success, Bufalino began to publish novels, essays, and poetry on a regular basis.

In his novels, particularly *The Plague-Sower* and *Lies of the Night,* Bufalino's characters search for answers to their questions about love, fate, chance, and death through an exploration of their memories, with the threat of imminent death setting the tone for their musings. Bufalino's novels reflect his interest in the perception of time and history as well as his conviction that the contemplation of one's memories can serve as a useful vehicle for self-understanding. In his essays, Bufalino addresses similar concerns, examining the nature of memory itself and lamenting the ravages that time has inflicted upon rural Sicily and its traditions. Bufalino also expresses concern over the increasing precariousness of modern life, a concern reinforced daily by Comiso's distinction as the site of the principal American cruise-missile base in Italy. Although a few critics have criticized the style in Bufalino's novels and essays as overly formal and his extensive use of literary allusions as pretentious erudition, most have praised him for his bold images and metaphors and his rich, carefully constructed prose, which Michela Montante has described as "spontaneous, fluid, harmonious, and capable of conveying universal ideas in a sharp and semi-ironic fashion."

PRINCIPAL WORKS

Diceria dell'untore   (novel)   1981
   [*The Plague-Sower,* 1988]
L'amaro miele   (poetry)   1982
Museo d'ombre   (essays)   1982
Argo il cieco, ovvero, I sogni della memoria   (novel)   1984
   [*Blind Argus; or, the Fables of the Memory,* 1989]
Cere perse   (essays)   1985
La luce e il lutto   (essays)   1988
Le menzogne della notte   (novel)   1988
   [*Night's Lies,* 1990; also published as *Lies of the Night,* 1991]

CRITICISM

Joseph Siracusa   (review date Autumn 1982)

[*Siracusa is an American critic and professor of Spanish and Italian. In the following excerpt, he discusses the theme of* The Plague-Sower *and praises Bufalino's style.*]

[*Diceria dell'untore*] is set in a tuberculosis sanatorium situated in the fertile Conca d'Oro, just a few miles out of Palermo. The events described in it occur in the summer of 1946 and are narrated by the protagonist—a projection of the author, who actually spent a period of his life struggling against the insidious disease that not only was ravaging his lungs, but had also made him a social outcast in his native Sicily, not unlike those infamous *untori* accused of spreading the plague in seventeenth-century Milan.

Ostensibly the novel deals with the protagonist's disease and with his intense love affair with the mysterious Marta, a patient he describes as "una delle più fradice" in the sanatorium. In reality, however, the novel is much more than a study of decay or an array of morbid anecdotes about the vagaries of temperament among patients and physicians. It is (*The Plague-Sower*) a moving and detailed description of the protagonist's search for answers to fundamental questions—life, love, chance, death, et cetera. Bufalino's book is indeed a fine developmental novel, one in which the narrator, a symbol of humankind, develops and grows into a better and wiser man through the experience of the sanatorium.

Although this novel may bring to mind others describing a similar situation such as Mann's *Magic Mountain* or Cela's *Pabellón de reposo,* any comparison will be futile, since Bufalino is at every moment unique, a writer who has read all kinds of books only to forget them at the moment of recreating his via dolorosa in an unmistakably Sicilian cultural context. Even though it was written in the 1970s, at the time of the *glaciazione neorealista,* the present novel is light-years removed from its esthetic canons. Every page displays such a variety of artistic devices that the reader's interest is never allowed to flag. Its remarkable language—even-tempered, rich in musical modulations—makes great use of daring images and metaphors, often as baroque as those used by the common people in his native Sicily, the land where the hyperbolic statement is more often the norm than the exception.

> *Joseph Siracusa, in a review of "Diceria dell'untore," in* World Literature Today, *Vol. 56, No. 4, Autumn, 1982, p. 667.*

Joseph Siracusa   (review date Summer 1983)

[*In the following excerpt, Siracusa describes the evolution of* Museo d'ombre *from a series of nostalgic reminiscences into a sequence of philosophical meditations.*]

[*Museo d'ombre*] consists of a collection of highly incisive vignettes in which [Bufalino] offers the reader a delicate evocation of people, gestures, sayings, vanished occupations and places he knew as a child some fifty years ago in his native town of Comiso.

As the author himself tells it, he had originally conjured up the shadows of his personal museum out of a nostalgic desire to restore somehow their fading colors, "allo stesso modo di chi imbalsama o imbelletta il viso di un caro estinto." Later, however, these innocent reminiscences about a rural world which is rapidly disappearing took on an unexpected dimension, providing him with an apt vehicle for some philosophical meditations on life, death, the ravages of time and the bittersweet fruits of memory. Such a development was especially prompted by one single event that in a few months changed what had previously been an idyllic, mafia-free, fertile area of eastern Sicily into the biggest atomic missile base in all of Europe. Convinced then by the awesome presence of these monsters of terror and destruction that life on our planet is becoming more and more precarious with each day that passes, Bufalino decided that he had to publicize the historical-imaginary portrait of life in his hometown, a veritable Sicilian Spoon River, in order to point out those small bits of simple wisdom that made life in the 1920s a worthy and bearable ex-

perience. In contrast to modern life, man was then part and parcel of a tacit pact with the forces of nature, an arrangement that made him stoically accept even his own natural demise "come un persuasivo destino, una scadenza regolata da una misteriosa, maestosa equanimità."

[Bufalino's] remarkable language—even-tempered, rich in musical modulations—makes great use of daring images and metaphors, often as baroque as those used by the common people in his native Sicily, the land where the hyperbolic statement is more often the norm than the exception.

—*Joseph Siracusa*

All in all, Bufalino in this slim and, to all appearances, simple book succeeds in compressing a great deal of personal experiences and insights into the human condition. He achieves this by the skillful use of a sober, finely crafted prose and also by an unusual ability to profile a character or a place in a few vivid details.

> *Joseph Siracusa, in a review of "Museo d'ombre," in* World Literature Today, *Vol. 57, No. 3, Summer, 1983, p. 441.*

Michela Montante   (essay date Winter 1987)

[*In the following excerpt, Montante favorably reviews Bufalino's collection of essays* Cere perse.]

The title of Sicilian author Gesualdo Bufalino's new collection of essays [*Cere perse*] uses the word *persa* in the sense of "volatile." Disappearance is, in fact, the destiny of all newspaper articles, but by collecting his many scattered articles according to his own scheme, Bufalino hopes to save them from this common fate and open up his true self to the reader.

The book is divided into five sections: "La parola ansiosa," "Occasioni siciliane," "Il lettore di venture," "Svaghi," and "Potpourri di memoria e morte." The articles of "La parola ansiosa" are an exhortation to write in good style, to use the right adjectives and verbs, and to avoid words which convey only an approximate meaning. Bufalino emphasizes also the use of the subjunctive, which seems to be disappearing from the Italian language. Finally, he launches an appeal to writers to avoid the publication of meaningless books that cloud readers' minds and leave them without time to return frequently to the classics.

In section 2 Bufalino writes as a keen critic of literary and visual art and as a devoted son of his land. In an essay on Vitaliano Brancati thirty years after the latter's death, Bufalino finds Brancati one of the most modern and deeply tragic writers in Italian literature. Two other pieces in the section show Bufalino's enormous esteem and friendship for his fellow Sicilian writer Leonardo Sciascia; one of the two traces Sciascia's career from the time when he was an elementary-school teacher who raised his voice against Sicily's malaise, to the man of today, the "poliziotto di Dio" who tries to understand the world and dares only to sigh and utter a few words interspersed with long "silences." Another two articles focus on the sixteenth-century painter Pietro Asaro and the contemporary artist Piero Guccione; yet another is dedicated to Bufalino's hometown of Comiso and constitutes an invective against the Americans who settled there following the installation of a nuclear-power plant but who made no attempt to adjust to local customs, with disastrous effects.

Many essays in the third section offer insights on French writers: the Comtesse de la Fayette, Baudelaire, Flaubert, Giraudoux, and Gide. Articles on Borges and Manzoni round out the section. Part 4 contains only three essays: a humoristic yet sad description of insomnia; a debate about whether it is better to spend one's vacation in one's own town or to travel and exhaust oneself; and a commentary on the Italian income-tax form 740, which Bufalino sarcastically calls a work of art, whose style varies from dry prose to lyric poetry and whose content is open to many misunderstandings. The fifth section begins with an appeal for peace in the world and ends with an article on memory.

In his essays Bufalino stands out as a man who graciously shares with his readers his intellectual and existential experiences. He comes across as a person of vast learning, whose knowledge ranges from film to music, from history to literature. He is passionately fond of French writing, especially Proust's work. His own prose is spontaneous, fluid, harmonious, and capable of conveying universal ideas in a sharp and semi-ironic fashion. (pp. 84-5)

> *Michela Montante, in a review of "Cere perse," in* World Literature Today, *Vol. 61, No. 1, Winter, 1987, pp. 84-5.*

Peter Hainsworth   (essay date 7 October 1988)

[*In the following excerpt, Hainsworth comments favorably on* La luce e il lutto, *a collection of Bufalino's essays.*]

La luce e il lutto (*The Light and the Grief*) is [Bufalino's] most recent collection of occasional prose-pieces on Sicily and the Sicilians. The viewpoint is personal, anecdotal, affectionate, the writing elegant and intelligent. As the title suggests, death and violence are not forgotten, but it is mostly a less dramatic Sicily which is evoked, a Sicily which retains much of its character, but which is losing many of its traditions along with its poverty. Bufalino has some evocative pieces on how his much-loved native town of Comiso is adjusting itself to being the main American cruise-missile base in Italy. But while the present has brought new problems, the past can also cast itself in a novel light. Apparently in the local dialect *mafioso* was once the word used to describe a shy but flamboyantly beautiful girl. If Bufalino has his own myth, it is of a Sicily which was, and might still be, *mafioso* in this sense as well as the other.

Peter Hainsworth, "Sicilian Myth and Reality," in The Times Literary Supplement, *No. 4462, October 7, 1988, p. 1096.*

Leonardo Sciascia   (essay date 1988)

[*Sciascia was a highly distinguished Italian novelist, essayist, and dramatist whose works focus on Sicilian society. He played a prominent role in Bufalino's literary career as the individual who convinced Bufalino to publish his first novel. In the following essay, which served as his introduction to* The Plague-Sower, *Sciascia discusses the nature of Bufalino's fiction.*]

Years ago a major journalist, from a major European newspaper, told me about an odd interview he had conducted at the beginning of his career with a famous Chinese general. The interview was probably never published, or if so, was published in the guise of an amusing "professional failure," which was how he recounted it to me.

This journalist thought himself to be somewhat experienced with the world of the Chinese, which has always been a rather "difficult" world for a European, especially then, when China was particularly restless and uncertain of its destiny. Thus he accepted what the general told him as a perfectly reliable account, intelligently analytical and truthful in its intentions. He jotted down note after note, filled with joy at the thought that the interview would seem so extraordinary, even unique, to his readers. Everything the general said was precise, rationally linked, plausible, and true. But when the interview was over, and he had shut his note-filled pad, the general took his leave with the following statement: "A word of advice: Never believe a Chinaman," smiling subtly and giving him so mischievous a look that the journalist understood he was referring to the extraordinary things he had just told him.

I use this anecdote as a kind of fable, or reading-key, for the oeuvre of Gesualdo Bufalino—for every book, essay, article, or aphorism he has ever written. "Never believe a writer": such an exhortation seems, however, contradicted by another: "Always believe in literature." But there is no contradiction. What Bufalino means (though he has never explicitly said so) is that one must never believe writers who want to be believed for what they describe or avow, for their "truthfulness" (worse still if it is the "truthfulness" of *verismo*); and that a writer attains the truth of existence only through mystification, games, ambiguity, deception—deception in itself, of oneself, of feelings, things, and facts. "Mountebank of my own soul," an Italian "crepuscular" poet once called himself (Giuseppe Antonio Borgese termed "crepuscular" a group of poets who were somewhat Symbolist, masochistic, and melancholy, but also capable of irony and mockery; Bufalino himself shares a certain vein of such "Crepuscularism").

Even one who considers himself far from this sort of notion of literature and who in being a writer implies a profession of faith "in the magnificent destinies and paths" of man in history, cannot ignore—or in any case sense the prickly premonition—that such a profession of faith is an illusion with little likelihood of becoming "action," and that in a writer, in short, one would do better to believe the "lies" than the "truths," since after all it is precisely "untruths" which, in a writer, are changed into "truths," and are in fact "truths"—though "truths" which are in turn changeable, mutable, and which would not be "truths" if they were fixed. A book, indeed, is a theatre of "untruth"—"untruth" that has become "truth." As the author is writing it, he gradually moves away from the idea or reason for which he started writing it; and when he finishes writing it he no longer knows whether that idea or reason is really given shape or presence therein. In other words, he no longer knows why he wrote it, how he wrote it, what elements of reality, experience, unconscious memory, or incidental emotionality have had a part in it, what darknesses of consciousness, sentiment, or the senses, or what illuminations of mind have nourished it; nor does he know if he wrote it for himself or for others, for a self that includes others or for the others who are himself. Thus when one asks the author the whys and wherefores, lo, he adds "untruth" to "untruth"; to which are then added the "untruths" of the critics and readers. Hence in short, in making a book become "truth," many "untruths" converge.

I have used the word "author" here with Pirandello in mind. Since today more than ever the inclination is toward a geographical dislocation in modern and contemporary Italian literature, toward a regional and regionalistic centrifuging which certainly exists but which, especially as concerns Sicilian writers (without whom, it must be said, Italian literature today would count for little), is applied as an ethnic category, coming very close to being a kind of racism and giving rise to such idiotic designations as that of "the Sicilian clan"; and since, therefore, once must speak (and it is right to do so, though cautiously) of a nature and tradition particular to Sicilian narrative, one cannot help but think of Pirandello, who is the highest datum point in such a topos and who, in his vision of life, is the most Sicilian of all—which also goes to show how the highest degree of Sicilianness coincides with the greatest universality.

Pirandello has behind him Heraclitus, Empedocles, and Gorgias, and before his eyes that *great theatre of the world*—inexhaustible, full of contradiction and conflict, wavering between being and appearing—that is Girgenti, that small town (Spoon River, Our Town, etc.) in western Sicily. Bufalino instead has behind him Pirandello and before his eyes a library—or sometimes a labyrinth, sometimes a chessboard; or a labyrinth and chessboard at once, anguish and game. Which is not to say that the reality of Comiso (the town in which he was born and lives) does not find its way into this labyrinth and chessboard, complicating matters and moving a few pawns; however, his coming "after Pirandello" consists in his having transferred that wavering of the world, those contradictions, those oppositions without synthesis, those unreconciled and irreconcilable conflicts into the author himself, into his being as writer, into his writing—which for him too, as for Pirandello, constitutes nearly the totality of life.

For this first book in particular (but is it really his first?), but also for the others that he subsequently published, Bufalino has made marginal notes, declarations and confes-

sions which seem, indeed, to tend toward—in approximative terms—a kind of "introverted Pirandellianism," a Pirandellianism inside the writing, inside the being-as-writer. A Pirandellianism of a sort that Pirandello himself did not feel: for Pirandello, all the world's wavering, vacillating, and writhing do not touch the Author—who is reality's amanuensis, but also its demiurge. For Bufalino, on the other hand. . . . Here, for example, is an admission he made, about this very book: "I must confess that the first chapter I wrote (it is not the first in the definitive order, and there is no need to say which one it is) was born of a difficult game, the challenge of finding plausible interconnections among fifty words chosen beforehand for their common tone, color, and evocative charge. Something a bit less maniacal than the mathematics of Raymond Roussel, and the legitimacy of which I would not hesitate to defend—since, in my case, the connections between the provided *fiches* was neither fortuitously rhythmic (as in obligatorily rhymed sonnets) nor esoteric nor cabalistic, but born of a kinship and coalition of expression and music. . . . "

A dizzying confession . . . and enough to make any translator's head spin. (xi-xv)

Leonardo Sciascia, in an introduction to The Plague-Sower *by Gesualdo Bufalino, translated by Stephen Sartarelli, Eridanos Press, 1988, pp. ix-xv.*

Harriett Gilbert   (essay date 21 June 1990)

[*Gilbert is an English novelist and critic. In the following review, she comments on Bufalino's language and techniques in* Night's Lies.]

Conjurers are said to outwit us by using elaborate distraction techniques. They joke; they shuffle the playing cards; they engage us in shaggy-dog anecdotes; and all the while the key to their trick is being turned home right in front of us: click.

A literary magician, Gesualdo Bufalino plays similar games with his readers. *Night's Lies* is an elegant fiction, a dexterous, eye-catching riffle of aces, kings, queens, jokers and knaves behind whose cover the author is carefully preparing a narrative shock. And, when he springs it in the final chapter, a major reaction is to want to go back and begin reading over again, not because the ending seems false but because you would like to see how it's *achieved.*

The story, simply, is this. A student, a baron, a soldier and a poet are imprisoned on an island fortress somewhere off Italy. We are in the mid-19th century, a time throughout Europe of revolution, nationalist struggle, the battle for rights, and our heroes are due to be executed for having attempted to murder the king. On the eve of their execution, the prison governor offers them a deal: if one of them . . . *one* . . . will betray their leader, then all four conspirators will be released, sent abroad for a while and eventually allowed to slip home.

Having already refused to betray their leader under torture, the four merely spit at this suggestion, but the governor elaborates his plan. The men are to spend their last night of life in vigil in the prison chapel. After the vigil, as night pales to dawn, each will privately mark on one of the four blank papers provided either a cross, a defiant refusal, or else the name that will save both him and his comrades. If they avoid this test, he persuades them, they will never know whether they *might* have cracked and will mount the scaffold unsure if their deaths are honourable, or a fraud.

Once in the chapel, the four are confronted by a fifth man, also to be executed: the notorious bandit and holy blasphemer Cirillo. His recently tortured face bound in rags, Cirillo joins in the men's conversation and proposes that they should pass the long night by telling him stories about themselves, so that each can assess if 'the lives you have lived are worthily concluded by this stoic death; or whether, on the contrary, it does not sound an untoward false note.' So the student, the baron, the soldier, the poet all tell of one major event in their lives—events during which their political ardour is seen to be jostled by personal vice—with each of these narrative chapters followed by a chapter containing the questions, comments and judgments of the other prisoners.

If its structure is that of a formal debate, then the novel's language is also punctilious, lightly dusted with Latin quotations and words such as 'tantivies', 'glaired', 'montgolfier' with which the reader may not be on intimate terms. This quirk may have something to do with the fact that the author spent most of his life as a teacher—before, at 60, becoming a prize-winning novelist—but, if so, then the students of Sicily were privileged. Far from being oppressive, exclusive, the stylisation is wittily engaging, charming us into a world of ideas, abstractions and intellectual debate with none of the usual thumping of tubs and insistence that politics, ethics, religion and death be approached with solemnity.

Besides, there are strands that connect us, still, to the concrete and sensual world. Throughout the novel, Bufalino steps back from the intricate debates of his protagonists to show us the moon through the windows of the chapel, the sea that rises and roars on the rocks: those last slender links to life, the real world, that the four men will either relinquish or not for a possibly corrupted ideal. When the student Narcissus finishes his story 'of love, and of music, and moonlight', his sudden explosion of terror, of doubt about his death's usefulness, has as great an impact emotionally as intellectually.

The novel is also alert with small unexpectednesses. It's the bloodthirsty soldier Agesilaos, for instance, whose story most obviously tries to examine the roles played by God, religion and sin in men's actions. The soldier's tale is also concerned with the intertwining of personal hatred—in his case, for the man who by raping his mother caused him to be born—with a more disinterested hatred of political oppressors. Similarly, the other men's tales are a complex of psychoanalytic, political and philosophical enquiry. Has one the right to make uninvolved, uninformed bystanders martyrs to a cause? Can muddied waters give pure results? Is freedom something that people actually *want*?

In effect, the book is a sceptical survey of human (or, more precisely, male) beliefs, aspirations and values, a survey conducted throughout with integrity and wit. But what is revealed in the final chapter, while true to all that's preceded it, washes back to lift everything up to a higher and more exciting position: one in which it is suddenly clear that scepticism may also have faith, self-knowledge courage, and honour a sense of humour. In the end, Bufalino's most skilled sleight of hand is to have produced, from so careful a structure, so visionary and generous a climax.

Harriett Gilbert, "Midnight Feasts," in The Listener, *Vol. 124, No. 3170, June 21, 1990, p. 35.*

Pat Conroy

1945-

American novelist and nonfiction writer.

The following entry focuses on Conroy's novel *The Prince of Tides* (1986). For further information on Conroy's life and works, see *CLC,* Volume 30.

INTRODUCTION

Conroy is known primarily for his best-selling novels *The Great Santini, The Lords of Discipline,* and *The Prince of Tides,* all of which have been adapted for film. In these works Conroy blends fiction, myth, and personal revelation, drawing heavily upon his experiences growing up in a military environment in the southeastern United States. His works often concern a character's coming of age and address such issues as racism, authority, family values, loyalty, and personal integrity.

Born in Atlanta to a conservative Catholic family, Conroy was raised in various locales along the southeast coast, notably Beaufort, South Carolina. Conroy has described his father, a Marine Corps fighter pilot, as gruff and ill-tempered, and his mother as socially ambitious. Various fictionalized portraits of his parents, as well as of himself and his siblings, appear throughout his work. In 1963, after graduating from high school in Beaufort, Conroy enrolled at the Citadel, a military academy in Charleston, South Carolina, where he served as editor of the college literary magazine. Conroy's experiences at the academy, particularly his relationship with Lieutenant Colonel Thomas Nugent Courvoisie, Assistant Commandant of Cadets, also known as "The Boo," formed the basis for his first book, *The Boo,* a romanticized account of his cadet years.

After graduating from the Citadel in 1967, Conroy taught English at several area high schools, and in 1969 he accepted a position teaching disadvantaged black children on Daufuskie Island off the South Carolina coast. Conroy's experiences there, which culminated in his dismissal due to unorthodox teaching methods, led to his writing *The Water Is Wide,* a caustic retelling of his battles with student illiteracy and an intolerant school administration. The work was adapted for film in 1974 as *Conrack.* Following the publication of *The Water Is Wide,* Conroy returned to Atlanta and has since published several best-selling novels.

In his novels *The Great Santini, The Lords of Discipline,* and *The Prince of Tides,* Conroy used personal experience to examine issues related to loyalty, authority, and family relationships, particularly among men. The relationship of a father and son is explored in Conroy's first novel, *The Great Santini.* Bull Meecham, who calls himself "The Great Santini," is a marine fighter pilot who obscures the line between military and family life, dominating his wife and children with ruthless discipline and blind egotism. The novel chronicles the struggle of Meecham's son Ben to free himself from his father's tyranny and culminates in a highly competitive game of one-on-one basketball between the boy and his father. Ben wins the game and becomes the first member of his family to beat his father in any contest, an achievement symbolic of Ben's passage into manhood. *The Lords of Discipline* takes place at the Carolina Military Institute, an all-male academy based primarily on the Citadel. In this work Conroy explores the power struggles and viciousness often associated with military life. Will McLean, the narrator and a senior cadet, is assigned by his superiors to protect the Institute's first black student from hostile, segregationist forces within the student body. In order to carry out his assignment, Will must confront many of his fellow cadets, and his conflicting impulses between group loyalty and personal integrity are a source of the novel's dramatic tension. In addition, Conroy's juxtaposition of scenes of understanding and sympathy among the cadets and his graphic depictions of hazing practices at the Institute suggest the mixture of love and brutality that exists in this society of men.

In *The Prince of Tides* Conroy follows Tom Wingo, an unemployed high school English teacher and football coach, on a trip from coastal South Carolina to New York City, where he helps his twin sister Savannah recover from a nervous breakdown and suicide attempt. At the request of Savannah's psychiatrist, Tom relates episodes from the Wingo family history, revealing a bizarre and horrific past that includes disturbing incidents of their father's brutish behavior, the rapes of several family members, and the death of their brother. Despite these tragedies, critics have observed, the novel retains a sense of optimism due to the love that the Wingo children have for each other and the idea, expressed by Judy Bass, that "one's future need not be contaminated by a monstrous past." Although Conroy's fictional works have been faulted by some critics as implausible and melodramatic, they are often admired as courageous, imaginative, and ironically humorous exposés on such topics as military discipline, racial intolerance, paternal domination, and family relationships.

PRINCIPAL WORKS

The Boo   (nonfiction)   1970
The Water Is Wide   (nonfiction)   1972
The Great Santini   (novel)   1976
The Lords of Discipline   (novel)   1980
The Prince of Tides   (novel)   1986

CRITICISM

Brigitte Weeks   (review date 12 October 1986)

[*In the following excerpt, Weeks provides a generally favorable assessment of* The Prince of Tides, *noting what she considers minor weaknesses in style and plot.*]

As soon as Henry Wingo appears, on the very first page of *The Prince of Tides,* we know we are in Conroy country. The violent, abusive, insensitive brute of a Marine pilot, who terrorized his family as Lieutenant Colonel Bull Meecham in *The Great Santini,* has a new name and he's now a fighter pilot turned shrimper, but he hasn't changed. There's a similar supporting cast of rebellious children (Luke, Tom and Savannah Wingo), a long-suffering wife Lila, and a bunch of Southern Gothic extras that would put Steven Spielberg to shame. But the Wingos are painted in grimmer colors than the Meechams were and their family life is even more violent, though still punctuated by episodes of almost manic hilarity.

Taking, for his fifth novel, the same kernel of clearly autobiographic material that dominated *The Great Santini* (this book too is dedicated to his father and other family members) and flickered in and out of *The Lords of Discipline,* Conroy develops the story of the self-torturing Wingos into a novel that is monstrously long, yet a pleasure to read, flawed yet stuffed to the endpapers with lyricism, melodrama, anguish and plain old suspense. Given all that, one can brush aside its lapses like troublesome flies.

The story centers on the summer when 37-year-old Tom Wingo leaves South Carolina and goes to New York City. His mission there is to save the sanity of his suicidal twin sister Savannah by delving into memories of their shared childhood for her psychiatrist. (This creates a structural imbalance that almost derails the novel. The 50-minute-hour device is tired and the Manhattan scenes are pale shadows of the South Carolina drama. Fortunately, we lose sight of the psychiatric trappings almost at once.)

Savannah is by now a successful feminist poet—her second book is called *The Prince of Tides.* Tom's marriage is in limbo and their elder brother Luke is dead in mysterious circumstances which are revealed only at the very end of the saga. The evil geniuses of Tom's tale to the psychiatrist are their father, Henry Wingo, brute and Philistine, and Lila Wingo, the beautiful, adoring mother who betrays her children, her husband and, in the end, herself. The saving grace is the tight triangle of love that holds the three children together. Their relationship with each other, convincing and moving, lightens the somber mood of the novel.

The details of what happened on the South Carolina island of Melrose where the Wingos grew up should not be spelled out here, for we are in the hands of a fiendishly skilled storyteller. Conroy's plot twists and turns. Extravagant foreshadowing, especially of Luke's death and his mother's treachery, leads the reader down many false paths and even a partial list of his subjects boggles the mind: mental illness, racial hatred, marriage, the Vietnam War, child abuse, conservation, psychiatry, feminism, nuclear war, sports and, of course, the South.

"I know exactly who I am," says Tom as a boy. "I'm Tom Wingo, southern born and southern made." It is not, however, the usual manners, inhibitions and drawl of the Southerner that dominate this book, even though Tom Wingo postures as a good ol' southern boy in the drawing rooms of New York. The author's heart belongs to the land, the water, the winds, and the wildlife of the Carolina marshland. . . . (pp. 1, 14)

With his feet set firmly on his native earth, Conroy is, above all, a storyteller. His tales are full of the exaggeration and wild humor of stories told around a camp fire. When the young Wingos set out from their island to get revenge on a woman from nearby Colleton who has cruelly snubbed their mother, they don't just play any old Halloween prank on their victim. While she and her husband are on vacation, the kids smuggle a large, very dead loggerhead turtle into her house, drag it up to the master bedroom, ensconce it in the four poster bed, turn up the heat—and leave.

At times Conroy's intensity and gift for the nightmarishly grotesque become almost overpowering. One has to set the book down and check in with the familiar living-room furniture. His obsession with intruders bent on rape, recurring here from *The Great Santini,* and mirrored in the most violent of the hazing scenes from *The Lords of Discipline* has escalated from scary to horrific. The encounter on the isolated island between the children, their mother and three escaped convicts rivals in terror and gore anything Stephen King could conjure.

The echoes back and forth between *The Great Santini* and *The Prince of Tides* are pervasive, but the mood has changed. Bull Meecham was allowed more voice in *The Great Santini,* given more credit, allowed occasional displays of affection and died a hero's death. Henry Wingo is an outcast from his family, a failure at everything he puts his hands to and ends up in a federal penitentiary for running dope.

Despite his success as a novelist, Conroy implies that America has failed to fulfill his expectations in some profound way. Bitter humor is the only defense he gives Tom against mediocrity and middle age. "Mom, why don't you get a job bottling guilt? We could sell it to all the American parents who haven't mastered the fine art of making their kids feel like s—t all the time. You'd be a shoo-in to win the patent," he snarls at his once-beloved mother. His parents' marriage finally disintegrates, and that too is somehow the fault of our particular society: "In some ways, there was something classic and quintessentially American in their marriage. They began as lovers and ended up as the most dangerous and unutterable of enemies. As lovers, they begat children; as enemies, they created damaged, endangered children."

Words pour from Pat Conroy, creating a world full of passion, taking the reader into the soft inner souls of his characters. Some times he stumbles, and strays off course. The words slip out of control. When Tom meditates on his mission to Manhattan, he sounds like a pompous commencement speaker: "If I could summon the courage to tell it all, by speaking without forestallment, by humming the melodies of all those dark anthems that sent us marching so resolutely toward our appointments with a remorseless destiny . . . " But it's easy to forgive these lapses. Conroy gets carried away by the sound of his own voice, but the storyteller soon returns. Most often, the words are just right, cramming layers of meaning into a small sentence, as when Tom thinks of his grandmother's decline: "The capillaries in her brain seem to be drying up slowly, like the feeder creeks of an endangered river."

The terrain is rough in Conroy country and the climate stormy, but the views are often spectacular. *The Prince of Tides,* his largest and darkest novel, will unquestionably establish Pat Conroy as a popular novelist of depth and distinction. (p. 14)

Brigitte Weeks, "Pat Conroy: Into the Heart of a Family," in Book World—The Washington Post, *October 12, 1986, pp. 1, 14.*

Gail Godwin (review date 12 October 1986)

[*In the following review, Godwin finds the plot and style of* The Prince of Tides *excessively hyperbolic.*]

The Southern-boy protagonists of Pat Conroy's fiction have twin obsessions—oppressive fathers or father figures, and the South. Against both they fight furiously for selfhood and independence, yet they never manage to secede from their seductive entrappers. Some fatal combination of nostalgia and loyalty holds them back; they remain ambivalent sons of their families and their region, alternately railing against, then shamelessly romanticizing, the myths and strictures that imprison them.

After Bull Meecham, the self-aggrandizing hero of *The Great Santini,* crashes his F-7 and is buried with military honors, his oldest son, who has often prayed for his death, dons the father's flight jacket and is overwhelmed with love for him. In *The Lords of Discipline,* a corrosive fictional exposé of racism and brutality in a Southern military college, the narrator, a graduate of the college, tells us: "I want you to understand why I hate the school with all my power and passion. Then I want you to forgive me for loving the school."

The same ambivalences are rife in *The Prince of Tides.* The Southern-boy narrator, Tom Wingo, is now in early middle age. A fired high school teacher and football coach, he describes himself as a Southern-made and Southern-broken failure, "the most dishonest person I've ever met. I never know exactly how I feel about something." But he also claims that it is the Southern part of him "which is most quintessentially and fiercely alive," and that his Southern memories "surround the lodestar of whatever authenticity I bring to light as a man."

In contrast, Tom's twin sister, Savannah, is "one of those southerners who were aware from an early age that the South could never be more for them than a fragrant prison administered by a collective of loving but treacherous relatives." Having fled the low country of South Carolina right after high school, she is now a famous poet, living in New York and writing poems that make the language "sing and bleed at the same time" about growing up as a shrimper's daughter. "The South kills women like me," she tells Tom. However, safe in Greenwich Village, she periodically tries to kill herself.

It is her latest suicide attempt, followed by a severe psychotic withdrawal, that lands her in Bellevue, summons Tom to New York and provides the novel's narrative device. Savannah's psychiatrist, Dr. Susan Lowenstein ("one of those go-to-hell New York women with the incorruptible carriage of lionesses"), asks Tom to stay in New York for an extended period and tell her "all he knows" about Wingo family life. "From beginning to end," he promises, over a candlelit dinner at Petite Marmite. For the rest of the book, the chapters alternate between Tom's narratives of "the grisly details of our epic childhood" and his increasing romantic involvement with his sister's psychiatrist.

The Wingo family configuration bears resemblances to previous parent-sibling setups in Mr. Conroy's work, but this time everything is bulging with symbol and jacked up to the lofty realm of myth. The bullying Henry Wingo is another Santini, with a shrimp boat instead of an F-7, but the negative aspects of fatherhood and manhood that he personally embodies now extend to the bigger Bad Daddies of business, politics and the narrow-minded authoritarianism of government. The beautiful Lila Wingo belongs to that species of Southern mothers described in *The Lords of Discipline* who "rule their families with a secret pact of steel," and whose sweetness, deadly as snakes, "has helped them survive the impervious tyranny of Southern men." But her beguiling, undermining poisons have now leached beyond the domain of a specific family and stand for treacherous womanhood in all its manifestations, as well as the Southern way of life.

In the Wingos' "grotesque family melodrama," as Tom calls it, each of the three children has been assigned an unchangeable role. Savannah is the gifted lunatic who bears the accumulated psychotic energy. Luke, the older brother, is the strong, simple man of action, "The Prince of Tides" in Savannah's book of poems by that name, who becomes a local martyred folk hero after waging a one-man guerrilla war against the heaviest father of them all, the Atomic Energy Commission, which appropriates his hometown and the family's island to make plutonium for hydrogen bombs. And Tom is "the neutral country, the family Switzerland," a go-between with "the soul of a collaborator," who has been "tamed by mortgages, car payments, lesson plans, children, and a wife with more compelling dreams and ambitions than my own."

The ambition, invention and sheer energy in this book are admirable. But many readers will be put off by the turgid, high-flown rhetoric that the author must have decided would best match his grandiose designs. And as the bizarre, hyperbolic episodes of Wingo family life mount up, other readers are likely to feel they are being bombarded by whoppers told by an overwrought boy eager to impress or shock.

But readers who have a high tolerance for the implausible, the sentimental and the florid will pad happily off to bed for a week or so with this hefty tale of a Southern family "that fate tested a thousand times" clasped cozily to their chests, and read about the birth of twins in a hurricane, and a boy shooting the last bald eagle (his father makes him eat it and wear the feathers to school), and dead siblings stored in the freezer with the shrimp until burial time, and the pet tiger that rips the faces off rapists; and, progressing parallel to all this Wingo memorabilia, the satisfying, present-time story of a sassy, middle-aged Southern boy who sweeps the "breathtakingly beautiful" New York psychiatrist off her feet, teaches her unhappy son to play football, and comes to better terms with "the beauty and fear of kinship, the ineffable ties of family," so he can return home to "try to make something beautiful out of the ruins," as his sister has done with her poems, and raise his children "in a South stolen from me by my mother and father."

"With all due respect," Dr. Lowenstein asks Tom in their first meeting, before she succumbs to his charm, "why should we entertain the opinion of a white southern male?"

"Because, Doctor," Tom retorts provocatively, "when I'm not eating roots and berries . . . and when I'm not slaughtering pigs out back at the still, I'm a very smart man."

The thing is, beneath all his anguished ambivalence and excessiveness, Mr. Conroy is a smart man too. "I have a need to bear witness," his narrator tells us in *The Lords of Discipline.* "I want a murderous, stunning truthfulness. I want to find my own singular voice for the first time." In *The Prince of Tides,* the smart man and serious writer in Pat Conroy have been temporarily waylaid by the bullying monster of heavy-handed, inflated plot and the siren voice of Mother South at her treacherous worst—embroidered, sentimental, inexact, telling it over and over again as it never was.

Gail Godwin, "Romancing the Shrink," in The New York Times Book Review, *October 12, 1986, p. 14.*

R. Z. Sheppard   (review date 13 October 1986)

[*In the following excerpt, Sheppard mildly admonishes Conroy for implausible narrative devices in* The Prince of Tides.]

The *Prince of Tides,* Pat Conroy's high-blown family saga of coastal South Carolina, began to stir interest in May at the American Booksellers Association convention in New Orleans. Introduced by Walter Cronkite, Conroy regaled publishing executives and retailers with funny stories about his career and family. With just the right amount of country-boy shuffle, he told how his father, a rough Marine Corps fighter pilot, and his mother, a genteel Georgia beauty, gave new meaning to the word incompatibility. Conroy reminded everyone that his father was the model for the eruptive hero of his 1976 novel *The Great Santini.* He then disarmed his listeners by talking frankly about the close relationship between his life and his fiction.

Writers are usually touchy about discussing this subject. But faced with an eager and influential audience, Conroy suggested a truth common to most readers: they are less interested in distinctions of fact and fiction than in rousing stories and lively characters. *The Prince of Tides* provides plenty of both. There is the time Grandma tried out a coffin at the local funeral home and nearly frightened Ruby Blankenship to death. There is Grandpa, who can water-ski 40 miles and carries a 90-lb. cross through town every Good Friday. Conroy can be shameless in his extravagances of language and plot, yet he consistently conveys two fundamental emotions: the attachment to place and the passion for blood ties.

Literally and figuratively, the Wingos of "Colleton, S.C.," are crazy about one another. Father Henry is a shrimper whose feelings for his family are well disguised with verbal and physical abuse. His wife Lila despises his brutality and low status and dreams of moving up in Colleton society. Eldest Son Luke, the Rambo of the salt marshes, returns from Viet Nam to wage a one-man guerrilla war against the construction of plutonium production plants. Brother Tom is an ex-high school football coach struggling with the aftermath of a nervous breakdown and a failing marriage. His twin sister Savannah is a successful poet and, fortunately, a failed suicide.

The Wingos are players in a ramshackle tragicomedy supported by a dubious narrative device. After Savannah tries to kill herself in Manhattan, Tom comes to town and spends the summer talking to his sister's psychiatrist, the beautiful and unhappily married Dr. Susan Lowenstein. He is a charming Southern storyteller who fills his 45-min. hours with lyric and grotesque tales of his low-country family life. He also plays the defensive redneck to Lowenstein's assured Jewish intellectual, a match-up that begins as a clash of stereotypes and ends as beautiful chemistry. But it is never clear who is paying the psychiatrist's $75-a-visit fee and why she is more interested in Tom's yarns than in Savannah's feelings. . . .

Conroy tempts fate and the limits of his talent when he plays at being William Styron, John Irving and perhaps even Mark Twain, if Dr. Lowenstein's couch is considered as a raft on which Jew and Gentile drift toward enlightenment. There is also a reckless blend of Bobbsey Twins adventure and revenge fantasies usually associated with drive-in-movie horror festivals. Would you believe that after Lila, Savannah and Tom are raped by three escaped convicts, the family's pet Bengal tiger bursts in and rips the criminals into small pieces? Would you believe that no one finds out about this because Lila insists on cleaning up the mess before Henry comes home? What you can believe is that *Prince of Tides,* no small amusement, will be on the best-seller lists before you can say chutzpah and grits.

R. Z. Sheppard, "The World According to Wingo," in Time, New York, Vol. 128, No. 15, October 13, 1986, p. 97.

Lamar York   (essay date Spring 1987)

[*In the following excerpt, York discusses the theme of coming of age as evidenced in Conroy's first four works.*]

In the "Introduction" to the 1981 paperback reprint of *The Boo,* Pat Conroy wrote that "by reading *The Boo* you will become acquainted with the most primitive archaeological fragments of a writer's beginnings." . . . Whether he knew when he first wrote *The Boo* in 1970 that he would go on to write more books, it is unmistakable that he knew in 1981 that writing had been his intended career all along. Each of his three successive books, *The Water Is Wide* (1972), *The Great Santini* (1976), and *The Lords of Discipline* (1980), has as its protagonist a young man struggling to emerge from adolescence into his adult identity as an artist.

After writing three more books setting forth the coming of age of his artist protagonist, Conroy then went back to the first of his books and wrote in the 1981 preface to that book of his own recognition of what had been the earliest beginnings of his characters as himself, the writer. He wrote *The Boo,* he says, out of his own innocence, in "those sweet incorruptible days when I lived in Beaufort, South Carolina, taught some wonderful kids on Daufuskie Island, was deeply in love with my wife, and thought I would be happy forever. I had not learned to write then and had not even tried. I had no intimation that my writing and my nature were such inseparable communicants." But he did know, even then, that what he had written was not just revenge on behalf of his friend, Colonel Courvoi-

sie, or just an alumnus' recollection of his school days. What he had done was, he knew, to begin his life as a writer: "When I wrote the chapter at the end of the book entitled 'Me and the Boo,' I heard the resonant, unmistakable sound of my voice as a writer for the first time. I felt the full authority of the writer's scream forming in my chest, felt the birth of the artist in the wild country of the spirit, and knew it was somewhere in me and was deciding it was high time to begin moving out." Conroy's recognition here of his own origins as a writer has about it the same brash quality of his last two heroes, Ben Meecham and Will McLean, both of whom articulate lofty goals while those about them indulge in schoolboy routines. (pp. 34-5)

Conroy outlined in his 1981 "Introduction" most of the main points he would delineate in the stories of Will McLean, Ben Meecham, and Conroy himself, teaching on Daufuskie Island. His writing is personal, mostly autobiographical, which he explained in the 1981 "Introduction": "prose, all my prose, was a letter to the world telling what happened to me last summer. *The Boo* was my longest letter to the world." He also explains in the new "Introduction" how important place, and love of that place, is to his work, as it usually is in Southern storytelling. In the book itself Conroy said of the setting that "the Citadel cherishes the belief that the more hardship endured by the young man, the higher the quality of the person who graduates from the system," yet the day comes when "the cadet looks in the mirror, and in a moment of madness, decides he loves the place." But the special quality that place offers is, for Conroy, a sense of isolation. The Citadel was to become his place of splendid isolation in *The Lords of Discipline,* better even than remote Daufuskie Island in *The Water Is Wide,* or out of the way Beaufort in *The Great Santini.* But in the "Introduction" to the reprinted *Boo* it was the very love of language that provided the most palpable sense of isolation at the Citadel: "I . . . knew that I wrote the language with more facility than other cadets at the Citadel which infused me with no surfeit of confidence over my gift. In the barracks, a proven inability to function in the English language was unassailable proof of virility. Awkwardness with the written word was as natural to Citadel cadets as speed among impalas."

Finally, in the 1981 "Introduction" Pat Conroy deals with the greatest hurdle facing the artist he would become, the necessity to tell the truth. In staking out first Charleston and The Citadel for his first and fourth books, then Beaufort for his second and third books, he has, wherever his future books may be set, delineated the South Carolina coast as his special place, his own postage stamp of earth. And if, he says, he could tell the truth about this one place, he could tell the truth about his observations of people in any place: "if I could tell the whole truth about The Citadel, then I could write an accurate and withering description of the entire human race." One compelling aspect of Conroy's writing that he gives no hint of in his artist's apologia preface is how hard each of his protagonists would struggle with themselves in order to tell the truth. The struggle they each face is the same—their need to be liked, even loved, or at least admired. The need for approval, Conroy asserts clearly in each of his next three books, is the single greatest impediment to the absolute truthtelling necessary to the artist. Each of his protagonists comes to realize his need for approval and to deal with it in ways Conroy offers as the ritual of the coming of age of the artist as teacher, athlete, and cadet. (pp. 35-6)

In *The Water Is Wide* one of the themes of the emerging young artist as Southerner is how the hero confronts the task he has set for himself. In later books Conroy would tell the story of Ben Meecham's beating his Dad in basketball, and of Will McLean's story of surviving the rigors of The Citadel. Here, he tells the story of learning to teach school. (p. 37)

The main theme, however, in *The Water Is Wide,* a theme Conroy develops with each of his next two heroes, Ben Meecham and Will McLean, is the problem the artist faces of wanting, by virtue of his art, to change the world and make it better, rather than simply to tell the truth about what he sees in people and their behavior. He calls it, here and in the next two books, the problem of his own "do-gooderism." It is what leads him to Daufuskie Island: "I sat in the back of the boat and decided once and for all to take the job. Yamacraw was a universe of its own. The lushness of the island pleased me and the remarkable isolation of the school appealed to the do-gooder in me. Only a thoroughbred do-gooder can appreciate the feeling, the roseate, dawnlike, and nauseating glow that enveloped me. I had found a place to absorb my wildest do-gooder tendency. Unhappy do-gooders populate the world because they have not found a Yamacraw all their own." But setting out to teach the children of Daufuskie quickly turns into more of a task than even the well-meaning Conroy intended: "I had stumbled into another century. The job I had taken to assuage the demon of do-gooderism was a bit more titanic than anticipated. All around the room sat human beings of various sizes and hues who were not aware that a world surrounded them, a world they would be forced to enter, and enter soon."

Conroy's attack on the isolation of the children of Daufuskie quickly turns to an attack on the school system that will do nothing to alleviate the isolation. He writes an angry letter to the school superintendent who had hired him for the job on Daufuskie, a letter written "in a fit of Conroy passion, the tiny bellicose Irishmen residing in my genes and collective unconscious urging me on and whispering to me that a great injustice was being perpetrated and that it was up to me to expose this condition."

But, by 1968, while his first book is still two years away, Conroy says that he was "getting tired of my own innocence" when "something happened to me in April that also changed my life. . . . the lone rifleman murdered Martin Luther King, Jr." By the time he comes to teach on Yamacraw, Pat Conroy is at full tilt against racism, still expecting more to change the world than to record its emotions. He arranges an outing on the mainland for his students, who enjoy themselves and are well received in a white community. He thinks the world is beginning to change: "I thought later that perhaps . . . I had concocted a shallow arena for the betterment of race relations, that what we had done was better for us (some crowning achievement we could point to and say, 'Look what we have done for the improvement of mankind'). . . . We wanted to do so much, wanted to be small catalysts in the transformation of the disfigured sacramental body of the South, which has sired us. I was a cynic who needed desperately to believe in the salvation of mankind or at least in the potential salvation."

The situation began to change for Conroy just when and as it did for so many Southerners. He did not just read about the beginnings of the Civil Rights movement, however, because "by some miracle of chance, I was playing a high school basketball game in Greensboro, North Carolina, on the day that black students entered a dime store for the first nationally significant sit-in demonstration. I was walking past the store on the way to my hotel when I heard the drone of the angry white crowd." (pp. 38-9)

The strength of the combined racism and educational bureaucracy help Conroy to see that what he needed in order to write the truth is just to see it, not create it in his writing. He confronts both of these unchangeables, and begins to learn to see the world as the writer, taking it all in. Then, in a last mistake, he thinks he has straightened out the schoolboard because they return him to the position on Yamacraw even after the superintendent has fired him. He thinks he has won: "but that was when I was young. I underestimated the dark part of mankind that is rarely seen in the light of day. I failed to reckon with the secret beasts that reside in the lightless forests of men's souls. The beasts were watching me at the first board meeting, and in the flush of victory I failed to hear the baying of those hounds in the unlighted thickets ahead. . . . It was Homer who had written again and again about the dangerous folly of mortals challenging the gods."

In *The Water Is Wide* Conroy has described his own coming of age as a teacher, a journey he offers as a metaphor for the coming of age of the artist. He shows his coming of age in this arena of the artist just before launching into Ben Meecham's struggle to survive under a strong code of discipline. But Conroy also finds in his own epic battle with isolation, racism, and anti-intellectualism that he has formulated a philosophy, just as his later fictionalized protagonists would. He learns that "life was good, but it was hard," and with that preparation, Conroy went on beyond two works of autobiographical non-fiction to write two distinguished works of fiction describing the initiation of a young Southerner who would become the artist that is Conroy himself.

On one level, *The Great Santini,* Conroy's first novel, is a poignant Southern initiation story. As in *The Water Is Wide,* the theme of isolation is strong this time in Ben Meecham's transfer to John C. Calhoun in Ravenel, South Carolina for his final year of high school. A strong sense of place comes from his new friend Toomer Smalls, the crippled black flower peddler, who teaches him from the "textbook of the river . . . things he would never have known, the calculus of approach and recall that ruled every living thing in the tight, contained beauty of returning river . . . [where] all fish, the greatest and the smallest, listened to the testing of the tide in their every nerve ending, in every bone, and in every cell." (pp. 40-1)

The most immediate arena for Ben's initiation is the basketball court. For him, "the basketball was a part of him, an extension of him because of the long years of dribbling around trees, through chairs, down sidewalks, past brothers, away from dogs, past store windows and before the eyes of men and women who thought his fixation was demented at best." But when he finds no real competition at Calhoun High School, he soon returns to the more real task of adolescence in this novel, beating his father, a battle which merges with the game of basketball. Soon after arriving in Ravenel, the fictional Beaufort, Ben decides that the time has come to challenge his father on the court. (p. 41)

But neither basketball nor his father provide Ben with his real antagonist in this story of the coming of age of the artist. Ben includes neither attributes of his father nor of basketball expertise in his description of the perfect "God of Ben Meecham." His real antagonist, as it had been for Conroy in *The Boo* and *The Water Is Wide,* is his own sense of the need to be good, to gain the approval of everyone. The chief manipulator of Ben's need for approval is his sister Mary Anne. In the opening pages of the novel, while the family is still enroute to their new home in Ravenel, Ben tries to stop an argument between his brother and sister. But what Mary Anne hears from him is "the voice of sublime perfection. Was that the godly one? The sainted brother? The perfect son?" She is expert at telling Ben why he does the things he does: " 'Is that the voice of perfection?' " she asks him. " 'Is that he that hath fed on honeydew? Is that my saintly, sugarcoated brother, projected hero of the first game? The patron saint of jump shots?' " She is the character who enunciates the real nature of Ben, the problem he must overcome in order to see into human nature and tell the truth about it. He asks her, " 'Do you think either one of us will ever write?' " and she tells him " 'No. We won't write any books. Writing books is something you talk about when you're very young and continue to talk about all your life until you die.' " But she had told him, only moments earlier, the real reason he wouldn't write books: " 'You've got to have people love you. . . . you've got to have their approval. . . .' "

Mary Anne is more capable than any other character of letting Ben see the nature of his problem. Her relentless attack on his approval-seeking behavior heightens when he takes her to the Junior-Senior Prom: " 'There are two things about you I can't stand, golden boy. One is your sickening fake modesty. The other is your goodness. . . . You can't stop being good. You can't be satisfied with being an average nice guy, you've got to be the nicest guy that anyone will ever meet. But I've noticed that you're always good in ways where people can see it and compliment you on it.' " Mary Anne is also capable of showing Ben why his need for approval encourages dishonest responses in others, rendering him incapable of seeing people through artist's eyes for what they really are. " 'You and Mom can hurt people more with your piety than Dad ever hurt with his temper. . . . You know why Dad hits you. . . . he sees her piety in a male face and sometimes he can't help but hit it. If he can beat it out of you, he thinks maybe that some of it will be drained out of her.' "

And Ben knows, too, just as Conroy did in *The Water Is Wide,* that he needs to be good. He knows that at heart he is merely well-behaved. He complains to his mother of the injustice of his father's harsh treatment: " 'it's not like I was a juvenile delinquent and went around slashing tires and smoking cigarettes. When we lived on the base I never got in trouble with the M.P.'s. . . . I didn't do anything and yet I got knocked all over the place.' "

Ben tries to warn Mary Anne early on in the novel that he sees this move to Ravenel, just as he is beginning his last year of high school, as a matter of survival, every one for himself. " 'Look, Mary Anne,' " he had told her early in the novel, " 'my one goal this year is to survive without him mopping the floor with me. I'll play his little games as long as his fists don't bounce off my head every night. It looks to me like you're going to have to learn the same thing.' " But by the end of the novel, only three pages before the end, Ben finally realizes how his do-gooder ways have already distorted relationships, especially with Mary Anne. Their father is dead, Ben is driving them back to Atlanta, and Mary Anne sits in the back seat of the car, flicking tears at him from a spoon as she had done to their father on the original trip to Ravenel. He finally understands not only how right his sister is, but how she has been the chief victim of his need for approval. "For his whole life, Ben had thought that he was her most significant ally, but lately, he had come to look at himself differently. He was beginning to suspect and recognize his own venomously subtle enmity to his own sister. Because he had been afraid, he had said 'yes' to everything his parents wanted, . . . had danced to the music of his parents' every dream, and had betrayed his sister by not preparing them for a girl who would not dance. But Ben knew that there was a girl named Mary Anne in the back seat who could teach Lillian and all the other lovely women in the world things about beauty they would never know. He had always thought that Mary Anne had been harmed by the coldness of her father and the beauty of her mother. It was only lately that he was having small moments of clarity, of illumination, and seeing himself for the first time as the closest of Mary Anne's enemies, the kindest of her assassins."

On the first page of *The Lords of Discipline,* Pat Conroy writes that this book will tell "the history of my becoming a man." More importantly, this book is, more assuredly than the previous ones, the story of the coming of age of an artist. It features a unique isolation. After one book about Charleston and two about Beaufort, South Carolina, Conroy returns in this fourth book to Charleston. Charleston, the city, is as much a character as any antagonist Will McLean faces. It is "a dark city, a melancholy city, whose severe covenants and secrets are as beguiling as its elegance, whose demons dance their alley dances and compose their malign hymns." (pp. 41-3)

McLean has the same need of approval that Conroy confessed as a teacher on Yamacraw in *The Water Is Wide,* that Mary Anne accused Ben Meecham of in *The Great Santini.* "I was," McLean says, "the most preachy, self-righteous, lip-worshipping, goody goody person I have ever known. My ideas were gaseous emanations rising out of a natural, inexhaustible well-spring of piety." McLean tells the reader why the need to do good has to be overcome in order for the artist to tell the truth: "my goodness is my vanity, my evil. It does not well up naturally out of me but is calculated and plotted. . . . Sometimes I will reveal this to friends so they will like me and praise my honesty, but in actuality, I am presenting them with a mariner's chart of my character." (pp. 44-5)

In his greatest test as a do-gooder, McLean comes to the ultimate use of it, brooding for days after his roommate Pig's discharge and suicide: "In those dreams I satisfied my own sick and overextended need to be my own greatest hero, I had a passion for the undefiled virtuous stand and a need to sacrifice myself for some immaculate cause. . . . Who else would I take as prisoners of my high sanctity before my life was over?" But Pig's case has already been the means of his breaking the cycle of do-gooderism and delivering himself from the need for approval by doing the right thing no matter what. In defending Pig before the student Honor Court, McLean has realized that no country, institution, or ideal is worth a single individual. He comes to the truth of the artist, that only the individual is ever too holy to violate: "If I could help Pig get out of this room unharmed and safe, I would tell any lie I could and I would tell it under oath. I would commit an honor violation as easily and simply as I adjusted my uniform belt in the morning." And though for Pig it is too late, for McLean it is not. He sheds his overwhelming need to do the right thing in order to look good. Now he is ready to tell the truth as he sees it. McLean asks the Commandant of the Corps to sign his diploma, in addition to the President and Trustees. "I want the name of a man I can respect on my diploma, Colonel." But the Colonel returns the diploma to McLean, saying, " 'There already is.' And he pointed to my name."

Pat Conroy's four books, especially the last three, remind the reader of the familiar dictum that Southern storytelling is either about young people growing up or old people who have become like children again. Southern novels are seldom about statistically average middle class wage earners in the suburbs. Conroy's novels are clear evocations of the special quality of adolescents coming into manhood in the recent South. But in each he offers an autobiographical protagonist who has to acquire a greater need to face the truth than he has to be liked. Each protagonist has the same problem, that of having to learn acceptance of the world as it is, without judging it or trying to reform it. In each book, Conroy suggests that art begins when the artist recognizes the most natural state of mankind, always in need of grace, yet nevertheless ready to have its story told by the artist. (pp. 45-6)

> *Lamar York, "Pat Conroy's Portrait of the Artist as a Young Southerner," in* The Southern Literary Journal, *Vol. XIX, No. 2, Spring, 1987, pp. 34-46.*

David Toolan   (essay date 22 February 1991)

[*In the following excerpt, Toolan explores the spiritual and psychological underpinnings of Conroy's work.*]

Pat Conroy no longer calls himself a Catholic—nor does he regret his exit from the fold. "I have never had a single day when I wished to be Catholic again," he has said. But Catholic antibodies run in his blood, feed his imagination, in much the same way that the palmetto groves, tidal creeks, and salt marshes of his boyhood Georgia and South Carolina low country do. As he testifies:

> I left the church but she has not left me. This seems to be the universal condition of ex-Catholics. . . . I loved Gregorian chants, the sight of nuns at prayers on Good Friday, the Sanctus bells, the covered forms of saints during Lent, the drum roll of the Confiteor with all the sadness and elegance of a dead language filling the church and entering my bloodstream at the ear, and the sunburst of gold when the priest raised the monstrous chalice at the Consecration. I loved the ceremony, the adherence to tradition, the astonishing continuity of it all. The church equipped me with a limitless arsenal of metaphor. I have never recovered from the vividness of its imagery, from the daze of its language.

Never recovered indeed. Nor does he appear to want a complete cure. That "arsenal of metaphor" fortifies all his pages, and puts us on notice that the story is a passion narrative in which nothing less than a soul's loss or gain is at stake. Few signs of modernist anomie are to be found in Conroy country; nor is there any fancy postmodernist narrative fragmentation or sudden interruptions of the author telling you this is a fiction. His stylistic mentor is the flamboyant Thomas Wolfe. No minimalist he. Conroy doesn't hoard or save anything till later, but, as Annie Dillard advises, spends it all, right away, every time.

I hear that his next book will be on the Holocaust. But to date all of Conroy's hero-narrators have been Catholic, and in a Bible Belt milieu of red necks and scions of "old families," this makes them eccentric outsiders. Belonging does not come easily but must be earned by trial and ordeal. The stories, then, are romances in the medieval sense, adventure stories, tales of young knights errant braving the odds on the playing field, outwitting giants, rescuing damsels in distress, or taking on the lost causes of put-upon Jews and blacks. Dramatic high points come with moments of glory on the basketball court or football field—marvelously described—where the young athlete, till then a cipher in the crowd, acquires "a face, a name, and an identity." At the same time Conroy's heroes are firmly rooted in the ethos of the Southern tidewater of their birth, in their families, and in the peculiar traditions of their faith.

In a sense what these tales track is but a single life, one boy's rough rite of passage—through the betrayals of high school, college, first job, and marriage—to an adult ethic of honor and loyalty. It is not exactly everyman's story, for the hero is of a certain Appolonian type: intuitive, duty-bound, vacillating, his own worst critic, and given to either/or choices that will prove his courage or cowardice. Ambiguity is anathema. Unless he finds a proper enemy or an underdog to defend, energy and action fail him. If there is a spiritual path here—and there is—it is Percival's quest for the Grail, the way of the free-lance warrior/adventurer, which relies on the choice of worthy opponents; the hero must test the weight of his youthful idealism, his loyalties, loves, and hopes—his theological virtues—against various adversaries: a tyrannical father (*The Great Santini*), a conspiracy of military school bullies (*The Lords of Discipline*), institutionalized poverty and racism (*The Water Is Wide*), or the betrayals of his mother and his own heart (*The Prince of Tides*). Along the way he is aided by wisdom-figure sisters or respected male mentors, usually coaches or imaginative teachers of English or history. (Conroy's first, self-published book, *The Boo,* was a memoir of a tough but colorful college teacher.)

Undoubtedly, a large slice of Conroy's autobiography feeds into these stories. His first novel and in some ways my favorite, *The Water Is Wide,* is a *roman à clef,* a thinly disguised account of the author's year (1969) teaching eighteen impoverished black grammar school children, fifth through eighth grades, on Daufuskie Island (called Yamacraw in the book) off the South Carolina coast. (The film version, titled *Conrack,* starred Jon Voight.) *Water* tells what it was like (engrossing and harrowing) to teach children whom the twentieth century had passed by. Most of them had never left their island, didn't know what country they lived in, couldn't read or count, didn't know the Atlantic Ocean lay beside them, thought the Civil War was fought against the Germans and Japs, hadn't heard that JFK and Martin Luther King, Jr., were shot, and still believed the earth was the center of the universe.

Conroy's emerging educational philosophy: "Life was good, but it was hard; we would prepare to meet it head on, but we would enjoy the preparation." His descriptions of epic battles with school superintendents ("not evil men . . . just predictably mediocre"), and what he did with these pupils, exposing them to classical music and taking them to Washington, D.C., made me wish I'd had him as a teacher at that age. "I lacked diplomacy and would not compromise," he admits. "I could probably still be with the Yamacraw kids had I conquered my ego."

Unmistakably, one also hears the author's personal history in his next book, *The Great Santini.* The satire of CCD classes, notably the nuns' lectures on sex and how they made a boy feel—that the Prince of Darkness has staked a claim to his loins—obviously comes from one who has been there. And, as a nomadic military brat himself, Conroy surely knew young Ben's longing "for a sense of place, of belonging, and of permanence . . . [and] friends whose faces did not change yearly." Indirectly in this novel, he began to tell his mother's story with the seemingly benign Lillian Meecham, "Santini's" wife, who sees only what she chooses to see and subtly reinforces the code of her tyrannical husband—whose prototype is clearly Colonel Donald Conroy, U.S.M.C. Ret. (both parents are heralded in the dedication as "grandest of fathers and Marine aviators" and "grandest of mothers and teachers"). This despite the fact that, in this as in the other novels, the young hero's childhood has been "one long march of fear."

The theme of the *The Great Santini* is courage. It presents a classic Oedipal struggle, the tale of a boy ("the son as challenger, the son as threat, the son as successor, the son

as man") pitted against an overbearing, Marine pilot father. . . . (pp. 127-28)

The next novel, *Lords of Discipline,* focuses on the meaning of honor. It celebrates the wonder of male bonding, a boy's first love (she, an upper-crust damsel in distress, shamelessly jilts him), and his enduring affection for the most beautiful of Southern cities. It draws on Conroy's experience of plebe hazing and "four years of fear" as a cadet at The Citadel in Charleston, South Carolina, from which he graduated in 1967. The widowed mother here—who belongs to "that taloned species who speak with restrained and self-effacing drawls . . . and rule their families with a secret pact of steel"—has sent her son off to a paranoid's delight, the kind of place where catastrophic expectation is foreordained. The young hero, Will McLean, takes on the role of protector of the school's first black student, and consequently finds himself up against the "refrigerated intelligence" and ego (it would "fit snugly in the basilica of St. Peter's in Rome") of the college president, General Bentley Durrell, and his sadistic cadet minions, a kind of secret Ku Klux Klan within what is called the South Carolina Military Institute. We all wish we had foes as coldly monstrous.

> At first [says Will McLean], I thought I had wasted my college years, but I was wrong. The Institute was the most valuable experience I have ever had or will have. I believe it did bring me to manhood: the Institute taught me about the kind of man I did not want to be. Through rigorous hardness, I became soft and learned to trust that softness. . . . I want you to understand why I hate the school with all my power and passion. Then I want you to forgive me for loving the school.

We do understand: The endurance of male friendships under adversity. And that opposition makes him feel alive, checks his grandiosity, gives coherence and weight to the mercurial dreamer, the eternal youth in him.

In a school full of cracker patriots, Will has a "negative attitude," is a guilty, knee-jerk liberal, and opposed to the war in Vietnam. Thanks to his violent father, he admits, "Rebellion came naturally to me. It is the tyrant's most valuable gift." But underneath his bravado and defensive sarcasm lies the self-doubter's inevitable "Yes, but. . . ." In retrospect, Will senses something phony, compulsive, in his outlaw's rescuing operations. "I felt I had a power," the boy almost shouts, "I could put myself in the place of others and ask myself how I would feel if I were in their place." He does have that power. But he does not quite see the ocean of fear he swims in, only the cost of his disobedience. Having habituated himself to suspect the motives of the authorities, whoever they are, he turns that suspicion against himself in the form of self-loathing. You might anticipate that young Will, if he turned up in another Conroy novel, would be moving ahead by fits and starts, with the debris of unfinished projects all around him—unhorsed, swamped, plagued by doubts.

This is exactly the condition that Conroy faces in *The Prince of Tides* with Tom Wingo, who regales us with the saga of a "family with a fatal attraction to the extraordinary gesture."

"As a family we were instinctive, not thoughtful. We could not outsmart our adversaries but we could surprise them. . . . We functioned best as connoisseurs of hazard and endangerment. We were not truly happy unless we were engaged in our own private war with the rest of the world."

The line is familiar by now. The setting: South Carolina's barrier islands, whose magic beauty Conroy lets us smell and taste. The suicidal Mary Anne, sister of the hero Ben in *The Great Santini,* in a sense reappears here, more fully formed, as Savannah, the sister who has escaped to become a successful poet in New York (the South is death, she tells us, for women who don't choose to hide their intelligence). Her amnesia and schizophrenic collapse will propel her twin brother Tom to remember their troubled growing up at the hands of a violent but weak father and a powerful mother, Lila Wingo—whose character, here fully rounded, is shaped by Conroy's own mother, the woman he credits with having given him "the gift of tongues."

As Conroy explains in an *Atlanta Journal* article:

> My pretty mother had been hurt because she had been born poor. I never knew a woman who lusted so openly for gentility, for the grace and prestige of a family history she would never have. During her whole life, she burned to be what she could never be. So *Gone with the Wind* became the King James Version of her own reclamation and remaking of herself in the image of Scarlett O'Hara. . . . When my mother married a Conroy, whose family originated in the Irish county of Roscommon, she thought she was being true to the spirit of her heroine O'Hara. . . . I never saw the cunning strategies she employed . . . as she turned me into a Southern male with her seal of approval stamped along the high margins of the packaging. Nor did I notice the distinctive moment my mother began the long, curious process of turning me into a Southern writer who would tell my mother's story to the world.

"No Southern man will ever understand himself," he adds, "until he learns how the South cripples its women. . . ." As she lay dying of leukemia in 1984, Conroy's mother asked him if he was writing about her, "to make me beautiful." He did.

He also made her a force to be reckoned with: a common shrimper's wife but also a superb gourmet cook, and a kind of Cumean Sybil who discerns the dreams of animals, wears many masks, and spins deadly webs. Lila Wingo's campaign to seduce a local land baron is worthy of a Douglas MacArthur. In time their collusion with bureaucrats from the Atomic Energy Commission will destroy the children's beloved island home and their town by the river. Papa goes to jail and Mama (divorced now) gets her mansion and phony pedigree, but her uncompromising, too-good-to-be-true son Luke, an ex-Green Beret who remains true to the quixotic Southern code of lost causes, will secede from the Union. A good-natured Rambo, more brawn and pure instinct than brain, he's the perfect athlete

and martyr-for-a-cause that Conroy's central heroes are not.

The many anecdotal digressions make *The Prince of Tides* Conroy's most richly textured family saga to date. In fact, the diversions—various escapades of the siblings (like placing a dead loggerhead turtle in a local patrician's bed), grandmother Tolitha's funeral arrangements, grandfather Amos's water skiing stunts and Good Friday "way of the cross," and finally the riveting horror story of a giant rapist by the name of "Callinwolde" who twice terrorizes the family (the second time to his bloody regret)—are alone worth the price of admission. (The book will be on celluloid soon.) One has no trouble accepting the verdict of surviving Wingo brother and sister that "our life in the house by the river," however scarring, has been "relentlessly interesting"—and "somehow magnificent."

But there are really two main stories here, one of a damaging but magic childhood, the other of the adult narrator's odyssey in New York. When we first meet him, Tom is anything but happy. The theatrics of youth are over. He is thirty-five years old and grieving for his dead brother, out of work, "bushwhacked" by the women's liberation movement, "sick of being strong, supportive, wise, and kingly," and haunted by "the terrible knowledge that one day I would be an old man still waiting for my real life to start." His wife Sallie, whom he has put through medical school on his teacher/coach salary and is now making a hundred grand a year, doesn't need rescuing. Choosing sides, us *vs.* them, at this juncture doesn't work so neatly. It means dropping out, quitting—and as we learned in *Lords of Discipline,* that's forbidden. Real men don't quit. But if Tom is a sample, when on leave from a war they do close down, shut their Sallies out, and retreat into bitterness and self-pity. They become W. B. Yeats's "unfinished man with his pain, brought face-to-face with his own clumsiness."

I never read Conroy without thinking of him as illustrating Ernest Becker's now classic rendition of the Oedipal struggle in *The Denial of Death* (1973). Becker's thesis was that the modern autonomous self—the grail of Conroy's young heroes—is a "vital lie," a denial of our creatureliness. Behind all the striving to become independent, a shaper of one's own destiny rather than a passive object of fate, Becker argued, lies the terror of death—symbolized by the engulfing world of mothers, vulnerable flesh, and the earthly. Fleeing death, we "partialize" ourselves, construct our own prisons. The emerging self typically strikes a bad bargain, building up character armor and trading off feeling, sensitivity, and wonder at the vast, numinous universe (the "softness" of Conroy's heroes) in return for an identification with some cultural project that falsely promises to guarantee one's own immortality.

Of course Conroy's men-in-the-making are unwilling to make this lethal trade-off—and the high drama of his books consists in the *non serviam,* "their great refusal to become the Man of Iron." "I am not Santini," cries Ben at the close of *Santini.* The last word in *Lords of Discipline,* as the hero Will McLean graduates, is his crediting "the system" for proving to him that "I was not one of them." But these refusniks do not know so well how to say yes. And we (and they) mistrust their daredevil bravado for what it conceals about their hearts.

In any case, come the cessation of hostilities, they do not seem any better off than (or different from) the grisly old despots they have defied—wounded, impotent Fisher Kings all. What emerges, as Ernest Becker claimed, is something right out of Kierkegaard: a dread-filled vacuum, the sickness unto death. Taken unawares, they are also thus poised for a leap of faith, as the threshold of what Becker called "legitimate foolishness." Which is just where we find Tom Wingo in this novel.

The free-lance adventurer, the man of action he thought he was—who is clearly differentiated in this book as Tom's naive, Silvester Stallone-like, and celibate brother Luke—has returned from the chase, settled into cooking perfect soufflés, and feels "tamed by mortgages, car payments, lesson plans, children, and a wife with more compelling dreams than my own. . . . I have the soul of a collaborator. A Vichy government has set up headquarters in that soul." He is scourging himself for not being what his fanatic older brother was. He fears his own emptiness, vacuity, boredom, "the death-in-life of the middle class," and doesn't know who he is or what he wants. On top of all that, he sees his mother, whom he both admires and fears, in all the women he has ever slept with.

So the second story woven into *The Prince of Tides* is the one of Tom's comeback, his resurrection from the dead, and his acceptance of limits and ambiguity. The opportunity is provided by Susan Lowenstein, his sister's therapist. The contretemps provides Conroy fans with the usual outrageous entertainment (and includes a moving testimony to the vocation of coaching). The healing love affair with Susan represents new territory for the hero and the author, Conroy's first bid at portraying a mature sexual relationship.

That relationship, one is led to believe, would not have bloomed if a new man hadn't already been rising from the closed tomb of Tom's despair. The poet in him comes again to the surface, which for him means roots, his connection to a particular place, the "Southern part of me which is most quintessentially alive," that is both wound and anchorage.

In remembering the noble savage, his brother Luke, he recalls something else: that precious animal element, a certain call of the wild that is indistinguishable from the summons of the creator and is answered to in the gut.

The Prince of Tides reads like a hymn, a celebration of ties that no longer bind, or of Wallace Stevens's line that "The imperfect is our paradise." At the close Tom is still unemployed, still dreaming of the gorgeous "Lowenstein." But he seems to accept, however ambivalently, that he has no

duty to pretend that he was made in the image of his martyred brother. Instead, he reowns the regenerative sea; it is part of him, runs in his blood. He will count on the constancy of returning tides. Reunited at the end with his ex-con father, his wife, and daughters, Tom Wingo does not break out into a warrior's song. He is off his horse, on foot—a prince still, but unguardedly human.

> I had come to this moment with my family safely around me and I prayed that they would always be safe and that I would be contented with what I had. I am Southern made and Southern broken, Lord, but I beseech you to let me keep what I have, Lord. I am teacher and coach. That is all and it is enough.

Don't be fooled. However lyrical he is at this point, this is still the prayer of a man who is sure he dwells in a fearfully *un*safe world. Unlike his brother who never once failed, he is not innocent. And if you want the theology that charts this sort of maturity, for this type of person, read Paul Tillich's *Courage to Be* again. Conroy's is the Catholic version, juiced by devils, angels, and a good deal more laughter. (pp. 129-31)

> *David Toolan, "The Unfinished Boy & His Pain," in* Commonweal, *Vol. CXVIII, No. 4, February 22, 1991, pp. 127-31.*

FURTHER READING

Bass, Judy. "A Prince of Pain." *Chicago Tribune Books* (19 October 1986): 3.

   Reviews *The Prince of Tides,* describing the work as "a brilliant novel that ultimately affirms life, hope and the belief that one's future need not be contaminated by a monstrous past."

Eder, Richard. Review of *The Prince of Tides,* by Pat Conroy. *Los Angeles Times Book Review* (19 October 1986): 3, 11.

   Faults *The Prince of Tides,* above all, for its unjustifiably inflated story. Eder implies that Conroy could have fashioned a worthwhile novel had he limited himself to describing life in the South Carolina tidewater town which forms the heart of the story.

Leviton, Joyce. "Shaping His Pain into Novels, Pat Conroy Gets His Reputation, His Fortune—and His Revenge." *People Weekly* 15, No. 4 (2 February 1981): 67-8.

   Overview of Conroy's personal life as it pertains to his work.

Additional coverage of Conroy's life and career is contained in the following sources published by Gale Research: *Contemporary Authors,* Vols. 85-88; *Contemporary Authors New Revision Series,* Vol. 24; *Contemporary Literary Criticism,* Vol. 30; *Dictionary of Literary Biography,* Vol. 6; and *Major 20th-Century Writers.*

Réjean Ducharme
1941-

French-Canadian novelist, playwright, and screenwriter.

The following entry presents an overview of Ducharme's career through 1992.

INTRODUCTION

Ducharme is considered a major figure in contemporary French-Canadian literature. The author of complex and challenging fiction, Ducharme is known for the surreal quality of much of his work and for his sophisticated use of language. Critics often remark on his original treatment of themes of alienation, despair, and the search for identity in the modern world.

Little biographical information is available about Ducharme, who shuns almost all publicity. Born in 1941 in Saint-Félix-de-Valois, Quebec, Ducharme seems to have lived most of his adult life in Montreal. Critics were impressed by the sophistication of his first novel, *L'avalée des avalés* (*The Swallower Swallowed*). In the wake of excitement that followed the publication of this work, French reporters traveled to Montreal to obtain more information on Ducharme; however, they found he invariably changed his hotel address every two or three days to avoid being located. To date, the only authorized photograph of Ducharme is one which he sent to his publisher to include on the book jacket of *The Swallower Swallowed.* So absolute was Ducharme's refusal to meet journalists that many French critics questioned his existence and asserted that his name was a pseudonym for another author. They only accepted Ducharme's existence after he wrote letters to a number of reviewers, and after his publisher allowed the press to examine Ducharme's manuscripts. When Ducharme's play *Ah! Ah! (Ha! Ha!)* won a Governor General's Award in 1982, Ducharme's mother accepted it for him. During the 1980s, Ducharme published no new works; his only public gesture was his participation in an art show under an assumed name, Roch Plante.

The Swallower Swallowed concerns a young girl whose rage at adult authority and hypocrisy gives her the feeling that the world wishes to "swallow" her, and that she, in turn, must "swallow" it in self-defense. His next two novels, *Le nez qui voque* and *L'océantume* (both of which were written before *The Swallower Swallowed*) also describe the psychological journey from adolescence to adulthood, and like much of Ducharme's work, present characters who find themselves at odds with the world around them. In *Le nez qui voque,* a boy traumatized by his approaching adulthood purposely deceives and ridicules others in order to distance himself from a world he loathes. *L'océantume* describes a young woman who lives with her family aboard a boat stranded in a river. She eventually leaves her

family and, with a young friend, journeys downriver toward the ocean in order to sever her ties with her past. Many critics consider these three works a trilogy of adolescent rebellion. It is not only in these three novels, however, that Ducharme deals with the tribulations of young people. Appearing in the same year as *L'océantume,* the dramas *Le Cid maghané* and *Inès Pérée et Inat Tendu* also treat the problems of young adults who attempt to establish their identities in the context of an unsympathetic world. *Le Cid maghané,* set in a Montreal ghetto, is both a parody of Pierre Corneille's *Le Cid* and a satire on French-Canadian identity, with young men modeling their lives on characters from American comic books and movies. The two childlike adults in *Inès Pérée et Inat Tendu* search for food, security, and love in a dark comic world which ultimately destroys them.

La fille de Christophe Colomb is a surreal novel in verse. This work concerns a woman who is the offspring of Christopher Columbus and a chicken. After the death of her parents, she finds herself torn between the human and animal worlds, and in her attempt to reconcile the two, prompts a war which destroys humanity. In his more realistic works, Ducharme portrays individuals who find themselves alienated from others. For instance, the drama *Le marquis qui perdit* deals with France's loss of Quebec to the English, and emphasizes the alienation associated with loss of national identity. Ducharme's *L'hiver de force* (*From Wild to Mild*), traces a couple's quest to find a simpler life. They reject the consumer society of twentieth-century North America and refuse to produce or own anything, even to the point of homelessness. *Les enfantômes* purports to be the memoirs of a middle-aged man whose physical and mental development ceased during childhood, and who wonders why he no longer grieves for his mother or his twin sister, both of whom died when he was very young. In Ducharme's drama *Ha! Ha!,* two bickering couples ridicule one another as part of an elaborate game, until one of the female characters jumps out a window while the other three shout phrases reminiscent of children's games implying that she is the loser. In 1990, after a silence of nearly a decade, Ducharme published *Dévadé,* a novel set in the 1970s in which a group of young adults try to cope with insecurity and helplessness.

Critics often praise Ducharme for his linguistic playfulness, including his use of bilingual puns and neologisms, and his interjection of unusual situations into his works. Eccentric narrators are another device Ducharme utilizes in his fiction: the protagonist of *The Swallower Swallowed* attempts to invent her own language, and the memoirist of *Les enfantômes* purposely writes in an attic lit only by a flickering candle rather than in a well-lit room. As D. J. Bond points out, Ducharme's works leave many readers both "bewilder[ed]" and "spellbound" by their presentations of language, theme, and image. Because of the complexity of Ducharme's language, few of his works have been translated into English. However, he remains one of the most critically acclaimed French-Canadian writers. Charles Foran describes Ducharme as "Quebec's most celebrated novelist, a figure of near-mythic status."

PRINCIPAL WORKS

L'avalée des avalés (novel) 1966
    [*The Swallower Swallowed,* 1968]
Le nez qui voque (novel) 1967
Le Cid maghané (drama) 1968
Inès Pérée et Inat Tendu (drama) 1968
L'océantume (novel) 1968
La fille de Christophe Colomb (novel) 1969
Le marquis qui perdit (drama) 1970
L'hiver de force (novel) 1973
    [*Wild to Mild,* 1980]
Les enfantômes (novel) 1976
Ah! Ah! (drama) 1978; published as *Ha ha!,* 1982
    [*Ha! Ha!,* 1986]
Les bons débarras (screenplay) 1979
Les beaux souvenirs (screenplay) 1981
Dévadé (novel) 1990

CRITICISM

The Times Literary Supplement   (review date 18 April 1968)

[*In the following excerpted review, the critic discusses* L'avalée des avalés (The Swallower Swallowed) *as a treatment of adolescent psychology.*]

At the very outset [of *The Swallower Swallowed*] Réjean Ducharme puts the reviewer on the spot. His novel is not "about" anything. Nietzsche in the *Birth of Tragedy* has a remark which is relevant here and which in English might run: "Art is not an imitation of nature but a metaphysical complement to it—something created with the express purpose of dominating it". To say that the book is "about" a young French Canadian girl called Bernice before and at the stage of puberty, that she is half-Jewish, that her parents squabble, that she is sent away from her Usher-ish home on an island in a great river—the Saint Lawrence?—to live with strictly orthodox Jewish relatives in New York, and that at the end she finds herself in an embattled Israel—to say all this is really to convey nothing of the book's quite remarkable quality.

And to go on to say that every young child lives in a world of fantasy is to beg the question. Every young child *is* its world. In this book the grown-ups loom up and just as suddenly fade, ogres one minute, irrelevant bores the next. There are imaginary conversations with imaginary confidantes who can be killed in motor accidents and come to life again, and who are just as "real" as brother Christian who wants to be a javelin-thrower; there are wild adventures that peter out; there are sudden cruelties; blood temperature shoots up and wild visions jostle frighteningly in the forefront of the brain. This is Bernice and her world. Not an imitation of the "real" world, but a metaphysical complement to it.

> "*Juveniliad,*" *in* The Times Literary Supplement, *No. 3451, April 18, 1968, p. 391.*

D. J. Bond   (essay date Winter 1976)

[*In this excerpt, Bond analyzes the difficultes Ducharme's characters encounter in establishing their own identities.*]

The first impression which strikes the reader of Ducharme's novels is one of amazement and even bewilderment, provoked by the rapid style, the flood of words, the disparity of themes, the arbitrary succession of thoughts, chapters and textual divisions, and the generally disordered nature of the works. The reader is soon spellbound, and comes to accept docilely and with growing wonderment the strange world into which he has been drawn. It would be wrong, however, to allow the novelty and enchantment of the language to hide the fact that there is a serious theme, or to be blinded by the chaotic construction to the presence of this theme in all the novels. The problem of individual identity is, I believe, the unifying element in Ducharme's fiction. All his heroes and heroines are looking for an identity, for something they can call *me.* This search is carried out in the knowledge that any such identity is both infinitely precious and fragile. It must be found, cherished and protected against all that would destroy it, and, in Ducharme's world, everything does conspire to destroy it.

His main characters are children [*L'Avalée des avalés* (1966), *L'Océantume* (1968)], adolescents who cling to childhood [*Le Nez qui voque* (1967), *La Fille de Christophe Colomb* (1969)] or adults who remain remarkably childlike in their behaviour [*L'Hiver de force* (1973)]. Their perception of the world, of other people and of themselves shows the child's uncompromising clarity of vision, his refusal of masks and comfortable assumptions. Their reaction to what they see is also the child's: swift, direct and often violent. Yet they are not *just* children. What Ducharme depicts is the anguish of all human beings faced with the problem of identity and of defending the self in a hostile environment. He uses children because the child has not learned to disguise his anguish or to drown it in the cares of making a living and pursuing success. What he really describes, however, is an anguish which lies in the heart of all men, and his children are representatives of mankind.

All of us are struck, for example, at one time or another, by the ludicrous fact that much of what we consider our identity is due to an accident of birth, that we have a cultural identity imposed on us by the surroundings in which we are born and grow up. Ducharme's children are acutely aware of this too. Mille Milles, the hero of *Le Nez qui voque,* ponders in amazement the Negro he can hear in a nearby hotel room ejecting a woman who will not sleep with him. Had this man been born in mediaeval Europe, he would have thrown himself at the woman's feet and treated her as a princess.

Cultural identity is imposed on us, yet it is something which most of us see as precious and which we are prepared to defend. It is significant, of course, that the problem of cultural identity should be raised in the works of Québecois, belonging, as he does, to a culture threatened by engulfment. It is no surprise to find that Mille Milles is deeply conscious of being a Québecois, and that he reads avidly of his nation's past. He is full of a sense of Quebec's loss of prestige in the modern world, and of the threat posed, not just by Canada's English culture, but by Americanisation. At one point, he produces a burlesque hymn of praise to Canada, depicting it as Americans see it: a land of cold, of lakes, Eskimos and otters. He points out, however, that, while Americans may be too afraid of the cold to live in Canada, they have managed to buy up most of it and impose American habits on Canadians. (pp. 31-2)

Mille Milles refuses to turn in desperation to France as the source of his language and culture. He reaffirms that he is a Québecois, condemns the French for having betrayed Quebec, mocks them for leaving because it was too cold, and tells them it is no use coming back to "civilise" Quebec now that central heating has been invented. He rejects French identity. . . .

At least Mille Milles has a cultural identity, precarious and threatened though it may be. Ducharme's other char-

acters cannot even be sure to what culture they belong. Iode Ssouvie (*L'Océantume*) lives in Quebec, but her mother is Cretan and her father Dutch. Bérénice Einberg (*L'Avalée des avalés*) also lives in Québec, but her father is Jewish and has forced his religion on her. Her mother is Polish, and both she and Bérénice's brother are Catholics. The family is divided by race and religion, and the parents squabble over the religion of the children. Colombe Colomb (*La Fille de Christophe Colomb*) is the daughter of Columbus, the adventurer from the Old World who discovered the New World. She seems to have no place in either of them.

If these characters have difficulty in defining themselves as part of a culture, their difficulty in defining themselves as individuals is even more acute. They feel that their identity is immensely fragile and threatened by the world around them. (p. 33)

Revolt is pushed to the point where it becomes an attempt to create a private world. Ducharme's characters shut themselves up within themselves and become what Iode calls an independent republic. One often finds them closing their eyes and shutting others out. Bérénice (who lives, significantly, on an island) says: "Je suis seule. Je n'ai qu'à me fermer les yeux pour m'en apercevoir." The best way of being totally free of restraint, she maintains, is "rayer le monde de sa vie." When others become importunate, she (and the other characters) simply ignore them. Both Bérénice and Iode remain impassive under the rain of threats from the teacher, as though she simply were not there. Iode tells herself: "Fais l'aveugle, le sourd et le muet. Que tout reste bien enfermé! Que je reste à l'abri au fond de moi-même! Que je me garde intacte, entière." At such moments, Ducharme's characters seem to achieve their ideal of being self-sufficient, fixed in identity, just like the tree Mille Milles admires.

Mille Milles, Colombe, André and Nicole are more passive in their resistance than Bérénice and Iode, so their revolt even more obviously takes the form of withdrawal. Mille and Chateaugué retreat into the protection of their room, which becomes a kind of sanctuary. (Hence their sense of outrage when the sanctity of the room is violated by the police and spectators after Chateaugué's accident.) Their room is small, and can therefore be easily made their own, for Mille, when he ventures outside, always feels swallowed up by the wide world. . . . He and Chateaugué have also locked themselves up in the world of suicide, having made a pact to kill themselves when their money runs out. As a visible sign of their pact, and a mark which distinguishes them from others, they paint their lips black. Their world is also one of purity, in which they try to refuse the sexual obsessions of adults. Chateaugué represents in Milles' eyes all that is pure, uncontaminated virginity (or "virginitude," as he calls it, by analogy with "béatitude"). The constant reminder of this purity is the bridal gown they steal from a shop window, the gown Chateaugué will wear when they are married in death. (pp. 37-8)

Much has been said and written about Ducharme's use of language, but it is surely in the context of this attempt to create a new reality that it is best viewed. All Ducharme's characters are fascinated by words, although one at least (Bérénice) points out that words can never convey precise meaning. Mille Milles adores words as something beautiful in themselves, things which have an identity independent of any meaning one may attribute to them, and he enjoys splitting words into syllables, separating them into component sounds, finding new meaning in their sounds, and creating puns. Chateaugué exclaims in exasperation: "Tu regardes ce que je dis. Tu n'écoutes même pas ce que je dis."

From the realisation that words are imprecise in conveying meaning, yet independent in themselves, springs the idea that language means whatever one sees in it, whatever one wants it to mean. "Ce qui compte," says Iode, "c'est ce qu'on veut dire, non les paroles dont on se sert pour le dire." Hence words are an important tool in the creation of a new and private reality. Characters like Iode use words to create a world of their own where outsiders cannot penetrate, and Bérénice even goes so far as to invent her own language, "Bérénicien." Their language thus becomes a violent and destructive arm used against the outside world.

Nothing but total autonomy will satisfy such natures, nothing but freedom of all limitations imposed by the outside world. The desire for freedom is imagined by Iode to be a huge eagle bearing her aloft from the earth, which would hold her down. There is one symbolic scene where both she and Asie Azothe are carried up by a balloon, and they are filled with a sense of exhilarating freedom. Mille Milles and Chateaugué find freedom in their suicide pact, which liberates them from all the limitations imposed by life, but especially from the fear of ever becoming adults.

Free they may be, but, because their freedom depends on denial of all but themselves, Ducharme's heroes are terribly lonely, and their solitude inspires them with fear. Bérénice speaks for them all when she says: "Je suis seule, et j'ai peur." Yet they embrace their solitude with pride and flaunt their difference from others as a badge of glory. "Je trouve mes seules vraies joies dans la solitude. Ma solitude est mon palais," Bérénice persuades herself. Her solitude becomes like the tank in which, during her period in the Israeli militia, she hides at night. There, all alone, she feels secure and comfortable, protected, as it were, from the outside world by the armour plate of the tank. So precious does her solitude become to her that she refuses to share it with Gloria, the other militia girl who tries to become her friend. "L'espace dans lequel je suis, où que je sois, personne ne peut y pénétrer. Je suis seule!" she informs the interloper. . . .

There is usually, however, one special person, one friend (or, perhaps, "accomplice" would be a better word) who is allowed to enter the palace of solitude. For Bérénice, it is Constance Chlore; for Iode, Asie Azothe; for Mille Milles, Chateaugué. (André and Nicole Ferron are so closely united, on the other hand, that it is hardly a case of one of them accepting another, for there is no dominant partner.) This friendship is created against the outside world and relies on shared secrets and surreptitious communication of the kind Iode and Asie Azothe practise when their teacher's back is turned. Bérénice and Con-stance Chlore use the number 239 as a kind of code, while Iode and Asie use the name Cherchell to designate themselves, and Mille Milles and Chateaugué call themselves Tate.

Bérénice, Iode and Mille always remain the dominant partner in their friendships, and there is obviously something of an attempt to swallow the weaker one. (This element is absent, however, from the relationship of André and Nicole.) They choose as their accomplice someone who is totally different from themselves. Iode is ugly, dirty, and rejected by her family, while Asie Azothe is pretty, popular and adored by her eight brothers; Bérénice is rejected and spiteful, while Constance Chlore seems (at least, at the beginning) happy and well-adjusted; Mille Milles sees himself as ugly and impure, while Chateaugué is, in his eyes, beautiful and pure. Behind this choice of a partner who is so different one suspects a desire, on the part of the dominant partner, to define himself or herself against someone who is a direct opposite, to create a personality by contrast. It is also clear, especially in the case of Iode and Asie Azothe, that the weaker partner initially represents a threat because she is so different. She has, therefore, to be swallowed in self-defense. The threat posed by Asie Azothe accounts for Iode's violent reaction when she first meets her, for she realises she could easily give in to Asie's charm.

Together, these couples face the world (in Colombe's case, she and her animals face the world), and they are inevitably seen as subversive and a menace. The world, therefore, pursues and persecutes them in an attempt to obliterate this threat to its certainties. Bérénice says of her enemies: "Ce n'est pas pour rien qu'ils veulent m'abattre. Ils savent que je les hais, que je hais ce qu'ils ont fait, que je hais ce qu'ils ont fait de la vie qu'ils m'ont donnée avant de me la donner." They react to Iode's threat by treating her as mentally disturbed and having her locked away. She replies that she prefers madness to being as they are. They turn on Colombe and try to annihilate her animals, so she, in self-defense, has to annihilate humanity.

There is often no defense against the hostility of the world, and Ducharme's characters feel overwhelmed by persecution. It is as though there is no place for them where they can be left alone, so they dream of leaving home, of setting off and finding somewhere where they will be happy. They all dream of travelling and do, in fact, manage to travel a great deal. "Partir. Il faut partir" says Bérénice. She drags her brother off on an unsuccessful attempt to stow away on a ship whose destination is unknown, takes Constance Chlore all around New York on public transport in the middle of the night, and finds herself, at the end of the novel, in Israel. Iode dreams of an expedition to Tierra del Fuego, leads another expedition to "rescue" Asie Azothe from her holiday camp, and follows Faire Faire Desmains around France; Colombe and her animals travel the world over; as for Mille Milles, although he does little actual travelling, his very name indicates his restless nature and the fact that he is at home nowhere.

Travel is yet another attempt to take in or swallow the outside world. Yet it also smacks of escapism, of an attempt to avoid one's problems. (As, indeed, does the wish to shut out the outside world and create one's own reality.) Bérénice, in her more lucid moments, realises that these are not solutions. She condemns religion, sex, opium and other "voyages vers le haut" because they weaken the individual. Men, she says, must be strong and face their anguish. . . . All of Ducharme's characters glimpse that there can be no escape from the anguish caused by the problem of identity and the world's attacks on the individual's identity. "Partir, ce n'est pas guérir, car on demeure," says Bérénice, pointing out that the individual can never escape himself and his anguish.

The anguish which Bérénice, Iode, Mille Milles, Colombe, André and Nicole all feel proves that there is no escape. Outside reality still breaks through to them and causes them to suffer in their soul, as Bérénice puts it. Both she and Iode refer to this suffering as "ennui," and it does frequently bear a marked resemblance to Baudelaire's sense of mortal "ennui." Even Nicole and André, however long they stay in bed, cannot escape it. Mille Milles describes it as an unsatisfied yearning. . . . (pp. 38-41)

The revolt which Ducharme depicts in his novels inevitably comes to naught because it is too negative. It proposes nothing to replace the reality it seeks to destroy. It is merely a reaction against a state of affairs considered intolerable, an attempt to deny that reality by opposition to it. It is, therefore, totally dependent on the reality which it seeks to oppose. His characters cannot destroy the reality they oppose, or they themselves would cease to exist. . . . The secret, personal world of Ducharme's characters, and the identity they try to forge for themselves, are posited as the exact opposite of what they see around them, and can only exist in terms of what is around them. "Je veux une Milliarde, un monde offensif, agressif, méchant," says Iode, for she knows that, otherwise, she cannot define herself. Hence, even if one tries to swallow up the outside world, one is still part of what is being swallowed up. Bérénice puts it this way: "La vie ne se passe pas sur la terre, mais dans ma tête. La vie est dans ma tête et ma tête est dans la vie. Je suis englobante et englobée. Je suis l'avalée de l'avalé."

The cornerstone of the secret world, the anti-reality which Ducharme's characters try to erect, is their use of language. Yet, as Mille Milles realises, words have no effect on the objects of outside reality, for, if one tells a mountain that it is only a tiny hill, it will still remain a mountain. Words can, however, affect other people, but, in order to do that, they must be intelligible to them, must be a means of communication, must recognise the presence of others. Mille Milles admits that he has an imperious need to communicate with others, but that, fearing to approach them directly in case he is swallowed by them, he writes down his experiences. The language he uses (and which all of Ducharme's characters generally use) is, therefore, although unusual in many ways, intelligible to others. He has, by the very act of writing, made a compromise with others.

The only two characters in Ducharme's novels who appear to have preserved their identity and shut out a hostile world are Chateaugué and Colombe. Yet, in both cases, it results in a loss of identity. Chateaugué only remains

pure of contamination by killing herself, and thus becoming nothing. Colombe's solution is to annihilate humanity, but that leaves her totally alone, with no others against whom she can react and affirm her identity. As Mille Milles points out, one cannot exist in a vacuum.

It would seem, then, that there is no solution to the problem of affirming an identity and defending it against a hostile world. The best there can be is a partial solution, and Ducharme himself seems to have opted for that. He has used literature to create a world which is, if not completely autonomous, at least partly so. It has been suggested that his work is an attempt to destroy traditional novel forms, and, if this is true, one must see his work as a reaction against an existing reality. It produces, however, a somewhat more satisfactory result than his characters' reaction against the world. Although initially dependent on the novel forms against which it reacts, his fictional world, once created, can stand on its own as an independent reality. (pp. 43-4)

D. J. Bond, "The Search for Identity in the Novels of Réjean Ducharme," in Mosaic: A Journal for the Comparative Study of Literature and Ideas, *Vol. IX, No. 2, Winter, 1976, pp. 31-44.*

Peter France   (review date 14 May 1976)

[*France describes Ducharme's style in* Les enfantômes *and his theme of painful longing for childhood.*]

Les Enfantômes is a search for time past. It is a book of wandering, the wandering of the Québécois Vincent Falardeau through a chaotic life and of his middle-aged mind as he seeks to rejoin the boy he once was. At the end of the book a note from Réjean Ducharme tells us that Vincent "wrote these crazy memoirs in an attic, lit by a candle stuck in a bottle of Seven-Up, he liked the lighting to be weak and shaky". This candle sets the tone; flickering, casual, anti-literary. The story gives the impression of being spontaneous, inconsequential and uncontrolled, moving unexpectedly from scene to scene and person to person. Broadly, the narration follows a downward path from some time in the 1940s to 1974, and there are references to contemporary events or styles which give clues to the dating of particular sequences, but inside this overall chronology there are shifts and surprises. The language too is never allowed to settle in any one mould, moving to and for between the formal and literary ("Ce fut son apogée"), the lyrical, the conversational, the truculent and the near-incoherent. The European reader's eye is inevitably caught by the everyday language of Montreal, but this is perhaps less important than the Queneau-like play on words (seen first in the title, as in the titles of Ducharme's earlier books, *L'Océantume, Le Nez qui voque*) and the frequent movements of lyrical vehemence in the middle of a casual, selfconscious and often parodic narration.

Les Enfantômes is like a literary equivalent of a Godard film, complete with jump-cuts, talismanic references to great art (the wind in an open car is like the flags on Bosch's "Ship of Fools"), verbal provocation, and half-mocking addresses to the reader/spectator. And, as often with Godard, a single dominant tone underlies the apparent incoherence. Here it is one of desperate nostalgia, nostalgia for childhood and its wild freedom, nostalgia for the mother, but above all for the loved sister Fériée. We learn dimly that both mother and sister have killed themselves and that the aging Vincent lives in guilt at surviving them and even greater guilt at no longer feeling their deaths. It was with Fériée that Vincent shared his lost paradise, a paradise that he tries to keep alive in the "marvellous island" of imagination; it is her figure that dominates all the women who flicker through these pages.

In a note accompanying his first novel, *L'Avalée des avalés,* Ducharme wrote: "S'il n'y avait pas d'enfants sur la 'terre, il n'y aurait rien de beau." Here too, many years later, one still reads a desperate refusal of adult seriousness and boredom, partly represented by Vincent's English Canadian wife Alberta Turnstiff. As in most French Canadian novels there are plenty of allusions to national problems, but these do not serve any political commitment, only a general rejection of the oppressive world. No doubt all sorts of objections could be made to this out-and-out romanticism, but rather than preach it seems better to enjoy the vigorous movement of the language in what the narrator, perhaps remembering Céline, calls his descent to the end of his rope.

> *Peter France, "The Island of No Return," in* The Times Literary Supplement, *No. 3870, May 14, 1976, p. 578.*

R. T. Neely   (review date Spring 1977)

[*Neely offers a brief but laudatory review of Ducharme's* Les enfantômes.]

Réjean Ducharme has written a charming novel [*Les enfantômes*] about love and the past, about the ideal woman, about the life of French-speaking Canada in the postwar period. It is not totally irrelevant to point out the literary traditions of the Proustian portrait of an epoch, of the Stendhalian psychology of love and the flashes of Gallic wit along with the hints of cynicism and tragedy carefully covered by a sense of humor showing a basically healthy perspective.

It is impossible to describe the flavor of the book except in the poorest of generalities: a dialogue among the most natural and believable characters, a series of situations at once comic and serious, a rain of dialectal French and American slang of the 1940s and 50s and other elements which conspire to depict a whole epoch and an entire generation. The title is a well-chosen neologism evoking the narrator's attitude. (pp. 248-49)

The novel is warm, cynical, as well as romantic and fanciful. I know nothing about the author's life but can testify that this novel is able to touch and to please. (p. 249)

> *R. T. Neely, in a review of "Les enfantômes," in* World Literature Today, *Vol. 51, No. 2, Spring, 1977, pp. 248-49.*

> **Leduc-Park on Ducharme's *L'hiver de force*:**
>
> [In Ducharme's *L'hiver de force*] the use of language affords him an opportunity to enjoy and to play (*jouir*), which places him in the company of such fellow revellers as Joyce and Beckett, Queneau and Céline. The apparent flexibility of the excesses of this playful type of writing are consistent with the diversity and vitality of a language uninhibited by the rigidity of standard French, whereas, the antihero and his companion are inflexible in their refusal of material comforts and in their discarding of possessions, demonstrating a rare kind of frugality and integrity. The reader/consumer, who is more often than not used to being subjected to aggressive advertising, identifies with these two protagonists who will not compromise. This constant play of opposing forces makes for a dynamic text and tempers its pessimism.
>
> *Renée Leduc-Park, in her "Repetition with a Difference in Réjean Ducharme," translated by Renée Leduc-Park and Margaret Gray McDonald,* Yale French Studies, *1983.*

Camille R. La Bossière   (essay date 1982)

[*In the following excerpt, La Bossière discusses the lonely metaphysical voyage experienced by many of Ducharme's characters.*]

Of Québec's writers of the sixties, none stages with an imagination, an inventiveness, and a learning greater than Réjean Ducharme's historical drama of rebirth to solitude in the less spacious theatre of his *patrie*. . . . Since Ducharme's fictions of the sixties, *L'Avalée des avalées* (1966), *Le Nez qui voque* (1967), and *L'Océantume* (1968), are spoken by children who assault society, who fiercely and with an enormous erudition proclaim their autonomy from any code or world not of their own making, [Yvan G.] Lepage's observation [that Ducharme's works are less the product of an individual than of Quebec culture in general], simple at face value, comprises a profound irony: it recalls a society of *révoltés* who would destroy society. . . . If Ducharme's fictions are less the work of an individual than of a society, they are the work of a society insisting on the absolute independence of the "I" from the "We." This, perhaps, is the irony at the centre of "les problèmes inhérents à la 'renaissance'." It is certainly at the centre of Ducharme's fictions of the sixties, where the individual's solitude is a condition of the radical freedom he or she aspires to.

"The heroic voyage of our time" is "the voyage into man's spirit," writes Robertson Davies. It is, he urges, the great Canadian voyage to self-knowledge paralleling the explorations of Magellan, Vasco da Gama, and Columbus. Ducharme's characters are such voyagers, though they sail without benefit of compass in an element without external referents. A voracious consumer of Renaissance travel books, the diabolical rebel Bérénice would be a world unto herself in *L'Avalée des avalés.* Sailing in the abyss which is the mirror of the self, she protests to all would-be intruders, "Il n'y a que moi ici," "Rien n'importe que moi ici-bas." Bérénice repeats a dozen times: "Je suis seule." In *Le Nez qui voque,* Mille Milles, who, like Cartier, de La Salle, Lewis and Clark, would set out to discover the "splendeurs du Nouveau Monde," undertakes a similar voyage in the abyss: "Me reviolà seul avec mes chimères." Referring to Cartier, Columbus, Vasco da Gama, and Martin Alonzo Pinzon (Columbus's chief rival), Iode too would set out to discover the world in *L'Océantume.* She looks forward "d'être engloutie . . . jusqu'au plus vrai de ma solitude, d'explorer les silences sous-marins." The Ducharmian voyage continues into the seventies. Like Ducharme's daughter of Christopher Columbus, who jettisons compass and smashed rudder after the taking of a passenger ship, the protagonist of his *Les Enfantômes* (1976) imagines himself in "la nef de Bosch" bound for nowhere, his destination "loin au fond de mon trou."

For the Ducharme character, the age of revolution, discovery, and invention is the age of solitude. It is an historical coincidence long familiar to thinkers in "la grande lignée" of Saint-Denys Garneau's meditation. "Il n'a pas bien appris son Moyen Age et sa Renaissance, à l'école"— words from *Le Nez qui voque*—do not describe Ducharme. For some, though, writers reflecting this tradition are merely old-fashioned. André Brochu suggests this view in his ribald and uproariously high-spirited metafiction *Adéodat I* (1973): "vive la bonne chanson, la Canadienne et ses morpions, le cotillon, la danse carrée, Réjean Ducharme et compagnie." (pp. 112-14)

Camille R. La Bossière, "Of Renaissance and Solitude in Québec: A Recollection of the Sixties," in Studies in Canadian Literature, *Vol. 7, No. 1, 1982, pp. 110-14.*

Jonathan M. Weiss   (essay date 1986)

[Weiss presents a survey of Ducharme's plays, exploring his use of symbolic language and imagery.]

Ducharme is best known as a novelist, and for good reason; he has published five novels in prose and one in verse, but so far only two of the five plays he has written since 1968 (*Inès Perée et Inat Tendu* and *Ah! Ah!*) have been edited. This situation arises not from any lack of quality in the plays themselves but rather from the manifest desire on the part of the author that dramatic texts, which are merely the "pretext" for the performance, not become fixed works of literature. Even if Réjean Ducharme takes little interest in the production of his plays (he once asked to be considered "as a dead author") his texts are really working documents for an eventual performance.

In a sense, it is ironic that Ducharme is known principally as a novelist, since, in all his prose works, he essentially writes *against* the novel. Ducharme's attitude toward literature is to refuse to accept that writing involves the description of reality. Ducharme believes that "the novel is related to passionate love, to possessive love, to urban life and its network of interests, to dubious historical occurrences." This attitude is rooted in a rejection of everything the modern, adult world has to offer; like Salinger's Holden Caulfield, Ducharme's youthful characters perpetually see the hypocritical, seamy side of adult life and are

digusted by possessiveness, sex, pollution, and selfishness. They search for a new way of seeing things that brings into focus not so much what things are but what they can become in the human mind. This perspective is what Ducharme calls "falseness"; it is essentially a poet's way of looking at the simplest object and transforming it: "look at a cabbage and imagine that when it's ripe each of its leaves will fall off by themselves and begin to fly, to sing, to be a goldfinch." Without the connivance of the reader, of course, this transformation is impossible. Ducharme wants his readers to listen to the *voice* of his characters rather than to believe in their descriptions of reality in order to "follow the path of 'falseness,' of the imaginary, of the perpetually new miracle of existence."

Ducharme rejects not only the passive reader but the passive narrator. His characters are desperately looking for some kind of *action* that will remove them from literature. Bérénice Einberg, heroine of *L'Avalée des avalés* (*The Swallower Swallowed*), finds herself suffocated by everything around her:

> Everything swallows me. When my eyes are closed I'm being swallowed by my stomach . . . When my eyes are open, I'm swallowed because I can see . . . I'm swallowed by the river which is too large, the sky which is too high, the flowers which are too fragile, the butterflies which are too fearful, my mother's face which is too beautiful.

Bérénice, like all Ducharme's narrators, is trying to find a way out of the restricted world which she observes around her. But more important, she is trying to escape the limitations that the novel form puts on her as a character/narrator. To avoid being "swallowed" by the reality she sees, she must constantly keep that reality in motion either by subjectively transforming it or through some act of violent destruction. As Bérénice puts it, "that's what I need to do to be free: swallow everything, spread myself into everything, encompass everything, impose my law on everything, master everything . . . But I'd rather destroy everything."

Ducharme's hostility to the traditional novel form and to the passive reader implies the necessity of a genre that is not constrained by the written word and in which action takes the place of contemplation. It seems likely that one of Ducharme's principal motivations in writing plays is precisely to replace the printed page with the movement of the drama. Moreover, theater is the antithesis of the *real*. Everything on the stage is *false,* from the actors who ask us to believe they are characters to the pieces of wood and cardboard that magically become a castle. In the theater every performance gives evidence of "the perpetually new miracle of existence."

Ducharme's first play, *Inès Pérée et Inat Tendu,* was first produced in 1968. The title is a pun (*inespéré* means "unhoped-for" and *inattendu* means "unexpected") and indicates that here, as in all Ducharme's works, words and their meanings are extremely important. The names of the characters in the play (Isalaide Lussier-Voucru suggests *l'eussiez-vous-cru?,* which means "would you have believed it?"; Mario Escalope is a pun on *Marie-salope,* a dirty woman, and *escalope,* a veal cutlet), the dialogue, and even the stage directions ("Première Rake," "Deuxième Make") have a multiplicity of senses that, far from being gratuitous, are at the very center of Ducharme's intentions. We have seen how joual plays an essential role in the plays of Tremblay, who through its use asserts his solidarity with Quebec's working class. In a similar vein, but with a different purpose, Ducharme's use of puns and word games is a refusal of traditional middle-class theater. But Ducharme isn't particularly interested in the working class (or in any other class), and it is out of disaffection with the world in general that he chooses to turn words over and over, to play with them rather than to use them merely as tools. By playing with words, by exploring them, Ducharme explores the possibilities of change and ambiguity. Tremblay uses joual as a way of finding roots, a personal and social reality; Ducharme uses puns to remove words from their usual meanings and to escape being pinned down by any reality.

Inès Pérée is a young woman dressed as a bathing beauty (but wearing boots and a rubber glove). Inat Tendu, her companion, is a young man dressed as a bank clerk. Together they roam the earth searching for someone to take them in, to welcome them into their home. Like all of Ducharme's protagonists, they are permanent adolescents; they live together but have never made love and have a relationship based on friendship. They are not entirely human ("I wasn't born. I found myself on earth all of a sudden, with Inat, my hand is his," says Inès); they have no notion of work ("Life is free. I have never paid for it and I never will," says Inat); and they carry with them a violin and a butterfly, symbolic of their "good ideas," their ideals of music and beauty which will be perfectly useless to them and of which they will soon be deprived.

In fact, what Inès and Inat need to survive on earth is neither a butterfly nor a violin but brute force, and of this they are virtually incapable. Their search for a welcome is not like begging for alms but rather is like claiming one's due: "We didn't care to look for charity, but to take our share from you, to take our place next to you," says Inat. Their adventure consists of three stages, in each of which they meet people who threaten to destroy their innocence and idealism. In the first step, in the "disused funeral chapel" of a veterinary clinic, they encounter Isalaide Lussier-Voucru who, as her name implies, is ugly (*laide*) beyond belief (she is a veterinarian infested with as many fleas as the dirtiest of animals). Not only does Isalaide treat Inès and Inat with a cruelty bordering on sadism, but she does so as representative of the established order, of the fraternity of professionals who judge some people normal and some abnormal: "you are abnormal enough to be committed and I'm as normal as a normal school," she tells Inès. The veterinary hospital is a disguised mental clinic, and Isalaide's boss and erstwhile lover is Dr. Mario Escalope, a traumatized Italian psychiatrist who gets sexual pleasure from stealing and runs an insane asylum from which no one escapes. "The only way an inmate [he says *passionaire* instead of *pensionnaire*] will get out of my establishment is over my dead body. I'm too good at making them feel good," he says, and his involuntary (?) Freudian slip reveals the basic opposition between his way of seeing

human existence and that of the two searching adolescents. Inès and Inat believe in passion—if not in passionate love, at least in passionate *life*—and they are thwarted at every juncture by people who, like Isalaide and Mario, reduce life to a system of controlled reactions and predictable behavior. Or, to put it another way, Inès and Inat represent poetry, and poetry implies dissatisfaction with the state of the world, a kind of anguish that the psychiatrist, preoccupied with making people feel good, cannot accept. Mario Escalope says of Victor Hugo's poems: "they short-circuit the neurons, they screw up my science of exercising influence".

To escape from the evil Dr. Escalope, from Isalaide and from the cruel miniskirted nurse Pauline-Emilienne who throws cans of pet food at them, Inès and Inat would need only to assert themselves, to let each of their persecutors stew in their psychological juices, and to run for the door. But Inat is too tired and he soon falls asleep, and Inès has an irresistible urge to find a mother, a point of origin, a past to which she can attach her very fragile present. Having never been born ("I've always been as I am", Inès is fascinated by the fetal life of Isalaide's daughter: "What did the baby do when he was in your body? Did he explore you like a geography lesson? Did he pull himself up to your mouth and then slide down to your feet? She declares her love for Isalaide and asks to be adopted: "When a boy and a girl knock at your door, and tell you they are your children, you have a duty to be their mother". At the same time Inès is terrified of being alone with Inat, and of their having to build their own life, as orphans, from nothing: "Sometimes I tell Inat: 'Let's build our own house.' That's when I'm discouraged. What a horrible thing to have to live in one's own house".

In the behavior of Inès and Inat toward the menace of Dr. Escalope and Isalaide we can see two of the themes that lie behind all of Ducharme's theater, and indeed a great part of Quebec literature: defeatism and the search for an identity. Inat solves his problems by refusing to face them. On the surface, he is polite, nonviolent; when the situation gets too difficult for him, he can always sleep. Inès, on the other hand, is not only a more aggressive character but is actively searching for a *space* in which she can settle. It is not by accident that, in the quote above, Ducharme has used spatial images. Isalaide's fetus is seen by Inès as exploring his mother's body in the same way as Champlain came down the St. Lawrence to explore Quebec. Ducharme's imagery here joins the tradition of Quebec literature that, from the novelist Savard to the poet Miron, is searching for a *pays,* a land whose space can be explored, mapped, made familiar. Inès cannot conceive of building her house in a void, without roots in the past or in the land. Unfortunately, her choice of an adoptive mother is ill advised, since Isalaide, even if momentarily sympathetic, will, by the end of the play, turn against Inès and Inat and join their oppressors.

"Children have come and they have rung the hour of terror," says Isalaide at the end of the "Premier Rake", and, as the play progresses, the sage of Inès and Inat begins to take on apocalyptic overtones, like a black version of Saint-Exupéry's *Le Petit prince.* It is not by accident that, once having encountered the world of psychology, Inès and Inat find their second challenge in the world of religion, in the cell of Sister Saint-New-York-des-Ronds-d'Eau to which they have escaped after a period of internment in Dr. Escalope's mental hospital. Inès is without her violin, Inat without his butterfly; these objects were stolen from them by the psychiatrists along with their "good ideas." The couple is rapidly becoming a shadow of its former self. Drugged at the hospital, their minds emptied both of anguish and ideas, Inès fills the void within her with junk food; when she has eaten enough chips and drunk enough coke, she feels "well stimulated, full of wicked energy". As she becomes cruder, more violent (but without purpose or direction), Inat becomes even less aggressive, even more detached, preferring to elevate his soul rather than to fight for his right to exist: "I'd rather have a crown than a mouthful of bread. And your crown falls when you bend down to pick up a morsel of bread".

At first Inès and Inat seem to have found a kindred soul in Sister New-York. Her ideas, a kind of naive and romantic ecology, are not without resemblance to their rebelliousness: "The word belongs to the forests and the forests aren't made for those who cut down trees, oh no! They're made to grow, to give more and more shade to lovers, who are so hot, and so that fearful birds can build their nests higher up". But Sister New-York immediately adds, "I am the servant of the R.M.B.: the Reverend Mother Banker", thus calling attention to her real nature, indicated visually by the revolver she carries, the safe in the middle of her cell, and by her tendency to show off her thighs (her defense is that "Christ certainly showed his thighs on the cross". Sister New-York's links with wealth and capitalism on the one hand (the "New-York" of her character), and her ostentatious display of her body to Inat on the other, make her a double threat: the adolescent ideal Inès and Inat represent accepts neither sex nor money. Inès's newfound violence is sparked and she finally goes into action, tying up the ever-present Pauline-Emilienne. But a new character enters, a gentleman thief named Pierre-Pierre Pierre who, accompanied by Isalaide's daughter, the "firewoman" Aidez-Moi (help me!), quickly grabs Sister New-York's revolver and turns the tables on Inès.

Pierre-Pierre Pierre is part of the third and final threat to the existence of Inès and Inat. He is, despite his good manner, violent and materialistic: "We have come to take everything," he asserts and his philosophy is based on force, disharmony, and the work ethic. In the third act he finally lives up to his name. He has already subjugated, by his mere presence, Isalaide who had begun to emulate the adolescents by roaming the world carrying the violin and butterfly Mario had stolen; slowly but surely Pierre-Pierre begins to close in on Inès and Inat. He takes up his place in a bathtub in the middle of Sister New-York's cell in which he has replaced the crucifixes with pictures of sex and violence. Inès, dressed as a cowboy, fires her pistol in the air and orders him to raise his hands, but he merely ignores her and she puts away the gun. Inat threatens to hit Pierre-Pierre Pierre, but he gets confused and says "je t'éponge" (I sponge you off) rather than "je te ponche" (I punch you). Smiling, Pierre-Pierre presents Inès and Inat with something to eat—eggs. But as Ines and Inat

look closely, the eggs reveal themselves to be stones (*pierres*): "Pebbles! We've come all this way for pebbles!". It is the final disappointment, and even if Inat makes a last desperate effort to break open the stones and find a meaning in them ("maybe they contain something, a sign, a message?", the game is irrevocably lost. Inès and Inat, dying of hunger, fall to the ground and expire.

The two themes which I have already mentioned—the search for a space and a tendency toward defeatism—can be seen as typical of a nationalist current in Quebec literature. But Ducharme is very subtle, and his protagonists are motivated not so much by nationalism (either in the sense of Abbé Groux or of René Lévesque) as by a naive desire for freedom. They are searching for a welcome, an *acceuil,* but they refuse the charity of Sister New-York or the work ethic of Pierre-Pierre Pierre because they want to be accepted for what they *are* rather than for any usefulness they might have for someone else. They insist on this aspect of their search which sets them apart from more common mortals: "We aren't made of the same water as other people . . . The land is ours as much as theirs. They didn't make it; they didn't earn it". For Inès and Inat the idea of a country, a land with specific borders, is inconceivable; their journey is in a land without limits, from house to house "in a straight line" leading toward the ocean. The space they claim for themselves is that of limitless imagination, and this space is as necessary to them as air, food, or water.

The dramatic structure of *Inès Pérée et Inat Tendu* is closely related to the play's meaning. It is above all a play of *words* (some critics have gone so far as to suggest that Ducharme's plays are better as literature than as performances—a conclusion with which the playwright would probably disagree), but of words in free play, free to have a variety of meanings (one could find, for example, numerous senses to the words *inespéré* and *inattendu* within the thematic context of the play). Affinities with Ionesco and Beckett, and especially with Boris Vian's *Les Bâtisseurs d'empire,* will be immediately evident: Ducharme's theater contains elements both of the absurd and of surrealism. The world of Inès Perée and Inat Tendu has no specific point of reference in our world. The elements that compose our everyday reality are completely detached from their contexts, set loose on stage to be whatever the playwright wants them to be. Even the protagonists are not like us; they are not the recognizable Quebecois adolescents of Jean Barbeau's *Ben-Ur.* Ducharme's plays refer principally to themselves, and as such, they are "a window on another world" whose contours are those of a desperate search for a way out of an oppressive universe.

Le Cid maghané and *Le Marquis qui perdit,* Ducharme's next plays (produced respectively in 1968 and 1970), are a departure from the kind of theater the playwright had created with *Inès Pérée et Inat Tendu* in that they are parodies of other works rather than original creations. Ducharme himself claimed, having written *Le Cid maghané,* that this play wasn't really his: "I only wrote one play (*Inès Pérée et Inat Tendu*) since the *Cid,* as messed up as it is, isn't written by me but rather by some Castro whose first name I can't recall and by Pierre Corneille." Despite this quip, Ducharme's purpose in writing these plays was very serious indeed; behind the parodies, the gags, and the laughter lie some very sombre reflections.

Ducharme wrote *Le Cid maghané* (*maghané*, messed up) to make the classic French play "more understandable here, less serious and uglier." In fact, it is the coexistence of two very different centuries and civilizations that impress us first. The play is to be done "en costumes d'époque dans des meubles 1967"; some lines are to be declaimed *à la française* whereas others are to be spoken *à la québecoise*. Parodies of Corneille's verses abound. For example, Don Diègue's exhortation to Rodrigue: "Va, cours, vole et nous venge" (Go, run, fly and avenge us), becomes "Quick, my son! Take the bus, take a taxi, take the train, take the plane, hurry up, go ahead, break him into a thousand pieces." The heroic and noble sentiments of Corneille's characters become the common sentiments of common people. The confrontation between Rodrigue and Chimène in act 3, scene 4, in which Chimène finally avows her love for Rodrigue ("va, je ne te hais point" (Go, I hate you not) becomes, in Ducharme's version, a burlesque and juvenile love scene in which Rodrigue tickles Chimène's feet, Elvire throws herself onto the couple, the three of them roll together on the floor, and Chimène ends up by making a date with Rodrigue for a night at the local motel ("OK, bum, OK creep. Eight o'clock. Motel Sunset"). And the scene corresponding to act 4, scene 3, where Don Fernand pardons Rodrigue and says to him "henceforth be the Cid," becomes a barter in which Rodrigue demands of the king something more tangible—a new car.

In a sense, it is ironic that Ducharme is known principally as a novelist, since, in all his prose works, he essentially writes *against* the novel.

—*Jonathan M. Weiss*

As in most parodies, complexities of character are reduced to caricature. Rodrigue, in Corneille's play, is very reticent to carry out his father's wishes to fight with Don Gormas and, in act 1, scene 6, makes the painful vow to "venge a father and lose a mistress." No such thoughts torment Ducharme's Rodrigue. His deliberations are reduced to: "this business isn't all that complicated. I lose my honey anyway, whether I kill my honey's father or not. I'd be really nuts not to kill my honey's father." L'Infante, in the seventeenth century version, is caught between the knowledge that Rodrigue loves Chimène and that the rules of her society make any marriage between herself and Rodrigue impossible; at the end of the play she generously exhorts Chimène: "accept without sadness / this generous victory from the hands of your princess." No such generosity inspires the heart of Ducharme's Infante. Her rivalry with Chimène has made her a quarrelsome character who does not hesitate to express her jealousy to Chimène: "What have you got that I haven't got? What

did you do to him so that he doesn't look at me anymore?" There is certainly an element of exaggeration in Ducharme's characatures, but it is the childish naïveté of the characters that dominates and provides a link with *Inès Pérée et Inat Tendu.* Characters end each scene by giving each other a "petit bec," the kiss of friendship, as if they were children rehearsing a play just for the fun of it. Rodrigue has a slogan—a king of macho warning—that he, like the Lone Ranger, repeats before going into action: "Qu'ils viennent les maudits si c'est pas des peureux!" ("Let the bums come on if they're not chicken"). One often has the impression that the play is an interpretation of Corneille by children who understand concepts of love, honor, and death only in their own very simplified way.

Despite first appearances, however, Ducharme's *Cid* is not a simple parody of Corneille. In fact, the play, which until about midway seemed a straightforward line-for-line parody, suddenly takes off on its own and changes considerably from the Corneillean plot. The most important of these plot changes concerns the development of the characters of Rodrigue and Cimène. Rodrigue does not come to bid his "last adieu" to Chimène "in full daylight" but rather does so in the middle of the night, in her room. She is in pajamas and he is drunk. To prove his courage, and in preparation for his fight with Don Sanche, Rodrigue decides to descend the fifty steps from the apartment to the street on skis. This feat costs him a broken leg, and the injury, on top of his inebriated state, makes Rodrigue no match for Don Sanche. Chimène, sure that Rodrigue has been killed, feels none of the pain and despair of Corneille's character but rather a great relief, as she says to Elvire: "How I wish you could put your hand on my soul and touch the marvelous peace that is settling upon it second by second." In fact, contrary to Corneille's play, Don Sanche *has* killed Rodrigue ("The pocket-size Cid is dead! Long live the king-size Cid!", and Rodrigue's body, "in skis and boxing gloves, with catsup spread over it" is brought to the middle of the stage at the play's end.

Rodrigue's death is not the only point on which the end of Ducharme's play differs from Corneille's. Whereas Corneille's king establishes order and satisfies both the need for honor and love by sending Rodrigue to battle for a year, Ducharme's king is not nearly so powerful. Not only does he have problems with his telephone service and with a police force on a perpetual coffee break, but he is incapable of imposing any kind of order on his society. Ducharme's play ends in perfect anarchy. Characters insult each other and a free-for-all ensues during which the women gain the upper hand. The king vainly tries to establish order by drawing his sword, but he is quickly disarmed by the valet Blackie who says to him: "Quit waving your sword around or I'll stick it in your nose." The play ends with all the actors dancing a *ronde* around Don Rodrigue's body while singing *O Canada*.

These plot changes indicate that Ducharme's intentions go far beyond dressing *Le Cid* in modern clothing. By presenting a king who is powerless, by ending the play in disorder, by giving us a Rodrigue who is full of hot air and drink, Ducharme (as most of the critics remarked) holds the mirror to Quebec society. He sees a society that resembles the world of the western movies more than the well-ordered France of Louis XIV. The real courage of Corneille's Rodrigue is replaced by the comic-book bombast of Ducharme's character: "Nothing can harm the Cid. I can catch Indians' arrows with my bare hands just like tennis balls," boasts Rodrigue.

To be sure, Ducharme is not the only Quebec dramatist to comment on the tendency to use American comic-book heroes as role models; Jean Barbeau's *Ben-Ur* is perhaps the bitterest satire of a young man who uses comic books to hide from reality. But what characterizes Ducharme and sets him apart from Barbeau is the emptiness of his characters. Underneath Rodrigue's boasts, behind Chimène's great right arm which, like that of Muhammad Ali, knocks out most of the noblemen in the play's last scene, there is only a gaping void. Ducharme's characters *are* the masks they wear and nothing else; they are, as one critic put it, "disjointed puppets." The most striking example of this aspect of the play comes in the scene corresponding to the Infante's introspective monologue in Corneille's play. Ducharme's Infante tries but is incapable of uttering her monologue; instead, she lets her mask drop and appears to the audience as an actress: "it's not the Infante who is speaking to you, ladies and gentlemen, it's Antoinette Buffon, actress." Not only does this technique remind us that we are in the theater (as opposed to Corneille who demands complete suspension of disbelief) but it also reveals an actress whose personal life is as painfully empty as that of the women in Tremblay's *Les Belles-soeurs*. Her boyfriend has left her and she last saw him on television being interviewed on his reaction to the high cost of bureau drawers:" I cry into my tube of toothpaste when I brush my teeth and I cry into my ashtray when I smoke," she sobs. Incapable of remembering her lines in the play, Antoinette Buffon pours out her soul and shows us an alienation that the seventeenth century ignored: that of people living alone in apartments, waiting for the telephone to ring, seeing their former lovers through the intermediary of television.

As in *Inès Pérée et Inat Tendu,* however, Ducharme also expresses a personal philosophy in *Le Cid maghané.* Ducharme uses *Le Cid* as a pretext to create his own Corneillean situation, that is, one in which there is no way out. *Le Cid* is a tragedy despite its happy ending; for Corneille, the fact that Rodrigue was "a man more virtuous than wicked, who, through human weakness, . . . meets a misfortune that he doesn't deserve" was sufficient to give the play an Aristotelian sense of tragedy. But Ducharme rejects the tragic element in *Le Cid.* His Rodrigue lacks the physical and moral superiority of Corneille's and the fundamental honor / love conflict is reduced to a childish but deadly game. Ducharme's Chimène is not concerned with avenging her father's death but with finding the macho heroic man of her dreams: "the really virile and masculine man I'm looking for is not to be found here," she declares. The duel she sets up between Rodrigue and Don Sanche will, she believes, give her boyfriend the chance to prove his masculinity, but when he leaves her apartment too drunk to fight, she has no feeling of regret: "Ouf! Another good deed done!" This lack of tragic element creates a darker and more pessimistic play than that of Corneille.

Rodrigue knows the rules of the game and has ignored them: his death is deserved and inevitable.

If *Le Cid maghané* turns its back on history by the confusion of costumes and decor, and by its plot changes, *Le Marquis qui perdit* (the Marquis who lost—a reference to Marquis de Vaudreuil, who, in 1759, lost New France to the English) is an attempt to re-create the history of the British conquest of North America). It can also be seen as an attempt to *conquer* history in order partially to avenge the conquest not only by England but equally by France (before and after 1760), by the old generation of Quebecois (defeatist—with some exceptions), and by women (the matriarchy of a Marguerite Bourgeoys). It is the most political of Ducharme's plays since it puts into question popularly accepted myths regarding Montcalm's heroism, Levis's sanity, and the reasons for which France was defeated in the first place.

Ah! Ah!, arguably Ducharme's best play, represents both a continuation of, and a departure from his previous dramatic works. Unlike *Le Cid maghané,* or *Le Marquis qui perdit,* it is not a parody. Yet there are hints of these two plays in some of the lines as well as in some of the themes. There are also affinities with *Inès Pérée et Inat Tendu,* especially in the emphasis Ducharme puts on the cruelty that human beings inflict on each other. Overall, however, the play presents us with a much more ambiguous situation than Ducharme had used before; it is both real and unreal and seems to transcend any single categorization as a philosophical, psychological, or social drama.

This is how the publicity department of the Théâtre du Nouveau Monde summed up the play:

> Roger and Sophie are living together; Bernard, a childhood friend of Sophie, and Mimi, his supernumerary, pay them a visit. In a setting at once filled with real elements and detached from exterior reality, transcending time and space, they will love each other, hate each other, destroy each other

The plot is deceptively simple, the characters and decor deceptively realistic. Sophie and Roger are the classic couple in their late thirties; she is "passionate, complex," he is "rather ugly, rather blubbery." Bernard and Mimi are younger, wealthier, better looking (he is a "handsome, well-dressed man"). The apartment seems normal enough (thick purple carpet, Tiffany lamp, expensive but tasteless furniture). But there are items that are unusual, strange: next to the modern stereo set and lazy-boy chair there is a tall ashtray with small flashing lights on top; Roger wears too many rings and his language is hopelessly confused; Roger and Sophie sometimes speak while holding their noses. Roger's moods vary from serenity to violence and he is completely unpredictable. Sophie has to pay Roger each time she wants to make love; she earns this money pushing mescaline. Bernard becomes morose, drunk, helpless. In the midst of all this Mimi, the youngest of the four, is a scapegoat for the others who take pleasure in making her suffer.

"A great Quebec tragedy," said one of the critics. To some extent *Ah! Ah!* is a sort of French-Canadian *Who's Afraid of Virginia Woolf?* in that it defines the relationship between people as a battle for domination. But Ducharme has another interest besides psychology: games, play, theater—all used by people to escape from the present and from reality.

During the second act, Mimi tells of a nightmare:

> There were lots of people, like at Dorval Airport during the holidays. But no one was waiting for anyone or for any planes. We were all paying attention to ourselves . . . We were watching out not to hurt each other but there were too many of us to avoid bumping into others or hitting them . . . At the beginning everyone was polite. When we accidentally touched each other we said hello, we smiled, we said excuse-excuse-me-I-didn't-do-it-on-purpose . . . But suddenly it all changed. Nothing really happened but we noticed that all those who had been touched had marks on them which ate through their clothes like burning wounds . . . Then we heard them announce on the loudspeaker that it was an epidemic . . . We all wanted to leave, we fought and pushed to get out. It was hideous. Because the more we bumped into each other, the more marks we got . . . Then someone yelled out: Stop-stop-it's-not-the-end-of-the-world-it's-only-a-game-of-tag. But it was too late. I looked at myself, I was completely rotten.

This dream is a précis of the play as it appears to Mimi and, because she is the underdog, the audience interprets the play from her point of view. As she so clearly sees, contacts between people, despite attempts to be polite, exist only at the level of aggressiveness. People are looking to exercise their power and they need a willing victim; Bernard and Sophie take turns playing this role with Roger. Roger dominates all the characters. He possesses, psychologically and physically, both women; he obliges Sophie to recite newspaper clippings with her nose plugged; he tears Mimi's skirt while she tells her dream; he obliges Bernard to drink from the toilet; he keeps all the money in the stuffing of his sofa. Sophie takes her revenge on Mimi whom she treats as a child; Bernard (like Rigaud) takes his revenge out on the bottle. What sets Mimi apart from the others and what explains her emphasis on physical wounds is her exaggerated sensitivity. "I'm a strange person . . . When someone touches me it hurts," she explains to Sophie, but rather than finding sympathy she gets nothing but derision: "Oh, when you're as sensitive as that, it's no longer sensitivity, it's . . . it's . . . I won't say innocence . . . you're terribly suspect," says Sophie. What enable Roger, Bernard, and Sophie to disdain Mimi's sensitivity is their ability to play the game. "It's a game! It's not for real! We're pretending! That doesn't hurt!" says Sophie to Mimi but the latter is unable to distinguish game from reality until the end of the play ("I'm a good enough actor . . . artress, artist . . . to be on the stage"). By then it's too late—she has lost her innocence and has become, as in her dream, "rotten"—and she will leap to her death at the end of the play while the others yell to her "it doesn't count . . . Ah! Ah! . . . TAG!"

The game that Roger, Bernard, and Sophie play is called,

throughout the play, *le phone,* and this deformation of the word "fun" is significant. The game is *phoney,* of course, but it is also alienating. It keeps people at a distance from each other, just as the telephone, at numerous times during the play, allows characters to converse without seeing their partner. *Le phone* is also a deadly game. Sophie goes so far as to compare the sound of her voice to that of a machine gun, but this gun is filled with words, not bullets, and Roger has taught her how to protect herself from words. He knows how to make words into objects. The lights on his ashtray flash, he plugs up his nose to deform the sound of his voice, and he recites: "Sh h h h sh't'ava pourtant ben nana ben n'avarti!". The message ("But I had warned you") is lost in voluntary alienation. Roger and Sophie empty themselves of all feeling and fill themselves with words which, like the newspaper clippings rolled into balls that they throw in the air, gradually come to dominate the entire play.

It is not some perverse desire to play deadly games that motivates the characters in *Ah! Ah!* but rather a very clear vision of themselves as irretrievable losers. Like Ducharme's Rodrigue or like Inès and Inat, the personages here are looking for some way out of the inevitable failure of their lives. Inès and Inat had, in the beginning at least, their "good ideas"; no such ideals are present in *Ah! Ah!.* Sophie compares life to a hockey game being lost: "Our greatness can be measured in the empty hockey rink, in the multitude of inhabitable solitudes which have reverted back to the bleachers. It's a matter of losing the match and *may our cry alone fill up the entire amphitheater*" (my emphasis). The loss is accepted—even more, it is proclaimed as the human condition. All that is left is the game that, in turn, becomes its own pleasure. Roger's quote from the Polish playwright Witkiewicz is apt: "something within me revels in this endless sacrifice, in this bottomless mediocrity."

There is a second level of meaning to *Ah! Ah!.* The entire drama can be seen as a play within a play with Roger as the director. Sophie implicitly recognizes that the play has been planned out in advance and that she is but an actress reciting a part: "and to think that . . . the drama was all written, corrected, censored, performed." She goes on to pay homage to her director: "Master, you have shown me that I was full of my role, full and round like a ball, that I had only to let myself roll." Roger is apparently certain that he is in complete control of the play: "I write my life in advance: I choose it before anyone else does it for me . . . I am a creator, my creator: I PREDICT MYSELF!". But although he is a director he is also an actor and is as imprisoned by his words, his lines, as other characters. He and the others accept to play their roles to the end ("isn't acting fun [*"le phone"*]?" asks Sophie.

It is impossible here to distinguish between games and reality, between actors and the roles they play. The game is all the more deadly serious because there is nothing else. We see here a transposition, on the level of theater, of the image/substance dialectic that was at the basis of *Le Cid maghané* and *Le Marquis qui perdit.* In these two plays the search for an identity became the search for an image; if Rodrigue or Montcalm were powerless in fact, at least they could try to transcend that reality and to become fiction. In *Ah! Ah!* it is the play itself that provides the images and enables the characters to believe in some (fragile) existence. Lacking any existence outside of their games, the play (in its strictest sense) becomes the only reality.

More than any of Ducharme's other dramatic works, *Ah! Ah!* is self-conscious theater. The playwright uses the phenomenon of theater to explore not only the lives of his fellow Quebecois but to explore his own purpose as a dramatist. If life is a series of empty and false contacts with others, then theater becomes a privileged form of expression because it allows an audience to perceive both the false and the real, and to distinguish the false—the game—from what is real (the illusion-making machine called theater). In the end the *real* disappears. As soon as an actor appears on stage, he loses his identity as a human being and becomes a character. This process is all the more evident when, as in *Le Cid maghané,* a character reveals herself to be an actress. We the audience know that the actress (appropriately named Antoinette Buffon) is just as fictitious as the character she is supposed to play; even if the real actress were to use her real name and tell us the real story of her life, we would accept her story as essentially theatrical, that is, as something invented. The stage has a magic power that turns everything upon it into an illusion, into game, and it is this magic that Ducharme uses to create a dramatic universe in which the false envelops the real and becomes the only mode of human existence.

Ducharme's contribution to Quebec theater, like his contribution to the world of fiction, is considerable and exists as much, if not more, on the level of structure and technique as on that of theme. His theater is far from literary; it is "a theater of victory over words, a theater of cruelty and innocence, a completely *theatrical* theater." The comparison with Artaud's theater of cruelty is not without foundation. Like Artaud, Ducharme is interested in a theater of metaphysics, where the very existence of human beings is put into question. That this theater contains political overtones is inevitable; a Quebecois's existence as an individual presupposes, in the eyes of most artists and intellectuals, his existence as a member of a French-Canadian nation which has not yet gained control of its own destiny. Or, to put it another way, Montcalm's and Rodrigue's defeats are part of the reason that Roger, Sophie, Bernard, and Mimi play their games to the death. But Ducharme is one of the least *engagé* of Quebec writers, and the significance of his plays can be appreciated in any society. This is not the least of his merits. (pp. 77-93)

> *Jonathan M. Weiss, "The Deadly Games of Réjean Ducharme," in his* French-Canadian Theater, *Twayne Publishers, 1986, pp. 77-93.*

Marc Côté   (review date March 1987)

[*Côté considers philosophical allusions in* Ah! Ah! (Ha! Ha!) *and objects to some of the play's plot devices.*]

According to the back cover of *Ha! Ha!* "Réjean Ducharme gives us this riotous play about power, politics and the couple. [He] shows us the art of dissembling through speech." To read the script, however, is to be confronted with four characters who sound the same and whose lives never manage to touch or even interest the reader.

The play, in its original French, won the 1982 Governor General's Award. Jean-Pierre Ronfard, an important Montreal director, calls *Ha! Ha!* one of the great works of contemporary playwriting. . . .

What can be considered great are the many references by the author, through the mouths of his characters, to theatre theory: the reader is constantly assaulted with reminders that this is only a play, that theatre is like a game of tag (wherein the person who's "it" has the plague—is this supposed to be a reference to Artaud?) and that what separates the audience from the action is the thin line at the edge of the stage.

Meanwhile, the plot stumbles forth with characters vomiting, crying, yelling, screaming, laughing, drinking, necking, ripping their own and others' clothing off; alarms go off and police-car lights turn round, shining bright red. A charming array of behaviour designed, no doubt, to keep the audience watching. Or the reader reading.

> *Marc Côté, in a review of "Ha! Ha!" in* Books in Canada, *Vol. 16, No. 2, March, 1987, p. 25.*

Patrick Coleman   (essay date Spring 1989)

[*In this excerpt, Coleman argues that although it is sophisticated and entertaining,* Ah! Ah! (Ha! Ha!) *lacks underlying unity of plot.*]

As Jonathan Weiss points out in his *French-Canadian Theater,* [the structure of Ducharme's play *Ha! Ha!*] recalls that of Albee's *Who's Afraid of Virginia Woolf?* Two couples—Roger and Sophie, Bernard and Mimi—engage in a series of power plays, complicities, and role reversals, all culminating in the victimization and expulsion of Mimi, the youngest and most naïve of the characters. The games are masterminded by Roger, a paunchy, nihilistic parasite. His sometimes half-hearted, sometimes calculatingly sadistic machinations are given literary overtones (by reference to poetic figures) and political dimensions as well (from time to time, he holds his nose as he delivers a "[b]rittle speech from the . . . drone". This is Ducharme's familiar world of disenchanted creativity and envious resentment at lost innocence. As usual, there are many funny moments, and on a moment-by-moment basis the interplay of characters is lively and well-outlined. Considered as a whole, though, I think the play fails to cohere.

The chief problem with the play is that we are never convinced that the characters' lost innocence was real or worth preserving, narrow and intolerant as it may have been. Mimi's expulsion has none of the complexity and pathos Ducharme brings to such a process in his film script for *Les bons débarras* ("Good Riddance"). Perhaps the absence of any children or genuinely childlike character in *Ha! Ha!* is partly to blame for the play's emotional void. In the second part of the play, Mimi does come into her own with an extended account of a dream. She tells of being caught in an airport full of people waiting for no one, and about the horrible wounds that appeared wherever they touched each other. This is a powerful image, but the dream comes very late in the play, and it remains an isolated moment. It fails to suggest a second level of existence that would have given a deeper resonance to the games we see unfold on stage.

The same half-heartedness can be found on the dramaturgical level, too. The play is divided into two roughly equal parts, whose separation is marked by a slight change of set. The stage directions tell us that the furniture in Sophie's living room has been shifted around to give the room "that 'big surprise party in honor of Lucie' look", Lucie being the wife Roger abandoned when he took up with Sophie. We are also told that at "the back, clearly visible" are "Polaroid-type photos of two girls (8-9-10 years old) blown up into posters." This device reminds us of the giant postcard that forms the backdrop for Michel Tremblay's *A toi, pour toujours, ta Marie-Lou.* Ducharme's posters, however, are much less effective, since nothing is really made of them in the play, nor does Lucie's absent character exert any genuine influence on the action. Perhaps his intent is a parodic one; no doubt concepts such as memory, illusion, presence, and absence have lost any structuring function in his degraded universe. By the same token, the ritual scapegoating of Mimi that the play enacts is deprived of any real force.

It might be argued that *Ha! Ha!* is all the more resolutely and self-consciously theatrical in focusing on the characters' power games in themselves, and on the process of play-acting, as Ducharme leaves the chips to fall where they may. Looking at his career as a whole, we could indeed make the case that the theatre represents for him an escape from, or at least an alternative to, the obsessively monological narrative strategies of the novels. That is, the theatre gives Ducharme the opportunity to introduce contending voices into a vision whose central impulse is to control meaning (or its disruption). *Ha! Ha!* certainly dramatizes various distortions of voice. Whether it does more, whether it has found a counterpart to the asceticism of discourse that in the best novels redeems the obsession, is doubtful. (pp. 146-48)

> *Patrick Coleman, "Brittle Speech," in* Essays on Canadian Writing, *No. 37, Spring, 1989, pp. 146-49.*

Charles Foran   (essay date February 1992)

[*Foran comments on* Dévadé's *striking imagery and discusses the difficulty of translating Ducharme's works into English.*]

Set in the 1970s, [*Dévadé*] chronicles a group of *rada*—a Ducharme coinage for outcasts—who wander a wintry Montreal in alcohol and drug hazes, unable to articulate the source of their malaise or envision the future except in the most fragmented terms. The protagonist, Bottom (the character's own translation of Lafond, with Shakespearean undertones), is an ex-convict whose job is to tend to *La Patronne,* an eccentric, wealthy woman confined temporarily to a wheelchair. Services include the sexual, and the relationship between mistress and servant is parasitic, though scarcely worse than contacts between other characters. Ducharme provides no plot to direct these

people, and Bottom's yearnings for a more meaningful existence are undercut by his own insights into his condition: "This isn't a life. With the filth I throw in, it's a garbage can."

Even readers familiar with Roch Plante [a pseudonym Ducharme used as an artist who worked with rubbish] were shocked by the image. Garbage as a metaphor, in art work or in a novel, is potent. *Dévadé* despairs for its misfits; befuddled, unable to connect with anyone or anything, they stand little chance of extricating themselves from the mire. Gone are both the jocosity of *L'Hiver de force* and the demonic will of Bérénice Einberg. What saves the novel from nihilism is Ducharme's obvious compassion for these lost souls. His characters, like those in a Samuel Beckett play, suffer, despair, but carry on.

As well, the book is remarkably written. Perhaps the most textured of Ducharme's novels, *Dévadé* is a joyful assault upon the conventions of French. Sentence fragments, new words, alliterative runs, bilingual puns ("Little by little I lost my Lady Chatterley's Laveur complex," Bottom tells us), and shifts in tense keep the narrative off balance and unpredictable. Though jarring, the rhythm is highly addictive. (p. 66)

How hard is Ducharme to translate? A sampling of titles alone hints at the difficulties. Most of the books employ neologisms and sound associations. *L'Océantume* plays with the ocean and *amertume* (bitterness): "Bittersea" would do. *L'Hiver de force* blends the French phrase for straitjacket, *camisole de force,* with the notion of a symbolic winter: "Strait Winter" is an approximation. *Les Enfantômes,* a lovely binding of *enfants* and *fantômes,* works well as "The Ghost-children." *Dévadé* is more problematic. An *évadé* is an escaped prisoner, but *dévadé* carries greater import. "Devasion" is interesting, though it loses the reference to Bottom's stint in prison. Other titles, including *Le Nez qui voque* ("The Equivocating Nose"?), would probably have to be changed.

All of which suggests that Ducharme may be best left in French. For a major writer, language is rarely a mere conduit; it is integral to the creative impulse, often to personal identity. To some extent, Ducharme is his language; the prose in his novels reflects discernible moods, ranging from whimsy to rage, ironic detachment to earnest entreaty. These moods, in turn, constitute a personality, a compelling form of literary intimacy. (p. 67)

> *Charles Foran, "Ghost Writer," in* Saturday Night, *Vol. 107, No. 1, February, 1992, pp. 15-18, 66-7.*

FURTHER READING

Leduc-Park, Renée. "Repetition with a Difference in Réjean Ducharme." *Yale French Studies* No. 65 (1983): 201-13.

   Leduc-Park examines Ducharme's use of language, focusing on *L'hiver de force* and its relation to popular Quebec culture.

Additional coverage of Ducharme's life and career is contained in the following source published by Gale Research: *Dictionary of Literary Biography,* Vol. 60.

Frantz Fanon

1925-1961

Martinican essayist.

The following entry presents an overview of Fanon's life and work.

INTRODUCTION

A political essayist, Fanon is chiefly remembered for *Les damnés de la terre* (*The Wretched of the Earth*), a prose collection denouncing colonialism and racism in the Third World. In this and other works he urged native Africans to reclaim their land and culture by revolting against their European oppressors. Although critics have often faulted Fanon for his advocacy of violence to achieve political liberation, *The Wretched of the Earth* is broadly regarded as a powerful indictment of racial subjugation.

Fanon was one of eight children born into a light-skinned, middle-class family on Martinique, a French-controlled island in the West Indies. According to his brother Joby, Fanon was a sensitive but difficult child who often fought with his peers and consequently was often told by his mother to "stop acting like a nigger." As a child he learned to speak French, sing patriotic French songs, and read French literature and history. Like other Martinicans, he regarded himself as French rather than black and grew up hearing that native Africans were "savages." In 1943, inspired by General Charles de Gaulle's call to defend France during World War II, he joined the French army. There he encountered blatant racism—black soldiers were often given poorer quality rations and were often the first to be sent into battle—and decided that France, and consequently, the whole of white-dominated society, considered him a black man. Disillusioned by his growing awareness of racism, Fanon returned to Martinique in 1946. About this time he met fellow West Indian writer Aimé Césaire and briefly embraced the philosophy of *négritude,* a movement founded by Césaire and Léopold Sédar Senghor that promoted pride in black people, black culture, and black art. For the next year, Fanon campaigned for Césaire's election to the French National Assembly.

In 1947 Fanon traveled to France to study psychiatry. After successfully completing his medical training and passing his doctoral examinations, he left for French-controlled Algeria in 1952 to serve as the psychiatric director of the Blida-Joinville Hospital. A year after his arrival, the Algerian War erupted, and Fanon surreptitiously began lending his services and writing talent to the Algerian Front de Libération Nationale (FLN), a group of native revolutionaries who sought Algerian independence from France. After participating in a strike with other doctors sympathetic to FLN, Fanon was expelled from

Algeria in 1957. Settling in Tunisia, he continued to protest French colonialism, chiefly through his writings in underground newspapers. Fanon attracted powerful supporters as well as enemies as his political influence grew. After surviving numerous assassination attempts on his life, he was stricken with leukemia in the late 1950s. Deliberately ignoring his condition, Fanon sought treatment very late, first in the Soviet Union and then in the United States. Just prior to his death in 1961 in Washington, D.C., he completed *The Wretched of the Earth.* In accordance with his wishes, his body was returned to Algeria for burial.

Fanon wrote four books during his lifetime, each addressing the effects of colonialism and racism. His first book, *Peau noire, masques blancs* (*Black Skins, White Masks*), is an essay collection in which he examines black life in a white-dominated world. In this work, Fanon draws upon his experiences as a psychiatrist to profile the white colonizer and the colonized African and to discuss the psychological effects of racism on both groups. Linking to colonialism the mental disorders and sexual dysfunctions he observed in both black and white patients, Fanon urged blacks to throw off their white masks—or their attempts at assimilation—and embrace their "blackness," which would restore their mental health and dignity. In his lesser-known essay collections *L'an V de la révolution algérienne* (*A Dying Colonialism*) and *Pour la révolution africaine: Ecrits politiques* (*Toward the African Revolution: Political Essays*), Fanon continued to explore the effects of racism and colonialism on individuals and black society.

Fanon's reputation as a literary and political figure rests chiefly upon his posthumously published essay collection *The Wretched of the Earth*. This volume has been praised as a manifesto for Third World revolution that has inspired many contemporary liberation groups, including the Black Panthers and the Black Liberation Army. In this work Fanon argued that Western countries had exploited the resources and people of the Third World and that a violent revolution was the only feasible path to political and cultural liberation. Since the "wretched of the earth," the poorest of the poor, were the only group uncorrupted by Western materialism, Fanon argued, only they were worthy of leading the revolution. Although he expressed a horror of violence in his writings and cautioned against harboring hatred for whites, he encouraged blacks to arm themselves in the effort to reclaim their land and dignity. In his view, violence was the only option left to the black man, whose "back is to the wall, the knife . . . at his throat, or more precisely, the electrode at his genitals." Fanon also believed that violence for the "wretched" was a positive force: "Violence frees the native from his inferiority complex and from his despair and inaction; it makes him fearless and restores his self-respect."

Discussion of *The Wretched of the Earth* has dealt chiefly with Fanon's proposal for the decolonization of Third World countries. Albert Memmi, for example, argued that Fanon had overestimated the leadership role of the Third World poor and, like many commentators, found his theory of violence "disturbing and surprising for a psychiatrist." Others, however, have proclaimed Fanon a hero whose work has energized civil rights movements across the world. In response to the charge that Fanon glorified violence, Césaire argued that Fanon proposed violence in an attempt to create a nonviolent world: "[Fanon's] violence, and this is not paradoxical, was that of the nonviolent. By this I mean the violence of justice, of purity and intransigence; . . . his revolt was ethical, and his endeavour generous."

PRINCIPAL WORKS

Peau noire, masques blancs (essays) 1952
   [*Black Skins and White Masks,* 1965; also published as *Black Skins, White Masks,* 1967]
L'an V de la révolution algérienne (essays) 1959; also published as *Sociologie d'une révolution* (*L'an V de la révolution algérienne*), 1966
   [*Studies in a Dying Colonialism,* 1965; also published as *A Dying Colonialism,* 1967]
Les damnés de la terre (essays) 1961

   [*The Damned,* 1963; also published as *The Wretched of the Earth,* 1965]
Pour la révolution africaine: Ecrits politiques (essays) 1964
   [*Toward the African Revolution: Political Essays,* 1967]

*These works were published posthumously.

CRITICISM

Robert Coles   (review date 18 September 1965)

[*Coles is an American psychiatrist. In the following excerpt, he favorably appraises* The Wretched of the Earth, *particularly extolling Fanon's social, political, and psychological insights into colonialism and rebellion.*]

Frantz Fanon was born in Martinique and educated in France to be a physician and specialize in treating mental disorders. At 27 he tried to describe the feelings of a Negro living in a predominately white world (**Black Skin, White Masks**). Soon thereafter he was summoned to Africa, there serving with the French during the "internal" war, the rebellion of the Algerians against the mother country. Instead he deserted to the foe, convinced that colonialism must die. He worked as a doctor for the rebels, and wrote passionately for them, publishing **Year Five of the Algerian Revolution** and this present volume [**The Wretched of the Earth**], which is a study of the political and economic nature of racism and colonialism as well as an analysis of what they both do to the minds of their victims. In 1961, at 36, Fanon was dead of a cancer he knowingly ignored in order to work as a revolutionary. As he so often observed, the oppressed live short lives. (p. 20)

[**The Wretched of the Earth**] tells what is happening to those lives now (as colonialism relinquishes its grasp on them) and it does so in a singular way, mixing the doctor's and psychiatrist's concern for the health of the individual with the political rebel's interest in institutional change and the street fighter's canny sense of tactics and power.

Before we can hear Fanon, we have to contend with Sartre, whose preface shows all too clearly how little of the book's spirit he has absorbed. The Parisian intellectual tries to outdo Fanon's anger, and at the same time wants to give it direction. Where Fanon cries his specific outrage at European sins, then goes on to abstain hating Europe as such, or Europeans in general (he took on French patients in Algeria) Sartre forecasts the doom of Europe with uninhibited enthusiasm and wrath, showing not the slightest effort—and he is a philosopher—to differentiate between the West's past behavior, its present struggles, or the honest future it just might have. He writes "to bring the argument to a conclusion," then follows that remark with what is the least charitable assault on Europe ever written, one that fairly quickly focuses—of all places—on

Paris and its "narcissism." (It is the philosopher, not the psychiatrist, who gets tied up with language like that.)

Just as Fanon cannot escape the purposes of Sartre, the colonial peoples in general have found themselves caught in the blunt competition of the Cold War. Fanon desperately wants a way out for Africans, calling it a "Third World" that will hopefully avoid commitment either to Washington, Moscow or Peking. For him, a Stalin would be merely another imperialist.

In the major portion of the book Fanon talks mainly to—though sometimes about—this beloved Third World. I suppose, sitting at my comfortable desk, I can dismiss many of the pages as repetitious and tiring. Again and again the poor are exhorted to rise up, to break away from their jailers. (Again and again the jailers have hunted them down; and so the repetition I find in the book has been experienced by others.) The violence, the brute force that once enslaved people and still holds them at sword's point is relentlessly exposed. The violence in the violated, potential vengeance run amok, is not neglected either.

Fanon's "wretched" have yet to find true freedom, and he knew it when he died, in spite of the so-called "sovereignty" granted one nation after another in Africa. Are those countries, or the many "republics" of Central and South America, free when they are at the various mercies of foreign stock exchanges, industrial complexes, and a nondescript assortment of mercenaries, spies, agents, and what have you—in the clutch, troops—whose activities probably match the most lurid fantasies any of us can make up?

What distinguishes this book, turns it from a blazing manifesto to an authentic and subtle work of art, is the author's extraordinary capacity to join his sharp social and political sense with the doctor's loyalty to the individual, whatever his particular worth or folly. As a result, fierce hatred—to hell with the merciless exploiters, still bleeding their victims—is qualified by an alarmed recognition that native tyranny can replace its foreign predecessor. Indeed, the author systematically exposes such dangers as ultranationalism in the newly liberated countries; the cult of the leader; the kind of excessive regard for the "spontaneity" of the people that results in disorder all around; the mystification that ideas like "negritude" can produce; and the extreme betrayal threatening millions in the countryside of Africa at the hands of the colonial-trained native civil servants—to Fanon they are a rigid, arrogant crew—who try to take over the new governments when the Europeans make their reluctant or relieved departure.

It is in the book's last section that Dr. Fanon reveals his skills as narrator and artist. Shunning any temptation to avoid confusion and ambiguity, the gray in life, he gives us instead a terrifying glimpse into the mental disorders associated with both colonialism and the revolutions that aim to end it. The crushed people are brought to life as only the novelist or clinician can do it, by detailed descriptions of their private lives, their fears and terrors. One price of rebellion, the mental pain, is revealed, as are the tortures rebellion evokes from the desperate colonial authorities, many of whom eventually collapse, prey to their own bestiality.

Fanon is impressively and painstakingly willing to see hurt and suffering on all sides, guilt everywhere, the entire population saturated with anxiety and nightmares. Children cringe; natives lunge, then collapse in panic; some of the oppressors, at last unnerved and petulant, are seized with remorse. People are tortured, pressed for information, left cowering, not for hours or days, but for the long months they, their families and their doctors must confront.

It is an awful spectacle; and in many ways the justice Fanon does to the mind of the native African under such circumstances resembles what Conrad did to the white man's in *Heart of Darkness*. Western man shares "the horror, the horror" of his nature with millions of others in all corners of the globe. Terror and madness will unite ruler and sufferer if it must come to chaos before brazen tyranny is ended. Insofar as we realize that fact, and act on what we realize, we will live safer and less corrupt lives. For all the resentment and hurt in him, Dr. Fanon had that message for us when he wrote this book, and it is a healing one. (pp. 20, 22-3)

Robert Coles, "What Colonialism Does," in The New Republic, *Vol. 153, No. 12, September 18, 1965, pp. 20, 22-3.*

Roger Barnard   (essay date 4 January 1968)

[*In the following excerpt, Barnard evaluates Fanon's theories on colonialism and the use of violence to achieve political and social liberation.*]

Frantz Fanon was a very brave and honest man who was exceptional in his love and respect for the oppressed. He was a Negro psychoanalyst and one of the leading spokesmen for the revolution which wrought, by much bloodshed and innumerable atrocities, independence for Algeria. He demonstrated his personal commitment by his professional work in Blida in Algeria, by throwing in his lot whole-heartedly with the FLN, and by his writing, which amounts to four published books to date: *The Wretched of the Earth, Studies in a Dying Colonialism, Black Skin, White Masks* and *Towards the African Revolution.* He left the French-run mental hospital in 1956, and devoted the brief remainder of his life to the cause of Algerian freedom. He did not live long enough to see an independent Algeria.

As a writer, he is distinguished by his passionate seriousness, and by his extremely penetrating insights; his books bleed with emotion, rage, indignation and searing disgust at the degradation, dehumanisation and torture imposed on the oppressed coloured peoples of this world by their western colonial masters. His writing is neither easy nor systematic, and one senses that his books were wrung from him by his experience: they are neither tracts, nor essays, nor treatises, nor convenient assemblages of cold fact, but much more like a continuing series of intellectual explosions.

There are virtually no transitions: he wrote like a man fuelled by the implicit belief that history itself provided the elements of continuity in his work, moving from reflections on violence in the colonial and international contexts to the deceptions of decolonisation; from the political machinery before and after independence to the existence of the national bourgeoisie; from national consciousness and culture, to mental disorders in their relationship with colonial war, to the movement forwards to a truly revolutionary socialist world.

Yet beneath this dazzling ferment of ideas, all of Fanon's work has one unchanging central figure: that of "the colonised" (*le colonisé*). Who is *le colonisé?* He is any man, woman, or child who has been brought up in one of the poor, "underdeveloped" regions of the Third World, under the domination, whether covert or overt, of people from the rich regions with different coloured skins. Most of *les colonisés* are non-white—like Fanon himself, who was from Martinique—and they form the majority of the population of the globe. *Les colonisés* are the products of the colonial system—or, when stripped of its humanitarian propaganda, of the forcible domination of one group of men by another. "The settler (*colon*) and the colonised are old acquaintances. As a matter of fact, the settler is right when he makes the claim that he knows 'them.' It is the settler who *made* and *continues to make* the colonised."

Fanon believed that the success of the fight by the colonised for independence lies wholly in the total change of the existing social order. And according to Fanon, the only possible (and indeed, desirable) revolutionary method necessarily involves a murderous and decisive confrontation between the protagonists. With great bitterness, Fanon presented the popular stereotypes that are created round the figure of the native—laziness, necessary savagery, mental debility, puerility, lack of emotivity, and so forth—and then insisted that because of the repressive social system in which the colonised native is forced to live, he is bound irrevocably to manifest much of his tension in the form of aggression.

However, in the stages preceding the revolutionary uprising, he utilises the mechanism of avoidance in his dealings with the colonial "superior," and he vents his aggression against his fellow natives. Then, too, much is released, canalised, transformed or conjured away by drawing on myth and fantasy, and by indulging in orgiastic dance and pantomime in order to relax the "muscular tension." "These disintegrations of personality, these doublings and dissolutions, discharge a basic economic function in the stability of the colonised world."

Gradually, however, there comes to be an alienation from these practices, and during the struggle for freedom the forms of aggression alter drastically. In the final analysis, Fanon equated the absolute line of action with violence. In his theory of violence, he rebelled against the violence which is inner-directed, but he exhorted and celebrated the violence which is outer-directed. The death of the settler is the defined goal, and freedom is found through the violent thrust outwards, rather than inwards. The degree of the thrust is in direct proportion to the violence that is exercised by the threatened colonial regime. Thus, there is terror, counter-terror, violence, and counter-violence, an escalating whirligig of atrocities and bloodletting. Gen-

erally, there is some kind of sudden end in a vast and all-conclusive repression which serves to mobilise the masses. "For the native, life can only spring up again out of the rotting corpse of the settler."

Fanon did not mean to say that violence is the creation of colonialism, which is how he is too often interpreted, but on the contrary, that colonialism itself is a form of violence—what is more, an extremely brutal form of violence that has been developed predominantly by the most tightly organised and most effectively violent human societies. "Colonialism is not a thinking machine, it is not a body endowed with reason. It is violence in the state of nature, and it can be defeated only by greater violence."

As Fanon saw it, colonialism has done everything in its power to separate, segregate and regionalise the colony, and to smash solidarity; contrariwise, the employment and practise of violence cements together that which has been torn apart, for violence is all-inclusive, it integrates, unifies and cleanses. (This is in fact exactly similar to what the Italian futurists were proclaiming in 1914, and it is also the "intellectual" backbone of organised fascism.) The masses become more sophisticated, less easily duped and tricked, and they are finally loosed from their deep-rooted inferiority complex and freed from generations of inaction and induced acquiescence.

This was Fanon's dominant theme, certainly, but he had others too. He discussed at length the growth and evolution of political parties, and the development of a national party in an "underdeveloped" nation. He was at pains to stress the error of using the European left-wing party as the model. The excessive emphasis on the urban working class, meaningful in Europe, serves only to alienate the majority of people, the rural masses, in an "underdeveloped" nation. Rural people are suspicious of "urban folk," and the colonial regime capitalises on this antagonism in its struggle against the growing revolutionary nationalism.

Fanon was concerned, too, to describe the rift between the native intellectual and bourgeoisie, and the mass. In his view, the national parties consist, for the most part, of intellectual and commercial elites which dabble faint-heartedly in philosophical and political discussion about self-determination. They are not radical. They do not aim at total change. They do not act. They are "violent in words, and reformist in action." In the main, the people who form the national parties in the Third World are precisely those who have begun to profit somewhat from the very system which burdens the masses. They nurture the illusory hope of assimilating into the colonial world.

Therefore, argued Fanon, if the power remains in the hands of the national bourgeoisie, the revolution is doomed to failure from the word go. By this token, the national party must not be the only relevant political bureau, and it must not depend on the cult of leadership. Leading members, declared Fanon, should avoid centralisation in the capital, and the emphasis should be on extreme decentralisation. The nation should be divided into many areas and the party should be represented through one of its members in a political bureau in each area. But even here, there must not be administrative power. Rather, the aim is to contact the rural masses. The party and the government must truly be in the service of the people: they must detribalise, educate and unite.

If, unfortunately, the national bourgeoisie remains at the helm after independence, it will look for aid to the former mother country and to foreign capitalist investment. Gradually, predicted Fanon, the "economic channels of the young state sink back inevitably into neo-colonialist lines, and the budget is balanced through gifts." But unity cannot be achieved or maintained this way. The only way to do it is by the "upward thrust of the people, in defiance to the interests of the bourgeoisie." Fanon's opinion was that the country can move forward only if it nationalises the middleman's trading sector. "This means organising wholesale and retail cooperatives on a democratic basis, and decentralising these cooperatives."

Finally, Fanon claimed that in the context of the cold war, and during the slaughter and insurrection prior to independence, the cries emanating from the Third World are heard and are of great importance. There is the loss of the colony as a consumer market, but—hopefully—there is at the same time increasing political and diplomatic support for progressive countries and peoples. "For Europe's sake, for our own sake, and for the sake of humanity, comrades, we must take on a new skin, develop a new kind of thinking, try to create a new kind of man."

The major value of Frantz Fanon's work lies primarily not in his generalisations, which are often devastatingly acute, but above all in the relationship of his ideas to direct experience: though Fanon refined and extended them in his later books, all his notions are grounded fundamentally and from the start in the perspective of the Algerian revolution, which was the crucial "watershed" event in his life. In this respect, it may not be unfair to assert that Fanon was perhaps taken in by his own propaganda: that is to say, though he recognised clearly the dangers of a preening dictator, and though he wanted the masses to participate, yet throughout his work the single-party state remains an unquestioned assumption—and in such a set-up, it is inevitable that the masses act out a burlesque of involvement without the concrete reality of decision-making.

A brief glance at the course taken by the Algerian revolution, which in fact ran counter to most of Fanon's prophetic claims, will suffice to demonstrate my meaning. In Algeria, the peasantry contributed men, sweat and blood for an anti-colonial war. Once the war was won, the peasantry tended to disperse, relapsing into local interests and seeking individual small-scale ownership of the land. It was too weak, too poor, too diffuse to remain or become the leading force for social change in the newly liberated country. The bourgeoisie (what there was of it) having been shattered, and the working class pushed aside, what remained was primarily the party of nationalism, led by men who were dedicated, up-rooted, semi-educated and ruthless: an independent force above the weakened classes and the direct negation of what Fanon hoped to see, so much so in fact that Colonel Boumedienne has recently been able to push through the reintroduction of national conscription in Algeria.

As far as his influence goes, Fanon's role has been pretty close to that of a teacher, despite the tarnishing of his vision in Algeria: he sketched out some broad-based strategies of action for the dispossessed and he showed very clearly how the oppressed—tortured and tricked into resenting their own existence—can nevertheless be mobilised to change their status. Later theorists, writers and activists—for example, Ché Guevara, Stokely Carmichael and Régis Debray—have taken his basic analysis one stage further, and they have revised some of his tactical prescriptions.

Yet it is still true that Fanon's work has had, and continues to have, an enormous fascination for, and impact on, a whole generation of radicals and intellectuals on both sides of the Atlantic.

The Wretched of the Earth, still his best-known book, was acclaimed in France and Britain when it first appeared and in America it has become something of an activist's bible for many sections of the "new left." Much the same thing is happening with *Towards the African Revolution,* published very recently. *Black Skin, White Masks,* which describes from the viewpoint of a psychoanalyst the inner feelings and sufferings of the oppressed, made the "recommended" column of the best-seller list for weeks in America. Strangely enough, *Studies in a Dying Colonialism,* perhaps his most subtle and well-organised book, seems to be little read anywhere.

One disastrous result of this popularity has been the development round the legend of Frantz Fanon of a darkly menacing, anti-west, anti-white myth. I suspect that this myth draws its power not so much from the actual ideas of Fanon, and his insistence on the therapeutic value of violence for rebellious blacks, as from its LeRoi Jonesian ability to evoke shame and pain in the bosoms of white middle class masochists. For, when all is said and done, the inescapable fact remains that Fanon was writing from the bottom, looking up. His was not the viewpoint of the European liberal, sympathetic to the aims of the revolution, but deploring its excesses and seeking the non-violent way out, nor was it even the viewpoint of a French sympathiser with the revolution like Jean-Paul Sartre, whose introduction to *The Wretched of the Earth,* though eloquent, was too much concerned with the rationalisation of France's quilt and the self-lacerating shame of many French intellectuals.

However, in his ready acceptance of Fanon's emphasis on the use of violence as the means to liberation, Sartre did put his finger on the raw nerve for many white radicals. Casting aspersion on the thinking of Camus, Sartre wrote: "A fine sight they are, the believers in non-violence, saying that they are neither victims nor executioners . . . if the whole regime, even your non-violent ideas, are conditioned by a thousand-year-old oppression, your passivity serves only to place you in the ranks of the oppressors."

What to make of it? Though Fanon wrote, in *Towards the African Revolution,* that "no man's death is indispensable for freedom," the fact remains that he preached violence, including violence against civilians, as the legitimate resource of the oppressed. He knew full well that the white western nations, primarily America, establish and maintain their imperial control either by open and direct military force and the powerful weaponry of advanced technology, or by violence institutionalised in economic and commercial exploitation. Therefore, he argued, the conquered have the absolute moral right to employ equivalent violence in order to end that rule; further, he asserted that they will refuse to allow their conquerors the right to define for them what kinds of violence are to be considered legitimate.

My own position on Fanon's exaltation of violence is somewhat tricky, by reason of the pacifist and libertarian anti-state philosophy that I hold. I am not shocked (though I do not support them) that foul injustices are done in the course of colonial revolutions, for it is not the case that a just situation has suddenly become unjust. My own non-violence is not so absolute that I would categorically deny that there may be times when a man can see nothing better to do than to take up arms (say, in Brazil, or South Africa, or Vietnam), since to do anything else would be to betray some very particular values—liberty or justice, for example—that are even more fundamental than respect for human life.

What is terrible, however, is if violence goes on and on, or if it is casual or callous, or if it becomes organised in such a way that the killing of judicial prisoners or military captives is an accepted part of it, or if you find yourself turned into a soldier, a creature of war. This way is terribly dangerous, and revolutionaries everywhere do well to fear it.

I think that this is where Fanon's theories of violence can be criticised and said to be basically wrong, as the outcome of the Algerian revolution testified. Organised violence on the part of the colonised natives and peasants may well be sociologically and psychologically necessary; nevertheless, it remains true that all violence tends to be reactionary and to bolster the status quo, whatever may be the avowed objectives of those who employ it.

The central point to be grasped, then, is that the utilisation of violence by revolutionaries invariably sets up ends which absorb the original revolutionary goals and nullify them—and in the process, both the wielders and the recipients are made unjust. This is not any kind of subjective judgment, by the way, but objective and inarguable fact, attested to by historical experience time after time in the last 200 years. And, as Brecht sadly wondered, how on earth do unjust men build the worthwhile society? Still, there it is: this is the sort of "double bind" that is inherent in the use of revolutionary violence. The question is, are you prepared to accept those binds? Fanon clearly was.

However, I believe that if the future is not yet closed, and if there are significant present choices to be made, then there are some genuine tasks ahead for western radicals who wish to aid the colonial revolution in the Third World. Frantz Fanon never did believe in this: he wrote us all off—pacifists, anarchists, radicals, revolutionaries, left-wing democrats, liberal reformists, or whatever—for he believed that nobody in the western mother countries could be absolved from the continuing tortures and suffer-

ings inflicted on the colonised peoples. If it is the case, as seems pretty clear, that all the crimes committed by all sides in all colonial wars derive from the one fundamental wickedness of a domineering rule that is imposed and maintained from above, then it may well be (though I hope and work otherwise) that this rule is not finally accessible to any appeal save that of violence.

For good or for ill, it is probably true that you and I can do little or nothing about the growing violence in the Third-World; the victims of our collective greed and selfishness will listen to each other, and then act, which is perhaps as it should be—for one of the more worthwhile lessons to be learnt from marxism is that the failure of revolutionary violence at the appropriate historical moment may in fact bring on the all-embracing violence of fascism: the repressed material accumulates and then erupts on such a scale as to annihilate everything in its path, including the seeds of new departures.

If we are to be of any help at all to Fanon's les colonisés, it will be in two ways: (a) by striving to transform Britain and America from aggressive and exploitative nation-states into rational free societies which will cooperate peacefully in solving economic problems in the Third World; and (b) by providing a continuing critique of coercive power, political authoritarianism, and institutionalised violence.

And the best way to provide that critique is for us to begin applying it to our own society. I like to think that Frantz Fanon might at least have come to agree with that. (pp. 11-13)

> Roger Barnard, "Frantz Fanon," in New Society, Vol. 11, No. 275, January 4, 1968, pp. 11-13.

Ronald Segal   (review date 17 May 1968)

[Exiled to England for his anti-government views, Segal is a South African writer and critic. In the following excerpt, he concurs with Fanon's analysis of "the colonised mind" in Black Skin, White Masks.]

Black Skin, White Masks is an early book by Frantz Fanon, author of the now widely celebrated The Wretched of the Earth, who was born in Martinique; practised psychiatry in Algeria, where he associated himself with the nationalist struggle against France; and died of leukaemia at the age of 36 in 1961. Here already are the ideas he subsequently developed to such effect: the psychic ravages of colonialism, on colonisers and colonised alike; the betrayal of colonial revolution by mimics of the metropolitan dominion; violence as an essential instrument of liberation; the 'restructuring of the world' as the sole answer to racism.

In an incisive critique of Manoni's influential Prospero and Caliban (1956), he dismisses the argument, so congenial to the metropolitan rich and resourceful, that colonial racism is the product not of the best in European civilisation, but of the artisans, the clerks, the petty traders, the lower ranks of the civil service and army, who are the vulgar of white empire. Quoting Francis Jeanson's indictment of the

French over Algeria in 1950, he promotes that 'post-Nuremberg morality' which is so much a part of young radicalism in Europe and America today, and which power and profit, not least in Britain, so blandly disregard—no, despise:

> You pride yourselves on keeping your distance from realities of a certain kind: so you allow a free hand to those who are immune to the most unhealthy climates because they create these climates themselves through their own conduct. And if, apparently, you succeed in keeping yourselves unsullied, it is because others dirty themselves in your place. *You hire thugs,* and, balancing the accounts, it is you who are the real criminals: for without you, without your blind indifference, such men could never carry out deeds that damn you as much as they shame these men.

Fanon's analysis of the white racist mind is concerned principally with sexual roots:

> . . . the Negrophobic woman is in fact nothing but a putative sexual partner—just as the Negrophobic man is a repressed homosexual . . . the white man behaves toward the Negro as an elder brother reacts to the birth of a younger . . . when a white man hates black men, is he not yielding to a feeling of impotence or of sexual inferiority? Since his ideal is an infinite virility, is there not a phenomenon of diminution in relation to the Negro, who is viewed as a penis symbol? . . . Projecting his own desires onto the Negro, the white man behaves 'as if' the Negro really had them.

I am sure that there is much truth in all this; that the sexual sickness which whites project as the threat of the Negro's supposed superior potency, so that to persecute him is to castrate him, has a place in the development of attitudes to colour, perhaps above all among the Anglo-Saxons.

But this part of the truth Fanon spoils by over-feeding. Racism is also the exultation and excuse of power. For civilisations constructed from the morality of might, the mastered required contempt to establish the righteousness of the masters. It was the vulnerability of the coloured that constituted their vice, as conquest became a virtue that was made for many—if manifestly not all—its own reward. Empire promoted a mass metropolitan acquiescence in conditions that would otherwise far sooner and more fiercely have been challenged. The British poor may not have been the equals of the British rich; but they were, by Hope and Glory, the superiors of the savages whom they, also after all, ruled. No one who has followed the course of foreign policy under Labour governments can fail to recognise the allurements and compensations of the imperial image. And the usefulness of a distraction or a scapegoat is equally relevant—as the mood of Britain today amply demonstrates. The shadow of the coloured immigrant comfortably falls over the decay of the social services; the persistence of poverty; high unemployment and slum housing; the triumph of successive governments, Conservative and Labour alike, in perpetuating the systematic inequalities of welfare capitalism.

Fanon is at his best in exploring the colonised mind: the exchange by blacks of their human meaning for the counterfeit currency of white myths; the longing to be accepted on the very terms of white superiority that inevitably make such acceptance impossible; the self-hatred, the self-contempt, the self-mutilation. 'It is the racist who creates his inferior.' From this psychical self-torture, violence is the instrument of liberation. Fanon quotes Aimé Césaire, a fellow Martinican who is one of the great poets of the French language and of the revolutionary mind:

> We broke down the doors. The master's room was wide open. The master's room was brilliantly lighted, and the master was there, quite calm . . . and we stopped. . . . He was the master . . . I entered. 'It is you,' he said to me, quite calmly . . . It was I. It was indeed I, I told him, the good slave, the faithful slave, the slavish slave, and suddenly his eyes were two frightened cockroaches on a rainy day . . . I struck, the blood flowed. That is the only *baptism* that I remember today.

What is Fanon's answer? He rejects the confinement of history, the locking of man 'into a world of retroactive reparations'. He cries:

> The disaster of the man of colour lies in the fact that he was enslaved. The disaster and the inhumanity of the white man lie in the fact that somewhere he has killed man. And even today they subsist, to organise this dehumanisation rationally . . . The Negro is not. Any more than the white man . . . The tragedy of the man is that he was once a child.

Further and further it seems to recede, the vision that man should meet man to discover and love him. Fanon replies to all those who work so destructively to secure the sterile peculiarities of their race: 'I can imagine myself lost, submerged in a white flood composed of men like Sartre or Aragon, I should like nothing better. . . . What have I to do with a black empire?' But what does white empire foster, if not black empire? And so white power for its own sake produces black power for its own sake in a continuous repudiation of humanity. The Negro is, as is the white man. The violence of liberation becomes the violence of rule. The separate civilisations deface each other to achieve a common barbarism. How will we stop this cannibalism in our blood? For the worst of what we are doing in this country is not to them, or to us, but to all, in a consuming of the human purpose. That we do so in vanity and greed is hideous enough. That we claim to be doing so in the cause of preserving our standards, of progress and peace, is the ultimate perversion. Mirror, mirror, on the wall. . . . Where is the face of Prospero? We are the Calibans we make. (pp. 656-57)

Ronald Segal, "Caliban Speaks," in New Statesman, *Vol. 75, No. 1940, May 17, 1968, pp. 656-57.*

J. E. Seigel   (essay date Winter 1968-69)

[*Seigel is an American educator who specializes in the study of modern European history. In the following essay, he discusses how Fanon's writings were informed by his personal experiences.*]

Until recently, few Americans had heard of Frantz Fanon. His death in a Washington, D. C., hospital in 1961 went practically unnoticed in this country. Now, suddenly, he is a presence in our lives. His last book, ***The Wretched of the Earth,*** is cited as the handbook of the revolution in our midst; his life and thought feed the stream of our fate. Yet it remains difficult to get a clear picture of him. Militant blacks (and some of their white cousins) see their hopes in Fanon; frightened whites see their fears. The two opposing perspectives reinforce each other: both give an image of a determined apostle of violence and a romantic, even messianic revolutionary. Yet Fanon was more than this, and the parts of his life this image neglects also speak to our condition. Fanon felt the split between blacks and whites to the depths of his soul, but his zeal was to overcome it, not to solidify it. He gave himself wholeheartedly to the anticolonial rebellion in Algeria, but he feared and hated violence even while he glorified it. Fanon has been made the symbol of conflict; we must see that he also stood for reconciliation. To do so is to move a step closer to reconciliation ourselves.

Frantz Fanon grew up in Martinique, where he was born in 1925. He always remembered his West Indian origins, even while trying to identify himself first as a Frenchman, and later as an anti-French Algerian rebel. He studied medicine and psychiatry in France, and was sent to direct a psychiatric hospital in the (still French-ruled) Algerian city of Blida. Meanwhile, he had written his first and most personally revealing book, ***Black Skin, White Masks.*** According to Simone de Beauvoir, who knew him shortly before his death, "when the Algerian war broke out, he was torn in all directions at once; he hated to give up a status it had cost so much to attain, yet all colonized peoples were his brothers; he recognized the Algerian cause as identical with his own." After a period of surreptitiously aiding the rebels, he resigned his French post and openly joined them. Until he died in 1961 Fanon worked for the Algerians, writing articles and editing a newspaper, serving for a time as ambassador to Ghana, traveling through Africa to encourage solidarity among anticolonial movements. It was apparently in Ghana that he first fell ill with a sickness later diagnosed as leukemia. He sought the help of specialists, first in Russia and then, reluctantly (for he viewed America as racist and imperialist), in the United States. While he lay dying in a Washington, D. C., hospital, his last work, ***The Wretched of the Earth,*** appeared and received accolades in the French leftist press. After his death his body was flown back to North Africa and buried with national honors by the Algerian National Army of Liberation.

The jumbled pattern of Fanon's life prepares us for his thought: he was a man of contradictions. In contrast to the one-dimensional image put forth by some of his disciples, he was far from being an unquestioning apostle of violence. In ***Black Skin, White Masks*** his mood was often angry, but it was above all searching, inquiring, mistrustful of irrational enthusiasm. "These truths do not have to be hurled in men's faces," he declared. "They are not intended to ignite fervor. I do not trust fervor. Every time

it has burst out somewhere, it has brought fire, famine, misery . . . and contempt for man." Of course Fanon did not always hold to this view. But the Fanon who did not trust fervor must be confronted if we are to understand the Fanon who later preached violence.

Black Skin, White Masks is a complex book. It is a rich and unshapely mixture of personal reminiscence, philosophical analysis, literary criticism and psychiatric case history, all tied together by a single theme: the fact of being black in a white world. Fanon sought to delve into blackness, to make it yield up the painful reality behind the masks it wears in the world, and finally to overcome it, to find the means by which blackness could be made irrelevant by merging it in the larger fact of humanity. "To us, the man who adores the Negro is as 'sick' as the man who abominates him. Conversely, the black man who wants to turn his race white is as miserable as he who preaches hatred for the whites. In the absolute, the black is no more to be loved than the Czech, and truly what is to be done is to set man free."

Fanon's road to these conclusions was rough and painful, and he had not really traveled it as completely by the time he wrote his book as these quotations suggest. Yet he had read the signposts, learned the directions, and arrived at a point that gave a clear view of the goal. He knew that in a white world to be human is to be white. The black who grows up in this world learns the lesson just as whites do: wanting to be a man he tries to be a white. But this is denied him. Through their fear and distrust, whites remind him that he is black. "Whether concretely or symbolically, the black man stands for the bad side of the character. . . . The archetype of the lowest values is represented by the Negro." Man is civilized, rational, the Negro is primitive, genital. The black who has had this consciousness forced on him has two choices, either to reject his own self, or to spurn the world that created the dilemma. Only the second alternative seems to offer hope. Seizing it, the Negro turns on the white world and celebrates blackness, desperately cultivating those parts of himself that cannot be mistaken for white. But this attempt to storm his way into full humanity must fail: it excludes at the start all those parts of man that the white world has appropriated for itself. It is not a means of reaching manhood but a truncating of humanity. Painfully the black who has set out along this path must find his way to a different one, where blackness can become not a fractional humanity but a form of fully human existence.

For Fanon himself this itinerary led through the concept of *négritude,* the intense and sometimes frenzied pursuit of black consciousness championed by Léopold Senghor, which inspired many African writers in the late forties and fifties. Fanon's discovery of *négritude* was a discovery of tribal culture and African history in its many aspects, of the sculpture of African natives, of rhythm, of emotion, of the occult, but also of the gentleness, unity and social harmony of the African societies described by early European explorers. Yet on a deeper, personal level, Fanon by 1949 had begun to see it also as something else. The stress on emotion and primitivism was a rejection of the rationality on which white civilization was based, and it led toward a rejection of all rationality. "I had rationalized the world and the world had rejected me on the basis of color prejudice. Since no agreement was possible on the level of reason, I threw myself back toward unreason. It was up to the white man to be more irrational than I. . . . I am made of the irrational. I wade in the irrational." Later, in *The Wretched of the Earth,* Fanon commented further on this stage in his own and other Negroes' development. Negro writers caught up in it had produced some good poetry, but the kind of thinking it encouraged was "sterile in the extreme." The search for blackness degenerates into banal exoticism, a cult of the sari and the pampootie. "Going back to your own people means to become a dirty wog, to go native as much as you can, to become unrecognizable, and to cut off those wings that before you had allowed to grow."

Fanon earned the right to reject this phase in the evolution of black consciousness by the torture of his own passage through it. In *Black Skin, White Masks* the pride and hope of his first acceptance of *négritude* still shines through the dense torment of his later rejection of it. It was Jean-Paul Sartre who destroyed the foundations of Fanon's belief in *négritude.* Sartre's essay, "Orphée Noir," published in 1948 as a preface to an anthology of Negro and Madagascan poetry, identified *négritude* as an antiracist racism that could only be a stage on the way to a higher consciousness. What would replace the "subjective, existential, ethnic idea of *négritude,*" in Sartre's view was the "objective, positive, exact idea of proletariat." Only a society without class oppression could eliminate race oppression, the French philosopher argued, and the Marxism of many young Negro writers was a sign of their own recognition that *négritude* was inadequate by itself. Sartre therefore concluded that *négritude* was "the root of its own destruction . . . a transition and not a conclusion, a means and not an ultimate end." To Fanon this conclusion first appeared as "a blow that can never be forgiven." How could the black thinker and writer value his own emerging consciousness if he were forced to regard it as a mere minor term in the Hegelian dialectic? "In all truth, in all truth I tell you, my shoulders slipped out of the framework of the world, my feet could no longer feel the touch of the ground."

That Fanon's emerging black identity could be so deeply shaken by Sartre's arguments is a sign that he may already have felt unsatisfied with certain aspects of it. Fanon reveals himself throughout his writings as an intellectual, a man who lived much of his emotional life in the realm of thought. The power of Sartre's arguments over him is one sign of this. For such a man, the elements of *négritude* that Fanon himself would later associate with a cult of irrationality may have created conflicts even while they seemed to answer deeply felt needs. These elements had to be exorcised. Fanon responded to Sartre's challenge by seeking to reconstruct his black identity in a manner that eliminated them. "What had been broken in pieces was rebuilt." It was rebuilt with certain pieces left out, and with others occupying different places from those they had before. Fanon could not build a self-consciousness for himself without making the fact of blackness the central element. What he could do was forge an attitude toward his black-

ness that regarded it not as a particular aspect of humanity in which certain human qualities flourished while others languished, but rather as a particular form of humanity containing the whole range of human potentials just as any other form did.

> In effect, what happens is this: As I begin to recognize that the Negro is the symbol of sin, I catch myself hating the Negro. But then I recognize that I am a Negro. There are two ways out of this conflict. Either I ask others to pay no attention to my skin, or else I want them to be aware of it. I try then to find value for what is bad—since I have unthinkingly conceded that the black man is the color of evil. In order to terminate this neurotic situation, in which I am compelled to choose an unhealthy, conflictual solution, fed on fantasies, hostile, inhuman in short, I have only one solution: to rise above this absurd drama that others have staged around me, to reject the two terms that are equally unacceptable, and through one human being, to reach out for the universal.

Black Skin, White Masks was Fanon's attempt to "reach out for the universal." In addition to recounting his own development and setting it in the general context of "Negro psychopathology," Fanon pursued human universality by exposing and combating various attempts to make the Negro something other than a species of humanity. Combining Hegel and Sartre with Freud and Jung, Fanon saw the Negro not as a product of biology, but of history and case history. Like the Jew of Sartre's *Anti-Semite and Jew,* the Negro of Fanon's analysis is a creation of those who oppress him. In one chapter Fanon denied the contention of the French psychologist Mannoni that African natives had a peculiar psychology that gave them a need for subjection to others. In another, he studied the black hero of René Maran's novel *Un homme pareil aux autres.* Jean Veneuse's inability to accept the love of the white girl he loved could not be taken as a sign that the gap between black and white was unbridgeable, Fanon argued. Rather, Veneuse suffered from a peculiar psychological malady, an "abandonment neurosis," which produced a fundamental lack of trust in himself. Veneuse's blackness was not the cause of his inability to love and be loved (except as it affected his childhood experiences), but the sign of it, the metaphorical expression of his incomplete humanity. "His color is only an attempt to explain his psychic structure." Of course, important differences between Negroes and whites existed, Fanon recognized. As a psychiatrist he was struck by the absence of the Oedipus complex among African natives. But this phenomenon meant only that Freud's concepts were tied to the experience of Europeans, not that Negroes were more or less manly than whites. Such recognitions would, Fanon believed, allow the Negro progressively to rise above the dilemma created by white society. He offered his book as "a mirror . . . in which it will be possible to discern the Negro on the road to disalienation."

Yet, as suggested above, if Fanon in 1952 was on the way to overcoming his alienation as a black man, he had not arrived at the goal. *Black Skin, White Masks* is a tortured book. The desire to merge blackness with a wider humanity even made the cry "I am a Negro" more violent in the face of white society's dehumanization of blacks. Black emancipation was still in the future; to achieve it would require a struggle in which the black joined his cause with that of all others who were oppressed. Here Fanon hinted at the positive value he would later place on struggle and conflict as a test of manhood and will. The possibility of a meaningful struggle led him to prefer the situation of Negroes in America to that of those in France. In France the Negro had no chance to test his identity or prove his manhood. "In the United States, the Negro battles and is battled. There are laws that, little by little, are invalidated under the Constitution. There are other laws that forbid certain forms of discrimination. And we can be sure that nothing is going to be given free." Yet, as these lines suggest, Fanon's position was not that of a black nationalist or a Marxist revolutionary. "I have no wish to be the victim of the *Fraud* of a black world," he wrote, and "I am not a prisoner of history. I should not seek there for the meaning of my destiny." The final words of the book neither proclaimed nor envisioned ultimate solution; instead they were a prayer for human growth: "O my body, make of me always a man who questions!"

Black Skin, White Masks has beauty, poetry and insight, but its most striking quality is its incompleteness. Fanon believed he had glimpsed the solutions to the awesome problems that beset him, but the mere sight of them gave him no resting place and no certainty that he would ever find one. The torment of Fanon in his twenties is easily—perhaps too easily—labeled today: it is a classic case of what Erik Erikson has taught us to call an identity conflict. Using Erikson's terms, we may say that Fanon's crisis had not reached any viable solution in *Black Skin, White Masks,* but had only arrived at the aggravated self-consciousness that Erikson calls "identity consciousness." "Identity-consciousness is, of course, overcome only by a sense of identity won in action. Only he who 'knows where he is going and who is going with him' demonstrates an unmistakable if not always easily definable unity and radiance of appearance and being." It is precisely this "sense of identity won in action" that Fanon could not achieve on the basis of the position put forth in *Black Skin, White Masks.* He could recognize that the concept of *négritude* as others understood it posited the Negro as (to use another of Erikson's terms) a "pseudospecies," and he could proclaim his solidarity with a wider humanity. But where could he find the members of that humanity who would join with him in the actions that would cement their oneness? Fanon's attempt to proclaim himself a *black man* (giving equal emphasis to both words) at the time he wrote *Black Skin, White Masks* could not put an end to the neurotic situation white society imposed on him: it could only re-create unendingly.

We know the vehicle that finally lifted Fanon out of this vicious and tragic circle: the Algerian revolt. If the account of Fanon's thinking put forward here is correct, then his hesitation before openly joining the Algerian cause may have a significance not suggested in the passage quoted above from Simone de Beauvoir. To join the revolt was not just to give up his status in the French civil service, it was to give up his hold on the wider values of uni-

versal humanity represented by French culture in order to cast his lot unconditionally with the oppressed. In the writings that came out of his Algerian experience Fanon no longer tried to overcome his alienation from white Europe: he reveled in it. Especially in *The Wretched of the Earth* (which its American publisher calls a "handbook for the black revolution"), but also in *A Dying Colonialism,* Fanon turned his back on Europe and blasted black intellectuals who could not shake their fascination with white culture. These writings give none of the sense of incompleteness of his earlier work. The mood of searching and questioning has been replaced by an all-determining commitment. Through participation in the Algerian struggle Fanon found a sense of identity won in action which his earlier attempt to assimilate himself to Europe could not provide.

The new perspective meant a revision of the analysis of "disalienation" given in *Black Skin, White Masks.* The individualist diagnosis worked out there was replaced by one that stressed the relationship between the intellectual and the people. Now it was not an internal psychological crisis that led black writers and thinkers to a rejection of white culture; rather, "at the moment when the nationalist parties are mobilizing the people in the name of national independence, the native intellectual sometimes spurns these acquisitions which he suddenly feels make him a stranger in his own land." This movement of rejection led to the stage of *négritude,* which Fanon criticized here for its negative character as he had before. What condemned it in his eyes now, however, was not its truncated view of humanity, but its concentration on a people's past rather than their present. In order to overcome the limitations of this stage the writer had only one course open to him: to become a leader in the revolutionary struggle and thus to fight for freedom and the creation of a national community.

The best-known aspect of *The Wretched of the Earth* is indeed a central feature of the book: its glorification of violence. "Decolonization is always a violent phenomenon." Violence is a necessary and welcome aspect of revolutionary struggle. The violence of the revolutionaries is the only response to the settlers' compartmentalization of colonial society. Violence creates community where none had existed before. Violence is the native's natural reaction to praise of Western culture, in whose name he had been oppressed. We are far removed from the younger Fanon who "did not trust fervor"; the old identity of questioning intellectual has been suppressed. In place of (what he now described as) "the idea of a society of individuals where each person shuts himself up in his own subjectivity, and whose only wealth is individual thought," Fanon affirmed his discovery of "the substance of village assemblies, the cohesion of people's committees, and the extraordinary fruitfulness of local meetings and groupments." The glorification of violence was a celebration of mass action, an inversion of the personal stance he had taken before.

Fanon moved away from his earlier individualism in another sense. No longer the analyst of interior experience, he turned sociologist and political scientist. The terms of the discussion were post-Marxian: economic realities were determining, but they in turn derived from the racial structure of colonial society. Fanon made use of Marxist categories, but he had no patience with the Marxist faith that history itself would bring victory to the oppressed. Engels' attempt to fit tactics to stages of historical development was puerile. Parts of Fanon's analysis are closer to Lenin (or perhaps to Mao) than to Marx. This is particularly true of his view of the native middle class. Small and weak, composed not of powerful businessmen but only of their agents and intermediaries, from taxi drivers to traders and small wholesalers, the native bourgeoisie had strictly limited aims and capacities. Living only in the cities, the middle class could not express the needs of the rural masses. In its view decolonization meant only taking over colonialist businesses for itself—nationalization—not the social and political development of the whole country. If the revolution were to succeed in moving the country toward a genuine transformation, it had to involve the peasants of the countryside as well as the traders and workers of the towns. These peasants needed the help of intellectuals who recognized the limitations of urbanized natives, but the intellectuals could not be the major revolutionary force or constitute a Leninist-type party.

The violence of the anticolonial revolution would take place in the "international context" of the Cold War, and Fanon admitted that only in this context could colonial revolts succeed. The superior force of the colonial power could not be overcome by the weaker insurgents; instead the Europeans, for reasons of their own internal and international situation, would find the struggle no longer worth its cost and throw in the towel. Fanon proclaimed himself a socialist, but he refused to equate the native struggle against colonialism with the fight between socialism and capitalism. He recommended gratitude to the socialist countries for their aid against imperialist powers, but he coupled it with a plea that the Third World refuse to become a factor in the East-West competition, concentrating instead on the development of its own values, method and style. The looming international question to Fanon in 1961 was not between socialism and capitalism, but between the rich and the poor.

Thus the determined revolutionary of *The Wretched of the Earth* and *A Dying Colonialism* differed profoundly from the brooding, inward author of *Black Skin, White Masks.* Yet the two writers were after all the same man, and their identity is not hard to discover. Beneath the social and political analysis of decolonization there remained the earlier concern for overcoming the dehumanizing effects of alienation and fragmentation. For a time the anticolonial struggle would magnify black feelings of separation from whites, but its final outcome would be the destruction of black racism, not the intensification of it. In *A Dying Colonialism* Fanon wrote of white Europeans who joined the Algerians in the face of French actions during the rebellion, and he accepted them with enthusiasm. A description of the same phenomenon in *The Wretched of the Earth* led to the declaration that, "In their weary road toward rational knowledge the people must also give up their too-simple conception of their overlords. The species is breaking up under their very eyes." As some whites join the rebels in their struggle, the "primitive Manichaeism of the settler" is overthrown. In another sphere, the revolution itself destroys both the basis and the need for a racist culture: "To believe that it is possible to create a black culture is to forget that niggers are disappearing, just as those people who brought them into being are seeing the breakup of their economic and cultural supremacy." Fanon was still trying to "reach out for the universal."

One of the clearest pieces of evidence for the continuity between the younger and the older Fanon is the description Simone de Beauvoir gives of his state of mind when she knew him in 1961. Her picture accords so well with the image that emerges from his writings that we must quote it extensively:

> Though an advocate of violence, he was horrified by it; when he described the mutilations inflicted on the Congolese by the Belgians or by the Portuguese on the Angolans—lips pierced and padlocked, faces flattened by *palmatorio* blows—his expression would betray anguish; but it did so no less when he talked about the "counterviolence" of the Negroes and the terrible reckonings implied by the Algerian revolution. He attributed this repugnance to his condition as an intellectual; everything he had written against the intellectuals had been written against himself as well. . . . It was evident that he found it distressing not to be fighting the battle on his native soil, and even more so not to be an Algerian-born. "Above all, I don't want to become a professional revolutionary," he told us anxiously. . . . He had a passionate desire to send down roots.

One thing this revealing portrait may show is that Fanon had never really resolved the crisis of forging an identity for himself. He could neither accept nor rid himself of his essentially European role of intellectual; he assumed the related career of professional revolutionary with even greater reluctance. We have already taken note of Fanon's own analysis of the antirational style of the black intellectual who turns against European culture. This is not the dominant style of *The Wretched of the Earth,* but it sometimes breaks through, as in the assertion that, because Europeans have long taken raw materials from Africa, Asia and Latin America, "Europe is literally the creation of the Third World." This kind of extravagance may have satisfied one side of Fanon's character, but it recalls a style of thought he previously decried. Many of Fanon's earlier contradictions remained unresolved, including his love-hate relationship with Europe. The conclusion of *The Wretched of the Earth* is a deep well of ambivalence toward the European experience and its values. "When I search for Man in the technique and the style of Europe, I see only a succession of negations of man, and an avalanche of murders." Yet "All the elements of a solution to the great problems of humanity have, at different times, existed in European thought." The struggle to create a new man must be carried out "for Europe, for ourselves, and for humanity."

Most people will probably find Fanon's attempt to bridge the gap between violence and civilization by a romantic faith in revolution not only unsatisfying but dangerously simplistic. Already his name has been linked with one of the bogeymen of modern European history, Georges Sorel. But Fanon should not be confused with Sorel. His advocacy of violence is not a "myth" in Sorel's sense: it was not put forward as a substitute for a searching analysis of what revolution means, concretely, for all the individuals and groups who are caught up in it. On the contrary, Fanon's account of revolution, of the social divisions and antagonisms it brings out, of the mental disorders it breeds, of its horror as well as its promise, deserves a prominent place in the literature of modern social analysis. Fanon sometimes gave way to a messianic hope that the revolution he had joined would "make man victorious everywhere, once and for all," but he did not abuse that hope to justify revolutionary actions on the basis of some ultimate, cosmic significance. He never wallowed in the hate revolutionaries must sometimes feel; his view of the postrevolutionary world was no mere inversion of the compartmentalized, "Manichean" society that had oppressed him.

The point, then, of this discussion of Fanon has been to try to wrest him away from the *terribles simplificateurs* who seek to equate him unconditionally with the advocacy of violence in *The Wretched of the Earth.* It is not possible to say how many of those who claim to follow Fanon actually resemble him in the depth of their inner conflicts, or how many may someday learn to see themselves in Fanon's picture of the irrational style of black antiwhite thought. Fanon's adoption as a spokesman by militant blacks in our country is both a reminder of a painful present and a warning of a troubled future. But in meeting the challenge this poses, we would do well to consider whether, hidden behind the rhetoric of black militancy, there does not remain something of Fanon's hunger "to reach out for the universal." (pp. 84-96)

> J. E. Seigel, "On Frantz Fanon," in The American Scholar, Vol. 38, No. 1, Winter, 1968-69, pp. 84-96.

Black Panther leader Bobby Seale on Fanon's influence on the Black Panthers:

One day I went over to [fellow Black Panther Huey Newton's] house and asked him if he had read Fanon. I'd read *Wretched of the Earth* six times. I knew Fanon was right and I knew he was running it down—but how do you put ideas like his over? . . . So I brought Fanon over one day. That brother got to reading Fanon, and, man, let me tell you, when Huey got ahold of Fanon and read Fanon (I had always been running down about how we need this organization, that organization, but never anything concrete), Huey'd be thinking. Hard. We would sit down with *Wretched of the Earth* and talk and go over another section or chapter of Fanon, and Huey would explain it in depth. . . . Huey was one for implementing things, and I guess this is where the Black Panther Party really started.

Bobby Seale, in his Seize the Time, *Random House, 1970.*

Edmund Burke III   (essay date Winter 1976)

[*In the following essay, Burke presents an overview of* The Wretched of the Earth, *noting that the work is "far more important for the myths it has helped generate than for the quality of its analysis" of colonialism in the Third World.*]

Frantz Fanon's *The Wretched of the Earth,* first published in 1961, is probably the most widely read of the books to emerge from the Third World upheaval of the post-war period; it has been translated into sixteen languages and has reached an international audience. Initially, it was widely hailed as the most passionate and brilliant analysis of the process of decolonization. Rereading the book today, one realizes how much the world has changed in the interval: we now see the extent to which Fanon was a man of his times and the extent to which he was a throwback to the Romantic nationalists of the nineteenth century. Far from having been the Marx of the African revolution (and there were some who mistook him for that), Fanon now emerges more clearly as having been its Mazzini. For the strength of *The Wretched of the Earth* rests less on the incisiveness of its analysis than on the violence and inspiration of its rhetoric. It is a call to arms, not a scholarly autopsy. In the end, it seems more appropriate to apply to it the methods of literary criticism than those of political science. Despite its many contradictions and excesses, *The Wretched of the Earth* remains a remarkable achievement. The universalism of Fanon's imagination and the forcefulness of his language have given the work an appeal that has already made it a modern classic.

In some ways, what one makes of the book depends on what one makes of Fanon himself. By the details of his biography, Frantz Fanon was a kind of black Everyman, a marginal man who was nonetheless able to transcend his marginality. He was born in 1925 into a middle-class black family in Martinique in the French West Indies. Intensely conscious of his race, but also irrevocably within the orbit of French society by virtue of his education and class position, he found himself unable unambiguously to throw in his lot with either. Like others of his background, Fanon fell under the influence of Aimé Césaire, the Martiniquean poet and politician, and of the movement of *négritude* of which Césaire was a leader. He was to remain deeply marked by this early encounter, although *négritude* came increasingly to seem shallow and parochial to him as time went on. His first book, *Black Skin, White Masks,* published in 1952, publicly revealed this ambiguous break with Césaire. It also shows something else—the manner in which Fanon was able to use this ambivalent position among cultures and races to develop a series of penetrating insights into the psychology of racism and colonial domination. His continual preoccupation with these themes was later to give rise to some of the most incandescent passages in *The Wretched of the Earth.*

The life of Frantz Fanon contains a number of additional paradoxes for our reflection. Outwardly, he was the very model of the successful young professional, a psychiatrist of undoubted talents and ambition. He completed his medical degree in 1953 and soon thereafter was posted to the mental hospital at Blida, a small city near Algiers, with the position of *chef de service.* When the revolution broke out at the end of 1954, he was initially slow to take sides. But by 1956 his growing involvement with the rebels led him to resign his position and openly to join the revolution. Even after he became an editor of *El Moudjahid,* the F.L.N. newspaper in Tunis in 1957, however, he continued to practice medicine.

The fact that Fanon was a psychiatrist was to have a major impact on his analysis of the Third World revolution. On the one hand, it was to make him more sensitive than most to the sufferings of individuals in the grip of the colonial system and of the ambivalences of colonizers and colonized. On the other hand, it was to lead him to underestimate the importance of social and economic structures and, consequently, to overrate the possibilities of change. Fanon remained a deeply committed partisan of the cause of Algerian independence until his death. His duties for the F.L.N. brought him into continual contact with the leaders of the independence movements in black Africa, and he was thus able to renew his commitment to the Pan-African dream and to black liberation. In 1960, he served for a time as F.L.N. representative to the All-African People's Conference in Accra, Ghana. In the end, of course, Frantz Fanon was neither an Algerian nor an African. This fact gave his treatment of both movements a curious ambivalence, at once the sympathetic supporter and the clear-sighted critic. Like Albert Memmi, whose *Colonizer and Colonized* presents an analysis of French colonialism which in important ways parallels his own, Fanon was the perpetual outsider. Unlike Memmi, he was able to transcend his marginality to take part in the struggle. *The Wretched of the Earth* can be seen as a kind of synthesis of his life's experience.

The favorable reception of *The Wretched of the Earth* needs to be understood in terms of the movements of decolonization in the postwar world. The steady, ineluctable retreat of European colonialism evoked a feeling of excitement and expectancy throughout Asia and Africa. For a time all things were believed possible; it was the dawn of a new age, of a new chance for humanity. It was at the apogee of this wave of enthusiasm that *The Wretched of the Earth* was published. The forcefulness of its language, its condemnation of colonialism and justification of armed resistance elicited an immediate response throughout the Third World. The book echoed the hopes and fears of its times, and it did so with an idealism that is hard to imagine being expressed today.

The Wretched of the Earth needs also to be situated within the political and intellectual context of postwar France. French intellectuals, already bitterly divided over the Cold War and Stalinism, found themselves in the early nineteen-fifties at odds over decolonization as well. The Algerian war further intensified this conflict. On the Left, the battle was joined between the supporters of the F.L.N. and the French Communist Party. As a leading F.L.N. publicist, Fanon wanted to widen the base of support in French left-wing circles for the insurgents, and *The Wretched of the Earth* was the political manifesto by which he sought to accomplish this task.

The book is the product of an intellectual milieu, as well as a political debate—the cafés of Saint-Germain-des-Prés and postwar Marxism and Existentialism are never far from its pages. The influence of Jean-Paul Sartre, one of the few leading French intellectuals to display an active sympathy for the aspirations of Third World peoples, is especially to be noted. Fanon frequented Sartre's circle in the early nineteen-fifties, and, as has been shown by Irene Gendzier, Sartre's essay *Anti-Semite and Jew* exercised a considerable influence upon Fanon's approach to racism and colonial domination. It was therefore especially fitting that the first edition of *The Wretched of the Earth* should contain a preface by Sartre.

Tracing intellectual influences on Fanon is a frustrating game, for he freely appropriated concepts which appealed to him, frequently without fully understanding them. His Sartreanism is of this sort, and so is his Marxism. Fanon cannot be described as an orthodox Marxist, although he utilizes Marxist categories and his thought tends to be dialectical. His analysis is indeed impregnated with a kind of folk Marxism which appears to have struck an immediate chord with many of his readers. One suspects that it was less the originality of *The Wretched of the Earth* which assured its success than the way in which it stated what was already widely believed by those for whom it was written.

Another reason for the book's appeal is that, like other classics, it permits a wide range of interpretation. The list of those who claim to have been influenced by it includes (among others) African nationalists, Palestinian commandos, and the Bangladesh guerrillas of 1971-72. It enjoyed particular success among black militants in the United States. For a time it was regarded by the Black Panthers as their "Bible." Third World groups found in it a sympathy for their sufferings, justification for their struggles, and encouragement to persist in overcoming all obstacles. In a sense, the book is a kind of mirror; one sees in it who one is. The quasi-literate militant is carried along by the flow of the language and never led to take the analysis very seriously. Others, with more education and experience, are encouraged to meditate on the pitfalls of bourgeois nationalism, but miss the section on national culture. The liberal critic is horrified by the passages on violence, which he takes as confirmation of his fears of Third World nationalism. Armchair theorists of revolution disparage the book as pre-political. Its heart is in the right place, but its analysis is hopelessly soft-headed, if not dangerously voluntarist. In this way, everyone can have the Fanon he chooses. Somewhere, presumably, Fanon himself is smiling.

It is important to realize that *The Wretched of the Earth* was written by a man who knew that he had but a few short months to live. The greater part of the book was written over a ten-week period in the spring of 1961. Previously, Fanon had planned to write a book that would show the relevance of the Algerian revolution to black Africa. Stricken with leukemia toward the end of 1960, he abandoned that earlier project to address himself to a far more ambitious task, a general study of the Third World upheaval. *The Wretched of the Earth* is thus, in effect, Fanon's revolutionary will and testament, a final personal exorcism of the demons which haunted his life. The first chapter, "On Violence," already contains in embryo the main themes that would be developed subsequently. It is almost as if, fearing that he would never be able to complete the manuscript, Fanon sought to disgorge it all in these first few pages. The argument is extremely difficult to follow, as it is presented in an abrupt, violent, and convulsive fashion that eludes all but the most careful of readings. The writing is here at its most searing, an extraordinary outpouring of white-hot emotion—sarcasm, anger, and contempt.

It is clear that Fanon had a very personal sense of language, and this has a great deal to do with the impact the book has had on its readers. Fanon had little patience with most of what passes for intellectual discourse. As he wrote to the French editor of his first book, ***Black Skin, White Masks,*** in response to a request for clarification on a point in the text, "I cannot explain that phrase more fully. I try, when I write such things, to touch the nerves of my reader. . . . That's to say irrationally, almost sensually." It seems to me that his style had its roots in the popular culture of Martinique. It is as if *The Wretched of the Earth* were written more to be declaimed like some enormous and terrifying prose poem than it was to be read. No one who has ever encountered the book has come away unmoved.

One key to what the book is about is contained in the final chapter. Here, we are given a vision of the future of mankind, of a new golden age. The chapter begins with some corrosive remarks on the decadence of Western civilization:

> When I search for Man in the technique and the style of Europe, I see only a succession of negations of man, and an avalanche of murders.

> The human condition, plans for mankind, and collaboration between men in those tasks which increase the sum total of humanity are new problems, which demand true inventions.

Then there follows a series of exhortations:

> Let us decide not to imitate Europe; let us combine our muscles and our brains in a new direction. Let us try to create the whole man, whom Europe has been incapable of bringing to triumphant birth.

> Two centuries ago, a former European colony decided to catch up with Europe. It succeeded so well that the United States of America became a monster, in which the taints, the sickness, and the inhumanity of Europe have grown to appalling dimensions.

> Comrades, have we not other work to do than to create a third Europe? The West saw itself as a spiritual adventure. It is in the name of the spirit, in the name of the spirit of Europe, that Europe has made her encroachments, that she has justified her crimes and legitimized the slavery in which she holds the four-fifths of humanity.

Finally, there come the visions of the future:

> It is a question of the Third World starting a new history of Man, a history which will have regard to the sometimes prodigious theses which Europe has put forward, but which will also not forget Europe's crimes, of which the most horrible was committed in the heart of man, and consisted of the pathological tearing apart of his functions and the crumbling away of his unity.

> . . . For Europe, for ourselves, and for humanity, comrades, we must turn over a new leaf, we must work out new concepts, and try to set afoot a new man.

The notions that the confrontation between European civilization and the societies of the Third World would produce a new man and a new chance for humanity were commonplaces of African writings in French at the time. In Fanon, they become part of a new golden age which would be attained through the success of the Third World revolution. In this sense, *The Wretched of the Earth* is a utopian work, a mighty hymn to the advent of the new man, freed from colonialism, racism, national chauvinism, and class oppression. If we view the work as a whole, rather than taking individual sections out of context (the better to criticize them), it is here that we must start.

The Black Panthers were more correct than they knew when they regarded Fanon's book as their "Bible." I would insist on the biblical metaphor. Even though Fanon was not a Christian, the work is permeated with salvationism, albeit of a secular kind. Indeed, I would go even further and suggest that to read the book in its entirety is, in a sense, to undergo a conversion. The argument is not always easy to follow; each succeeding chapter negates and supplants the main points in the one that comes before. By this method, one progresses from the crippling Manichaeism of the colonial experience to the pitfalls of national consciousness and finally to the vision of the new man. The individual who conscientiously follows this path achieves a kind of secular salvation or, in Fanon's terms, he becomes politically educated. The book is thus a spiritual guide for an unspiritual age on how to achieve revolutionary beatitude. Like a sermon in a Southern Baptist church, *The Wretched of the Earth* shows us the fires of hell and the glories of the world to come, warns us of the dangers along the way, and encourages us to lend our energies to the work of the Lord. We emerge from the experience transformed, no longer the same men and women.

Like most such experiences, however, there is the letdown of the morning after—the realization that our faults and those of society are not so easily corrected. Given Fanon's suspicions of fancy words and high-flown phrases (by which the bourgeois nationalist leaders deceive the people), there is a chilling irony here. How to warn the people of the intoxication brought by words, when one is intoxicated by them oneself? In the end, one begins to doubt that Fanon has managed to escape from his own rhetorical trap.

The Wretched of the Earth is filled with ideas which flow in many different, often contradictory, directions. Despite the rhetoric, there is an orderly progression to the argument, although it is difficult to perceive at first, so dazzling are its individual passages. If the purpose of the book is didactic—what Fanon calls (following Césaire) the inventing of souls—its structure rests on four interwoven levels of analysis, which are successively introduced in the first four chapters. The levels progress from the psychological (the analysis of colonialism), to the societal (the study of spontaneity), to the political (the unreliability of the national bourgeoisie), to the cultural (the call for a national culture). Allied to this is a parallel temporal progression, in which we are led from the colonial system, to armed struggle, to independence (with its disappointments), to an authentically national culture (which can only arise from the revolution). The fifth chapter documents (using Fanon's case notes) the violence of the colonizer, thereby reinforcing the original diagnosis. Finally the conclusion, with its visions of the new man, provides an inspiring *envoi*.

There is little doubt that *The Wretched of the Earth* will in the end prove far more important for the myths it has helped generate than for the quality of its analysis. Chief among these myths is the liberating force of violence in the anti-colonial struggle, which, taken out of context, has been used by a variety of groups to justify programs based solely on killing. Is violence psychologically liberating to the native? The question is never directly posed, but the answer Fanon gives seems to be affirmative. But is it? To deal with what Fanon in fact says requires confronting the structure of his argument as well as his own personal ambivalences.

The section on violence comes toward the end of the first chapter and follows the discussion of the colonial system. The colonial world, we learn, is a Manichean world, a dualistic world, in which the settler stands for all that is good and the native for all that is evil. It is also a world built on violence—first on the bayonets of the conquering armies, then on the psychological violence inflicted on the native to keep him in his place by convincing him of his unworthiness. The impact of the colonial system leads to the disintegration of native society and with it the personality of the native. The argument thus far is built around a series of oppositions: colonizer/colonized, West/non-West, settler/native, disintegrated/integrated. At first these cancel each other out; they are equally false, as Fanon remarks in one place. Then the argument shifts so that these dichotomies become the thesis and antithesis of a dialectic. A synthesis is therefore possible; it represents an escape from the colonial stalemate. The way out is through violence. Because the system was established and perpetuated through violence, it must be destroyed through violence. Fanon even makes the point that the more settlers there are, the more violence there will be. Only in this way can the native reintegrate his personality and the synthesis of the dialectic be achieved. The need for violence thus derives from the logical structure of Fanon's argument. Violence is (in his theory) good therapy; it is also the best guarantee that the people will remain immune to the mystification of their leaders.

The subject of violence is resumed in the next chapter, but treated from a slightly different angle. There, we learn that violence, while it may be an understandable response to

colonial domination, is far from being an adequate one. The phase of spontaneous violence must be quickly superseded. For a war of national liberation to be successful, violence must be disciplined to its needs; it cannot be left uncontrolled. Fanon, as a psychiatrist, was well aware of the destructive impact that violence can have on its perpetrators as well as on its victims. He presents the case histories of a number of torture victims and of their torturers. The former are Algerians, the latter are French. Both suffer lasting psychological damage. He begins his discussion of the psychological impact of torture with the case of an African nationalist who, during the independence struggle, planted a bomb which took the lives of a number of Europeans. Years later, he was still tormented by anxiety and suicidal impulses on the anniversary of the deed. Even in a just cause, we learn, violence is not liberating.

A second myth to emerge from *The Wretched of the Earth* is that of the peasantry as the primary revolutionary force in the colonial world. Based on a misreading of the wider relevance of the Algerian revolutionary experience, Fanon's analysis on this point appears to have led astray more than one would-be guerrilla leader. Why does Fanon select the peasantry? The answer is clear when we examine the text more closely; the logical imperatives of his argument require it. The peasants, as opposed to the bourgeois leadership of the nationalist movement and the urban working classes (both of which have lost contact with the old ways and are therefore the most inclined to individualistic behavior), are the most integrated and thus the best disciplined group. They are therefore most suited to be in the vanguard of the revolution. The original argument of the liberating qualities of violence has been transformed, but the interplay of opposites continues here: integrated/disintegrated, rural/urban, bourgeois/peasant. Fanon's assertion of the primacy of the peasantry in wars of national liberation thus stems from a logical rather than a sociological analysis of the colonial situation.

It is now all but forgotten that Fanon's views of the peasantry were received with ridicule and disbelief. French Communists stoutly condemned the heretical notion that the peasantry, and not the working class, would produce the revolution. Western liberal analysts systematically discounted the rural populations, placing their bets instead on the development of political parties in the cities. Only later, as knowledge of the Chinese and Vietnamese revolutions began to spread and the Cuban revolution came to power through the mobilization of the rural masses, did this consensus begin to change. Algeria was clearly a case of a peasant-based revolutionary movement, and Fanon sought to underscore this fact in his analysis, the better to make some polemical points.

Given Fanon's commitment to the cause of Algerian independence, it was not surprising that he tended to use the Algerian model in his views on the decolonization of the rest of Africa. This has earned him a great deal of adverse criticism, for conditions in Algeria were in important ways quite different from those that pertained in most of black Africa. Juridically part of France, Algeria had almost a million European settlers in 1954 (and some nine million Muslims). The European impact on native society was vastly greater than elsewhere in Africa, and the regime was far more discriminatory and repressive. The prospects for a peasant uprising on anything like the Algerian scale were minimal in other parts of Africa. It is even possible to question Fanon's understanding of the Algerian situation, for his knowledge of Arabic was rudimentary at best and his grasp of the intricacies of Algerian Arab-Islamic culture seems on some points to have been rather precarious. Given Fanon's intentions and the level of generalization on which *The Wretched of the Earth* is written, these are not crippling weaknesses, but they do lessen confidence in his judgment.

One of the most prescient parts of the book is the analysis of the national bourgeoisie. Most of French Africa had been independent for only a few years when Fanon wrote his scathing denunciation of the nationalist elite who had come to power there: the new leaders of Africa are notable chiefly for their ability to manipulate slogans, the better to profit from their office. The people, when they realize that their leaders are primarily interested in filling their pockets, cry treason. But, says Fanon, the treason is not national, it is social. From this, he draws two conclusions. The first of them is that one does not have to be white to be an exploiter, the second, that nationalism is not in itself a sufficient program. Fanon's penetrating criticism of bourgeois nationalism is one of the great achievements of the book. But while we credit Fanon with uncommon foresight in his analysis of the bourgeoisie, we must also recognize that he seriously underestimated its power. According to his analysis, the national bourgeoisie occupied no productive function in the life of the nation and was thus simply an ersatz class whose early disappearance could be anticipated. Time has not borne this out. Today Lumumba is dead, and it is Mobutu who rules Zaire in a grisly parody of the authentic revolution.

One of Fanon's greatest weaknesses lay in his impatience with the study of social and economic structures. This led him to underestimate the staying power of the national bourgeoisie, in particular its connections with the army and its access to external sources of support against domestic rivals. At a time when three quarters of Africa is ruled by military men, it seems in retrospect remarkable how little Fanon has to say on the role of the army in his new Africa. In all fairness, however, others writing at the time were not notably more perceptive. The first of what was to become an avalanche of military coups did not take place until 1963 in Togo.

Fanon had some proposals about how a country might hope to avoid domination by its national bourgeoisie and pursue a different political path. Basically, Fanon's suggestions are unremarkable. They are the standard ones proposed by theorists of revolution. Having first demonstrated the inadequacies of spontaneous violence, he then indicates how the bourgeois nationalist, by virtue of his class interests, will be unable to address the real problem—namely, social inequality. In order to bring about a more just socio-political system, Fanon suggests, first, that a trustworthy political party be formed, one that will genuinely represent the people (and not merely one that claims, like the bourgeois parties, to represent them); sec-

ond, that the party's decision-making apparatus be decentralized insofar as possible, in order to place power in the hands of the people; third, that the intellectuals come into close contact with the people, but in such a way that the people still feel that they are in charge; and fourth, that political education be undertaken. Fanon states, "The purpose of political education is to invent souls." The phrase is borrowed from Césaire. Here, the argument shifts abruptly. The party now becomes nothing less than the mechanism that will create the new man; his appearance will mark a new beginning in the history of mankind. This new man—political man—is the creation of the intellectuals. It is totally an accident that just where Fanon is being the most straightforwardly descriptive, we suddenly find ourselves plunged into his utopian dream of the revolution?

It is characteristic of Fanon's thought that in the end he should opt for culture rather than material conditions as the crucial factor in bringing about the revolution. This is made clear in the chapter "On National Culture." It has been a source of debate among Marxists. It is perhaps a reflection of Fanon's consciousness of the fragility of political order in the new Africa that for him the crucial problem is that of legitimacy. If the political legitimacy of the government of national liberation is not to be called into question, then it must be supported by an authentic national culture. Fanon takes great pains to distinguish between the kind of revolutionary culture he is speaking of and the pseudo-national cultures most African states have contented themselves with: folklore, *négritude,* a truncated and self-interested version of the national past. The revolution, if it is not to lose itself in chauvinism, racism, or other errors, must seek to evolve a national consciousness which can transcend narrow nationalism. Only thus, Fanon argues, will it be possible to attain a new humanism. Unlike those who view the struggle in strictly political terms, he sees the revolution above all as a cultural phenomenon, a position approaching that of Mao Tsetung, or perhaps more appropriately here, the Guinean President Sékou Touré. It is Fanon at his most theoretical, but also at his most universalist and humanitarian.

The Wretched of the Earth is a book of a particular moment in history, but also a stage of development of political consciousness in the Third World. With the liberation of most of Africa, its popularity is in decline and its utopian vision no longer seems convincing. The two major myths to which the book gave rise, that of the liberating qualities of violence and that of the primacy of the peasantry in the liberation struggle, still have their adherents, but they lack persuasive force in the harsher political environment of the mid-seventies. Yet while the book has reduced appeal, its language still has a capacity to startle and capture the attention of new discoverers. The upheaval in the Third World and among American domestic minorities persists, although new forms of struggle have emerged. It seems safe to predict that Fanonist ideas will continue to find supporters among the desperate and the downtrodden. To a remarkable degree, *The Wretched of the Earth* can still put us in touch with the hopes and fears of an age and with its lost illusions. In its pages that springtime of the nations, the nineteen-fifties and early

-sixties, lives again. Because of its rhetorical brilliance, but also its universalism, *The Wretched of the Earth* will continue to be read long after other more parochial writings from this period and perspective have been forgotten. (pp. 127-35)

> Edmund Burke III, "Frantz Fanon's 'The Wretched of the Earth'," in Daedalus: Journal of the American Academy of Arts and Sciences, Vol. 105, No. 1, Winter, 1976, pp. 127-35.

Emmanuel Hansen   (essay date 1977)

[*Hansen is a Ghanaian educator and writer who has written several books on African politics and government. In the following excerpt, he studies the impact of Fanon's writings on international political thought.*]

When Frantz Fanon died in December 1961, he was relatively unknown except among his fighting Algerian comrades, a small group of French leftists who had been attracted to his writings, and a handful of radical Africans. Today, in the United States and to a less extent in Western Europe, his name in some quarters is a household word. Even the Russians, who for a long time have ignored his writings, are now beginning to break their silence about him. His books still continue to sell in thousands, and among some black militants and certain white radicals his words have acquired the status of canonical pronouncements. Books and articles about him are appearing with increasing frequency. Of all black writers and intellectuals he is perhaps the most written about. In Algeria places have been named after him, and in the United States and Italy research centers have been erected in his memory. He has taken his place, alongside Herbert Marcuse, Ché Guevara, and Régis Debray as intellectual and ideological mentor of the New Left and a guru of black militants.

Ironically, in Africa, where he spent a large portion of his adult life dedicating himself fanatically to the fight for African liberation, he is relatively unknown except in academic circles.

Why does Fanon claim our scholarly attention? A number of reasons can be given: his impact, his intriguing personality, his life as a model for the black intellectual, and the importance of his message.

There are specific areas in which one can talk about the influence of Frantz Fanon. He provides an ideological frame of reference for explaining the oppressive conditions of blacks and other nonwhite peoples in a white-dominated world. In this connection Fanon's impact as an ideological mentor is particularly felt by the Black Panthers. Bobby Seale writes [in his *Seize the Time*]:

> One day I went over to his house and asked him if he had read Fanon. I'd read *Wretched of the Earth* six times. I knew Fanon was right and I knew he was running it down—but how do you put ideas like his over? . . .
>
> So I brought Fanon over one day. That brother got to reading Fanon, and man, let me tell you, when Huey got ahold of Fanon, and read Fanon

> (I had been always running down about how we need this organization, that organization, but never anything concrete), Huey'd be thinking. Hard. We would sit down with *Wretched of the Earth* and talk, go over another section or chapter of Fanon, and Huey would explain it in depth. It was the first time I ever had anybody who could show a clear-cut perception of what was said in one sentence, a paragraph, or chapter, and not have to read it again. He knew it already. He'd get it on the streets.

The influence of Fanon in providing ideological coherence for black radicals is also recognized by Eldridge Cleaver [in "Fanon," *Saturday Review,* 17 July 1971]:

> The feelings and thoughts and passions that were racking us were incoherent and not connected until we read Fanon. Then many things fell together for us harmonizing our attitudes and making it possible for us to organize into a political organization.

Marx and Engels have talked of how the oppressed could free themselves by revolution in the form of a class conflict, but black militants have always had trouble trying to relate class conflict to the race question. Fanon does not subsume the race question entirely in class terms as certain Marxists tend to do. In *The Wretched of the Earth,* he declares:

> In the colonies the economic substructure is also a superstructure. The cause is the consequence; you are rich because you are white, you are white because you are rich. This is why Marxist analysis should always be slightly stretched every time we have to do with the colonial problem.

Due to his recognition of the race question, black radicals even of socialist persuasion find more ideological comfort in Fanon than in Marx and Engels. They regard Fanon as being more "relevant" to their particular situation. This has led Zayd Shakur to say [in the *Saturday Review* article cited above]:

> They [Marx and Lenin] were dealing with European phenomena and they were concerned with whites. Fanon took it to another level. He set down the dialectical contradictions that most oppressed black people are confronted with in a colonized situation.

Another area where Fanon's impact is noticeable is in providing inspiration for the oppressed and urging them to rebellion and revolution. If we are to believe a statement attributed to Dan Watts, editor of *Liberation Magazine,* and quoted in the *Chicago Sun Times* after the riots in Newark and Detroit, every black rebel is inspired by Fanon.

> You're going along thinking all the brothers in these riots are old winos. Nothing could be further from the truth. These cats are ready to die for something. And they know why. They all read. Read a lot. Not one of them hasn't read the Bible . . . Fanon. . . . You'd better get this book. Every brother on a rooftop can quote Fanon.

[quoted in "The Americanization of Frantz Fanon," *Public Interest,* No. 9, 1967]

The point Watts is making here is that Fanon's inspiration has provided blacks with the will and determination to rebel and fight against their oppression. It is not only among blacks in the United States that Fanon's influence in providing inspiration for rebellion has been noticed. In Canada, French-speaking Canadians have been invoking the name of Fanon to back their claim for self-determination for Quebec by the use of revolutionary violence. They view the situation in which they find themselves, as French-speaking Canadians forming a minority of the population in which the English-speaking dominate all aspects of social, economic, and political life, as approximating to that of an internal colonial situation. Whether this perception is correct or not is immaterial. What is important is that their self-image is that of a people living in a colonial situation, and this image is shaped into a framework by their reading of Fanon.

Fanon has also had some impact on political science literature with regard to the analysis of problems faced by the underdeveloped nations of Africa. Of the writing about Africa that owes an intellectual debt to Frantz Fanon, one may mention the work of Bob Fitch and Mary Oppenheimer. The authors accept Fanon's view that colonial rule is violence pure and simple, and that "authentic" decolonization can only come about by armed revolution. With this as the basic theme, they try to explain the problems and the demise of the Nkrumah regime, using social classes as units of analysis in the same way as Fanon does in *The Wretched of the Earth.* Another area where one can discern the intellectual debt to Fanon is in the current writing about oppressive conditions of blacks in the United States. Among these one may mention the work of Stokeley Carmichael and Charles Hamilton, and also that of Robert Allen. Those writers treat the black community as an internal colony and delineate the same relations that operate between the colonizer and the colonized in the underdeveloped countries of Africa. They also treat the black revolt in the United States as a struggle for self-determination, in the same way as colonial peoples are struggling for self-determination. The model is taken from Fanon's works.

Fanon's writings have also had some impact, if only indirectly, on African leaders grappling with the practical problems of development. Among these may be mentioned Julius Nyerere, president of Tanzania, who was so impressed by René Dumont's work on Africa that he made it required reading for his cabinet, and invited Dumont to Tanzania to address government officials, politicians, and students at the university. Dumont deals in his book with some of the issues raised by Fanon in *The Wretched of the Earth,* and makes references to him. It must here be added that Tanzania has perhaps gone further than any other African country in effecting social change along the lines suggested by Fanon. The emphasis on the peasantry and on rural development, the goal of socialist development, the insistence on participatory democracy in the single party system, the decentralization both of the government and the party, the strenuous efforts to bridge the elite-mass gap and to prevent the birth

of a bourgeois caste, and the attempt to create entirely new structures to serve the ends of man are all measures of which Fanon would wholeheartedly approve.

Fanon has also had some impact on Algeria's leaders. In a speech in August 1963, Ben Bella, the former premier of Algeria, declared:

> In the name of the government I must declare that he (Fanon) has not only been our comrade in the struggle but our guide, since he has bequeathed to us through his spiritual and political testament, an ideology that guarantees the Algerian revolution.

[One] area in which Fanon's influence can be delineated in Algeria is the emphasis placed on the Revolution as a primarily peasant revolution, rather than one guided and dominated by the trade unions and the cities. Having said that, one has to add that the current regime in Algeria is far from the Fanonist ideal.

One important reason Fanon claims our attention as a subject of serious inquiry is the issues of his writings and the way he deals with them. He presents a serious commentary on significant human problems. The question of the psychological alienation of the black man in a white-dominated world, his inferiority complex, the quest for whiteness, the depersonalization, the feeling of hopelessness, of nonbeing, that Fanon deals with are all current problems of people living in the underdeveloped countries. In places like Rhodesia, South Africa, the dependent countries, and even the independent countries, these problems are still manifest. The forms in which they manifest themselves may be slightly different, but they are the same everywhere.

Underdeveloped countries face a host of problems. To mention only a few, there are problems of how to overcome illiteracy, poverty, and disease. There are problems of achieving national integration; of fashioning nation-states out of a collection of different ethnic groups; of transforming colonial economic structures into self-sustaining economies; of preventing corruption and authoritarianism; of building effective political parties that will function as transmission belts carrying information to and from the national leadership; of creating a sense of dedication and commitment to the nation; of building social and political institutions that will enable man to express and to maintain his freedom. These are some of the crucial problems Fanon deals with, which we call collectively problems of development. But Fanon's interest transcends the immediate problems of underdeveloped countries. His central concern is freedom. He recognizes that the quest for freedom does not end with the creation of free states. He agrees with Marx that the state can be free without man being free. The quest therefore leads to the creation of social and political institutions that will allow man to express his freedom. And it is this generality of his concern that gives added significance to his thought. We may disagree with some of his prescriptions or with his analysis, but we cannot ignore the issues he raises. Admittedly, other writers have dealt with some of these issues, but not with the same universalistic appeal or the same dramatic forcefulness that characterizes Fanon's writings.

Fanon deals with the above questions not in a cold, detached academic way but as a committed writer who is anxious, even impatient, to correct what he sees as wrong. For him analysis is not an end in itself. It is important only as a precondition to prescription and social action. (pp. 3-9)

> *Emmanuel Hansen, in his* Frantz Fanon: Social and Political Thought, *Ohio State University Press, 1977, 232 p.*

FURTHER READING

Biography

Geismar, Peter. *Fanon.* New York: Dial Press, 1971, 214 p.
　Critical biography of Fanon based on interviews and Fanon's writings.

Gendzier, Irene L. *Frantz Fanon: A Critical Study.* New York: Pantheon Books, 1973, 300 p.
　Biography of Fanon, covering his childhood in Martinique to his militant activities in Algeria. Gendzier concludes with a discussion of Fanon's influence in the Third World.

Hansen, Emmanuel. "Frantz Fanon: Portrait of a Revolutionary Intellectual." *Transition* 9, No. 46 (October/December 1974): 25-36.
　Profile of Fanon, focusing on his life and work as a "professional revolutionary."

Memmi, Albert. "The Impossible Life of Frantz Fanon." *The Massachusetts Review* XIV, No. 1 (Winter 1973): 1-39.
　Biographical essay by an acquaintance of Fanon.

Criticism

Bondy, Francois. "The Black Rousseau." *New York Review of Books* VI, No. 5 (March 1966): 26-7.
　Describes *The Wretched of the Earth* as a work that elevated Fanon to "the rank of hero and saint of 'negritude'."

——. "Frantz Fanon." *Encounter* XLIII, No. 2 (August 1974): 25-9.
　Evaluates Fanon's views about political liberation.

Forsythe, Dennis. "Frantz Fanon: Black Theoretician." *The Black Scholar* 1, No. 5 (March 1970): 2-10.
　Lauds Fanon as a great hero who has energized contemporary liberation movements across the world.

——. "Frantz Fanon—The Marx of the Third World." *Phylon* XXXIV, No. 2 (June 1973): 160-70.
　Compares the political ideas of Karl Marx and Fanon.

Gendzier, Irene L. "Frantz Fanon: In Search of Justice." *The Middle East Journal* 20, No. 4 (Autumn 1966): 534-44.
　Discusses Fanon as a political figure and examines how his writings, particularly *The Wretched of the Earth,* have influenced African politics.

Grohs, G. K. "Frantz Fanon and the African Revolution." *The Journal of Modern African Studies* 6, No. 4 (December 1968): 543-56.
　Identifies and studies the four periods of Fanon's life: "His origins in the French colony of Martinique, his studies in the 1950s in Paris, his qualifications as a doctor and a psychiatrist, and his constant fight, up to the last day of his life, for the Algerian revolution."

Kessous, Naaman. "Fanon and the Problems of Alienation." *The Western Journal of Black Studies* 11, No. 2 (Summer 1987): 80-91.
　Examines the connection between colonialism and alienation in *Black Skin, White Masks* and *The Wretched of the Earth.*

Nursey-Bray, Paul. "Race and Nation: Ideology in the Thought of Frantz Fanon." *The Journal of Modern African Studies* 18, No. 1 (March 1980): 135-42.
　Discusses Fanon's ideas on race and national culture.

Obiechina, Emmanuel. "Frantz Fanon: The Man and His Works." *Ufahamu* III, No. 2 (Fall 1972): 97-116.
　Explores Fanon's impact in the Third World, concluding that his life and works "constitute one of the great landmarks in the recent history of Africa and the Third World."

Parry, Albert. "Fanon and the Black Panthers." In his *Terrorism: From Robespierre to Arafat,* pp. 301-21. New York: Vanguard Press, 1976.
　Discusses the influence of Fanon on the Black Panthers and the Black Liberation Army.

Sutton, Horace. "Fanon: The Revolutionary as Prophet." *Saturday Review* (17 July 1971): 16-19, 59-60.
　Examines the impact of Fanon's life and writings in the United States and Africa, describing the author as both "a prophet of violence" and "the harbinger of hope."

Zolberg, Aristide R. "Frantz Fanon." In *The New Left: Six Critical Essays on Ché Guevara, Jean-Paul Sartre, Herbert Marcuse, Frantz Fanon, Black Power, R. D. Laing,* edited by Maurice Cranston, pp. 119-36. New York: Library Press, 1971.
　Discusses a selection of essays from *The Wretched of the Earth.*

Additional coverage of Fanon's life and career is contained in the following sources published by Gale Research: *Black Literature Criticism; Black Writers;* and *Contemporary Authors,* Vols. 89-92 [obituary], 116.

Betty Friedan

1921-

(Full name Betty Naomi Friedan) American nonfiction writer, journalist, and activist.

The following entry provides an overview of Friedan's career through 1992.

INTRODUCTION

A renowned figure in the women's movement, Friedan first gained prominence in the early 1960s as the author of *The Feminine Mystique*. In this best-selling work, she argued that the "feminine mystique," the belief that women gained fulfillment only from marriage and motherhood, is responsible for the boredom, fatigue, and dissatisfaction that has pervaded the lives of many American women. *The Feminine Mystique* has been credited with revitalizing interest in the women's movement, and in the years following its publication Friedan has founded the National Organization for Women, lobbied for the passage of the Equal Rights Amendment, and served as a prominent and frequently controversial activist for women's equality.

Born in Peoria, Illinois, Friedan attended Smith College, where she studied psychology with the noted Gestalt psychologist Kurt Koffka. Upon graduation she won a research fellowship at the University of California at Berkeley, yet faced with the necessity of sacrificing marriage and motherhood in pursuit of an academic career, she turned down the fellowship and took a nonprofessional job in New York City. She married soon after and began working as a newspaper reporter. Fired from this position after requesting a second maternity leave, Friedan became a free-lance writer for women's magazines. Noticing that editors frequently eliminated references to her subjects' careers from her articles, Friedan began interviewing housewives about their lives. This research formed the basis of *The Feminine Mystique*.

In 1966 Friedan cofounded the National Organization for Women (NOW) and served as its president until 1970. Under her guidance, NOW lobbied for the legalization of abortion, the passage of the Equal Rights Amendment, and the equal treatment of women in the workplace. Friedan, however, came into frequent conflict with radical feminists over the issue of lesbianism as a political stance, which she opposed on the grounds that it alienated mainstream women and men sympathetic to the movement. Political infighting between Friedan and such prominent activists as Gloria Steinem and Bella Abzug disrupted the 1973 National Women's Political Caucus, and Friedan later indirectly accused them of manipulating the balloting to prevent the participation of her supporters. Friedan discussed this controversy and chronicled her early involvement with the women's movement in *It Changed My*

Life, a collection of her speeches and previously published writings interspersed with retrospective commentary.

In *The Feminine Mystique,* Friedan argued that the post–World War II boom of suburban homes and labor-saving appliances produced a generation of women who "changed the sheets on the beds twice a week instead of once, took the rug-hooking class in adult education, and pitied their poor frustrated mothers, who had dreamed of having a career." Friedan maintained that the lack of fulfillment from these domestic routines resulted in the widespread boredom, depression, and anxiety reported by American women, as well as an increase in the number of women addicted to tranquilizers and alcohol. To combat these problems, Friedan advocated increased educational and career opportunities for women. Widely read and discussed, *The Feminine Mystique* played an influential role in drawing supporters to the feminist movement, and it remains her best known work.

In *The Second Stage,* Friedan discussed the emergence of the Superwoman myth—the image of the woman who effortlessly juggles her career, marriage, and children. Describing this phenomenon as the "feminist mystique," Friedan warned that the Superwoman, as far removed from reality as the perfect housewives depicted in the magazines of the 1960s, could have lasting negative effects on the women's movement. Militant feminists objected to the book's implied message that women have succeeded in gaining equality to the degree that men could now play a significant part in the women's movement, and charged that Friedan had lost touch with basic goals of the movement which she had helped to establish. Erica Jong, however, observed that Friedan's "understanding of the doubleness of things, her refusal to be conned by slogans, her insistence on psychological truth rather than political polemicizing, her insistence on seeing the feminist movement in historical perspective, her refusal, in all instances, to throw out the baby with the bathwater, make the reading of [*The Second Stage*] a supremely optimistic experience. For those of us seeking a new direction for feminism, it is here."

PRINCIPAL WORKS

The Feminine Mystique (nonfiction) 1963
It Changed My Life: Writings on the Women's Movement
    (nonfiction) 1976; revised edition, 1985
The Second Stage (nonfiction) 1981; revised edition,
    1986

CRITICISM

The Yale Review (review date Spring 1963)

[*In the following review, the critic faults the "strident and angry tones" of* The Feminine Mystique.]

The Feminine Mystique is another in the succession of crusading efforts to assert that "women are 'human beings' before we are women" in the words of Virgilia Petersen's cover blurb. Pearl Buck seconds this tribute enthusiastically: "this is a sound, sensible book and now that the absurd feminine mystique is set forth so clearly, we can discard it and let a woman be a woman." It would seem by now that it has been amply demonstrated that women are both human beings and women. Mrs. Friedan's grievance, however, is not that women haven't been allowed to be women. It is that they have not been allowed to be "just people." "Vive la différence" is a goad to her blood pressure. Her ideal is a world where men and women are not differentiated as such, but pursue education, tasks, careers, and roles in ways which do not relate to the accident of their belonging to different sexes.

This is all very well—and we have heard it before. But it is a long time since we have heard it in such strident and angry tones. Mrs. Friedan is enraged by those who have weakened Feminism as a fighting faith, by accepting what

she scornfully calls the "feminine mystique." She traces this subversive doctrine to Freud and his influence—veritable opium for women in her view—that woman's primary fulfillment must come from love, marriage, and motherhood, and not from the satisfactions of a career in business or one of the professions. She concedes that it is necessary to function as a female for some reasons, and that trying to manage both roles—with subsidiary ones involved in each world—is a great struggle, and a feat when achieved. But all women must engage in the struggle—cost what it may—and stop deluding themselves that there is anything special about being a female besides the label. She herself is proof of this—as are many other strong, effective, energetic, able women. All women, she asserts, are capable of doing the same, if only they refuse to give in to the corrupting and corrosive idea that accidents of physical and emotional growth may not always permit people—men or women—to achieve the ability to keep an equilibrium in the handling of several roles at one time in a really satisfactory way.

The book claims that modern psychological insights have led in many instances to a lowering of educational standards in some institutions; and it is full of information about the incidence of dissatisfaction among married women. The causal connection in the first instance may be debated. As for the latter, the author seems to have discovered later than many of her readers how prevalent this discontent has been and for how long. She has many facts and many references, so that this is a handy book to have if one can overlook the rather drilling insistence of the style. It is a pity that Mrs. Friedan has to fight so hard to persuade herself as well as her readers of her argument. In fact, her passion against the force of the irrational in life quite carries her away. Her "New Life Plan for Women" is not particularly revolutionary—it is being acted upon by many women. Her insistence on certain forms, timing, and procedure, and the defensive way in which she advances many arguments cannot but alienate many who would agree with much of the substance of what she says, even if there are differences of emphasis.

It seems, however, to be characteristic of the issue of woman's role and woman's education that few people will accept fully the opinions or solutions of others—and humor never intrudes into this world. All of which serves to keep the subject alive and worth a publisher's interest.

> *A review of "The Feminine Mystique," in* The
> Yale Review, *Vol. LII, No. 3, Spring, 1963, p.
> xii.*

The Times Literary Supplement (review date 31 May 1963)

[*In the following review of* The Feminine Mystique, *the critic discusses Friedan's views on the educational and vocational opportunities available to women and praises her book as a lively and vigorous analysis of feminist issues.*]

It is the incontrovertible assertion of [**The Feminine Mystique**] that women should be educated and treated as individuals rather than functionaries whose jobs are predestined by nature. Why such a truism should be so much in dispute that it needs as long and as vehement a justification as this volume is, according to Mrs. Friedan, the fault of a postwar cult which she aptly names "the feminine mystique".

This mystique, she says, insidiously maintains that the highest value and only commitment for women is "the fulfilment of their own femininity". And that means the glorification of "Occupation: housewife" from natural childbirth and breastfeeding to baking your own bread, having majored in home economics. The mystique is Victorian homelife made roseate by the women's magazines and the ad-men, and made intellectually respectable by pseudo-Freud. It grew up partly as a reaction against feminism, and partly in a search for security after the last war, but principally through a mistaken choice. The women of America (Mrs. Friedan is American) thought that they had to choose outright between marriage and a career. Thus instead of studying pure mathematics at college they learnt how "to play the role of woman", and once they were inside the home the salesmen saw that they stayed there, penned.

The results, we are told, of early marriage and interests centred exclusively on the home are frustrated, stunted wives, nagged husbands and passive, smothered children. Contrary to common belief, Mrs. Friedan argues, the more education a woman has, the happier is her marriage likely to be and the more often is she likely to achieve orgasm in sex. Moreover, women who have jobs feel less tired than those who stay at home, do their housework in less time and consult the analyst less frequently.

This mystique, then, is an *angst* of America, where more girls start (but do not all finish) college and where parent-teacher associations and dishwashers both proliferate. But the symptoms detailed are evident here, in less overt but equally dangerous form, to take but the one example of the long, heated and often obscurantist correspondence which took place a few years ago in *The Times* on how girls should be educated. The problem is without doubt real and great, and the important question is what to do about it.

"A massive attempt", says Mrs. Friedan,

> must be made by educators and parents—and ministers, magazine editors, manipulators, guidance counsellors—to stop the early-marriage movement, stop girls from growing up wanting to be "just a housewife", stop it by insisting, with the same attention from childhood on that parents and educators give to boys, that girls develop the resources of self, goals that will permit them to find their own identity.

Agreed. But once a girl has chosen her satisfying career is it that easy for her to pursue it? Mrs. Friedan would grant that the most deeply committed professional woman will not be willing to hand her children of pre-school age to the care of another, even if there were adequate mother substitutes or creches available. Most women, then, face a period in their lives when they will have and want to spend at least part of their time at home. The difficulty,

somewhat underestimated here, is how to get into gear for the rest of the time.

Mrs. Friedan feels that if a woman is determined enough she can keep up her vocation. The creative arts can, to some extent, be practised on a part-time basis; so can medicine, teaching and journalism. But the trouble is that on neither side of the Atlantic is there enough part-time employment of a responsible nature.

There remains in addition, and discussed little by Mrs. Friedan, that large section of the female population which, in [Great Britain] at any rate, never aspires beyond the minimum statutory education. The Crowther report and every subsequent relevant analysis have shown that at each stage fewer girls than boys feel the urge to seize the educational ladder. These early leavers are even more susceptible than college girls to the ills of boredom and vacuity after even earlier marriage and with the aid of more and more automation in the home. Here again it is political action that is needed, from better initial education (less emphasis on typing and cookery in secondary modern schools?) to training schemes for those in their thirties and forties.

If, then, there is still a feminist fight to be fought it is for the right to work. And if they are to win it women must have all the ammunition they can of the calibre of this book. Mrs. Friedan may lack detachment but this is live sociology and her vigour is contagious.

> *"White Woman's Burden," in* The Times Literary Supplement, *No. 3196, May 31, 1963, p. 391.*

Sylvia Fleis Fava   (review date December 1963)

[*In the following review, Fava expresses reservations about the psychological approach she perceives in* The Feminist Mystique, *but commends the work as an important and original study of the prevailing myths concerning the role of women in American society.*]

It is remarkable how the power of sexual topics to shock or excite argument has diminished in the past decade. The one issue that still guarantees an emotional, morally-laden response is sexual but not "sexy"—the role of women, especially educated women, outside the home. Significantly, *The Feminine Mystique* [is] a recent and most welcome addition to the debate. . . . (p. 1053)

The book's thesis is that since the 1940's the ideal role held before American women has shifted from independence, careers, and fulfillment of special capacities to an emphasis on "the feminine mystique." "The feminine mystique says that the highest value and the only commitment for women is the fulfillment of their own femininity. . . . Beneath the sophisticated trappings, it simply makes certain concrete, finite, domestic aspects of feminine existence . . . into a religion, a pattern by which all women must now live or deny their femininity." The housewife-mother role as the be-all of feminine existence is roundly taken to task by Friedan.

Friedan, by training a psychologist and by occupation a

journalist, supports her thesis mainly with data from these fields. The feminine mystique is prevalent enough that it is necessary to add that she is married and the mother of three. She describes how the mystique developed in the women's magazines; in Freud's Victorian view that "anatomy is destiny"; in advertising; and in the tendency of the functionalist approach in social science to emphasize adjustment. An item of interest to sociologists is the content analysis of the leading women's magazines showing the emergence of the "happy housewife heroine" in the post–World War II period. The behind-the-scenes description based on Friedan's own participation in this field has no counterpart that I know of.

The author documents the psychological difficulties resulting from the feminine mystique—boredom, family problems, psychosomatic complaints, and so on, and asks whether we want this straitjacket imposed on our women. Her answer, that we should take women seriously as individuals, not as women, resounds throughout the book; I heartily agree with it. The value position makes this an important book, worthy of the wide reading and discussion it is already gaining. There is one *caveat,* however. Friedan tends to set up a counter-mystique; that all women must have creative interests outside the home to realize themselves. This can be just as confining and tension-producing as any other mold.

The main reservation I have about the approach taken in the book is that it is so heavily psychological. This is clearest in the last chapter, in which Friedan discusses what can be done to change the feminine mystique. She recommends changes in individual woman—less attention to home-making, more commitment to serious education and creative work. These changes in attitude would culminate in a "new life plan." This neglects the fact that the changed attitudes and plans must be acted upon in the context of the total society. The woman who develops the new life plan will find few institutionalized channels by which it can be put into effect. Negroes, too, have begun to change their attitudes and goals and to find that this is not enough without facilitating changes in social institutions. This does not deny the necessity of bringing about social change, but in the process the psychological frustration and conflicts may be as great, though of a different kind, as those experienced before the individual decided on a new life plan.

Friedan has put her finger on the key problem of American women today: recognition as individuals. Her psychological approach does not offer a complete solution but *The Feminine Mystique* makes it abundantly clear that sociologists should analyze the systemic implications. We know surprisingly little about the social causes and consequences of women's roles in our society. (pp. 1053-54)

Sylvia Fleis Fava, in a review of "The Feminine Mystique," in American Sociological Review, *Vol. 28, No. 6, December, 1963, pp. 1053-54.*

Jane Howard   (review date 27 April 1974)

[*In the following review of the Tenth Anniversary Edition of* The Feminine Mystique, *Howard discusses the social impact of Friedan's writings and her role in the women's movement.*]

I was assigned to 8A, by the window. On the aisle, in 8B, sat a long-legged, roving-eyed businessman. I assume that's what he was, because when he wasn't flirting with the stewardess he kept fussing with graphs and charts he pulled from a fancy briefcase. Somewhere over Ohio the stewardess wheeled us our lunch, a predictably dreary one, and offered us daffodils to brighten our trays. The daffodils, to my wonder, were real. 8B, to my further wonder, didn't want his. He turned it down so vehemently that I couldn't help asking what he had against flowers.

"People might get the wrong idea," he said. "They might think I was some kind of faggot."

"Oh come on," I said. "You can't be serious." But he was. So help me.

"I wouldn't expect *you* to understand," 8B said. "I saw what book *you* were reading."

I had in fact been reading the new Tenth Anniversary Edition of that celebrated polemic *The Feminine Mystique,* whose original version sold 57,000 hardcover and 1,700,000 paperback copies, gave Betty Friedan's name the status of a surefire household word, and, more than any of the torrent of feminist documents that followed, set the women's movement in motion. The new edition has an introduction and an epilogue drawn from the piece Friedan did a year ago for *The New York Times Magazine,* in which she assessed the movement's effect on womankind in general and her own life in particular. The *Times* called her article **"Up From The Kitchen Floor."**

8B could not have known it, and probably wouldn't have wanted to, but his attitude illustrated one of Friedan's most recurrent points. Men, she keeps saying in her book and wherever else she crusades to "lead other women out of the wilderness," are not the enemy; they're fellow victims. They are as much entrapped by false notions of what's manly as women are by the compulsion to be, as the song has it, as soft and as sweet as a nursery.

In her hair Friedan wore not a gardenia but a smart ecumenical headband the day she went to the Vatican to trade medallions with, and try to raise the consciousness of, the Pope himself. That encounter, alas, happened too late for her epilogue, in which she explains why she's been too busy to write a sequel to *The Feminine Mystique.* It's quite some decade she's had for herself, since her first diagnosis of "the problem that has no name"—the epidemic discontent of middle-class American women whom she found, by the droves, "in the state of sexual larvae [prevented] from achieving the maturity of which they are capable."

She has picketed the White House, been subpoenaed, helped to "liberate" the Oak Room of the Plaza Hotel for women at lunchtime, talked herself hoarse from 1000 lecterns and before innumerable television cameras, and overcome her fear of flying. Not all her adventures have been upbeat. "A lot of people treated me like a leper," Friedan said when she came back from the 25th reunion of her high school class in Peoria, Illinois. "The other guy in my class who'd made good, a state senator, refused to be photographed with me. All of a sudden it wasn't convenient for my kids' cousins to play with them, either."

What had she written that so threatened Peoria? That sex and motherhood and domesticity were nice, but not everything; that shopping for things was no fit *raison d'être* for a grown-up intelligent woman; that it was nasty for an industry to scheme to give future customers "positive fur experiences"; that Sigmund Freud's equation of anatomy with destiny had been taken too seriously; that Margaret Mead was a hypocrite to preach a subservience to men she never practiced herself. Most of all, Friedan declared, women urgently needed not merely to be educated, but to make lifelong use of what they had learned.

She said all this at undue length, and with more passion than style, but her effect was and still is persuasive. "American women lately have been living much longer than men," she observed, "walking through their leftover lives like living dead women. Perhaps men may live longer in America when women carry more of the burden of the battle of the world, instead of being a burden themselves." She might also have quoted from a letter Jung wrote to Freud in 1909, remarking that "in America the mother is decidedly the dominant member of the family. American culture really is a bottomless abyss; the men have become a flock of sheep and the women play the ravening wolves—within the family circle, of course." Give women some access to a few other circles, the Friedan message goes, and maybe there wouldn't be so many dangerous matriarchs around, or so much wasted energy.

You might think her colleagues in sisterhood would rally to Friedan's support, in gratitude for the harsh and early light she shed on such matters, but not all of them have. The movement's momentum has been so dizzying that some feminists see Friedan as "hopelessly bourgeois," practically a Helen Hokinson caricature. She is no heroine among lesbians, nor does their cause much interest her. She hints that some among them, along with radicals who see the movement as a class struggle, may be plotting to take over the whole operation, perhaps in collusion with the CIA. They hint right back that she is a reactionary who could have carried the movement much farther than she has chosen to do. She was hissed at a conference of OWL (Older Women's Liberation), for urging her sisters to "stay reality-oriented, instead of debating clitoral versus vaginal orgasms."

Nobody's perfect. "Betty is impossible sometimes," writes [Bella Abzug], the author of the autobiographical *Bella!,* "because she tends to regard herself as 'the' leader of the women's movement." It might have been a nice gesture, readers of her *Times* piece last year wrote to say, if she had shared a little of the credit with Simone de Beauvoir, and with the other cofounders of NOW (the National Organization for Women) and the strike and march on August 26. Jill Johnston's letter mentioned something about "sexual McCarthyism."

And all along there have been men, like my companion in seat 8B, who squirm at the very sight of Friedan's name. A frailer spirit, amid such eclectic crossfire, might have

crumpled in defeat, but Friedan's has not. Far from it. A suburban housewife when *The Feminine Mystique* came out, she is now a Manhattan divorcée, ensconced, as she tells us in her epilogue, "high in an airy, magic tower with open sky and river and bridges to the future all around." The future she envisions, both personally and politically, will most assuredly not exclude men. However middle-class and shrill she may seem, and whatever her excesses and shortcomings, I think she's on the right track. Her book is worth rereading. (pp. 25-6)

> *Jane Howard, "Tenth Anniversary Edition,"*
> *in* The New Republic, *Vol. 170, No. 17, April*
> *27, 1974, pp. 25-6.*

Eliot Fremont-Smith   (essay date 28 June 1976)

[*In the following essay, Fremont-Smith contends that while* It Changed My Life *is weakly organized and overly long, the views on feminism expressed in it are valid.*]

It is pertinent that last week's publication gala for Betty Friedan's *It Changed My Life: Writings on the Women's Movement* was held in the spacious and poshly svelte executive offices, high above 57th Street, of what is probably the world's most successful cosmetics corporation, Avon Products, Inc.

It is pertinent in two ways. Betty Friedan alluded to one of them in her "remarks" (she's an effective speaker) to the assembled throng of celebrants and well-wishers: She had nothing against cosmetics, she said, nothing against women making themselves up in ways both men and women thought attractive. She said this jokingly and in passing, a necessary acknowledgment to cool whatever flames of protest the setting might ignite (none were visible, however; it was a fairly classy crowd). Those who had read the book might have detected a personal edge as well.

In the book Friedan tells how, during the battle with Gloria Steinem and Bella Abzug over the control and direction of the National Women's Political Caucus in 1972, she was hurt and, in effect, "paralyzed" by snide comparisons of her and Steinem's looks and antifeminist press suggestions that she was "jealous" of Steinem "because she was blonde and pretty and I was not." (She lost the Caucus battle—and another later over control of NOW—by what she considers ruthless and dishonest subterfuge, and by Abzug's determination to snuff out a potential rival: Friedan had thought of running for the Senate in '74 or '76.)

In any case, the cosmetics connection fits. Cosmetics may or may not be the second-oldest profession, but it's what a lot of people use and care about, people Friedan wants in the movement, not insulted or hectored out of it. *It Changed My Life*—the title derives from both Friedan's own experience and grateful readers' letters about her 1963 book *The Feminine Mystique,* perhaps not quite the Rosetta Stone Random House makes out but certainly one of the important consciousness-raising classics of the movement—has mirroring polemical themes: *for* an inclusive or "mainstream" movement for equality and liberation that American women everywhere, including middle-class wives, mothers, and homemakers, can feel a part of, and *against* militant or "separatist" elements committed to exclusionary politics—radical or lesbian or whatever—that she feels subvert the fundamental aims of women's, and men's liberation. Thus, all too simply, to be against cosmetics *per se* is to be simply against the grain (a vanity itself), a milder-seeming but symbolically potent expression of the antimale, antisex craze (to confuse antisexism with antisex *is* a bit nutty) that, with the help of the antifeminist and porn-prone media, became the movement's most raucous voice in the early '70s.

Not just in Kansas or Fernwood, Ohio, but here, too. Friedan is well aware of the viciously misleading campaign conducted by anti-ERA forces in New Jersey and New York [in 1975] but (and I think she is correct in this) the success of that campaign, the devastating defeats of ERA in these supposedly enlightened states, would not have been possible had not the movement seemed to have grown rabid and exclusionary. Women (men, too) are not going to vote for something perceived as being against men, against wives, against marriage, against homemaking, against family and children. There are enough fears and prejudices that ERA and the causes of equal rights and pay and opportunity and self-esteem must overcome without adding the burden of what seem to be basic, natural, animal, human, social predispositions.

Though taking some delight in having been denounced as a "heterosexist," Friedan is careful to spell out that she is not antilesbian; but she argues that lesbian rights is a civil liberties issue, not the cutting edge of a successful national women's movement. Similarly, she is uninterested (at length, because this too has been so diversionary) in vibrators, the relative political merits of vaginal versus clitoral orgasms (assuming these are meaningfully distinguishable, which they probably are not), and other myopic crotch phenomena which may be important to the macho porn industry and to therapists for upper-class despondents, but are not, she thinks, of central concern to the great majority of women she would like in an equality movement for all. She's after something wider and more humble, and thus, by her, more beneficial.

Which suggests the other Avon connection—Avon being very lower-middle-class ("Avon calling") and, with Fuller, the great doorbell-ringing success story of our time. To put it in a reverse way: Friedan thinks there is no reason for the movement, specifically NOW which she founded, to be *less* inviting or *gem utlichkeit* than, for God's sake, a cosmetics business is. The cause, after all, is totally decent, can be argued against on moral grounds only by hard-core Biblical literalists (even thought-to-be-Fundamentalist Jimmy Carter is not against), and a fanatical fringe of antiabortionists (those who go all the way in denying totally a woman's rights over her own body, and there are not many of them). In a symbolic nutshell: Let the buyers of Avon products in on, feel part of, the movement, and women's rights cannot be stopped. Alienate them and it's going to be a needlessly long, frustrating, vulnerable, and possibly, in any short run beyond presently "liberated" careerists and intellectuals, doomed struggle. Friedan is haunted by previous women's movements

that have made noise, won battles, then been totally forgotten; 50 years after the suffragist movement women had to reconstruct from the discarded pages of official American and British history the fact that women (and men, too) had previously worked together for an entirely just cause.

It Changed My Life is a much too long, seemingly unedited collection of Friedan's writings over the last decade, interlarded with current appraisals and recollections. (It is a documentary of sorts; as such, the absence of an index is inexcusable.) There is bitterness and chagrin (the political infighting chapters—chagrin in the sense that she was in effect driven out of the movement for a time) and some distortion (there is little acknowledgment that the movement had another beginning independent of NOW that affects it still, out of political caucuses in the civil rights, anti-Vietnam, and left political movements of the 1960s that produced Witch, Redstockings, the Radical Feminists, etc.—so that the splintering of the movement wasn't simply inside what Friedan had started).

There is also a lot of good sense. Among other things, Friedan wants to get rid of the holier-than-thou (and unsaleable) notion that women in power can use power better or more beneficently than men do or can (*viz.,* dictator Indira Gandhi). She argues that the *right* to equal opportunity for power is what is inalienable, not that humankind won't have to cope with abuses of power willy-nilly. And there is a nice—forgive me—warmth to her prose, both personal and polemical: She wants us to *get together* in a cause that is right and good for all of us, women, men, children, grandparents, single people, everybody.

Friedan ends her book with a call for a rather vaguely defined "stage II" or "new yes" by which I believe she means the above: One person's sense of freedom and dignity spurs everybody else's sense of freedom and dignity; claustrophobic and unfair sex-role discrimination (and the operative word is neither sex nor role but discrimination—not that homemaking is less worthy than a career, but that it is not properly acknowledged in our society, or shared in, or negotiated over, or paid for) hurts women most obviously first and foremost but hurts us all.

As a man, a husband, a father, it is very difficult for me not to side with Friedan on virtually all of this. As a middle-class citizen with intellectual pretensions, a professional, a journalist, a "mainstream" liberal Democrat (unlike Friedan I was for Bobby over Gene, and was possibly wrong; like Friedan I thought it a mistake to place the women's movement on the edge of the McGovern effort where it simply lost twice; possibly unlike her I shall probably vote for Bella in the fall, for mostly nonwomen's movement reasons)—ditto.

These aspects do not entirely color my opinions: I'm a dog-owner, too, and think people who take their dogs to playgrounds to defecate are dangerously demented and belong somewhere else, like Bellevue. (What is the matter with dog lovers, that they think dog shit is not something to clean up? Parents of human infants don't as a rule leave babyshit around public parks and thoroughfares.) But they do, without a doubt, color them somewhat. Friedan, culturally and to some degree politically, speaks my lingo.

She is criticized for being too white-upper-middle-class in outlook, too much a "lady"—and, in truth, she doesn't seem as sensitive on this point as one might expect. The real roots (beyond the pill, which made all else possible) of the current movement were the affluence of the 1950s and 1960s and the concurrent boom in education for women, which together (and with new media communication) allowed and stimulated the kind of self-examination that Friedan, by class, would have come to anyway. A lot of Redstockings militants and/or politically ambitious tacticians who happen to be women might not have—so there is a gap both in rhetoric and in experiential empathy. There is an underside to privilege, as there is to Avon, that is not wholly deserving of applause.

Friedan is also too intolerant (only slightly, but given the politics of the movement slightly is a lot) of certain militancies not under her aegis that have also changed our lives. For example, an entirely personal phenomenon, Susan Brownmiller's *Against Our Will* which, discounting polemical idiocies (an overbearingly literal and sometimes brutish natural history of human male/female relationships in terms of rape) nonetheless made me see how little I had questioned, even though they were more frightening than pleasant, certain long-held fantasy-assumptions about male and female sexual roles. The sex part has to be muted for an effective national movement because it is enormously complex and also subject to stupid and deliberately offensive interpretation (vibrators really are *not* what life and love are about); yet, it is as fundamental as class considerations (probably more so) and the sense of human dignity and decency that the women's movement, like civil rights, calls forth.

The vagueness of Friedan's "new yes" is exactly in this area, the interface of calculated political strategy and sexual drive and feeling and self-identification. The *politics* of the movement can (and should) let this pass for the moment; the *philosophy* cannot. What we've been offered so far in the latter is neither intellectually nor emotionally acceptable: a bunch of mutilating or joke-prone no's (depending on who or what you think you are), diverse mechanical stimulators for the Mafia and the lonely, a replay of romantic gush about prostitutes (which always used to be a male sexist hang-up, the notion of the whore as Mother Earth if not plain mom or sis), and essentially vacuous crud about androgyny that can stand up to about 30 seconds of Rodgers and Hart.

Essential things first: A wide-based movement that has more "yes" in it than "no" can get ERA, which is an important legal beginning: in this I am all for Friedan. I doubt that the current movement will disappear from history as previous women's movements have, but I think that without the essential things first we may be denied for an unconscionable time the chance to come to terms with and break the hidden chains that bind us—in such perverse and hurtful ways—together, but for continuing separation, misunderstanding, fear, and hate. (pp. 43-4)

Eliot Fremont-Smith, "Ding-a-Ling! Friedan Calling," in The Village Voice, *Vol. XXI, No. 6, June 28, 1976, pp. 43-4.*

Stephanie Harrington   (review date 4 July 1976)

[*In the following review of* It Changed My Life, *Harrington faults Friedan for failing to answer the "politically sensational questions" she raises concerning Gloria Steinem and Bella Abzug and their alleged subversion of the 1973 National Women's Political Caucus.*]

Reading Betty Friedan's new book [*It Changed My Life*] is like ambling down memory lane, retracing the last 12 years of developing feminist consciousness and political action, through groves of insights long since elaborated, of speeches past, of articles previously published, of documents already reported. Grateful for the refresher course, you proceed through little patches of newly written connective commentary towards a breezy review saying, "And that's the way it was 10 years ago today." Then, abruptly, you realize that you have been led smack into a mass of political charges that leave your head reeling with any number of paranoid possibilities.

Did supporters of Bella Abzug really sabotage the New York State Women's Political Caucus? Of course, Friedan never actually says they did. She just says that they opposed a state structure, that the state caucus registration list was mysteriously stolen, that the state caucus couldn't be effectively put back together for two years, and that, "meanwhile, the Manhattan Political Caucus, which Bella controlled, in effect spoke for the whole state."

Did Abzug and Gloria Steinem "go into the [National Women's Political Caucus] to deliver it to McGovern . . . for their own political payoff or to defuse political organization of women in '72"? Friedan never actually says they did. She just says that "certain women" did. And she says it in a paragraph in which she attacks Steinem and Abzug for the way in which they organized N.W.P.C. activity at the 1972 Democratic Convention. In the same paragraph she says, "Again, I'm not sure whether genuine differences in ideology and thus tactics were involved—maybe political feminism versus political opportunism—or something more sinister."

Did Abzug and Steinem manipulate the 1973 N.W.P.C. national convention to close out Friedan and her faction, going to the extreme of tampering with ballots to be sure that Friedan would not win a place on the steering committee? Friedan never actually says that they did. She just points out that "the officers elected were women who would stay in Texas most of the time, or, having no independent constituency of their own, could be easily controlled by Bella and her cohorts. . . . " She never actually says Abzug and Steinem were responsible for ballot tampering. She just reports that before an N.W.P.C. national board meeting, at which her lawyer was "to present her findings of improper election procedures . . . Bella, Gloria and Olga Madar from U.A.W. descended on me in a menacing, moralizing cohort, and told me to keep my mouth shut." And four paragraphs later she writes:

> But nationally it seems to many as if the fix is in. If we had known then what was revealed when the Watergate "dirty tricks" were exposed, and the subsequent revelations of C.I.A.'s "Operation CHAOS" and the F.B.I.'s acknowledged massive infiltration of the woman's movement,

I might not have dropped the matter [of the N.W.P.C. steering committee election] so easily . . . I was scared. Political infighting is one thing; outright illegality, tampering with votes, contempt for ordinary standards of honesty, and intimidation . . . is something else. Above all, I felt helpless because the perpetrators of those "dirty tricks" were sister leaders of the women's movement, and sometimes they even got black or Chicano women to do the actual dirty work for them.

In fact, I was scared enough . . . to stay away, for the next three years, from any confrontation whatsoever with Gloria Steinem or Bella Abzug. . . .

Well, this is heady stuff. Is she saying Steinem and/or Abzug have C.I.A. or F.B.I. connections? If so, why doesn't she say it plainly? If her own experiences lead to that conclusion and, despite insufficient hard evidence to prove it, she feels she has an obligation to alert other women, why doesn't she say precisely that? (Steinem's admitted work for a C.I.A.-financed foundation in the late 1950's and early 1960's is a monkey she has not yet been able to shake from her back. In May 1975, Redstockings, a radical feminist group, raised the question of whether Steinem had continuing ties with the C.I.A. Steinem, of course, denies it. In her section on the International Women's Year Conference in Mexico City, Friedan refers to these charges against Steinem and, without either questioning or supporting them, says that, for the good of the women's movement, they should be taken seriously and investigated.) Why does Friedan operate in the half-light between innuendo and substantiated accusation, juxtaposing names and her version of events and letting the implications fall where they may? Or is this sequential, suggestive style the literary contribution of Random House's legal department?

Friedan says that *It Changed My Life* is her valedictory to organized feminist politics, and she seems to have decided to leave that world not with a whimper but a bang. But indications are that, although the N.W.P.C. and individuals whose names are named may offer a rebuttal, the tentative reaction on the receiving end is to let the whole thing blow over as quietly as possible and thus spare the movement destructive notoriety and save Friedan from a self-inflicted reincarnation as Suzy Knickerbocker. Of course, my friend the conspiracy theorist says, "Isn't that just what you would do if you had something to hide?"

You can't be too paranoid these days (as demonstrated in Friedan's report on the International Women's Year Conference, which reads like a spy thriller). However, some beguilingly pedestrian answers to Friedan's exotic charges, stated or implied, are available:

The organizing meeting of the New York State Women's Political Caucus was disrupted by a group that had nothing to do with Abzug and the Caucus didn't get itself together for two years because, according to its first chairperson, New York is a big state and it was difficult to organize a political cross-section of women who had other commitments. Gloria Steinem was N.W.P.C. spokesperson at the 1972 Democratic Convention because she was elected to that role over Friedan and others by the N.W.P.C. policy council. There was a recount in the steering committee election at the 1973 N.W.P.C. convention because the original tally became so irreparably confused by fractional voting that the ballot boxes were sealed and delivered to an independent accounting firm for a recount. And Friedan didn't make the steering committee because, although she was among the top 10 in the voting, she was not one of the top five Democrats, and there was a limit of five steering committee seats per party. The charge that "black or Chicano women" did "the actual dirty work" probably refers to the fact that of the three vice chairpeople supervising the election, one was black and one Chicano.

But to examine all the charges and explanations is clearly beyond the scope of a book review. If most of this space has been spent questioning Friedan's version of events, she cannot complain, since she has raised politically sensational questions that she must know will not go unnoticed, and she has failed to spell out or document her answers. (p. 7)

But Friedan can't be allowed to divert our attention from the fact that her first book, *The Feminine Mystique,* broke ground for renascent American feminism, and that now, when *a priori,* psychodramatic revolutionary zeal is the vogue, she has had the courage to be a middle-class extremist, determined not to frighten off women with rhetoric equating feminism with lesbianism or with the overthrow of men. Her goal has been to mobilize them by urging them to break out of domestic isolation. Her pragmatic gospel calls on women to win, in proportion to their numbers, policy-making positions in industry, labor unions, the churches, the educational system, the professions, the political parties and government on all levels and to join with men in a sex-role revolution that will restructure the institutions of our society so that women can play an active part in determining its life and their own. It is an approach that has resulted in not only abortion reform and Congressional passage of the Equal Rights Amendment, but in the election of ever-increasing numbers of women to political office and in government action against sex discrimination in employment, education, finance and the tax structure.

Now, when a political fight must be waged against the backlash that has defeated state Equal Rights Amendments, stalled the Federal E.R.A. and threatens abortion reform, Betty Friedan, that tenacious theorist of revolution as the art of the possible, is too valuable a resource to waste—or to be allowed to waste herself. (p. 8)

> *Stephanie Harrington, in a review of "It Changed My Life," in* The New York Times Book Review, *July 4, 1976, pp. 7-8.*

Sara Sanborn   (review date 24 July 1976)

[*In the following review, Sanborn finds* It Changed My Life *disappointing, but praises Friedan's contributions to the women's movement through her work as an activist.*]

Every woman in America, whether she knows it or not,

owes Betty Friedan a debt of gratitude. I can't say (as I think she would like her readers to) that she created the women's movement; as events proved, the right people, ideas, time, and place had already been collected by history. But Friedan sounded the kick-off signal in 1963, with *The Feminine Mystique,* and she performed the writer's unique service by saying out loud what the rest of us had only nervously thought.

Things have never been the same since.

Her second book [*It Changed My Life*], after thirteen years of organizing and action "in the mainstream" (as she stresses), is something of a history of the movement—and something of a valedictory to it. Primarily a collection of previously published writings and speeches, interspersed with recollections and commentary, this book should be profoundly reassuring to women who fear that the movement is the enemy of family and femininity. It will (if it's read at all) doubtless be jeered at as namby-pamby by the more radical feminists, who wrote Friedan off years ago. To those broadly concerned with the women's movement and women's changing estate, it will probably prove both interesting and disappointing. With me, I'm sorry to say, disappointment has the edge.

To begin with, the speeches reprinted here, stirring as they doubtless were at the time, now wear the outdated air of most campaign oratory after the fact. Further, to read one is pretty well to read them all. They do have a certain historic interest, as we now count history, but it is largely that of an exhibition of campaign memorabilia—one look is enough. Their careful preservation here (for what purpose? to persuade women living in 1976?) is in line with a self-justifying, even self-regarding, tone that runs through the book, as though Friedan were afraid we might forget our debt to her. There is a buried quarrel here with other feminists that is often alluded to but never really described or discussed, and the persistent but opaque references to wrongs committed by Gloria Steinem or Bella Abzug compound one's confusion about the purpose of the book.

There are ripe insights here for the gathering—Friedan's knowledge, for instance, that the "pathology" produced by demeaning sex roles (women's rage, hostility toward men, separatism) does not equal liberation from those roles; or her awareness that however much our daughters may benefit from the women's movement, "We did it for ourselves," and the doing of something for ourselves is the mark of our maturity. However, these good points and others like them lie in a bed of conceptual cotton, a muzzy background of vague good intentions that cannot substitute for a philosophical base.

Friedan started her career as a writer for housewives' magazines and began to incubate *The Feminine Mystique* (which took her five nervous years to write) when she realized that the seraphic vision of feminine life in the likes of *The Ladies' Home Journal* did not equal the life she and other women were actually leading. However, the mental habits of the ladies-magazine writer have stayed with her. This book is marked by a failure of penetration and analysis that amounts to a refusal to work in those terms, and

by a glorification of the purely and sometimes trivially personal that at times rises to soap opera. Her highest epistemological standard is every woman's own experience, and her highest hope for the future "a new YES to life."

In her own way, Friedan invokes warm-puppy verities as cloudy and sentimental as those of the Fluffy Fifties. She insists, for example, on the socially redemptive value of happy sex relations as though making love really were an alternative to making war. In the chapters that set forth her visits with Indira Ghandi, Simone de Beauvoir, and Pope Paul, she unwittingly makes the strongest case for the women's movement by showing herself a total Innocent Abroad, scarcely able to imagine the realities of power, painfully parochial and fastened on the personal. To Pope Paul she handed a women's-equality symbol, telling him happily that it was "a different kind of cross."

It is not necessary to be a radical feminist, a Marxist, or a conservative Catholic to find this book intellectually unsatisfying. But I should make a clear distinction (which I am not sure Friedan made in the writing) between her book and her work on behalf of women. I suspect that as a writer Friedan had one important book in her, and this one isn't it. I think that as an activist and a political mover, she's worth an auditoriumful of the people who pushed her out of active leadership in the National Organization for Women, which she helped found, and who have now proved themselves incapable of organizing a scavenger hunt. Friedan's understanding of, and sympathy for, the majority of American women—who want to love men and children and don't want to squeeze into the corset of an alien ideology—made her a tremendously effective speaker and activist. It may be that her years in that work dissipated her capacities as a writer, that enhancing the political possibilities narrowed the philosophical ones. In any case, we need her now, when men and women who could be educated and reassured by her are marching against the Equal Rights Amendment.

The best chapters in this book, and the most telling, are the first and last: "The Way We Were—1949" and "Scary Doings in Mexico City" (1975). The long way we've come in between, for better or worse, is in no small part Friedan's doing. More power to her.

> Sara Sanborn, "Warm-Puppy Feminism," in Saturday Review, *Vol. 3, No. 21, July 24, 1976, p. 26.*

Anne Bernays   (review date 8 August 1976)

[*In the following review, Bernays praises* It Changed My Life *as a history of the women's movement, but objects to what she perceives as the "distinctly women's magazine taint" of Friedan's writing.*]

There are two books here [in *It Changed My Life*]. One is set in type. The other can be read only between the lines. The first is conscious, the second inadvertent. It is not really surprising that the unconscious stream in this book delivers a message as substantial as its conscious presentation.

The history (my typewriter chokes over what Betty Friedan renders as "herstory") of the women's movement, galvanized by her 1963 book, *The Feminine Mystique,* makes genuinely stirring reading. Friedan has by now assumed a new persona: Mother of Us All. I, for one, feel fortunate to be among her daughters. *The Feminine Mystique* changed the lives of a generation of American women who, once Pandora's box was open, were never the same again. A thoroughly researched analysis of what is wrong with us, Friedan's first book named and probed the "nameless problem" that plagues women; it demonstrated how we are manipulated by a psychically stunting mystique as pervading as oxygen. Friedan was an accomplished magazine writer when, 13 years ago, she took on education, Freud, advertising, television and women's magazines. It showed: her approach and her prose were seamless. Moreover, her exposure of injustices to women carried a profoundly emotional appeal.

What happened then? The thing solidified, got leaders who formed collectives, wrote manifestoes, did grubby work for salutary ends, marched, spoke, got elected, demanded, legislated, rallied, met again, founded the National Organization for Women, wrote some more, grew. And then it began to fall apart.

Friedan claims that she did not "set out deliberately to found the women's movement." But once it coalesced, she viewed it as totally committed to social change within the system—a foot in the door here, a bill passed there, and so on. Some of her followers, however, "deviationists" such as Gloria Steinem, began to leave around what Friedan calls a "sexual red herring"—a peculiarly inappropriate image. To Friedan it stank, chiefly because it diverted the movement from serious political action and put its focus on lesbianism, the orgasm debate and, ultimately, women's psychosexual existence with men—and preferably without them. The movement ground to a halt, passing up the opportunity to scoop in all those American women out there who were—justifiably, I suppose—frightened off. These women needed their men, and they liked their orgasms, however flawed. This is the story that Friedan means us to see.

The covert message is far more poignant. Writing now, Friedan says, "I seemed increasingly to be at ideological, and tactical odds with Bella Abzug and Gloria Steinem and Brenda Feigen Fasteau and other self-styled radicals." A bitter understatement. What, in fact, seems to have happened is that Steinem—not society, Freud, television, or underarm goo—became for Friedan the Enemy. A classic power struggle on the surface, but it had to do with things more basic and vulnerable than ideology or tactics. "I was no match for her," Friedan writes of Steinem, "not only because of the matter of looks—which somehow paralyzed me—but because I don't know how to manipulate, or deal with manipulation." In other words, "I'm just an ugly little girl who can't deal with the realities of political power or the accommodations it demands." This is a devastating confession. If she were going to lead, why in hell didn't she *learn* how to manipulate people?

There's something else about this book Friedan's children will find unsettling: she has reverted to type. Her prose—

and reflexively some of her basic attitudes—have a distinctly women's magazine taint, so that you begin to suspect that her first book was a freak accident, however inspired. As to her appeal on the last page for a "new YES to life"—well, I wish she hadn't said it.

But if, as I believe, history—even hindsight as history—is validation, then I can only regret Friedan's lapses in taste, and value this book for the words that in their time produced what we're all really after: affirmative action. Especially recommended: the "Statement of Purpose" for NOW; the 1970 "Call to Women's Strike for Equality"; "Critique of Sexual Politics"; and a chilling analysis of "female chauvinism," viz., "If I were a man, I would strenuously object to the assumption that women have any moral or spiritual superiority as a class, or that men share some brute insensitivity as a class. This is male chauvinism in reverse; it is female sexism. It is, in fact, female chauvinism."

Anne Bernays, "Love Her or Leave Her," in Book World—The Washington Post, *August 8, 1976, p. F7.*

Hilary Spurling (review date 8 July 1977)

[*In the following review, Spurling lauds* It Changed My Life *as a compelling history of the women's movement.*]

It is presumably no accident that Messrs Gollancz, should have chosen to publish Betty Friedan's call to arms [*It Changed My Life*] at a point almost exactly midway between St Sexburga's Day and the feast last month of that even greater patron of militant Anglo-Saxon feminism, Sexburga's sister, the sainted virgin Etheldreda. Etheldreda was an East-Anglian princess who married two kings and refused to sleep with either until in 673, after 20 years or so of male intimidation ranging from moral blackmail to brute force, she fled from her second husband's armies to sanctuary at Ely, then a virtually inaccessible swamp, where flocks of defaulting wives, widows and virgins promptly joined her, and where the fervour of her own virginity became not only a legend in her lifetime but a force to be reckoned with for nearly 1,000 years after her death. She has always seemed to me a distinctly modern type: not simply in her implacable attitude to men (though here, too, one may see aspects of the stern sisterhood described by Ms Friedan, which seeks to eliminate man altogether and elevate lesbianism to the first principle of the women's movement), still more in her understanding that the liberation of women might become, if properly organised, a formidable source of power.

It is in this respect, rather than in her loathing of the marriage bed, that Etheldreda resembles Ms Friedan. One of the most fascinating parts of *It Changed My Life* describes the writing of her first, famous manifesto, *The Feminine Mystique,* and its electrifying effect in 1963 on the wives and mothers of America. Its author became a celebrity overnight, ostracised by her suburban neighbours ('the children were kicked out of the dancing-class car pool') but idolised by thousands more, whose passionate letters of support led eventually to the founding of the women's movement in America and Europe. No one could have predicted the scale of these complaints from unknown prisoners at the kitchen sink ('Here I am: I feel like an appliance! I want to live!'), nor the comprehensive scope of their resentment, anger and frustration. Admittedly, Ms Friedan writes at times as though housewives held exclusive rights to bitterness and boredom; even so, there can be small doubt that the book released something she herself describes in almost mystical terms:

> I believe . . . it's an unprecedented new kind of power in the world, one that threatens the old control of political and economic power by church and state in ways we ourselves are only dimly aware of.

This is the language of revolution and, like all able revolutionaries, Ms Friedan deals in dreams ('The new dreams, the real dreams women must make come true themselves') as much as in rational analysis: one is not surprised to learn that on one occasion she reduced an audience of hostile college boys to tears, and on another touched the heart of the Pope in person. Equality for women in her book will not only promote personal fulfilment, economic emancipation and moral independence; it will also increase the sum of happiness for both sexes (special benefits—'less nagging, less guilt, fewer problems'—promised for men), strengthen the marriage bond and lower the divorce rate; and, if it won't actually make your hair curl, it will certainly act against old age, loneliness and fading looks, not to mention being well on the way to abolishing war itself (by removing 'the frustrations built into our sexual roles that made us explode in violence and want to napalm all the green life in Vietnam, and club the long-haired young').

All this rests partly on faith, but partly on a grasp of practical priorities at the farthest remove from that ideological insistence on the moral superiority of women as a class which is shared, oddly enough, by both the radical lesbian sisters who hold it rank treachery to consort with men, and by the apparently highly organised viragos of such all-American institutions as Total Womanhood or the Pussycat League. No one could set her face more resolutely against extremists of either persuasion than Ms Friedan. Hers is a peaceable revolution to be brought about by education, for which she predicts precisely the consequences—increased independence, self-reliance and self-respect—once foretold with dread by opponents of the 19th-century New Woman.

Indeed, one is forcibly struck again and again by parallels between her arguments and those of what one might call the hoop-trundling school ('Why can't people let girls dress dolls and trundle hoops, as they used to?') led by Charlotte M. Yonge more than a century ago. Both are above all concerned with the feminine mystique. Both confidently prophesy its destruction if girls once start to think. And both are preaching to the same congregation, since the sex-object schooled in self-repression, the subservient wife and selfless mother described so feelingly by Ms Friedan possess all the characteristics of Miss Yonge's 'average woman of the higher type . . . made to learn; to lean; to admire; to support; to emphasise every joy; to soften every sorrow of the object of her devotion'. The Victori-

an line of duty—so unenticing at the time that Miss Yonge was regularly obliged to devise spectacular punishments like brain fever, destitution and death for girls who flouted it—turns out in short to be at bottom none other than that round of car pool, cookie jar and coffee morning, dancing class and scout pack to which in recent years the women's movement has given such unequivocally sinister connotations. No wonder if housewives from Rome to Rio prefer to see themselves as, in Ms Friedan's phrase, the heroines of 'herstory': 'Women's life now for us all means moving on unmapped roads, with signposts non-existent or none too clear, mapping it as we go . . . "

This is stirring stuff, and so are the grand set scenes in which, as the book fans out from the domestic to the international front, we find the women's movement forced to pit itself alone against the combined reactionary forces of the FBI, CIA and international communism. But one would be hard put to find a shrewder, more level-headed and resourceful strategist than Ms Friedan, nor one half so eloquent; and it would be a stony heart which did not rejoice to think that, even 13 centuries later and on another continent, St Etheldreda rides again.

> *Hilary Spurling, "Mstique," in* New States-man, *Vol. 94, No. 2416, July 8, 1977, p. 57.*

Webster Schott   (review date 1 November 1981)

[*In the following review, Schott praises* The Second Stage *as an insightful analysis of the problems facing women in the 1980s.*]

Betty Friedan's **The Second Stage** is the right book at the right time. She sees the problems facing women now. She has ideas about how to deal with them. And the thrust of her solutions push the women's movement back toward the mainstream of American thought about where the good life takes place—in that small group of familiars called the family.

Eighteen years ago in **The Feminine Mystique** she said, "The problem that has no name stirring in the minds of so many women today is not a matter of loss of femininity or too much education, or the demands of domesticity. It is far more important than anyone realizes. It is the key to . . . new and old problems which have been torturing women and their husbands and children, and puzzling their doctors and educators for years. . . . We can no longer ignore that voice within women that says: 'I want something more than my husband and my children and my home.' "

It was 1963. In the decade and a half that followed, a confluence of forces beyond anyone's imagination—massive use of oral contraceptives, a monstrously inflationary war in Vietnam, more inflation from OPEC oil and federal fiscal policies, and the informed will of our first post–World War II generation of college-educated women—gave American females some of what they wanted.

They organized themselves to gain access to power outside the family. They learned how to change the behavior of institutions. Because they had acquired control over their childbearing bodies they could enter business, industry, and government with plans to stay. They got some of what they wanted because standards of living would fall without wives and mothers at work. Moreover the U.S. economy could not face foreign productivity unless women worked.

Women flew from the kitchen, and today about 52 percent of all women between 19 and 59 years old are employed. Friedan cites one study showing nearly 90 percent of all women over 40 work. Only 11 percent of all U.S. families consist of dad on the job, and mom at home with the kids. Fifty-eight percent of all mothers of school children work. The change has affected American life all the way from the size of grocery stores to the frequency of church services. The family of Right-to-Life and presidential fantasy no longer exists.

But Friedan senses "something off, out of focus, going wrong" as women try to live the fuller life of economic participation and equality that she, Gloria Steinem, and others in the women's movement fought for. "I sense the exhilaration of 'superwomen' [women who've broken through to the executive suite and enjoyed the tokens of professional and political equality] giving way to a tiredness, a certain brittle disappointment, a disillusionment with 'assertiveness training' and the rewards of power."

Right. Things have gone awry, and at least half of *The Second Stage* is description and analysis of the women's movement off the road, while the Moral Majority, Ronald Reagan, and various Neanderthal forces bear down with a wrecker.

Many of the gains of the 1960s and 1970s are in jeopardy. The Equal Rights Amendment is short of ratification, and time ends next June. Congress is threatening to amend or circumvent the Constitution in order to void the 1973 U.S. Supreme Court decision affirming women's right to abortion; this especially strikes at "the personhood of women" because oral contraceptives and intrauterine devices have proved dangerous or defective. An array of federal entitlement programs equalizing access, protection, or compensation have been crippled or reversed by Ronald Reagan and an intimidated Congress. If the economy fails or falters, women will lose jobs faster than men. Women's freedom is economically contingent. Therefore it can be lost.

Even women's gains are illusory. Women earn an average of "fifty-nine cents to every dollar men earn, the average male high-school dropout today earning $1,600 more a year than female college graduates." Some of the largest corporations in America have admitted pay discrimination against women. In some states women must prove, in court, the equitability of their contributions to a marriage in order to share in property after divorce. In 1979, 8 million women headed households, half of them on less than $10,000 a year, and a third on less than $7,000.

Women themselves, says Friedan, have placed the gains of the women's movement at risk. "We must at least admit and begin openly to discuss feminist denial of the importance of family, of women's own needs to give and get love and nurture, tender loving care," she says. Burning bras and operating as if their freedom was to be won in bedroom battles, women have let the Moral Majority and

Right-to-Lifers claim family as their property. Gay separatists have diverted the movement into sexual politics. Victors and activists have been corrupted by power. Upon election to Congress, appointment to government, elevation in the corporation, women have abandoned the issues and constituencies that brought them to power and have compromised or acquiesced on women's issues to stay there. Fifty-two percent of the U.S. population are women, but women failed their U.S. senators in the 1980 election. Nearly all women's rights supporters lost.

Friedan knows what's wrong with the movement. She also knows what women want because she is a clinical psychologist by training, and she founded and served as first president of the National Organization for Women.

Friedan says women want what we all want—everything, or as much of it as we can get. They want to work and to choose when to have children. They want to participate fully in all aspects of the world around them—business, politics, education, sport, social service—but they also want freedom to do that for which they are uniquely qualified. They want to be able to bear and rear children, and they want help from men and the institutions men have made.

The basic question our society must answer, says Friedan, is this:

> Must—can—women now meet a standard of perfection in the workplace set in the past by and for men who had wives to take care of all the details of living and—*at the same time*—meet a standard of performance at home and as mothers that was set in the past by women whose whole sense of worth, power and mastery had to come from being perfect, all-controlling housewives and mothers?

Her answer has to be "no" because woman has a double set of needs: "Power, identity, status and social security through her own work or action in society, which the reactionary enemies of feminism deny; and the need for love, identity, status, security, and generation through marriage, children, home, the family, which those feminists still locked in their own extreme reaction deny. *Both sets of needs are essential to women, and to the evolving human condition.*"

Friedan is less clear about how both sets of needs can be met. But the women's movement has gone beyond the "feminist mystique" of the pill and unshaven legs. It has entered what she calls "the second stage: the restructuring of our institutions on the basis of real equality for women and men, so we can live a new 'yes' to life and love, and *choose* to have children."

The gains of the past must be preserved and advanced—ERA, job equality, full sharing in family assets, control over childbearing. But now we must change how we work and live. Friedan says women and men need flexible working hours so one or the other can see the kids off to school or greet them when they come home. We need a national policy for maternity and paternity leaves so women can bear children without loss of job or seniority, and men can truly become parents.

She says women must press for new alternatives to child care, "using services and funds from a variety of sources (public and private, companies, unions, churches, city state, federal agencies, but always parent-controlled), demanding tax incentives and innovations like a voucher system."

She tells us that "the second stage has to focus on a domestic revolution within the home and extending, in effect, the concept of home. We have to take new control of our home life, as well as work life." Men and women must share roles at home. But they need new physical and special designs in housing and neighborhoods to take into account the changing, shifting needs of women and men, singly or in couples, with or without children. And Friedan calls for new kinds of buildings and communities in which kitchens, dining rooms, recreational areas are shared while each family has private space. Sweden offers models.

She has other good ideas, like child allowances, job rehabilitation for mothers, and community family service centers. She has read her Paul Goodman, Karl Menninger, and Milton Friedman. But what she doesn't have—and probably can't devise at this time—is a strategy or even a tactic to convert the second stage into action.

The prognosis isn't good. Women voted against themselves in 1980. Friedan cites surveys showing women don't want day-care centers and we spend less on such services than most industrialized countries. She pretty well proves that women start acting like men when they get men's power. The Congress is a near-perfect example.

She knows what women are up against: "In all known political terms, the women's movement as we knew it has come to a dead end; the problems are insoluble."

But she has hope. It lies with men. She believes the women's movement has led men to ask new questions about their own lives—what work is for, what families mean, what love does. And she thinks a convergence of mutual interest may "provide a new power and energy for solutions that seem impossible today." I suspect economics more than idealism will do it.

There are things wrong with Friedan's **The Second Stage.** Most of them are matters of style or taste. Friedan's case histories fatten the book in the absence of program proposals. She tells us too often that she is at the power center of the women's movement, talking to big shots and lecturing at West Point. Her material is repetitive, disorganized, and written in a hurry.

But one only notes the flaws to dismiss them. **The Second Stage** is intelligent, compassionate, and pertinent. It's an education. And it provides a course of action, especially for men. If we don't want for our mothers, wives, and daughters the freedom we have, why is it worth having? If we are not partners with women, what are we? (pp. 1, 14)

Webster Schott, "Where Do We Go from Here?" in Book World—The Washington Post, November 1, 1981, pp. 1, 14.

Herma Hill Kay   (review date 22 November 1981)

[*In the following review of* The Second Stage, *Kay critiques Friedan's views on the "feminist mystique" and the "second stage" of the women's movement, but praises her underlying emphasis on individual self-realization.*]

It is a commonplace that in most societies throughout history the division of household labor has corresponded to gender. Any society that attempts to change this pattern must be prepared to experience the turmoil that accompanies basic social reorganization. If significant groups within the society oppose this fundamental alteration of traditional sex roles, as they now do in the United States, the turmoil is likely to be exacerbated. Thus, it is not surprising that those who are trying to break the old pattern in their own lives should feel the tension most keenly. They are, after all, accurately perceived as threats to established ways, as agents provocateurs. But the strain extends as well to those whose comfortable habits are disturbed in the process.

In [*The Second Stage*], Betty Friedan confronts these constraints—as though for the first time—and finds them startling. In conversations with young women around the country, she finds an "unarticulated malaise" suggested by a questioning of whether it is really possible to combine marriage, children and career. From men who overidentified with their jobs only to discover that human satisfaction had eluded them, she hears warnings about "dead ends for women" if they, too, follow this path.

Given such distress signals, and the continuing political backlash against the women's movement (apparent in the stalled effort to ratify the Equal Rights Amendment), Mrs. Friedan concludes that the women's movement has created a "*feminist* mystique" that threatens to become every bit as confining as the "feminine mystique" she identified in her earlier book. If it was necessary in the "first stage" of the women's movement to break out of the "feminine" mystique, with its image of a woman "completely fulfilled in her role as husband's wife, children's mother, server of physical needs of husband, children, home," then in the "second stage" it will be necessary to go beyond the "feminist mystique," which has limited women to a reactive stance, as they press their "grievances against men in office and home, school and field, in marriage, housework, even sex."

The cost of this feminist reaction against male domination, Mrs. Friedan now believes, is that many women felt forced to abandon or deny their human needs for home, mate and children. She argues that by turning their backs on the family, many members of the women's movement abandoned that institution to the opponents of feminism, who have effectively used the defense of traditional family values as a platform from which to attack the Equal Rights Amendment, procreative choice and homosexuality. In **The Second Stage,** Betty Friedan makes a bold attempt to regain control of the family policy agenda. Her strategy calls for a joint effort by men and women to redefine what is meant by success at home and on the job so that the needs of both sexes for achievement, intimacy and nurturance can find adequate expression. She reports on research that contrasts "Alpha," or "masculine," leadership styles, which draw on quantitative analysis, with "Beta," or "feminine," ones, which, according to at least one scientist from the Stanford Research Institute, are based on more "intuitive" thinking and a "contextual" power style. Mrs. Friedan responds by calling for a type of leadership marked by fewer confrontations and greater adaptability.

It is possible to applaud this strategy without embracing the reasoning that produced it. For example, it seems premature to identify a second stage in a social movement when the original goals of the "first stage" of the movement are still disputed and largely unrealized. It turns out that what Mrs. Friedan means by the "second stage" is an effort to enlist the aid of men to attain some of those original goals—namely, the emancipation of women from the home as a primary source of personal identity and the restructuring of the marketplace to accommodate the human needs of both male and female workers. Hence, one may fairly conclude that no significant completion of the "first stage" of the movement has occurred.

A second weakness in the argument is the dichotomy Mrs. Friedan poses between "feminine" and "feminist" mystiques, and, as she puts it, the resulting need for "a dialectical progression from thesis-antithesis (feminine mystique-feminism) to synthesis." The "dialectical progression" seems more a forensic device than either a description of actual experience or a valid analysis of the direction the women's movement has taken. The dichotomy seems artificial, and the categories too narrow. Neither the suburban housewives described in *The Feminine Mystique* nor the radical feminists who, as portrayed in *The Second Stage,* perceived man as "the enemy" represented large numbers of American women. For one thing, both groups were composed largely of white, middle-class women; even within that subgroup, certainly the revolutionaries and possibly the suburbanites were far from a majority. Still, Mrs. Friedan is right to insist that the experiences of both groups have been influential beyond their mere numbers. What is misleading is her assumption that either category is capable of containing all women or even one woman throughout her lifetime. A synthesis may indeed be needed, but if so, it must reflect more elements of the female experience than can be isolated from either the "feminine mystique" or "feminism."

Finally, it seems unnecessary to invoke new models of masculine and feminine leadership—even with the caveat that neither model is "innate" to a particular sex—to make the point that a certain amount of flexibility is needed in a period of transition. If men truly want to escape the pressures of their work and the rigidities of their lives, they will find ways to permit women to share these burdens, even as they allow themselves to enjoy an expanded role within the family.

Mrs. Friedan's new plea for cooperation between men and women cannot disguise the fact that the women's movement has always represented a struggle for liberation from an ascribed and limited status. Like any other liberation movement, whether that of racial minorities or homosexuals, its basic theme is freedom to choose one's own destiny.

But in all such efforts it soon develops that the power to make decisions about one's life without the means to implement them is an illusion. For all disadvantaged groups, the means of implementation include access to education, jobs and social status. In the case of men, the scope of choice can be broadened if race and sexual orientation are eliminated as permissible grounds for legal or social disapproval. But we have learned that we cannot establish freedom of opportunity for women merely by eliminating gender as the stated or unstated basis for distinction. The United States Supreme Court's determination in 1976 in General Electric Company v. Gilbert that distinctions (for purposes of job-related disability plans) based on pregnancy are not based on sex showed us the limitations of the "sex-blind" argument. If women workers are to have opportunities for advancement equal to men, and if the human race is to survive, we must find ways to prevent women from being disadvantaged if they choose to have children.

Two kinds of initiatives would help. One is public and includes the enactment of laws (already begun in the 1978 Congressional reversal of Gilbert) to prevent employers from treating pregnancy less favorably than other disabilities. The courts must also recognize that such laws do not prevent state legislatures or employers from taking further steps to neutralize the economic impact of pregnancy through, for example, paid maternity leaves—even if such leaves are not available to men.

The other kind of initiative, stressed by Mrs. Friedan, is a private one. If a couple wishes to raise a family, it is simply inefficient for two people sharing a household both to work outside the home. The available options are relatively few. Broadly, they include the use of paid help or shared parental responsibility for child rearing. The cost of the first option limits its usefulness, but it clearly permits the greatest flexibility for both partners. If the Government provided children's allowances, or if employers arranged for child-care facilities as part of fringe-benefit packages, this choice might be possible for more families. Virtually every modern industrial society except our own has adopted such a solution in one form or another. Mrs. Friedan doubts whether such programs are "politically viable" today in the United States, but the political climate may change, and, in any event, women workers should continue to press for these solutions.

The second option, having both parents share in child rearing, is perhaps the more promising one for most families, but it entails significant practical problems. The major obstacle is the present organization of the work force, which assumes 8-hour shifts and even longer hours and more irregular away-from-home schedules for people who reach the higher ranges of executive and professional work. Individual willingness to share child-care responsibilities means nothing unless the work place is restructured to facilitate and even reward such initiatives.

Mrs. Friedan's perception that this is the goal toward which both men and women must direct their efforts is a sound one. Her further proposal, that families should create a different model of housing, one that would permit several families to share common kitchen, dining and child-care areas, while having separate apartments for privacy, is a valuable option for those drawn to communal living. Care must be taken, however, lest the "communal mystique" become as confining as Mrs. Friedan now finds both the "feminine" and "feminist" ones. The underlying theme of this book—and it is a valid message—is that both men and women need to be free to discover their own "personhood" and to build a new society on that discovery without preconceptions and in the absence of social compulsion. (pp. 3, 33)

> *Herma Hill Kay, "Do We Suffer from a Feminist Mystique?" in* The New York Times Book Review, *November 22, 1981, pp. 3, 33.*

Catharine R. Stimpson (review date December 1981)

[*In the following review of* The Second Stage, *Stimpson finds Friedan's views on the women's movement naive, zealous, and overly simplistic.*]

If **The Feminine Mystique** was Betty Friedan's Old Testament, **The Second Stage** is her New. She has revised her vision of history to offer us her gospel and our redemption. Her good news is that "virtually all women today" want both families and "their own equality within and beyond it, as long as family and equality are not seen to be in conflict." Because that message is appealing, Friedan, no fool, will have many converts. I wish to confess my partial belief in **The Second Stage,** and my profound agnosticism.

Like many prophets, Friedan writes as if a force larger than she had driven her to her toil. "I did not intend to write another book on the woman question," she begins. Having given in to the pressure of events and emotions, she will, a latter-day Jacob, "wrestle anew" with the Women's Movement. She claims that she will bear with realities that few of us have been willing to own up to.

Friedan's historical contributions to feminism give her stance an immediate authenticity. They also complicate the passion with which she denounces the movement she helped to found. She still supports women's rights, but in this prolix and repetitive text, her anger persistently undermines her praise.

Friedan asserts that feminism has passed through a first stage. There it demanded "full participation, power and voice in the mainstream"; the recognition of women's personhood; and a woman's control over her own body, which she wisely renames the right to choose being a mother in dignified, supportive circumstances. She accurately describes the economic, social, and demographic forces behind feminism's contemporary resurgence. She knows that history and necessity create us as much as we create ourselves.

Unfortunately, Friedan flattens out the complexities of women's history. She says that "sexuality, motherhood . . . used to be women's only sources of power. . . . " Her oversimplifications are most embarrassing in her treatment of minorities. Only occasionally mentioning minorities, as well as the Third World, she erases race as a vital part of America.

The Second Stage then charges that first-stage feminism has gone astray, a distressing fact that first-stagers are insufficiently sheepish about. Some specific complaints are cogent: women do suffer and strain to balance public and private lives; feminists have been insensitive to the feelings that many women have about maternity and domesticity.

However, Friedan's zealous rhetoric vilifies the Women's Movement far more dramatically than she perhaps meant to. The inventor of the invaluable phrase, "feminine mystique," now discovers a "feminist mystique." The former kept women in the home; the latter keeps them out of it. Indeed, feminists have repudiated not only the family, but a womanhood it tenderly frees. Endorsing a retrograde theory that women have a universal nature, an essence, a hidden mystery, an inner spaciness, Friedan blames feminists for denying "their own need as women to love or to have children. . . . "

Those whom the feminist mystique has blinded now stumble along two paths. Some buy into the system and become little men. (**The Second Stage,** often claiming an originality it does not always possess, overlooks the reality that many people of varying ideologies have long warned that a movement that calls for participation in the mainstream might lead some women into a bog.) Others, she laments, have become enamored of sexual politics, of such issues as pornography. They have so inflamed feminism's reputation that they threaten the passage of an Equal Rights Amendment. Friedan scolds: "Sexual war against men is an irrelevant, self-defeating acting out of rage."

Such a flurry of accusations cries out for more proof than Friedan offers. Though she summons up some studies and statistics, she is her own witness. Her evidence is her experience. Obviously, that life is inseparable from contemporary feminism, but **The Second Stage** inadequately reveals how much it is taking sides in arguments that have haunted the movement since the 1960s; how much and in what ways Friedan is going public with what some might have treated as family quarrels that demand clarity and charity rather than polemic and self-interest.

Let me give two examples. Since the Houston Conference in 1977, Friedan has been publicly more supportive of lesbians than she once was. Yet, she apparently still wants the issue to go away. **The Second Stage** labels sexuality a private matter. Since lesbianism is a sexual practice, it belongs in a private, not a political, sphere. Brushing it all back into the closet, Friedan refuses to realize how much queer-bashing is the Red-baiting of this decade. She also profoundly believes that women really ought to be with men, especially with the New Adams that are emerging to join the New Eves in the replanted Garden of the sex-role revolution.

Next, Friedan has far more faith than others that the American system is capable of reform. She encourages us to make capitalism work for us. She inflates a legitimate suspicion of some Communist states into a flirtatious evasion of left-wing thought in general. She borrows some Marxist notions, but when she appropriates Dolores Hayden's work on ways in which we might redesign the home (*The Grand Domestic Revolution,* 1981), she avoids the socialism in Hayden's explicit socialist feminism. She goes on to preach that if we practice new values, we can fear atomic war a little less. After a fascinating visit to a military academy, she blandly gushes in a conclusion many may find reassuring:

> I leave West Point as the first female cadets are about to graduate, feeling safer somehow because these powerful nuclear weapons that can destroy the world and the new human strategies therefore needed to defend this nation will henceforward be in the hands of women and men who are, with agony, breaking through to a new strength, strong enough to be sensitive and tender to the evolving needs and value of human life. . . .

Happily, errant feminists are not Friedan's only villains. She wars with people on all sides. She deplores, rightly, the last gasps of a threatened machismo; huge bureaucracies; a linear habit of mind that prefers product to process, abstract to concrete, isolated thing to the thing in a web of relationships; the rise of the New Right. She is witty about Phyllis Schlafly, that "paper tigress," but she cannot stop herself from a comparison between radical lesbians and some conservative women. Both hate themselves, and other women.

Friedan's peace plan is for us all to enter "The Second Stage." Women's liberation will give way to human liberation, women's politics to human politics. We will link, rather than sever, family and work. Both domains will embody the values of equality and nurturance. She cites well-known tactics, such as flexitime, that might enable men and women to traverse the realms of home and job with ease.

An ambitious woman, she wishes to reconstruct more than feminism. As if she were writing the platform for an alternative party, she urges us to incorporate "feminine" modes of thought into leadership positions; to renew grass-roots politics and democratic pragmatism; to be altruistic and serve the community. If we do so, we may even glimpse the face of God. She writes: "The most important effect of transcending those old sex roles may be an evolution of morality and religious thought. . . . "

The Second Stage dismays me. I, too, believe in personhood, families, communities, justice, morality, and even, I must murmur, the mystical and the sacred. I, too, long for survival and for vision. Yet, *The Second Stage* is an erratic prescription for survival, a skewed vision. No doubt I am mired in the first stage. No doubt I am too "immature" to climb toward the cozy, yet uplifting, reaches of the second. Yet, if I am to evolve, to realize that 19th-century dream of a progressive human process, I hope I have the miseries of the first stage really healed; I hope that I will be alert to race, to sexual complexity, to the realities of economic structures, and to the temptations of masking my rage against a historical moment in victim-blaming, partial revelations, and messianic oratory. (pp. 16, 18, 21)

> *Catharine R. Stimpson, "From Feminine to Feminist Mystique," in* Ms., *Vol. X, No. 6, December, 1981, pp. 16, 18, 21.*

Margaret O'Brien Steinfels (review date 18 December 1981)

[*In the following review, Steinfels argues that* The Second Stage *fails as a serious analysis of the choices and conflicts facing contemporary women.*]

Twenty years ago, Betty Friedan provided college-educated, suburban housewives with a label for "the problem that had no name"—the *feminine* mystique. She now offers to their heirs, college-educated, urban career women, another label for a new problem—the *feminist* mystique. In short form the feminist mystique sums up the excesses of the woman's movement, the anti-male, bra-burning, separatist forays of sexual politics that have come to be serious liabilities in our present less indulgent political atmosphere.

Two slogans, two poles, and the outcome is two women's movements: the one Mrs. Friedan helped to found, and the one that found itself in reaction to hers—Mrs. Schlafly's.

Over the last decade women who fit the ideal image of neither movement have felt out of place in both. Most women in this country are married; most have children; most work and are paid less than a man doing equivalent work. Most work, not because they have been liberated from the feminine mystique, but because most families can no longer live on one income. Most women think there should be equal pay for equal work; that women should have equal opportunities for education, jobs, and advancements. Most women, when polled, believe that abortion should be legal, but not available on demand; and, although not most, a very significant number of women, have helped to defeat the Equal Rights Amendment (ERA). A third woman's movement, nicely fitted between the other two would accommodate the real interests of most women in this country. Mrs. Friedan's recent writing, now gathered in this book, suggested that she had become acutely aware of that fact.

The Second Stage is an effort to reoccupy the territory her woman's movement unwisely abandoned to Mrs. Schlafly and the Radical Right—family, children, men, intimacy, and (in the oft-repeated phrase) "life-cherishing values." Although acknowledging the power of the anti-woman woman's movement, Mrs. Friedan does not seem to fully understand what the first woman's movement did to bring on the formation of the second.

The excesses of sexual politics that gave a tawdry image to her woman's movement were the work, she says, of bad companions—the media, women refugees from the radical student movement, and counter-culture earth mothers. While getting in her licks at the bad companions, she also apologizes and urges a more sober assessment of what women and men must face in the Reagan years. Apologies and reassessments notwithstanding, Mrs. Friedan seems to believe that it is an image problem and not matters of substance that divide women on the woman question.

In fact, the issues that Mrs. Friedan sees as the bedrock of woman's liberation, passage of the ERA and preservation of abortion on demand, are precisely the issues that brought the second woman's movement into existence. Abortion and the ERA are the political children of upper and upper-middle class men and women who believe both measures are an unalloyed benefit to all women. But in different ways both measures subtly threaten working class and traditional-minded women and men who resist the shifts in power that each measure entails.

Unfortunately these concerns are not the focus of *The Second Stage,* but another dilemma recently brought home to Mrs. Friedan: In our culture the individual worth of men and women is measured by their work, while the primary sources of emotional satisfaction for most adults come from families, spouses, children, and life in small groups. The first woman's movement must attend to these realities that too often tug and pull in opposite directions.

In her travels, Mrs. Friedan has picked up this new refrain: too many choices, too much to do. Powerhouses at work, successful career women are fearful of having children and losing their place on the career ladder. Coeds free to go to law school, to medical school, to marry, bemoan the range of choices that lie before them. Supermoms whose days and nights at work and at home are scheduled like battleplans down to the last minute feel they have no time to sit back and enjoy any of it.

But for every woman who has too many choices, surely there are many with too few. Mrs. Friedan pays some attention to older divorced women left without husbands, without skills, without careers or pensions, and with too few economic and social choices before them. But overall we hear very little in these pages about women forced to take low-paying jobs, to leave children without adequate care, to forego having children, or raising them alone, because the men in their lives won't support offspring. In short, we hear a great deal from the women who are the success stories of the first woman's movement and very little from those who carry the burdens of liberation, but receive very few of its benefits: women who must work, but have no career; women who have children, but no childcare; women who have relationships, but no commitments.

Unsettled by the problem of too many choices, rather than too few, Mrs. Friedan is off in all directions in search of new answers, new research findings, new ways of looking at things. She is off to West Point, off to meetings with rabbis and priests, off to international conferences. She is, I regret to report, simply off.

Those alive and reading in 1963, when *The Feminine Mystique* was published, will remember the endless yardage of popular prose laced with pseudo-psychology and sociology, chapter after chapter badly patched from old magazine articles. *The Second Stage* adds to that style the worst of social scientese and journalese: a pastiche of Freudianism and laundered sociobiology, the lame-footed anecdote that parades as evidence, the personal encounters that are inflated into revealing trends.

Reviewing West Point cadets, male and female, marching to lunch, Mrs. Friedan tweaks her host, an army major, and points an anti-military finger, "Do they actually line up and march like that when they have to fight?" But, in fact, she does not oppose the military life for men or women. At the Baltimore session of the White House Conference on the Family, she feels she has resolved a priest's difficulty with abortion by a semantic sleight of hand: everyone could support "the choice to have children." Attending a meeting at the Stanford Research Institute International, she delights in finding that the Beta style, "based on synthesizing, intuitive, qualitative thinking and a 'contextual,' 'relational' power style," is receiving serious attention. The Beta style long practiced by successful feminist leaders is hailed by corporate managers as a welcome balance to the overly analytic, rational, quantitative, and masculine Alpha style.

Although hardly attending the real problem of real differences, Mrs. Friedan's political agenda for the second stage is the conciliation of polarities, of males and females at West Point and elsewhere; of pro-choice and pro-life activists; of liberals and conservatives, of . . . you name it. "Improbable as it may seem, we could bridge the old conservative-liberal chasm, if we realize the true potential of that elusive new male-female, second-stage mode."

Many have stood perplexed between the first woman's movement and the second, finding truth and error in each camp. Others have called for conciliation or, at least, the grounds for agreeing to disagree. Perhaps those confusions and pleas inspired this book. But in writing it, Mrs. Friedan too often occupies the high ground of rhetoric, extolling life-cherishing values instead of exploring the genuinely contradictory definitions of those values held by the two woman's movements. When acknowledging differences, she papers them over. Rather than clarifying and sharpening areas of agreement and disagreement, she obfuscates. It may be churlish to say so, but I doubt that Mrs. Friedan will be among the founders of the third woman's movement, but then neither will Mrs. Schlafly. (pp. 726-28)

> *Margaret O'Brien Steinfels, "All the World's a Stage," in* Commonweal, *Vol. CVIII, No. 23, December 18, 1981, pp. 726-28.*

Megan Marshall   (review date 20 January 1982)

[*In the following review of* The Second Stage, *Marshall questions Friedan's assumptions about the success and future of the women's movement.*]

It took just a few thousand words excerpted from Betty Friedan's agenda for the women's movement in the 1980s, *The Second Stage,* in the *New York Times* to draw fire from the feminist press. The suggestion by the founder of NOW that women had secured their place in the working world and, despite the ERA stalemate, could now afford to join men in a "Second Stage" movement for reforming the family brought instant charges of collaborationism. "Betty Friedan would destroy feminism in order to save it, and beat the Moral Majority by joining it," wrote *Village Voice* staffer Ellen Willis in a letter to the *Times.* And in *Working Papers,* Suzanne Gordon accused Friedan of being "willing to smooth out feminism's radical edges, thus making it respectable and acceptable to Peoria and to corporate America."

But is it really so shocking to hear Friedan take up the cause of the family? It is easy to forget that Friedan, whose *The Feminine Mystique* touched off the modern women's movement in America, was always a staunch defender of the family. Her chief argument in *The Feminine Mystique* was that the bored, depressed housewife of the 1950s was good for no one—not her husband, not her children, not herself. Could Friedan help it if her book inspired bitter bedroom debates, consciousness-raising groups, a new rationale for divorce, even a separatist lesbian culture? These were never her concerns.

It's not so surprising that we haven't heard much from Friedan in print since the 1963 publication of *The Feminine Mystique.* It took more radical thinkers to carry on where she left off, to define and chart the long history of the unequal male-female power relation that Friedan first identified in the 1950s. But now that those strident voices have quieted, or turned to issues outside the mainstream of American women's concerns—pornography, lesbian culture, women's spirituality—Friedan has taken the chance to win back her audience. Her method is once again to uncover a "problem with no name" afflicting much of female America—not the Feminine Mystique, this time, but the Femin*ist* Mystique. And the problem is a real one.

The discovery came, Friedan writes in *The Second Stage,* as she began listening to the "daughters" of the women's movement express

> an uneasiness, almost a bitterness that they hardly dare admit. As if with all those opportunities that we won for them, and envy them, how can they ask out loud certain questions, talk about certain other needs they aren't supposed to worry about—those old needs which shaped our lives and trapped us, against which we rebelled?

In other words, the independent working woman who won her freedom in the 1970s is, understandably, getting homesick.

If only the remedy were as simple as Friedan's prescription for the depressed housewife of the 1950s: get a job! As her feminist critics are so quick to remind her, the overworked, underpaid woman of the 1980s can't solve her problems by simply turning back to the kitchen. And Friedan doesn't need to be told that the lid will never be shut on the Pandora's box of the working woman's woes. (*The Second Stage* will disappoint feminists eager to label Friedan a neo-Marabel Morgan.) But in attempting to embrace the complexity of the modern woman's problems, Friedan has come up with a program in *The Second Stage* that is no less than utopian—and, sadly, not much more workable than Total Womanhood.

To understand what Friedan is proposing in *The Second Stage,* one must make a few rather large assumptions along with Friedan: that women have secured a place in the job market alongside men; that men are willingly taking on child care and homemaking responsibilities now that they are no longer the sole breadwinners; that, in short, the inequities of the "first stage" of the women's movement are in the past. Our problem now, as Friedan sees it, is how to "live the equality we fought for." In the "Second Stage" of the women's movement, says Friedan, both women and men will fight to "take back the day": to reform the workplace and the home so that balancing job and family commitments will be easy, even fun. Part-time, flex-time, job-sharing, company-sponsored day care, tax credits and vouchers for child care, extensive maternity and paternity benefits, new home designs to permit communal housekeeping and cooking arrangements—all these are part of the Second Stage agenda.

None of these unquestionably appealing reforms is in itself a new idea. What is new here is Friedan's notion that such reforms can and will be accomplished through a quiet, community-based movement of "job protestors" of both sexes. Unfortunately, only the most starry-eyed of optimists will be able to accept those important first assumptions: that women now have enough power in the workplace to make effective demands; that enough men will join women in fighting for household reforms. Even the suggestion that all *women* may be ready to work together seems little more than wishful thinking in a time when pro-lifers and pro-choicers aren't even speaking to each other. Worse, it is unlikely that the same men and women who are so oppressed by their work loads will take time out for protest. And can we believe that in our current economic climate, American business will listen any more closely to worker demands than it did when profits were certain and unemployment low?

But readers of *The Second Stage* will soon discover that Friedan is her own worst enemy. The book she's given us is neither the field manual nor the manifesto needed to accomplish her reforms. As if shying away from the bitter response she has already provoked with this book, Friedan has expressed most of her ideas as rhetorical questions—whole paragraphs of them—dizzying her readers where she might have inspired them. And, perhaps hoping to win support from all factions, Friedan insists on crediting all sides of every issue. But she only succeeds in contradicting herself. Friedan would have us believe that men and women will seek reforms for the family because the working world offers only drudgery or fierce competition:

> 'good jobs' . . . have become scarce. In the last twenty-five years, more than three out of five new jobs are in retail trade or services where 'many jobs are part-time and wages extraordinarily low.'

But elsewhere she urges readers to join in the movement with the news that

> more and more, the kinds of work that will be required of people will involve creative, innovative, and decision-making responsibility. . . . This kind of work can often be done as well at home or under a tree as in an office.

When it comes to establishing those two basic premises of the Second Stage, Friedan's equivocations are just embarrassing. On women's gains in the workplace she says, "the breakthrough against sex discrimination has made a real difference for women"—and then, in practically the same breath, "who can be sure that the barriers of sex discrimination won't be raised again in the current political climate?" And, on men's willingness to take responsibility in the home: "Men are now seeking new life patterns as much as women are"—but, later, "on the economic bottom line, after nearly twenty years of the women's movement, it becomes clear that most women are still saddled with the work they used to do in the family."

But if we could use a bit more straight talk from Friedan-the-writer, we hear altogether too much from Friedan-the-public-speaker. She quotes freely from her own statements at rallies and conferences as if she were calling on an impartial expert. And we can't help wishing she'd handed over the gossipy anecdotes about Bella, Gloria, Phyllis, Marabel, and the gang to a biographer.

When she wrote *The Feminine Mystique* 20 years ago, Friedan could get away with cribbing from her own experience: her life as a housewife *was* like the lives of the women she was writing for and about. But how many women can identify with the new Betty, with her house on Long Island and *pied-à-terre* in Manhattan, whose "family," she says, now "stretches from California to Cambridge." Friedan has based her vision of the Second Stage on the evidence she collected from that bicoastal family on her speaking tours—but the result is a peculiar assortment of confessions, testimonials, and diatribes from "troubled sisters," hecklers, and groupies. Can we learn anything for certain about the new world we live in from this random collection of anecdotes of husbands who willingly babysit their children and wives who burn out on high-powered careers—a world, we know from Friedan's own equivocations, that is far less certain than the world of the Feminine Mystique?

It is a symptom of Friedan's quandary that the only heroine she can point her readers to is Joan of Arc. With full seriousness she counsels working wives and mothers who are troubled with competing demands from work and family to remember what "Joan of Arc said, facing the flames: 'All that I am I will not deny.' " But surely, for all that Joan was, she could never be a symbol of fulfilled motherhood. Nor even, at the time of her burning, a unifier of men and women. Still, Friedan is on to something here, for the image of Joan at the stake may fit those troubled feminist "daughters" who set Friedan thinking about the Second Stage—women so committed to a cause, be it careerism or women's rights, that they have become estranged from men and deprived of families. If only Friedan had come up with a program the Joans of the 1980s could trust! Still, we can hope that the readers of *The Second Stage,* like those of *The Feminine Mystique,* will take matters into their own hands, advancing the cause of women as much in the next two decades as in the two just past. (pp. 32-4)

> *Megan Marshall, "What Women Want in the 1980s. . . ," in* The New Republic, *Vol. 186, No. 3, January 20, 1982, pp. 32-4.*

R. Emmett Tyrrell, Jr.   (essay date February 1982)

[*In the following excerpt from an editorial in which he nominates* The Second Stage *as the worst nonfiction book of the year, Tyrell derogates Friedan as an "egregious pest."*]

Friedan is one of our foremost national pontificators, which is to exalt her above a multitude. The Republic may not be abundant with learned minds—higher education has seen to that—but it is full of fanatics vehemently pontificating quackery in the abstruse. In the early 1960s the authoress's bugaboo was "the feminine mystique," with its idealization of the concubine and the garbage disposal. Now her bugaboo is "the feminist mystique," a "reactive mystique" whose aversion to family life played right into the hands of Ronald Reagan and "the far right." Her solution is a "second stage" that comes down smartly in favor of "the choice to have babies." Friedan has discerned "that core of women's personhood that is fulfilled through love, nurture, home." The family "is the nutrient matrix of our personhood." Hence, the second stage will be "generative," and even observant of "the grounding . . . realities of daily life." This glad and glorious morn will keep the harried forces of patriarchy on the run, however, for the second stage will be lived in strict accordance with the Beta "mode." That is the feminine "mode" characterized by "synthesizing, into intuitive, qualitative thinking" that comprehends the "relational." These are her findings! She has taught these mysteries at Temple University, Yale University, The New School for Social Research, and Queens College. She has been a Senior Research Associate at the Center for the Social Sciences at Columbia. The Ford Foundation funds her "researches."

The plangent stupidity of this egregious pest, then, is not unfamiliar. It is the wisdom of our pop thinkers, the yahoos who liven things up on college campuses, in foundations, in the churches, wherever nervous breakdowns are admired and the growing-changing-experiencing ethic prevails. She has no more bugs in her coco than any of the other *philosophes* who write those moronic books about body language and future shock and the rights of puppy dogs. That she was—as Anne Crutcher points out in these pages—asked to lecture at the United States Military Academy against manliness and on behalf of an army populated by "sensitive and yearning and vulnerable" George Pattons is but an indication of how far this doltishness has been allowed to travel in modern America.

Friedan has achieved a lot. She has spoken to an entire generation of young women and left them miserable, filling housewives with doubt and embarrassment while sending the professional gals out to scrimmage for their daily grub. The spectacle has fortified the prejudices of every misogynist. Though the working gals have multiplied in number, they have not multiplied in any achievements not directly tied to politics and to government coercion. In most areas of male endeavor there are no more female prodigies than ever before, and in some areas of endeavor, for instance international athletic competition, American women have lost their edge to the women from the least liberated lands of all. Now Friedan suggests the gals have babies, but that the carping continue not only against men but also against the corporations.

I do not believe that she could have achieved so much had she not been so invincibly stupid through all these years. . . . In our age, basic stupidity has replaced talent and learning as the engine for intellectual achievement. (pp. 4-5)

R. Emmett Tyrrell, Jr., "The Worst Book of the Year," in The American Spectator, Vol. 15, No. 2, February, 1982, pp. 4-5.

Betty Friedan with Paula Gribetz Gottlieb (interview date February 1982)

[*In the following interview, Gottlieb and Friedan discuss the social issues which prompted Friedan to write* The Second Stage.]

[*Gottlieb*]: *What prompted you to write* **The Second Stage**?

[Betty Friedan]: I have a continuing commitment to the women's movement—after all, I helped start it—and I felt that without this second stage, *The Feminine Mystique* would be aborted. Women could be stuck halfway through, and there might be a real reaction against the women's movement in the next generation. During the past few years I've traveled around the country, talking and lecturing, and I began to worry when I met women—young and not so young, especially women in their 30s—with awful conflicts about having children. They told me they were not going to have children, but I could tell they weren't very happy about the decision. Childbearing seems to me such a strong value of life. That worried me. Then this superwoman stuff began to worry me, too.

So, on the one hand, I was working this out theoretically in my university lectures and, on the other hand, I was observing younger women who had a whole new set of problems. I wrote a few articles about it, and I also raised some of these questions in my teaching and lecturing. I began to have an increasing uneasiness that something was going wrong. And I saw that the official feminist agenda, the first-stage agenda, was just not where these women were—they had other needs and problems to deal with.

What is the "feminist mystique" and why is it so dangerous?

A mystique is an image that short-changes the reality of an idea or denies part of its totality. The feminine mystique that I wrote about tried to define women solely in terms of marriage, motherhood, sexual relationships and service of home. It ignored the woman as a person and, therefore, it limited, truncated, women's possibilities. Now there is a danger that feminism, too, is becoming a mystique. There's a tendency to throw the baby out with the bathwater and to deny that part of the personhood does indeed come from traditional sources of women's identity.

When I said there was a danger of a *feminist* mystique, I meant an agenda so concentrated on that which had been denied—the ability and need of a woman to move as a person, in her own right—that it denies that there are other aspects to her life. We had to break through the feminine mystique, but this is not to deny that those other aspects are also part of the personhood of woman. What is needed now is an integration of the two.

Just as the feminine mystique was a pseudo-glorification of the housewife that really denigrated her, so in a certain sense the feminist mystique glorifies career. It is a pseudo-glorification that makes woman a prisoner of that career—passive to that career and shortchanged by it.

In your new book you call for the woman's movement to embrace the idea of family. Why is this so important?

We have to embrace our own roots in the family, our responsibilities to the family and our needs for family. And I mean families in all their diversity and in the realities that they change over time. We must understand that this is as important a side of our lives as our careers are.

The Moral Majority, the radical Right, people like Jesse Helms [Republican Senator, NC], use the concept of family demagogically, and they play to real needs of people. I think that people are concerned about families. I don't believe that young people today have a good enough choice on whether to start a family or not. The reality that parents have to work outside the home is not taken into account by society in terms of the family. So we don't have the necessary restructuring of hours and aids in child care.

It is for the welfare of families that you need things like child care. It's a lie to wave the flag of family and then to prevent action on new solutions that real families—especially children—now need.

But it is our own paralysis and our blind spots that have enabled the Moral Majority to become so powerful. They don't represent any majority of people in the United States, but they certainly have taken up the flag for family life and God, and those are real values for most Americans.

You can't counter real values by not recognizing them, because if you don't recognize the real needs then you're dealing in obsolete, truncated terms yourself. After all, there hasn't been a really strong effort on the part of the women's movement, on the part of many feminists, to embrace the necessities of families today.

We have created a vacuum that the Moral Majority walked into. You don't fight the banners of people who say they are for the right to life. I say we are for abortion, but that's like being for mastectomy. We are for the choice to have children, for affirming the generative roots of women in families. We want to make it a good choice, good for the children in families as well as for the life of the woman herself.

You seem very optimistic about the changes in the workplace that you see as inevitable. Why?

As the number of women in the work force approaches 50 percent and as the majority of women are now working, the reality of work life has to lead to restructuring work—restructuring jobs as well as restructuring homes. Half the people in the work force give birth to children, and the other half now are expected to share the burdens of child rearing. And it's about time.

Furthermore, everything we know about technological development and the development of work and what's likely to happen in the next stage indicates that flexitime will evolve naturally.

The first stage of the Industrial Revolution may have required that people on the assembly line perform robotlike jobs, but things are changing. I've had interesting discussions with people working for the telephone company who demanded a whole new approach to the quality of work life. They insisted that they be given more autonomy in controlling their own work, instead of punching a time clock. People are insisting on more control over their work lives, and these issues go beyond just women.

With a greater percentage of women in the work force, child-care structures will change. What is your vision of the future of parenting in the US?

The reality is that parenting is going to have to be shared between the mother, the father and the government.

The image of the soulless federal day-care system, of handing your child over to the state, is horrifying to women because their roots are in family and the idea of motherhood is so crucial to their identity. But women are facing up to reality. They can't keep running a home and take care of the children as their mothers did if they're also going to work outside the home. So what we need is diverse options for ensuring good care of children, giving mother or father some option to take parental leaves and reduce their schedules, or something like Milton Friedman's concept of the negative income tax or the voucher system, which the conservatives are suggesting for other purposes. We should institute a child allowance, which other nations do. Every person who takes primary responsibility for the care of a child or a dependent adult would receive a certain allowance paid as income, like a tax rebate. If the mother and father jointly share the responsibility of the child, then it should be paid to both. When they both work, then the child allowance is used to help pay for child care. Child care can be offered for profit or not for profit, by unions, by community agencies, by the local community using empty school buildings, or use a federal block grant for it. The single solution that we used to talk about in the early days is not feasible anymore: 24-hour child care, free for the children of all income levels, paid for by federal taxes. It was a dream. What's really important is that there should be a diversity of child care in the community that parents can control.

Why do working women feel that they have to be superwomen?

I call that "female machismo," and it stems from their mothers and grandmothers. When the man had to define himself solely as the one who could beat up the other man or who scored bigger in the rat race of success, he had to hide his own humanness by excessive machismo.

When the woman had to define her whole identity in terms of the house and the children, it had to be a perfectly run home and there had to be perfectly controlled children. And the superwoman syndrome evolved from these exaggerated pressures, not from the actual double burden of working in the office and in the home. In the rat race, men were willing to conform to excessive demands because that was supposed to be their whole identity. But in addition to these career standards, women have excessive standards at home (which don't necessarily have anything to do with the real needs of a healthy child or a livable home), handed down from those kinds of communities where the mothers derived their only power, status and control from the home.

How will the increased number of women in the workplace affect men and the nature of work?

The battle of the first stage was for women to break into a man's world. But in the second stage we're going to see the value of woman's world, only it's no longer going to be woman's world or man's world—they're both going to be shared.

There's nothing wrong with ambition in women or with aggression, with assertiveness, with success. Let us all enjoy whatever of it we can. One of the reasons for the tendency of men to fall into the machismo trap and to have a gray and linear identity was because they were defined solely in terms of rat-race success. If in that competitive world everything rests on success, then men are passive to that, and underneath they really are cowering.

What is liberating for men is to find other aspects of their identity—this is the other half of the women's movement. They can find their feelings, their real identity in the family in terms of the emotional relationships and the nurturing that strengthens anybody, not just the competitive drive.

But then how ironic if the woman would shortchange those parts that have been her strengths, that have given her flexibility and sensitivity, even probably longer life, fewer ulcers, strokes, and heart attacks. How tragic if she would sacrifice those nurturing and nurturing parts of her personhood and let herself be boxed in by that narrow definition of career and success that makes her passive and helpless to the demands of the corporation.

What would you advise a Working Woman *reader?*

I'd say to her, "Don't exchange one half-life for another." We had to react against something, break through one mystique, break through a barrier, and we haven't completely finished that job yet. But it is not a good bargain to put yourself totally at the mercy of one half of life. Everything we know teaches us that the self rests on the twin roots of work and love.

Abilities are also needs. You need to use your ability. Aside from the economic needs, there are psychological needs—for status, identity, participation in the world, some sense of meaning—and the abilities themselves must be used by women and men.

Could you sum up the message of **The Second Stage***?*

We must begin to ask new questions and, even though we don't have any answers, the asking will free the women now feeling in an unquiet way that they may be shortchanging themselves. It will free women just to see that there are problems with both the standards they have been accepting at work and at home. And that they have every right to want the fullness of life in both places. But in order to put it all together, they must begin to question the standards and seek new solutions that go beyond the agenda of the first stage of the women's movement. And these new solutions are going to be every bit as important to men in the next stage. (pp. 130, 132)

> *Betty Friedan and Paula Gribetz Gottlieb, in an interview in* Working Woman, *Vol. 7, No. 2, February, 1982, pp. 130, 132.*

Mary Warnock   (review date 30 July 1982)

[*In the following review, Warnock finds Friedan's message in* The Second Stage *valid if not particularly applicable to the lives of British women.*]

Betty Friedan, whose **The Feminine Mystique** was published twenty years ago, has taken another look at the Women's Movement; or rather, if the claims implied both in the blurb and by herself are to be accepted, she has taken a first detached look at what she herself created and has written a mid-term report on her own child. **The Second Stage** has one very simple theme: for women, the achieving of independence and a satisfactory life does not entail antagonism to men. Men should now be seen, not as the enemy, but as the trusted ally.

This agreeable message is dragged out to considerable length. The style is flabby and tends to be rhetorical; and the book as a whole, being deeply American, translates uneasily to England, despite an explanatory introduction by Carolyn Faulder and Sandra Brown. Though in this introduction women are called on to "seize the initiative now by making their feminism a world stage for action", the British reaction to the second stage may well be that it is a fuss about nothing, a mountain made out of a molehill. Loud denigration of men, the shrill cries of those drawing up demarcation contracts over the housework, the crackle of burning bras or eye-brow pencils, none of these sounds were ever heard more than faintly in this country, and, when they were heard, they were dismissed as coming from the lunatic fringe (or that useful scapegoat "the small disruptive minority"). Equally, the defenders of family life against the feminists have not needed to be as insistent as they have been on the other side of the Atlantic.

But it would be wrong to dismiss all the problems discussed in this book as irrelevant or exaggerated. Even if, in America, there has been a greater degree of polarization, the feminist *contra* family, it cannot be denied that feminism, the "raising of consciousness", has had an enormous effect on English women, even the most dutiful and conservative. And the problem of reconciling a proper job, demanding ambition and the display of a bossy nature, with family responsibilities and the tendency to *give in,* which is the mark of the successful wife, exists now, and has existed ever since the end of the Second World War. Moreover there is here, almost as commonly as in America, a type of "male" who is built up by the advertising profession, the man who will dominate, conversationally, sexually, in the committee room and on the road. It is particularly noticeable for us, on this side of the Atlantic, that

when Margaret Thatcher dominates conversation, as she sometimes does, refusing absolutely to listen to the voice of others, she is thought of as being "unfeminine"; and Mrs Friedan herself, in an *Observer* interview, spoke of her as exhibiting "the male model of leadership". Conversely, though Mrs Friedan does not place enough emphasis on this, there is still in existence the woman who lets the side down by insisting that "her husband wouldn't like it" if she stayed late at work, came to a staff-meeting after school, or lifted a heavy piece of equipment: the Little Woman is by no means dead.

Mrs Friedan is right to argue that the area within which these deeply ingrained attitudes must now be changed, if they can be, is the family; and if we are to be realistic, the concept of the family itself ought also to change. For it is no longer the case, and has not been for a long time, that the "true" or most typical family, consists of an earning father, a home-bound mother and two or three children. There is a vast number of families where both parents work; there are single-parent families; there are people living together unmarried, with or without a child. The very word "family" has become suspect because of the false image it suggests. It has become an ad-man's word, inextricably bound up with cornflakes and safe television viewing. But in this country it hasn't quite such guilt-producing power as it has in the United States. The demand for perfection, for perfect good-humour, understanding, cleanliness and "niceness" . . . the domination of the dainty, has not had so powerful an effect here as in America. Perhaps the British are simply better prepared to put up with a bit of squalor, dirt and untidiness than their American cousins. If so, this is probably why feminism has not, here, had to be so violent.

But if the concept of family life is indeed to change, whether by the greater participation of men in domestic life, or if housing is redesigned so that the extended family can become a reality, with neighbours actually sharing the work and the amenities, as Mrs Friedan suggests, it is economic rather than feminist factors that will change it. Unemployment may turn out to be the great equalizer. It is no good being male, aggressive and ambitious if there is no job in which to display these characteristics. Indeed it is intolerable to be ambitious if there is a risk of remaining unemployed. Far better, and nicer, to decide that work isn't everything, and opt for a greater quality of life; and if this involves sharing the shopping, sitting in the launderette with your book, or taking the babies to the park in the mornings, so much the more enjoyable. Men and women may well find themselves *faute de mieux* in the same boat.

At the end of the second stage, Betty Friedan speculates about the consumer-market in such an equalized state of affairs. If women are no longer "kept"; if they are no longer frustrated by their powerlessness outside the home, will they continue to demand more and more possessions? "Having", she implies, has been a substitute for "doing". If "personhood" (her word) goes with a less acquisitive mood, will Capitalism survive? My guess is that it will. But it would have been worth pursuing this line: The Economic Consequences of the Peace.

> *Mary Warnock, "Peace between Sexes," in*

The Times Literary Supplement, *No. 4139, July 30, 1982, p. 822.*

Mary Kenny (essay date February 1983)

[*In the following excerpt, Kenny compares* The Second Stage *to* The Feminine Mystique.]

Twenty years after her first book, in 1982, Betty Friedan published a fresh look at the women's movement which she called *The Second Stage*—a very different kind of book in a very different kind of time. The recession was accepted as a depressing fact of life: unemployment and inflation had become grave in every country in the world. Many of the radical movements of the 1960s had taken a bitter turning: the students' rebellions in Western Europe had laid the ground for the terrorism of the Baader-Meinhof gang and the Red Army Fraction. The "flower children" of America had given way to drugs, bombsters, and the fringe horrors of a Charles Manson. The civil rights movement of Northern Ireland had opened the door to the IRA. Among women, nothing as bloodthirsty had happened, but the price of what freedom had been won was often high.

In Britain, divorce had quadrupled over a period of twenty years. Women who once "chose" to seek liberation in work were now obliged to slog it out in the market-place just to keep up with the demands of inflation. (Ironically, the working wife was one of the contributory causes of inflation, as two-income families unwittingly pushed up the price of houses and other commodities to the detriment of single-income families.) Abortion, which had been expected to fade away with better contraception, rose in England and Wales from 49,000 in 1969 (the first year the Abortion Act was fully operative) to 130,000 in 1980. The pattern was similar in the United States, as in most developed countries.

What Betty Friedan saw when she came to *The Second Stage* was not a picture of women who were "underachieved" in their suburban homes, but a picture of women who were stretched to the limit: under stress, competing with their husbands (and ex-husbands) in the employment market, often vying with their teenage children for jobs, reeling from the fatigue of trying to keep home and work together, greatly disadvantaged by the breakdown of the family which the women's movement had helped to engineer. In *The Feminine Mystique,* Betty Friedan had noticed that the married women who had careers were supported by the housewives in their circle (if a child was sick, or there were problems at home, neighbours would help). In *The Second Stage* she noted that there were no housewives left at home to provide any support at all. In place of the bewildered housewife with the fake cake-mix, she found an ailing New York career woman alone in her apartment; her neighbour, also an overstretched Superwoman, was "too busy" to drop by with a carton of milk. (Telling details. Betty was always good at that.)

As for "housework", it also figured in Betty's recantation. Had it only been a series of menial tasks fit for morons; or was it also about caring for the people one loved? Marriage may have been a male plot to keep women in their place, but most women still seemed to want it. The sexual revolution had produced freedom for women; it also produced an increase in rape, violence against women, exploitation, pornography, and an epidemic of herpes. (Shulamith Firestone had claimed that a woman's freedom could only really be achieved when her babies were conceived and developed in laboratories; this was becoming eerily true with *in vitro* fertilisation and the prospect of fetal development artificially.) Women who had rallied for abortion demonstrations were now, Betty Friedan noted, frantically trying to have babies, often "against the biological clock." And the most distressing phenomenon was that men seemed to have changed scarcely at all.

The Second Stage is an older, sadder, more disillusioned book; it is also less neat, less specific, less certain in its conclusions and prescriptions. What women need now, Betty proclaims vaguely, is the ability to alter men and the right to produce their children joyfully as and when they want to. Evidently nobody has yet mentioned to her that nature does not award rights. (pp. 28-9)

Mary Kenny, "In the Driver's Seat," in Encounter, *Vol. LX, No. 2, February, 1983, pp. 28-9.*

Betty Friedan (essay date January-February 1991)

[*In the following essay, Friedan discusses contemporary issues facing the women's movement.*]

I argued in *The Feminine Mystique* that American women are being hoodwinked by an elaborate myth which seeks to persuade them that marriage and a career are incompatible and that domesticity offers them the best chance for fulfillment.

For over a year now, two years maybe, we have been experiencing a dangerous tendency toward a *new* feminine mystique. Recent events having to do with Barbara Bush and Wellesley College (her being chosen as its commencement speaker) made me feel a lot more seriously about its impact. In the confused discussion, it seems to me there has been a symptomatic and dangerous polarization of women against women—a distortion not only of the choices Barbara Bush once had but of the choices facing women today.

Twenty-five or 30 years ago, nobody really asked, "What do you want to be, little girl, when you grow up?" We asked ourselves, "What do I want to be when my children grow up?" But the headiness that began in the 1960s brought the whole sense of *personhood* of woman—not the either-or but the yes, of course, marriage, motherhood. It's a headiness of being taken seriously enough, of being able to take ourselves seriously enough to sense that we could choose—that we could have a life that would use our education, our talents, our abilities, and that we could move in society ourselves. That made all the difference.

We began to empower each other to fight for real equality. The personhood of woman had to come first. We had to be able to say, "I am a person." As Nora said when she left the doll's house, "I am a person. I am a person just like you are. And until I find out what kind of person I can be, I am not sure how good a wife and mother I can be." So we broke out of the old mold. We empowered each other to begin to move for true equality and to define for ourselves the personhood of woman. By our actions and then by our words, we began to move into the professions.

Today there is a new set of problems. The women who work outside the home, through a combination of new opportunity, new vision and ambition, and new inflation-bred economic necessity, are now the overwhelming majority. And they do not wait until after the children are in school to begin. A majority of women with children under six, with children under three, now work outside the home. And while some of us won the battles, and others marched and opened doors of access, a backlash was beginning—a backlash against women's rights.

For a while, there was talk that our daughters were no longer interested in women's rights. With impunity they thought they could take back the very basic right to choose. And they found out differently. We marched— and our daughters marched with us—and we made "choice" the hottest political issue in the November 1988 elections.

For 10 years now, the political mentality of this nation has said it is not the responsibility of government to meet the needs of people. This is not a political problem. It is a personal problem, especially if you are a woman. Don't talk to us about child care; don't talk to us about parental leave. The social programs that existed must be deregulated and abandoned, because government has only one responsibility: to maximize the profits of the corporation. Government says it has no responsibility to people. And Democrats think they have to sound like Republicans in order to get back into the White House.

The whole Wellesley debate seems to have been between feminists who say, "Do your career just the way a man does and don't have children," and others who say that women can make a choice and stay home full time and take care of the children, as Barbara Bush did. In fact, she didn't make a choice; she took the course that was open to her. Similarly, there is no choice open to many women today. They do not have the luxury of staying home full time and taking care of children. But this is not my point. This is not where it is at. We are the only advanced industrial nation besides South Africa without a national policy of child care and parental leave.

We have given the corporations a great source of cheap labor—wonderful, overskilled labor that never has to be promoted beyond mid-level if offered just a little flexibility. With flex time, with maternity leave or whatever, women pay the price of being out of the mainstream and out of the promotion line. A pseudo-solution. A no-win solution.

We get excuses instead of child care and parental leave from the Republican administration. Yes, women are supposed to hold down two jobs now, and nothing else has changed. We have not gone on to the second stage: a restructuring of home and work. Now we must challenge and correct the blind spot.

We must analyze the choice which decided elections in November 1988. It was a choice not just about abortion but also about the decision to have children; the choice to have children before you are 40 and, therefore, the need for parental leave and child care. I challenge the leaders of the women's movement to expand their sense of choice so they will fight with the same passion for parental leave and child care with which they fought for access to abortion. I challenge them to understand that these are not just personal problems. Women who think strongly about being mothers and women who know they want professions and careers must not polarize each other. Instead, they must join together in a new second stage of the women's movement. Yes, my sisters and daughters, into the breach once again—and march, march, so that we can have real choices. Otherwise, there is no win in the feminine mystique. (pp. 26-7)

> *Betty Friedan, "Back to the Feminine Mystique?" in* The Humanist, *Vol. 51, No. 1, January-February, 1991, pp. 26-7.*

FURTHER READING

Criticism

Call, Joan. "Women's Choices as Seen by H. L. Mencken and Betty Friedan." *Menckeniana,* No. 107 (Fall 1988): 9-11.
Notes similarities between the views of Friedan and those of Mencken as expressed in his *In Defense of Women.*

French, Marilyn. "The Emancipation of Betty Friedan." *Esquire* 100, No. 6 (December 1983): 510-14, 516-17.
Biographical and critical overview of Friedan's work as activist and writer.

Friedan, Betty. "Feminism Takes a New Turn." *The New York Times Magazine* (18 November 1979): 40, 92, 94, 96, 98, 100, 102, 106.
Presents Friedan's views on issues facing the women's movement for the 1980s.

———. "Twenty Years after *The Feminine Mystique.*" *The New York Times Magazine* (27 February 1983): 35-6, 42, 54-57.
Retrospective view of the women's movement.

Howard, Jane. "Angry Battler for Her Sex." *Life* 55, No. 18 (1 November 1963): 84, 86-88.
Brief profile and photo essay on Friedan.

Interview

Kurtz, Paul. "Humanism and Feminism: New Directions." *The Humanist* XXXIV, No. 3 (May-June 1974): 10-13.
Interview in which Friedan and Jacqueline Ceballos, a former regional director of NOW, discuss such topics as economic goals for women, feminism and religion, and the evolution of the women's movement.

Additional coverage of Friedan's life and career is contained in the following sources published by Gale Research: *Contemporary Authors,* Vols. 65-68; *Contemporary Authors New Revision Series,* Vol. 18; *Contemporary Issues Criticism,* Vol. 2; and *Major 20th-Century Writers.*

Paul Fussell

1924-

American nonfiction writer, essayist, critic, and editor.

The following entry provides an overview of Fussell's career through 1992.

INTRODUCTION

Although he began his writing career as a specialist in eighteenth-century literature, Fussell has reached a widespread popular audience with his nonfiction studies on warfare, travel, and social class. His studies are noted for their extensive scholarship and accomplished prose style as well as their often polemical tone. His first major work, *The Great War and Modern Memory,* which examines the cultural impact of World War I on the modern era, was awarded the National Book Critics Circle Award and the National Book Award. Fussell's commentary on military subjects is informed by his combat experience during the Second World War, and he has described himself as a "pissed-off infantryman, disguised as a literary and cultural commentator." Ronald B. Schwartz observed that Fussell "fashions himself as a kind of thinking man's John Wayne, wielding prose with a certain fetching swagger and acid humor, and blaming it all on nothing less than his stint as a combat platoon leader in WWII."

The son of a wealthy corporate lawyer, Fussell was born in Pasadena, California. While attending college, he enrolled in the Reserve Officer Training Corps, and in 1943 began training as an infantryman. The following year he was shipped to France as a second lieutenant in charge of a combat rifle platoon. In March of 1945, Fussell was severely wounded in the back and legs by a burst of shrapnel. Although he was later found to be partially disabled, Fussell was assigned to the 45th Infantry Division, which was then preparing for an invasion of Japan. Shortly before the invasion was to take place, the United States dropped atomic bombs on Hiroshima and Nagasaki, thus ending the war. After demobilization, Fussell returned to college under the GI Bill, earning a master's degree and a doctorate from Harvard, and began a teaching career in 1951.

During the first twenty years of his academic career, Fussell wrote several books on eighteenth-century literature and poetic theory. Although critics disputed some of Fussell's interpretations and conclusions, particularly in *The Rhetorical World of Augustan Humanism* and *Samuel Johnson and the Life of Writing,* these works were praised as valuable and thought-provoking contributions to literary scholarship. In his first best-selling work, *The Great War and Modern Memory,* Fussell explores the cultural impact of World War I on twentieth-century life, focusing on "the British experience on the Western Front from

1914 to 1918 and some of the literary means by which it has been remembered, conventionalized, and mythologized." Analyzing a variety of literary works as well as unpublished war memoirs, he argues that the dominant change brought about by the war is the irony that has since pervaded modernist culture. According to Fussell, traditional romantic forms of art and literature which depicted war as glamorous and heroic proved inadequate to express the realities of mass destruction and suffering. In the opinion of some critics, Fussell overstated the influence of the war on western culture, but most complimented *The Great War and Modern Memory* as a stimulating and novel assessment of the often unrecognized significance of World War I.

Fussell's next work, *Abroad: British Literary Traveling between the Wars,* examines British travel writing from 1919 to 1939 as a distinct literary form, suggesting "what it felt like to be young and clever and literate in the final age of travel." According to Fussell, the adventurous traveling and sophisticated travel writing of the interwar era have been largely replaced by pre-packaged mass tourism and unimaginative guidebooks. Some reviewers found his attitude toward tourism unnecessarily condescending; however, several commentators commended Fussell for reviving interest in the accomplishments of travel writers.

In *Wartime: Understanding and Behavior in the Second World War,* Fussell argues that although World War II was necessary, it was abominable. As he explains in his preface: "The damage the war visited upon bodies and buildings, planes and tanks and ships, is obvious. Less obvious is the damage it did to intellect, discrimination, honesty, individuality, complexity, ambiguity, and irony, not to mention privacy and wit. For the past fifty years the Allied war has been sanitized and romanticized almost beyond recognition by the sentimental, the loony patriotic, the ignorant, and the bloodthirsty. I have tried to balance the scales." In addition to examining literature, memoirs, propaganda, and journalism, Fussell cites numerous examples of needless slaughter and military blunders to present a realistic portrait of life during the war. Noting the contrast between the despair of demoralized soldiers in the field, who, Fussell posits, were primarily fighting for their own survival, and the way their struggle was presented as a high-minded, ideological cause, he concludes that "the real war will never get in the books." Although some reviewers felt that Fussell failed to emphasize the political necessity of the war and a few viewed him as a Nazi sympathizer, most nevertheless applauded his efforts to debunk the myths surrounding the Second World War.

Class: A Guide through the American Status System examines the nature of class distinctions in the United States, generally focusing on the middle and upper classes. Fussell finds that differences between the classes primarily depend on various preferences for certain types of clothes, housing, automobiles, and other possessions and includes a do-it-yourself test to determine which social class the reader occupies. In *BAD; or, The Dumbing of America* Fussell denounces everything that he finds "phony, clumsy, witless, untalented, vacant, or boring that many Americans can be persuaded is genuine, graceful, bright, or fascinating." Some critics found portions of these books amusing, but most considered them elitist and condescending towards the middle class.

In addition to his full-length critical studies, Fussell has published numerous essays on literature, warfare, travel, and social class. The title of *The Boy Scout Handbook, and Other Observations* is taken from a piece in which he performs a rhetorical and literary analysis of the ninth edition of the official boy scout handbook, asserting that it is "among the very few remaining popular repositories of something like classical ethics, deriving from Aristotle and Cicero." The final essay in the volume, "My War," details Fussell's personal experience during the Second World War. In the title essay of *Thank God for the Atom Bomb, and Other Essays,* Fussell asserts that although the decision to drop atomic bombs on Japan was a "vast historical tragedy" it saved the lives of at least a million servicemen, including his own, and argues that most of those who object to the decision were either too young for military service or in no position to suffer the consequences of staging a land invasion. While some critics found his arguments for using atomic weapons offensive, many respected Fussell's complex moral outlook regarding the event.

Fussell has also edited the war memoirs of Siegfried Sassoon and Alfred M. Hale, as well as *The Norton Book of Travel.* After compiling *The Norton Book of Modern War,* a critical anthology of literary responses to twentieth-century warfare, Fussell commented: "I found it so depressing, really, that I'd like to write a cheerful book, about the circus or the theater or something a little elevating. I'm tired of writing about mass murder and its meaning. After a while, you're persuaded that it doesn't have any meaning."

PRINCIPAL WORKS

Theory of Prosody in Eighteenth-Century England (criticism) 1954

Poetic Meter and Poetic Form (criticism) 1965; revised edition, 1979

The Rhetorical World of Augustan Humanism: Ethics and Imagery from Swift to Burke (criticism) 1965

Samuel Johnson and the Life of Writing (criticism) 1971

The Great War and Modern Memory (nonfiction) 1975

The Ordeal of Alfred M. Hale [editor] (memoirs) 1975

Abroad: British Literary Traveling between the Wars (criticism) 1980

The Boy Scout Handbook, and Other Observations (essays) 1982

Class: A Guide through the American Class System (nonfiction) 1983; also published as *Class,* 1984; also published in England as *Caste Marks: Style and Status in the U.S.A.,* 1984

Siegfried Sassoon's Long Journey: Selections from the Sherston Memoirs [editor] (memoirs) 1983

The Norton Book of Travel [editor] (anthology) 1987

Thank God for the Atom Bomb, and Other Essays (essays) 1988

Wartime: Understanding and Behavior in the Second World War (nonfiction) 1989

BAD: or, the Dumbing of America (nonfiction) 1991

The Norton Book of Modern War [editor] (anthology) 1991

CRITICISM

The Times Literary Supplement (review date 16 February 1967)

[*In the following review, the critic favorably appraises* The Rhetorical World of Augustan Humanism *but finds the second part of the work weaker than the first.*]

Dr. Fussell has written an intelligent and important book—or rather, two books, the second somewhat less good than the first. The subtitle [of ***The Rhetorical World*** *of Augustan Humanism*] is "Ethics and Imagery from Swift to Burke", and (oversimplifying his scheme a little) the author devotes his first book to a discussion of the eighteenth-century humanist ethic as it reveals itself in the six writers he takes as constituting "the central nervous system" of the age, and his second to a study of the way in which their preoccupations reveal themselves in shared patterns of imagery. Dr. Fussell is well aware of the important differences between his chosen writers (the others being Pope, Johnson, Reynolds and Gibbon), but he is here attempting a synthesis, and he succeeds in showing how humanist calls sombrely to humanist across a whole century.

Acknowledging the imprecision of the term "humanist", Dr. Fussell devotes an excellent opening chapter to listing a dozen main attributes of humanism, distinguishing the eighteenth-century variety as "a more or less diminished and secularized version of the Christian humanism of the English Renaissance", and stressing the importance of Locke and (particularly for Johnson) of the Raphael-Adam conversation on the limits of human inquiry.

As he points out, the great humanists were already a bit old-fashioned, at war with many of the "official" assumptions of their progressivist and sentimental age. Unable by definition to leave serious moral subjects alone, they all in their different ways express severe moral discomfort in a world rapidly turning "modern" about them. They are beset by enemies, including mechanism, the rationalism of Hobbes and Descartes, the sentimentality of Shaftesbury and Hutcheson, the new enthusiasm both scientific and religious, Grub Street and all its ways, and all the "new utopian flippancy about man and his mortal state" summed up in the figure of the wretched Soame Jenyns. The counter-tradition, running from Defoe to Burns and Blake, includes such men as Addison, Thomson, Young and Cowper—though the difficulty of drawing firm lines is exemplified by the fact that Dr. Fussell places Goldsmith in this team, while later quoting several examples of Goldsmith clearly wearing the humanist jersey.

For the humanist, man is a paradox. Pope's summary of him as "Sole judge of Truth, in endless Error hurl'd: / The glory, jest, and riddle of the world!" echoes the words of that earlier great humanist, Hamlet. Man is a failure, who must see himself as a social animal because he is too frail and incomplete to exist by himself. His problems are mostly insoluble and—for the majority of humanists, perhaps—there is no help to be obtained from outside; and yet his dignity lies partly in his capacity for apprehending or contriving such problems. His spirit or *anima,* the possibility of a limited redemption through choice or free will, his ability to use his memory and power of abstraction in order to liberate himself from slavery to matter, place and time—these are the weapons in the humanist's armoury, and account for so many of his preoccupations, artistic and otherwise.

Dr. Fussell shows how much of eighteenth-century literary theory derives from the self-distrust of the humanist—the reliance on the authority of the literary past, the doctrine of genres or "kinds", the duty to instruct through pleasing, the insistence on objectivity and impersonality,

the painstaking rhetorical attention to be exercised by the artist. Such phrases as "the grandeur of generality" are seen less as critical observations than as moral and philosophic articles of faith, and Dr. Fussell rightly points out that the deeper one penetrates into the heart of his central figure, Johnson, "the more one perceives that what at first looks like personal singularity is actually often some manifestation of Renaissance humanism slightly disguised".

Apart from the clarity of the thought and the deftness of expression, what gives this first section of the book much of its force is Dr. Fussell's own involvement, his evident sense of commitment to what he feels as the moral beauty of the great Augustans. Occasionally his enthusiasm carries him too far; when (in a phrase he uses of Johnson) he gets his humanist steam up it is hard to stop him. Thus, he speaks of Pope's question "Why has not Man a microscopic eye? / For this plain reason, Man is not a Fly" as "suggestive of the imagery of *King Lear*", but the resemblance is surely trivial. Again, Cowley's deathbed prayer ("O Lord, I believe; help my unbelief . . . ") is described as "humanist", but its origin in St. Mark's Gospel is not particularly so. Elsewhere Dr. Fussell seems to have been led into overstatement and sometimes distortion; but one's local disagreements do not detract from the sense of a considerable and original achievement in this part of his work.

The second and longer section attempts to show how the Augustan humanists used, to the point of obsession, images or image-systems drawn from five main groups— warfare, architecture, clothes, insects, and travel; a concluding chapter deals with the use of elegiac motifs, and ends (rather in the manner of Caroline Spurgeon) with the evocation of a peopled landscape made up of the dominant humanist images.

The most valuable aspect of this part is its insistence on the importance of figurative language in eighteenth-century writing, prose as well as poetry, and on the necessity for the modern reader to be alive to this metaphorical quality. Much Augustan imagery admittedly seems unexciting and has passed into cliché or lies buried in the Latin root meaning of words; but the reader who will acquire or regain the sensitivity to language possessed by the great Augustans will be well rewarded, and may indeed find himself travelling within the countryside described in Dr. Fussell's "moral geography".

Here again, Dr. Fussell is aware of the dangers of overstatement. He recognizes, for example, that the humanists do not have a monopoly of military imagery, of seeing life as a battle or a siege; but, this caveat made, he nevertheless pushes some of his points too far. Thus it is surely wrong to see "veteran" in Johnson's line "Superfluous lags the vet'ran on the stage" as in any sense a military image, even though Johnson's Dictionary gives "an old soldier" as one of the definitions. The trouble with image-collecting is that it is too easy to be led away by zeal. One finds what one is looking for. If one is looking for humanists, one can find them behind every bush; if one has already decided that the creature behind the bush is not going to be a humanist, then the situation must be reinterpreted.

An example will illustrate the difficulties. The insect-figure is, we are told, a touchstone of eighteenth-century humanism; putting it crudely, a writer is or is not a humanist according to his handling of insects, real or imaged. Clearly where Swift or Pope is concerned the insect-figure operates for the most part unambiguously (though there is something almost Keatsian about the way Pope can feel empathy with the spider; and ants and bees, of course, have always to be excepted from generalizations about the unpleasantness of insects). Cowper, on the other hand, is not properly contemptuous of insects, and has not observed them properly, and therefore is not a humanist—or rather, because he is not a humanist he is not properly contemptuous. A passage from "The Task" (in which, we are surprisingly told, "Cowper is engaged in bringing to birth Sterne's Uncle Toby") is cited in support, with the stern comment "Any reader of *King Lear* knows that flies are not 'gay' ". Apart from the fact that one could argue that the small gilded fly lechering in Lear's sight *is* gay enough in its own terms, the reasoning seems very confused here, and has a question-begging tinge to it.

Similarly, Dr. Fussell is troubled by Robert Hooke. The discoveries of the microscopists were "modern" and anti-humanist, but because Hooke's Preface to *Micrographia* ends on an apologetic note which seems to admit that fleas and mites are not as splendid and worthwhile as horses and lions, we are told that "even the naturalist Hooke feels the orthodox (humanist) contempt for things so small, mercurial, evanescent, and hideous as insects", close to the bottom of the moral hierarchy as they are. Yet surely if there is one emotion Hooke does *not* feel it is contempt for the creature or its maker. Almost every insect described in his wonderful book is called beautiful, or lovely, or pretty. Dr. Fussell calls the great engraving, of the flea "especially revolting"; but Hooke's description begins "The strength and beauty of this small creature . . . ", and he can even speak of the blood in its guts as "of a very lovely ruby colour". Which side does this leave Hooke on? Presumably he is an anti-humanist who has allowed himself to slip into a humanist pose in his Preface; and yet his attitude to the Creator is very close to that of Pope, and both men know all about the Great Chain of Being.

The touchstone, then, may be of uncertain efficacy; there are many places where one could dispute in similar fashion and produce counter-examples and exceptions. But to stress this is to be less than fair to Dr. Fussell, who does not, after all, claim that a humanist shall be known by his images alone. The second part of his book is admittedly tentative; its main purpose is to illustrate the insights of the first part and the author does make out a fair case for demonstrating how and why characteristic Augustan humanist images differ from those of, say, the Romantics. He has attempted to "write a work less of literary or historical scholarship than of interpretation, suggestion and recommendation", and he has succeeded admirably.

"Humans and Insects," in The Times Literary Supplement, *No. 3390, February 16, 1967, p. 128.*

Frank Lentricchia, Jr.   (review date May 1967)

[*In the following excerpt, Lentricchia praises Fussell's approach to discussing poetic theory in* Poetic Meter and Poetic Form.]

With Paul Fussell's *Poetic Meter and Poetic Form* we get back to the idea that poetry is a complex and "very exacting art" which demands exacting skills from its readers. This book might be required reading for all students of poetry because it makes wonderfully clear the relationship of metrics to the formal achievement of meaning. And that is why, as Fussell says more than once, we are interested in the difficult subject in the first place: a sophisticated grasp of it is not an end in itself—he is no formalist—but a means to the enrichment of the total critical process. It can be said without reservation that Fussell's command of his subject and his never-failing common sense will guarantee that enrichment for anyone who takes the time to read his book.

Each of Fussell's chapters is shaped by the assumption that "art works by artifice, by illusion, and by technique, . . . through, that is, a mastery of the conventions appropriate to the art". And this is to say that, as a non-romantic, Fussell never forgets that art and nature are distinct, that the verbal medium of the poems we turn to over and over again exist primarily as self-contained systems of intricately related verbal and metrical pressures. This literary theory, though it bristles with logical difficulties, has the great virtue of postulating a verbal poetic which, properly applied by the critic, will keep him from making his primary responsibility such secondary problems as the relation of literature and culture, or the relation of literature to various brands of politics and philosophy. Too often, the lure of the humanist calling produces a gross misreading of the artist under consideration. We dare not make generalizations about the relations of poetry and life *before* we have probed the complex structure of artifice in which the artist embeds his tone and meaning. Fussell teaches us just how complex that structure is. (pp. 122-23)

Frank Lentricchia, Jr., "Attitudes toward Literature," in Poetry, *Vol. CX, No. 2, May, 1967, pp. 119-23.*

Walter Allen   (review date 10 May 1971)

[*In the following review of* Samuel Johnson and the Life of Writing, *Allen questions Fussell's definition of literature and his view of Johnson as the archetypal writer while praising the work as a well-written analysis of Johnson's writings and beliefs.*]

According to the publishers, [*Samuel Johnson and the Life of Writing*] is the first book ever to deal with Johnson wholly as a writer. It is in any event an uncommonly good one; witty and elegant, with admirable analyses of Johnson's prose as well as of his beliefs, and infinitely arguable. For the issues it raises go beyond Johnson the individual writer: Mr. Fussell is offering "Johnson as an example of 'the writer,' " Johnson as the archetypal writer, and it is with this, of course, that argument starts.

Mr. Fussell begins by pointing out, as has become almost obligatory when writing of Johnson in our time, that he was a much more complex character than the Johnson of the popular imagination, that "fictive substitute called 'Dr.' Johnson" which was the invention of Boswell and Macaulay, who between them turned him into a "combination of Mr. Punch, John Bull, and a sort of Lord North of criticism, with overtones of creepy, half-sane religious superstition and brutal literary 'prejudices.' "

"What makes his life so interesting," Fussell says in his opening paragraph, "is the unlikeliness of it all."

> He was an ugly, brilliant, neurotic boy from the English Midlands who somehow got through seventy-five years of pain and misery, becoming in the process one of the most sophisticated and versatile of English writers. Just before his death he looked back and saw his existence as "a life radically wretched."

Again:

> Everything about his character and manners was forcible and violent: whether eating, drinking, or lovemaking, reading, writing, or arguing, he found moderation all but impossible, and consequently tended to overvalue it as an ideal principle and to urge it too often upon others. The key to his character is his impetuosity, impatience, and irrationality.

As for his "characteristic way with literature," it was "a violent oscillation between total boredom and idleness, on the one hand, and, on the other, a total engagement that left him exhausted and frightened."

Then there were the consequences of what is tantamount to his religious conversion at Oxford. Of him at this time Fussell writes:

> . . . he was a vigorous, sensual, and emotional youth, but now, thanks to Law's *Serious Call,* also a guilt-ridden one. His violent appetites seemed dangerously at war with his desire to contain them. Strain set in, and he became so melancholic that sometimes he feared he would simply go mad. His compulsive tics and swayings and mutterings became more conspicuous. He even talked of suicide. Forever after he labored under a conviction that he could very easily lose his mind and that his sanity depended almost wholly upon his own self-control.

And the tally of his miseries is not complete. There is the sense of special obligation that against all odds of illness God has allowed him to live. There is too, though Fussell does not mention it, what seems to me plainly his sexual masochism, which comes out in his relations with Mrs. Thrale and was at once, one assumes, the product of guilt and the cause of further guilt.

What is permanently fascinating is the contrast between the extremes of his temperament and the formal order of his writings. There are similar contrasts in Swift and Pope. All three seem to us now, in the nature of their personalities, almost excessively "romantic," but their art is the negation of romanticism. Why? The answer must lie in the disposition of 18th-century society and its expectations of literature. Fussell indicates one aspect of this when he writes: "In the eighteenth century a writer does not 'develop' the way we assume nineteenth- and twentieth-century writers do. Joyce's *Dubliners* is not like *Finnegans Wake* in the way Johnson's earliest work is like his last. The pattern of the literary career conceivable in Johnson's time does not imply development and change—it implies intensification." And there is something else, allied to this: the notion of originality and of the writer's duty to be original was unknown. The great difference between the world of the 18th century and ours is that the 18th century's was a closed world, one in which, in fundamentals, everything was known—which is why Pope could write:

> *True wit is nature to advantage dressed.*
> *What oft was thought but ne'er so well expressed.*

Invention was possible, but not originality.

It was not to be so for long, and what has happened since is what makes our situation so different from the 18th century's. We know that everything is *not* known, that at any given moment truth and knowledge are provisional. The difference between our times and Johnson's may be summed up in a sequence of very obvious names, names that are signs for much else also: Darwin, Marx, Frazer, Freud, Einstein, Jung, Heisenberg. Which is why Fussell on the nature of literature won't entirely do and why his presentation of Johnson as the archetypal writer has to be questioned.

What constitutes literature? Fussell asks, and answers himself:

> Simply this: the decision of an audience that a piece of writing is "literary." An act of what observers will consent to consider literature can take place only when an individual talent engages and, as it were, fills in the shape of a preexisting form that a particular audience is willing to regard as belonging to the world of literature.

Well, yes. The statement has a splendid no-damn-nonsense air about it. But is it more than partially true? What induces the observers, the "audience," to make the decision? Isn't it, and as a simple matter of literary history hasn't it been for the best part of two centuries now, very often the writer himself? How long has it been since a competent observer said William Blake was mad? Isn't the fact of the case that indicated by Wordsworth in his letter to Lady Beaumont?

> Never forget what, I believe, was observed to you by Coleridge, that every great and original writer, in proportion as he is great and original writer, in proportion as he is great and original, must himself create the taste by which he is to be relished; he must teach the art by which he is to be seen. . . .

For Fussell the individual talent "fills in the shape of the pre-existing form." The pre-existing form is the genre. Johnson's "life of writing," Fussell tells us, "took place in the midst of a heady profusion and variety of forms." That the 18th century had a greater sense of genre than we have is no doubt true; but I think Fussell exaggerates the profusion and variety of the genres available to Johnson as compared with those available to our contemporaries. More important, though, is that he sees genres in all too easily definable terms, as his metaphor of the writer filling in pre-existing forms suggests. It is as though the genre were a mold to be filled up with so much molten metal.

> The making of literature is a matter of the engagement of a vulnerable self with a fairly rigid coded medium so though that it bends and alters only under the most rigorous pressure which only the rarest of spirits among writers can exert. The idea of the "coded medium" is a modern way of conceiving of a relatively fixed literary genre. *This coded medium comes inevitably from outside the writer:* otherwise it fails to transmit signals recognizable to the observer.

I suppose the notion that a vulnerable self may be able to exert rigorous pressure on a medium that is not only fairly rigid but also tough may stand; but surely some media are not nearly so rigid and tough as the argument demands. The novel, for instance, is almost infinitely plastic. As for Fussell's italicized sentence, in what sense, apart from the typographical arrangement that indicates that we are in the presence of verse, do the actual poems that are "The Prelude," "Song of Myself," "The Waste Land," Pound's Cantos and Ted Hughes's "Crow" come from "outside the writer"? These were new works, almost one might say new genres, but readers have learned to read them by the very act of reading them. While it is obviously true that genres, pre-existing forms, condition the works that are written in them, it is surely even more obviously true that the genres themselves are bent, altered and finally shaped by those who use them.

For Fussell 18th-century patterns of writing and 18th-century expectations of literature seem to be the norms. I don't think they are, either for the two centuries that have followed or for the Elizabethans and Jacobeans. He is on safer ground when he describes how Johnson filled up *his* genres. He sees Johnson as a writer by default; unable to be a lawyer and having failed as a schoolmaster, he took to Grub Street. But his approach to writing, as Fussell convincingly shows, was a lawyer's. To write was to execute a brief; the act of writing was an exercise in rhetoric in which sincerity and the desire for self-expression scarcely entered.

This is to oversimplify, which Fussell does not do. There were times, as he shows, when for Johnson the claims of sincerity were paramount, and then his "acute awareness of necessary artifice" was cracked as it were in consequence. Fussell's example is the famous criticism of "Lycidas," in which Johnson "chooses to forget that a poem is only a poem, and that by definition the poet is a contriver of effects, not an experiencer of emotion." Indeed, what in the end Fussell seems to me to show us is a Johnson who triumphed over the tyrannies both of genre and of his forensic, rhetorical conception of literature. One might say self-expression crept in. He saw writing as an "elucidation of general human nature" and lacked any "paradigm for open autobiography or confession." Nevertheless, the elucidation of general human nature was intimately related, perhaps based upon, his insights into his own nature. It

is this that gives him his authority as a writer. As Fussell says in his last sentence:

> Johnson's species in the *Lives* of the poets is the writer as representative man, obliged by his frailty to imitate and to adhere to genres and conventions which he has not devised; tormented by the hunger of the imagination only to be always defeated of his hopes; and finally carried away by the very stream of time which it has been his ironic ambition to shape, and by shaping, to arrest.

In this sense, surely, Johnson is a prime example of the writer. Yet the caveat is still necessary. "Writer" is in any case an ambiguous word; and our notions of what constitutes a writer, of what we expect from literature, have changed radically since his day. They have become vaguer, even more ambiguous, at once narrower and wider. This may be seen in the shift in emphasis in the teaching of English that has taken place in universities in the past thirty years. Increasingly literature is construed as "imaginative" literature, poetry, fiction, drama. The quintessential writer is now the poet, in the extended meaning of the word. I think it time the balance was redressed and I hope Fussell's book may help the process. But plainly Johnson, though a poet, was much more a writer at the level of journalist, a writer primarily for periodicals. It is anything but a disappearing breed, but the gap between the journalist and the poet grows wider. A 20th-century equivalent of Johnson, both in his sense of the writer's responsibility and in his professional willingness, almost as a point of professional honor, to try all the genres open to him, would be G. K. Chesterton. One would not, I think, see him as the prime example of the writer. Nor can we any longer see Johnson in that role.

There remains Fussell's book. It raises fundamental questions and it teaches us to read Johnson with greater understanding. If it leads us to read more deeply into Johnson, so much the better. What the rewards will be Fussell's quotations from him indicate. (pp. 601-03)

> *Walter Allen, "Grand Cham of Letters," in* The Nation, *New York, Vol. 212, No. 19, May 10, 1971, pp. 601-03.*

A. Bakshian   (review date 10 August 1971)

[In the following review, Bakshian finds that Samuel Johnson and the Life of Writing *is largely "a cover for airing personal prejudices and pet theories only marginally concerned with the title character."]*

Professor Fussell has resorted to that ancient academic ruse of writing about someone famous, as a cover for airing personal prejudices and pet theories only marginally concerned with the title character. The first 34 pages of [**Samuel Johnson and the Life of Writing**] are an adequate summary of Johnson's life as a writer, but, from there on, it is muddy going. The author takes a few valid swipes at the Romantic school of literature and criticism, which pretends to a new level of "creativity" and "individual inspiration" while looking askance at the less egocentric, less pretentious work of men like Johnson. But then Professor Fussell launches into a sea of twaddle about the writer as the prisoner of genre and other fevered notions, with poor Sam Johnson simply rattling along for the ride. Still, in the midst of much silly and artificial codifying and microanalysis, some real glimmerings of understanding and appreciation for Samuel Johnson seep through. His amazing versatility as a writer has too often been overshadowed by his legendary status as a "character," thanks to the efforts of Boswell and a second wave of men like Macaulay, who disliked Johnson's Toryism and intentionally limned him as a colorful crank. Professor Fussell does not. The real Johnson was, no doubt, an eccentric, even a neurotic, but he was also a sound conservative and a devout Christian in an age that scoffed at both. Fortunately, his prowess as a conversationalist and an advocate were such that he held even the beautiful people at bay. "There is no arguing with Johnson," Oliver Goldsmith once said, "for when his pistol misses fire, he knocks you down with the butt end of it." Were the Great Cham of English letters alive today, he would probably dismiss Professor Fussell with words he once used on James Boswell: "Sir, you have but two topics, yourself and me. I am sick of both."

> *A. Bakshian, in a review of "Samuel Johnson and the Life of Writing," in* National Review, *New York, Vol. XXIII, August 10, 1971, p. 880.*

John J. Roberts (review date Spring/Summer 1977)

[*In the following excerpt, Roberts praises* The Great War and Modern Memory *as an ambitious attempt to assess the impact of the First World War on modern life but finds some of Fussell's conclusions overly speculative, particularly his assertions concerning the influence of postwar literature on popular culture.*]

The modern world began in 1914, according to Paul Fussell, and the change was as stark as that from Eden to the fallen creation; men went to war in prelapsarian naiveté and found only vicious ironies. "The innocent army fully attained the knowledge of good and evil at the Somme on July 1, 1916," Fussell declares. "That moment, one of the most interesting in the whole long history of human disillusion, can stand as the type of all the ironic actions of the war." And that sentence can stand as a good introduction to *The Great War and Modern Memory,* both its strengths and its weaknesses. The book sports crisp, elegant prose, muscular and lithe, frequently allusive; it is always a joy to watch a wordsmith crafting prose, and Fussell's stylistic achievement is the more admirable because of the tremendous number of note cards he obviously had to mold and meld into his running narrative. Something like awe is elicited by the amount of research that must have gone into this book to inform the vast array of topics covered.

However, as the comment on the Somme also indicates, Fussell prodigally scatters assertions and speculations which range from brilliant to outrageous. When he shows how thoroughly Great War diction has come to permeate the civilian vocabulary (barrage, bombard, crummy, lousy, sector, rank and file, over the top, no man's land), we wonder why we never thought of it ourselves. And yet,

with a straight face this same Fussell assures us that "Peculiar to military language is the use of terms with significant unintended meanings which to the outside may easily seem ironic," or that "What we can call gross dichotomizing is a persisting imaginative habit of modern times, traceable, it would seem, to the actualities of the Great War." Just as every language presents ironic meanings to outsiders, just as gross dichotomizing is unfortunately a persistent human habit at all times, so history refuses to split compliantly into Pre-War and Post-War. And even if history were so inclined, urging July 1, 1916, as the watershed founders on the eyebrow-elevating claim that on this one day the innocent army became "fully" initiated.

When the enormity of the task Fussell set himself is considered—nothing less than accounting for the specific origin of the *Zeitgeist* of our remarkable century—it becomes obvious that complete success was never a possibility, and with that in mind we develop considerable respect for how much this book does accomplish. Fussell's fundamental insight into the significance of the Great War is surely valid, so much so that even the temptation to overstate his case is quite understandable. The 1914-18 experience was, after all, an immersion in hyperbole and exaggeration; to cite but one illustration, it was in the Great War that men learned genocide on a massive scale. Fussell puts the War's losses at 6½ million, while other recent estimates approach 10 million dead and 21 million wounded: Passchendaele alone cost 420,000 casualties and the notorious Somme 600,000. Like the numbers in the national debt, such figures balloon into abstractions too amorphous for comprehension. (pp. 390-91)

Paul Fussell establishes the formative impact of the Great War on modern literature, and goes far towards substantiating his claim that the general cast of modern life was set in the trenches. It is his contention that the knowledge of the Front suffused the collective unconscious of Western man; but had that actually transpired, it is unthinkable that the repeated atrocities and violence of our war-ridden century would have been tolerated. A great many of the trench survivors were silent; many others revised their experiences to fit the official version; those who recognized and retained the nightmare clearly and expressed it honestly were, of course, the literary and intellectual remnant, men like Graves and Blunden and Sassoon. Indeed, one could with Fussell's own extensive files of note cards construct a more coherent argument that the Great War altered the perceptions of artists and thinkers but not of most men. The War brought a crisis in language, Fussell points out, because neither hyperbole nor the old, genteel literary vocabulary could cope with the new horrors, and the result was that irony has become the dominant literary mode. Quite true, but irony is not the characteristic means of expression for most men. Popular language and popular entertainment have remained fixed in the older conventions of romance and heroism and virtue triumphant. The popular Hollywood conception of warfare is John Wayne's, even as the best-known verse from the Great War, a favorite with veterans as well as homefolk, has turned out to be John McCrae's "In Flanders Fields," a striking instance of second-rate art prostituted to the service of pro-war propaganda.

Fussell's case, ultimately, rests upon the existence of a unified sensibility following the War, and precisely here is the deciding weakness in his marvelous book. For the twentieth century is the record of anything but a unified Western sensibility. We suffer from a plethora of cultures and subcultures, and what our sociologists bravely call the pluralistic society threatens to collapse about us in a million shards and fragments. Seldom have artists and intellectuals lived in a world so far removed both from the people and from the centers of power, let alone from each other, and these cleavages represent in large measure the tragedy of our time. The origins of these yawning gulfs extend back at least to the Romantic alienation, but of the several causes surely the Great War has not been sufficiently acknowledged. It is a commonplace in the academy that *The Waste Land* is the most important single poem in recent English, and that poem certainly is indebted to the Great War and the trench experience—but how many of our citizens have read it? How many, for that matter, have heard of Mr. Eliot? Fussell holds that the absurdities of *Catch-22* and the obscenities of *Gravity's Rainbow* are the most appropriate way of apprehending and presenting what the Great War did to us, and he may be right—but how many people read Pynchon, and of those who know Heller how many understand? No, Fussell has passed too many years within ivied walls; it is a likely assumption that most of our citizens, if confronted with Heller and Pynchon, Mailer and James Jones, would not see beyond the absurdities and obscenities. Fussell argues that the Great War destroyed the old myths and gave birth to new ones, and so it did, but only for those with ears to hear and eyes to see. (pp. 401-02)

> *John J. Roberts, "Red Sweet Wine of Youth: Poetry and the Great War," in* Parnassus: Poetry in Review, *Vol. 5, No. 2, 1977, pp. 390-403.*

Douglas Kerr   (review date October 1977)

[*In the following review of* The Great War and Modern Memory, *Kerr objects to some of Fussell's conclusions about post–World War I literature while praising his analysis of wartime memoirs.*]

[*The Great War and Modern Memory*] is not just a survey of the literature of the Great War, but an enquiry into the way the war is remembered, and the way that memory has helped to shape modern understanding. We are accustomed to think of the war as a shared trauma which invalidated, for those who lived through it, a whole system of interpreting experience, and which in turn called in question a whole literary tradition. Professor Fussell's book has plenty to tell us about this: but more interesting is his attempt to show how, while life is feeding materials to literature, literature returns the favour by conferring forms on life. The experience of the Great War, as it has been remembered, seems to Professor Fussell a fascinatingly literary one; and he confesses with revealing candour that 'sometimes it is really hard to shake off the conviction that this war has been written by someone'.

He examines war memoirs, prose fiction, 'war poetry', letters, anecdotes, military history, rumour, propaganda, journalism, and scores of unpublished amateur memoirs from the archives of the Imperial War Museum. The result is the most comprehensive account to date of Great War writings. It is especially valuable in showing how many of the conventions of Great War writings are not confined to writers of a high literary consciousness, but are also to be discovered in the humbler records of the literary other ranks.

Professor Fussell's inspection of his texts is always informative and interesting. The book is organized thematically: the sheer bulk of the evidence dictates this. Thus in one chapter he sketches the 'dichotomising habit' which war is bound to inculcate in soldiers (variations on the radical wartime distinction between 'us' and 'them') illustrating its appearance in a wide spectrum of war writings; and this leads into an account of the more ambiguous exploitations of this theme in Sassoon's Sherston trilogy. The chapter 'Arcadian Resources' yields a just and generous treatment of Blunden's *Undertones of War;* but only after an impressive demonstration of the part pastoralism plays in many other war writings, and not only among the more literary writers.

Earlier in the book, Professor Fussell considers Dawn. After exploring some pre-1914 literary treatments of dawn and sunset, he looks at examples of the representation of break of day (and nightfall) in the trenches, both times of day particularly invested with significance by the ritual 'stand-to'. Dawn over the trenches, he suggests, has become part of the collective national memory, even for those who never experienced it; and the traditional equation between dawn and renewed hope has been irrevocably soured. And he goes on to quote from a poem completed four years after the war, 'Under the brown fog of a winter dawn . . . ', whose daybreak reveals a land laid waste and inhabited, like Sorley's dreams, by countless ghosts ('I had not thought death had undone so many').

It is fascinating to see the Great War dawn considered as a sort of genre painting which may be 'remembered' in later writings and actually modify later perception. But it is difficult to know what status to give to Professor Fussell's claim that 'dawn has never recovered from what the Great War did to it'. There are wilder surmises. He notes as 'a persisting imaginative habit of modern times' the tendency to dramatize the frustrations and fears of modern life into the person of some identifiable Enemy. ' "He" is the Communist's "Capitalist", Hitler's Jew, Pound's Usurer, Wyndham Lewis's Philistine, the Capitalist's Communist. He is Yeats's "rough beast".' This habit of 'gross dichotomising', it seems to Professor Fussell, is 'traceable . . . to the actualities of the Great War'. There is enough truth in this to make it very misleading. Certainly the Great War (indeed any war) provides a handy metaphor for this kind of dramatization. But it is only one of many available models; and the habit of gross dichotomizing is not by any means peculiar to the twentieth century.

Professor Fussell is at his best writing about the classic memoirists, Graves, Sassoon, and Blunden. He shows how all three, under the disguise of 'memoirs', produced narratives that are highly organized, each for a particular kind of ironic effect; and while only Graves is actually convicted of lying, the prose records of the war experience of these three poets are a good deal closer to fiction than they encourage the reader to believe. Professor Fussell tells us that frequently the memorialist's understanding of the irony attending events is what enables him to recall them; and this discovery is supported as much by citation of the 'amateur' memoirs from the Imperial War Museum as by the canon of War Literature.

An insistence that irony is the proper and only decent mode for recalling the war leads Professor Fussell, curiously enough, to quarrel with David Jones's *In Parenthesis.* While acknowledging the work to be in many ways a masterpiece, Fussell is suspicious of the referential apparatus that informs it, the way the action is linked to heroic literary and mythic traditions, and sees it as an attempt to romanticize the war, and even to validate it by suggesting that it is firmly 'in the tradition'. This is a charge worth making; though if Professor Fussell is right, it does not mean that *In Parenthesis* is a failure, but only that it fails to be a certain kind of war literature. In any case I suspect that to confront the situation of private soldiers on the Western Front with that of Launcelot or Henry V, as Jones does, is to bring into play immediately that very irony which Professor Fussell prizes in other, less ambitious war writings.

The Great War and Modern Memory is impressive in its scope, and bold in design. Everyone will find something to quarrel with in it. It is a very welcome contribution to the subject. (pp. 928-30)

> *Douglas Kerr, in a review of "The Great War and Modern Memory," in* The Modern Language Review, *Vol. 72, No. 4, October, 1977, pp. 928-30.*

Louis K. MacKendrick   (review date Spring 1978)

[*In the following review, MacKendrick praises* The Great War and Modern Memory *as a well-documented and entertaining analysis of the influence of World War I on modern literature.*]

It is difficult not to admire *The Great War and Modern Memory* very highly, for rarely do social history, distinguished literary criticism, synthesis, organization, a serious but not heavy style, and inherently interesting material come together so smoothly. Fussell's perspectives are always clear, and generously illustrated by citation, commentary, statistics and facts, and vivid details of trench life on the European Front between 1914 and 1918. Instruction and—it must be acknowledged—entertainment parade closely and familiarly.

Fussell's subjects are the experiences of warfare, British literary memorials of World War I, and the occasions where "literary tradition and real life notably intersect," where attitudes which became available for subsequent writing were systematized and raised into consciousness. Nine chapters, each sub-divided self-explanatorily, focus the *kinds* of experience and literary practice into neat modes and themes that, despite their apparent conve-

nience, do not lose the sense of a totality of imaginative response to the War.

The prophetic ironic perspective of Thomas Hardy, which Fussell sees as dominating both the re-creation of frontline actuality and post-bellum writing, begins *The Great War and Modern Memory,* as received certainties and language were irrevocably dislocated. "The Troglodyte World" examines the life and literature of the trenches and efforts to preserve ritual meaning, particularly in writing about the sunrise-sunset "stand-to's, "an attempt to make some sense of the war in relation to inherited tradition."

With "Adversary Proceedings" the first of Fussell's memoirists, Siegfried Sassoon (*Memoirs of George Sherston*), epitomizes an exploration of the "binary vision," the mode of antithesis in the War's writers, in a singularly persuasive chapter. Its successor, centering on an analysis of David Jones's *In Parenthesis,* likewise treats the persistence of legend, rumour, the sacrificial theme, conversions, rebirths, and metamorphoses as rationalizations of the intolerable, ". . . unprecedented meaning . . . had to find precedent motifs and images"; the model became *Pilgrim's Progress,* a rich source of archetypes for contemporary usage.

"Oh What a Literary War" surprises, demonstrating "the unparalleled literariness of all ranks who fought the Great War" with their presiding genius, the *Oxford Book of English Verse.* As with the dependence on older models of myth, ritual, and romance, Fussell claims that such allusion was primarily consolatory. An associated "problem of factual testimony" is a joyous summary of British euphemism and "heroic grandiosity," for " . . . the presumed inadequacy of language itself to convey the facts about trench warfare is one of the motifs of all who wrote about the war." "Theater of War", stressing the "caricature scenes" of Robert Graves's splendid memoir, *Good-Bye to All That,* studies the War literature's tendency to "melodramatic self-casting," again by way of accomodating new, unreal existences: "Most people were terrified, and for everyone the dramaturgic provided a dimension within which the unspeakable could to a degree be familiarized and interpreted." Fussell concludes the chapter with an extensive look at a modern instance, Anthony Burgess's *The Wanting Seed* (as Joseph Heller's *Catch-22* and Thomas Pynchon's *Gravity's Rainbow* are often cited throughout, the last thoroughly in the final chapter, as examples of the persistence of the Great War's patterns and images into modern writing).

"Arcadian Recourses" (memoirist: Edmund Blunden, in *Undertones of War*) seeks out the pastoral, again "a way of invoking a code to hint by antithesis at the indescribable; at the same time, it is a comfort in itself. . . . " The pastoral, too, assists ironic perception, and both are present in "the greatest poem of the war", Isaac Rosenberg's "Break of Day in the Trenches." The penultimate chapter, "Soldier Boys," delicately presents the homoerotic note in some Great War writing. Fussell is at pains to emphasize the chaste, sentimental, and protective nature of such relationships in the literature; as exemplar, Wilfred Owen's verse is searched fairly for its sublimation and sensuous particularity, though an undismissable colour is now added to our understanding of that poetry.

Fussell concludes by nominating war memoirs as a kind of fiction and, Northrop Frye in hand, suggests the development in the War's writing from plausibility through irony to myth. It is continuation that occupies him here and elsewhere, and several clearly defined themes emerge which Fussell claims as determinants for the conduct of subsequent writing. These include anxiety; the appearance of the War's data as metaphor, the predominance of euphemism as "the special rhetorical sound of life in the latter third of the twentieth century", the persistent adversary habit of "simple distinction, simplification, and opposition," and "paranoid melodrama, which I take to be a primary mode in modern writing."

The Great War and Modern Memory is an eminently readable book. It is not a survey of great and lesser names (though, as well as those above, Brooke, Eliot, Gurney, Kipling, Nichols, and Read are here) but a highlighting of literary types and postures. Its syntheses, patterns, and motifs are exact and well-supported, rarely strained. Most importantly, it gives a distinct sense of what the War was *like,* its habits and defenses, in both viewing and vision. (pp. 168-69)

> *Louis K. MacKendrick, in a review of "The Great War and Modern Memory," in* The Southern Humanities Review, *Vol. XII, No. 2, Spring, 1978, pp. 168-69.*

Alfred Gollin   (review date 1979)

[*In the following excerpt, Gollin praises* The Great War and Modern Memory *as "a brilliant study that makes an outstanding contribution to our understanding of life and literature in the present century."*]

The First World War is still known as the Great War. Its results dominate our lives to this day. Unlike earlier conflicts that were fought by relatively small aristocraticly led armies the manhood of nations was involved in the gigantic sieges and battles of the Great War. It was also a war of material in which the industrial populations of Germany, France, Britain and the United States were pitted against each other in the production of warlike stories and equipment on a scale never dreamed of before. Contemporaries believed at first that the war would end quickly because it seemed obvious that no national economy could endure such burdens for very long. The British were convinced it would be over by Christmas. The Germans staked all on their Schlieffen Plan, designed to win them a lightning victory in the West. Within a few months, however, trench warfare began. It soon became clear to some, if not to the highest Allied Generals, that a war of attrition had set in. Winston Churchill, a participant in these mighty struggles, wrote: "Two and even three British or French lives were repeatedly paid for the killing of one enemy and grim calculations were made to prove that in the end the Allies would still have a balance of a few millions to spare. It will appear not only horrible but incredible to future generations that such doctrines should have been imposed by the military profession upon the ar-

dent and heroic populations who yielded themselves to their orders." The British lost more than 700,000 men, killed either in the Naval or Military Service; there were more than five million French casualties; six million Germans, killed or wounded; and six million Russians.

After the war the various governments produced their official histories. Military experts wrote independent accounts of the struggle in thousands of books, articles, essays, and pamphlets. There were biographies of all the civilian and military leaders and war memoirs by the hundreds. Recently, the British Government has opened its official archives and for the past few years researchers have been exploiting this tremendous collection of material, housed in the Public Record Office in London, in order to re-write the history of the war in the light of modern knowledge and historical scholarship. Paul Fussell deals in his *The Great War* with the literature that was written as a result of men's experiences in the trenches of 1914-1918. The book is a brilliant study that makes an outstanding contribution to our understanding of life and literature in the present century.

Trench life was a gruesome and searing experience. It inspired or provoked the British writers and poets who are dealt with in Fussell's book. In the trenches the British were usually worse off than the Germans. The British Generals were convinced that their next attack, and they were always planning offensives and attacks, would result in a rupture of the German Line, and a victorious march to Berlin. Therefore, the British trenches were regarded as temporary positions, they were not dug deeply enough; their dugouts were sometimes too shallow; they were not drained adequately. The Germans knew better. Their positions were deep under the earth, carefully engineered, and provided with amenities unknown in the opposing line. In quiet times lice, rats, mud, filth and death were the British troops' portion. "Georgian complacency," quotes Fussell, "died in the trenches." When the front was active the scene was even worse. Sir John French and Sir Douglas Haig assured themselves times without a number that a frontal assault would succeed if it were preceded by a heavy enough artillery barrage. The plan never worked. At Passchendaele, in 1917 there were nearly 400,000 British casualties. They gained three or four miles of useless mud and slime in a salient overlooked by the German guns on three sides. The worst episode in the entire history of the British Army occurred on 1st July 1916 when 60,000 men were lost in a single day with no genuine objectives gained. Fussell writes of the British: "The innocent army fully attained the knowledge of good and evil at the Somme on July 1, 1916. The moment, one of the most interesting in the whole long history of human disillusion, can stand as the type of all the ironic actions of the war."

The writers and poets were compelled to express in literature their reaction to these monstrous occurrences. Fussell ranges over their works with deep insight and profound scholarship. Although he concentrates on Sassoon, Graves, Wilfred Owen, and David Jones, he stresses that in the British ranks "an astonishing number took literature seriously." He explains that in 1914 there was virtually no cinema, no radio at all, and certainly no television:

"amusement was largely found in language formally arranged . . . in books and periodicals . . . in . . . clever structuring of words." Even louse-hunting, he points out, was called "reading one's shirt." Lloyd George, the British Prime Minister, was convinced that if the war were ever described in accurate language people would insist that it should be stopped at once. Fussell states, however, that the war was "indescribable in any but the available language of traditional literature." Analysis of the resulting literature is the subject of his absorbing book. (pp. 107-08)

> *Alfred Gollin, "The British Experience from One War to the Next," in* Modernist Studies: Literature and Culture 1920-1940, *Vol. 3, Nos. 1, 2 & 3, 1979, pp. 107-10.*

Bruce Allen   (review date Spring 1982)

[*In the following review of* Abroad: British Literary Traveling between the Wars, *Allen finds some of Fussell's comments on travel writing unconvincing or unnecessarily condescending but commends the book for its well-written prose and interesting subject matter.*]

[In *Abroad,* an] eclectic, far-ranging, and notably witty examination of British travel writing from 1918-1939 we observe an almost frighteningly urbane cultural critic making ingenious connections (and in a few cases, I'm afraid, pulling unclassifiable rabbits out of possibly nonexistent hats).

Fussell's central thesis is that "the great flight of writers from England in the 20's and 30's" toward sun-warmed foreign lands expressed much more than the traditional general desire to escape homebound stuffiness (climatic and social); the impulse was now a weariness with "wartime Philistinism" as well as with the war itself—and a conviction that elsewhere was (simply by virtue of being elsewhere) the place to be, if not utopia. He argues further that this newly revived genre necessarily fell back on bad days with the recurrence of world war and a "darkening" of the "zest" that had produced that revival.

The opening chapters note the onetime belief in travel as an educational tool, and the classic form of the travel book (as "a repository of wonderful lies"); analyze chauvinistic conventions, both inhibitive and stimulating ("the English sense that abroad is odd," "the British traveler as outrageous person"); and include a long interpolation lamenting contemporary conditions that have made travel all but impossible, and emphasizing the author's own disillusioning experiences.

Fussell finds evidence of the passion for "abroad" not just in written literature but in movies, radio programs, and popular songs. He presents brief pointed commentary on the comparative usefulness of the guidebooks of Tauchnitz, Baedeker, Fodor, and Fielding. But the core of the book comprises his chapters on representative travelers, and what their experiences meant to them. If the sections on "teams, either social or erotic" (D. H. Lawrence and Frieda, Auden and Isherwood) seem a little shopworn, they are more than balanced by Fussell's acute readings

of all-but-forgotten books like Graham Greene's *Journey Without Maps* ("a virtual autobiography in little") and Robert Byron's *The Road to Oxiana* [i.e., Persia] ("an artfully constructed quest myth in the form of an apparently spontaneous travel diary" which "juxtaposes into a sort of collage the widest variety of rhetorical materials"). He is wonderfully sensitive to the appeal of that outrageous iconoclast Norman Douglas, and perceives beneath Evelyn Waugh's choleric self-portraiture "a hero of British skepticism and empiricism."

Elsewhere Fussell comments with needless condescension on much of what he quotes, and strains unconvincingly for resonant inferences (can one say that postwar travel restrictions helped produce "a loss of amplitude, a decay of imaginative and intellectual possibility"?; or that blurred, indistinct passport photos contributed to modern man's sense of anxiety?). I have trouble too with Fussell's efforts to define the genre, particularly with his insistence that "a travel book is ultimately very difficult to distinguish from a fiction."

And yet quite clearly there is something to his conclusion that the patchwork structures of many of these books have a real relationship with "the unravelling and dissolving of forms" that is literary modernism. If I find *Abroad* ultimately only half-convincing as argument, I would nevertheless recommend it to you for the fluidity and grace of Fussell's prose, and the intrinsic interest of his many rediscoveries. One final disagreement: the author declares his book an elegy for a lost genre. I'm not persuaded it's lost, and I think he may have done better recovery work than he realizes. (pp. xlv-xlvi)

> *Bruce Allen, "British Literary Travelers between the Wars," in* The Sewanee Review, *Vol. XC, No. 2, Spring, 1982, pp. xlv-xlvi.*

Thomas Mallon   (review date 12 November 1982)

[*In the following review, Mallon praises the wit, style, and insight of the essays collected in* The Boy Scout Handbook, and Other Observations.]

If the word were not so often connotative of illiteracy, it would be tempting to call Paul Fussell a "sociologist" of books. In this collection of essays [***The Boy Scout Handbook, and Other Observations***] one finds him gingerly explaining literature in terms of the real circumstances from which it springs and in which it gets read. He takes on such jobs as exposing the racial sanitizing of Booth Tarkington's *Penrod* in our squeamishly enlightened age; celebrating the "classical ethics" of "The Official Boy Scout Handbook"; explaining the exhausting mania that drives the machinery of South African sex censorship (**"Smut-Hunting in Pretoria"**); and discoursing upon the reasons for our current appetite for things Edwardian. He can read photographs and places with the same casual brilliance he brings to a text. The essays in each of this collection's five parts—"Americana," "Hazards of Literature," "Going Places," "Britons, Largely Eccentric," and "Versions of the Second World War"—come from a steady faith in what empiricism and common sense can do when leavened by language that has wit and precision.

It is all done with a fine lack of stuffiness. Fussell finds, for example, that the supposed polarity of Whitman and Poe is actually bridged by the "bit of P. T. Barnum in both"; and if their descendant Harry Crosby "had studied and thought and practiced all his life he might—just might—have become a fourth-rate Hart Crane." Fussell would, one feels, rather like a book than dislike it, but when his duty is to put it down he does it: "Not all Dr. Ober's essays are ridiculous. Some are pointless . . . " He has a nice un-academic fondness for contractions and mild profanity and jazzy parentheses. (One parenthetical cavil of my own: in the name of good taste and humanity can we retire the use of the term "final solution" in any other context but its appalling original one?) The only pedagogical baggage he brings to this book from his job at Rutgers is the occasional use of the examination: **"Notes on Class"** and **"Can Graham Greene Write English?"** come with exercises and quizzes appended. So read carefully; there will be a test.

His travel pieces make agreeable reading, but he is really better when talking about characters who have gotten themselves mixed up with literature—operators and frauds and crazies from Boswell to Baron Corvo to Somerset Maugham. He knows, contrary to university practice, that "personality never hurt any piece of writing." His own writing has plenty, and it is of the wry, exasperated, and grumpily humane variety.

Anyone familiar with *The Great War and Modern Memory* (1975), Fussell's magnificent study of the ironic consciousness that emerged from the First World War—a sort of brilliant extended overstatement with which all future scholarship will have to cope—will be eager to read his critical and personal reflections on the Second. Most of the pieces in the last section of this book first came to life as reviews (of Herman Wouk; of the re-issued *Yank;* of Time-Life's photo history of the war), but an overall view of the war emerges from them and coheres: namely, that although it was "necessary it was absurd and cruel, reasonable in intent but botched in particulars, a task for professionals bungled by amateurs." He prefers authors who recognize it as "a murderous farce," however high-minded the Allies' aims.

Fussell is bent on extirpating sentimentality and myth from present retrospection. One of his techniques for doing so is to pay attention to ghastly details: "In photographs dead sailors are often more shocking than dead soldiers if their feet show, because they wear quasi-civilian shoes and nice thin 'dress' socks. We don't expect them to be treated so badly." If you doubt this, remember how this summer the photographs of dead horses in Hyde Park seemed somehow more terrible than the ones of limbless bandsmen in Regents Park.

In the final piece in the volume, **"My War,"** Fussell is very hard on his own youthful illusions; they had to be shot out of him in France on March 15, 1945. He came back thoroughly transformed: "Indeed, the careful reader will have discerned in all the essays in this book a speaker who is really a pissed-off infantryman, disguised as a literary and cultural commentator."

Trying to remember something as simultaneously necessary and absurd demands a brave double vision. Fussell emphasizes the absurdity because he has so often seen the necessity rendered with limp nostalgia. But I wonder how easily the perception of nobility will die. I have stood near my father's marker (#764, Section 4) in the veterans' cemetery in which he was buried in 1980, and felt private thoughts give way to the abashed civic realization of how little I, and many of my generation and sort, have been called upon to do. Camouflaged from the draft a decade ago in our coats of student ivy, we are not comfortably settling into our lives. When I consider my father's and Fussell's generation, and then look at my own and myself, it's hard not to think what a falling-off was there. I suspect this is the last mood Fussell wants his clear-eyed and de-mythologizing book to summon; but it's the mood I was put in nonetheless. As one of the great modern students of irony, he will, I hope, understand and forgive.

Thomas Mallon, "Honorable Discharges," in National Review, *New York, Vol. XXXLV, November 12, 1982, p. 1428.*

Christopher Hawtree   (review date 5 February 1983)

[*In the following review of* The Boy Scout Handbook, *Hawtree finds Fussell's essays "agreeably diverting" but faults the lack of variety in the volume.*]

If one were unfortunate enough to live in America there would be less need to look through this collection of essays [in *The Boy Scout Handbook*]. Most of the pieces were published in magazines there, and if they had come one's way would have made an agreeably diverting read. However, like many journalists and others before him, Professor Fussell has more of a hopeful eye on *The Round Table* than a realistic one on the remainder-shops to which essays and photographic studies of royal tours are the first to percolate. His book about the Great War and his various studies of the 18th century make enjoyable criticism; these essays, too, are written with a vigour and frequent good sense rarely found in American academics, but the cumulative effect is wearying over 284 pages. He lacks here the continuous, varied interest of Edmund Wilson's best collections.

'Poets are seldom good for any thing except in rhime,' remarks Cowper in a letter; Paul Fussell, 'persuaded by the performance of George Orwell', thinks that professors might do otherwise. In *The Boy Scout Handbook,* with some recycling in the Boswell and travel sections, he covers subjects often far removed from the lecture-hall, and perhaps his experience of a world distant from the Inner Temple and Olney allows him to get away with it. As he observes in the moving and even comic essay, **'My War'**, with which the book ends, 'the careful reader will have discerned in all the essays in this book a speaker who is really a pissed-off infantryman, disguised as a literary and cultural commentator'. This masterly reminiscence describes school in the Thirties where, 'fat and flabby', he hated to 'invite—indeed, compel—ridicule' by showering after gym; he escaped such humiliating washing by joining the infantry R.O.T.C., later doing the same at college. By now the war involved America, and those who had opted for this infantry corps found that they were committed to it even if, like Paul Fussell, they might have expected an administrative post. 'These hillbillies and Okies, drop-outs and used-car salesmen and petty criminals were my teachers and friends.' The account of their time in France, his flab sweated off, for the final, protracted stages of the European war excellently conveys naïvety turning to disillusion: he stumbles over dead Germans, catches pneumonia after an ill-clad winter and is wounded in the leg during a battle that has seen his friends tumble as bloodily as animals in a makeshift abattoir; the subsequent infection almost lasts until the bomb has fallen on Nagasaki. Most bravely of all, perhaps, he quotes from his letters home: their embarrassing fatuity gradually turns to something better when the sight of almost everyone on stumps instead of legs instills an attraction to Pope and Swift. He has 'ever since . . . been trying to understand satire, and even to experiment with it himself'.

A salty belligerency, described in the blurb as 'rich ironic wit', fills the book. The degeneration of language in America, from petrol-tankers being marked 'flammable' because 'in' was muddled with 'un', to basic ignorance in the editors of scholarly texts, is a prevalent theme. His few pages on Evelyn Waugh's *Letters* form an incisive understanding of the seriousness of his satire and its relation to a sense of honour: 'he is that rarity, a writer who cares about language. He knows that writing is an affair of words rather than soul, impulse, "sincerity", or an instinct for the significant'. He points to Waugh politely telling Graham Greene that he should use 'buttress' in place of 'cornice' in *The End of the Affair,* a change duly made. Professor Fussell's review of *Ways of Escape,* however, which ends with a two-page examination-paper inviting candidates to correct Mr Greene's grammar, has the bombast of Michael Geare as Quentin Oates 'reviewing the reviews' in *The Bookseller.* It is pleasing to see that Mr Greene has ignored him in preparing the paperback's text. Most bizarrely he proposes the notion—twice—that Mr Greene, like Maugham, has worked in MI5 for longer than is realised and that the writing of entertainments serves as a cover. To make up for such crudities he provides an entertaining discussion of letters, with all the stock locutions, sent by authors to newspapers that have printed hatchet-reviews: again one marvels at the tearful sensitivity of May Sarton and Jan Morris. (One Sidney Smith makes a couple of appearances here.) His letter from the recipient of a needlessly laudatory review ('. . . your readers deserve better than this') is as neat a satire as his fantasy of the perfect town in which to recuperate is overloaded—Orwell's pub in *The Moon under Water* is more persuasive.

Professor Fussell's convalescent wish for a bookshop with 'all the volumes of . . . the World's Classics as they existed in 1949' is pleasant. A recurring enjoyment of such things is enough to make him an honorary Englishman, but is hardly enough to install him at Twickenham. The £10 which this book costs would be better put towards the 700-page edition of Evelyn Waugh's journalism due out in the autumn. (pp. 23-4)

Christopher Hawtree, "Fusillades," in The Spectator, *Vol. 250, No. 8065, February 5, 1983, pp. 23-4.*

Ronald B. Shwartz (review date July 1983)

[*In the following review of* The Boy Scout Handbook, and Other Observations, *Shwartz praises Fussell as a gifted critic but finds his stance as a "pissed-off infantryman" overly self-dramatized.*]

Paul Fussell is a chaired professor of English who doesn't take literature—or much else—sitting down. It's been said that he is "untrammeled by reticence," but that puts it too daintily. In fact and by reputation, he is a bull in the china shop of American letters, and no wonder: he fashions himself as a kind of thinking man's John Wayne, wielding prose with a certain fetching swagger and acid humor, and blaming it all on nothing less than his stint as a combat platoon leader in WWII: "The careful reader," he writes, "will discern in all the essays in this book a speaker who is really a pissed-off infantryman, disguised as a literary and cultural commentator . . . I entered the war when I was nineteen, and I have been in it ever since."

The careful reader may also discern that Fussell's portrait of the artist as ex-GI is more than a tad overdrawn and smacks of self-dramatization. But it's precisely his flair for such brash insight, for the dazzling connection, that marks the 34 pieces in [*The Boy Scout Handbook, and Other Observations*] and proves him to be a gifted critic and more than a garden-variety gadfly. And it's the measure of his quirky sensibility that his chief interests—books, manners, war, and travel—are so often viewed from the acute angle of out-of-the-way if not downright frivolous texts: *The Boy Scout Handbook,* for example, whose ninth edition he subjects to a book review, and then there are black-and-white photos from *Life* magazine, a censor's guide to taboo novels in South Africa, and even some cookie-tin lids from a bakery in Georgia, which provide quaint fodder for a study in historical revisionism.

Does Mr. Fussell climb such molehills and turn them into mountains "because they are there"—or is it because no card-carrying critic of somber mien ever has? "A serious moment in cultural history," he says, "occurred a few years ago when gasoline trucks changed the warning word on the rear from Inflammable to Flammable. Public education had apparently produced a population which no longer knew In- as an intensifier." Is it (as he claims) a merger of literary and social commentary, or rather a coy flouting of both, when he divines a link between two modern-day "prose genres"—classified "personal" ads and protest letters by authors aggrieved by bad reviews: "They are not as distinct generically as one might imagine at first glance. They share the convention of shameless self-satisfaction. Each constitutes a little arena of a very twentieth century sort of insecure egotism and self-concern, and a critic would be hard pressed to decide which bespeaks the more pitiable dependence on external shows of esteem."

Even when it comes to more sacred literary fare—like Waugh, Maugham, and James Boswell—Fussell's slant is off-center and mischievous, and a far cry from *explication de text.* What we get, instead, is a gallery of clowns, cads, and loons and their dark comic frailties, with criticism just a front for the juicier stuff of caricature and psychobiography: the "neurotic" temper of Waugh's collected letters, the "positively Hearst-like *chutzpah*" of Maugham, Boswell's life as "one of the most memorable satyrs of all time." It is highly amusing stuff but it all starts to sound like gossip-mongering in a smooth doctoral tongue. There is the "terrible truth" that Graham Greene cannot write English and there is Nabokov's "constant pursuit of the *outré*" Poe, too, it seems, has "an urge toward the *outré*"—a phrase not unbefitting Fussell himself, who seems to create authors in his own image. It's as if erudition, which Fussell has in spades, were a license to entertain whatever the cost.

There is, moreover, a prissiness here vaguely reminiscent of Gore Vidal, but Fussell's only avowed mentor is George Orwell. Like Orwell, he revels in the tell-tale signs of class structure and social status. But the claim to kinship ends there. He is by far the snootier, has notably less moral vision, and is less at home with tenderness. And Orwell, while ironic, is always serious—Fussell's irony can't decide how serious it is or what it wants to do when it grows up: obesity, he states, is four times more visible among the lower class, "as any observer can testify who has witnessed Prole women perambulating shopping malls in their bright, very tight jersey trousers. Not just obesity but the flaunting of obesity is the Prole sign, as if the object were to give maximum aesthetic offense to the higher classes and thus achieve a form of revenge."

The last and longest piece in this collection, **"My War,"** is also the best, and it points up the trouble with even the most brilliant of the others—namely, the infantryman's "disguise." Recounting his grim first hours of combat in Alsace, France, Fussell finally remembers (instead of simply acting out) emotions for which the term "pissed-off" is apparently just a frail euphemism. Not that he ever fully abandons the hard, tinny, and rather loveless edge to his accomplished sentences. Inside that gruff exterior might be a largely gruff interior. But the heady candor and precision of this final, in all ways climactic essay suggest that almost everything else is indeed just so much high-grade fluff by a man who knows better and can't help it. If only he would quit acting as if he wanted to donate his wit to the Smithsonian. If only he'd let the old soldier fade away. (pp. 39-40)

> *Ronald B. Shwartz, in a review of "The Boy Scout Handbook and Other Observations," in* The American Spectator, *Vol. 16, No. 7, July, 1983, pp. 39-40.*

Mary R. Lefkowitz   (review date 6 July 1984)

[*In the following review of* Caste Marks, *Lefkowitz discusses Fussell's views on social class in America.*]

The Classics department at Wellesley still possesses a contraption called a stereopticon that enables one to view through binocular lenses double-imaged sepia postcards of classical sites as they appeared one hundred years ago. Through this device young women, confined by geography and financial restraints to the second-state Piranesis in their classroom, saw all they would ever see of ancient Europe. But now that going abroad is easier (and cheaper) than going to California, armchair travel has been replaced by armchair sociology; instead of gazing at illustrations of monuments, we peek through metaphorical keyholes into the houses and lives of our fellow Americans.

Today's stereopticon is the catalog(ue). Anyone who has a steady job has a credit card; the card-owner's name is made known to scores of advertisers-by-mail; magazines and pamphlets arrive daily, filled with tempting coloured illustrations of clothes, furniture, appliances, "collectibles", for work, play, home, garden and perhaps most sacred of all, cars. Sitting in one's living-(ie, drawing-) room or possibly even on the lavatory, one can leaf through thousand of "offerings" from companies all over the country, each promising personalized care from their smiling employees. But since the purveyors of the mailing lists have only a general notion of their customer's disposable incomes, inevitably one receives stacks of information about what one could not conceivably want to buy: Frugal Frannie's Fashion Sweaters (ie, jerseys) in pink polyester with simulated pearl collars; electronic door-chimes that can be set to play different tunes; seven-piece sets of silver-with-magenta-trim nylon luggage that might impress the skycap (ie, porter) at the airport, if you can find one.

Since the catalogues keep pouring in, many people must actually buy these things. But now, thanks to Paul Fussell, I have some notion why. Taste, according to Fussell [in his *Caste Marks: Style and Status in the USA*], is a function of class. In order to move up or down a notch one needs to change not how much one spends but rather the catalogues one buys from. The wearers of pink polyester sweaters with pearl collars are high proles who want to show directly how they spend their money. Their lower-middle neighbours might have tuneful doorbells or "collect" commemorative china thimbles. Upcoming middle-class executives would sport the matching luggage. It is the upper-middles and lower-uppers (since real uppers, Fussell believes, don't do much of anything but inherit) who restore old houses, wear clothes made of natural fibres, and conceal the extent of their property behind high fences, long driveways, and the intricate layers of clothing described in *The Preppy Handbook.*

In England, at least once upon a time, one could tell what class a person was by how he spoke and where he was educated. In America you can learn more from his possessions and his environment. Class, Fussell insists, despite all efforts, can never be concealed completely. Successful executives betray their middle-class origins by stating that they "live" by the advertisements in the *New Yorker;* lower-uppers display an indifference to the appearance of their cars that the acutely self-concious middles could not tolerate and the ostentatious proles could not comprehend. One could tell that President Kennedy was not upper-class (for all his family's wealth) because he wore two-button suits. But since he went to Harvard he inevitably had more "class" than Presidents Nixon or Reagan who, whatever they wear, still went to no-name schools.

If all else fails, Fussell offers keys to language and pronunciation. These should be of particular use to the foreigner, since regional variations are not reliable indicators of class; more can be determined from tendencies toward euphemism (*home* instead of *house, passed away* instead of *die*), multiplication of syllables (*obligate* instead of *oblige, processes* to rhyme with *indices*), accentuation of foreign words, especially placing the stress on the final syllable of any French word—all characteristics of the middle class.

Only the people who strive to avoid the classifications inherent in every aspect of American life can escape detection. These rare persons, designated as "X's", are usually the satirists and critics who live outside of or off society, the artists, poets, actors and academics. Fussell claims that "it's only as an X, detached from the constraints and anxieties of the whole class racket, that an American can enjoy something like the Liberty promised on the coinage". But I wonder if these revolutionaries, so long as they feel constrained to comment on the rest of us by their eccentric behaviour, can ever truly manage to be free. In their struggle to be different they too achieve a uniformity, with their pseudo-prole jug wines, Vietnamese food, kitschy furniture, patched (but clean) jeans, straight talk spiced with foreign words (correctly pronounced) and learned obscenity and vulgarity. Presumably, if the X doesn't contrive constantly to be listening to the proles and middles and analysing conformist social mores, he might end up by forgetting to wear his cowboy hat to a mid-town Manhattan dinner-party and slipping inconspicuously back into his parents' social class.

In case you don't know what class you or your friends belong to, Fussell provides exercises at the back of the book to test your sensitivity to class inferences, and fake Ann Landers letters with pungent answers to plaintive questions (the response to "Have a Good Day" is "Thank you, but I have other plans"). There is also a scale to evaluate class by taking an inventory of the contents of living-rooms. The score can be improved by owning or displaying foreign-language books, the *TLS* (because it is both intellectual and English), original works of art by "recognized practitioners" (except Picasso), antiques and frayed oriental rugs. But points can be taken away if you can see a bowling ball with its cover, oil-painted photographs of the owner's children (or paintings *by* them), framed high-school diplomas, or cases with collections of commemorative objects, such as bronze statues of straining athletes (special edition cast in honour of the Los Angeles Olympics). The living-room test seems pretty accurate, though an upper limit should have been set on desirable items like original paintings, to restrain *nouveau riche* overkill. Sometimes, too, Fussell seems to insert some of his own personal prejudices, as when he insists that polyester is middle-class rather than simply convenient, or that purple, now chic, once royal, is a distinctly prole colour. Also the test reveals that he expects his book to be enjoyed not just by the élite Xs but by normal upper-middles. But then they are the only other Americans who actually read anything other than newspapers, best-selling novels, and, of course, catalogues, and who believe that they can find some significance in familiar surroundings and the conventions of ordinary life.

Mary R. Lefkowitz, "Class of '84," in The Times Literary Supplement, *No. 4240, July 6, 1984, p. 749.*

Thomas Mallon   (review date September 1988)

[*In the following review, Mallon praises the essays in* Thank God for the Atom Bomb, *focusing on Fussell's complex moral outlook in the title essay.*]

Paul Fussell's growing readership looks to him for news of three territories he has made very much his own during the last dozen years: war, travel, and status. Books like **The Great War and Modern Memory, Abroad,** and **Class** have displayed a happy regression in literary-career terms. Professor Fussell, respected scholar of eighteenth-century literature at Rutgers and, more recently, Penn, has become a cultural and moral commentator of considerable reach: he is more like Swift and Burke and Johnson now than when he was writing books about them.

Having become famous for a book on the First World War, Fussell has lately been turning more and more of his attention to the Second—a war that was bad for literature, because it lacked the distinguishing thing of the First: irony. "The high-minded loquacity of all those poets of the Great War! Entirely a different scene from the style of the Second War, which is silence—silence ranging from the embarrassed to the sullen." From Vietnam, fought in a "postverbal age," one must expect even less: "how is it that we know ('for certain,' it's tempting to add) that no weighty, sustained poems, or even short poems of distinction, are going to come out of it? . . . Is it perhaps that we secretly recognize that real poetry is, as Hazlitt called it, 'right royal,' aristocratic in essence, and thus unlikely to arise from the untutored or the merely street-smart?"

If some of what Fussell has to say about travel seems a little obvious this time out, he does offer the useful coinage *touristees,* for "South Sea islanders, the lifetime junk-dwellers of Hong Kong, the villagers of India, the young women of China who spend their lives making tiny stitches on horrible embroidered pictures to sell to tourists. *Touristees* are the geeks of the contemporary world . . . " In any case, the postverbal age is also, he tells us, a post-touristic one: we no longer expect to acquire wisdom from travel, just as the deconstructionists tell us we shouldn't look for it in literature.

Fussell is fond of Linnaean classification, even when it comes to offering an anatomy, as it were, of nudism: "Nude, older people look younger, especially when very tan, and younger people look even younger—almost like infants, some of them. In addition fat people look far less offensive naked than clothed . . . the eye is repulsed much less than in normal vacation life by those hideous 'resort' clothes." Turning his slightly embarrassed eye from highly formal cavorters on the Adriatic to spectators at the Indianapolis 500, he finds three social classes:

> the middles, who on race day, in homage to the checkered flag, tend to dress all in black and white and who sit in the reserved seats; the high proles, who watch standing or lolling in the infield, especially at the turns, "where the action

is"; and the uglies, the overadvertised, black-leathered, beer-sodden, pot-headed occupiers of that muddy stretch of ground in the infield at the first turn known as the Snake Pit.

Even though the aphoristic and allusive Fussell has something wise to say on nearly every page ("It's amazing the way a bikini, even if both top and bottom are present, looks grossly obscene in a nude context, nastily coy and flirtatious"), *Thank God for the Atom Bomb* is probably not as varied and stimulating as his previous gathering of essays, *The Boy Scout Handbook and Other Observations.* Readers may find him straining a bit in ones like **"On the Persistence of Pastoral"**: "It is curious that as a venue of pleasure and relaxation, a place from which you return 'refreshed,' the beach began to be popular only when the demise of formal literary pastoral had taken place." I would say such things as automobiles and Robert Moses are more to the point here. I would also, as the recognized leader in American scholarship on the British poet Edmund Blunden (up to now a non-competitive sport), take issue with Fussell's description of Blunden's "unabashed patriotism." Blunden was abashed about roughly everything, including national identities. But Fussell is absolutely right in reasoning that Blunden's chief disqualification as a "modernist" is a fondness for people. (Surely no one has offered George Orwell a higher compliment than this one from Fussell: "It's impossible to imagine him being interested in Wallace Stevens.")

For Fussell, one's values as man and writer are not to be separated. Orwell, too, found those things forever joined: "As [Orwell] sees it, there are two moral defects which issue in bad writing: one is laziness, the other pretentiousness." Like most good poems, most good essays usually end up being inquiries into the powers and limits of language itself. Whether writing about nudism, chivalry, or auto racing, Fussell finds that diction unlocks mindset:

> In their enthusiasm to forward a noble *cause* in a suspicious, nasty-minded world, *naturists* have been vigorous devisers of euphemism. *Naturist* has by now virtually ousted *nudist,* which itself could be supposed a sort of euphemism for *nakedist.* Lest the idea of a *naturist beach* seem too jolting to the conventional, naturists have come up with *free beach,* or *clothing-*or-*swimsuit-optional beach. Sunbathing* is popular as a disarming synonym for *nudism,* and among the cognoscenti no elbow nudge is needed to suggest how it differs from *sunning,* which is what you do with a bathing suit on.

On poetic diction a year after Gallipoli: "Even though the war had been going on for two years and three months, to sentimentalists and Tories one still did not carry a rifle, one *bore arms.* The enemy was still *the host,* the battle *the tumult,* and actions *deeds,* rendered variously as *valiant, gallant,* or *noble.*" Even the Indianapolis 500 is "a language event" full of name-branded garb: "A person unable to read . . . would get very little out of Indy." Like Orwell—in fact, as a nice subtle touch within his essay on Orwell—Fussell can make his discriminating language even more precise by numbering his points.

Language, however polluted, is the only river on which

truth can ride, and honest men will face up, unselectively, to each definition and dependent clause—even the one the National Rifle Association leaves off its inscription of the Second Amendment on the facade of its offices on Rhode Island Avenue in Washington: "A well-regulated Militia, being necessary to the security of a free state . . . " Fussell sends the whole NRA a Swiftian draft notice. Surely they can close-read their own amendment if he, wounded veteran, can do that to his own decoration: "The American Purple Heart Medal still says 'For Military Merit' on its obverse, although one earns it not for any action or decision but for having one's body accidentally penetrated by foreign objects."

The really superb essay in this volume is the title one, **"Thank God for the Atom Bomb,"** which is finally not so much about the bomb, or even war, as it is about ambivalence—the honest ability to live uncomfortably in moral shades of gray. Though in the foreword Fussell oversells the controversial nature of this collection, this essay is genuinely worthy of that adjective.

In the spring of 1945, Fussell "was a twenty-one-year-old second lieutenant of infantry leading a rifle platoon. Although still officially fit for combat, in the German war [he] had already been wounded in the back and the leg badly enough to be adjudged, after the war, 40 percent disabled." Being still "officially fit" meant that he could figure on being part of the imminent invasion of Japan, which was expected to last a full year and incur one million American casualties from the "universal national kamikaze" being prepared to meet it. That noted military tactician John Kenneth Galbraith is typical of appalled retro-moralists in thinking the bomb was unnecessary: The Japanese would have surrendered in "two or three weeks." But as Fussell points out:

> At the time with no indication that surrender was on the way, the kamikazes were sinking American vessels, the *Indianapolis* was sunk (880 men killed), and Allied casualties were running to over 7,000 per week. "Two or three weeks," says Galbraith. Two weeks more means 14,000 more killed and wounded, three weeks more, 21,000. Those weeks mean the world if you're one of those thousands or related to one of them.

The New York Review of Books asks, "Was the Hiroshima Bomb Necessary?" when it should, Fussell says, be asking, "Was It Effective?" Nowhere in the essay does he lose sight of his own life-and-death self-interest in the matter; he refuses to pretend he isn't grateful for something that probably saved his life. (At this point I have to thank God for the college draft deferments that let me sit out Vietnam reading Keats, and now let me spend this Sunday afternoon fifteen or twenty years later writing this essay before getting up to the fridge for a Rolling Rock. Unlike the atomic bomb, which can be debated strategically, draft deferments seem now, as we knew they were then, incontrovertibly immoral. I like to think I would have voted against them in a referendum—but I suspect I wouldn't have.)

The dropping of the bomb was, Fussell contends, "a vast

historical tragedy," but not a disaster—since tragedies have two sides and disasters only one. In the book's most useful aphorism, he declares: "Understanding the past requires pretending that you don't know the present." Fussell is talking about the remove of forty years, but the law applies equally to a remove of forty seconds, the time it may take to realize that what you thought was an F-14 was really an airbus. The only thing morally relevant is that forty seconds ago you thought it was an F-14.

Paul Fussell's sensibleness (as opposed to "sensitivity," in its present corrupt usage) amounts to a sort of sensibility—shaped by his study of writers like Johnson and Orwell, his imaginative reconstruction of the First World War, and his direct experience of the Second. Our only light amidst the snares is language, and we must shine it constantly. Foolish critics will describe Fussell as a "curmudgeon," which is all wrong, since curmudgeons just occupy the opposite end of the spectrum from those calling themselves "sensitive": neither group thinks; each just twitches. Fussell belongs to that small intelligent group in the middle who believe that the only real courtesy you can pay your fellow man is to use your brains.

We all live on the moral seashore, the waterline of right and wrong shifting and disappearing with each new tide of events. The only way to keep any sort of responsible footing is to pay attention to the disagreeable details of the events themselves. How well I remember discussions with my liberal academic colleagues several years ago about intermediate-range nuclear missiles. I took the position that the only way we'd get rid of Soviet weapons of this kind (something that didn't preoccupy them much anyway) was for the Western countries resolutely to deploy their own intermediate-range weapons. Then maybe both would be negotiated away. You remember: build up to build down. My colleagues' reaction to this argument was to label it grotesque, following that with all the usual sensitive stuff about "enough weapons to kill everyone fifty times over," etc., etc. The only word that made them smile, like children in from the rain, was "freeze." Of course, if we'd gotten a freeze then, what we'd have now is a Europe with Soviet missiles, as opposed to the far more missile-less Europe we're about to see. But what I most remember, and what's relevant here, is my colleagues' unwillingness to look at facts. No, let me change that word, since each side in any argument tends to use "facts" when it means "outlooks." What they would not look at was *information.* They did not care to acquaint themselves with the names of these missiles, their particular destructive capacities, their location, and the like—boning up on such stuff was, remember, grotesque. They preferred the cultivation of their own finer feelings to such study, and retreated with their nonnuclear umbrellas further up the moral beach, where the sand is never wet.

I suspect that Paul Fussell would actually have been opposed to the position I took on these missiles, but I want, presumptuously, to claim him as a kind of ally because of his statement that war "requires choices among craziness-es." In fact, one could say the same for most instances of human behavior. That he looks closely enough to do the choosing is his true claim to be that much devalued thing,

a critic. These days, at least in academic precincts, critic usually means hermeneutical snake-oil salesman. Fussell can be proud of living up to the definition the word could be said to have had from Johnson's time through, roughly, Orwell's: Critic—an on-the-spot moral philosopher. (pp. 38-40)

Thomas Mallon, in a review of "Thank God for the Atom Bomb and Other Essays," in The American Spectator, *Vol. 21, No. 9, September, 1988, pp. 38-40.*

Jeffrey Hart   (review date 29 September 1989)

[*In the review below, Hart lauds* Wartime: Understanding and Behavior in the Second World War *as a masterpiece.*]

A wise reviewer will go to almost any length to avoid such words as I am going to use, lest his reader suspect that he is smoking something strange or else is secretly receiving an emolument from the book's publisher. But the truth is the truth, and here goes. Paul Fussell's [**Wartime: Understanding and Behavior in the Second World War**] is a masterpiece. It brings us important new cultural knowledge, a rare achievement. Its overall thesis is powerful and persuasive. Its local insights are numerous and very rich. You turn the final page with a sense of melancholy, for now you have read it and, alas, there is no more.

Fussell's argument is that we do not *know* the war that was fought between 1939 and 1945, and for two reasons. First, all the regular organs of information—government statements, press, radio, advertising, motion pictures, and the "literature" produced by such writers as MacLeish, Sandburg, Millay, and countless others—concealed the nature of the "real war" through sentimentality and propagandistic high-mindedness.

Second, the horror of combat reached a pitch that was incommensurate with the human imagination. Even a book like **Wartime,** which makes a heroic effort at honesty, cannot finally communicate the existential reality. In the end, silence is the commensurate language of World War II.

> If you asked a wounded soldier or Marine what hit him, you'd hardly be ready for the answer, "My buddy's head," or his sergeant's heel or his hand, or a Japanese leg complete with shoe and puttees, or the West Point ring on his captain's severed hand.
>
> It was common throughout the Okinawa campaign for replacements to get hit before we knew their names. They came up confused, frightened, and hopeful, got wounded or killed and went right back to the rear on the route by which they had come, shocked, bleeding, or stiff. They were forlorn figures coming up to the great meat-grinder and going right back out of it like homeless waifs, unknown and faceless to us, like unread books on a shelf.

But no photograph, either official or in such publications as *Life,* showed an Allied soldier dismembered. Even relatively honest journalists like Ernie Pyle cooperated with the "war effort," and mortal American wounds were always clean and dignified.

Then there were the still larger lies, which even now have penetrated the historiography of the war. The troops

> knew that despite the advertising and publicity their arms and equipment were worse than the Germans'. They knew that their automatic rifles (World War One vintage) were slower and clumsier, and they knew the Germans had a much better light machine gun. They knew that despite official assertions to the contrary, the Germans had real smokeless powder for their small arms and that they did not. They knew that their own tanks, both American and British, were ridiculously under-armed and under-armored, so that they were inevitably destroyed in an open encounter with an equal number of German Panzers . . . And they knew that the greatest single weapon of the war, the atomic bomb excepted, was the German 88-mm. flat-trajectory gun, which brought down thousands of bombers and tens of thousands of soldiers. The Allies had nothing as good, despite one of them designating itself The World's Greatest Industrial Power.

Perhaps as shocking—or even more so given the widespread view that in World War II at least the "issues" were clear—is Fussell's chapter "The Ideological Vacuum." Few of those fighting it could discern what the war was all about. For most men, it was simply a bad job that had to be got through.

> Randall Jarrell says: "99 of 100 people in the army haven't the faintest idea what the war's about. Their two strongest motives are a) nationalism . . . and b) race prejudice—they dislike Japanese in the same way, though not as much as, they dislike Negroes."
>
> "The Marines didn't know what to believe in," Robert Sherrod reported from Tarawa, "except the Marine Corps."
>
> John Hersey asked the Marines on Guadalcanal "What are you fighting for?" . . . "To get the goddam thing over and get home."

Here we see a sharp difference between the two world wars. Men like Hemingway went over idealistically in 1918. Hemingway was a Wilsonian, shattered by what he experienced. His understated prose communicates hurt and rage. In World War II there were no illusions to begin with. Asked in 1940 what he felt about the war, E. M. Forster replied: "I don't want to lose it. I don't expect Victory (with a big V!) and I can't join in any build-a-new-world stuff. Once in a lifetime one can swallow that, but not twice."

Fussell's highly original chapter "Fresh Idiom" brings to bear his formidable talents as a literary critic. The troops who knew the facts created a subversive idiom and an oral tradition of rebellious songs as a way of protecting the integrity of their experience from the sea of official lies. Virtually all of this material is obscene, but cleaner than the lies. For instance this song, sung to the tune of "John Brown's Body":

> We'd been flying all day long at one hundred
> f-----g feet,
> The weather f-----g awful, f-----g rain and f-----g
> sleet;
> The compass it was swinging f-----g south and
> f-----g north,
> But we made a f-----g landing in the Firth of
> f-----g Forth.

In the real war, the pilots were not exactly "Coming In on a Wing and a Prayer," as the popular song had it.

Those who lived through the Second World War here at home, and those who are too young to remember the war and have been brought up on scholarly "histories," will experience this splendid book as a cold shock of intelligent perception.

To all of this, I have only one addition to make. Fussell focuses on the experience of the "real war" at combat level, as he himself experienced it in France. However, was there not also a "real war" at the highest planning levels? And did not this provide a rationale, at least, for all the horror?

What the Roosevelt Administration saw during the 1930s was the rise of two new would-be imperial powers: 1) Japan, which was consolidating its hegemony in Asia through the Greater East Asia Co-Prosperity Sphere, and looking to pick up British, French, and Dutch possessions (with their resources of rubber, oil, and tin), and even threatening the Philippines and Australia; and 2) Germany, with the military potential to build a Continental system that might stretch from the English Channel to the Black Sea, perhaps extending its commercial and political influence to Latin America. The regimes in Tokyo and Berlin would be autarkic, xenophobic, and implacably hostile to American interests. The international environment would be poisonous.

Pearl Harbor was therefore not "unprovoked aggression." Roosevelt had been pouring arms into China and, in 1940, cut off oil to the Japanese fleet. Our destroyers in 1940 were chasing U-boats up to a thousand miles into the Atlantic. The *rationale* from a cold-eyed perspective in Washington was geopolitical and based upon power calculations, admittedly not such considerations as could easily be communicated by Betty Grable or Archibald MacLeish. (pp. 57-8)

> *Jeffrey Hart, "You Can't Even Talk about It,"* in National Review, *New York, Vol. XLI, September 29, 1989, pp. 57-8.*

Paul Fussell with Roger J. Spiller   (interview date November 1989)

[*In the following interview, Fussell discusses his experience as a soldier during World War II and its influence on his writings.*]

[*Spiller*]: *As you make very clear in* **Wartime,** *the memory of the Second World War has taken a beating at the hands of "euphemizers" and "Disneyfiers," so let's do a pop quiz: What do Walt Disney, Henry Luce, and Edna St. Vincent Millay have in common?*

[Fussell]: Ignorance preeminently. Ignorance about the conditions, the real conditions, of human life, as experienced by almost everybody in the world except Americans—who've never been bombed. Who have an abundance of food and goods. And who have never had the experience of most Europeans of almost starving for a six-year period.

Such people as you mentioned seem to me to lack imagination of other people's predicaments and consequently to view the world optimistically, as if the whole world were like Southern California, full of sunshine and good fellowship and fun and superficial pleasures. It's the absence of a tragic sense that I'm suggesting, which is very hard to get over to most Americans because they never really have had the experience, which is highly tragic and ironic. They can't even imagine it. If they would read more *Oedipus Rex* and *King Lear,* under decent instruction, it would help.

This is why my literary interests parallel my political and social and critical interests. It's all one big package. I love teaching eighteenth-century literature because it's ironic and skeptical, and it doesn't hold that people need to be protected against the condition of human foolishness.

Wartime *is a book that seems to look forward as well as backward. The first of September, 1989, was the fiftieth anniversary of the Polish invasion, which inaugurates for the next six years a great line of fiftieth-anniversary commemorations. Could* **Wartime** *be taken as a cautionary tale for all those who would launch celebrations?*

There's nothing wrong with celebrating the resounding victory, which was moral as well as military, of the Allies in that war. There's nothing wrong with that as long as it is accompanied with an appropriate understanding of the disaster the whole thing visited upon Europe.

Friends who have read pieces of **Wartime** *wanted me to ask whether Fussell thinks he may have gone too far in the other direction—that your picture of this war is simply too grim.*

No. It would be impossible to go too far in the other direction. War as an institution is so nasty and so vile. I quote Cyril Connolly in the book, saying something that I agree with entirely: that one must never forget that the war *was* a war, and therefore stupid, destructive, opposed to every decent and civilized understanding of what life is like.

So I don't think I went far enough. I didn't go farther because you want to revolt the reader only up to a certain degree; otherwise you wipe out the effect you're trying to create. So part of it is a question of literary tact. I could write a whole book about the disposal of human bodies in Europe, which would be fascinating, but I think nobody would like to read it except medical doctors and funeral directors.

Would you say then that since 1945 the nation really has not come to grips with the actualities of that war?

I do say so. And many of the reasons for that are praise-worthy, actually. It was the beneficence, say of the GI Bill, from which I profited. It helped pay for my Ph.D. work at Harvard. The beneficence and benignity of that tended to suggest that human nature was benign, whereas the war itself had argued the opposite, that human nature has a very dangerous leaning toward wickedness, original sin, vileness, and delight in destruction and sadism. So it was partly American decency, which is always to be praised and celebrated, that helped wipe out some of the viler memories of that war, and it set us back on a highly American optimistic track again.

How much of that optimism would you be willing to see in our later involvement in the Southeast Asian wars?

I think it had a lot to do with it, because it was assumed that anything we did must have been done from benign motives, since people imagined that repression of what was called communism in Southeast Asia was somehow serving the causes embodied in the Declaration of Independence and the Constitution. But I remember that the original entry into the South Vietnam quagmire was justified in President Kennedy's inaugural speech, where he said that we will bear any burden, et cetera, et cetera, in order to advance the cause of freedom. The problem was that we misidentified the South Vietnamese government as being connected in any way with the cause of freedom.

But at its start, the war could be conceived of as a fairly noble enterprise. It was only as it turned sour that people began to see ways in which it was not. No war starts out vicious. It starts out as an attempt to clean up something that is vile and to redress some injustice. Hitler invaded Czechoslovakia on the excuse of rescuing the Germans there—giving the action a plausible color. Nobody ever says, "Look, I'm going to invade your country because I feel like it," or "because I'm an invader," or "I want what you've got."

And then the war changes shape?

It inevitably escapes control because that's the nature of modern war. If bombs won't do the job, then you invent atomic bombs, and if they won't do the job, then you invent hydrogen bombs. War takes charge, in other words. And war knows nothing about the ideological reasons that have propelled it. The war is an engineering operation.

Your division, as we have noted, went into the line on November 16, near St.-Dié.

The Germans set fire to St.-Dié, angering us very, very much. Just after we attacked, there was an outpouring of priests and nuns from St.-Dié, soliciting help for the people who'd lost everything in this fire the Germans had set.

After the war I found out something very interesting, which has had a lot to do with my sense that more is going on in the Army than you think is going on. Just before the attack I was assigned to a house between the lines, calling down mortar fire on the Germans who'd been silhouetted by the fire they'd laid. I got an order from battalion to send out a patrol with an NCO and three or four men to see how deep the river was between our positions and the Germans. So I sent out my best sergeant and three or four of the six or eight men I had with me, and they went out for a couple of hours and reported that the river was nine inches deep and was very easy to cross without bridging equipment.

I sent the news back to battalion. The attack took place the next morning, and it was not terribly successful. They did achieve their mission, but with many casualties. After the war I was in a German town and I found this sergeant and we drank some beer together and he said, "You know, I want to ask you something. You know that night you sent us out, do you really think we went down to that river?"

And I said, "Yes, I did. I really did."

He said, "But of course we didn't. When we went out of the house we were scared to death. We went down from the house about fifty yards, we lay in the grass for about two hours, we all agreed on the story about the river."

I said, "Okay, thanks for telling me." That happens much more often, I think, than most people are aware.

November and December 1944 were bad enough, the weather getting worse there in the mountains. Then, in the third week in January, according to the reports, your outfit was hit by what looked like a panzer division.

We saw no tanks, but we saw a lot of troops. I think they were SS. They were very young and angry and National Socialist. That attack actually took place about five hundred yards to my right in a snowstorm. I wasn't aware of it at all. I had been warned that an attack was very likely, and I was looking out of my slit with my field glasses, and indeed I was seeing troops on the hill far away, German troops in line, moving from left to right, which I reported. The response was, "Well, they're too far away for us to do anything about it; keep us informed."

Those German troops were going through our line on my right, but I was utterly unaware of it. I heard a lot of firing to the rear, but you know, you always hear firing in all directions. And you're not certain where the rear is. It might be your right flank, which might bend back to another adjoining battalion. The line was never given on a map to a platoon leader. The company commander probably doesn't exactly know where it is.

Still, I would have numerous bright ideas. The Germans would carouse in a house within easy range, right in front of us. And I said to my company commander, "Look, may I get a bazooka and get out there some night and give them a big surprise? We'll send a shell right through the wall; we'll kill some of them." And the guy said, "No, you'll just stir them up—it will make things worse. If we sit here quietly, we'll be relieved in three or four days and we won't have any more casualties, and some new people will come up and deal with the situation." That's the sort of thing you get.

So you don't have much patience with explanations of wartime behavior that depend upon ideology and cause.

If you've been in combat more than ten minutes, you know that it is about survival, and it's about killing in order to survive, and one forgets the presumed ideological motives when one is performing these operations. You're captured by combat, and the only way to get out of the capture is to reduce the threat to your own personal safety, which is to kill the enemy. That's what you're doing in combat.

You did stir up the Germans at some point. When were you wounded?

The first day I was wounded was the first day I was on the line. When I was wandering around innocently and I hadn't yet heard of the 88-millimeter self-propelled gun, a fragment hit me on the elbow. It wasn't bad enough to require much treatment, but it happened. The second time was also a self-propelled gun; it looked like a tank. It hit a tree above me. I was lying on top of a bunker with another officer and my platoon sergeant, both of whom were killed by the same shell. And I was hit in the thigh and in the back.

That was the day of the attack of the 7th Army, ending ultimately in the crossing of the Rhine, but by that time I was in the hospital, and I stayed there until the war was over.

And since then you've been working up to this book.

Well, I suppose so. The first version of it was **The Great War and Modern Memory,** which is essentially the result of my own war experience and my attempt to make sense of it. Interestingly, I think the idea of that book came to me unconsciously in 1945 when I found myself in Alsace conducting my own platoon war against the Germans in concrete emplacements left over from the First World War. We used those bunkers just as they had been used a generation earlier. I got very interested in the First World War as a sort of prolegomenon to the Second. I wasn't ready to write about my own war, so I thought, I'll put some of my awareness of what combat is like in a quasi-scholarly account of the relation of the First World War to general culture. That's why I did that book.

I remember opening your **Great War and Modern Memory** *to the dedication page and seeing: "To the memory of Technical Sergeant Edward Keith Hudson, ASN 36548772, Co. F., 410th Infantry, killed beside me in France, March 15, 1945." I thought that here at last might be a different kind of book about the Great War.*

Let me say a word about that dedication. I have always tried to get telling details into my books. In the piece I just finished writing for **The Norton Book of Modern War,** I talk about the immense numbers of people involved in the Second World War and the consequent anonymity. When the battle cruiser *Hood* blew up fighting the *Bismarck,* everybody on it, 1,419 men, was killed, except three men. My wife sometimes helps me with research, and I have her the job of finding out the names and ranks of those three men, because I wanted to make the point that these numbers mean nothing when they're detached from individuals. She actually found the names, and I've got them in there.

In the same way—in that dedication to the memory of Sergeant Hudson—I wrote the Army to get his serial number because I knew that would make a very subtle ironic point about this guy's relation to the whole proceeding, and it took them about a year to find it. I'm always anxious for details like that because you convince the reader of your own probity and the verisimilitude of what you're getting at. You're not making this up. You're an accurate and responsible reporter, and the more of that you convey to the reader the better he'll be prepared to receive the things in your book that are not reporting, that are interpretations.

Historians sometimes get very angry at what I do, and what I have to say is that although I use historical data, I'm essentially writing an essay. One critic thought he was dumping on *The Great War and Modern Memory* when he called it a gothic elegy, but I agreed with him: it is a gothic elegy. If I were really working in history, it probably wouldn't be readable. One has to color it emotionally. One has to make the reader cry and laugh to get anywhere with the sort of work that I want to do.

You've said that though you're a professor of English literature, you've mostly gone through life as a pissed-off infantryman. That refusal to concede anything to sentimentality seems to be disappearing in American letters and certainly in modern American life as the wars recede. What is on the horizon?

Well, I'm not sure that when the Vietnam War veterans get to be my age—I'm sixty-five—we won't have some superb material. Their experience would have been processed through memory, and we'll get some real literature instead of just grievances and complaints. It takes about a lifetime for you to decide in what form you're going to couch your own response to these experiences, and I think this is why it wasn't until my present age that I decided to write about the second war.

Memory, public and official and academic, occupies a great deal of your attention in all your work. I take it you've concluded that memory is so fragile and subject to manipulation and corruption that it is always to be regarded with skepticism and that sometimes these corruptions are so deeply entrenched that they can be uprooted only by satire.

By satire or by documents. Although not a historian, I've learned to distrust almost everything except documents dating from roughly the moment of the event they describe. I treasure the remark by Wright Morris, the novelist—a great observation: "Everything processed by memory is fiction." It has to be; otherwise it doesn't have the form that it requires if you're going to recall it from memory. It has to be a coherent thing, and that means it's got to have plot imposed on it. I've written a lot about how ironic plots make possible wartime memory.

Well before this book was finished, you said that you were still trying to bridge the gap between experience and writing about experience. Has **Wartime** *done that?*

No, because I wasn't writing about myself, really. When I started writing the book, I put in a lot of personal stuff—sort of shocking stuff that I wanted to remind people of and that I wanted to validate by indicating that I myself had experienced it. At one point we were on an exercise at Fort Benning, very near our graduation as infantry officers, the climactic exercise involving paratroops and live artillery and so on, and we were aware of an anomalous explosion up in the air, up in the sky, about five thousand feet. It proved to have been the moment when a shell hit

a Piper Cub that was observing artillery fire. Nothing came down but a shoe, with a foot in it, to our horror and astonishment. And I wanted to testify about that.

I originally had that in the book when I was talking about military blunders. I let a friend, a former student of mine, read that text, and he said, "No, that doesn't belong in there. Either you've got to write an objective account or you've got to write a personal account. But you can't bring them together." So I removed all that stuff.

You wrote in two earlier essays, "My War" and "Thank God for the Atomic Bomb," as well as in **Wartime,** *that direct experience is crucial to understanding the actualities of war, and you've agreed with Walt Whitman that "the real war will never get in the books."*

Eugene Sledge wrote about his experience with the Marines in a book called *With the Old Breed at Peleliu and Okinawa,* and it is one of the finest memoirs to emerge from any war. One reason I like it so much is that Sledge, having really fought, knows that even the people back at battalion headquarters, and sometimes company headquarters, have no idea what's going on three hundred yards to the front and that the troops treat them with something of the same contempt that they reserve for the people at home. They don't know what's going on, and now knowing, they make you do things that they would never make you do if they knew what those things meant. Like sending out night patrols, for example, which are hopeless, at least with Americans. The Germans might be able to do them, and the Japanese, but not Americans. We're not prepared psychologically for that kind of military work, especially in small units. As I point out in the book, the terrible thing about that war is that it was fought by amateurs, necessarily; it was the first war any of us had ever been in, and nobody knew what he was doing. Even General Eisenhower had never fought in a war before. We were all sort of making it up as we went along.

You mentioned Sledge and his comrades' animosity toward the rear echelons. There's a line in Harold Leinbaugh and John Campbell's book The Men of Company K *that essentially defines the rear as "anybody whose foxhole is behind mine."*

Well, it depends. Anybody who doesn't favor an M-1 rifle is a sissy, I would say. If you favored carbines, it indicated that you weren't a serious combat person and that you were some distance behind the line, because nobody on the line would be content to try to defend his life with a carbine. It's a tiny little thing; it's like a .22. So we regarded even the 60-millimeter mortar section as rear area, because they were so unlikely to get shot at, you know. Counterbattery fire might fall near them, and they would have to move, but they were terribly safe. I had men that would have cut off their arms to be sent back to the sixties, because they were three hundred yards behind.

There is a kind of continuity among soldiers, in whatever war, of imputing tremendous abilities and virtues to their enemy.

Well, I'm still doing it with the Germans, for whom I have intense military respect, which I developed on the line in that winter. They're incredibly good officers. Their junior officers were much better than ours, partly because they were desperate, and they didn't loaf and they didn't screw around the way we did. We knew we were going to win the war and they weren't certain they were going to lose it, until quite a way into 1945, so maybe they fought better.

And they were more disciplined than we were. They took the war more seriously than we did, and they made more out of slimmer resources than we did. We had much more ammunition, we could shoot it off all the time. We never did anything without laying this incredible barrage on the Germans, partly to scare them, partly to assert our own superiority, and we had it in abundance. There was only a week or so when ammunition was short, but if you just phoned in and said, "I'd like a concentration here," it would come. But the Germans had to proceed much more skillfully to make up for deficiencies, both in men and in material.

Another thing that has helped disguise the true nature of the war was the strictures imposed on the wartime correspondents. Anything that didn't conduce to the war effort was simply not to be written down.

Right. But much of the censorship was self-censorship, and it was generated by genuine patriotic and moral feeling; it was not really imposed. It was a sense that everybody must get on the team because the issues were so important. And so it's a sort of honorable censorship.

It's not easy to believe that the cause of the war would have been forwarded, or that the war would have ended earlier than it did, if people had been told about body parts flying around on the battlefield and horrible things. They were not told them. So I may imply in the book that the self-censorship was a sort of violation of the spirit of the war, but in a sense it was not. Because the object in the war was to win it as fast as possible, and if lying would do it, if false comfort would do it, if fraudulent representation would do it, these were weapons as honorable as any other.

So it's a very complicated question. I don't know how it would have aided the war if people had known more of the truth about what combat involves than they were told. That would have aided the cause of universal truth and the development of the human intellect, but it wouldn't have won the war any faster. It probably would have slowed it down.

Of course, in later wars there was a great deal of tension between public information officers and the representatives of the media, an adversarial relationship.

The Vietnam War might be still going on if it had been a constitutional war, which would have made it possible to exercise treason statutes against those who were impeding the war effort. But because it was not a declared war, they had to be allowed entire freedom, and consequently they ruined the war effort. The moral is, Don't fight undeclared wars. The Constitution has carefully forbidden them, and every one that we've fought has ended very badly. Even the Korean War ended by killing a vast number of people

and accomplishing nothing. It ended where it began and devastated both sides of the country.

So the Founders—excuse my sentimentality, but I care deeply about this—the Founders realized from experience in Europe that a war, bad as it is, must be popular. Everybody must be behind it or it won't work. There must be wide popular support for it. So they carefully wrote into the Constitution that war is declared by the Congress. They had no idea that what they also said (largely to honor George Washington), that the President would be the commander in chief of the Army, was going to be used by people like Ronald Reagan as a way of frustrating the popular will.

In this, as in your other works, you attain a mastery of your subject by drawing from unconventional sources.

You get interested in everything that bears upon it—old files of *Life* magazine, *The Saturday Evening Post,* and so on, which I'm fascinated by, and any sort of ephemera that seems to shed light on the subject. When you work with such material, you become extremely sensitive to it; your whole life then is devoted to awareness of these things you may not have noticed before. Consequently you become conscious of popular music and the way popular music always expresses the popular will; otherwise it won't succeed. You become conscious of the fact that advertising is the real American literature, and that's where you go to find people's secret hopes and dreams embodied, and so I did a lot on advertising, radio commercials, things like that.

I also like to get away from literature. I've learned how to interpret literature, and it's fun for me to learn how to interpret other sorts of documents. I can say wonderful things about sonnets, but there's no fun because I know I can do it. But to say something about a Rinso ad is a challenge.

Did you wonder what **Wartime** *might be like if you were a German, a Japanese, a Russian, an Italian?*

No, I haven't, but it's interesting. The book probably couldn't be done, because it has to be by somebody who won the war; otherwise the news that the event was not entirely happy isn't astonishing. The Germans wouldn't be at all astonished to be told that their war was nasty. They were bombed; they know it. Everybody there lost a relative or two or a whole family and all their possessions, so to bring to their attention that the war was vile wouldn't be interesting.

But the very fact that we won the war gives the war a sort of happy atmosphere that needs to be trimmed down a bit. It violates what actually happened in the war.

Before reading the book, I rather expected I would find a chapter on heroism and cowardice.

I don't know why I didn't do anything with that. It just wasn't a subject that interested me. I might have attempted a definition of heroism and cowardice—I dealt with that topic a bit in the section on fear, where people brought themselves finally to recognize that fear was inevitable.

During the war the medics were quick to say, and you say in your book as well, that to anyone who's been on the line, there isn't any such thing as getting used to combat. I take it you think that in such circumstances terms like bravery *and* cowardice *really aren't useful.*

I think *sick* or *well* is better, or *innocent* or *experienced.* I mean, everybody innocent is going to give the impression of courage, as I did the first six weeks on the line. I gave the impression I was incredibly brave, because I was stupid and ignorant, and I would lead patrols and I would volunteer for things and place myself in great danger, to the immense annoyance of my platoon, whom I was jeopardizing by these gestures. Gradually that security begins to wear away until you end just on the brink of what would look like cowardice. You try to give the impression that you're more in control than you know you can be. I think if I had stayed a week longer without being wounded, I probably would have broken down right on the line. I did break down in the hospital after about three or four days.

After you finally realized that you had escaped?

Well, knowing that I had gotten my sergeant killed, feeling guilty that I hadn't given the right orders to save more of my people. The artillery barrage that got us was predictable. We were coming out of the woods, and there was an open space in front of us that we were going to have to cross, and this self-propelled gun was in the woods across the way. It saw our skirmish line beginning to approach, so systematically—some would say Germanically—it began firing from its right to left, and it dropped a shell about every fifty yards in sequence. The one that hit me was about the eighth shell, and you could have seen the pattern by the second or third shell, and I should have. I got my men into the dugouts, so fewer of them were hurt than might have been, but somehow I froze with my sergeant and this machine-gun officer on top of the dugout. We didn't see what was happening. And by the time we perceived it, by the time the penultimate shell hit fifty yards to our left, we realized the next one was going to hit us. But by that time it was too late to do anything. And to have run into the bunker at that point would have been to risk a panic, so we simply stayed there and got hit. There are many reasons why you get hit, and some of them involve questions like that. You know, both ignorance and getting hit are better than what might have happened otherwise. So we just stayed there.

You quote a very affecting passage from Robin Maugham's Come to Dust *in which just after a tank battle in North Africa he sits down to read Boswell's* Life of Samuel Johnson *while a trapped soldier screams. I showed this passage to a friend of mine who had fought in Vietnam, and it immediately brought to his mind one day when he ate a can of C-rations while studying a beautiful severed hand that lay immediately nearby.*

Well, one has to eat. You know, I had a very good platoon sergeant who got wounded and who came back. I saw him again in the Alps when we were occupying there in Austria, and we got drunk one night. I said, "Look, I know you disapproved of me many times, but tell me the time

you disapproved of me the most, what I did that annoyed you most."

He said, "It was the time you'd come back from helping Lieutenant Goodman," who'd been shot in the back. I had helped him and put a couple of pads on him, and my hands were covered with blood, and there was no place to wash them, and I was very hungry. And I opened a can of C-ration cheese, great yellow cheese, and with these bloodied hands, which I didn't even notice, I ate the cheese. He said, "At that point I really almost gave up on you. I thought you were incredibly insensitive and bloody-minded and so on," and I said, "Well, I never even noticed." I had to do these two things: One was to help Lieutenant Goodman and get him back to the medics before he died of bleeding, and the other was to eat my cheese. And I did them both.

If someone innocent of combat reads **Wartime**, *what do you hope he will take from it?*

I hope it will move him to conscientious objection or else impel him cunningly to get into a noncombat branch of the service, if that's possible. It wasn't possible for me, partly because I didn't want to disgrace myself. I was enrolled in Army ROTC in college, and my unit was an infantry unit, and I was enrolled in it for many, many reasons. It was easier than gym. I never liked physical exercise all that much, and I enjoyed certain things about the military. I enjoyed its formality. Formality has always attracted me in literature. I prefer ordered verse to free verse, for example. I prefer eighteenth-century understandings of literary structure to loose understandings.

Knowing what I know now, I would not have been in the infantry. I might have been in the ordnance, which my father was in the First World War. He spent the war riding a horse around an ammunition dump near Bordeaux, a dump of which he had charge. He made a daily inspection around it and had a perfectly satisfactory war. Now, of course, I'd try to get in intelligence or OSS or something involving some kind of intellectual talent. But I was too young in those days to have such pretensions. I was just as bright then as I am now, but nobody knew it.

James Jones has argued that history is too much the story of the top downward. Would you agree?

Well, to a degree, but I talk a lot about the top as well. I talk about Churchill's drinking, and I talk about the difficulty of making top decisions. I end the book, certainly, with a focus at the top. I'd treated the leader class in the book with a degree of disdain up to that point. But I thought I would end by indicating that there is very much another side to it.

You end the book by quoting Eisenhower's revisions to his famous Normandy message, when he drafted a public statement that was to be released in case the invasion failed on the beaches.

He started by trying to sort of sneak out of responsibility by saying, "The troops have been withdrawn," as if some distant, anonymous agency had made the decision. Then he caught himself—I used the word *nobly*—caught himself at it and decided that he had to earn the privilege of leadership by accepting all responsibility, which few people realized. So he said, "If any blame or fault attaches to this attempt, it is mine alone." I thought that was wonderful. (pp. 130-38)

Paul Fussell and Roger J. Spiller, in an interview in American Heritage, *Vol. XL, No. 7, November, 1989, pp. 126, 130-32, 134, 137-38.*

Samuel Hynes   (review date 13 November 1989)

[*In the following review of* Wartime, *Hynes praises Fussell's effort to demythologize the Second World War but finds fault with his failure to acknowledge the political necessity of the conflict.*]

The Second World War has never acquired an honorific title. It hasn't been called The Second Great War, or The Even Greater War, or The War to End Anything. It goes on being simply The Second World War. The naïveté that could associate the violent deaths of millions of human beings with greatness died on the western front in the First War, and men went to the second unencumbered by the big abstractions. Eisenhower might call his invasion of Europe a Crusade if he wanted to, but nobody listened. It was just a job that had to be done.

Nearly half a century after the end of hostilities, the Second World War has not generated a myth as moving or as literary as the first one did. Nobody has said that "The Poetry is in the Pity," nobody has written an *All Quiet* or a *Journey's End*. There is no dramatic shape to the second war's story, no peripeteia, no conversion from innocence to bitter wisdom, no irony, no outrage. In their place is the sustained conviction that great moral issues were at stake, and the awareness of the scale of the thing, that it was fought mightily over vast spaces. It isn't really much of a *story,* and it's not surprising that there is still no canon of World War II literature.

For most people these two elements, the moral issues and the scale, define the myth of the Second War. This seems to be the case whether one fought in the war or not. John Updike, for example, who was a child when the war ended, wrote this version of the myth last summer:

> This war, at least for Europeans and North Americans, has become the century's central myth, a vast imaging of a primal time when good and evil contended for the planet, a tale of Troy whose angles are infinite and whose central figures never fail to amaze us with their size, their theatricality, their sweep.

This is a romanticized and aestheticized version of the war, putting it into literary and theatrical terms in a way that obscures the war's real issues; but it seems to be the way many people imagine it. And the drama was there, all right: there were heroes and villains. And what is more important, they never changed; at the end of it all, the armies went home (at least *our* armies did) still certain that the same goods were good, the same evils evil.

It is against this reading of the war, at once reductively moral and theatrical, that Paul Fussell directs the argument of *Wartime.* His concern is not with narrative history—there are no battle pieces here and no analyses of strategy, and virtually no chronology; he is out not to tell the story, but to dismantle the myth. "For the past 50 years," he writes in his preface, "the Allied war has been sanitized and romanticized almost beyond recognition by the sentimental, the loony patriotic, the ignorant, and the blood thirsty. I have tried to balance the scales." Fussell intends to disperse altogether the notion that the Second World War was a "Good War," and to put in its place an anti-myth—one that will be *un*sentimental, *un*patriotic, informed, and—what's the opposite of bloodthirsty?—pacific. He aims to persuade his readers to alter their understandings, and to accept his view that the war they think of as justified and necessary was in fact as stupid and as meaningless as, in *its* myth, the First War is seen to be.

I can't think of anyone better equipped for this problematic task than Fussell is. He is the author of a justly admired study of the First World War, *The Great War and Modern Memory;* he is a fastidious scholar (take a careful look at the notes to *Wartime*); and he is an elegant writer, one of the few contemporary critics whose prose actually gives pleasure. And he has another qualification that is at least as important: he has been a soldier. He served as an infantry platoon leader in France, and was wounded in action. It is a demonstrable fact that the best books about war have been written by men who fought, and that the best view of battle is from ground level in the middle of it: you might call this the Willie-and-Joe Principle. Of course there have been exceptions—there was Homer, there was Stephen Crane—but not many. War, one must conclude, is very nearly unimaginable; most men must live it before they can begin to understand it.

One other fact about Fussell is crucial to this book (and for that matter to all his books): he is an ironist by nature and by training. He began his writing career as an 18th-century scholar, with books like *The Rhetorical World of Augustan Humanism,* and you can see in his later, non-academic books—*Abroad, The Boy Scout Handbook and Other Observations, Class,* and *Thank God for the Atom Bomb*—that his choice of a field was an inevitable one. For Fussell shares with the great Augustans their rational and superior posture toward humanity, their disdain for whatever is popular and common, and their distrust for mass feelings. These attitudes, in their highest expressions, have produced the greatest satirists in our language; at their lowest they produce condescension, snobbery, and curmudgeonly huffing. Fussell has come near to both ends of that continuum in his time, and there is something of both in *Wartime.*

It was the ironist in Fussell, addressing the great ironic episode of modern history, that made *The Great War and Modern Memory* the fine and moving book that it is. It is essentially a book about rhetoric—the rhetoric of the First World War—and how it was altered and made ironic by events. Because the story of that war has an ironic twist to it, Fussell was at home in it, and could write a book about it that is very personal, not so much criticism as a kind of displaced war memoir—as though instead of writing about his own experiences in his own war he had chosen to write about the previous war, but in a strongly emotional way. You see that personal involvement at once, in the book's dedication:

To the Memory of
Technical Sergeant Edward Keith Hudson
ASN 36548772
Co. F, 410th Infantry
Killed beside me in France
March 15, 1945.

Consider all that is implied in these lines: male comradeship in arms, shared combat in a foreign land, the violent death of a friend in battle. There is a whole idea of war here—and a rather romantic one, I'd say. It's interesting that Fussell could attach those feelings to the Great War, and not to his own war; there is nothing so personal in *Wartime.*

Fussell begins his assault on the Myth of the Good War in *Wartime* with the errors, the misconceptions, and the ghastly blunders of the war. This is shrewd strategy—for what can one say in defense of "precision bombing" or the casualties that our own weapons inflicted on our own troops, or of The Great Dakar Fuck-up? But the heart of his case lies not in the misuses of men, but in the misuses of language; *Wartime* is another book about rhetoric. Its thesis is that during the Second World War thought, and thought's instrument, language, were degraded and corrupted. "The damage the war visited upon bodies and buildings is obvious," Fussell writes. "Less obvious is the damage it did to intellect, discrimination, honesty, individuality, complexity, ambiguity, and irony, not to mention privacy and wit."

Many of the terms in that last sentence are from the vocabulary of Fussell's Augustans: Swift and Pope would have shared his concern for discrimination, irony, and wit. But they are also a vocabulary of our own century, which together define a particular modern style—the mode of discourse that has descended in English and American culture from imaginative writers like Eliot and Joyce and Woolf, and from critics like Empson and Tate and Blackmur. Modernism, in short: the High Ironic Style of our century. And not only a style, an ideal of civilization and a system of values that went with it—private, cultivated values to support the gifted individual marooned in our unsympathetic, democratic century. One can argue that the Second World War was the end of that high style and that idea of civilization, and that Fussell, writing out of a Modernist sensibility, condemns the war because it made such sensibilities anachronistic.

Certainly Fussell sees the war as the enemy of those values and of that style. War dehumanizes, war subjects thought to "debilitating simplifications," war is gullible and believing and unironic, war suppresses individual identity, and turns men into regiments. His greatest enemies are the degraders of language, and his best chapters are arraignments of the lies of governments, and of the terrible homogenizing of terms, and therefore of feelings, in wartime. There are original, inventive chapters on how the troops used language: "Chickenshit, An Anatomy," and "Fresh Idiom," which deals with, among other things, the songs of the services, including "The Fucking Great Wheel," which even President Bush is said to have sung in his day.

Fussell's war heroes are not men under arms, but the writers, many of them civilians, who fought back with style and taste against war's decivilizing force. His literary masters have long been Evelyn Waugh and Kingsley Amis, two fierce satirists, both of whom served in the war (without distinction), and who survived to write ironically about it. Both appear in *Wartime,* and are praised for their ironic vision of war's chickenshit. *Brideshead Revisited* in particular is offered as a model of the conflict that Fussell sees in the war, between military crudity and the felicities of elegance and taste.

But the real hero of the book—and a most unlikely one—is Cyril Connolly, minor novelist and reviewer, sybarite and exquisite-manqué, procrastinator, self-absorbed whiner, failed genius. Connolly's career as a whole is a dreary story, but he had one period of high achievement, the war years, during which he founded and edited the literary monthly *Horizon* in London. It was the best high-brow English journal of its time, one of the best of any time. Fussell describes *Horizon* as "one of the most civilized and civilizing of periodicals," and so it was; but what makes Connolly the hero of this book is that he carried on his mission while the V-1s buzzed overhead and the bombs fell on London. He and *Horizon* were a civilizing force, opposing war's brutality in the only way that civilization can, by going on being civilized. And, one might add, Modernist.

The place of Connolly and *Horizon* at the center of *Wartime* brings into focus what Fussell's book is really about: it is a celebration of an idea of civilization, and a denunciation of war, civilization's antithesis and enemy. And because, in Fussell's view, war won, it is also a sort of elegy for lost values—the last civilized Modernist, like H. G. Wells's last Martian, howling alone on Primrose Hill.

In one of Bill Mauldin's great war cartoons, Willie says to Joe: "You'll get over it, Joe, I wuz gonna write a book exposin' the army after the war myself." Willie got over it, but Fussell has not, and the persistence of his rage against the war, 50 years after, is perplexing. One possible explanation is that the real object of his wrath is not war itself, but the stupidity of human beings in not seeing it as *he* does—the true satirist's rage against humanity, for being "the sentimental, the loony patriotic, the ignorant, and the bloodthirsty."

Another possible explanation is in a remark of Connolly's that Fussell approvingly quotes. Writing about Henry James, Connolly observed that he was a "symbol of a certain way of life, a way that is threatened not only by the totalitarian enemy but by the philistine friend." Connolly felt that dual threat; and so, I think, does Fussell. But what do those two terms "totalitarian" and "philistine" have to do with one another? Both, one might say, are enemies of civilization. But one is repressive and lethal, the other simply tasteless. One is the political terror of our age, the other merely the price of democracy. You can only merge them if you turn the war into a paradigm case of the modern process of social leveling, and say that the trouble with the Second World War was its vulgarity. And to do that you must deny that the war had any political causes or meanings.

Here we come to the major weakness of **Wartime:** that it expresses no political sense at all. Consider this passage in which Fussell condemns the war:

> It was a savage, insensate affair, barely conceivable to the well-conducted imagination (the main reason there's so little good writing about it) and hardly approachable without some currently unfashionable theory of human mass insanity and inbuilt, inherited corruption.

Is Original Sin really an adequate account of the causes of the Second World War? What about Nazism, Fascism, Stalinism, Japanese militarism? To be what Fussell describes himself as being, "the historian of emotion and attitude," is perhaps not an adequate basis for understanding the war's significance.

"America," Fussell writes, "has not yet understood what the Second World War was like," and his conviction that this is true has been his motive for writing his book. In the middle of my reading of **Wartime** I took time off to go to a reunion of my old Marine Corps squadron. I'm not usually a reunion-going type, but I went this time, and as I looked around at those friends of 45 years ago, I wondered whether they understood their war, and whether they would understand Fussell's version of it. What, I wondered, would they make of a passage like this one:

> It's thus necessary to observe that it was a war and nothing else, and thus stupid and sadistic, a war, as Cyril Connolly said, "of which we are all ashamed . . . a war . . . which lowers the standard of thinking and feeling . . . which is as obsolete as drawing and quartering."

Most of them would not have heard of Cyril Connolly, but whether they had or not, they would not understand why he should have felt ashamed of the war that they had fought. They would say, I thought, that it was sometimes stupid and sometimes not, sometimes sadistic and sometimes simply violent, because war *is* violent. But, they would add, the Japanese had attacked Pearl Harbor, the Germans had conquered France, the crematoriums of the concentration camps were smoking. They would agree among themselves, I thought, that the war had been, if not a "Good War," then a war so obviously necessary that there was nothing to be argued about. And to Connolly's remark about lowering the standard of thinking and feeling they would probably ask what that standard would have been in a Nazi Europe, a Japanese Asia?

Speaking for these old friends, I am obviously speaking for myself. And in so speaking I am taking issue with a writer I admire. But to take issue is to acknowledge the troubling impact of this powerful though to my mind wrong-headed book, and to suggest that it has importance for contemporary readers. For Fussell is surely right in thinking that our war generation and the generations that have followed have taken the Second World War too complacently as a pure moral act against an absolute evil. I think it was Russell Baker who wryly called it "the last nifty war," and most of us must feel something like that bland satisfaction with our nation's last unambiguous victory. Fussell's version of the war doesn't, perhaps, exactly "balance the scales," but it is a useful corrective. Nobody who reads it will come away thinking about the war complacently. (34, 36-8)

> *Samuel Hynes, "Blood, Sweat, and Vulgarity," in* The New Republic, *Vol. 201, No. 20, November 13, 1989, pp. 34, 36-8.*

Ray Monk   (review date 16-22 November 1990)

[*In the following review of* Killing in Verse and Prose, and Other Essays, *Monk praises Fussell's view on travel and literature but finds his argument for dropping atomic bombs on Japan offensive.*]

"This is not a book to promote tranquillity, and readers in quest of peace of mind should look elsewhere." So announces Paul Fussell in the stridently polemical foreword to [**Killing in Verse and Prose, and Other Essays**]. His list of intended targets—he goes so far as to describe them as "the enemy"—is long, and includes: "habitual euphemizers", "artistically pretentious third-rate novelists", "writers who bitch about the reviews they receive" and "humorless critical doctrinaires with grievances (Marxist, Feminist, what have you)".

Fortunately, the foreword's adversarial tone is at odds with the values expressed in the essays themselves, one of which indeed celebrates the life and work of Edmund Blunden precisely for his refusal to become embroiled in what Fussell describes as the modernist "Adversary Culture". Nor do the targets on Fussell's list feature as prominently as one might expect (though one of the essays, it is true, includes an ill-tempered attack on Andrea Dworkin for her refusal to accept bad reviews). More conspicuous are the themes of war and travel, about which Fussell has written so compellingly in his two best-known books, **The Great War and Modern Memory** (1975) and **Abroad** (1980). The much slighter pieces reproduced here reveal hitherto unperceived relations between the two subjects. Whether he is writing on war or travel, one feels strongly Fussell's sense that the twentieth century has fallen from grace, a fall represented on the one hand by the contrast between the paucity of great literature in the Second World War and the abundance of it in the First, and on the other by the degeneration of the tradition of literary travel (epitomized, say, by D. H. Lawrence in Sardinia) into the mass stupidities of the tourist industry.

There is another connection between the two themes: the modern world, the world created by the Great War, is so horrible, so antithetical to art and literature, that the impulse to travel, to get away from it all, is—particularly for a writer—the most natural and perhaps the only possible response. Fussell's essays on "the fate of chivalry" and "the persistence of pastoral" strike an elegiac note. Chivalry, he writes, "has proved unsuited to the world we have chosen to create". The pastoral can persist in this world, not in poetry, but in tourist slogans, for example Club Méditerranée's description of their holidays as "the antidote to civilization". Extending this line of thought, but in a lighter vein, **"Taking It All Off in the Balkans"**—one of the most enjoyable essays in this collection—celebrates the nudist beaches of Yugoslavia as "an attainable version of superpastoral".

As readers of Fussell's previous work will know, he is at his best when rummaging through the forgotten literary remains of our culture and holding up for scrutiny exhibits which others would pass over without comment. This he does to great effect in **"Writing in Wartime: The uses of innocence"**, on *My Sister and I: The diary of a Dutch boy refugee,* which, at its publication in January 1941, was acclaimed as "the most moving document that has yet come out of the war". Fussell exposes it as a fraud: the work not of Dirk van der Heide, a twelve-year-old Dutch innocent, but of Stanley Preston Young, a New York journalist and playwright. It is a captivating piece of literary detective work.

By contrast, Fussell is at his worst as a polemicist. Pride of place in this collection is given to **"Thank God for the Atom Bomb"**. Fussell's argument is the familiar one that the bombing of Hiroshima and Nagasaki was justified because it prevented the deaths of hundreds of thousands of American, British and Japanese soldiers. What offends is Fussell's startlingly crude *ad hominem* means of defending the argument. Against J. K. Galbraith's plea that the Japanese were ready to surrender anyway, he merely draws attention to the fact that by working in an administrative capacity during the war Galbraith avoided "having his ass shot off". Similarly, countering the historian Michael Sherry, he notes that "when the bombs were dropped he [Sherry] was going on eight months old, in danger only of falling out of his pram". Quite shamelessly, he reproduces **"An Exchange of Views"** between himself and the writer Michael Walzer. Walzer's case is that the atomic bombing was not only morally repugnant but militarily unnecessary; Fussell's reply is that in 1945 "Michael Walzer, for all the emotional warmth of his current argument, was ten years old."

Ray Monk, "Searching for Superpastoral," in The Times Literary Supplement, No. 4572, November 16-22, 1990, p. 1230.

Christopher Buckley (review date 13 October 1991)

[*In the following review, Buckley comments on the amusing aspects of* BAD: or, The Dumbing of America *and notes what he views as Fussell's thorough distaste for twentieth-century American life.*]

Jeremiads about the decline of America are not in especially short supply, but when the Jeremiah is Paul Fussell, author of the masterly *Great War and Modern Memory,* attention must be paid. *Bad* is his *summa contra America.* What he likes about the United States would comfortably fit under a gerbil's paw. Mr. Fussell makes his home in Philadelphia, where he is a professor of English at the University of Pennsylvania, but after more than 200 pages of excoriation you're left to conclude that on the whole he would rather be somewhere else—like, say, England, where he spends a lot of time.

Bad is an alphabetically organized denunciation of everything that is "phony, clumsy, witless, untalented, vacant, or boring that many Americans can be persuaded is genuine, graceful, bright, or fascinating. . . . For a thing to be

really BAD," he posits, "it must exhibit elements of the pretentious, the overwrought, or the fraudulent."

For example, Mr. Fussell continues, "Bathroom faucet handles that cut your fingers are bad. If gold-plated, they are BAD. Dismal food is bad. Dismal food pretentiously served in a restaurant associated with the word *gourmet* is BAD. Being alert to this distinction is a large part of the fun of being alive today, in a moment teeming with raucously overvalued emptiness and trash."

Mr. Fussell's uppah-case "BAD" takes some getting used to, typographically, but you soon settle down to an enjoyable, if depressing, tour through what he calls this country's "Paphlagonia." Say what? It's a conceit based on the British philosopher David Hume's reference to the backward Roman province in Asia Minor where "the people were extremely ignorant and stupid, and ready to swallow even the grossest delusion." Its capital is Salt Lake City, "the very pulsating heart" of the U.S. of P.

His special disdain for Mormons derives from his conviction that "the dumbing of America" originated during the "creeping nincompoopism"—as one contemporary put it—of the 1830's, when Joseph Smith was visited by the Angel Moroni. It climaxed, he says, in 1978, when 913 followers of Jim Jones drank flavored cyanide in the jungles of Guyana. A half-dozen lacerating references to Ronald Reagan, as well as several to his successor, introduce an element of nearly mortal despair over our collective predicament. Vice President Dan Quayle is hardly mentioned—a strange omission, you might think, in this context, unless Mr. Fussell did not want his English friends to accuse him of broad satire.

His BAD mansion has many rooms, and in them you'll find Chrysler's "Corinthian" leather, made in Newark; John F. Kennedy International Airport in New York (hear, hear) and the Albert Speerish Kennedy Center in Washington; the statue added on for political reasons to the Vietnam Veterans Memorial; novels by anyone less than middle-aged; our habit of interrupting one another; American engineering (the French and Japanese have their fast trains, the Swiss invented Velcro; "The American achievement—I know it's bad taste to mention this—is the *Challenger,* brought to you by faulty manufacture, inept and dishonest quality control, and lying and evasion for the sake of big bucks"); processed cheese (natch); the national pathology of euphemizing our language into meaninglessness ("*shower activity* for rain, *nonperforming loans* for *bad debts*"); People magazine and USA Today; Leonard Bernstein; Andrew Lloyd Webber's Broadway productions; Pachelbel's Canon in D; the United States Navy; the "creepy metal mannequins" of the sculptor J. Seward Johnson; television (and how), "a grossly proletarian medium . . . a place where nothing exciting or interesting can possibly happen" (like when the Challenger blew up?); waiters who insist on a first-name basis, and that 35-foot-long white limousine.

Here and there you can hear the tree limbs cracking underneath an excess of weight. Call me a philistine—he will, he will—but I sort of like Lincoln Center. Does the "medical evidence" really suggest that one in 10 Americans is "insane"? And is *The Washington Post* truly a "second-rate newspaper"?

Mr. Fussell's loathing for television—which he nominates as the chief cause, along with the collapse of the public secondary school, of our slippery slide—has an amusing flash point: once, while rehearsing for a talk show about culture, he was asked to substitute "an easy synonym for *anthropological,* a term, I was assured, way over the heads of the audience."

His policy prescriptions sound a bit like the platform of a Cuomo-Tsongas ticket: nationalize the airlines, abolish nuclear energy, stop exploring space while children go hungry, raise the capital gains tax and "get the homeless into a new Civilian Conservation Corps," presumably with all that capital gains windfall. On the private sector side of things he wants us to "start a few sophisticated national newspapers," reinstall Latin in the high schools and have the guts to tell BAD restaurateurs that no, we have *not* enjoyed our dinner, thanks all the same.

He has seen the future, and it is broken. "The new Goddess of Dullness is in the saddle, attended by her outriders Greed, Ignorance, and Publicity." You can say that again, bub. America in the late 20th century ain't no place for an 18th-century man. (pp. 9, 11)

> *Christopher Buckley, "Creeping Nincompoopism," in* The New York Times Book Review, *October 13, 1991, pp. 9, 11.*

Gertrude Himmelfarb   (review date 28 October 1991)

[*In the following review, Himmelfarb disparages* BAD: or, The Dumbing of America *as a pretentious primer in "social correctness" and discusses the elitist attitudes of Fussell's earlier works.*]

Finally we have the book that we have long awaited: a primer in SC (Social Correctness), to complement PC (Political Correctness). In [*BAD: or, The Dumbing of America*], Paul Fussell provides us with a guide to correct thinking on a multitude of important subjects: advertising, airlines, airports, architecture, banks, behavior, beliefs, books, and so on through the alphabet, ending prematurely with television, thus depriving us of his views on undertakers, vivisection, women, xenophobia, youth, and zoolatry.

More specifically, what Fussell has given us is a guide to what is bad about our advertising, airlines, airports, architecture, and so on—or rather, what is BAD about them. And because almost everything about them is BAD, we are invited to conclude that much of America itself is, as Fussell's title pithily puts it, *BAD.* Lest we miss the point, or are among the "millions of BAD people" too obtuse to know how BAD things are, his subtitle makes it clear: "The Dumbing of America."

"Bad" would not be so bad. "Bad" is what everyone knows to be bad—"dogdo [sic] on the sidewalk, or a failing grade, or a case of scarlet fever." "BAD," by contrast, is what only superior folk like Fussell know to be BAD: "something phony, clumsy, witless, untalented, vacant, or

boring that many Americans can be persuaded is genuine, graceful, bright, or fascinating." Bad is universal; BAD is pre-eminently American. "The great crappiness," Fussell tells us in his graceful, witty way, "is essentially American."

As a checklist of Socially Correct opinion, and as a cross-reference of the Socially Correct and the Politically Correct, this book is invaluable. The introduction gets us into the spirit of things by suggesting some of the finer political nuances of BADness. Thus Lawrence Welk is a "low" example of BAD and George Bush a "high" example; the Vietnam War was not a "bad" war, but a "really BAD" war; and Lyndon Johnson and William Westmoreland were the "admen" ("BADmen"?) for that BAD war. From this promising beginning, we go to the first entry, Advertising, which is "the *sine qua non* of BAD," and which became "really deep BAD" in the Reagan period, when pretty girls began to be displaced by flags and patriotic themes were used to tout nuclear energy and the cigarette industry.

The next item, airlines, displays the same mixture of the political and the social. "The United States," it opens, "is the only highly industrialized country with privately owned airlines, which means that profit-grabbing and the attendant fraud will dominate their operations, inviting them to engage in BAD in a big way." (This may have to be revised in a later edition as other countries carry out plans to privatize their airlines, having discovered that government ownership is no guarantee against badness, let alone BADness). But capitalism is only one reason for the BADness of airlines. Another is the "proletarianization" of air travel since the Second World War. Fussell quotes Paul Bowles, who recalls the good old times (the 1930s) when he had his own cabin, complete with bed, sheets, and blankets, and who no longer wants to travel, "now that the world had worsened." Fussell sympathizes with him. Air travel, which was once "almost elegant, or at least pleasant," has become extremely disagreeable, with boring, vulgar people crowding the planes and airports, queuing up for the toilets, incapable of engaging in "civilized human intercourse" or of maintaining a "civil distance" from their neighbors. "Social conditions," we are advised, "are probably the worst on planes making the New York-southern Florida run."

Banks are BAD for the same reason, now that everyone is using them. Once built like "marble temples" or "the grander sort of Episcopal churches," they have come to resemble "lower-middle-class motel offices with mock-friendly housewives in charge." Because there are too many clients to be known personally to these housewifely tellers, the depositors are treated like "proles," made to wait in roped-off lines, suffer the indignity of having their signatures checked, and subjected to canned music (Handel, Mozart, or even worse).

Not all cities are BAD; only a large number of them. Fussell names the worst of them, from Atlantic City, New Jersey, to Juneau, Alaska (thoughtfully providing the states for the sake of his illiterate readers). But there are a host of others—all those cities where one can't get a decent meal (by the standards of the *Mobil Travel Guide*) or a drink ("it's hard to imagine what any civilized person might be doing in Salt Lake City"), or where SAT scores are low and there is no public transportation (we are not told how many people in such cities own cars). Washington, D.C., is singled out as an especially "impressive" example of a BAD city. It lacks a decent theater, has a second-rate newspaper ("complete with horoscopes and funnies"), and is full of embassies and consulates occupied by "very dull people . . . quite devoid of originality, wit, or charm."

And so on through the alphabet. Hotels in the old days, before the advent of Holiday Inns and Howard Johnsons, were only "bad to fair," but now they are "almost uniformly BAD." Again Washington gets special mention for its most famous hotel (unnamed, perhaps for reasons of libel), where a Pentagon contract may be "consummated over BAD booze in a BAD bar, for 100,000 monkey wrenches at $75 each." Then there are the BAD movies that contribute to the "infantilization of the electorate" and thus "the election of Ronald Reagan and George Bush and the agitation over flag desecration." Or the BAD Naval Missile Firing responsible for the crash of the Pan Am 747 at Lockerbie, Scotland. Or the BAD newspapers, like *USA Today,* which also happens to be "the perfect emblem of Reaganism." Or the BAD People, such as Jessie [sic] Helms, Richard Nixon, Ed Meese, Oliver North, William Bennett, Robert Bork, Jimmy Swaggart, Jim Bakker, Zsa Zsa Gabor, Fawn Hall, and George Steinbrenner. Or BAD Public Sculpture, of which the "prime example" is the Statue of Liberty, "that archetypal manifestation of the national yearning for kitsch." Or BAD Restaurants, where the discerning diner is repelled by the "one-half polyester" napkin or the misspelled *"Crème Anglais."* Or, finally, BAD television, "a grossly proletarian medium," which is bad when it serves its primary function of selling diapers and denture cleaners, but becomes BAD when it attempts to deal with books, ideas, or "civilized discourse."

What is obvious in this compendium of the BAD is not only the mutual reenforcement of PC and SC, but the dependence of this SC, Social Correctness, upon another SC, Social Class. This is not surprising in view of Fussell's earlier book *Class,* published in 1983, which dealt in great detail on the differences of dress, speech, food, houses, recreations, and other vital signs that distinguish proletarians from the middle classes and both of these from the upper classes. (At a time when even Marxists have abandoned "proletarians" as patently inappropriate for American workers, Fussell insists upon the term, generally in the derisive form of "proles." "Working classes" he regards as a British euphemism.)

In the earlier book, as in the present one, Fussell's animus is directed more against the "middles" than against the "proles." Although he loses no opportunity to ridicule the proles, with their T-shirts emblazoned with lewd messages and ball caps with beer labels, he professes to find them pathetic, whereas the middles are "loathsome." (The upper classes are merely "fatuous.") In that book, too, it is the ubiquitous polyester that symbolizes the essence of BADness: the "crappy polyester shirt" for men, the "pur-

ple polyester pantsuit" for women, the "small percentage of polyester in an Oxford-cloth shirt" discerned by the "elite eye" (alerted to it by that other definitive class guide, *The Official Preppy Handbook*). After remarking upon Reagan's "Los Angeles (or even Orange) County Wasp-Chutzpah" style of dress, which makes him look "like a prole setting off for church," Fussell "hesitates even to speculate about the polyester levels of his outfits." (Outfits? Surely that is a prole, or worse, a middle-class, word!)

One sometimes wonders what country Paul Fussell inhabits. Did the upper-middle-class American woman, circa 1983, "invariably" appear in a "skirt of gray flannel, Stuart plaid, or khaki; a navy-blue cardigan, which may be cable-stitched; a white blouse with Peter Pan collar; hose with flat shoes; hair preferably in a barrette"? And do the middle classes (now, then, or ever) drink "martoonis" rather than martinis, and frequent restaurants where grilled salmon is invariably accompanied by slices of canned grapefruit? And do they speak of living rooms as "living forums," of bedrooms as "sleeping chambers," of shoes as "footwear," and of glasses as "eyewear"? (These euphemisms are attributed to the people themselves, not to advertisers.) And is a plastic Popeye a common adornment on TV sets in prole households?

More important, one begins to wonder about the entire enterprise. Fussell, after all, is a serious literary critic and historian, who prides himself on being (unlike most of his countrymen) intelligent, cultivated, and sensitive. Why, then, is he so obsessed with the mundane and meretricious aspects of life? Why does he spend so much time in BAD hotels and restaurants, read so many BAD books, watch so many BAD movies and television shows, consort with so many BAD people? And why does he then compound all of that BADness by writing about them? Surely this itself is a species of vulgarity that approaches the very essence of BAD. If it is the height of pretentiousness, and therefore of BADness, on the part of the middle classes to try so strenuously to differentiate themselves from the proles, why is Fussell's elaborate exercise in differentiation not also a mark of pretentiousness and BADness?

The explanation may lie in the special "category" that Fussell devised, in his earlier book, for himself and his kind. He called it "category X." The people in this category exist outside the class structure. They are bohemians, artists, intellectuals, expatriates, even "the more gifted journalists." An "X" person can be contradictory, outrageous, even vulgar without becoming *déclassé,* because he belongs to no class; indeed he is obliged to defy all the conventions to prove that he belongs to that superior "category." Thus, when an invitation calls for "black tie," he appears in a dark suit ("of a distinctly unstylish, archaic cut"); or when a suit is called for (at a funeral, perhaps?) he omits the tie. By the same token, he has license to indulge in all those BAD things that are reprehensible in others.

A simple-minded reader of this book, recalling Fussell's contempt for advertising as the *"sine qua non"* of BAD and of the "publicity enterprise" as the "propelling" force behind all that is BAD in modern life, might suppose that the author would have instructed his agent and publisher to refrain at least from the more vulgar forms of advertising and publicity. Yet the reviewer of Fussell's book has been advised, by means of a handwritten (or possibly, worse yet, a pseudo-handwritten) card signed by his agent or publisher's representative, that the author would be in the States during the last weeks of October for "publicity," and that he would be available for interviews.

One's first thought is that the book is an elaborate leg-pull, an example of that large genre of humorous books that aspire to the best-seller list. Occasionally one suspects a mischievous, even comic intent in some of Fussell's illustrations of the "dumbing of America," such as the appalling fact that most Americans, in this day of mass college education, do not know that formal academic attire is called a "gown" rather than a "robe" and a "hood" rather than a "sash"—"just as they've not heard of Chapman's *Homer* or Spinoza or the Great Chain of Being." To one reader, at least, that sounds very funny. But when Fussell goes on about this for several paragraphs, returns to it later, and cites it as an example of the abysmal "public ignorance" and lack of "cultural literacy" of a national Pulitzer Prize-winning newspaper, the reader begins to take it seriously. A humorous book should surely be good-humored and witty. But this is conspicuously ill-humored and heavy-handed.

Moreover, it is too insistently political to be funny—although here too, in its solemn adherence to every cliché of PC, some readers might find it comical. The final paragraph of the book so neatly amalgamates PC and SC that it is a parody of both genres. BAD has gone so far, Fussell concludes, that nothing can slow it down—not even blowing up the teachers' colleges and nationalizing the airports, curbing the national impulse to brag and raising the capital gains tax, teaching people to sneer at advertising and putting the homeless in a Civilian Conservation Corps, encouraging diners to speak out against BAD food and abandoning the remnants of the "self-congratulatory cold war psychosis." Because none of this is likely to happen, "the only recourse is to laugh at BAD. If you don't, you're going to have to cry."

Fussell is right. Laughter may be the reader's only recourse—but laughter not so much at BAD as at *BAD.* How else can we bear to read, again and again, his indictment of America:

> The great crappiness is essentially American.
>
> The USA is the world headquarters of moral pretension.
>
> America's main contribution to the world is BAD. It is the thing that we are best at.
>
> Actual American life as experienced by most people is so boring, uniform, and devoid of significant soul, so isolated from traditions of the past and the resonances of European culture, that it demands to be "raised" and misrepresented as something wonderful. BAD thus becomes an understandable reaction to the national emptiness and dullness.
>
> How about a country which spends billions of dollars on "exploring" outer space when millions of the poor and hungry sleep, like the natives of Calcutta, on its city streets? How about a nation in which tens of millions are so culturally and spiritually empty that their main way of defining themselves and achieving self-respect is to "go shopping"? What about a country slavering to Americanize Eastern Europe, nurturing there the values that bring us white stretch limos, Donald Trump, Jim and Tammy Bakker, Leona Helmsley, and Messrs. Milken and Boesky?

After almost 200 pages of this, it is not reassuring to be told, in a single paragraph two pages before the end of the book, that "not everything in America is bad or BAD," that there is enough "taste" left to "keep Muhammad Ali generally out of sight" and to recognize, "if only implicitly and by silence," that the Vietnam War was a "scandal." Fussell goes so far as to concede that there are some good things, and even VERY GOOD things, in America: its open borders ("when they've not been compromised by follies like the McCarran-Walter Act"), the "assumption" that its citizens are free, and the First Amendment, which together make up "a package of values so admirable as to be almost worth dying for."

"Almost" worth dying for, but not quite. That equivocal note reminds us that Fussell is better known as the author of two influential books on the two world wars, both of which convey the message that neither of those wars was worth dying for.

The first of these, *The Great War and Modern Memory,* published in 1975, was an impressive if not entirely persuasive work. Describing in graphic detail the horrors of trench warfare, and quoting copiously from the poems, memoirs, and fiction of contemporaries (many of them participants in the war), the book powerfully reinforced what was by then the conventional view of the First World War: that it was barbarous, murderous, and unnecessary. The book was praised for its skillful exploitation of the literary evidence and its imaginative treatment of the war as a literary construct, in terms of language and rhetoric, myth and ritual, theater and romance, image and symbol, irony and satire. Irony is, in fact, the constant refrain of the book. A subheading in the first chapter, "The War as Ironic Action," could well serve as the title of the whole.

Two years ago Fussell published a sequel called *Wartime: Understanding and Behavior in the Second World War.* Using the same kinds of sources and techniques, he came to much the same conclusions: this war, too, was barbarous, murderous, and unnecessary. This time, however, the critics were far less well disposed to Fussell's ironies, finding fault with the evidence and the thesis. Still, the book is instructive in ways that the author never intended. For it unwittingly reveals the shortcomings not only of the earlier book but, much more important, of a mode of analysis that has become increasingly fashionable in recent years: the use of literary concepts—irony, for example—to "demythologize" or "demystify" the subject under analysis. In the case of history, irony serves as an invitation to the historian to impose his "critical" or "ironic" imagination upon the events and characters in history, quite as if they were events or characters in a novel. If one did not know that Fussell is a professor of English, the author of such much-admired works as *Theory of Prosody in Eighteenth-Century England* and *The Rhetorical World of Augustan Humanism,* one could deduce it from his books on the two world wars.

When *The Great War* was published sixteen years ago, such an approach to history was sufficiently novel to excite admiration, and the thesis itself was sufficiently familiar to allay criticism. That war had already been demythologized—in political and human terms, however, rather than literary and aesthetic ones. Historians had taken account not only of the casualties and the follies of the war, but also of such other pertinent facts as national and imperial rivalries, the balance of power in Europe, the nature of the contending regimes, and the implications of the victory of an authoritarian power over a liberal one. Fussell offers no such political accounting, no countervailing force to the tragic "irony" of the war. Regarding the war itself as a form of "ironic action," and "irony as the appropriate interpretive means" for understanding the war, Fussell presents the reader with the simple scenario: "In the Great War 8 million people were destroyed because two persons, the Archduke Francis Ferdinand and his Consort, had been shot." It is this disparity between cause and effect that condemns the war as utterly meaningless, as "sheer madness."

Other historians who have a similarly bleak view of the First World War have come to it not only by way of a more complicated analysis of cause and effect, but also by seeing it in the perspective of the Second World War. For the first war is all the more meaningless by contrast to the second, which was all too meaningful; here there is no doubt of the facts of German aggression or of the consequences of a Nazi victory. For Fussell, however, the two wars are much of a piece. His only uncertainty is which war was slightly more meaningless. At one point in the earlier volume he has the second war offering "even more preposterous ironies" than the first, though a few lines later the first was "more ironic than any before or since." In the later volume he credits the first war with "presumably clearer ethical purposes" than the second, although he does not make much of this. What he does make much of, however, here as in the earlier volume, is the familiar theme of irony.

While the Second World War provides Fussell with no such powerful "ironies" as trench warfare, it does suggest to him "more preposterous" ones, such as those detailed in the chapter on "Chickenshit" (the military "obsession" with haircuts and the like) or in the chapter on "Drinking Far Too Much, Copulating Too Little" (the soldier's "anodyne" to "absurdity and boredom and chickenshit"). And if the leaders of the second war were not the bungling "Old Men" of the first war, who senselessly destroyed millions of lives, they were cheap rhetoricians who shamelessly degraded the language. Thus Winston Churchill, that "perpetual schoolboy," is criticized for being unable to "reprehend" (a curious word in this context) "Axis evil" without sounding a note of "self-righteousness, even priggishness." And all those speeches that have been immortalized—Churchill's "We will fight on the beaches," de

Gaulle's "France has lost a battle but she has not lost the war," Roosevelt's "A date which will live in infamy"—are derided as phrasemaking "in the tradition of advertising display copy."

Fussell deplores the "ideological vacuum" in which men fought without knowing what they were fighting for. As for those men who did happen to know what they were fighting for, who found purpose and virtue in the Allied cause, they are ridiculed for vapid "high-mindedness." An entire chapter is devoted to such egregious displays of "high-mindedness"—Eisenhower, for example, praying to God to bless "this great and noble undertaking," or the sailor writing his father to reassure him that now that he has the great Red Army on his side, "the fight for freedom" would go on and "a free people will win."

If there is a hero in Fussell's book on the Second World War, it is, appropriately enough, a writer: Cyril Connolly, one of the few independent spirits, we are told, to resist the prevalent "self-congratulatory mode." In fact, Connolly resisted so well that he described the war, in a passage quoted approvingly by Fussell, as a war of which "we are all ashamed," which "lowers the standard of thinking and feeling," and which is opposed to "every reasonable conception of what life is for, every ambition of the mind or delight of the senses." Here Fussell's own sense of irony deserts him, as he lavishes praise on a man who did not serve in the war but who "almost died from longing for France," and whose greatest suffering came from an "acute and anguished sense of wartime deprivation, not just from food and drink and subtlety but from Continental and Mediterranean travel." (In almost exactly the same words and in his own voice, Fussell makes this the main theme of his chapter on "Deprivation.")

Nor is there any ironic note in his admiration for Connolly's *The Unquiet Grave,* published pseudonymously toward the end of the war, in which Hitler is mentioned once in passing ("Marx with his carbuncles, Hitler with his Beer-Hall"), and which nostalgically recalls the pleasures of which the author has been unhappily deprived: truffles, freshly roasted coffee, the smell of brioches. This "descant of deprivation," Fussell finds, is a fitting accompaniment to Connolly's "sober excursus on the worldwide neurosis which issues in wars, especially this one." Fussell is equally enthusiastic, and unironic, about *Horizon,* the journal that Connolly edited during the war—a "brave anomaly," a noble attempt to keep culture alive in the midst of "the horrors and the darkness—and a paper shortage so severe as occasionally to reduce *Horizon* to sixty gray, crummy pages." Fussell remarks upon the "unlikelihood, if not the impossibility, of a phenomenon like *Horizon* appearing in the wartime U.S.A." In fact, of course, America had just such a journal, as Connolly himself certainly knew, since many of his writers were published in *Partisan Review*— Stephen Spender, Arthur Koestler, and most memorably George Orwell, whose "London Letters" appeared regularly throughout the war.

World War II, then, was BAD, and for some of the same reasons that America is BAD. If Fussell's America is not as "stupid and sadistic" as his war, it is irredeemably stupid and vulgar. Indeed, the BADness of America, we are told—the "genuine deep BAD"—dates from the end of the war. Connolly is quoted very little in Fussell's book, but his voice is discernible throughout. It is the voice of the aesthete and the snob repelled by the barbarous hordes clamoring at the gates.

In this glossary of BAD, one entry (a "genuine deep BAD" one, as Fussell would say) is unaccountably missing. This is "BAD faith": recognizing the pretensions of others but not of oneself, elevating social gaffes into spiritual failings and lapses of taste into moral evils, and compounding the banality of a radical-chic PC with the snobbery of a tory-chic SC. (pp. 27-31)

> Gertrude Himmelfarb, "The BAD-mouthing of America," in The New Republic, *Vol. 205, No. 18, October 28, 1991, pp. 27-31.*

Joseph Epstein (review date 20 December 1991)

[*In the following review, Epstein finds* BAD; or, The Dumbing of America, *petulant, humorless, and snobbish.*]

For Americans of an eschatological bent who are also burdened by a powerful sense of their own sinfulness, Paul Fussell's new book brings immensely cheering news. If Professor Fussell is even half correct in his assessment of life in the United States, hell, after living here, is likely to be, as we gringos say, a piece of cake. The America that appears in *BAD* is wretched indeed. Life in the country Fussell has limned is disgusting, stupid and vicious; its people, ugly, vulgar and vile. The place is a confederacy of dunces, an Eden populated almost entirely by snakes. Decidedly, it is no country for old men, nor young ones, women, girls, or well-behaved pets. Next to America, hell, as noted, has to be considered, unequivocally, sheer upward mobility.

Is Professor Fussell's picture of American life recognizable to those of us who for the most part live rather contentedly in the United States? It is recognizable, though dimly, perhaps one does better to say darkly. It is recognizable, I should say, as the vision of a man who arises from bed constipated, dyspeptic, hungover, and—to go technicolor for a bit—red with rage, green with envy, blue with disappointment, purple with snobbishness, and what a shame that humourlessness hasn't a colour to represent it, for it, too, needs to be tossed upon the palette Fussell uses to paint the country of his birth and upbringing and mildly successful academic life. He is a man fully and perpetually fed up—"ticked to the max", as American kids often say—loaded for bear, and heart-attack angry. Not, one should think, an ideal companion at breakfast. Nor one to whom blithely to say, as Americans in their immitigable cheerfulness are frequently wont to do, "Have a nice day".

Probably best, too, not to have Fussell as a house guest. But, if you must, don't, whatever you do, pick him up at an American airport (he despises everything about American airlines and aeroplanes); don't arrive wearing a Greek fisherman's cap (he thinks them ridiculous, fit only for Greeks who fish); on the ride home don't play Elgar or Percy Grainger on your automobile tape deck (he finds

their music pretentious in the extreme); and—oops—don't refer to your house or your apartment as your "home" (he is death on what he considers sappy euphemisms); don't serve him anything even faintly resembling the provender that passes for delicacies in restaurants that style themselves "gourmet", don't remark upon the wine, don't use one of those American butterfly corkscrew wine-bottle openers (feeble pretensions again, also ignorant technologizing); and, above all, don't, in imitation of certain expensive American hotels, leave a mint or a chocolate on his pillow (unless you want to call in the paramedics to treat him for full-out apoplexy). Like Holden Caulfield's parents in *The Catcher in the Rye,* Fussell is "touchy as hell".

Extreme petulance, lavished on small enough objects, if brought off in sufficiently grand or deliriously comic style, can be very amusing. But to be so, it ought also to be pure; it can be compulsive, even obsessive, but it oughtn't to proceed from politics or mean-hearted snobbery or give the least hint that it issues from pathetic psychological motivation. The prejudice behind this petulance is generally most attractive when it is isolated and implausible; plausible prejudice, which is what H. L. Mencken called criticism, makes little sense when the object of one's petulance is a wine opener or a man's cap or a chocolate upon the pillow. Worst of all is when one has erected a theory upon which to dangle all the objects and causes of one's perturbation.

Fussell, regrettable to report, has such a theory. His is a theory that sets out to explain the truly egregious, which he refers to as BAD, all loathsome capitals, to distinguish it from the merely (lower-case) bad. Bad, Fussell begins by telling us, is "something no one every [how unfortunate to have a typographical error in the first sentence of a book about shoddy goods and thinking] said was good", whereas BAD is "something phony, clumsy, witless, untalented, vacant, or boring that many Americans can be persuaded is genuine, graceful, bright, or fascinating". In Fussell's view, boring is BAD, pretentious is BAD, euphemistic is BAD, not appreciating irony is BAD, unearned informality is BAD, and BAD, too, is much else in America, from public signs to television to US Naval missile firing.

Fussell includes in his inventory of the contemptible those items that he finds "banal, stupid, or sub-adult". He finds the United States a vast thesaurus of such items. "America's main contribution to the world is BAD", he writes. "The great crappiness is essentially American", he adds, "for reasons that will become clear as we go along." They don't become all that clear, as it happens, unless you are someone who believes that the fall of man began with the election of Ronald Reagan to the presidency of the United States. Fussell's book gives the distinct impression that he believes this is precisely when the fall took place. He is a man who will cross a crowded road against the traffic light to say something unpleasant about Ronald Reagan. A junky newspaper is "emblematic of Reaganism"; we are living in "the post-Reagan atmosphere of open greed disguised as a good thing"; then there is the "infantilization of the electorate" that resulted in, among other things, "the election of Ronald Reagan and George Bush"—such droppings festoon the pages of Fussell's book. Elsewhere, in support of his quite unoriginal political observations, he quotes rather second-line left-wing writers—Todd Gitlin, Barbara Ehrenreich, Mark Crispin Miller—on behalf of his case against American television or advertising or education. Although *BAD* is a book abristle with old-fashioned left-wing clichés, Fussell's argument with America, one senses, is more personal than political.

There is something quaint if never touching about Fussell's anger. Imagine a man going blue in the face about advertising in the year 1991. To be angry at contemporary advertising is like yelling at fungus; better, when one comes upon it, to walk around it. In his tirade against advertising, Fussell writes: "To have a fraud, you have to have a large distance between the touted grand appearance and the commonplace actuality, a distance perhaps perceivable by the disillusioned customer after buying the item but never before." I fear that indictment might apply more aptly to, say, Rutgers University, where Fussell taught for many a year, and to several other American universities of extravagant pretension, than to, say again, a lite beer. One wants to say to Fussell, red-faced with anger as he seems, in the spirit of a contemporary American beer advertisement, "Hey, pop open a cool one, baby. It don't get much better than this."

"To be angry", Hugh Kingsmill used to say, "is to be wrong." Fussell stays angry throughout *BAD,* and, because he does, his entire book feels wrong. Everyone will have his own notion of the bad, including a text defaced by altogether too many upper-case letters, but he is under an obligation, if he is going to go public with it, not to go about, as Fussell does, like a man who has flunked out of charm school. Fussell badly misconceives the role of curmudgeon, if that is what it is he thinks he is playing. Mencken could attack his countrymen with much greater, and deadlier, verve and accuracy, and not come out of the exercise stinking from the sweat of his own hatred. In Mencken could always be sensed the love of life; and his intellectual sword was brandished against those who, through simplifying life with empty explanations of complex mysteries, or through setting up laws with which they themselves could not live, diminished life in its richness and in its possibilities for pleasure. But one senses no such love of life in Fussell—only a dreary distaste for it. Poor fellow, cut adrift in America: he cannot grin and he cannot bear it.

> "To be angry", Hugh Kingsmill used to say, "is to be wrong." Fussell stays angry throughout *BAD,* and, because he does, his entire book feels wrong. Everyone will have his own notion of the bad, including a text defaced by altogether too many upper-case letters, but he is under an obligation, if he is going to go public with it, not to go about, as Fussell does, like a man who has flunked out of charm school.
>
> *—Joseph Epstein*

What he particularly cannot bear turns out to be the middle class in America. In an article about him some years ago in the gossip magazine *People,* Fussell was quoted as saying, "The middle class is the real danger. It's uneducated, it's self-righteous. It's large enough to determine style and then impose it on me. It's large enough to get everybody in this country saying things like 'Have a nice day', causing my stomach to turn. It's my enemy. More than the people in the Kremlin. They're very bad, too, but at least they're not here." One important difference, of course, is that in the United States one can write a poor book like *BAD* and laugh all the way to the bank, while to do so at the time that Fussell said this would, in the Soviet Union, have resulted in his crying all the way to the Lubyanka.

Fussell is himself of the middle class. His father practised law; he makes his mother, whom he describes in the same *People* article as a "club-woman", sound like the pathetically constricted Mrs Bridge in Evan Connell's novel of that name. He grew up in Pasadena, California, not a good address. The *People* article makes plain that Fussell is not pleased about his antecedents. His hatred of his own class supplies the energy and animus for this book. To hate one's own social class is, inevitably, a form of self-hatred. The nice thing about self-hatred in olden days was that at least one kept it to oneself. No longer.

When, in *BAD,* Fussell gets around to attacking magazines, he doesn't attack *People.* Nor does he go after the television and radio talk shows on which he appears to promote *BAD.* But then the objects of his attack throughout his book are notably easy, and never entail a possible conflict of self-interest. He attacks both middling and low-status and large state American universities, for example, but not Harvard, Princeton, and Stanford, which have a special hollow prestige all their own. He savages junky newspapers, but the *New York Times,* which has its own plangent awfulness characterized by its false air of disinterestedness, is never mentioned. Selective anger of this kind is not impressive, especially for a man pretending to wield an intellectual machine-gun. But even when agreeing with Fussell, so unappealing is the tone that one feels inclined to rethink one's position.

BAD is an act of unamusing snobbery. Snobs can be quite amusing, of course, at least when they have genuine style. Evelyn Waugh was a snob with genuine style. His snobbery also had a romantic element to it; he wanted to live in a past that perhaps existed only in his own mind, but his distaste for the present was real and issued in hilarious bits, such as his once remarking that he would not vote for the Tories who, having been in power for many years, had not during all that time turned back the clock a single minute. Fussell is an example of a snob without style. Reading Fussell, not only in this book but in his earlier books *Class* (published in Britain as *Caste Marks*) and *Abroad,* the latter about British literary travelling and travel writing between the wars, one is reminded again of

Hugh Kingsmill, who said of snobbishness that it "is the assertion of the will in social relations, as lust is in the sexual. It is the desire for what divides men and the inability to value what unites them."

Fussell, in his books, is a downward-looking snob, chiefly interested in putting as much space as possible between himself and the class from which he derives. The downward-looking snob is happiest when using his own small attainments to put down others. Thus, in *Abroad,* Fussell writes: "One who has hotel reservations and speaks no French is a tourist", adding later in the same paragraph that "the resemblance between the tourist and the client of a massage parlor is closer than it would be polite to emphasize", which is, of course, precisely what that sentence does. The point to grasp here is that Fussell cannot possibly himself be included in the swinish category of ordinary tourists. How much more elegantly, and with what admirable comprehension of the complicatedness of modern travel, did Henry James, in one of his essays on travel in Italy, put the question when he said that he wished to visit a particular monument early in the day before the arrival of "my detested fellow pilgrims".

It may not come as bad news to Fussell to learn that he is a snob. In *Class,* he clearly puts himself in what he there calls the "X category", which is reserved for those people of talent and high intelligence who are able to escape social class altogether. As Fussell puts it, "you earn X-personhood by a strenuous effort of discovery in which curiosity and originality are indispensable". Often, it should be known, entry to category X "requires flight from parents and forbears". But the rewards are, above all, freedom. "X category", Fussell says, "is a sort of unmonied aristocracy." He then goes on to describe the details of life as lived in this class apart from all classes. Nobody would call it elegant or handsomely ordered; as described in the pages of *Class,* it sounds rather like being a full-time graduate student, with more boozing and without the pretence of scholarship. Greatest of all its pleasures, as so often with Fussell, seems to be the power of put-down it confers:

> When an X person, male or female, meets a member of an identifiable class, the costume [his casual clothes] no matter what it is, conveys the message, "I am freer and less terrified than you are", or—in extreme circumstances—"I am more intelligent and interesting than you are: please do not bore me."

Life in X category sounds, not to put too fine a point on it, messy and dreary. Alienated from one's family, contemptuous of most of one's countrymen, without religion or loyalty to any institution, one's enjoyment limited to the narrow pleasures of expressing one's insolence, endless turgid little ironies, and sense of superiority. Apropos of his X category towards the close of *Class,* Fussell quotes E. M. Forster's on the "aristocracy of the sensitive, the considerate, and the plucky". But the X category sounds much more a lost collection of the insensate, the inconsiderate, and the devastatingly unlucky.

Of greater import than Fussell's aesthetically displeasing and sociologically preposterous volume, his *BAD* book, is the standing of the book as a prime document of X-category culture. Fussell makes the X category sound an elite corps, but in fact it has many thousands of members, the vast majority trained by, and most remaining within, the contemporary American university, where they find a home for their unhappiness and an attenuated sense of community in their shared distaste for their countrymen. Much of the old X-category snobbish emotion used to find a home in Anglophilia and Francophilia, but now neither a weakened England nor a meanly inhospitable France is any longer quite able to support such snobbery. So the X-category culture that is the name of Paul Fussell's desire lives on, its members essentially expatriates in their own country. Here they breathe with difficulty, as through a thin reed, trying to find sustenance in what they deem to be their good taste, enjoying their multiple ironies and the quite unearned belief in their own superiority.

It's all pretty bad; and I don't mean BAD; I really mean sad. (pp. 9-10)

> *Joseph Epstein, "Bad-mouthing America," in* The Times Literary Supplement, *No. 4629, December 20, 1991, pp. 9-10.*

FURTHER READING

Criticism

Dahlin, Robert. "Paul Fussell." *Publishers Weekly* 218, No. 14 (3 October 1980): 8-9.
> Brief overview of Fussell's career, focusing primarily on *The Great War and Modern Memory* and *Abroad.*

Fantasia, Richard. "Legible Status." *American Book Review* 7, No. 4 (May-June 1985): 7-8.
> Comparative review of Fussell's *Class* and Benita Eisler's *Class Act.* Fantasia comments: "In contrast to *Class Act,* Paul Fussell's *Class* is consistently, and intentionally humorous. . . . [While] the acidic style of his observations often infuriates, his eye is keen to the symbolic forms of class divulged in everyday manners and gestures, producing some surprising insights."

Hardin, James. Review of *Sunrise with Seamonsters: Travels & Discoveries 1964-1984,* by Paul Theroux, and *Abroad: British Literary Traveling between the Wars,* by Paul Fussell. *South Atlantic Review* 51, No. 3 (September 1986): 98-102.
> Discusses books by Theroux and Fussell at length, concluding that "[*Abroad*] is an erudite piece of literary criticism but also a work of cultural anthropology, sociology, and anecdote that will be read with profit by those interested in the cultural life of the twenties and thirties. But the existence of the stories of Theroux, among others, shows that Fussell is too pessimistic about the future of travel literature."

Mano, D. Keith. "Paul Fussell." *People Weekly* 19, No. 5 (7 February 1983): 60-2, 67.
> Biographical and critical overview of Fussell.

Sheed, Wilfrid. "Upward Mobility: How to Be an X." *The Atlantic* 252, No. 4 (October 1983): 104-06, 108, 110.

Review of *Class: A Guide through the American Status System,* focusing on Fussell's discussion of "X people," or those who reside outside the ordinary class structure.

Additional coverage of Fussell's life and career is contained in the following sources published by Gale Research: *Bestsellers* **90:1;** *Contemporary Authors,* **Vols. 17-20, rev. ed.;** *Contemporary Authors New Revision Series,* **Vols. 8, 21, 35; and** *Major 20th-Century Writers.*

Seamus Heaney

1939-

(Full name Seamus Justin Heaney) Irish poet, critic, essayist, translator, and editor.

The following entry presents criticism of Heaney's works from 1979 to 1991. For further information on Heaney's career, see *CLC*, Volumes 5, 7, 14, 25, and 37.

INTRODUCTION

Heaney is widely considered Ireland's most accomplished contemporary poet and has often been called the greatest Irish poet since William Butler Yeats. In his works, Heaney often focuses on the proper roles and responsibilities of a poet in society, exploring themes of self-discovery and spiritual growth and addressing political and cultural issues related to Irish history. His poetry is characterized by sensuous language, sexual metaphors, and nature imagery.

The eldest of nine children, Heaney was raised a Roman Catholic in Mossbawn, County Derry, a rural community in Northern Ireland. He once described himself as one of a group of Catholics in Northern Ireland who "emerged from a hidden, a buried life and entered the realm of education." At age eleven, Heaney left his family's farm to study at Saint Columb's College in Londonderry, Northern Ireland, where he had received a scholarship. In 1957 he attended Queen's University in Belfast, where he was introduced to Irish, American, and English literature and was particularly influenced by such artists as Ted Hughes, Patrick Kavanagh, and Robert Frost, whose poetry reflected their local backgrounds. Heaney commented: "From them I learned that my local County Derry [childhood] experience, which I had considered archaic and irrelevant to 'the modern world' was to be trusted." While in college, Heaney contributed poems to university literary magazines under the pseudonym Incertus. After graduating from Queen's University with a first-class honors degree in English language and literature and a teaching certificate, he held positions as a secondary school teacher and later returned to Queen's University as a lecturer. During this time he also established himself as a prominent literary figure with the publication in 1966 of *Death of a Naturalist,* his first volume of poetry. As a Catholic living in Belfast when civil fighting erupted between Protestants and Catholics in 1969, Heaney took a personal interest in Ireland's social and political unrest, and he began to address the causes and effects of violence in his poetry. In 1972 Heaney moved from Belfast to a cottage outside Dublin and began writing full time, producing such pastoral works as the Glanmore sonnet sequence. He returned to teaching in 1975 as head of the English department at Caryfort College in Dublin. Heaney has traveled frequently to the United States to give poetry readings and has ac-

cepted teaching positions at Harvard and Oxford Universities.

Heaney's earliest works evince sensuous memories associated with nature and with his childhood on his family's farm. In such poems as "Digging," from *Death of a Naturalist,* Heaney evokes the Irish countryside and comments on the care and skill with which his father and ancestors farmed the land. Nature is also a prominent theme in his next volume, *Door into the Dark,* in which several poems focus on the work of rural laborers. Critics have praised the poem "Undine," for example, in which Heaney describes the process of agricultural irrigation in the context of myth and sexuality.

Much of Heaney's poetry addresses the history of social unrest in Northern Ireland and considers the relevance of poetry in the face of violence and political upheaval. Included in his collections *Wintering Out* and *North,* for example, are a series of "bog poems" that were inspired by the archaeological excavation of Irish peat bogs containing preserved human bodies that had been ritually slaughtered during the Iron Age. Heaney depicts the victims of such ancient pagan rites as symbolic of the bloodshed caused by contemporary violence in Ireland. In such poems as "Ocean's Love to Ireland" and "Act of Union," Heaney portrays the English colonization of Ireland as an act of violent sexual conquest. Critics have noted that Heaney also addresses Ireland's cultural tensions and divisions through the linguistic duality of his poetry, which draws upon both Irish and English literary traditions.

Irish history and myth are frequently incorporated in Heaney's works, including his prose poem *Sweeney Astray,* which is based on the medieval Irish tale of King Sweeney, who was transformed from a warrior-king into a bird as the result of a curse. Some critics have interpreted the figure of King Sweeney as a representation of the artist torn between imaginative freedom and the constraints of religious, political, and domestic obligations, reflecting Heaney's concern with the role of the poet in society. Irish history is also an important motif in a sequence of allegorical poems entitled "Station Island," included in his collection of the same title. Patterned after Dante's *Divine Comedy,* the sequence portrays a three-day spiritual pilgrimage undertaken by Irish Catholics to Station Island. While on the island, the narrator encounters the souls of dead acquaintances and Irish literary figures, who inspire him to reflect on his life and art.

Some critics believe that Heaney's most effective poetry emphasizes personal themes of self-determination and poetic imagination. While many of the poems in *Field Work*—including such elegies as "The Strand at Lough Beg," "A Post-Card from North Antrim," and "Casualty"—continue to address the unrest in Northern Ireland, they incorporate a personal tone as Heaney depicts the loss of friends and relatives to the violence. Critics have also praised the privately emotional tone of *The Haw Lantern,* a collection that includes parables of Irish life and a series of poems entitled "Clearances" in which Heaney explores memories of his relationship with his mother. In such poems as "From the Republic of Conscience" and "From the Canton of Expectation," he meditates on spirituality in the context of a menacing political climate. *Seeing Things* also diverges from Heaney's previous emphasis on politics and civic responsibility, returning to the autobiographical themes of childhood experience and Irish community ritual. Feelings of loss and yearning are prominent motifs in the collection, as many poems evoke celebratory images of Heaney's deceased father, who appears frequently throughout the volume. Critics have cited "Squarings," a sequence comprising four sections each containing twelve twelve-line poems, as exemplary of Heaney's stylistic and technical virtuosity. Although some commentators have faulted *Seeing Things* for its presentation of elusive images and themes that eschew critical interpretation, many have praised the volume for its imaginative qualities and its focus on visionary transcendence experienced through ordinary life events.

PRINCIPAL WORKS

Death of a Naturalist   (poetry)   1966
Door into the Dark   (poetry)   1969

Wintering Out   (poetry)   1972
North   (poetry)   1975
Field Work   (poetry)   1979
Poems: 1965-1975   (poetry)   1980; also published as *Selected Poems 1965-1975,* 1980
Preoccupations: Selected Prose 1968-1978   (essays)   1980
Station Island   (poetry)   1984
Sweeney Astray: A Version from the Irish [translator and adaptor]   (poetry)   1984
The Haw Lantern   (poetry)   1987
The Government of the Tongue: Selected Prose, 1978-1987   (essays)   1988
The Cure at Troy: A Version of Sophocles' Philoctetes   (drama)   1990
Seeing Things   (poetry)   1991

CRITICISM

Seamus Heaney   (essay date 1974)

[*In the following excerpt from an essay written in 1974, Heaney discusses poetry as a process of self-discovery and cultural understanding, the means of finding a poetic voice, the development of his poetic career, and the differences between technique and craft in writing.*]

I am uneasy about speaking under the general heading of "innovation in contemporary literature." Much as I would like to think of myself as breaking new ground, I find on looking at what I have done that it is mostly concerned with reclaiming old ground. My intention here is to retrace some of my paths into that ground, to investigate what William Wordsworth called "the hiding places":

> the hiding places of my power
> Seem open; I approach, and then they close;
> I see glimpses now; when age comes on,
> May scarcely see at all, and I would give,
> While yet we may, as far as words can give,
> A substance and a life to what I feel:
> I would enshrine the spirit of the past
> For future restoration.

Implicit in those lines is a view of poetry which I think is also implicit in the few poems I have written that give me any right to be here addressing you: poetry as divination; poetry as revelation of the self to the self, as restoration of the culture to itself; poems as elements of continuity, with the aura and authenticity of archaeological finds, where the buried shard has an importance that is not obliterated by the buried city; poetry as a dig, a dig for finds that end up being plants.

"Digging," in fact, was the name of the first poem I wrote where I thought my feelings got into words, or, to put it more accurately, where I thought my *feel* had got into words. Its rhythms and noises still please me, although there are a couple of lines in it that have the theatricality of the gunslinger rather than the self-absorption of the digger. I wrote it in the summer of 1964, almost two years after I had begun to dabble in verses, and as Patrick Kavanagh said, a man dabbles in verses and finds they are his life. This was the first place where I felt I had done more than make an arrangement of words: I felt that I had let down a shaft into real life. The facts and surfaces of the thing were true, but more important, the excitement that came from naming them gave me a kind of insouciance and a kind of confidence. I didn't care who thought what about it: somehow, it had surprised me by coming out with a stance and an idea that I would stand over:

> The cold smell of potato mould, the squelch and
>   slap
> Of soggy peat, the curt cuts of an edge
> Through living roots awaken in my head.
> But I've no spade to follow men like them.
>
> Between my finger and my thumb
> The squat pen rests.
> I'll dig with it.

As I say, I wrote it down ten years ago; yet perhaps I should say that I dug it up, because I have come to realize that it was laid down in me years before that even. The pen/spade analogy was the simple heart of the matter, and *that* was simply a matter of almost proverbial common sense. People used to ask a child on the road to and from school what class you were in and how many slaps you'd got that day, and invariably they ended up with an exhortation to keep studying because "learning's easy carried" and "the pen's lighter than the spade." And the poem does no more than allow that bud of wisdom to exfoliate, although the significant point in this context is that at the time of writing I was not aware of the proverbial structure at the back of my mind. Nor was I aware that the poem was an enactment of yet another digging metaphor that came back to me years later. This was a rhyme that also had a currency on the road to school, though again we were not fully aware of what we were dealing with:

> "Are your praties dry
> And are they fit for digging?"
> "Put in your spade and try,"
> Says Dirty-Face McGuigan.

Well, digging there becomes a sexual metaphor, an emblem of initiation, like putting your hand into the bush or robbing the nest, one of the various natural analogies for uncovering and touching the hidden thing. I now believe that the **"Digging"** poem had for me the force of an initiation: the confidence I mentioned arose from a sense that perhaps I could work this poetry thing, too, and having experienced the excitement and release of it once, I was doomed to look for it again and again.

I don't want to overload **"Digging"** with too much significance. I know as well as you do that it is a big coarse-grained navvy of a poem, but it is interesting as an example—and not just as an example of what one reviewer called "mud-caked fingers in Russell Square," for I don't think that the subject matter has any particular virtue in itself; it is interesting as an example of what we call "finding a voice."

Finding a voice means that you can get your own feeling into your own words and that your words have the feel of you about them; and I believe that it may not even be a metaphor, for a poetic voice is probably very intimately connected with the poet's natural voice, the voice that he hears as the ideal speaker of the lines he is making up. I would like to digress slightly in order to illustrate what I mean more fully.

In his novel *The First Circle,* Solzhenitsyn sets the action in a prison camp on the outskirts of Moscow where the inmates are all highly skilled technicians forced to labor at projects devised by Stalin. The most important of these is an attempt to invent a mechanism to bug a phone. But what is to be special about this particular bugging device is that it will not simply record the voice and the message, but that it will identify the essential sound patterns of the speaker's voice; it will discover, in the words of the narrative, "what it is that makes every human voice unique" so that no matter how he disguises his accent or changes his language, the fundamental structure of his voice will be caught. The idea was that a voice is like a fingerprint, possessing a constant and unique signature that can, like a fingerprint, be recorded and employed for identification.

Now, one of the purposes of a literary education as I experienced it was to turn your ear into a poetic bugging device, so that a piece of verse denuded of name and date could be identified by its diction, tropes, and cadences. And this secret policing of English verse was also based on the idea of a style as a signature. But what I wish to suggest is that there is a connection between the core of a poet's speaking voice and the core of his poetic voice, between his original accent and his discovered style. I think that the discovery of a way of writing that is natural and adequate to your sensibility depends on the recovery of that essential quick which Solzhenitsyn's technicians were trying to pin down. This is the absolute register to which your proper music has to be tuned.

How, then, do you find it? In practice, you hear it coming from somebody else, you hear something in another writer's sounds that flows in through your ear and enters the echo chamber of your head and delights your whole nervous system in such a way that your reaction will be, "Ah, I wish I had said that, in that particular way." This other writer, in fact, has spoken something essential to you, something you recognize instinctively as a true sounding of aspects of yourself and your experience. And your first steps as a writer will be to imitate, consciously or unconsciously, those sounds that flowed in, that in-fluence.

One of the writers who influenced me in this way was Gerard Manley Hopkins. The result of reading Hopkins at school was the desire to write, and when I first put pen to paper at university, what flowed out was what had flowed in, the bumpy alliterating music, the reporting sounds and ricocheting consonants typical of Hopkins' verse. I remember lines from a piece called "October Thought," in which some frail bucolic images foundered under the chain mail of the pastiche:

> Starling thatch-watches, and sudden swallow
> Straight breaks to mud-nest, home-rest rafter
> Up past dry dust-drunk cobwebs, like laughter

> Ghosting the roof of bog-oak, turf-sod and rods
>   of willow . . .

and then there was "heaven-hue, plum-blue and gorse-pricked with gold" and "a trickling tinkle of bells well in the fold."

Well, anyhow, looking back on that stuff by Hopkins out of Heaney, I believe there was a connection, not obvious at the time but, on reflection, real enough, between the heavily accented consonantal noise of Hopkins' poetic voice and the peculiar regional characteristics of a Northern Ireland accent. The late W. R. Rodgers, another poet much lured by alliteration, said that the people from his (and my) part of the world were

>   an abrupt people
> who like the spiky consonants of speech
> and think the soft ones cissy; who dig
> the k and t in orchestra, detect sin
> in sinfonia, get a kick out of
> tin-cans, fricatives, fornication, staccato talk,
> anything that gives or takes attack
> like Micks, Teagues, tinker's gets, Vatican.

It is true that the Ulster accent is generally a staccato consonantal one. Our tongue strikes the tangent of the consonant rather more than it rolls the circle of the vowel—Rodgers also spoke of "the round gift of the gab in southern mouths." It is energetic, angular, hard-edged, and it may be because of this affinity between my dialect and Hopkins' oddity that those first verses turned out as they did.

I couldn't say, of course, that I'd found a voice, but I'd found a game. I knew the thing was only word play, and I hadn't even the guts to put my name under it. I called myself *Incertus,* uncertain, a shy soul fretting, and all that. I was in love with words themselves, had no sense of a poem as a whole structure, and no experience of how the successful achievement of a poem could be a stepping stone in your life. Those verses were what we might call "trial pieces," little stiff inept designs in imitation of the master's fluent interlacing patterns, little heavy-handed clues by which the archaeologist can project the whole craft's mystery.

I was getting my first sense of crafting words, and for one reason or another, words as bearers of history and mystery began to invite me. Maybe it began very early, when my mother used to recite lists of affixes and suffixes, and Latin roots with their English meanings, rhymes that formed part of her schooling in the early part of the century. Maybe it began with the exotic listing on the wireless dial: Stuttgart, Leipzig, Oslo, Hiversun. Maybe it was stirred by the beautiful sprung rhythms of the old BBC weather forecast: Dogger, Rockall, Malin, Shetland, Faroes, Finisterre; or with the gorgeous and inane phraseology of the catechism, such as "the solemnization of marriage within forbidden degrees of kindred"; or with the litany of the Blessed Virgin that was part of the enforced poetry in our household: "Tower of Gold, Ark of the Covenant, Gate of Heaven, Morning Star, Health of the Sick, Refuge of Sinners, Comforter of the Afflicted." None of these things was consciously savored at the time, but I think the fact that I still recall them with ease, and can delight in them

as verbal music, means that they were bedding the foundation of my ear with a kind of linguistic hard core that could be built on someday.

That was the unconscious bedding, but poetry involves a conscious centering on words also. This came by way of reading poetry itself, and being required to learn pieces by heart, phrases even, like Keats's, from "Lamia":

>   and his vessel now
> Grated the quaystone with her brazen prow . . .

or Wordsworth's

>   All shod with steel,
> We hiss'd along the polished ice . . .

or Tennyson's

> Old yew, which graspest at the stones
>   That name the underlying dead,
>   Thy fibres net the dreamless head,
> Thy roots are wrapped about the bones.

These were picked up in my last years at school, touchstones of sorts, where the language could give you a kind of aural gooseflesh. At the university I was delighted in the first weeks to meet the moody energies of John Webster—"I'll make Italian cutworks in their guts / If ever I return"—and later on to encounter the pointed masonry of Anglo-Saxon verse and to learn about the rich stratifications of the English language itself. Words alone were certain good. I even went so far as to write these **"Lines to myself"**:

> In poetry I wish you would
> Avoid the lilting platitude.
> Give us poems humped and strong,
> Laced tight with thongs of song,
> Poems that explode in silence
> Without forcing, without violence.
> Whose music is strong and clear and good
> Like a saw zooming in seasoned wood.
> You should attempt concrete expression,
> Half-guessing, half-expression.

Ah, well. Behind that was "Ars Poetica," MacLeish's and Verlaine's, and Eliot's "objective correlative" (half-understood), and several critical essays (by myself and others) about "concrete realization." At the university I kept the whole thing at arm's length, read poetry for the noise and wrote about half a dozen pieces for the literary magazine. But nothing happened inside me. No experience. No epiphany. All craft—and not much of that—and no technique.

I think technique is different from craft. Craft is what you can learn from other verse. Craft is the skill of making. It wins competitions in *The New Statesman.* It can be deployed without reference to the feelings or the self. It knows how to keep up a capable verbal athletic display; it can be content to be *vox et praeterea nihil*—all voice and nothing else, but not voice as in "finding a voice." Learning the craft is learning to turn the windlass at the well of poetry. Usually you begin by dropping the bucket halfway down the shaft and winding up a taking of air. You are miming the real thing until one day the chain draws unexpectedly tight, and you have dipped into waters that will continue to entice you back. You'll have broken the skin on the pool of yourself. Your praties will be "fit for digging."

At that point it becomes appropriate to speak of technique rather than craft. Technique, as I would define it, involves not only a poet's way with words, his management of meter, rhythm, and verbal texture; it involves also a definition of his stance toward life, a definition of his own reality. It involves the discovery of ways to go out of his normal cognitive bounds and raid the inarticulate: a dynamic alertness that mediates between the origins of feeling in memory and experience and the formal ploys that express these in a work of art. Technique entails the watermarking of your essential patterns of perception, voice, and thought into the touch and texture of your lines; it is that whole creative effort of the mind's and body's resources to bring the meaning of experience within the jurisdiction of form. Technique is what turns, in Yeats's phrase, "the bundle of accident and incoherence that sits down to breakfast" into "an idea, something intended, complete."

It is indeed conceivable that a poet could have a real technique and a wobbly craft—I think this was true of Alun Lewis and Patrick Kavanagh—but more often it's a case of sure-enough craft and a failure of technique. And if I were asked for a figure who represents pure technique, I would say a water diviner. You can't learn the craft of dousing or divining—it's a gift for being in touch with what is there, hidden and real, a gift for mediating between the latent resource and the community that wants it current and released. If I might be permitted a sleight of quote, as it were, I would draw your attention to Sir Philip Sidney's animad-version in his *Apologie for Poetrie:* "Among the Romans a Poet was called *Vates,* which is as much as a Diviner . . . " And I am pleased to say I came upon the coincidence myself, again unconsciously, by that somnambulist process of search and surrender that is perhaps the one big pleasure of poetry that the reader of it misses.

The poem was written simply to allay an excitement and to name an experience, and at the same time to give the excitement and the experience a small *perpetuum mobile* in language itself. I quote it here, not for its own technique, but for the image of technique contained in it. The diviner resembles the poet in his function of making contact with what lies hidden, and in his ability to make palpable what was sensed or raised.

The Diviner

Cut from the green hedge a forked hazel stick
That he held tight by the arms of the V:
Circling the terrain, hunting the pluck
Of water, nervous, but professionally

Unfussed. The pluck came sharp as a sting.
The rod jerked with precise convulsions,
Spring water suddenly broadcasting
Through a green hazel its secret stations.

The bystanders would ask to have a try.
He handed them the rod without a word.
It lay dead in their grasp till nonchalantly
He gripped expectant wrists. The hazel stirred.

What I had taken as matter of fact as a youngster became a matter of wonder in memory. I'm pleased when I look at the thing now that it ends with a verb "stirred," the heart of the mystery; and I'm also glad that "stirred" chimes with "word," bringing the two functions of *vates* into the one sound.

I suppose technique is what allows that first stirring of the mind round a word or an image or a memory to grow toward articulation, articulation not necessarily in terms of argument or explication but in terms of its own potential for harmonious self-reproduction. The seminal excitement has to be granted conditions in which, in Hopkins' words, it "selves, goes itself . . . crying What I do is me, for that I came." Technique ensures that the first gleam attains its proper effulgence. And I don't just mean a felicity in the choice of words to flesh the theme—that is a problem also, but it is not so critical. A poem can survive stylistic blemishes, but it cannot survive a stillbirth. The crucial action is pre-verbal: to be able to allow the first alertness or come-hither, sensed in a blurred or incomplete way, to dilate and approach as a thought or a theme or a phrase. Frost put it this way: "A poem begins as a lump in the throat, a homesickness, a lovesickness. It finds the thought and the thought finds the words." As far as I'm concerned, technique is more vitally and sensitively connected with that first activity where the "lump in throat" finds "the thought" than with "the thought" finding "the words." That first epiphany involves the divining, vatic, oracular function; the second, the making, crafting function. To say, as Auden did, that a poem is a "verbal contraption" is to keep one or two tricks up your sleeve.

Traditionally, an oracle speaks in riddles, yielding its truths in disguise, offering its insights cunningly. And in the practice of poetry, there is a corresponding occasion of disguise, a protean, chameleon moment when the lump in the throat takes protective coloring in the new element of thought. (pp. 263-72)

Technique, as I would define it, involves not only a poet's way with words, his management of meter, rhythm, and verbal texture; it involves also a definition of his stance toward life, a definition of his own reality.

—*Seamus Heaney*

When I called my second book ***Door into the Dark,*** I intended to gesture toward this idea of poetry as a point of entry into the buried life of the feelings or as a point of exit for it. Words themselves are doors; Janus is to a certain extent their deity, looking back to a ramification of roots and associations and forward to a clarification of sense and meaning. And just as Wordsworth sensed a secret asking for release in the thorn, so in ***Door into the Dark*** there are a number of poems that arise out of the almost unnamable energies that, for me, hovered over certain bits of language and landscape. The poem **"Undine,"** for example.

It was the dark pool of the sound of the word that first took me: if our auditory imaginations were sufficiently attuned to plumb and sound a vowel, to unite the most primitive and civilized associations, the word "undine" would probably suffice as a poem in itself. *Unda,* a wave; *undine,* a water-woman—a litany of undines would have ebb and flow, water and woman, wave and tide, fulfillment and exhaustion in its very rhythms. But old two-faced vocable that it is, I discovered a more precise definition once, by accident, in a dictionary. An undine is a water sprite who has to marry a human being and have a child by him before she can become human. With that definition, the lump in the throat, or rather the thump in the ear, *undine,* became a thought, a field of force that called up other images. One of these was an orphaned memory, without a context, obviously a very early one, of watching a man clearing out an old spongy growth from a drain between two fields, focusing in particular on the way the water, in the cleared-out place, as soon as the shovelfuls of sludge had been removed, the way the water began to run free, rinse itself clean of the soluble mud, and make its own little channels and currents. And this image was gathered into a more conscious reading of the myth as being about the liberating, humanizing effect of sexual encounter. Undine was a cold girl who got what the dictionary called a soul through the experience of physical love. So the poem uttered itself out of that nexus—more short-winded than "The Thorn," with less red*undant* energy, but still escaping, I hope, from my incoherence into the voice of the undine herself.

> He slashed the briars, shovelled up grey silt
> To give me right of way in my own drains
> And I ran quick for him, cleaned out my rust.
>
> He halted, saw me finally disrobed,
> Running clear, with apparent unconcern.
> Then he walked by me. I rippled and I churned
>
> Where ditches intersected near the river
> Until he dug a spade deep in my flank
> And took me to him. I swallowed his trench
>
> Gratefully, dispersing myself for love
> Down in his roots, climbing his brassy grain—
> But once he knew my welcome, I alone
>
> Could give him subtle increase and reflection.
> He explored me so completely, each limb
> Lost its cold freedom. Human, warmed to him.

When I read it once in a convent school, I said it was a myth about agriculture, about the way water is tamed and humanized when streams become irrigation canals, when water becomes involved with seed. And maybe that's as good an explanation as any. I like the paraphrasable extensions of a poem to be as protean as possible, and yet I like its elements to be as firm as possible. Words can allow you that two-faced approach, also. They stand smiling at the audience's way of reading them and winking back at the poet's way of using them.

Behind this, of course, there is a good bit of symbolist theory. Not that I am in any way consciously directed by symbolist prescriptions in my approach to the composition of poems, but I am sympathetic to a whole amalgam of commonplaces that might vaguely deserve that label, from Rimbaud's notion of vowels as colors and poetry as an alchemy of sounds, to Yeats's notion of the work of art as a "masterful image." And the stylistic tenets of imagism as well as the aesthetics of symbolism I find attractive: to present an image, "an intellectual and emotional complex in a moment of time." I suppose all this was inevitable, given a conventional course in English literature that culminated with Eliot and Yeats.

In practice, however, you proceed by your own experience of what it is to write what you consider a successful poem. You survive in your own esteem not by the corroboration of theory but by the trust in certain moments of satisfaction that you know intuitively are moments of extension. You are confirmed by the visitation of the last poem and threatened by the elusiveness of the next one, and the best moments are those when your mind seems to implode and words and images rush of their own accord into the vortex. Which happened to me once when the line "We have no prairies" drifted into my head at bedtime and loosened a fall of images that constitute the poem **"Bogland,"** the last one in *Door into the Dark.*

I had been vaguely wishing to write a poem about bogland, chiefly because it is a landscape that has a strange assuaging effect on me, one with associations reaching back into early childhood. We used to hear about bog-butter, butter kept fresh for a great number of years under the peat. Then when I was at school the skeleton of an elk had been taken out of a bog nearby, and a few of our neighbors had got their photographs in the paper, peering out across its antlers. So I began to get an idea of bog as the memory of the landscape, or as a landscape that remembered everything that happened in and to it. In fact, if you go round the National Museum in Dublin, you will realize that a great proportion of the most cherished material heritage of Ireland was "found in a bog." Moreover, since memory was the faculty that supplied me with the first quickening of my own poetry, I had a tentative unrealized need to make a congruence between memory and bogland and, for the want of a better word, our national consciousness. And it all released itself after "We have no prairies . . . "—but we have bogs.

At that time I was teaching modern literature in Queen's University, Belfast, and had been reading about the frontier and the West as an important myth in the American consciousness, so I set up—or, rather, laid down—the bog as an answering Irish myth. I wrote it quickly the next morning, having slept on my excitement, and revised it on the hoof, from line to line, as it came.

> We have no prairies
> To slice a big sun at evening—
> Everywhere the eye concedes to
> Encroaching horizon,
>
> Is wooed into the cyclops' eye
> Of a tarn. Our unfenced country
> Is bog that keeps crusting
> Between the sights of the sun.

They've taken the skeleton
Of the Great Irish Elk
Out of the peat, set it up
An astounding crate full of air.

Butter sunk under
More than a hundred years
Was recovered salty and white.
The ground itself is kind, black butter

Melting and opening underfoot,
Missing its last definition
By millions of years.
They'll never dig coal here,

Only the waterlogged trunks
Of great firs, soft as pulp.
Our pioneers keep striking
Inwards and downwards,

Every layer they strip
Seems camped on before.
The bogholes might be Atlantic seepage.
The wet centre is bottomless.

Again, as in the case of **"Digging,"** the seminal impulse had been unconscious. I believe what generated the poem about memory was something lying beneath the very floor of memory, something I connected with the poem only months after it was written, which was a warning that older people would give us about going into the bog. They were afraid we might fall into the pools in the old workings, so they put it about (and we believed them) that *there was no bottom* in the bogholes. Little did they—or I—know that I would filch it for the last line of a book.

There was also in that book a poem called **"Requiem for the Croppies,"** which was written in 1966 when most poets in Ireland were straining to celebrate the anniversary of the 1916 Rising. Typically, I suppose I went farther back. Nineteen sixteen was the harvest of seeds sown in 1798, when revolutionary republican ideals and national feeling coalesced in the doctrines of Irish republicanism and in the rebellion of 1798 itself—unsuccessful and savagely put down. The poem was born of and ended with an image of resurrection based on the fact that some time after the rebels were buried in common graves, these graves began to sprout with young barley, growing up from barley corn the "croppies" had carried in their pockets to eat while on the march. The oblique implication was that the seeds of violent resistance sowed in the Year of Liberty had flowered in what Yeats called "the right rose tree" of 1916. I did not realize at the time that the original heraldic murderous encounter between Protestant yeoman and Catholic rebel was to be initiated again in the summer of 1969, in Belfast, two months after the book was published.

From that moment, the problems of poetry moved from being simply a matter of achieving the satisfactory verbal icon to being a search for images and symbols adequate to our predicament. I do not mean liberal lamentation that citizens should feel compelled to murder one another or deploy their different military arms over the matter of nomenclatures, such as British or Irish. I do not mean public celebrations or execrations of resistance or atrocity—although there is nothing necessarily unpoetic about such celebration, if one thinks of "Easter 1916." I mean that I felt it imperative to discover a field of force in which, without abandoning fidelity to the processes and experience of poetry as I have outlined them, it would be possible to encompass the perspectives of a humane reason and, at the same time, to grant the religious intensity of the violence its deplorable authenticity and complexity. And when I say religious, I am not thinking simply of the sectarian division. To some extent the enmity can be viewed as a struggle between the cults and devotees of a god and a goddess. There is an indigenous territorial numen, a tutelar of the whole island—call her Mother Ireland, Kathleen Ni Houlihan, the poor old woman, the Shan Van Vocht, whatever—and her sovereignty has been temporarily usurped or infringed by a new male cult whose founding fathers were Cromwell, William of Orange, and Edward Carson, and whose godhead is incarnate in a rex or caesar resident in a palace in London. What we have is the tail end of a struggle in a province between territorial piety and imperial power.

Now, I realize that this idiom is remote from the agnostic world of economic interest whose iron hand operates in the velvet glove of "talks between elected representatives," and remote from the political maneuvers of power-sharing; but it is not remote from the psychology of the Irishmen and Ulstermen who do the killing, and not remote from the bankrupt psychology and mythologies implicit in the terms Irish Catholic and Ulster Protestant. The question, as ever, is "How with this rage shall beauty hold a plea?" And my answer is, by offering "befitting emblems of adversity."

Some of those emblems I found in a book that was published here, appositely, the year the killing started, in 1969. And again appositely, it was entitled *The Bog People*. It was chiefly concerned with preserved bodies of men and women found in the bogs of Jutland, naked, strangled, or with their throats cut, disposed under the peat since early Iron Age times. The author, P. V. Glob, argues convincingly that a number of these, and, in particular, the Tollund Man, whose head is now preserved near Aarhus in the museum at Silkeborg, were ritual sacrifices to the Mother Goddess, the goddess of the ground who needed new bridegrooms each winter to bed with her in her sacred place, in the bog, to ensure the renewal and fertility of the territory in the spring. Taken in relation to the tradition of Irish political martyrdom for the cause whose icon is Kathleen Ni Houlihan, this is more than an archaic barbarous rite; it is an archetypal pattern. And the unforgettable photographs of these victims blended in my mind with photographs of atrocities, past and present, in the long rites of Irish political and religious struggles. When I wrote this poem, I had a completely new sensation: one of fear. It is a vow to go on pilgrimage, and I felt as it came to me—and again it came quickly—that unless I was deeply in earnest about what I was saying, I was simply invoking dangers for myself. It is called **"The Tollund Man."** (pp. 275-80)

. . . . .

Something of his sad freedom
As he rode the tumbril
Should come to me, driving,

Saying the names

Tollund, Grauballe, Nebelgard,
Watching the pointing hands
Of country people,
Not knowing their tongue.

Out there in Jutland
In the old man-killing parishes
I will feel lost,
Unhappy and at home.

And just how persistent the barbaric attitudes are, not only in the slaughter but in the psyche, I discovered, again when the frisson of the poem itself had passed, and indeed after I had fulfilled the vow and gone to Jutland, "the holy blisful martyr for to seeke." I read the following in a chapter on "The Religion of the Pagan Celts" by the Celtic scholar Anne Ross:

> Moving from sanctuaries and shrines . . . we come now to consider the nature of the actual deities . . . But before going on to look at the nature of some of the individual deities and their cults, one can perhaps bridge the gap as it were by considering a symbol which, in its way, sums up the whole of Celtic pagan religion and is as representative of it as is, for example, the sign of the cross in Christian contexts. This is the symbol of the severed human head; in all its various modes of iconographic representation and verbal presentation, one may find the hard core of Celtic religion. It is indeed . . . a kind of shorthand symbol for the entire religious outlook of the pagan Celts.

My sense of occasion and almost awe as I vowed to go to pray to the Tollund Man and assist at his enshrined head had a longer ancestry than I had at the time realized.

I began by suggesting that my point of view involved poetry as divination, as a restoration of the culture to itself. In Ireland in this century it has involved for Yeats and many others an attempt to define and interpret the present by bringing it into significant relationship with the past, and I believe that effort in our present circumstances has to be urgently renewed. But here we stray from the realm of technique into the realm of tradition; to forge a poem is one thing, to forge the uncreated conscience of the race, as Stephen Dedalus put it, is quite another, and places daunting pressures and responsibilities on anyone who would risk the name of poet. (pp. 281-82)

> *Seamus Heaney, "Feelings into Words," in The Poet's Work: 29 Masters of 20th Century Poetry on the Origins and Practice of Their Art, edited by Reginald Gibbons, Houghton Mifflin Company, 1979, pp. 263-82.*

Seamus Deane   (essay date 1985)

[*Deane is an Irish critic and poet who has written extensively on Irish literature. In the following essay, he asserts that Heaney's works are characterized by a quality of boldness tempered with caution and discusses Heaney's treatment of violence in Northern Irish history.*]

As he tells us in his essay **'Feeling into Words'**, Seamus Heaney signed one of his first poems 'Incertus', 'uncertain, a shy soul fretting and all that'. Feeling his way into words so that he could find words for his feelings was the central preoccupation of his apprenticeship to poetry. In a review of Theodore Roethke's *Collected Poems* he declares that 'An awareness of his own poetic process, and a trust in the possibility of his poetry, that is what a poet should attempt to preserve'. The assurance of this statement is partly undercut by the last phrase. It strikes that note of uncertainty, of timorousness which recurs time and again both in his poetry and in his prose. His fascination with the fundamentals of music in poetry, his pursuit of the central energies in another writer's work, his inspection of the experiences, early and late, which guarantee, validate, confirm his perceptions, his admiration of the sheer mastery of men like Hopkins or Yeats, all reveal a desire for the absolute, radical certainty. But this boldness has caution as its brother. For all its possibilities and strengths, poetry is a tender plant. Heaney dominates a territory—his home ground, the language of Hopkins, an idea of poetry—in a protective, tutelary spirit. Images of preservation are almost as frequent as those of nourishment. The occlusions of life in the Northern state certainly contributed to this. It was not only a matter of saying nothing, whatever you say. For him, there is no gap between enfolding and unfolding. It is a deep instinct, the reverence of an acolyte before a mystery of which he knows he is also the celebrant. Hence the allegiance to the mastery of other writers is indeed that of an apprentice. But he is indentured, finally, to the idea of poetry itself and is awed to see it become tactile as poems in his own hands. His boldness emerges as he achieves mastery, but his timorousness remains because it has been achieved over mystery.

This duality is visible in his first two books. Writing in a medley of influences—Frost, Hopkins, Hughes, Wordsworth, Kavanagh, Montague—he emerges from the struggle with them with a kind of guilt for having overcome them. This sense of guilt merges with the general unease he has displayed in the face of the Northern crisis and its demands upon him, demands exacerbated by the success of his poetry and the publicity given to him as a result. Although political echoes are audible in *Death of a Naturalist* and in *Door into the Dark,* there is no consciousness of politics as such, and certainly no political consciousness until *Wintering Out* and *North.* It would be easy, then, to describe his development as a broadening out from the secrecies of personal growth in his own sacred places to a recognition of the relations between this emergent self and the environing society with its own sacred, historically ratified, places. This would not be seriously inaccurate, but it is unsatisfactory because it misses one vital element—the source of guilt in Heaney's poetry and the nature of his search for it.

His guilt is that of the victim, not of the victimizer. In this he is characteristic of his Northern Irish Catholic community. His attitude to paternity and authority is apologetic—for having undermined them. His attitude to maternity and love is one of pining and also of apology—for not being of them. Maternity is of the earth, paternity belongs to those who build on it or cultivate it. There is a politics here, but it is embedded in an imagination given to ritual. That which in political or sectarian terms could be called nationalist or Catholic, belongs to maternity, the earth itself; that which is unionist or Protestant, belongs to paternity, the earth cultivated. What Heaney seeks is another kind of earth or soil susceptible to another kind of cultivation, the ooze or midden which will be creative and sexual (thereby belonging to 'art') and not barren and erotic (thereby belonging to 'society' or 'politics'). Caught in these tensions, his Ireland becomes a tragic terrain, torn between two forces which his art, in a healing spirit, will reconcile. Thus his central trope is marriage, male power and female tenderness conjoined in ceremony, a ritual appeasement of their opposition. One source of appeasement is already in his hands from an early age—the link between his own, definitively Irish experience and the experience of English poetry. There was a reconciliation to be further extended by Kavanagh and Montague in their domestication of the local Irish scene in the English poetic environment. But what was possible, at one level, in poetry, was not possible at another, in politics. Part of the meaning of Heaney's career has been in the pursuit of the movement from one level to another, always postulating the Wordsworthian idea of poetry as a healing, a faith in qualities of relationship which endure beyond the inclinations towards separation. Yet such has been the impact of the Troubles in the North, that Heaney's central trope of marriage has been broken, and in *Field Work* (1979) a new territory has been opened in pursuit of a reconciliation so far denied, although so nearly achieved.

In the early volumes, poems commemorated activities and trades which were dying out—thatchers, blacksmiths, water-diviners, threshers, turf-cutters, ploughmen with horses, churners, hewers of wood and drawers of water. These, along with the victims of historical disasters, the croppies of 1798, the famine victims of 1845-7, are, in one light, archaic figures; in another, they are ancestral presences, kin to parents and grandparents, part of the deep hinterland out of which modern Ireland, like the poet, emerged. These figures have skills which are mysterious, even occult. Banished, they yet remain, leaving their spoor everywhere to be followed, like **'Servant Boy'** who leaves his trail in time as well as on the ground:

> Your trail
>
> broken from haggard to stable,
> a straggle of fodder
> stiffened on snow,
> comes first-footing
>
> the back doors of the little
> barons: resentful
> and impenitent,
> carrying the warm eggs.

In commemorating them, Heaney is forming an alliance between his own poetry and the experience of the oppressed culture which they represent (the Catholic Irish one) and also between his poetry and the communal memory of which their skills, as well as their misfortune, are part. *Death of a Naturalist* and *Door into the Dark* are not simply threnodies for a lost innocence. They are attempted recoveries of an old, lost wisdom. The thatcher leaves peo-

ple 'gaping at his Midas touch'; the blacksmith goes in from the sight of motorized traffic 'To beat real iron out'; the diviner 'gripped expectant wrists. The hazel stirred.' And the Heaneys had a reputation for digging:

> By God, the old man could handle a spade.
> Just like his old man.

For the inheritor, the poet, his matching activity is the writing of verse, a performance which has to be of that virtuoso quality that will make people stare and marvel at this fascinating, almost archaic, skill, still oddly surviving into the modern world. The sturdy neatness of Heaney's verse forms in the first two volumes and the homely vocabulary emphasize this traditional element, enabling us to treat them as solid, rural objects, authentically heavy, not as some fake version of pastoral. But the alliance I spoke of has yet deeper implications.

In Part 2 of **'A Lough Neagh Sequence'** (from *Door into the Dark*) we are given what, for want of a better word, may be called a description of an eel:

> a muscled icicle
> that melts itself longer
> and fatter, he buries
> his arrival beyond
> light and tidal water,
> investing silt and sand
> with a sleek root

That sibilant sensuousness, however spectacular, is not devoted entirely to description. It gives to the movement of the eel an almost ritual quality, converting the action into a mysterious rite, emphasizing the sacral by dwelling so sensuously on the secular. This mysterious and natural life-force becomes the root of the soil into which it merges before it is disturbed again by something like 'the drainmaker's spade'. Heaney's fascination with the soil, for which he has so many words, all of them indicating a deliquescence of the solid ground into a state of yielding and acquiescence—mould, slime, clabber, muck, mush and so on—ends always in his arousal of it to a sexual life. Quickened by penetration, it responds. A spade opens a canal in which the soil's juices flow. A turf-cutter strips it bare. It converts to water as a consonant passes into a vowel. Even there, there is a sexual differentiation, the vowel being female, the consonant male; and in the sexual differentiation there is a political distinction, the Irish vowel raped by the English consonant. Thus a species of linguistic politics emerges, with pronunciation, the very movement of the mouth on a word being a kiss of intimacy or an enforcement. Variations on these possibilities are played in *Wintering Out* in poems like **'Anahorish'**, **'Gifts of Rain'**, **'Broagh'**, **'Traditions'**, **'A New Song'**, **'Maighdean Mara'**, and in **'Ocean's Love to Ireland'** and **'Act of Union'** in *North*. It might be said that the last two poems from the later volume go too far in their extension of the subtle sexual and political tensions of the others, turning into a rather crude allegory what had been a finely struck implication. However, the close, intense working of the language in all these poems derives from this activation of the words in terms of sexual and political intimacies and hatreds. In addition, many poems display an equal fascination for decomposition, the rotting process which is part of the natural cycle but which signals our human alienation from it. Fungoid growth, frog-spawn, the leprosies of decay in fruit and crop, are symptoms of 'the faithless ground' (**'At a Potato Digging'**) and this extends to encompass soured feelings, love gone rancid, as in **'Summer Home'** (from *Wintering Out*):

> Was it wind off the dumps
> or something in heat
>
> dogging us, the summer gone sour,
> a fouled nest incubating somewhere?
>
> Whose fault, I wondered, inquisitor
> of the possessed air.
>
> To realize suddenly,
> whip off the mat
>
> that was larval, moving—
> and scald, scald, scald.

The language of Heaney's poetry, although blurred in syntax on occasion, has extraordinary definition, a braille-like tangibility, and yet also has a numinous quality, a power that indicates the existence of a deeper zone of the inarticulated below that highly articulated surface:

> As if he had been poured
> in tar, he lies
> on a pillow of turf
> and seems to weep
>
> the black river of himself.
>   (**'The Grauballe Man'**, *North*)

When myth enters the poetry, in *Wintering Out* (1972), the process of politicization begins. The violence in Northern Ireland reached its first climax in 1972, the year of Bloody Sunday and of assassinations, of the proroguing of Stormont and the collapse of a constitutional arrangement which had survived for fifty years. Heaney, drawing on the work of the Danish archaeologist P. V. Glob, began to explore the repercussions of the violence on himself, and on others, by transmuting all into a marriage myth of ground and victim, old sacrifice and fresh murder. Although it is true that the Viking myths do not correspond to Irish experience without some fairly forceful straining, the potency of the analogy between the two was at first thrilling. The soil, preserving and yielding up its brides and bridegrooms, was almost literally converted into an altar before which the poet stood in reverence or in sad voyeurism as the violence took on an almost liturgical rhythm. The earlier alliance with the oppressed and archaic survivors with their traditional skills now became an alliance with the executed, the unfortunates who had died because of their distinction in beauty or in sin. The act of digging is now more ominous in its import than it had been in 1966. For these bodies are not resurrected to atone, in some bland fashion, for those recently buried. They are brought up again so that the poet might face death and violence, the sense of ritual peace and order investing them being all the choicer for the background of murderous hate and arbitrary killing against which it was being invoked. In **'The Digging Skeleton (after Baudelaire)'** we read:

> Some traitor breath

> Revives our clay, sends us abroad
> And by the sweat of our stripped brows
> We earn our deaths; our one repose
> When the bleeding instep finds its spade.

Even in this frame of myth, which has its consoling aspects, the violence becomes unbearable. The poet begins to doubt his own reverence, his apparent sanctification of the unspeakable:

> Murdered, forgotten, nameless, terrible
> Beheaded girl, outstaring axe
> And beatification, outstaring
> What had begun to feel like reverence.
>   (**'Strange Fruit'**, *North*)

The sheer atrocity of the old ritual deaths or of the modern political killings is so wounding to contemplate that Heaney begins to show uneasiness in providing it with a mythological surround. To speak of the 'man-killing parishes' as though they were and always would be part of the home territory is to concede to violence a radical priority and an ultimate triumph. It is too much. Yet how is the violence, so deeply understood and felt, to be condemned as an aberration? Can an aberration be so intimately welcomed?

> I who have stood dumb
> when your betraying sisters,
> cauled in tar,
> wept by the railings,
>
> who would connive
> in civilized outrage
> yet understand the exact
> and tribal, intimate revenge.
>   (**'Punishment'**, *North*)

Heaney is asking himself the hard question here—to which is his loyalty given: the outrage or the revenge? The answer would seem to be that imaginatively, he is with the revenge, morally, with the outrage. It is a grievous tension for him since his instinctive understanding of the roots of violence is incompatible with any profound repudiation of it (especially difficult when 'the men of violence' had become a propaganda phrase) and equally incompatible with the shallow, politically expedient denunciations of it from quarters not reluctant to use it themselves. The atavisms of Heaney's own community are at this stage in conflict with any rational or enlightened humanism which would attempt to deny their force. Heaney's dilemma is registered in the perception that the roots of poetry and of violence grow in the same soil; humanism, of the sort mentioned here, has no roots at all. The poems **'Antaeus'** and **'Hercules and Antaeus'** which open and close respectively the first part of *North,* exemplify the dilemma. Antaeus hugs the ground for strength. Hercules can defeat him only by raising him clear of his mothering soil.

> the challenger's intelligence
>
> is a spur of light,
> a blue prong graiping him
> out of his element
> into a dream of loss
>
> and origins . . .

This is surely the nub of the matter—'a dream of loss / and origins'. Origin is known only through loss. Identity and experience are inevitably founded upon it. Yet Heaney's loss of his Antaeus-strength and his Herculean postscript to it (in Part II of *North*) is only a brief experiment or phase, leading to the poem **'Exposure'** which closes the volume. In **'Exposure'**, the sense of loss, of having missed

> The once-in-a-lifetime portent,
> The comet's pulsing rose . . .

is created by the falseness of the identities which have been enforced by politics. This is a moment in Heaney's work in which he defines for himself a moral stance, 'weighing / My responsible *tristia*', only to lose it in defining his imaginative stance, 'An inner emigré, grown long-haired / And thoughtful', and then estimating the loss which such definitions bring. To define a position is to recognize an identity; to be defined by it is to recognize loss. To relate the two is to recognize the inescapable nature of guilt and its intimacy with the act of writing which is both an act of definition and also the commemoration of a loss. The alertness to writing as definition—the Hercules element—and the grief involved in the loss that comes from being 'weaned' from one's origins into writing—the Antaeus element—dominate Heaney's next book, *Field Work.* But it is worth repeating that, by the close of *North,* writing has itself become a form of guilt and a form of expiation from it.

In *Field Work,* all trace of a consoling or explanatory myth has gone. The victims of violence are no longer distanced; their mythological beauty has gone, the contemplative distance has vanished. Now they are friends, relations, acquaintances. The violence itself is pervasive, a disease spread, a sound detonating under water, and it stimulates responses of an extraordinary, highly-charged nervousness in which an image flashes brightly, a split-second of tenderness, no longer the slowly pursued figure of the earlier books:

> In that neuter original loneliness
> From Brandon to Dunseverick
> I think of small-eyed survivor flowers,
> The pined-for, unmolested orchid.
> ### ('Triptych I, After a Killing')

In this volume, that gravid and somnolent sensuousness of the earlier work has disappeared almost completely. Absent too is the simple logic of argument and syntax which had previously distinguished the four-line, four-foot verses he had favoured. Atrocity is closer to him now as an experience and he risks putting his poetry against it in a trial of strength. In **'Sibyl'**, Part II of **'Triptych'**, the prophetic voice speaks of what is happening in this violent land:

> I think our very form is bound to change.
> Dogs in a siege. Saurian relapses. Pismires.
>
> Unless forgiveness finds its nerve and voice,
> Unless the helmeted and bleeding tree
> Can green and open buds like infants' fists
> And the fouled magma incubate
>
> Bright nymphs . . .

Forgiveness has to find its nerve and voice at a time when the contamination has penetrated to the most secret and sacred sources. The ground itself is 'flayed or calloused'. It is perhaps in recognition of this that Heaney's voice changes or that the tense of his poems changes from past to future. What had been the material of nostalgia becomes the material of prophecy. The monologue of the self becomes a dialogue with others. The poems become filled with voices, questions, answers, guesses. In part, the poet has gained the confidence to project himself out of his own established identity, but it is also true, I believe, that the signals he hears from the calloused ground are more sibylline, more terrifying and more public than those he had earlier received. The recent dead make visitations, like the murdered cousin in **'The Strand at Lough Beg'** or as in **'The Badgers'**, where the central question, in a very strange poem, is:

> How perilous is it to choose
> not to love the life we're shown?

At least a partial answer is given in the poem in memory of Robert Lowell, **'Elegy'**:

> The way we are living,
> timorous or bold,
> will have been our life.

Choosing one's life is a matter of choosing the bold course, that of not being overwhelmed, not driven under by the weight of grief, the glare of atrocious events. Among the bold are the recently dead artists Robert Lowell and Sean O'Riada; but the victims of the recent violence, Colum McCartney, Sean Armstrong, the unnamed victim of **'Casualty'**, are among the timorous, not the choosers but the chosen. Among the artists, Francis Ledwidge is one of these, a poet Heaney can sympathize with to the extent that he can embrace and surpass what held Ledwidge captive:

> In you, our dead enigma, all the strains
> Criss-cross in useless equilibrium . . .

Perhaps the poet was playing aspects of his own choice off against one another. Leaving Belfast and the security of a job in the University there, he became a freelance writer living in the County Wicklow countryside, at Glanmore. In so far as he was leaving the scene of violence, he was 'timorous'; in so far as he risked so much for his poetry, for the chance of becoming 'pure verb' (**'Oysters'**), he was 'bold'. The boldness of writing confronted now the timorousness of being there, gun, not pen, in hand. The flute-like voice of Ledwidge had been overcome by the drum of war, the Orange drum. But this, we may safely infer, will not happen to Heaney:

> I hear again the sure confusing drum
>
> You followed from Boyne water to the Balkans
> But miss the twilit note your flute should sound.
> You were not keyed or pitched like these true-
>   blue ones
> Though all of you consort now underground.

In **'Song'** we have a delicately woven variation on this theme. Instead of the timorous and the brave, we have the mud-flowers and the immortelles, dialect and perfect pitch, main road and by-road, and between them all, with a nod to Fionn McCool,

> And that moment when the bird sings very close
> To the music of what happens.

This is the moment he came to Glanmore to find. It is the moment of the *Field Work* sequence itself, four poems on the vowel 'O', envisaged as a vaccination mark, a sunflower, finally a birthmark stained the umber colour of the flower, 'stained to perfection'—a lovely trope for the ripening of the love relationship here. It is the remembered moment of **'September Song'** in which

> We toe the line
> between the tree in leaf and the bare tree.

Most of all, though, it is the moment of the Glanmore sonnets, ten poems, each of which records a liberation of feeling after stress or, more exactly, of feeling which has absorbed stress and is the more feeling. The sequence is in a way his apology for poetry. In poetry, experience is intensified because repeated. The distance of words from actuality is compensated for by the revival of the actual in the words. This paradoxical relationship between loss and revival has been visible in all of Heaney's poetry from the outset, but in these sonnets it receives a more acute rendering than ever before. The purgation of the ominous and its replacement by a brilliance is a recurrent gesture here. Thunderlight, a black rat, a gale-warning, resolve themselves into lightning, a human face, a haven. As in **'Exposure'**, but even more openly, the risk of an enforced identity is examined. But the enforcement here is that desired by the poet himself, the making of himself into a poet, at whatever cost, even the cost of the consequences this might have both for himself and his family. The fear of that is portrayed in the Dantesque punishments of **'An Afterwards'**. But in the sonnets there is nothing apologetic, in the sense of contrite, in the apology for poetry. This is a true *apologia*. It transmits the emotion of wisdom. What had always been known is now maieutically drawn out by these potent images until it conjoins with what has always been felt. The chemistry of the timorous and the bold, the familiar and the wild, is observable in Sonnet VI, in which the story of the man who raced his bike across the frozen Moyola River in 1947 produces that wonderful final image of the final lines in which the polarities of the enclosed and the opened, the domesticated and the weirdly strange, are crossed, one over the other:

> In a cold where things might crystallize or
>   founder,
> His story quickened us, a wild white goose
> Heard after dark above the drifted house.

In such lines the sense of omen and the sense of beauty become one. In *Field Work* violence is not tamed, crisis is not domesticated, yet they are both subject to an energy greater, more radical even, than themselves. By reiterating, at a higher pitch, that which he knows, his familiar world, Heaney braves that which he dreads, the world of violent familiars. They—his Viking dead, his dead cousin and friends, their killers—and he live in the same house, hear the same white goose pass overhead as their imagina-

tions are stimulated by a story, a legend, a sense of mystery.

It is not altogether surprising, then, to find Heaney accompanying Dante and Vergil into the Inferno where Ugolino feeds monstrously on the skull of Archbishop Roger. The thought of having to repeat the tale of the atrocity makes Ugolino's heart sick. But it is precisely that repetition which measures the scale of the atrocity for us, showing how the unspeakable can be spoken . . . **'The Strand at Lough Beg'** is enriched in the same way by the reference to the Middle Irish work *Buile Suibhne,* a story of a poet caught in the midst of atrocity and madness in these specific areas:

> Along that road, a high, bare pilgrim's track
> Where Sweeney fled before the bloodied heads,
> Goat-beards and dogs' eyes in a demon pack
> Blazing out of the ground, snapping and squealing.

Atrocity and poetry, in the Irish or in the Italian setting, are being manoeuvred here by Heaney, as he saw Lowell manoeuvre them, into a relationship which could be sustained without breaking the poet down into timorousness, the state in which the two things limply coil. Since *Field Work,* Heaney has begun to consider his literary heritage more carefully, to interrogate it in relation to his Northern and violent experience, to elicit from it a style of survival as poet. In this endeavour he will in effect be attempting to reinvent rather than merely renovate his heritage. In his work and in that of Kinsella, Montague and Mahon, we are witnessing a revision of our heritage which is changing our conception of what writing can be because it is facing up to what writing, to remain authentic, must always face—the confrontation with the ineffable, the unspeakable thing for which 'violence' is our helplessly inadequate word. (pp. 174-86)

> Seamus Deane, "Seamus Heaney: The Timorous and the Bold," in his Celtic Revivals: Essays in Modern Irish Literature, 1880-1980, Faber & Faber, 1985, pp. 174-86.

Neil Corcoran   (review date 26 June 1987)

[*In the following review of* The Haw Lantern, *Corcoran discusses Heaney's emphasis on the relationship between writing and experience, the concept of literature as a morally responsible act, and the value of poetry as a means of coping with political oppression.*]

The god Hermes figures centrally in **"The Stone Verdict"**, one of Seamus Heaney's new poems, and there are good reasons for regarding him as the presiding genius of *The Haw Lantern.* Responsible for ensuring the departure of the souls of the dead to the underworld, he shadows the book's various memorial poems, notably the sonnet sequence **"Clearances"**, written in memory of Heaney's mother. His name apparently deriving from the root for "stone" ("God of the stone heap", Heaney calls him), he stands over the book's frequent uses of stone as image, symbol and emblem; its resisting, dangerous obduracy is almost as necessary to *The Haw Lantern* as the yielding, preservative malleability of bog peat is to *North.* Above all, as the patron of writing and speech, whose signature may be read out of both "hermetic" and "hermeneutic", he is very much the god of a book which sometimes enigmatically foregrounds the acts of writing and interpretation themselves, and whose strict moralism has its roots in the poet's "representative" speech.

The word "writing" (or one of its cognates) occurs ten times during the book's thirty-one poems, and there are frequent glimpses of the writer writing. These include, outstandingly, a prayer to his mother in the prefatory poem to **"Clearances"** that she might teach him to "strike it rich behind the linear black", as she once taught him how to split a coal block, and a poem in which a poet-analogue, the "stone grinder", tells us how "I prepared my surface to survive what came over it— / cartographers, printmakers, all that lining and inking": some of these new poems are slyly knowing about their own future as critical palimpsest. This address to the act of writing makes newly and sophisticatedly salient the familiar vein of self-commentary in Heaney's poetry, and *The Haw Lantern* is, despite a title which oddly conjures up an earlier Heaney mode, a book very much of its literary-critical moment. Opening with a poem called **"Alphabets"** and closing with one called **"The Riddle"**, it offers a more demanding scrutiny of writerly procedures—of "script" and "story"—than anything in Heaney's career to date.

In **"Alphabets"** the scripts are the complicatingly various ones of English, Latin and Irish which the young Heaney acquires in the classroom, first of all understanding his alphabets through his experience ("the forked stick that they call a Y"), and then interpreting his experience through script and print ("Balers drop bales like printouts where stooked sheaves / Made lambdas on the stubble once at harvest"). This exchange between world and word, experience and text, is uneasy and haunted by loss in *The Haw Lantern;* the poems have a very contemporary sense of how writing is elegy to experience. Indeed, what seems to me the book's finest poem, **"Hailstones"**, discovers an exact figure for this in its first section when, it risks one of the central buzz-words of deconstruction:

> I made a small hard ball
> of burning water running from my hand
>
> just as I make this now
> out of the melt of the real thing
> smarting into its absence.

The Haw Lantern elsewhere reminds us that for Heaney the idea of writing as hurt "absence" has its specific cultural and linguistic signification: the Irish script—"this other writing"—which **"Alphabets"** describes as a "new calligraphy that felt like home", is a poignant, perilously almost absent sign of "whatever might have been" as it writes itself in the "running sand" at the end of **"A Shooting Script"**.

But **"Hailstones"** also makes it plain that Heaney's new writing inscribes more than merely absence. In its third section it connects the original "smarting" experience of childhood with later sexual experience when it imagines the way everything says *"wait"* after a hailstorm:

> For what? For forty years

> to say there, there you had
> the truest foretaste of your aftermath—
> in that dilation

> when the light opened in silence
> and a car with wipers going still
> laid perfect tracks in the slush

The poem defends itself here as the arena in which the healingly interpretative powers of memory can be celebrated, in which apparently discrete experiences can be brought into significant relation by the almost surprised Rilkean delight of "saying there". The present perfection of the poem **"Hailstones"**, which will continue to lay down its trace in time, its own perfect tracks in the slush, supplants and acts as consolation for the "perfect" hailstones of the poem's second section which were "in no time dirty slush".

The Haw Lantern is full of another kind of "saying" too: of saw, fable, instance, riddle and parable. **"The Riddle"** itself is a punningly titled poem: its "riddle" is at once the wire mesh in which someone in "that story" tried to carry water, and the riddling questions which this poem asks about "that story" ("Was it culpable ignorance, or was it rather / a *via negativa* through drops and let-downs?") It is a poem, therefore, about how you interpret a "story", and about how interpretation is a morally responsible act. Many poems in the book interpret old stories, particularly those of an earlier generation's classrooms: Constantine's miraculous writing in the sky; Diogenes and his lamp; Penelope at her shuttle; Socrates on his death-bed versifying Aesop; Wolfe Tone on the sea. There is also an example of that primary interpretative act, translation, in a version of the description of Scyld's "ship of death" in *Beowulf.*

Heaney's own contributions, in a group of "parable" poems, to this tradition of taletelling supply *The Haw Lantern* with its most interesting stylistic development, and they demonstrate a new kind of poetic intelligence. These poems follow the invitations and promptings not of image but of fable, and they are written mainly in a bare, almost prosaically discursive form. Moralizing the fate of Ireland and the poet's responsibility, but unpresumptuously disguising their didacticism in allegory, they inherit some of the procedures of that post-war East European parable poetry which Heaney has recently glancingly discussed in his Eliot memorial lecture on Auden. They are diagnostic, analytic, dispassionate, admonitory, forensic and post-mortem. Nevertheless, their fables have something of the intent, not entirely unamused wryness of, say, Zbigniew Herbert's. In **"Parable Island"** the "missionary scribes", those "old revisionists", derive "the word *island* from roots in *eye* and *land*", and those who gloss the ancient texts enter into the battle between "subversives and collaborators" about the true "island story". In **"From the Canton of Expectation"** the post-war history of Ireland is figured as a grammar of changing verbal moods; pushing through optatives and imperatives, the poem ends up longing for the realistic heroism of the indicative. And **"The Mud Vision"** discovers contemporary Ireland as the posthumous, depleted betrayer of an ambivalent but potentially energizing visionary moment when it had been "as if a rose window of mud / Had invented itself out of the glittery damp / . . . sullied yet lucent".

Such poems, with their ingenious allegorical worlds, constitute a new kind of political poetry for Heaney, and they make it clear that writing has, for him, a moral compulsion even deeper than the aesthetic compulsion of **"Hailstones"**. **"From the Frontier of Writing"** articulates exactly this when, after describing Heaney's encounter with an army patrol, it turns the literal into the metaphorical: at the "frontier of writing", the experience "happens again". The title of this poem may allude covertly to all those frontiers in Auden's early work, and the poem itself could be regarded as an implicit challenge to the Auden view, in his elegy for Yeats, that "poetry makes nothing happen". In Heaney, if poetry makes nothing happen, it does at least make something "happen again". In repeating the experience of political oppression, the poem effects, even if only for the poet, a temporary release from it: at the literal frontier Heaney is "as always . . . / subjugated, yes, and obedient". But at the frontier of writing he suddenly breaks "through, arraigned yet freed". Modernism and postmodernism have given us numerous instances in which writerly self-consciousness is a nightmare of disabling confinement, even where, as in Beckett, being disabled itself becomes newly and weirdly enabling. In Heaney, however, such self-consciousness is the means of transforming the guilt and burden of writing into the true freedom of responsible speech; the poet is still called to account ("arraigned") but now only at the bench of what another of these poems calls the "Republic of Conscience".

When *The Haw Lantern* is not so carefully self-preoccupied, there are some disconcerting moments of less significant repetition: when, for instance, **"A Postcard from Iceland"** tries to do again what the lovely **"Polder"** did definitively in *Field Work,* and when **"Holding Course"** is a supernumerary and vaguely embarrassing addendum to that volume's marriage poems. Some of the **"Clearances"** sonnets too, for all the strength of their portrayal of Heaney's loving but uncertain relationship with his mother, are perhaps a little tired with their own facility. The best of *The Haw Lantern* is more estrangingly demanding and spare, and almost frighteningly assured in the way it carries its own commentary along with it: as the end of **"Alphabets"** does when the great globe itself appears (as a world in a text must) made of strange letters, but wearing the face and name of its writer. (pp. 681-82)

> *Neil Corcoran, "From the Frontier of Writing," in* The Times Literary Supplement, *No. 4395, June 26, 1987, pp. 681-82.*

John Hildebidle   (essay date Autumn 1987)

[*Hildebidle is an American poet, short story writer, critic, and editor. In the following essay, he asserts that the collections* North, Field Work, Sweeney Astray, *and* Station Island *represent Heaney's decade-long exploration of personal experience and Irish history in which he contemplates the role of the poet in the world.*]

Full of recollections and echoes, *Station Island* insists that it be taken as a retrospective view of Seamus Heaney's ca-

reer. As such, it is very much of a piece with his prior work, which has from the beginning been regularly and productively visited by the ghosts of the past. But there is, I think, a more particular reason for looking at the book in the light of the three which precede it—*North* (1975), *Field Work* (1979), and *Sweeney Astray* (1984). The four volumes, taken together, represent a decade-long effort on Heaney's part to find or to create some coherence out of the varied "pasts" which have affected his life, and out of the peculiar present of Ireland as well. They amount to a sustained meditation on the place of the poet in the world, in the hope of resolving the cruel choice which Yeats proposed, a choice between the work and the life.

North is a book especially concerned with history; or rather with histories. There is the political history marked by the colonizations of Ireland by Danes, missionaries, Normans, and most importantly by the English, colonizations which are transformed into acts of sexual conquest in a sequence of poems (**"Ocean's Love to Ireland," "Aisling,"** and **"Act of Union"**) very near the center of the volume and which of course underlie the contemporary conflicts in the poems in Part II. The book as well incorporates the mythic cultural history of Heaney's Ireland, both in the "bog poems" that follow upon those in *Door into the Dark* and in the pair of poems **"Antaeus"** and **"Hercules and Antaeus,"** which frame Part I of the book and which propose a fundamental image of conflict and rootedness. Heaney's effort to find or to define his own place in literary history becomes explicit in the evocation of writers as varied in time and character as Baudelaire, Walter Ralegh, Yeats, and Wordsworth, as well as in the dedication of many poems to Heaney's contemporaries. And finally, the personal history which had been the substance of so many of the poems in Heaney's first three books is at last drawn together, especially in the powerful long poems in the second half of *North,* which amount to an autobiographical meditation on the intersection of the poetic and the political.

But categories quickly lose their distinctness, as for instance in **"Funeral Rites,"** where the small necessary acts of burying one's own dead connect both with the Viking burial of the hero Gunnar and with the sadly repetitious and minimal ceremonies occasioned by "each neighbourly murder" in the Northern Ireland of the mid-1970's. To distinguish between various myths—personal, tribal, political, cultural, historical—is in fact to misrepresent the character of the book, which is fundamentally concerned with interconnection. The problem which dominates the book is how, and why, and to what end one may speak verse in a tragically interwoven world, one in which, as Heaney argues at several points in *Preoccupations,* even vowels and consonants have an apparent political import.

One might fairly define the theme of *North* by way of the borrowed dictum, "whatever you say, say nothing." The source is any Belfast shop-window, where posters remind all sects that any speech is dangerous. Heaney slightly revises the line to "whatever you say, you say nothing," a version which does much to explain the particular darkness of *North.* Many of the voices to be heard in Heaney's later poetry, and especially in **"Station Island,"** object to that dictum, seeing it both as an abdication of responsibility and as a simple untruth: in Ireland, even to say nothing is to take a side. In any case, for a poet who continues to speak (and Heaney's output has not flagged since *North*), the line will not serve as a resting-place. But the inevitable conflict between the sense of powerlessness which the line states and the effort in *North* as a whole to make "music" out of "what happens" (as Heaney puts it later, in **"Song"** in *Field Work*) is in fact the generative tension of the book, and of Heaney's work since.

The apparent solution to that conflict in *North* (and in Heaney's own life, since he is no longer a resident of the North) is to abandon the context in which the conflict exists—to seek a protective and yet still productive geographic estrangement. **"Exposure,"** the final section of the concluding sequence **"The Singing School,"** provides a richly open ending to the volume. Heaney has fled to his new (but, as a note in *Field Work* tells us, only temporary) home, in Co. Wicklow. The flight leaves him "an inner émigré"—which captures both Heaney's sense of being forced back on himself and his recognition that to move to the South is to move within, rather than truly between, lands. That new position brings a kind of freedom (he is "neither internee nor informer"), at least the freedom from making one sort of impossible choice. Thus he has perhaps been empowered; he has at least "grown . . . / thoughtful." The question which the poem propounds— and which, we realize, the whole book has tried to answer—is "How did I end up like this?" That question is complicated by the number of voices Heaney still hears, and which will come to dominate, indeed to determine the shape of, **"Station Island"**: "I often think of my friends' / Beautiful prismatic counselling." But the question misrepresents the case, since Heaney has not, at this point, "ended" anywhere. And what is he to do next?

Whatever relief the poem may offer—and it opens with a lovely evocation of the Wicklow landscape, in which the violent forces operating in so many of the prior poems seem blessedly absent—still this is no unequivocally comfortable place. The time is December and night, the place outdoors, the voice alone. The poem ends with a richly mixed image of a "wood-kerne," escaped and lost. Surely no escape can put to rest the itch of what Heaney a few lines earlier calls "my responsible *tristia*"; and the very title of the poem is a complex image. It would seem that Heaney has escaped that landscape in which he would be, still, exposed to what he calls in one of his essays "predatory circumstances." But too long a stay in this new outdoors could very well lead to the death-by-exposure which so many migrants suffer. He can hide—using "protective colouring"—but to do so may continue the restriction of his view. The goal of this escape is, perhaps, a different kind of exposure: an openness both to the new and to the significance of the old.

But what if that opportunity to confront the new involves a separation from all those things which have given rise to poetry? The question which the final lines of *North* necessarily leave moot is whether and how Heaney might still write once his poetic and geographic and familial roots are at some remove. He has, of course, never been strictly an admirer of the old ways. The much-anthologized **"Digging,"** to take only one instance, had asserted a continuity between his poetic work and the labor of his fathers; but it is a continuity that contains as well an inescapable distance, since his digging with the pen will never be more than analogic to the digging he sees his father doing. But never, before **"Exposure,"** had the distance been so absolute, or its risks so badly stated.

If *Field Work* is, in part, an answer to the conundrums of **"Exposure,"** it is, to use a word Heaney himself uses in **"Casualty,"** a "tentative" one. That tentativeness appears less in the manner of his speech (which confidently manipulates form and language) than the unsettlements in what is being said. The title of the book suggests a return to the rural, richly typological landscape of *Death of a Naturalist,* but Heaney's home-place is explicitly present only in **"The Strand at Lough Beg."** And that one return, which confronts "random sectarian killing," is anything but reassuring.

The landscape may still be full of familiars and relics, but what is clear even without the prior evidence of *North* is the degree to which escape is a necessary step. The sequence of memorial-poems to Colum McCartney (**"The Strand at Lough Beg"**), to Sean Armstrong (**"A Postcard from North Antrim"**), and to a nameless fisherman (**"Casualty"**) emphasizes the murderous actuality of Heaney's former home; and worse yet the unpredictable intrusion of violence even into relatively unpolitical lives. One thing which distinguishes these poems from the attention paid to the contemporary Troubles in *North* is the relative clouding of sectarian lables. Heaney acknowledges his own politics, but only early on, in poems such as **"The Toome Road"** and **"Triptych."** Now the sects turn on themselves. The tribe which slays the fisherman is "ours"; bomber, victim, and elegist are all Catholic. In **"Triptych,"** Heaney's sybil proclaims a dark fate for the whole of Ireland, including that part to which Heaney has "escaped": "Our island is full of comfortless noises."

Thus the nature and potential of Heaney's escape from the North is heavily qualified from the beginning; and the note of escape brings a countervailing sense of abandonment and betrayal, which culminates in Dante's story of Ugolino, with which Heaney closes the book. Ugolino's sin of betrayal places him very near the absolute bottom of hell, in the ninth circle. He suffers eternally just below the betrayers of kinsmen (a charge which Colum McCartney will level at Heaney himself in **"Station Island"**), just above the betrayers of friends (and Heaney, for all his affection for the dead fisherman, had, as he admits, "missed his funeral"), in the midst of those who have betrayed their nation.

Dante's curse falls not only on Ugolino but on his homeland; he calls down a purifying flood upon Pisa for including within its atrocity the deaths not only of the traitorous Ugolino but also of innocent children. The betrayal, in other words, is cruelly doubled: the person betrays the State, and the individual and often innocent human life is betrayed by the political forces within the State. Heaney uses the poem in part as a charge against Ireland (and surely not only the North), which has shed so much blood to no apparent effect. But the focus of the poem is on Ugolino himself, the collaborator, and thus a man who tried, in a term Heaney applies to Francis Ledwidge, to achieve an "equilibrium," albeit one which proves, in the end, to be "useless." Ugolino's punishment is eternal cannibalism; he "lives" in hell "soldered" to his arch-rival Archbishop Roger (we might observe that all parties to this violence are Catholic), "gnawing him where the neck and head / Are grafted to the sweet fruit of the brain."

It is not far from that appalling image to the picture Heaney constructs of himself in the first poem in *Field Work,* "Oysters." There, what begins as an account of a friendly, if extravagant, meal turns unexpectedly into a poem about anger, trust, and voracity. The oysters at first allow Heaney to step into a portentous star-scape like that which, at the close of **"Exposure,"** he had feared losing. But his transport arises from victimization; the oysters are "alive and violated," "ripped and shucked and scattered." Heaney on the one hand can take pleasure in "toasting friendship, / Laying down a perfect memory" like a rare wine. Yet that human gesture brings him to anger.

The poem's final stanza is indeed enigmatic. The connection between poetry and freedom, both creatures of "clear light" and perhaps even of "repose," is an important foreshadowing of the Sweeney figure, an altogether (and yet rarely reposing) free singer. But the poem speaks of "poetry *or* freedom," as if the two were in fact at odds, as if the freedom from threat which is the altogether-recognizable human impulse behind Heaney's search for a new home may in fact be the foe, not the fellow, of art. The condition of repose and freedom is in any case denied, in large part by the poet's own learning and imagination; he cannot help imposing on the events of the day a bookish memory of an old, imperially Roman "glut of privilege." Ultimately, the poet here is an omnivore; the hope is not for memory or friendship but for a digestion (and gestation) into language. One wonders how "pure" any word so born could be said to be.

Often in *Field Work* Heaney suggests the dark, even traitorous character of the poetic vocation. In his elegy to Lowell, he defines "art's / deliberate, preemptory / love and arrogance." *Deliberate* takes us back to **"Oysters"**; and Heaney's frequent talk, in his poems and in his essays, of poetry as a kind of visitation should not blind us to the willed and crafted nature of his work. Even in his love-lyrics, which often depend upon a kind of incantation, one cannot escape the sense of the observing, recording, reshaping poetic eye and hand. "Love and arrogance" can serve to label the doubleness of Heaney's position, at once attached and detached, at home (or wishing to be so) and astray (or hoping to remain so), both confident (about his art) and tentative (about the human connections it records).

Part of that doubleness shows in poems of marital disaffection. In **"An Afterwards,"** the making of poetry is at the heart of the central figure's estrangement from his family—just as, in **"Casualty,"** it is Heaney's role as poet that stands between him and the slain fisherman. As he will often do in *Station Island,* Heaney cedes the poem to an accusing other voice—his wife's?—who consigns the poet

to the ninth circle of hell (where Ugolino suffers) and who insists that the "perfection of the work" has, as Yeats feared, led to a sacrifice of the (domestic) life. Worse yet, the betrayal of the home is only the first; neither art nor life is served in the end: "you left us first, and then those books, behind." The same note of accusation is sounded by a dream-consciousness in **"A Dream of Jealousy"**; there the wounded beloved cannot be healed by "these verses / Nor my prudence"—by either speech or silence, in other words. It is against the hard background of this self-imaging that the powerful love verse of such poems as **"Field Work"** must be read. And even there the poet's memory plays him false, misremembering in small ways the beloved.

To the poet-as-traitor and the poet-as-devourer must be added the poet-voyeur, as when "At my window over the hotel car park" Heaney watches young lovers, only to find himself "like some old pike." All these predatory versions of the "arrogance" of the artist are of course only part of the story. But the recurrence of such unsettling images complicates the search throughout *Field Work* for a home; one wonders what place could serve to house this creature of love and threat.

Heaney places at the center of *Field Work* the sequence of Glanmore sonnets, which are the fullest account in the book of a home. Like many another such evocation in his work of the possibly comforting place, the sequence closes ambiguously, in a dream of love and death and a clear remembrance of "our separateness"—a memory which is placed "years ago in that hotel" and thus separate from the 'home' landscape of the poems. In an earlier poem, he had posed a pained question: "How perilous is it to choose / not to love the life we're shown?" Now, as if in answer, he makes the substance of the sonnets from precisely what, almost accidentally, is before and around him: weather, trees, a rat at a window, even the litany of names from a radio weather forecast. The poems pronounce the relief to be sought and found in words, as when, in the seventh of the sonnets, the names of places and of vessels bring him to a sense of (momentarily) completed escape and comforting residence. But earlier in the sequence, words—even the apparently innocent "elderberry"—argue not for rest but for alienation and loss, which can only in part be overcome by a persistent verbal memory and the assertion that "We still believe what we hear." In any case moments of confident loud speech are offset by the defensiveness of such lines as "I won't relapse / From this strange loneliness I've brought us to," and by the intrusion of terror, haunting, and self-interrogation. Even having escaped, the poet still wonders, seeing a rat at the window, "Did we come to the wilderness for this?" Safely south, the habitual worries of the North remain: "What would I meet, blood-boltered on the road?" And again, "What is my apology for poetry?"—where *apology* captures both the defensive anxiety of the modern meaning of the world and the prideful assertiveness to be heard in the echo of Sidney's *Apology for Poetry*.

The first of the Glanmore sonnets can serve as a final *locus* of the complications of the book as a whole. The poem begins with language, even with sound ("Vowels ploughed into other"), and reminds us of the erotic power Heaney finds in the words which visit him. The image of ploughing is an old one for him, and one which as in **"Digging,"** attaches his work as artist with the hand-work of his agricultural forebears, and thus to what he calls, in *Preoccupations,* "the ordinary rituals of life." There is a note of formal elegance as well in the way in which the vowels of the opening line—especially the varying *o* sounds—do persist in "ploughing" into the consonantal field throughout the poem, down to the final word. The poem is carefully placed in the present (as if the ghosts of memory had, for the time, been put to rest) and in a landscape which is general enough not to insist on its distance from Mossbawn. The season is mild and promising (very early spring), and all visible work points toward fruition. In this place Heaney can imagine both the "good life" and the paradigmatic congruence of art with the most natural of human acts.

But that imagining is only potential; it is what "could be," not what is. He is himself (as he wished to be in **"Oysters"**) quickened; but he is as well "gorged," and while what provokes him is a Dantean rose, it is "redolent," as if with the odor of its own death. All that he can propose for now is to wait. Such waiting in part flies in the face of the oddity and temporariness of the landscape. In place of the music of what happens, there is an absence of sound, a silence which is vulnerable to the customary noises of farming. Heaney's own ploughing then is in its way at war with the actual ploughing that will allow the true fruition of this farmland.

What transpires is a visitation by yet more ghosts. They bear a clear force of ritual and religious meditation, taking up their stations as Heaney himself will in **"Station Island."** They too carry the promise of quickening, sowing their seeds. Yet those seeds are "freakish Easter snows": unseasonable, out-of-place, and (as snow) potentially deadly to any true growth. The ghosts are particularly "mine"—a statement of ownership perhaps, a sense of special vocation or, it may be, only of special torment. In any case the poem ends with Heaney in isolation, the communal sense hinted at in the word "our" now having, it seems, fallen away. It is no surprise to learn, in the poem which follows the sonnet sequence (**"September Song"**), that Heaney is now an émigré from Glanmore as well.

Heaney calls Glanmore his "hedge-school"—the old, surreptitious but indomitable culture of Celtic learning, long "staffed" with wandering bards. In *North,* he had called Belfast his singing school; that school, too, he had in the end abandoned. After four years at Glanmore, the record of which is both the sonnets and the book which contains them, he has perhaps finished his schooling altogether. But what then is to be done with what he has learned? If "the end of art is peace"—the motto at the heart of **"The Harvest Bow"**—then his art is, at the conclusion of *Field Work,* not yet at its end, either for the nation or for Heaney himself.

Sweeney Astray is, at first glance, the clearest outgrowth of Heaney's formal schooling. The introduction Heaney appends to his "version"—he is scrupulous in not presenting it as a straightforward translation—makes clear the

particular complex of appeals which Sweeney's story offers to Heaney. Sweeney is, first of all, not strictly speaking a mythic figure at all, but rather "a literary creation" and thus—like the Heaney of *North*—"an historically situated character." His historical moment is, like the present, the locus of a sharp conflict, the "tension between the newly dominant Christian ethos and the older, recalcitrant Celtic temperament." Today, of course, the Christian and the Celtic—especially, the Catholic and the Celtic—are so identified that it takes an accurate historical consciousness to recall with what pain and violence that identity was achieved. The linking of Celtic and "recalcitrant" is important. It will, as we will see, give Heaney a possible key to the paradoxical wish to be "responsible" to his own Irishness while refusing, as one of the **"Station Island"** ghosts—also named Sweeney—advises him, to join any procession: the possibility, in other words, of being most true to the Celtic temperament precisely by remaining at odds with all sectarian definitions of it. Sweeney's tale, which exists at the intersection of history, literature, and myth, becomes in Heaney's version an exploration of that free escape which is, in his prior poetry, at most one side in a continuing war of the self.

Indeed, Heaney makes explicit the value of Sweeney as a figure of the artist (and especially, one suspects, the Daedalian artist), and does so in terms which with little revision could serve as a characterization of the central figure in *Station Island:* "displaced, guilty, assuaging himself by his utterance," which relief, for both Sweeney and his translator, is only momentary, and summoned most fully by the poetry of place and name, of landscape and language. Sweeney's troubled escape—or as we might call it, in terms that will apply to *Station Island,* his estrangement—is complete. Home, family, tribe, even the bodily shape of a man are all gone. In the person of Sweeney, the "creative imagination," which has often seemed in Heaney's poetry to be a kind of betrayal of the human and communal demands of life, can be set loose from "constraints of religious, political, and domestic obligation"—freed, in other words, from exactly those predatory circumstances which are at work in almost all of Heaney's poetry.

But the paradoxical appropriateness of that "escape" is that it represents, for Heaney, a simultaneous *meeting* of obligations. The act of translation represents Heaney's acceptance of a place in the ongoing, almost institutionalized recovery of the "Irish" past that has engaged the effort of writers from Synge and Yeats, through Frank O'Connor and Flann O'Brien, down to Kinsella and Montague; and the beauty of the translation serves as yet another demonstration of the particular richness of Irish poetry. That this recovery and transmission must occur by way of the imperial language might seem ironic, and might even today be politically suspect, if the point is to honor the recalcitrant Celtic temperament. But on the other hand the fact that Heaney can find a way reasonably to English this poem suggests that there is a way to stop fighting the war of language, to rest more comfortably at last in the role of an Irish poet writing exclusively in English.

The poem serves in personal ways as well. There is a biographical and topographical connection, by way of "a family of tinkers, also called Sweeney, who used to camp in the ditchbacksalong the road to the first school I attended"—a family which will return, twice, in *Station Island.* That persistence, into life, of the mythic Sweeney, is indicated by an accident of naming (but to Heaney, correspondences of language are never accidental) and a similarity of migration. It offers yet one more opportunity for Heaney to connect his own life to some indomitable tradition—but in this case one of unattached wandering, not respectable and settled farming. Sweeney is himself a singer of places, a talent for which his mobile life offers particularly rich material, and those places are Heaney's as well, both the North of his childhood and the Wicklow of *Field Work.*

If his account of his own childhood in the prose reminiscence **"Mossbawn"** is at all accurate, Heaney has long imagined himself as a Sweeney-figure, a wary watcher in the trees. And to that intimately personal web of connections is added an intriguing political possibility. For Sweeney may not be Irish at all, in the end; there is the chance that his tale is in fact "a development of a British original," making Sweeney a citizen of two mythic cultures, assumed usually to be inevitably at war. Counterbalancing the utterly free Sweeney, the untrammelled artist, is a thoroughly rooted Sweeney, and one who offers, Heaney tentatively suggests, a new and potentially useful kind of equilibrium: "Sweeney's easy sense of cultural affinity with both Western Scotland [the ancestral home of Ulster Protestantism] and southern Ireland [may be] exemplary for all men and women in contemporary Ulster."

Having broached that optimistic possibility, Heaney steps back from it, and indeed from the broad claims he has made for the poem, and argues that it "makes its immediate claims more by its local power to affect us than by any general implications we may discover in its pattern." *Local* here bears a nicely double weight, as place-within-the-poem and as place(s)-which-the-poem-names. We might observe that it is Heaney's version of the entire work that seems to need defense; certainly many of the individual lyrics within it will stand as poetry and incantation. But the larger patterns which Heaney both proposes and dismisses are in fact clearly visible in his "version" as a whole; and the tale stands as a representation of a mind in transit from the dislocations of *Field Work* to the meditations of *Station Island,* where Heaney will detach Sweeney from his traditional literary home and unashamedly use him as persona and metaphor. Even the modest prunings which Heaney the scholar acknowledges will not, to the modern eye, make Sweeney's tale a tidy one; his wanderings are circular and repetitious, characters like the mysterious hag appear and disappear, the whole story has two endings, and Sweeney himself, as the story advances, shows a disposition to go back and recapitulate. But the apparently loose threads of the tale cannot obscure the fundamental—to both Sweeney and Heaney—question of trust and responsibility. The word *trust* recurs throughout the poem, but in an oddly negative way, often in conjunction with its cousin *faith:* keeping the (new) faith and living up to (old) trusts are both to be avoided.

Sweeney's battle against the new priestly creed brings upon him a punishment that is both inward and outward; driven from his own kingdom and denied any permanent "natural asylum," he is at the same time "exiled from [him]self." In one sense, he pays the price of his "sin," and the Christian ethos wins out, not altogether convincingly, in the end, when he asks forgiveness (something Sweeney has not seemed to crave before) and wins a kind of sainthood. But through most of the poem, the moral weight is all behind the Celtic, the impious, and the irresponsible. The whole notion of trust (and "trust" was somehow a part of Heaney's anger in **"Oysters"**) is a trap, a means by which Sweeney may be re-attached to human society, at the cost of his ability to sing. Again and again Sweeney's music draws his enemies: soldiers, priests, kinsmen, wife. From such approaches Sweeney must always flee, just as the poem must break away from lyric into prose narration. That flight allows him to sing again, even if all he has to sing about are the cruel winds of winter, as he does some nine times.

The movement of the hero in *Sweeney Astray* may seem, especially to one whose knowledge of Irish geography is sketchy, almost random, although he does return again and again to one adopted home, the edenic Glen Bolcain—a dangerous return, since his fondness for the place is what allows his deceitful kinsman Lynchseachan to find him. The crucial movement, however, is not geographical; and it is orderly, or at least falls into a pattern of movement back-and-forth, toward the human, toward memory, toward old attachments, and then rapidly away, to "freedom." For a bird-man with a hatred for the Church, Sweeney spends an astonishing amount of time near churches; that is in fact where his first flight, to Kilreagan, takes him, to "an old tree by the church," and so too does his last and fatal journey, to St. Mullins in Wicklow. Sweeney's place of refuge is not the open and unpopulated wild, but a tree at the edge, where he—like Heaney himself, as a child—finds a point of concealment and observation.

But the customery entanglements are never far away (Heaney's own tree was in sight both of a shrine of St. Patrick and of an occupying army). In Sweeney's tale, marriage is so sour as to be utterly poisonous. But now the betrayer is not the singer but the spouse: Eorann, Sweeney's wife, who prefers good sense and good manners to the demands of vocation, and who has "broken trust, / unmade it like a bed." Women in general in the poem—as so often in early Irish poetry—are sinister. More often than not they have a concealed net near at hand. But all domesticity is the real snare; however much Sweeney may "dread the cold space of plains," he knows too that his ancestral house is a place where he'll be tied and mocked. So also the "normal" domestic emotions: Lynchseachan's plot, the only snare which captures Sweeney, is based on that deceiver's ability to summon up Sweeney's love of parents, wife, and children.

In the person of Sweeney, then, the tension between art and life is, especially in domestic but also in political terms, played out, but with an absence of the guilt on the part of the singer which forms the substance of earlier poems like **"An Afterward."** The condition of exile from self, the role of inner émigré, however painful, is clearly necessary here. The rejection of the obligations of kingship, martial virtue, marriage, fatherhood, are vital and productive, even if not altogether voluntary. The figure of Sweeney, and the story his poem tells—not to mention the poetry his story includes—are, then, an elaborate exploration of one answer to the puzzles of **"Exposure"** and the sense of migratory rootlessness so common in *Field Work.* In Sweeney's estrangement the betrayals outlined in Heaney's verse autobiography since *North* are justified.

But that justification occurs only in a world long-dead and half-mythic; the answers which *Sweeney Astray* provides to Heaney's long argument with himself, and between himself and his element, are only metaphoric, only imagined. To find a way in which the metaphoric Sweeney may be brought 'home' to the world of the actual, the world of contemporary Ireland, is, in large measure, the work which *Station Island* undertakes, in the context of an extended reconsideration of all of Heaney's work of the past decade, and indeed to a degree of his work *in toto.*

The book explicitly presents itself as a Dantean venture, a descent into "St. Patrick's Purgatory," the Irish devotional shrine at Lough Dearg. The movement down, spiritually and psychically, is at the same time a movement backwards in time, once again into Heaney's own life and into the history and myth of Ireland. The parallel to the *Divine Comedy* suggests that the descent will not be permanent, the purgatory not (for the poet-hero) a stopping-place but a field of transition, even a route out of Hell. The book's plot—to use a clumsy word term for it—involves not only a trip but a transformation; Heaney himself, the central figure in Parts One and Two, becomes in Part Three a revived Sweeney, now at large in a new, and indeed a modern, world. The Dantean hope of progress is thus complicated by the degree to which that third part of the exploration is, yet again, a return; but the return at least allows, indeed demands, a new vantage point, an adoption by Heaney of Sweeney's wary and perceptive marginality.

The complexities of movement are proposed in the very first poem, **"The Underground,"** which begins as a memory, apparently a happy one, of a moment when Heaney and his wife, "honeymooning, moonlighting," rush up the stairs at a London Tube stop near the Albert Hall. The joy of the memory seems, on first reading, to prompt a kind of learned playfulness. The speaker of the poem manages to see himself, in a short space, as a nameless god and Hansel and Orpheus. But the priapic deity who appears first—"a fleet god gaining / Upon you before you turned to a reed"—is, in his way, rapacious and threatening; his embrace would bring not love but, for the beloved, a loss of all humanity. Thus the beloved's flight is as much away from as alongside the speaker. So too we should recall what a dark story "Hansel and Gretel" is—a tale for children, to be sure, but one which incorporates abandonment, foiled escape, and betrayal. And the final Orphean echo suggests that the beloved is permanently trapped in a nether region, an entrapment caused by the curiosity of an anxious husband.

The poem darkens considerably just about half way along, when the speaker shifts his attention from the marital *then* to the isolated "now." It is at this point that he becomes Hansel, "retracing the path back," only to find not a home (as Hansel hopes to) but a distinctly Eliotic purgatorial place, "a draughty lamplit station / After the trains have gone." There he stands, "bared [or, we might say, once again exposed] and tensed"—but at the same time, and by way of a pun, "all attention." What he awaits is "your step"; but he (or is it she?) would be "damned if I look back."

The topography of the poem has been utterly contorted. At that final moment, to look back would be to look in exactly the direction that was so breathlessly and promisingly forward in the opening stanza: prospect and retrospect are somehow now the same. And the possibility of damnation is all the more cruelly near if we keep in mind the fact that—chronologically—the poet just has looked back, and shortly will again. If hell is the price of such looking, he has already earned it, and his beloved's following footstep might take her there as well.

The whole first part of *Station Island* continues the theme of dangerous but necessary retrospect. Thus Heaney observes a dying man who is himself, apparently in the hope of comfort, re-viewing his home landscape and his past (**"Looking Back"**). And the poet looks repeatedly not only into his own past (the prevailing tense of these poems is the preterite), but further back still, by way of relics and topography, of imagined recreations of other lives and of mythic creatures. The degree to which he is at the same time looking back at his poetic life can be measured by the ease with which many of these poems place themselves alongside poems in earlier volumes. Thus **"A Hazel Stick for Catherine Ann"** recalls **"The Diviner"** in *Death of a Naturalist;* **"The Sandpit"** echoes so many of his poems of Mossbawn and digging, as well as his tributes to the "ordinary rituals" of work. **"Remembering Malibu"** repeats the mood and very nearly the location of **"Westering"** in *Wintering Out* and **"The Skunk"** in *Field Work.* **"An Ulster Twilight"** revisits the land of *North* and, in its consideration of sectarian division and the ominous figure of a policeman, particularly recalls **"A Constable Calls"** in that volume. And finally, **"A Bat on the Road"** is another of a long string of evocative, precise, and dark animal poems which stretches back to the title piece of *Death of a Naturalist.*

I do not mean to say that this part of *Station Island* is merely repetitious. Just as Heaney presumes, correctly, that his "glosses" on Sweeney in Part Three can stand apart from *Sweeney Astray,* so too these poems work individually without the burdens of their bibliographic past. In some cases Heaney is clearly revising—**"An Ulster Twilight"** moves carefully toward a *rapprochement* with at least one Ulster Protestant, and thus is in a way an answer to earlier poems like **"Docker"** or **"Protestant Drums, Tyrone, 1966."** There is often something reassuring in the echoes one hears in these poems. For Heaney, relics still function (and will continue to do so in Parts Two and Three) as points of reference and as the focus of what Thoreau called "in-sight and far-sight." So too will attachments to friends and fellow writers and family, and the erotics of marriage and language. Heaney seems in these poems particularly to be searching for stability. He finds it more often in things than in people—sloes are "bitter / and dependable" (perhaps, in fact, dependable because bitter), a gourd is "reliably dense." But then too ghosts can be "reliable," as they are for Hardy. More clearly than ever, what stability there is can be found in small, repeated, painstaking acts of work and survival—wood-working, for instance, or ironing.

These points of anchorage stand out all the more clearly in a world of transition, which he calls at one point a "miasma of spilled blood." There, freedom is to be craved, no matter how hard it is to find and to sustain a "free state of image and illusion," no matter how much freedom (which is almost always a freedom of *movement*) may seem, as Heaney imagines it is for Chekhov, a "burden." Movement at least brings one into contact with an imaginative landscape in which "the deer of poetry" may not, for once, "scare." Heaney feels drawn two ways, attracted and repelled, encountering again and again "dream fears I inclined towards"; he addresses loving poems to his family but admires as well "a migrant solitude." He says, in apparent exasperation, "I still cannot clear my head / of lives in their element"—but the element is his as well as theirs. What is to be longed for, it seems, is persistence. Thus the migratory Brigid holds together her family on a voyage of exile that parallels Heaney's own, from the North to Wicklow (**"A Migration"**); thus Hardy stubbornly makes of his ghosts a body of work that can overcome speechlessness and "resist" the too-easy appeal of "the words of coming to rest" (**"The Birthplace"**); thus Chekhov on Sakhalin is, however hesitantly, at the threshold of work that is both socially useful (his monograph on convict life will prompt penal reform) and artistically great.

The woman whom Heaney recalls ironing embodies what he hopes for—she is at the same moment "dragged upon. And buoyant." So too is the self which Heaney at times achieves, most centrally in **"Making Strange"**—a self who can be a reliable guide because he can find a viable place of estrangement, especially in language, a place where he can be "adept and dialect" and communicative. But the final shape this figure takes is that of Sweeney, "The King of the Ditchbacks," who follows the Scriptural advice and abandons his riches to become a trespasser. As Part One closes, Heaney sees himself first in "the limbo of lost words," then stripped down and adopting a protective "dissimulation." At that point he is ready for the penitential encounters of Part Two.

The central poem-sequence **"Station Island"** is, in one sense, a long, ritualized self-accusation, a mortification of the artistic flesh, but it is also a vehicle by which Heaney controls and confronts his ghosts, and thus defines more particularly the heritage he wants to take on, which is not necessarily the one which his culture and upbringing, not to mention his adult experience as a poet, would apply to him. One of the many artifices of this sequence is to grant to the visiting ghosts most of the powerful lines. The poet himself seems to speak little, just as in the *Divine Comedy*

the character Dante seems almost preternaturally (for a poet) silent and slow to learn.

The technical mastery of the poems is particularly important, because it allows Heaney implicitly to defend poetry of a highly crafted kind even while he hears (and allows us to hear) it being questioned. The homage to Dante which is apparent in the premise of the sequence is explicitly rebuked by McCartney, who accuses Heaney of having "whitewashed ugliness" by employing "the lovely blinds of the *Purgatorio*"; but it is supported both by translation (in poem VI) and by the frequent use of a supple English *terza rima*. McCartney's rebuke in poem VIII is itself, ironically, couched in a careful variation of the *ottava rima* stanza. The sequence as a whole is in fact very close to what Heaney says *Sweeney Astray* is, in the original—"a primer of lyric genres." The particular forms are recognizably Heaney's—stanzaic free verse in poem I, rhymed quatrains in poems III and X, blank verse in much of poem VIII, sonnets in poems VI and IX.

Against that array of what Heaney has in his essays called discipline, there is an increasing power of feeling in the first nine poems, moving to a "bottom" of self-doubt and self-loathing in poem IX. Each of the ghosts to that point has contributed to the descent, as have the two poems (III and VI) where Heaney confronts not shades but the memories of his own life. The various visitors recapitulate the guises apparently available to Heaney himself: the migratory tinker Simon Sweeney, an illiterate man of place and movement; the folklorist and "turncoat" Carleton, who insists on the virtue of memory; the young priest who has tried to carry an Irish faith into foreign parts; schoolmasters, who invoke as well the poet Kavanagh; an archaeological bog-digger, a sectarian activist hunger-striker, and several sectarian victims. The ghosts raise again old questions of obligation and silence, rebuke the ignorance which remains in Heaney, despite his learning, and demand that he wonder whether any change is possible. And they propose renunciation, suggesting the curative effects of a "last look" at Catholic Ireland. But they also ask to what place Heaney might flee, as if in answer to the young priest's charge in poem IV, that Heaney's visit to Lough Deargh is false in the extreme.

The accusation which marks the crisis is McCartney's—the charge that Heaney's apparent effort (in particular, in **"The Strand at Lough Beg"**) to fulfill, poetically, his obligations to home, family, and tribe, has actually been an avoidance. That calls into question all the rich bulk of elegiac record in Heaney's poems, and it is directly after that that Heaney touches bottom—and begins to rise. But in a sense Heaney has already defended himself—has, in a new way, kept his eye on the facts, while still making music—in poem IV, which gives speech to the bloody victim of a night-killing. In that poem Heaney's attention is not on the poet's response but on the victim himself, and not on the life but on the death. For the first time, I think, in Heaney's long career as an elegist, the poem ignores the metaphoric healing to be sought in a placing of a life in its element, in order to keep its eye and ear on the direct and painful account of the ugly, deforming wound. Certainly there is no whitewashing. And interestingly, the particular party—if any—of which the victim is a member, is not a part of the record. We may presume the man is Catholic but we are not told so; he is no more and no less than an individual being wakened in the night to be shot for no explicit reason. That is, I think, the furthest Heaney has yet gone in making poetry (and in form, it is Dantean poetry) of the omnivorous modern world. In so doing he has finally been true to the dictum, borrowed from Willa Cather, which had been offered to him as long ago as 1962: "Description is revelation!"

Heaney's way back up is both a movement forward and a circling back. The vehicles of restoration are, not surprisingly, relics: an old brass trumpet in poem IX, a mug in poem X. And the penance is an abandonment, briefly, of his own voice, by way of a translation from John of the Cross in poem X. Having fulfilled the ritual, in poem XII he meets—now on the ground of the real world, a tarmacked car-park—one last tutelary figure: Joyce. The ghost is a relatively new one for Heaney, who in his essays, for instance, has focused his attention, understandably, on Hopkins, Wordsworth, Yeats, and Kavanagh. Joyce urges (rather deceptively, given the retrospect in his own works) not memory but forgetfulness, and more importantly, independence and an abandonment of the formulae of Irish poetic/political rhetoric—a message which recovers the wisdom offered at the beginning of the sequence by tinker Sweeney: "Stay clear of all processions."

Joyce is in fact a kind of literary Sweeney, a polymathic, highly schooled, and yet thoroughly grounded king of the ditchbacks, whose physical distance from his home sharpened, rather than obscured, his view both of the fact and the whole. Heaney, by having Joyce speak in Dante's *terza rima,* conjoins those two masters—two more schoolmasters, really. And both can serve as exemplars of a new stance in relation to the historical situation. We should recall that Dante—as Heaney himself remarks in *Preoccupations*—was immersed in, and indeed plagued and exiled by, the political conflicts of his own time, and as well a poet who had moved through the more 'personal' utterance of the *Vita Nuova* to the vision of the *Divine Comedy.* Similarly, Joyce may be said to have progressed from the autobiographical (in *Stephen Hero* and *Portrait*) into something more objective. And just as Sweeney takes to his tree in part to have an unobstructed view, Dante and Joyce both made of their exile the opportunity to record—and to transform—the minutiae of an historical moment. By a similar kind of straying Heaney may hope at last and less painfully to see and to say something more than nothing.

Station Island explicitly moves, in Part Three, to Sweeney—but only to Sweeney's voice. In other words, it is a shift of perspective and speech rather than of material, since the substance of the **"Sweeney Redivivus"** poems remains recognizably the material of Heaney's life: one more climb up the childhood tree (**"In the Beech"**), the recognition of the "murders and miscarriages" of Irish life (**"The First Kingdom"**), of the pressures of life amid the "spiteful vigilance of colonies" (**"Drifting Off"**), of the hand of clerics and schoolmasters with their seductive weapons of language (**"The Cleric," "The Masters," "In Illo Tem-**

pore"). What Sweeney's voice empowers Heaney to do is to articulate most directly his answer and his rejection of the self, of trust and obedience (**"Alerted"**), in favor of a figure which is made explicit in **"The Artist,"** where the virtues are "anger," "obstinacy," "coercion / of the substance from green apples," a "hatred of his own embrace," and finally "fortitude." The estrangement laid out in these poems is not, however, complete; Sweeney's flights are balanced by **"Sweeney's Returns,"** and the richness of landscape remains, as in **"Holly,"** a powerful rooting, as do the relics of the past (**"The Old Icons"**). But now at least those elements of betrayal so worrisome earlier are to be praised as "dear-bought treacheries / grown transparent now, and estimable."

In the book's final poem, **"On the Road,"** Heaney, in Sweeney's voice, offers one (temporarily) last assessment of things as they are. He is once more (or should we say, still?) in motion, but no longer so concerned with arrival, since "all roads [are] one." Shades still visit him, but now the question (a Biblical one: "What must I / do to be saved?") has an answer ("Sell all you have"). He recalls one more ascent, made as a child climbing a chapel roof, protectively, we suspect, outside the sanctuary itself; that is the way of "scaling heaven." But it is also, when it needs to be, a route of return. The latter part of the poem shifts to the future and the conditional; "would" is now the ground-note. Heaney has long returned, roosted, migrated, meditated, but not by way of a verb-form that carries with it so much force of choice, intention, and control. There is now a road yet to be travelled, not just a road back; what is at hand is now "a book of changes."

It would be presumptuous in the extreme to predict where Heaney/Sweeney will go next. But at the least this final poem answers **"Exposure"** by proffering a way out of the limits of self-consciousness. The old powers will not be abandoned, but the poet is now abroad in a slightly more hopeful landscape, on which is outside the self and in which the "deer of poetry" is no longer "dumbfounded," no longer stricken by silence, but ready to break cover into a new life.

The song of the self has, for more than a decade, been a richly productive terrain for Heaney. Yet it is one that it may be he has at last exhausted (I do not mean the word judgmentally). All along, aware that, as he puts it in *Preoccupations,* "poetry is secret and natural, [but] it must make its way in a world that is public and brutal," to the work of healing the self Heaney has added the task of healing the community, of encompassing fully and directly a culture which seems, especially to those outside of it, incurably riven, eccentric, even mad. But attention to the nightly news prompts the reflection that Ireland may, in its contour if not its details, be truly "normal" and representative. Whatever shifts in vantage point he may have undertaken, it is hard to imagine that Heaney has yet finished with the question of how to live, as individual and poet—how to live *usefully,* in a torn and contentious world of exposure, exile, murderously politicized speech, and irreconcilable obligation. (pp. 393-409)

John Hildebidle, "A Decade of Seamus Heaney's Poetry," in The Massachusetts Review, *Vol. XXVIII, No. 3, Autumn, 1987, pp. 393-409.*

Ian Hamilton (review date 1 October 1987)

[*An English author of several volumes of poetry, Hamilton is best known for his criticism, which is collected in his* A Poetry Chronicle: Essays and Reviews *(1973). In the following review of* The Haw Lantern, *he considers the poetic distance that characterizes Heaney's work and interprets Heaney's role as a bardic poet.*]

'About the only *enmity* I have is towards pride.' Seamus Heaney said this in an interview, and since we know him to be the most over-interviewed of living poets, perhaps he shouldn't be forced to say it again here. Put in its context, though, this too-worthy-sounding protestation has much to reveal about the disposition of Heaney's work so far, and can even be read as a riposte to those critics who complain that, for all its verbal richness and its moral courage, his work is strangely without personality.

In the interview, Heaney was talking about his Catholicism, about how his sensibility had been formed by the dolorous murmurings of the rosary, and the generally Marian quality of devotion afforded by the Roman Church—a Church to which Heaney, even in his twenties, continued to go for confession and which 'permeated' the whole life of his Northern Ireland childhood. Thanks to this Church, its doctrines and its rituals, Heaney's sensibility was from the start centered in relation to what he calls a 'feminine presence'. It was this presence that induced in him his 'only enmity':

> A religion that has a feminine component and a notion of the mother in the transcendental world is better than a religion that just has a father, a man, in it. I also—just in my nature and temperament, I suppose—believed in humility and in bowing down, and in 'we' rather than 'I'. I hate a *moi* situation, an egotism, a presumption, a *hubris,* and I'm used to bowing down to the mother as a way of saying that. About the only *enmity* I have is towards pride.

When people complain about the absence of 'personality' in Heaney's work, they are at some level complaining also that the '*moi* situation' has been skirted or suppressed, and that as a result his poems lack the sort of sharply individual human *tone* that Larkin has, or Frost, or Lowell. I have heard it said that Heaney's work is 'teachable but not memorable', that lines of his don't linger in the mind, and it certainly seems to be true that admirers of his do tend to remember images or situations or stylistic brilliances rather than cries from the heart or haunting melodies. He has written few 'inter-personal' poems that are any good, and he is better at addressing the dead than he is at confiding in the living.

Of course, when Heaney started writing—in the late Sixties—there was '*moi*-poetry' aplenty to be haunted by, and we can now see that the literary-historical moment was precisely right for the eventual, if not imminent appearance of a poet for whom none of all *that* held any magnetism. A new Auden, a new Stevens might have seemed to

be the answer, and shortly there were indeed new Audens, new Stevenses to choose from. But neither intellectualism nor playfulness nor mere perfection of technique would be enough to reclaim glamour for the impersonal, or anti-personal. The only real challenge to the over-intimate would have to come from a poetry that risked its opposite: the too-theatrical. A poetry to be listened in on would be most effectively displaced by a poetry that dared to resurrect some of the art's discredited rhetorical/theatrical presumptions. (These, it should be said, had by the early Seventies been 'discredited' not just by the aching whispers of Confessionalism but also by cute performance stars and by sloganisers of the 'Left'.)

In terms of the desirable 'next step' for British poetry, Seamus Heaney had some obvious natural advantages. After all, confessional poetry was unlikely to seduce a Catholic. And, for the wishing-to-be-humble, there was no great allure either in the mock-humilities of the Larkinesque. Even so, Heaney did not at first seem to offer much of a challenge to anything, or anyone—he was too like Ted Hughes, minus the Lawrentian, black-magical ingredients, and he was a shade too youthfully delighted with the plopping, slopping, thwacking sounds of spade on soil, or milk in pail, etc. (Donnish critics have always loved this onomatopoeic side of Heaney, though: maybe because it gives them the chance to exhibit their own 'sensibilities'— 'You'll notice how the "thwa-" of "thwack" is shyly answered by the "plu-" of "plump".')

And yet, if one looks back now at Heaney's first two books, *Death of a Naturalist* and *Door into the Dark,* it becomes evident that he had already there commenced a sort of rebellion against the *moi,* against the autobiographical 'I', the nervously-wracked victim 'me'. The voice he spoke in, or rather the voice in which his poems spoke, already had a tinge of bardic anonymity, a suggestion that the self had indeed been humbled, but momentously: Seamus Heaney the man was being elected, so it seemed to him, into the role of Seamus Heaney, poet.

If this makes him sound like George Barker, it absolutely shouldn't. What is attractive about Heaney's response to his vocation is that he is never entirely happy that it is *he* who has been called: a childhood spent wondering how to avoid the priesthood had perhaps ill-prepared him for such singularity. And it is the marvelling near-reluctance with which he acknowledges his own election that silences, or ought to silence, any post-Movement tendency to scoff.

Like Dylan Thomas, like Graves, Heaney assumed the noble vestments, but he did so with an engaging awkwardness, a persuasive lack of flourish. One of the fascinations of Heaney's work, read from the beginning until now, is in observing how he shifts this way and that to find a genuinely comfortable fit, a non-fake, non-proud way of living in the sacred robes he knows he has the obligation and the right to wear. He can neither fling them off nor swap them for the more workaday gear which, in certain moods, he might feel more 'at home in'. But there is always a touch of 'Why me?' in his sometimes effortful transcending of the 'me', and this has given him a rare sturdiness of posture—rare, that is, for the 'chosen' sort of poet he's become. Indeed, it could be said that one of Heaney's principal achievements is that he has redignified the bardic stance.

There are those who would say that he has been helped in this by having something to be bardic *about,* by having arrived on-stage at a place and time when it was possible for him to say: 'To forge a poem is one thing, to forge the uncreated conscience of the race . . . is quite another and places daunting pressure and responsibilities on anyone who would risk the name of poet.' Certainly, it is hard to think of how an English poet could get away with saying this: but with Heaney 'getting away with it' does not arise.

A Heaney without the Troubles that erupted just as he was finishing his second book, *Door into the Dark,* would maybe have been all vocation and no job: archaeological, etymological, nostalgic, literary-grandiose and 'good on nature'. He might even have fallen victim to some Irish version of the thin-spined Californian-meditative which showed faint signs of enticing him around the time of his third volume, *Wintering Out.* From his first two books, it's hard to tell. These were much concerned with the *discovery* of his vocation, with measuring the distances between his sort of digging and that of the farm-folk he'd grown up with, and with registering a sense of awe at the mysteries which seemed to lie ahead. When he has spoken of this period he has usually portrayed himself as almost-passive: the poems were already *in* him, he would say, and his task was to uncover them, to excavate, or even just to make himself available to their arrivals. He was also reading a lot of modern poetry, late in the day and in something of a hurry, it might seem, as if to seek directions, signs. The dark behind the *Door in the Dark* was, simply, dark.

The Troubles did erupt, though. Heaney wintered out the first few months, tinkering with place-names and imperilled Irish crafts, but he sensed from the start—from 1969—that the bard's moment had almost certainly arrived, that from now on 'the problems of poetry' had changed 'from being simply a matter of achieving the satisfactory verbal icon to being a search for images and symbols adequate to our predicament'. Again, it is 'our' predicament, not his, although as a liberal, blood-shed-hating Northern Ireland Catholic with strong ties to the British, both personal and cultural, he could hardly have felt all that 'representative'. The 'we' at this point could so easily have surrendered to the *moi,* and Heaney could respectably have withdrawn to the margins of his maddened tribe. He could even have done this without handing in his robes.

But he didn't, and his poetry since then has been a moving drama of discomfiture, of trying to reconcile the 'magic' aspects of his calling with, so to speak, the 'duties' of the tribal bard. He has never been confident that the two can be reconciled and whenever he has had to make the choice he has almost always chosen to safeguard the 'mystery' of his vocation. There have been wobbly moments, as in the second part of *North,* where he has tried to confront the 'Irish thing' in ordinary speech, as Seamus Heaney, but all in all he has held honourably fast to the objective he set himself at the beginning of the Seventies: 'to discover a

field of force in which, without abandoning fidelity to the processes and experiences of poetry . . . it would be possible to encompass the perspectives of a humane reason and at the same time grant the religious intensity of the violence its deplorable authenticity and complexity'. These words must have been arrived at with some anguish, and much care. It is not easy, perhaps not even possible, to speak of 'deplorable authenticity' without seeming to favour the 'authenticity' aspect of that formulation.

Heaney has looked for his 'field of force' in some out-of-the-way places, as remote sometimes from the present tense as he could reach: not in order to seek comfort from the past—unless there is comfort in knowing that history is comfortless—but to bring back 'befitting emblems of adversity'. Befitting they have been, and delivered with a curt or stoic shrug, as if to say: 'What can I say?'

> I am Hamlet the Dane,
> skull-handler, parablist,
> smeller of rot
>
> in the state, infused
> with its poisons,
> pinioned by ghosts
> and affections,
>
> murders and pieties,
> coming to consciousness,
> by jumping in graves,
> dithering, blathering.

It was with his fifth book, *Field Work,* that Heaney found a voice that is neither bleakly antiquarian nor awkwardly portentous. By this time the Troubles really had become *his* troubles. Friends and relatives of his were being killed: the *moi* could no longer be prevented from intruding some of its own nervous cadences. In poems like **'The Strand at Lough Beg'** and **'A Postcard from North Antrim'**, Heaney sounds that 'heartbreak' note which Robert Lowell used to talk about. Maybe Lowell talked to *him* about it. *Field Work* has an elegy in memory of Lowell ('the master elegist'), and the two poets saw each other often during the mid-Seventies. In this book, even the 'love-poems' (a genre Heaney says he hates the sound of) are unaffectedly meant to be listened to by the beloved—and thus listened-in to by the rest of us. But it's Heaney's Irish elegies that hurt the most:

> Across that strand of yours the cattle graze
> Up to their bellies in an early mist
> And now they turn their unbewildered gaze
> To where we work our way through squeaking
>   sedge
> Drowning in dew. Like a dull blade with its
>   edge
> Honed bright, Lough Beg half shines under the
>   haze.
> I turn because the sweeping of your feet
> Has stopped behind me, to find you on your
>   knees
> With blood and roadside muck in your hair and
>   eyes,
> Then kneel in front of you in brimming grass
> And gather up cold handfuls of the dew
> To wash you, cousin. I dab you clean with moss
> Fine as the drizzle out of a low cloud.

I lift you under the arms and lay you flat.
With rushes that shoot green again, I plait
Green scapulars to wear over your shroud.

Field Work, to my mind, is the book of Heaney's which we ought to remember (how can we not?) when there are grumbles about 'anonymity' or 'suppression of the self'. His *moi* poems are all the stronger, all the more hard-won, it seems to me, not because they go against his notion of a tribal role but because—at their best—they don't: it's just that, in these poems, the 'I' lurks behind the 'we', and vice versa. And the elegy is, of course, the perfect form for such lurking, or entwining: an intimacy meant to be made public.

In *Station Island* (1984), Heaney returned to pondering the 'poet's role', but with a new despondency. He enlists the assistance of other artists, from Dante to James Joyce, and yearns guiltily for the 'clumps' and 'clunks' and 'clogs' of his most youthful verses. Not so guiltily, though, that he cannot welcome some jeering Joycean advice:

> 'Keep at a tangent.
> When they make the circle wide, it's time to
> swim
> out on your own . . . '

After all, what had those grand elegies in *Field Work* actually *done,* except perhaps to 'saccharine' with literature the suffering of those they claimed to mourn? The Dantesque apparitions contrived by Heaney in *Station Island* are accusatory, and our instinct (also contrived by Heaney?) is to spring to the defence of the accused, to tell him to

> Let go, let fly, forget.
> You've listened long enough. Now strike your
> note.

In the 'Sweeney' versions and translations which appeared in this country at the same time as *Station Island* the central fantasy is one of flight—of elevation *and* liberation.

Heaney's new book, *The Haw Lantern,* does strike one or two new notes, but it is slight and low-powered, by his standards. It shows signs not so much of high vocation as of obedient professionalism: a Phi Beta Kappa poem for Harvard, a poem for William Golding on his 75th birthday, a poem for Amnesty International, Irish Section, on Human Rights Day, 1985. And there are signs, too, that Heaney has set himself to learn from the oblique, clandestine parables and allegories which poets of Eastern Europe use to fox the censors. I am not sure that he has a light enough touch for modes like these (and in any case does their 'lightness' not thrive on necessity?), but perhaps for the moment they offer a relaxing middle path between the druid and the *moi.* A sense of exercise prevails throughout the book, except in the group of sonnets written in memory of the poet's mother, who died in 1984. These are touchingly uneven: fondly anecdotal, with some strongly sentimental moments, but sometimes almost breathtakingly ill-made:

> She'd manage something hampered and askew
> Every time, as if she might betray
> The hampered and inadequate by too
> Well-adjusted a vocabulary.

Or is Heaney himself attempting to avoid a similar betrayal? Certainly, throughout the sequence, there is a reluctance to reach for anything that might be thought of as poetic grandeur.

'Silence' and 'emptiness' are what these sonnets register, and one senses that silence and emptiness are at the emotional centre of this book. Weariness, also. Dutifully, mechanically almost, Heaney continues to be full of words, and full of worries about what to do with them. But he has been tired of such worries for some time: those robes, it seems, will never fit. In a poem called **'From the Frontier of Writing'** he describes being stopped at an Army roadblock where 'everything is pure interrogation.' When he is eventually let through, he feels

> a little emptier, a little spent
> as always by that quiver in the self,
> subjugated, yes, and obedient.

The same kind of thing happens, he says, at the 'frontier of writing': the writer is interrogated, guns are aimed at him, data about him are checked out, he could easily get shot. If all goes well, though, he's allowed to cross the frontier, 'arraigned yet freed'. Seamus Heaney has been arraigned often enough, by himself and by others' expectations of him. Why is it so hard to think of him as ever being 'freed'—he who has dared to 'risk the name of poet'? (pp. 10-11)

> *Ian Hamilton, "Excusez-moi," in* London Review of Books, *Vol. 9, No. 17, October 1, 1987, pp. 10-11.*

The whole relationship between a writer's spiritual/emotional condition and the kind of wordstuff and form-making that's going on in his work is an interesting one. . . . Part of my gradual education of myself has been to think that there is a deep relationship between the nature of the creature and the worth of the art.

—*Seamus Heaney, in an interview with Randy Brandes in* Salmagundi, *Fall 1988.*

J. D. McClatchy   (review date 21 December 1987)

[*McClatchy is an American poet and critic. In the following review, he considers the balance between "masculine and feminine modes of imagination" in Heaney's poetry collections preceding* The Haw Lantern. *Commenting on* The Haw Lantern, *he praises the collection's variety and discusses Heaney's concern with language and his expression of spiritual and political themes.*]

It would be fair to say that Seamus Heaney is now the most successful and widely read contemporary poet in English. He stands as that rare colossus who can best ride both the Atlantic and the Irish Sea. In all three literary cultures, and at a comparatively early age, he is a critical touchstone. His books are big sellers, and his readings thronged. In Ireland, he is considered a national hero. The English, temperamentally suspicious of hype, have had to whisk him to appearances by helicopter. In America, he is a Harvard professor.

He has succeeded in part because, while continuing to please his admirers, he has always flown the nets of their expectations. Those Irish readers whose ambition it was that he take the place of Yeats have been disappointed by what Heaney himself has characterized as his "timid circumspect involvement" with the continuing Irish troubles, by his disavowal of any grandiloquent encounter with conscience in favor of the "sensings, mountings from the hidden places," the roots and graftings rather than the great chestnut bole. Those seeking a new Patrick Kavanagh have been disconcerted by Heaney's self-conscious suavities and by his persistent concern for the private life of memory, the erotics of domesticity.

Americans have always welcomed an Irish bard on stage, but this one doesn't preen or croon. Like Frost, he has charged the traditional verse-line with new, buoyant tasks, but prefers not to pursue the psychology of character beyond a canny, sympathetic moralism. Like Lowell, he has perfected a wholly personal idiom and turned his own past into a general history, but he has little of Lowell's metaphysical compression or far-ranging curiosity. To be sure, he appeals to those readers tired of the garrulous weightlessness of so much recent American poetry, formless and woolly.

Still, he sometimes seems an odd alternative here, more delicate and oblique than any American counterpart. If he has abided by Valéry's warning that profundity is a hundred times easier to get than precision, and made his poems exact with Irish terms and rural lore, to American ears he remains an exotic. He is essentially a *local* poet, for whom (in his own formulation) "place symbolizes a personal drama before it epitomizes a communal situation." This doesn't always travel well; the resonance of certain words, key events, the whole geography of an Irish imagination is hard to appreciate fully. For the American edition of *The Haw Lantern,* in fact, Heaney has added a lean page of explanatory notes. Even more would have helped.

Heaney has eluded the claims and the ambitions others have set for him by being always "in between." This is his own term for a series of accidents—having been born a Catholic in the North, then settling as a Northerner in the South, and always being an Irish poet in an English culture. From the start he's been poised between the bog and the demesne—that is, between the half-lit romantic heritage of a wrecked Irish language and culture, and the imposing heritage of English lyric poetry. And his task has been to ruffle the lyric's decorum. He has wanted to "make it eat stuff that it has never eaten before . . . like all the messy and, it would seem, incomprehensible obsessions in the North," and to give it a new accent, disrupt its complacent graces. His early books certainly announced a "guttural muse," a lilting or grating music drawn into clipped stanzas from a rich, peat-packed word-hoard. And with

North (1975) he found his analogous way to write of the brutality and enduring anguish, the "tribal, intimate revenge" exacted by life in Northern Ireland.

The aim of his art, and the true achievement of his style, though, is not discord but balance, the sometimes estranging harmonics of conflicting demands and bequests. When, in the fine essays collected in *Preoccupations* (1980), Heaney writes about this balancing act, time and again, he describes it in terms of masculine and feminine modes of imagination—forging and incubation. The differences are embedded in language and in consciousness itself: "I think of the personal and Irish pieties as vowels, and the literary awareness nourished on English as consonants." Writing is an encounter between, or a union of, a masculine ascendency of will and shaping intelligence, and a native feminine topography of emotion and image. Heaney, for whom words are music before they are discourse, would no doubt characterize himself as working primarily in this "feminine" mode, where

> the language functions more as evocation than as address, and the poetic effort is not so much a labour of design as it is an act of divination and revelation; words in the feminine mode behave with the lover's come-hither instead of the athlete's display, they constitute a poetry that is delicious as texture before it is recognized as architectonic.

We may be uncomfortable with Heaney's old-fashioned terms, but they do remind us that he has continually tried to adjust our view of his work away from its pretexts and argument and toward its texture, that soft way in which experience is lined with language. And if by "feminine" we understand a Words-worthian "wise passivity," a nurturing of "the buried life of feelings," then we are closer to Heaney's reasons for abjuring any hard political line. He has been less a poet of ideas than of place, less a poet of the heights than of the hearth. Or perhaps it would be more accurate still to say that he is a poet of the *body,* fascinated by physicality, the world's body of remembered places, the feel and scent and sound of the beloved. If Yeats found a style to resist his surroundings, Heaney has found one to savor and celebrate his.

When there is a note of nostalgia thrumming beneath his poems, it serves to remind those who hear it of how often he writes—still, always—as the outsider, the "inner émigré." Like Sweeney, the poet's rhymesake and mythological king-turned-bird keening in the treetops, and also like his master James Joyce, Heaney is an exile. In his case, it is an exile from the country to the city, from the community into the writer's solitude, from the solipsism of childhood into the mortal distractions of adulthood.

At his best, Heaney is the plaintive rhapsodist of that exile. He is primarily an elegiac miniaturist, a lyric poet with an impeccable ear and astonishing gifts for the surprising word, the heart-stopping phrase. At the start his lyre was strung very tautly, and a little primly. In *Field Work* (1979) he relaxed his line, and also broadened the appeal of his work. He had learned, as he later said of this book, "to trust melody, to trust art as reality, to trust artfulness as an affirmation." The political poems at the front of the book, among his very best, yield to domestic and pastoral subjects that affirm the restorative power of the quotidian and of the natural world.

What he did next, in **Station Island** (1984), was pitch these same themes higher, and reverse his emphasis. The title poem sets out to be the long poem about the matter of Ireland that many of Heaney's readers—especially Americans, with their appetite for ambition and risk—must have longed for. It is a stunning piece of work, richly and dramatically imagined, if not altogether the large-scale triumph some wanted or claimed.

Perhaps even more to be pondered and praised is the book's concluding sequence, **"Sweeney Redivivus,"** a series of sometimes hermetic but always exquisite lyrics that eerily blend moments of Heaney's own past—early joys and sorrows, his loss of faith, his acquired art—with the voice of the legendary bird-king hero. This group parallels the "Bog sequence" in **North** that first brought Heaney fame but is composed with much more originality, canniness, and tender authority. It declares that here is a poet who, having mastered the traditions, might now set out to change them over in his own image. In this book of changes, he proved that a new "spirit broke cover / to raise a dust / in the font of exhaustion."

Those whose expectations for Heaney's new book have thereby been raised are likely to find **The Haw Lantern** something of a disappointment. I would say it had been written with damp powder, except for my lingering suspicion that the poet himself may deliberately have wanted, by means of this rather slight book of mostly occasional poems, to defuse again the megaton reputation many have made for him. The presiding figure here, the haw lantern itself, is described as a "small light," a humble red hip on its twig, glad of "not having to blind them with illumination."

On the other hand, I do not want to underrate Heaney's remarkable gifts, or the many fine poems here. The book has an exhilarating variety: ballad and translation, riddle and dramatic monologue, complaint, blessing, eulogy, dream vision, love poem. Everywhere he writes with a cadenced ease. Consider this last part of **"Hailstones,"** the memory of a sudden storm of childhood:

> Nipple and hive, bite-lumps,
> small acorns of the almost pleasurable
> intimated and disallowed
>
> when the shower ended
> and everything said *wait*.
> For what? For forty years
> to say there, there you had
> the truest foretaste of your aftermath—
> in that dilation
>
> when the light opened in silence
> and a car with wipers going still
> laid perfect tracks in the slush.

The sensations are tangibly described, yet still shot through with symbolic lights. The flintlike Anglo-Saxon words give way to softer Latinate terms, just as the experience itself sinks into thought, and as the child's primary world gives way to the old heart's persuasions. Then at the end, its epiphany earned, how convincingly he turns the poem back in on itself—the memory of tire tracks having become the lines of the very poem we're reading.

The Haw Lantern opens with other poems about childhood, not so much evocations as little preludes about the growth of the poet's mind. He is concerned with how the child he was came to words and stories, and so to a magical view of the world, subject to spells and transformation—to poetry itself. The poet John Montague once said that the whole Irish landscape is a manuscript its people have lost the skill to read. Whenever Heaney writes about the countryside, he treats it as a text. It comes as no surprise that here he maps his language as well.

This concern with language is continued in the book's half-dozen allegorical poems. These are a new route for Heaney. With titles like **"From the Republic of Conscience"** and **"From the Canton of Expectation,"** they are not specific historical accounts, but meditations on spiritual conditions in a menacing political climate. They have fictive energy but can seem vague in effect. The purpose of allegory, wrote Coleridge, is to convey in disguise "either moral qualities or conceptions of the mind that are not in themselves objects of the senses," so that their difference is everywhere present to the eye, and their likeness suggested to the imagination. The most vivid of Heaney's parables returns to the subject of a poem in an earlier collection—getting stopped in his car by a border patrol. Now it's become a version of the writer's—any writer's—imperiled conscience:

> So you drive on to the frontier of writing
> where it happens again. The guns on tripods;
> the sergeant with his on-off mike repeating
>
> data about you, waiting for the squawk
> of the clearance; the marksman training down
> out of the sun upon you like a hawk.
>
> And suddenly you're through, arraigned yet
>   freed,
> as if you'd passed from behind a waterfall
> on the black current of a tarmac road
>
> past armour-plated vehicles, out between
> the posted soldiers flowing and receding
> like tree shadows into the polished windscreen.

The heart of the book is, as before, elegiac. One of the most affecting poems is his tribute to Robert Fitzgerald, on whose death in 1984 Heaney succeeded to the Boylston professorship at Harvard. **"In Memoriam: Robert Fitzgerald"** uses that great translator's own Homeric figures to render a homage passionate in its restraint. Here is the conclusion, Fitzgerald's death portrayed as his hero's moment of victory:

> After the bowstring sang a swallow's note,
> The arrow whose migration is its mark
> Leaves a whispered breath in every socket.
> The great test over, while the gut's still hum-
>   ming,
> This time it travels out of all knowing
> Perfectly aimed towards the vacant centre.

The book's centerpiece is **"Clearances,"** a sequence of eight sonnets plus a prayer written in memory of Heaney's mother. They will recall the ten brimming **"Glanmore Sonnets"** in *Field Work,* which taught the hedge-school lessons of an idealized farm life. Because of its subject, **"Clearances"** is more austere. Anecdotal memories of his mother have the stillness of genre scenes:

> When all the others were away at Mass
> I was all hers as we peeled potatoes.
> They broke the silence, let fall one by one
> Like solder weeping off the soldering iron:
> Cold comforts set between us, things to share
> Gleaming in a bucket of clean water.
> And again let fall. Little pleasant splashes
> From each other's work would bring us to our
>   senses.

His mother is portrayed as a rather stern and simple woman. Neither mother nor son much understand "each other's work." At home he would "decently relapse into the wrong / Grammar which kept us allied at bay," while she seems to have had a secret respect for words and his way with them. At her deathbed:

> The space we stood around had been emptied
> Into us to keep, it penetrated
> Clearances that suddenly stood open.

These are difficult scenes and feelings to write about, much harder certainly than any political issue. Heaney's reined-in emotion is all the more wrenching. When, in the final sonnet, the heft and hush of a felled tree have become "a bright nowhere, / A soul ramifying and forever / Silent, beyond silence listened for," we are in the presence of a poet with his ear to the heart of things. (pp. 36-9)

> *J. D. McClatchy, "The Exile's Song," in* The New Republic, *Vol. 197, No. 25, December 21, 1987, pp. 36-9.*

Helen Vendler   (review date Fall 1988)

[*Vendler is an American critic who is highly regarded for her insightful explications of poems and for her comprehension of individual aesthetic principles. Her most noted work,* Part of Nature, Part of Us: Modern American Poets *(1980), is recognized as an extensive and informed view of contemporary American poetry. In the following essay, Vendler discusses "From the Canton of Expectation," "The Haw Lantern," and "Alphabets" as illustrative of Heaney's broadened poetic vision.*]

There are two significant moments in the life of the lyric artist. The one I cannot take up here is the moment of the incorporation of the unbeautiful: that is a topic in itself. The other moment is the one when the gaze of the artist widens beyond the private concerns of the self. I want to turn to the evolution of the widened gaze as Seamus Heaney imagines it in three recent poems, published in *The Haw Lantern* (1987). There are many ways to the widened gaze, and Heaney's early poems suggest that one way is through consciousness of territorial borderlines that reflect conflict or difference. It is not until we perceive a group different from our own that we confront the choice of political inclusion or exclusion—that we even conceive of the possibility of a widened look at the world. Though Heaney's early poems had noticed the uneasy ac-

commodations between Ulster Protestants and Ulster Catholics, it was in his volume *North* that he looked beyond his own province to map a whole arc of Northern countries linked by a common history of sectarian and political violence. In *The Haw Lantern* he takes the gaze yet further, from geography into allegory. Now the terrain is not Ireland, not "the North," but rather the unspecified "canton of expectation"; and in another poem of this series, the frontier is not that of a nation or a territory, but rather the uneasy border of conscience (the unknown extension of an inner terrain).

The gaze can be widened, too, not simply by territorial difference, but in a second way—by the appearance, on the horizon of conscience, of an exemplary figure (one that Wallace Stevens would call "the impossible possible philosopher's man, / Who, in a million diamonds, sums us up"). This "major man" is a figure of ethical probits and accomplished human possibility. We have met him before in the poems of Seamus Heaney: in **"Chekhov on Sakhalin"** he was Anton Chekhov, visiting the penal colony on the island of Sakhalin in order to witness and write about penal conditions; in **"Station Island"** it was James Joyce. In the title poem of the new volume, the exemplary figure of ethical warning is the archetype of all such figures, the Greek philosopher Diogenes, searching with his lantern for one just man.

There is a third way of widening the gaze. If the first is territorial, and the second ethical, the third is linguistic: one extends one's vision by learning, in the fullest sense, languages. I will come back to that when I turn to the recent poem **"Alphabets,"** but for the moment I want to look at **"From the Canton of Expectation."** I have said that in this poem Heaney turns to allegory; and the movement from mimetic, or historically specific, writing to the writing of allegory is one of the most decisive a writer can make. That move represents the belief that poetry is, as Aristotle said, more philosophical than history—that personal history is merely illustrative, contingent, and transient, while the truth of the human condition is shared, recurrent, necessary. While the events in the canton of expectation may resemble events in Ireland, they equally, in the form of parable, may resemble events in, say, Poland. This is the reassuring view of the use of allegory. But there is another view, which would see a written allegory as the trace of an earlier felt despair. In every allegory, written parable has displaced historical event, smoothing out to some degree the idiosyncratic, the local, and the particular in favor of the widely-shared, the intelligible, the ahistorical. Writing is used to efface the pangs of immediate experience; universal timeless "nature" or "necessity" soothes the irritability of the ungovernable personal present.

In **"From the Canton of Expectation,"** what is kept of the contemporary historical scene resides in the language of the uneducated and religious elder generation as it is mimicked in the poem—a language of the passive and the martyred; a language optative, latinate, ceremonious. This language is set over against the rude imperatives of the younger, secular, educated generation—active, revolutionary, nervous, impatient. We hear the Latinate words of the elders—*expectation, resignation, vouchsafe, credit-*

able, humiliation, exaction, confirmed, prescribed, generation, impervious, De profundis, anathema, corroborated. Against these words we hear the crowbars of the violent young—political, unmannerly, in a hurry. But against both the resigned optative of the elders and the rude imperative of the young the poem sets a third possibility— the calm indicative of Noah as he prepares the ark, the saving ship that will "rise when the cloudburst happens." Noah neither despairs with the old nor forces the issue with the young.

In the resort to parable, there is, poetically speaking, both a gain and a loss. The gain lies in the fact that, as Jesus knew, we may recognize ourselves more accurately in a parable than in an historical narrative of our lives. The loss is felt in the absence of the odd, the intransigent, and the unintelligible as they appear in historical specificity. Seamus Heaney is a poet who has continued to write a poetry of many intimate particulars—family usages, seasonal events, personal elegy. Perhaps in consequence, he succeeds in preserving, even in his most mythical or allegorical moments, an intimacy with the language and customs of historical reality. The cunning and weariness here of the elder generation, their circumlocutions and defensiveness, their routine bravado and their pious aphorisms, mean that although the story of defeated political hopes and easy religious evasions may be a universal one, the language in which it is couched here is devastatingly particular to Ireland, and gives the parable its local acidity and sting of contempt. Perhaps the poem should have remained purely contemptuous—contemptuous of the old with their aggrieved complacency, contemptuous of the young with their intemperate activism. But if the gaze were to open and widen beyond the self only to have contempt for others, of what use would that widening be? "I yearn," says Heaney's speaker; and he yearns for Noah, the one just man who will meet and survive the deluge, and stock the culture afresh. Contempt and yearning are both dark poles for a writer, but they are complementary, rather than identical, darknesses.

In the poem **"The Haw Lantern,"** Diogenes looks at, and through, the speaker and others with his lantern of a possible, or impossible, righteousness. One is expected, by Diogenes, to incorporate the stone or pit of fortitude as well as the blood of human frailty, to withstand being pecked-at as well as to continue ripening. This is perhaps the widest opening of the gaze, as the poem looks out to two limits—the extreme of human deficiency and the extreme of human perfectibility. Diogenes' scrutiny is a test no one passes, but it continues to haunt the poet's mind.

Heaney's mode in **"The Haw Lantern"** is, surprisingly, that of the metaphysical emblem. His thorn-apple, his haw-lantern, is a cousin of Herbert's rose, "whose hue, angry and brave, / Bids the rash gazer wipe his eye." Unlike the allegorical parable, the metaphysical emblem as literary form is bright, visual, particular; it speaks of thorns, of the eye pricked by sensation, of the drop of blood exacted by insight. It marks the brilliant point where vision has both its sensual and its saving meaning; and consequently its rhetoric is often modest and self-obliterating, as it defers to the image seen in the eye's in-

stantaneous grasp. The troubles in Ireland are generally interpreted in terms of Christian sectarianism; it seems to me significant that in invoking Diogenes, Heaney turns for authenticity to a pre-Christian standard of justice.

I now return to the third way (after the territorial and the ethical) of widening the gaze, the linguistic one—the mastery of languages, including, but also going beyond, one's mother-tongue. In the smiling, tender, and beautiful poem **"Alphabets,"** Heaney recounts his own socialization by language into the human world. He does this in a pure lyric measure, the rhyming quatrain. The other poems I have mentioned invoke the discursive tradition, written as they are in something like blank verse; and they hover near sonnet length, in their stanzas of thirteen, fourteen, and fifteen lines (**"The Haw Lantern"** especially resembles a sonnet reversed, with a short opening and a longer close). But the naively joyous slant rhymes of the long poem **"Alphabets"** deliver us into the poetic world of the child, whom we see as *tabula rasa,* a slate upon which consciousness will appear through language.

We watch as the child first learns English, the mother-tongue; and then Latin, with its elaborate historical and religious extensions of experience; then the lost mother-tongue, Irish, with its aura not only of the monastic scriptorium but of a native Muse; then Greek, with its differently-shaped letters—lambdas, deltas, omegas—which the child assimilates to the familiar rural landscape— sheaves, potato pits, horseshoes. Through these several languages come prophecies and resolutions—the divine promise that one would conquer by a sign (remembered from the story of Constantine), the Renaissance magus's resolve to hang a globe in his house so as always to think of the planet, "not just single things."

Years ago, as a student, I heard I. A. Richards say to us, earnestly, "Think of the planet!" No one had previously urged me, or any young woman I knew, to think of the planet. We were to think of our future houses, our husbands, and our children. Perhaps because it took me so very long to heed Richards at all, I value those poems that urge that larger look. When many languages are known, Heaney implies, the heart's sympathies may widen to include the whole world, a world seen from the astronaut's window as a single radiant vowel—"the risen, aqueous, singular, lucent O."

Heaney's poem reminds us that even the largest gaze is an eventual consequence of the child's first conscious mirroring of the self in a word, as the child in the poem, before he goes to school, sees with his "wide pre-reflective stare" the plasterer's trowel print out, on the gable of the house, the letters of the family name. From the single name to the entire world is the measure of the natural, necessary, and creative trajectory of language. The lyric charm of **"Alphabets"** keeps it firmly in the historical singular of one sensibility; but future readers of the poem will surely see in it analogies to their own transformation through languages from provincial children to citizens of the planet.

It is always hard to say in what way a poem is modern, but these poems might suggest a few generalizations. A poem can be modern in suggesting that Christians might look to paganism for probit; or in surveying the world with an astronaut's eye; or in returning, with a bow to Czeslaw Milosz's "The World," to naive quatrains; or in satirizing a current nationalist idiom of worn-out piety; or in finding a way to invent a metaphysical emblem from a native thorn-tree; or in altering the prosody of the pentameter. **"From the Canton of Expectation," "The Haw Lantern,"** and **"Alphabets"** come from the center of a politically disturbed and religiously exhausted moment in Ireland. Heaney hopes to find, in the differing alphabets of his culture,—classical, Christian, and allegorical—elements that can unite human beings politically while allowing them a legitimate aesthetic, philosophical, and linguistic pluralism.

"Alphabets" calls its readers to go beyond the provinciality with which they all began, to adopt the astronaut's inclusive view, to bring to actuality the possibilities of that "magnified and buoyant" planet that exists only in hope. The arks and lanterns of these parables by Seamus Heaney decline, by their conscious allegory, a specified political intent; but in their conscious modern pluralism, they contribute to the perpetually reinvented alphabet of twentieth-century culture. (pp. 66-70)

> Helen Vendler, "On Three Poems by Seamus Heaney," in Salmagundi, No. 80, Fall, 1988, pp. 66-70.

Elmer Andrews   (essay date 1988)

[*Andrews is an Irish screenwriter and critic. In the following essay, he surveys important themes in Heaney's poetry.*]

In a 1981 interview with John Haffenden, Heaney remarked 'It's possible to exacerbate . . . I believe that what poetry does to me is comforting . . . I think that art does appease, assuage.' In **Field Work** the poet, newly 'landed in the hedge-school of Glanmore', renews his commitment 'to raise / A voice caught back off slug-horn and slow chanter / That might continue, hold, dispel, appease'. **'The Harvest Bow'**, one of the best poems in this volume, ends by quoting Coventry Patmore, 'The end of art is peace.' Heaney expresses a view of poetry as secret and natural even though it must operate in a world that is public and brutal. He has found himself caught in the sectarian crossfire with fellow Catholics pressing him to write political verse and liberal critics congratulating him on not taking sides.

For Heaney the great question is:

> How with this rage shall beauty hold a plea
> Whose action is no stronger than a flower?

His answer is also from Shakespeare—lines from *Timon of Athens* which have become, he says, 'a touchstone' for him:

> Our poesy is as a gum which oozes
> From whence 'tis nourished.

The concept of nourishment becomes a central preoccupation. The first part of his **Preoccupations: Selected Prose 1968-1978** discusses the things which have nourished his poetry and contributed to the development of a poetic voice which, like Wordsworth's, emerged out of a music overheard in nature and in childhood.

Preoccupations begins with the word 'Omphalos', the Greek word for a navel, or a central point. Significantly, it is the sound of the word which first recommends it to his attention: he immediately relates it to the sound of water gushing from the pump in the yard of the farm where he was brought up. The source of his imaginative power, we are to understand, lies in his rural childhood experience that is centered and staked in the image of the pump. The pump, like his poetry, taps hidden springs to conduct what is sustaining and life-giving. The centre of the poet's imaginative world is also the centre of family and community life: the women of five households came with their big enamel buckets to draw water from that pump. Its rhythms are the elemental rhythms of nature itself, that continue undisturbed by the American bombers returning to their base nearby, indifferent to the great historical events of the 1940s. The pump is a symbol of the nourishment which comes from knowing and belonging to a certain place and a certain mode of life.

For Heaney, a sense of self depends, among other things, on a sense of place and a sense of history, something which is typical of the Irish writer and derives to some extent from the Irish writer's desire to protect and preserve what is threatened and diminished. Possession of the land, like possession of different languages, is a matter of particular urgency in Ireland. The Revival of the late nineteenth century marked a re-discovery of confidence in the writer's own place, his own history and his own speech, English and Irish. After Yeats, and the exhaustion of the heroic-romantic myth of Ireland, new directions were called for. What was required was a readjustment of social and poetic strategies which would allow the writer to express his own most authentic experience. With Patrick Kavanagh, an alternative to the esoteric, mythological systems of the writers of the Revival was affirmed. Kavanagh's demonstration of the poetic validity of the parish, as opposed to the nation viewed as a spiritual entity, his interest in the local and ordinary, had a decisive influence on Heaney. And, from the other side of the cultural and religious divide there was the Ulster regionalist experiment of John Hewitt, whose 'lifelong concern to question and document the relationship between art and locality has provided all subsequent Northern writers with a hinterland of reference should they require a tradition more intimate than the broad perspectives of the English literary achievement'.

That larger tradition had, of course, its own useful models to offer, most conspicuously Wordsworth, being 'perhaps the first man to articulate the nurture that becomes available to the feelings through dwelling in one dear perpetual place'. Wordsworth wrote out of a tradition which, as Kavanagh admiringly explained, divorced English literature from England the nation, leaving the writer free to 'go on quietly unconcerned, undeceived by the latest reports on anything', free to evolve his own individual myths, his own sustaining structures to nourish his inner life and help him to express it. Kavanagh yearned for a myth and failed to find it (an artistic dilemma which he states explicitly in his poem 'A Personal Problem'). Heaney's career becomes a strenuous effort to reconcile the vital abundance of Kavanagh with an explanatory or consoling myth-making faculty: he wants to be a celebrant of instinct and mystery and, at the same time, through the ritual of art, to aspire to the intelligence and mastery of a Yeats or a Hopkins, whose austere genius he considers with warm and sympathetic understanding in 'The Makings of a Music', 'The Fire i' the Flint' and 'Yeats an Example?' in *Preoccupations.*

Poetry is born out of the watermarks and colourings of the self. But that self in some ways takes its spiritual pulse from the inward spiritual structuring of the community to which it belongs; and the community to which I belong is Catholic and Nationalist.

—Seamus Heaney

Heaney's poetic career, however, begins with modest ambitions, by his delving into his own childhood past. But gradually he extends his excavation of self to place it in relation to a communal past. He likes to think of his poems as 'soundings' that probe the landscape for a shared and diminished culture. He attempts to define and interpret the present by bringing it into significant relationship with the past. Dominated by a sense of nature's powers, he sees history, language and myth as bound up with nature, with territory and landscape. The landscape is sacramental. He is peculiarly responsive to the emblematic character of natural objects and processes. They evoke in him a deep sense of the numinous. He is open to intuitions that relate human female psychology and sexuality to the landscape. Landscape becomes a memory, a continuity, a piety, a feared and fecund mother, an insatiable lover.

This sacral vision of place has its origins in his childhood apprehension of nature on and around the family farm, which he recalls in the first part of *Preoccupations.* Lost among the pea-drills, he finds himself in a 'sunlit lair':

> . . . a green web, a caul of veined light, a tangle of rods and pods, stalks and tendrils, full of assuaging earth and leaf-smell.

The experience of another 'secret nest' in the hollow of a birch tree introduces the image of the wood-lover and tree-hugger which underlies the Heaney/Sweeney identification of recent work:

> Above your head, the living tree flourished and breathed, you shouldered the slightly vibrant bole, and if you put your forehead to the rough pith you felt the whole lithe and whispering crown of willows moving in the sky above you.

He remembers bathing naked in a moss-hole:

> . . . treading the thick-liver mud, unsettling a smoky muck off the bottom and coming out smeared and weedy and darkened.

This incident is recalled as a 'betrothal' and an 'initiation', the ritual intensity of Heaney's language indicating an involvement with nature through which his religious and sexual impulses also find expression.

Beyond the security of the farmyard lay 'forbidden grounds', the 'realm of bogeys', the haunt of recluses and mystery men who lived on the fringes of the bog. As childhood perspectives widen, the physical landscape assumes a social and historical dimension as well. He comes to recognize division as well as community. Mossbawn, the name of the family farm, lay between Castledawson and Toome, between English influence (Castledawson) and native experience (Toome), the demesne and the bog. The demesne was Moyola Park, an estate occupied by Lord Moyola, formerly Major James Chichester-Clark, the ex-Unionist Prime Minister of Northern Ireland. The bog was where hoards of flints and other relics had been found, reminders that this was one of the oldest inhabited places in the country. Mossbawn itself is a name made up of two words: 'Moss', a Scots word brought to Ireland by the Planters; and 'bawn', the name the English colonists gave to their fortified farmhouses. Mossbawn—the Planter's house on the bog. Heaney comments, however, that the preferred pronounciation was Moss bann, that *bán* is the Gaelic word for white, and that the name may therefore mean the moss of bog-cotton: 'In the syllables of my home I see a metaphor of the split culture of Ulster.' Mossbawn is bordered by the townlands of Broagh and Anahorish, 'forgotten Gaelic music that leads back to the ancient civilization that was destroyed by soldiers and administrators like Spenser and Davies'. At the same time, Heaney acknowledges that his own perceptions have been conditioned significantly by the English tradition. The countryside of Grove Hill and Back Park which also bordered the family farm is recognized as 'a version of pastoral', and while 'Grove and Park . . . do not reach me as a fibre from a tap-root', they are part of 'the intricate and various foliage of history and culture that I grew up beneath'.

From an early age there was another love in Heaney's life as well as that of nature: 'I was in love with words themselves'. Words as verbal music is another source of assuagement, and it is the poet's delight in words which more than anything else nourishes his poetry. 'The secret of being a poet, Irish or otherwise', Heaney says, 'lies in the summoning of the energies of words'.

In *Preoccupations* he traces his love of words back to childhood as he does his love of nature. He recalls his first experience of how words as bearers of history and mystery began to invite him: listening to his mother recite lists of affixes and suffixes, Latin roots with English meanings, rhymes that had been part of her schooling. Then there was the 'exotic listing' of Stuttgart, Leipzig, Oslo, Hilversum, on the wireless dial; the 'beautiful sprung rhythms' of the old BBC weather forecast: Dogger, Rockall, Malin, Shetland, Faroes, Finisterre; 'the gorgeous and inane phraseology' of the Catechism; the litany of the Blessed Virgin. At school there was his introduction to the classic canon of English poetry, the 'roadside rhymes' chants that were scurrilous and sectarian, and the reading of Irish myths and legends. Later came the conscious savouring of the music of an English education: Keats, Webster, Anglo-Saxon verse, Wordsworth and Hopkins, who receives a special mention because of the similarity between his energetic, hard-edged, consonantal music and Heaney's own Ulster dialect.

All this he mentions as contributing to the process of finding a poetic voice. That voice, he explains, is composed of two elements. There is that part of the poetry which takes its structure and beat, its play of metre and rhythms, its diction and allusiveness, from the literary tradition. And there are also those 'intonations and appeasements' offered by a poet's music which are instinctual, unconscious and pre-verbal, made up of the kinds of noise which assuage him, pleasure or repel him, drawn from the world around him. They are the inklings and echoes which reach him from 'all the realms of whisper'. Heaney speaks of the private and cultural 'depth-charges' latent in certain words and sounds and rhythms and kinds of rhyme. There is a 'binding secret' between words, 'which delights not just the ear but the whole backward abysm of mind and body'. One is reminded of Eliot's 'auditory imagination':

> The feeling for the syllable and rhythm, penetrating far below the conscious levels of thought and feeling, invigorating every word; sinking to the most primitive and forgotten, returning to the origin and bringing something back.

The personal and Irish pieties Heaney thinks of as vowels, and the literary awareness nourished on English as consonants. His poems, he hopes, will be 'vocables' adequate to his whole experience.

One way in which Heaney describes the process of turning feeling into words is as an 'oozing' that starts with the 'gazing heart', the 'listening ear', a 'wise passivity'. Poems come up out of the dark, organically oozing up into consciousness:

> I have always listened for poems, they come sometimes like bodies come out of a bog, almost complete, seeming to have been laid down a long time ago, surfacing with a touch of mystery. They certainly involve craft and determination, but chance and instinct have a role in the thing too.

The voice in Heaney's poetry is the voice that is found to express what Eliot termed 'a dark embryo'. It originates in a primary generating surrender to the poet's *données*. Discussing the difference between 'technique' and 'craft', Heaney says:

> The crucial action is pre-verbal, to be able to allow the first alertness or come-hither, sensed in a blurred or incomplete way, to dilate and approach as a thought or a theme or a phrase. . . . That first emergence involves the divining, vatic, oracular function.

This is technique. Technique is what allows the first stirring of the mind around a word, a rhythm, an image or a memory to grow towards articulation, articulation not necessarily in terms of argument or explication, but in terms of 'its own potential for harmonious self-reproduction'.

The second activity is 'the making function' that depends on 'craft'—the 'thought' finding the words. Sometimes, Heaney admits, it is not easy to distinguish between feeling getting into words, and words turning into feeling. His title, *Door into the Dark,* he says, was a gesture towards the idea of words themselves being doors.

Wordsworth is Heaney's primary model of the poet as diviner. Wordsworth is attentive to the invitations of 'the mind's internal echo', and sets out to discover the verbal means which will amplify his original visionary excitement into 'a redundant energy / Vexing its own creation'. Heaney begins a discussion of his own poetry in **'Feeling into Words'** by quoting from *The Prelude:*

> The hiding places of my power
> Seem open; I approach, and then they close;
> I see by glimpses now; when age comes on,
> May scarcely see at all, and I would give,
> While yet we may, as far as words can give,
> A substance and a life to what I feel:
> I would enshrine the spirit of the past
> For future generations.

Heaney embraces these lines as a statement of his own view of what poetry means to him:

> Implicit in those lines is a view of poetry which I think is implicit in the few poems I have written that give me any right to speak: poetry as divination, poetry as revelation of the self to the self, as restoration of the culture to itself; poems as elements of continuity, with the aura and authenticity of archaeological finds, where the buried shard has an importance that is not diminished by the importance of the buried city; poetry as a dig, a dig for finds that end up being plants.

The Wordsworthian method of composition is contrasted with the Yeatsian view of poetry:

> When he talked about poetry, Yeats never talked about the "ooze" or "nurture." He always talked about the "labour" and the "making" and the "fascination of what's difficult."

Heaney develops this contrast between 'receiving' and 'making' into a view of poetic creation as either a 'feminine' or 'masculine' activity:

> From Shakespeare's ooze to Eliot's dark embryo, we have a vision of poetic creation as a feminine action, almost parthenogenetic, where it is the ovum and its potential rather than the sperm and its penetration that underlies their accounts of poetic origins. And out of this vision of feminine action comes a language for poetry that tends to brood and breed, crop and cluster, with a texture of echo and implication, trawling the pool of the ear with a net of associations.

Poetry to Keats, says Heaney, has a physical equivalent in a mother's birth pangs. But Hopkins brings to his craft a "siring instinct":

Keats has the life of a swarm, fluent and merged; Hopkins has the design of a honeycomb, definite and loaded. In Keats the rhythm is narcotic, in Hopkins it is a stimulant to the mind. Keats woos us to receive, Hopkins alerts us to perceive.

Hopkins strikes his fire from flint and, unlike the organic 'oozy marshlight' of symbolism, Hopkins' poetry is fretted rather than fecund, maintaining a design rather than releasing a flow, exuding a masculine brilliance and revealing the presence of 'powerful and active thought' that disciplines the music and takes charge of the language and emotion. It is possible for the two opposing spirits of poetry to be reconciled: Yeats is said to prove 'that deliberation can be so intensified that it becomes synonymous with inspiration'.

Everywhere in his writings Heaney is acutely sensitive to the opposition between masculine will and intelligence on the one hand, and, on the other, feminine instinct and emotion; between architectonic masculinity and natural female feeling for mystery and divination. It is the opposition between the arena of public affairs and the intimate, secret stations of 'the realms of whisper'. He uses it to describe the tension between English influence and Irish experience ('The feminine element for me involves the matter of Ireland and the masculine strain is drawn from involvement with English literature'). It underlies two different responses to landscape, one that is 'lived, illiterate and unconscious', and one that is 'learned, literate and conscious'. Early poems like **'Digging'** and **'Follower'** establish his troubling self-consciousness about the relationship between 'roots and reading', the lived and the learned. In attempting to resolve these contrarieties, the example of Patrick Kavanagh was invaluable. Kavanagh, the son of a country shoemaker in Inishkeen, Co. Monaghan, made the move from his native parish to London in 1937, and then in 1939 to Dublin, where he spent most of the rest of his life. Kavanagh's career seemed to Heaney to parallel much in his own, especially the conflict between 'the illiterate self that was tied to the little hills and earthed in the stoney grey soil and the literate self that pined for "the City of Kings / Where art, music and letters were the real things" '. 'The Great Hunger' was of special interest because of the balance Kavanagh achieved between 'intimacy with actual clay' and 'the penalty of consciousness'. The poem was a model of the poet's imaginative self-sufficiency within his own parish. Kavanagh's assertion that 'parochialism is universal, it deals with fundamentals' gave Heaney confidence in the poetic validity of his own preoccupation with his County Derry childhood. From Kavanagh's most successful work he could learn from a poet whose management of ironic points-of-vantage on his material promoted the expression of more subtle, complex feelings about the relationship between poet and place.

The pervasiveness of the masculine/feminine opposition in Heaney's writings about himself and other poets originates in a deep-seated sense of his own divided feelings and experience. His poetry reflects the attempt to reconcile the tension. The poem, Heaney says, should be a 'completely successful love act between the craft and the gift'. But it is the gift, the initial incubatory action, he keeps reminding us, which is for him the crucial stage in the creative process. A poem, he believes, can survive stylistic blemishes that are due to inadequate craftsmanship, but 'it cannot survive a still-birth'. Poetry is essentially a mystery, a corpse from the bog, a whispering from the dark, a gift from the goddess. The poet is passive receiver before he is an active maker.

There are times, however, when Heaney has felt guilty or exasperated with this essentially passive role and has wanted poetry to do something; when he wished to be a man of action making direct political statements rather than an equivocator, a parablist, a supplicant or withdrawn aesthete. From the beginning, from that opening image in the first poem in his first volume, **'Digging'**, the shadow of a gunman is present, as if to convince us that the pen can be as mighty as the gun. He compensates for his failure to follow men of action by making promises: he'll dig with his pen he says. The theme does not become prominent until *North,* where art and the role of the artist come under his tormented scrutiny. By then Ulster was in a state of war.

Despite the lapse of confidence in art which *North* evinces—and the intensity of the anguish it occasioned should not be underestimated, as the last poem in *North,* **'Exposure'**, would testify—the great bulk of Heaney's prose statements, comments to interviewers and reviews of other writers are made from the point of view of a poet. When he turns to fellow poets, he tends to focus on their use of language, their verbal music, before theme or meaning. He never comments from the point of view of a politically committed spokesman, rarely even from a strictly academic viewpoint. He registers his appreciation of poetry as 'self-delighting buds on the old bough of tradition'. He takes the politically committed artist to task, in this case the Marxist, for attempting 'to sweep the poetic enterprises clean of those somewhat hedonistic impulses towards the satisfactions of aural and formal play out of which poems arise, whether they aspire to delineate or to obfuscate "things as they are" '. Typically, Paul Muldoon qualifies as 'one of the very best' for 'the opulence of the music, the overspill of creative joy', for his exploitation of 'the language's potential for generating new meanings out of itself . . . this sense of buoyancy, this delight in the trickery and lechery that words are capable of '.

'During the last few years', Heaney stated in 1975, 'there has been considerable expectation that poets from Northern Ireland should "say" something about "the situation" '. Heaney's comment on this demand was that 'in the end they (poets) will only be worth listening to if they are saying something about and to themselves'. Poetry for Heaney is its own special action, has its own mode of reality. In his review of the Russian poet, Osip Mandelstam, who had found it impossible to make an accommodation with Soviet realities under Stalin, Heaney writes:

> We live here in critical times ourselves, when the idea of poetry as an art is in danger of being overshadowed by a quest for poetry as a diagram of political attitudes. Some commentators have all the fussy literalism of an official from the ministry of truth.

What Heaney's review asserts is the urgent need to fight

for the very life of poetry in a world which seems increasingly to discount it. He elevates the artist's work above the moralist's. The principle of the autonomy of art frees the artist from tendentiousness, vulgar moralizing and political propagandizing. A cut below the surface, however, are the whole world's concerns which, by virtue of the poet's 'aesthetic distance', can be treated with a kind of passionate detachment, a concerned disinterestedness. Heaney speaks as an apologist of the 'religion of art'. The Mandelstam review begins with this impassioned pronouncement:

> "Art for Art's Sake" has become a gibe because of an inadequate notion of what art can encompass, and is usually bandied by people who are philistines anyhow. Art has a religious, a binding force, for the artist. Language is the poet's faith and the faith of his fathers and in order to go his own way and do his proper work in an agnostic time, he has to bring that faith to the point of arrogance and triumphalism.

Inevitably, however, politics come into communication with the poetical function. But only legitimately so when the political situation has first been emotionally experienced and reduced to subordinate status in an aesthetically created universe of symbols. If Heaney's poetry automatically encompasses politics, he is careful that it should not serve them. In this respect the Yeatsian aesthetic is exemplary. There is a passage from Yeats's essay, 'Samhain: 1905', part of which Heaney quotes at the beginning of *Preoccupations*:

> One cannot be less than certain that the poet, though it may well be for him to have right opinions, above all if his country be at death's door, must keep all opinion that he holds to merely because he thinks it right, out of poetry, if it is to be poetry at all. At the enquiry which preceded the granting of a patent to the Abbey Theatre I was asked if *Cathleen ni Houlihan* was not written to affect opinion. Certainly it was not. I had a dream one night which gave me a story, and I had certain emotions about this country, and I gave those emotions expression for my own pleasure. If I had written to convince others I would have asked myself, not "Is that exactly what I think and feel?" But "How would that strike so-and-so? How will they think and feel when they have read it?" And all would be oratorical and insincere. If we understand our own minds, and the things that are striving to utter themselves through our minds, we move others, not because we have understood our thought about those others, but because all life has the same root. Coventry Patmore has said, "The end of art is peace," and the following of art is little different from the following of religion in the intense preoccupation it demands.

Like Yeats, Heaney writes political poetry; but, also like Yeats, he is not political in any doctrinaire sense. As a man like any other man, politics are part of his life: being a poet does not separate him from the concerns of common humanity. What being a poet means is that his concern cannot simply be with abstract ideas, but with ideas suffused and shaped by emotion, and absorbed at the deepest levels of consciousness. The Yeatsian declaration that poetry is 'expression for my own pleasure' is echoed by Joyce's shade in **'Station Island'**, when he advises the poet, 'The main thing is to write / for the joy of it.' Art and politics may come from different imaginative 'levels' of the personality if the art is good, original, deep, authentic enough: if the latter is the case (that is, in the case of good writers) the artistic insight is prophetic, 'true', at a deeper level, and for a longer time, than any political idea can be,

In an interview with Seamus Deane, Heaney sought to explain the political nature of his poetry:

> Poetry is born out of the watermarks and colourings of the self. But that self in some ways takes its spiritual pulse from the inward spiritual structuring of the community to which it belongs; and the community to which I belong is Catholic and Nationalist. I believe that the poet's force now, and hopefully in the future, is to maintain the efficacy of his own "mythos", his own cultural and political colourings, rather than to serve any particular momentary strategy that his political leaders, his para-military organization or his own liberal self might want him to serve. I think that poetry and politics are, in different ways, an articulation, an ordering, a giving form to inchoate pieties, prejudices, worldviews, or whatever. And I think that my own poetry is a kind of slow, obstinate, papish burn, emanating from the ground I was brought up on.

Heaney will not renounce tribal prejudice as the rational humanist would urge, but write out of it in such a way as to clarify his own feelings, not to encourage—or discourage—prejudice in others. That would be propaganda—the didactic achieved at the expense of the poetic. 'We make out of the quarrel with others rhetoric', Yeats has said, 'but out of the quarrel with ourselves, poetry.' Clearly, Yeats, like Heaney, was preoccupied with the opposition between the divided selves of the poet, between the poet as poet and the poet as a human being like other human beings. 'In most poets', writes C. Day Lewis, 'there is an intermittent conflict between the poetic self and the rest of the man; and it is by reconciling the two, not by eliminating the one, that they can reach their full stature.' Heaney strives for such a reconciliation—a reconciliation between primitive piety and rational humanism, between illiterate fidelity to origins and a sense of objective reality, between the feminine and the masculine impulses.

Long years of debating this synthesis for and in his own poetry have promoted some large and luminous insights into the work of other poets. Heaney is remarkably acute to the way the making of a music by other writers betrays their concern either to flee external pressures on creativity, or to find an ideology in which to lodge their own casual, vagrant impulses. In his essay, **'Envies and Identifications: Dante and the Modern Poet'**, he begins with the idea that all poets turn to the great masters of the past to re-create them in their own image. Eliot, he says, discovered the political Dante, the poet with a 'universal language', the artist as seer and repository of tradition, one who was prepared to submit his intelligence and sensibility to the disciplines of 'philosophia' and religious orthodoxy: 'Eliot's ultimate attraction is to the way Dante could turn values and judgements into poetry, the way the figure of the poet as thinker and teacher merged into the figure of the poet as expresser of a universal myth that could unify the abundance of the inner world and the confusion of the outer.' This was the 'stern and didactic' image of Dante which Eliot discovered in the struggle to embrace a religious faith.

Mandelstam, on the other hand, in the effort to free himself from the pressures of Stalinist orthodoxy, discovers a different Dante: 'Dante is not perceived as the mouthpiece of an orthodoxy but rather as the apotheosis of free, natural, biological process, as a hive of bees, a process of crystallization, a hurry of pigeon flights, a focus for all the impulsive, instinctive, non-utilitarian elements in the creative life.

For Heaney's own part, Dante is the great model for the Irish poet who would explore the 'typical strains' the consciousness labours under in that troubled land: 'The main tension is between two often contradictory commands: to be faithful to the collective historical experience and to be true to the recognitions of the emerging self.' He responds to the Dante who 'could place himself in a historical world yet submit that world to scrutiny from a perspective beyond history', who 'could accommodate the political and the transcendent'.

Heaney's own poetic preoccupations as revealed in his interpretative approach to Dante may, finally, be pursued with the help of psychoanalytic vocabulary, especially as it has been developed in the light of structuralist and post-structuralist theories of discourse. Separation from the Edenic past, from the organic society, from home and heritage, from origins, from the female matrix of being, from the 'life-force', is enforced by having to come to terms with the masculine realities of the wider, public world. Heaney's struggle for a 'bi-sexual' form of writing sets up a play of unconscious drives, of deep symbols and rhythms, of silences and absences, a 'ghost-life' issuing from 'all the realms of whisper'; and these irruptions of unruly energy counterpoint and colour received social meaning and value. The fluid and diffuse, evocative, vowel-based, eroticized element in his poetry offers a resistance to the male metaphysical world of abstraction, division and fixed essence. Modern society is what the post-structuralist would call both 'phallocentric' and 'logocentric' (to use the terms expounded by the French philosopher Jacques Derrida): 'phallocentric' because it is a male world, and the phallus is the symbol of certain, self-present meaning; and 'logocentric' because it believes that its discourses can give us total and immediate access to the essence and presence of things. Heaney's poetry includes a force within society which disrupts and opposes it—a force embodied by, for example, the figure of Sweeney or Antaeus. There is in his poetry a kind of pleasureable excess over precise meaning, a libidinal gratification within the systematizing or mythologizing structures which transgresses or interrogates their limits. This feminine mode of discourse is both 'inside' and 'outside' the masculine 'symbolic order' of linguistic, social and sexual power: in a similar way, the indigenous Gaelic reality is represented within a colonial framework, fixed by the sign, image

and meaning of another culture, yet because it is also the 'other' or 'negative' of that social order always possesses something which eludes representation.

In dismantling the unified subject, in fracturing and throwing it into contradiction, Heaney poses some radical questions to existing society, but this does not lead to the proposal of a new kind of politically activated subject nor to a wholesale scepticism which acknowledges only the infinite play of textual inscription. His feminine mode of being and discourse is not an alternative to the male, authoritarian 'symbolic order' (not that that in itself would constitute a politically revolutionary gesture), but an internal limit of its conventional, privileged value. The perennial image is that of the mutual embrace. In the early **'Lovers on Aran',** the poet wonders whether it is the fluid, timeless, female sea which 'possesses' the land or the hard, male arms of rock thrust out by the land which force the sea's submission:

> Did sea define the land or land the sea?
> Each drew new meaning from the waves' colli-
> sion.
> Sea broke on land to full identity.

Poetry is such an act of love. In its embrace the intractable raw materials of experience are brought into relationship with each other in a way which promotes 'new meaning' and 'full identity'. Implied here is a notion of poetry which is empiricist, humanist and organicist. Empiricist in that knowledge is seen as the product of experience, personal and historical (as opposed to the modern structuralist emphasis on the arbitrary and conventional nature of language which leads to the view that knowledge is not at all the product of experience): Heaney insists on the referential function of poetry, on being 'faithful to' and 'true to' experience. Humanist in that his belief in art's relevance to life confers upon poetry a role once ascribed to religion or philosophy: it can help us cope with the problems of everyday existence. Poetry achieves this status because it both includes reality within itself and at the same time, by virtue of its organic form, resolves the conflicts of mind and history, creating in us a state of equilibrium rarely afforded by other kinds of experience. It is not something to galvanize us into action because it remains an essentially contemplative mode; it is not the vehicle of an irredeemable alienation because it recreates what is found to be lacking in the world. Heaney's project is the achievement of that momentary peace—that sunlit space, that 'home' or 'haven'—in which all oppositions are harmonized in the self-contained, transcendent poetic symbol. For a sceptical, defensive, displaced poet, torn by conflicting dogma and troubled by the nightmare of history, constantly threatened with the dissolution of the self yet deeply suspicious of the more obvious forms of ideological control, the Romantic symbol with its offer of totalization and timelessness exerted a profound attraction.

The morality of Heaney's symbol is not something to be grasped as a formulated code or explicit ethical system: it is rather a sensitive preoccupation with the whole quality of life, which encourages us to reverence the world for what it is, to respect the sensuous integrity, the rich variousness of its manifold objects and processes. It is rooted in the 'concrete' life and its 'immanent' meanings, which he comes to know with experiential, intuitive or, as Leavis would say, 'irresistible' certainty. Poetry is a re-discovery of the 'life-force'. On this last point, Heaney seems happy (as Leavis was) to celebrate intuitively what he takes to be a vibrant, universal presence, but what in reality is a vague, Romantic idealist fiction championed before him by writers such as D. H. Lawrence and Martin Heidegger who used it to justify rampant sexism, racism and authoritarianism. This only serves to highlight the way that Heaney's poem, like the Romantic symbol, is imbued with a transcendent mystical authority that is not to be challenged. His poem is the product of a thoroughgoing irrationalism closely linked with the religious impulse. Heaney's organicism, reflected in his ubiquitous invocation of natural analogues for poetry, and in his notions of the poem's autonomy and teleological unity, is fundamentally theological: the poet imitates the generative activity of nature or the 'life-force', if not the creative act of God. (pp. 1-16)

> Elmer Andrews, in his The Poetry of Seamus Heaney: All the Realms of Whisper, *The Macmillan Press Ltd., 1988, 219 p.*

Helen Vendler   (review date 13 March 1989)

[*In the following review, Vendler favorably assesses* The Government of the Tongue, *emphasizing Heaney's views on the works of several major poets and his interpretation of the role of poetry in relation to life, society, and the self.*]

In 1970, a year after the intensification of hostilities in Northern Ireland, the Irish poet Seamus Heaney had a dream:

> I was shaving at the mirror of the bathroom
> when I glimpsed in the mirror a wounded man
> falling towards me with his bloodied hands lifted
> to tear at me or to implore.

Once the necessary narcissism of the youthful art-mirror was invaded by an ambiguous national—even familial—horror, Heaney's work began to exhibit an anxiety that has never left it, in spite of his move, in 1972, from Ulster to the Republic. His new collection of essays, *The Government of the Tongue,* opens with an allegorical primer of this anxiety:

> Both Art and Life have had a hand in the formation of any poet, and both are to be loved, honoured and obeyed. Yet both are often perceived to be in conflict.

The first half of this new book belongs chiefly to Life. Several of its essays praise modern poets who have been called upon to exhibit exceptional moral courage under totalitarian regimes (Mandelstam, Holub, Herbert). Other essays hold up for inspection post-colonial poets such as Kavanagh and Walcott. (There is also a brilliant essay on Larkin's visionary moments; it springs from Heaney's interest in the assertion of value in the absence of any proof of the existence of such value—a question not unrelated to resistance to state control.)

The second half of *The Government of the Tongue*—four essays delivered in 1986 as the T. S. Eliot Memorial Lectures at the University of Kent—belongs chiefly to Art. Writing on Auden, Lowell, and Plath, Heaney pays homage (not without criticism) to three contemporary poets of the English language who were, to his mind, exemplary in their aesthetic practice. Heaney does not pretend to solve the dilemma put to the poet in every era by the demands of life and of art, and at least two of the examples he cites (George Herbert and Sylvia Plath) seem to me less than adequately represented for the purposes of his argument. But to follow the darts and feints of Heaney's mind as he worries his own case through these surrogates is immensely instructive.

In his first collection of essays, *Preoccupations* (1980), Heaney was engaged in coming to terms with some of his early masters—Wordsworth, Hopkins, and Yeats. He went to school to them to learn ways, both conceptual and linguistic, of treating his original givens—rural life, Catholicism, Irish nationality. His essays on his predecessors—bravura pieces of characterization, the best in recent memory—ended up defending a Wordsworthian and Keatsian "wise passiveness" (absorptive, hidden, receptive, yielding) against the Hopkinsian and Yeatsian tendency to force-march language into compliance with an authorial will.

The Irish troubles, however, put pliability and privacy into question as literary values. When Heaney was subjected to considerable pressure at home to take a public stand, he responded by anthropologizing the Irish conflict. In his incomparable volume *North* (1975) he published poems referring to centuries of tribal warfare in a whole swath of northern countries, from Scandinavia to Ireland, and the long-preserved violence of historical memory took on symbolic form in poems about slaughtered bodies exhumed from the bogs of Jutland and Ireland alike. The long view was a countermeasure to those whose memories went back only to the plantation of Ulster.

Heaney may have been drawn to a poet like Zbigniew Herbert by Herbert's comparable historical allusions to totalitarianism in Roman times. All writers under political pressure find historical allusion and allegory congenial forms, since they are oblique and non-referential in any legal sense. One solution to censorship—one that Herbert and Holub have adopted in Eastern Europe—is to write in parable, and Heaney himself has written in parables in his most recent volume of poems, *The Haw Lantern.* Nonetheless, this solution—though interesting and fruitful stylistically—does not entirely satisfy Heaney as an answer to his central question: "What must the poet do in a politically troubled time?" It smacks too much of the political address.

Heaney's title—*The Government of the Tongue*—has, as he says, two meanings. In Heaney's first meaning, the writer's tongue takes governance over the world by exercising its transcriptive power and by its conferral of value. In Heaney's second meaning, the political world, perturbed by descriptions of itself not to its liking, attempts—by pressures ranging from censure to execution—to govern the tongue of the poet. And the poet's spirit, if it yields up its inner freedom, can engage in self-censorship and a disabling self-governing. In writing about these matters Heaney explicitly disavows comparison of his own free position with that of poets writing under totalitarian regimes, but he makes it clear that open speech is rarely welcome in any divided community.

Heaney's critics in Ireland have come from many sides. He has been accused of cowardice (being insufficiently political) and of propaganda (being too political), of complicity in violence (by seeing sectarian murder as endemic in the North since the Vikings), and of complicity in the status quo (by refusing to lend his voice to sectarian politics). He has accused himself (in **"Exposure"**) of evasion of responsibility and (in **"Station Island"**) of prettifying assassination with the absolution of verse.

[Poetry] holds attention for a space, functions not as distraction but as pure concentration, a focus where our power to concentrate is concentrated back on ourselves.

—*Seamus Heaney*

What attracts Heaney to poets like Holub and Herbert (and Milosz) is their success in dealing with a relatively intractable subject matter. The poets of Eastern Europe have proved that even the most volatile social concerns can, and must, be brought under the government of the tongue if they are to be represented at all. At the same time, and at a deeper level, Heaney wonders whether, in order for the poet to act politically, it is necessary for him to represent history in poetry. Here his mentor is Mandelstam, who, after five years during which he was unable to compose, discovered for himself that writing about anything at all—provided one writes as a free man uncoerced by political prudence—is itself a rebuke to the totalitarian attempt to govern the writer's tongue, to direct writing toward certain approved subjects. In writing on Mandelstam, Heaney speaks out for the unlimited freedom of lyric to take up private subjects as well as public ones, as long as it does so without respect to social pressure.

Human fearfulness under the threat of social disapproval—not to speak of the threat of punishment or death—assures the conformity of most writers to the will of the totalitarian state. Those who have resisted coöptation have been enrolled in what Heaney calls "a modern martyrology" of art. Though he equally admires, in a moral sense, non-poets who resist immoral state pressure, what he values in the poets who resist is their preservation of "cultural memory" (so that authentic poetry does not cease to exist), their "indicative mood" of bold presentation, and the "fate and scope" of their wide social concern. Contemporary Western lyric poetry, by contrast, can seem confined within private walls and damned to the conditional mood of wish, yearning, and indeterminacy. It

seems afraid to take on the question of the collective social fabric.

The central question, which Heaney does not sufficiently address with respect to collective ideology and art, is whether some artists at all times and all artists at some times can work happily within a civic or ecclesiastical ideological consensus. The numerous Madonnas and Masses of supreme aesthetic quality suggest that "living" ideologies, as long as they are believed in, are not so aesthetically oppressive as dead (totally codified, governmentally imposed) ones. The view of the artist as a living critique of ideological consensus is, of course, an attractive one to us, post-romantics as we are, and can perhaps be applied retrospectively even to some Renaissance artists working within an ideology like Christianity, where Heaney sees only "acceptable themes . . . given variously resourceful treatments." To me it seems that a critique of received forms of religious expression is visible, for instance, in the work of George Herbert, whom Heaney prefers to regard as one who "surrendered himself to a framework of belief and an instituted religion; but in [Herbert's] case, it happened that his personality was structured in such a way that he could dwell in amity with doctrine." Amity and surrender are not the marks of any strenuous art; and Herbert deserves better praise than the "felicity or correctness of a work's execution" which is all that Heaney allows the Renaissance poet working within the Christian consensus. We need a better theory of what it means to an artist to struggle with an ideology from within, as a believer.

In treating the Eastern European poets, Heaney necessarily works from translations. When he turns, in the second part of *The Government of the Tongue,* to modern poets writing in English whom he admires, a palpable change of emphasis, from society to self, appears in his pages. Imaginative arts such as poetry, Heaney concedes, are "practically useless," but he adds, "They verify our singularity, they strike and stake out the ore of self which lies at the base of every individuated life." Here it is the transcription not of the social fabric but of the private self—and a special sort of self, the "individuated life"—that is at stake. Knowingly or not, Heaney in this vocabulary breaks definitively with most of the literary theory that is interested in the social function of literature. Such theory refuses precedence to the "imaginative arts" (as Heaney calls them) of language, and puts writing that exhibits poesis on the same footing as all other "texts." This move, which is a political one, wishes to allocate to all texts equal cultural interest. Of course, this sociological view of writing allows no particular privilege to what Heaney calls "singularity" and to the "individuated life"—those qualities indispensable (but not sufficient) for identifiable literary style.

There have been singular and individuated selves who never wrote a word. But without a singular and individuated moral self there has never been a singular and individuated literary style. The writing self does not have to be virtuous in the ordinary sense of the word; but it does have to be extraordinarily virtuous in its aesthetic moves. It must refuse—against the claims of fatigue, charm, popularity, money, and so on—the *idée reçue,* the imprecise word, the tired rhythm, the replication of past effects, the uninvestigated stanza. It is this heroic virtue in the realm of aesthetic endeavor that courses in great authors exist to teach (as courses in "texts" do not). And Heaney stands by this aesthetic arduousness, which he finds in each of his authors. Human testimony—from the poor, the uneducated, the prudishly conventional, the genteelly euphemistic, the propaganda hacks, the well-meaning sincere—is not uninteresting. It *is* interesting. But it does not convey the morality of the imaginative effort toward aesthetic embodiment. That morality is almost unimaginably exhausting.

In pointing out Lowell's deliberate breaking of his own style not once but twice, Plath's sedulous youthful work on poetic form, and Auden's pursuit of the Anglo-Saxon underpinnings of English, Heaney pays tribute to the sheer toil toward competence, on the one hand, and toward freshness, on the other, that is the indispensable preparatory work for poetry. The fact that Auden and Lowell and Plath all came from a privileged elite is not for Heaney an issue; it is axiomatic for him that privilege, somehow acquired, is necessary to becoming an accomplished artist. He does not confuse the political work of a just society (insuring that talent has access to training) with aesthetic judgment (which can only say whether or not a writer has successfully deployed the moral, imaginative, and linguistic resources needed for the art work in hand). Nor is Heaney diffident about the ranking of aesthetic efforts. He understands what his chosen writers are up to, can see where and how they succeed, and is entirely willing to demonstrate and defend what he sees. Practical criticism consists in just that evidential demonstration, but it is rarely had from one who knows the medium and its potential glories and pitfalls as well as Heaney.

In Heaney's Auden essay we catch a deflected glimpse of his own aims as a writer of prose. There he praises the critical "responses and formulations" of the poet Geoffrey Grigson as the sort that "count for most in the long poetic run, because they are the most intrinsically sensitive to the art of language." Some Auden critics, he remarks, have concentrated on the history of ideas, whether in commenting on Auden's "shifting allegiances to Marx and Freud" or, more recently, in finding Auden's texts metaphysically self-deconstructive. "It may be," Heaney continues, "that Grigson's way of talking about poems is not as strictly analytical as this, but the way it teases out the cultural implications and attachments which inhabit any poem's field of force is a critical activity not to be superseded, because it is so closely allied, as an act of reading, to what happens during the poet's act of writing." The art of Heaney's criticism is never to lose touch with the writing act, the texture of the lines on the page. And his next sentence is one that, revealingly enough, would never be uttered by a historian of ideas or a deconstructive critic: "A new rhythm, after all, is a new life given to the world, a resuscitation not just of the ear but of the springs of being." That sentence leads him into a splendid and energetic glance at the early Auden.

In canonizing an English Anglican, an American Brahmin, and a female expatriate American, Heaney stands aside from the depressing literary politics in which Marxists puff only Marxists, women puff only women, blacks puff only blacks, and so on, with a consequent loss of credibility for the whole enterprise of literary judgment. Of course, the fraternity of artists has its familial bonds, and Heaney has not hesitated to praise, with generational solidarity, admirable work by other Irish artists and other post-colonial writers. But he has reserved his extended and investigative critical writing for major writers, and in them he observes, with an insight impossible to anyone but a poet, their subtlest as well as their broadest powers. Space allows me only one brief example: Heaney's remarks about the way Lowell ends poems. He quotes a sample of last lines, and goes on:

> Closing lines like these would tremble in the centre of the ear like an arrow in a target and set the waves of suggestion rippling. A sense of something utterly completed vied with a sense of something startled into scope and freedom. The reader was permitted the sensation of a whole meaning simultaneously clicking shut and breaking open, a momentary illusion that the fulfilments which were being experienced in the ear spelled out meanings and fulfilments available in the world. So, no matter how much the poem insisted on breakdown or the evacuation of meaning from experience, its fall toward a valueless limbo was broken by the perfectly stretched safety net of poetic form itself.

Heaney's adverse criticism of his three poets—always courteous, but not the less incisive for that—suggests values that he is too sophisticated to prescribe but is nonetheless disappointed not to find in them. He regrets that Auden forsook his original wildness of language: in later Auden "the line is doctrinaire in its domesticity, wanting to comfort like a thread of wool rather than shock like a bare wire." Lowell in the late sonnet trilogy massed his shock troops too oppressively for a human scale: "To confront the whole triptych is to confront a phalanx. I feel driven off the field of my reader's freedom by the massive riveted façade, the armoured tread, the unconceding density of it all." Plath, instead of enlarging herself into myth, reduces powerful ancient myths to the confines of her own personal history: "In 'Lady Lazarus' . . . the cultural resonance of the original story is harnessed to a vehemently self-justifying purpose, so that the supra-personal dimensions of knowledge—to which myth typically gives access—are slighted in favour of the intense personal need of the poet." One may not always agree with Heaney, but one is moved to profitable thought by his metaphorically vivid judgments.

Heaney's volume tosses and turns between "the hedonism and jubilation" of the poetic act and the affront to human misery presented by that hedonism. In the most original moment of this very original book, Heaney finds a way into the space between creative hedonism and human suffering. He quotes the Gospel of John, in which the scribes and Pharisees bringing before Jesus a woman taken in adultery ask whether they should obey the Mosaic law and stone her:

> This they said, tempting him, that they might

have to accuse him. But Jesus stooped down, and with his finger wrote on the ground, as though he heard them not.

So when they continued asking him, he lifted up himself, and said unto them, He that is without sin among you, let him first cast a stone at her.

And again he stooped down, and wrote on the ground.

And they which heard it, being convicted by their own conscience, went out one by one, beginning at the eldest, even unto the last: and Jesus was left alone, and the woman standing in the midst.

When Jesus had lifted up himself, and saw none but the woman, he said unto her, Woman, where are those thine accusers? hath no man condemned thee?

She said, No man, Lord. And Jesus said unto her, Neither do I condemn thee: go, and sin no more.

Heaney finds here an allegory for poetry:

> The drawing of those characters is like poetry, a break with the usual life but not an absconding from it. Poetry, like the writing, is arbitrary and marks time in every possible sense of that phrase. It does not say to the accusing crowd or to the helpless accused, "Now a solution will take place," it does not propose to be instrumental or effective. Instead, in the rift between what is going to happen and whatever we would wish to happen, poetry holds attention for a space, functions not as distraction but as pure concentration, a focus where our power to concentrate is concentrated back on ourselves.

> This is what gives poetry its governing power.

This remarkable exegesis of Jesus' mysterious and uninterpreted writing finds a way to place art where it must be situated in order to be correctly judged—within human action but at least partially disengaged from direct dispute with it. Propaganda and political action enter the dispute confrontationally. Poetry exists within it, marking (as one of the poet's many invoked senses would have it) the epoch, taking its measure. Heaney comments that when Osip and Nadezhda Mandelstam died, "nothing died with them." They still mark their time.

The writing about poetry done by a poet like Heaney is done out of need—the need to find ways to create a work and a life that are as yet only imagined. There is a later, colder writing concerning poets, done by others after their death, in which their moral choices and their relation to the politics of their age take on a historical interest rather than an existential urgency. At that moment, the values of the second half of this volume come into decisive dominance: Did the poet find an individuated language for a morally individuated self? During the poet's lifetime, however, the thousand daily choices of what is said and done in the moral life (actively and broadly conceived) exert a compulsion at least equal to that of language. The two halves of this volume—the first more responsible to

the lived life, the second more responsible to the morality of style—declare that (as for Wallace Stevens) "It was not a choice / Between, but of." Heaney's recent powerful volumes of verse, *Station Island* and *The Haw Lantern,* when they are read in the light of these essays, can be seen to exhibit in terse and symbolic form the poetic strategies Heaney has been finding to mark the time of his time. (pp. 102-07)

> *Helen Vendler, "A Wounded Man Falling towards Me," in* The New Yorker, *Vol. LXV, No. 4, March 13, 1989, pp. 102-07.*

John Bayley   (essay date Spring 1989)

[*Bayley is an Indian-born English poet, novelist, and critic who is noted for his insightful and original analyses of such writers as Leo Tolstoy, Alexander Pushkin, and George Eliot. In the following essay in which he places Heaney's works among Modernist poets, Bayley discusses Heaney's approach to poetry, emphasizing the detached quality of his verse and his awareness of the distinction between the emotional and intellectual aspects of poetry.*]

Maurice Blanchot, the most pretentious if also at times the most suggestive of poet-type critics, has observed that *la negation est liée au langage.* A word is the memorial to what it signifies. Death is implicit in the distinction between sign and self. Clever, eh? Well, striking at least. But where the morale of contemporary poetry is concerned it may be rather more than that. Everyone has remarked on the apparent inability of poetry to assert its speech with authority over the great horrors of our age. An awareness among poets similar to Blanchot's, however much less conscious and formulated, may be the reason? Defeatism about language is in the air, and of all users of the language poets are most sensitive to it. They are also sensitive to critics, the only audience they can rely on. And many critics—George Steiner for one—have told them that their art is no longer capable of responding to what is happening around them in life.

All they can pronounce is an elegy, in words which cannot convey the true matter of what they signify, but only raise a consciously inadequate memorial to it. Persons of intelligence and discernment may also feel thoroughly inhibited today about putting headstones and epitaphs in churches and churchyards; and this signifies the same defeatism that poets feel? Restraint and good taste are the only hope: their very inadequacy argues the only way we have now of being sincere. Just a name and a date and the right sort of stone. There is a striking parallel here with the inhibitions in a poet's words. We do not live any more with and among the dead, as if they were still alive, because we are aware that what we say about them only recognises extinction by drawing attention to our own survival.

Seamus Heaney is a poet whose consciousness of these things has become his chief strength as a poet. His poetry is continually aware that it does not live in its own area of discourse, but only visits it. His poetry is a pilgrimage to its own subject, like the journey of the pilgrims in **"Station Island"**. Afterwards it returns to real life for breakfast. And yet Heaney has converted what might in this item sound like weakness and inadequacy into a source—a source for poetry—of honesty and strength. The essential flavour of his poetry is one of diffidence, a quality as distant as possible from the overbearing and energetic stance of Yeats, and perhaps deliberately so. Yeats's whole ego was devoted to living in his poetry: so much so that when he tells us "Once out of nature I shall never take / My bodily form from any natural thing / But such a form as Grecian goldsmiths make" . . . he persuades us, at any rate momentarily, that this is a genuine desire and ambition, and that he has every expectation of finding it fulfilled. To live in his verse was for Yeats an act of the will, but for many poets of our time and during the last century—one could cite such otherwise contrasting figures as Emily Dickinson and A. E. Housman, Philip Larkin and Paul Celan—it seems the most natural thing in the world.

Natural how? and in what ways that Heaney, for example, is not? There is always in Heaney's poetry, I think, as, in its very different way, in Geoffrey Hill's, a note of apology. Both poets seem to have taken sober and rational thought about what might be said against them and their poetry; and they seem to have taken it, in a sense, before the poetry itself has been written. Such an effect, in the context of their own special skill and personality, is oddly impressive. The meeting with the ghosts of earlier poets and writers in **"Station Island",** is an echo of Dante, amongst other echoes, including those from "Little Gidding"; but what makes it especially typical of Heaney is the note of withdrawal, the true humility which sets aside the man writing from the poetry he writes. The recognition of death and separation is implicit in the distinction between the words of the poetry and the poet himself. Analogously the modern stone in the churchyard, or the new tablet on the church wall, do not identify with their subject but seem to say: this is the proper and decent thing to do, though death is not a subject about which anything now can be said. Heaney's poetry has strange delicacy, as well as humility, in suggesting that poetry nowadays has to be written about things—like patriotism, affection, belief itself—about which there is in fact no longer anything to say.

Such a tone is most literally and truthfully elegiac in its practical demonstration that, in Blanchot's words, negation is tied in with language. An age which feels this, and a poet of the age who expresses it, however unconsciously, have absorbed the first lesson of Modernism, which was: think before you write; study before you do so. Since you cannot be spontaneous, do not attempt to imitate or to cultivate spontaneity. Do not live, or affect to live, in "poetry", but in the house of learning, from which the good poetry of this age must proceed. Write notes on it, or in it; and think with T. S. Eliot rather than feeling with Harold Monro.

The message has been learnt to the third or fourth generation: a Geoffrey Hill or a Seamus Heaney have come to take it for granted. Not so Philip Larkin, who was in silent, or sometimes not so silent, reaction against the Modernist assumption. He lived over the shop, lived in the poems that came to him, in the same sense that A. E. Housman had done. Death was a holy terror to him, not

a subject for historic reverie in verse, and there being "nothing to say" is itself a matter of the starkest import. The fact of death that accompanies us through life, and makes life "slow dying", means nothing—or everything.

> And saying so to some
> Means nothing, to others it leaves
> Nothing to be said.

The cousin's ghost, who speaks with such care and precision to Heaney in **"Station Island",** may forfeit in so doing this kind of immediacy, but through him the poetry gains in denseness and delicacy of reference. Heaney's individuality is of a strangely passive sort, as if he were urged in different directions by external forces which the poetry keeps in equilibrium by a wise passiveness, rather than by an adroit or wary control. This gives the poetry its special quality, but the poet pays a price for his neutrality in seeming at the side of what he writes. Like most poets in the Modernist tradition his sense, and learning, and skill detach him from the kind of central emotional obsession that wells up in the verse of a Larkin or Housman. Hence in Heaney the tone of gentleness, of unassertiveness, and of something wistful too, as of a poetry apologising for its own civilised qualities.

None of that savagery which is cultivated by Yeats or by Sylvia Plath, who will themselves into the centre of their poetry as a personal obsession. Other non-Modernist poets—Housman and Larkin again, or Dickinson, or Marianne Moore—seem to live in it without effort, as their native environment. In a brilliant but bewildering piece in *Essays in Criticism* (January 1987), from which I have borrowed some of my examples, John Kerrigan shows a puzzling lack of awareness of the surely basic difference between poets like the Modernists, who live outside their sophisticated, referential, and highly group-conscious verse, and those who live inside it with the confidence born of total solitariness. There are giant figures who can do both, as Eliot does in *The Waste Land,* a poem related as much to Dante and to Pound on the one hand as to Housman or Burns on the other; but Heaney, like Hill, is surely a poet whose readability comes from the precision with which both chart their own difficulties in approaching from outside the poetic area.

Once there, there is, in a curious way, nothing to be said: the effect of the poetry lies in the mode of approach and the mode of uncertainty. Kerrigan's essay on "Knowing the Dead" . . . assumes concord and indivisibility between such an extraordinary poem as Celan's *Engführung—Lies nicht mehr—schau! Schau nicht mehr—geh!*—with its absolute existence in the primitive terror brought by the vertiginous unmeaning of the Holocaust, and the thoughtful elegies of poets who live well outside such areas of recall and of memory. It is the basic difference, if you like, between Romanticism—the spontaneous overflowing of powerful feelings—and the much wider, more perennial notion of poetry as the *Sprachgefühl* of civilisation, the repository of intelligence, perception, personality, in its highest linguistic form. The distinction was made by Housman when he claimed that poetry was different from the things the poet was saying, the things *in* poetry. The difference is clear and obvious in Wordsworth, and at the other end of the scale it is equally obvious in such a poet as John Betjeman: whose "total" and atavistic voice, overflowing about Leamington Spa or Miss Joan Hunter-Dunn, is quite different from his expository, pseudo-Augustan, pseudo-Victorian tones. Heaney is one of the very few poets—indeed perhaps the only poet writing in English today—whose poetry seems able *in itself* to take cognizance of the distinction, and to give such an awareness continuous and unique expression. And this is a very remarkable achievement. (pp. 32-6)

John Bayley, "Living in and Living Out: The Poet's Location for the Poetry," in *Agenda,* Vol. 27, No. 1, Spring, 1989, pp. 32-6.

William Bedford   (review date Winter 1991)

[*In the following review of* Seeing Things, *Bedford asserts that the collection explores visionary and inexplicable aspects of life, and he praises the highly imaginative qualities of the poems but criticizes their elusiveness.*]

Seeing Things begins with Aeneas's request for 'one face-to-face meeting with my dear father' and a poem in which [Philip] Larkin surprises Heaney by quoting Dante. The surprise is obviously rhetorical—the visionary in Larkin is the theme of Heaney's essay **"The Main of Light"**—and the ghost of the father has haunted Heaney's work ever since *Death of a Naturalist.* What is avowedly new here—'Me waiting until I was nearly fifty / To credit marvels'—is the *challenge* of the visionary: the way it provides the dramatic structure of the first half of the collection, and the actual material, the technique in a sense, of the second half. *Seeing Things* is a brilliantly organised collection, a conversation between two modes of being, and the very irony of the title announces the post-modernist delight of the argument, the deeper anguish of the tension for the modern mind.

In the first half of the book, the most familiar device is for the visionary to emerge through the ordinary. In **"Markings,"** a game of football settles into the 'fleetness, furtherance, untiredness' of time that 'is extra, unforeseen and free.' Again, in **"Three Drawings,"** 'booting a leather football' raises the question 'Was it you / or the ball that kept going / beyond you, amazingly / higher and higher / and ruefully free?' **"Wheels within Wheels"** has the young Heaney spinning the wheels of his bicycle through water until the 'space between the hub and rim / Hummed with transparency.' These poems all hint at glimpses of the visionary, the child-like moments of displacement, which *because* they are childish contain their own saving distance, something gentler than irony. **"Man and Boy,"** seeing Heaney's own father as a boy, has a deeper resonance, a yearning for the past which could be purely human:

Blessed be down-to-earth! Blessed be highs!
Blessed be the detachment of dumb love
In that broad-backed, low-set man
Who feared debt all his life, but now and then
Could make a splash like the salmon he said was
'As big as a wee pork pig by the sound of it.'

a reality which leads to the visionary possibilities of:

He has mown himself to the centre of the field
And stands in a final perfect ring
Of sunlit stubble.

and the lovely recreating memory of:

My father is a barefoot boy with news,
Running at eye-level with weeds and stooks
On the afternoon of his own father's death.

The tension of all of this lies precisely in the rootedness of the experience, the humour, the sense of loss which deepens experience into something beyond the ordinary. I don't know if that is what the visionary is, but for the post-modernist mind, that is how it seems to operate within these poems. In the title poem, **"Seeing Things,"** we have 'Inishbofin on a Sunday morning / Sunlight, turfs-moke, seagulls, boatslip, diesel,' an insistence upon the concrete which guarantees the experience as the boat guarantees the voyagers—'That quick response and buoyancy and swim'—and yet keeps us 'in agony,' the suspense of '*Claritas,*' as:

All afternoon, heat wavered on the steps
And the air we stood up to our eyes in wavered
Like the zig-zag hieroglyph for life itself.

a clarity which leads into the third section of the poem where the poet's 'undrowned father' is seen in a moment of displacement, 'his ghosthood immanent':

That afternoon
I saw him face to face, he came to me
With his damp footprints out of the river,
And there was nothing between us there
That might not still be happily ever after.

This could be the 'making strange,' the *ostranenie,* of art, or of suffering or of the visionary moment: the glimpses of the real we are sometimes given through the ordinary, the moments when time stills and our senses come 'tumbling off the world.' Whatever the meaning, the experience is wonderfully given in these poems, and given even with a gleeful sense of fun, a humour that might be delighting in the self-parody of '*glar* and *glit* and floods at *dailigone,*' a stateliness that is self-mocking and has always been the watchful consciousness in Heaney's work. There are risks of course: this is not the rooted poetry I personally loved in *Field Work,* and the **"Glanmore Revisited"** sonnets suffer from a certain self-consciousness about all this looking back which was not there in the original, wonderful marriage-poems. But Heaney knows all this. In **"Fosterling,"** he sets the terms of the ambition himself: the poetry 'Sluggish in the doldrums of what happens,' which might be exactly the criticism made of his early work; the challenge of the marvels for which the poet has waited so long:

Like the tree-clock of tin cans
The tinkers made. So long for air to brighten,
Time to be dazzled and the heart to lighten.

We need not accept the judgment to grasp what is being hazarded in the second half of the volume.

The second half of *Seeing Things,* titled **"Squarings",** consists of forty-eight twelve-line poems arranged in four sections: **"Lightenings"**, **"Settings"**, **"Crossings"**, and

"Squarings". In the third poem of the first section we have a definition of squarings:

> Squarings? In the game of marbles, squarings
> Were all those anglings, aimings, feints and
>   squints
> You were allowed before you'd shoot

and in poem twelve of the first section, a definition of lightenings as a 'phenomenal instant when the spirit flares / With pure exhilaration before death'. **'Settings'** are perhaps more obviously embodied in the poems themselves:

> Hazel stealth. A trickle in the culvert.
> Athletic sealight on the doorstep slab,
> On the sea itself, on silent roofs and gables.

as are **'Crossings,'** where an encounter with a fox ends with the poet talking about rebirth and recognising that to achieve this he has to 'cross back through that startled iris." The definitions are of course reductive. In the actual texture of the sequence, the practice of the poems, everything comes together, so that the opening poem might be said to operate on all four levels simultaneously:

> Shifting brilliancies. Then winter light
> In a doorway, and on the stone doorstep
> A beggar shivering in silhouette.
>
> So the particular judgement might be set:
> Bare wallstead and a cold hearth rained into—
> Bright puddle where the soul-free cloud-life
>   roams.

The difficulties are obvious. They are the difficulties hinted at in the thirty-seventh poem, where Heaney has the sage Han Shan telling us that 'Cold Mountain is a place that can also mean / A state of mind.' They are difficulties which have Heaney himself admitting that 'Talking about it isn't good enough.' And the whole point, of course, is that 'talking about it' is precisely beside the point. You can show the experience, but not much else. This leaves the reader with the job of deciding what has been *done*. We are being asked to address something which can't be explained.

I think Heaney has hazarded his own definition elsewhere. In his Inaugural Lecture as Professor of Poetry at Oxford, **"The Redress of Poetry,"** he has some fascinating things to say about George Herbert, and this particular passage struck my attention when I was reading *Seeing Things:*

> I want to profess the surprise of poetry as well
> as its reliability, its given, unforeseeable thereness, the way it enters our field of visions and animates our physical and intelligent being in
> much the same way as those bird-shapes painted
> on the transparent surfaces of glass walls or glass
> doors and windows must suddenly cross the line
> of the real bird's flight. In a flash those shapes
> register and transmit their unmistakeable presence so the birds then veer off instinctively and
> thereby avoid collision with the glass.

That he should be drawn to talk about Herbert, and not Vaughan or the Eliot of *Four Quartets,* is of course a function of the particular lecture, but the comparison might be helpful to our understanding of this second half of *Seeing Things.* I would always have thought Herbert a poet

of obvious interest to Heaney, and in that sense, these new poems were a surprise when I first saw some of them published in *Agenda.* Having read the whole sequence, I can't feel that they are successful, although I don't fully know what 'success' would mean in this context. They aren't quite mystical poems in the sense Vaughan achieved, nor do they have the tension I personally find in *Four Quartets.* That poem always suggests to me that Eliot knew he hadn't achieved the mystical union he sought, and that the tension between belief and experience is what makes *Four Quartets* a great poem. The poems in **"Squarings"** are not mystical or religious in either of these senses: here, we have the mind which won't let go, the conscious intellect organising the visionary experience—or perhaps even the *occasions* for the visionary experience, if one may trespass perhaps where the reader ought not to go. At the very least, they give the impression of being occasions.

I cannot believe in these poems as epiphanies, because they are being analysed in the process of being written. The saving grace of humour, which works so well in the first half of the collection, here becomes intrusive, so that the voice which cries 'What'll you have?' doesn't ease the tension, it merely causes embarrassment, the same kind of embarrassment one feels in the presence of Joyce's ghost in *Station Island.* There are wonderful images throughout, 'Shifting brilliances' which are perhaps what the sequence is after, but the meaning somehow evades me, and the elusiveness makes me long for the emotional power of the earlier poems.

Seeing Things seems a transitional book to me, full of marvellous things, and yet straining after an illumination I can't find *felt* in the poems. It may be that I haven't the sensibility for what Heaney is *after*—or senses he is missing—but he seems an inescapably post-Christian poet to me, yearning for a dimension and a seriousness postmodernist playfulness somehow doesn't allow. He seemed to be reaching for that seriousness in the political allegory of *Station Island* and *The Haw Lantern* and the essays of *The Government of the Tongue,* but this collection is a lunge in another direction. I find the poems about his father intensely moving and consoling in the way great poetry has always been consoling—to do with order and recognition—but beyond that, the vision won't come, or it isn't felt: at least, a vision which is anything more than the illumination that is always offered by real poetry, that making strange which itself makes us tumble 'off the world.' That is more than enough for me, though the power of Heaney's imagination is such that he leaves one feeling convinced one has missed the point. (pp. 57-62)

William Bedford, "Two Irish Poets," in Agenda, *Vol. 29, No. 4, Winter, 1991, pp. 57-62.*

Michael Hofmann   (review date 15 August 1991)

[*In the following review, Hofmann praises Heaney's* Seeing Things *for its straightforward style and its focus on autobiographical themes, asserting that the collection represents Heaney's return to Irish influences and culture.*]

Seeing Things, Seamus Heaney's ninth volume of new

poems, is aimed squarely at transcendence. The title has a humble and practical William Carlos Williams ring to it, but that is misleading. It is better understood as having been distilled from 'I must be seeing things', said seriously, and with a fair amount of stress on the 'I must'.

The greatest difficulty for the poet is how to go on being one. Randall Jarrell set it out like this at the end of his essay on Stevens:

> A man who is a good poet at 40 *may* turn out to be a good poet at 60; but he is more likely to have stopped writing poems, to be doing exercises in his own manner, or to have reverted to whatever commonplaces were popular when he was young. A good poet is someone who manages, in a lifetime of standing out in thunderstorms, to be struck by lightning five or six times; a dozen or two dozen times and he is great.

This is poetry as catastrophe, as Minnesotan roulette, Heaney in his *The Government of the Tongue* quotes the Polish poet Anna Swir to similar but subtly different effect; according to her, the poet is 'an antenna capturing the voices of the world'. Compared to the chilling folly of Jarrell, this is both pat and heroic. It is more statuesque, less adventitious, less calamitous. It allows less room both for the will and for good luck: what it expresses is not so much the poet's real agony and uncertainty as his function in hindsight—a poet struck by lightning will have become an antenna of sorts.

Neither quotation bothers to work out the effect on the poet of popularity and fame, but it seems easy enough: such a poet might not be inclined (in Jarrell) to go out in the wet so often, or (Swir) he might stop retuning his receiver, and stick to a familiar frequency. In the introduction to his 1988 selection of *The Essential Wordsworth*, Heaney seems uncomfortable, even compromised, as he discusses the starchy, establishment figure of the older Wordsworth, 'in his large, not uncomplacent house', seemingly 'more an institution than an individual', 'an impression not inconsistent with the sonorous expatiations of his later poetry nor with the roll call of his offices and associations—friend of the aristocracy, Distributor of Stamps for Westmoreland, Poet Laureate'. In that padded, double-breasted construction, the double negative, Heaney would seek to offer criticism and mitigation at the same time, but in so doing he betrays his own anxiety.

I don't know whether Glanmore, the house where Heaney wrote much of *Field Work* (1979), is large and complacent or not (although I doubt it), but readers of *Seeing Things* learn that he has now returned to it as its owner-occupier, a condition which, with some more awkward doublespeak, he celebrates in the seven sonnets of **"Glanmore Revisited"**—in such lines as 'only pure words and deeds secure the house.' Of course, Heaney has also become the master of a 'roll call of offices and associations' of Wordsworthian distinction and dimensions, so it seems tempting to try on the 'institution' and the 'sonorous expatiations' for size as well. In the event, I don't think they fit. The new book is many things, among them Heaney's most plainspoken and autobiographical work to date. It is a departure in style, tone and purpose. So nix institution and expatiations.

As much as any poet alive, Heaney has understood the need to move on, to remake himself from book to book. (In that same essay of his Jarrell quotes Cocteau's advice to poets: learn what you can do, and then don't do it.) Blake Morrison has drawn attention to the way Heaney likes to use the last poem of one book to suggest the nature of its successor, a pattern skilfully maintained over many books, beguiling his readers with a glimpse of the future. At the same time, though, in myself at any rate, each new Heaney book since *Field Work* has provoked an uncertain response. Either it was the poems that were slow to take, or I was slow to take to them—even such (now) obvious favourites as **'The Underground'**, **'The Railway Children'** and **'Alphabets'**. In retrospect, this must have been because Heaney was always doing something slightly different—here was a popular poet who was (mercifully) less conservative than his readers.

Each of Heaney's books since *Field Work,* at all events, has had a different concern and a different presiding genius. *Station Island* (1984) had its Sweeney poems and its Dantesque sequence of colloquies with ghosts (suggested by **'Ugolino'** at the end of *Field Work*). *The Haw Lantern* (1987) had its allegories and parables, drily enthused by Eastern European poetry somehow filtered through Harvard and America. *Seeing Things* is Heaney's most 'Irish' book since *North.* While seeming to hark back to the whole of his career and to resume it—the seaboard and rustic settings and subjects, the translations from Dante and Virgil that frame it, the elegies for dead friends, the poems about driving and fishing (it is also Heaney's most 'sporty' book)—it takes its note from the penultimate poem in *The Haw Lantern,* **'The Disappearing Island'**, and its last line: 'All I believe that happened there was vision.'

The 'unsayable light' of an earlier poem (one of the original **'Glanmore Sonnets'**) is here said. 'The rough, porous / language of touch' that made Heaney famous is forsaken for what one might call the smooth slippery language of sight, the quickest and furthest, most abstract and disembodied, and most trusted and fallible of the senses. That sense of 'words entering almost the sense of touch', the deep historical familiarity for which Heaney strove earlier, has yielded to a kind of seeing that is halfdreaming. He takes up the cudgels against himself. He speaks quippingly of 'the thwarted sense of touch', and in **'Fosterling'** writes:

> I can't remember never having known
> The immanent hydraulics of a land
> Of *glar* and *glit* and floods at *dailigone.*
> My silting hope. My lowlands of the mind.

The equivalent in painting of the 48 12-line poems called **'Squarings'** that make up the second part of the book would surely be abstracts called Impressions, Improvisations or Compositions, numbered like the poems.

The Haw Lantern was pioneering in that it had at its heart a single physical or geometrical image or scheme, the hollow round or sphere which appears in a variety of guises:

as the haws of the title; the 'globe in the window' of another possible title; the letter O 'like a magnified and buoyant ovum' in the touching first poem **'Alphabets'**, about reading and literacy and literature and read to the students of Harvard. There is the O of **'Hailstones'**:

> I made a small herd ball
> of burning water running from my hand . . .

Then there are the many islands in the book, and there's the sequence called **'Clearances'** to the memory of his mother:

> I thought of walking round and round a space
> Utterly empty, utterly a source
> Where the decked chestnut had lost its place
> In our front hedge above the wallflowers.
> The white chips jumped and jumped and skited
> high.
> I heard the hatchet's differentiated
> Accurate cut, the crack, the sigh
> And collapse of what luxuriated
> Through the shocked tips and wreckage of it all.
> Deep planted and long gone, my coeval
> Chestnut from a jam jar in a hole,
> Its heft and hush become a bright nowhere,
> A soul ramifying and forever
> Silent, beyond silence, listened for.

The O is both something and nothing, origin and omega, mother and rooted sense of self. Heaney consigns himself to living with its equivocations, in the fullness of absence. The haw is not a lantern, but he will live by its light, 'its pecked-at ripeness that scans you, then moves on'. The round O's in the book evoke maternity, self-sufficiency and the integrity of conscience: the one image brings to coherence Heaney's personal loss in **'Clearances'** and the several meditations on the practice of his art.

Seeing Things has a similar geometrical *leitmotiv* or schema, and that is the straight line, or pattern of straight lines, dazzling as op art, and producing the sensation of depth. The lines are not adduced from such obvious sources as waves, layers of rock or clouds at sunset; they are rooted in experience and have more to do with a way of seeing, or even a way of being.

Here is the transcendence of *Seeing Things,* the simple and miraculous escalation from a sixth sense to a seventh heaven, the lovely delusive optics of sawing and cycling and barred gates. The miraculous is produced by patience, by attentiveness, by repetition and work; there is no secret hinge the world swings on the way there is in Edwin Muir, a poet whose name has come up recently in Heaney's essays. The lines—for once not ploughlines, not lines of verse—have their meaning, just as the sphere or circle of *The Haw Lantern* did. The meaning is not as intricate, or as deeply argued, as it was there, but here again it has to do with mortality, and with the generations of men. In 1986, Heaney's father died, leaving the poet in the front line of the senior generation. The straight lines in *Seeing Things,* the visionary buzz, seem to me to be connected to Heaney's sense of the passing generations. The mower, the gate, the spinning-wheel, all have associations with death, as does the phenomenon of 'lightening', defined as 'A phenomenal instant when the spirit flares / With pure exhila-

ration before death'. The book begins and ends with the descents to the underworld undertaken by Aeneas and Dante. At the same time, though, the dazzling, silvery lines are an epiphany, a standing vibration, and, for all their confusion, a stay against confusion and mortality. They are a paradox, the contemplation of something physical and at hand, giving rise to a long view of the human struggle, a metaphysics of light:

> Heaviness of being. And poetry
> Sluggish in the doldrums of what happens.
> Me waiting until I was nearly fifty
> To credit marvels. Like the tree clock of tin cans
> The tinkers made. So long for air to brighten,
> Time to be dazzled and the heart to lighten.

The straight line, the dazzle of abstract and op art, are the symbol and message—it seems an appropriate word—of the book, while its human content is drawn immediately from Heaney's life. Experiences from childhood, his courtship and wedding, the death of his father and memories of him, the birth of his children, the painting of his portrait (the one by Edward Maguire that appears on the back of *North*), the acquisition of a bed, a house, the lapidary events of a life—and not a public life, or even necessarily a writing life: all are recounted and alchemised, worked into dazzle, overbrimming, 'sheer pirouette', 'a dream of thaw', the marvellous, 'like some fabulous highcatcher / coming down without the ball'.

In the second section of the book, Heaney displays his new form, the 12-line poems made up of four tercets and known as **'Squarings'**. The 48 poems fall into four sections of 12, each one of 12 lines: squarings. He has perhaps found a compendious form for the work of his fifties, his version of Lowell's unrhymed sonnets and Berryman's *Dream Songs*. The poems are impressive for their freedom, their firmness of purpose, and their skilful arrangement—Berryman's and Lowell's forms retained, by contrast, the randomness of daily writing.

Naturally, not all of them are as good as the best ones—I would nominate v, xvii, xviii, xxviii, xxxiii and xlv—but there is nothing fuzzy about any of them, even the most mysterious. Their principle is the same transcendence as in the book as a whole: they are like homing devices, or Geiger counters, infallibly orientated towards the abiding surplus energy of the moments they describe. The aim is not to provide an adequate (and static) verbal icon, but to reflect in words some continuing effect, a vibration, a recurring figure, and this is how they end: 'Above the resonating amphorae', 'In a boat the ground still falls and falls from under', 'Another phrase dilating in new light', 'Sensitive to the millionth of a flicker', and lastly: 'That day I'll be in step with what escaped me.' These are more aftershocks than tied ribbons; they speak of the poems having located the source of the indestructible energy Heaney was after. Here, in full, is xxvii:

> The ice was like a bottle. We lined up
> Eager to re-enter the long slide
> We were bringing to perfection, time after time
> Running and readying and letting go
> Into a sheerness that was its own reward:
> A farewell to surefootedness, a pitch

Beyond our usual hold upon ourselves.
And what went on kept going, from grip to give,
The narrow milky way in the black ice,

The race up, the free passage and return—
It followed on itself like a ring of light
We knew we'd come through and kept sailing
                                        towards.

Here is the iterative motion, the abandon, the astrophysical in the playful, that characterises these poems. The adjacency of being and non-being. CERN in Geneva ought to like them.

Stylistically, *Seeing Things* is plain as plain, sometimes 'awful plain' (Elizabeth Bishop, 'The Moose'). The gutturals of early Heaney are long gone, and now also the suave Latinity—or Latin suavity—of what one can now call his mid-period. The poems have the most pedestrian beginnings, often stumbling over themselves, with humdrum idioms, and words repeated in the first lines, and rarely anything like a spark. An index of first lines would look dismaying. Occasional shafts of cleverness, against such a background, are almost wounding to the reader: 'Like Gaul, the biretta was divided / Into three parts' might look well on some poets, but one's jaw drops on seeing it here. There are still the puns—more and more like tics—which now seem characteristic of Heaney, but which he may have got from Muldoon or Lowell. They are puns without the spice of puns, where the second meaning is only an amplification, an organ-stop, of the first, like 'the free passage' in the lines I've just quoted. Because of its preoccupation with dazzlement and with energy, language in *Seeing Things* tends to be straightforward, unobstructive, building step by step towards its illuminations, without much in the way of decoration or distraction. One-word sentences and sentences without verbs abound, line-breaks can be so-so or worse, and, in going for clarity rather than elegance, he has even permitted himself several of those notably ugly adjective-preposition compounds that our parents and guardians always warned us against: 'un-get-roundable weight', 'stony up-againstness', 'seeable-down-into water'. This wilful crudity and quiddity is evident in **'Field of Vision'**:

She was steadfast as the big window itself.
Her brow was clear as the chrome bits of
                                        the chair.
She never lamented once and she never
Carried a spare ounce of emotional weight.

In anyone but Heaney, and anywhere but here, this would be brutally demeaning, the person (twice) in terms of the thing, and then the vicious locution of the last line. I think it is the only passage in the book where pursuit of its dazzling philosophy has caused Heaney to be ruthless. As composed and constructed as his books always are—and as other people's hardly ever are—and with a surprisingly thoroughgoing devotion to the insubstantial for a book with that title, *Seeing Things* has taken Heaney to the edge of a new freedom, and to a set of poetic positions that are the very opposite of those with which he started out a generation ago. (pp. 14-15)

Michael Hofmann, "Dazzling Philosophy," in

London Review of Books, *Vol. 13, No. 15, August 15, 1991, pp. 14-15.*

Rand Brandes   (review date Fall 1991)

[*In the following review, Brandes discusses the scope of Heaney's* Selected Poems 1966-1987, *commenting favorably on revised versions of poems contained in that volume. He then considers Heaney's collection* Seeing Things, *emphasizing its theme of loss and commending its fresh perspective on ordinary truths.*]

One can imagine Seamus Heaney zipping through the stratosphere at Mach-2 somewhere over the Atlantic in his space-age scriptorium. Fingertips on the keyboard, searching the word-hoard, he gazes out of the Concorde's window when he thinks he sees something drifting on the vast blue, a boat. After a series of loose associations—the ship of death, Aeneas, the ferryman, water, weight, buoyancy, crossings, loughs, the sea—he enters:

All the time
As we went sailing evenly across
The deep, still, seeable-down-into water,
It was as if I looked from another boat
Sailing through air, far up. . . .

Momentarily disoriented, he wonders how far it is from here to the Broagh Road, Mossbawn, his father's house and the threshold of the past, to the "ground of [his] being" and the marble games, bicycles, and sledding of his youth. Taking a deep breath and scanning the screen, he continues in another file:

Out of that earth house I inherited
A stack of singular, cold memory-weights
To load me, hand and foot, in the scale of things.

Then, eyes closed, he types:

The places I go back to have not failed
But will not last.

and

Running water never disappointed.
Crossing water always furthered something.
Stepping stones were stations of the soul.

He says to himself: "It steadies me to tell these things," as the jet touches down and he stuffs the laptop into his eel-skin briefcase—the text of *Seeing Things* inscribed on the hard drive.

Seamus Heaney may in fact be "Seeing Things" from the dizzying heights of literary stardom. Launched into bardic space, Heaney's *Selected Poems 1966-1987* records his lift-off in *Death of a Naturalist* and steady ascent through *The Haw Lantern,* while his new collection of poems (and one of his best), *Seeing Things,* confirms that his rockets are still firing and that he will stay in orbit. Still, no one feels more uncomfortable about Heaney's astronavigating than Heaney himself, which may account for the strange sense of melancholy and exhaustion one feels underlying *Seeing Things.*

Despite his stellar life, it is amazing how little of the space age and contemporary commercial reality, or Harvard and Oxford, or his globe-trotting and diplomatic hobnob-bing is reflected in Heaney's work. *Selected Poems* and *Seeing Things* reflect Heaney's inclination to gaze through and beyond the post-industrial, global village to his rural childhood in Derry. Of course, Heaney has often tackled the Troubles and the nightmares of Irish history, but he has more emphatically argued for the self-determination of the imagination and the responsibility of the lyric to its original impulses and influences—which for Heaney are private, (trans)historical and neo-pastoral. Heaney's poetry stays close to home and to traditional values; his poems often feel the weight and support of the rectifying lesson. In *Seeing Things* his deceased father's house, metaphorically, embodies the values themselves which have shaped Heaney's life and work:

> A paradigm of rigour and correction,
> Rebuke to fanciness and shrine to limit.

Heaney's *Selected Poems* is a monument to discipline, a discipline which is refined and re-imagined in the brilliant gaze of *Seeing Things.*

What does one say about a Selected poems, even Heaney's? Like a "Greatest Hits" CD, *Selected Poems* to a certain extent simply confirms the critics' choices. In *Selected Poems* one encounters the canonical Heaney, the culturally conservative and technically proficient Heaney, the meta-poetic Heaney as archeologist or pilgrim. Rightfully, therefore, *Selected Poems* ignores many of the earlier, critically overburdened poems and provides a generous sampling of the post–*Fieldwork* material—material that has not yet been completely worked over or trivialized. In addition, the collection profits from the inclusion of both a selection of prose poems from Heaney's *Stations* (1975), which were not published in the U.S., and the entire, slightly yet significantly revised **"Station Island"** sequence.

The most significant revisions in **"Station Island"** occur towards the end of the sequence in Sections X and XII. In Section X Heaney simply tightens the poem by eliminating one stanza and modifying the last three stanzas. These changes make the poem less narrative and more dramatic, which intensifies the poem's concluding epiphany and gives it the lyrical punch of the other poems. Section XII is the sequence's closing poem in which the poet/pilgrim encounters the ghost of Joyce. When first published, this section raised the eyebrows of some critics who felt that Heaney was anointing himself by calling for comparisons with Joyce. In the *Selected* version Heaney attempts to place more distance between himself and Joyce by changing "let others wear the sackcloth and the ashes" to "[you are] so ready for the sackcloth and the ashes." This change does less to implicate others by making the condemnation more self-referential. Heaney also rejects the heavy-handed command to the poet/pilgrim to "get back in harness." In addition and most importantly, Heaney drops the stanzas which allude to Stephen Dedalus' diary entries on April 13, Heaney's birthday:

> there is a moment in Stephen's diary
> for April the thirteenth, a revelation
>
> set among my stars—

In these revisions Heaney retains Joyce as a mentor and spokesperson for aesthetic freedom, but he erases the metaphoric paternal line from Joyce. Heaney has felt the heat produced by other poems, such as **"Punishment,"** and has not revised them. So the motives behind the revisions in Section XII are more complicated than simple critical sensitivity. Ultimately, the revisions produce stronger poems, which is justification enough for their inclusions.

The addition of seven of the original 21 prose poems from *Stations* to *Selected Poems* gives an edge to the book and provides a representative selection of the collection and a look at the less traditional, more experimental Heaney. Though published in 1975 and placed in *Selected Poems* between *Wintering Out* (1972) and *North* (1975), *Stations* was actually begun in California in 1970-71 and only completed in the "hedge-school" of Glanmore in 1975. Heaney says that he did not finish them immediately, because upon his return to Belfast he found his signals jammed by the Troubles, and also because Geoffrey Hill's collection of prose poems, *Mercian Hymns* (1971), anticipated if not out-maneuvered his tentative explorations of a genre with which he felt uncomfortable. Covering some of the same thematic ground of the opening paragraphs of **"Mossbawn"** from *Preoccupations,* the *Stations* prose poems attempt to approach Wordsworth's "spots of time," according to Heaney. One of the most interesting pieces is **"Cloistered,"** in which the poet recalls his boardingschool days where he was like the "assiduous illuminator himself," his "hands cold as a scribe's in winter." The poem's master metaphor of the scribe anticipates Heaney's constant allusions to writing *as* writing, to writing as inscription, and to the word *as* word, as in **"Viking Dublin: Trial Piece,"** *Sweeney Astray,* **"Sweeney Redivivus,"** and **"Alphabets."** There is one unacknowledged change in **"Cloistered"** which makes the ending less melodramatic. Heaney deletes the original final sentence of **"Cloistered"**: "I was champion of the examination halls, scalding with lust inside my daunting visor." We find a much more subdued poet in the final prose poem from the *Stations* selection and from the original volume, **"Incertus"**:

> I went disguised in it, pronouncing it with a soft
>   church
> Latin c, tagging it under my efforts like a damp
>   fuse.
> Uncertain. . . .

It is difficult to imagine an "uncertain" Heaney, especially in the context of *Selected Poems.* Still, it is important to remember that there was *Stations* before *Station Island* and *Door into the Dark* before *Seeing Things.*

There are appreciatory poems to other poets such as Ted Hughes and John Montague, dedicatory poems to Philip Larkin, John Hewitt and Richard Ellmann among others, a sonnet sequence **"Glanmore Revisited,"** two translations that frame the collection, and a number of outstanding poems to his father who died in 1986. Yet, unlike the previous volume, *Seeing Things* is divided into two parts. The first contains the above poems (excluding the last translation), while the second part, titled **"Squarings,"** comprises four sections of twelve poems each, with each poem being made up of twelve lines. Heaney has always been concerned with form, but this concentration on technical perfection in this volume, at this point in his life and career, reflects a more fundamental longing for control and an ordered and meaningful life as suggested in a poem from **"Squarings"**:

> 'Down with form triumphant, long live,' (said I)
> 'Form mendicant and convalescent.'
>
> (xxxviii)

But what can form heal? And what about perfect form as the poet asks the ghost of Yeats: "How habitable is perfected form?" Certainly, form can kill, can rob the poem of its potential lyrical spirit, its emotional intensity. Keats's and Wordsworth's sonnets on the sonnet and their celebration of the liberating power of form, the limits of our perceptions and understanding the world in relation to the power of the imagination to take us beyond those limits and to return us regenerated and recommitted to live, where we learn that

> whatever is given
> Can always be re-imagined

even where politics and ideologies are involved.

Like the tough nut of *The Haw Lantern, Seeing Things* is an intentionally understated title—no *Wind among the Reeds* for Heaney. The title, *Seeing Things,* undercuts possible poetic inflation at the risk of evoking the prosaic. The obvious duplicity of the title, seeing things "clearly," and seeing things that are not "there," is deceptively simple:

> clear truths and mysteries
> Were inextricably twined.
>
> **("The Golden Bough")**

Seeing Things is also about seeing things again from a different and hopefully enabling perspective both in time and space, and it is about keeping a sense of perspective, and of self-knowledge. This knowledge produces a "new momentum" that "enters" the poet:

> Like an access of free power, as if belief
> Caught up and spun the objects of belief
> In an orbit coterminous with longing.
>
> **("Wheels within Wheels")**

This liberating "power" is balanced by a

> Heaviness of being. And poetry
> Sluggish in the doldrums of what happens.
>
> **("Fosterling")**

One of the strongest poems in the collection, **"Fosterling,"** has an epigraph from John Montague's poem "The Water Carrier": " 'That heavy greenness fostered by water'." Originally appearing in an anthology dedicated to Montague, **"Fosterling"** playfully affirms Montague's influence, while also parodying Heaney's "the music of what happens," a phrase translated from an ancient Irish text that also appeared in *The Book of Irish Verse,* which Montague edited in 1974.

In *The Haw Lantern,* the sonnet sequence **"Clearances,"** written in memory of Heaney's mother, to a certain extent sets the private emotional tone of the volume. In *Seeing Things,* the poet's father is the presiding spirit and emotional reference point for the volume. In *The Haw Lantern,* the poems to the mother were for the most part grouped together, thus increasing their impact by the sheer weight of their mass. Throughout *Seeing Things,* however, the father reappears in poems like a restless spirit, and thus the sense of loss is suspended throughout the volume. In **"Clearances"** Heaney focuses on the close, yet apprehensive relationship with the mother. In *Seeing Things,* the father is more emotionally distant, yet just as central to the poet's life. Poems which refer to the poet's father are among the most successful in the book. **"Man and Boy"** is a realistic tribute to the father and his world. The father is a stoic character who is afraid that he will spoil his children:

> the sweet time
> Made him afraid we'd take too much for grant-
> ed.

He was a

> broad-backed, low-set man
> Who feared debt all his life.

One of the finest Heaneyesque passages also appears in the poem where

> A mower leans forever on his scythe.
>
> He has mown himself to the center of the field
> And stands in a final perfect ring
> Of sunlit stubble.

The poem concludes in a manner reminiscent of **"Follower"** from *Death of a Naturalist,* when the father carries the son who metaphorically carries the father himself in his memories and poetry.

More closely echoing **"Follower"** is the father who appears in section three of the volume's title poem, **"Seeing Things."** In the earlier poem the slightly romanticized and mythologized father of the poem's opening stanza is "An expert" with the horse-plough, but in **"Seeing Things"** Heaney de-mythologizes the father by recalling a time when the horses

> reared up and pitched
> Cart and sprayer and everything off balance.

The "once upon a time" fairy tale opening of the poem is disarming and leaves the reader unprepared for the catastrophe. However, it provides a perfect set-up for the poem's ironic ending where the fallen father is "face to face" with the son who recognizes that

> there was nothing between us there
> That might not be happily ever after

In other poems the father appears as a judge of character and performance. And although his spade is mentioned, his emblems in *Seeing Things* are the ash plant (walking stick), which he wields "like a silver bough," and the pitchfork:

> He loved its grain of tapering, dark-flecked ash
> Grown satiny from its own natural polish.
>
> **("The Pitchfork")**

The search for the dead father, and the desire to bring him back, informs the spiritual and mythological framework of *Seeing Things,* beginning with the volume's opening translation from the *Aeneid:*

> I pray for one look, one face-to-face meeting
> with my
>   dear father.

There are many other fine poems in the volume, especially from **"Squarings,"** such as poem xvii about the "foul-mouthed god of hemp," the rope man, and poem xxviii, which describes the pleasures of sledding:

> The ice was like a bottle. We lined up
> Eager to re-enter the long slide
> We were bringing to perfection.

In addition, poem xxx recaptures the subtle yet expansive beauty of **"The Harvest Bow"**:

> On St. Brigid's Day the new life could be entered
> By going through her girdle of straw rope
>
> The open they came into by these moves
> Stood opener, hoops came off the world.

Heaney has kept to his strengths in these poems by relying heavily on pleasurable childhood experiences, communal rituals, and descriptions of archaic characters. This is the stuff of some of Heaney's best poetry, and at the risk of appearing slightly archaic himself, he has fearlessly returned to it.

In the end, *Seeing Things* must be measured by the high standards Heaney himself has set. *Seeing Things* is one of Heaney's most accomplished works, but it is not flawless. For instance, even if one acknowledges that the poetic return to the Glanmore cottage contributes to the book's buoyancy, the sequence **"Glanmore Revisited"** lacks the earthy authenticity and the metapoetic depth of the original **"Glanmore Sonnet."** Also, although **"Squarings"** must be praised as an important addition to Heaney's repertoire of stylistic variations, the four sub-sections lack solidarity, and occasionally the poems themselves are indistinguishable. Still, these are minor kinks in a long and strong chain.

Although Heaney's *Seeing Things* covers familiar ground, it is not simply a return to an earlier mode of operation; it is a more complex process of seeing things again—things that were overlooked or hidden before, and "new" things. *Seeing Things* is about looking through "things" and being looked through oneself—about what is visible in the invisible. As Heaney writes of the facade of the Orvieto cathedral in Section II of **"Seeing Things"**:

> The stone's alive with what's invisible.

Seeing Things records the poet's struggle to stay true to himself and his vision, yet to be open to that which is beyond him.

Heaney may have been launched into space in *Selected Poems 1966-1987,* but he is not lost in space. *Seeing Things* records the poet's journey into "the heartland of the ordinary." And like the mysterious mariner in the already much acclaimed poem viii in **"Squarings,"** the "or-dinary" for Heaney is really "the marvellous as he had known it." (pp. 30-1)

Rand Brandes, "The Scale of Things," in Irish Literary Supplement, *Vol. 10, No. 2, Fall, 1991, pp. 30-1.*

Robert Tracy   (review date Fall 1991)

[*Tracy is an American critic and translator. In the following review of* The Cure at Troy, *he discusses the play's theme of isolation.*]

The Cure at Troy enthusiastically received at its Derry premiere and subsequent performances throughout Ireland, is Seamus Heaney's first play, his version of Sophocles' last play but one, *Philoctetes.* Heaney is always subtle, and the change of title, dropping the protagonist's name to hint at a future curing, healing, hints at the way he has slightly re-directed the play's energies to make it an oblique commentary on contemporary Ulster.

Irish playwrights have been busy adapting the classics lately, to use them as metaphors for their own predicaments. In the 1980s, we have had versions of *Three Sisters* by Brian Friel and Frank McGuinness; McGuinness' *Peer Gynt;* Thomas Kilroy's *Seagull;* Brendan Kennelly's *Medea* and *Antogone;* Tom Paulin's *Antigone* (*The Riot Act*) and *Prometheus Bound* (*Seize the Fire*). Since *Sweeney Astray* (1984), Heaney has been meditating about the artist's freedom from politics, and the austere loneliness of that freedom. *Philoctetes/ The Cure at Troy* is a play about isolation. Philoctetes' people have abandoned him to a solitude he hates. In that solitude he becomes Other, a magic presence essential to his people's success. There are strong affinities with Sophocles' last play, *Oedipus at Colonus,* which Yeats adapted to express his own isolation and talismanic necessity. Like Sweeney, Oedipus and Philoctetes have left behind their roles as king and warrior. Apollo's hand is upon them; the god of prophecy, who is also god of poetry and of archery, has set them apart from ordinary life.

Prophecy has told the Greeks that Troy will fall only to the combined efforts of Achilles' son Neoptolemus, the man of reckless bravery, and Philoctetes, the man of art, who wields Hercules' (and Apollo's) magic bow. Philoctetes has been marooned on Lemnos, because a snake has bitten him during a ceremony at Apollo's enclosure, and his comrades cannot stand the stench of the wound nor the sound of his continual lamentations. Now Odysseus, the man of guile, has come to persuade or force him to join the Greeks against Troy. Odysseus refers often to "the cause," as recruiting officers will do. He corrupts young Neoptolemus ("new fighter") by teaching him to trick Philoctetes and so capture him ("I know all this goes against the grain / . . . you'll be ashamed / but that won't last"). An older man enlists a youngster in an ongoing struggle, its origin somewhere in the past. The Ulster analogy is tempting.

There is a double tension in the play: between Odysseus' guile and Neoptolemus' sense of honor, and between Neoptolemus' eagerness and Philoctetes' sullen hatred. A schemer to the last, Odysseus exits unredeemed ("I'm going back / To outline all the charges"). But Philoctetes' hatred is cured when Neoptolemus refuses any longer to participate in the plot, and freely returns the bow. By doing so, he cures his wounded honor. "You are back to your old self," Philoctetes tells him; "Your father's son."

Though Philoctetes comes to trust Neoptolemus, and so break out of his fierce isolation, he still will not join the cause. "You are to come / Of your own free will to the town of Troy," Neoptolemus tells him, " . . . and you're to be / The hero that was healed and then went on / To heal the wound of the Trojan war itself / . . . Stop just licking your wounds. Start seeing things." The god Hercules must finally speak through the Chorus to send him to Troy:

> Go, Philoctetes, and with his boy,
> Go and be cured and capture Troy.
> Asclepius will make you whole,
> Relieve your body and your soul.
>
> Go, with your bow. Conclude the sore
> And cruel stalemate of our war.
> Win by fair combat. But know to shun
> Reprisal killings when that's done.

These appearances of gods to settle matters are always awkward for modern audiences. Heaney neatly solves the difficulty by letting the Chorus Leader speak as Hercules. At the same time, his solution works to resolve both the play's and some of Heaney's own antinomies. Philoctetes has been a cave-dweller on his island, kenneled in the earth, like the Antaeus figure of Heaney's earlier poetry, "cradled in the dark that wombed me," associated with water, darkness, bogs, digging in the earth. Heaney's Antaeus succumbs to "sky-born" Hercules, associated with air, light, flying. As former master of Apollo's bow, Hercules is a man of art. At the beginning of the play, Heaney adds a choric statement to remind us that the Chorus speaks as poetry itself. The Chorus condemns gods, heroes, and resentful victims alike as "fixated, / Shining with self-regard like polished stones, . . . Licking their wounds / And flashing them around like decorations." At once hating it and "a part of it," the Chorus, "a borderline between / The you and the me and the it of it," reminds us that only poetry, another "borderline," can break those fixations, thaw frozen attitudes:

> Poetry
> Allowed the god to speak. It was the voice
> Of reality and justice. The voice of Hercules
> That Philoctetes is going to have to hear
> When the stone cracks open and the lava flows.

In a Greek play, the god speaks what must be, inexorably destined. Heaney's god speaks through a woman, the Chorus Leader, to remind us that poetry can merge antitheses. But only as poetry. The voice promises victory, and also healing, outside the play, in a play we cannot see. The Cure that Heaney's title promises remains a promise, words not yet realized. Poetry and theatre can make everything right. But outside the theatre, in the ravaged streets of Derry, the audience are on their own, with only a vision of change and healing. "No poem or play or song / Can fully right a wrong / Inflicted and endured,"

the Chorus chants, as a distant volcano (another Heaney addition) begins to flash and rumble:

> The innocent in jails
> Beat on their bars together.
> A hunger-striker's father
> Stands in the graveyard dumb.
> The police widow in veils
> Faints at the funeral home.
>
> History says, *Don't hope
> On this side of the grave.*
> But then, once in a life-time
> The longed-for tidal wave
> Of justice can rise up,
> And hope and history rhyme.
>
> So hope for a great sea-change
> On the far side of revenge.
> Believe that a further shore
> Is reachable from here.
> Believe in miracles
> And cures and healing wells.

By framing Sophocles' play in a prologue and epilogue of his own devising, Heaney undermines the older play's endorsement of joining a cause, when Hercules promises that Philoctetes will be cured if he will agree to kill. Sophocles ended with a three-line speech for the Chorus: "Let us all leave together / Once we've prayed to the Nymphs of the Sea / For a safe journey back." Heaney gives Philoctetes a final exultant speech: "I feel I'm a part of what was always meant to happen, and is happening now at last. Come on, my friends." "What's left to say?" asks the Chorus, then answers its own question:

> Suspect too much sweet talk
> But never close your mind.
> It was a fortunate wind
> That blew me here. I leave
> Half-ready to believe
> That a crippled trust might walk
>
> And the half-true rhyme is love.

Even the Chorus is only "Half-ready to believe." *Believe / love* can never be more than a half-rhyme, *hope / history* puzzles the nimblest rhymer. But language can triumph over its own intractability. Philoctetes agrees to enter a future that exists only in language. For ten years—the length of Philoctetes' exile on his island—Field Day's pamphlets have explored the misuse of language in Northern Ireland, and the myths that govern attitudes there. *The Cure at Troy* does not prescribe a cure, but only reminds us that a cure is possible—or imaginable. "May I have the fortune to preside over an Ireland at a time of exciting transformation," declared President Mary Robinson in her inaugural address; "when we enter a new Europe where old wounds can be healed, a time when, in the words of Seamus Heaney, 'hope and history rhyme.' " (pp. 31-2)

Robert Tracy, "When Hope and History Rhyme," in Irish Literary Supplement, *Vol. 10, No. 2, Fall, 1991, pp. 31-2.*

John B. Breslin   (review date 7 December 1991)

[*Breslin is an American critic and a Roman Catholic priest. In the following review of* Seeing Things, *he discusses the collection's focus on the death of Heaney's father, its theme of visionary insight glimpsed through ordinary experiences, and Heaney's use of a new form that incorporates personal memory and literary history.*]

I first heard several of the poems in this latest collection by Seamus Heaney, *Seeing Things,* when he read them to a small class I was teaching at Trinity College in Dublin over a year ago. During this past August, I heard him read more of them at the conclusion of an arts festival in Kilkenny. Between the two readings, the book was published in England and Ireland and appeared for several weeks on the Irish best-seller list, a rare achievement for any poet.

But then, Seamus Heaney is no ordinary poet. In a country that has traditionally taken its poets—and its footballers—seriously, for praise or blame, Heaney has long been accorded world cup status. His success abroad has something to do with that; he now holds simultaneously the chair of poetry at Oxford and the chair of rhetoric at Harvard. But in the words of Fintan O'Toole of the *Irish Times,* through it all Heaney remains "hype-proof," and so does his poetry.

Since the publication of *Station Island* in 1984, Heaney has been exploring new forms to express a vision that has grown more astringent but no less celebratory. In "Sweeney Redivivus," the final section of that collection, Heaney used the voice of the exiled and cruelly charmed poet-king (whose story he had previously Englished in *Sweeney Astray*) to express his own disenchantment from the thralls of received opinion—about belief or art or his own role as poet. The book's last poem **("On the Road")** sets him a lonely vigil before a prehistoric carving of a deer with "a nostril flared / at a dried-up source." It concludes with this at once ascetic and aesthetic response to Jesus' offer of discipleship to the rich young man, a text Heaney uses to punctuate the poem:

> I would meditate
> that stone-faced vigil
>
> until the long dumbfounded spirit
>   broke cover
> to raise a dust
> in the font of exhaustion.

That "would" is a favorite Heaney auxiliary verb, announcing an intention consigned to an indefinite future. What might come from such a discipline? A newfound voice from an exhausted spring? In any case it would be a baptism peculiarly his own.

Seeing Things, Heaney's second collection of new poems since *Station Island,* continues to provide new answers to those questions, but, as we might expect, they are elliptical and aslant, teasing us *into* thought. Many of the poems celebrate his father whose death, he said in Kilkenny, propelled him into a whole new awareness of adulthood as life in a roofless universe, a prospect both liberating and terrifying. Vistas keep opening up in these poems:

> young footballers play on heedless

> of the dark:
> It was quick and constant, a game that never
>   need
> Be played out. Some limit had been passed.
> There was fleetness, furtherance, untiredness
> In time that was extra, unforeseen and free.

Or these lines from two other linked "sports" poems that celebrate the same kind of release, at once ecstatic and somehow bereft. The first is called **"The Point"** and ends:

> That spring
> and unhampered smash-through!
> Was it you
>
> or the ball that kept going
> beyond you, amazingly
> higher and higher
> and ruefully free?

The other, titled **"A Haul,"** invokes northern mythology to complement the angling poem that comes between them; Thor and Hymer let the world-serpent get away, and Thor is left

> at one with space,
> unroofed and obvious—
> surprised in his empty arms
> like some fabulous high-catcher
> coming down without the ball.

A sonnet from **"Glanmore Revisited,"** a series that harkens back to *Field Work,* gives this unroofed experience a domestic setting and, again, a biblical resonance; the speaker recalls a disagreement about putting in a skylight in their cottage; he preferred the "claustrophobic, nest-up-in-the-roof / Effect . . . all hutch and hatch":

> But when the slates came off,
> extravagant
> Sky entered and held surprise wide open.
> For days I felt like an inhabitant
> Of that house where the man sick of the palsy
> was lowered through the roof, had his sins for-
>   given,
> Was healed, took up his bed and walked away.

Notice that the poet does not identify with the sick man, only with a fellow lodger, one who observes and records the miracle. But the same interplay of vigorous activity and passive acceptance that marked the "football" images recurs here; transcendence, like healing or poetic inspiration, is a gift—and usually a surprise, like grace. What we do is either preparation or response.

For the poet, a good part of the preparation is technical, constantly refining the craft and experimenting with new forms. Are there not myriad ways to catch a ball, hook a fish, see the light? The second half of *Seeing Things* offers such an experiment: 12-line poems with four three-line stanzas each. Heaney said he tried one during a fallow period, liked it, tried another, got to 12, then thought of squaring that for 144! This proved too ambitious, so he settled for 48 in four groups of 12 and called the whole section, as well as one of its parts, **"Squarings."**

Since the form is so consciously geometrical, it is tempting to look for a similar ordering of themes. Certainly there are correspondences, echoes, allusions back and forth—

and once again the poet's father appears frequently; but the thematic sequencing here is loose, working against the strict formality of the stanzas. Occasionally one poem generates another, as in the parenthetical "correction" of his first description of Thomas Hardy as a young boy "experiment[ing] with infinity" by playing dead among the sheep: (*I misremembered* begins the next poem. Each has its own perspective to contribute to these meditations on place and time. The "misremembered" posture of young Hardy flat out on the ground stirs a ripple among the sheep

> that would travel eighty years
> Outward from there, to be the same ripple
> Inside him at its last circumference.

The "correct" image is of Hardy playing sheep himself on all fours, [*seeking*] *the creatures face to face* in a proleptic parody of the social gatherings of his *renowned old age—* all *blinks and murmurs and deflections* to which Hardy will respond by imagining himself a ghost as he makes the rounds. What links the young Hardy to the old is precisely this ripple of the imagination, caused here by a gesture compounded of equal parts shyness and audacity. Once started, this ripple expands indefinitely yet retains the same center, a defining moment to be recovered in memory and in verse. Childe Hardy as sheep and aged Hardy as ghost meet and embrace across Heaney's squarings.

Other of these squarings explore more personal memories and display Heaney's characteristic skill in verbalizing the visual as in this Rembrandt-tinged memory of his father with a lantern, checking his supplies:

> his right hand foraging
> For the unbleeding, vivid-fleshed bacon,
> Home-cured hocks pulled up into the light
> For pondering a while and putting back,
>
> That night I owned the piled grain of Egypt.
> I watched the sentry's torchlight on the hoard.
> I stood in the door, unseen and blazed upon.

In these poems the way to the visionary is through the ordinary that, attended to imaginatively, invariably proves extraordinary. Heaney has found a freedom in this new form that allows him to forage at will through his own hoard of personal memory and literary history. He seems a bit rueful at the end of the sonnet that closes the book's first movement: *Me waiting until I was nearly fifty / To credit marvels,* but the release such crediting provokes seems well worth the wait: *So long for air to brighten. / Time to be dazzled and the heart to lighten.* (pp. 438-39)

> *John B. Breslin, "Vision and Revision: Seamus Heaney's New Poems," in* America, *Vol. 165, No. 18, December 7, 1991, pp. 438-39.*

FURTHER READING

Agenda: Seamus Heaney Fiftieth Birthday Issue 27, No. 1 (Spring 1989): 1-80.
Contains poetry and a lecture by Heaney as well as essays by such critics as John Bayley, Neil Corcoran, and William Bedford.

Brown, Duncan. "Seamus Heaney's 'Book of Changes': *The Haw Lantern.*" *Theoria* LXXIV (October 1989): 79-96.
Asserts that *The Haw Lantern* is "a highly experimental volume" in which Heaney departs from the local Irish concerns evidenced in his previous works and notes that "*The Haw Lantern* is characterized by an openness to a variety of literary influences, felt particularly in the range of poems in different styles and on different themes."

Burris, Sidney. *The Poetry of Resistance: Seamus Heaney and the Pastoral Tradition.* Athens: Ohio University Press, 1990, 165 p.
Examines pastoral elements in Heaney's poetry and considers the relationship between the pastoral literary tradition and political resistance.

Corcoran, Neil. *Seamus Heaney.* London: Faber and Faber, 1986, 192 p.
Presents a critical introduction to Heaney's works and includes biographical material and a select bibliography.

Curtis, Tony, ed. *The Art of Seamus Heaney.* Bridgend: United Kingdom, 1982, 180 p.
Thematic and chronological overview of Heaney's career through *Station Island.* Curtis states: "This collection of essays is formed, quite deliberately, of distinct, diverse and sometimes opposed views regarding Seamus Heaney's work."

Fry, August J. "Confronting Seamus Heaney: A Personal Reading of His Early Poetry." *Dutch Quarterly Review of Anglo-American Letters* 18, No. 3 (1988): 242-55.
Discusses the development of themes and style in Heaney's first three volumes of poetry in an effort to better understand "the world of this man's poetry."

Hart, Henry. *Seamus Heaney: Poet of Contrary Progressions.* Syracuse: Syracuse University Press, 1992, 219 p.
Examines Heaney's delineation of personal and political crises, highlighting pastoral and anti-pastoral elements, history, myth and apocalypse, and the representation of psychological and imaginative forces in his poetry.

Johnston, Conor. "Seamus Heaney, Sweeney, and *Station Island.*" *Éire-Ireland* XXII, No. 2 (Summer 1987): 70-95.
Considers Heaney's "response to community and to his poetic vocation" as central themes in *Sweeney Astray* and *Station Island.*

Kelly, H. A. "Heaney's Sweeney: Poet as Version-Maker." *Philological Quarterly* 65, No. 3 (Summer 1986): 293-310.
Analysis of *Sweeney Astray,* comparing it to the original medieval Irish narrative *Buile Suibhne* and assessing the literary merit of Heaney's adaptation.

Kinzie, Mary. "Deeper Than Declared: On Seamus Heaney." *Salmagundi,* No. 80 (Fall 1988): 22-57.
Studies political and spiritual themes as well as the style and structure of Heaney's works.

Longley, Edna. " 'Inner Emigré' or 'Artful Voyeur'?: Seamus Heaney's *North.*" In her *Poetry in the Wars,* pp. 140-69. Newcastle upon Tyne: Bloodaxe Books, 1986.
Close analysis of *North,* emphasizing Heaney's poetic

representation of Irish consciousness, politics, and history.

Macrae, Alasdair. "Seamus Heaney's New Voice in *Station Island*." In *Irish Writers and Society at Large,* edited by Masaru Sekine, pp. 122-38. Gerrards Cross, Buckinghamshire: Colin Smythe, 1985.
    Examines the poems in *Station Island* and considers the relation of the modern poet to his society, asserting that "there is manifested in the volume . . . a new, acute awareness of dangers, tensions, questions in writing the kinds of poems [Heaney] has."

McGuinness, Arthur E. "Seamus Heaney: The Forging Pilgrim." *Essays in Literature* 18, No. 1 (Spring 1991): 46-67.
    Discussion of masculine or "forging" qualities in Heaney's *Field Work* and *Station Island.*

Mendelson, Edward. "Poetry as Fate and Faith." *The Times Literary Supplement,* No. 4,448 (1-7 July 1988): 726.
    Review of *The Government of the Tongue,* exploring Heaney's views on several major poets and his thoughts concerning contemporary poetry and politics in Ireland.

Molino, Michael R. "Heaney's 'Singing School': A Portrait of the Artist." *The Journal of Irish Literature* XVI, No. 3 (September 1987): 12-17.
    Discusses the section entitled "Singing School" in Heaney's *North,* asserting that the poems reflect Heaney's life experiences and his role as a poet.

Morrison, Blake. *Seamus Heaney.* London: Methuen, 1982, 95 p.
    Early study of Heaney's works through *Field Work,* asserting that "Heaney's poetry has been seriously misrepresented, not least by its admirers. A proper response to Heaney's work requires reference to complex matters of ancestry, nationality, religion, history and politics."

Rudman, Mark. "Voluptuaries and Maximalists." *The New York Times Book Review* (20 December 1987): 12.
    Review of *The Haw Lantern,* praising Heaney's lyrical style and noting the addition of experimental poems "in which Heaney grapples with abstraction in a way he has not previously attempted."

Sacks, Peter. "Unleashing the Lyric: Seamus Heaney." *The Antioch Review* 48, No. 3 (Summer 1990): 381-89.
    Analyzes Heaney's interpretation of the relationship between art and life and the poet's response to suffering in *The Government of the Tongue.*

Tamplin, Ronald. *Seamus Heaney.* Philadelphia: Open University Press, 1989, 114 p.
    Introductory guide to Heaney's poetry through *The Haw Lantern.*

Tapscott, Stephen. "Poetry and Trouble: Seamus Heaney's Irish Purgatorio." *Southwest Review* 71, No. 4 (Autumn 1986): 519-35.
    Considers the influence of the Irish poetic tradition in Heaney's poetry.

Vendler, Helen. "Second Thoughts." *The New York Review of Books* XXXV, No. 7 (28 April 1988): 41-5.
    Review of *The Haw Lantern,* focusing on the collection's theme of emptiness and absence. Vendler states: "Heaney is a poet of abundance who is undergoing in middle age the experience of natural loss."

Additional coverage of Heaney's life and career is contained in the following sources published by Gale Research: *Concise Dictionary of British Literary Biography, 1960 to the Present*; *Contemporary Authors,* Vols. 85-88; *Contemporary Authors New Revision Series,* Vol. 25; *Contemporary Literary Criticism,* Vols. 5, 7, 14, 25, 37; *Dictionary of Literary Biography,* Vol. 40; and *Major 20th-Century Writers.*

Norman Mailer

1923-

American novelist, short story writer, nonfiction writer, screenwriter, filmmaker, and journalist.

The following entry contains recent criticism on Mailer's life and career. For further information, see *CLC*, Volumes 1, 2, 3, 4, 5, 8, 11, 14, 28, and 39.

INTRODUCTION

A prolific and highly controversial figure who has resisted identification with any particular literary group, Mailer is regarded as one of the United States's most prominent contemporary writers. Praised for the scope and diversity of his works, he is respected for conventional novels in which he examines the conflict between the individual will to power and overwhelming social and political restraints, as well as for his provocative nonfiction and "nonfiction narratives," in which he combines factual reportage with such literary devices as stream-of-consciousness, extended dialogue, and multiple points of view to lend immediacy to the events he describes.

Mailer was born to Jewish parents in Long Branch, New Jersey, but moved with his family to Brooklyn in New York City at the age of four. Enrolling in Harvard University at the age of sixteen, he studied aeronautical engineering and cultivated an interest in writing. Mailer was inducted into the United States Army a year after graduating in 1943 and voluntarily went ashore as a rifleman with a reconnaissance platoon during the invasion of Luzon in the Philippines. Following his discharge in 1946, he drew upon this experience in his first novel, *The Naked and the Dead,* which proved a major critical and popular success.

Mailer attended the Sorbonne in Paris under the G. I. Bill before returning to the United States in the mid-1950s. With Daniel Wolf and Edwin Fancher he cofounded the leftist newspaper *The Village Voice,* for which he wrote a regular column beginning in 1956. Although his reputation as a fiction writer flagged following the largely hostile critical reception that attended his novels subsequent to *The Naked and the Dead,* Mailer achieved national celebrity in 1959 with *Advertisements for Myself,* a compendium of essays and writings from his career. In some of these pieces Mailer admitted to his increasing experimentation with drugs and alcohol. In 1960, his personal life became public when the media reported his arrest for wounding his wife Adele with a penknife following a drunken party in his Manhattan apartment. He later received a suspended sentence when she refused to press charges. In the years following the incident, Mailer became as famous for his public rebelliousness as for his literary works. In Provincetown, Massachusetts, he was arrested for taunting and fighting with police, and at Birdland, a fashionable New

York nightclub, he was again incarcerated for belligerently arguing with a bartender over his liquor tab. While Mailer's penchant for publicity has prompted many critics to consider him opportunistic or self-aggrandizing, others, such as Philip H. Bufithis, have asserted that for Mailer such public demonstrations serve as inspiration for his writings. His arrest for crossing the U.S. Federal Marshal's line during an antiwar march on the Pentagon, for instance, became the subject matter for his nonfiction narrative *The Armies of the Night: History as a Novel, the Novel as History.* Since the 1980s, Mailer has become more conservative in his private and public life and has served as president of PEN (the International Association of Poets, Playwrights, Editors, Essayists, and Novelists).

Mailer's novels, particularly those written early in his career, often focus on individuals who challenge social or political restraints in their search for self-actualization. This theme is delineated in "The White Negro," a frequently anthologized essay first published in 1957 and later included in *Advertisements for Myself.* In this piece Mailer considers the African-American, whom he views as capable of placing the needs of the self over those of society, as a model for the American "hipster," a violent "philosophical psychopath" immune to traditional institutions of social control. Mailer had previously explored the conflict between the individual will and established power in *The Naked and the Dead,* which focuses on a fourteen-man infantry platoon that leads the invasion of a Japanese-held island in the Phillipines during World War II. Writing in an unsentimental narrative voice, Mailer discourages sympathy for any one character, focusing ambiguously on a likable liberal commander who is violently betrayed by an immoral and ambitious sergeant. The theme of the individual's struggle against conformism appears in less radical form in *The Deer Park,* in which a socially conscious film director attempts to revive his creative powers after being blacklisted by Hollywood producers for refusing to testify as a "friendly witness" for a Congressional investigative committee. The narrator of *An American Dream* typifies Mailer's "philosophical psychopath" in that he embraces what Mailer called "the affirmation of the barbarian" by murdering his estranged wife and disappearing from public life. By casting off his respectable social identity as husband, professor, and author, the protagonist of this novel hopes to emerge as a new being.

Mailer's recent novels include *Tough Guys Don't Dance,* a conventional crime thriller that Mailer also adapted for film and directed, and *Harlot's Ghost,* in which he imagines the inner workings of the United States Central Intelligence Agency in relation to such events as the Cuban missile crisis and the Bay of Pigs. The first installment of a longer work, *Harlot's Ghost* is narrated by Harry Hubbard, a ghost writer of planted texts for the C.I.A. who divines the department's purpose from his mentor, the apostolic cold-war philosopher Hugh Tremont ("Harlot") Montague. During the course of this long novel, Harry encounters evidence suggesting that the C.I.A. is a haven for ivy-league elitism that has little or no effect on world events.

Mailer received the greatest praise of his later career for nonfiction narratives in which he relates factual events from his own perspective. His first such work, *The Armies of the Night,* garnered a National Book Award as well as a Pulitzer Prize and drew frequent comparisons to Truman Capote's "nonfiction novel" *In Cold Blood* (1965). In his narrative, Mailer remains scrupulous to the facts attending an antiwar march on the Pentagon that took place in 1967, yet endows the book with his own subjectivism by comically inflating his role in the event. *The Executioner's Song,* for which Mailer received a second Pulitzer Prize, examines the life and death of convicted murderer Gary Gilmore, who at his own request received the death penalty in 1977. By shifting between the viewpoints of doctors, lawyers, police, and journalists as well as Gilmore's friends and relatives without denying subjective involvement with his material, Mailer was credited with having transcended the inherent limitations of the nonfiction narrative. In the late 1960s and early 1970s, Mailer wrote a wide variety of nonfiction works that established him as a preeminent writer in that genre. In *The Presidential Papers* and *Cannibals and Christians* Mailer offers extended critiques of American politics and society. *The Prisoner of Sex* is a treatise on Mailer's various sexual relationships in which he responds to Kate Millett's celebrat-

ed attack on his presumed sexism in her study *Sexual Politics* (1970), while *Genius and Lust: A Journey through the Major Writings of Henry Miller* is a critical appreciation of American novelist Henry Miller, whom Millett had attacked on similar grounds. In addition, Mailer also wrote *Marilyn,* a novelized biography of Hollywood actress Marilyn Monroe, and *Of Women and Their Elegance,* a fictionalized interview between Mailer and Monroe.

PRINCIPAL WORKS

The Naked and the Dead　(novel)　1948

Barbary Shore　(novel)　1951

The Deer Park　(novel)　1955

*The White Negro: Superficial Reflections on the Hipster (essays)　1957

Advertisements for Myself　(short stories, verse, nonfiction, and nonfiction novel)　1959

Deaths for the Ladies (and Other Disasters)　(poetry) 1962

The Presidential Papers　(essays)　1963

An American Dream　(novel)　1965

Cannibals and Christians　(essays)　1966

The Deer Park: A Play　(drama)　1967

The Short Fiction of Norman Mailer　(short stories) 1967

Why Are We In Vietnam?　(novel)　1967

The Armies of the Night: History as a Novel, the Novel as History　(nonfiction novel)　1968

Miami and the Siege of Chicago: An Informal History of the Republican and Democratic Conventions of 1968 (nonfiction novel)　1968

Of a Fire on the Moon　(nonfiction novel)　1970; also published as *A Fire on the Moon,* 1970

Maidstone: A Mystery　(screenplay)　1970

The Prisoner of Sex　(nonfiction)　1971

Marilyn: A Biography　(nonfiction)　1973; revised edition, 1975

Genius and Lust: A Journey through the Major Writings of Henry Miller　(criticism)　1976

The Executioner's Song　(nonfiction novel)　1979

Of Women and Their Elegance　(fictional autobiography) 1980

The Executioner's Song　(screenplay)　1982

Pieces and Pontifications　(essays and interviews)　1982

Ancient Evenings　(novel)　1983

Tough Guys Don't Dance　(novel)　1984

Tough Guys Don't Dance　(screenplay)　1987

Harlot's Ghost　(novel)　1991

---

*The title essay of this work is reprinted in *Advertisements for Myself.*

CRITICISM

Jean Radford   (essay date 1983)

[*In the following essay, Radford defends Mailer's use of literary experimentation throughout his career, asserting that "his attempts to forge new connections for narrative form are both significant and valuable."*]

Among students of the American novel, it is a truth universally acknowledged that Norman Mailer is a man in possession of much talent in want of achievement. Starting in 1948 as one kind of a writer, he developed into a stylistic chameleon (realist, allegorist, journalist), crossing generic border-lines (with essays, short-stories, criticism and the novel), raiding a number of ideological positions (marxist, existentialist, left conservative, Zen) and in the course of his progress losing and gaining more points in the critical 'Bimmler' than almost any other contemporary American novelist.

I want to suggest, first, that this intellectual and stylistic mobility is important not merely for American literature but for the future possibilities of the novel form; to suggest that Mailer's changing literary strategies are not simply expressive of his personal qualities as a writer, but are symptomatic of the social and aesthetic problems faced by *all* contemporary writers. The great divide between those novelists who have turned toward fantasy and fabulation on the one hand, and those preoccupied with 'faction' and non-fiction modes on the other, is now too striking to ignore. In the last year, the major literary prizes around the world reflect this division: the Nobel Prize for literature going to Gabriel Garcia Marquez for his *One Hundred Years of Solitude* and in Britain the Booker Prize being awarded to Thomas Keneally's non-fiction novel *Schindler's Ark.* In this re-run of what some critics describe as the old antagonism between romance and realism (or, going further back, as the distinction between the 'true' and the 'real' made in Plato's *Republic*), Mailer's position astride this divide, his forays since the 1950s into journalism and 'non-Literary' discourse and his attempts to forge new connections for narrative form are both significant and valuable.

Secondly, I would argue that Mailer's recent work *The Executioner's Song* (1979), is not just a commercial interruption of the 'large social novel' about America which he has been promising for some fifteen years now, but is itself a major achievement and a partial realization of that project. In the account of the Utah murderer Gary Gilmore and his execution, he has assembled a new repertoire of literary devices through which he mounts a panoramic documentary on American culture. The montage of voices, produced from hundreds of interviews with those involved in the Gilmore case, has in effect released Mailer from the limitations of his personal voice and vision and provided him with a new means to address the contradictions and nuances of his world. Apart from the compulsive readability of this 1000-page fiction, *The Executioner's Song* is remarkable among his works for the almost complete absence of Mailer's personality; there is no authorial verdict on the events narrated, no distinctive Maileresque 'style' separable from the multitude of narrating voices. Mailer remains almost invisible, behind or beyond his handiwork, working in Joycean fashion with a very rich verbal palette and working, it seems to me, brilliantly. Not perhaps since *The Naked and the Dead* has he come as close to writing an epic on the American way of life.

Mailer started writing while still at Harvard in the early '40s and the influence of various '30s writers—Farrell, Dos Passos and Steinbeck—is evident in *The Naked and the Dead.* This novel in four parts describes the capture of a small island in the South Pacific from the Japanese in World War II: it offers a detailed realistic account of an Intelligence and Reconnaissance platoon from the initial landing, in combat, through a reconnaissance patrol to the conclusion and aftermath of battle. Intercut with this narrative are the inter-chapter biographies of the platoon members, in a manner which recalls the techniques of *USA.* The debt is not merely a technical one either, since many of the ideas in the book are clearly continuous with the social vision of Dos Passos's trilogy. The patrol is used as a microcosm of American society, and the racial and sexual attitudes of the enlisted men with their power-hungry dreams are used to represent the corruption of the American dream. The conversations between the neo-fascist General Cummings and his liberal Lieutenant, Hearn, dramatize the political alternatives which Mailer envisages for post-war America. The juxtaposition of the fragmented physical ordeals of the private soldiers with Cummings's highly structured overall conception of the war, is itself one of the themes of the novel: the undemocratic nature of an army engaged in fighting against fascism.

Where the writing about combat is brisk and effective, and strongly reminiscent of Hemingway, the somewhat determinist presentation of character in the 'Time Machine' sections is a legacy of the naturalism of the '30s, which Mailer assumed along with the more experimental newsreel style of the social commentary. As he revealed in the *Paris Review* (1948) interview, the characters in *The Naked and the Dead* were carefully researched. He kept a long dossier on each man, had charts to show which characters had not yet had scenes with others, and used his sociological data methodically. It was for the 'social realism' of this large cast of characters that the arch-realist George Lukács was to hail Mailer as a contemporary realist in his *The Meaning of Contemporary Realism*:

> *The Naked and the Dead* marks a step forward from the trackless desert of abstractions towards a portrayal of the actual suffering of actual people during the Second World War. Arbitrary though much of the detail is, and retrograde though the author's subsequent development has been, the merits of that achievement . . . should not be overlooked.

Lukács's comment is typical of critics who see Mailer as a renegade realist; it not only fails to understand his subsequent achievements but actually misrepresents his first novel. Mailer's own statement, in *Current Biography* (1948) is much more relevant:

> In the author's eyes *The Naked and the Dead* is

not a realistic documentary; it is rather a 'symbolic' book of which the basic theme is the conflict between the beast and the seer in man.

The novel in fact operates in a mixture of narrative modes and is both realist and 'symbolic'. Although the realist/naturalist elements are dominant in *The Naked and the Dead,* the allegorizing impulse which was to prevail in his second novel *Barbary Shore* (1951) and later again in *An American Dream,* is present from the first. If Mailer's allegiance to 'the real' emerges in the characterization of Valsen, Polack, Minetti and the others, the reconnaissance trip and the assault on Mount Anaka become an allegorical quest in which the nature of man and man's relation to Nature are examined. The allegorical element is underpinned by the finding of the Japanese officer's diary which functions as a sub-text to the theme of the beast and the seer: 'I ask myself—WHY? I am born, I am to die. WHY? WHY? What is the meaning?' Thus while the conflicts between Hearn and Cummings about the merits and demerits of different social systems represent the political, Mailer introduces another level—the existential questions—which pulls the mimetic description of character and event back toward the mythical-symbolic pole. It is this complex negotiation between the rival claims of myth and realism, *within* each of his novels and from one book to another, which makes his writing so resonant.

Abandoning the omniscient technique of *The Naked and the Dead,* Mailer in his next two novels shifts from third- to first-person narration. Although the thematic concerns of *The Naked and the Dead* are developed—in his treatment of the failure of the Russian Revolution to provide an alternative to the American Dream and the nature of Hollywood as the dream-factory of America—neither *Barbary Shore* nor *Deer Park* is as effective as a fictional treatment of these issues. In *Barbary Shore* the fictional world of the Brooklyn boarding-house and its inhabitants collapses into a chapter of political speech. The unifying motifs—the images of the revolution betrayed—cannot support the weight of Mailer's ideological argument. Lovett, the first-person narrator and a writer who has lost his memory, is the surrogate for the writer who has rejected the borrowed authority of Mailer's composite voice in *The Naked and the Dead* and not yet found an alternative. The same difficulties with voice and point-of-view are evident in *The Deer Park.* The novel begins in the first-person, as Sergius O'Shaughnessy gives a prolonged introduction of himself, the setting and characters. Only in Part II does the main storyline begin and O'Shaughnessy recedes into a witness-narrator role. In the third part of the novel, the narrator's role and authority decrease still further—('I have the conceit I *know* what happened'). Here he is referring to the Eitel-Elena affair which is told in the third-person, although O'Shaughnessy's tone colours the presentation. In effect the point-of-view becomes that of a first-person narrator with omniscient powers but the uncertainties of the narrative method begin to tell on the novel. The psychological realism of Eitel's characterization is insufficiently integrated with Marion Faye's apocalyptic visions and Sergius's mystical view of Time as 'the connection of new circuits', and the fiction falters between these three centres of consciousness. It was however an important experiment for the writer struggling to find his own voice—as Mailer comments in *Advertisements for Myself*:

> . . . the style of the work lost its polish, became rough, and I can say real, because there was an abrupt and muscular body back of the voice now. It had been there all the time . . . but now I chipped away . . . I felt as if I was finally learning how to write. . . .

The short stories, essays and articles published as *Advertisements for Myself* (1957) and *Presidential Papers* (1963) are part of that explosion in literary journalism which Tom Wolfe was later to call 'The New Journalism'. In these essays Mailer brings all the resources of fiction to bear, working on his new 'muscular' style, experimenting with point-of-view strategies, stretching his language to include the kind of demotic American which he had previously kept within quotation marks. Where in *The Naked and the Dead* the literary and the colloquial divide into description and dialogue, the purple passages and the 'fuggin', here the two modes are brought together. *Advertisements,* like Lowell's *Life Studies* published the same year, is a form of autobiography which tells the story of a writer and his struggle with available forms. It is also a reconnaissance trip by a writer who like the hero of the story **'The Man Who Studied Yoga'** feels he can no longer employ the anonymous omniscient narrator of the classic realist text. When Sam Slovoda is asked by one of his friends why he has given up his projected novel, Sam says he cannot find a form. He does not want to write a realistic novel, he says, 'because reality is no longer realistic'. Again, rather like Robert Lowell, Mailer was at this point reproached by some critics for narrowing his scope from the epic sweep of his early work to the confessional mode; but there is no real contraction evident in the range of his concerns. His problem is rather to devise new methods of addressing the 'non-realistic' realities of America, to construct a narrator within the fictional frame, with a voice large enough to carry his creator's ideas about the world to a reader 'changed utterly' from the reader of nineteenth-century realist fiction. This problem, clearly, is not peculiar to Norman Mailer. It is perhaps *the* most urgent and difficult task facing the twentieth-century novelist. Within the most realistic tales, the narrating subject is seemingly removed from the frame of action, a voice (as in *The Naked and the Dead*) charged only with the duties of representation, a presence that strives to appear solely as absence. Mailer's attempts to represent that 'absence', to acknowledge his own voice within the text and to give that narrating subject a fictional existence, found its most radical expression in *Armies of the Night*—but not before he had made an excursion into a rather different realm.

An American Dream (1965) which originally appeared in monthly instalments in *Esquire* magazine, marks a return to an older narrative tradition. It is a 'romance' which rather than aiming at minute fidelity to 'the real', in Hawthorne's words [as expressed in *The House of Seven Gables*], presents 'truth under circumstances . . . of the writer's own choosing and creation'. Stephen Rojack, Mailer's first-person narrator-hero, is an American pilgrim in quest of rebirth and regeneration in an allegorized but recognizably American setting. The novel opens with a reference to Jack Kennedy and closes with a phone-call to Marilyn Monroe and claims 'a certain latitude, both as to its fashion and material' which relates it not merely to the 'ideal' dreamlike world of the fable but to the violent thrillers of American popular fiction. Whatever one thinks of Mailer's views about power and sexuality this is a brilliant dramatization of them. The suspense and economy of the narrative-line, the range of characters, the use of classical myths and gothic atmosphere, are all highly effective. As a negotiation of traditional and popular forms, as a sustained structure of interlocking metaphors, *An American Dream* is one of Mailer's most controlled pieces of writing. It succeeds in almost every way that *Barbary Shore,* his earlier allegory, failed. The one question it does not resolve is the author's need to break away from the first-person mode of narration which he discusses in *Advertisements*:

> For six years I had been writing novels in the first-person . . . even though the third-person was more to my taste. Worse I seemed unable to create a narrator in the first-person who was not overdelicate, oversensitive, and painfully tender, which was an odd portrait to give because I was not delicate. . . .

Neither Rojack nor DJ, the first-person narrator of *Why Are We in Vietnam* (1967), can be called 'delicate' and with his audiovisual media hero, DJ, Mailer manages to expand his narrator's voice into a polyphonic, polymorphous choir of American speech. Like the singer Shago Martin in *An American Dream,* his voice is 'not intimate but Elizabethan, a chorus, dig?'.

It was not, however, until *The Armies of the Night* (1968), published exactly twenty years after his first novel, that Mailer moved back to third-person narration—and here it is a third-person with a difference. The authorial position is represented as neither the 'I' of his essay work, nor as an author-surrogate narrative persona like Rojack or DJ, but through the creation of a character called Norman Mailer. This simple device—calling his hero by the same name as the author whose name appears on the cover of the book—has several advantages: Mailer has a subjective vantage-point from which to expound his most pressing concerns, but at the same time the device forces a new distance into the expression of those ideas. He is able to write about the problems of America as he sees them with a new flexibility and irony, and the stridency which mars so many of his essays is absent here. The author's voice is neither excluded from the fictional frame, nor inflated to fill it, instead it is partially 'objectified' by Mailer writing in the third-person about 'Norman Mailer'. As an attempt to bridge the fiction-autobiography, novelist-reporter dichotomy which had dominated his writing for more than a decade, *The Armies of the Night* represents a major advance.

The sub-title 'History as a Novel—The Novel as History' indicates the nature of the undertaking: the attempt is to write both a history and a novel about the anti-Vietnam war march in Washington in October 1967—and in doing so to make certain points about the interrelationship between fictional and historical modes of writing. The first

section ('History as a Novel') is in his own words 'nothing but a personal history which while written as a novel was to the best of the author's memory scrupulous to facts'. In the second section ('The Novel as History') Mailer uses a more 'historic' style to write what he calls a kind of 'collective novel' about the battle of the Pentagon. The point of cross-cutting between the terms 'novel' and 'history' in this way is presumably to subvert the traditional distinction between the novel—imaginative, subjective writing—and history—factual, objective writing; to argue that in so far as history is *written* (and not just *events*) it shares certain characteristics with other forms of writing. Mailer is not suggesting that nothing exists outside discourse (which would be a rejection of ontological realism and hence idealism) but that since we cannot know 'history' except through discourses about it, historical discourse has no more privileged a relation to 'the real' than does the novel. He thus moves freely between the novelistic and the historical modes, enriching his factual account with fictional techniques—as in the speech which he inserts into the mouth of the commanding officer in 'A Palette of Tactics':

> . . . the point to keep in mind, troopers, is those are going to be American citizens out there expressing their Constitutional right to protest—that don't mean we're going to let them fart in our face—but the Constitution is a complex document with circular that is circulating sets of conditions—put it this way . . .—they start trouble with us, they'll wish they hadn't left New York unless you get killed in the stampede of us to get them.

Through this creative reconstruction, a device commonly used in classical histories, Mailer gives an 'interiority' to characters on the other side of the battle. The characters encountered by the protagonist—Lowell, Dwight Macdonald, the Marshall and the Nazi together with a host of students, demonstrators and jailbirds—are vividly presented. But to get beyond the limitations of Mailer-the-protagonist's point-of-view, to present a more inclusive 'historical' account, Mailer-the-writer invokes his authorial prerogative of omniscience. The point is neatly made: the historian is an omniscient narrator of 'collective novels'.

Like the Constitution, then, *The Armies of the Night* is 'a complex document'. It is a culminating point in the history of Mailer's literary career: another volume in the muted autobiography of the writer which runs through his work, an essay at the big novel about America in war and peace, and further than this, it is a reaffirmation of the novel as a form and a philosophical justification of the 'novelistic' approach to experience. The exchange between Robert Lowell and Norman Mailer at a Washington party before the march is a dramatic prologue to this argument. When Lowell tells him he thinks him the best journalist in America, Mailer's retort is an affirmation—not just of Mailer—but of the role of the writer:

> 'Well, Cal,' said Mailer using Lowell's nickname for the first time, 'there are times when I think of myself as being the best writer in America'.

The choice of the word 'writer' (not novelist) is his assertion of the unity of his literary activity which takes in both fiction and journalism, and his refusal of the categories of 'artistic' and 'non-artistic' forms of writing. If *An American Dream* is a bid to combine the conventions of 'serious' allegory and popular fiction, *The Armies of the Night* makes the same attempt in relation to journalism and the novel. As Rojack confronts the need to make connections between the 'intellectuals' guild' and the 'horde of the mediocre and the mad' who, in his view, people the American continent, so the hero of *The Armies of the Night* defines his responsibility to connect 'the two halves of America . . . not coming together'. Both Rojack and 'Mailer' in the later book, are writers walking the parapet between the intellectual and the popular, and Mailer with his dream of making 'a revolution in the consciousness of our time' is too ambitious a writer to settle for a minority 'art' audience.

More than ten years after the Pulitzer prize-winning *Armies of the Night,* Mailer was awarded a second Pulitzer Prize for fiction for his 'true life story' *The Executioner's Song* (1979). His work during this period continues the shift away from 'pure' fictionality in a series of engagements with popular culture—writings on sport, sexual and party politics, the space programme and the media. He uses this material, as he used the geographical and sociological descriptions in *The Naked and the Dead,* to pursue his existential questions about good and evil, the meaning of life and death. Despite some powerful short pieces like the essay entitled **'The King of the Hill'**, too often Mailer extrapolates from the detail of his material to make familiar generalizations about mystery, Dread and the technologizing of America. There is a repetitive quality about *Of a Fire on the Moon, The Prisoner of Sex* and *Marilyn* which suggests that this working-through of positions was becoming compulsive and his metaphorical flights as stylistic tic. There was also his failure to complete the big novel about America; Mailer was 800 pages into this new novel (since entitled *Ancient Evenings* and reputedly set in Egypt) when he began to write the story of Gilmore.

Apart from the financial imperatives, the story—which in an interview he described as ' . . . a found object . . . gold'—offered him a chance to develop his interests in reincarnation, the experience of working-class America and the role of the media. It also promised a new and enlarged audience, new scope and a new hero—a figure very different from himself. Most importantly, perhaps, the wealth of documentary material provided a bedrock of detail which resisted recuperation and operated as a check on Mailer's generalizing habit:

> The more I worked, the more I began to feel I didn't have the right to generalize on the material. In the past, of course, I always have. I usually had more in me to say than proper material with which to express it, so that it was natural to overflow into essays. But at this point in my life, I thought, well, the people who have chosen to listen to what I've said have registered it, I've sort of used up my audience, and I thought, well, I want another audience, I want those people who think I'm hard to read.

It is this effort to reach and represent the popular—'the mediocre and the mad who listen to popular songs and act upon coincidence', as Rojack characterized them in *An American Dream*—which informs the narrative strategy of *The Executioner's Song.* Unlike Truman Capote in *In Cold Blood,* Mailer does not use his own voice or point-of-view on the events narrated. Instead, the tale of Gilmore's release from jail in April 1976 through to his execution in January 1977 is told almost entirely in the language and from the point-of-view of those involved with Gilmore during this period. Only the use of the third-person signals the presence of the narrator, indicating that the first-person pronouns of the recorded interviews have been transposed into the third-person—that 'I was six when I fell out of the apple tree' has become 'Brenda was six when she fell out of the apple tree.' Not only have the usual tags 'she said' or 'he said' been omitted, the narrator's voice is virtually effaced in favour of the diction, syntax and grammar of the original 'speakers' or interviewees.

One important consequence of this technique is that the vast cast of characters, from East and West, are present not simply as secondary figures whom the narrator 'objectifies' for the reader in his own voice, but to some extent retain their subject-positions in the discourse. Thus their perspective, their angle on Gilmore is not qualified or situated by the narrator's 'voice-over' but by the juxtaposition of accounts: of Brenda's with Nicole's, that of the family with that of police and prison officials, the psychiatrist's with the journalists and so on. Gilmore himself, as David Lodge noted, is never used as a reflector of events. He is always the object of other characters' perceptions and when his actions are described by the narrator—for example in the two unwitnessed murder scenes—it is without any interiority. This different tactic has two effects: first it maintains the enigma of Gilmore's character, and second it reduces identification. His position as 'hero' is not endorsed by the adoption of his point-of-view—he is allowed to speak directly only through the letters and interviews which, since these appear in italics, are typographically marked off from the rest of the narrative.

The narrative organization which denies Gilmore any privileges with voice, also refuses the reader any privileged relation to an omniscient narrator of the kind Capote permits in his non-fiction fiction. Compare, for example, the description of the murderer's sister's house in *In Cold Blood* with the description of Nicole Barrett's house:

> The house, like the others on the slanting hillside street, was a conventional suburban ranch house, pleasant and commonplace. Mrs Johnson loved it; she was in love with the redwood panelling, the wall-to-wall carpeting, the picturewindows fore and aft, the view that the rear window provided—hills, a valley, then sky and ocean. And she was proud of the small back garden.
>
> Her little place was the oldest building on the block, and next to all those ranch bungalows lined up . . . like pictures in supermarket magazines, the house looked as funky as a drawing in a fairy tale. It was kind of pale lavender stucco on the outside with Hershey-brown trim. . . . In the backyard was a groovy old apple tree with

a couple of rusty wires to hold the branches together. She loved it.

Although both Capote and Mailer are using 'setting' for thematic purposes, and both descriptions depend, more or less, on the character's vocabulary and point-of-view, the degree of objectification is very different. In Capote's novel, the narrator who calls the house 'pleasant and commonplace' is clearly distinct (and distant) from the Mrs. Johnson who 'loved it'; in Mailer's description no such evaluative distance is present. This is noticeable not only in individual passages, or their use of setting, but in their presentation of the major characters. Both Capote and Mailer, for example, sketch their childhood histories, and include psychiatric reports on their subjects, but whereas Capote's text gives a certain authority to the psychological explanation for the murders, Mailer not merely refuses to give the 'professional' report on Gilmore any more status than any other point-of-view, he positions the psychiatric commentaries within a medical-legal debate on Gilmore's sanity so that they themselves become objects of scrutiny. Within *Executioner's Song* there is no single authoritative voice or consensus of views, and certainly no voice from the 'intellectual's guild' to give the reader a guided tour of middle-America, directing and explaining, instead, using a form of 'free indirect speech' Mailer ensures that it is the voices themselves ('an Elizabethan chorus, dig?') that are foregrounded.

Read as a play for many voices, it is not just another non-fiction novel about a murderer, but a novel about the state of the nation—or rather about the state of the nation's language. *The Executioner's Song* is therefore 'about' Gary Gilmore only in the sense that Joyce's *Ulysses* is 'about' 16 June 1904 and the sub-titles of two halves of the book 'Western Voices' and 'Eastern Voices' direct us toward this kind of reading.

'Western Voices', the first half, presents the smalltown thief and murderer who in Mailer's words 'was quintessentially American and yet worthy of Dostoevsky', and tells how he falls in love with a girl 'who is a bona-fide American heroine'. The latest in a long line of Mailer's homicidal heroes, Gilmore is heroic not for the way he lives but in the manner of his death. For he is the beast who begins to 'grow' (Mailer's word) into a seer when he chooses to die for his immortal soul rather than damage it further by serving another life sentence in prison in the West. His girlfriend, Nicole, is a feminine counterpart, self-destructive where Gilmore is destructive; her similarity to Mailer's other sexually 'wasted' waifs clearly establishes her as a bona-fide Mailer heroine—like Cherry and Marilyn, a victim who suffers, but this time survives her man. Not merely does Mailer not generalize about his material as he does—disastrously I think—in *Marilyn,* the effect of the fictional strategy (her presentation in 'free indirect speech') is such that there is less sexual objectification than with almost any other Mailer heroine since Elena Esposito of *Deer Park.* By allowing her to, as it were, 'speak for herself' the text effectively distances itself from the sexual objectification it describes. This is another of the complex effects produced by Mailer's narrative strategy.

The second half of *The Executioner's Song,* entitled 'Eastern Voices', in a sense continues the story of Gilmore—his imprisonment, refusal to appeal against sentence, and his eventual execution. But it tells another story of how an enterprising, unscrupulous writer called Larry Schiller—of some talent if small achievement—collected the material for a book on Gary Gilmore. The means whereby Schiller negotiated with Gilmore, his relations and lawyers, his interview techniques and sub-contractual relations with other agents and reporters, as well as his personal life, are then recounted—again from various points-of-view. Almost all of Mailer's novels have contained a figure of the writer (Hearn in *Naked,* Lovett in *Barbary Shore,* Sergius and Eitel in *Deer Park,* Rojack in *Dream,* DJ in *Why* and Mailer himself in *Armies of the Night*) and the second half of *The Executioner's Song* continues the saga of the writer and his conditions of existence in a commercial, media-ridden world. Further, the second half of the novel in effect lays bare the devices whereby the first half—Gilmore's story—has been constructed. It partially 'deconstructs' that story by narrating the story of the writer, Schiller, behind whom, as the direct heir to his labours, stands—none other—Norman Mailer! (A fuller 'deconstruction' would have to include the tale of the two-and-a-half years that *he* spent writing *The Executioner's Song* but, as it is, that story is split off into the Afterword to the main text.) In addition, certain passages in *The Executioner's Song* ironically allude to these processes and problems in writing; when for example Mailer presents Barry Farrell, a writer subcontracted by Schiller to conduct an interview with Gilmore, he raises the whole question of authorship:

> It looked to Farrell as if Gilmore was now setting out to present the particular view of himself he wanted people to keep. In that sense he was being his own writer. It was fascinating to Barry. He was being given the Gilmore canon, good self-respecting convict canon.

The intricacies of narrative form—the question of who is doing what to whom in the writing and reading of fiction—are playfully put before the reader here. In *The Executioner's Song,* as in all his earlier writings, we can read the 'true-life story' of an American novelist and his struggle to find the best possible form.

Too serious a writer to play nineteenth-century 'artist' with the novel, Mailer broke with conventional realism after his very first full-length work. The sequence of experiments which followed represent his belief that 'preserving one's artistic identity is not nearly so important . . . as finding a new attack on the elusive nature of reality' that 'primarily, one's style is only a tool to use on a dig'. Mailer's achievement is not just the individual novels, considerable though many of these are, but the use to which he has put his talent. He has attempted to take the novel out of its canonized existence—the good self-respecting 'art' canon—back into relation with other forms of writing, in the firm belief that only an alliance between the different literary practices—journalism, autobiography, history etc.—will safeguard the novel-form from the assaults of the non-literary mass-media forms which in the twentieth century dominate Western culture. He has thus proved a radical not merely in his politics, but in the sense that he has tried to return to the roots of the novel. For, according to one formulation,

> The novel develops from the lineage of non-fictitious narrative forms—the letter, the journal, the memoir or biography, the chronicle or history; it develops, so to speak, out of documents.

Mailer's non-fiction novel draws precisely on these sources and *The Executioner's Song* is in my view an achievement which suggests that he has the talent, and the stamina, to go forward from there. (pp. 222-36)

> *Jean Radford, "Norman Mailer: The True Story of an American Writer," in* American Fiction: New Readings, *edited by Richard Gray, London: Vision Press, 1983, pp. 222-37.*

Denis Donoghue   (review date 29 July 1984)

[*Donoghue is an Irish critic and educator. In the review below, he finds Mailer's novel* Tough Guys Don't Dance *unconvincing in plot and characterization.*]

The first question [in *Tough Guys Don't Dance*] is, Did Tim Madden, drunk and drugged, murder Jessica Pond? If not, who did? And in any case, how did Jessica Pond's severed head turn up in Madden's marijuana patch in Truro?

Norman Mailer's new novel is a murder mystery. The scene is Provincetown, Mass., on Cape Cod—"And for fall, winter and spring, nothing is superior to little old P-town"—the time is November, all the visitors have gone. Madden, an ex-bartender, is a writer of sorts. He has also done three years in jail for drug-running. His wife, Patty Lareine, has left him, so he is hitting the bottle in The Widow's Walk bar. Things get blurred when he blunders into a conversation between a California lady and her sexually ambiguous escort. In no time at all another female head turns up, severed and blond—"Any lady who chooses to become a blonde is truly blonde," according to one of the novel's more charming passages. Two hundred pages later we have assembled, by my count, seven corpses, not including Madden's dog, Stunts, killed by Spider Nisseh's knife.

Mailer reported, in *Pieces and Pontifications* (1982), that he had thought of writing a novel for which Provincetown and its environs would make a proper setting. "Living in Provincetown on the edge of those rare, towering and windy dunes . . . I had begun to think of a novel so odd and so horrible that I hesitated for years to begin it." He imagined "a group of seven or eight bikers, hippies and studs plus a girl or two living in the scrub thickets that sat in some of the valleys between the dunes." In any event, he didn't write the book. His mind lit out for Alaska, and the book became *Why Are We in Vietnam?*

Again, in **"Advertisements for Myself on the Way Out"** Mailer imagined a millionaire pimp, Marion Faye, planning a murder to take place in a house in Provincetown. The third section of that piece is a description of the town and the dunes: "There are few places on the eastern seaboard where one could bury a man as easily and leave one's chances so to nature, for the wind could leave the corpse under twenty feet of fill, or as easily could discover the cadaver before the cells were cold."

Mailer didn't write the novel he projected, but he continued to think of Provincetown as a strangely suggestive place—"in winter the town is filled with spirits"—a place, he said, "for murderers and suicides." He recalled that "a few years ago, a young Portuguese from a family of fishermen killed four girls, dismembered their bodies, and buried the pieces in twenty small and scattered graves." The town, he said, "is so naturally spooky in mid-winter and provides such a sense of omens waiting to be magnetized into lines of force that the novel in my mind seemed more a magical object than a fiction, a black magic." Deducing a theory of fiction from these intimations, Mailer speculated that "the novelist fashions a totem just as much as an aesthetic, and his real aim, not even known necessarily to himself, is to create a diversion in the fields of dread, a sanctuary in some of the arenas of magic."

Tough Guys Don't Dance isn't the odd and horrible novel Mailer thought of extracting from the dunes of Cape Cod. There are no bikers or hippies, no easy riders. The studs come from the rising bourgeoisie. But the spooks are fully acknowledged, sensed at large in the landscape and beneath the sand. The ghosts of whaling captains mingle with those of the Pilgrim Fathers who landed first near Provincetown before going on to Plymouth. Mailer's plot and characters don't correspond to anything in his account of the projected novel of Provincetown, but I imagine the general atmosphere of the novel arises from his first intention.

It is my impression that in *Tough Guys Don't Dance* Mailer planned to relax after the appalling exertions of *Ancient Evenings.* Or to rotate his crops. Think of a novel by Dashiell Hammett and transpose it into Mailer's more flamboyant style. Then, to thicken the mixture far beyond any requirements of mystery novels, think of Mailer reaching back to *Barbary Shore,* the story **"The Time of Her Time"** and *An American Dream* for sundry allusions and pontifications. Then you have a fairly accurate notion of an evident intention. Some of the correspondences between the new novel and earlier work are unmistakable. The repeated motif of climbing Provincetown Monument corresponds to the accepted risk of the parapet in *An American Dream.* And so forth.

But the comparison with Hammett doesn't extend beyond Mailer's general intention. Hammett was far more equably in possession of his genre than Mailer is, so he engaged his narrative without fuss. Mailer has let his obsessions dominate the narrative, to the extent of confounding main roads with side issues, highways with detours. Where Hammett was cool, Mailer is loose, his self-indulgence all too assertively a matter of putting his obsessions yet again on show.

I have a small theory, touching upon Mailer's fiction as a whole. I take it that the formative cast of his mind is naturalistic, in the sense of the naturalism that Yeats described by saying that "the romantic movement with its turbulent heroism, its self-assertion, is over, superseded by a new naturalism that leaves man helpless before the contents of his own mind." Suppose, without being too intelligent about it, that the contents of one's mind are mostly given, inherited like one's parents or the condition of growing up a Jewish boy in Brooklyn, or imposed by the circumstance of a war in the Pacific. Then, with talent to the degree of genius, it would be almost natural to write *The Naked and the Dead,* a novel in its main qualities naturalistic, close kin to Dreiser's fiction if locally responsive to Dos Passos's. I take Mailer to be a naturalist, according to this typology.

But a more accurate account of his mind would allow for a certain refusal of naturalism, in the form of a scruple or some revulsion against its authority. Such a mind would retain romanticism's self-assertion, not as a settled conviction but as a sporadic gesture of recalcitrance, representing the mind's refusal to coincide with its official character. Against the accepted force of circumstance and contingency, the mind would exert, intermittently, a force equal, opposite and correspondingly extreme; setting two admitted violences in combat. In those intermittences, the whole human story would amount to a man's will and what it opposes. Or to a sensed complicity between one's will and what Madden calls "that strange will so external to myself," which drives him beyond any action his will would recognize as its chosen form. It would be natural for such a mind to give as much credence to ghosts as to bodies, to hallucinations as to verities, to dream play as to ratiocination. It would work as nonchalantly by improvising as by following the established procedures of cognition. So, in the new novel, Madden is thrown into a world of demonic combat, a frantic compound of "that fiend who dwells in the sweet kundalini of our spine," otherwise named as "the unmanageable in myself," recognized in sinister communion with "the nearness of the Devil waiting to receive me" and, succinctly for once, as "something other."

Mailer during his service in the United States Army in World War II.

Within this structure of interests—the simultaneous presence of naturalism and the unofficial romanticism that scorns it—we can locate Mailer's favorite ensemble of emotions: fear, anxiety, dread, desire, guilt. In these, the organism is at war with itself and relishes the war. I think of O'Shaugnessy's phrases in **"The Time of Her Time"**— "the clear bell-like adrenalins of clean anxiety" and "the rarer amalgams of guilt."

The most typical episode in *Tough Guys Don't Dance* occurs when Madden, accompanied by Stunts, discovers the severed heads in his marijuana patch and carries them back to his car. He is attacked by the villains, Nissen and Stoodie, Nissen with a knife, Stoodie with a tire iron. The details of the fight can't be paraphrased. Madden survives it and drives home. "Shall I tell you the virtues of such a war?" he offers. In fact, he doesn't recite them, but reports that "if not for the war by the side of the road, I could never have slept." As it was, "I slumbered as well as any of those who were dead."

"Though a quarrel in the streets is a thing to be hated," the poet Keats said, "the energies displayed in it are fine; the commonest man shows a grace in his quarrel—by a superior being our reasonings may take the same tone—

though erroneous they may be fine." Madden, Mailer's surrogate in this respect, would offer a Keatsian justification for his violence, if the question were raised. Mailer would justify it further by seeing it as heroic resistance not only to evil at large but to the naturalism that demeans his energy. So a fight with thugs becomes "the war." The justification is then developed as a particular style of exorbitance, not so much depicting reality as usurping it to enforce a transfigured sense of human possibility. It is as if Mailer were intermittently what his sense of reality would hardly allow him to be for long, a visionary, floating as free of history and order as of contingency.

Style—"the labial tortures and languors of words," as Mailer once called it—is the only form in which this visionary desire can be appeased: in his case, a neo-Elizabethan style in which sentences scorn the reality they ostensibly annotate. His theory would say that a sense of reality, in that conventional phrase, is merely a bad habit, and should be defeated by exerting nearly any violence upon it. But scorn, too, can be a bad habit when its gratifications are not earned. It is hard to put up with Madden's grandiloquence when, instead of saying "I couldn't face it," he says "I preferred to molder in the last suppurations of cowardice." Or "The thought of being knocked cold was an anodyne dear as nepenthe." How dear is nepenthe? "I made myself a drink to coat the double barrels of my fatigue." To what the what?

It is hard to put up with these exorbitances, but Mailer's achievement in other books makes it worth trying. I think I understand why Mailer refuses to let his sentences be replaced by their meaning. The high style, which sobriety is apt to rebuke as a Mardi Gras of metaphor, is Mailer's way of forcing the reader to sense continuous turbulence between the words; or at least to feel tension between the local meaning the reader is inclined to settle for, and the scornful rival meaning the sentences insist on. The reader is asked to respond to a fury in the words. I read such sentences as tokens of a desperate, because unmoored, spirituality; as "notes from underground," or frantic gestures to intuit a vision for which the only evidence is one man's compulsive need of it. The sentences require the kind of indulgence asked of readers of Yeats's poems, which run to astrologies and spiritualities hardly better authenticated than Mailer's insistent motifs. Most readers are willing to let Yeats's forms of nonsense clear a space, against conventional pressure, for his imagination.

But what I mostly feel, reading *Tough Guys Don't Dance,* is the wretched inadequacy of the novel to the intention it clearly enough avows. There are good things in the book, notably a warmly imagined relation between Madden and his father. There is a handsome scene in which Madden recalls that, as a boy, he lost a fight his friends said he should have won and his father said, "That's friends; you lost it in the last round." There are vivid descriptions of town and beach. And a few good jokes. But the novel as a whole is frigid, less a work of relaxed skill than a mechanical assertion of Mailer's will in the forms it habitually takes when the temperature is low.

The main trouble is that Madden is preposterously unequal to the work he is supposed to do. He is hardly imagined at all. His name merely brings together the already well-documented sequence of Mailer's obsessions: God, the devil, magic, asserted presences, assorted voices, what Mailer once called "the animism of the wind and an old house," fantasies of power, the melodrama of murder as "the cure for all the rest." In *The Naked and the Dead* and even more tellingly in *An American Dream* and *Why Are We in Vietnam?* hallucinations exerted pressure, much to their advantage, upon an official world in every sense hostile to them. The occult deliverances of a mind upon no authority but its own were scandals, justified by their critical relation to the forces they contended with. But in *Tough Guys Don't Dance* they are not required to contend with anything. Monstrous familiar images swim yet again to Mailer's eye, but no convincing reality is set against them. The book is a rigmarole of notions supposedly elucidating Madden's consciousness, but in fact borrowed for the occasion from the discursive books in which Mailer has repeatedly asserted them. This wouldn't matter if Mailer had imagined, for his hero, not Madden but himself; or a character as fully present through his notions and obsessions as Mailer is. But Madden is nothing, compared to what he needs to be. And since he is nothing, the reality

he supposedly mediates, the other characters we receive through his bloodshot eyes, are negligible.

No diversion is created, this time, in the fields of dread, no sanctuary in any of the arenas of magic. (pp. 1, 32-3)

> *Denis Donoghue, "Death on the Windy Dunes," in* The New York Times Book Review, *July 29, 1984, pp. 1, 32-3.*

Jack Beatty   (review date 27 August 1984)

[*In the following review, Beatty characterizes* Tough Guys Don't Dance *as a commercially motivated "embarrassment" that "makes painful reading, especially for those of us who honor Mailer's power as a writer and a visionary."*]

You have felt the urge. You're sitting at your desk, surrounded by hills of unpaid bills, when suddenly it hits you: you'll take a month off, write a mystery, and make a modest killing. Most of us resist that urge. Unhappily, Norman Mailer did not. *Tough Guys Don't Dance,* Mr. Mailer's first try at the mystery genre, is an embarrassment—and a warning. If a writer of Mr. Mailer's large talent and even larger ambition can't manage a mystery, what chance have you got?

Tough Guys is set in Provincetown, in gray November. (Mr. Mailer captures the emotional geography of the Cape in winter with a concreteness of detail and evocativeness of imagery that deserts him when he puts his prose to other tasks.) The hero is a 40-year-old ex-bartender and writer named Tim Madden; and the subject is murder, or it would be if Mailer had kept his well-known obsessions—with cancer, courage, and the interpenetration of spiritual forces—from blighting the few shoots of suspense that pop their heads above the thick surface slush of philosophy.

As the novel opens Mr. Madden's wife, Patty Lareine, has left him, for reasons that remain unclear to me, and to console himself he seduces a woman he meets in a local bar, even though she is accompanied by another man. I say seduces, but really all he does is expose himself to her. He being a Mailer man, the sight is impressive; she being a Mailer woman, it is irresistible.

The next day he awakes with an amnesia-inducing hangover to confront the following realizations: that blood is smeared over the front seat of his Porsche, that the Provincetown Police Chief is curious as to the whereabouts of Patty Lareine, and that the foot locker where he hides his dope now also contains the head of a blonde. Is it the woman from the bar or Patty Lareine? Hysterical, Madden flies from the locker without finding out. Meanwhile other characters are being introduced and, in the manner of horror films, quickly killed off. Soon the locker contains two blonde heads. Just in the nick of time, Madden's dad, a garrulous longshoreman and Maileresque philosopher, arrives to help his son clear his name and discover the real murderer.

The chief suspects are the Police Chief, Patty Lareine's ex-husband and sundry Provincetown toughs, including one man who films his copulations with his lover: "It was awful to see. He used to urinate on her, there also for us to see on the TV screen. He had grown a wispy-light-brown D'Artagnan mustache which he would tweak like a villain while he hosed her down. . . . " And more in that vein. Mr. Mailer's male characters are nearly all mouthpieces for him, so vanity dictates that he make them at least a tad interesting. Not so his women. As in pornography, they are merely sexual appendages.

The writing is laced with campy implication; one can see why *Vanity Fair* ran two excerpts from the novel. "On the Cape, in winter, nothing ever came right to the point," a sentence reminds, just as we are getting fed up with the plot's refusal to do just that. On the other hand there are such unintentionally revealing sentences as "My mind was yawing like a wind in the hills." Well, I wouldn't have put it quite that cruelly. And of course there are the old familiar Mailer phrases " . . . you could sit down and take a taste of the marrow of the mood . . . "; and the too familiar Maileresque identifications with criminality, " . . . I gained (could I term it that) some small measure of compassion for all who are afflicted by the compulsion to go out and do what is absolutely not to be done—whether it is the seduction of little boys or the rape of adolescent girls. . . . " One has to keep reminding oneself that this novel is the work of a man now past sixty, for nothing in it would.

Dull, turgid, bare of wit, *Tough Guys* makes painful reading, especially for those of us who honor Mailer's power as a writer and a visionary. Perhaps if candidates were paid large sums of money to run for public office, Mailer could afford to make a fool of himself by launching another campaign for mayor of New York. That way he would get it out of his system, and would not need to repeat this successful experiment in literary humiliation.

> *Jack Beatty, "The Faked and the Dead," in* The New Republic, *Vol. 191, No. 9, August 27, 1984, p. 40.*

James Campbell   (review date 19 October 1984)

[*In the review below, Campbell views* Tough Guys Don't Dance *as unsuccessful due to deficiencies of plot and Mailer's failure to differentiate his protagonist's voice and character from his own.*]

[In *Tough Guys Don't Dance*], Timothy Madden, hard drinker, would-be writer, amateur nude photographer, lately deserted by the wife he first met at a swap, wakes up one morning to the familiar hangover plus a nagging suspicion that he may have murdered a woman the night before, if not two (the optional one being the deserter). The women have disappeared, the inside of Madden's car is covered in blood, and buried in his private marijuana patch he finds a severed head which he can look upon long enough only to remark that, like both the missing ladies, it is blonde. Which, if either, is it? and whodunit?

As the opening to a thriller, this is promising. But Norman Mailer has trouble with plots, as he admitted during an interview with me in 1983. "They never come naturally to

me. I have to work them out bit by bit, and eke them out." For that reason, it has been noted, his talent is less well suited to fiction than to journalism, where the narrative procedure is often fixed by the course of actual events. The book which best illustrates this talent at work is *The Executioner's Song*, which Mailer, however—unhappy at being merely America's finest journalist—attempted to disguise as "A True Life Novel."

Tough Guys Don't Dance shows how that old plot trouble continues to worry him. After the first chapter, which has Madden musing on the first pilgrims who landed nearby, and comparing their hopes with his own deeds (which once earned him a spell in prison), the story lumbers from step to step with little sense of its own direction. Clumsy coincidences move it on, as much as sudden recollections of hidden clues and the introduction of important new characters late in the game. By these means, Madden pieces together the fragments of his nightmare, and his creator attempts to suggest how it might be part of a greater dread which has clouded the American Dream for good.

The novel of that name was Mailer's last attempt to write in what the blurb-writer calls his "tough, raw, uncompromising style." As there, the cast in *Tough Guys Don't Dance* consists mainly of blondes ("angels or bitches"), faggots, and men who are "as powerful as a Kodiak bear"; the bar-room jokes prove once and for all that a sense of humour has no place in a tough guy's armoury, and the sexual element is puerile, even by Mailer's standards: black men have big penises; one character likes to urinate on his wife while video-taping the performance which he then shows publicly; another says "I honour you because you are man enough to fuck your wife." Everybody seems to have slept with everyone else's wife, though they don't always remember having done so. "Despair," aphorizes Madden, "is the emotion we feel at the death of beings in us."

Or at the collapse of the writer in us. How can Mailer write as badly as this? "Although Patty Lareine was trim to bursting in her build, peppy as a spice jar, he modulated the moxie of her personality down to more delicate herbs." One reason must be the much-repeated publicity item of the great number of wives and children he is obliged to clothe and feed, but the deeper affliction is one which he has suffered since the start of his career: Mailer is corrupted by his own brilliance. No other American writer of his generation informs his writing with such a rich fund of ideas, yet Mailer is frequently seduced by a thought before it has been tested. In the writing of fiction this has proved to be disabling.

Tough Guys Don't Dance provides new skin for a lot of old anxieties, familiar from previous novels and from the essays (which is their proper home): the relationship between social behaviour and cancer; the action of man on earth influencing the struggle between God and Satan; plus many sexistential speculations. This hints at Madden's greatest flaw as a literary creation, which is that he has no narrative voice separate from that of his creator. And there are other similarities: both are writers, boxing aficionados, woman hunters, heavy drinkers, drug takers (formerly, in the creator's case), familiar with life in prison, and liable to attack their wives. Madden is not Mailer, certainly, but Mailer is charmed by what he claims to deplore, and cannot resist the murky atmosphere of Madden's mind. In attempting to moralize over it, he has succeeded only in adding to the round of dirty jokes.

> James Campbell, "From Dream to Dread," in
> The Times Literary Supplement, No. 4255,
> October 19, 1984, p. 1178.

Carol Iannone   (essay date October 1985)

[*In the essay excerpted below, Iannone examines why Mailer has enjoyed major support from intellectuals of his generation.*]

If there is one thing the case of Norman Mailer teaches us, it is that ideas matter, that they shape the common life both of the individual and of the culture. For the ideas propagated by Norman Mailer, along with those of such figures as Norman O. Brown and Paul Goodman, exercised a tangible influence in dragging America out of the Eisenhower years into the Aquarian age of the 60's and beyond. And in advancing those ideas, Mailer had the enthusiastic support of a perhaps surprising number of the major intellectuals of our time.

At this point it may be hard to see just what was so magnetic about Mailer in the first place. To date, his prolific but uneven output has yielded a number of notable books, but he can hardly be said to have borne out the ecstatic expectations that many once attached to him (and some still do). The fact is, however, that it was not entirely in terms of literary excellence that he exercised his appeal on people languishing in the supposedly arid air of the late 50's; he spoke, rather, to a hungering need for getting the life of the mind into touch with the life of the instincts. As Irving Howe sums it up for the "New York intellectual group" in Peter Manso's *Mailer: His Life and Times,* a 700-page compendium of reminiscences by family, friends, associates, and colleagues, "We were essentially rationalistic people for better or worse—he was still able to get at certain things we could not. We admired it, I think even envied it. He was our genius." (p. 60)

To be sure, not all the members of the "New York intellectual group" that adopted Mailer as "our genius" were blind to the morally disturbing aspects of his work, the life of the instincts being notorious for disrupting more ordinary decencies. Specifically, his now legendary essay, **"The White Negro"** (1957), celebrating what he called "hipsterism," offered as an example the courage that might drive two strong eighteen-year-old hoodlums to beat in the brains of a middle-aged candy-store keeper, thereby attacking the institution of private property and "daring the unknown." This was greeted at the time by Norman Podhoretz as "one of the most morally gruesome ideas I have ever come across, and which indicates where the ideology of hipsterism can lead." But a year later Podhoretz expressed sympathy "with Mailer's latest effort to maintain a sense of huge possibility, even if one is totally out of sympathy with some of the doctrines he has recently been preaching." And William Phillips, the editor of *Partisan Review,* observes in *Mailer* that "while 'The White Negro' was considered intellectually nonacceptable, it was still acceptable for purposes of fictional exploration." Thus, although no one really ignored the ugliness of some of Mailer's ideas, he seemed to operate under a kind of extra-moral extenuation. The reprehensible notions advanced in **"The White Negro"** could be understood somehow as a necessary element in the dissection of the world of the instincts that it was Mailer's assigned mission to undertake.

For his part, Mailer was glad enough to assume this public role as "genius" of the irrational, which he may have recognized as his ticket to greatness. After the tremendous success of *The Naked and the Dead,* according to Barbara Probst Solomon in the Manso book, Mailer had panicked at getting "caught short being a leftover Dreiser or Dos Passos." And as Mailer himself comments here:

> Writing **"The White Negro"** emboldened me to raise more questions. . . . It gave me the courage to make remarks of the order of "I shall attempt to answer the question of "—the oft-quoted sentence in which I list all those things— "murder, suicide, orgy, orgasm, incest," and so forth. My true purpose as a writer, I recognized, might be to tackle questions like that. They were going to be my frontier, and if I had any chance at all of becoming a great writer it was to move in that direction.

Not long after **"The White Negro,"** however, Mailer's real-life flirtations with violence (which had to that point found outlets in drinking and brawling), passed over into the nearly fatal stabbing of his second wife, Adele, and it began to be clear just how much the public and private selves had fused. Mailer's lawyer, Joseph Brill, declared at the time that "This is a talent that must be protected," and Mailer himself pleaded his own cause by telling the judge, "If you put me in Bellevue, it will be an indictment of my *work* as the work of a crazy man" (emphasis added).

While not everyone went so far as the friend who felt that Mailer "finally did to Adele what should've been done years earlier," or as his mother, who reflected, "If Norman would stop marrying these women who make him do these terrible things . . . ," there were many who believed he could not be held responsible for his deed, who saw him as a victim of uncontrollable forces, who worried less over the state of his soul than over the state of his career. In *Mailer,* playwright Maria Irene Fornes seems alone to have glimpsed how profoundly Mailer's public role had superseded ordinary moral considerations:

> Norman I saw about two months after the stabbing. I wasn't close to them anymore, but he told me that at first they said that Adele had fallen on something, on broken glass, but then he'd decided the next day, "After all I couldn't hide behind a woman's skirt." To me that was really so sad and ugly. I mean, he stabbed her. An ordinary person commits a stabbing, he doesn't have this choice, whether to hide behind this or that. I'm talking about Norman's privilege, that even in a moment of despair he is reacting in a privileged manner. . . . It's like saying "I won't go

to jail in Alabama, I'll go to jail in West New-port."

Fittingly, however, the entire episode—which did indeed include some time in Bellevue—failed to put even a dent in Mailer's career; on the contrary, it helped to solidify his reputation as a fearless explorer of the self. Yet from the vantage point of today it must be said that as his sense of himself as a public figure grew stronger, his understanding of himself seems to have grown ever fainter. Although many speak of his courage, perhaps the most important act of courage, that of genuine self-discovery, seems to have remained beyond him, and the various autobiographical reflections gathered in such works as ***Advertisements for Myself, Cannibals and Christians,*** and so forth, while full of self-revelation, appear devoid of self-insight. Even his famous autobiographical style, in which he speaks of himself, dissociatedly, in the third person, tends to feed this escape from self-confrontation.

It should thus scarcely have been surprising that some two decades after he stabbed his wife Mailer found himself involved in another, oddly similar, legal and moral imbroglio. For some time since the late 70's he had been in correspondence with a prisoner named Jack Henry Abbott who had spent twenty-five of his thirty-seven years behind bars, in part for having killed a man. Thanks largely to a letter written by Mailer attesting to the prisoner's literary talent, Abbott was set free on parole despite psychiatrists' warnings about his tendency to violence. During Abbott's first weeks out of prison, he lived in a halfway house on the Bowery—in his words, "the most violent and bombed out area in New York City." But his life was not confined to the Bowery; a book of his prison memoirs, *The Belly of the Beast,* was published to great acclaim, and he was a frequent guest at the Mailer home in New York and at least once in Provincetown. He was, however, also growing more hostile and restive, and had begun to carry a knife. One night outside a Greenwich Village restaurant, he plunged it into the heart of a twenty-two-year-old man named Richard Adan—an aspiring actor and playwright, a newlywed working part-time as a waiter in his father-in-law's restaurant. Adan's last words were, "You didn't have to kill me."

The detective assigned to this case, William Majeski, had "seen a lot of bodies," but he found that

> this was different. Although Adan was twenty-two, he looked younger, and his face, the expression, was angelic. Also there was a tremendous amount of blood. The knife had gone to the heart, and apparently just about every drop of blood in his body had been pumped out. There was literally a pool going from the body across the sidewalk to the curb and out into the gutter.

Claims by Abbott that Adan had intended him harm turned out to be quite false; as this book makes clear, Abbott was filtering events through a prison paranoia. Indeed, according to Abbott's lawyer Ivan Fisher, Mailer himself said to Abbott over the phone, "Look, I don't care what you say, you killed a decent guy. You keep talking about what a crazy he was, but I checked him out. That kid was sweet as hell. Admit you did a lousy thing, admit you're gonna have to pay for it. . . . Stop lying to yourself."

Perhaps a little like Voltaire, however, who reportedly refused to discuss his free moral views at the dinner table lest his servants overhear and rob him, Mailer spoke one way to Abbott in private while in public his story was different, relying heavily on the principle of literary extenuation. "Culture is worth a little risk," he asserted, adding, "I'm willing to gamble with a portion of society to save this man's talent." Nor did he neglect to mention the extenuating circumstances springing out of America's "fascist" heart—an *idée fixe* for Mailer—in particular the prison conditions Abbott had suffered and in general the "violence" of our state and our institutions.

Mailer did issue enough statements of self-blame—if none of self-shame—to satisfy a number of his admirers, from Liz Smith to George Plimpton. Others among his erstwhile supporters had fallen away over the years, in varying degrees of disgust and disagreement, and the Abbott episode merely confirmed their more sober view. Disturbingly, however, some still seem caught in the Mailer mystique. Thus, Irving Howe's remark on the Abbott affair— "My guess is that I wouldn't think Abbott's as talented as Norman does, but it's not criminal to make a mistake"— almost makes it sound as if Mailer's failure here were one of literary judgment.

At another point, Howe castigates himself for not having fought with Mailer over the storekeeper passage in **"The White Negro"** (first published in Howe's magazine *Dissent*)—actually, this is not the only celebratory passage on violence in the essay—and wonders aloud, "Would he still defend that sentence about the eighteen-year-olds 'daring the unknown' by murdering a fifty-year-old storekeeper? That seems to me crucial. That's where it begins, you see." Similarly, Diana Trilling muses, "What are we allowed to get away with by calling it literature rather than life? Was Norman's hipster, his 'White Negro,' entirely a figure of speech? I'm not at all sure, and I don't think Norman himself has quite figured that one out either."

Why do Howe and Mrs. Trilling still trouble themselves over this issue? It would seem that more than enough evidence has accumulated to show that Norman Mailer has trafficked in ideas that are evil, and that have borne fruit after their own kind. Too, Mailer has had ample opportunity to repudiate "that sentence" and others like it; the fact that he has not done so hardly entitles him to the continuing benefit of the doubt. It would seem to suggest not that he isn't "sure," or that he hasn't "quite figured that one out," but that he is, and that he has.

Mrs. Trilling's perseverance seems especially baffling since she emphatically observes of the infamous sentence that it was "bad writing because it was bad thinking because it was bad being." But she was apparently impressed with Mailer's behavior on the Dick Cavett show during the Abbott affair, feeling that he had come a long way from his "hipster" days. (A transcript of the interview reveals that despite obligatory breast-beating, Mailer withdrew nothing and in fact reiterated his views on individual violence being in many ways a natural response to the "violence of the state.") Mrs. Trilling's words close [*Mailer*]; in them she terms Mailer "the best writing artist of our time" and expresses encouragement for his "excursions into dissidence." Although she is careful to call for balance—"My superego friends could use the correction in Norman just as Norman needed the principle of control which they might teach him"—her position depressingly suggests that nothing at all has been learned since the 50's.

One of the women recorded in this book reveals a great deal about Mailer's life and times when she remarks: "We were all terribly Scott Fitzgeraldish, very dramatic and romantic . . . having high times. It didn't occur to me that anybody was really going off the wall." Yet Fitzgerald saw through his own boozy romantic destructiveness, while Mailer seems less to resemble Fitzgerald than he does one of Fitzgerald's fictional characters, the ones who break and smash things and then retreat unreflectingly back into money and privilege. To Jack Henry Abbott, after the Adan stabbing, Mailer confided that he had felt the same "compulsion of fate" when he stabbed his wife Adele, "that it was irreversible, the logic of events" (in Abbott's words). This, presumably, is the same logic according to which playing with fire means that someone will get burned. Yes, ideas do matter. Even, or perhaps especially, bad ones. (pp. 61-2, 65)

> *Carol Iannone, " 'Our Genius': Norman Mailer & the Intellectuals," in* Commentary, *Vol. 80, No. 4, October, 1985, pp. 60-2, 65.*

Maurice A. Mierau   (essay date Fall 1986)

[*In the following essay, Mierau compares Mailer's treatment of an antiwar march on the Pentagon in* The Armies of the Night *to Mikhail Bakhtin's "concept of the Medieval Carnival, or the Carnivalesque, which both parodies official norms and religious formulas and functions as a renewing mechanism for the whole community."*]

"I'm not so sure I want a revolution," said Norman Mailer less than four months after the completion of *The Armies of the Night,* "some of those kids are awfully dumb." Mailer's ambivalences, evasions and self-deceptions about his role as a political prophet have rarely been as cogently expressed. These ambivalences, however, exist as much in Mailer's "nonfiction novel" as they do in his casual remarks, and they are evidence of a consistent failure in *Armies* of the political in favor of the mythic and the esthetic. Andrew Gordon, commenting on the book [in his *An American Dreamer: A Psychoanalytic Study of the Fiction of Norman Mailer*], proposes that "form is, among other things, a system of defense," and he goes on to cite Mas'ud Zavarzadeh's belief that the form Mailer's "defense" takes is a kind of literary "schizophrenia." If, as Robert Merrill claims [in his *Norman Mailer*], *Armies* is indeed a "powerful synthesis of Mailer's artistic and prophetic ambitions," formal "schizophrenia" should not be any part of it. Yet it is apparent that any "nonfiction novel" is at odds with itself in ways that contradict grandiose ambitions on the part of its author; thus Gordon perceptively entitles his chapter on *Armies* "Mailer vs. Mailer."

In his ambitious attempt to wed, however, schizophrenically, history and the novel, cosmic vision and politics, prophecy and personal comment, Mailer resorts to a form that Sacvan Bercovitch has written about as "the American Jeremiad" [in his book of the same title]. The American jeremiad, according to Bercovitch, is rooted in early New England sermonizing and electioneering, where it began to function as a fusion (often self-contradictory) of sacred Christian mission and secular ambition. He describes Mailer's book in terms of the jeremiad's characteristic self-contradictions, seeing *Armies* as "a self-enclosed bipolar vision," which makes it something of what he terms the "anti-jeremiad," or "the denunciation of all ideals, sacred and secular, on the grounds that America is a lie." Of course, there is a fundamental ambiguity, if not contradiction, in this definition, since no one who gets worked up enough to write or deliver a jeremiad is utterly without idealism or hope. Mailer's novel is a bravura exercise on this ambiguous ground, and the political (non)implications of this exercise need to be pursued.

The double-edgedness of the American jeremiad finds its great locus, writes Bercovitch, in American literature: "American writers have tended to see themselves as outcasts and isolates, prophets crying in the wilderness. So they have been, as a rule: *American* Jeremiahs, simultaneously lamenting a declension and celebrating a national dream. Their major works are the most striking testimony we have to the power and reach of the American jeremiad." This double movement of the jeremiad, "lamenting" and "celebrating," is very close to Mikhail Bakhtin's concept of the medieval carnival, or the carnivalesque, which both parodies official norms and religious formulas and functions as a renewing mechanism for the whole community. This conjunction between the jeremiad and the carnivalesque is important in that it provides a powerful tool for interpreting American literary and cultural history. Bercovitch, for example, observes that "The American Puritan jeremiad was the ritual of a culture on an errand—which is to say, a culture based on a faith in process. Substituting teleology for hierarchy, it discarded the Old World ideal of stasis for a New World vision of the future." Given this definition of the jeremiad in the New World, it is not at all far-fetched to say that Bercovitch sees the New World as a carnivalesque one in the Bakhtinian sense, for Bakhtin defines the carnivalesque [in his *Rabelais and His World*] as follows: "As opposed to the official feast, one might say that carnival celebrated temporary liberation from the prevailing truth and from the established order; it marked the suspension of all hierarchical rank, privileges, norms, and prohibitions. Carnival was the true feast of time, the feast of becoming, change, and renewal. It was hostile to all that was immortalized and completed." In other words, the carnivalesque and marketplace forms of expression of the classical medieval period were at base anti-European just as, in Bercovitch's formulation, was the Puritan errand. The belief in the "progress of man" held by the participants in these medieval carnivals is comparable to the belief in "the progress of the kingdom of God" evinced by Bercovitch's Puritans.

Linda Hutcheon is, to my knowledge, the only scholar who [in her *A Theory of Parody: The Teachings of Twenti-*

eth-Century Art Forms] has made a connection between Bakhtin's concept of the carnivalesque and the writing of Norman Mailer, probably because she departs from Bakhtinian orthodoxy in her refusal to see the carnivalesque as historically bound to the medieval period. Hutcheon notes that Mailer, like Bakhtin, uses "the carnival as a metaphor for recognized and legitimized freedom, existing within, though against, the accepted norms." This paradoxical metaphor is also located (and unconvincingly rectified) by Fredric Jameson, who [in his *The Political Unconscious*] questions the idea that carnivalesque forms can be an overturning of hierarchies when the carnival itself is a kind of officially sanctioned pacifier, a mere holiday granted by the authorities. Hutcheon's concept of "authorized transgression" sums up the contradiction: the carnival is "authorized" or "legitimized" by the authorities at the same time that it is opposed to authority or "accepted norms" (*Theory of Parody*).

Bakhtin solves this methodological contradiction in a most undialectical way. Although he quotes Marx, Engels and Lenin (often at the ends of chapters, as afterthoughts), he is clearly more a myth critic than a historical materialist. His emphasis on the idea of renewal or rebirth through carnival is clearly transhistorical: witness his remarks on "the perspective of ever-changing and renewed time." Bakhtin makes a connection between the medieval carnival and the "pagan" one that makes him sound like a Soviet version of James Frazer: "Even more significant is the generic link of these festivals [the carnivals] with ancient pagan festivities, agrarian in nature, which included the comic element in their rituals." Tony Bennett, in the face of all this evidence, insists [in his *Formalism and Marxism*] that Bakhtin provides a critical approach that is "historically and not aesthetically formed"; however, the idea of "renewal" and "rebirth" through carnival is *not* a historical materialist fact or category—it derives from the plane of the ideal, or the mythic. For Bakhtin writes that "They [festivals and feasts, the carnivals] must be sanctioned not by the world of practical conditions but by the highest aims of human existence, that is, by the world of ideals. Without this sanction there can be no festivity." And he goes on to say that carnivals "were the second life of the people, who for a time entered the utopian realm of community, freedom, equality, and abundance." It is clear that carnival represents for Bakhtin a temporary (esthetic/social) escape from the world of hierarchies and the status quo, and that its revolutionary potential is sharply delimited.

It is not hard to establish that the form of *The Armies of the Night* is closely related to the carnivalesque. [Mas'ud] Zavarzadeh writes [in his *The Mythopoeic Reality: The Postwar American Nonfiction Novel*] that "The barriers, as Alfred Alvarez has observed in his essay on *Armies,* between fact and fiction, life and art, are . . . broken down." This breaking down, according to Bakhtin, is a typical feature of the carnivalesque:

> It belongs to the borderline between art and life. In reality, it is life itself, but shaped according to a certain pattern of play.

> In fact, carnival does not know footlights, in the

sense that it does not acknowledge any distinction between actors and spectators.

By placing his book on "the borderline between art and life," between the novel and history, Mailer, at least initially, makes a revolutionary esthetic and political gesture; he is "deterritorializing" the normally mutually exclusive categories of the novel and the historical narrative account. In spite of the limitations of the carnivalesque form, *Armies* represents an attempt to use that form in order to address both the cosmic, or the mythic, and some part of the range of things designated by the "political," those things that would interest a historical materialist. Because of Mailer's persistence in employing the carnivalesque mode, his work suffers from the same kind of political ambivalences inherent in the form as Bakhtin describes it.

Proceeding into the largely uncharted territory of *Armies* with a Bakhtinian map, I propose to explore six key Bakhtinian areas of the carnival: the scatalogical, the act of drinking, the act of eating, comic reversals and descents, clowning and fooling, and the carnival or saturnalia itself.

The first scene of *Armies,* Mailer's intentional debasement (in hindsight) of the art of public speaking at Washington's Ambassador Theater, is a virtuoso example of what *Time* described as "an unscheduled scatalogical solo." The importance of the scatalogical is immense in *Armies*; Andrew Gordon notes that Mailer "uses anal imagery and scatology as a means, if you will, of unearthing buried truth . . . ". This, Bakhtin writes, is also the technique of Rabelais:

> It is characteristic for the familiar speech of the marketplace to use abusive language, insulting words or expressions, some of them quite lengthy and complex. The abuse is grammatically and semantically isolated from context and is regarded as a complete unit, something like a proverb. This is why we can speak of abusive language as of a special genre of billingsgate. Abusive expressions are not homogenous in origin; they had various functions in primitive communication and had in most cases the character of magic and incantations. But we are especially interested in the language which mocks and insults the deity and which was part of the ancient comic cults. These abuses were ambivalent: while humiliating and mortifying they are at the same time revived and renewed.

Mailer's "near to unprintable views" in *Armies* often take on "the character of magic and incantations." He is substantially in agreement with Abbie Hoffman not only about ends but also about means—in this case, the "levitation" of the Pentagon in order to exorcise it of evil spirits: "the Novelist was working up all steam in the 'Out, demons, out.' " For Bakhtin, carnivalesque magic of the sort Mailer describes (invoking gods from Anubis to Christ), in its linking of the sacred and profane (also a feature of the jeremiad), Christ and Tyrone Power, is a kind of excremental vision transcended through its own process. Bakhtin discusses "the ambivalent image of excrement, its relation to regeneration and renewal and its special role in overcoming fear." He continues: "Excrement is gay matter; in the ancient scatalogical images . . . it is linked to the generating force and to fertility. On the other hand, excrement is conceived as something *intermediate between earth and body,* as something relating the one to the other."

Mailer's quotation from *Time* fills us in on further scatalogical details. In it Mailer is described as "spewing obscenities," relating "in detail his search for a usable privy on the premises," and explaining why LBJ "is as full of crap as I am." He also indulges "his all-purpose noun, verb and expletive: '**** you'" and insists that "true liberty . . . consisted of his right to say shit in *The New Yorker.*" The ritual role of all this scatology lies in overcoming Mailer's fear of public speaking and in (mythically or biologically) "fertilizing" the Ambassador by urinating on it. The importance of micturation as an assertion of an anti-authoritarian and anti-rational position is discussed extensively by Bakhtin. This is paralleled in *Armies*: Mailer's confession to wetting the men's room floor may lead the audience, he proposes, to "a restorative view of man." His use of "piss" and "shit" in his Ambassador speech are also important in this regard, and the discussion of foul language and *The New Yorker* begins a typically carnivalesque link between words (language) and waste (the products of the body, food). The anti-authoritarian impulse here is especially obvious: " 'We're going to try to stick it up the government's ass,' he shouted, 'right into the sphincter of the Pentagon' "; and "what was magnificent about the word shit was that it enabled you to use the word noble . . . ". Bakhtin writes that in various medieval parodies the rectum was considered "the entrance to the underworld." Thus it is appropriate that scatology and mythology should coincide in Mailer's treatment of the Pentagon as hell, a place to be exorcised (if possible) of its evil denizens. The White House gets similar carnivalesque treatment when Mailer quotes a hippie plan to have "a lad of nine . . . climb the fence and piss, piss . . . ".

Mailer presents himself as a drinker (and a drunkard) in the first scene of the novel, where he quotes *Time*'s accusation that he was "slurping liquor." Bakhtin reminds us that Rabelais, too, begins his great medieval carnival with the image of a drinker: "Gargantua was born shouting 'Drink, drink, drink!' " The drinking theme in *Armies* is clearly linked with the scatology (urination in particular) and is also connected with the "uncrowning . . . thrashing" (Bakhtin) and general humiliation of the traditional hero in the carnivalesque world ("Mailer" in Washington, in this case). Mailer confesses that "years ago he had made all sorts of erosions in his intellectual firmament by consuming modestly promiscuous amounts of whiskey, marijuana, seconal, and benzedrine." In a (linguistic) carnivalesque reversal, the use of the world "firmament" reminds us of its opposite, fundament, the place from which the substances used to ravage the intellect are eventually drained or excreted. The exaggerated and swaggering air of Mailer's confession is also carnivalesque; Bakhtin observes that "exaggeration, hyperbolism, excessiveness are generally considered fundamental attributes" of the carnival style.

There is an almost Rabelaisian obsession with food in *Armies.* Mailer tells us that pacifists are "vegetarian" but that he "enjoyed his food and ate with large appetite, an ability he almost always possessed no matter how much he had drunk the night before . . . ". There is, moreover, such a thing as a "more or less vegetarian prose," probably caused by "spiritual flatulence." One could go on and on; the book abounds with such examples.

Images of eating, dismembering and devouring are, according to Bakhtin, typically carnivalesque: "This element of victory and triumph is inherent in all banquet images. No meal can be sad. Sadness and food are incompatible (while death and food are perfectly compatible)." Given this information, it is no surprise that "Mailer's heart . . . sank, not to his feet but his stomach." Again, the connection between food (or the digestive, lower-body processes) and language is insisted on: "a good heavy dinner on half a pint of bourbon was likely to produce torpor, undue search for the functional phrase, and dry-mouthed maunderings after a little spit." Bakhtin also makes this connection explicit: "The power of food and drink to liberate human speech is proved by the fact that schoolmen's and clerics' talks were invaded by a wide range of 'colloquial' parodies . . . ". The schoolmen in *Armies* are the politicians, the police, the media, and other officials. Mailer's speech must be liberated from their oppressive forms of discourse by his liberal recourse to food and drink, especially to drink. Some of Mailer's images of eating and digestion are inevitably negative. For example, the lurking injuries and deaths for the young people in the March are a kind of "Cancer Gulch with open maw," and "totalitarian food" can in-corporate the healthy body politic with its peculiar cancer.

In carnival, we expect as well comic reversals and descents, upon which Bakhtin comments: "We find here a characteristic logic, the peculiar logic of the 'inside out,' of the 'turnabout,' of a continual shifting from top to bottom, from front to rear, of numerous parodies and travesties, humiliations, profanations, comic crownings and uncrownings." The first clear example of such a carnivalesque reversal in *Armies* occurs early on, when Mailer explains that "he had given his own head the texture of a fine Swiss cheese" by overindulging in drugs. Another occurs later when he says that his hangover "left his brain like a fresh loaf." These grotesque reversals bring together heaven (the head) and earth (food, the rump/rear). Again effecting a grotesque shift, Mailer mentions a reviewer who tried to "disembowel" one of his novels. The import of such shifts as these is made clear by Bakhtin who theorizes that "the accent is placed not on the upward movement but on the descent."

Nevertheless, Mailer's exchange with Robert Lowell shifts from abuse to praise ("headmastermanship") in what Bakhtin would describe as a carnivalesque movement: "abuse is followed by praise," says Bakhtin, just as "death is followed by regeneration." The "Beast" that Mailer discovers within himself at the Ambassador is a traditional sign of a descent into one's lower, more depraved self (the self that takes care of foul language and micturation). Mailer's drunken introduction of Lowell as a poet not from the "bottom" but from the "top" is also congruent with the image of descent. Mailer's phrase "the voice of their abdomen" once again links body with language, as does his idea that LBJ's "Upper Rhetoric" is "located three inches below and back of Erogenous Zone Clitoric."

There are a number of very important sacred parodies in *Armies.* Sacred parodies, according to Bakhtin, usually connect images of food and digestion with religious stories or rituals through a reversal process. Mailer, for example, describes Dickie Harris and the black radicals at the March as "imbibing the bread" of the white enemy, thus parodying a communion, with perhaps a touch of the feeding of the five thousand thrown in ("Anyone like some food?"). When Mailer describes the Pentagon as "chalice and anus of corporation land" he again degrades the sacred by juxtaposing it with the body.

There are also a few "mock wars and killings," as Bakhtin terms them, in *Armies,* the most important being between Lowell and Mailer. The parodic invocation of the "matador" is also a kind of summons to a mock war.

The "fool's garden" of bourbon is a phrase that Mailer uses to alert us to his self-presentation as a fool, a travesty. Thus the theme of crowning and uncrowning which Bakhtin identifies as essential to the carnival is announced with the mock-title "Mailer, Prince of Bourbon." Bakhtin considers the "feast of fools" to be another important form of the carnivalesque: "Nearly all the rituals of the feast of fools are a grotesque degradation of various church rituals and symbols of their transfer to the material body level: gluttony, drunken orgies on the altar table, indecent gestures, disrobing . . . ". It is disturbing to note here, however, that Enid Welsford's account of the fool includes his eventual expulsion as scapegoat after a ritually determined period of time. This raises the question whether Mailer makes himself into a cultural exile (and hence renders himself powerless) through his assumption of the role of the fool in this carnival.

Obviously one of the essentials for participation in the carnival (or readerly enjoyment of that participation) is a sense of sin or transgression. When Mailer says that he met people who were "utterly lobotomized away from the sense of sin," it is clear that such persons, lacking the necessary set of taboos, will not be able fully to participate in carnival. Another jarring note in the proceedings is their beginning date: "somewhat early in September"—not the right time for a carnival, according to Bakhtin, who suggests May Day. These dissonances at the start lead to the ultimately tragic conclusion of the March: the brutal beatings and arrests of hundreds of demonstrators. Carnival turns into "saturnalia," and these are not at all the same things, as Mailer knows.

Although there are various fragmentary jeremiads earlier in *Armies,* the first extended one is on the subject of "liberal academics." These "liberal technologues" are guilty of more or less the same things that Bercovitch tells us people are always guilty of in jeremiads: "False dealing with God, betrayal of covenant promises, the degeneracy of the young, the lure of profits and pleasures . . . ". The sermon/jeremiad on the "common democratic man" and his speech-habits is the first significant conjunction of the carnivalesque and the jeremiad in the book, although there

are hints at it earlier (in the opening scene, for instance). The point at which these two movements are most strikingly superimposed on one another, however, is in Mailer's speech about his wife, her "unspoken love for Jesus Christ," and Vietnam. Mailer's mocking (but half-serious) appeal to his wife's wisdom is utterly typical of the carnivalesque, for Bakhtin observes that in Rabelais "Womanhood is shown in contrast to the limitations of her partner (husband, lover, or suitor); she is a foil to his avarice, jealousy, stupidity . . . false heroism [probably the most important for Mailer], and abstract idealism. . . . She represents in person the undoing of pretentiousness, of all that is finished, completed, exhausted. She is the inexhaustible vessel of conception, which dooms all that is old and terminated [the Vietnam War, in Mailer's conceit]."

While Mailer's use of the figure of his wife renders the speech carnivalesque, his appeal to a consensus, a specifically American and Christian consensus, also joins his "Novel as History" with the great tradition and ritual of the American jeremiad [as Bercovitch has noted]:

> The ritual of the jeremiad bespeaks an ideological consensus—in moral, religious, economic, social and intellectual matters—unmatched in any other modern culture. And the power of consensus is nowhere more evident than in the symbolic meaning that the jeremiads infused into the term America. Only in the United States has nationalism carried with it the Christian meaning of the sacred. Only America, of all national designations, has assumed the combined force of eschatology and chauvinism.

In thus allying himself with the quintessentially American as embodied in the jeremiad, Mailer manages to end his book by delivering his metaphor in what looks, superficially, like a hopeful manner. Bercovitch, however, has this to say about the underlying tension (or contradiction, in my terms) of the jeremiad form: "Not infrequently, their affirmations betray an underlying desperation—a refusal to confront the present, a fear of the future, an effort to translate 'America' into a vision that works in spirit because it can never be tested in fact." Mailer critics on the whole have been insensitive to this tension and tend to read the endings of both Books One and Two as unironic and optimistic. Even a cursory examination of Mailer's political opinions as expressed throughout the book make this conclusion questionable. In characterizing himself as a "left conservative," Mailer can make carnivalesque comments on the political sphere, such as "America, that hog's trough of Paradise." His own politics are a "private mixture of Marxism, conservatism, nihilism, and large parts of existentialism" and, although his level of commitment increases later in the book, his political statement does not satisfactorily answer Dickie Harris' question about what the American left should do after the carnival of a mass protest, just as Bakhtin never tells us how a society is changed after the medieval carnival.

A last, desperate attempt at the jeremiad (itself a desperate form) is a powerful literary device, very funny and cute (although none of Mailer's critics have noted its humor), but it avoids the question of the continuing political (non)implications of the novelist, "Mailer." Perhaps Mailer has anticipated what Gerald Graff has called [in an essay in *Boundary 2,* Vols. XII/XIII, 1984] the "poststructuralist two-step," a doubtful rhetorical trick that flourishes in the following atmosphere: "In the twentieth century, this ambiguous, quasi-anarchistic, largely literary-artistic strain of 'radicalism' [post-structuralism] has become pervasive, its prestige increasing roughly in proportion to the decline of an actual political Left with a realistic chance of exercising general influence." If God, the rhetorically convenient God of Mailer's final metaphor, that is, continues to writhe in his bonds, who will release the old vision of America? And if it was wrong from the start, as Bercovitch's definition of the anti-jeremiad suggests, who will come up with a new one? Certainly not Mailer in *The Armies of the Night;* he is a "left conservative," as thoroughly committed to "the absolute existence of witches" as he is to the teachings of Karl Marx. (pp. 317-25)

> *Maurice A. Mierau, "Carnival and Jeremiad: Mailer's 'The Armies of the Night'," in* Canadian Review of American Studies, *Vol. 17, No. 3, Fall, 1986, pp. 317-26.*

Gerald Peary (essay date Spring 1987)

[*In the article excerpted below, Peary talks with Mailer on the film set of* Tough Guys Don't Dance *and provides a critical overview of Mailer's previous screenwriting and directorial efforts.*]

In the late 1960s, between winning 'New Journalism' works such as *Armies of the Night* and a losing race for Mayor of New York City, Norman Mailer wrote, cast, financed, directed and starred in three full-length, low-budget movies, *Wild 90, Beyond the Law* and *Maidstone.* These pictures weren't exactly *The Naked and the Dead,* nor were they intended to be. They were made in fun, in the spirit in which Mailer challenged Gore Vidal to a boxing match or debated with Germaine Greer at New York's Town Hall on the liberation of women. And mainly untried actors, extremely sketchy scripts and bouncy, improvised *cinéma-vérité* style shooting seemed fine for Mailer's purposes.

When Mailer made his 60s trilogy, all released in 1968, he claimed that his inexperience and amateurishness were actually virtues against the fossilised mainstream cinema. (Rare films he did admire: *The Maltese Falcon, The Asphalt Jungle, On the Waterfront, Midnight Cowboy.*) He boasted that his primitivist approach could 'give a sense of the bewildering surface of cinematic reality, which was finer by far than the work of all but the very best film artists.'

In November 1983, Mailer was invited to Brookline, Massachusetts, for a special tribute by Boston's Institute of Contemporary Art. For this first-time retrospective of films he hadn't seen in years, he helped to dig out the old prints and agreed to speak at a screening of *Maidstone.* The film was an experiment, he said, and he hoped people would watch it charitably. 'I'm curious to find out whether it's ten years ahead of its time or twenty years behind it, or whether it went clear off into a time that never exist-

ed.' With that, Mailer marched off the stage of Brookline's Coolidge Corner Moviehouse and *Maidstone* was shown: his self-starring, self-promoting, admittedly self-indulgent saga about a pornographic film-maker who runs for President. When he returned to talk afterwards, Mailer was smiling. He had found it a pleasant surprise. 'It's better the fourth or fifth time,' he assured a sceptical crowd, 'especially if treated as a family movie.'

He admitted that his film became increasingly chaotic and incoherent, 'The actors were fresher at the beginning,' he said. 'But I made the whole film on three hours sleep a night. By the last days, I was a general suffering from combat fatigue.' He was sorry that the audience didn't get the chance to see the original three-hour version, which was never released. 'It was kind of good. Also easier to follow. Also, very boring.'

Maidstone at any length is *Citizen Kane* next to Mailer's first film, *Wild 90,* the embarrassment of the Boston tribute. *Wild 90* is a one-set, stagnant *No Exit* in Brooklyn, with three Mafia thugs lying low in a warehouse. Two of them talk pidgin Peter Falk; the third, the Prince (Mailer), sounds like some strange mixture of Rod Steiger and Aldo Ray. Mailer's Prince has bleary, punchy eyes and thick boxer's hands. He snarls a lot; he gets smart with the cops; he talks tedious nonsense that only an Andy Warhol could have loved; he engages in a sustained barking contest with a German shepherd. Finally, the Prince looks straight into the camera and addresses whatever audience may still be out there: 'You've been watching all this courtesy of the CIA.' The Prince ends the movie by reading a poem credited to Norman Mailer.

In 1983, Mailer admitted to discomfort about anyone forced to watch *Wild 90.* But he remained proud of his next picture, *Beyond the Law,* the only one of his films to attract any good reviews when it was released. He also liked his acting turn in the film.

Dressed as a plainclothes policeman, with a hat squashed down on his head, Mailer is surprisingly effective as a hardnosed Irish lieutenant who conducts police interrogations in the old-fashioned way of tough dicks since the Inquisition. . . . In fact, there are flashes of genuine brilliance in *Beyond the Law:* the brutal interrogations become so lifelike that you want to beg a dime to call a lawyer. Unfortunately, the film drags badly in the second half, when Mailer starts chasing dames.

As Mailer explained in Boston, it was the semi-success of *Beyond the Law* which led him to believe he could shoot *Maidstone* in five days. Not since Gatsby arrived in East Egg had the stolid, respectable part of Long Island been subjected to such an invasion of parvenus and pranksters as Mailer's *Maidstone* company. Everybody who mattered in his life flocked there to be in the film: boxing pals; fair weather friends from Provincetown, Massachusetts; two ex-wives; his current (now also ex-) wife Beverly Bentley; and a crowd of Mailer children.

With *Maidstone,* Mailer jumped impetuously ahead to make an *8½* with only his third movie. The slim plot; secret police surrounding Norman T. Kingsley (Mailer), film-maker and presidential candidate, are hoping to as-

Mailer at the October 1967 march on the Pentagon, which became the basis for his Pulitzer Prize–winning nonfiction narrative Armies of the Night.

sassinate him before he beats out Richard Nixon and Hubert Humphrey in the 1968 election. But the film is mainly remembered for its coda, a legendary moment of painful reality intruding on fiction. Rip Torn, who played Kingsley's brother, suddenly went for Mailer's head with a toy hammer, and perpetrated this act of violence before a running camera. Surprised and bleeding, Mailer retaliated by sinking his teeth in Rip Torn's unguarded ear. There is a forgotten wild card in the lore surrounding the most dubious battle since Mohammed Ali-Sonny Liston. As we see clearly in the film, Mailer's wife, Beverly Bentley, joined in the squabble too, clobbering Torn. Two against one; and so much for anyone's image of a macho Mailer. (pp. 105-06)

In fall 1986, Mailer, now 63 years old and serious, tries movies again. For the first time in his life, he is directing a scripted film, with a professional cast and crew and with significant money behind it. Cannon Films has provided a $6 million budget for Mailer to write and direct a 35mm film of his 1984 novel, *Tough Guys Don't Dance.*

The book was written, and also set, in Mailer's summer home of Provincetown, at the end of Cape Cod. Here, Eugene O'Neill wrote his plays, and the Pilgrims first landed. 'I love Provincetown and I thought it would be a wonder-

ful place to make a film,' Mailer says. So instead of returning in the autumn to his Brooklyn home, he stayed on to shoot *Tough Guys*. . . .

'In the earlier movies, I wouldn't really call myself a director,' says Mailer. He is between camera set-ups in the attic office of his home, and *Tough Guys* interiors are being shot downstairs. 'I didn't spend any time with the cameramen; I'd leave it up to them what to film. There were no scripts, and I worked as an actor. I wanted to, so that I could push the stories one way or another from the centre of the action. Afterwards, I took forever editing them. *Maidstone* had 45 hours of sound and film, and it took me three years to get it down to ninety minutes.'

Was it worth the trouble? Mailer acknowledges the criticism of his 1968 trilogy, but he also feels an affection for the films. 'They had great stuff but they also had great flaws. The sound was substandard. That's what sank them finally. You could hardly hear them. Those movies were done mostly without professional actors, because I didn't have scripts. But my conclusion is that you can't do a scripted movie without professionals, unless you have an unlimited budget. If you're working on a tight budget, as with *Tough Guys,* you had better have real pros because the irony is that, once the production begins, you have no time to spend with the actors. The lighting takes so long, the sound has to work, and so on. We were lucky to have two weeks of rehearsal before we began.' (p. 106)

'Next to the really hard-boiled school,' [Mailer] says about *Tough Guys,* 'it's more medium-boiled. Of the genre I'm invading, the film I most respect is *Chinatown,* a wonderful picture with a wonderful script.' He sees *Tough Guys* as, 'A commercial film which with luck will find a reasonably large audience. You want it to be seen as an art film twenty years after it was made, not two weeks after it comes out.' . . .

After five weeks of non-stop shooting, Mailer seems to be confident, amiable and having quite a good time. Could it be that film directing is . . . easy? 'Easier than writing novels, anyway. Writing is so lonely, and it demands everything in you. You never quit the work. As a novelist, I dream about the book and just worry all the time. It's like being in debt and trying to keep up payments. It's like being in prison. I sleep better as a film-maker than I ever did as novelist.' (p. 107)

> Gerald Peary, "Medium-Boiled Mailer," in Sight and Sound, *Vol. 56, No. 2, Spring, 1987, pp. 104-07.*

David Denby   (review date 28 September 1987)

[*In the following review, Denby assesses Mailer's film* Tough Guys Don't Dance *as heavy-handed and unconvincing.*]

I can think of few male writing acquaintances of my age or younger who haven't tried to steal something—a metaphor, a mood, a charge of feeling—from the fiction and journalism of Norman Mailer. The writers who form your taste in college and right after become influences to honor, guard against, and (if you are sane) stamp out. Given such convolutions of sentiment, the prospect of reviewing a movie directed by Mailer—***Tough Guys Don't Dance,*** an adaptation of his own novel—becomes a job rather like that of grading your father's term paper. And what if your father happens to be a master of revels, a genius, and a fool?

Mailer's potboiler, ***Tough Guy's Don't Dance,*** published in 1984, was a delirious experience—a kind of cracked existential murder mystery that might have been conceived by a tender-souled nephew of the Marquis de Sade. Please don't misunderstand: The style and texture of the book couldn't have been further from pornography. There were, for instance, lovely ruminations on the scenery and history of Cape Cod, passages suggestive of a long-suppressed lyrical talent; and a generous sympathy for the depressed, burnt-out hero, a failed writer, pages that offered a surprisingly close acquaintance with the emotions of defeat. Still, the way that Mailer manipulated his lurid cast of killers, studs, and ravenous women was worthy of the systematic author of *The 120 Days of Sodom.* By the time the many layers of story came together in the hero's mind, everyone, it seemed, had screwed everyone else, and at least seven men and women and a dog had been gathered to the earth. What a gaudy imagination Mailer loosed on the world! Severed heads, shrieks at a séance, the savor of "dirty" sex . . . at times, his fantasies became indistinguishable from the trash-writer's convention of unending lust, unending greed. He mixed high and low skills recklessly together.

I was hoping for some sort of ecstatic terrible movie—spangled with absurdity, perhaps, but fun. The dreary truth, however, is that Mailer doesn't have the moviemaking skills to create a scandalous film. His hand is too heavy; he's too ambitious, too obsessed, too serious for his own bizarre material. The movie is meant to have a *noir*ish flowing narrative, something experienced as both nightmare and trance, and it comes complete with the *noir* convention of voice-over narration. But at the same time, Mailer offers views of Provincetown that are somberly and statically beautiful—as tasteful as Woody Allen in a classical mood—and after a while, one thinks that the glowing light of the northern Cape is wrong for a tale of murder and obsession. Certainly *noir* is the product of the modern city. Mailer can't create visually the spooks and echoes of his text—witches cackling, sailors' bones rattling below. The dialogue becomes heavy with portent.

In some indefinable way, the actors don't fit into their settings, and the words they say—the wilder lines from Mailer's book—rarely fit into their mouths. In the book, the characters, however outrageously imagined, are enveloped in Mailer's prose, writing that never loses its special pitch of warmth, its purchase on sweet reason, and so the lewd, grabby women, the philosophical hardballs, and tormented homosexuals exist happily in the reader's fantasies. But Mailer the director can't prop them up the same way, and the characters, now larger than life, are almost gross and sometimes ludicrous, like dirty-talking refugees from *Dynasty.* Their words pop out too emphatically, with an air of shocking us that becomes laughable. (pp. 138,140)

David Denby, "Making Book," in New York Magazine, *Vol. 20, No. 58, September 28, 1987, pp. 136, 138, 140.*

Gabriel Miller   (essay date 1989)

[*Miller is an American critic and educator who often contributes to film and literature journals. In the following essay, Miller delineates social and political themes in Mailer's early fiction.*]

In one of the ***Presidential Papers*** Mailer wrote, "Our history has moved on two rivers, one visible, the other underground; there has been the history of politics which is concrete, practical, and unbelievably dull . . . and there is the subterranean river of untapped, ferocious, lonely and romantic desires, that concentration of ecstasy and violence which is the dream life of the nation." Much of Mailer's writing, like much of the American writing from which he consciously borrows, is concerned with such dualities. As he declared in **"The White Negro,"** Mailer finds the twentieth century, for all its horror, an exciting time to live because of "its tendency to reduce all of life to its ultimate alternatives." This fascination with dynamic polarities is reflected in Mailer's style as well, as he has struggled in his modeling of language and form to fuse the real, political/social world with the world of dream and myth. In reading his novels chronologically, one can trace Mailer's process of borrowing and merging different styles, then discarding them, and experimenting with others in quest of a voice that will be most compatible with his own recurrent themes and emerging vision. Mailer's central subject is the relationship between the individual will and a world that attempts to overwhelm and extinguish it. Intimately connected with this spiritual warfare is the subject of power, particularly political power, and the individual's need to resist the encroaching forces of totalitarianism. Mailer's early fiction clearly warns that modern man is in danger of losing his dignity, his freedom, and his sense of self before the enormous power of politics and society.

These concerns are already apparent in his first novel, ***The Naked and the Dead*** (1948), which despite its brilliant, evocative scenes of men at war, is ultimately a political novel. Mailer describes his attitude about the Second World War in **"The White Negro"**:

> The Second World War presented a mirror to the human condition which blinded anyone who looked into it . . . one was then obliged also to see that no matter how crippled and perverted an image of man was the society he had created, it was nonetheless his creation, his collective creation . . . and if society was so murderous, then who could ignore the most hideous of questions about his own nature?

The Naked and the Dead elaborates this harrowing perception of the individual who exemplifies and perpetuates what is wrong with the society he inhabits. In this first novel Mailer equates the army with society and thereby explores the fragmented nature of that society, which has militated against social development, revolutionary or otherwise. In so doing, Mailer demonstrates his own loss of faith in the individual's ability to impose himself creatively, perhaps redemptively, on the oppressive condition of the post-war world.

The novel exhibits a hodgepodge of styles and influences: the works of James Farrell, John Steinbeck, and John Dos Passos inform its structure and form. Herein the thirties novel, with its emphasis on social engagement and reform, collides with a pessimistic, even despairing world view, as Mailer blends naturalism with symbolism, realistic reportage with nightmare images and hallucinatory dream landscapes, documentary portraits with political allegory. The dramatic thrust of the novel, however, springs from Mailer's fascination with his three central figures: General Cummings, Sergeant Croft, and Lieutenant Hearn.

Cummings is presented as a despotic fascist, wholly preoccupied with the power he wields over the island which his troops occupy. When Hearn accuses him of being reactionary he dismisses the charge, claiming that the war is not being fought for ideals but for "power concentration." His plan to send a patrol to the rear of the Japanese position to determine the validity of a new strategic theory is prompted by raw opportunism, and it results in the death of three men. Croft, on the other hand, is a brave but illiterate soldier who embraces the war cause to satisfy his lust for killing and conquest. He is Cummings' collaborator, carrying out the general's orders without question. It is Croft who leads the men through jungles and swamps to pit them and himself against Mt. Anaka, even after the Japanese have surrendered (though the patrol does not know it), to further his own ambitions.

Hearn is the character who bridges the gap between the soldiers and command. Although he represents the liberal voice in the novel and so seems ideally positioned to embody the moral center in this desperate society, he emerges as a rather vague and empty character, even less sympathetic than most in Mailer's vast array of characters. This surprising deficiency in Hearn is surely intentional, as Mailer introduces an intelligent and sometimes outspoken man only to emphasize how ineffective he is. Resented both by the commanders and by the soldiers, he is eventually killed for no purpose; such is the fate of liberalism in Mailer's universe.

The political argument develops primarily in dialogues between Cummings and Hearn, whom Cummings is trying to convert to his autocratic views. This overt confrontation of ideologies, a staple of the political novel and a device Mailer would repeat less successfully in his next novel, provides an abstract gloss on the narrative, while the use of the "Time Machine" episodes to delineate the lives of the men more subtly equates the structure of society with the army. America is thus portrayed as a place of social privilege and racial discrimination, as exploitive and destructive as the military organization that represents it. Mailer presents the individual as either submitting to these repressive forces or attempting to maintain some spiritual independence. The fates of Hearn and, to some degree, Red Valsen, a Steinbeckian hobo and laborer who struggles to preserve his private vision, indicate that defiance is fruitless. Both men are destroyed, while Cummings and Croft, in their ruthless drive to power, prevail and triumph.

However, this schematic simplification does not reflect the complexity of Mailer's view, conveyed in some aspects of the novel that undercut the apparent political formula, most notably his narrative style. Mailer recounts his tale in a tone of complete objectivity, his authorial voice remaining detached and disinterested. Considering the moral dimensions of his story, this lack of anger or indignation is disorienting, and the effect is strengthened by Mailer's unsympathetic treatment of Hearn and the vibrant images of Cummings and Croft, who seem to fascinate him. Clearly Cummings' egoism repels Mailer, but it also attracts him, for in this island tyrant he perceives also the individualistic impulse to reshape and recreate an environment and in so doing, to form a new reality. Cummings thus possesses a kind of romantic aura as a dreamlike projection—which Mailer will recast in different forms in his subsequent fiction—of the active response to life which Mailer advocates in principle, if not on Cummings' specific terms. Croft, too, seeks a channel in which to funnel his powerful drives. Both men see evil as a vital force and their apprehension of it (not only in people, but in nature as well) provides them an energy and a decisive manner that the weaker, idealistic characters lack.

Still, at this point in his career Mailer did not want to exalt Cummings and Croft at the expense of Hearn. Therefore, in his climb up Mt. Anaka, Croft is left finally with feelings of despair: "Croft kept looking at the mountain. He had lost it, had missed some tantalizing revelation of himself. Of himself and much more, of life. Everything." At another point Mailer sums up Croft thus: "He hated weakness and he loved practically nothing. There was a crude unformed vision in his soul but he was rarely conscious of it." This man has energy but no form. Mailer the novelist is himself searching for the kind of form necessary to shape his vision. The liberal philosophy of a Hearn is rejected as insufficient to the challenges of modern history. It lacks the energy and daring of Croft and Cummings, but they still frighten Mailer, and he refuses to align himself with their authoritarian methods. Concluding the novel with Major Dalleson, a mediocre bureaucrat, enjoying the monotony of office details, Mailer instead pulls back from taking a definite position on the struggle he has chronicled. As Richard Poirier points out, he "has not yet imagined a hero with whose violence he can unabashedly identify himself."

After completing *The Naked and the Dead,* Mailer went to Paris, where he met Jean Malaquais, an anti-Stalinist Marxist philosopher and novelist. They spent countless hours discussing politics and philosophy, during which Malaquais laid the groundwork for Mailer's broader understanding and thinking about politics. By the time Mailer returned to America he had come to believe in collective political action and the necessity of the artist's direct engagement in the political sphere. He put this new creed into practice by working vigorously in the 1948 presidential campaign of Henry Wallace, who was running on the Progressive Party ticket against the incumbent Harry Truman and Republican Thomas Dewey. Wallace's campaign was marked by much controversy and dissent, as many leftist intellectuals felt that Wallace was deceived by the Communists and so refused to vote for him. Mailer, however, remained loyal to Wallace, whose candidacy was effectively repudiated by the electorate, with only 2.37 percent of the vote. This overwhelming defeat ended Mailer's involvement in collective political action; in bitter disillusionment he later dismissed the whole affair, commenting [in Hillory Mills's *Mailer: A Biography*], "The Progressive Party, as an organization, was almost as stupid as the army."

Mailer's political orientation is presented in a very direct way in his second novel, **Barbary Shore** (1951). Making plain his disenchantment with Stalinism, he also reasserts his view that liberalism is dead, the proletariat in despair, and the right in control. Not only is the liberal dream dead, but so is the the Marxist vision, which the novel maintains was mankind's last hope, now blasted by the Stalinist subversion of socialist ideals. Russian communism and American capitalism are both seen as reactionary and repressive; privilege and oppression are now ascendant.

In his second novel Mailer is attempting to cut himself off from the past and forge his own personal vision, and although he will not succeed here, **Barbary Shore** nevertheless heralds a bold departure. In structuring this work Mailer abandons the omniscient narrative technique of **The Naked and the Dead,** adopting in its place the first-person narrator, a device to be retained in his subsequent fiction. Mickey Lovett is an amnesiac, a psychic casualty of war who becomes part of a nightmarish present. He has no real past—though he manages to recollect bits and pieces as the novel progresses—and so must make a commitment to the present. The novel's action takes place in a rooming house in Brooklyn Heights, where Lovett's relationships with its various inhabitants form the story, which is told partly in realistic and partly in symbolic/allegorical terms.

This narrator's amnesia opens the way for a significant stylistic ambivalence, as Lovett's probing of self and memory infuses his story with numerous surreal, dreamlike moments. It is clearly implied in the book's first half that the world cannot be fully understood by rational means; the "subterranean river" is always winding its way through consciousness, undercutting any reliance on reason alone. In these sections Mailer achieves his best writing, for his obsessions with individual psychology and motivation seems to interest him more than the political novel he obviously wants to write. When the action switches from Lovett's relationships to the confrontation between Hollingsworth, a government agent, and McLeod, a former revolutionary Socialist, the novel becomes didactic, much of it devoted to arguments about politics and history. Ultimately **Barbary Shore** becomes more a polemic than a novel as Mailer loses his grip on his fictional voice and his book's design.

As a novelist Mailer does not fully break free from the past, for this book owes much to Hawthorne's *The Blithedale Romance,* which is also concerned with a failed attempt to create a new and better world. Mailer's skepticism about the viability of social progress and the allegorical structure of his work parallel Hawthorne's, as does his choice of the name Hollingsworth for his villain. In *Blithedale,* Hollingsworth, a reformer of criminals, is revealed to be an egoist who is blind to the complexity of human nature and incapable of real love. Mailer's Hollingsworth is a government undercover agent who is in the building to investigate McLeod and to recover from him a mysterious "little object" which disappeared from the State Department some years ago. This Hollingsworth also likes to present himself as a humanitarian, but he is exposed as a fascist, equally incapable of love. Another strong echo is provided in Mailer's use of the symbolically and ironically named Guinevere, a temptress who draws Hollingsworth, McLeod and Lovett into her orbit, much like Hawthorne's Zenobia.

Furthermore, Mailer's narrative method recalls Coverdale, the narrator of *Blithedale* (which is Hawthorne's only novel narrated in the first person). Hawthorne has Coverdale fashion his material, as Hawthorne writes in the preface, like a play, "where the creatures of his brain may play their phantasmagorical antics, without exposing them to too close a comparison with the actual events of real lives." Lovett/Mailer attempts to organize and shape his material in a similar way. In **Barbary Shore** Mailer has deliberately narrowed his canvas from the expanse of his first novel to a small cast whose actions are situated almost exclusively in the small boardinghouse. Here they are carefully manipulated as they come and go, performing their allegorical and political functions as they act out their various parts in the story. It is also a convenient device for Lovett, who has lost his past, to try to structure and so control his present as he structures the novel he is writing.

The novel's political expression centers around McLeod, whose career represents in microcosm the recent history of Russian socialism. Affiliated with the Russian Communist Party for nineteen years, he embodies the altruistic ideal of Trotskyism now degenerated into Stalinism and incriminated in the Nazi-Soviet pact, the purges, and the labor camps. McLeod, who had come to be known as the "hangman of the Left Opposition," abandoned the Party and came to America where he worked for the State Department. His leftist sympathies causing him to leave that job, he has assumed a new identity and married Guinevere, and he is now hiding out in the Brooklyn boardinghouse, where he spends time studying history and striving to understand through rigorous Marxist analysis why the revolution went wrong.

Guinevere, unlike her husband, remains ignorant of politics. Sexually vital and self-indulgent, she attracts all the men in the novel. In the novel's allegorical scheme her union with McLeod emphasizes the degeneration of the intellectual Marxist ideal as it merges either with materialism or, more broadly, with the lack of social engagement that she represents.

McLeod's antagonist is Leroy—Mailer puns ironically on the French word for king—Hollingsworth, a reactionary who seems more sinister than General Cummings because he disguises his fascist views behind a friendly manner. Like Hawthorne's Hollingsworth, however, he is a cold, vapid, robot-like functionary whose power Mailer sees as signalling the approach of Barbary. McLeod connects

Hollingsworth with an advancing "state capitalism" which conjoins "state profit and state surveillance" and in which "the aim of society is no longer to keep its members alive, but quite the contrary, . . . how to dispose of them," and indeed, Mailer's Hollingsworth displays no moral comprehension nor intellectual depth. Greedy and sadistic, he merely serves the system that empowers him, and his elopement with Guinevere at the novel's end constitutes the author's ultimate comment on the fate of America, merging the fascist with the materialist.

The other central player in Lovett's vision is Lannie Madison, a young woman spiritually formed by the ideals of the Russian Revolution. A Trotskyite, she has been decimated psychologically by the war and its aftermath, and she is now a pathological remnant of her former self. Like Guinevere, she casts a spell over Lovett, reminding him of his own radical days, when he, too, was fired by a vision of human progress and betterment. Now bitterly reproaching herself for being foolish enough to hope for a better world, Lannie views the post-war society as a larger version of the concentration camps, similarly dedicated to the eradication of individualism and emotion. She blames McLeod for the betrayal of the ideals of the revolution.

Lovett, too, is a former Trotskyite, and he describes his early devotion in terms at once realistic and dreamlike:

> I was young then, and no dedication could match mine. The revolution was tomorrow, and the inevitable crises of capitalism ticked away in my mind with the certainty of a time bomb, and even then could never begin to match the ticking of my pulse . . . For a winter and a spring I lived more intensely in the past than I could ever in the present, until the sight of a policeman on his mount became the Petrograd proletariat crawling to fame between the legs of a Cossack's horse. . . . There was never a revolution to equal it, and never a city more glorious than Petrograd. . . .

The passage is haunting and suggestive, like the feeling it describes, because it vividly characterizes the spiritual fervor of the youthful idealist, while its images convey the elusive intensity of the ideal itself. This Petrograd is an eternal city, a symbol of human perfectibility, yet beyond human reach. Lovett's amnesia, the novel suggests, results not only from the war but also from the death of his ideals and his devotion to an ennobling cause, which has cut him off both from his sense of self and from his past.

Barbary Shore concludes with McLeod's suicide, as Hollingsworth and Guinevere run off together and Lannie is arrested by the police. McLeod has, however, willed the "little object," the subject of Hollingsworth's search and the emblem of his own endangered Marxist ideals, to Lovett. Thus it is left to Lovett to keep the socialist dream alive while awaiting the apocalyptic war to come. The novel ends on a note of pessimism as Mailer echoes Fitzgerald:

> But for the present the storm approaches its thunderhead, and it is apparent that the boat drifts ever closer to shore. So the blind will lead the blind, and the deaf about warnings to one another until their voices are lost.

The final line also concludes Chapter One, and the resulting suggestion of cyclical movement underscores Mailer's cynical view of human possibilities.

That pessimistic perspective is most prevalent in the dream-like sequences which evoke the narrator's personal sense of loss, but it is also supported by the political collapse narrated in realistic, historical terms. Again, Mailer portrays the human race as spiritually bankrupt, unable to grow or evolve beyond the state of Barbary. The spiritual malaise of the modern world colors much of the novel's prose, ultimately picturing a dark and barren landscape where no dreams may take root. In the face of this enveloping gloom, McLeod's legacy to Lovett seems weak and ultimately, as Mailer never specifically defines it, merely symbolic. Probably Mailer's belief in politics is only symbolic as well: at this point in his career he surely seems to be saying that political solutions have no practical value. If McLeod leaves anything to Lovett, it is a renewal of feeling, a rejuvenation of the psyche, but the effect of this endowment on Lovett's troubled spirit remains unexplored. In Mailer's later work, on the other hand, the individual's spiritual/psychological vitality will become paramount, and it will be linked not to political urges but to existential ones.

Like *Barbary Shore* Mailer's next novel, *The Deer Park* (1955), is a first-person narrative by a spiritually dislocated would-be novelist. Sergius O'Shaugnessy is both an orphan and a victim of historical disaster: a wartime bomber pilot, he became sickened by the recognition of his role as a killer. Revolting against the horror of this "real world," he suffered a nervous breakdown and then retreated to the fictitious community of Desert D'Or, a Palm Springs-like enclave situated near the cinema capital of Southern California and on the edge of the western desert. There Sergius drifts in search of some meaning to compensate for the emptiness of his world. Creatively and sexually impotent—Mailer's emphasis on sex in this novel signals an important shift in his thematic concerns—Sergius finds a perfect haven in Desert D'Or, which is full of aimless people like himself. Most prominent among these lost souls are Charles Francis Eitel, once a powerful Hollywood director, and Marion Faye, a drug dealer and pimp.

Eitel occupies the political center of the novel. Once recognized as a gifted artist who made socially responsible films in the thirties and as a committed radical who fought for democracy in Spain, he refused to cooperate with the House Committee on Un-American Activities in its Hollywood witch-hunts in the 1940s and 50s. There-upon blacklisted by the industry, he forfeited his power and his identity, and when Sergius meets him, he is hiding out in Desert D'Or, ignored by its more prosperous citizens. Eitel's loss of artistic and sexual potency represents for Sergius the betrayal of past values, which he feels he has lost as well, and so Eitel's future becomes a matter of personal significance to him.

The destructive power of the congressional committee makes it an obvious example of the totalitarian nature of American life, but the energy of evil permeates the novel's setting in another way, for Desert D'Or is a place of extraordinary sexual license. The title of the novel refers to Louis XV's infamous Deer Park, a description of which is used as an epigraph which reads in part: "Apart from the evil which this dreadful place did to the morals of the people, it is horrible to calculate the immense sums of money it cost the state." The carnal atmosphere of the isolated desert community is not for Mailer representative of America, a sexually repressed society; instead he implies that the libertine life enjoyed by the inhabitants of Desert D'Or is their reward for supplying the American public with movie myths about its democratic ideals. Charles Eitel once measured himself in rebellion against such a world.

In his exile Eitel is given a chance to recover his sense of self through his relationship with Elena Esposito, a failed dancer and actress who remains, nonetheless, a natural and courageous woman. With her his sexual potency is restored, and he begins work on an ambitious script which he hopes will reclaim his integrity as an artist. However, this burst of personal and artistic fortune does not last, as Eitel, becoming fearful of the risks his renewed vitality exposes him to, finally capitulates to the pressure of Hollywood. He confesses before the committee, recanting his youthful ideals, and is allowed to make a watered-down version of his original script. This apostasy blights his relationship with Elena, and she leaves him for a time.

Interestingly, the autocrat-figures in *The Deer Park,* the studio heads and producers, while formidable in power and prestige, are represented in a generally comic fashion. Their despotic control of the creative community seems neither frightening nor appalling, as was the grim dedication of Hollingsworth. Eitel well knows how to handle Herman Teppis (a studio head) and Collie Munshin (a producer and Teppis' son-in-law), although he fails to challenge their authority in any meaningful way. By undercutting the Hollywood power structure with such deliberate ridicule, Mailer seems to be opening the door for a character to defeat the oppressive system, but Eitel is a broken man, no longer possessed of the stamina needed for sustained rebellion. His capitulation before the committee signals an end to Mailer's preoccupation with politics as a solution.

Mailer's prescribed alternative to Eitel is Marion Faye. As Richard Poirier perceptively points out [in his *Norman Mailer*], "Faye is the secret center of *The Deer Park*. . . . The truth was simply that perversity and power interested [Mailer] far more than those efforts at health which led to limpness or defeat." This partiality for vigor in preference to virtue, apparent in the subtexts of Mailer's first two novels but suppressed because it discomfited him, here rises to the surface for the first time: Eitel is defeated because he has lost his passion and his courage. Of little worth now are his refining powers of intelligence, a certain amount of compassion, and a large residue of guilt; according to Faye, these "vices" only weaken men and turn them into "slobs." In a deceptive world of compromise and illusion, more forceful modes seem called for, and Marion Faye believes in pushing himself to the limits of experience, seeking the "experience beyond experience"

that will empower him to overcome all obstacles to his existential freedom. He cultivates this mystical bravado by leaving his doors unlocked, thus exposing himself to the metaphoric threads of the desert and the very real threats of his local enemies; in fact, he hopes to open a door to some authentic experience at the precipice of reality. He enjoys driving at great speed to a mountain top where he looks out over the desert, the gambling city, and the atomic testing grounds. This last sight fills him with loathing for the military and the political leaders who justify its destructive power. At the same time, Faye yearns for the cataclysm it promises, for he recognizes in Desert D'Or a prime locus of the rationalized immorality of modern society, and he dreams of its violent destruction. Anticipating the perverse attitude Mailer would formulate two years later in **"The White Negro,"** Faye is, in fact, a deliberate psychopath, regarding irrational violence as a means to exercise some control under repressive conditions. Perceiving that a violent act committed without regret or regard for social restraints can give him unlimited power and authority, he replaces the guilt that infuses Eitel's life with a numbing apathy. Faye, however, is too wholly a nihilist, repudiating all feeling, to represent an acceptable alternative to the defeated idealism of Eitel.

The central intelligence who strives to make sense of these psycho-socio-political phenomena is, again, the narrator, Sergius O'Shaugnessy. Like Mailer, Sergius views the world as a divided landscape:

> I had the idea that there were two worlds. There was a real world as I called it, . . . and this real world was a world where orphans burned orphans. It was better not even to think of this. I liked the other world in which almost everybody lived. The imaginary world.

The escapist, "imaginary" world of Desert D'Or teaches him, however, that this, too, can be a painful and destructive place. At the end of the novel Sergius imagines Eitel sending him a message to confess that he has lost his artistic drive, his belief that the created world is "more real to us, more real to others, than the mummery of what happens, passes and is gone." He then urges Sergius,

> So . . . try for that other world, the real world, where orphans burn orphans and nothing is more difficult to discover than a simple fact. And with the pride of an artist, you must blow against the walls of every power that exists, the small trumpet of your defiance.

From the voice of an exhausted generation of idealists, the young man thus receives the charge to persevere in the artist's quest for individual truth and validity against the oppressive forces of delusion and distortion.

After much tribulation, Sergius finally leaves Desert D'Or, to travel in Mexico and then settle in New York. At last he has cut himself off from politics—"I was still an anarchist, and an anarchist I would always be"—and devotes himself instead to sex. Concluding with the injunction, "Rather think of Sex as Time, and Time as the connection of new circuits," he (and Mailer) have clearly rejected engagement in the fortunes of a larger society in favor of the pursuit of personal relationships. In this novel

Mailer seems to be moving in new directions, seeking to refocus his attention to the individual rebellion against repression rather than the society-wide political activism that has yielded him no solutions in the past. Unfortunately, the central voices here remain weak, perhaps because he is still struggling for definition and real commitment to his new ideas. Faye, while provocative, is too extreme a character to command sympathy, and even Sergius is not a very compelling personality. Passive and unresponsive, he projects no convincing sense of the emotional consequences of his experience.

In examining Mailer's early fiction it is important to consider his masterful short story, **"The Man Who Studied Yoga"** (1952), written after the disillusionment expressed in *Barbary Shore* but before *The Deer Park.* Here Mailer writes for the only time about "normal" middle-class characters, Sam and Eleanor Slovoda, who are presented as a mature, well-adjusted couple. Sam is an ex-radical and aspiring novelist who makes his living writing continuities for the comics; Eleanor thinks of herself as a painter, but is also a housewife and mother. The story's central event occurs when they host a dinner for some friends, one of whom brings along a pornographic film, which they all watch and discuss. After the guests leave, the Slovodas run the film again and make love as they watch it. Then, his wife having fallen asleep, Sam thinks about his unrealized life as a writer and as a man. The film has reminded him of longings which are never to be satisfied, of the frustrations which underlie his comfortable life. In contrast to the sedate existence of these characters is one guest's tale of Cassius O'Shaugnessy, the man who studied yoga. A world-traveler who has spent his life testing himself against a variety of experiences, he occupies the moral center of the story. His example of self-realization highlights by comparison Sam's own inability to express or extend himself or to relieve his anxieties. Apparently he is doomed to live out his life in conformity to social convention and to be forever secretly despairing and frustrated.

Sam is clearly a more prosaic middle-class model for Eitel, and the story of Cassius a preparation for the extremist alternative of Marion Faye. However, Mailer would specifically elaborate on the response to life he was working toward in his early fiction in his famous essay, **"The White Negro"** (1957). Therein he declares that it is the fate of modern man to live with death, which is the heritage of the Second World War. The only response to such a situation is "to accept the terms of death, to live with death as immediate danger, to divorce oneself from society, to exist without roots, to set out on that unchartered journey with the rebellious imperatives of the self." The exemplar of this condition of instinctual consciousness is the urban American Negro: by replacing the imperatives of society with the more vital and life-affirming imperatives of the self, the Negro makes it impossible for social institutions to account for him in their own terms. This form of rebellion is for Mailer the essence of "hip":

> So there was a new breed of adventurers, urban
> adventurers who drifted out at night looking for
> action with a black man's code to fit their facts.
> The hipster had absorbed the existentialist syn-

apses of the Negro, and for practical purposes could be considered a white Negro.

The hipster, then, defies "the collective murders of the State" by becoming a psychopath. The strength of the psychopath is that he knows what is good or bad for him and knows that he can change "a negative and empty fear with an outward action." He is an existentialist in that his values are determined by his inner psychological needs. His energy derives from the orgasm: "Orgasm is his therapy—he knows at the seed of his being that good orgasm opens his possibilities and bad orgasm imprisons him." Thus Mailer finds sources for energy and being in the self, and so he turns away from society towards an inner world which contains the seeds of his well-being. Poirier explains: "The 'Negro' is the child in all of us, but the child after Freud, and the essay is a call to us to become 'children' not that we might escape from time but that we might re-engage ourselves with it."

Mailer's first attempt to explore this inner, subconscious world in his fiction was *An American Dream* (1965), an extraordinary tour de force in which his language and style attain a new level of poetic suggestiveness, bridging the two worlds of external and internal reality. It is, again, a first-person narrative, told by Stephen Richards Rojack, a war hero, former congressman and professor of psychology, who recounts a thirty-two-hour psychic journey in which his old self is destroyed as he struggles toward spiritual and psychological rebirth. His odyssey begins with the murder of his estranged wife, Deborah, who represents for him an anti-life force. To be reborn involves immersing oneself in the destructive element, so Rojack must court death and so gain a heightened awareness of life. In order to free himself of the shackles of societal conformity, he must push himself to the limits of experience. Symbolically Rojack realizes this self-liberation when he visits his father-in-law, Barney Kelly, high atop the Waldorf Towers, where Kelly has summoned him to discuss his daughter's death. In order to free himself of Kelly, a man of enormous wealth and power, Rojack realizes that he must go to the terrace and walk the parapet: the performance of this act symbolizes his self-renewal.

Rojack thus makes of himself the kind of primitive being who is in contact with his non-rational self, and Mailer apparently envisions him as a prototype of the heroic new individualist who will emerge in modern America to assault the repressive state. The subconscious being a state outside time and civilization, Rojack arrives there in classic American literary fashion when he "lights out" for the prehistoric jungles of the Yucatan and Guatemala at the end of the novel.

Since *An American Dream* Mailer has written only three novels—*Why Are We in Vietnam?* (1967), *Ancient Evenings* (1983), and *Tough Guys Don't Dance* (1984)—reaffirming in each case his devotion to individual consciousness as the rightful sphere of aesthetic concern. In his early work the social world retained sufficient importance that Mailer felt obligated to serve the demands of mimesis even while moving away from it; in the later fiction that ambiguity is resolved in favor of a subjectivity that supersedes realism. It seems clear that the Norman

Mailer of the past twenty years is more comfortable in the realm of non-fiction, where the demands of social and political reality force him to keep a tighter rein on the extravagant energies of his imagination. In works such as *The Armies of the Night* (1968), *Of a Fire on the Moon* (1971), and *The Executioner's Song* (1979), Mailer's narrative talents and his prodigious capacities as an observer of American social and political life merge into a fluent and compelling whole. Perhaps he realizes that the "big book" about America that he has longed to write will have to unite the two voices, the realistic and the romantic, in a coherent and sustained vision. So far the ability to do so seems to have eluded him. (pp. 79-91)

> *Gabriel Miller, "A Small Trumpet of Defiance: Politics and the Buried Life in Norman Mailer's Early Fiction," in* Politics and the Muse: Studies in the Politics of Recent American Literature, *edited by Adam J. Sorkin, Bowling Green State University Popular Press, 1989, pp. 79-92.*

Mailer on the problems of being a writer:

Every good author who manages to forge a long career for himself must be able to build a character that will not be unhinged by a bad reception. That takes art. . . . The young writer usually starts as a loser and so is obliged to live with the conviction that the world he knows had better be wrong or he is wrong. On the answer depends one's evaluation of one's right to survive. Thanks to greed, plastics, mass media and various abominations of technology—lo, the world *is* wrong. The paranoid aim of a cockeyed young writer has as much opportunity to hit the target as the beauty queen's wide-eyed lack of paranoia. So occasionally this loser of a young writer ends up a winner, for a while. His vision has projected him forward, he is just enough ahead of his time. But dependably that wretched, lonely act of writing will force him back. Writing arouses too much commotion in one's psyche to allow the author to rest happily.

Norman Mailer, "The Hazards and Sources of Writing," in Michigan Quarterly Review, *1985.*

Barbara Lounsberry (essay date 1990)

[*In the essay excerpted below, Lounsberry examines several of Mailer's later nonfiction narratives, including* Genius and Lust, The Prisoner of Sex, Marilyn, *and* The Executioner's Song.]

Norman Mailer is an artist of epic prose. Across his career he has insistently described himself as a novelist rather than as a nonfiction artist, despite the fact that in both quantity and quality his greater contribution has been to literary nonfiction. Mailer's remarkable achievement has been to explore and expand the boundaries of many of the nonfiction genres: autobiography (*Advertisements For Myself*); biography (*Marilyn, The Executioner's Song, Of Women and Their Elegance*); history (*The Armies of the Night*); the essay (*The Prisoner of Sex*); scientific and technical writing (*Of A Fire On The Moon*); and travel, political, and sports writing (*Miami and the Siege of Chicago, St. George and the Godfather, The Fight*).

Perhaps one reason Mailer insists he is a novelist is that he knows his strength is not in research, in the fact-gathering side of literary nonfiction. His greatest works of nonfiction have come from events in which he was an active participant (*The Armies of the Night*), or when extensive research has been done for him (*The Executioner's Song*). Indeed, in *Miami and the Siege of Chicago* so uncommitted to legwork was Mailer that he chose to stay home one evening and watch the 1968 Republican convention on television rather than experience the event firsthand. At this and other conventions he admits to missing the import of key events.

If Mailer is not a dedicated fact-gatherer, he compensates with his genius for shaping and styling the facts, once they are amassed. His greatest gift as a writer is for metaphor, which he employs as a probe of his subject and as a tool for enhancing intimacy with his readers and stimulating mental and social activity. Mailer's metaphors are his means of enlarging his subjects and introducing new ideas. As Aristotle observed, "it is from metaphor that we can best get hold of something fresh" (*Rhetoric*). (p. 139)

If *The Armies of the Night* represents Mailer's rite of passage from youth to manhood, the middle period of his nonfiction career involves adult love affairs with women and literature. *Genius and Lust,* published in 1976, offers the key to the earlier volumes in this period, for in *The Prisoner of Sex* (1971) and *Marilyn* (1973) the work of Henry Miller provides the inspiration. "Never has literature and sex lived in such symbiotic relation before," Mailer writes of Miller in *Genius and Lust.*

Mailer's anxiety before Miller's oeuvre is daringly confessed in a metaphor depicting Miller as a giant elm and Mailer in a state of desire—even penis envy:

> Miller, his work embraced, which is to say swallowed in four or five weeks, and then re-read over another month or two, can sit in one's mind with all the palpability of a huge elm lying uprooted in your backyard. The nobility of the trunk and the relations of the branches are all on the ground for you to examine and try to compare. . . . Fibers of root-hair emerge from the soil like ideas drawn into wires. One hallucinates: every scent comes off every crotch of the roots—wholesale corruption may beckon here along with organic integrity.

Mailer speaks of "the irrigation Henry Miller gave to American prose," and the passage above even suggests a homosexual scenario with Mailer embracing and swallowing Miller whole.

Later, in his section titled "Crazy Cock," Mailer will write: "To enter Miller's mind is to write like him. Sometimes, his writing even has the form of a fuck." These sentences can be taken as a gloss for *The Prisoner of Sex,* which is nothing less than rhetorical intercourse with the women's movement in homage to and emulation of Miller's *Tropic of Cancer*. The sexual scenario of *The Prisoner of Sex* introduces readers to an impotent, unnaturally attacked male ego in Section I and progresses to foreplay in Section II. In Section III Mailer trades rhetorical thrust for thrust, rhetorical orgasm for orgasm, in a *menage a cinq* involving feminist critic Kate Millett, Henry Miller, D. H. Lawrence, Jean Genet, and himself, and the final section concludes with a single, soulful rhetorical "fuck"—an entry into the womb's prison for the prize. If *The Prisoner of Sex* is read, then, not as a profound exploration of the issues raised by the feminist movement, but as a rhetorical "gang-bang" of feminists in general, and as an extended session of rhetorical intercourse with Kate Millett in particular, *ultimately for the purposes of art,* a more accurate assessment of the book's achievement can be made. In truth, the rhetoric of sex throughout the volume points to this reading, and readers would be well advised that the most interesting action occurs at the level of sexual metaphor rather than that of political and social ideas.

In "The Prizewinner," the book's opening section, Mailer confesses that he would like to begin a discourse on women's liberation from the elevated podium of a Nobel Prizewinner—but he cannot. "Failed Prizewinner" is more accurate, and Mailer's diction makes clear he is in a state of ennui, indeed—let us face it—in a state of impotence:

> It was simply that his ego *did not rise* very often these days to the emoluments of the Prizewinner. His mood was nearer to the dungeon. For his battered *not-so-firm ego* was obliged to be installed in Provincetown through a long winter to go through the double haul of writing a book about the first landing on the moon while remaking himself out of the loss of a fourth wife. (emphases added)

Mailer finds that the women's movement will provide provocative enough stimulus for him to "rise" to the occasion and make himself anew. In fact, his animus rises when women take the initiative in the rhetorical intercourse:

> While the Prizewinner was packing lunches this picknicking summer, the particular part of his ghost-phallus which remained in New York— his very reputation in residence—had not only been ambushed, but was apparently being chewed half to death by a squadron of enraged Amazons, an honor guard of revolutionary (if we could only see them) vaginas.

The feminists are trying to emasculate him. Kate Millett is trying to "snip off" Henry Miller (and D. H. Lawrence) as well. Mailer projects himself as a weak and innocent hero under unnatural attack. "On *came* the ladies with their fierce ideas," PW (the Prizewinner) cries at the end of the section (emphasis added). Yet Mailer promises to make his mark deep: "For the PW was now off on a search and knew that the longer he looked, the less we would see of him."

The second section of *The Prisoner of Sex,* titled "The Acolyte," chronicles Mailer's approach to the womb. First he must penetrate "all that prior thicket of polemic and concept which revolved around Freud, penis envy,

and the virtue or vice of the clitoral orgasm. Sexual theories undulated like belly dancers in every bend." Feminists are shown here beckoning and arousing Mailer. He then initiates (reluctantly) his (rhetorical) descent: "the damnable descent of the PW into the arguments of liberated women was obliged to continue. The mysteries of the feminine orgasm, as revealed by their literature, continued to wash over him." Mailer continues outraged at feminists' achieving "satisfaction" first. "What abuse a man had to take!" he exclaims as he prepares to take the sexual offensive in the third, "Advocate," section.

Here Mailer "bangs" at Millett's rhetoric for a while and shows her banging at Henry Miller. Mailer defends Miller and then says, as if pausing for a cigarette, "Let us relax a moment on the moralisms of Millett." Round two is not far away, however, for Mailer soon says: "Henry won't be allowed to rest for long. Squirt bomb at the ready [i.e., rhetorical orgasm], Millett is laying for him." At the end of this subsection, Mailer depicts Millett as trying to emasculate *Miller's* ghost-phallus in her "confetti-making . . . ideological mincers."

In the Lawrence section the orgy begins anew. In terms of Mailer's anxiety regarding Miller's influence this section is particularly important, for (as Mailer asserts twice in *Genius and Lust*) Miller was never able to finish his own work on Lawrence. Mailer is thus able both to complete and surpass Miller's work. As the orgy continues Mailer first sees women "withdraw" respect from men; then Millett is pictured as "embolden[ed]," trying to be "more manly than the men," wanting "to push past the argument" with her "social lust," her "cerebral passion." Soon Millett and her cohorts are "*case-hardened* guerilla[s]," yet Mailer foolishly believes that a dose of D. H. Lawrence will render them impotent: "which stout partisan of the Liberation would read such words and not *go soft* for the memory of some bitter bridge of love they had burned behind" (emphases added).

Millet, however, proves perdurable, and Mailer describes her rhetoric as if it were toxic orgasm: her words "poisoned [Lawrence's prose] by the acids of inappropriate comment." Mailer, however, will show her how it is properly done: "Take off your business suit, Comrade Millett. . . . it is hardly the time for a recess." Mailer feels little need to bang at Millett over Genet, and so closes "The Advocate" section as he prepares to go alone toward that ultimate prize/prison of the womb.

The action of this final section, titled "The Prisoner," takes place predominantly within the uterus. The thought of unification of egg and sperm, man and woman, "rouse-[s]" Mailer. And when he quotes from his own *An American Dream,* the hero does find "new life [beginning] again in me," through intercourse with a woman. It is, Mailer's narrator acknowledges, "like a gift I did not deserve." Mailer's hero discovers that the meaning of love is that "we would have to be brave," revealing Mailer's own hope for new literary life in this bold rhetorical intercourse with the women's movement, hope for new life as a gift (prize) he does not deserve. He thus ends his "portentious piece" in parentheses (the typographical equivalent of the womb) with the suggestion that he is merely imitating God's own desire to "go all the way."

Thirty-four episodes of explicit sexual intercourse are included in the Miller excerpts chosen by Mailer for *Genius and Lust.* Seven of these are from *Tropic of Cancer,* the volume that begins with "the prison of death," yet moves within paragraphs to woman, and intercourse, and Miller proclaiming: "I am still alive, kicking in your womb, a reality to write upon." Mailer's close of *The Prisoner of Sex*—"he had been able to end a portentious piece in the soft sweet flesh of parentheses)"—is a subtle remodeling of this statement. Mailer describes the Miller of *Tropic of Cancer* as "the man with iron in his phallus, acid in his mind, and some kind of incomparable relentless freedom in his heart," and this would be a good description of Mailer's unrelenting persona in *The Prisoner of Sex.* So fervid indeed is Mailer regarding his literary enterprise that he calls to mind Miller's words in *Tropic of Capricorn:* "It came over me, as I stood there, that I wasn't thinking of her anymore; I was thinking of this book which I am writing, and the book had become more important to me than her. . . . I realized that the book I was planning was nothing more than a tomb in which to bury her."

This last sentence might apply as well to *Marilyn,* which represents Mailer's homage to Miller's post-*Tropic of Cancer* fiction. Monroe represents for Mailer the June/Mona/Mara figure that would haunt, and ultimately elude, Miller throughout his life. Mailer writes in *Genius and Lust*:

> The mysteries of his relation with Mona have so beguiled him that he has spent thirty-six obsessive years living with her and writing about her and never succeeds, never quite, in making her real to us. . . . She hovers in that space between actual and the fictional where everything is just out of focus.

This last is true of Mailer's *Marilyn* as well; in fact Mailer's continuing obsession with Monroe, as shown in *Of Women and Their Elegance* and the play *Strawhead,* suggests the persistent influence of Miller (as well as Monroe) on his artistic imagination.

It is only by viewing Marilyn Monroe as Mailer's Mara/Mona that *Marilyn* comes into sharp focus. Three times Mailer compares Monroe with Valentino, describing her as the female incarnation of love. This equation becomes more meaningful when we learn that Mona, in *Sexus,* changes Henry Miller's name to Val, another "diminutive of Valentine."

In that same excerpt Miller teases Mona about her stomach, which was becoming "rather generous." He is quick to add, however, that he is "not critical of her opulent flesh. . . . It carried a promise, I thought." Twice in *Marilyn* Mailer reprises this observation with the same approbation. Monroe's stomach, he writes, "popped forward in a full woman's belly, inelegant as hell, an avowal of a womb fairly salivating in seed"; "she has a belly which protudes like no big movie star's belly in many a year, and yet she is the living bouncing embodiment of pulchritude."

Mailer further follows Miller in seeing in his Marilyn an incarnation of America. In an excerpt from *Tropic of Capricorn* that Mailer reproduces twice in *Genius and Lust* Miller depicts himself as passive, and Mona in the dominant, phallic role. She is America of two oceans and buffaloes in between, America of opulence and poverty, America of Broadway and gangsters, an American "sword" cutting him through. Mailer opens *Marilyn* with a similar, though shorter apostrophe. Marilyn "was every man's love affair with America," he writes, yet it seems to me he surpasses Miller in developing this metaphoric equation throughout his volume. In at least twenty-eight passages in *Marilyn* he presents Monroe as a "magnified mirror of ourselves." For the emigre photographer André de Dienes, Marilyn is the Girl of the Golden West. In *The Seven-Year Itch* she is "an American girl . . . as simple and healthy as the whole middle of the country, and there to be plucked." Indeed, she is ice cream, "the cleanliness of all the clean American backyards." Shifting from geography to economic class, Mailer notes that Marilyn's visit to Korea becomes a "newsman's love affair: G. I. Joe meets America's most gorgeous doll." Her marriages to Joe DiMaggio and Arthur Miller are workingmen's dreams, and in her final days Marilyn comes to resemble "the brothers and sisters of America's most well-known Irish family," the Kennedys. She remains the "First Lady of American ghosts."

Yet Marilyn is also "the secret nude of America's dream life" and America as "an insane swamp" with a void in its sense of identity. Here Mailer, following Miller, begins to suggest that it is the very multiplicity of Monroe's roles that makes her not only representative of America, but also ultimately ungraspable. Given this admission, it is finally Monroe as artist, assuming roles, that interests Mailer more than Monroe as ungraspable America, and this is also true of Miller and his Mona.

In *Marilyn* Mailer speaks only fleetingly of Monroe's narcissism; in *Genius and Lust* he will devote a whole section to the subject in respect to Mona and Miller. Once again this later volume casts light on the former; indeed, the following lines hint at part of the attraction of both Miller and Monroe for Mailer: "The narcissist is always playing roles, and if there is any character harder for an author to create than that writer greater than himself, it may be a great actor. We do not even begin to comprehend the psychology of actors." Narcissism is "an affliction of the talented," Mailer writes, and in *Marilyn* and *Genius and Lust* he speaks of Monroe, Mona, and Miller as in the *prison* of narcissism in need of another person/role to break them free. Mailer attempts this liberation for both Marilyn and Miller; simultaneously he must hope (and believe) that they are big enough subjects to take him out of *himself.* As he writes in *Genius and Lust*: "If one can only break out of the penitentiary of self-absorption, there are artistic wonders, conceivably, to achieve."

June/Mona/Mara, however, ultimately eludes Miller— and Mailer acknowledges the same of both Marilyn and Miller. Even on Marilyn's last day on earth Mailer speculates that "in some part of herself she has to be calculating a new life that will be grander than she has known." And he closes *Marilyn* with Monroe's mysterious "Guess where I am?" (pp. 168-74)

The Executioner's Song, Mailer's 1979 volume chronicling the macabre life, love, and death of Utah murderer Gary Gilmore, unveils a new facet of Mailer's artistry. Not only is Mailer conspicuously absent as a character in this volume, but he uses metaphor in a completely new manner. Indeed, he employs metaphor for rhetorical effects opposite those for which he has wielded metaphor in all his previous work.

Readers of this Pulitzer Prize-winning "true life novel" immediately become aware of the volume's short sentences and large white spaces. The remarkable, though somewhat unnerving, achievement of *The Executioner's Song* is that while Mailer has employed metaphor as means to knowledge (and action) in all his previous nonfiction, in *The Executioner's Song* he uses it to suggest "not knowing" or the failure to know, and in this way it suggests the end of the line for Mailer's "ages of man"— the stage beyond death and re-birth, that of the ultimate unknown.

Readers accustomed to the rich, original, and extended metaphors in Mailer's previous volumes are struck first by the relative sparsity of metaphor in this 1,050-page book. The majority of metaphors that *do* appear can be characterized as simple and often banal, for Mailer is employing substitutionary narration. He is imitating the accents and diction of his subjects. Banal language is that which has lost power through overuse, said Hemingway, and indeed the majority of the Western and Eastern voices in this work speak in the weakest metaphoric cliches. "Poor as a churchmouse" (Bessie), "drunk as a skunk" (Gibbs), "out on a limb," "stabbed in the back" (Brenda), "off the wall" (Gilmore), "up the wall" (Farrell), "climbing the walls" (Schiller), "clutching at straws" (Gilmore), "spinning his wheels" (Farrell) represent only a small sampling of such cliched speech. And it is not only the poor, uneducated, and disaffiliated whose voices are those of vacant cliche; the educated lawyers and journalists employ them as well.

Joining this metaphor-of-cliche is the banal metaphor-of-slang through which Mailer also authenticates his saga. Gary Gilmore is "cruising for a bruising," Roger Eaton's "ass is grass," and the whole tragedy to Dr. Woods is "the pits." Such metaphors not only help to create the general air of unpleasantness in the world Mailer is depicting, but also disclose a lack of original perception on the part of its inhabitants. Humans fall into cliched speech because it is at hand, thus obviating the need for deep reflection on experience. The metaphor of slang and cliche in *The Executioner's Song,* therefore, reveals the lack of cerebration in the cast of characters and forms one of many impenetrable barriers for the reader seeking deeper knowledge of the events. John Garvey has written that "if future readers want to know how America sounded in the 1970s they can come to this book." If this is true, and in some respects it is, the volume brims with social criticism.

Mailer's art, of course, lies in his ability to capture this banal idiom. Perhaps even more to his credit, however, are

the series of simple, homespun metaphors that further enhance the Western atmosphere of the Utah setting. Bessie, Gilmore's mother, had been raised "root straight down," and talking to Nicole was "like sitting on the back porch for all of a hot July afternoon." However, even the thoughts of New York-born entrepreneur Larry Schiller are presented by Mailer in homespun terms. "Schiller needed more money the way a farmer without a tractor needs a tractor," Mailer writes, noting that Schiller figured there must be "tons of meat and potatoes" in Gilmore's letters. Through use of these tropes Mailer forces readers to perceive his story through the consciousness of the Western inhabitants.

Discord in Gary Gilmore's ambiguous character is first sounded through these homespun metaphors. Gilmore is both of and not of his region. Born in Texas and raised in Utah and Oregon, he is undeniably a son of the West, yet he has been separated so long from society that he is not at home in the contemporary West. Schiller's first impression of Gilmore is that he "looked like he wouldn't be comfortable in a restaurant with a tablecloth," and a certain irony and tension are created precisely through the ordinary metaphors Mailer fashions to depict Gilmore's inordinate emotions. "The more [Gilmore] spoke [of the police], the angrier he got. It came off him like an oven with the door open," Mailer writes. When Gilmore leaves Nicole Baker, the great love of his life, "he dropped her off . . . as easily as going down to the grocery for a six-pack." Such metaphors make Gilmore's saga both familiar and frightening.

Anthropologist Victor Turner has written [in his *Dramas, Fields, and Metaphors*] that when people's backs are to the wall, subconscious models (metaphoric paradigms) are what sustain them. A further index of the shallowness of the majority of Mailer's characters is that their models are derived primarily from popular culture rather than from any deeper historical or philosophical tradition. Gilmore tells his lawyer Dennis Boaz, "It's like I'm the Fonz and you're Richie," and Boaz, in turn, thinks of Utah Attorney General Robert Hansen as "a Clark Kent character." Police informant Gibbs's foremost desire is to appear on the Johnny Carson Show. Even when richer paradigms are suggested it is only to be undercut. Mailer begins his portraits of Gilmore's victims by saying that Colleen Jensen "had once been told she looked like a Botticelli. . . . Yet she hardly knew Botticelli's work."

It should not be surprising, therefore, that one of the largest metaphoric systems in *The Executioner's Song* involves parallels to the great American myth, the "western." Near the beginning of the volume Mailer writes: "Overhead was the immense blue of the strong sky of the American West. That had not changed." Indeed, the popular myth of the West seems to be the subconscious model by which the majority of characters in the volume operate. Bessie Gilmore is the granddaughter of pioneers on both sides of her family, and when Gary returns to Utah from the Maycomb, Illinois, prison Mailer reminds us that he retraced "practically the same route" his Mormon great-grandfather followed. Gilmore is named for cowboy movie star Gary Cooper, is described as a "loner," occasionally speaks in a Texas accent, and thinks of himself as "a Texan forever," despite the fact that he lived only the first six weeks of his life in Texas. Considerable evidence exists in Mailer's text to suggest that Gilmore conceives of himself as a Gary Cooperlike, taciturn, high-noon cowboy. Gilmore plays poker and goes to the Silver Dollar Bar, and we can feel Mailer's hand shaping the Western equation in the following richly metaphorical passage: "When [Gary's] stories got too boiled down, when it got like listening to some old cowboy cutting a piece of dried meat into small chunks and chewing on them, why then he would take a swallow of beer and speak of his Celestial Guitar. He could play music on it while he slept."

A significant shift from guitar-strumming cowboy to hunted Western "critter" occurs, however, after Gilmore's crimes. At the moment of his capture Gilmore appears to Lieutenant Peacock to be "a wildcat in a bag," and Brenda tells him, "I didn't know any other way to round you up." Gilmore's whole strong-man struggle with the American legal system might be seen as an effort to reverse this metamorphosis from cowboy to hunted animal, to regain his humanity, yet despite his heroics, Mailer titles the chapter describing his execution "The Turkey Shoot."

The truth is that Gilmore is not the only one enacting an inner Western scenario. Mailer is careful to record that practically every character in the volume comes from a ranch background. Max Jensen, the first of Gilmore's victims, feeds and brands cattle in the weeks before he dies, and even the Mormon chaplain Cline Campbell grows up "thinking of himself as a second Butch Cassidy," as someone who could shoot "from the hip." The "lair" of Judge Ritter, the non-hanging judge who stays Gilmore's execution, is a hotel with nineteenth-century decor, "real elegant Wild West," while Ritter's hanging counterpart, Judge Bullock, we are told, probably set the execution at sunrise "to put a little frontier flavor into the judgment." At the execution Ernie Wright, director of the Board of Corrections, is "practically gallivanting with his big white cowboy hat." (pp. 181-83)

Operating as a substructure of this pervasive Western motif is a related series of metaphors and conflicts built around the myth of the American strong man. In fact the words "strength" and "strong" appear an inordinate number of times across the volume. Both physical strength and mental toughness seem to be Gary Gilmore's ruling passions. He tells Lieutenant Nelson that prison "demanded you be a man every step of the way," and he later asks of his brother: "Do you know how strong you have to be, year after year, to keep yourself together in this place?"

At the beginning of the volume, when Gilmore is released from prison, displaying physical superiority seems excessively important to him. He is dismayed when Brenda's brawny husband beats him in a casual contest of strength, as well as later when his Uncle Vern bests him in arm wrestling. Some readers have viewed Gilmore's murder of Ben Bushnell in the motel next to Vern's home as his way of showing his soft-spoken but powerful uncle how tough he can be. Indeed, this is an interpretation Mailer stressed in his 1982 teleplay of *The Executioner's Song.* Gilmore's

last words to Vern at his execution seem to support this interpretation. Having failed to impress Vern with his physical strength, Gilmore settles for mental fortitude at his hour of death. "I want to show you," he tells Vern, "I've already shown you how I live . . . and I'd like to show you how I can die."

Such a "strong man" obsession might also illuminate other Gilmore actions. The Utah legal system is embodied in Attorney General Robert Hansen, a man whom Mailer depicts (through lawyer Judy Wolback's eyes) as being "a strong, righteous . . . good-looking man with a stiff, numb face, dark horn-rimmed glasses." When we recall that Gary's early attorney, Dennis Boaz, has characterized Hansen as Clark Kent (i.e., Superman), we see the foe Gilmore determines to engage for his final (legal) wrestling match. In this final showdown Gilmore shares traits with Judge Willis Ritter, the judge who stays his execution. Both Ritter and Gilmore are loners; both are fighting the Mormon and legal establishments, and both have shown remarkable ability to come back from physical setbacks—Ritter from heart attacks and surgery; Gilmore from his battle with the prison drug Prolixin and from suicidal drug overdoses. Thus facing Superman Hansen are Gilmore and "the toughest Federal Judge in the State of Utah. Conceivably the toughest in the nation."

Yet Ritter is not strong enough to beat Hansen and the Utah legal system, and though perhaps perversely victorious in achieving his wish to die, Gilmore obtains only Pyrrhic victory. His courage in death, however, should not be undervalued. In many ways Gilmore exhibits the bravery Mailer admires in his fictional heroes. Bravery does not come easily to Gary. He writes to Nicole about the need to be strong and overcome fear. In fact Nicole's own strength in defying the establishment is one of the qualities that draws Gilmore to her.

In the final hours and minutes of his life Gilmore certainly exhibits admirable strength of will. We learn from Doug Hiblar that Gary may have persuaded his mother not to attend his execution because "it would take from [his] strength if he saw her." Schiller notices that, though strapped into the execution chair, Gilmore "was still in control," and despite his famous banal final words ("Let's do it"), Gary's bearing, according to Vern, reflects "the most pronounced amount of courage, he'd ever seen, no quaver, no throatiness, right down the line." Cline Campbell, in fact, reports that "Gilmore was so strong in his desire to die right, that he didn't clench his fist as the count began," and as the bullets sound we are given this "as if" metaphor, transforming Gilmore's last moments into a subtle salute to Mailer's beloved Hemingway: "When it happened, Gary never raised a finger. Didn't quiver at all. His left hand never moved, and then, after he was shot, his head went forward, but the strap held his head up, and then the right hand slowly rose in the air and slowly went down as if to say, 'That did it, gentlemen'."

Some will claim that the heart of *The Executioner's Song* is this laconic Western strong-man refrain. The metaphoric systems certainly are present for such a reading. This would make *The Executioner's Song* another Mailer exploration of American machismo. But what is new and remarkable in *The Executioner's Song* is Mailer's ultimate abandonment of these very models which have preoccupied him. In this volume Mailer presents the Western myth without endorsing it; indeed, he undercuts such glib interpretations by offering them through the unreliable voice of Dennis Boaz: "Now that they had agreed to work together, Boaz began to ponder the tougher side of Gary. Macho to a certain extent. Of course, he had had to use a gun to prove his power. . . . 'Gary's on a real macho trip, that's for sure,' Boaz said."

Mailer implies that the truth of Gary Gilmore is more than machismo—and maybe less. Through the more reliable voice of Barry Farrell he even sounds the view that Gilmore was not tough at all, that he was fundamentally a punk. Such conflicting views only serve to increase the mystery that is Gary Gilmore, the mystery abetted by the short paragraphs and blank white space, by the empty metaphors of cliche and slang, and the deceptively simple homespun comparisons. (pp. 184-86)

Alongside the banal and homespun metaphors, Mailer creates a series of what can only be called metaphors of imprecision—a use totally opposite his previous precise, probing, and expanding mode of metaphorizing. Mailer writes that on the night of the Jensen murder April Baker, Nicole's sister, "walked around Craig [Taylor] like he was a barrel or something." Grace McGinnis, a Portland spiritualist who might, we think, be able to offer some insights, offers only this after a three-hour conversation with Bessie: "They covered a lot of the universe." In her moments of fearing Gilmore the closest even Nicole Baker can come is: "He's a bad package"—contents apparently unknown. More than 500 pages later Barry Farrell expresses his own frustration at Gilmore's bland responses to his most probing questions of a similar metaphorical context: "Resolute refusal, thought Farrell, to attach value to any detail. Life is a department store. Lift what you can." Thus, despite the proliferation of vivid particulars across 1,050 pages, we are given few conclusive perceptions about *this* "universe," about life as a department store, and the bad package that is Gary Gilmore. This is not a flaw in the work, but deliberate design—a design persistently frustrating any precise understanding of Gary Gilmore.

The reader arrives at resignation in the face of the unknowable, however, only after a long pursuit and after assailing numerous blank walls. This process, as Mailer confessed to William Buckley, was his own:

> This material made me begin to look at ten or twenty serious questions in an altogether new fashion, and it made me humble in that I just didn't know the answers. I mean, I've had the habit for years of feeling that I could dominate any question pretty quickly—it's been my vanity. And it was an exceptional experience to spend all these months and find that gently but inevitably, I was finding myself in more profound—not confusion—but doubt about my ability to answer, to give definitive answers to these questions. . . . I thought it might be very nice for once just to write a book which doesn't have answers, but poses delicate questions with a great deal of evidence and a great deal of mate-

> rial and let people argue over it. . . . I've always leaned on the side that literature, finally, is a guide—that it explains complex matters to us, it gives us a deeper understanding of our existence. And I felt that maybe the time had come—at least for me in my own work—to do a book where I don't explain it to the reader, and in part I can't explain all of it to the reader.

Thus the largest linguistic system in *The Executioner's Song*—encompassing even the grand American Western metaphorical paradigm—is that affirming the inability to know. *The Executioner's Song* is filled with people who cannot comprehend the world. Bessie Gilmore admits that "she never asked why" she and her husband lived the drifting life they lived, and when she receives Gary's letters from prison "he spoke of violence with a gusto she could not comprehend. It was altogether outside every conversation or understanding they had ever had of each other." Debbie Bushnell, wife of the slain Ben, seems to possess a similar insubstantial comprehension of life. Debbie "lived in a world of two-year-olds and four-year-olds," Mailer writes, and in language that hints at the rhetorical function of his textual breaks he explains that after Ben's murder, Debbie "kept trying to get the new thing together, but there had been too many breaks. Seeing the strange man in the motel office was a break in her understanding. Then the instant when she saw Ben's head bleeding. That was an awfully large break."

The breaks in understanding indeed are everywhere: in April Baker's drug-damaged psyche as much as in the failure of the magicians to reach the spirit of Harry Houdini, Gilmore's "kin," on Halloween. Gary Gilmore and Nicole Baker are children exhibiting this same cosmic bewilderment. At the beginning of their relationship, Mailer writes, "Nicole got the impression that [Gary] was just like her and could hardly comprehend what was happening." When Lieutenant Nelson asks Gilmore why he committed the murders he first says, "I don't know," and then "I can't keep up with life." And it isn't just these child-like Westerners who are confounded, although certainly Mailer offers some criticism of their lack of sophistication. Mailer also implies that some issues are beyond comprehension. He reports psychiatrist Woods's admission that "the best-kept secret in psychiatric circles was that nobody understood psychopaths, and few had any notion of psychotics." Death, of course, is particularly incomprehensible. In his summation at Gilmore's mitigation hearing Gilmore's lawyer states: "I don't excuse what Mr. Gilmore did, I don't even pretend to try to explain it," and when the death sentence is read in court Mailer offers one of his acutely imprecise "as if" metaphors: "It was as if there had been one kind of existence in the room, and now there was another: a man was going to be executed. It was real but it was not comprehensible."

Nor is Gary Gilmore, the bringer of death, comprehensible finally to anyone in the volume. One by one the American institutions forced to deal with him prove helpless: the family, the police, the legal system, the psychiatric profession, the church—and most certainly the fourth estate. Gilmore is a man of many masks and contradictions. Before he is released from prison Brenda observes that he has "a different face in every photograph." Barry Farrell makes the most thorough, though ultimately futile, analysis, locating twenty-seven Gilmore poses.

Gilmore even eludes the man most obsessed with securing his story, Larry Schiller; in fact *The Executioner's Song* differs profoundly from *The Armies of the Night* in Mailer's insistence that even literature cannot encompass Gilmore. *The Executioner's Song* thus takes Mailer to the final stage in his "ages of man": to the unfathomable unknown beyond death. This may explain why Mailer has attempted no major works of nonfiction since 1979. Having completed his ages he has nowhere else to go.

Where, then, might his vision of re-generation conceivably take him in the years to come? It seems to me that what remains is to begin the cycle again. Intriguingly, this is precisely what Mailer appeared to be doing in *Ancient Evenings,* his novel of reincarnation. Yet this is fiction rather than nonfiction. To my mind what will be required for Mailer to begin a new generation of nonfiction is the proper circumstance. He needs either to participate in a major American event or to find another researcher like Larry Schiller who will bring whole bodies of material to him. Furthermore, he would seem to benefit from an inspiriting American predecessor. Given another major American author (like Whitman, Miller, Hemingway, and Melville) to haunt him, he is capable of giving birth to himself anew. (pp. 186-89)

> *Barbara Lounsberry, "Norman Mailer's Ages of Man," in her* The Art of Fact: Contemporary Artists of Nonfiction, *Greenwood Press, 1990, pp. 139-89.*

John Simon (review date 29 September 1991)

[*A Yugoslavian-born American film and drama critic who believes that criticism should be purely subjective, Simon has been both praised as a judicious reviewer and censured for his often vitriolic commentaries. In the following review of* Harlot's Ghost, *Simon acknowledges Mailer's gift for improvisatory writing but faults the novel for its excessive length.*]

Norman Mailer travels far in his writings. With one book he is in contemporary Utah, with another in ancient Egypt. Now he is on present-day Cape Cod; now, in his latest, all over the world from the late 1940's to the assassination of President John F. Kennedy and beyond. He travels far and, generally, not light. *Harlot's Ghost,* his new novel, runs to more than 1,300 pages, and where you expect to find THE END, you get instead TO BE CONTINUED.

This information can affect you in two ways. You may feel that this epic novel, which means among other things to explain United States foreign policy over the last few decades from the point of view of the Central Intelligence Agency (or, more specifically, three of its employees), is such a spell-binding re-creation of momentous events that the length of the first installment is well earned, and the wait for the second, however long, amply justified. Or you may feel that Mailer, though he writes as if privy to the

secret thoughts and private conversations of the makers of history, from John F. Kennedy to Fidel Castro, from Allen Dulles to J. Edgar Hoover, from Maj. Gen. Edward G. Lansdale to Howard Hunt, must make most of this up, then bend it to fit in with his fictional characters—who tend to pale by comparison—only to end up with an arbitrary, lopsided, lumpy novel that outstays its welcome. And keeps on outstaying it.

The three central characters, all inventions, interact intimately with major and minor historical figures in a device hallowed by much illustrious fiction, but especially in vogue since E. L. Doctorow's *Ragtime,* in whose movie version, incidentally, Mailer played a supporting role. The trio—all New England blue bloods—comprises Hugh Tremont Montague, an urbane, icily fascinating, lethal top-level C.I.A. official; his much younger, beautiful wife, Hadley Kittredge Gardiner, a Radcliffe graduate from an academic family, herself a mid-level C.I.A. operative; and Herrick (Harry) Hubbard, second-generation C.I.A., protégé of Hugh, later godfather of Hugh and Kittredge's son, still later lover and, subsequently, husband of Kittredge, only to be thrown over in turn. (I am not giving away too much, since all of this happens early in the story, which starts with its end, sort of, to progress toward its middle, sort of, with hints of what will come later if the author and we live that long.)

Harlot's Ghost, then, begins with a prologue-cum-epilogue in which Harry talks about family prehistory, much of it taking place at the Keep, a residence of the Hubbards on a Maine island, haunted by the ghost of Augustus Farr, a pirate of olden days. The Keep is eventually bought by Hugh Montague, whose C.I.A. code name is Harlot—unusual, but then Hugh is altogether extraordinary—where he lives with Kittredge and their young son, Christopher. Hugh has not only taught Harry, who is his C.I.A. colleague Cal Hubbard's son, how to climb rocks; he has also watched over Harry's career at the Agency. Harry worships him, but he is also consumed with love for Kittredge, who in some strange, perverse but platonic way responds and flirts with him. Years have gone by, and Kittredge has become Harry's mistress. In a climbing accident, Christopher is killed and Hugh breaks his back and ends up in a wheelchair.

Unforgiving, Kittredge marries Harry, who once saved her from suicide. Lovemaking with Kittredge is "fabulous," what with Harry introducing her to the joys of French sex, whereas Hugh never went beyond Italian. But though copulation with Kittredge is "a sacrament," Harry cheats on her with Chloe, a waitress, with whom it is "like kids in the barn." One stormy night, Harry drives back to the Keep over slippery roads that nearly kill him, only to find Kittredge in a terrible state. Chloe calls Harry in a panic; her place has been mysteriously ransacked. Word has come that Hugh has died in a sailing accident; his decomposing body has been fished out of Chesapeake Bay. Or was it murder?

Arnie Rosen, a colleague of Harry's from the C.I.A., has arrived with three men to watch the Keep. They are waiting for Dix Butler, an ex-colleague and perfect blond brute, vicious and irresistible. He has become deviously super-rich after leaving the Agency, and is apparently on his way to the Keep. More strange things happen. The Keep burns down with Arnie in it. Kittredge disappears with the bestial Dix, with whom she has fallen helplessly in love.

This is the stuff of popular fiction; one is reminded of Daphne du Maurier's *Rebecca.* But Mailer decks it out with extraordinary twists and turns that only someone sure of his greatness would dare inflict on a reader who demands his widow's mite of credibility. The chaste Kittredge, who has known no other man besides Hugh and Harry (unless we count the ghost of Augustus Farr, who "submitted [sic] me to horrors"), and who is now happily married to Harry, visits with Hugh an orgy farm that Dix runs near Washington, and sleeps repeatedly with that ruthless fellow, who, as a C.I.A. man, would torture the spies who worked for him: urinate on them when tied up in an S & M joint, force their heads into his unflushed toilet bowl. As she says, "With Dix Butler, I can't explain why, I feel very close to Christ."

After this opening section, we learn how Harry hid out in the Bronx for a year and wrote a long memoir, provisionally entitled *The Game,* of the years leading up to these events. Then, under an assumed name, he leaves for the Soviet Union, where he expects to find Harlot a revered defector, pampered by the K.G.B. Ensconced in Moscow's Hotel Metropole, Harry rereads *The Game* on microfilm; this account constitutes the bulk of "Harlot's Ghost." In its first part, we follow Harry through his school years (at exclusive St. Matthew's), college years (at Yale) and, more important than either, apprenticeship with Hugh on those vertical rock faces. After grueling training at the C.I.A., he puts in time working in the Agency files, where, under a cryptonym, he falls afoul of William King Harvey, the historic Berlin station chief and the first nonfiction figure that Mailer brings to deeply disquieting life.

Part Two takes us to Berlin, where Harry becomes Harvey's assistant, beneficiary of his confidences as well as of his rages, during which this walking arsenal with weapons

Mailer and the feminist author Germaine Greer at a debate between Mailer and four advocates of women's liberation held at New York City's Town Hall in March 1971.

secreted all over his anatomy imperils anyone near him. Harvey's pride and joy is a tunnel he has had secretly dug from West into East Berlin. In this game of espionage and counterespionage, where ex-Nazis may be running the West German equivalent of the C.I.A., and every German is a double agent if not something more complicated, Mailer's two specialties—the fiction of paranoia and polymorphous-perverse fiction—have themselves a ball. The climax is a visit to a homosexual S & M dive to which Dix takes Harry; after that, in a particularly harrowing scene, Dix tries, unsuccessfully but deeply affectingly, to rape or seduce the still virginal young man.

Mailer comes up with a truly ingenious plot device: Harvey assigns Harry to track down the cryptonymous C.I.A. file clerk who, as Harvey sees it, defied his authority; reluctantly, Harry must trail himself. This is a variation on one of the great detective plots, from "Oedipus Rex" to that remarkable Elio Petri film, *Investigation of a Citizen Above Suspicion.* Saved by Hugh from Harvey's ire, Harry lands back in Washington.

Part Three is taken up mostly with Hugh's parallel lectures to high-echelon and lower-echelon C.I.A. personnel on the techniques of espionage and counterespionage. Here Mailer indulges his penchant for windy metaphysics and metapolitics, as well as his eagerness to show off his learning and verbiage. The learning is sketchier than he realizes, the verbiage riddled with grammatical and lexical errors, but the pontification proceeds undaunted: "Our discipline is exercised in the alley between two theaters— those separate playhouses of paranoia and cynicism. . . . Are [we] trying to analyze no more than an error by our opponents, a bureaucratic fumble, a gaffe, or, to the contrary, do we have before us an aria with carefully chosen dissonances?" Hugh gets grander and grander, but Harry's reactions may be grandest of all—as when Hugh's use of the word "artist" for a counterspy elicits from his disciple a comment about "using the word with as much nesting of his voice as an old Russian lady saying *Pushkin.*"

The C.I.A. does go in for musical analogies. Thus Allen Dulles, from the audience, interrupts Hugh's lecture with an operatic trope for Communist fallibility: "When we have to listen to an awfully vain tenor who can never hit his high note, we do grow fond of him after a time. His very inability finally offers the dependable pleasure." This is true neither to tenors nor to the tone of Allen Dulles— nor, I should think, to the tenor of C.I.A. discussions; but it may be Mailer's plea for his own *modus operandi.* Throughout the book he has a tendency to get carried away with his imagery, as when Hugh, Kittredge and Harry attend one of Lenny Bruce's performances, and suddenly "the most incredible sound issued unexpectedly from Kittredge. She could have been a horse who had just seen another horse trot by with a dead man in the saddle." Does a horse care? They shoot people, don't they?

Next, in Part Four, Harry is posted to Montevideo, Uruguay, where he is no longer an apprentice as in Berlin, but a budding spymaster working under none other than E. Howard Hunt, a formidable figure whose "long pointed nose had an indentation just above the tip that suggested a good deal of purpose in his trigger finger." One would have to be a graduate of the C.I.A. to figure out that connection. In any case, Harry thrives at the cold war game, Western hemisphere style. He has a torrid affair with Sally Porringer, the wife of one of his colleagues (and one of Mailer's most touchingly delineated characters), gets involved with Uruguay's most spectacular courtesan (a hermaphrodite who underwent a sex operation into womanhood), and plays havoc with the staff of the Soviet Embassy (all K.G.B. types) by bugging the bed in which one high-level Russian conducts a liaison with another one's wife.

This Uruguayan section, encompassing the years 1956 to 1959, affords Mailer a chance to display his knowledge of the uneasy interaction between American diplomatic personnel and the C.I.A. guys for whom they must provide cover, even as other sections enable him to impress with his insights into the rivalry between the C.I.A. and the Federal Bureau of Investigation. He has not only thoroughly done his homework (in an appendix he lists 80 odd relevant books he has perused), he has also integrated that material with his own inventions. These include Harry's correspondence with his mentor, Hugh; another with his platonic beloved, Kittredge; and occasional communications from Arnie Rosen, one of Harry's smartest colleagues, stationed back in Washington. Rosen, doubly uneasy in the C.I.A. as a homosexual and as a Jew, is nevertheless one of its shrewdest operatives, as well as one of Mailer's most winning creations.

Mailer's C.I.A., it must be noted, is very strong in the humanities. The talk here is full of erudite references to Alexander Calder, Henry Miller, Henry James, Hemingway, Melville, Kant, Lautréamont, Joyce, Kierkegaard, the Oxford English Dictionary, T. S. Eliot, Proust, "Medea" (in the Gilbert Murray translation), Pindar, Martin Buber, etc. Cal, Harry's father (who, significantly, shares a nickname with Robert Lowell), eulogizes both Dashiell Hammett and William Faulkner upon their passing. It is comforting to think that C.I.A. personnel, no longer needed as cold war fighters against a now democratic Soviet Union, will be able to slip easefully into a new role as preservers of humanistic culture.

Harry's education in Uruguay ends, and he is transferred to Miami for Parts Five and Six, dealing respectively with the Bay of Pigs and the Cuban missile crisis, leading up to Operation Mongoose, the attempt, between 1961 and 1963, to eliminate Castro by various undercover means. Here Mailer really comes into his own and vividly evokes the internecine intrigues among the C.I.A., the F.B.I., the Pentagon and the State and Justice Departments. Hugh, Harry, Kittredge, Hunt, Butler and Rosen are joined by such new players as General Lansdale, Jack and Bobby Kennedy and Modene Murphy, an amalgam of Marilyn Monroe and Judith Exner, who provides Harry with the chance to steal a woman who is variously the mistress of Frank Sinatra, President Kennedy and the gang lord Sam Giancana—the earnest of his ascent into manhood as well as secret agenthood.

Good as Mailer is at evoking straightforward action—a clandestine nocturnal operation by sea and land against Cuba is a gem any novelist could be proud of—he promptly lets his obsessions spoil his game. Through almost all his fictions, Mailer pursues, manicly or maniacally, power and sex, i.e., achieving supremacy in some profession such as politics or the military, and possessing the most beautiful women in the world. A Stendhal could make some magisterial fiction even out of this, but in Mailer the hang-ups are too naked, puerile, perverse.

The ultimate power becomes the ability to kill others ("the sense of realization you can get killing another human," "There's an awful fascination to be found in eliminating one's fellow man"), the sexual pinnacle is to have the world's most desired woman ("the sort you have to be ready to kill for") according you, preferably, oral and anal sex, and, best of all, a willingness to go to bed with you and another woman. (Hard to get, that.)

The crowning refinement, of course, is to supplant your own father—by overcoming him in a test of strength, and by taking his woman away from him. Here Harry, Mailer's alter ego has two fathers: Cal and Hugh. He finally defeats Cal in a foot race and makes off with Hugh's wife, Kittredge. (True, she leaves him later for Dix, but not to worry: Dix is yet another authorial stand-in, the artist as Devil incarnate.) And Harry becomes Hugh's—Harlot's—ghost: "I now see myself as his Shade." He tracks Hugh, it seems, to the Soviet Union and, I would guess, bests and supersedes him in the sequel. Already this first installment ends with the affirmation "Harlot . . . was my embodiment."

This not always successful supersession of the powerful but slightly corrupt father figure has been a paradigm of Mailer's fiction since the start: Lieutenant Hearn and General Cummings in *The Naked and the Dead*; Sergius O'Shaughnessy and Charles Francis Eitel in *The Deer Park,* and so on. It is touching in its way; it reminds one of *Bambi*, whose young deer hero eventually reincarnates his father, the mighty antlered stag whom he has always looked up to in awe.

But there are aspects of Mailer's fiction that are less endearing. I am not even thinking of such minor absurdities as the fixation on bodily effluvia and odors (thus the Nazi maid in *An American Dream,* whom the hero possesses anally, exudes "a thin high constipated smell"; Ingrid, the German bargirl who initiates Harry, has "a thin avaricious smell . . . stingy, catlike"), which reached its apogee in *Ancient Evenings.* More troublesome is the shopworn mysticism that Mailer keeps peddling as brand new; in the Egyptian novel, and again here, it takes the form of a dualism as hoary as Zoroastrianism (Ormazd versus Ahriman) and as recent as Freudianism (superego versus id). It becomes particularly obstreperous and tiresome in *Harlot's Ghost,* where Kittredge keeps evolving—for the C.I.A., no less, but also for her own and Harry's delectation—a theory of two principles in human nature, the masculine Alpha and the deeper, feminine Omega.

Long before the story—whose two manuscripts even bear the labels Alpha and Omega—is over, so much has been subjected to the Alpha-Omega treatment that we begin to empathize with dough at the mercy of the cookie cutter.

Hardly has Mailer uttered a powerful epigram, such as "Irrationality is the only great engine of history," and already he is off on "I see the Company [C.I.A.] as one huge Alpha and Omega."

It is not easy to be sure that Mailer's much-headlined life doesn't color one's judgment, but the author of *Harlot's Ghost* does come across as a punch-drunk writer trying to outbox all competition, real or imaginary. Who else would commit to print such writing as "Miami, soft as a powderpuff, murderous as a scorpion, lay suspended like Nirvana"? Or, featuring that favorite among his many archaisms, inversion: "Sex on marijuana was bizarre. Large and occult was its arena. Beautiful were the curves of the belly and breast, and eloquent was the harmonium of universal sex." And much, much more, down to such unidiomatic hiccupings as "You are not witting to Swedish chirurgery?"

So, too, Mailer here espouses just about all known and several unknown forms of fiction: *Bildungsroman,* epistolary novel, diary novel, phone-call novel, gossip-column novel, philosophico-political novel, pornographic novel and adventure story rotate into our field of vision. He comes closest to another highly gifted, overexuberant ex-Harvard man, Thomas Wolfe, whose voluminousness he certainly has. What he lacks is his editor. (pp. 1, 24-6)

> *John Simon, "The Company They Keep," in* The New York Times Book Review, *September 29, 1991, pp. 1, 24-6.*

Christopher Hitchens (review date 7 November 1991)

[*In the review excerpted below, Hitchens interprets* Harlot's Ghost *as a continuation of Mailer's earlier deliberations on "violence and perversity and low life."*]

I once got into trouble with Norman Mailer by asking him, on an every-man-for-himself chat-show with Germaine Greer, about his fascination with the Hubert Selby side of life. Boxing gyms, jails, barracks, the occasions of sodomy. The *practice* of sodomy. He appeared riveted, in book after book, by its warped relation to the tough-guy ethos. Had this ever been a problem for him personally? I miscued the question, and Mailer thought I was trying to call him some kind of a bum-banger. He later gave an avenging interview to the *Face,* asserting that he was the victim of a London faggot literary coterie, consisting of Martin Amis, Ian Hamilton and myself. (Amis and I contemplated a letter to the *Face,* saying that this was *very unfair* to Ian Hamilton, but then dumped the idea.) Now here is Mailer attempting the near-impossible [in *Harlot's Ghost*]: that is to say, a novel about the interstices of bureaucracy which, without any Borgesian infinite libraries or Orwellian memory holes, can summon the sinister and the infinite. . . . And here is Harry Hubbard, his outwardly insipid narrator. Hubbard is a white-collar type of CIA man, a 'ghost' writer of planted texts, who is vicariously thrilled by the knowledge that he is working with ruthless men. He meets this 'other half' of the Agency, Dix Butler, a cruel exploiter of local Berlin agents, and has a gruelling soirée with him on the Kufurstendamm which culminates when

'Let me be the first,' he said, and he bent over nimbly, put his fingertips to the floor and then his knees, and raised his powerful buttocks to me. 'Come on, fuck-head,' he said, 'this is your chance. Hit it big. Come in me, before I come back in you.' When I still made no move, he added, 'Goddamnit, I need it tonight. I need it bad Harry, and I love you.'

This blunt offer, which stirs Hubbard more than he wants to admit ('two clumps of powered meat belonging to my hero who wanted me up his ass, yes I had an erection'), enables him to summon the heft to take his first woman that very night. Ingrid turns out to have some qualities in common with her fellow Teuton, the German maid Ruta in *An American Dream*: 'She made the high nasal sound of a cat disturbed in its play . . . but then, as abruptly as an arrest, a high thin constipated smell (a smell which spoke of rocks and grease and the sewer-damp of wet stones in poor European alleys) came needling its way out of her' (*An American Dream*). 'A thin, avaricious smell certainly came up from her, single-minded as a cat, weary as some putrescence of the sea . . . pictures of her vagina flickered in my brain next to images of his ass, and I started to come' (*Harlot's Ghost*).

Berlin and bildungsroman, you say. OK, so he's a camera: get on with it. But, self-plagiarism apart, I think that Mailer is distilling an important knowledge from his many earlier reflections on violence and perversity and low life. As Balzac knew, and as Dix Butler boasts, the criminal and sexual outlaw world may be anarchic, but it is also servile and deferential. It is, to put it crudely, generally right-wing. It is also for sale. (Berlin has seen this point made before.) Berlin was the place where the CIA, busily engaged in recruiting hard-core ex-Nazis for the *Kulturkampf* against Moscow, first knew sin. First engaged in prostitution. First thought about frame-ups and tunnels and 'doubles' and (good phrase, you have to admit) 'wet jobs'. More specifically—because this hadn't been true of its infant OSS predecessor in the Second World War—it first began to conceive of American democracy as a weakling affair, as a potential liability; even as an enemy.

Mailer strives so hard to get this right that he's been accused of not composing a novel at all. But as the pages mount one sees that this is one writer's mind seeking to engage the mind of the state. *The Imagination of the State* is the name of a CIA-sponsored book on the KGB and fairly early in *Harlot's Ghost* its eponymous figure 'Harlot', a James Angleton composite, says of the Agency that 'our real duty is to become the mind of America.' How else to link the Mafia, Marilyn Monroe, the media, the Congress, Hollywood and all the other regions of CIA penetration? 'The mind of America'. A capacious subject. As Harry minutes while he's still a green neophyte: 'In Intelligence, we look to discover the compartmentalisation of the heart. We made an in-depth study once in the CIA and learned to our dismay (it was really horror!) that one-third of the men and women who could pass our security clearance were divided enough—handled properly—to be turned into agents of a foreign power.' Which, in one sense, they already were. As Kipling made his boy spy say, you need 'two separate sides to your head'. The boy, of course, was called Kim.

A continuous emphasis, then, is placed on the concept of 'doubling' and division. It's expressed as a duet between 'Alpha' and 'Omega' which may not be as obvious as at first appears, since 'Omega' was the name of the most envenomed Cuban exile organisation. Homosexuality 'fits' here—even, on one occasion, androgyny—as being supposedly conducive to concealment and ambivalence. Same-gender infidelity, too, can be conscripted. So can the double life led by the 'businessmen' and 'entertainers' linked to organised crime. But Mailer calls his novel 'a comedy of manners' because it treats of people who have been brought up 'straight', as it were, and who need a high justification for dirtying their hands. One of the diverting and absorbing features of the book is its fascination with the WASP aesthetic. Not for nothing was OSS, the precursor of the CIA, known during its wartime Anglophile incubation as 'Oh So Social'. A proper WASP—former CIA Director George Herbert Walker Bush swims into mind—can have two rationales for entering the ungentlemanly world of dirty tricks. One is patriotism. The other is religion. Hubbard finds a release from responsibility in both:

> I eschewed political arguments about Republicans and Democrats. They hardly mattered. Allen Dulles was my President, and I would be a combat trooper in the war against the Devil. I read Spengler and brooded through my winters in New Haven about the oncoming downfall of the West and how it could be prevented. . . .
>
> (pp. 6-7)

[This excerpt] can be read as an avowal of Manicheism and thus as the ideal statement of the bipolar mentality. I've heard and read many CIA men talk this way, though usually under the influence of James Burnham (and Johnnie Walker) rather than Osvald Spengler, and found it easy to see that their main concern was sogginess on the domestic front—the enemy within. Hence the battle, not just against the Satanic 'other', but for the purity of the American mind. And, since the Devil can quote Scripture, it's an easy step to mobilising the profane in defence of the sacred. *Facilis descensus Averno.* 'The Agency' becomes partly a priesthood and partly an order of chivalry. . . . The norm at Langley, Virginia is Episcopalian, though Mormons and Christian Scientists and better-yourself Catholics are common in the middle echelons, and Mailer has a go at creating a Jewish intellectual agent who is also, perhaps avoidably, the only self-proclaimed shirt-lifter. (p. 7)

This is ideal psychic territory for Mailer, who surveys with an experienced eye the Balzacian cassoulet of hookerdom, pay-offs, cover-ups, thuggery, buggery and power-worship [that have characterized recent American politics]. . . . 'Give me a vigorous hypothesis every time,' exclaims Harlot/Angleton at one point. 'Without it, there's nothing to do but drown in facts.' His protégé Hubbard wonders whether it's ideologically correct to be too paranoid, or whether there exists the danger of not being paranoid enough. Mailer registers these oscillating ambiguities brilliantly in the minor keys of the narrative and in the small encounters and asides. He does less well when he tries to

supply his own chorus and commentary, as he attempts to do by means of a lengthy epistolary sub-text. Hubbard, 'on station' with the real-life E. Howard Hunt in Uruguay, writes long confessional letters to Kittredge, Harlot's much younger and brighter wife and a classic Georgetown bluestocking. One sees the point of going behind Harlot's back, but this exchange is improbably arch and overly literal, bashing home the more subtle filiations and imbrications that are the real stuff of the novel.

'Large lies do have their own excitement,' as Hubbard shrewdly notices. There must have been CIA men who whistled with admiration at the scale of Adlai Stevenson's deception of the UN over Cuba, and who disgustedly or resignedly went through the motions of reassuring Congress that things were above board. . . . Mailer summons their sense of illicit delight very persuasively. Crucial to the skill and thrill was, of course, knowing how far they could go and then going just that crucial bit further. There were laws and customs and codes to be negotiated and circumvented, and these were men with law firms in their families. As Cal, Hubbard's leathery old warrior WASP of a father, puts it, while seeking to lure President Kennedy into further complicity over Cuba:

> 'Always look to the language. We've built a foundation for ourselves almost as good as a directive. *"Subvert military leaders to the point where they will be ready to overthrow Castro."* Well, son, tell me. How do you do that by half? . . . Always look to the language.'
>
> Two weeks later, Jack Kennedy sent a memo about Cuba over to Special Group. 'Nourish a spirit of resistance which could lead to significant defection and other by-products of unrest.' 'By-products of unrest,' said Cal, 'enhances the authorisation.'

I can just hear him saying it. By *looking to the language* you find that the secret state, in addition to a mind, possesses a sense of humour and a sexual sense also. The Agency knew, as Angleton's hero knew in *Murder in the Cathedral,* that potentates are very flirtatious and need to have their desires firmed up—hence the mentality, very commonly met with among intelligence agents, of aggressive self-pity. The public hypocrisy of the politicians convinces them that they do the thankless, dirty, dangerous tasks: getting the blame when things go wrong and no credit when they go right. (The CIA memorial at Langley has no dates against the names of agents missing in action.) Thus great fealty can be recruited by a superior who sticks by his thuggish underlings. As Kittredge writes to Hubbard, when the excellently-drawn Bill Harvey, a psychopathic station chief, has run afoul: 'Helms did go on about the inner tensions of hard-working Senior Officers accumulated through a career of ongoing crises and personal financial sacrifice . . . Helms may be the coldest man I know, but he is loyal to his troops, and that, in practice, does serve as a working substitute for compassion.' Or again, annexing real dialogue for his own purpose, Mailer uses an occasion during the Commission hearings when Warren himself asked Allen Dulles:

> 'The FBI and the CIA do employ undercover

men of terrible character?' And Allen Dulles, in all the bonhomie of a good fellow who can summon up the services of a multitude of street ruffians, replied, 'Yes, terribly bad characters.'

'That has to be one of Allen's better moments,' remarked Hugh Montague.

It's some help to be English, and brought up on Buchan and Sapper, in appreciating the dread kinship between toffs and crime.

Yet this gruff, stupid masculine world is set on its ears by one courtesan. 'Modene Murphy', who is Mailer's greatest failure of characterisation here, is perhaps such a failure because she has to do so much *duty*. In the novel as in life, she has to supply the carnal link between JFK, Frank Sinatra and the mob leader Sam Giancana. (Ben Bradlee, JFK's hagiographer and confidant, says that one of the worst moments of his life came when he saw the diaries of Judith Campbell Exner and found that she did indeed, as she had claimed, have the private telephone codes of the JFK White House, which changed every weekend.)

Because it's not believable that this broad would write any letters, Mailer's epistolary account of Modene takes the form of recorded telephone intercepts between her and a girlfriend. These are read by Harry, whose general success with women is never accounted for by anything in his character as set down. He both gains and loses the affection of Modene: the gain seemingly absurdly simple and the loss barely registered. Perhaps Mailer was faced with a fantasy/reality on which he couldn't improve, but one could hope for better from a friend of 'Jack' and a biographer of 'Marilyn'. Incidentally, what was Modene like in the sack? 'Its laws came into my senses with one sniff of her dark-haired pussy, no more at other times than a demure whiff of urine, mortal fish, a hint of earth—now I explored caverns.' This is perhaps not as gamey as *An American Dream* ('I had a desire suddenly to skip the sea and mine the earth'), but evidently Mailer's olfactory nerve has not failed him. Still, one occasionally feels ('Modene came from her fingers and toes, her thighs and her arms, her heart and all that belonged to the heart of her future—I was ready to swear that the earth and the ocean combined') that he is pounding off to a different drummer. At one point, losing his grip entirely, he makes Hubbard exclaim: 'I could have welcomed Jack Kennedy into bed with us at that moment.'

These elements—volatile, you have to agree—all combine to make Kennedy's appointment in Dallas seem like *Kismet*. It's a fair place for Mailer to stop, or to place his 'To Be Continued'. Ahead lies Vietnam, of which premonitory tremors can be felt, and Watergate, and Chile . . . But the place of covert action in the American imagination, and in the most vivid nightmare of that imagination, has been so well established that it will be impossible—almost inartistic—for future readers and authors to consider the subjects separately. (pp. 7-8)

Christopher Hitchens, "On the Imagining of Conspiracy," in London Review of Books, Vol. 13, No. 21, November 7, 1991, pp. 6-8, 10.

Wilfrid Sheed   **(review date 5 December 1991)**

[*Sheed is an English-born American critic and fiction writer who has served as a columnist for* The New York Times *since 1971. In the review excerpted below, Sheed defends Mailer's novel* Harlot's Ghost *as a flawed but impressive portrait of the CIA.*]

If Norman Mailer's own character Harlot were reviewing [*Harlot's Ghost*]—and what better occupation for a retired superspy with the most devious mind in the West?—he would probably deduce by way of background that the author has spent a suspicious amount of time preparing us to expect the worst of this book, no doubt to ensure that when it got here we would hold our breath at every curve and dip in the plot—oh my God, he's not going to make it. "Mailer and the CIA"—by now the very phrase is enough to strike terror in the heart of a stunt man or soldier of fortune, let alone a cautious, bet-hedging reviewer.

Since two can play at this game—and since you can't just leap into reviewing a book of 1,310 pages—let me string out the suspense a little by reminding late arrivals of exactly why Mailer's campaign of disinformation worked so well. To begin with, the subject. The CIA is like a china shop disguised as a rumpus room and the Mailer of legend is at least half bull. Since practically nothing about any spy agency, even a leaky one like the CIA, can ever be proved one way or the other, it looks as if the novelist can do whatever he likes with it; and the CIA's own conceits have already set formidable standards for fantasy. You wouldn't suppose that you could go too far in making up stories about the dreamers who once actually plotted to make Fidel Castro's beard fall out—causing him to lose face, so to speak, by gaining it. The sky inside these people's heads would appear to be the limit.

But, of course, there are limits even in there, and laws of probability, and the fact that they are not plainly visible makes the writer's task harder, not easier. If you play tennis without a net, you had better be awfully good at imagining nets, all the way down to the net-cord shots, and at devising rules that make sense in a situationless situation. And who would want to impose rules on an imagination that has given us over the years theories about cancer and sex, unfairly but fatally reminiscent of General Jack D. Ripper himself—or to home in closer to our topic, a mind that proposed just eighteen short years ago founding "a people's CIA," to guarantee everyone a piece of the paranoia.

Of course, we knew that Mailer knew better. For all his apparently riotous living, much of which seemed to take place on television, none of his synapses seemed to be missing yet and he certainly hadn't passed that point of no return for writers, the loss of energy. Even the weakest of his only-kidding books, *Tough Guys Don't Dance,* fairly hummed with the stuff, but quite pointlessly, like a powerful machine that has spun out of control and is careering off the walls of the lab. After a while you stop expecting anything great from it and just wait for it to run down.

By the time of Watergate at the latest, Mailer seemed so far sunk in playfulness and the need to be original that he couldn't give a straight answer to anything. And as if to round off this spree, he finally disgorged a novel that was so hellbent on being great that it skipped goodness altogether. Unless *Ancient Evenings* really is an inspired guess about primitive consciousness (and we'll never know), it has to stand on its linguistic-cum-psychological ingenuity. And even Hemingway at his most afflated never talked of going one on one with *Finnegans Wake*.

Yet in retrospect, *Ancient Evenings* may have been a good book to get out of one's system, like a giant kidney stone. It was, to the point of parody, the kind of quasi-masterpiece that is in no hurry to be appreciated: if the critics don't like it now, maybe they will twenty years from now. Or a hundred. It will still be there, a stake in the future. So *that's* taken care of.

If Harlot is still with us—and if he ever guessed right about anything, which history gives reason to doubt—he would have noticed at least one good omen in those same years, namely *The Executioner's Song,* a documentary style of book, in which the author seems to be testing how much he can efface himself from a text, how much he can *not* show off. The operation was so thoroughgoing that the reader found himself thinking at times, "This is great stuff—but why does it need Mailer?" But of course it was great precisely because of Mailer, whose best writing has always been self-effacing, possibly to his annoyance.

The chronology suggests that *Executioner* was partly designed to buy indulgence for *Ancient Evenings,* but if so, the price was way too high. What it did do was give its author a workout in American realism, far off his usual celebrity writer rounds, and us a reminder that the machine was as powerful as ever, and that Mailer could still control it whenever he chose to.

After just a few pages of *Harlot's Ghost,* it becomes clear that he chooses to very much this time. And after a stretch of cranking and sputtering it also becomes reassuringly clear that the whole crazy contraption is working as well as if not better than ever.

The slow and somewhat "literary" opening, full of arcane New England botany and topology—the narrator's "roots" in the most literal sense—is actually something of a decoy, and it seems only fair to warn the reader that it builds toward a climax that will just have to hang out there until the next volume. Although Mailer strikes some notes in this section that will reverberate through the whole enterprise, there are in sum an awful lot of words for a rather modest effect—a strategy more Conradian than Hemingwayesque—and I couldn't help wondering, as the narrator wound into his "Last night I dreamed I went to Manderley again" account of returning to an excessively haunted house for the climax that never quite comes, whether Mailer wasn't intentionally slowing the reader down here and elsewhere (slow patches are dotted throughout, like speed bumps) to assure us that this will not be a page-turner, it will not be slick.

Anyway, slick the book certainly is not. But a page-turner it is for a great deal of the time, and none the worse for it. The best sequences in the book, all of which involve the CIA in action, require a certain breathlessness, as the operatives spin through their madcap motions faster than the

speed of thought; as with the Red Queen in *Alice* this is the pace they have to maintain in spyland just to stay in the same place.

And the same place is very much where Mailer's version of the CIA wants to stay—that is to say, right in the middle of a cold war that is built to last until Armageddon at the earliest (after which we'll probably need an even larger budget), a cold war that bustles with activity and goes absolutely nowhere so that you can confidently enter your son's name for it at birth at the same time you're entering it for Yale. And never mind for a moment the relative probability of this version—suffice it to say that this is the kind of cold war we actually got, whether we got it Mailer's way or not, and that the testimony in the recent Robert Gates hearings has been the best testimonial Mailer's conjectures could possibly have hoped for. Unless several very impressive witnesses were lying, the real-life CIA put up a last-ditch struggle to save its cold war as grim as anything in the annals of welfare.

The heart of the novel concerns a properly Skull and Bonesy generational laying on of CIA hands. The hero, or Alice figure, one Hedrick (Hal or Harry) Hubbard, is a son of the pioneers, two of them in fact, his earthly father Cal being a straightforward, hard-drinking old Samurai who demands only the occasional display of superhuman courage to win his love, or at least his attention, and his spiritual one being Harlot himself, aka Hugh Tremont Montague, the company mystic and cold war metaphysician who wants a bit more—namely a leap of faith and a sense of transcendence, both symbolized by rock-climbing, which he and Hal solemnly undertake together as an ethereal rite of passage.

Like any good apostle Harlot burns to pass on his vision to a younger version of himself, but as, I suggest, is his wont, he guesses badly, wrong about both his disciple *and* his vision, since all he winds up actually passing on to young Hal is his own wife, who lands in the youngster's bed after a thousand pages or so of footsy; and if he is still alive, he has been obliged to watch the whimpering end of the real cold war from a wheelchair, to which his rock-climbing has dispatched him, a victim for life of his own metaphor. Thus perish all spy organizations, one might wish.

Although Mailer does not push the symbolism of those events anything like as hard as this account may make it sound, Hal's cuckolding of his godfather never quite makes sense on any *but* the symbolic level, any more than his love for his rather goatish father does. Never mind for now. A narrator doesn't have to know why he does what he does. What is clear to us at least is that young Hal is a far cooler breed of cat than his elders—so much so that his real father asks him despairingly why he is in the agency at all and he answers, "Because I like the work."

With this answer the book is, for my money, saved. If he had said either "I'm in it because I want to be like you," or, self-deludingly, "I really hate Communism, you know," it would have unleashed everything that is second-best about the novel. What made Mailer famous and worth writing about in the first place was neither his knowledge of the human heart, which is variable, nor his global theories, but his overpowering intuition of men at war—with each other, with civilization, but best of all with and within the organizations created by and for themselves.

The Naked and the Dead became easy to underestimate the minute after it had left the room and the impact had worn off. But for all its faults, it hit one like a pile driver the first time around, and here the same theme is back, with the bugs removed. And if it doesn't hit quite as hard now, this is partly because the world had grown older and we're used to Mailer and all the little mailers by now, but partly because it keeps on running long after the reader has lost his first wind, and because the impact seems at times to be packed in the thick cotton of a romance that starts out as an interesting possibility and ends up as a plot device. But if you follow Hal Hubbard's instructions, and keep your eye on the work, you will find there the kind of intensely imagined world that only the very best novelists can create or sustain—leaving one to wonder where the author has been all these years. Like James Jones, his literary brother in arms, he comes to life at regimental reunions in whatever guise, and his strength comes surging back.

Hal's "I like the work" would have had to seem a dangerously watered-down and facetious way of looking at things to either of his fathers. The founders of the CIA needed a great big vision to get this thing off the ground, and to justify a spy agency in peacetime, but in the giddy first years of the cold war the air was thick with visions, and while Harlot by elimination is based mostly on James Angleton (if he isn't Angleton, who is?) there are times when he could easily pass for Whittaker Chambers in full rhetorical sail.

But second-generation bureaucrats need no such infusions of hot air to keep their department aloft and the appropriations coming. They know by heart, because it is all around them in their infancy, the great principle of stasis and stability in our democracy, which of course is that it needs a mighty effort to get something like the CIA, or the farm program, or anything at all started but a Herculean one to get it stopped. So they know they are safe to enjoy their work, which, under all its accretions of circumlocution and top-secret paper, has long since become its own justification.

And what work it is. For four hundred or so inspired pages Mailer portrays the CIA strutting its stuff in two very different regions ("theaters" would be the appropriate word), and anyone who can find a significant difference between their work and what is normally known as play deserves to be debriefed and turned into a mole before the other team finds out.

In Berlin, the game consists mostly of the constant turning and unturning of agents, so that no one on either side can begin to tell you which of "their people" are actually "our people," or to what degree. The best possible insurance policy for an ambitious German of any age or sex who wants to get in on the fun is to sell his services to both sides simultaneously. But what makes it unmistakably a game

is that none of this Len Deighton street theater makes any serious difference—none that can be found now, anyway, as one traces the real ups and downs of the cold war.

As ringmaster Bill Harvey—the actual name of the Berlin station chief—explains over his fifth martini or so, we already know all we need to know about the Russians (he is talking in the 1950s), to wit that they are years and years away from being able to invade Western Europe—a piece of information that must have been very hard to miss (just concealing all of the broken-down train lines would have been beyond anything we know of Russian capacities). Meanwhile the CIA's task is simply to keep the pot bubbling, and the public entertained, so that there will still *be* a CIA when World Communism makes its big move for the souls of men.

If Harvey is right, it seems fair to extrapolate that many if not all of these fabulous CIA operations were simply cold war make-work, a WPA for Yalies and would-be Yalies, who would naturally need a Holy War to justify living off the government teat, to use their own phrase. And if this seems unduly cynical, once again one can only say that the operations certainly *look* like make-work for all the difference most of them made to the course of history. And anyway the estimate doesn't come from Mailer, who is cautious to a (most welcome) fault with his own conjectures; it comes, like a burp, from the liverish Harvey who is a bit of an outsider himself, a former FBI defector in our own little cold war between agencies and the only operative uncouth enough to see through the exquisite Kim Philby. And Harvey's putative drunkenness is itself a species of disinformation. Is he planting rumors today or genuinely blurting?

Whatever the real William Harvey may have been like, Mailer's recreation is a true likeness of *someone,* and whoever it is is made to order for that spy novelist's gold mine, postwar Berlin. A James Bond who is built like a pear and has to throw up periodically, Harvey comes across as at once grandiose and seedy, a dandy who can fart at will and an all-round bilious interloper at the CIA branch of the Yale drama school. If the game is to acquire information that you don't need as sensationally as possible, he will by God go all the way and build a tunnel right under the enemy's ass to get it—just the kind of caper to make one a legend in the agency, which is all, one suspects, that most of these people really want.

And to match Harvey excess by wretched excess, Mailer has fashioned Dix Butler, an authentic wild man of the Fifties, yawping and clawing for experience like Jack Kerouac or, less primitively, like Henderson the Rain King, as the schoolmarms close in on him. The game for the likes of Dix Butler is to stay in booze money without either having to wear a suit or quite break the law, and once again the CIA is the ideal answer, like a government grant, and Berlin the perfect playground. Since virtually every Berliner is a potential agent waiting for someone to turn and unturn him, Butler is free to roar through bars and bordellos to his heart's delight, bullying and seducing as the mood takes him while the agents fall out of the trees either way, and writing it all off to limitless expenses. At European prices, even graduate students used to feel like conquerors in those days. But here is the real swaggering thing, and Butler's triumphal rambles constitute a quite brilliant choice by Mailer as foreground to the whole crazy "we may all be dead tomorrow, so what'll we do tonight" atmosphere of a great city perched on the edge of the cold war, halfway between terror and boredom. ("Don't tell me we may all be dead tomorrow *again*?")

Even in the CIA, all good things and postings come to an end—but if you play your cards right, they are replaced by more good things, and our narrator Hal Hubbard next finds himself in Uruguay, where a different kind of play is going on, as different as Wagner from Puccini, but not without its giggles.

Operatic is probably the only word to describe the Latin political style as rendered by Mailer, or even by Castro, and once again, Mailer and the CIA have chosen a most suitable American to insert into the plot. Howard Hunt is the author's second "real" character of any consequence, and once more Mailer has probably tailored him to his own specifications, leaving only the name and a persona that doesn't jar too grossly with the facts. At any rate, Mailer's version is a very model of Yankee *bella figura,* the kind of dude who likes nothing better than to conduct his dirty business while hosing down his polo pony or exchanging gorgeously insincere after-dinner speeches with his hosts about the undying love between our great countries. Hunt's normal agenda is as busy and vacuous as a day in the life of a Jane Austen heroine, and the high point of his bureau's activities during Hubbard's stay is the taping of an adultery in the Russian embassy, the publication of which will, it is hoped, cause one of the Russians to defect in a rage, though with what object nobody bothers to ask any more. It will simply give us someone else to debrief, re-brief and worry about and a temporary psychological edge—in Uruguay! Still it must be done. An agency can't just *sit* there.

The tape of the adultery, transcribed in the pidgin Russian of a bad translation, is funnier than Mailer has ever shown signs of being, as if the general mellowing and cooling off of vanity much noted in cover stories have finally brought him to the point where most writers begin. Humor if it's ever going to get there usually declares itself early, so a late-blooming humorist would be something to celebrate—especially this one, our intrepid conqueror of new worlds who only occasionally makes it.

A skeptic might pause here to point out that it's hard not to be funny about the CIA, and outside of the fact that, as every comic knows, it is never hard not to be funny about anything, he would have a point. Yet at the same time one's blood runs slightly chilled at the thought of grown men cackling like schoolboys over some of the pranks that pass for high policy in the CIA. The upper classes at play have always been a daunting sight to normal people, and when the sainted Harlot himself descends from the clouds in the last act and lights up with glee over a scheme to "turn" a Jewish homosexual agent into a Christian hetero one in order to seduce information out of a homely secretary, one may feel that pig-sticking can't be far behind.

And this is Mailer's real subject, whatever he thinks it is

himself: Dink Stover goes to Berlin, to Cuba, to Vietnam—but taking with him everywhere the sense of an old boys party at two in the morning where, amid the roar of laughter and crash of glass, somebody accidentally gets killed. One of the ways in which Mailer has been disinforming us most fiendishly about his own seriousness is the frequency with which he seems to have been dining out himself lately. But clearly this has been field work of the most exacting kind, a grueling excavation into the mind of the dining classes; and if he hasn't always got the sound of these people quite right, this can perhaps be traced to one last damning piece of evidence Mailer has given us over the years, namely those peculiar little movies he made back in the Sixties, which suggested that, to put it tactfully, his ear for dialogue is not absolutely pitch perfect.

But dialogue has never been what Mailer is about; he wants nothing less than the souls, the essences of his subjects, in relation to which their dialogue is just the froth at the top of the mug. And the souls of the CIA might be looked for along the following lines.

In an officially classless society like our own, the ruling class has to be a shadowy affair by definition, a secret society unto itself whose members identify each other—but who can be sure?—by such outward signs of inward grace as accent and personal style (clothes are too easy to learn, and only weed out the troglodytes) and, above all, by "being in the know," by being plugged into the central dynamo. If you got your information from a source in Washington, you barely pass, if you got it from "Tuppy" or "Boots" himself, you win this one cleanly. But if you do too much of either of these things, you're trying too hard and you return to "go."

The ideal ploy is, of course, to be perceived to be in the know while you talk about inscrutable nothings, hollyhocks, and hunting dogs—in other words to sound as English as possible. To be rumored to be in the CIA can be a source of immense social power in some circles, akin *mutatis mutandis* to being something or other in the Mafia. So of all the clubs this class has so far formed, to declare itself while giving nothing away, this government agency with the untraceable expense account is the purest and most platonic. *We* know who we are, and you just know that we're someone pretty important. Perfect.

But the game doesn't cease once you're in the club: members must continue working on their style and their insideness until they die or drop from sight. In a piece of acute and assuringly accurate social observation, we find Kittredge Montague mocking Howard Hunt's alleged snobbishness in a letter to Hal the narrator.

It seems that Hunt's family, of which he seems so proud, is nothing like as good as *hers,* fancy that. It's not, as her facetious tone makes urgently clear, that things of that kind really matter at all, but if Mr. Hunt wants to play by those rules—well, it does give her a heaven-sent chance to inform us of how very good *her* family is, without seeming to boast about it. I mean it *really* doesn't matter, does it, either to her *or* the CIA? But Hunt (Mailer's version) has given the impression that it matters to him, so just like that he has lost the game. He has blurted, in manner if not words, and shown his credentials, instead of assuming he doesn't need to and just breezing on in. And since imposters and *arrivistes* have certain obvious advantages at intelligence over people who have never had to work at their manners, it is only fair that blue-bloods should seize such openings.

What is particularly haunting about this sequence, outside of the touching unself-consciousness with which real top people like Kittredge give their own game away again and again for novelists like Mailer—and Truman Capote—to snap up (it must seem to them like talking in front of the servants), is that you would have to be quite a ways inside the club yourself to see any difference whatever between Kittredge's lofty family and Hunt's inferior one. (I can only say, in the same "isn't it all too silly?" spirit, that they both seem pretty trashy to a Sheed of Aberdeen and Sydney.)

But in the eyes that count, Howard Hunt is a minor-league gentleman perfectly suited to a minor-league country like Uruguay, where loud colors are more likely to impress the locals than the grays and nuances of a real big-league gent—whom only another gent can truly appreciate anyway. And here toward the end of our hero's apprenticeship the book reaches its first natural stopping place, with our traveling salesman-like representative, the alleged Hunt, matching style for style with the local blowhards, while over the transom and under the door seep the first emanations from Castro's *and* Batista's Cuba (culturally it is still both at once), which promises to be a really weird theater, if the first messengers are anything to go by: Chevi Fuertes, a café philosopher and double agent who is quite capable of turning and unturning himself from side to side by just listening to himself talk, and the fabulous Libertad, a transvestite courtesan who turns men, as it were, to putty in her hands.

If Harvey was perfect for Berlin and Hunt for Uruguay, what manner of creature could the agency have up its sleeve for such a theater as this? No one, as we shall see to our regret, only the same ones recycled, as Mr. Gates is being recycled right now—but here I wish that Mailer had rung down the curtain on Volume One with the question still in the air; in fact I'm tempted to do so for him, by stamping his own phrase "to be continued" on this review before both the review and the book have to go wheezing together around the track one more time.

However, it probably wasn't practical for him, in publishing terms, to stop, with all the comic strip events—the Bay of Pigs, the Missile Crisis, Jack Kennedy—still in front of him, and it isn't practical for me. But if you don't imagine an intermission about here, you may have the impression that the author is gasping for breath in the second half, whereas he is simply shuffling sets and characters and starting over with a slightly different kind of book.

By continuing the same one without pause, Mailer sacrifices several things, the most obvious being much chance of a careful reading by the first round of reviewers, who are guaranteed to use some of the space usually designed for analysis to groaning amusingly over the book's length.

To a busy reviewer, who is not paid by the hour or the ton of manuscript, the word "long" automatically means "too long," and if such a one does read all the way to the end it will likely be with a sarcastic impatience that relatively few books can stand up to (see *Moby-Dick*).

Fortunately, readers who pay for their books don't much mind how long they are, and for the material covered *Harlot's Ghost* is not too long at all. Insofar as the subject of the novel is the CIA and its doings, one feels that it has barely gotten started by the end, and the coy "to be continued" is properly frustrating; but as a study of a group of people, it has meanwhile gotten steadily weaker and weaker, until some of the principals barely limp across the pseudo finish line and one doesn't mind a bit if they decide to take a good long rest before starting up on their next rounds.

The most conspicuous casualty in length is the romance between Hal Hubbard and his godmother, Harlot's wife, Kittredge. This was quite a stunt to attempt in the first place. It is hard for most male writers to render a female character at novel length, especially with the audience primed to jeer as it is with Mailer, and to some extent one may feel he has solved the problem by cheating a little and taking what used to be called a man's mind and just adding skittishness. But this is to quibble. Anyone, man or woman, attempting to describe Katherine Hepburn, let alone Eleanor Roosevelt, would encounter even more disbelief. Indeed, any character held up to this kind of scrutiny begins to look kind of funny, so Mailer's women never have a chance.

But by normal community standards, Kittredge is real enough and even likable enough (tastes will differ, as in real life). But Mailer is not content to leave her lifting the lightweights: she must also be captivating enough to keep our young narrator, who is many years her junior and lubricious to boot, in unconsummated thrall for the length of an Irish courtship almost entirely on the strength of her letter-writing ability, which, unlike her bewitching presence, is right out there on the page for us to be bewitched by, or not, ourselves.

As with any loony endeavor, the wonder is that this affair works at all. The note of private-joke casualness struck by any two strangers writing to each other is as hard to capture as a random number in math; yet, with our complicity, Mailer makes Kittredge's letters sound real and plausibly attractive and sufficiently idiosyncratic right through the Uruguayan period, which means halfway through the book.

After which, forget it, as you might suppose. By the time Jack Kennedy has come and gone, the two lovers just seem to be shoveling information at each other in whatever voice comes to hand, and their occasional declarations of love sound perfunctory and no longer make sense to anyone but themselves. What on earth do they think they're in love with at this point? We have reached the stage where the onlookers have completely given up on the couple. He may still be charmed by her caprices and changes of mood, but we don't have to be. And whatever Kittredge decides to do next, be it, as the opening suggests, switching gears and taking off with Dix Butler, or merely flying to the moon, is all the same to us.

And the same goes double for her much advertised Alpha and Omega interpretation of personality. This gender-lite contribution to the world's stock of dualisms—yin and yang, animus and anima, etc.—is almost the only trace in the book of Mailer's spitballing period when he was spraying the landscape with theories, and feminist critics may make what they will of the fact that he hands it to a woman. But it surely should be taken as a sincere compliment, a gift from the heart, because the theory is vintage Mailer. Note, by way of trademark, that there is no personality permitted, no life lived, within the extremes: either your Alpha is on top today or your Omega, and Lamda and Upsilon might as well pack up and go home. Anyone consulting the rich jumble in his own head may be relieved to learn that it all boils down to two distinct, fully articulated personalities—not one self to get drunk and the other to go to church, but each to do both, with varying degrees of willingness and profit—because from the inside one could swear there are a dozen or so bits and pieces of personality rattling around in there with one disheveled spokesman fronting for the lot of them to the outside world.

In other words, the theory, as baldly stated, seems at once both too schematic and too vague, and no better or worse than a hundred other theories that the owners don't even bother to patent. The test of course is where Kittredge, a paid psychologist for the CIA, goes with it, and the answer I fear is just about nowhere, except to apply it to assorted events with predictably imprecise results: so-and-so's Omega was really running wild today, it obviously hasn't talked to his Alpha in months (but then what can you expect of a Gemini whose star is in Pisces?).

The only use for this jabberwocky worthy of the rest of the book would be to cite it as an example of the crazy things the CIA was willing to pay money for in those days. And if the author didn't mean it that way, this is neither here nor there. The point is the Alpha-Omega doesn't matter a straw to the real business of the novel. The only excuse for introducing it in the first place was presumably to provide some intellectual underpinning for a tale of divided souls. But this is not the primary work of the novelist anyway, which has fortunately been done so well and thoroughly in scene after fine scene that no amount of jawboning can fatally harm it.

The labyrinthine psyches of the feral American Dix Butler and the serpentine Chevi Fuertes sprawl all over Kittredge's blueprint obliterating the lines, and when the two or more of their personalities are finally brought together the shock of battle, of self colliding uncomprehendingly with self, almost explodes off the page. And this is just one of several epic male encounters, to which Mailer now brings the insights of age combined with the alertness mixed with apprehension of youth and of a time in life when one might, especially if one was Mailer, find oneself suddenly thrust into the very center of such scenes.

So well does Mailer convey the latent menace of the unhousebroken male that one of his most powerful confrontations can actually get away with occurring offstage in the best Aristotelian manner, without losing an ounce of fire power. The mere thought of Bill Harvey and Harlot being alone in the same room brought back memories to me at least of gazing spellbound at the headmaster's door and wondering what's happening in there, and what they will both look like immediately afterward. So it's deflating to think that whatever it was could have been reduced even conceptually to a couple of Greek letters playing on separate seesaws. But here as elsewhere, one feels that Mailer the novelist and observer has scooted so far ahead of Mailer the thinker that the old philosopher can barely see his gifted partner's back, although he still keeps trying to jump on it.

Harlot's showdown with Harvey is one of the imposing peaks that defines the shape of the putative Volume One. But it is a defect of the novel and of the agency as well that both characters should be dragged into Volume Two, the Cuba volume, where they manifestly don't belong. In the case of Harlot no real harm is done. Although Latin America isn't his circus, Harlot can make mischief and subplots anywhere he goes, and the worst that happens from the novel's point of view is that the reader mildly wishes that he, with his bag of tricks, and his wife Kittredge with her theories, would just go away for a while and let us concentrate on this new stuff. Harlot is presented as a man of a thousand faces, but he's always wearing the same old one when we see him.

But the case of Bill Harvey is serious and constitutes perhaps the book's most convincing criticism of the CIA. It is a feature of large organizations in general (for some reason, the Jesuits come to mind) that they like to keep their best people moving around and around until all the stars wind up in the wrong place—where if these best people are Jesuits they will learn humility and if they are agents they will from time to time imperil the free world, or at least inflict twenty or thirty years' worth of damage on it.

In such organizations, when Parkinson's law of upward failure is blocked vertically, it simply branches out sideways. Bill Harvey and his sidekick Dix Butler in Cuba, two Wagnerians in Puccini-land, neither know nor want to know that in this part of the world fighting words are actually an honored alternative to fighting, and that the last thing Castro or JFK wants is for anyone to be crass enough to act on Fidel's arias. But what do politicians know about these things? thinks Harvey, from deep in the bag, his regular habitat, as it seems to be half of the agency's. The CIA has its own wisdom; and Harvey, fresh from playing God in a *real* theater, knows better than anybody. Name a country, and he'll tell you what's good for it.

So it came to pass, in Mailer's book at least, that Harvey and Butler, or cold warriors just like them, pretty much took Cuban policy by the scruff and hauled it into their own sphere, rocking the boat so hard that diplomacy was impossible and incidentally giving their president a much more fiendish fight than he ever got from Castro—although Mailer, on his best behavior throughout, doesn't offer a specific assassination theory, but just surrounds the event with Cuban-CIA intrigue and leaves it up to us.

Fortunately a novelist doesn't have to prove anything at all, just make it convincing, and by echoing and embellishing Philip Agee's diary of those days [*Inside the Company: CIA Diary*], Mailer at least establishes (charmingly) a convincing setup for his version; the buzz of politics and toy soldier preparation with the Cuban refugees, the huge concentration of agency attention and personnel, and the nonstop unofficial raids on the Cuban coast to keep the pot boiling—all this just for a Bay of Pigs? Since that halfhearted fiasco is the most reliable guide we have to JFK's own wishes, it is tempting to say that Mailer wouldn't have to prove his case even outside a novel. If the agency *didn't* want more war with Cuba than Kennedy did, then neither his moves nor theirs make any sense at all.

What Kennedy did want may possibly be deduced from his own rather dreamy choice of *deus ex Pentagon* to the Cuban mess, namely the quiet but ugly American himself, Edward Lansdale, surely the ultimate misplaced star of the cold war. Lansdale was by now in the position of somebody who had bet Truman to win in 1948—an expert forever, even if he never bet right on anything else as long as he lived. Having successfully won the obviously somewhat special hearts and minds of the Filipinos, Lansdale, the Kennedy boys figured, could do it anywhere, and before he was through, this peace-loving soul would have wandered into and slightly exacerbated hostilities in both the Caribbean and Southeast Asia.

If this cross between a Bible salesman and minor college professor (Mailer's version is kinder than Graham Greene's) ever indeed had a chance in Cuba—and early returns suggest that he was completely at sea—the hostility of the agency quickly took care of that: for all its glamorous trimmings, the CIA had long since become a rock-ribbed bureaucracy that knew just how to deal with hotshots from upstairs, and of all the hearts and minds that Lansdale ever failed to work his charms on, none proved colder or more impenetrable than those of his countrymen, Bill Harvey and the boys at the club.

Meanwhile, back at the White House our president is making elaborately sure that no future novelist will ever have far to look for love interest, and it takes only the slightest of segues for our narrator to find himself spang in the middle of a Kennedy love caper.

Of all the real names in the book, the author makes the best case for using Kennedy's. He says you can't just invent a sexy, forty-two-year-old president, any more than you can invent a Frank Sinatra. And Mailer has the good sense not to march these lions on stage but to leave them mostly in the *oratio obliqua* (extremely obliqua at times) of a flaky, hard-drinking air hostess named Modene Murphy, who is definitely the kind of woman Mailer can describe well, although doing so will probably not advance his cause with feminist critics. Within the limits of celebrity mimickry, Mailer acquits himself ingeniously, dashing off a charming and somewhat Shavian Kennedy, a warm-blooded version of Shaw's Julius Caesar toying good humoredly with a considerably hipper Cleopatra. (Nothing is harder than for an older novelist to capture a young character just right, and Mailer's Castro also sounds a touch too world-weary for his age in the few lines he's

given: or maybe it's just the cares of state talking. In any event, both characters represent possible readings; neither is a travesty.)

There are no real travesties to be found in the book even when the characters seem to beg for it. Mailer had obviously decided he can get more out of them with the utmost seriousness and seeing them as far as is humanly possible as they see themselves. If he seems at times to have stayed inside them a little too long and gone over to their team halfway, that's the chance you take when you work this close to your subjects. And the reward is the best Faustian deal a novelist could hope for, a slew of convincing portraits, even down to the bit parts, the faces at the embassy, the voices at the bar.

If, to suggest another equally impractical redrawing of the book's boundaries, **Harlot's Ghost** were to begin with the narrator's arrival in Berlin, properly introduced, and end with the Bay of Pigs, it would be a much harder book to carp at. During most of this span, the author is safely within what athletes call "the zone" where, at least in terms of what he is attempting, he can do no wrong. If he announces an anecdote, or starts a scene, you have the sense that this is just what the story needs at this point. And even the CIA craft mumbo jumbo, which earlier in the book had reminded me of a slightly breezier version of Melville on whales, seems like part of the fun.

Which means that the reader is in the zone too, and helping. And so what if a character occasionally forgets his or her obligations not to sound *too* much like the author and barks out something in purest Mailerese ("believe this," someone will say in mid-sentence, or "be very sure that . . . "). Just as one doesn't notice the terrible prose in the last twenty pages of an Agatha Christie novel, so too whatever mistakes Mailer inevitably makes in this impressively long stretch of first-rate work are swept up in the action all the way to the Bay of Pigs, which Mailer describes in the manner of Stendhal at Waterloo: by the time the participants know what is happening, the battle is long since over. And they have the rest of their lives to discover that what seemed to them like the whole universe, or at least the glorious start of a major war, is perceived as a minor embarrassment on its way to a footnote by the outside world.

It can't happen too often that history offers such a perfect climax to what an author has been saying. The Bay of Pigs has almost everything Mailer's CIA is made of: hot air and hocus pocus, fecklessness and waste. The one thing it lacks, unfortunately, is the one thing that would let Mailer off the hook for good, namely finality. The Bay of Pigs didn't change the CIA or even chasten it; it simply made the boys mad, to the roots of their schoolboy souls, and eager to make themselves seem even more necessary, to the roots of their bureaucratic souls.

No doubt to end the book here would be false to the facts, and to the nature of the subject. Still, it would be good for the novel, which after all, is not a perpetual motion machine, but is designed from the outset to go a certain distance, and not a heck of a lot further. Even a novel about the Hundred Years War has to end sometime, but *Har-*

lot's Ghost runs right over the sides of the frame as the author tries to cram more and more history into a manifestly finite picture. The natural size has actually been established quite firmly by the opening sequence: as we enter an appropriately sinister country house, Harlot has either just died or defected, and Hal, Bix, Kittredge, and one other key character have been assembled and frozen there, as in a game.

Whatever else it does, the book obviously has to go back and lead the characters step by step into the house and unfreeze them and show why any of this matters: which means, at the very least, that it has to keep us interested in them. Yet faced with a choice of delivering on that pledge or giving us a sizzling account of the Cuban Missile Crisis, Mailer doesn't hesitate.

Nor at this point should we perhaps want him to. By the time Khrushchev and Kennedy face off over the missiles, Harlot is just improvising like an old vaudevillian anyway, and not growing into the rich strange character we've been promised, while Hal and Kittredge are barely hanging on to each other like marathon dancers, in case the author should need them sometime. And the house, which has been so portentously described along with its ghost, disappears altogether. Meanwhile, Hal's father Cal has undergone a quirky surge of life as a character, and Mailer has the wit and good sense to place any conjectures about Marilyn Monroe's death squarely in Cal's tipsily romantic skull. But Cal won't even be in the big-bang scene that opens the book, so this is just more garnish. And the author's own interest in resolving his story may be divined from his announcement that he plans to dash off a book about Picasso before he gets round to it. And if Picasso should lead to Matisse, or possibly to a novel about bullfighting (take that, Papa)—well, 1,310 pages is a lot of good behavior to make up for.

So we may never know what happened. Yet *Harlot's Ghost* would not be the first book to contain a disastrous structural flaw (in the case of *Tender is the Night,* the flaw is almost a landmark by now). And the many excellent pages of this one should not be buried under its mistakes. Mailer writes English by ear and he swings for the fences, so his gaffes can be spectacular, but so can his successes, and I noted more apt and pleasing phrases than in any other Mailer book I can remember.

Beyond that, he has written a surprisingly well-orchestrated picaresque novel—more Deighton than le Carré, if one must have these slatternly comparisons—about a masonry within a masonry, namely about the Ivy Leaguers at the heart of the CIA who have been put on unlimited expenses to do what they do best, which is to dissimulate from morning to night, practicing on their wives and children and each other and occasionally on their opposite numbers from Russia for the big game that never comes, and secondly to have fun doing it—fun which seeps down through the ranks like laughing gas so that even the recruits from State Tech find themselves dashing off facetious memos in no time as part of their class apprenticeship.

No one, including Mailer, would suggest that this is the whole story about the CIA, most of whose work consists of clipping and pasting, as Miles Copeland's book, *Without Cloak or Dagger,* plonkingly reveals, or even the whole story about covert action. In his epilogue, Mailer claims only to be writing about his own CIA, a valid psychological structure based on the facts and concerning which he has some striking and remarkably wise insights, as if he has finished sowing his intellectual wild oats once and for all.

However, granted that a man should be allowed to do what he likes with his own CIA—and perhaps the less literally accurate he is, the better for him—one flaw remains, even in terms of Mailer's own construct, the seriousness of which readers may decide for themselves.

The reason the CIA attracted or at least neutralized so many left-centrists, who would have seemed its natural critics, was its apparent enlightenment and levelheadedness in a crazy-house time. Indeed when Joe McCarthy came sniffing around the CIA and Allen Dulles sent him packing, Dulles almost seemed to be winking at us—you'd be amazed at who we're hiding in here. The CIA was indeed anti-Stalinist—wasn't everyone?—but it wasn't insane on the subject, which was enough to make it seem like Voltaire in that atmosphere.

Much of this was undoubtedly flim-flam, designed to do exactly what it did, silence the little magazine folk, but some of it surely wasn't. A certain degree of sophistication, of coolness, has to have been at the very core of a CIA man's self-definition, his unmistakable proof that he wasn't an FBI man or other primitive. And the whole point of the real life James Angleton was that he was considered a crank by the illuminati of the agency, for his uncoolness about Communism, and those sappy enough to follow him were referred to by same as "fundamentalists," for taking up with such a Messiah. The drama of Angleton was that he was so good at getting, or faking, results that the agency had to go along with him anyway, until he almost took it over the edge.

But you would guess none of this from Mailer, who makes no attempt to differentiate Harlot's anti-Communism from that of the other spooks except to make it more high-flown. The others, when they talk about it at all, sound like run of the mill John Birchites. But Harlot sounds like—Spengler!

This seems to me a fat pitch missed, and a good story untold, but it's not quite the flaw I'm referring to, which is not so much the lack of philosophical smarts within Mailer's CIA (who finally cares?), as the complete lack of interest in, or apparent knowledge of global geopolitics. It is one matter to make the game the thing to the temporary exclusion of everything else, but it's another to deny these men even a few minutes of speculation about particular political situations—hardly a single politician is named the whole time we're in Berlin for instance—as if their work existed solipsistically completely outside of local politics while they gaze solemnly at something called World Communism and prepare themselves for the Big One. By leaving out part of their brains, Mailer has allowed his characters to seem a little less serious, a little more cartoony than they need have, but he has made up for it in ways that only he could have, and has given us, if you pick your pages carefully, a quite remarkable book about them. (pp. 41-8)

Wilfrid Sheed, "Armageddon Now?" in The New York Review of Books, Vol. XXXVIII, No. 20, December 5, 1991, pp. 41-8.

Bruce Bawer   (review date January 1992)

[In the following excerpt, Bawer acknowledges instances of admirable writing in Harlot's Ghost but generally faults Mailer's novel as deficient in characterization and plot.]

Harlot's Ghost consists of two texts. In the first, the "Omega manuscript," Mailer's alter ego, Harry Hubbard, relates the circumstances under which he learned, in 1983, of the apparent death of Hugh "Harlot" Montague, his godfather and CIA mentor and the ex-husband of his wife and cousin, Kittredge (also a CIA agent). Widely regarded in the Company as a "burnt-out case," Harry has an unadventurous job: he works on pro-CIA thrillers and serves as Harlot's ghostwriter (which accounts for one of the title's many meanings); he's also supposed to be drafting a definitive study of the KGB, but has instead been compiling a secret memoir of his career. That memoir, the "Alpha manuscript," which constitutes over nine-tenths of Harlot's Ghost, begins in 1955, when Harry—the Yalie scion of an old New England clan (though his mother was a "Jewish princess")—follows in the footsteps of his dad, an old OSS hand, by joining the Company.

Harry's early CIA years are busy ones: in Germany, he takes part in the Berlin tunnel escapade; in Uruguay, he works for a pre-Watergate Howard Hunt; in Miami, he's in on the Bay of Pigs operation. In place of Judith Campbell Exner—the real-life bed-mate of Sinatra, Kennedy, and Mafioso Sam Giancana—Mailer gives us a stewardess named Modene Murphy, who sleeps not only with those three worthies but also, naturally, with Harry (who, according to Kittredge, is "just as pretty as Montgomery Clift"). He's privy to the inside skinny on Marilyn Monroe's death, the J. Edgar Hoover-Bobby Kennedy rift, and the JFK assassination—all of which, though "Alpha" takes us only as far as 1965 (the story, we're told, is "TO BE CONTINUED"), seems to point toward a Grand Unified Conspiracy Theory that before we're done, assuming Mailer writes a sequel, will take in the deaths of RFK and Martin Luther King, Watergate, Iran-Contra, the Savings and Loan scandal, etc., and thereby solve the riddle of America, Mailer's love and obsession, once and for all.

Or so (one suspects) Mailer hopes. In point of fact, though none of his books has offered so panoramic a view of the world according to Mailer, Harlot's Ghost doesn't come anywhere near to being, as its dust-jacket claims, "the culmination of one of America's great literary journeys, a novel to fulfill Mailer's lifelong obsession with the mystery of America." Quite simply, the further one gets into this book the less it reads like a novel; gradually, all one's hopes of character development, suspense, and dramatic conflict are crushed by the steamroller of amorphous, diaristic narrative (much of it in the form of letters be-

tween Harry and Kittredge—who, during the period covered by "Alpha," is still Mrs. Montague, a chastely adoring Cousin Daisy to his earnest young Nick Carraway). Even grammatical rules are steamrollered. Mailer routinely employs the incorrect form "equally as," replaces "I" with "myself," says "so soon as" instead of "as soon as," and dangles modifiers (including one in the book's very first sentence). Throughout the book, his prose wavers from wordy to workmanlike, its generally flat tone often giving way to a synthetic-seeming portentousness, heavy on highfalutin abstractions and artificial syntax, with which Mailer's longtime readers will not be unfamiliar: "I had signed up with him [Harlot] as if he were fate itself. There are more metastases in guilt than in cancer itself. . . . I was like an iron filing skittering about on a plate as magnets are shifted beneath. Powerful as gods are those magnets." Mailer has never been known as an exquisite stylist; if the writing here is especially slovenly and redundant, however, one has the impression that it is because he has been more than usually fixated on filling pages. Just as many an architect has sought to build not the most beautiful but the tallest skyscraper, it seems clear that the guiding aspiration here was less to write something great than to write something big.

It seems clear, too, that Mailer wants us to see Harlot's Ghost as mirroring America's bigness, in the same way as, say, An American Tragedy or U.S.A., and wants us to see the CIA—whose operatives live in an atmosphere of betrayal and subterfuge and uncertainty, and who must, from time to time, do evil in order to serve good—as the ultimate symbol of America's moral ambiguity, an emblem as equivocal as Hawthorne's scarlet letter and Melville's white whale. Mailer goes out of his way to incorporate allusions to native literary touchstones: Harry hikes up Mount Katahdin, apparently in order to make us think of Thoreau; Kittredge's first name is Hadley, an apparent hommage to Hemingway's first wife; Hunt suggests that Harry use the name of Robert Jordan (the hero of For Whom the Bell Tolls) as a cover; and Harry compares kissing Kittredge to "picking up a great novel and reading the first sentence. Call me Ishmael." To Harry, the "primary fact" is that he is a Hubbard, descended from Bradford and Fidelity Hubbard, who came to Massachusetts in 1627; and the name Bradford, of course, brings to mind William Bradford, who in his History of Plymouth Plantation established the idea of America as a setting for sacred drama, in whose settlers the "worke of God" was "manifest."

This Puritan view figures crucially in Harlot's Ghost. Harry, Hugh, and Kittredge are all Christians who labor on behalf of "this Christ-inspired civilization" and who, if they do something evil in the line of duty, see it as "transcendental wickedness that partakes of goodness because its aim is to gain the rightful day." Harlot, who calls his CIA lectures the "High Holies," is described as "a manifest of the Lord" by Harry, who proclaims: "What a man of the cloth he would have made!" Kittredge quotes Harlot to the effect that "we were blessed in our work at the Agency because the best and the worst in ourselves could work together on a noble venture." And she herself is plainly supposed to sound like a Puritan-style Manichaean when she declares that "[i]f God is trying to tell us anything, it is that every idea we have of Him, and of the universe, is dual. Heaven and Hell, God and the Devil, good and evil. . . . " Significantly, Mailer's epigraphs—from Ephesians, Vanbrugh, and Roethke—all refer to the struggle, in either society or the soul, between good and evil.

Make no mistake: Mailer's aim here is not to paint his characters as self-righteous, unreflecting zealots. On the contrary, Harry is constantly aware that "[w]e cannot know the moral value of our actions. We may think ourselves saintly at the exact moment we're toiling for the Devil. Conversely, we can feel unholy and yet be serving God." Harlot warns Harry about both "cheap patriotism" and "cheap Christianity," and is frank about the likenesses in theory between Christianity and Communism, saying that "what's satanic about Communism" is that it "trades on the noblest vein in Christianity. It works the great guilt in us." A Soviet spy notes that while Russians speak of losing their souls, Americans speak of "free-floating anxiety"—but Harry and company *do* worry about losing their souls. Quoth Kittredge, after a project of hers ends in failure and death: "We live in a great moral trusswork, after all. To fight the Opponent, we will dare evil ourselves, and I feel as if I have. Only I did not come back with a compensating good. . . . Have I endangered my soul?" For all their soul-searching, however, Harry, Harlot, and Kittredge share the conviction that there *is* a vital difference between America and the Soviet Union, and that it comes down to the difference between faith and atheism. As Kittredge puts it:

> With all our abominations and excesses, we are a superior society to the Soviets because there is an ultimate restriction upon our behavior—we believe, most of us Americans, in God's judgment upon us (even if it is the last thing one can ever talk about). I cannot emphasize how crucial such a last inner fear, such a modesty of the soul, is to the well-being of society. Without it, the only thing infinite about human beings becomes their vanity, which is to say, their contempt for nature and society. They generate an inner belief that they know a better way to run the world than God. All the horrors of Communism come out of the vanity that they know that God is only a tool employed by the capitalists.

What is one to make of this apparent Trinitarian boosterism by a secular Jew? Surely one can imagine a novelist making out of the materials of *Harlot's Ghost* a profound and provocative work about the moral and spiritual challenges of *Realpolitik*. But Mailer has not done so. Taken though he is with the drama of Christian rhetoric, it is clear that he employs it not because it has a deep and heartfelt meaning for him but because he thinks this sort of oratory appropriate to a would-be Great American Novel. CIA veterans have said that Mailer's understanding of the agency is superficial and unconvincing; the same holds for his understanding of Christian theology. Certainly the spiritual reflections of Harry, Harlot, and Kittredge often recall not Augustine or Aquinas but earlier Mailer novels. Harry, for instance, sounds less like a Millerite than a standard-issue Mailerite when he says that at prep school "God was lust to me," and notes that, in plan-

ning Bay of Pigs, he realized that "I would mourn Fidel if we succeeded, mourn him in just the way a hunter is saddened by the vanished immanence of the slain beast. Yes, one fired a bullet into beautiful animals in order to feel nearer to God." Ditto Kittredge (whose CIA work consists mostly of psychological studies testing her theory that human consciousness has two components, a rational "Alpha" and a faith-driven "Omega") when she professes "that God is present when we make love" and "that somewhere in sexual excess—at least for good people, brave people—there is absolution." The Mailer of this novel is, in short, still very much the Mailer of yore, who in his heart of hearts acknowledges only two sacraments: sex and violence. Certainly the Mailer machismo hasn't ebbed: in a line that no one but the author of *An American Dream* could write with a straight face, Harry tells his mistress, "The mark of how much I feel for you . . . is that I love my wife, do you understand, I do love her, yet I still see you." And who but the author of *Marilyn* could have created the double agent who tells Harry that "the glamour attached to the possession of nuclear missiles" is "equal to sex with a movie star"?

If "God was lust" during Harry's preppie days, it was, he explains, because he was "introduced to carnal relations during my first year by an assistant chaplain of St. Matthew's." (This happened, incidentally, in a hotel on Washington's H Street, the letter "H"—as in Harry, Harlot, Hunt, heaven, hell, and Hemingway—being of huge, if obscure, import here.) Ever since that signal event, one gathers, Harry has been fighting off a yen for men. His colleague Dix Butler says, "Half of our agents are queer. It comes with the profession." (Both gays and spies, you see, "lead a double life.") Indeed, homosexuality is almost as pervasive in these pages as espionage. Harry makes nervous jokes on the subject, writing Kittredge that a colleague "chose to talk in a lisp as if we were planning a homosexual romp. (God, what if the KGB had a tap? Think of all those fey agents who would be thrown at me in months to come. Hubbard, the jewel of the Andes!)." In Uruguay, his mistress demands that he "prove to me you're not a queer," and later declares: "I bet you are a faggot. Deep down!" It was after spurning a pass by Dix that our hero found a woman and lost his virginity, during which encounter "[p]ictures of her vagina flickered in my brain next to images of his ass, and I started to come, and continued to come, and to come from the separate halves of me, and had a glimpse of the endless fall that may yet be found on our way into the beatitudes." What's going on here? The men-without-women theme has, of course, been popular with American novelists ever since Cooper sent Natty Bumppo into the woods with his faithful Indian companion; many an American hero has been a boy at heart, a Huck Finn who prefers male company and sees women as a threat to his freedom. Doubtless Mailer thinks he is giving us a 1990s version of this motif, a vision of the American male as torn to the depth of his soul between opposing urges, his bisexuality a metaphor for humankind's moral dualism. But what one comes away from this novel with, alas, is a picture of an aging author so desperately insecure about his own manliness, so threatened by women (and inclined to value them not for themselves but for their attachment to certain men), and so helplessly tethered to a pubescent boy's outsized horror of homosexuality, that he is incapable of addressing the topic of sex without coming off as a buffoon. Homosexuality is not a major theme here, then, so much as a running joke—a joke that only Mailer seems not to get.

It should be said that here and there in **Harlot's Ghost** one finds passages to admire—less, perhaps, for their literary merit than for the characters' frank expression of views that one does not expect to see treated sympathetically in a Mailer novel. Harlot attends a performance by Lenny Bruce, whose comedy foreshadows, for him, a bleak future where nothing is private or sacred; and Hunt speaks about how "Americans abroad are engaged in Envy-Control. We've shown the globe a way to live that's clean and prosperous, so they hate us all over the world." Certain episodes, moreover—an espionage class, a simulated KGB interrogation—represent an engaging use of CIA lore and lingo. Yet the debits here far outweigh the credits. There is too little showing and too much telling—in the form of chatty letters, facile Irving Wallace-type gimmicks (such as Harlot's lectures) for shoveling in research, and (by novel's end) excerpts from 1963 *New Republic* articles about Kennedy and Castro. Consequently, with few exceptions, Mailer's people and their emotions—notably Kittredge's oft-avowed infatuation with Harry—don't become real to us. Nor is the spy-world *mise en scène* delineated as convincingly or unsettlingly as in, say, John Le Carré, or the mystery of Harlot's supposed death, once established, ever returned to, let alone resolved. Though Mailer takes on some promising materials, then, he fails utterly to make a novel out of them. (pp. 58-61)

Bruce Bawer, "Big & Bad," in The New Criterion, *Vol. X, No. 5, January, 1992, pp. 58-63.*

FURTHER READING

Bibliography

Adams, Laura. *Norman Mailer: A Comprehensive Bibliography.* Metuchen, N.J.: Scarecrow Press, 1974, 151 p.
    Extensive listing of both primary and secondary materials on Mailer.

Biography

Manso, Peter. *Mailer: His Life and Times.* New York: Simon & Schuster, 1985, 718 p.
    Detailed "authorized" biography containing numerous photos and reminiscences of Mailer by his friends and fellow writers.

Mills, Hilary. *Mailer: A Biography.* New York: Empire Books, 1982, 477 p.
    Extensive critical biography.

Rollyson, Carl. *The Lives of Norman Mailer: A Biography.* New York: Paragon House, 1991, 425 p.
    Critical biography covering all aspects of Mailer's life and career through 1990.

Criticism

Alter, Robert. "The Real and Imaginary Worlds of Norman Mailer." In his *Motives for Fiction,* pp. 46-60. Cambridge, Mass.: Harvard University Press, 1984.
    Defends Mailer's attempts to write about factual political realities in works of fiction.

Amis, Martin. "Mailer: The Avenger and the Bitch." In his *The Moronic Inferno and Other Visits to America,* pp. 57-73. London: Jonathan Cape, 1986.
    Reprints several previously published articles on Mailer's public life.

Anderson, Chris. "The Record of a War." In his *Style as Argument: Contemporary American Nonfiction,* pp. 82-132. Carbondale: Southern Illinois University Press, 1987.
    Compares Mailer's and Tom Wolfe's treatments of the American space program in their respective works *Of a Fire on the Moon* and *The Right Stuff.*

Arlett, Robert M. "The Veiled Fist of a Master Executioner." *Criticism* XXIX, No. 2 (Spring 1987): 215-32.
    Examines the theme of execution in Mailer's works to illuminate his stylistic treatment of social and political realities in *The Executioner's Song.*

Begiebing, Robert J. *Acts of Regeneration: Allegory and Archetype in the Works of Norman Mailer.* Columbia: University of Missouri Press, 1980, 224 p.
    Detects allegorical and symbolic elements in Mailer's writings.

Braudy, Leo. "*Maidstone: A Mystery* by Norman Mailer." In his *Native Informant: Essays on Film, Fiction, and Popular Culture,* pp. 60-3. New York: Oxford University Press, 1991.
    Reprints a brief favorable review of Mailer's published transcript of *Maidstone,* an improvised film released in 1971.

Edmundson, Mark. "Romantic Self-Creations: Mailer and Gilmore in *The Executioner's Song.*" *Contemporary Literature* 31, No. 4 (Winter 1990): 434-47.
    Compares Mailer's romantic artistic aspirations to those of Ralph Waldo Emerson and refutes the prevalent critical opinion that Mailer's avoidance of a "high romantic style" in *The Executioner's Song* implies a break with romantic thought.

Girgus, Sam B. "Song of Him-Self: Norman Mailer." In his *The New Covenant: Jewish Writers and the American Idea,* pp. 135-59. Chapel Hill: University of North Carolina Press, 1984.
    Compares Mailer's philosophy with that of Walt Whitman, characterizing his works of new journalism as inherently metahistorical in that they represent "a literature that is synonymous with American culture and history."

Hersey, John. "The Legend on the License." *The Yale Review* 75, No. 2 (February 1986): 289-314.
    Briefly examines *The Executioner's Song* in an essay lamenting the failure of modern writers to clearly distinguish between fact and artistic invention in their works.

Jaehne, Karen. "Mailer's Minuet." *Film Comment* 23, No. 4 (August 1987): 11-17.
    Chronicles Mailer's directing of the film version of *Tough Guys Don't Dance.*

James, Clive. "Mailer's *Marilyn*." In his *First Reactions: Critical Essays, 1968-1979*, pp. 227-40. New York: Alfred A. Knopf, 1980.

Reprints a negative review of Mailer's biography *Marilyn*.

Kernan, Alvin B. "The Taking of the Moon: The Struggle of the Poetic and Scientific Myths in Norman Mailer's *Of a Fire on the Moon*." In his *The Imaginary Library: An Essay on Literature and Society*, pp. 130-61. Princeton, N.J.: Princeton University Press, 1982.

Examines mythic elements in Mailer's nonfiction narrative *Of a Fire on the Moon*.

Leigh, Nigel. "Spirit of Place in Mailer's *The Naked and the Dead*." *Journal of American Studies* 21, No. 3 (December 1987): 426-9.

Asserts that Mailer's inclusion of a map of the island of Anopopei in *The Naked and the Dead* is not incidental but is rather "a crucial part of the novel's design, functioning both as a controlling metaphor of the book and a guide to the process of reading it."

———. "Getting It Wrong: The Cinema of Norman Mailer." *Journal of American Studies* 24, No. 3 (December 1990): 399-402.

Surveys Mailer's unsuccessful efforts at filmmaking.

———. *Radical Fictions and the Novels of Norman Mailer*. New York: St. Martin's Press, 1990, 280 p.

Examines political and social views expressed in Mailer's novels.

Mayer, Hans. "Women's Liberation and Norman Mailer." In his *Outsiders: A Study in Life and Letters*, translated by Denis M. Sweet, pp. 123-30. Cambridge, Mass: MIT Press, 1982.

Ponders Mailer's confrontation with women's liberation in *The Prisoner of Sex*. Originally published in German in 1975.

McLaughlin, Robert L. "History vs. Fiction: The Self-Destruction of *The Executioner's Song*." *CLIO* 17, No. 3 (Spring 1988): 225-38.

Maintains that despite his adherence to facts, Mailer's tendency to undercut "the reliability of each of his source materials" in his nonfiction narrative *The Executioner's Song* "self-consciously destroys the idea of history as a vehicle for conveying truth."

Messenger, Christian K. "Norman Mailer: Boxing and the Art of Narrative." *Modern Fiction Studies* 33, No. 1 (Spring 1987): 85-104.

Traces the concept of sport in the writings of Mailer, who is considered to have "told us more about the meaning of aggressive male competition and the roots of its compulsion than any other current American writer."

Olster, Stacey. "Norman Mailer after Forty Years." *Michigan Quarterly Review* XXVIII, No. 3 (Summer 1989): 400-16.

Scrutinizes Mailer's ethics as reflected in his writings up to *Tough Guys Don't Dance*.

Pizer, Donald. "Norman Mailer: *The Naked and the Dead*." In his *Twentieth-Century American Literary Naturalism: An Interpretation*, pp. 90-114. Carbondale: Southern Illinois University Press, 1982.

Characterizes *The Naked and the Dead* as "a work in which Mailer has successfully created a symbolic form to express the naturalist theme of the hidden recesses of value in man's nature despite his tragic fate in a closely conditioned and controlled world."

Taylor, Gordon O. "Of Adams and Aquarius: Henry Adams and Norman Mailer." In his *Chapters of Experience: Studies in Twentieth-Century American Autobiography*, pp. 1-15. New York: St. Martin's Press, 1983.

Compares Mailer's view of history in *The Armies of the Night* to that of Adams's in *The Education of Henry Adams*.

Wenke, Joseph. *Mailer's America*. Hanover, N.H.: published for the University of Connecticut by the University Press of New England, 1987, 271 p.

Surveys Mailer's views of American society and politics.

Wilson, Raymond J. "Control and Freedom in *The Naked and the Dead*." *Texas Studies in Literature and Language* 28, No. 2 (Summer 1986): 164-81.

Explores elements of existentialism in Mailer's novel.

Interview

Farbar, Jennifer L. "Mailer on Mailer." *Esquire* 105, No. 6 (June 1986): 238-40, 243-44, 246-49.

Discusses Mailer's philosophical evolution as a writer.

Leeds, Barry H. "A Conversation with Norman Mailer." In *Conversations with Norman Mailer*, edited by J. Michael Lennon, pp. 359-77. Literary Conversations Series, edited by Peggy Whitman Prenshaw. Jackson: University Press of Mississippi, 1988.

Discusses the novel and film versions of *Tough Guys Don't Dance*, as well as Mailer's novels *Ancient Evenings*, *The American Dream*, *The Naked and the Dead*, and *The Executioner's Song*.

Bill Moyers

1934-

(Born Billy Don Moyers) American television journalist and nonfiction writer.

The following entry covers Moyers's print adaptations of his television documentaries through *Global Dumping Ground* (1990).

INTRODUCTION

A distinctive television journalist, Moyers is renowned for such documentary programs as "Bill Moyers' Journal," "The Fire Next Door," "The Vanishing Family," "The Secret Government," "A World of Ideas with Bill Moyers," and "Joseph Campbell and the Power of Myth." Moyers first gained widespread attention, however, as the author of *Listening to America,* a chronicle of his 13,000-mile journey across the United States during the summer of 1970. Since that time, largely through the medium of television, Moyers has become a well-known personality, praised for his earnestness, erudition, and thought-provoking discussions.

Moyers was born in Hugo, Oklahoma, to a working-class family. When he was a few months old, the family moved to Marshall, Texas, where he spent his youth. As a child during the 1940s, Moyers was deeply influenced by journalist Edward R. Murrow, whose radio broadcasts of the events of World War II were reported with dramatic intensity. In 1952, after displaying an aptitude for reporting during his high school years, Moyers enrolled at North Texas State College to study journalism and public affairs. In the spring of his sophomore year, Moyers wrote to Senator Lyndon B. Johnson, offering to help with the senator's reelection campaign. Johnson hired Moyers for a summer internship, and, impressed with Moyers's work, persuaded him to transfer to the University of Texas at Austin. There Moyers studied journalism and theology, worked as assistant news director at a local television station, and preached part-time at two small Baptist churches. Moyers received his bachelor's degree in journalism in 1956 and spent the following year at the University of Edinburgh in Scotland as a Rotary International fellow. Although Moyers returned to the United States to prepare for the ministry at Southwestern Baptist Theological Seminary, by 1959 he had decided that he was better suited for a career in public affairs.

From 1959 to 1967 Moyers advanced steadily in his political career, serving as special assistant to Senator Johnson, executive assistant during Johnson's vice-presidential campaign, deputy director of President Kennedy's newly created Peace Corps, special assistant to President Johnson, and, finally, Johnson's press secretary. In 1967, over Johnson's strenuous objections, Moyers resigned as press

secretary to become publisher of *Newsday,* one of the largest suburban daily newspapers in the nation. Under Moyers's tenure, *Newsday* garnered thirty-three major journalism awards, including two Pulitzer Prizes. However, by 1970 Moyers had so altered the newspaper's conservative editorial perspective that *Newsday*'s owner sold the paper, leaving Moyers unemployed. At this time, *Harper's* magazine offered Moyers a cover story if he would travel across the United States documenting his talks with people and gathering the mood of the nation. The article led to Moyers's first book, *Listening to America,* which was published in 1971 to critical acclaim. Based on the success of *Listening to America,* Moyers landed a job hosting a television news documentary for a New York City public television station that eventually evolved into the national program "Bill Moyers' Journal," a weekly show that addressed political and social issues. The winner of five Emmy Awards, the "Journal" ran from 1971 until 1976 and again from 1978 to 1981. From 1976 until 1979 Moyers served as chief correspondent of "CBS Reports," and for five years between 1981 and 1986 he was a senior analyst and commentator for "CBS News." Since that time Moyers has become a well-established figure in public television.

Moyers's works focus primarily on social and political issues. In *Listening to America* he documented his discussions with everyday Americans on such topics as the Vietnam War, youth, drugs, racism, unemployment, labor unions, law enforcement, and conservation. "Joseph Campbell and the Power of Myth" presents a series of six one-hour discussions between Moyers and mythologist Campbell conducted during 1985 and 1986. Aired in 1988, the year after Campbell's death, this series and its companion book launched widespread interest in Campbell's life and ideas on religion and myth, and astounded skeptics who thought the subject matter would meet with public indifference. Equally successful and even more sweeping in scope was Moyers's forty-one-part series "A World of Ideas," which consisted of conversations with such figures as historian Henry Steele Commager, pediatrician T. Berry Brazelton, and novelist Chinua Achebe on diverse issues. A follow-up series, "A World of Ideas II," contains an additional twenty-nine interviews with various thinkers. Other print adaptations of television documentaries by Moyers include *The Secret Government,* an exposé of the Iran-Contra scandal of President Reagan's administration, and *Global Dumping Ground,* which records the fallout of the international trade in toxic waste.

Moyers's work for television and the print medium has generally been well-received. Although some critics have agreed with Tom Wolfe's assessment that Moyers weakens his journalistic perspective through "stupefyingly empty generalizations" and "nice soft woolly concepts," most critics applaud Moyers's sense of topical balance, skill at simplifying difficult issues, sincere interest in his subject matter, and ability to draw out his subjects.

PRINCIPAL WORKS

Listening to America: A Traveler Rediscovers His Country (nonfiction) 1971
*The Power of Myth (interview) [with Joseph Campbell] 1988
*The Secret Government: The Constitution in Crisis (nonfiction) 1988
*A World of Ideas: Conversations with Thoughtful Men and Women about American Life Today and the Ideas Shaping Our Future (interviews) 1989
*A World of Ideas II: Public Opinions from Private Citizens (interviews) 1990
*Global Dumping Ground: The International Traffic in Hazardous Waste (nonfiction) [with the Center for Investigative Reporting] 1990

*These works were published as companion volumes to Moyers's television series.

CRITICISM

James Dickey   (review date 14 March 1971)

[*Dickey is an American poet, novelist, critic, essayist, and screenwriter who is perhaps best known for his novel* Deliverance *(1970). In the following excerpt, he outlines the social value of* Listening to America.]

"The best lack all conviction, while the worst / Are full of passionate intensity," said Yeats, and, from wherever we happen to be standing, we look at the current social and political scene and nod. Bill Moyers, former Special Assistant to Lyndon Johnson, and then publisher of *Newsday,* has had a look himself. Last summer he traveled 13,000 miles around the country. He is interested in no such extremes as best and worst; he is practical, and believes that this country and its present condition can be known and understood, and its problems in some way handled.

Listening to America is very much—it is exclusively—a "now" book. Its overtones and implications, however, may be something more than that. I doubt very much if there is or will be, of the traveling-around-asking-questions-to-all-kinds-of-people type of book, a more relevant (ah!) one than this. A great deal of its value stems from Moyers's own personality, and his gifts as a reporter. All through his long, earnest voyage over the United States he is flatly faithful to what he sees and hears, and he does indeed listen well.

And he is, in a very real sense, a man of faith: of faith in America—its institutions and its way of being in and dealing with the world—in its people and their basic resourcefulness and honesty. He also relies on an unfailing faith that if people will just *talk* to each other, get together on issues, everything can be worked out. There is little hint of the possibility, looming more and more these days, that there are conditions that nothing can help, like, say, the extinction of the grizzly bear or the destruction of the Everglades or the assassination of the Kennedys and Martin Luther King. Or the incredible boredom of American life, for which there appears to be no cure possible, or even thinkable.

The good thing about Moyers's book is that it is just systematic *enough.* It is not a survey, or even a "sampling." Though most of the time Moyers knows whom he wants to listen to and how he can be found, he is also refreshingly open to caprice: "I noticed a sign which announced 'Piqua, Home of Donald Gentile, World War II Air Force Ace, 1920-1951.' I grew suddenly preoccupied with Donald Gentile."

He goes to the Piqua, Ohio, cemetery to look for Gentile's grave. He can't find it, but he does manage to locate the great Mustang pilot's 78-year-old immigrant father, and one of his most moving interviews results. I like to think that Moyers remembers the afternoon with Patsy Gentile as life-giving human time, as I do my experience of reading about it. It is an account of the best kind of sympathetic exchange between strangers, and one cannot experience it without realizing how closed-off and uncreative one's own conduct has been, and for years.

Nevertheless, the majority of the exchanges deal with politics and society. Moyers wants to hear what people are thinking about The War, Youth, The Drug Culture, The Racial Problem, The Small Town Dependent on a Single Industry, Minorities, Unemployment, Labor Unions, Schools, The Police, Conservation. He believes with his very heart-bone in democratic process: in the interchange of ideas, in individual speaking-out, in the political power of the strongly-motivated single person, and above all in organization, and he wants to see for himself how (or if) these things are working out *really*. (p. 2)

In the meetings he attends, with the individuals with whom he converses, it is surprising how often the word "power" occurs. The conviction throughout the book is that something can be done about inequalities, about the ecology, labor abuses, unemployment, if power can be acquired by the right interests, whether blacks, Chicanos, Chinese, whether laid-off aircraft workers or employees of textile manufacturers being undersold by the importers of Japanese goods.

Except in one or two instances, there is no hint that voting power and institutional process cannot be invoked to bring about more desirable situations in specific localities. Moyers's questions to his interviewees demonstrate abundantly that he believes in the American political dream, and their answers indicate that they do as well, even to members of the drug culture and conscientious objectors sent to prison for refusing to be inducted into the armed services.

What to make of this? One thing I made of it is that the uneasy possibility that we may need some radically new form of government is not yet troubling mass America as much as I thought it might be. The second conclusion is something I should already have known: that for the majority of people truth resides in the platitude, not in the high idiosyncratic lightning of the genius-ridden phrase. "I think those people in Washington know what they're doing," "A man's got to respect the laws," "What I call the law is the will of the people."

How bad is this? How good is it? Moyers believes it's more good than bad. Thomas Jefferson would have agreed with him, though Alexander Hamilton, the flayer of the "great beast" of the people, would not have. Yet the fact remains that the very soul of America is committed irrevocably to the opinions, formulated in clichés of masses of human beings only half-equipped to think. Moyers has done well to go to them and reaffirm this, for better or worse. (pp. 2, 37)

> *James Dickey, in a review of "Listening to America," in* The New York Times Book Review, *March 14, 1971, pp. 2, 37.*

Tom Wolfe   (review date 25 April 1971)

[*Wolfe is an American author credited with developing New Journalism, a form of writing that unites characteristics and techniques of journalism and fiction. His best-known works in this style include* The Electric Kool-Aid Acid Test *(1968) and* The Right Stuff *(1979). In the following excerpt, Wolfe comments on what he considers Moyers's inability to ask probing questions of his subjects and his problematic handling of valuable material in* Listening to America.]

Bill Moyers was thirty-two years old and still the boy wonder of the White House that day in August, 1966, when he got on the telephone to pass along a message from his Daddy Warbucks, Lyndon Johnson, to Harry F. Guggenheim, owner of *Newsday,* the Long Island newspaper. Captain Harry, as he was known, was on the beach sunning his seventy-five-year-old shanks out in Cabaña Heaven at the time, and all at once he asked Moyers to come to work for him. To everybody's surprise, Moyers accepted. The Captain made him publisher of *Newsday* and indicated he would bequeath Moyers control of the newspaper when he died. Moyers said goodbye to Johnson, amid friendly tears, and moved to Long Island.

But soon he alienated first Johnson and then Guggenheim by playing up to New York State's most powerful Democrat, Bobby Kennedy, and steering *Newsday's* policies more toward the Kennedy wing of the Democratic Party. In May of 1970, while Moyers was off in Europe, Guggenheim sold *Newsday* to the Los Angeles *Times,* and left Moyers out in the cold.

Moyers now had to figure out how to reintroduce himself into American politics. He hit upon, among other things, a first-rate idea for a book. Most politicians' books, whether John Kennedy's *Profiles in Courage,* Eisenhower's *Crusade in Europe,* Johnson's *My Hope for America,* or Nixon's *Six Crises,* are, at bottom, variations on the masterpiece of the genre, Trujillo's *The Basic Policies of a Regime,* which is a 210-page illustration of Shaw's epigram: "Principles without programs equal platitudes." Moyers, on the other hand, headed out across the United States, not as a statesman dispensing answers but as a reporter concerned with finding out what his countrymen thought about the problems of the day.

Indeed, the best things in **Listening to America** are the slices of life that Moyers got because he had the enterprise to leave his "narrow strip of the Eastern Coast," as he calls it, and go all over the country talking to people. . . .

Which is to say that Moyers-as-reporter turns up his share of good material. But he also runs into his share of trouble handling it. It is almost as if, bereft of his great patrons, he were suddenly back where he started out seventeen years ago; namely, in the University of Texas journalism school. He succumbs to such amateurisms as Tape Recorder Guilt. The first time a reporter uses a tape recorder, the thought of using only a minute fraction of the great heap of transcriptions he ends up with may seem a waste too monumental to bear. So he stuffs them into the story by the handfuls. Of the 342 pages in **Listening to America,** 154 are made up of people rattling on from one to eight pages at a stretch.

In order to put these talkathons into some kind of perspective, Moyers will insert a few stupefyingly empty generalizations at the beginning: "Next to loneliness, the national disease is homesickness," "A city has a beginning and an end; suburbs go on forever," and then try to wrap them up with a Pregnant Symbolic Detail at the end, such as: "In her right hand she gripped a plastic Santa Claus."

By far his biggest problem, however, is diffidence. One of the hardest jobs in journalism is making yourself walk up to total strangers and ask questions. Too often Moyers gives in to the convenient vice of talking instead to friends, friends of friends, official spokesmen, experts—and cab drivers. In San Francisco's Chinatown, for example, he starts off with a marvelous cornball gasper about how he spent "two nights in a Chinatown tourists never see," then proceeds to offer nothing more than five pages of tape-talk by a Chinese teacher he knew before he got there.

But Moyers's most profound timidity seems to be political. He seems to have questioned his sources solely in terms of nice soft woolly concepts every newspaper reader by now can slip into like an old Sears car coat: Generation Gap, Middle America, the Establishment, Bossism, Minority Rights. . . . When it comes to the taboo subjects of our times, such as class, status, and ethnic hostilities, Moyers is as gun-shy as the old pols who prefer to write about principles rather than programs. It is not only the reader but also Moyers who suffers because of his play-it-safe approach. After 13,000 miles back and forth across the U.S.A., Moyers ends up looking like the pleasant but banal young tour guide many Americans have spent too much time with on the Gray Line already.

> *Tom Wolfe, "I Hear America Talking," in* Book World—The Washington Post, *April 25, 1971, p. 4.*

Roger Sale   (review date 12 August 1971)

[*Sale is an American educator, editor, and critic. In the following excerpt, he suggests that Moyers's journalistic impartiality is inadequate to the task he has set himself in* Listening to America.]

Calvin Trillin writes for *The New Yorker,* Bill Moyers for *Harper's;* both live in or near New York. Yet because Trillin is originally from Kansas City and Moyers from east Texas, when the news and pressures of the Sixties led them to think something large was happening in the country, they set out, away from the big city, toward the heartland, which had once been home. Somehow, they seemed to imagine, their considerable journalistic "eastern" skills might be combined with their back home ways and knowledge to produce a record of what was happening. They wanted to talk to people, to see things, nothing big except in so far as it impinged on ordinary people. Presumably theirs was an impulse like Eugene McCarthy's when he came out of the committee room and said that what he'd heard was so crazy he had to go to "the people." These men knew what they could learn from the big city, and somehow that was not enough.

The impulse is understandable and honorable; it partakes of much that good men can believe in about American democracy. But the result in each of these books is not very satisfactory, because the combination they sought, of journalistic habits with the impulse to withdraw from the sphere in which those habits were learned, turned out to be impossible, perhaps in ways neither could have foreseen. As the people and events "out there" are rendered to make them clear to the readers of *The New Yorker* and *Harper's,* most of what these writers sought gets lost.

Of all journalistic forms, the *New Yorker* sketch is one of the most thoroughly established and least capable of adjustment. There are thirty-two such sketches in Trillin's *U.S. Journal,* and he knew while writing and we know while reading each one that after about two thousand words the piece will end soon; a short sketch runs six pages, a long one eight. As he travels about the country Trillin must look for whatever can neatly be subsumed into the form: no confusions, no mysteries. (p. 9)

Bill Moyers had nothing like Calvin Trillin's obligation to be strict to a form, but he gets into similar difficulties nonetheless [in *Listening to America*]. His great weakness is that he seems not to have remembered or recognized the consequences of his being Bill Moyers, former director of the Peace Corps, LBJ's best adviser in the days before Vietnam turned to quicksand for American schemers, trustee of the Rockefeller Foundation. Moyers can get lots of doors opened to him, and the very ease with which he can get those doors opened limits him as Trillin's format limited him. Go to a political convention and talk to the bosses, go to Earlham or Antioch and talk to the president of the college, go to a small town and talk to the mayor and the newspaper's editor, go to a ghetto and talk to the black leaders and take a ride in a patrol car—come to Seattle and talk to executives of the Boeing Company in an interview I couldn't get in a hundred years.

If, as well, you are a decent man and have the ability to listen, these people will talk easily. But they all end up giving set speeches because all are as articulate as one might expect and all want to talk to Moyers. As a result, they are all rather predictable and after a while the scenarios of Moyers's travels seem to write themselves.

The most striking example of this comes during Moyers's visit to Lawrence, Kansas. He had stopped there and interviewed the people he knew could give him an angle: the editor of the paper, the ex-druggie who runs a semi-clinic for kids whose lives have gone blurry, the former mayor who knew how to become involved in the university and the drug scenes. Then, that night, a policeman shot a young black and hell broke loose. Here, if ever, was a chance for Moyers to lose his composure, to be frightened, to try to describe the way trouble smells. But instead Moyers is impeccable as he interviews all sorts of new people: a number of policemen, the president of the University of Kansas, blacks of many different persuasions, hippies who demonstrated in protest of the shooting.

Each one of these people says so precisely what we would predict he'd say that it begins to seem that Moyers's sympathy and skill at interviewing make his impartiality seem like blindness, a disease: I don't know what the world is coming to; They're going too far; It's about time; If it's not a revolution, what is it; It ain't too late to start killing niggers; We don't want any more trouble; You better keep passing through, honey. To read this episode is to feel that had Moyers traveled incognito, or allowed himself to open up more to what he felt, then he might not have found it so easy to talk to all those people and something more surprising might have happened.

The VFW in Richmond, Indiana, is not happy about Vietnam but tries to conduct business as usual; the hugely successful rancher in Wyoming thinks he lives in a great country; farmers in eastern Washington are angry about radicals on the Washington State campus; a cop in San Francisco sees terrible blindnesses and ravages among the footloose young; the Chicanos in south Texas are acting up. It just is not news.

The habits of reportial listening become so ingrained that when Moyers wants to open up he can't find his own voice and simply adopts someone else's. He begins his account of Houston by saying he finds it "one of the most exciting cities in the country" because it is "astir with the future." It sounds very promising; we all know LBJ did a lot of boondoggling and have wondered if that meant death or life for Houston. But this is how Moyers goes on:

> Off in the distance I could see new buildings glistening in the sun and steel shells of others under construction. Some predictions say it will one day be our largest city. The absence of fixed boundaries in the charter has allowed wild annexation of peripheral townships and acreage, and already 1.3 million people live in a metropolis of some 450 square miles lying a flat 41 feet above sea level. Still the city continues to spread. Its people earn $6 billion a year.

The Chamber of Commerce is talking, not Moyers. Whatever excites him about Houston, it can't be that.

Bill Moyers is fascinated and disturbed by America, and his restlessness and desire to know and tell about it are admirable. He does not want to gobble up his subject, and, given his 13,000 miles of traveling, his sense of scale is good enough. But we should, after 342 pages, get more than the familiar outlines of these fascinations and disturbances, and we don't. Perhaps a clue to why comes on page 342:

> People are more anxious and bewildered than alarmed. They don't know what to make of it all: of long hair and endless war, of their children deserting their country, of congestion on their highways and overflowing crowds in their national parks, or art that does not uplift and movies that do not reach conclusions; of intransigence in government and violence; of politicians who come and go while problems plague and persist; of being lonely surrounded by people and of being bored with so many possessions; of being poor; of the failure of organizations to keep the air breathable, the water drinkable, and man peaceable. I left Houston convinced that liberals and conservatives there shared three basic apprehensions: they want the war to stop, they do not want to lose their children, and they want to be proud of their country. But it was the same everywhere.

That is a fair enough, even an intelligent enough, state-

ment of the obvious truths Moyers has elicited. But that Moyers can do no more than this is perhaps best revealed in that telltale phrase about the people in Houston: "liberals and conservatives." The obvious point is that the labels are too crude to fit even the people in Houston with whom Moyers talked. But perhaps Moyers's real trouble is that he would not have dreamed of talking to someone without trying to get his side of an issue, or of leaving town without trying to talk with someone of an opposing persuasion.

Issues make news; the good reporter listens to both or all sides. Behind that, America is the sum of all the issues and all the sides. These are the assumptions with which Bill Moyers and Calvin Trillin work, and they are so deeply assumed that they are probably not noticed by their authors. But, if I may be so bold, I think they are the assumptions of what Willie Morris calls the Big Cave that is New York, of the *Times,* of the television networks. Scrupulosity, impersonality, and fairness are great virtues indeed, as can be attested by anyone who lives somewhere in the America out there where he is subject to the narrownesses and caprices of bush journalism.

Furthermore, CBS and the *Times* have placed us all in their debt with their recent reports on the knavery and the evil clownishness of the last two administrations, and we needed organizations as powerful as these to do the uncovering. When it comes to reporting on the feds there just aren't enough I. F. Stones to go around, and even he could not have gotten the scoops that CBS and the *Times* got. But the subject at hand is not the feds but the people of America, and I would like to suggest that the kind of reporting offered by the *Times* and the networks, by Bill Moyers and Calvin Trillin, is practically by definition inadequate and inappropriate for the task. (pp. 9-10)

> *Roger Sale, "Hello Out There," in* The New York Review of Books, *Vol. XVII, No. 2, August 12, 1971, pp. 9-10.*

Sandra Lieb   (review date 15 November 1988)

[Lieb is an American educator and editor. In the following review, she finds The Secret Government *compelling though lacking in substantive analysis.]*

This adaptation of the Emmy-winning public-television program [Moyers's *The Secret Government*] is a ringing indictment of "an illegitmate, White House-inspired network of spies, profiteers, mercenaries, ex-generals, and superpatriots," who freely make war abroad and threaten rights at home, accountable to no one. Focusing on the Iran-Contra scandal and incorporating excerpts from his 1973 Watergate documentary, Moyers traces the growing imperial presidency as well as many covert operations since the National Security Council was formed in 1947. There are secret wars discussed here, assassination attempts, governments overthrown, arms profiteering, and illegal contra aid—all without the knowledge of Congress. Moyers tells this incredible story with the fast, compelling pace of television news. But this is still a script; the treatment is general and brief, the declarative sentences seem simplistic on the page, and the contrast to the thoughtful and eloquent afterword Moyers has provided here makes one wish he had expanded this adaptation into a fuller book.

Sandra Lieb, in a review of "The Secret Government: The Constitution in Crisis," in Booklist, Vol. 85, No. 6, November 15, 1988, p. 536.

A public emerges when citizens take part, not when they merely watch. Citizenship is more than voting; it means participating in the dialogue of democracy. Television, the modern commons, could make this possible.

—Bill Moyers, in his introduction to A World of Ideas II: Public Opinions from Private Citizens, *1990.*

Alex Raksin   (review date 16 April 1989)

[*In the following review, Raksin offers a generally favorable assessment of* A World of Ideas.]

Reporting events and political rhetoric without examining underlying trends and ideas, nonfiction programming on television is not renowned for its subtlety of thought. For a few months beginning last September, however, Bill Moyers managed to imbue the airwaves with a more reflective spirit in the PBS series, "A World of Ideas." Regular readers of literature will be familiar with many of Moyers' subjects—from Isaac Asimov to Derek Walcott—but [his book *A World of Ideas*], based on edited transcripts of the show, should still be of interest, for Moyers doesn't lower the level of dialogue for TV. On the contrary, he consistently focuses these conversations through thoughtful comments and enlivens them by playing provocateur.

Moyers is clearly fond of this latter role. In his interview with Northrop Frye, for instance, he playfully puts the Canadian literary critic on the defensive by confronting him with a number of stereotypes (e.g., "Canadians are so friendly that they even say, 'Thank you' to a bank machine"). In many other dialogues, Moyers takes just the opposite role, tempering his subjects' extremes of optimism and pessimism. While Joseph Heller paints a bleak picture of American politics, for instance ("It is the function of a leader in a democracy, if he wishes to be a leader, to manipulate the emotions and ideas of the public"), Moyers gently counters Heller's cynicism ("But, like taxes, isn't politics the price we pay for civilization?"), leading Heller to acknowledge that "There's no other government that we can envision that we would prefer to democracy."

Moyers' conclusion is a minor problem in these pages. Attempting to avoid partisanship, he claims that the only consensus most of these thinkers reach is that "we can best negotiate the future through a multitude of shared acts."

In fact, Moyers' subjects agree on many issues, such as the need to require our politicians to speak more spontaneously. Were Moyers to have stressed these areas of agreement, he might have been able to give his world of ideas greater clout in the world of action, since squabbling intellectuals are usually the first to be ignored in politics. One gathers that Moyers would favor such influence, for as he writes, "the men and women who shared their ideas in the series are public thinkers. Their Ivory Tower is just a mailing address; they are at home in the world."

Alex Raksin, in a review of "A World of Ideas," in Los Angeles Times Book Review, *April 16, 1989, p. 6.*

Alison Friesinger Hill   (review date 4 June 1989)

[*In the following review, Hill pronounces* A World of Ideas *a well-balanced, inspirational collection of conversations.*]

Forty-one interviews, well-edited transcripts from the recent public television series of the same name, compose *A World of Ideas.* The subjects have been chosen from diverse fields and include the historian Forrest McDonald, the novelist Chinua Achebe, the geneticist Maxine Singer, the linguist and author Noam Chomsky and the movie executive David Puttnam. Mr. Moyers does an excellent job drawing out each of his subjects; there is a pleasing balance, both of overall areas and of topics covered within the interviews. Although Mr. Moyers imposes few constraints, he does have an overall agenda, albeit a broad one. He is inquiring into contemporary values and concerns, within the United States and in global society. The men and women interviewed address these issues on their own respective territories, as it were: the pediatrician T. Berry Brazelton stresses the importance of family; the psychiatrist Willard Gaylin believes we need a "rediscovery of community"; the sociologist Anne Wortham wants greater respect for individuals; and the educator Sara Lawrence Lightfoot sees education as the paramount issue. Not surprisingly, every person interviewed speaks as if his or her concerns were the most imperative. Because of this and the huge number of ideas presented, there is a danger of the reader being left confused and skeptical in a cacophony of strident voices. But this remarkable group presents articulate, intelligent, energetic plans; the various solutions to a wide world of problems serve not to bewilder but to inspire.

Alison Friesinger Hill, in a review of "A World of Ideas," in The New York Times Book Review, *June 4, 1989, p. 23.*

James Gardner   (review date October 1989)

[*In the following excerpt, Gardner reviews* A World of Ideas *and examines the reasons for Moyers's success.*]

A World of Ideas, the series of interviews that Bill Moyers conducted on PBS last winter, has now been gathered together in book form. This new format is generally more satisfying than the original broadcasts because it permits us to study more closely those arguments that possess real substance, and to skip over much cant and attitudinizing. Thus, while the broadcasts were generally duller than polite people were willing to concede at the time, these transcripts do provide some moments of genuine intelligence and illumination.

The book consists of forty-two "conversations with thoughtful men and women about American life today and the ideas shaping our future." It is divided into two parts, "Our Changing American Values" and "American Values in the New Global Society." The roster of names is remarkably and perhaps even shrewdly comprehensive, containing not only celebrities but also many personalities from science and law who are apt to be unfamiliar to most readers. Feminists, blacks, Hispanics, Asians, and even Canadians will find no reason to feel left out, while conservatives, who are not always well served by public television, will be comforted that writers like Peter Berger and John Lukacs have been included. The only significant omissions would seem to be musicians and visual artists, and with the glaring exception of Noam Chomsky, controversial political spokesmen from the far Left or the far Right.

In general, these interviews are most valuable when the subjects have some very specific expertise to bring to the discussion, and when they are allowed to use that expertise in all its specificity: the pediatrician T. Berry Brazelton on contemporary child care, Arturo Madrid on the condition of Hispanics, and William Julius Wilson on the condition of blacks in contemporary America. However, the interviews are most entertaining when their subjects turn out to be live wires whom Moyers, despite his best efforts to the contrary, cannot contain within his narrow orbit: men like Tom Wolfe and Isaac Asimov who, bless him, seems sublimely oblivious of all the contemporary orthodoxies to which "thoughtful people" are supposed to subscribe.

Least interesting of all, and unfortunately in the majority, are those "thoughtful" people whom Moyers has obviously selected because they intuitively share his own leftist centrism, generalists who are theoretically "interesting" but who in fact could not invent a genuinely provocative statement if they set their minds to it for weeks in advance: F. Forrester Church, pastor; Vartan Gregorian, president of Brown University; Sara Lawrence Lightfoot, educator; and many more.

The popular success of *A World of Ideas,* as of most of the other projects with which Bill Moyers has been associated over the years, evidently results from the distinctive chemistry generated among the three parts in the equation— Moyers, his subjects, and his audience. It is this equation that, ultimately, is the most interesting aspect of what, with only slight exaggeration, may legitimately be called "the Moyers phenomenon."

The first and most essential component of the equation is, of course, Moyers himself. For many Moyers addicts who are more interested in the interviewer than in his subjects or what they are saying, the present volume is likely to be something of a disappointment—this, for the very reason that the book is superior to the telecasts, namely that Moyers, who was irremovably omnipresent on the screen,

imposes himself far less in print. Yet even in print Moyers—the Thinker as Everyman—remains a presence, and his addicts will get some measure of the fix they came for in this volume.

What is perhaps most striking and least obvious about Moyers is his utter mirthlessness. A Southerner who is ever eager to invoke his deeply religious upbringing, Moyers seems to take everything absolutely in earnest. Here is a man without ironies, for whom the opportunity to discuss ideas is "truly joyous."

In one of his earlier and most successful endeavors, *The Power of Myth,* Moyers interviewed the mythologist Joseph Campbell, who had much to say about the power of archetypes. Those meditations seemed especially pregnant to Moyers, no doubt because he himself traffics conspicuously in archetypes.

Thus—and here we come to the second component of the equation—so many of the personages included in *A World of Ideas* seem to be there not because they have any intriguing or important or original ideas to express, but because they conform obediently to one of several archetypes of what Moyers apparently imagines a thinker looks and sounds like.

There is, for example, the patriarchal Grand Old Man, the exalted father figure, embodied in the historians Henry Steele Commager and James MacGregor Burns, and the literary critic Northrop Frye. There are those elegant, soft-spoken "Noble Savages" like the Nigerian novelist Chinua Achebe and the Caribbean poet Derek Walcott. There is the slightly oddball and alarmingly hirsute Jewish Explainer, represented by the novelists E. L. Doctorow and Joseph Heller, who are called upon to provide a kind of comedic interlude to the more ponderous meditations that are going on around them. There is the Liberated Woman, who is not thereby precluded from being attractive or having a family (the historian Elaine Pagels, the philosopher Martha Nussbaum, and the novelist Louise Erdrich).

Finally, to complete the equation, we come to the audience, the viewers of public television. These are people caught up in careers and in "getting and spending," who are apt to feel that "the world is too much with us," and for whom it is reassuring to know that there are certain remote corners of the country where ideas are still discussed and taken seriously.

And yet along with this commendable sentiment, there is at work here a less lovely element, one that is only occasionally exposed, an oddly complacent, never fully articulated suspicion of unearned superiority. For to watch Moyers and his guests is to join effortlessly in a process of wrinkling one's nose at the supposedly meretricious glitz of mainstream American life.

It is this ability of Bill Moyers to persuade his millions of viewers of their essential apartness from the workaday pursuits and preoccupations of their own society that, surely, is the secret of his success. He has squared the circle and brought into being a miracle: elitism for the masses. (pp. 70-1)

James Gardner, "The Thinker as Everyman," in Commentary, *Vol. 88, No. 4, October, 1989, pp. 70-1.*

Bill Moyers with *American Film*   (interview date June 1990)

[In the following interview, Moyers discusses journalism, television, politics, and the role of storytelling in society.]

Bill Moyers acquired his love of conversation as a boy in Marshall, Texas, a half-century ago. Although he would grow up to become a broadcast journalist of the first rank with ground-breaking PBS series like *Bill Moyers' Journal* and *A Walk Through the 20th Century,* it's Moyers' love of conversation that has been his greatest gift to the medium.

In his series "A World of Ideas," consisting of half-hour talks with preeminent Americans in fields ranging from ethics to literature and science, Moyers provides a safe haven for the reasoned, the impassioned and the informed. Virtually alone among the thousands of hours of programming beamed into American homes, Moyers' half-hour corner of the broadcast spectrum gives the country a chance to celebrate thinking.

The late scholar of mythology Joseph Campbell was one of the most inspiring intellects captured by Moyers on video. In "Joseph Campbell and the Power of Myth," Moyers served as the nation's surrogate student to a master storyteller. Their talks proved among the most popular hours ever broadcast on public television and led to a book that remained on the *New York Times* best-seller list for more than a year.

[American Film]: Could you tell us why you chose the world of television?

[Moyers]: I was saying earlier that coincidence is God's way of remaining anonymous. It's as Joseph Campbell said in the series, "When you're living your life, it doesn't appear to have any pattern to it, [but] when you look back, it appears as if, after all, a perfectly composed rhythm brought you from there to here." And when I look back, I think of my life as a series of coincidences, of God's way of remaining anonymous. And the biggest coincidence in my coming to television is that I got fired from the job that I had been doing.

I was publisher of a newspaper on Long Island called *Newsday.* When it was bought, by the *Los Angeles Times,* one of the conditions of the elderly, senile gentleman who was selling it was that they fire me. [Laughter] And they did.

And there I was, at 36, having been seven years in government, a cub reporter on a newspaper—I had worked my way through the University of Texas doing local news for the radio and television station—and then I published this paper for three years. And I had no skills. I didn't know what to do. And the phone rang, and Willie Morris, who was the editor of *Harper's* magazine, said to me, What are you going to do? I said, I don't know. He said, I'll tell you what: If you'll go and get on a bus, and travel the country

for three months, I'll give you the whole magazine in November just to write about your experiences. And I thought, Well, that's good. I didn't ask him what he would pay me [laughter], which shows you how desperate I was to have something to do.

I got on that bus, and I spent three months traveling the country—20 years ago this summer, in fact; it was 1970. I wrote *Listening to America*—my wife suggested the title—and they put it on the cover of *Harper's,* and a book came out of it in January of the year, which became a best-seller. It was pure reporting. (p. 17)

The late Samuel Beckett had a wonderful line, "In reading, a voice comes to you and whispers, Imagine." Imagine. Doesn't happen in television, because you can't stop if imagination summons you. You have to go on, because we're doing the work for you.

—*Bill Moyers*

In your program with Joseph Campbell, he said that "to look at our society's mythology is to look at the front page of The New York Times." *Where does journalism fit into supporting or developing or fighting against the mythology of our society?*

Well, we don't make the mythology. But we do put the front page there. And it's a limited front page. We don't put everything there or on the evening news. But we gather the stories that then reflect or become the mythology. Other people make the myths. The media today is a vast publicity machine for this explosion of fame that, I think, is the characteristic of the '80s. You know, this is a terrible game to play, but I think historians 100 years from now will look back and see the '80s as the decade in which fame literally went through the roof—our fascination with fame, with people who are celebrities.

And the media, on the whole, is the engine driving that. We put it out there, but we don't make the mythology. The mythology is made by the interpreters, by the people themselves, who read into what we report far more than we, as prosaic scribblers, see. And that's really what journalists are, whether it's with a pen or with a video camera. We're scribblers. The mythology comes from elsewhere.

Could you comment on how the shrinking sound-bite and the emphasis on flash over substance has affected presidential politics in this country, particularly since your days with President Johnson?

I think the American political discourse today is very banal, and I think it's in large part because of television.

When I spoke to a group of journalism students recently, I passed out Lincoln's Gettysburg Address. I said, You have two assignments: Pick out the nine-second sound-bite, and pick out the 14-second sound-bite. Turn them into a report for the evening news. It might read, "Four score and seven years ago," and then trail the voice down and say, "President Lincoln spoke to a vast crowd today, but his speech was not as well received as that of Edward Everett Hale, who spoke immediately before and had the audience cheering . . . " and cut to the sound of the audience cheering and all that [laughter]. I mean, you should see the sound-bites. Try it some time. Try it.

Ethnically, culturally, intellectually, historically, psychologically, we are a complex society, and that cannot be conveyed through sound-bites. So our political speech has become banal, in large part, because of this.

We did research on the sound-bites for these series of documentaries that they call *The Public Mind*. And we show an excerpt. In the 1968 campaign, a protester at Columbia University challenged Senator Muskie, who was running for vice president, to let him speak. And Muskie turned the microphone over to him, and the protester, a young student, got up and spoke, and more than 60 seconds of his speech was on the evening news that night. No presidential candidate got that much time in 1988.

What does that do to our speech? Imagine if you had to romance your love in sound-bites [laughter]. It would be, "How do I love thee," and then you cut to the correspondent, "He went on to list nine ways that he loved." Look what it would do to the language of love. And it's the same with the language of governance and politics. You cannot get complex ideas honored in television today.

Even with longer sound-bites, I wonder if you wouldn't agree that television is ill-suited to complex thought because of the fact that it allows no time for reflection.

Television is limited in that respect. The late Samuel Beckett had a wonderful line, "In reading, a voice comes to you and whispers, Imagine." Imagine. Doesn't happen in television, because you can't stop if imagination summons you. You have to go on, because we're doing the work for you. We're controlling the pace of the run, of the race, for you. With a book, you can turn back and say, What did it say? You can make comparisons, which is one of the chief functions of all intelligence, of critical thought. To say, Wait a minute: He said this on page four, but he said that on page nine. How do you reconcile, if you can reconcile, the contradiction? Can't do that on television. It's one reason why debates don't really work on television, because you can't stop and get the rhythm of the reply. So I try to draw out a person's thoughts, hoping that you will follow up.

The technology of television flattens everything out. And in flattening things out, it goes to the lowest common denominator, which is devoid of all nuance and subtlety and history and context so that it becomes consensus-creating, even though it is not intended to impose a consensus on people. (pp. 19-20)

I think the Campbell series is dearest to my heart. Could you talk a little bit about the writing process and the place of myth and fairy tales to empower the writer—to give him

information and images that will release him to his art form?

It's all story, isn't it? It's all story. Before there was cuneiform, they sat around the campfire, and they told stories. They had just killed the buffalo and they were fixing its meat, and somebody said, What if we killed the last buffalo? What if there's no more buffalo? Then morning would come, and the buffalo would come—Boy, there must be a big buffalo up there who keeps sending us little buffalo— and they developed creation stories that way.

It's all story. Whether it's verbal, whether it's visual, whether it's linear with words, it is still a way we have of trying to make sense of ourselves and the universe around us. There are good stories and bad stories, and good storytellers and bad storytellers—some in print and some with cameras and some orally.

As I sat with my father recently, he just talked about his boyhood in east Texas. My God, what a storyteller he was. Fourth-grade education, but what a storyteller. It's all story. There isn't anything worth doing, in my judgment, except telling stories. The oral tradition is the oldest, and the video medium is the newest, but it's always a matter of story.

Most of our information is fed to us from television not only in sound-bites but in little visual bites, too. We're literally put into the point-of-view that whoever's shooting wants us to have. And I wonder if education—teaching children the power of television and how it is manipulative at times—can maybe help change that?

We advocate that in *The Public Mind*. The New York Times chastised me for returning to "academic experts"— literally that term—for these shows, but I think of the teacher as someone whose whole life has been given to pioneering insights about a certain field. Crispin Miller at Johns Hopkins, or Stuart Ewen at Hunter College, or Herbert Schiller at the University of California, San Diego— they all argue for teaching visual literacy. So that this next generation of kids can begin to think, Who is sending me a message? and, Why did they choose this particular medium to send the message? Why is the camera angle here instead of there? When Oliver North went before Congress, his people insisted that the network cameras be a little below him so that you'd see this jutting Marine's jaw looking up with that bold and courageous defiance at this tribe of elders up there who are about to pass sentence on him. He made that theater by the angle of the camera. I think young people are going to have to be taught visual literacy in the same way I was taught by Inez Hughes to diagram sentences.

Some of the choices you make—camera angles, the questions you ask—are these conscious decisions, something you learned, or just part of your personality?

Who knows? I mean, I was a good student. I wasn't a scholar, but I really was a good student. I knew how to take notes, I knew how to listen to teachers, I knew how to get teachers to feed me. . . . That goes all the way back to junior high.

I really do believe, with a few exceptions, that most of the people I've met are better than they seem. And if you want to do the best you can for somebody else, make him or her feel as good as he or she really is. I really do believe that if I could sit one-on-one with the most inarticulate person in this room, in a couple of hours, I would understand something of the essence of that person. I believe we have these higher and lower angels. I have my lower angels, and somebody can bring them out. I have my higher angels, and it takes help to reveal them.

The function of political leadership is to listen to what we value. It's also true with television. But I know an SOB when I see him [laughter]. Johnson used to say, If you can't walk into a room and tell instantly who's for you and who's against you, you don't belong in politics. He learned that in life. (p. 44)

> *Bill Moyers and 'American Film', in an interview in* American Film, *Vol. XV, No. 9, June, 1990, pp. 17-20, 44.*

Merry Ann Moore   (review date Winter 1990-91)

[In the following excerpt, Moore summarizes the thrust of Global Dumping Ground.]

It must have been tempting for the folks at the Center for Investigative Reporting (CIJ) to portray the international trade in hazardous waste as the good versus the bad and ugly. But in *Global Dumping Ground: The International Traffic in Hazardous Waste,* the companion book to CIJ's first independent television documentary, CIJ reporters manage to cover many gray areas of an issue with manifold legal, economic and sociological nuances. The thriving trade in hazardous chemicals—some legal, much not—is responsible for more than 2.2 million tons of toxic garbage crossing international borders yearly. Our toxics regulatory structure concentrates not on reducing waste, but on controlling it. The 1,800-or-so *maquiladoras*—American factories located across the Mexican border—have largely failed to comply with an agreement requiring them to return waste, and little doubt exists that this material is dumped—the New River from the Baja into the Imperial Valley is among California's most polluted.

Global Dumping Ground is at its most intriguing—and outraging—when profiling the profiteering businessmen who stimulate the international toxics trade. These "waste brokers," no questions asked, arrange transport to foreign fields. The "pioneering" Colbert brothers, New Jersey waste brokers, obtained material from the U.S. government and resold it to developing countries, from DDT to rolls of lead-contaminated paper to be sold to an African country as toilet paper from the Treasury Department. Townspeople near Juarez, Mexico store their drinking water in a U.S. container which held a liquid formula of sodium hydroxide. Zulu villagers downstream from a British processing factory in South Africa drink water with a mercury concentration 1.5 million times higher than the World Health Organization standard.

Many African countries have assimilated the idea that nature is something to overcome from the West; a constituency dedicated to protecting its land from harmful chemicals is frequently absent. Racism plays a part; in the U.S. and elsewhere, there is a correlation between where hazardous waste is disposed of and who lives there.

> *Merry Ann Moore, "Trashing Trash," in* San Francisco Review of Books, *Winter, 1990-91, p. 54.*

The Times Literary Supplement   (review date 8 November 1991)

[In the following excerpt, the critic offers a qualified appraisal of Global Dumping Ground.]

Global Dumping Ground is a spin-off from an American television documentary. . . . It is short, snappy and grim, though its provenance—the Center for Investigative Reporting—promises more in the way of original revelations than it delivers. (Most of the book's data appear to have been gleaned from a careful scrutiny of the world's press rather than from intrepid primary research.) The story begins in 1987, when a smallholder near the port of Koka in Nigeria stumbled on a nice little earner: he received $100 a month for storing mysterious tins on his plot of land. He died in 1990, as did nineteen of his fellow villagers, after eating contaminated rice. The tins contained 4,000 tonnes of toxic waste from Italy, including 150 tonnes of PCBs (Polychlorite Biphenyls), and they eventually cost 11 million dollars to repatriate. The annual international trade in toxic garbage now exceeds 2.2 million tonnes. *Global Dumping Ground* traces many of these tonnes to their producers—often government installations in developed countries—and follows their peregrinations, both inside and outside the law—to Third World nations and others that should know better than to receive such noxious imports but whose regulations are feeble. Conspicuous among the latter is the United Kingdom. The book is flatly contemptuous of Britain's fragmented system of by-laws and their haphazard enforcement, laws which permit hazardous waste to be mixed with ordinary rubbish and dumped in landfills—whose number in 1988 totalled 4,156 in comparison with just 325 in the United States.

> *S. M., in a review of "Global Dumping Ground," in* The Times Literary Supplement, *No. 4623, November 8, 1991, p. 32.*

FURTHER READING

Biography

Bouton, Katherine. "Bill Moyers: The Quest for Quality TV." *Saturday Review* 9, No. 2 (February 1982): 16-18, 20. General discussion of Moyers's background and his television career. Remarking on what motivates him in his work, Moyers says, "The stewardship of air time is critical. It's not the ability to change the course of things directly, but you can change a person's view of the world. You can affect the quality of his day."

Ferguson, Andrew. "The Power of Myth: Bill Moyers, Liberal Fraud." *The New Republic* 205, Nos. 8 & 9 (19 & 26 August 1991): 22-5.

> Provocative exposé implicating Moyers in dishonorable activities while serving as an aide in the administraton of President Lyndon Johnson and quesioning the financial ethics of his relationship with public television. (See Moyers's 1991 citation below.)

Moyers, Bill. "An Open Letter to the Editor from Bill Moyers." *The New Republic* 205, No. 15 (7 October 1991): 14-15.

> Two-page advertisement paid for by Moyers as a response to Andrew Ferguson's article in *The New Republic* (19 & 26 August 1991), which Moyers characterizes as an "abominably inaccurate attack." (See Ferguson citation above.)

Zurawik, David. "Bill Moyers: On the Road with the Hero of a Thousand Televisions." *Esquire* 112, No. 4 (October 1989): 139-40, 142, 144-46, 148.

> Personal account of Moyers and his career.

Criticism

Lindberg, Tod. "The World According to Moyers." *National Review* XLI, No. 4 (10 March 1989): 22-5.

> Essay which faults Moyers's television series "World of Ideas" for its "fuzzy-left political agenda." Lindberg perceives Moyers as "a public televangelist on a mission of salvation—saving the children, saving the planet, saving viewers from themselves."

Moyers, Bill. Introduction to *A World of Ideas II: Public Opinions from Private Citizens*, edited by Andie Tucher, pp. xxi-xiv. New York: Doubleday, 1990.

> Presents Moyers's views on the proper role of television in society.

Additional coverage of Moyers's life and career is contained in the following sources published by Gale Research: *Contemporary Authors*, **Vols. 61-64;** *Contemporary Authors New Revision Series*, **Vol. 31; and** *Contemporary Newsmakers: 1991 Cumulation.*

Richard Selzer

1928-

American short story writer and essayist.

The following entry is an overview of Selzer's career.

INTRODUCTION

A practicing surgeon for most of his life, Selzer draws on his medical experience for much of the material in his short stories and essays. In these works, Selzer focuses on the beauty and transcendence that he finds in the harsh realities of disease and suffering. Critics have praised Selzer for his lyrical prose and his ability to intertwine fiction with nonfiction.

Selzer was born and raised in Troy, New York. His father, an unsuccessful general practitioner, died suddenly when Selzer was fourteen, leaving behind an unpublished novel about an affair between a doctor and a prostitute. Selzer's mother regarded the book as scandalous and destroyed it soon after her husband's death. Critics consider these events important for a full understanding of Selzer's work. Although Selzer grew up in a conservative Jewish household, he was fascinated by Roman Catholic beliefs and rituals and often attended Catholic services during his youth. Both Jewish and Catholic religious symbols appear frequently in Selzer's writing. After graduating in 1948 from Union College in New York, Selzer earned a M.D. from Albany Medical College in 1953. Military service interrupted Selzer's residency at New Haven Hospital, requiring him to spend the next two years in Korea and Japan. His year in Korea, which Selzer described as "a powerful experience," provided the inspiration for his story "Korea," which has received considerable critical attention.

Selzer began writing at the age of forty in an attempt, he has said, to translate his "helplessness and despair as a surgeon into an affirmative act of creation." His first works, which were horror stories, appeared in *Ellery Queen's Mystery Magazine* and were later collected in *Rituals of Surgery*. Selzer became the object of critical attention with the publication of his second book, *Mortal Lessons: Notes on the Art of Surgery*. Realizing that the emotional involvement necessary for his work as a writer conflicted with the detachment required of him as a surgeon, Selzer retired from surgery in 1984, although he continues to volunteer for INTERPLAST, an organization of surgeons who perform plastic surgery in poverty-stricken third world nations. His experiences as a volunteer surgeon have provided material for some of the essays and stories in *Confessions of a Knife, Letters to a Young Doctor,* and *Taking the World in for Repairs.*

Although Selzer has written on non-medical topics, such as the legends of medieval saints and his travels in Italy, his most distinctive works focus on some aspect of medicine. Often forced to confront the grotesque and traumatic manifestations of disease, Selzer's characters search for love, transcendence, and the meaning behind their suffering. In "Sarcophagus," for example, a surgeon whose patient bled to death when a cancerous aorta ruptured during exploratory surgery struggles to find meaning in the patient's suffering which he has transferred onto himself. While some critics find Selzer's subject matter distasteful and fault his prose as overly ornate, others have praised his effective use of symbolic imagery, his success in conveying the mystical nature of his characters' experiences through the interweaving of fact and fantasy, and his skillful fusion of disparate images. Typical of Selzer's prose style is the description in his essay "The Knife" of a scalpel as a cello bow, a tulip, and a tool for entering the body. Charles Anderson asserts that by means of such figurative language, Selzer creates "an alternative to contemporary medical discourse, . . . reeducating himself, re-creating his world, and making that new world accessible to patients, colleagues, and outsiders alike."

PRINCIPAL WORKS

Rituals of Surgery   (short stories)   1974

Mortal Lessons: Notes on the Art of Surgery   (essays)
   1977

Confessions of a Knife   (essays)   1979

Letters to a Young Doctor   (essays and short stories)
   1982

Taking the World in for Repairs   (essays and short stories)   1986

Imagine a Woman, and Other Tales   (short stories)
   1990

CRITICISM

David B. Morris   (essay date Spring and Summer 1980)

[*Morris is an American educator and critic. In the following essay, he examines the relationship between
beauty and pain in Selzer's stories.*]

The modern history of beauty contains a moment of profoundest change. In 1757 human understanding of the
beautiful passed from philosophy and religion into the
possession of psychology and aesthetics. It is a change
from which we have still not recovered.

Edmund Burke—then an unknown Irishman in his twenties—is the theorist chiefly responsible for changing Western ideas of beauty. His *Philosophical Enquiry into the Origin of our Ideas of the Sublime and Beautiful* (1757)
founded the infant discipline of aesthetics on a division as
relentless and fatal as the Cartesian split between matter
and thought. In the *Enquiry* beauty loses all its ancient
(classical and Christian) associations with knowledge,
truth, goodness, and wisdom. Plato, for example, considered beauty the proper goal of love. The true lover is a na-
scent philosopher—the true philosopher an enlightened
lover—because the passion for individual beauty leads finally to the love of truth (philosophy) itself. "Man seeks
to be near beauty," as Paul Friedländer summarizes the
view espoused by Socrates, "because the soul's wings grow
at the sight of beauty." In Burke's *Enquiry* the soul has
lost its wings, and the lover has lost his soul. "We must
conclude," writes Burke, "that beauty is, for the greater
part, some quality in bodies, acting mechanically upon the
human mind by the intervention of the senses." Beauty,
it turns out, is whatever produces the sensation of love,
and what produces the sensation of love is anything appropriately small, graceful, varied, soft, colorful, undulating,
delicate, mild, sweet, muted, or elegant. It is not coinci-
dental that most of these qualities meet in the female figure. For Burke, beauty (in a choice which would have baffled the Greeks) is exclusively feminine. Missing but implicit is the standard accoutrement of parasol and corset,
lisp, fainting spells, and tears. "Beauty in distress," adds
Burke, as if winking to the new entrepreneurs of senti-

ment, "is much the most affecting beauty." The beautiful
here stands completely defrauded of any cognitive or spiritual power: helpless, domestic, and trivial. Burke believed
that he had advanced knowledge by discovering the psychological laws and social purpose of beauty—as the force
which unites solitary individuals in a community of love—
but his real achievement was to reduce the beautiful to a
list of arbitrary forms and qualities. It occupies the exhausted category which we find reserved today for movie
stars, sunsets, rainbows, swimsuit competitions, old works
of art, and little fuzzy animals who don't bite.

With such an inheritance, it is hardly surprising that beauty is no longer among the primary aims or subjects of serious art. Artists who elect to pursue the beautiful reclaim
it—like Baudelaire and Picasso—through deliberate strategies of dismemberment.

Richard Selzer in his brief story **"Raccoon"** narrates the
first-person account of a surgeon who visits a female patient as she recovers from recent abdominal surgery. She
ignores his tactful knock, secluding herself in the toilet at
some secret act. Worried, violating her secrecy, the surgeon finds her seated, bent forward, with her arm plunged
elbow-deep in her freshly opened incision. A razor blade
lies on the floor. He hurries her back to bed, appalled, and
hastily begins to suture the wound, all the while grasping
for an explanation of the terrible scene he has witnessed.
The woman remains calm. Then the surgeon experiences
a moment of revelation: "All at once I knew what it was,
what she was reaching for, deep inside. It was her pain!
The hot nugget of her pain that, still hissing, she would
cast away. 'I almost had it,' she said. 'You should have
waited,' she said."

Pain, mysterious, elusive, compelling, is one of Selzer's recurrent subjects. As a practicing surgeon he might be considered a specialist in pain. Painlessness is now among our
national obsessions: anesthesia has become, like television,
a household god, and at the first sign of discomfort we
rush for our pills and doctors. Suffering we prefer to en-
trust to professionals. What we ask from the professionals,
prior even to cure, is something to kill the pain. For Samuel Johnson, Burke's great contemporary, pain was a one-
word definition of living. Smallpox, toothache, childbirth,
kidney stone, syphillis, and gout marked the ages of man
with successive torments. (Selzer writes a fine essay on the
once-dreaded **"Stone."**) Every era, of course, has its tormenting maladies—cancer and insanity are the familiar
modern plagues—but we have managed a peculiar refinement upon disease. We sleep through harrowing operations; we soothe our conscious hours with utopian chemicals, often designed to simulate unconsciousness. Pain is
understood mainly as something to be gotten rid of. Tolstoy's Ivan Ilych at the approach of death screamed continuously for three days in a voice so terrible that you
could not hear it through two closed doors without horror. (This was a passage to enlightenment.) Today, while
under-developed nations battle starvation, Western man
is astonishing for how many of his fellow countrymen, at
any single moment, are free from the intensest suffering
of hunger, injury, and disease. A numbness to pain has become (in ways historically unprecedented) our habitual

state. Into this analgesic world, pain intrudes with the sudden shock of authenticity, as if nothing in human life were so real, so believable. We *know* we are in pain, even if we inhabit a universe of doubt. The unexpected intrusion of pain, like an ingot hissing deep within the abdomen, seems almost a reminder of forgotten knowledge.

In **"The Hartford Girl"** Selzer takes his subject from the newspaper rather than from the hospital. He quotes a clipping which contains the following account: "A sixteen-year-old girl slashed her wrists and arms and then rushed to the steps of a Roman Catholic church poking a razor to her throat while a crowd of three hundred persons cheered and screamed, 'Do your thing, sister.'" Like the hospital, the newspaper is a cultural repository for vignettes on the indifference and brutality of urban life. Selzer avoids the trap of cliche by implicating his narrator in the scene as a fascinated voyeur. Unable either to intervene or to stop watching, the narrator witnesses more than a senseless parable of modern horror. In their Dionysian frenzy, the citizens of Hartford reenact a form of primitive rite. Memories of blood sacrifice work like an aphrodisiac as the crowd surges round the girl, exposing what the narrator calls "our changeless ancestral themes." At last she collapses. After the tardy officials of reason (a priest and policeman) remove her, people still linger, murmuring, bending toward the dark blood-pooled steps, but now "strangely spent, melancholy"—as if drained of their sudden and archaic lust. The narrator, understandably, finds it difficult to release his thoughts from the abhorrent yet mesmerizing spectacle. Less understandable is the abstracted comment which the girl evokes in his final two sentences: "It is months later. Still, whenever I think of beauty, I think of her."

What idea of beauty is it, we must ask, which coincides with the image of a suicidal girl dazed and bleeding before a savage crowd? The question proves central to much of Selzer's work.

Pain is the unlikely medium through which Selzer attempts to recover some of the ancient resources of beauty. Burke had annexed pain to the sublime (with its new glorification of everything vast, obscure, wild, infinite, overpowering, and terrible), leaving beauty to command the softer feelings and forms. Beauty and pain, for Burke, occupy divided worlds. A glance backwards can indicate the force of Burke's influential division. Aristotle, who for over one thousand years provided the standard physiological account of pain, offered in his *Poetics* a theory of tragedy in which pain and beauty achieve a subtle, necessary concord. Through a catharsis of pity and fear, pain ultimately carries the spectator to a state of intellectual, emotional, and aesthetic clarification. Knowledge and beauty replace the confused accidents of history, and it is pain which provides the essential raw material for the transmutations of tragic art.

Selzer, in exploring the buried connections between beauty and pain, enters a region which most readers have never viewed first-hand: the *inside* of the human body. This inner landscape, luxuriant with mystery and danger, is closed to all but the surgeon, whom Selzer represents as a kind of priestly naturalist: "A surgeon, who feels the

slow slide of intestines against the back of his hand and is no more alarmed than were a family of snakes taking their comfort from such an indolent rubbing. A surgeon, who palms the human heart as though it were some captured bird." As often, Selzer's prose internalizes the familiar world of nature and transforms it into images of strangeness, reflecting the surgeon's access to a secret, cognate understanding. Through a novitiate of special training, the surgeon (like the priest) is separated from the laity by virtue of forbidden knowledge: "At last one emerges as a celebrant, standing close to the truth lying curtained in the Ark of the body." Yet the mysteries revealed to the surgeon prove unremittingly secular: "There is no wine, no wafer. There are only the facts of blood and flesh." In the damaged and perilous interior of the body, in the space abandoned by metaphysics and outlawed by taboo, Selzer discovers the origin of a strenuous aesthetic. Gazing at our most intimate deformities, he finds in fat and fluid and tissue and bone—in man as sheer mass and matter—the potential for a beauty Burke would not instruct us to discover. Brutal and plain and painful facts always possess for Selzer the possibility of transcending themselves. "To *perceive* tragedy," as his (Aristotelian) narrator remarks of our capacity for vision, "is to wring from it beauty and truth." Beauty, for Burke, is subject to laws of form and sensation. For Selzer what beauty requires is an act of human understanding.

The body—*inside* the body—is where for Selzer our understanding of the beautiful begins. Like Whitman, whose rhythms and phrases occasionally surface in Selzer's prose, he brings us back to the body as mystery and fact. We learn to know ourselves in a new dimension. And it is through this fresh encounter with the body—especially as the scene or locus of pain—that Selzer brings us to question what might constitute beauty. It exists here, deep in the black cavities of matter, or nowhere. Beauty, as we learn the contours of Selzer's aesthetic, cannot separate itself from the vision of a "bloodless limb turned rotten and festering." It is not a quality of form but a quality of vision: a way of seeing, of feeling, of understanding. We may come to recognize it in the speechless and savage passion which binds a father to his blind, malformed son. We must, if we can, accept it in the desperate rage and exhaustion which drive Selzer's protagonist to sew the head of a violent patient to the mattress, passing heavy stitches through each ear lobe, so that surgery may continue. Our conventional (Burkean) sense of beauty often defeats love by creating an automatic recoil from images of deformity and pain. The surgeon's dispassion is not simply an instrument, as crucial as knife or clamp, for working daily amid the terrors of disfeatured flesh. Selzer writes of the surgeon's knife as almost an extension of his body—surgery as a pitiless act of love—and dispassion becomes the vehicle of an intimate and inaccessible knowledge. It is the poet—gifted with language as well as vision—who becomes Selzer's model of the true physician: "the poet who heals with his words, stanches the flow of blood, stills the rattling breath, applies poultice to the scalded flesh." Some poets may find this description of their craft extravagant. Selzer, however, holds to an ideal which defines poetry—like medicine at its best—as a discipline of understanding and vision, which can recognize in mute, inexplicable pain the possibilities of knowledge, healing, and beauty.

The medical understanding of pain is in its infancy. Indeed, medicine is just beginning to enlarge its view of pain as something beyond the most common symptom of illness: "an unpleasant sensory and emotional experience associated with actual or potential tissue damage, or described in terms of such damage" (IASP Subcommittee on Taxonomy). The recent development of "pain clinics" offers a new forum for considering pain not as the sign of something else (a traditional symptom referring to a hidden source) but as the thing itself. It imparts to pain a new ontological status. Pain becomes the primary phenomenon to be studied and treated and understood—while the disease to which it may or may not refer is secondary. It is mainly chronic pain (as distinguished from acute pain, whose duration is limited and etiology clear) which is now under study. This study is especially difficult because, while pain centers us in the body, even the authors of the standard definition allow that pain is "always subjective" and "always a psychological state." Chronic pain seems to suffuse the uncharted spaces where body, mind, and emotions intersect. How do we begin to *know* such an amorphous creature? How do we separate pain from the other demons—guilt, fear, depression, terror, desire—which share its dominion and perhaps give it visible shape? What kinship exists between the experience of Lear as he holds the body of his murdered daughter Cordelia and the patient who reports violent pain in the space once occupied by an amputated limb? Such questions may direct us—as does Richard Selzer—to a study no less crucial to doctors than to writers. What happens to us (what changes do we undergo?) when we enter the subjective and psychological body of pain?

Selzer offers us at least one firm answer. We gain access to a new manner of speech, almost a new linguistic system. As his narrator says with the brevity of one who knows: "Pain invents its own language." This unfamiliar tongue expresses both a new range of experience (for which our normal words prove inadequate) and the separation which divides every patient from the world of health. It delineates the borders of a private experience from which all but the sufferer are shut out. Pity and compassion may comfort both the patient and the comforter, but they provide no reliable entry into the individual world of pain, which they merely circle, endlessly. (As Wittgenstein asserted: "Pity, one may say, is a form of conviction that someone else is in pain.") The narrators in Selzer's writing are empathetic figures—acute in their awareness of suffering—but they too share a curious detachment as spectators. Reading Selzer is to understand how seldom even the most heroic physician manages to penetrate, *inside,* the suffering of another human being. The best of us, as can be said of Selzer's narrators, are concerned observers, not native speakers, in the region of another's pain. We hear a strange language spoken which we cannot quite understand. "Never mind," advises Selzer's narrator, "we shall know it in our time."

The failure of language, in the presence of extreme pain, is a serious obstacle to diagnosis and treatment, giving rise to elaborate medical questionnaires which attempt to locate what is essentially wordless on a grid of metaphorical terms. Is your pain pulsing, flashing, stabbing, sharp, crushing, wrenching, hot, dull, taut, exhausting, suffocating, terrifying, cruel, blinding, unbearable, penetrating, tearing, cold, or dreadful? The question seeks to make us the spectators of our own pain. We experience the physician's puzzled view from outside. Yet, pain is sometimes the occasion for a relationship between surgeon and patient which ultimately, in Selzer's fiction, makes detachment impossible. In **"Sarcophagus"** the patient remains unconscious throughout. "We do not acknowledge his struggle," explains the surgeon-narrator. "It is our own that preoccupies us." The patient's pain, now blocked by anesthesia, gives way to the painful dilemma of the surgeon who attempts to heal him.

In **"Sarcophagus"** the narrator-surgeon confronts a situation beyond healing. A cancerous aorta ruptures during exploratory surgery. The surrounding tissue crumbles with tumor, preventing all efforts to repair the irreparable damage. "There is nothing to do." Nothing, that is, but decide to shut off the oxygen. "It is the act of an outlaw, someone who does not know right from wrong. But I know. I know that this is right to do." After excruciating minutes the patient dies. At issue, however, are not the familiar, tangled questions of medical ethics. The moral or legal implications of the surgeon's act interest Selzer less than a kind of primitive transference, as in voodoo or black magic, wherein pain shifts its location from patient to doctor. "It was terrible," confesses the surgeon, "his refusal to die." The pain now has embedded itself within the surgeon—it is *his* terror—and detachment, like dispassion, cannot be maintained. His participation in the terrible intimacy of death dooms him to further struggle as he works over the events which so unexpectedly have claimed him, too, in their pain. Yet action, like language, seems to recede toward a realm of the private and incommunicable. It is as if meaning cannot be brought back, to our garrulous world of health, from a region so utterly primitive, alien, silent, and stark. "I close my eyes and see again the great pale body of the man, like a white bullock, bled. The line of stitches on his abdomen is a hieroglyph. Already, the events of this night are hidden from me by these strange untranslatable markings." It is the nature of their work—not their temperament—which transforms so many of Selzer's surgeon-narrators into solitaries.

Pain initiates us into a new—or forgotten—knowledge. It beholds, at its most intense, an unknown world of its own construction.

When, in the final act, after his visions of solace have been shattered, Lear enters carrying the body of Cordelia, it is a moment of inconceivable pain. In this extended moment of blind agony Lear utters but three words, a single, repeated monosyllable: "Howl, howl, howl!" The speech seems composed of imperatives, like his opening commands addressed to his daughters and attendants, kingly discourse. But at least one director has interpreted Lear's three words differently. Lear, in this version, is not issuing commands, not even impersonal orders, as when earlier he had commanded the winds, cataracts, and hurricanes. The word "howl" is not spoken as a command; instead, Lear *howls* it. Language is no longer a form of social ceremony or mode of reference. It is an action, a lone howling, a reduction of speech to its most primitive kinship with animal cries. Its desolate repetition bears no similarity to the fractured sense and syntax of his intermittent madness, which still acknowledged a world of shared experience. Imagine a world in which there is nothing but pain. How would we speak of it? How endure it? For its duration, which can seem endless, Lear's howling suspends all movement, all speech, all thought. Holding his daughter in his arms, the old king stands as a visible icon of pain, intolerable and incommunicable.

The relation between beauty and pain does not offer comforting insights. In addition, Selzer's genre is the brief story, the essay, the prose fragment, the *pensée,* the sketch, where neither character nor action finally sustain us. A certain bleakness and shock are costs necessarily exacted by his vision and forms. What is characteristic of Selzer's bleakness, however, is the suggestion that pain can lead us beyond its own dark privacies. It is as if only through pain can pain truly be transcended. Unlike Beckett, whose speakers increasingly lose contact with their own anatomy, Selzer creates a fiction where only in and through the body is knowledge possible. His is not a slow and reflective literature of ideas. His stories generate such immediacy, speed, and suspense as to seem, on the contrary, all plot. Certainly the possibilities of knowledge and of beauty which he makes available are not for the tender-hearted. But an aesthetic which can gaze into the wreckage of human tissue, in order to secure its deepest values, offers us something less brittle than formalism. Selzer takes us forward and back, well beyond Burke, to a region where beauty and pain begin to recover, together, their lost heritage of meaning. (pp. 124-30)

> *David B. Morris, "Beauty and Pain: Notes on the Art of Richard Selzer," in* The Iowa Review, *Vol. 11, Nos. 2 & 3, Spring & Summer, 1980, pp. 124-30.*

Selzer on how he began writing:

I started writing when I was forty. I had never written a word before that. In fact, it was always tedious for me to write a letter. I'd always been a reader, but never a writer. And one day—I suppose it was part of the mid-life crisis— you see, it's not all bad, you can make a discovery about yourself if you're not careful—I felt a certain restlessness. And so I sat down and wrote and it turned out to be a short story, the retelling of the old Biblical story of Jonah and the whale. Since I was a surgeon, I knew what the inside of the stomach looked like better than the Biblical author. So I wrote that. And I knew immediately that I was a writer; and I made a commitment to it in the same way I had made a commitment to become a surgeon, and that is that I would write every day.

> *Richard Selzer, in an interview from* The Centennial Review, *Winter 1981.*

Enid Rhodes Peschel   (essay date 1980)

[*Peschel is an American critic and educator. In the following excerpt, she assesses Selzer's use of religious imagery and symbolism in his descriptions of surgery.*]

Richard Selzer is a surgeon-poet. He is the author of two books that have received wide critical acclaim: ***Rituals of Surgery*** (short stories, 1974), and ***Mortal Lessons: Notes on the Art of Surgery*** (essays, 1976). . . . Selzer's religious rearing was Jewish, that type of Conservative Judaism that is very close to Orthodox, but early in his predominantly Catholic home town he witnessed and was drawn to the rituals and the beliefs of the Roman Catholic religion. Many were the times when young Selzer would slip into a church in Troy to observe and to absorb the rites and the mystery. Selzer is not a Catholic convert: he is deeply drawn to the mystical elements in both Roman Catholicism and Judaism. Interweaving, mingling with his Jewish background, his attraction to Roman Catholicism gives his writings substance, shape, and power; and a sense of sacredness at once pain-filled and uplifting.

When Selzer was fourteen, his father died. His father's life, and more than that, his father's death, are the major influences in Selzer's own life. For Julius Selzer was not only a physician: he also tried his hand at writing. During the depths of the depression, from 1934 to 1937, Julius "went furtive—through his empty waiting room, to his desk— and took up his pen to write fiction," writes Selzer in his humorous and revealing essay **"Down from Troy."** Selzer was never able to read his father's manuscript; his mother thought it too scandalous and destroyed it after Julius died. But Selzer has been told that his father's novel was about a doctor who falls in love with a prostitute and during that time becomes an atheist; ultimately he loses the girl and regains his faith. A doctor, the longing for love, a condemned love, and a spiritual search—the themes of his father's novel will become the major themes of Richard Selzer's own writings as well.

Selzer says he wishes he could have read his father's manuscript, wishes he could hold it now. "It is one of my lifelong regrets that the manuscript has not been preserved. Now that I too have been reduced to the anguish of writing, it should be my holy scripture, my beacon, and my emblem. . . . Ah, if only I could weep over *his* metaphors, fondle the pages where his alphabet was spilled." Selzer longs to follow his father's mind and imagination ("*his* metaphors"). He craves to recapture an essence that is bodily as well: he would "fondle"—touch lovingly, tenderly, caressingly—the pages whereon his father wrote. Through his father's lost novel, which for the son becomes a sacred scroll, the symbol, too, of his own moral truth (it would be his "emblem"), Selzer imagines—believes—he would rejoin his father's spirit, and flesh.

Because of his quest at once spiritual and physical for his father, Selzer searches for answers in the human body itself. It is there that he seeks for truth. A "heart, a lobe of the liver, a single convolution of the brain . . . would tell all the frailty and strength, the despair and nobility of man," he writes. This truth, which he believes "lies hidden in the body," he seeks to explore and to reveal with his scalpel, and with his words.

In the first three and lyrically intense chapters of **Mortal Lessons** (**"The Exact Location of the Soul," "The Surgeon as Priest," "Lessons from the Art"**), Selzer dwells at length upon several wounds—wounds that hurt and heal both the patient and the surgeon. Let us examine two of them.

"I invited a young diabetic woman to the operating room to amputate her leg," he announces. The word "invited" is ironic: the surgeon mocks his own authority, his seeming graciousness. The word intimates too that he allured or enticed this young woman indecently, seductively almost, into the room where he would stand over, and penetrate, her body. He describes the festering limb clinically and metaphorically:

> She could not see the great shaggy black ulcer upon her foot and ankle that threatened to encroach upon the rest of her body, for she was blind as well. There upon her foot was a Mississippi Delta brimming with corruption, sending its raw tributaries down between her toes. Gone were all the little web spaces that when fresh and whole are such a delight to loving men. She could not see her wound, but she could feel it. There is no pain like that of the bloodless limb turned rotten and festering. There is neither unguent nor anodyne to kill such a pain yet leave intact the body.

The wound first appears like an animal: large, coarse, unkempt ("the great shaggy black ulcer"). Then it is a river mouth brimming with "corruption": the word suggests the physical, and the moral. This mouth would befoul—or engulf—both the woman and the surgeon. The delta-wound's "raw tributaries" evoke the river, the ulcer, pus, and pain. The spaces between the woman's toes are gone, overrun with putrefaction: there is no place here for love. Or so it would seem.

Why does the surgeon dwell at such length upon this festering flesh? Is he repelled, revolted by the rotted limb? To some extent, yes. But he also suffers physically, emotionally, and morally with the woman, whose pain is so terrible that nothing can overcome it that would not also harm or destroy the rest of her.

Priestlike, the surgeon "anoints" the limb:

> For over a year I trimmed away the putrid flesh, cleansed, anointed, and dressed the foot, staving off, delaying. Three times each week, in her darkness, she sat upon my table, rocking back and forth, holding her extended leg by the thigh, gripping it as though it were a rocket that must be steadied lest it explode and scatter her toes about the room.

The accursed limb is now sanctified, for the surgeon's anointing of it is both medicinal and spiritual—a healing act, a holy act. Still the woman is not cured; and therefore neither is the surgeon who suffers for her, and with her. "Who can gaze on so much misery and feel no hurt?" asked Selzer earlier in the book. There must be an operation. "There must be an amputation in order that she might live—and I as well. It was to heal us both that I must take up knife and saw, and cut the leg off. And when

I could feel it drop from her body to the table, and see the blessed *space* appear between her and that leg, I too would be well." His own life, his own health, are bound to hers, and to that festering limb.

When the woman is put to sleep in the operating room, undergoing thereby a symbolic death, her leg is uncovered. Now the surgeon is startled, overcome with gratitude, and with love. "There, upon her kneecap, she has drawn, blindly, upside down for me to see, a face; just a circle with two ears, two eyes, a nose, and a smiling upturned mouth. Under it she has printed SMILE, DOCTOR." No, the surgeon is not the hero, nor really the healer, here; but the patient is—heroine and healer, in her deathlike and transcendent state. Whereas the surgeon-priest merely cleansed and anointed her limb, the patient has done more: cleansed, anointed, sanctified—and therefore healed—with her humor and compassion, his spirit. The wound has bound them together and joined them in an act of love. In the body, seen through the wound of surgery, lies the truth: the frailty—and the strength—of man.

On a symbolic level, this amputation scene may be read as the surgeon's (or at least as Selzer the surgeon's) castration anxieties. The limb he must sever in order to heal himself appears to him festering, foul, putrid; or "a rocket that must be steadied lest it explode and scatter" its contents. But after the amputation-castration he will feel relieved, gladdened, even consecrated: the *"space"* that will appear between the body and that limb he calls "blessed."

"So, I have learned that man is not ugly, but that he is Beauty itself," writes Selzer immediately after this amputation scene. Both men and women are for him "exuberant bloody growths." The word "bloody" implies sloppiness, ugliness, a wound. But blood also evokes beauty, and blessedness: the lifeblood, or the Blood of Christ. "Growths" suggest tumors and disease, but also life that matures and develops—exuberantly, luxuriantly.

The wound, according to Selzer, and the suffering it begets make both the patient and the surgeon receptive to grace. "I would use the defects and deformities of . . . [people] for my sacred purpose of writing, for I know that it is the marred and scarred and faulty that are subject to grace." These words reveal Selzer's compassion for, his suffering with, the maimed, the outcast. Their pain, he believes, opens them to grace. All people, both virtuous and miscreant, are subject to grace according to the doctrines of the Church; but it is the faulty—the physically, emotionally, morally, and spiritually wounded—who particularly interest Selzer. And so this surgeon who perceives beauty in the diseased, who loves these people and identifies with their defects, who sympathizes so thoroughly with their pain that he feels it as his own pain, becomes, like them, "subject to grace." Grace is granted by God. Grace is God's unmerited love and favor toward human beings, enabling them to reach toward God, enabling them to become pure and morally strong. Grace implies beauty, holiness, and love: Grace is man's assurance of God's love. One receives grace as a gift from God, and through the sacraments of the Church, which for Selzer become the sacraments of surgery.

Why does Selzer envision surgery in terms of the Roman Catholic sacraments? The sacraments, he has said, guarantee what he craves—God's love and forgiveness. His surgery, therefore—symbolized by the sacraments of surgery that he performs and in which he participates—is actually his search for God and for love; and for his father who, like the God who grants grace, will love him and forgive him.

Immediately following his words about grace, Selzer writes, "I would seek the soul in the facts of animal economy and profligacy." Purporting to describe the scientific and natural—economy and waste in nature—these words imply as well the moral ("the soul"), and the immoral ("profligacy"). By linking the immoral and the moral, they reinforce Selzer's ideas about the marred and scarred and faulty who are subject to grace. "Yes, it is the exact location of the soul that I am after," Selzer continues with a combination of arrogance, humor, and longing. "I have caught glimpses of it in the body diseased. . . . It is as elusive as the whippoorwill that one hears calling incessantly from out the night window, but which, nesting as it does low in the brush, no one sees. No one but the poet, for he sees what no one else can. He was born with the eye for it." And that is why Selzer dwells at such length upon the festering limb, the ugliness of the wound. This surgeon-poet seeks, by means of his aesthetics of ugliness—his perceiving beauty in what is traditionally regarded as repulsive—nothing less than a holy communion. Only the poet, he believes, (and the blind diabetic woman is certainly such a poet) can truly see and transmit that "grace": the beauty, love, and divinity embedded in the living, festering, wounded—and exuberantly bloody—human body.

A second wound, also repulsive, also in a way blessed in the truths it reveals to him, opens further vistas into Selzer's psyche: his mind, his heart, and his soul. Once, he says mockingly, but pridefully as well, he thought he had found "the exact location of the soul." It lay in a suppurating wound. Selzer's words dramatize, re-create the ambiance. It is late at night. The doctor has been called to treat a young man recently returned from excavating Mayan ruins in Guatemala. In the man's left upper arm, a wound: "a clean punched-out hole the size of a dime." The surgeon studies it. "The tissues about the opening are swollen and tense. A thin brownish fluid lips the edge, and now and then a lazy drop of the overflow slips down the arm." At first, the hole seemed clean; then indications of pain are noted. Finally the opening appears repulsive as the surgeon remarks the "brownish fluid" suggesting pus, or blood, or excrement. Symbolically now the wound is vaginal, or anal.

With confidence, and some complacence, the surgeon makes a speedy diagnosis: "An abscess, inadequately drained." Easily, he can handle this.

Suddenly, revulsion, like a wave of nausea, sweeps over him. "What happens next is enough to lay Francis Drake avomit in his cabin," writes our surgeon-explorer. For now the wound becomes a "crater" from which looms all the Evil of the universe. His words capture and transmit his horror, his feelings of frenzy: "No explorer ever started in wilder surmise than I into that crater from which there now emerges a narrow gray head whose sole distinguishing feature is a pair of black pincers. The head sits atop a longish flexible neck arching now this way, now that, testing the air. Alternately it folds back upon itself, then advances in new boldness. And all the while, with dreadful rhythmicity, the unspeakable pincers open and close." The "dreadful rhythmicity" of the creature's pincers reflects visually the horror gripping the surgeon, the dreadful rhythms of his throbbing pulse.

Darting forth, now retreating, the creature seems a "beast"; the wound is its lair. Taut and terrified, the surgeon is a "high priest" determined to vanquish this evil—all Evil. He will wait, and he will conquer:

> Here is the lair of a beast at whose malignant purpose I could but guess. A Mayan devil, I think, that would soon burst free to fly about the room, with horrid blanket-wings and iridescent scales, raking, pinching, injecting God knows what acid juice. And even now the irony does not escape me, the irony of my patient as excavator excavated.
>
> With all the ritual deliberation of a high priest I advance a surgical clamp toward the hole. The surgeon's heart is become a bat hanging upside down from his rib cage. The rim achieved—now thrust—and the ratchets of the clamp close upon empty air. The devil has retracted. Evil mocking laughter bangs back and forth in the brain. More stealth. Lying in wait. One must skulk. . . . Acrouch, strung, the surgeon is one with his instrument; there is no longer any boundary between its metal and his flesh. They are joined in a single perfect tool of extirpation. It is just for this that he was born. Now—thrust—and clamp—and *yes*. Got him!

The beast with its "malignant purpose" that suggests physical and moral evil appears horrifying, yet strangely alluring, to this surgeon-priest. Momentarily it even seems beautiful as he imagines its "iridescent scales." Then it becomes loathsome again, a snakelike creature, or a phallus "injecting God knows what acid juice." Despite his nausea and fear, the surgeon smiles inwardly as he grasps the irony of the situation and coins a clever phrase: his patient is the "excavator excavated." But the irony in this tale turns—symbolically, strikingly—against the surgeon.

With its pincers opening and closing continuously, the phallic creature that hides, waits, then shoots forth is an image—hideous—of the surgeon joined to his surgical instrument: the pincerlike ratchets of his clamp opening and closing ceaselessly as he waits, skulks, and thrusts and thrusts again. More, the surgeon becomes, like the "devil"-beast, an image of ugliness and of evil. But in him these characteristics are internalized: his heart "is become a bat hanging upside down from his rib cage"; and "evil mocking laughter bangs back and forth in the brain." The poet's pounding plosive *b* sounds echo, amplify the surgeon's pounding heart. The irony is fierce: the high priest-surgeon who would combat, conquer Evil is imaged by the evil, foul, phallic creature that he angrily seeks to cut down and destroy in order to heal both his patient and himself.

When the surgeon finally grasps the creature in the jaws of his hemostat, he feels exultant, exalted. The beast appears to him "the whole of the evil of the world," and he will "kill it. For mankind." Here the surgeon is not merely priest: "Here is the surgeon as Savior indeed," announces Selzer with arrogance and deliciously self-deflating humor.

Extracted from the wound, the demon drowns in the specimen jar and is carried by the victorious, somewhat vainglorious, surgeon to the medical school. There the pathologist tells him that the creature is the larva of a botfly. It was about to burrow its way out of the wound and would have died anyway. His surgery was really unnecessary.

"No, it is not the surgeon who is God's darling. He is the victim of vanity," says Selzer in summation. "It is the poet who heals with his words, stanches the flow of blood, stills the rattling breath, applies poultice to the scalded flesh." For the surgeon-would-be-healer here was actually imaged by the Evil he sought to overcome. And at best he was someone who speeded along, slightly, the course of nature. True healing for Selzer comes from love and from the poet: from words, which to his mind are like the Holy Spirit. The surgeon-healer must be for him the surgeon-poet.

What emerges from Selzer's lengthy descriptions of these two wounds—the diabetic's festering leg and the excavator's excavated arm—is that because of his experiences of them, the surgeon is transformed. In the case of the diabetic woman, the physician is uplifted and healed not by his own acts, but by his patient's: her courage, and humor, and compassion. In the botfly case the surgeon's own courage and humor help him face his task. Too, they bring home to him his own importance, and his own unimportance. He learns that as a surgeon, even as the surgeon-"priest," he has only limited powers to heal. For a priest is but one who performs a sacred ritual or who ministers; not godlike, he is merely a servant of God. What he can do he does by cutting. The rest is left to the body, and to the poet. The wounds reveal to him the sacredness not of the surgeon but of the flesh and of life. The surgeon's place in Selzer's universe is, paradoxically, very small.

A third wound grants Selzer the vision—tragic and transcendent in this case—of one of the sacraments. A man of letters is lying in the intensive care unit of a hospital. He was struck suddenly with "the look of the Wound," writes Selzer. He seemed to *see* something for the first time, to understand "something that had eluded him all his life." Lying there, dying there, the man is tended—dutifully, lovingly—by a nurse. In Selzer's eyes, she appears a wife joined to this man through the obligations, the rights, and the love-filled devotion of the sacrament of matrimony:

> In the room a woman moves. She is dressed in white. Lovingly she measures his hourly flow of urine. . . . The man of letters did not know this woman before. . . . But this nurse is his wife in his new life of dying. They are close, these two, intimate, depending one upon the other, loving. It is a marriage, for although they own no shared past, they possess this awful, intense present,

this matrimonial now, that binds them as strongly as any promise.

The metaphorical marriage joins the patient and the one who tends him in the love—intense, sorrowful, and exalting—of the nursing relationship. It is a pain-filled but privileged state, one that permits a person to transcend himself through a wound and through love, to give himself. For Selzer, love is always inseparable from suffering; by extension, then, so is the sacrament of matrimony. But according to Selzer it is pain precisely, and not joy, that enables a human being to surpass himself, and in so doing to come to know redemption and grace.

Surgery, therefore, is Selzer's search for grace. It is not an easy quest, and one does not practice surgery easily. There is a taboo against entering the human body, laying it open. It is an act of violence, like a rape. Not surprisingly, the opened body evokes strong ambivalences in Selzer: revulsion and attraction, "horror and fascination." It appears an object of holiness, or of dread and potential punishment.

A man under spinal anesthesia is looking into his own opened abdomen. "This man is violating a taboo. . . . How dare he look within the Ark!" exclaims Selzer, drawing upon his Jewish background by referring to the enclosure in the synagogue, the Ark, in which the sacred scroll, the Torah, is kept. "But it is too late; he has already *seen;* that which no man should; he has trespassed." That man has seen only once. But the surgeon has elected to see again and again this tabooed, this terrible and wonderful territory: the body of his patient, which is the image of his own body, and of the truth concealed within it—all the strength and the frailty of man. It is enough to drive one mad, or to make one blind. "The hidden geography of the body is a Medusa's head one glimpse of which would render blind the presumptuous eye." Mythic, monstrous: the body is the Medusa's head that the surgeon must observe—and even grapple with—day after day. And because of his ordeal, he believes he will be cursed, and blessed.

Sometimes the entry into the body is portrayed by Selzer as an erotic act: violent sometimes, like a rape; sometimes loving. "The flesh splits with its own kind of moan. It is like the penetration of rape." But he also writes, "One enters the body in surgery, as in love, as though one were an exile returning at last to his hearth, daring uncharted darkness in order to reach home." Requiring physical and spiritual courage, the act described here is a search for love, for unity, and for communion. The erotic for Selzer is never far from the spiritual: Eros joined to Agape.

Opened, the abdomen becomes in Selzer's eyes the site and the substance of a divine transubstantiation, the place and the means of a Mass. Not the traditional transubstantiation of the Roman Catholic Church (the consecrated bread and wine transformed mystically into the Body and Blood of Christ), but the actual body and blood of his patient appear transubstantiated for Selzer into the Body and Blood. And they permit him thereby to commune with divinity.

Central to the Mass, and to the sacrament of Holy Communion that it celebrates, are the ideas of sacrifice (literally "making sacred," from the Latin *sacer,* "sacred," and *facere,* "to make"; one gives up something of value for the sake of something with a greater claim), and salvation: God the Son gave His Body and Blood to God the Father, in order to save man. "Sacrifice," "sacrament" and "sacred" all derive from *sacer.* By describing surgery in terms of a Mass, the ceremony that reenacts Christ's crucifixion and is actually called the "sacrifice of the Mass," Selzer blends images of the Roman Catholic religion with figures from his Jewish heritage. The Old Testament priest sacrificing an animal-victim to God may be seen, after all, as a kind of surgeon-priest. And so for Selzer's surgeon-priest, the patient evokes at once an Old Testament animal sacrifice as well as a Christ figure who saves the surgeon spiritually through the symbolical sacrifice of his body and blood on the operating table: his body and blood that become the Body and the Blood.

Selzer's depiction of surgery as a metaphorical Mass also combines images of the sacrament of Holy Communion with words suggesting the sacrament of baptism. The opened abdomen, he writes, "is the stillest place that ever was. . . . This is no silence of the vacant stratosphere, but the awful quiet of ruins, of rainbows, full of expectation and holy dread. Soon you shall know surgery as a Mass served with Body and Blood, wherein disease is assailed as though it were sin." This silence teems with life, with beauty, and with terror: It is a sacred silence. The "holy dread" suggests Selzer's feelings for the Old Testament Jehovah: hopefulness combined with fear. The Mass is the assurance of grace. But the Mass, like the Old Testament sacrifices, reenacts a ritual death. The "awful [implying both awe and horror] quiet of ruins" evokes splendor, stillness, and solitude. The rainbows call forth beauty, hope, and holiness: the covenant between God and Noah—the flood and the chosen one's escape in the ark; the promise that there will be no more floods to destroy the earth. God's wrath, followed by God's forgiveness. In this ambiance surgery suddenly becomes an act of Holy Communion. The Mass, like the Last Supper, is "served." The surgeon is joined mystically with the patient-Christ, and surgery has become a means to salvation. Christ gave Himself to save man: the patient upon the altar of surgery saves the surgeon spiritually—the surgeon who is operating to save, literally, the patient's life. Salvation from disease is equated in Selzer's mind with salvation from sin: the operation appears to him a symbolic baptism. Just as he seeks to purge his patient's body of disease "as though it were sin," so the surgeon-priest is in a sense purified by his sprinkling with, or immersion in, his patient's sanctified blood. It is a surgical, and a spiritual, bathing.

For Selzer, therefore, the body and blood of his patient, transubstantiated into the Body and Blood, purify the surgeon-priest and exalt him; and unite him through the reenactment of sacrifice and salvation—the awful/awe-ful Mass of Surgery—with the godhead and with grace.

Sometimes the symbolic sacrifice of the patient becomes a real sacrifice: a death, and a rendering sacred. For always the surgeon is confronted with the possibility of death. Selzer describes a terrifying experience, the one he as a surgeon fears above all others: an operation during which the patient dies on the operating table. The operation described is supposed to be a routine one, but suddenly the patient begins to hemorrhage, uncontrollably. "The surgeon suctions away the blood; even as he does so, new red trickles; his eyes are full of it; he cannot see." The blood—like the Medusa's head of the opened body—blinds him. Then it infiltrates him, fills his own eyes. Not a baptism now, but a drowning. The surgeon has become in some ways like his patient: the blood that surges in the patient's abdomen floods his own eyes. He feels himself drowning, "his hand sunk in the body of his patient." Part of him too will die during this operation.

The surgeon is frightfully, fearfully, alone. The carnivore wound would suck him in, its "mouth" devour him even as he tries to suction away the blood. "No matter how many others crowd about the mouth of the wound, no matter their admiration and encouragement, it is *he* [the surgeon] that rappels this crevasse, dangles in this dreadful place, and he is *afraid. . . .* " A mountain climber, he is totally responsible: totally dependent upon himself and upon forces outside of himself *over which he has no control.* "The surgeon cuts. And all at once there leaps a mighty blood. As when from the hidden mountain ledge a pebble is dislodged, a pebble behind whose small slippage the whole of the avalanche is pulled. Now the belly is a vast working lake in which it seems both patient and surgeon will drown." The lake of blood is at once horrid and holy: horrid because it means that the patient will die, that the transfusions being poured and poured in are gushing out of his body even faster than new blood can replace them. But it is holy because the surgeon is overwhelmed with a feeling of awe and with the recognition of his own insignificance. And holy as well because it evokes the Blood shed for others.

The surgeon realizes that the man on the operating table has died. Selzer writes, "Now there is no more sorrowful man in the city, for this surgeon has discovered the surprise at the center of his work. It is death. The events of this abdomen have conspired to change him, for no man can travel back from such darkness and be the same as he was." The death and the guilt—the sense of sacredness and of sacrifice—will remain with him, forever.

"To *perceive* tragedy is to wring from it beauty and truth," writes Selzer. The tragedy of illness, the tragedies of his patients' deaths, permit him to *seize,* to *receive,* to *understand* (as the Latin *percipere,* the root of "to perceive," implies) beauty and truth. Sickness, suffering and death touch his life and transform it; and grant him through knowledge, pain, and sorrow the gifts of compassion and of grace.

Surgery for Selzer is a sacred occupation. Like his writing, surgery reflects his search—physical, emotional, and spiritual—for love and for his father. His search for his father is actually his longing for a father figure who will love him: It is not unlike a quest for God. Selzer remembers that when his father died it was then that he decided he also would become a doctor. It is not so much his father's presence, but rather his father's absence, that has directed, determined—driven his life. Surgery, Selzer has said, more than other types of medicine, immerses one in the body. His surgery, therefore, reenacts symbolically his loss of, and his search for, his father: the wound inflicted by his father's death; and his own attempts, by immersing himself in the bodies of his patients, to rejoin the flesh, and so the spirit, of his father. Surgery, like his "sacred purpose of writing," becomes for him a means to reach out toward salvation: to commune through a wound and through suffering with his father, with divinity, and with Love.

There are three major aspects to Selzer's portrayal of surgery: the profane or artistic (the art, the skill of cutting); the sexually symbolic (the entry into the body as an act of love, or a rape; the reenactment on his patients' bodies of the surgeon's castration anxieties); and the sacred (his blending of the Jewish with the Roman Catholic). Combined with the first two aspects, Selzer's portrayal of the sacred is what makes his vision of surgery unique: haunting, powerful, uplifting. For Selzer, in fact, the surgical experience encompasses symbolically the seven sacraments of the Roman Catholic Church.

The most important sacrament for Selzer's vision of surgery is Holy Communion. The operation, which in some ways resembles the animal sacrifices described in the Old Testament, appears to him a Mass during which the body and blood of the patient are transubstantiated into the Body and Blood. The patient becomes a symbolic Christ figure who enables the surgeon standing at the altar of surgery to transcend himself mystically: to commune with divinity, and to know grace. Through the sacred bodies of his patients, Selzer also seeks to rejoin—by means of the fleshly wound of surgery and the symbolic death on the operating table—his own father. The surgical wound is reminiscent of the wound caused him when his father died, and the patient narcotized upon the surgical table recalls the sleep of death: The wound and death that will join him with Love.

Although Holy Communion is the most dramatic and most important rite of surgery as portrayed by Selzer, aspects of the six other sacraments are also present. The surgeon's being bathed in his patients' blood is for him a kind of baptism, a spiritual purification. The sacrament of matrimony is present in his depiction of the love and marriage that unite the patient and the one tending him in the nursing relationship. Extreme unction, also called anointing of the sick, is evoked as the surgeon-priest anoints the dying, festering flesh of the young diabetic woman.

Confirmation, full membership in the church (of physicians), and the taking of holy orders are represented as well. The surgeon undergoes a long apprenticeship, a real novitiate, to become a priest of his profession. Here the imagery is as much Jewish as Roman Catholic: "I must confess that the priestliness of my profession has ever been impressed on me. In the beginning there are vows, taken with all solemnity. Then there is the endless harsh novitiate of training, much fatigue, much sacrifice. At last one emerges as celebrant, standing close to the truth lying curtained in the Ark of the body."

Finally, Selzer's writings may be seen as his symbolic confession and penance: his admissions of guilt and of anguish; his deflating of the surgeon's ego and importance; his making amends for his past. Throughout, it is fascinating to see that Selzer the surgeon forever humbles the surgeon while also of course praising his art and his mission of healing. But the surgeon, maintains Selzer, is not the true healer. More than healer, the surgeon for Selzer is the servant of healing, and the one who may be healed. He writes: "The truly great writing about doctors has not yet been done. I think it must be done *by* a doctor, one who is through with the love affair with his technique, who recognizes that he has played Narcissus, raining kisses on a mirror, and who now, out of the impacted masses of his guilt, has expanded into self-doubt, and finally into the high state of wonderment." This doctor may come "upon the knowledge that he has done no more than meddle in the lives of his fellows, and that he has done at least as much harm as good." Here Selzer accuses the doctor—himself—with having loved not life or his patients, but his art and his own ego. Yet the guilt, weighty and impacted, he says, will fester and drive him to doubt himself. And in so doing it will permit him to enter a higher state of wonderment and belief: not in himself, but in something greater—more human, and more divine. Linked to his surgery, Selzer's writings are a confession and an expiation; and a reaching out for forgiveness and for grace.

Surgery is at once an art for Selzer and a religion. The surgeon's skill and technique are essential. But these, though necessary, are not enough. Surgery for him is profane and sacred, erotic and spiritual: a searching, through the blood and the body of his patient, for his father and for healing; for truth, for love, and for salvation. The surgeon in Selzer's eyes is a priest who is the servant of healing, and so of humanity. He is the would-be healer who is healed himself—joined with love and with divinity—by means of the grace accorded him through the sacraments of surgery. (pp. 66-77)

Enid Rhodes Peschel, "Richard Selzer and the Sacraments of Surgery," in Medicine and Literature, *edited by Enid Rhodes Peschel, Neale Watson Academic Publications, Inc., 1980, pp. 66-77.*

Gayle Whittier   (essay date Summer 1989)

[*In the following excerpt, Whittier discusses creation as a subject in Selzer's works through an exploration of the distinct roles Selzer assigns to women and men involved with surgery and writing.*]

The craft of surgery and the art of poetry reciprocate throughout Richard Selzer's work. Having spent his professional life "literally within the body of another human being," he finds that "surgery or pain, the infliction of pain, is a self-inflicted wound." Writing heals this wound, in part by allowing the writing surgeon to construct, rather than violate, a body: "And I write in longhand, for a number of reasons. One is that I like to feel the words coming out of the pen, because it's like a secretion from the body. . . . Some of the rhythms, I think, of the prose in *Mortal Lessons*—it has the rhythm of the body. Heartbeat and the breathing and the sounds of the organs—I've tried to capture those in my essays."

Selzer on the similarities between writing and surgery:

You know, writing the pieces that I do—short stories, essays, memoirs—the short pieces—they're rather like surgical operations in themselves. There's a beginning, a middle, and an end. You make the incision, rummage around a little bit, and then stitch it up. Since the new instrument I had picked up was a pen, I immediately felt at home with it: it's about the same size as a scalpel, has the same circumference, if you will. It sits differently in the hand; nevertheless, it was an instrument so like unto the one I had used all my life, that it was not a stranger, but a distant cousin to the knife. In the use of each, something is shed. When you use the scalpel, blood is shed; when you use the pen, ink is shed. I liked holding the instrument in my hand, rather than typing, because I was able to watch the word issuing from the end of my hand, as it were, as though it were a secretion from my own body, something that I had not only made, but done, as though it were coming out of me. And that intimacy with the word as it was being written became very important to me. A notebook and a pen, that's really all it was.

Richard Selzer, in an interview from
Salmagundi, *Summer 1990.*

In his early work especially, Selzer's densely allusive, imagistic, and melodic prose, with its frequent appeals to the readers' several senses, builds a verbal body which, through the writer's style (*stylus,* correlative of the surgeon's scalpel), opens to reveal the mysteries of surgery to a layman otherwise uninitiated. If the revelation of the mystery is too direct, however, or if it is simply visual but not verbal, it plummets the onlooker into a taboo, as when Selzer's spinally anesthetized patient glimpses his own viscera in the overhead lamp of the operating room. The surgeon, "deeply employed" in his abdomen, glances up and meets his eyes. "Watch him. This man is violating a taboo," Selzer tells us. "How dare he look within the Arc!" that is, the covering which protects the sacred scroll of the Torah. For what is glimpsed is not simply the inner body, but the word-within-the-body. [In her essay "Richard Selzer: The Rounds of Revelation" (*Literature and Medicine: Toward a New Discipline,* ed. Kathryn Allen Rabuzzi)] M. Teresa Tavormina reminds us that "this explication of the body's book, like other hermeneutics, is itself often veiled, shrouded in its own sophistication," for if wordless vision violates, it remains true that literally naming the patient can incapacitate the doctor: "I should not have spoken his name aloud! No good will come of it. The syllable has peeled from me something, a skin that I need."

Yet the act of writing can also be directly analogous to the removal of foreign tissue from a diseased or invaded body, since, as surgery excises, writing exorcises the demons surgery leaves in its practitioner. In Selzer's latest collection, a character suggests,

> Why don't you try writing it down? . . . Just putting it into words on a page will make it recede. . . . I read somewhere that there is an an-

cient magic in writing a sorrow down, then burning the paper upon which it is written. It makes the affliction go away.

The speaker refers to her mother's obsessive love for a young man, a passion not unlike that violent desire to *see* and commune which Selzer often associates with surgery. Writing, then, may both augment and diminish the profession of medicine. "The writing has made me a better doctor, because it has made me look at my patients with the dilated pupils of a poet. . . . But it has also drained from me some strength with which I distance myself."

In view of the reciprocity between writing and surgery, it is not surprising to find that Selzer's own metaphors for the creative process densely relate to his surgical endeavor. Like the surgeon, who leaves the scar as a "signature," not of himself but of the surgery, so the poet often leaves a metaphoric or narrative cicatrice tracing both the stages of the story's creation and his/her own psychic journey over the same aesthetic terrain. Over the whole of Selzer's oeuvre, one finds paradigmatic narrative strategies and motifs anatomizing the creative process for this particular writer; in their evolution, they trace how the act of writing itself acts dynamically upon the writer.

The dominant western model for artistic creativity is phallocentric. The male artist engages in transcendent intercourse with a female Muse and, departing from biological analogy, is impregnated by her; after great labor, he delivers a "brainchild." Perhaps because it opens, demystifies, and causes the body to bleed, surgery too is often seen as a masculinizing and heterosexual transaction. . . . (pp. 278-80)

Possibly the traditional genderizing of surgery explains why, among all medical specialties, it is among the most resistant to the inclusion of women, and why, in America, more surgery is performed on women than on men. For it follows that, if surgery masculinizes the doctor, it feminizes the patient. In a sense, the surgical body is always feminine, the medium upon which the surgeon "writes" his opening bloody line even as the poet writes through the Muse and writes the female body itself, reflecting and usurping female reproductive functions and making woman the "thing inscribed." Accordingly, the opened body in Selzer's work often shares cultural stereotypes of women as landscape, food, or "Mother Earth."

In her brilliant analysis of Selzer's early **"Korea,"** Enid Rhodes Peschel notes that the story "opens with the image of a woman; it will close with one. The two tableaux are studies in contrasts. The woman first seen has bulging eyes and an enormously enlarged thyroid; Sloane will operate successfully on her. The woman at the end of the story is Shin, whom Sloane has abandoned. She is in labor with the child he has unknowingly fathered. Sloane must cut into her in order to save the child; he cannot save her." Peschel asserts that **"Korea"** may be read as "the symbolic story of the birth of the artist," Selzer himself. If this is so, then the two surgeries mark a shift from one kind of bodily knowledge and use to another. The woman with her bulging eyes and asexual goiter can be saved; the woman with her distended belly cannot. The artist's birth requires that this gravida die and that birth itself be appropriated as a male function (Caesarean). Out of this transference and destruction, comes sound or voice, the writer's crucial element, first in the baby's "gurgling sound, a cry, a life, and a death" (the mother's), and then in the voiceless noise of a stick falling to the floor. In Peschel's interpretation, Selzer as artist is delivered in the course of these events, a delivery in which Shin becomes "Korea raped. I did it, we're doing it, we're screwing this country," while the bond between the two countries and the two people persists in the living child. This artistic birth requires literal human sacrifice, namely, the sacrifice of the woman whose childbirth is taken over and conducted by the man (artist) even as, in the traditional story of a man and his muse, the male artist ultimately gives birth to the spiritual child, the artifact. Selzer himself might agree with Peschel's analysis, since he found Korea a "powerful experience. . . . In a sense I awakened as a writer long before I ever started to write because of that experience in Korea."

Yet the traditional pattern of using women as a bridge to the artifact or using the artifact as a woman's body is both retained and augmented in Selzer's personal aesthetics of creativity. M. Teresa Tavormina, for example, notes that his early loss of his physician father made his medical study, in Selzer's own words, "a boy's search for his father . . . finding him through his work." (pp. 280-81)

As he recalls it, Selzer's loss of and search for his father involves a cry without a response, which perhaps illuminates the frequency of male dialogue as an essential achievement in his own stories. To add to his loss, Selzer later discovered that his mother had destroyed the manuscript of his father's novel. "It is one of my lifelong regrets that the manuscript has not been preserved. Now that I too have been reduced to the anguish of writing, it should be my holy scripture, my beacon, and my emblem. . . . Ah, if only I could weep over *his* metaphors, fondle the pages where his alphabet was spilled." Here the writer's need is both anatomical (letters spilled like blood or semen, metaphors that can be "fondled") and artistic, a need not simply for the father as man, but the father as himself a writer. Perhaps, too, his mother's censorship of the father's testament, his novel, influences the relative muteness of women in those stories which focus on creation: the silencer silenced. In any case, Selzer's search for his lost father reshapes the traditional poet-Muse scenario in his work. Woman becomes transitory material through which the writer moves, her normal procreative functions pathologized, appropriated, or displaced; but after passing through her "body," the narrator comes to *voice,* often engaging in dialogue with another man or men. Selzer's is not simply one more example of the literary exploitation of female bodies poeticized to secure male communication in a "tradition." His is a personal and memorial communion with his own dead father whom he seeks first in the operating theater, then in narrative.

The early story **"Abortion"** in *Mortal Lessons* introduces this paradigm of creativity along with other delineations of Selzer's metaphoric scar across the body of his work. The theme of the story is consciousness or its denial, in this case, denial of the human likeness of the aborted fetus. Selzer's persona is virtually anonymous at the beginning

of the piece, his tone greatly distanced from his material; he speaks in the documentary overvoice familiar from newscasts and horror movies, generalizing, in fact, that "horror, like bacteria, is everywhere." Almost at once, however, the focus changes and the voice gradually incarnates the spectacle of a "rain of fetuses" falling on "73rd Street near Woodside Avenue" in New Haven on the morning of August 6, 1975. This documentary attitude suggests a factual and journalistic exposé. But Selzer's sensibility takes over. The fetuses have tumbled from a broken hospital garbage bag ironically labeled "hazardous waste"—"waste" insofar as they are disposable humans; "hazardous" since their disposal must be hidden from view, made invisible, to spare society the witnessing of the end result of the act. At first, the fetus seems as foreign, as "other," as the transitional female is in Selzer's work: "It is a foreignness on the pavement," but only until one sees and feels that "such a gray softness can be but one thing. It is a baby, and dead." By individualizing and renaming the fetus as "baby," Selzer causes his readers to *feel* and *know* it as human, in their own image. He makes them envision this resemblance with their own minds' eye, and, more closely, in imagined *touch*.

In the abortion procedure the narrator decides to attend, however, the fetus is never literally expelled. Instead, it is imaginatively recreated and absorbed by Selzer's protagonist. Relying first on the Western sense of vision as the supreme faculty for obtaining "truth," he *sees* the introduced needle jerk and is himself jerked awake, suddenly conscious. Despite the doctor's counter-naming this as merely a "reflex," Selzer's narrator's imagination is touched. Tonally, he steps back to enter the womb and describe the fetus at the end of the fifth month, the date of this late abortion. "Hair is on the head. There are eyebrows, eyelashes. Pale pink nipples show on the chest. Nails are present, at the fingertips, at the toes." Having thus verbally "made" a fetus himself, the teller next assigns "it" his own male gender. "At the beginning of the sixth month, the fetus can cry, can suck, can make a fist. He kicks, he punches. . . . " Vigorously endowed with activity, the fetus seizes life in a traditionally aggressive male manner. "His grip is very strong. He could support his weight by holding with one hand." The identification between the gymnast fetus and the narrator, who is actively undergoing change himself, culminates as the speaker enters a waking dream. "I close my eyes. I see the inside of the uterus." Here vision deepens from the literal to the imaginative, from the medical to the artistic, from the isolated to the communal, as the narrator himself regresses into a prenatal (i.e. dream) state in which he again renames the fetus, this time as a "sleeping infant."

The womb, too, is beautified, in "ruby gloom," while the prenatal life it harbors enjoys a passive, peaceful, virtually Edenic condition: "I see the creature curled upon itself. Its knees are flexed. Its head is bent upon its chest. It is in fluid and gently rocks to the rhythm of the distant heartbeat," Selzer writes, in lines which themselves gather into a lulling rhythm. The narrator's identification with the fetus becomes total when the fetus is most vulnerable, imminently threatened with death, at which point sight yields to the more intimate sense of touch. "The needle comes closer in the pool. The point grazes the thigh, and I stir. Perhaps I wake from dozing. The light is there again. I twist and straighten. My arms and legs *push*. My hands finds the shaft—grabs! I *grab*. I bend the needle this way and that. The point probes, touches on my belly. My mouth opens. Could I cry out? All between is a commotion and a churning. There is a presence in the pool. An activity! The pool colors, reddens, darkens." The life of the fetus is recapitulated in the life of the prose itself, shortening sentences lending a quality of to-and-fro struggle as the fetus tries to fend off the invading needle. The prose becomes, in every sense, reflexive.

The intimate relationship between the fetus and the artifact Selzer constructs makes "Could I cry out?" a crucial question. On the literal level, as the abortionist later relates, the answer is yes, the fetus can cry, and it can be heard once it is out in the air. But while the fetus is still within the womb, now threatened, he is deprived of being heard even as he is being deprived of life. He lacks the writer's vital faculty, and yet the writer speaks for the fetus. Across the identification between them, voice has been transferred. Vocally, at least, the abortion itself is aborted by the author. A space opens on the page after Selzer's depiction of the fetus's death wound, a visual reminder of the concomitant extinction of words themselves. Then the narrator leaves the dream, opens his eyes, and witnesses the rest of the procedure. No longer in Eden, he too has fallen into consciousness.

What, however, of the woman on and in whose body the ritual of abortion is performed? She is typical of otherness both by gender and nationality, a Jamaican whose race extremizes, even literalizes, the "foreignness" that, in a phallocentric culture, woman represents to man. She is also characteristically almost voiceless, her one exclamation an "Oh!" which permits authorial (male) interpretation: "But I guess it is not pain that she feels. It is more a recognition that the deed is being done." Her bond with another woman present, a nurse, is silent, based on a shared "secret" which remains unspecified and untold, alien to both the narrator and to us his readers. At one point her identity shrinks to that of a pregnant belly "cleansed a magical three swabbings." To the end of her story, her presence is made known by body language rather than speech. She "lies on the table submissively, and now and then she smiles at one of the nurses as though acknowledging a secret," or she "grimaces," or "smiles again and seems to relax," "settles comfortably on the table," "shakes her head," "gazes at the ceiling," etc., finally effectively disappearing from the account. Her active part in the abortion, the labor and expulsion which will occur eight to twelve hours later, is whited out by her literal absence and also by the medical lie: " 'There,' says the doctor. 'It's all over. It wasn't too bad, was it?' " For her real function has been to enable the narrator's experience, not her own; and her body, having served both its limited procreative and artistic purpose, dissolves into the narrative. It is *this* body which is "aborted" artistically. The fetus is, again through the auspices of a compensatory art, "saved."

A casual reader of **"Abortion"** may try to interpret it politically, noting that the fetus is assigned the male gender it commonly receives in anti-abortion tracts; that the woman's experience is ignored; that there is no female spokesperson in the account; and that men claim voice both in the narrative and in the making of the narrative itself. The (male) fetus's will to live contrasts dramatically with his mother's passivity, and, given the late date of the abortion, the mother herself implicitly is indemnified as indecisive or irresponsible. What is more, when Selzer's narrator tries to justify abortion, his last-minute rationales sound specious, if not actually untrue to the motivations of real women seeking to abort in America.

> I know. We cannot feed the great numbers. There is no more room. I know, I know. It is a woman's right to refuse the risk, to decline the pain of childbirth. And an unwanted child is a very great burden. An unwanted child is a burden to himself, I know.

So the writer evokes the *audible* coverings that obscure the act he has just witnessed.

But the political reading is an incomplete one, doomed, in fact, to the ambiguities in the story itself. Only on an aesthetic level does the same textual evidence provide a solid interpretive scenario. The foreignness of the patient, for example, is less a comment on her recency or immigrant status than what Tavormina calls "Selzer's appreciation of the external alien beauties of the Orient . . . intriguingly similar to his fascination with foreign presences inside the human body. . . . In Japan and Korea, of course, the 'foreign' was the native, and a visitor might well be expected to make himself permeable to its otherness." In **"Korea,"** giving up that "otherness" and then emerging from it vocally takes place "in another country" and through a sexual connection. In **"Abortion"** the foreignness is imported, so to speak, as the otherness of the female body which may be either encouraging or hostile to fetal life. (The Korean War was hostile to life, but encouraging to Selzer's art.) Concomitantly, the muteness of the woman in **"Abortion"** serves as a foil for the dialogue between men.

The patient's story is left incomplete, nor is the literal fetus ever expelled, since the fetus has been rescued, that is, recreated, as an artifact by the author-teller of the account. As **"Abortion"** ends, Selzer's language turns increasingly self-conscious and literary; the fetus is now endowed with "the sprout and pouch of man," and at its imagined conception the "naked pearl" of an earlier description (**"The Exact Location of the Soul,"**) recurs, this time in a yolk which is also archaic and matrimonial, a "dowry." (For Selzer, one suspects, marriage is above all a physiological act; the genesis of a new creature marries its parents not in a ceremonial, but in a biological way.) Now the fetus partakes of art as much as of nature, as Selzer emphasizes with his use of a specifically literary term, "persona."

> It is a persona carried here as well as a person . . . a signed piece, engraved with a hieroglyph of human genes.

By this last-minute likening of the fetus to an artifact, something from the realm of *man*-made things, he aborts the abortion, transcends his own identification with what is aborted, and extends his own essay, his creation, into a future.

Selzer's artistic purpose becomes even clearer if we consider how many possible end-lines **"Abortion"** contains. For example, if the piece stopped at the line, "I saw life avulsed—swept by flood, blackening—then *out*," it would imitate the very process the story describes. The story would *become* the abortion in this case. Or Selzer might have chosen as a final sentence one from the penultimate section of the essay: "It is a persona carried here as well as a person, etc. . . . I did not think this until I saw. The flick. The fending off "; the last image would be of the actual fetus, not the imagined one. Repeatedly, then, he has chosen to stop, to bring us to a halt as readers, and then to continue the forming of the story beyond a terminal point. He thus includes and surpasses conventional expectations. Unsurprisingly, the story concludes with the practicing doctor describing to the observer an abortion which failed, which, in fact, generated both voice and life.

> We stand together for a moment, and he tells of
> an abortion in which the fetus cried after it was
> passed.

Here the voices of the two men unite over the voice of the fetus, this one an "accident" or a "miscalculation" who lives. On the verbal level only, the two doctors have "saved" this fetus as their final narrative bond; on the literal plane, ironically, one of them, a doctor who often encounters the surprising fragility of life, finds that the tenacity of life has defeated his medical purpose.

Specific elements in **"Abortion"** recur in other of Selzer's stories of the art of surgery and the surgeries of art. The pathologizing of the female body for example, persists from his earliest to his latest work. In particular he associates pregnancy with disorders. The Korean woman Shin dies in Caesarean childbirth, a correlative of Sloane's "anomie," while in **"Semiprivate, Female"** a comatose foreign woman is depicted as consumed both by fever *and* by the fetus which she herself has symbolically consumed:

> The patient in the next bed is an emaciated
> woman, a Filipina in the sixth month of a preg-
> nancy. There is a frost of ashes about her mouth.
> Each night she is swept clean by a fever that has
> burnt up every bit that is not essential—blood,
> saliva, tears, tissue. Only the mighty fetus, rav-
> ing to be born, is not touched. Even as the child
> buds and splits and specializes, the woman
> grows daily less differentiated until she is some-
> thing rudimentary, a finger of flesh, unfulfilled,
> unformed, that will surely die of its one achieve-
> ment. She resembles a snake that has swallowed
> a rabbit and is exhausted by her digestion.
> Through the translucent, dark-veined belly, the
> legs of her meal, moving.

The pathology of a pregnancy and a disease which makes the mother "something rudimentary" is countered by art, in this instance, the author's carefully designed alliteration of "a finger of flesh, unfulfilled, unformed," which emphasizes the *form*ality of language, and his differentiated and satisfying rhythms which bring the passage to a close.

Even when the pregnancy itself is not pathological, how-ever, as in the **"Maternity Ward"** section of **"Rounds"** in *Letters to a Young Doctor,* it is presented contextually as an unnatural distortion of the "natural" heterosexual bond which creates the child. Of two women, one laboring, one assisting, whom the narrator glimpses in passing, he remembers chiefly their street quarrel, the one "fat and with a furious fat-man's face," the other "slim and mean-eyed." One has "close-cropped hair" while the other's, "ivory," hangs to her waist. They seem, at first, to be female lovers imitating male-female roles, especially when the "masculine" one speaks as if betrayed by a lover in "words that barked up from her windpipe in solid lumps: 'Fuckin' whore,' she yelled." Both the bodies *and the words* of the pair sicken the narrator.

> I thought then of the ovaries and uteri of these
> two, and felt sick . . . (with) all the punching
> and blood, all the "fuck" in the air. There was
> a real possibility that I might vomit.

Nevertheless, he stays to witness, drawn by his usual compulsion to *see.* Later, the strangely sexual commerce of the two women, sisters, as it happens, is "tamed" by the narrator's familiarizing it from his own male heterosexual standpoint: "It was like spying on the faces of women in orgasm while they know nothing but their own passion." What is most violent and terrible about these women is explained by their sisterhood, and how they help each other through a sexual situation in which men are displaced, "husbandless childbirth."

Where one or more "husbands" attend it, however, birth is romanticized, reclaimed as a (male) artifact. In **"The Virgin and the Petri Dish,"** a meditation on in vitro fertilization, Selzer archaizes and idealizes the process of a conception involving not one, but two men, the sperm donor and the gynecologist. His classical allusions are to male deliveries, Zeus's stealthy impregnation of Danae, thigh-born Dionysus, the births of Venus and Athena (but not, say, Haphasistos, Juno-born). Gradually the meditation culminates in the typical dialogue between two men, the romantic narrator with his burden of sacred metaphors, and the pragmatic gynecologist who declares, "No ethical problems here," but " . . . only a matter of plumbing." The doubly male conception then generates the narrator's witty entertainment of its enshrinement in art:

> Instead of an archangel holding a lily and whis-
> pering, they will show a masked gynecologist
> holding a laparoscope; instead of Mary, kneel-
> ing, ecstatic, a covered glass dish. . . .

While the author ends with praise for the pagan goddess Ishtar (thus nearly avoiding the ethical problems Judaism and Christianity locate in in vitro fertilization), and while he praises life whatever its source of conception, the real narrative emphasis here is on a conception that takes place entirely in a male imagination, otherwise enabled by a technology culturally defined as male.

Literal foreignness also characterizes the birthing or birth-related woman in many of Selzer's later accounts. Enid Rhodes Peschel sees this foreignness as the otherness to which the artist surrenders in order to accomplish the artifact-in-progress; he loses or crosses the boundary between self and other, typified by a union with the country which, microcosmically, the woman contains and which, macrocosmically, contains her. (In at least two stories, **"Korea"** and **"Taking the World in For Repairs,"** the American doctor suffers from an indigenous illness, malaria and dysentery, respectively, and these illnesses play a catalytic role in the development of the narration. He becomes, as it were, infected with the new place, and takes it into his body in a form which demands to be recognized.) By rendering the "other," woman, doubly "other" as foreign, Selzer possibly negotiates her otherness which, as geography, is easier to deal with than the dark and ill-remembered cavern of the maternal body—and more accessible to a literary tradition in which epic journeys lead male protagonists to wisdom.

Female muteness is a related phenomenon. Needless to say, a foreign woman is not likely either to speak as often or to be heard as readily as an English-speaking one who is, at least potentially, the linguistic equal of the writer. She thus permits male *vocal* dominance. This remains true even when the persona spies on an all-female medical team, as in **"Amazons,"** where the women issue brief directions for "towels," "clips," "drape," except for the *anesthesiologist,* the one who silences the patient and puts out feelings of pain; she wordlessly "whispers," "soothes," and "croons as though to a child."

Where a male doctor himself incorporates foreignness as otherness, however, his portrayal is positive, one of sensitivity and even priestliness. The Tibetan healer Yeshi Dhonden performing diagnosis by hand and ear, enters a trancelike state similar to the waking dream that overtakes the artist. He licenses Selzer's persona and narrator to envy, to wish to become, the female patient to whose body he *listens* attentively, as if it were a text composed of words. And after his visit, what remains is his echo. "Now and then it happens, as I make my own rounds, that I hear the sounds of his voice, like an ancient Buddhist prayer, its meaning long since forgotten, only the music remaining. Then a jubilation possesses me, and I feel myself touched by something divine." So, too, the Indian doctor of **"Fetishes"** receives his patient's vulnerability with an emotional understanding surpassing the limits of culture and language; as her husband's gift to him, a shaman's charm, passes into his hands, the patient thinks she sees "fire," the visual correlative of the "something divine" in the Yeshi Dhonden account. (Even here, however, men hear each other, while the women merely imagine or see.)

As Selzer's work matures, the elements in his creative paradigm migrate and change in emphasis. Pathological childbirth, for example, is displaced in two later stories by pathologies of the menopausal or post-menopausal woman. In **"'The Black Swan' Revisited,"** Rosalie von Trummler's acceptance of menopause is compared to her daughter's acceptance of spinsterhood (presumably the result of her clubfoot); but, since she has fallen in love with a young man, she mistakes the return of bleeding for her rejuvenation rather than the cervical cancer it signals. Gynecological pathology also marks **"Fetishes,"** in which another post-menopausal woman, Audrey Blakeslee, undergoes a total hysterectomy in connection with the removal

of an ovarian cyst (benign). The ghost of the pathological childbirth lingers in that Rosalie has a deformed child and Audrey, none. And each woman suffers from what is considered to be a female vice, a kind of vanity which catalyzes the male bond through concrete artifacts, Audrey's false teeth and Rosalie's gold earrings.

The male bond, dialogic in Selzer's earlier work, also changes, in his later stories, turning more narrowly on artifacts or artistic pursuits which the men share. Seeing an emaciated old woman fixing gold earrings to her ears, the narrator of **"'The Black Swan' Revisited"** is inspired to retell Thomas Mann's similar work. Selzer actually dedicates the story to Mann, placing himself in dynastic sequence with the older writer, his spiritual or artistic "forefather." In **"Fetishes"** Audrey's false teeth, a secret kept from her husband for years, first bond her and the Indian doctor; subsequently, her anthropologist husband (an expert in foreignness?) gratefully offers the same doctor a real fetish, once given to him by a shaman of the Asmat people—and representative of the story's theme of deception and candor, since the charm is double-faced, with images of a parrot and a monkey on obverse sides. This exchange occupies the last paragraphs of the story, and is, in fact, its culminating event; it displaces Audrey from central focus to periphery, so that the exchange of artifacts between two men is the last thing "seen" both by her and by the readers. The shaman's charm emblematizes the male/male dialogic exchanges of the early stories, and the foreign doctor is identified with the woman because he shares and keeps her improbable secret. The secret is that her teeth (vagina dentata?) are "false," while her real sexual organs have been removed and proven "benign."

Selzer also minimizes the inclusion of the dream phase of creation in these late stories, though it never completely disappears. In **"Korea"** Sloane's malarial dream leads Sloane to "lose his identity, his ego, join with nature, with Korea" [Enid Rhodes Peschel, " 'A Terrible Beauty Is Born': Richard Selzer's 'Korea'," in *Le Mythe d'etiemble: Hommages, etudes et recherches*], its counterpart, the dream he enters while Shin is in labor, is broken by a staccato word "Stat," an American medical term, the voice of his original culture interrupting the changed psychic state he attains. In **"Abortion"** "I close my eyes" signals the narrator's entry into the imagined uterus and prenatal life, while, in the later **"Amazons,"** "Perhaps I fall asleep. . . . perhaps I dream . . . " permits his retrogression to an archaic vision of the Amazonial initiation rites making warriors of young women. In all these accounts, Selzer's dream inverts the Adamic deep sleep during which Eve was separated from Adam's flesh. Selzer's use of dream and trance recognizes woman as already separated and cut off, as "other." He must reincorporate himself with her and then also pass *through* her into the bond of male dialogue. But where male bonds are intrinsic to the entire narrative, as in **"The Virgin and The Petri Dish,"** dramatic meditation forms the whole of the essay. Alone, without a male counterpart to befriend him dialogically, the narrator either views women as inscrutably perverse (**"Maternity Ward"**) or he over-romanticizes them (**"Amazons"**).

In Selzer's last two collections, however, he focuses on creation in larger and more specific ways. ***Taking the World in for Repairs*** contains two stories or essays explicitly instructing the reader **"How to Build a Slaughter-house"** and **"How to Build a Balcony,"** while, in the same collection's title story and the previous collection's **"Imelda"** Selzer's own professional "halves" as surgeon and artist combine in accounts of the plastic surgeon's endeavors. Selzer's perspective on plastic surgery is *not* that it simply improves on faulty nature; instead, it perfects a previously imperfect *art* which includes the procreative process. Thus Imelda's people have "museum feet" and she herself is "a figurine, orange-brown, terracotta, and still attached to the unshaped clay from which she had been carved." (In this, Selzer resembles the mature Shakespeare, whose triune aesthetic set art over nature over art.)

Levels of artifice interweave subtly and complexly in **"Imelda."** The title itself evokes both a sound and an image, two rudimentary elements of art; her name, now a title, is the "one word" the plastic surgeon has heard Imelda speak (she thus epitomizes the earlier foreign, almost speechless women); it is the name of the patient or "figurine"; it is the photographic image on the slide; and, finally it becomes the name of the story itself. On the chained strength of this single word, and not simply on the body of the girl herself, the male bonds in the story depend.

Male bonding dominates **"Imelda,"** opening and closing her story, framing, as it were, her portrait. The real "subject" of the account is Hugh Franciscus, doctor-as-god, "coat monkishly starched" and with "the appearance of a prophet." As a professional "father," an instructor in medical school, he seeks out the narrator, his student, on the basis of a language skill: the narrator speaks Spanish and will therefore be useful as an interpreter in Honduras, as an extension of Franciscus's voice. (The narrator, in turn, will later interpret Franciscus himself and will use his skill in language to write the story we read.) Like Renaissance sonnet cycles, also entitled by the names of specific women, **"Imelda"** really emphasizes the reactions of men involved in the same *art*.

"Foreignness" now becomes a predominantly geographical concept, mediated by the narrator's knowledge of Spanish, for Imelda herself is barely sexual, "her breasts making only the smallest imprint in the cloth, her hips none at all." In a gesture from the harem, however, she covers her face in shame and modesty until the plastic surgeon seizes the cloth to reveal her cleft palate, "a nude, rubbery insect" on her face. Even before the plastic surgeon can begin his transformation of his insect, the narrator begins an analogous process in his transformative prose. Within lines the "insect" gives way to a slightly more attractive image of Imelda as "a beautiful bird with a crushed beak." But the two processes—the narrator's transformation by prose and the surgeon's by scalpel—are not yet synchronized, and the surgeon's directive freezes the imaginative flow of the writer as it does Imelda's image: "Take her picture."

During Imelda's surgery, each doctor discovers a new bond with the other: that of failure. The surgeon's skill, hardly tried, cannot prevail against the unexpected malignant hyperthermia which flames up in the patient. The narrator's linguistic skill, his call for "hielo" (ice), fails too, because his word lacks any referent in this rural, undersupplied place. As a result of Imelda's death, the locus of metaphoric divinity shifts from the doctor to her mourning mother in a dress "like a cassock," while Franciscus now seems to shrink until he is "scarcely taller than she. There was a place at the crown of his head where the hair had grown thin. His lips were stones." Disempowered as creator, he turns into artifact. "At that moment he was like someone cast, still alive, as an effigy for his own tomb." Yet even as the doctor sinks beneath the weight of an acknowledged mortality, Imelda's mother reaffirms, even enhances his priestliness, for she holds an absolute belief in his recreation of an imperishable body (the image): " . . . she was happy now that the harelip had been fixed so that her daughter might go to heaven without it," and "the doctor is one of the angels. He has finished the work of God. My daughter is beautiful." The surgeon has gone in the night to the morgue and repaired the girl's dead face. He has practiced his art on death's artifact.

For the narrator, this is the point at which he enters one of those "certain dreams (that) illuminate a whole lifetime of past behavior," just as Franciscus, bowed under failure, formerly has "closed his eyes." The incident makes the plastic surgeon, his putative father, *known* to him, and what he recognizes in him is the "dire necessity" of the artist at his work. As a result of this empathetic recognition, the plastic surgeon's art and that of the author-teller now coincide, so that Selzer spends a lingering and generous interval on the imagined reconstruction of Imelda's face, art out of art. The detail with which he describes the surgeon's work lends it a quality of ritual and order, the same order denied in Imelda's untimely and quixotic death. The doctors' crafts reciprocate even more deeply in that, were it not for the surgeon's art, unseen at the time of its performance, the author's narrative could not move forward; were it not for the narrator's slides, the surgeon's *product* would remain invisible; and, were it not for Selzer's prose, the *process* of the plastic surgery would never be "seen" by the readers. Among these three men, then, two of them fictional or fictionalized characters, and one the writer of the fiction itself (subject, persona and author), there is not simply the bond of gender and medical profession, but an interdependence of skills as **"Imelda"** reconstructs Imelda's reconstruction.

Through the art form of photography the girl herself even seems to come back from the dead, "extracted from the shadow, suspended above and beyond all of us like a resurrection" in the before-and-after slides Franciscus screens for medical personnel. Yet that same resurrecting art threatens to uncover the "father's nakedness." The next slide is the one taken in the morgue. Franciscus will be exposed, the narrator tells us. Significantly, the narrator-son withholds this slide and goes on to the next case, protecting the surgeon's image, but not before Imelda's photographic still life has melted into the sound of her spoken name. After this point, the account trails off into a nostalgic and eulogistic recapitulation of Franciscus's decline into age, until voice itself is put out. "I would like to have told him what I now know, that his unrealistic act was one of goodness, one of those small, preserving acts done, perhaps, to ward off madness . . . But, of course, it's too late now." Yet the author has performed just such an act himself, redeeming, then commemorating, his professor. While the death of Franciscus interrupts the literal dialogue between them, the bond between the men frames and even creates Imelda's portrait, inspiring the story which we ourselves read. Selzer seems here to have found a male muse and to have remade the "transitional" woman as artifact (story) itself.

In the title story of *Taking the World in for Repairs,* Selzer returns to the world of volunteer plastic surgeons, this time in Peru. No mere reworking of **"Imelda,"** this account's emphasis is on the shifting and tragic imbalance between rich and poor and the inability even of these volunteers—"Within two weeks they will have performed more of these operations than most surgeons will do in a lifetime"—to accommodate all the potential patients in an overscheduled fortnight's work. A sense of urgency pervades both INTERPLAST and **"Taking the World . . . ,"** both of which move in episodic rush from one human need to another. The story wrests its readers from scenario to scenario at a quick pace like that of the surgical team. As the flow of the prose pours forward, blocks of documentary detail push against the slower "cameo" stories on individual cases which, in this work, are brief and frequent, all seeming to lack the patient dramatic development of **"Imelda"** and to be as unfinished as the flesh of the patients itself. They come and go without leaving ponderous and artful "meaning" behind them. This is the world of **"Imelda,"** but of "Imelda Unbound." In fact, Selzer recollects the earlier story by repeating its memorable image of the harelip as a "nude, rubbery insect," now appearing on the face of a seven-year-old boy. Here, as in **"Imelda,"** an operating emergency occurs for want of supplies, but here, oxygen is found—stolen, really, from the recovery room, for every sufficiency in ths poor country begets a deficiency elsewhere. The miracle is not that a face, a hand, should be reconstructed, but that a backup supply exists at all.

Selzer's emphasis, then, cannot be on the leisurely study of a single person's damaged or remade face, nor can his story shape itself according to the conventions of a leisurely art. There is neither reason nor time to lavish romanticized descriptions on conception where fecundity abounds and, with it, human misery. In the midst of **"Taking the World . . . ,"** Selzer pauses only briefly to encapsulate the very matter of physical creation in his own prose:

> A short lesson in embryology: Mesenchyme is that all-purpose undifferentiated tissue of which we are largely made early in fetal life. Mesenchyme is not stationary, but flows, folding upon itself, rising in ridges, incorporating within itself little sacs and hollows. Within the first trimester of pregnancy it happens sometimes, far oftener in Peru than in America, it seems, that the mesenchyme destined to form the upper jaw, the lip and the palate fails either to fuse in the midline of the face, or even to migrate to the midline of the face. And so there is a cleft where there should have been an uninterrupted smooth and attractive joining.

The motion of this prose itself keeps extending, spreading from clause to clause, so that mesenchyme is both the subject and the emblem for the very structure—or structurelessness—of **"Taking the World. . . . "** The story, too, flows forward, folds back on itself, forms "sacs and hollows" of little incompleted dramas, against which the dispensary of Honorio Delgado stands as "an instrument with which to confront life, a rock . . . firm against the incessant lapping of fate." The whole shape of the story is cataclysmic and, not surprisingly, its central drama turns out not to be in the surgery, but in nature, where the volunteers' car accidentally bumps another one over a ravine. Even the terrain of the ravine with a river running below it evokes mesenchyme imperfectly joining on the midline of a face, an analogy Selzer intensifies through his comparison of stone and flesh:

> We pick up stones and toss them over the side. The one I throw sounds like the impact of flesh. A noise like that could kill you. I would not go down there again for Saint Francis himself.

Instead of adopting the birth process as a paradigm of creativity, Selzer artistically submerges himself in the mesenchyme of things, the nearly formless yet vital matter which spills and fails or seals a face into its human image. His story does not replicate the process of birth, but the process of the first cellular formation after conception has taken place.

In yet another late variation on his earlier paradigms of creativity, Selzer enables male dialogue through a *speaking* female member of the staff. The narrator's Spanish cannot secure a smooth communication with his Peruvian counterpart, so the patient's spasm and the spastic dialogue coincide:

> "Calculo in choledochus!" the surgeon shouts at me.
>
> "Si! !Si!" I shout back. He then tries to pass a dilator down into the duodenum. It will not go.
>
> "Otro calculo?" I suggest.
>
> "No!" he thunders. "Espasmo!"

In a second gall bladder surgery, the narrator, rushing through the operation because of his own incipient attack of *turista,* diarrhea, suddenly finds that the patient is bleeding excessively. This hemorrhage shocks him out of his bilingual status into his native speech and the recognition that he is indeed in a "foreign" place. Nationality invades the international community of surgeons and dialogue is only restored when a third language, French, and a second sex, female, interprets for them.

> "Jesus," I say in English. "She is bleeding all over South America." I say it again, this time, for some reason, in French. Then it is that Maria, the scrub nurse, who has up to now been silent, says, all but inaudibly, *"Je parle francais."*

Here the two-way speech between men, so frequent towards the end of other Selzer stories, becomes triadic, including, for the first time, a woman's voice not simply incidentally, but centrally. "Her very words are hemostatic for the patient, antidiarrhetic for me." When she is teasingly elevated to divine status—"Et Maria est mon ange gardien . . ."—and ordered to translate the compliment for the benefit of the operating team, she proves to be "more than a match for the whole lot." Her "foreign" language mediates between two others, English and Spanish, as the interpreter of the earlier **"Imelda"** now finds himself in need of interpretation. The operating theater's drama becomes a drama of vocalization and communication on another plane.

Thus, as the act of writing shapes the writer, so Selzer's metaphoric and narrative homage to the process of creativity expands, changes, and shifts over the course of his work, from personal lack to the tragic loss underlying all human experience. He both varies the heterosexual muse/poet paradigm he inherits from Western tradition and invents a new vision of human community based on daily acts of modest heroisms and on the exchange of artifacts to consecrate them. He merits the place he achieves among those other physicians for whom writing was and is a "cure" for the wounds of surgery and a way to become, as Selzer desires in **Mortal Lessons,** a doctor. (pp. 282-301)

Gayle Whittier, "Richard Selzer's Evolving Paradigms of Creativity," in The Centennial Review, *Vol. XXXIII, No. 3, Summer, 1989, pp. 278-301.*

Selzer on why he retired from surgery:

In the operating room, the patient must be anesthetized in order that he feel no pain. The surgeon too must be "anesthetized" in order to remain at some distance from the event: when he cuts the patient, his own flesh must not bleed. It is this seeming lack of feeling that gives the surgeon the image of someone who is out of touch with his humanity, a person wanting only to cut, to perform. I assure you that it is the image only. A measure of insulation against the laying open of the bodies of his fellow human beings is necessary for the well-being of both patient and doctor. In surgery, if nowhere else, dispassion is an attribute. But the surgeon-writer is not anesthetized. He remains awake; sees everything; censors nothing. It is his dual role to open and repair the body of his patient and to report back to the waiting world in the keenest language he can find. By becoming a writer, I had stripped off the protective carapace. It was time to go. A surgeon can unmake himself; a writer cannot.

Richard Selzer, in his "The Pen and the Scalpel," The New York Times Magazine, August 21, 1988.

Charles I. Schuster   (essay date 1989)

[*Schuster is an educator and critic. In the following essay, he focuses on Selzer's nonfiction, praising him for his ability to fuse disparate images and intertwine fiction and nonfiction.*]

In **"Surgeon as Priest,"** the second essay in **Mortal Les-**

sons, Richard Selzer describes the diagnostic abilities of Yeshi Dhonden, personal physician to the Dalai Lama. Unlike his American counterparts, Yeshi Dhonden peers at no X-rays, draws no blood. Instead, after two hours of bathing, fasting, and prayer, he enters the female patient's room and for a long time gazes at her. Then he takes her hand and feels her pulse, cradling her hand in his for thirty silent minutes. Finally, he pours a portion of her urine into a wooden bowl, whips the liquid until a foam is raised, and inhales the odor three times. He speaks no word to her, nor her to him, except for her "urgent and serene" calling of " 'Thank you, Doctor' " as he leaves to share his diagnosis with the physicians of the Yale School of Medicine. In the conference room, he speaks, his words translated by an interpreter:

> He speaks of winds coursing through the body of the woman, currents that break against barriers, eddying. These vortices are in her blood he says. The last spendings of an imperfect heart. Between the chambers of her heart, long, long before she was born, a wind had come and blown open a deep gate that must never be opened. Through it charge the full waters of her river, as the mountain stream cascades in the springtime, battering, knocking loose the land, and flooding her breath. Thus he speaks, and is silent.

> "May we now have the diagnosis?" a professor asks.

> The host of these rounds, the man who knows, answers.

> "Congenital heart disease," he says. "Interventricular septal defect, with resultant heart failure."

I restate this story because it stands as a central paradigm for Selzer's work. As Selzer makes clear, Dhonden is surgeon as priest, a man so holy that his spirit can "enter" the body of his patient. Dhonden is also lover, a physician who gives the serene beauty of himself, so much so that Selzer declares he is envious—not of Dhonden but of the patient: "I want to be held like that, touched so, *received.*" Dhonden furthermore possesses the humility necessary to all fine surgeons and stands as a warning against what Selzer later will label "the gauleiter mentality of some of the surgeons," that vulgar, meaty pride which suffocates the sensibility. In typical fashion, Selzer has yoked disparate concepts together here—the physical and the spiritual, Western analysis and Eastern intuition, medicine and religion—and he has maintained them in, to use one of his favorite terms, a resonance. But I call attention to this one episode for another reason. And that is to claim that Selzer himself is Dhonden. Not in any literal way, of course, for Yeshi Dhonden is no figment of Selzer's pen. Like Dhonden, however, Selzer makes of science an art. Like the Dalai Lama's personal physician, Selzer elevates his craft, transforming the bloody drabness of the operating room into religious ecstasy, poetic possibility. Under his gaze, blood and flesh become sacrament; surgeon becomes Christ and Judas, healer and murderer. It is this kind of unresolvable conflict and tension that vitalizes Selzer's work.

Selzer seldom perceives object as object. He has instead a poet's vision, the ability—even the compulsion—to transform reality through image. In a recent interview, Selzer described his thinking during a breast operation: "I noted that her breasts reminded me of the blue and white china teapots on my grandmother's shelf. They were so fragile, that I was always afraid that I would break one, and here I was going to break one now." For Selzer, the breast and the teapot merge, and yet neither loses its identity in the other. Such thinking may not aid the surgeon, but it is of incalculable benefit to the artist. Like Baudelaire—and the French symbolists to whom he is greatly indebted—Selzer reorders reality, creating correspondences between the delicacy of a woman's veined breast and the rare, fragile china placed out of the careless reach of the child. This is the observation of the surgeon as priest, seer, and poet. Even more than Yeshi Dhonden, Selzer practices medicine through art and mystery, transforming objects into metaphor and symbol.

In Selzer, an object frequently becomes enriched with multiple associations. The surgeon's scalpel, for example, is called "the knife," a common synonym but one which nevertheless signals violence and potentially murderous intent. But this dead metaphor does not suffice. Within the first paragraph of his essay, **"The Knife,"** Selzer creates an association of the scalpel with the bow of a cello, a tulip, a slender fish, and a "terrible steel-bellied thing" with which the surgeon conspires. Each association creates interpretative possibilities. As cello bow, the scalpel is seen as an instrument that plays upon the strings of the human body, making music, creating art. The surgeon, concomitantly, becomes musician, artist. Sensitivity is required, a delicacy of drawing bow across strings of gut. The play of possibilities complements Selzer's themes of surgeon as artist and surgery as a fusing of surgeon and patient into one cooperative relationship of mutual dependency. As a tulip, the scalpel is transformed into an object of pure delight, frivolity, and delicacy. It is, as well, an object or token of love. And the tulip, I would wager, most commonly conjures up an image of a blood-red flower at the end of a long stem. This, too, is of a piece with the scalpel "drawing across the field of skin," leaving a trail of blood. Finally, the scalpel works silently beneath the surface of things like a fish. And it travels quickly, almost swimmingly, across and inside the flesh, not only like a fish but like some sinister alien object, a "terrible steel-bellied thing." It is true that Selzer only names these associations, developing them slightly if at all in this opening paragraph, but that is part of his power as an artist. These associations are invitations to create contexts for terms left bare in Selzer's prose. The scalpel is not simply an instrument; it is an emblem, a mysterious totem, like a thyrsus or a crucifix, to which the reader can affix subjective interpretations.

Selzer continues to create multiple significance for the scalpel throughout **"The Knife."** An operation, writes Selzer, is "an entry into the body," so that knife becomes sexual instrument in an act of physical penetration—it is penis honed to a razor-thin edge. This association of scalpel with sexual organ, of surgery with lovemaking, immediately gives way to religious imagery. The knife has be-

come chalice, the operation a literal communion in which the body and blood are altogether body and blood: "Not surplice and cassock but mask and gown are your regalia. You hold no chalice, but a knife. There is no wine, no wafer. There are only the facts of blood and flesh." The surgeon, moreover, is accorded a mystic vision of an ancient world. He becomes "a traveler in a dangerous country." But knife is more. It is also the dread double-headed axe, for the surgeon is "like an executioner who hears the cleric comforting the prisoner." It is wild and fierce, untameable, an animal—"It grins. It is like a cat. . . ." It joins with the surgeon "like the Centaur—the knife, below, all equine energy, the surgeon, above, with his delicate art." "In a moment it is like the long red fingernail of the Dragon Lady." It is the peer among the instruments, the sneering lord.

But all these figurative attempts do not suffice; in the last section of the essay Selzer returns to the basic question: "What is it, then, this thing, the knife. . . ." His initial response is to find refuge in objectivity, in a brief discourse on the historical origins of the knife followed by the most objective and scientific description that yet appears in the essay. Why place this dictionary-like attempt here at the end of an emotionally charged series of complex allusions and associations? It is, I would argue, an example of rhetorical irony, of Selzer indirectly claiming once more that the meaning of *knife* is not conveyable in these terms. The scalpel's physical characteristics, the description it is given as handle and blade with "a narrow notched prong," appear ludicrous now after the previous celebration of scalpel in all its power. Selzer himself seems aware of this, for by the third sentence, art and association have once again intruded upon scientific detachment. "Without the blade," Selzer explains, "the handle has a blind, decapitated look. It is helpless as a trussed maniac." The reader is immediately thrust back into a more literary context, a poetic rendering of this mysterious object. And Selzer's answer to "What is it, then, this thing, the knife" becomes in large part a climactic restatement in slightly different terms—it is knife, and beast, and penis, and death, and life:

> Now the scalpel sings along the flesh again, its brute run unimpeded by germs or other frictions. It is a slick slide home, a barracuda spurt, a rip of embedded talon. One listens, and almost hears the whine—nasal, high, delivered through that gleaming metallic snout. The flesh splits with its own kind of moan. It is like the penetration of rape.

> The breasts of women are cut off, arms and legs sliced to the bone to make ready for the saw, eyes freed from sockets, intestines lopped. The hand of the surgeon rebels. Tension boils through his pores, like sweat. The flesh of the patient retaliates with hemorrhage, and the blood chases the knife wherever it is withdrawn.

Afterwards, like some brute animal it lies "spent, on its side, the bloody meal smear-dried upon its flanks." There can be little doubt, I think, of the sexual suggestion of "spent," a verb used frequently in eighteenth- and nineteenth-century literature. Like a phallus, the knife here is exhausted but capable of renewal.

What is remarkable in this essay, I think, is the profusion of images and associations that are poured into a very few pages. Nor is **"The Knife"** atypical. The essay that follows it in *Mortal Lessons,* **"Skin,"** opens by describing its subject as "baklava," "scabbard," an "instrument," a means by which we are "bagged and trussed," and a covering that "upholsters," all of which is followed by the "seamless body-stocking" image that opens the succeeding paragraph. Moreover the opening clause, "I sing of skin . . . ," evokes Virgil and sets up comic expectations that **"Skin"** belongs somewhere within the heroic tradition. Indeed, the language here is clearly mock-heroic with its comparison to the dawn and its highly descriptive, parallel phrases. The body itself is an item of furniture; the armpit is transformed into a "grotto." Our body becomes an interior landscape, each perforation "with its singular rim and curtain."

That Selzer makes continuous recourse to images and allusions suggests two possibilities concerning his writing. First, it implies a limitation of expositional language, of the linear, denotative, explicative use of words. This explanatory mode simply will not suffice. Selzer's at times almost uncontrollable use of allusion and image suggests the lengths to which he is compelled to write in order to create a personal code, a meta-language that can express the center of his mystical, affective experience. Selzer pushes language to its limits. When accepted words of the English language are insufficient, he invents others: *siffling, apter,* and *slidder.* He stretches syntactical boundaries by inverting his word order and piling phrases and Latinate constructions into his essays. (For example, in *Mortal Lessons,* "First from his fingertips did the rich blackness fade—to no mere cocoa or tan, but to such a white as matched the fairness of a Dane"). He enriches his prose with a profusion of figurative tropes and stylistic usages—simile, metaphor, asyndeton, aposiopesis, hyperbole, anaphora. This is a writer who pushes rhetoric to its limits. It is thus fair to say that the profusion of images and allusions contributes to Selzer's overall attempt as an author to bypass conventional linguistic forms. Selzer's language strives for connotation, association, implication, signification beyond sign. This is not always the case, of course, for every writer must provide sufficient linear exposition to provide a context for the reader. But as the brief description of the scalpel at the end of **"The Knife"** illustrates, expositional prose frequently fails. Its explicit nature disallows hypothetical and imaginative responses on the part of the reader. Such language oversimplifies; it is too stipulative, too parched, too bare of the contradictory impulses that feed Selzer's work. The images and allusions represent, therefore, a deliberate and continuing attempt to signify the unsignifiable.

Second, I would suggest that the neologisms and seemingly random and grotesque images also contribute considerably to the impression Selzer's work gives of originating in dream and nightmare. When he first began writing professionally, Selzer composed between 1 A.M. and 3 A.M. and he acknowledges that he tapped his dream life as he

wrote. One can feel the tempo of dream in much of his work. Objects flower into vivid images: a slug is extolled as lover; a Civil War doctor looks into a peach orchard and sees a mortally wounded Pegasus collapsing to the earth; the young Selzer punches a young bully in the chest and then watches him first cough up meaty gobs of blood and, over the period of a year, succumb to a tubercular death. These are the images of dream and restless sleep. The profusion of them, moreover, is dictated in large part by association, just as are the symbols of dream. In **"Longfellow, Virgil, and Me,"** for example, Selzer notes that one of his teachers "gorged us with Latin." The verb, apparently, triggers an association, for Selzer extends the metaphor: "We were geese being primed for pâté," and the image of students as geese continues until the teacher becomes Medea "slaying her children"—perhaps serving them up to a figurative Jason as pâté de fois gras. Back and forth career the tropes and associations like the subliminal events in a dream state. The effect in Selzer is to add a dimension of interpretive possibility: things in Selzer are not only themselves but, to use Freud's terms, "hieroglyphics, whose symbols must be translated, one by one, into the language of the dream-thoughts." Nor is there a one-to-one ratio of image with meaning. Often Selzer's tropes are nonspecific; they are signs of an inchoate sensibility, images for which no fully specific language is available.

Selzer, in this respect, can be likened to Keats, a poet who has significantly influenced him. Keats, in a well-known passage from an 1817 letter to his brothers, George and Thomas, writes: "It struck me what quality went to form a Man of Achievement especially in Literature and which Shakespeare possessed so enormously—I mean *Negative Capability,* that is when man is capable of being in uncertainties, Mysteries, doubts, without any irritable reaching after fact and reason." The poet must be able to sustain the ambiguity of dream, the confusion of a sensibility overcharged by experience. The literal, the unitary and isolatable event, is denied by such a writer in order that he may express the complications of an unresolvable world. In another well-known passage from his letters, Keats argues that the poetical character "has no self—it is everything and nothing—It has no character—it enjoys light and shade; it lives in gusto, be it foul or fair, high or low, rich or poor, mean or elevated—It has much delight in conceiving an Iago as an Imogen. What shocks the virtuous philosopher, delights the camelion Poet." Selzer, too, is a "camelion Poet" to whom no action or event is so terrible as to be unreportable. His words and images pluck slices out of the profusion of life played out about him. That they are contrastive, contradictory, and at times wholly created by the occasion of the prose is part of Selzer's expression of his negative capability.

Out of this binary impulse both to reach beyond the literal and tap the subliminal power of dream, Selzer has introduced into his work a particular kind of figurative trope which has, to my knowledge, never been fully characterized in critical study. It has its roots, I am convinced, in the work of Poe, Dickens, the romantics, and the French symbolists, within which the evocation of dream and the desire to capture affective, ineffable experience are as strong as they are in Selzer. What characterizes this trope is the conjoining of two independent and distinct entities which are then bound and held together by one shared feature while simultaneously maintaining all their difference. In other writers, this kind of comparison takes the form of simile, metaphor, or analogy. But Selzer yokes the two terms together without the use of explicit "like" or "as" and without extending the vehicle. My term for this kind of trope is "fusion" or "fused image," and it appears frequently in Selzer's work.

For example, in **"Down From Troy,"** Selzer writes humorously and lovingly about his boyhood in Troy, New York, and about his relationship with his general practitioner father. After his expositional opening, he tells an Edgar Allan Poe tale of descending with his brother down the forbidden stairs into the cellar where they discover an old chest in the gray and moldy gloom. In typical fashion, Selzer describes this journey as a return to the mythic womb and an Orphean expedition, but these are mockheroic allusions here for comic effect, not fused images. What the two boys find inside the chest are two skeletons "lying athwart each other in terrible disarray." Immediately they convince themselves that these are the bones of two murder victims, patients, perhaps, of their father's haphazard practice. Swearing each other to secrecy, Selzer and his brother afterward "haunted the house like spectres . . . we failed to thrive, lost weight, became spidery and full of sighs." The boys became skeletal. Selzer makes this identification explicit, stating "that in some subliminal way, far below the threshold of consciousness, those two skeletons had become us, that by some strange inconsistency of time, Billy and I had come face to face with our own mortal remains." The two brothers have merged with the skeletons, and yet the skeletons remain skeletons, the brothers brothers. This is no simile, no metaphor, no allusion. It is a fusion of separate identities in which neither is lost.

The power of the fused image is that it locates itself ambiguously, between the literal and the figurative. It possesses no clear border, thus denying the reader any clear ground for response. In **"The Belly,"** for instance, Selzer describes the effects of an overacidic stomach:

> Rubor, Tumor, Dolor, Calor (Redness, Swelling, Pain, Heat), the Four Horsemen of Peptic Apocalypse come riding hard, galloping across the midriff, pillaging, raping tissue, laying waste. On and on they stampede, unchecked by antacid, surcease, even sleep, their lust sated only by the triple calamities of Obstruction, Hemorrhage, and Perforation.

In this example of fusion, Selzer takes four physiological effects (Latinate terms and all) and personifies them into literary-biblical figures without losing the interpretive weight of either tenor or vehicle. The semantic tension makes itself felt in the words themselves: the phrase "laying waste," a dead metaphor, gains by the identification of waste with rot, excretion, and products of physical corruption. These horsemen not only "lay waste" in the sense of siege and destroy but also in the most literal sense of producing waste, brooding and hatching it out of the bowel. In the next sentence, the tenor and vehicle seesaw in somewhat the following manner:

Tenor *(physiological-scientific)*	*Vehicle* *(Four Horsemen-Literary)*
	On and on they stampede,
unchecked by antacid, even sleep,	surcease, their lust sated only by the triple calamities of
Obstruction, Hemorrhage, and Perforation	

The sentence pitches back and forth, with the three final terms coming full circle in the sense that they, like Rubor, Tumor, Dolor, and Calor, are both physical symptoms and literary personifications. Moreover, this description is, like the passage in Revelation from which it draws its inspiration, a prophetic vision except that this one ironically describes the problems of overacidity.

Placed as it is between two quite technical, scientific descriptions, this example of fusion suggests its own genetic roots. Selzer is a surgeon who is also a writer, but he is also a writer who practices surgery. (In fact, he is now a retired surgeon and a full-time writer.) He is a doctor and humanist, a man of science and of letters. He considers himself as a writer to be an artist seeking aesthetic effects, a surgeon explaining the delicate intricacies of his profession, a resident doctor teaching his students, a mystic who wants to turn our thoughts to soul and spirit, a devotee of Poe who seeks to immerse us all over again in the formless horrors of our childhood. These impulses make themselves apparent in the tables of contents of his books: he includes treatises on medical subjects, personal essays, excursions into the grotesque, anecdotes, didactic addresses to particular and public audiences. As an artist, Selzer is invigorated by a host of irreconcilable intentions which create irreconcilable effects in the writing. In **"Belly,"** he develops a descriptive explanation of the effects of acidity, suddenly interrupting this mode with the fusion example of the four horsemen. And this fusion participates within the text as both exposition and metaphor, situating itself uneasily between the two, bridging the passage that precedes it with the one that follows, both of which are highly expositional. The fused image thus complicates the reading, heightens the effect without wholly giving way to the figurative, artistic, humanistic impulse. It mixes elements without blurring their identity. It captures the multiplicity of Selzer's mind and art, the irreconcilability of his contradictory interests and intentions. And by this very power and ambivalence, it creates powerful moments in the text.

Perhaps its most climactic usage is in **"The Masked Marvel's Last Toehold,"** an account Selzer offers in *Confessions of a Knife.* This book, the successor to *Mortal Lessons,* blends fiction with nonfiction, so that the reader is at times unsure of the mode of a particular piece. But in the case of **"The Masked Marvel,"** Selzer has made himself clear: this is nonfiction. Selzer describes the experience in the first person, as surgeon ministering to patient. And his patient in this case is Elihu Koontz, a seventy-five-year-old diabetic amputee who, as a young man, lumbered around the wrestling circuit as "The Masked Marvel."

Selzer opens the essay with a brilliantly impressionistic description of the gnomish old man who once basked in his physical, muscular power but who now sits in a hospital bed staring at the "collapsed leg of his pajamas." This theme of strength and health amputated by time and disease echoes through the essay. Koontz is a man living backward, a refugee of popular culture still carrying his old clippings and photographs, celebrating his gloried past. He is a wrestler once and always, a point that Selzer returns to at the end of the narrative. Koontz's admission of his past identity pushes Selzer himself backward, to a night in Toronto's Maple Leaf Gardens where the featured wrestling match was "The Angel vs. The Masked Marvel." Typically, Selzer's narrative is vivid, filled with the violence of the action. Witness his description of The Angel:

> The shaved nape rises in twin columns to puff into the white hood of a sloped and bosselated skull that is too small. As though, strangled by the sinews of that neck, the skull had long since withered and shrunk. The thing about The Angel is the absence of any mystery in his body. It is simply *there*. A monosyllabic announcement. A grunt. One looks and knows everything at once, the fat thighs, the gigantic buttocks, the great spine from which hang knotted ropes and pale aprons of beef. And that prehistoric head. He is all of a single hideous piece, The Angel is. No detachables.

Selzer's exaggerated terms make of the angel a mythic antagonist; he is a combination of Antaeus, *Tyrannosaurus rex,* and Moby Dick. And the Marvel, through nearly all the heroic battle, is victimized by this brainless, brutish power, especially by the Angel's use of the toehold, which twists his foot downward, straining bone and ligament to the cracking point. Selzer, the young boy, is horrified, but his uncle roars to the Angel, "Break it off! Tear off a leg and throw it up here!" The uncle's shout reverberates through the story. It is the scream of a madman, a calling forth of the primeval urge for sacrifice and mutilation. Selzer's response is more plaintive, more civilized. "That's not fair," he states, as the Marvel's toes are twisted further. Selzer and uncle, in their opposing loyalties, mirror Marvel and Angel, even as the wrestlers themselves ironically participate in what Tom Wolfe calls single combat warfare (*The Right Stuff*). The wrestlers signify opposing forces, though not particularly of good and evil. If anything, the Angel suggests direct, open brutality while the Marvel, because of his mask and secret identity ("No one knows who The Masked Marvel really is!") implies mystery and the ominous unknown. Theirs is a highly ritualized struggle. Moreover, it is a parodic battle. Wrestling, in our culture, is strength and showmanship. It is theatre. There is within Selzer's depiction of this match the unstated irony of the play of it all, the sense that the whole affair has been scripted. The agony of the toehold is both real and totally false; the violence of the match is, for the contemporary reader, at best mock-heroic. But from within the point of view of the essay, the point of view of the young boy and his uncle in the Gardens, everything that unfolds is high melodrama and utterly credible. They are not watching a performance, but a gladiatorial fight to the finish. It is at this point, when the Marvel has been almost totally subjugated, that the Angel does something unspeakable: he turns, while maintaining the toehold, and begins to pull off the Marvel's mask. Young Selzer's response is instantaneous: he screams for someone to stop the Angel. In an instant it is over—the Marvel miracu-

lously kicks free, pins the Angel, and arises victorious and mysterious still.

All this Selzer remembers, and it leads him to the climax of the essay where a complicated fusion contributes to the power of the narrative. I quote it here in its entirety:

> Once again, I am in the operating room. It is two years since I amputated the left leg of Elihu Koontz. Now it is his right leg which is gangrenous. I have already scrubbed. I stand to one side wearing my gown and gloves. And . . . I am masked. Upon the table lies Elihu Koontz, pinned in a fierce white light. Spinal anesthesia has been administered. One of his arms is taped to a board placed at a right angle to his body. Into this arm, a needle has been placed. Fluid drips here from a bottle overhead. With his other hand, Elihu Koontz beats feebly at the side of the operating table. His head rolls from side to side. His mouth is pulled into weeping. It seems to me that I have never seen such misery.
>
> An orderly stands at the foot of the table, holding Elihu Koontz's leg aloft by the toes so that the intern can scrub the limb with antiseptic solutions. The intern paints the foot, ankle, leg, and thigh, both front and back, three times. From a corner of the room where I wait, I look down as from an amphitheater. Then I think of Uncle Max yelling, "Tear off a leg. Throw it up here." And I think that forty years later I am making the catch.
>
> "It's not fair," I say aloud. But no one hears me. I step forward to break The Masked Marvel's last toehold.

History has repeated itself with a merciless vengeance. Only this time the outcome is not playfully mock-heroic. Koontz, the wrestler, is wrestling still, held, "pinned," helpless. Just as before, Selzer affirms that "It is not fair." Just as he had as a boy, his response to Koontz's pain is "It seems to me that I have never seen such misery." The scene, the agony, the action, the phrases repeat themselves like a twice-dreamt nightmare, identical in theme if not in detail. Past and present merge; the match in the Gardens has fused with the scene in the operating room. Koontz's misery defines temporal boundaries. And Selzer himself has fused. He has become the Masked Marvel victorious once again ("And . . . *I am masked*"). He has become the Angel, who at long last is obeying Uncle Max's vehement demand. And he has even become his uncle, now about to make the catch. Selzer, here, by tearing off the Masked Marvel's leg, has most clearly allied himself with Angel and uncle, yet he is the Marvel as well. Indeed, the line "No one knows who the Masked Marvel really is" suggests that in some subliminal way the hooded wrestler is not Koontz at all. He is unknown, nameless, all of us, Selzer himself. What accounts for the Marvel's mythic proportion is not his strength or, like the "Angel," his neck and "bosselated skull," but his mysterious identity. He is a cipher, an etymological blank. He is the nameless, unrecognizable force inside us all. We are the Masked Marvel, in the same sense that we are all mysterious superheroes—Batman, the Lone Ranger, Spiderman. His strength and cunning, his ability to overcome the Angel's toehold, his final vulnerability and defeat make him a focus of our projected subconscious. In a very real sense, Selzer is looking down at the table as if into a mirror.

Selzer's use of fusion blurs lines of identity; boys become skeletons but remain boys; Selzer becomes Marvel and Angel and uncle while remaining altogether himself as surgeon. The reader, as emotional and imaginative participant in the text, experiences similar ambiguous relations between self and other. It is in this tension, this resonance between opposite and apposite, that Selzer's genius as a writer is particularly apparent. He is, in Mikhail Bakhtin's terms, a "dialogical" writer, with all the various textual manifestations that such an orientation necessarily produces. In coining the term *dialogical,* Bakhtin attempts to describe an authorial presence which deconstitutes itself. A dialogical text is an aesthetic creation in which plurality and polyphony replace a single, rigidly conceptualized voice or point of view. Dialogical texts are characterized by comingled voices, by open-ended ideological speculations submerged within a textual framework, by the presentation of consciousness as multiple and ceaselessly contrastive. Selzer's use of fusion is one aspect of this dialogical quality. Another aspect is the frequency with which he merges his authorial voice with that of characters, literary figures, subjects—simultaneously maintaining a voice or style with multiple accents, tones, and orientations. It is as if Selzer engages in the trope of fusion and then enlarges it to embrace an entire work.

Of all the irreconcilable impulses colliding within Selzer's work, however, perhaps the most significant from a formal point of view is his inability, his unwillingness, to separate the fictional from the nonfictional. His work, he claims, has "a central core of truth" even though he uses many "fictional techniques" to recover it. For most readers the distinction between real and unreal modes of telling is a significant one. Human beings have created a phenomenologically divided world where experience is filtered through oppositions such as good and evil, up and down, in and out. In reading, this emphasis gets expressed as the question, "Is this true or not? Is this fiction or nonfiction?" The answer to that question allows most readers to gauge their responses to a work, to classify the experience of their reading as being of the world or of the imagination.

Selzer consistently confounds that expectation. It is as if he is engaging in dialogism ontologically, as it were, by refusing to accede to the conventional limitations of the fictional/nonfictional generic distinctions that guide most of us through experience. Although *Rituals of Surgery* is a collection of fiction, the stories contain a good bit of surgical and physiological fact. *Mortal Lessons,* a work of nonfiction, reveals Selzer using numerous fictional techniques, especially shifts in point of view, to achieve his ends. *Confessions, Letters to a Young Doctor* and *Taking the World in for Repairs,* include both essays and short stories, at times in ways that make it difficult to perceive to which category a title should be assigned. Cast loose between two equally indistinct shores, readers must devise their own chart to steer by. They must become more willing to sustain doubt and ambiguity, more capable of supplying their own direction within the parameters established by the

work itself. For no essay (story? narrative?) is this more true than **"Pages of a Wound-Dresser's Diary,"** which, in fact, is a fusion of the nonfictional and fictional held in perfect tension.

"Pages" recreates the experience of a Civil War doctor-surgeon stationed aboard a steamboat plying the Mississippi from Pittsburgh Landing to St. Louis. It is less a story than a narration, a slice of experience which contains at its center a delicate tale of the love the doctor discovers for a young lifer who ultimately dies of his wounds. This sketchily drawn tale exemplifies Selzer's depiction of war: the doctor's passionate but concealed love represents a hopeful and healing prospect, while the boy's death is a small part of the fabric of wholesale death and dismemberment which the war weaves all around them. **"Pages"** is marked by features typical of Selzer's art: grisly depiction of wounds, illness, and medical treatment; short narrative scenes strung together without transition, a blending of reality with dream and nightmare; the use of neologisms and archaisms such as "musicked," "clackety," and "chunter," which, along with the phrasing and frequently inverted word order, achieve a heightening of the style; a general lack of dialogue; and a substantial amount of direct and indirect allusion, such as the link of the doctor and the Mississippi to Charon on the Styx. But it is the story's uneasy relationship with the actuality of the Civil War that gives an added twist to its power. Written in the first person as a series of undated journal entries, **"Pages"** recreates the experience of a Civil War doctor. The names of ships and ports, the detailed descriptions of river and wounded soldiers, the felt language of the narrator as he recounts experiences and visions all combine to achieve a remarkable verisimilitude. Nor is this any accident. For at the center of this fictive account lies a series of actual letters written by a young Civil War doctor to his brother and sister while he was stationed aboard a steamboat on the Mississippi. Now housed in the Beinecke Library at Yale, these letters were offered to Selzer to read by his friend, Archie Hannah, the curator of the Americana Collection. Selzer's description of the experience of reading this material is informative: "I read about 300 of this man's letters. He wasn't a writer by any stretch of the imagination, but he was a letter writer and a recorder. Everything was written down in these letters. If something floated by in the river, he reported it in one of his letters. So that by reading them one was suddenly . . . well, they had an enormous power by themselves, even though he wasn't what we think of as a writer. After I had read 100 of them I totally identified with this man. He was 25 at the time, and I was then on that steamboat myself. It required absolutely no transformation, no transmutation. I felt myself to be in the position of that man, and I knew then that I would write something."

What Selzer wrote, however, did not just evolve out of a fusion of identity between a Civil War doctor and himself. He felt the need for an additional element to complicate the unfolding of the narrative. He found that element in the figure of Walt Whitman. According to Selzer's own admission:

> I wanted to write about the events that took place on this steamboat, and its effect on the doc-

tor, his role. But I also wanted to use language. And I remembered that Walt Whitman had been a wound dresser during the Civil War . . . and in fact wrote a poem called "The Wound Dresser." So. Now I had it. I had the way to get into this material that would satisfy me as a writer. . . . I wrote it in the form of a diary, fragmented, using the language that approximates Whitman. In fact my character I describe from a photograph of Whitman as wound dresser. I use the word "wound dresser" as the title. I was making no secret of the fact that I was relying on Whitman's life experience and applying it, applying the poetry, applying the poetic sensibility to the events in this young doctor's life.

With his idealistic and explicit love for his fellow man, his poetic sensibility both horrified and enraptured by the experiences that washed over him, Whitman assumes an importance in the fusion equal to that of the historical doctor and Selzer himself. **"Pages"** blends the languages, experiences, perspectives, and points of view of all three individuals to produce a story which is neither fictional nor nonfictional but an indivisible fusion of both.

Here, for example, is a short passage which functions as an independent section of the text: "Another dawn. I stand on the upper deck. A strange elation has seized me, so that I am unable to sleep, except fitfully. The *January* rocks at her pier to the rhythm of far-off Minnesota springs. It is a soothing, amniotic pulse. On the opposite shore, a great hairy cypress surmounts the stream, dangling tendrils in the water." One can feel here Selzer's rhythm: the opening fragment, the rhythmic rise and fall of the following sentences as they settle into what may best be described as a rough, quantitative dactylic meter ("rocks at her pier to the rhythm of far-off Minn-e-sota springs"). But the language is not his alone; it is possessed, as well, by the doctor and Walt Whitman. The opening fragment recalls the journal form of the historical doctor. The terms used to describe the scene—the "soothing, amniotic pulse" and the "dangling tendrils"—forge a link between this writer and Selzer by creating a physiological personification of the natural scene. The "strange elation" he feels, however, is his Whitmanesque love for the young fifer, the image of the cypress being as naturalistic and evocative as one of Whitman's poetic figures. Throughout **"Pages,"** the narrator writes in the elegiac tone of the continuously bereaved mother and father, mourning the death of so many children. The narrator emerges as a Whitmanesque persona who is himself like the cypress tree he describes, a tree associated since classical times with sorrow and death.

Later on, the narrator presents another scene which effects a stylistic identification of the doctor, Whitman, and Selzer.

> One of the wounded is a Rebel lieutenant from Alabama. There is a sucking wound in the left side of his chest. With each inspiration, air is expelled through this ragged opening despite that I have plugged it with oiled lint. His fever rages. He is dying, certain. I sit with him during his final hour, and, all the while, he talks of the reasons for the war, why it is necessary.

> At the last, he tears a brass button from his gray coat and places it in my hand. There is that telltale "give," the taut arms gone limpsy, the onrush of silence that fills the space abandoned by labored breathing, moans; and I, visiting such new silences every hour.

Again one hears the specificity of the historical doctor: the identification of the officer and his state, his desperately matter-of-fact statement about having "plugged it [the wound] with oiled lint," the somewhat old-fashioned use of "inspiration." The very phrasing of "despite that I have" syntactically reaches backward to the doctor's era. Yet the descriptions of the injury, the "sucking wound" and "ragged opening" suggest Selzer, particularly his love of horror and the grotesque. And the rhythms again are his, the use of the post-position adjective in "He is dying, certain." Yet "Whitman, the poet-narrator," is also present with his characteristic omission of conjunctions and transitions between sentences, and the poetic descriptions like "that telltale 'give' " and "the taut arms gone limpsy." And only a poet could offer that dramatic, evocative last phrase in which the "I," the loving and grieving poet-doctor, is left dangling, alone, modified by an expression of continuous and unending bereavement.

Even in so short an analysis, I think it is clear that the language here is hybrid. The narrator is anchored to this context of steamer, Mississippi, and Civil War in a way that transcends place names and incidental detail. His language has become an inscape to the historical-medical-poetic experience. The very presentation of the story as a series of fragmentary images, associations, conjectures, and evocations, transforms it into a prose poem, one in which the reader must reconstitute the work by creating subjective interpretations that provide necessary interpretive connections. **"Pages"** is thus like an extended asyndeton; it is a work in which semantic ligature is minimized. Like a William Carlos Williams poem, its concentrated focus on the experimental and empirical implies a metaphysics without stating it. By focusing on the vividly palpable, the affective response to all this horror is implied but seldom offered. Description becomes image, metaphor, and symbol but always within a language that locates itself inside a particular and poetic rending of the event.

What **"Pages"** reveals about Selzer's language in dramatic fashion is what is more generally true of it. Selzer's language is dialogic in the sense that Mikhail Bakhtin describes in his theoretical work. Fusion is simply one instance of the dialogic impulse in Selzer's art. The introduction within Selzer's language of words and phrases from Keats, Longfellow, Virgil, Whitman, Poe, and others is another, more obvious (and thereby perhaps less successful) form of the dialogic. Dialogism cannot be introduced by overtly interrupting words with another's. It enters into the very accents of the words themselves. As Bakhtin describes it: "The word, directed toward its object, enters a dialogically agitated and tension-filled environment of alien words, value judgments and accents, weaves in and out of complex interrelationships, merges with some, recoils from others, intersects with yet a third group; and all this may crucially shape discourse, may leave a trace in all its semantic layers, may complicate its expression and influence its entire stylistic profile" [*The Dialogic Imagination*]. Selzer's aesthetic power draws heavily upon this dialogism, or rather, the dialogism contributes to the aesthetic qualities of his prose. Selzer fuses fiction with nonfiction, tenor with vehicle, the language of one social and normative reality with that of another. The work won't settle down comfortably into one genre or category. Not only from book to book or essay to essay, but even within individual phrases and clauses Selzer's language, at its best, continually interacts with other languages, literary languages, scientific languages, humanistic languages—and with the entire social, ethical, and philosophical constructs which surround those languages.

The following paragraph from **"Bone"** illustrates this principle:

> But this man who thrust himself from the earth, who wore the stars of heaven in his hair, was guilty of overweening pride. In act most audacious, he had defied nothing less than the law of gravity. He was to pay dearly for such high imposture. The vertebrae, unused to their new columnar arrangement, slipped, buckled, and wore out. Next, the arches of the feet fell. The hip joints ground to a halt. Nor was payment extorted only from the skeletal system. The pooling of blood in the lower part of the body distended the fragile blood vessels beyond their limits. Thus bloomed the fruitage of hemorrhoids; thus are we varicose. Worse still, our soft underparts have given way. Under the sag of our guts, we bulge into hernia. We turn to soft lump.

The opening sentence situates itself in a sermonic mode; the speaker here has mounted a pulpit. The second sentence takes a step toward the melodramatic with the postposition adjective in its opening phrase, in its word choice ("audacious," "defied"), and its echoing the theme of *Paradise Lost*. There is a literary quality here—and throughout—of words put together for dramatic effect, of syntax straining for originality. Moreover, there is a mocking tone produced by a combination of over-statement and the insinuation into this voice of a posture of the overly-righteous, a kind of Chadbandian overearnestness. That tone emerges distinctly in the third sentence, with its frocked, haughty denunciation of "man" made in the high Victorian tones of commercial metaphor ("pay dearly"). The language then shifts quite radically to the scientific, with its description of the vertebrae, arches, and hip joints. But the language is in part colloquial as well ("wore out," "fell"), until it ultimately slips into cliche ("ground to a halt"), which escapes the charge of triteness by the very fact of its being, in this case, literally true. Through the remainder of the passage, Selzer interweaves the language of the medical-school classroom, commercial boardroom, poet's study, and neighborhood bar. And yet it is all *his* language, his style, reflecting though it does the languages and styles of a wide spectrum of usages.

A second example illustrates a different kind of dialogical impulse at work in Selzer's prose. In **"Longfellow, Virgil, and Me,"** Selzer confesses his love for these two particular poets and the important role they played in his literary de-

velopment. Earlier, in **"Bone,"** Selzer had imitated Longfellow's distinctive tetrameter verse with a ten-line poem followed by the declaration, "Homage to Longfellow! One now understands why he wrote this way. Once you start, you can't stop." In **"Longfellow, Virgil, and Me,"** he declares his debt even more directly: "Within my mind, there are two men to whom I remain belted by filaments of the imagination of such a tensile strength as to have withstood the distraction, the wear and tear of thirty years. These are Longfellow and Virgil (bacio mano)." Selzer's love for Longfellow has indeed become so internalized that his writing "can't stop" being influenced by the rhythms of that earlier poet. Here, in stanzaic form to illustrate my point, is the third paragraph of the essay:

> And, ah, that intrepid youth
> "who bore 'mid snow and ice,
> a banner with the strange device, Excelsior."
> Where, we died to know,
> was he going?
> What implacable fury
> hounded him up that mountain
> as the shades of night were falling fast?
> What did it mean, Excelsior?
> Was it the emblem of a promise given?
> Some cryptic warning?
> A terrible cri de coeur?
> It did not matter.
> The very syllables drove us mad with yearning.
> We longed to climb with him,
> side by side,
> sharing his passion and his agony,
> to take from his faltering arm that banner,
> and to wrap ourselves in Excelsior.

There can be no doubt that Selzer here is having fun with the rhythms and diction of Longfellow in his own prose. Those rhythms and that diction, however, have become internalized, so that at the end of the essay when he is concluding a delicate and humorous example of mistranslating Virgil, Selzer can write "Here was no mere gesture of gratitude, / but an exchange of the heart. / Between those two smiles / (0 measure them in quanta, / in light years) / a rainbow arced; / there was sealed a covenant, / a secret troth plighted." Here is no imitation of Longfellow's irregular trimeter, but an internalization of the diction and rhythm so that it has become merged within Selzer's own style. The identical argument can be made in connection with other writers of prose and poetry, such as Virgil, Keats, Whitman, and Poe. Their distinctive words, phrases, and rhythms echo, at times consciously but more often dimly and indistinctly, in Selzer's prose.

This then is the dialogic element in Selzer's prose. Bakhtin describes the effect that this quality has on other forms and genres by claiming:

> They become more free and flexible, their language renews itself by incorporating extraliterary heteroglossia and the "novelistic" layers of literary language, they become dialogized, permeated with laughter, irony, humor, elements of self-parody and finally—this is the most important thing—the novel inserts into these other genres an indeterminacy, a certain semantic openendedness, a living contact with unfinished, still-evolving contemporary reality (the

openended present). As we will see below, all these phenomena are explained by the transposition of other genres into this new and peculiar zone for structuring artistic models (a zone of contact with the present in all its openendedness), a zone that was first appropriated by the novel. (*Dialogic*)

For Bakhtin, *novel* is a term that transcends generic boundaries to include all literary forms concerned with "becoming," that is, with language in the process of stylistically creating itself out of the array of languages around it. Dostoevsky is a novelistic writer, according to Bakhtin, but so are Rabelais, Ibsen, and Byron. Selzer, I would claim, also can be characterized as a novelistic writer whose language is dialogized in the sense that Bakhtin claims for the most innovative and exceptional works of art. For this dialogic quality contributes substantially to the richness of interpretation, the "semantic open-endedness" that characterizes Selzer's prose.

Fusion and the dialogical are leaf and stem from the same root, and in a very real sense they sum up Selzer's art. In the beginning of this essay I suggested that Selzer is Yeshi Dhonden, that he makes of science an art. Selzer's gift as a writer is precisely this ability to fuse together disparate worlds of thought and experience. In his images, his words, his language, his conception of art, Selzer welds contrastive elements into a sculpted tension. His work is mercurial, unstable, unresolvable, ambiguous, ambivalent. It is ungraspable, like the song of Keats's nightingale—or like Keats's poetry itself. It is for this reason that I think Selzer's work will endure. At its best, it reflects the themes, languages, and traditions of literature and fashions them to its own vision of the world. The genius of Richard Selzer is not that he is a surgeon who is also a writer, but that he is an artist who also happens to practice surgery. And like his narratives, that opposition too is unresolvable. (pp. 3-27)

> Charles I. Schuster, "The Nonfictional Prose of Richard Selzer: An Aesthetic Analysis," in Literary Nonfiction: Theory, Criticism, Pedagogy, *edited by Chris Anderson, Southern Illinois University Press, 1989, pp. 3-28.*

Richard Selzer with Peter Josyph (interview date Summer 1990)

[In the following excerpt, Selzer discusses the merits of the short story as a literary form.]

[*Josyph*]: *What can a short story do that a novel can't?*

[Selzer]: Well of course one of the chief goals of a short story is to tell a story quickly and economically—to have the characters about whom it is written change, in some significant way, within a few pages. There is a feeling of compression about it. What it lacks in long, luxurious recounting, it makes up for in its rather bullet-like speed. I think a surgeon is particularly suited by temperament to the short story form as opposed to the novel, because the short story is rather like a surgical operation. It has a beginning, a middle, and an end—at least *my* stories all do: you make an incision, you rummage around inside for a

little while, then you stitch it up. Writing a short story is like taking out an inflamed appendix.

In fact, surgery resembles writing short fiction in many ways for me. I write in longhand, and holding a pen, which is about the same size instrument as the scalpel, seems right for me, anatomically; the way it sits in my hand is familiar. And there is that intimacy with the instrument. Of course, when you hold the scalpel, you cannot give it its head: most of surgery is holding back, restraining. After thirty years of restraining my instrument, when I picked up the pen I said: "Go! It's not blood, it's only ink." Suddenly the surrogate was off, and I had this marvelous freedom to grab great armfuls of language and run across the page. And in writing, the sheet of paper becomes the patient, in a certain sense. In both cases, you are dealing in wounds. The act of making an incision is the creation of a wound for the purpose of healing the patient. The earliest forms of writing were exactly that: taking up a sharp rock and gouging out hieroglyphs in a flat stone— making wounds, as it were, to tell a story.

The difference, of course, is that the surgical wound must heal, eventually, but the writer's wound does not. I'm speaking now not of the wound made on the page, but the writer's *own* wound that he is attempting to heal by the act of writing the story. And yet the writer's wound *must not* heal. He attempts to bridge over that wound with language, but it must not heal because if it ever did, the result would be the kind of finality or fossilization that would ruin the writer. It would be an act of self-destruction. I think probably what happens to many writers who burn out or lose the energy or the inspiration to write is that they have healed themselves in some way through the act of writing, and there is nothing left to say.

You once said that one of the problems you have with the contemporary short story is that no blood is shed on the page.

Yes, that's true. And that is why one is often unmoved by even the most accomplished pieces of prose. Of course, blood and ink, at least in my hands, have a certain similarity. When you use a scalpel, blood is shed; when you use a pen, ink is spilled upon the page. Something is *let* in each of these acts, and that is another bond between them. I always wondered why every surgeon didn't write, why I was one of the very few. After all, a surgeon does walk around every day in the middle of a dozen short stories, and it would seem to me that it would be irresistible to write them down as I have done. But I think one of the reasons it isn't so is that the surgeon must remain anesthetized to the philosophical, the literary, even the humane implications of his work, in order to be able to carry it out dispassionately, at the proper remove from the white heat of the event.

Is there a similarity between the short story and the case history? Does the surgeon himself write the case histories of his patients?

Yes, he asks the patient a number of questions and attempts to piece together a diagnosis. Often this is not exact, and he is left with two or three possibilities, which constitute what is called a *differential diagnosis.* Although now, with the new technology, this is most often solved outside of the operating room, when *I* was practicing surgery we were often called upon to do exploratory surgery to find out what was wrong and treat it at the same time. The short story writer, too, is carrying on a diagnostic act. He creates a character, he presents this character with a predicament, with various conflicts, barriers, acts of fate, and then he waits to see how this will develop and what the diagnosis will be. This is similar to the examination of a patient.

Unlike most practitioners of the short form in fiction, you seem content to stay with it.

I think that is a personal thing. I'm a restless, rather impatient writer: I want to get things done and see what happens. On the other hand, I'm a very slow writer. Each of my short stories takes me approximately six months to write. *One* short story, *six* months. That is because I write slowly, I write a great deal for each story, and then I boil it down in my laboratory. (pp. 321-23)

In the case of your only novel, you reversed a common procedure: instead of stretching a story into a novel, you dismantled the novel and published only an excerpt, "Korea," in your first collection, **Rituals of Surgery.**

Well, I realized as soon as I finished my so-called novel, that it wasn't a novel at all; it was a series of episodes, all set in the same place and linked together by the narrator. But each event, really, was a short story that stood by itself, and I didn't think it had the sweep and the continuity of a novel. In fact, I don't believe that most so-called novels written today *are* novels. They're *called* novels, but they're really episodic constructs more akin to a series of short stories with the same locale and characters. I much prefer the short fiction of Cheever and Updike to their longer works, I think probably for that very reason. The popular novelists are not really producing novels. I'm not saying that in a negative way, but I don't see them in the same way I see *War and Peace,* or *Anna Karenina,* or *Madame Bovary,* or even *The Magic Mountain.* Many of today's novels seem to have a staccato quality: when you begin a new chapter, it's a new story. (p. 323)

You once quoted a phrase from Hamlet *to express something key to the author's purpose in writing stories.*

Yes. It's the point in the play where Hamlet has sneaked back into Denmark from England and is horrified to witness Ophelia's funeral. After they place her in her grave, Laertes leaps in to embrace his sister for the last time, and he begins an oration on his sorrow. Hamlet, offended by this, says, "Who the hell is *he* to use this kind of high-blown language about *my* tragedy?" Or, as Shakespeare puts it, "What is he whose grief / Bears such an emphasis, whose phrase of sorrow / Conjures the wand'ring stars and makes them stand / Like wonder-wounded hearers?" Well, that is *exactly* what the writer tries to do, to make of his readers *wonder-wounded hearers.* To do this, the writer will use every stunt he can find in the whole abominable gymnastic of writing. I am constantly aware of that and try never to write a sentence that will not increase by a little bit the temperature of the piece, so that it becomes warmer with each line.

Are there any contemporary short story writers who wound you with wonder the way some of the nineteenth-century writers can?

Of course I am a nineteenth-century writer who somehow got born a hundred years too late. But I can name several: Kay Boyle, Elizabeth Bowen, and V.S. Pritchett. Those three are, I would say, my favorite short story writers: they succeed more than anybody. There is an Irish short story writer named Mary Levin whom I like very much. Also, William Pritchard. You can see that my choices, with the exception of Kay Boyle, are from Great Britain. I don't know why. I do like many of the short stories of Kipling. He's a great short story writer, much underrated. I like the stories of Maupassant, another underrated writer these days. D. H. Lawrence wrote about a dozen of the greatest short stories ever written. And I think that Thomas Mann's best works by far were his short fiction. *Death in Venice,* "Felix Krull," "Mario the Magician" were the best things he did.

I have a sense that many a contemporary writer feels this pressure that they are not legitimately writers unless they write a novel.

Yes, there is that prejudice abroad in the land.

Editors and agents contribute to that, don't they?

They do, they do. I've never had a publisher who didn't urge me to write a novel. They all want THE NOVEL. The short stories, they say, are all right, but you can never finally achieve the kind of wide recognition with short stories that you can with a novel. What these people are overlooking is that true novelists are very rare. Very good short story writers will try to fit themselves into the mold of novelists, and very often they will fail. I know my own genre, and that is the short story.

But your first book has three times as many stories as your latest, and the average length has increased from ten pages to forty.

Do you mean that if I live to be 300, I'll write a novel? No. I'm stretching out. I'm looking at more facets of the characters and events, whereas my earlier stories perhaps had fewer dimensions and could be told more quickly.

You began by writing stories of horror and suspense. What does that enable one to learn as a beginning writer?

Surgeons—as you know—we love horror! But when I first began to write, at the age of forty, I realized I had to teach myself this craft, and I chose the horror genre because it seemed to be the simplest. No philosophical implications, no complex characterizations, very little irony. All you had to do was evoke a shudder or two in your reader. So I did write horror stories, and they began to be published—in *Ellery Queen's Mystery Magazine.* I would urge any new writer to send his or her best work to that wonderful magazine. After a few years of that, I had, I thought, achieved a certain level of facility, so that I could reach out and go beyond the horror genre, although *Imagine a Woman and Other Tales* has been referred to by a number of reviewers as a book of horror stories, which *horrifies* me. The themes are dark, but how they can call them horror stories is a mystery to me.

The thing I liked best about both surgery and writing, in the beginning, was the craft. That's what drew me to surgery: I loved learning how to cut and stitch and clamp. The technical side of it thrilled me. Similarly, when I first began to learn to write, it was the suturing together of words into sentences, the selection of these words, the scattering of them on the page, that delighted me. The language was and still is *the* most important part of my writing. After the work had become incorporated into my body, I could go beyond this intense focus on the language, to approach the content, the ideas, the abstractions.

In time, as you began to draw more closely on your experience as a surgeon, did you begin to explore your own wounds?

Yes, every writer does that, don't you think? When you write a story you are, in a way, telling your own. Timidity is the greatest sin. A writer must tell his or her own worst secrets. But there is a difference between an autobiographical work and one which transforms your life into universal terms. A writer's first work is often a matter of getting something off his or her chest. It's the rite of passage that gives one the proper distance, puts one beyond a certain self-indulgence, so that one can write about the world, extracting from it the syrup of transcendence. Nevertheless, as you suggested, it is true that the line between my fiction and my non-fiction is rather blurry, just as the line is blurry between prose and poetry in my works.

You have told beginning writers of short stories to go to the poets for their models and inspiration: Poe, Scott, Dickinson, Moore—

And add to that Francis Ponge, who wrote these beautiful, tiny pieces—prose poems, I guess you'd call them.

It's interesting that you don't say Hemingway, Steinbeck, Carver—

No, I'm not in the minimalist style—

You're a maximalist?

Yes, I'm a nineteenth-century voluptuary. I use as much of the language as I can, instead of as little. I want to enjoy every bit of it.

But why the poets?

Because of their use of simile and metaphor. Metaphor is the secret language of the writer, the gateway to the reader's imagination. Also, poets are very aware of the rhythm and the sound of their lines, and for me, too, that's important in a story. I count a whole lot on the beauty of the language. Marianne Moore, with that marvelous awe she had for Nature, wrote: "What sap went through that tiny thread / To make the cherry red?" That's honesty, that's sincerity before the great extravaganza of life. You can't beat that, and in fact it's what I tried to do in writing about medicine, to retain that sense of awe she evoked in writing that line.

I recently read an editor's advice to the aspiring short story writer: "Don't try to be Thomas Hardy." By which he prob-

ably meant, try to be Raymond Carver. *Then you will read other editors who say: "No minimalism, please." By which they mean do* not *try to be Raymond Carver. But whether it's Carver, Hardy, Hawthorne, Hemingway, Poe, Selzer— isn't it that sense of wonder that we experience when the work is at its best?*

Oh, without it you can't achieve anything.

Look at Carver's "Cathedral": there's nothing minimal about that, certainly not in terms of its effect.

Marvelous. I am very fond of Raymond Carver's work. That I do not write in that way does not mean that I don't admire him tremendously. He was a master. But it's a matter of style, and a writer does not form or create a style. He discovers it. It is already there in his body, like a fingerprint, and he has to find it. I believe the writer who has a great deal of discomfort writing has not yet discovered his style and is trying to be something he is not.

What have you learned from reading your critics?

I have learned nothing that has helped me. I have only learned by doing the writing itself, and by reading. The commentary of the literary critics does not seem to hit the mark, whether it's favorable or unfavorable. I feel that it is written about someone else. I can't relate to it. (pp. 324-26)

In the series of our recent conversations that we have turned into a book, you recounted to me some of the same events that you have written stories about. What is the difference for you between the oral and the written form?

That's interesting. I do see myself in the continuum of writers who were originally troubadours, who sang or spoke their stories. There was an *aural* and an *oral* component to storytelling, as there is to this day in numerous other cultures, in some of the Arab nations, for example, where there is this marvelous tradition of the men—it is usually the men—standing up before the group and telling a story, displaying a great improvisational skill, which we who write everything down seem to have lost. That's one reason why I like to read my stories in public. It's wonderful to be read to: it returns one to the state of childhood. Also, lending my voice to the written works gives them a dimension they wouldn't otherwise have. I like to *italicize* with my voice; one can *say* an exclamation point if one knows how. I like to get out and confront my readers and make new ones.

There will be fewer readers in the world, perhaps, because of television and the computer, but there will always be that cadre of people who take sensual pleasure in picking up a book and opening it to page one and losing themselves in the magical act of reading a story. It is for these people that one writes. Not for fame, not for money. One writes stories to reach out and approach another human being. The other half must come from the reader, of course, or the short story doesn't exist. And I am very careful of my readers. When I'm writing a story, some part of my mind is always aware that someone is out there.

And you never want to cheat them, do you?

Never. No cheap shots, no short cuts, no tricks. I want them to *get* it, desperately.

And you make a tacit agreement with your readers which I think relates to your having gazed at the very limits of life as a surgeon: "I will show you something I know about, but you must be willing to follow me all the way." Most of your stories cannot be approached lightly. They aren't written that way.

No, they aren't. They're written in blood. (p. 327)

> *Richard Selzer and Peter Josyph, in an interview in* Studies in Short Fiction, *Vol. 27, No. 3, Summer, 1990, pp. 321-28.*

Merrill Joan Gerber   (essay date 18 November 1990)

[*Gerber is an American novelist, short story writer, and educator. In the following excerpt, she presents a highly critical assessment of* Imagine a Woman, and Other Tales.]

[In *Imagine a Woman*] Dr. Selzer abandons the measured tone of his scientific observations and speaks with a wilder voice—deeply emotional, frankly melodramatic and notably unmodern. In six long stories, most of them told in a self-consciously old-fashioned narrative style, the human psyche is pressed to the farthest reaches of its tolerance and beyond. His heroes and heroines fight for their lives in a nether world of bogs and bat caves and garbage dumps, doing battle with evil forces in the guise of psychoses, incurable diseases, poverty, radioactive debris and overwhelming grief. Medicine is not an answer to their despair, and sometimes it is the cause of it. (p. 32)

Dr. Selzer's images are heavy with meaning: an autistic boy lives in a bat cave and hides from the world (**"Pipistrel"**); a poor boy with tuberculosis lives in a garbage dump in Brazil and finds a piece of radioactive trash that he thinks is a blessed star until his fingers are burned off by it (**"Luis"**). In every story, the reader is denied the triumph of discovery because clues that might have been deftly placed are announced with fanfare.

Time passes erratically in these stories. Once the author has established some basic facts, usually grisly ones, he leaps to the next dramatic moment. No story has a conclusion that features a gently extracted resolution; rather, there are long chains of mini-climaxes, multi-epiphanies and unabashedly obvious revelations.

Dr. Selzer is a master of description, and he has the power to evoke primal feelings and fears. His compassion is enormous. But somehow, as he steps from the restrained reporting of a man of science into the freedom of fiction, he seems to lose sight of what makes a story come to life—the reader's delicate engagement in a partnership in which emotion is invited, not demanded. (p. 34)

> *Merrill Joan Gerber, "Fighting for Their Lives," in the* New York Times Book Review, *November 18, 1990, pp. 32, 34.*

Evelyn Toynton   (essay date 9 December 1990)

[*In the following review, Toynton provides a mixed assessment of* Imagine a Woman, and Other Tales.]

Since surgeons have a reputation for being the pure technicians of medicine—uninterested in their patients' human problems, much less the state of their souls—the writer-surgeon Richard Selzer's preoccupation with the mysteries of the spirit seems particularly beguiling, a sort of triumph for the Other Side. As with his first short story collection, ***Rituals of Surgery,*** illness plays a large part in the stories in his latest book [***Imagine a Woman, and Other Tales***], but their primary focus is on the spiritual journeys taken by the afflicted, or by those who love them.

In **"Whither Thou Goest,"** a widow becomes obsessed with the desire to hear the beating of her late husband's transplanted heart. In **"Pipistrel,"** a woman whose fiercely loved autistic son has escaped the persecutions of their neighbors by going to live in a cave, struggles to protect him from the search party pursuing him. In the title story, a woman dying of AIDS she contracted from her bisexual husband flees to a small French town and is tended lovingly by the local peasants. With the help of their ancient gods, they orchestrate her death as though it were a joyful ballet:

" 'Yes,' [Triton] said. 'You are ready. We will go now. Look! Here are the fish to welcome you, and the birds to see you off.' The last sound I heard was the soft applause of their wings. The next moment my head filled with green. A rush, a rapture, a delirium of green."

In each of these stories, we feel that Selzer's heart is indubitably in the right place: his affirmation of the mysteries of human experience, of the enduring and strange forms love can take, of the power of the spirit, is wholly admirable, the sort of humanistic perspective that is lacking in too much modern fiction. Above all, he seems to be saying, love matters, joy will triumph, the realm of the spirit is all around us.

So one would like to be able to report that these are fully satisfying stories, as uniformly excellent as their author's intentions. Unfortunately, that is only intermittently the case.

Perhaps the most powerful story in the book is **"Pipistrel,"** in which the mixture of pain, terror and exultation felt by the mother of the autistic child is evoked so vividly that the reader's empathy is fully engaged. All the bizarre and frightening things that take place towards the end of the story are rendered believable by the sheer urgency of emotion in the prose, as well as by what has gone before, and the transcendence of the ending seems thoroughly earned. It is an impressive accomplishment.

In some of the other stories, though, the mystery seems forced, and the level of intensity is not high enough to carry the conceit. For example, there is something faintly ludicrous about the tale of the woman and the heart—and Selzer's tone here is rather flat-footed, so that the reader is never seduced into suspending disbelief. Nor is it clear why the American protagonist of **"Lindow Man,"** after nursing his wife through a debilitating illness and then becoming a total recluse, should suddenly become obsessed with an English bog and a corpse that was discovered there. The solemn, quasi-mystical descriptions of his journey to the bog and his explorations in it are finally just irritating. It's as if we're supposed to accept that something terribly meaningful is going on without being so crass as to ask precisely what it is.

In the title story, too, the overlay of mysticism sometimes seems like an excuse for abandoning simple logic and realistic perception. The dying woman, writing to her husband, mentions that it has been a year since she left, while also referring to the fact that she is pregnant with his child. The peasants are all possessed of wordless wisdom. And the narrator's tone of serene aloofness seems unearned, the product not of painful struggle and eventual triumph but of effortless acceptance, just as the painless prettiness of first her baby's death and then her own seems too easy to be real.

Perhaps what is missing is a sense of these characters' mere humanity, as opposed to their spiritual essences. Too few of them emerge as distinct individuals rooted in ordinary existence. They seem to have been created in order to illustrate a lofty point, and thus they never seem wholly real. One gets no sense of their individual loneliness, their messy sadness and resentment, only of their transcendence of such things.

Maybe Selzer, who is retired from surgery now, wanted to forget the ugly woes of the body and concentrate wholly on spirit instead. But as all the great romantics knew, the soul and the body cannot that easily be separated out. If he had grounded his characters more in their bodies, in their human particularities and emotions, he might have managed to make us care more about their spirits, too.

Evelyn Toynton, "The Afflictions of Body and Spirit," in Book World—The Washington Post, *December 9, 1990, p. 7.*

FURTHER READING

Bibliography

Stripling, Mahala Yates. "Richard Selzer: A Checklist." *Bulletin of Bibliography* 47, No. 1 (March 1990): 3-8.
    Brief biographical sketch accompanying a bibliography of works by and about Selzer from 1971 through 1988.

Criticism

Anderson, Charles M. *Richard Selzer and the Rhetoric of Surgery.* Carbondale: Southern Illinois University Press, 1989, 160 p.
    Analysis of Selzer's work with particular emphasis on the short story "Jonah and the Whale" and the first three essays from *Mortal Lessons: Notes on the Art of Surgery.* Anderson interprets Selzer's writing as a response to the inherent tension in the modern physician-patient relationship and considers an appreciation of Selzer's use of metaphors key to understanding his work.

Beppu, Keiko, and M. Teresa Tavormina. "The Healer's Art: An Interview with Richard Selzer." *The Centennial Review* XXV, No. 1 (Winter 1981): 20-40.
    Interview in which Selzer discusses his career as a surgeon, his writing style, and the symbiotic relationship between his two vocations.

Carson, Ronald A. "Selzer's Surgeon as Seer." *Perspectives in Biology and Medicine* 24, No. 2 (Winter 1981): 284-89.
    States that Selzer gives surgeons priestly and poetic qualities in his essays and fiction.

Elbow, Peter. "The Pleasures of Voice in the Literary Essay: Explorations in the Prose of Gretel Ehrlich and Richard Selzer." In *Literary Nonfiction: Theory, Criticism, Pedagogy,* edited by Chris Anderson, pp. 211-34. Carbondale: Southern Illinois University Press, 1989.
    Illustrates three distinct types of voice in nonfiction prose, using Selzer's writing as an example.

Josyph, Peter. "Richard Selzer and the Whale: A Physician Heals Himself." *Salmagundi,* No. 87 (Summer 1990): 322-31.
    Interview in which Selzer describes how and why he became a writer and his decision's effect upon his private and professional life.

Peschel, Enid Rhodes. " 'A Terrible Beauty Is Born': Richard Selzer's 'Korea'." In *Le Mythe d'Etiemble: Hommages, etudes et recherches; Inedits,* edited by Angelique Levi, pp. 209-17. Paris: Didier Erudition, 1979.
    Analysis of Selzer's short story "Korea." Peschel contends that " 'Korea' may be read as the symbolical story of the birth of an artist."

————. "Eroticism, Mysticism, and Surgery in the Writings of Richard Selzer." *Denver Quarterly* 16, No. 1 (Spring 1981): 87-98.
    Thematic exploration of the search for love and transcendence in *Rituals of Surgery* and *Mortal Lessons.* Peschel concludes: "Invariably in Selzer's writings, love is set against a background of anguish: tensions, loneliness, disease, and death. But when love does appear, it emerges as an illumination that provides an instant, and often it is no more than that, of vision and transcendence."

Schuster, Charles I. "The Last Grand Rounds of Richard Selzer." *Pennsylvania Medicine* 88, No. 9 (September 1985): 42-48, 50.
    A first-hand account of the final Grand Rounds of Selzer's surgical career, including Selzer's views on writing, the relationship between art and science and his retirement from surgery.

Selzer, Richard. "The Pen and the Scalpel." *The New York Times Magazine* (21 August 1988): 30-31.
    Reflects on his decision to retire from surgery and become a full-time writer.

Tavormina, M. Teresa. "Richard Selzer: The Rounds of Revelation." *Literature and Medicine* 1 (1982): 61-72.
    Surveys Selzer's life and career as a surgeon and a writer, paying close attention to the interrelatedness of his two vocations and his thoughts on death and healing—both physical and spiritual—as expressed in his writing.

> Additional coverage of Selzer's life and career is contained in the following source published by Gale Research: *Contemporary Authors New Revision Series,* Vol. 14.

Ntozake Shange

1948-

(Born Paulette Williams) American dramatist, novelist, poet, and essayist.

The following entry provides an overview of Shange's career through 1992.

INTRODUCTION

Best known for her self-described "choreopoem" *for colored girls who have considered suicide / when the rainbow is enuf,* Shange has won praise for combining poetry, prose, music, and dance in the stage production of this work. In her dramas, novels, and poetry—which are often an amalgamation of different literary genres and media—Shange draws upon her experiences as an African-American woman to innovatively and passionately address racial, political, and feminist issues. She is particularly noted for her portrayal of black women and her criticism of the discrimination against them in American society. Shange explained: "I feel that as an artist my job is to appreciate the differences among my women characters. . . . Our personalities and distinctions are lost. What I appreciate about the women whom I write about, the women whom I know, is how idiosyncratic they are. I take delight in the very peculiar or particular things that fascinate or terrify them."

Shange was born Paulette Williams, the oldest child of a professional middle-class family. Her parents, a surgeon and a psychiatric social worker, encouraged their children's interest in music, literature, and art, and Dizzy Gillespie, Miles Davis, Chuck Berry, and W. E. B. Du Bois were among the frequent guests at their home. Shange began attending Barnard College at the age of eighteen. During the following year, angry and despondent after separating from her husband, she attempted suicide several times before focusing her rage against society and its treatment of black women. While earning a master's degree in American Studies from the University of Southern California, she took her African name: Ntozake, which means "she who comes with her own things," and Shange, which means "she who walks like a lion." Since then she has gained distinction as an educator, a performer/director, and a writer whose works draw heavily on the frustrations of being a black female in America.

Shange's first drama, *for colored girls who have considered suicide / when the rainbow is enuf,* explores the sufferings and joys of seven African-American women through a combination of poetry, prose, music, and dance. Plays combining poetry and dance had already been staged by Adrienne Kennedy, but, according to Mel Gussow, "Shange was a pioneer in terms of her subject matter: the fury of black women at their double subjugation in white

male America." Yet Shange was faulted for her unsympathetic treatment of African-American men, who are depicted as obstacles to the social and spiritual freedom of black women. Most critics, however, viewed the play as an affirmation of the human will to survive. Toni Cade Bambara maintained that Shange "celebrates the capacity to master pain and betrayals with wit, sister-sharing, reckless daring, and flight and forgetfulness if necessary. She celebrates most of all women's loyalties to women."

Shange has written numerous other plays, including *Spell #7* and her adaptation of a Bertolt Brecht drama, *Mother Courage & Her Children.* A series of poetic vignettes blended with song and dance, *Spell #7* is structurally and thematically similar to *for colored girls,* but it relies more on such conventional elements as dialogue and plot development. Shange changed the setting of Brecht's play from seventeenth-century Europe to the post-Civil War United States and portrayed Mother Courage as a black woman selling her wares during the battles between United States Cavalry units and Native Americans. In a common reaction to the drama, Frank Rich commented: "To fulfill her mission of resetting *Mother Courage* in black America, [Shange] seems to have seized on some events that superficially correspond to those of Brecht's play without carefully considering how those events would square with the true meaning of the original text."

In the early 1980s, Shange began to concentrate on writing novels and poetry. Her collections of poetry, like her theater pieces, are noted for their innovative language, including the use of nonstandard spellings and punctuation. Some reviewers have argued that these innovations present unnecessary obstacles to readers of such works as *Nappy Edges, A Daughter's Geography,* and *From Okra to Greens: Poems.* Explaining her lower-case letters, slashes, and spelling, Shange has said that "poems where all the first letters are capitalized" bore her. "I like the idea that letters dance," she added. "I need some visual stimulation, so that reading becomes not just a passive act and more than an intellectual activity, but demands rigorous participation." Her idiosyncratic punctuation in her view assures "that the reader is not in control of the process"; she wants her printed words to engage the reader in a kind of struggle and not be "whatever you can just ignore." The spellings, she said, "reflect language as I hear it. . . . The structure is connected to the music I hear beneath the words."

Her first novel, *Sassafrass, Cypress & Indigo*—an expansion of her novella *Sassafrass*—combines prose, poetry, recipes, magic spells, and letters to tell of three sisters and their relationships. Sassafrass is a weaver who cannot leave Mitch, a musician who abuses drugs and beats her. Cypress, a dancer in feminist productions, struggles against becoming romantically involved. Indigo, the youngest sister, retreats into her imagination, befriending her childhood dolls, seeing only the poetry and magic of the world. The music she plays on her violin becomes a rejuvenating source for her mother and sisters. "Probably there is a little bit of all three sisters in Shange," Connie Lauerman has suggested, "though she says that her novel is not autobiographical but historical, culled from the experiences of blacks and from the 'information of my feelings'." Shange's second novel, *Betsey Brown,* is a semiautobiographical work set in St. Louis during the late 1950s, when that city began to integrate its schools. Betsey is a thirteen-year-old black girl who enjoys a comfortable home life. When she is bused to an integrated school across town, she becomes increasingly aware of differences between blacks and whites. Shange is especially concerned with Betsey's reconciliation of her cultural heritage and her new environment. Many praised *Betsey Brown* for its depiction of the black middle class, and Claudia Tate also noted several changes in Shange's writing. "Most of Shange's characteristic elliptical spelling, innovative syntax and punctuation is absent from *Betsey Brown,*" wrote Tate. "Missing also is the caustic social victimization. . . . *Betsey Brown* seems also to mark Shange's movement from explicit to subtle expressions of rage, from repudiating her girlhood past to embracing it, and from flip candor to more serious commentary."

Critics have detected a change in Shange's attitudes over the years, but she herself has asserted that she is as angry as ever but not as powerless, "because I know where to put my anger, and I don't feel alone in it anymore." Deborah

R. Geis commented: "Shange has created a poetic voice that is uniquely her own—a voice which is deeply rooted in her experience of being female and black, but also one which, again, refuses and transcends categorization. Her works articulate the connection between the doubly 'marginalized' social position of the black woman and the need to invent and appropriate a language with which to articulate a self."

PRINCIPAL WORKS

for colored girls who have considered suicide/when the rainbow is enuf: A Choreopoem (drama) 1975
Sassafrass: A Novella (novella) 1976
A Photograph: A Still Life with Shadows/A Photograph: A Study of Cruelty (drama) 1977; revised as *A Photograph: Lovers-In-Motion,* 1979
Natural Disasters and Other Festive Occasions (poetry and prose) 1977
Where the Mississippi Meets the Amazon [with Thulani Nkabinda and Jessica Hagedorn] (drama) 1977
From Okra to Greens: A Different Kinda Love Story (drama) 1978
Nappy Edges (poetry) 1978
Black & White Two-Dimensional Planes (drama) 1979
Boogie Woogie Landscapes (drama) 1979
Spell #7 (drama) 1979
Mother Courage & Her Children [adaptor; from the drama *Mother Courage and Her Children* by Bertolt Brecht] (drama) 1980
Some Men (poetry) 1981
Three Pieces (dramas) 1981
Sassafrass, Cypress & Indigo (novel) 1982
A Daughter's Geography (poetry) 1983
From Okra to Greens: Poems (poetry) 1984
See No Evil: Prefaces, Essays & Accounts (essays) 1984
Betsey Brown: A Novel (novel) 1985
Ridin' the Moon in Texas: Word Paintings (poetry) 1987
Three Views of Mt. Fuji (drama) 1987

CRITICISM

Erskine Peters   (essay date Spring 1978)

[*In the following essay, Peters objects to the portrayal of African-American men in* for colored girls who have considered suicide/when the rainbow is enuf.]

While it is not altogether inexplicable it is quite unfortunate that Ntozake Shange's Broadway chorepoem, *For Colored Girls Who Have Considered Suicide/When the Rainbow is Enuf,* has been so enthusiastically and uncircumspectly received in the general White and Black press—

es. This theatrical event forbodes more crucial damning, and subtle implications for our Black children and youth than it has virtues or redeeming value for the adults who sit through it and about whom the work is ostensibly concerned. After examining more than a score of reviews, I have found heaps upon heaps of praises, most of which to me are actually dubious, quite ironic, and very often, outright ridiculous.

The ultimate portrayal of Black existence in Shange's work which depicts episodes and fantasies in the lives of adolescent Black girls who supposedly become women, differs very little from what any unaware intruding anthropologist or social worker of the 1950's would have offered in her quarterly report on life in the ghettos: 'the poor black woman, doing all that she can, suffers so much and most of all she has to contend with her inherently no-good nigger men.' Although the drama has many technical merits, many superb phrasings, and some talented depictions of types of characters, especially in the first half of the production, the discriminating viewer is soon overcome with a sense of disappointment and betrayal. He is particularly disappointed that the writer does not use her apparent skill to move beyond the superficial aspects of the Black male characters whom he thought or hoped were initially being satirized, and not simply *dished*. He feels betrayed after the giving of his laughter to the first half of the show because he was believing that the 'colored girls' could deliver a Black perspective. He was not necessarily expecting the play to deal with anything other than the lives of the 'colored girls,' but he was expecting that their lives would have been delivered with a consciousness of all the major factors that shape and have shaped Black existence in this hemisphere.

It is not at all my intention to give the impression that Black men and women don't have particular issues that need to be taken account of. Anyone Black could learn that simply from growing up in this society with a mother and father, or perhaps even more poignantly without the latter. But what is the purpose of the artist if not to pierce the heart of truth, to plunge beneath the surfaces, to illuminate so that those of us with more ordinary eyes may become more ably informed. In order for particular truths to point toward the greater Truth, or collective Truth, these particulars must be inclusive; otherwise truth is distorted. Neither is it at all my intention to say that negative images are not a concrete part of our reality; however, negative images as fundamental components of our existence don't necessarily produce negative resolutions, especially not in the hands of the artist, who is the healer, the renewer of life.

The Ba Tswana novelist Bessie Head understands this need when she shapes her short story "The Collector of Treasures" and relates the circumstances of a mother of three children who kills her irresponsible husband by cutting off his penis. While the story may not be the most superbly crafted, it does provide a historical context for the development or emergency of a particular type of male who takes no responsibility for his children and little for himself. In addition, to avoid the highly misleading oversimplification that Botswana society is bereft of account-

able males, the writer balances her depiction by providing us with a father image from the other end of the spectrum. All of which Ntozake Shange's play lacks, except for a rather romantic allusion to Toussaint L'Ouverture.

If Shange's play has thematic virtue and historic significance, as has been almost universally proclaimed, it would only be in relation to what Jessica Harris (even though she found no seriously compromising flaws), states about the pre-Broadway opening at the Henry Street Playhouse:

> When the curtain came down, Black women in the audience wept openly, for onstage they had finally seen an image of themselves that showed not just the strength or the anger but also some of the vulnerability and pain. [*Essence*, November 1976]

> The women were excited because for once they saw a picture of themselves they could recognize. It was a picture representing them not as whores or as matriarchs, not as superwomen or mighty mommas, but simply as women who want to be loved, who try to be kind and who might get tired and evil sometimes, but women who above all were real people with the full spectrum of emotions and reactions that real people have. This was a new presentation and as such met with enormous success.

In rightly trying to reveal other dimensions of Black womanhood besides the strong, hard, enduring, and surviving ones, Shange conversely portrays contemporary Black men basically as pasteboards or beasts. One wonders to whom it is she is appealing in her vulnerability and pain, since such conclusively negative images would have a very limited appeal to Black men. Is it possibly an obscured and latent appeal to the Great White Father? Perhaps it is this that prompts *New York Times* critic Clive Barnes to write as his concluding accolade for the work: "It could easily have made me feel guilty as being white and male. It didn't. It made me feel proud at being a member of the human race, and the joyous discovery that a white man can have black sisters." But herein lies so much of the danger for the future of Black children in White America: if the phenomenon of the profound frustration of 'colored girls' does not make an influential member of the oppressor group feel guilty, it should at least make him uncomfortable. As an oppressed people whose power is yet too unorganized, we cannot afford not to acknowledge that the social bureaucracy under which we live is abnormal and pervasively threatening. In fact, as one reviewer, Curtis Rogers of the *New York Amsterdam News* put it:

> . . .in her unrelenting stereotyping of Black men as always 'shucking' and 'jiving' . . . she, without realizing it, just as insistently caricatures Black women as being easily duped, and as emotionally frivolous. This is so because Ms. Shange's *Colored Girls* invariably take up with those Black men whom she damns as mean and trifling.

Any other major historic significance of this work which Mel Gussow of the NY *Times* described as "a play that should be seen, savored and treasured" is that it is quite reminiscent of the dubious and even treacherous meaning of D.W. Griffith's *Birth of a Nation* to film history. Black Americans have no particular plight if we ignore the facts that not only do Black people have to contend with elements of human nature as any other people, but that to a greater degree than White Americans, Blacks and other non-Whites have to content (consciously or unconsciously) with a culture dominated by White males who for some reason find one of their greatest threats in other males who cannot perpetuate their physical image. It seems that we would all know by now at least something about all of the blatant and subtle doings projected at the psyches of Blacks and Whites alike through and since the time of Black enslavement to thwart and dismantle all Black strength. To ignore these looming influences in any presentation is again fundamentally a damnation of our children.

It is apparent that some of the fundamental problems with Shange's play originate in the mere fact of the author's own youth (which might, though, have easily become an asset in this historical time, one would think). It does not take one very long to realize that the play is an attempt to deal not simply with problems of Black women, but also with some very serious crises that relate mostly to Ms. Shange's individual self. Kevin Sanders, who acknowledges that perhaps he as "a white man has no ground to judge a play by and about black women" nevertheless felt compelled to make the following insightful comment:

> When I first saw *Colored Girls Who Have Considered Suicide*, when it first ran at Joe Papp's theatre downtown, I thought it was disturbing in a way that was not intended; it seemed too much like a long and shrill harangue. . . . Too much of it is in the same key—over-wrought and overacted. There are not enough variations of tone and style, and it's concerned very much with the narrow and subjective spectrum of human experience.

One certainly found that throughout the performance the individual mental state of the author seemed to rumble and peep from beneath the surface as the truly crucial issue being dealt with. It is not at all unusual for first works to be of this nature. And we cannot ignore the dynamics of the individual self. But it is important to the profundity and precociousness of first works in which the individual artist casts herself or himself as the exemplar of a collective sensibility that he or she should have a clear idea of the extent to which it is himself or herself and not the collective that is being treated. Hence, the artist will not be as inclined as Ms. Shange, and others such as the early and sometimes later William Faulkner, for example, to project too much of his or her personal mental confusion upon their already oppressed subjects.

From Ms. Shange's obvious misapprehension of her own maturity derives the terribly warped perspective which controls the play. Most unfortunately, one of the moments at which this perspective speaks loudest is the highest point at which the thematic tension and technical elements converge, the climax. One of the seven heroines, Crystal, who has borne children by the callous Beau Willie Brown, now the epitome of contemporary Black manhood, stares as Beau Willie smashes their children to

death. In these moments the author does nothing less than carry out an insensitive and cruel act of exploitation upon her subjects and her audience. She does indeed do what Clive Barnes says in an intended tribute: "make the theater such an incredible marketplace for the soul." Beau Willie Brown, the epitome of the contemporary Black man, becomes in the eyes of the reviewers "the crazed lover" who "invades" Crystal's life.

Writes the reviewer in *Time Magazine:* "If they can see themselves through Shange's eyes, black men are going to wince. They are portrayed as brutal con men and amorous double-dealers." And wince we do in shocking and utter amazement at the play's shortsightedness. For this climax is the author's blatantly melodramatic attempt to turn the work into tragedy without fulfilling her obligations to explore or implicate the historical and deeper tragic circumstances. There is a very heated attempt to rush the play toward an evocation of pity, horror, and suffering. The application of such a cheap device at this critical thematic and structural point is an inhumane gesture to the Black community. As Barbara Mahone has said with explicit reference to this Ms. Shange:

> There [are] . . . talented artists around who are blinding us with their gifts for re-creation of some current truths, but in whose work the net social effect is negative. Often we don't realize immediately what's going down. But ultimately we are left with a bitter, paralyzing taste in our mouth—because the artists failed to transform our pains into good progressive energy. [*First World,* May/June 1977]

We might say of Melvin Gottlieb's assertion that "the essence of the show remains its pure and perfectly captured blackness," that he is simply uninformed, is speaking facetiously, or is being all and out ridiculous. But what does one think when he encounters in Black reviewers a peculiarly apologetic, defensive, and sometimes desperate promotion of the play without their speaking directly to its flaws. Roseann Pope Bell writes rather defensively in the *Black Collegian* [May/June 1977]: "The choreopoem cannot and is not [sic] a statement of Black-on-Black oppression, because nothing ever happens to Black women that doesn't happen to Black men, except that Black women have Black children even when the fathers are not Black." Whatever it is that is discomfiting about the play to Ms. Bell, she does not admit; however, she is so defensive throughout her essay that she soon feels the need to rewrite the play, or at least supply parts of the missing perspective. No such comprehending or sympathetic portrait of Black men ever emerges from *For Colored Girls* to even approximate what Ms. Bell states:

> . . .the failure of this great money-mongering society is photographed in the hallow-eyed stares of Black men who cannot share in even a modicum of the pride that would rage forth if they could adequately share in providing for their loved ones.

More appallingly, beneath the parenthetical apologies for their unarticulated apprehensions, several Black reviewers seem to conclude, "So what, the image of Black men is destructive? We're on Broadway!" Jessica Harris writes, "It is the first time that a Black woman playwright has dealt with young Black women and with their role in contemporary society in such a way that it was a commercially viable production (the idea of Broadway theatre is afterall to make a profit)." William Austin writes with concession that "Our emergence on the great white way should not be allowed to smother our sense of ourselves, our realities, our aspirations or our creativity. . . . Black Broadway is too good to let slip away" [*New York Amsterdam News,* October 9, 1976]. Even after admitting that in addition to the play's good qualities, it also aroused his anger, Curtis Rogers would also opt for Broadway:

> The point is that *Colored Girls* expresses a narrow and single dimensional view of both Black men and women. In this sense, it does not reflect truth. But, the ability to entertain, not the ability to state sociological truths is the measure and essence of good theater. *Colored Girls* is excellent theater.

Trazana Beverley, the actress who dramatizes Crystal's "victimization" by the beastly Beau Willie Brown, and Ntozake Shange, herself, have attempted to rationalize the play's flaws. Says Beverley "particularly in regard to the correct political interpretation one should make of *For Colored Girls*":

> We cite certain painful realities, and it draws us together as Black women in a common bond, but I don't want it to be thought that we are shutting the doors on any future relationships with black men. Some brothers fail to realize this." [*The Village Voice,* October 4, 1976]

And Ms. Shange has been quoted as saying:

> What I am trying to say is that I am right here directly speaking with God and the rivers. . . . Now if you can't understand what we're doing there's something wrong with you. [*The New York Times,* June 16, 1976]

As two highly sensitive Black women writers, June Jordan and Audre Lorde, have constantly demonstrated through their voluminous writings, the voice of Black feminism demands extraordinary insight and gifted powers of discrimination. Beyond their personal pain, women also have to see themselves in relation to the pain of the men. The purpose of feminism in any kind of revolutionary sense is for woman to put herself more profoundly in touch with others. Bessie Head ends "The Collector of Treasures" not with women encircling themselves, and not simply with women knowing the plight of a particular woman, but with men and women united against the extremes of irresponsibility. We would do well to remember what June Jordan has already stressed:

> . . . you cannot aid half a people; you have to seek to assist the men as well as the women of any oppressed group. (If my father dies without living, if my son shall by castaway, if my men believe that they must be violent or perish, then what may I know of fulfillment; who shall I be to claim happiness?) [*Ms. Magazine,* February 1977]

(pp. 79-84)

Erskine Peters, "Some Tragic Propensities of Ourselves: The Occasion of Ntozake Shange's 'For Colored Girls Who Have Considered Suicide/When the Rainbow is Enuf'," in The Journal of Ethnic Studies, *Vol. 6, No. 1, Spring, 1978, pp. 79-85.*

Andrea Benton Rushing   (essay date Autumn 1981)

[*In the following essay, Rushing argues that the portrayal of African-American women in* for colored girls *is primarily inspired by Shange's own experiences and does not reflect the lives of most black women.*]

None of the dramas Ntozake Shange wrote after *For Colored Girls* achieved the critical acclaim and popular success of her first choreopoem. *Boogie Woogie Landscape, Photograph: Still Life, Photograph: Cruelty* attracted scant attention. *Spell #7* has been praised by the *New York Times* and *New Yorker* reviewers, but black people have described it to me as unclear and muddled, and it has generated no special excitement, interest, or rancor. The cool reaction to Shange's later works leads me to reexamine *For Colored Girls.*

Ntozake Shange's enormously successful choreopoem, which opened in an East Village coffee house, moved first to the Henry Street Theater, then to the Public Theater, and then to Broadway, then to touring the country. This article is not a review of it (the play is already a popular and critical success), but an analysis of its significance which grows out of my long-standing interest in black women in black literature. What is there about this young and formerly unknown playwright's presentation of black women which has galvanized both black and white audiences? What kind of barometer is it of black women's thinking and feeling?

I saw the play in June 1976 at the Public Theater in New York before it moved to Broadway. Alerted by 1960's definitions of the black aesthetic, I wondered how I would like a play about which *New York Times* critic, Clive Barnes, had said, "It could easily have made me feel guilty at being white and male. It didn't. It made me feel proud at being a member of the human race, and with the joyous discovery that a white man can have black sisters." *For Colored Girls* was being lauded by professional theatre reviewers like Walter Kerr and by black women who had not been at all interested in the renaissance of Afro-American theatre in the 1960's—a renaissance which produced few women dramatists and, in plays like LeRoi Jones' (Imamu Baraka's) "A Black Mass" and "Madheart," was sexist in its treatment of black women. I had heard that *For Colored Girls* put down black men; I had even heard scurrilous talk about lesbianism, so I watched this Saturday matinee with intense curiosity.

When I saw it, the audience was mostly white, and both men and women seemed touched and pleased by the play. I wondered how and why it affected them. I also wondered what responsive chords the play struck in the working-class black women in the audience or the women older than the twenty- to thirty-year-old age range of the actresses. Finally, I wondered what made me feel that, for all its surface richness and emotional intensity, the play was missing something. . . .

As long as the choreopoem was on stage, I was under its spell. I cried, I smiled in recognition of its truth, I nodded my head in approval. I was thrilled to hear the cadence of black women's speech replicated on stage and to see the humor and anguish of our trials with our men lifted out of the morass of our individual lives for cooler and more compressed contemplation on stage. As soon as I stood in the lobby, my misgivings began. I was not troubled by the revelations of black women's pain: it is no secret that we have sores and scars, and theatre provides the kind of catharsis that can help us bear and transcend them. I was not troubled by the way in which black men were portrayed or even by the play's airing the tensions between black men and black women: *For Colored Girls* discloses nothing about that that hasn't been in *Ebony* and *Essence,* nothing I had not heard black women in widely disparate age groups, income brackets, and regions say—from my childhood on. Nor was I dismayed by the pro-lesbian thrust some Afro-American men had detected in the play: I have seen enough women's solidarity to know it does not have homosexuality as a necessary component.

For Colored Girls begins with "Mama's little baby likes shortnin' bread" and little Sally Walker coming out of our childhood to "shake it to the east and the west," has a black girl's pout about not being allowed in the adult room of the public library, and mentions getting one's hair straightened, and the black women in the audience are dislocated into delight because we simply have not seen ourselves on stage like this. Movies and theatre have alternated between portraying us as domestics like Beulah, stalwart matriarchs like Mama Younger in *Raisin in the Sun,* and hot-blooded exotics like Carmen Jones. Shange has studied black women's body language and speech styles carefully, and her version of us starts in nostalgia and then presents aspects of our adult lives at a time when we had given up hope of ever seeing ourselves transformed into stage art. That soothes us and makes it difficult for us to be alert to the play's premises, fascination, and solutions.

Even while I was watching the play, four scenes disturbed me. The first was the lady in brown's "cute" monologue about Toussaint. On the one hand, Janet League, whose performance in "The First Breeze of Summer" was masterful, seemed to avoid her own 'possibilities' in her syrupy delivery. On the other, Shange had been described as a feminist, but having a little girl translate her admiration for the epic Toussaint L'Ouverture into interest in a small black boy named Toussaint Jones hardly seemed so. The second was the lady in blue's "I usedta live in the world/then I moved to Harlem." I know too much about ghettoes, from having lived and worked in them, to be sentimental, but while calling Harlem "six blocks of cruelty/piled up on itself/ a tunnel closin' " may reflect Shange's experience the year *she* lived there, it leaves out the vibrancy and vitality of that chocolate city and tells only a fraction of Harlem's intricate story. The third was the lady in red's long monologue about Crystel and Beau Wille Brown (the scene most often cited in reviews), about a crazed Vietnam veteran who drops his son and daughter

from a fifth-floor tenement window because their mother will not marry him. Though reviewers praised Trazana Beverley's performance, I found the scene melodramatically played for sniffles and pathos and completely unrelieved by the laughing-to-keep-from-crying blues humor that informs other sections of the play. And Shange seemed, to one who knows a few unemployed Vietnam veterans, to be blaming the victim. The final disturbing scene was the resolution Shange comes to after her vigorous exposition of black women's blues. The seven "colored girls," the aspects of the rainbow, sing "I have found God in myself and I loved her, I loved her fiercely." It is an effective piece of theatre, but knowing something of Afro-American religion and of black women's past and present, I worried about its truth.

For Colored Girls is rooted in Shange's own life, so it is interesting to glance at the slices of her life she shares in her interviews and in the introduction to the printed version of the play, for a guide to the prism through which she refracts black womanhood. She was born in Trenton in 1948 and, like Lorraine Hansberry, was a daughter of the black middle-class: her father a surgeon, her mother a psychiatric social worker. She spent her formative years in St. Louis, had some clashes with her parents about playing with lower-class black children, graduated Barnard with honors, read widely—especially Russian novels, French (in the original), and Spanish with the aid of dictionaries. In a *New Yorker* interview she mentions Genet, McCullers, Millay, Melville, and deBeauvoir as influences. In an *Essence* interview she credits Margaret Walker, Ralph Ellison, Richard Wright, James Baldwin, Ann Petry, Jean Toomer, Claude McKay, LeRoi Jones, Owen Dodson, Ted Jones, Senghor, and Césaire with giving her something, making a space for her. In a *Ms.* self-interview she recalls a childhood of visits by her parents' friends from Nigeria, Togo, Cuba, Haiti, India, the Philippines, France, and Mexico and Sunday afternoon variety shows where her mother read from Dunbar, Shakespeare, Countee Cullen, and T. S. Eliot; her father played congas and did magic tricks, and the four children did soft-shoe and played violin, cello, flute, and saxophone. In all these interviews she mentions the childhood impact of black music, specifically rhythm and blues and Charles Parker and Dizzy Gillespie: Dizzy Gillespie, Chico Hamilton, Sonny Til, and Chuck Berry visited the family. Later she got interested in the music of Cecil Taylor and Albert Ayler. She has been unhappily married to a lawyer and has attempted suicide twice—the first time at 19. After Barnard, she did work in American Studies at the University of Southern California, worked with the Women's Studies Program at Sonoma State College, studied dance with Raymond Sawyer, Ed Mock and Halifu, performed in Halifu Osumare's "The Spirit of Dance" troupe, did poetry readings at San Francisco State College and with the Shameless Hussy poets; and was "isolated in . . . a very close community of creative women." While in the Bay area, she began a series of seven poems, modelled on Judy Graham's *The Common Woman,* which were to explore seven different kinds of nameless women who "assume hegemony as dictated by the fullness of their lives." The twenty-three poems of *For Colored Girls* is the result.

Shange has said she used "colored" in the play's title because it was a word her grandmother would understand. In interviews she has also talked about her suicide attempts—briefly, and interviewers have either assumed the reference to suicide in the play's title was symbolic or metaphorical, or have been too awed or polite or dense to ask my question: Why would a light-skinned black woman, from an intact supportive upper middle-class family, who got honors at Barnard try to kill herself? And what made her stop wanting to kill herself? True, these are personal questions, but Shange's interviews are full of the personal. Besides, answers to my question about suicide illuminate the audience appeal of *For Colored Girls.*

Although several social scientists, including Herbert Hendin, have written on black suicide the focus has usually been on black men. "Suicide: A Growing Menace to Black Women" (*Ebony,* September 1973) by J. Slater is the only article I know on black female suicide. It draws on statistics from Metropolitan Life Insurance Company; interviews with two suicidal black women at a Baltimore out-patient clinic; the unpublished autobiography of a twenty-six-year-old mother who killed herself with a combination of roach powder and tranquilizers; and interviews with four professionals—all male. Here are the statistics:

1) the suicide rate of black women is 14th highest among women in the world

2) black women's suicide rate has risen 80% in the past twenty years

3) black women's suicide occurs most frequently between the ages of 15 and 24

4) for nonwhite (sic) females current suicide rates are at the highest levels recorded during the past fifty years

5) between 1957 and 1967

a) the rate for nonwhite females almost doubled

b) the rate for white females rose about ⅛

c) the rate for nonwhite males rose about ⅛

d) the rate for white males changed little

Some of the professionals Slater consulted discussed the link between black suicide and black poverty, but since none of the women in *For Colored Girls* is poor, the insights of Ronald W. Maris (sociology professor at the University of South Carolina) and James Comer (psychiatrist at Yale) are much more helpful. Maris sees suicide as having a "negative self-image, low self-esteem, and feelings of isolation and rejection." He also says, "hopelessness and isolation resulting from failed social relationships often lead to suicide," while reminding us that "it is not just being alone that causes one to be suicidal, rather it is the process of how one came to be alone." Comer stresses the socio-cultural, and his comments are more extensive. "The caring, protective systems which black people once found in the church and in the extended family are not now so available to us," and the "decline of the black church" has had a devastating "psychic effect" on black women who once found "a sense of belonging and importance" there. Comer further says,

> The church had a built-in defense mechanism for black people. When you don't relate any longer to a protecting system like that, you are thrown out in the larger system which is a rejecting system. You're thrown into a competitive game whose rules say that you must "make it" to be an adequate person. But in the black church you didn't have to "make it," because you had an intrinsic worth and value in that system.

He ends with a grim forecast, "I think suicides among black women will continue to rise."

Examined in the context of Slater's article, all the assets of Shange's upper-class (by black standards) childhood crumble before two debits: she was geographically rootless because, as an Army officer, her father moved (and moved his family) often. She writes, "i waz accustomed to traveling, since we moved so many times: from trenton, to upstate new york, to alabama, back to trenton, to st. louis and again back to trenton, before i waz thirteen. i never expected to have any particular place to call home." She felt alienated from other black people because of her family's income (she learned black talk first from their black maids) and professional status and because her family disapproved of her lower-class playmates. I don't know whether Shange would consider her family "extended," but on the basis of *For Colored Girls,* I doubt it. None of her interviews discuss her childhood religious training, but it's hard to imagine an Army surgeon and psychiatric social worker in the kind of black church Comer refers to.

That *For Colored Girls* is autobiographical is nowhere more evident than in the kind of women Shange wrote about and in the play's splendid isolation from the power poles of black culture: the extended family and the black church—and from salient aspects of black literary and political history as well. During the performance one does not notice what a narrow range of black women Shange portrays because, in part, Shange has converted her study of Afro-American dance which taught her to accept "the ethnicity of my thighs and backside" into the body language of her choreopoem with dazzling effectiveness. Shange says, "dance as explicated by Raymond Sawyer and Ed Mock insisted that everything African, everything halfway colloquial, a grimace, a strut, an arched back over a yawn, waz mine. . . . I moved what waz my unconscious knowledge of being in a colored woman's body to my known everydayness." In *For Colored Girls,* we not only hear lines real black women speak delivered with acutely accurate inflections, we also see familiar strides and shrugs and sweeps and recognize the grammar of black women's bodies.

The women in *For Colored Girls* are single. Except for Crystel, they don't have children and the centeredness, despair, and joy that rearing them brings. They don't have brothers, fathers, or uncles, and, although the [printed] version of the play is dedicated to Shange's grandmother and great-aunt, the ladies of the rainbow have no mothers, aunties, grandmothers, sisters, cousins, godmothers, play aunts, or play sisters. They have no christenings, funerals or weddings to go to and be buoyed and challenged by, no neighborhood's pride to push them on to college, no families (nuclear or extended) to harass and nourish and soothe them. They are as isolated and alienated as the typical, middle-class, single white woman in contemporary urban America, and that is probably part of the reason the play succeeds with white audiences. It is full of "local color" in its use of contemporary black urban talk, black popular music like "Dancing in the Streets" and "Stay," renditions of black dances like "the Pony," but *the* problem it focuses on (mistreatment by an immature, insensitive man and managing the ensuing distress alone) are "universal" enough for white audiences.

For Colored Girls has no knowledge of that "old-time religion" that was good enough for mother, of the voices of Mahalia Jackson, Clara Ward, Albertina Walker, and Dorothy Love Coates. It is ignorant of black women on the mourner's bench praying struggling souls "through," serving on stewardess boards, superintending Sunday schools, frying chicken by the crate to pay off church mortgages. Its ladies of the rainbow in their bright chitons with their exquisitely articulated anguish don't know the "Old Ship of Zion," the "Beautiful Garden of Prayer," or "Amazing Grace." They are cut off from the tradition of faith which sustained a slave people through fire and brimstone and a half-free people through Reconstruction, lynching, legal segregation, second-class citizenship, and all the other travails of our stay in this Babylon.

None of the women in *For Colored Girls* even *refers* to a job, though the majority of African-American women over sixteen work outside the home. Shange's version of them contains no teachers, beauticians, social workers, nurses, or salesclerks; and certainly no barmaids, domestics, or diet aides. Since Shange is creating an artistic reality rather than dramatizing census data, her choreopoem does not have to replicate the work life of African-American women. It is, however, interesting to note the effect of her omission of this facet of our lives. By not mentioning work and the independence it gives black women (no matter how meager their income or how demeaning the work), Shange makes her characters seem much more vulnerable than black women usually do. Her focus is on black women's shared pain, so she blurs the economic differences between those women who cry the blues over a beer at a neighbor's tenement kitchen table and those women who can afford to soak their man-sorrow while sipping rum punch on a vacation beach. Finally, she can intensify the characters' exhilaration or devastation by pinpointing it all to one source: black men.

Although there is a lot of black music in the play, and that is one of its formidable assets, it's not the music of black women, not the sublime and vigorous blues tradition that reaches from Big Mama Thornton through Ma Rainey, Bessie and Clara Smith, Billie Holiday, Dinah Washington, Esther Phillips, Nina Simone, and Aretha Franklin. Their music is completely ignored as though there was no extant artistic vocabulary in which black women have given form to their griefs and joys. Shange's introduction to the [printed] edition of *For Colored Girls* mentions her

connection with the first anthology of Third World women writers and with a women's studies course at Sonoma on Third World women writers. Some of the ladies of the rainbow are writers, and the idea of creative black women being misunderstood and thwarted runs through the play, but *For Colored Girls* makes no mention of the dreaming and daring of black women writers past and present: not of Phillis Wheatley's writing couplets as a domestic slave in enlightened Boston nor of Frances Lee Harper, Margaret Walker, Zora Neale Hurston, Ann Petry, Gwendolyn Brooks, Paule Marshall, Alice Walker, Toni Cade, Toni Morrison, Mari Evans, Lucille Clifton, Audre Lorde, or Carolyn Rodgers.

Despite all that black women have suffered and *still* suffer at the hands of white men and white women, white people don't appear in *For Colored Girls* at all. The play is shockingly ahistorical both in ignoring white responsibility for our pain (which is another reason white critics and audiences can praise it) and ignoring black response to white oppression. Despite Shange's education in American Studies (or because of it?), the play makes no reference to past or present tensions between black and white Americans. It shows no knowledge of the Kerner Commission report about two separate and unequal nations existing in the United States; about working for "Miss Ann"; about white men's "prerogative" to take black women; about the myth of white women's purity constructed on the debased valuation of black women; or about the difference between what white men and women annually earn and what black men and women annually earn and what (if any *possible* thing) that has to do with the tenderness and the rage that compose black love. Shange writes, "Unearthing the mislaid, forgotten, | or misunderstood women writers, painters, mothers, cowgirls, and union leaders of our pasts proved to be both a supportive experience and a challenge not to let them down, not to do less than—at all costs not to be less woman than—our mothers, from Isis to Marie Laurencin, Zora Neale Hurston to Kathe Kollwitz, Anna May Wong to Calamity Jane." However, the ladies of the rainbow are alienated from Afro-American history in a way that makes it impossible for them to recall Sojourner Truth, Fanny Lou Hamer, Harriet Tubman, Mary Bethune, or Rosa Parks to see what we have *already* endured and accomplished (despite much more overwhelming odds than the blues about loving some man) as a guide for what we can be and what we must do.

Shange speaks directly from and to the experience of a growing (but still small) section of African-American women who are born into the middle- or upper middle-class (or attain it through education or marriage), are able to secure some college education and to travel outside their neighborhoods in New York, Chicago, Atlanta, or Philadelphia to California, Europe or the Caribbean. Though the black women in the audience may not have "considered suicide," they are familiar with the rootlessness, alienation, and isolation Shange portrays and are, to some extent, either as distanced as the ladies of the rainbow from the sustaining bedrock of black culture or as unable to work out a synthesis between traditional black culture and technocratic, impersonal, individualized, hectic, mobile modern America. They have experienced the despair, loneliness, low self-esteem, and negative self-image that Maris talks about, and this theatre event offers them ways to understand, manage, and transcend that pain. A dimension of the play's appeal to white audiences also becomes clear. Alienation and despair are keystones of modernism. The individual *angst* of *For Colored Girls* (and Shange's resolutely apolitical solution) touches modernist themes familiar to educated whites since the beginning of the twentieth century, though its ending on a defiantly hopeful note is, like the vivid colors of the women's dresses, part of African-American spirit. The unanswerable question is how Shange fastened on troubles with black men as *the* roots of black women's pain. To do so she had to ignore a range of other causes, including value conflicts between black parents and children which provided so much of the fodder for black drama of the 1960's; the impact of the new sexual freedom on black women; the frustrations which, as Comer points out, come in the wake of expectations raised by the women's movement and the continued rejection of black women by the larger system; and the oppressive fist of white America keeping black men and black women on the bottom rung—together. If fastening on black men as the cause of black women's blues is inaccurate and unfair, it is also effective (because of the very real tensions between black women and black men), and safely apolitical.

One of the most dramatic consequences of the political and cultural black nationalism of the 60's was a searing black examination of African-American culture which pronounced much of it hopelessly integrationist, irrelevant, and counter-revolutionary. The black family and black religion were focal in this re-appraisal. Radicals pronounced them hopelessly corrupt; revisionists concentrated on their resilience and adaptability and their ability to sustain African-American life and hope against colossal obstacles. We searched for our true black selves down myriad roads lined with gelees, tikis, naturals, and dashikis. We re-assessed rural Southern black life and became intensely curious about historical and contemporary Africa. Though Shange dissociated herself from the black nationalism of the 60's because of its sexism, she is (like all of us who came of age then) very much its heir. She wears gelees and noserings and, unlike Lucille Clifton, who writes:

> light
> on my mother's tongue
> breaks through her soft
> extravagant hip
> into life.
> Lucille
> she calls the light,
> which was the name of the grandmother
> who waited by the crossroads
> in Virginia
> and shot the whiteman off his horse,
> killing the killer of sons
> light breaks from her life
> to her lives . . .
>
> mine already is an Afrikan name

Shange changed her name from Paulette Williams because she didn't want a feminized masculine first name (she must not have known Herbert Gutman's contention that such first names were slaves' incest-guards) or a slave-master's last name.

For Colored Girls does not attack the black family and the black church frontally, but the solutions Shange offers the ladies of the rainbow indicate her evaluation of these institutions. While some of African-Americans experimented with communalism, polygamy, Hinduism, the Nation of Islam, and cults modelled on traditional African religion, Shange worked out other solutions.

In her *Ms.* self-interview Shange refers to her Bay area involvement with a "very close community of creative women." She also says, "i surround myself with essentially the same people wherever i go . . . we usedta call ourselves the COMIC-DU-WOP COMMUNE . . . poets mostly and some musicians. . . ." In the "pyramid" section of *For Colored Girls* the traditional pattern of women's friendships destroyed by competition for a man is challenged as three women resist that temptation and come together to grieve over the man who betrayed them all. Unlike African kinship systems based on extended family ties and marriage or the African-American slave-made networks based on kinship and assigning titles like "aunt," "uncle," "sister," and "brother" to outsiders and then treating them as family, Shange devises an alternative to the family based on shared coming-of-age rites, suffering, and peer relationships which, like a strong age-group or family, is impervious to outside attacks. In place of the psycho-social "cement" of the black church or hoo-doo, Shange has substituted the rainbow (God's promise to Noah, though Shange doesn't mention that allusion). "She remembered driving home in California after a discussion in a class she taught about Gabriel García Marquez, author of *One Hundred Years of Solitude*. She saw a huge rainbow over Oakland and she realized, she said, that women could survive if they decide that they 'have as much right and as much purpose for being here as air and mountains do. . . . We form the same stuff here that sunlight does, we are the same as the sky, we are here breathing, living creatures and we have a right to everything.' " The play's closing words, "I have found God in myself and loved her fiercely," chanted by the entire cast, affirm women's solidarity, healthy acceptance of one's blackness, and sense of the ultimate sacredness of one's soul and its ties to all living things.

For Colored Girls is an artistic triumph for Shange and the women who portray the ladies of the rainbow. It is also a stark reminder of all the talented African-American women artists still unheard of and unknown. But for all its strengths, its phenomenal success and the meagerness of African-American critical analysis of it disturb me. How can a play which ignores racism and capitalism as *the* powerful engines of black women's oppression; which glorifies an individualism and emphasis on personal happiness which (though profoundly American) run counter to traditional African-American concern with the extended family and the redemption and re-birth of African-Americans; which suppresses cultural strategies that have enabled African-American women to endure, create, and transcend amid the struggles and sorrows of 300 years on these shores; and which offers simplistic solutions to the problems it does confront, have attained such an extraordinary popular and critical success? What state are African-American women in if *For Colored Girls* is *the* mirror in which these beautiful ones recognize themselves? The play's success alerts us to the idea of alienation and private despair being accepted as the cause of African-American women's anguish and to the rejection of political solutions (from moderate ones to radical ones) in favor of young African-American women seeking their solutions in themselves and with other young women who have exactly the same troubles and scant resources. And those solutions frighten me.

I am not naive or nostalgic enough to believe that my grandmother's Jacksonville, Florida-seamstress-A.M.E.-Pansy-Blossom-Sewing Circle, married-at-fifteen experience and wisdom is a ready-made blueprint for the maze of my radically different life. Our generation *is* different from hers; we *are* pioneers. But if we reject our past as irrelevant, we are fools, and if we are so culturally integrated into America's melting pot that we don't know our history and our culture, we are to be pitied—and educated. (pp. 539-50)

[Today] as we juggle the benefits of the educational, economic, political, and cultural integration brought by the 60's against African-American cultural imperatives; as we struggle to synthesize and act on the insights of Pan-Africanism, Marxism, and feminism; as we acknowledge our debt to our mothers and our daughters, we must delve bedrock-deep into the written and oral record of how we got over, pare away the aspects of our history and culture which still shackle us, and revive and honor all that has sustained us. We must fix our eyes on the "new world comin'," and gird ourselves for the cultural and political struggles ahead—instead of considering suicide at all. (p. 550)

> *Andrea Benton Rushing, "For Colored Girls, Suicide or Struggle," in* The Massachusetts Review, *Vol. XXII, No. 3, Autumn, 1981, pp. 539-50.*

Sandra L. Richards (essay date Summer 1983)

[*In the following essay, Richards discusses what she terms as the "combat breathing" of Shange's characters, or their desire to both struggle against social oppression and transcend the limitations of human existence through art.*]

In 1976 *for colored girls who have considered suicide/when the rainbow is enuf* exploded upon the stage and established Ntozake Shange as a major force in American theatre. Since that time, she has written at least five other plays, three of which were published in 1981 under the title *three pieces.* One of the most outstanding features of Shange's dramaturgy to date is a dialectic between the felt constrictions of the social order and the perceived limitlessness of the natural order. On the one hand, there is an awareness of social oppression and commitment to struggle; on the other, there is a desire to transcend or by-

pass, through music and dance, the limitations of social and human existence.

My purpose is to analyze one aspect of this dialectic, an element which Shange terms "combat breath," and to sketch broadly the dimensions of the opposing entity, which I am describing as a will to divinity. The contours, if not the purpose, of this fighting spirit are easily recognizable, while a discussion of the will to divinity, with its heavy allegiance to an African world view, could easily be the subject of a paper in and of itself. By focusing primarily on combat breath, I hope to explain the reason that Shange's plays not only startle and energize but also infuriate and disturb many of her audiences.

Shange borrows the term "combat breath" from Frantz Fanon. In analyzing Francophone African colonies, the social psychiatrist had argued:

> There is no occupation of territory, on the one hand, and independence of persons on the other. It is the country as a whole, its history, its daily pulsation that are contested, disfigured, in the hope of final destruction. Under this condition, the individual's breathing is an observed, an occupied breathing. It is a combat breathing. [Frantz Fanon, *A Dying Colonialism*]

Implicit in Shange's reference to Fanon is the understanding that the struggle for liberation involves the entire community, that liberation for women necessitates a concomitant liberation or redefinition of the position of men.

For Shange, Fanon's additional characterization of combat breath as "the living response/the drive to reconcile the irreconcilable" is noteworthy because of its potential reference to poetic or spiritual realms. Despite the fact that Shange, like Fanon, often fuses concrete social reality with metaphoric, visionary projections, I will use the term in the more restrictive sense of an awareness of social determinants and commitment to change. By doing so, I hope to differentiate this reflex from its opposite.

The diametric opposite of Shange's combat breath is the will to divinity whereby individual protagonists seek to transcend corporal existence in order to merge with natural, cosmic forces. These characters completely forsake the troubled realm of social relations to gain entry into the more pleasurable world of private, spiritual communication. The underlying principles of such New World African religions as *voudoun, santeria,* and *candomblé* provide a useful paradigm for the spiritual axis found in Shange's plays, for common to them all is the belief that the world is a dynamic interplay of force fields. Language, music, and dance are *mojos;* that is, they are both energy or spirit-forces complete in and of themselves and potent modes for the manipulation of more profound insights. Through their manipulation one can apprehend and finally become identical with God/the gods.

Although the epistemology of experience within an African world view is inseparably cognitive *and* intuitive, Shange's protagonists, who are African people raised within the Western perspective, tend to feel that they must opt for one mode of knowledge over the other. Their Western heritage teaches them to see experience as fragmented rather than holistic and to value rational over emotional systems—hence, the dialectic of combat breath vs. will to divinity.

In *spell #7,* subtitled a "quik magic trance manual for technologically stressed third world people," Shange tackles the iconography of "the nigger." Underneath a huge black-face minstrel mask, a master of ceremonies promises to perform a different kind of magic designed to reveal aspects of Black life authentically. The minstrel performers move through the pain of dance steps and memories associated with Black entertainment for white America on to the release of more private, improvisational party styles. In doing so, they banish the hideous mask along with their stage personae, thereby creating a safe space in which to expose secret hopes, fears, or dreams. But two confessions, coming at the end of each act, puncture the whimsical or contained quality of most of the fantasies to reveal an almost overwhelming anguish.

The first involves a young woman who gives birth to a boy named Myself. Sue-Jean is ordinary, a "colored girl with no claims to any thing/or any one": As a Black person, she is defined by her poverty and low status, as a woman by her availability as a sexual object. In choosing pregnancy, Sue-Jean refuses to see herself as inert or inconsequential. She creates instead an active, engaged self. She pursues the traditional female modes of self-expression in planting a garden, canning, baking, and knitting: "sue-jean waz a gay & gracious woman/ . . . she waz someone she had never known/she waz herself with child/& she waz a wonderful bulbous thing." And she strives to ensure that her baby will be safe from "all that his mama/waz prey to."

But when Myself wants to do more than nurse or sleep, when the child begins to crawl and explore the world, when the male Myself as the embodiment of Sue-Jean's own self grows into open and ill-defined new realms, Sue-Jean kills the child and drinks his blood. She then returns to a state of pregnancy, but now it is an imagined pregnancy in which the anticipation of an impending birth is gradually superceded by the joyous feeling of being pregnant "& she forgot abt the child bein born/& waz heavy & full all her life/with 'myself'." Thus, for Sue-Jean, psychic paralysis or the liminality of being forever on the verge of self-expression is preferable to the old negative evaluations or the (my)self which must necessarily evolve in sometimes frightening and unpredictable ways.

In Sue-Jean, Ntozake Shange creates a figure whom critic Barbara Christian identifies as the contrary Black woman [in *The Black Scholar,* March-April 1981]. Because she is seen as abnormal, as the "other" essentially apart from whites and Black men, the Black woman has limited alternatives: She may acquiesce to social norms or struggle to keep inviolate an authentic, interior reality. Should she choose the latter course, her words or acts may appear hopelessly ineffective, desperate, or insane. The extent to which she is marked different and isolated from a community of people, the extent to which her actions seem eccentric is a measure of the power of convention. Thus, contrariness can be a public, political act, a sign of a woman's attempt to become whole.

In fashioning the character of Sue-Jean, Shange embraces the concept of the nurturing female with such vehemence that it implodes. In killing her child Myself, Sue-Jean makes actual the suicide which many women symbolically experience in sublimating their own identities to those of their children. In committing a murder generally thought to be contrary to all laws of "nature," she courageously asserts her independence. But this independence leads nowhere. She remains in a limbo in which the old formulations have been forever rejected, and no new visions seem possible.

The Sue-Jean character works primarily on the level of metaphor. One senses that it is not so much a reflection of an actual event as a fantastic projection of barely understood, unarticulated, self-destructive urges. Its capacity to disturb, its high content of contrariness, comes from the fact that it aptly captures profound, infantile fears concerning our mothers and ourselves, social taboos long since forgotten but not emotionally erased.

Maxine is another Shange character whose actions in the final segment of *spell #7* seem like a contrary, pathetically ludicrous response to the socio-metaphysical ills she would cure. As a young girl she lived in a house where ". . . trees that grew into my room had to be cut back once a year/this waz when the birds sometimes flew thru the halls of the house as if the ceilings were sky & i/simply another winged creature. yet no one around me noticed. . . ." Nor did they notice that this intelligent little Black girl celebrated phenomena like polio epidemics as evidence of divine protection because "if god had made colored people susceptible to polio/then we wd be on the pictures & the television with the white children. i knew only white folks cd get that particular disease."

When she becomes a young woman, however, her grandmother closes up the windows, and, together with her mother, they send her out into the world to be among "trouble" but not get into "trouble." Her loss of innocence is not confined to the personal realm of the mysterious "trouble" young men present, for Maxine learns that, contrary to her cherished childhood beliefs, Black people are not immune to the diseases and perversions manifested by whites. Her faith shattered, she buys gold, knowing that more than likely it comes from apartheid South Africa; as the atrocities perpetrated by Blacks mount, she buys more and more gold jewelry

> to remind the black people that it cost a lot for us to be here/our value/can be known instinctively/ . . . i buy gold/ & i weep. i weep as i fix the chains round my neck/my wrists/my ankles. i weep cuz all my childhood ceremonies for the ghost-slaves have been in vain. . . . no one understands that surviving the impossible is sposed to accentuate the positive aspects of a people.

What gives arresting uniqueness to the familiar themes of the loss of innocence and the repression of natural instincts, inflicted upon young females, is the element of contrariness. Maxine's purchasing gold is the adult counterpart to the childhood ritual of paying homage to unknown ancestors. Though these gestures seem naïve or tactically ineffectual, they symbolize Maxine's utter helplessness in the face of overwhelming dehumanization: They speak poignantly to the gnawing fear that the victims as well as the perpetrators have become completely brutalized by oppression; they reflect the desperate hope that humanity retains the ability to learn from experience and advance in accord with its noblest instincts. The visible evidence of African subjugation, these pieces of jewelry are chains binding Maxine directly to the enslavers and reinforcing their basis of power. Thus, like Sue-Jean, Maxine chooses a liminal state in which her childhood faith has been almost completely destroyed, and no adult strategies have been devised to resolve the crisis effectively.

Despite the public, political implications of contrariness, one may wonder how these pictures of wounded, stagnating women are an indication of Shange's combat breath. For an answer, one must examine the thrust which Shange's playwriting assumes, for most often she is not writing tidy plays in which a crisis is resolved within the structure of the play. Nowhere is this thrust beyond the theatre clearer than in *spell #7,* for the play attempts to create a liberated stage space supportive of Black self-expression. Because Sue-Jean's and Maxine's confessions threaten to reveal a pain almost beyond cure, the magician/master of ceremonies must halt the action in order to reassure his audience that it will indeed love his Black magic. Under his spell the cast takes up the refrain "bein colored & love it" and tries to manipulate it in order of conjure forth the joyous celebration of church. With the magician's defiant reaffirmation of the right of Blacks to exist as they choose to define themselves, the minstrel mask returns, and the audience leaves.

To a certain extent, Shange, like her fictional magician, performs a sleight of hand which theoretically allows the drama to end on a positive note, provided the communion between actors and audiences, brought into being by the refrain, becomes a sufficiently strong countervailing force against all the negativity represented by the minstrel mask. But given the earlier image of Sue-Jean and the final picture of a bejeweled Maxine, it is hard to imagine the actors ultimately being able to create a safe space for themselves and audiences. In a sense, in performance the play has two possible endings: It can culminate in hard-won triumph or in painful defeat, depending on the interaction of the energies of all those who have experienced the event.

Shange draws upon two distinct traditions in contemporary Western theatre. In her commitment to combat breath, she achieves some of the effects described in Bertolt Brecht's dramatic theories. Chief among the German dramatist's tenets is the view that theatre must be an analytical forum which exposes bourgeois illusions and stimulates audiences to think objectively about the causes of social and personal ills. By constructing most of her plays as a series of poetic monologues, occasionally interrupted by conventional dialogue, she takes advantage of the telegraphic, elusive quality of poetry to encourage audiences to listen with close, critical attention; the resultant episodic structure diminishes the audiences' empathetic tendencies by denying them the opportunity to gain a more rounded sense of character. Additionally, the women's

contrariness can function like Brecht's *Verfremdung* effect as an alienation device which keeps observers at a more objective, thinking distance from the characters. But because this contrariness also emotionally engages spectators, after a performance they are apt to demand answers to questions like, "Why are these women so strange; what does it mean? Is Shange describing reality accurately? How do I feel about what she describes?" Most importantly, in debating their responses to Shange's views, they can initiate a process of change in the world outside the theatre.

Thus, Shange's combat breath resides in her preference for raising issues, suggesting directions, and daring audiences to write their own endings. *spell #7* forces both performers and audience members to acknowledge the terrible distortion of their lives. Both in its on-stage images, and its residual aftereffects, it is an arrogant challenge to all to re-examine so-called coping strategies.

Ntozake Shange practices combat breath at tremendous risk. Posing questions touching upon complex, vaguely defined issues may be dissatisfying to a public accustomed to finding in literature ordered, albeit idealized solutions to problems, a public which tends to value more the positing of answers which alleviate anxiety. Having created emotionally resonant pictures of distress without offering equally compelling projections of health, Shange runs the risk that her audiences, angered at having confused feelings exposed, will reject the reminder of their anguish and vilify her.

Secondly, in the context of the United States she must reckon with the problem of audience: For whom does the playwright create Black magic? In dramatizing ostensible pathology, how does she avoid having a Black audience feel that it has been violated for the pleasure of whites? How does she depict truths painful to Blacks without being perceived, merchandized, and rewarded by the dominant, white-male ideology for simply confirming existing negative stereotypes? How does she direct to Black Americans questions about their humanity when they control few theatres or other communication outlets, and anything reaching them in numbers must pass through the filter of morally indifferent producers, theatre owners, critics, and publishers? By what critical standards does the Black community, and she as an individual, distinguish between a work genuinely nurturing Black people (and by extension, all peoples), and one supporting a mechanistic, anti-human system?

The second movement to which Shange seems indebted is that of French theorist Antonin Artaud and Black nationalist Amiri Baraka, whose 1964 essay "The Revolutionary Theatre" is derivative of Artaud's *The Theatre and Its Double.* In this tradition theatre is a locus for emotionally charged, eruptive forces which assault social complacency to expose victims who, nevertheless, contain within themselves seeds of their own regeneration. But while Shange's mode of playwriting shares similarities with Artaud's and Baraka's theoretical writings, I would contend that her style is actually rooted in an even older philosophical tradition, that of the African world view.

Briefly stated, because this perspective posits the universe as animated by the interplay of energy-fields or forces, power resides not only in men and machines, but also in props, costumes, lighting, and sets. All have the capacity to assert a *presence* akin to what we associate with actors/characters. Music and dance are particularly strong in their power to convey layers of sensate information lying beyond or outside linguistic, cerebral dimensions of the brain. They function as *mojos*. As spirit-forces, they have the power to amplify, contradict, or reaffirm the spoken word. As structures, they act as channels for enlightenment, setting the conditions whereby the individual penetrates to essence. In Shange's drawing upon this Black aesthetic lies the will to divinity, an impulse which her characters experience as an opposition to combat breath.

For the purposes of this paper, two examples of the will to divinity will have to suffice. Both occur near the ends of plays; both follow moments shocking in their level of self-inflicted violence; both raise issues which extend beyond the plays. I refer to the transition from "a nite with beau willie brown" to "a laying on of hands" in *for colored girls . . .* and to the shift from Maxine's adult method of atonement to the cast's refrain "bein colored & love it" in *spell #7.* In the first play, Crystal's story about the death of her children caps a long list of grievances against men; the other women have nothing to match Beau Willie's self-hatred and psychosis. Their collective consciousness flees in horror—first to a numbness and then to a gradual, contemplative realization of the source of their womanly strength.

In a spare, tentative language the women grope past an identification with other human beings toward a merger with natural entities:

> i fell into a numbness
> till the only tree i cd see
> took me up in her branches
> held me in the breeze
> made me dawn dew
> that chill at daybreak
> the sun wrapped me up swingin rose light every-
>   where
> the sky laid over me like a million men
> i waz cold/i waz burnin up/a child
> & endlessly weavin garments for the moon
> wit my tears

The women transform Crystal's "i found god in myself/& i loved her/i loved her fiercely" into a chant which emotionally validates what language alone has posited as fact. Their song—in production set to the rhythms of a spiritual—parallels the movement of the word, sounding at first hesitant, next gathering momentum through repetition, and then creating a soothing, trancelike state in which the actresses and the audience can experience the joy of their own (female) divinity. As a *mojo,* music here is a potent mode for conveying a non-cerebral, felt reality for which there is no rational explanation. Its beauty derives from its capacity to satisfy primal longings for a god, for that which is omnipotent and beyond comprehension, yet open to fragmentary penetration by fragile, finite human beings.

It is important to note the major challenge Shange undertakes, for it is a risk similar to that involved in combat breath. The playwright depends on the spontaneity of the moment and the people on both sides of the footlights to carry a significant portion of her "message." Like the pastor of a Black church or the *mae dos santos* of a *candomblé* house, she carefully structures her plays, utilizing the differing forces of language, music, dance, gesture, and other production elements in anticipation of the manifestation of a particular spirit. But inherent is the gamble that a sufficiently strong harmonizing force will appear to unify disparate elements, energize the audience/congregation, and release it back into the world able to withstand challenges and courageous enough to attempt the merger of the sacred and the profane.

Whether she in fact succeeds in this task in the closing moments of *for colored girls . . .* is open to debate. For many women a performance became a quasi-religious event in which the hurt of personal and group relations was subsumed by the recognition that their lives were being given public validation for the first time; they experienced a communal yet intensely private discovery of their own worth. For others, however, Beau Willie Brown was infuriating, for his story, placed at the end of shared complaints about men, came to represent all Black men and made the occurrence of a transcendent experience impossible. Often their complaint was that Shange had completely ignored the context from which a Beau Willie emerges, that she had transformed a man who is himself a victim of poverty, war, and racism into a monster for whom one need have no compassion. But when one looks at the text, one notices that references to these social factors are indeed present:

> there waz no air
>
> . . . . .
>
> . . .he kept tellin crystal/any niggah wanna kill vietnamese children more n stay home & raise his own is sicker than a rabid dog
>
> . . . . .
>
> he came home crazy as hell/he tried to get veterans benefits to go to school & they kept right on puttin him in remedial classes/he cdnt read wortha damn/so beau cused the teachers of holdin him back & got himself a gypsy cab to drive/but his cab kept breakin down/& the cops was always messin wit him/plus not getting much bread

Yet, given an emotional recoil from the horror of his actions, along with a pervasive American attitude which attributes any weakness to individual rather than social deficits, these critics may find it equally hard to hear Shange's combat breath and to be open to the closing transcendent moment.

Similarly, the nearly final moment of *spell #7* should function as a *mojo* for the apprehension of the human validity of Black peoples within the American context, for the playwright indicates in stage directions that the chant should become *"a serious celebration, like church/like home.*" For reasons already discussed it is doubtful whether this epiphany actually does occur in performance.

In both these examples of the will to divinity, the characters ricochet from a devastating social reality wherein they are totally vulnerable to an ecstatic spirituality wherein they are identical with an eternal, natural power. Though their spiritual impulse is characteristic of Black traditions, what is noteworthy is the fact that what these characters experience in that realm does not inform mundane existence. Looking into the very jaws of hell, they choose to flee, instead, on the rhythmic wings of music to a secure firmament. There is no synthesis, no resolution of the dialectic of combat breath vs. will to divinity which would produce a new, integrated sense of being.

Because Shange renders each pole with enormous vitality, the resulting roller coaster effect leaves us both energized and disturbed. Our experience of her plays is mildly psychotic: We feel two strongly contradictory moods but sense no means to mold them into a coherent whole. Though there is no resolution of these impulses in *for colored girls . . .* and *spell #7*, the art Ntozake Shange fashions is formidable, and the challenge to find solutions, profound. (pp. 73-8)

> Sandra L. Richards, "Conflicting Impulses in the Plays of Ntozake Shange," in Black American Literature Forum, *Vol. 17, No. 2, Summer, 1983, pp. 73-8.*

Jean Strandness   (essay date Fall 1987)

[*In the following essay, Strandness discusses the title characters of* Sassafrass, Cypress & Indigo *as new metaphors for women's experience.*]

Historically, what has been associated with the masculine has been deemed important; what has been associated with the feminine has been trivialized. In *Sassafrass, Cypress & Indigo,* Ntozake Shange, drawing from the personal realm of women's everyday experience and from the ancient or folk traditions of women's spirituality, incorporates a number of these "trivial" images, activities, and modes of expression—dolls, flowers, stones, feathers, apples, the moon, trees, the ocean, menstruation, dreams, spells, recipes, rituals for trance journeys, letters, journals, weaving, dancing, psychic healing—to depict the individual and the archetypal personalities of three sisters—Sassafrass, a weaver; Cypress, a dancer; and Indigo, a healer—and to evoke their world.

"Metaphorical systems," Barbara Godard notes, "encapsulate a group's heritage and trace its psychological and historical development. New metaphors are new phenomena, calling forth, containing and stylizing our experience. New metaphors imply cognitive developments and provide ways of disrupting [existing] symbolic systems through which ideology is represented to the individual." Shange, by reclaiming the old and developing new metaphors for women's experience, creates female characters who differ significantly from previous female protagonists in nineteenth and twentieth century literature. Shange suggests new patterns and modalities for living and, in so

doing, radically transforms the reader's perceptions of what it may mean to be human.

Structurally, *Sassafrass, Cypress & Indigo* may be viewed as a circle of concentric rings, as Shange introduces Indigo first, then Sassafrass, then Cypress, then returns to Sassafrass, and finally to Indigo again. This structure suggests the circular *temenos* (sacred space) in practices of women's spirituality and so emphasizes the depth of the connection between the sisters, as well as their interrelatedness. This structure also reflects the extent to which each woman is connected to the transpersonal realm, with Indigo at the center as most psychic, then Sassafrass, and then Cypress as most worldly of the three at the outermost edge. In this sense, the circular structure suggests gradations in the similarities they share, as well as clarifying their unique and different personalities. The circle motif suggested by the overall structure of the novel appears, too, at the conclusion of the novel when Cypress and Indigo return home to celebrate the birth of Sassafrass' first child as the two women and their mother, Hilda Effania, circle around Sassafrass to be with her in support and encouragement. Here, the circle of women can be connected with themes of interconnection, healing, and empowerment.

While the structure of *Sassafrass, Cypress & Indigo* may very well be viewed as a circle of concentric rings, it can also be viewed as a textured weaving with various recurring strands/motifs—letters from Hilda Effania to her daughters, recipes for special occasions, images and rituals of transformation, manifestations of aspects of the immanent, archetypal Goddess. Personal and transpersonal, warp and woof, weaving together, creating new patterns, reclaiming the past, transforming the present. That the structure of the novel is suggestive of a weaving complements the facts that Hilda Effania is a weaver, as is her oldest daughter, Sassafrass; that the relationship of the three sisters evokes an allusion to the Greek Moerae, the Triple Goddess, the weavers of destiny; and that the archetypal Goddess is sometimes viewed in a global, contextual way as "the interwoven fabric of being . . . the web of connection . . . the pattern."

In *Beyond God the Father,* Mary Daly states:

> Women have had the power of *naming* stolen from us. . . . To exist humanly is to name the self, the world and God. . . . Words which, materially speaking, are identical with the old become new in a semantic context that arises from qualitatively new experience.

In Shange's novel, Hilda Effania gives her daughters the names of three trees, which are used in dying cloth and also have healing powers—Sassafrass, Cypress, Indigo. Since Hilda Effania is a weaver who loves her profession, these names connote a special bonding between mother and daughter. Growing up, all the girls learn to dye, warp, and weave; thus, they see a manifestation of their own name in a piece of cloth, something useful and esthetic, and connect personally with the world. The roots and bark of these trees have traditionally held healing powers; and so too, eventually, each daughter in her own way becomes a healer, connecting with other people. Further, with its branches reaching into the sky and its roots into the earth, the tree is a universal symbol of a cosmic connection between heaven and earth. In the Creole mythology of Voudoun (the girls grow up in Charleston), the androgynous god Legba, "the initial procreative whole," may manifest itself as the Tree of Life, or the Crossroads, "the link between the visible, mortal world and the invisible, immortal realms." Similarly, each of the tree-daughters develops, in an individual way, the powers of the Tree of Life and her spiritual abilities to link with otherworldly realms.

Each daughter has a rich complex of connotations in her name from which to draw meaning: in giving her daughters the names Sassafrass, Cypress, and Indigo, Hilda Effania identifies their potential germ of connection with her, the material world, other people, and other-worldly realms. In naming them, Hilda Effania empowers her daughters.

Sassafrass exemplifies the classical Persephone archetype. Away from her mother's home, she falls in love with a Hades figure, Mitch, a seven-foot-tall, jazz saxophonist, whom she perceives as "the cosmic lover and wonder of wonders." She directs all of her creative energy towards him—cooking for him, creating macrame wall hangings of black heroes for their house, bolstering his ego, loving him. She becomes obsessed with pleasing him, sinking deeper and deeper into the shadow realm of her own psyche.

Initially, Mitch appears to embody the creative animus, to be a male muse. He urges Sassafrass to write: "Look, Sassafrass, I just want you to be happy with yourself. You want to write and create new images for black folks, and you're always sittin' around making things with your hands. . . . Now, Sassafrass, get into yourself and find out what's holding you back." Sassafrass does authentically want to write; she also wants to write to please Mitch—"Sassafrass was supposed to be a writer." Ironically, it is Mitch (and Sassafrass' participatory identification with him) that is blocking her in her ability to write.

In fact, Mitch is a male chauvinist—at a gathering of his friends, he boasts (in Sassafrass' presence), "Sassafrass' got some of the best pussy west of the Rockies, man, and I don't care who knows it, 'cause it's mine"!

His music expresses "pure rage and revenge"; Sassafrass listens to him practicing for hours. When she discovers he is a drug addict, Sassafrass describes feeling "lost in the depths of Hell" as a result. Although she loves Mitch, being with him paralyzes her; for Sassafrass, living with Mitch is like being in Hell with Hades.

Mitch devalues Sassafrass' weaving. He denounces a sequin-and-feather, vagina-shaped hanging Sassafrass has made in honor of Josephine Baker "because it wasn't proper for a new Afrikan woman to make things of such a sexual nature." But, in the end, it is through her weaving, her mother's craft, that Sassafrass finally taps into her creative potential as a writer.

After feeling unable to extricate herself from listening to one of Mitch's friends read from his new book, *Ebony Cunt,* Sassafrass, initially internalizing her anger, finally explodes in rage. It is the primal, archetypal cosmic rage of the Creole goddess Oshun, a rage against displacement and enslavement. In her fury, Sassafrass goes to her loom and "almost unconsciously," begins the process of warping it. As she does so, she chants, a woman coming into her power.

> makin cloth, bein a woman & longin
> to be of the earth
> a rooted blues
> some ripe berries
> happenin inside
> spirits
> walkin in a dirt road
> toes dusted & free
> faces movin windy
> brisk like
> dawn round
> gingham windows &
> opened eyes
> reelin to days
> ready-made
> nature's image
> i'm rejoicin
> with a throat deep
> shout & slow
> like a river
> gatherin space

The lyrical and poetic language of the chant is trance-like, suggesting a connection with the deep unconscious, suggesting Sassafrass' integration with her transpersonal Self.

This is a turning point for Sassafrass. Weaving feels "essential" to her. It links her with her heritage—"her mama had done it, and her mama before that." Weaving puts her in a frame of mind that opens her creative potential in words and language. For her, weaving and word-making are interrelated—"when women make cloth, they have time to think." Sassafrass feels whole, integrated, and authentically purposeful.

As a representative of the Persephone archetype, in weaving and finding her voice, Sassafrass has emerged from Hades and returned to the Mother (the feminine principle). She leaves Mitch and goes to live with her sister, Cypress, where she reads about ancient civilizations and begins to write. In the process, she is encouraged in her endeavors by psychic visions of Billie Holiday and Mamie Smith: "We need you, Sassafrass, we need you to sing best as you can; that's our nourishment, that's how we live."

Yet, like Persephone, Sassafrass is drawn back into Hades—she returns to Mitch. Eventually, the two move to a Creole Voudoun spiritual community. Here, Mitch complains, curses the deities, and does drugs. But Sassafrass participates fully in the community life, desiring to become a priestess of Oshun—"to heal, to bring love and beauty wherever she went." In a group ritual honoring Shango, Sassafrass' patron, she prays to have a child. After she is warned that the child will be cursed if she does not renounce the father, Sassafrass is possessed by the archetypal goddess Oshun and, in the throes of wrath, she grabs a jar of honey and pours it into the bell of Mitch's saxophone. She continues to spread it all over the horn, until he finally becomes silent.

The next morning she has a vision of her mother "lying on a bed of oranges, surrounded by burning yellow candles, eating honey." Freed from the bonds of Hades, Sassafrass returns home to her mother—"to find the rest of [herself]."

Until recently, as Annis Pratt observes, many female protagonists in nineteenth and twentieth century women's literature have identified psychologically with the values of a " 'horrible husband,' who stops her dead in her tracks. In women's experience, the gynophobic shadow and the animus are often fused in a masculine character who loathes the woman character every bit as much as she loathes herself, reinforcing her self-blame and dragging her into compliance with social standards. . . . Confronting the horrible husband, the female character falls into madness, determines to commit suicide, or lapses into a zombie-like state that precludes further development." Shange, by having Sassafrass *complete* the Persephone cycle, including the descent to the Underworld *and* the return to the Mother, alters and transforms this pattern. In fact, in her relationship with Mitch, Sassafrass, does practically become paralyzed—"Sassafrass was weak from Mitch's torrent. She sat so still her old fear of actually being a catatonic came back." But, by drawing on the psychological strength she gains from her weaving as a catalyst, the encouraging visions of Billie Holiday and Mamie Smith, the wrath of the archetypal goddess Oshun, and the sustained support of her mother—all of which could be linked with the Demeter archetype, Sassafrass completes the Persephone pattern and comes into her own power.

Cypress is a dancer. Connecting with her own talents was never a struggle for her, as it was for Sassafrass. As a young girl, she knew "dancing was in her blood . . . every step." For her, dancing is a sensual experience that connects her with the world—a dancer is "someone whose body interpreted the world." And, dancing connects her (and the audience) with the past, the ancestors.

> Deep drumming is heard from the street; folks turn their heads backwards. *The Kushites Returned* leap, sweep down the aisles, silk cloth flies in the air gleaming with silver threads, the painted dancers burst through the darkness. . . . It's so magic folks feel their own ancestors coming up out of the earth to be in the realms of their descendants; they feel the blood of their mothers still flowing in them, survivors of the diaspora.

For the future, for the children she does not yet have, Cypress creates four fine works of embroidery—"blocks of minute figures and arrows and circles in different colors," which represent some of the dance notations of *The Kushites Returned* and also seem to symbolize Cypress' continuing potential as a dancer.

Cypress manifests the archetype of Aphrodite, goddess of love, beauty, sensual pleasure, and marriage. Her home is always open and filled with "wine, cocaine, and lots of men." Initially, she represents that aspect of the goddess, who, in giving herself to many men, really remains autonomous.

Cypress then moves from L.A. to New York and becomes

part of a woman's collective. Here, she finds a "woman-being space" where she feels connected to women as she had never felt around any man. She meets Idrina who opens Cypress fully to love. "Cypress hadn't known-. . . that she could be loved, because she'd never let anyone close enough. Yet Idrina seemed to move right in and slay the dragons Cypress had spouting 'don't touch me,' simply by looking at her. Holding her."

Cypress' next lover is a man, Leroy. Shange describes their lovemaking as a sensual dance:

> the original aboriginal dance of all time/challenge the contradiction of perfected pirouette with the sly knowin of hips that do-right/stretch till all the stars n sands of all our lands abandoned/mingle in the wet heat/sweat & grow warm/must be she the original aboriginal dancin girl.

Eventually, Cypress and Leroy make plans to marry in her "mama's house."

In much of nineteenth and twentieth century women's literature, women are depicted as restricted, inhibited, or frustrated by social standards and/or their own internal guilt, in their sexual fulfillment. Shange's character Cypress stands as a remarkable contrast. Her love relationships, in their duration, are all depicted as unselfconsciously sensual, affirmative, and joyful. She seems to represent the original meaning of the word *virgin*—a woman (*gyn*) like a man (*vir*). "Such a virgin," notes Annis Pratt, "retained at all times the right to choose what to do with her body, whether to roam at will or stay home, whether to practice celibacy or engage in sexual activity." Cypress moves from being the lover of many men, to being the lover of a woman, to being the lover of a man she will eventually marry. For Cypress, as a manifestation of the archetypal Aphrodite, all phases of her sexual life are in character.

> *The lunar sphere moves with the deepest sound.*
> [Cicero]

Indigo manifests the archetype of Artemis: the Maiden, One-in-Herself, who never bonds with a man as a lover, though she has male companions; the goddess of childbirth, of wild things, of the moon. The novel begins:

> Where there is a woman there is magic. If there is a moon falling from her mouth, she is a woman who knows her magic, who can share or not share her powers. A woman with a moon falling from her mouth, roses between her legs and tiaras of Spanish moss, this woman is a consort of the spirits.
>
> Indigo seldom spoke. There was a moon in her mouth . . .
>
> Sometimes when someone else was talking, Indigo excused herself—her dolls were calling for her. . . . There wasn't enough for Indigo in the world she'd been born to, so she made up what she needed. What she thought the black people needed.
>
> Access to the moon.

The power to heal.

Daily visits with the spirits.

"Wherever we find interest in folklore in novels by black women," Marjorie Pryse observes, "we also find stages in the tradition's emerging perception that women have the ability to reclaim their 'ancient power.'" Drawing from the traditions of Creole Voudoun and women's spirituality, Shange's Indigo creates rituals for trance journeys to the moon; like Artemis, she is closely linked with the moon and its powers.

Indigo creates dolls who talk to her; they seem to symbolize her latent potential for becoming a midwife, Aunt Haydee's profession. When she reaches a point where she decides she is too old to keep the company of her dolls, Indigo creates a rite of passage in which she carries each doll to the attic while her mother sings a sacred song. "Indigo was excited, beginning and ending the largest segment of her life." Exemplifying the concern of many women that girls do not have rites of passage paralleling those of boys, Shange shows Indigo spontaneously inventing her own rituals—as many women today are doing.

When Indigo has her first period, Sr. Mary Louise takes off her clothes and bathes her "in a hot tub filled with rose petals: white, red and yellow floating around a new woman." Then, she tells Indigo to go out into the garden and let her blood flow among the roses. For Indigo, it is a moment "filled with grace." Afterwards, Indigo invents a menstruation ritual for her dolls.

MARVELOUS MENSTRUATING MOMENTS

(As Told by Indigo to Her Dolls as She Made Each and Every One of Them A Personal Menstruation Pad of Velvet)

When you first realize your blood has come, smile; an honest smile, for you are about to have an intense union with your magic. This is a private time, a special time, for thinking and dreaming. Change your bedsheet to the ones that are your favorite. Sleep with a laurel leaf under your head. Take baths in wild hyssop, white water lilies. Listen for the voices of your visions; they are nearby. Let annoying people, draining worries, fall away as your body lets what she doesn't need go from her. Remember that you are a river; your banks are red honey where the Moon wanders.

The language of Indigo's ritual connotes a primal return to a woman's authentic connection with nature and with her own spiritual power.

Uncle John, a friend of Aunt Haydee's gives Indigo a 'talkin' fiddle. He explains, "The fiddle be callin' our gods what left us . . . talkin wit the unreal what's mo real than most folks ever gonna know." Indigo plays rough blues on her fiddle, making it sound like birds and animals, wild sounds. Once, when she is threatened by two boys, the Geechee Capitans, instead of running, she stands firm and chants, "Falcon come in this fiddle. Falcon come in this fiddle. Leopard come in this fiddle. Leopard come in this fiddle. I'm on the prey. I'm on the prey"—Artemis, goddess of the hunt. The two boys retreat. Shange comments, "Indigo had a moon in her mouth after all." In the tradi-

tion of Creole Voudoun, Indigo has the ability to evoke the transpersonal protective powers of guardian spirits, or *loa*.

Using her psychic powers, Indigo turns the 'talkin' fiddle into an instrument of healing.

> . . .now she'd look at somebody. Say a brownskinned man with a scar on his cheek, leathery hands and a tiredness in his eyes. Then she'd bring her soul all up in his till she'd ferreted out the most lovely moment in that man's life. & she played that. You could tell from looking that as Indigo let notes fly from the fiddle, that man's scar wasn't quite so ugly; his eyes filling with energy, a tenderness tapping from those fingers now, just music.

By focusing intensely on the person she is playing for, she is able to connect and heal at the transpersonal level. This ability to focus intensely, with such concentrated attention, is characteristic of the archetypal personality of Artemis (stemming from Artemis' concentration in shooting the bow and arrow).

Indigo becomes a midwife. Working as an apprentice under Aunt Haydee, a wise woman, she learns to give birth and cure women and children.

> At first Aunt Haydee only allowed Indigo to play her fiddle to soothe the women in labor, but soon the mothers, the children, sought Indigo for relief from elusive disquiet, hungers of the soul. Aunt Haydee was no fool. She watched Indigo playing the fiddle one evening as the tide came in. It'd been a long time since a colored woman on Difuskie moved the sea. Some say it was back in slavery time. *Blue Sunday,* that was her name 'cause she was born on a Sunday & black as pitch.

Shange concludes her characterization of Indigo with this implied comparison to the legendary *Blue Sunday. Blue Sunday* was invincible and could be taken by no man—one man who tried lost a leg when she turned into a crocodile. She was never seen again by a white person but women of color heard her songs when they were in labor. When Indigo plays her fiddle for women in childbirth, she manifests the spirit, or *loa,* of *Blue Sunday.* Like the classical Greek Artemis, *Blue Sunday* is fiercely virginal and the protectress of women in childbirth. Like Artemis, too, she is linked with the power of the moon to move the sea.

When Aunt Haydee dies, she goes "to Our Lord on a melody only Indigo or *Blue Sunday* could know." Indigo keeps Aunt Haydee's ashes in "a funny bluish jar Uncle John'd given her when she was small." Within the context of Creole Voudoun, this jar provides a place for Aunt Haydee's spirit, or *loa,* whose power Indigo could continue to call forth. Since the *loa* is not viewed as the spirit of an individual, but as an ancestral spirit which can pass from generation to generation, it is also conceivable that Aunt Haydee's *loa* would transfer to Indigo, that Indigo would then manifest the spirit of the wise woman who had been her mentor. Shange seems to signify this possibility when she says, "Indigo moved into Aunt Haydee's tabby hut, just like she belonged there."

Outside the realm of fantasy literature, there is really no

precedent for a character like Indigo in nineteenth and twentieth century literature. Socially, she is sexually related to neither men nor women. Psychically, she would seem to have the characteristics of a strange, asocial misfit—a witch, even. But Shange's affirmative valuation of Indigo's psychic powers noticeably stands against and transforms a long history of negative connotations associated with such talents; Indigo "reclaims her ancient power," as she manifests, by the end of the novel, the spirit *loas* of her mentor, Aunt Haydee, and the legendary *Blue Sunday,* and the powers of the archetypal goddess, Artemis.

"Women," Nan Bauer Maglin states, "are now consciously exploring the previously unconscious bonds that tied them to both their real as well as their historical mothers and grandmothers. In relation to this, there is a growing body of literature of matrilineage; women are writing about their female heritage and their female future." Shange's **Sassafrass, Cypress & Indigo** is a remarkable example. Each of the principal female characters is strongly bonded to her natural mother and to a traditional women's profession (Sassafrass-weaving; Cypress-dancing; Indigo-psychic healing). Each is encouraged by the love and leadership of a mentor (Sassafrass-her mother; Cypress-Idrina; Indigo-Aunt Haydee). Each receives inspiration from legendary women of the past (Sassafrass-Billie Holiday, Mamie Smith, Josephine Baker; Cypress-the maternal ancestors of Black Nile dance; Indigo-*Blue Sunday*). Each manifests some aspect of the Triple Goddess Oshun of Creole Voudoun mythology (Sassafrass-Wrath, the ability to destroy [her relationship with Mitch] in order to move forward; Cypress-Generous Love, the ability to relate intimately with other people; Indigo-Virginity, the ability to contain one's energy and concentrate and focus it in order to transform the world—the *loa* of things as they *could* be, not as they are). Each exemplifies the personality and life pattern of one of the archetypal classical goddesses (Sassafrass-Persephone; Cypress-

Aphrodite; Indigo-Artemis). Each character provides readers with positive alternatives to normative female modalities in today's society as well as connections with women's traditions and spiritual heritage.

In a circle of concentric rings; in a narrative weave of recurrent images and motifs; in a four-dimensional prismatic net in which facets of the realm of time and the eternal, the physical and the spiritual, and the personal and the transpersonal reflect and illumine each other, Ntozake Shange evokes the world of three extraordinary sisters, Sassafrass, Cypress, and Indigo. And, in so doing, she helps to transform our world. (pp. 11-16)

> *Jean Strandness, "Reclaiming Women's Language, Imagery, and Experience: Ntozake Shange's 'Sassafrass, Cypress & Indigo',"* in Journal of American Culture, *Vol. 10, No. 3, Fall, 1987, pp. 11-17.*

John Timpane   (essay date 1989)

[*In the following essay, Timpane discusses Shange's dramatic works, contrasting their openness to various interpretations with their expression of the political concerns of the 1970s.*]

Ntozake Shange's four best-known dramatic works appeared in the late 1970s. Her most popular work, **for colored girls who have considered suicide/when the rainbow is enuf,** began as a cycle of seven poems in 1974, and by 1976 it had reached Broadway. **a photograph** appeared in different versions in 1977 and 1979, and **boogie woogie landscapes** appeared as a one-woman show in 1978 and in play form in 1979. **spell #7: geechee jibara quik magic trance manual for technologically stressed third world people** first appeared in 1979. This impressive burst of productivity took place largely during the Carter years; ten years later, these pieces, though not exactly dated, bear the stamp of a period of social transition, of frustrations and possibilities, of a sense of imminent change and the necessity for improvisation.

That decade's remove makes it clear that Shange's dramatic work, especially **colored girls,** represents a moment of crucial importance in black and American history. (An unrepeatable moment, I might add. One could no more write a **colored girls** now than one could write another *Brave New World.* In her own words, these are works "dealing with a period of time that hasn't existed . . . for very long" [**"Postscript"**] and that underwent almost immediate change.) Writers with whom she is often compared, such as Imamu Amiri Baraka and Nikki Giovanni, seem to speak of a different, earlier moment. Where these and other writers attacked the obstacles to black self-realization, Shange's dramas represent the tortured moment of becoming itself, *the* moment of emergence and discovery. Ambivalence and paradox mark this moment; a dynamic world full of potential inhabits the same sphere as an old dead world in which nothing can change. The future for Shange's characters fluctuates between a positive, realizable potential, such as Marx envisioned, and a negative emptiness, such as Benjamin envisioned, which must be filled by individual effort and suffering. The pro-

---

Shange on language in her works:

It's very scary to me as a woman that we're denied and defiled in language. That is a personal power to go from one language to another and continually find the same thing happening in romance languages and Germanic languages. It's really very scary. So for me, the challenge was to kill off these things and to trip it and trick it and use it in ways that "they're" not expecting but in ways that people speaking the language I speak would receive and feel a sense of joy in. Language is a liberator, though not in the way that George Washington Carver thought that an education would free you. I don't mean that language will allow us to function more competently with people who use the King's English. I mean that language will allow us to function more competently and more wholly in a holistic sense as human beings once we take hold of it and make it say what we want to say.

Ntozake Shange, in an interview with Neal A. Lester in Black American Literature Forum, *Winter 1990.*

---

cess of becoming is Shange's subject, "our struggle to become all that is forbidden by our environment, all that is forfeited by our gender, all that we have forgotten" (**"History"**).

In *spell #7, boogie woogie landscapes,* and *colored girls,* there is no one outcome to the process of becoming, no one unifying end—but there is the process itself, in which all are engaged. What is more, communal expression may well be the only outlet for a certain range of feelings, according to Shange: "in addition to the obvious stress of racism n poverty/afro-american culture . . . has minimized its 'emotional' vocabulary to the extent that admitting feelings of rage, defeat, frustration is virtually impossible outside a collective voice" (**"Foreword"**). Again and again, Shange's dramas wander through a maze of personal and collective experience, only to coalesce in a chant that unites the subjective and the intersubjective. The women of *colored girls* chant

> i found god in myself
> & i loved her/i loved her fiercely

and the actresses, singers, magicians, and gypsies of *spell #7* end with the chant "colored & love it/love it/bein colored," encompassing extremes of joy and pain. Even *boogie woogie landscapes,* which focuses exclusively on a single woman, ends with a chant:

> dontcha wanna be music/& ease into the fog
> dontcha wanna be like rain/a cosmic event/like
>   sound. . . .

None of these epiphanies—the discovery of a "god" within one's self, the acceptance and love of being black, or the urge to be like music—"solve" the future, but they are communal starting points for a large number of possible futures.

There is, however, a paradox about Shange's work. As mentioned, her works are inscribed with the tensions of a very specific time and place. Further, these pieces announce themselves as being "for" a particular audience, such as colored girls or technologically stressed third-world people. Those pieces contain a great deal of aggression toward an oppressive white culture, an aggression that begins with an attack on white English: "i cant count the number of times i have viscerally wanted to attack deform n maim the language that i waz taught to hate myself in" (**"Foreword"**). "The mess of my fortune to be born black & English-speaking" (**"Anna Fierling"**) has motivated her to cultivate nonwhite orthography, syntax, and what she has called verbal "distortions" (**"Foreword"**). Yet despite all this effort at exclusion, her works remain remarkably "open" texts—that is, they anticipate and welcome the indeterminacy of any dramatic text and the unavoidable variation of performance. As a result, a series of texts that are addressed to, dedicated to, and written for a particular audience nevertheless throw themselves open to a multiplicity of audiences and performances. In this essay, I will examine this openness and its consequences for such a politically committed drama.

Texts are defenseless, most of all the text for a drama. No text can defend itself against being misread or misunderstood; the meaning of the text may change or be forgotten or be butchered over time, and no one can do anything about it. Doubly so for a text for a drama, which is, at best, a trace of a suggestion about the way a group of people might choose to act out that text. Directors and troupes fling texts down and dance upon them. But *colored girls* seems to me to be the kind of "open text" that people have been writing about for the past critical generation. Its undeniable power as a piece of performance art derives from that openness, which is, ironically, its best defense against being "miscast," "mis-directed," or "misunderstood." Not that *colored girls* has no subject—on the contrary, it has a very self-conscious program—but it anticipates the inevitability of variation and welcomes it, not, I think, as a means of defense against variation, but as a willing gesture toward it. The text of *colored girls* sets down a rhythm, but only as an invitation to improvisation:

> dark phrases of womanhood
> of never havin been a girl
> half-notes scattered
> without rhythm/no tone
> distraught laughter fallin
> over a black girl's shoulder
> it's funny/it's hysterical
> the melody-less-ness of her dance
> don't tell nobody don't tell a soul
> she's dancing on beer cans & shingles

These are the first 10 spoken lines in the piece. There are no sentences until the seventh line, and the connections between the fragments are completely open to interpretation. Add to this that *colored girls* is a "choreopoem," meaning that the speaker will be dancing or moving in some fashion, also undetermined, while delivering the lines; the flexibility of dance is likely to open the possibilities of interpretation even further. The speakers/dancers—one cannot call them characters—are identified not by name but by color ("lady in purple," and so forth). At times, they speak for themselves as centered personas, and at other times they narrate or act out the lives of others. In this second function it is always clear that they are bearers of someone else's tale; there is always an alienation, for example, between the lady in purple, who declares she is "outside houston," and Sechita, whose story she tells later. As the play ends, the question of who these particular colored women really are has faded before their communal becoming.

Much in the history of *colored girls* contributed to Shange's discovery of the open form. For example, she evidently originally conceived of the women as anonymous entities: "the women were to be nameless & assume hegemony as dictated by the fullness of their lives" (**"History"**). From the beginning, the composition of *colored girls* was predicated on the unpredictability of performance—in a sense, the text apologizes for having to be written to give all the speaking and doing an origin. Such an origin is, after all, only a convention. Plenty of acting groups climb the stage nightly without a script. *colored girls,* despite its heavy program, gestures toward improvisational theatre. It was born in bars and jazz dives, and Shange has written of the early performances: "the selection of poems chang[ed], dependent upon our audience & our mood, & the dance [grew] to take space of its own" (**"History"**).

Jazz, dance, women's cooperatives, the Women's Studies Program at Sonoma State College, "The Raggae Blues Band giving Caribbean renditions of Jimi Hendrix & Redding" (**"History"**—certainly these are conditions of possibility under which performance was thrown open to all arts and audiences. Even the word "choreopoem," meaning a piece that is part dance and part language, was coined to describe a kind of writing that "fits in between all" genres and does justice to "human beings' first impulses," which are "to move and to speak" (**"Postscript"**).

Clearly, Shange and her associates were trying to give a great deal of autonomy to the work itself. She has written that "the most prescient change in the concept of the work" occurred when she gave up her role as director to Oz Scott. This, for Shange, was a way of subduing herself to the autonomy of the piece: "By doing this, I acknowledged that the poems & the dance worked on their own to do & be what they were" (**"History"**). Just as the piece seems to have anticipated the multeity of variations, so Shange, by resigning her directorship, anticipated the death of the author.

So far I have contrasted the political program in Shange's dramatic works with those works' openness. A closer examination of Shange's technique will reveal the paradox at closer range. Shange's most characteristic literary effects are those of collage. In the opening lines of *colored girls* and throughout her works, the fragment vies with the sentence, the image with the complete thought, as though the struggle between two grammars, one unofficial and one official, mirrors the struggle between two cultures:

> yr hair is acorns/you rest on glass/quick
> as a sailboat heeling/yr wine glass barely braizes
>   yr lips/
> vermelho   tambem/yr   nails   unpainted/
>   ridiculously inviting
> you sit here in carved glass/in mirrors/on light/
> in sepia caves (***boogie woogie landscapes***)

The aesthetic values of the fragment—those of disjunction, disruption, juxtaposition, sudden illumination or re-contextualization—are also political values. That is because the complete sentence, complete plot, and complete character—all the hallmarks of the rage for closure—are associated with a white European theatrical tradition. To choose the disruption and fragmentation of collage is a strike at those values:

> as a poet in the american theater/i find most activity that takes place on our stages overwhelmingly shallow/stilted & imitative. that is probably one of the reasons i insist on calling myself a poet or writer/rather than a playwright/i am interested solely in the poetry of a moment/the emotional & aesthetic impact of a character or a line (**"Foreword"**)

Shange sees her choice of the "poetry of the moment" as a choice against the European bias of white American culture:

> for too long now afro-americans in theater have been duped by the same artificial aesthetics that plague our white counterparts/"the perfect play," as we know it to be/a truly european framework for european psychology/cannot function efficiently for those of us in this hemisphere (**"Foreword"**)

If the European insistence on closure is not appropriate for white American playwrights, it is still less so for the poet in an Afro-American theatre.

Collage is inherently subversive in that the artist who employs collage hopes to make meanings by disruption and juxtaposition rather than by the ordered sequence of signs prescribed by the rules of grammar—which is as much as to say that collage proposes a syntax to replace the standard syntax. Because of its subversive character, collage is a way of opening up the canon. It is used to challenge preconceived notions, show unexpected connections, and call forth the richness and dynamism of existence:

> at the disco we shout the praises of the almighty
> i wrap my arms around you til the end (***boogie woogie landscapes***)

At its least successful, collage can become merely associational, merely automatic: Castro/Santa Claus/Santa Cruz/the True Cross. Its very danger is that the number of possible connections is so very large, virtually infinite, while the number of meaningful connections is much smaller. Despite much critical support over the last 20 years, synchronic techniques such as collage have severe drawbacks as artistic tools. Synchrony can furnish flashes of light but is less effective as a means of developing or sustaining a continuous fire. Thus, for Shange, as for any literary *bricoleur,* the challenge is to fashion and sustain a drama that is not a single narration but a series of conflicts and collisions. Shange's solution has been to balance the potential anarchy of collage with a consistent political purpose.

An element of collage exists even in Shange's main dramatic technique, that of call and response, the monologue delivered against a chorus of voices. The magician lou begins *spell #7* with a bitter pastiche of a minstrel show, posing as Mr. Interlocutor while the rest of the cast is frozen kneeling. The piece is built on a series of monologues interspersed with various forms of group expression. ***boogie woogie landscapes*** is essentially a series of dialogues between layla and six "night-life companions," six aspects of her dreams and memories. As voices collide, so do images from personal history, world history, fashion, and literary and pop culture. In its juxtapositions and emphasis on improvisation, call and response is a dialogistic form of collage.

A crucial distinction must be made here. Shange's collage is not the undirected and autonomous collage of surrealism, but a consciously motivated syncretism with a political agenda. After all, black history, be it African, Caribbean, or American, is characterized by collage and syncretism—just as white history is characterized by the myths of completion, racial unity, and progress. European theatre thus insists on closure, while Afro-American theatre, as projects it, insists on the rough edge, the open, the fragment. The actor alec in *spell #7* recalls the tensions between past and present in his childhood. His family had become "paler" as it moved toward St. Louis, in "linear movement from sous' carolina to missouri/freedmen/landin in jackie wilson's yelp/daughters of the manumitted swimmin' in tina turner's grinds." Here, images of slavery collide with those of pop music. Sechita in *colored girls* combines the black connection with Egypt and her present as a dancer in a Creole carnival in Natchez: "sechita/goddess/of love/egypt/2nd millenium/performin the rites/the conjurin of men/conjurin the spirit/in natchez/the mississippi spewed a heavy fume of barely movin waters." Here the connections emphasize the richness and paradoxes of black history—even as they narrate the bitter experience of black individuals. There are moments in Shange that verge on surrealism, such as when in *boogie woogie landscapes* Fidel Castro is envisioned doing a "revolutionary rhumba" and Jimmy Carter, the Secret Service, Leonid Brezhnev, and the Ayatollah Khomeini are seen dancing on the moon, but even here, the thrust of intention is too strong to overlook. These dignitaries dance on the moon, "all white n barren n free of anybody who looks like me," because they have shown themselves incapable of such spontaneity or rhythm on earth. Carter and Khomeini and Brezhnev are made ridiculous in order to elevate layla, who lacks these men's power but surpasses them in spirit and spontaneity. Conversely, in *colored girls,* ancient Egypt, mystery religions, and the Mississippi are invoked in order to ennoble Sechita, who, while glamorous, is really just a carny dancer avoiding the coins flung between her knees.

Further, Shange's counterorthography—specifically, her rejection of periods and capital letters and her idiosyncratic use of the virgule—allows her collages to be even more abrupt, even more violent, than they would be had they been expressed in standard English orthography. The virgule, after all, is used to show that several alternatives may be appropriate simultaneously: "i waz a peculiar sort of woman/wantin no kisses/no caresses/just power/heat & no eaziness of thrust" (*spell #7*). The proliferation of virgules in Shange shows that alternatives are always present, always in conflict or tension.

Thus, even though collage is an "opening" technique, it is tamed, as it were, by a strong political program. The tendency toward closure (Shange's politics) somehow coexists with the tendency away from it (Shange's technique). In light of that tension, what happens to what many viewers value most in her drama—its content? These are, we must remember, dramatic events that thousands of spectators have *used.* These people attended these pieces because they had heard, expected, or been told that this drama would variously identify, vindicate, and validate them. These works served and are serving a purpose. Accordingly, the intended audience for *colored girls,* for example, considers it a holy thing, an object of reverence. What happens to all that if we consider *colored girls* an open drama? Do we not deny that audience their special access, their special meaning?

As mentioned at the beginning of this essay, Shange's text shows the effort of exclusion. But I have never seen a performance of *colored girls* that singled out any kind of audience. In this way *colored girls* is distinctly democratic. There is plenty of *Publikumsbeschimpfung,* plenty of flaying of the male cock of the walk, plenty of moralism. But in these aspects, *colored girls* is firmly in the tradition of world drama, especially the tradition of the democracy of abuse as described by Bakhtin. Thus, the attacks against unfeeling males, stuck-up white women, the empowered classes, all these attacks that at times seem jejune or schoolgirlish in the text, work splendidly in performance because they establish that democracy of abuse. The characters in Shange's dramas abuse one another as a means of establishing the dignity of each player. One is not allowed dignity until one is dressed down in public—and I cannot think of a more ancient ritual. No one audience is singled out. The women of *colored girls* will speak to anyone who will listen; the singers and dancers of *spell #7* will perform for anyone—"we're doin this for you."

Is the chosen audience then deprived of their chosenness? Have we taken *colored girls* or *spell* or *boogie woogie landscapes* away from a particular group of people— women or blacks or black women—in giving it to whoever has ears and eyes? I don't see how. For one thing, an Afro-American woman wrote these pieces about and for colored girls and third-world people, her chosen audience, and any rights appertaining thereto are of course unimpeachable. The arrival of her work at a particular place and time was felicitous and crucial; it is rightfully valued by those it has helped. But that audience must, I think, take its place among all possible audiences, and its manifold interpretations of the manifold performances of *colored girls* or *spell #7* must take their places among all the other possible interpretations. Shange's most characteristic gesture is, as I have discussed, toward possibility rather than closure; her works evoke the complexity of human relations rather than the completion of given actions or characters. Her women, like her men, are unfinished and fallible and, therefore, worthy.

Shange's work suggests the kind of "canon" one might design for dramatic works. Let us not build a reading zoo and assign each work its cage. Instead, let us have a canon not of texts but of potential performance events. Perhaps we can say that a text of *colored girls* or *spell #7* or *boogie woogie landscapes,* like any script for any play, is just a template from which may be spun off a continuing series of performances. Let us identify pieces with texts that suggest the greatest possibility of variation while retaining an integral character; let us say that such texts make up a group that we cherish. I nominate, not the text, but the unended group of performances indicated by the text of *colored girls* for inclusion into this nonexistent canon. (pp. 91-101)

John Timpane, " 'The Poetry of a Moment': Politics and the Open Form in the Drama of Ntozake Shange," in Studies in American Drama, 1945-Present, *Vol. 4, 1989, pp. 91-101.*

Pinkie Gordon Lane   (review date Fall 1990)

[*In the following review, Lane discusses how* Ridin' the Moon in Texas *departs in style and subject matter from Shange's earlier works.*]

I don't know that I will make the best reviewer of Shange's most recent book [*Ridin' the Moon in Texas*] because I can't just read a page or two of a work and then make a value judgment about its substance. I enter the book, become part of it. It becomes part of me. And then what I believe, what I have experienced become metamorphosed into what I have to say about the book.

And so it is with Ntozake Shange's *Ridin' the Moon in Texas.* This collection of prose and poetry calls forth so many images that the reader will see him/herself in every page. It becomes an exposé of the reader's psyche. Now that's saying a lot for a slender volume that takes "old wine and puts it into new bottles." That is, Shange has employed the technique of using visual art as a takeoff for creating the substance of her verbal images. Thus, the book also contains color reproductions of exciting contemporary art in various media: painting, sculpture, and photography.

But, as the author herself points out, hers are not just descriptions of other artists' works. She has created a "verbal dialogue with . . . [their] works, finding, seeking out what a poet might find in a tapestry, or a sculpture, or a watercolor. . . . I speak to these sculptures, wood prints, and paintings as I would a friend over coffee or champagne. *Ridin' the Moon* is not a visual maze, but a conversation that goes on all night long, when the house shakes and the lights go out." Paintings and poems, she says, "are moments, capturing or seducing us, when we are so vulnerable. These images are metaphors."

Shange's book itself becomes an elaborate, extended metaphor. The title comes from a prose sketch (I will not call it a short story or even prose fiction, if we think of the word *fiction* in the generic sense of having plot structure, situation, and dénouement) inspired by photographer Patricia Ollison Jerrols. This sketch consists entirely of dialogue with no identification of speakers. It could easily have been a transcription of a back-of-the-corral verbal exchange (overheard by the author) between black rodeo cowboys talking about rodeos, horses, and women. However, Shange captures the ambience of the moment so that the disconnected bits of dialogue weave their own "tapestry" and take us into a world that few of us will ever know or experience except vicariously: " 'Listen honey, I'ma see about [a horse named] Dallas. He misses me if I'm gone more than an hour and before a race he just gets beside himself and I gotta snuggle up to him, specially fore I put that bridle through his mouth—.' " Those familiar with Shange's first box office success *for colored girls who have considered suicide/when the rainbow is enuf* will find in *Ridin' the Moon* none of the kind of material which infuriated some black male readers, who regarded the work as denigrating to the black male. In several ways, *Ridin' the Moon* is a departure from her earlier poetry/drama.

These short, disconnected pieces (unlike the earlier, loosely joined narrative) contain lyricism, metaphor, and verbal subtleties (even elitism) that range from the vernacular to the linguistically sophisticated. The book's subjects range from a eulogy for a friend to social criticism. "Somewhere in soweto there's a small girl / she's brown thin & frightened." These lines from **"Who Needs a Heart"** allow us

to experience what it is like living under apartheid in South Africa as seen from the perspective of a black child.

There are poems of love (**"Dream of Pairing"**), introspection (**"Where the Heart Is"**), and nature (**"Wrapping the Wind"**), in which these lines appear:

> the waves leave the dunes sculpted
> momentarily heaving and shifting
> sound across the paths the
> waves thrash . . .

The sheer virtuosity of Shange's subject matter makes this book a significant leap into the world of what it means to be a writer—one capable of deriving inspiration from every nuance of living, of feeling, of absorbing life as a source of material to be transformed into art.

The book rocks, it rolls; but it also soars ethereally, shifting gears with dizzying speed. Breathless in its Joycean stream of consciousness, it just as quickly plummets to mother earth, its choice of style being adapted to the mood and subject.

Shange speaks to the reader who is (forgive me) middle- and upper-middle-brow. Hers is *not* a populist art. Its range is far more visionary, more encompassing. It tries the imagination of the reader as much as the writer. Nor is hers a book for the careless or lazy reader. This is not a book for the reader with a set idea of how one writes a poem or of what the limits of prose fiction should be. This is not a book for the person who is looking for the obvious, the mundane, the hortatory, the didactic, the communal, or all the other clichés that hit and then comfortably slide off a consciousness that avoids verbal challenges or that looks for subject melanism. Such a reader will have to look elsewhere.

Rather this collection of prose and poetry by a black female writer ignores these mandates. As Shange says in her final (love) poem **"New Orleans Nuptials"**:

> speak any language/I'll know what you mean
> look elsewhere/I'll see what you see
> hold me, let me kiss you
> now/we approach heaven.

This volume lets us know Shange. "This is my life," she says, "how I see and, therefore, am able to speak. . . . *Ridin' the Moon in Texas* allowed me this remarkable privilege." (pp. 578-80)

> *Pinkie Gordon Lane, in a review of "Ridin' the Moon in Texas," in* Black American Literature Forum, *Vol. 24, No. 3, Fall, 1990, pp. 578-80.*

Ntozake Shange with Serena Anderlini   (interview date Fall 1991)

[In the following interview, Shange discusses her family background and artistic influences.]

[Anderlini]: You grew up partly in the north and partly in the south, in a family of professionals, who had a racial consciousness and were artistically inclined. Would you like to talk about it?

[Shange]: The neighborhood where we grew up during segregation—as if there wasn't any now!—had Haitians, Nigerians, people from Togo, Jamaica, Panama, Costa Rica, East India, the Philippines and Japan. We all had to live with each other because we couldn't live with the white people: my friends' parents were from countries that were still colonies. When we were almost teen-agers these countries attained so-called independence: we experienced colonial history; my parents told us about it, but it was also all around us.

What about black American history?

My parents used to be called 'race people.' Life was dedicated to the betterment of the race; heroes or achievers of any kind were seen in terms of how they portrayed the race in the eyes of the Anglo, who saw us as 'Sambo.' Black people a generation or two before me found 'Sambo''s images embarrassing—not realizing that maybe that art form was the foundation of what came after. Before the baby-boom—before those of us who were born during world war two and after—'Sambo' types were all there was. There was no respect for black opera singers, for black poets.

Paul Laurence Dunbar is a genius because of his dialect poems; but he was most proud of a sonnet he wrote because that to him meant that he was a poet: he could not accept that his dialect poems were classics, and they would remain so forever. There was so much prejudice and make-believe about black people at that time that the only way he could respect himself as a writer was by writing sonnets; that to me is very painful. I was raised to listen to his dialect poems, and Langston Hughes' and Chuck Berry's. I was raised hearing it and knowing about it.

The people that I come from on my mother's side of the family are called Geechees, from the area that goes from North Carolina to South Georgia. Geechees are very proud and very separate. They have a language, a culture, food, caste and class. You never stop being a Geechee; you never stop being a Carolinian. Immediately after the civil war black south-Carolinians had the highest literacy rate of any slaves following emancipation. Geechees are a very arrogant, insular community; some are blue-black, and some are like me. But they accept that, which seems interesting to me. They speak a language called Gullah, that my grandmother could speak.

Can you describe it?

Gullah is slave-trade language, like Papiamento. There is Portuguese, French, Spanish, English and African. It is the language of the slave traders and Africans, all mixed up together. The syntax is very strange. At least in Gullah and Papiamento—where they are the same—the rhythmic pulses of the sentences are African. But the places of the adjectives, or of the verbs are probably European, although it would be a mixture of, say, three languages.

Do you speak French?

Yes, French, Spanish and Portuguese.

Did you learn French as a child?

Yes. My mother told us that we could go anywhere in the world if we spoke French, which is true particularly in Africa. But I think that in the new world there were enough of us (third-world people, or people of color) to feel a sense of richness and nourishment, and that's why I learned Spanish. More people who were slaves speak Spanish than they speak English. If I wanted to be related to people like me—as opposed to Africans who were not part of the slave trade—I had to learn the foreign languages of the new world. I did that as an adult.

This is related to my identity crisis: the only thing I knew is that I was 'a child of the new world.' There is a propensity among Anglos or Europeans to see us Afro-Americans with some kind of boundaries, and not understand that for a child of the diaspora—which for us is slave trade—there are no national boundaries. I can decide to discuss Chile or to write about Cuba, and I do not feel that I am a 'tourist.' When there are black people, I know how to dance, I know the rhythms, I know the food, I know how to have comradery, and I can talk, and sing.

At what point of your life did you have frictions with your family?

I was embarrassed to be a middle class person at a time when the black proletariat was so active; the black people I was around were having bridge parties. Everybody in New York and Washington was burning down the city!

What were the expectations that your family set on you?

They wanted me to go to a seven sister college, graduate *cum laude,* marry a nice doctor and have five children and a wonderful house; and belong to a wonderful black Civic Group, go to church and raise my kids.

From today's perspective, how do you look back to that rejection of middle-class values?

I owe my parents most of what I am, a sense of value, a sense of responsibility to the race in some sense. Some people might think that I am 'a doctor's daughter,' and I have been privileged, true, but I also know how to get from Little Italy through Little Puerto Rico, to midtown to where the 'niggers' are. By myself. Without getting killed. And somebody said 'I'll give you some credit,' because there is not one scar in my face.

I am part of the same race as my family, but don't do the same things my mother does for 'the race.' I work with the Nicaraguan government in the literacy campaign, and with the *Trabajadores Liberales* in Cuba, Panama and Guatemala. I write things that I would call 'cultural aggression.'

Were you raised in any faith?

I was raised as a Presbyterian, a Congregational and a Unitarian. All of which I rejected as entirely too intellectual. Now I am active as a Methodist Episcopalian, and I also practice Santaria, which is a religion based on Catholic and Yoruban belief systems.

*Speaking about **colored girls**, years ago you said that it was a 'distillation of years of work in common.' What do you think today?*

Shange—The collective effort was that of 20 to 30 feminist writers in the San Francisco Bay area, to remedy and explain, explicate and extrapolate our situation as women. That was the collective effort. The work itself is individual. The stamina and the courage—if there is courage involved in it to tackle issues that might be painful or unattractive—comes from that collective effort, but the work itself is individual. Judy Grahn, Susan Griffin, Sonia Sanchez, Janice Marcantoni, Jessica Hagedorn, we were a collection of black, Asian and native American women working at the same time. We read our works at the same readings. For the most part they were about our own experiences. We gave each other the strength and the environment to do that.

Do you think that a similar situation would be possible today?

It would be impossible today. Those of us who are my age group—in their late thirties—are much more sophisticated than we used to be. We are also involved with families and relationships of some sort, and we are not as available to one another as we used to be. We all used to be single and free. Free to do whatever, and that's no longer true. It is also no longer true that there haven't been great frictions in the feminist movement, between gay women and straight women, for instance. But when I was working there was no such thing. That didn't exist. The literature itself didn't exist: now we have virtually twenty years of it; so the kind of excitement and exuberance and commitment that you could get in 1971 is not necessary right now.

Would you like to talk about the mainstream American public? How would you characterize it?

I am one of these people who have never condescended to an audience, and I have never not had one. I was trained by black poets before I was twenty-one, I was lucky enough to have that. And I know the significance of a national art and popular art. I have never intended to do anything but that, because it wasn't important to me to do anything but that.

You moved out of New York when **colored girls** *became a big commercial success. Did that have to do with some kind of brutality that success in this country entails?*

That's one of the reasons I left. I had to keep doing things I didn't want to do. The people would stop me in a goddamned laundromat to ask me for an autograph. All this had to stop.

When I used to go to writers' workshops we all went there as a jury of peers. Nobody paying any money. Nobody was the teacher. There was no degree. There was criticism, but that was all voluntary and free. I am interested in honest writing and writing that's felt. I worry that an institutional context is an anthitesis to a writer's reality.

Can you describe the difference between theatre and performance art?

I can change performance art when I want to. Before performance theatre we had the same thing every night. The same lines. I don't like that. *[C]olored Girls* was never the same at any reading that I did in California. My character moved every night, and she had more and more things around her. By the last two weeks I was really feeling very accomplished: I knew I had hit some new things.

Doing the same thing every night, that's not an adventure for me. I'd find out how I use my fingers, I'd find out how I held my cigarette. I discovered things.

Is **ridin the moon in texas,** *a performance piece?*

Yes. There is no set, it is not a drama: it's performance art. It defies some theatrical conventions in the sense that we have gone beyond that little story. It is not very long. I don't like to do any more work on it: I like it as it is. If I had to do it as a theatre piece, I'd have to think about relationships with so and so: do this and do that. You've got two women there that are related conceptually and emotionally to the first piece. The first piece is also the refrain of the last piece. So it's all tied together. But it's much more like music to me. It's much more like doing a concerto with four flutes, than it is like theatre. And also I can change it.

Take that out, put this in. And my actors have more freedom, their blocking is not going to determine the success or failure. Performance art is to pull pieces, and put pieces in at will. Which you cannot do in a theatre. And I need that. I need to get back to my own art form.

We are not using a conventional theatre. I know the setting that we are going to use, and I designed the piece for it. We will tape it and we will repeat it, but we will not distribute the tape as a finished product. And I could still decide to change the last piece.

A play has a form that has to be finished. A performance piece has an organic form, but it can even flow. And there doesn't have to be some ultimate climax in it. And there does not have to be a denouement.

And I am much more interested in this because as a writer I can do more with it. Writing plays is very confining.

Do you think that there is a women's culture?

Yes.

What is it?

I don't know, it's ours.

Let's put it this way, do you think that gender is cultural?

Yes, gender is cultural: we have menarche to deal with, virginity, menopause, pregnancy, childbirth; these things are unavoidable. And in some places they've been wise enough to have ritual and ceremony about significant events. It is unfortunate in our culture—meaning north American mainstream culture—that all this has been minimized to the point where little girls are even afraid to say that they are starting to menstruate when they should be very happy. Grown women are afraid to say that they are approaching the menopause, when that means that they have lived a whole successful life. They've lived so long that they can have this.

A whole thrust of feminist mothers and daughters are beginning to change that. We are having menstruation parties for our daughters, and menopause parties for our friends. Another element of our culture is how we take care of those around us. It's a nurturing element that has to do with menstruation, menopause, pregnancy and childbirth. We like to make things for people, we make quilts, dinner, rugs, curtains, bedspreads, plants, altars, things to fill our environment.

A psychologist from Columbia Presbyterian Hospital did a study of bag people, vagabonds, and they discovered that the men would come to one of those refuge houses with nothing. They'd come in there with their clothes in their bags, they eat the soup, they say the prayers, they go to bed. The women come with pictures, altars, crosses, jewelry, little totems of things that they put around. The same little weird thing, and they put it back in their trash-bag and take it to the next place they're going.

How was a woman of color defined when you were becoming a woman, and how do you think that has changed, and how do you think you have contributed to that change?

All I had to do is go to school, keep my virginity and marry a doctor. That was it. Because there have been so many years of writing by women of color, I can give my daughter a book by a black woman writer, by a native American woman or by an Asian American woman that she can read. When we started writing this wasn't there, and so there was an urgency. Right now there is an urgency to things, but not in the literature itself.

What is the urgency?

The urgency now is to deal with more subtle issues, more complex and hidden conflicts between men and women. We can look at how we abuse ourselves, or how we abuse our daughters, or how we neglect men who are trying to help us, or how we abuse them. I think it's more introspective, and more cosmopolitan.

But do you think that before the new feminist movement there had been better times for women?

If they were rich and French and white. If you could be Georgia O'Keeffe, and marry Stieglitz, and then he'd let you go off in New Mexico and paint. On the other hand, there is always Frieda Kahlo, but she didn't do so well, and we had to wait till she would die to figure out that she could paint.

There were many women in the art scene in the twenties, especially here, in this country.

This country was not good for women. Women did something that made this country better. The country did not write the plays, the country did not sign their name at the end of it, the country did not sit up at night revising things. These women did.

There was an opportunity for them to do so.

People 'take' their space. They do things, but nobody 'gives' an opportunity. I just don't believe that. You do things.

In Europe women were in patriarchal companies where the writer was always a man.

But they also did things without signing their names at times: that's why we have *Anonymous was a Woman.* Because there are always things that were written by women . . . and women who signed their names as men. That doesn't mean they didn't do it. It just meant that they didn't sign their names as women. I don't believe that we haven't always struggled. I think that there are periods when there is more strength than at other times. As long as the incidence of rape increases every month, in the United States where these people live, why do I care if they have published twelve more female writers? What difference would that make to me? Women's lives are important, art is important, but what is more important? What women did appears in the text. But the credit is given, say, to Moliére.

And that's not where the credit should go. In this country women signed because the producers could make money. It has nothing to do with us.

Do you feel that there is something called Texan culture?

Yes. We call it the Gulf Coast Art, and it's Hispanic, Creole, Cajun, oil field trash, the newcomers from New York, everybody. Our response to our own land. And one thing about Texas that I like is that they don't talk about the United States here. My daughter asked me was the United States in Texas, that made me feel good. Something more important than this miasma called the United States. I can take you for miles, and you will never see a white person. Texas was covered with trees because the slaves like to have all those trees. All these little towns out here were all plantations. We are around here, we didn't have any place to go.

As Gulf Coast artists, *sabemos que nosotros esperamos de victorias con cultura y armas* (we know that we expect to win by culture and arms), we fight on a dual front, with culture and weapons. Writing is cultural aggression, but it isn't robbing someone. It is getting back something that was ours, our lives, our brains, our dignity. I wrote a performance piece, **Sanctuary;** in Spanish it is called **Donde esta la casa de Dios.** It is bilingual because it is about Anglos and Salvadorans in the Sanctuary movement in southern Texas. A couple of Anglos decide to take in Salvadorans without papers. A Protestant family. There is that sentence in the Scripture that says 'where two or three of you gather, I shall be with thee.' These people are going to say it to the Sheriff and the national Militia that is trying to get the Salvadorans out. They'll say that 'you can't come in here because there are two or three of us gathered.' In south Texas this is a problem: we have people going to jail all the time. They take refugees that our government doesn't recognize as refugees.

You said at one time that you are a third world writer. What do you mean by that?

At a major conference in the Philippines in 1945 Du Bois and some intellectual and political leaders of colonized countries met and they pronounced us the third world. Since world war two was the war for democracy, why were Moroccans fighting for France?

Why were Puerto Ricans, Navahos, Blacks, Filipinos fighting for America? We couldn't vote, we couldn't own land. Fidel Castro, Amilcar Cabran, Ho Chi Minh, Lumumba, Nasser, were all products of that political phenomenon. We said—our races said—'this is it, and from now on either get out or we'll fight you till you do.' That conference has promulgated more revolutions and more changes of attitude toward people of color in the world than anything else I can think of. In 1904 W.E.B. Du Bois wrote that the issue of the twentieth century is the issue of color, and he was right. I happen to be of color, and I have taken my stand on that basis. Hopefully my writing affects that.

Afro-Americans from North America have been so Anglicized that they have been isolated from the entire hemisphere, and that to me is atrocity. My work is now approaching the point where I can't even write in one language. I really truly believe that subliminally language, whether you understand it or not, hits certain nerves, as if somebody touches you, and you feel better, or you feel pain.

I do bilingual or trilingual work, I am trying to get to that point where the force of the language itself will move you. Not the dictionary explanation of what this word means, but simply the force of the language itself. If in fact, as the Bible says, in the beginning there was the word, that means that as a writer I can be anywhere. There is power in simple sound, language is no more than sounds that we give meaning to. We don't have to have a literal translation: if we do then there is something wrong. In poetry and opera I think that it is so.

Don't you suffer when you write?

I wrote a piece for an actor who died of AIDS, and for a sculptor who was murdered by her husband. That wasn't easy to do: it is not even easy to talk about it. But it is all I could give them: they can live in literature, somebody might not forget them.

Imagination allows us to feel and express those things that might destroy us in any other form. If we couldn't write, if we couldn't sculpt, if we couldn't play music, we might kill somebody. I'd rather weep over a piece of paper and have to retrace over the letters, than have gone out and killed somebody.

In the European sense I think I am a romantic poet: I don't think I know where my lines come from, I don't claim all the rights to them, and I do feel myself as a medium sometimes—beyond me. I think that the unconscious—which sometimes expresses itself through artists—is a medium of other spirits—of other deities: to let us have things that we can't have rationally.

People who read are dealing with themselves: our responsibility is to write something that somebody can take and have it in their life. As long as any reader remembers a character, or a line from something that I wrote then I did enough of that, that's my job.

There are three political movements to which I am really committed and act within. That's the activity against South Africa, active support for Nicaragua, and active support for Swapo in Namibia. But I am not conversant in those cultures. I know what I am talking about when I talk about white Protestants in south Texas and Salvadorans. I know the decisions and the legal system involved here; I know how to verbalize or articulate the desires of the refugees: they lived with me so I know this. When I say that I am 'a child of the new world' this is what I mean. I could travel from Houston to Panama City or Santiago, and wherever I meet people of color, there is never any discrepancy of thought.

There is no reason to be afraid of one another. The Sanctuary piece gave me an opportunity to say that. I was the first Afro-American Anglo to be included in a Latin American Theatre Festival. In 1979 at the Public Theatre in New York. My work is not about Anglos, it's about the western hemisphere. The Europeans came here to conquer paradise, the Africans were dragged here to work, the native Americans had paradise. We are all here now, let's do something with it. Let's make this something.

But you write in English, the language that has been inherited from the colonizer. How do you feel about that?

'We must kill the King's English,' that's Judy Grahn's line. And forge the new language of the hemisphere. The name of America has been imposed and appropriated. Limited to white English speaking Americans. Who the hell do they think lives here? California is two-thirds third world, and so is Texas and New York.

How is your work received in other American countries?

I have been published in Nicaragua. I gave all my publishing rights for Latin America to the Sandinista government. I have been produced in Portuguese in Sao Paulo and Rio de Janeiro, with Brazilian actresses, who would call themselves people of color.

Do you think that there is a reverse racism? Perhaps that complicity you were describing . . .

My job is to take care of my people. If seventeen blacks from the gang called the Mummers in Los Angeles irrupted in here doing this little step they do when they go out together, the separation would immediately happen: I would be them. And I would be them with no shame.

Does this complicity also happen with women?

Yes, I think so. For me it does. (pp. 86-96)

> *Ntozake Shange and Serena Anderlini, in an interview* in Journal of Dramatic Theory and Criticism, *Vol. VI, No. 1, Fall, 1991, pp. 85-97.*

FURTHER READING

Criticism

Murray, Timothy. "Screening the Camera's Eye: Black and White Confrontations of Technological Representation." *Modern Drama* XXVIII, No. 1 (March 1985): 110-24.
    Uses works by Shange and other African-American

playwrights to explore "how the complexity of technological confrontation is developed with particular care and concern by Black American theatre."

Interviews

Lester, Neal A. "At the Heart of Shange's Feminism: An Interview." *Black American Literature Forum* 24, No. 4 (Winter 1990): 717-30.

> Text of an August 1986 interview focusing on Shange's views on feminism and relationships between men and women.

———. "An Interview with Ntozake Shange." *Studies in American Drama* 5 (1990): 42-66.

> Primarily focuses on Shange's use of language.

Additional coverage of Shange's life and career is contained in the following sources published by Gale Research: *Black Literature Criticism,* Vol. 3; *Black Writers; Contemporary Authors,* Vols. 85-88; *Contemporary Authors Bibliographical Series,* Vol. 3; *Contemporary Authors New Revision Series,* Vol. 27; *Contemporary Literary Criticism,* Vols. 8, 25, 38; *Dictionary of Literary Biography,* Vol. 38; and *Major 20th-Century Writers.*

Leslie Marmon Silko

1948-

American novelist, poet, and short story writer.

The following entry presents recent criticism on Silko's works. For further information on her career, see *CLC*, Volume 23.

INTRODUCTION

Silko is considered among the foremost authors to emerge from the Native American literary renaissance of the 1970s. In her works she blends such western literary forms as the novel and the short story with the oral traditions of her Laguna Pueblo heritage to communicate Native American concepts concerning time, nature, and spirituality and their relevance in the contemporary world. Her protagonists, often of mixed Laguna and Anglo heritage, must draw upon the moral strength of their native community and its traditions in order to overcome the often repressive, alienating effects of white society.

Of Laguna Pueblo, Plains Indian, Mexican, and Anglo-American descent, Silko was born in Albuquerque and raised on the Laguna Pueblo Reservation in northern New Mexico. As a child she attended schools administered by the Bureau of Indian Affairs and learned about Laguna legends and traditions from her great-grandmother and other members of her extended family. She graduated magna cum laude from the University of New Mexico in 1969 and briefly attended law school before deciding to pursue a writing career. In addition to working on her fiction, Silko has taught at several universities and colleges throughout the Southwest.

Silko's first novel, *Ceremony,* interweaves free-verse poetry and narrative prose. The story is set primarily in the years following World War II and revolves around Tayo, a veteran of mixed white and Languna heritage who returns to the reservation shattered by his war experiences. He ultimately finds healing, however, with the help of Betonie, an elderly man who, like Tayo, is an outcast from Laguna society due to his Anglo heritage, and T'seh Montaño, a medicine woman who embodies the feminine, life-giving aspects of the earth. Through them, Tayo learns that his community's ancient ceremonies are not merely rituals, but a means of achieving a proper place in the universe. To underscore this concept, Silko incorporates Laguna myths and historical incidents to reflect the Pueblo's abiding connection to the natural world, which counteracts the despair and alienation engendered by much of white society. Critics applauded *Ceremony,* echoing Frank McShane's estimation that the novel "is one of the most realized works of fiction devoted to Indian life that has been written in this country, and it is a splendid achievement."

Silko's next work, *Storyteller,* comprises poems from her earlier collection *Laguna Woman,* short stories, anecdotes, folktales, historical and autobiographical notes, and photographs. According to Bernard A. Hirsch, "this multigeneric work lovingly maps the fertile storytelling ground from which [Silko's] art evolves and to which it is here returned—an offering to the oral tradition which nurtured it." One story, "Yellow Woman," is based upon traditional abduction tales in which a kachina, or mountain spirit, kidnaps and seduces a young woman on her way to draw water. In Silko's version, a contemporary Pueblo woman realizes that her liaison with a cattle rustler is in fact a reenactment of the "yellow woman" legend. The boundary between her experience and the myth gradually dissolves as she becomes aware of her active role in the traditions of her community. Upon returning to her family, she hopes that the story of her affair will be passed on as a new episode in the visionary drama kept alive by oral traditions.

In *The Almanac of the Dead* Silko presents an apocalyptic vision of North America in which Native Americans reclaim their ancestral lands after whites, lacking the spiritual and moral force of the Indian world, succumb to crime, perversion, drug addiction, and environmental degradation. Some critics have objected to what they perceived as Silko's exaggerated portrait of corruption in Anglo-American society. Malcolm Jones, Jr., for example, observed that "in [Silko's] cosmology, there are good people and there are white people." However, most commentators have praised Silko's vivid characterizations and inventive plot, contending that while *The Almanac of the Dead* may perturb some white readers, it is a compelling portrait of a society founded upon the eradication of Native Americans and their cultures.

PRINCIPAL WORKS

Laguna Woman: Poems (poetry) 1974
Ceremony (novel) 1977
Storyteller (poems and short stories) 1981
The Almanac of the Dead (novel) 1992

CRITICISM

Per Seyersted (essay date 1980)

[*Seyersted is a professor of American literature at the University of Oslo in Norway. In the following excerpt, he discusses the main themes of Silko's novel,* Ceremony.]

Silko has said that in Alaska, far away from her own Southwest, she was depressed, and that for a time, writing was therapy for her, a way to stay sane with "the one thing that I had that was like a familiar friend" (*Persona*, 1980). One day she started a short story which in time grew into *Ceremony,* a book about a Laguna World War II veteran's quest for sanity, and she makes him achieve it through reopening the lifeline to the constructive elements in his roots.

When the book was published, the dustjacket was provided with this statement by Silko:

> This novel is essentially about the powers inherent in the process of storytelling. . . . The chanting or telling of ancient stories to effect certain cures or protect from illness and harm have always been part of the Pueblo's curing ceremonies. I feel the power that the stories still have to bring us together, especially when there is loss and grief. My book tells the story of an Indian family, but it is also involved with the search for a ceremony to deal with despair, the most virulent of all diseases—the despair which accounts for the suicide, the alcoholism, and the violence which occur in so many Indian communities today.

These dark aspects of modern Indian life are certainly seen in this book, especially in the younger reservation people who are most exposed to the outside influence. Silko does not soften the bitterness they feel at having been robbed by the whites of their land and at being treated in general as second-class citizens, and she makes us very much aware of the suffering among Navajos and other Indians who end up as alcoholics or prostitutes in the bars and back alleys of Gallup.

Worst off in a sense are those who for a time had been in a way integrated into the main society, the veterans who had been praised as patriotic Americans, only to be demoted to their previous status. Trying to drown their bitterness, they use their disability checks to get drunk in the bars just outside the reservation line on Route 66. Harley, Leroy, and Emo—all with Purple Hearts from Wake Island—sit in Dixie Tavern, bragging of the white women they had had; telling themselves that they had been the best soldiers in the US Army, they curse the Anglos whose war they had fought and who had "taken everything," while acting out this rage in violence among themselves.

When Tayo, the main character, is also filled with despair, the reason is not so much that he hates the whites as that he cannot accept himself. Born of an unknown white father and a mother with whom he had lived for some years among the Gallup prostitutes, he had been given by her to her sister in Laguna, and she had made it clear to him that his mother's lightfootedness was a disgrace to the family and that he is inferior to her son Rocky. Auntie encourages Rocky's plans to become a football star in the white world, whereas Tayo's duty is to help his uncle Josiah with his cattle.

However, flattered when Rocky calls him "brother" and wants him with him in the Army, he enlists, too, whereupon Auntie gives him the task of looking after his cousin. But he cannot prevent Rocky from being killed beside him in the Pacific, and when they are ordered to fire on some Japanese prisoners, he believes that one of them is Josiah and that he is responsible for his death as well, even though he did not pull the trigger. This extreme self-condemnation causes him to break down, and during a long stay in a veterans' hospital he survived by withdrawing from himself into what he believes is invisibility. Finally returning to his pueblo after six years, he blames himself for having survived, and also for the drought which has plagued Laguna since his uncle died and for the loss of the cattle which had run away. No longer caring whether he lives or dies, he one day nearly kills Emo. When the Laguna medicine man Ku'oosh, called in by old Grandma, unsuccessfully has given him the Scalp Ceremony, he is sent on to another medicine man, the Navajo Betonie who lives near Gallup.

The position of a medicine man is a very respected one. As Geary Hobson notes (*The Remembered Earth*), not only does it take decades to become a medicine maker, but "He or she must have confirmation of the community, a great sense of the community, a profound knowledge of animals and plants, a knowledge of pain and suffering, and a sense of power that can be found only in adherence to the old things." While tradition is important, this does not mean that the medicine of, for example, the Navajo holy

men is one and static: at Chinle, Silko found that it is manifold and developing. She reflects this in Betonie, who is
even more "progressive" than others in that, having traveled and gone to school in the white world, he adjusts to
the changes around him and keeps samples of white culture in his hogan alongside the traditional paraphernalia.

Given the fact that in Native American thought, the natural state of existence is seen as whole, we can understand
that, as Allen has reminded us (*Literature of the American
Indians*) "healing chants and ceremonies emphasize restoration of wholeness, for disease is a condition of division
and separation from the harmony of the whole. Beauty is
wholeness. Health is wholeness. Goodness is wholeness.
A witch—a person who uses the powers of the universe
in a perverse or inharmonious way—is called a two-hearts:
one who is not whole but split in two at the center of
being." No wonder that the circle or the hoop is an important symbol with Indians.

While Betonie does give Tayo traditional ceremonies, he
wins his confidence by encouraging him to speak of his Pacific experiences, suggesting that the reason he saw Josiah
in one of the Japanese was that 30,000 years ago they were
no strangers. Tayo also talks about the fact of his origin,
which Betonie can sympathize with since he is a mixed
breed himself. What he is giving Tayo is less a cure than
a recipe for a self-cure: while the white doctors' medicine
had drained memory out of him, Betonie tells him to accept the fact that things are complicated and look into
himself and remember everything.

This approach to healing does not imply a modern emphasis on the individual, however:

> There was something large and terrifying in the
> old man's words. He wanted to yell at the medi-
> cine man, to yell the things the white doctors
> had yelled at him—that he had to think only of
> himself, and not about the others, that he would
> never get well as he used words like "we" and
> "us." But he had known the answer all along,
> even while the white doctors were telling him he
> could get well and he was trying to believe them:
> medicine didn't work that way, because the
> world didn't work that way. His sickness was
> only part of something larger, and his cure
> would be found only in something great and in-
> clusive of everything.

This means that he is beginning to grasp what Betonie is
suggesting to him: that he is part of an unending history,
of a pueblo community now influenced by another, greater
community, of a set of constructive and destructive forces,
and that in order to achieve wholeness, he has to accept
the fact that things are complex and not static. As Betonie
says, "There are balances and harmonies always shifting,
always necessary to maintain. . . . It is a matter of transitions, you see; the changing, the becoming must be cared
for closely. You would do as much for the seedlings as
they become plants in the field."

Betonie also says that in order to achieve a balance the Indians should not look upon themselves as helpless, blaming all witchery—the destructive forces—on the whites:
" 'Nothing is that simple,' he said, 'you don't write off all

the white people, just like you don't trust all the Indians'."
And to bring home to him the idea that they *can* master
their own fates and "deal" with white people, with their
machines and their beliefs," he presents Tayo with a serio-
comic story or chant relating how the Indians had *invented* the whites. While most of the many other interspersed
mythic chants are Laguna originals, this one is more or
less made up by Silko. With this song Betonie sends Tayo
on his way to look for the cattle, telling him to keep in
mind the constellation of the stars which had appeared in
a sandpainting made for him.

Tayo's search for the cattle is a way of showing his worth
by repaying Josiah, and the encounters it leads him to with
a woman and a mountain both mark steps in his cure. The
meeting with Ts'eh is meaningful not only because she
loves him, but especially because he is able to love her. He
who had been kept at a distance by Auntie and who believed it had to be that way, now experiences a warm, almost wordless closeness which opens him emotionally and
makes him realize that he *was* indeed loved by his mother
and uncle, just as he loves them. When Tayo later meets
Ts'eh at the spring, she leads him further towards the natural when she shows him the marvels of things that grow.

Tayo's encounters with Ts'eh (and her companion, the
hunter) are both real and unreal. There is a dreamlike
quality about their tender meetings: she seems to know
about him without asking; she has the paraphernalia of a
medicine woman; and in short, she has many of the qualities of Spiderwoman, the Mother who also created the
land. When they make love at the spring she seems to be
merged with it: "he felt her body, and it was warm as the
sand, and he couldn't feel where her body ended and the
sand began."

This re-opening of Tayo's lifeline to nature is further advanced on Pa'to'ch, the high mesa where he finally finds
the cattle. When his horse stumbles and he lies on the
ground, he knows that "the dark earth loved him" and
that it is up to him to join it: "The magnetism of the center
spread over him. . . . It was pulling him back, close to
the earth, . . . and even with the noise and pain in his
head he knew how it would be: a returning rather than a
separation." The mountain becomes a metaphor for love
and also for the land. When Ts'eh looks at Pa'to'ch, Tayo
"could feel where she had come from, and he understood
where she would always be."

After the final encounter with Ts'eh, Tayo knows he has
to enter the normal world. He is aware that his friends are
after him (they cannot accept a half-breed who will not
join in their self-deceiving bragging), and he realizes he
has to face them. Before doing so, he watches the sunrise
at Enchanted Mesa, the famous landmark between Acoma
and Laguna:

> All things seemed to converge there: roads and
> wagon trails, canyons with springs, cliff paint-
> ings and shrines, the memory of Josiah with his
> cattle; . . . it was all so beautiful, everything,
> from all directions, evenly perfectly, balancing
> day with night, summer months with winter.
> The valley was enclosing this totality, like the
> mind holding all thoughts together in a single

moment. The strength came from here, from this feeling. It had always been there.

Given the fact of Silko's extensive use of Pueblo myths, including the one of Creation, one might guess that when it is Enchanted Mesa she lets Tayo see as a center where all things converge, this is related to the near-religious significance of this gigantic rock and the meaning of its Keresan name (Katsi'ma), which is "he who stands in the door" (John M. Gunn, *Schat-Chen*): she may well see this door as the one leading from our fifth world to the worlds of origin below. In any case, there is a remarkable juxtaposition in the book of this Pueblo sanctuary (and that of Mt. Taylor) and the opening-place for the white man's new technological era, Trinity Site, with its Christian connotations.

Indeed, as can hardly surprise, central in the novel is the opposition between traditional Pueblo ways and beliefs and those of Christianity, or rather, the influence of the new on the old. While the ancients "had known, with the simple certainty of the world they saw, how everything should be," the world had become entangled with the advent of the Europeans. "Christianity separated the people from themselves; it tried to crush the single clan name, encouraging each person to stand alone, because Jesus Christ would save only the individual soul; Jesus Christ was not like the Mother who loved and cared for them as her children, as her family." The clearest example here is Auntie, a "devout Christian" who wants to prove that, "above all else, she was a Christian woman"; that is, because she is ruled by narrow Christian moral norms, she is inordinately upset by the disgrace reflected upon her by her relatives and forgets the clan idea of keeping the group together and helping everyone.

It is significant that Auntie (in connection with Rocky) thinks in terms of "success." a concept which focuses on what is happening to the world of the Pueblos: whereas their emphasis had been on cultivation and conservation, on making things grow, the whites—ruled by their ideas of "progress" and "development"—carried out an exploitation of the land and its resources, leaving dumps behind them when other places became more profitable.

This development is also upsetting for the whites: if witches are defined as destroyers and witchery as de- rather than con-structive forces, then the whites certainly demonstrate such powers, to the point that they can now destroy the world. Silko's emphasis, however, is more on what they are doing to the Pueblos: some blame the Anglos for their ills, and others blame themselves for not being whites, and in both instances, it leads to dissatisfaction and isolation, also among the Indians themselves. Another fact is also crucial to the author: Pueblos should remember that at the emergence from Shibapu, all were given both positive and negative qualities. That is, there is some good in the whites and some bad in themselves. In other words, they should return to the balanced views they have always had, and in general remember all their old wisdom, which also included the knowledge that as things grow, they also change. In this way, they can regain the old wholeness and "the feeling people have for each other" and get rid of some of the witches, at least those now intending to kill Tayo.

When his friends have taken him to an abandoned uranium mine, he manages to hide behind some boulders, but when they torture the one he thought was his real friend, he is tempted to come forward and attack them. Just in time he recalls Ts'eh's warning that "they"—presumably all not possessing Pueblo wisdom—want to end his story, and he has the strength not to join in this Indian self-destruction. He has reached the end of his ceremony, and he can tell the holy men in the kiva what he has learned: "He cried the relief he felt at finally seeing the pattern, the way all the stories fit together—the old stories, the war stories, their stories—to become the story that was still being told. He was not crazy; he had never been crazy. He had only seen and heard the world as it always was: no boundaries, only transitions through all distances and time."

The last to speak in the book is old Grandma: " 'I guess I must be getting old,' she said, 'because these goings-on around Laguna don't get me excited any more. . . . It seems like I already heard these stories before . . . only thing is, the names sound different'." This passage suggests the author's rationale for including the many myths in the book. The old stories contain the truth, the old verities about universal emotions and experiences. In other words, the message to all of us is that there are no boundaries, in the sense that life is repetition of what has gone before. Furthermore, you should treasure the store of traditional material handed down to you, partly because it is an integral element of your identity, partly because it ties you more intimately to the land that is yours. In this sense, stories insure survival.

Ceremony, then, is a very ambitious book: like the 4,000-year-old *Gilgamesh* or the Biblical myths, it in a sense wants to cover all men and all time. It is very rich in themes and imagery. It is complicated in that the author repeatedly goes back and forth in time. She also splits up some of the stories, especially the central myth of the Ck'o'yo medicine man. At the same time, spread over the whole book, this myth of a witch fooling with magic significantly contributes to the structure of the novel, just as it perfectly suggests an important theme: looking at this newcomer's tricks, the locals become "so busy / playing around with that / Ck'o'yo magic / they neglected the mother corn altar," with the result that "Our mother / Nau'ts'ity'i / was very angry" and "took the / rainclouds with her." At the end of the novel, Tayo has learned enough about nuclear tricks to know that his road is to go and gather pollen, the source of growth.

Not everything is equally good in the book, but this was perhaps inevitable in such a complex first novel. Occasionally there are passages or scenes which seem contrived, and in certain descriptions of what the whites have done, Silko's expression comes closer to that of the activist than we would expect. But on the whole, it is a very successful book. In most cases her characterizations are excellent, and she is just as good with men as with women. She is a master in evoking the landscape and describing animals. In most parts of the novel there is an impressive verve and drive. She clearly masters the old lore and interweaves it very effectively with the main story. As Robert Sayre has said (ASAIL *Newsletter,* Spring 1978), to the three elements of the Indian experience—myth, history, and realism—Silko has added the "world of romance, . . . the necessary fourth world where the other three could be mixed and transfigured, transcended," showing "a willingness to accept it, not as real but as a unifying ideal." In sum, the book is a remarkable achievement. (pp. 25-34)

Per Seyersted, in his Leslie Marmon Silko, *Boise State University, 1980, 50 p.*

Silko on *Ceremony:*

This novel is essentially about the powers inherent in the process of storytelling. . . . The chanting or telling of ancient stories to effect certain cures or protect from illness and harm have always been part of the Pueblo's curing ceremonies. I feel the power that the stories still have to bring us together, especially when there is loss and grief. My book tells the story of an Indian family, but it is also involved with the search for a ceremony to deal with despair, the most virulent of all diseases—the despair which accounts for the suicide, the alcoholism, and the violence which occur in so many Indian communities today.

—*Leslie Marmon Silko, on the dustjacket of* Ceremony, *Viking, 1977.*

Jim Ruppert   (essay date Spring 1981)

[*In the following essay, Ruppert focuses on the intermingling of reality and myth in Silko's works.*]

Leslie Silko as a contemporary writer and a Laguna brings a new perception to the effort to topple [the boundaries of fiction], or rather an old one, older than American Literature. Her short fiction and her novel ***Ceremony*** are illuminated by the assumption that the story has a greater, truer reality than the objective reality of the world around us. In the story reality, the seeming simplicity and reality of objective actions and reinterpreted and woven into a larger scheme through which the actions take on a new and deeper meaning and their place in a mythic pattern emerges. The characters and the readers must believe as much as the author that the world exists in story which gives objective reality its meaning, or they are lost. Although the story may be stretched over eons, although it may move slowly and our understanding of it come only with great difficulty, we can understand it; we can enter into the story reality. Despite the hardships and the violent wrenchings of perspective required to do this, the attempt is necessary because it is only through entry into the story reality that each character is given his/her identity and perhaps ultimately so are we, the readers.

The **"Yellow Woman"** is an excellent example of the larger, all-encompassing reality of the story through which individual objective actions are reinterpreted and given new meaning. The contemporary girl by the river is incorporated into the traditional mythic Laguna story. In the Laguna story, Yellow Woman is near the river where she is surprised by a mountain spirit. The mountain spirit seduces her, and they go through a series of interesting adventures before she returns home, rather reluctantly to her husband and relatives. The original Yellow Woman of the Laguna tale is aware of the inevitability of her actions; it has been ordained since time immemorial. In Silko's story, a young girl is seduced by the river and swept away by someone who says he is a mountain spirit. She feels that an old Laguna story is patterning the encounter. The girl becomes confused and uncertain about her identity; is she the person she always thought she was, the one living in an objective mundane reality, or is she becoming Yellow Woman of the stories? She struggles to affirm that she is a girl with her own name and a family, to establish time boundaries and boundaries between objective reality and myths. "I don't have to go," she says to the man. "What they tell in stories was real only then, back in time immemorial, like they say." As she goes off with the mountain spirit man, she cries that if only she might see someone who knew her, who could place her in the objective reality, she would be sure of her identity. "I will see someone, and then I will be certain that he is only a man—some man from nearby—and I will be sure I am not Yellow Woman." But the reality of the story triumphs and following the Laguna story, she runs off with the man. She is seduced into the story and goes off into the mountains where time seems to matter little and where she sees the larger pattern. When she leaves her husband, a new meaning is given it, and on the mountain she sees the larger patterns of living: in her own words, she can see "the world."

The girl's merging into the story seems to occur in part because it is ordained (a fortuitous collection of particulars), but more important the girl projects the proper psychic framework of a balanced being, while she is wondering if Yellow Woman herself had a sense of a separate identity or knew she was to become a story. The girl at this time is able to live totally in the present, in the story flow. "This is the way it happens in the stories, I was thinking with no thought beyond the moment she meets the Ka'tsina spirit and they go." At this time, the girl is thinking about her identity, not about the past or the future, for identity, as all existentialists know, reveals a child of the present moment. As if understanding the girl's thoughts and anticipation of her words, the mountain spirit man says, "What happened yesterday has nothing to do with what you will do today, Yellow Woman." Her description of her departure emphasizes the power of the story and her non-willful entering into it. "They the girl's family will go on like before, except there will be a story about the day I disappeared while I was walking along the river. Silva had come for me; he said he had. I did not decide to go. I just went. Moonflowers blossom in the sand hills before dawn, just as I followed him." When she finally returns home, according to the traditional story pattern, she speaks of "my story" and wishes that old grandpa was still alive because, as a storyteller, he would understand the identity the story gave her. In an interview in *Suntracks,* Silko explains this function of stories in oral traditions.

That's how you know, that's how you belong,

that's how you know you belong, if the stories incorporate you into them. There have to be stories. It's stories that make this a community. People tell those stories about you and your family or about others and they begin to create your identity. In a sense, you are told who you are, or you know who you are by the stories that are told about you.

In **"Tony's Story,"** Tony's action in killing the cop is similar to the girl's entrance into her story. Tony does not kill in a conscious, premeditated manner. "The shot sounded far away and I couldn't remember aiming." Tony has the knowledge of story reality throughout the piece, but it is only at the moment of the killing that he himself enters story reality. The ceremonial burning and the gathering rain clouds make Tony's story subsume the newspaper reality of the killing. The identity of the culture hero evil-slayer and the destroyer/witch is determined by the story, and Silko would have us believe that these identities are more true and real than explanations of objective reality.

In **"Storyteller"** the reality of the story and the individual's identity are woven together into one story reality that patterns all others. The girl's revenge, the bear's revenge on the hunter, and the land's revenge on the Gussucks lose their separateness and merge at the end of the story. In the beginning, the girl is ignorant of her identity. The old storyteller begins a long story of the hunter and the bear designed to explain and ease the approach of the "final winter" and the killing cold. As the girl outlines her own story, she listens more closely to the old man's story. They seem to coincide. She knows that the larger story, the one of the coming of the final winter, of the final retribution, will soon be completed.

> Somewhere the sea and land met; she knew by their dark green colors there would be no boundaries between them. That was how the cold would come: when the boundaries were gone, the polar ice would range across the land into the sky.

Just as the land and sky will lose their boundaries, so too the girl loses the boundaries between objective reality and the story, between the present flow of the story and ideas of the past and future—all will be the story. When she runs out on the ice, she enters the story reality of no boundaries. She has no identity and doesn't know where she is. Finally, she recognizes the red tin, part of the story of her parents. Before this recognition, the story cold have ended incorrectly, but now she is guided by the story pattern and no longer confused by the dissolution of the boundaries. She is saved, and the storekeeper dies. After this, she has an identity, not only that of storyteller in the community, but also an identity created by the all-inclusive story of the destruction of the Gussucks.

What I think we see in Silko's short fiction is that the story has a greater reality than objective reality, and that this story reality can be entered by placing ourselves in proximity to the story and acting with no thought beyond the moment so as to enter the story. In story reality, we assume an identity meaningful not only for ourselves, but also for the community that lives through the story. Perhaps this all becomes clearer if we turn now to *Ceremony.*

When Tayo returns from the war, he is sick, sick in much the same way his people are sick, and the world is sick through the influence of the manipulators. We are soon made to understand through old Betonie that "his sickness was only part of something larger, and his cure would be found only in something greater and inclusive of everything." His cure will be long, slow and difficult like the telling of the story itself, but it can be of great benefit to the people, for his story will be merged with the larger one of the destroyers and the people. Or as Silko concludes, "In the novel, it's the struggle between the force and the counter-force."

If we agree that Tayo enters story reality in the novel, we may be tempted to say that it is through old Betonie's ceremony that he does so and hence the name of the novel. But near the end of the story, as the pattern and the proper ending is working itself out in the person of Tayo, Ts'eh, the mysterious mountain woman, observes that the Destroyers:

> Work to see how much can be lost, how much can be forgotten. They destroy the feeling people have for each other.

Tayo revives his hurt and the deaths of Rocky and Josiah, and she continues:

> Their highest ambition is to gut human beings while they are still breathing, to hold the heart still beating so the victim will never feel anything again. When they finish, you watch yourself from a distance and you can't even cry—not even for yourself.

This is the very sickness that has affected Tayo. His gutted feelings have been stimulated by Betonie, but it is not until the love of Ts'eh, the story woman of the mountains, that he is able to feel, to give himself to the flow of the story with no thought beyond the moment. At this point, he understands the larger story because he has entered it, as well as something of the false endings that the manipulators are trying to push on him. Through love, the boundaries dissolve between story-beings and real people, between the story as a true ongoing reality and our distinctions of time. As Leslie Silko puts it, "One of the large battles Tayo begins to have to deal with is to keep the end of the story right. They're trying to manipulate him into doing something that would change the way the story has to go. It goes back to the ceremony thing that started long ago, and, of course, it does on and on."

As Tayo struggles to conclude the story and the ceremony, the only honing device he has is the "feeling of the story" that he has received from Ts'eh and Betonie. With this to guide him, Tayo sees the world, its peoples and cultures as one huge swirling sandpainting and all the peoples of the world as one clan that must unite ceremonially to defeat the fate the destroyers have planned for mankind. "Towards the end, everything Tayo sees is what Arrow Boy saw, but in a different century and a different form. It's there, it almost has to be. There's just no way around it."

Tayo's identity comes from this understanding of the story's reality. He may be a savior or just a facilitator, but he must contribute his part to the ceremony. His strength at the end of the novel comes from this understanding. When he returns to the village, the old men understand the story. They want to know about the story woman he met in the mountains, and they conclude that they will be blessed again because he has seen her. His communal identity is secured because he is the one who has seen the woman in the mountains, who has brought the blessing, who has entered the story. They purify him, and the story has ended correctly. He is ready to gather the story-woman's seeds and to plant them as he promised. He has found himself.

However, when we put the book down, another important question can be asked. Has the reader understood the story? Has he entered the story reality? If the reader has, then he has an identity determined by the story either as a victim, a manipulator, or one of the aware people who must unite to defeat the destroyers. Let's hope we can all get the ending right.

It may be commonplace to say that Silko's work attempts to introduce dimensions of oral literature into written literature, and seeks a unification of the two in a new reality or a better explanation of the ordinary one, but her work at once stands out from modern fiction because of it and blends with it.

Of course, modern writers have injected and explored the mythic dimension in their works, but normally it has been in the creation of personal myths as with Yeats, the re-emergence of mythic patterns as structural aides to meaning as in Joyce and Lawrence, or the expose and potential salvation of a disintegrated culture as with Eliot. In the development of contemporary fiction, "self-conscious" fiction struggles to incorporate the consciousness of the writer writing the story into the story, thus creating a myth of the writer. The result is that fiction and reality merge into one sphere. Silko, while having a different mission in inviting the story reality into what appears to be a non-story world, picks up the thrust of contemporary art toward an understanding of performance. The telling of the story creates a reality that merges with the non-story reality. The storyteller functions as a catalyst and an intersection for the merger of story reality and objective reality. The performance of the story becomes part of the story and though we do not feel the presence of Silko herself, the result is the same—a vision of the world as a unity of fiction and reality. More specifically in *Ceremony,* the unity is of the non-story world and the reality of the story-in-the-making. This is in effect a self-consciousness of oral literature. The story is being performed, and created. It is the material for future legends and the archetype for future tellings; the world and the story have been welded together. (pp. 53-7)

Jim Ruppert, "Story Telling: The Fiction of Leslie Silko," in The *Journal of Ethnic Studies, Vol. 9, No. 1, Spring, 1981, pp. 53-8.*

Paula Gunn Allen (essay date 1983)

[*Allen is a Native American poet and critic of Laguna and Sioux heritage. Her influential studies of Native American women and their mythic, historical, and literary traditions include* The Sacred Hoop: Recovering the Feminine in American Indian Tradition *(1986). In the following excerpt from* Studies in American Indian Literature: Critical Essays and Course Designs, *which she edited, Allen separates Silko's female characters into two categories: those who serve the earth's spirit and those who wish to destroy it.*]

There are two kinds of women and two kinds of men in Leslie Marmon Silko's *Ceremony.* The figures of Laura, Night Swan, Grandmother, Betonie's Grandmother, and Ts'eh represent one kind of woman, while to some extent Auntie, Betonie's grandfather's wives, and grandfather's mother represent the other. Josiah, the Mountain Spirit, Betonie's grandfather, Ku'oosh, Betonie, Robert, and Tayo represent a kind of man associated with the first category of women, while Rocky, Emo, Pinky, Harley, and the witches represent men associated with the second. Those in the first category belong to the earth spirit and live in harmony with her, even though this attunement may lead to tragedy; those in the second are not of the earth but of human mechanism; they live to destroy that spirit, to enclose and enwrap it in their machinations, condemning all to a living death. Ts'eh is the matrix, the creative and life restoring power, and those who cooperate with her designs serve her and, through her, serve life. They make manifest that which she thinks. The others serve the witchery; they are essentially inimical to all that lives, creates, and nurtures.

While *Ceremony* is ostensibly a tale about a man, Tayo, it is as much and more a tale of two forces: the feminine life force of the universe and the mechanistic death force of the witchery. And Ts'eh is the central character of the drama of this ancient battle as it is played out in contemporary times.

We are the land, and the land is mother to us all. There is not a symbol in the tale that is not in some way connected with womanness, that does not in some way relate back to Ts'eh and through her to the universal feminine principle of creation: Ts'its'tsi'nako, Thought Woman, Grandmother Spider, Old Spider Woman. All tales are born in the mind of Spider Woman, and all creation exists as a result of her naming.

We are the land. To the best of my understanding, that is the fundamental idea that permeates American Indian life; the land (Mother) and the people (mothers) are the same. As Luther Standing Bear has said of his Lakota people, "We are of the soil and the soil is of us." The earth is the source and the being of the people, and we are equally the being of the earth. The land is not really a place, separate from ourselves, where we act out the drama of our isolate destinies; the witchery makes us believe that false idea. The earth is not a mere source of survival, distant from the creatures it nurtures and from the spirit that breathes in us, nor is it to be considered an inert resource on which we draw in order to keep our ideological self functioning, whether we perceive that self in sociological or personal terms. We must not conceive of the earth as an ever-dead other that supplies us with a sense of ego identity by virtue of our contrast to its perceived nonbeing. Rather, for American Indians like Betonie, the earth *is* being, as all creatures are also being: aware, palpable, intelligent, alive. Had Tayo known clearly what Standing Bear articulated—that "in the Indian the spirit of the land is still vested," that human beings "must be born and reborn to belong," so that their bodies are "formed of the dust of their forefather's [sic] bones"—he would not be ill. But if he had known consciously what he knew unconsciously, he would not have been a major agent of the counter ceremony, and this tale would not have been told.

Tayo's illness is a result of separation from the ancient unity of person, ceremony, and land, and his healing is a result of his recognition of this unity. The land is dry because earth is suffering from the alienation of part of herself; her children have been torn from her in their minds; their possession of unified awareness of and with her has been destroyed, partially or totally; that destruction characterizes the lives of Tayo and his mother, Auntie and Rocky, Pinky and Harley, and all those who are tricked into believing that the land is beyond and separate from themselves.

The healing of Tayo and the land results from the reunification of land and person. Tayo is healed when he understands, in magical (mystical) and loving ways, that his being is within and outside him, that it includes his mother, Night Swan, Ts'eh, Josiah, the spotted cattle, winter, hope, love, and the starry universe of Betonie's ceremony.

This understanding occurs slowly as Tayo lives the stories—those ancient and those new. He understands through the process of making the stories manifest in his actions and in his understanding, for the stories and the land are about the same thing; perhaps we can best characterize this relation by saying that the stories are the communication device of the land and the people. Through the stories, the ceremony, the gap between isolate human being and lonely landscape is closed. And through them Tayo understands in mind and in bone the truth of his and our situation.

Tayo is an empty space as the tale begins, a vapor, an outline. He has no voice. "He can't talk to you. He is invisible. His words are formed with an invisible tongue, they have no sound," he tells the army psychiatrist.

Invisible and stilled, like an embryo, he floats, helpless and voiceless, on the current of duality, his being torn by grief and anger. Love could heal him—love, the mountain spirit Ts'eh, the "wonder" being, who was the manifestation of the creator of the waters of life that flow from a woman and bless the earth and the beloved with healing, with rain. It is loving her that heals Tayo, that and his willingness to take up her tasks of nurturing the plant and beast people she loves. And he had loved her from "time immemorial," unconsciously. Before he knew her name, he had given her his pledge of love, and she had answered him with rain:

> So that last summer, before the war, he got up before dawn and rode the bay mare south to the spring in the narrow canyon. The water oozed out from the dark orange sandstone at the base

of the long mesa. He waited for the sun to come over the hills. . . . The canyon was full of shadows when he reached the pool. He had picked flowers along the path, flowers with long yellow petals the color of the sunlight. He shook the pollen from them gently and sprinkled it over the water; he laid blossoms beside the pool and waited. He heard the water, flowing into the pool, drop by drop from the big crack in the side of the cliff. The things he did seemed right, as he imagined with his heart the rituals the cloud priests performed during the drought. Here the dust and heat began to recede; the short grass and stunted corn seemed distant.

As Tayo completes his prayer and begins to descend the mountain, he sees a bright green hummingbird and watches it as it disappears: "But it left something with him; as long as the hummingbird had not abandoned the land, somewhere there were still flowers, and they could all go on." Forty-eight hours after Tayo makes his prayer, the sky fills with clouds thick with rain. The rain comes from the west, and the thunder preceding it comes from the direction of Mount Taylor, called Tse-pi'na in Laguna (Woman Veiled in Clouds), a mountain that is blue against the sky, topped in white when it rains or snows. Having prayed the rain in, Tayo must experience its power personally as the next step in the ceremony. The rain makes it necessary for Josiah to miss his date with Night Swan, so he sends Tayo to the nearby village of Cubero with a message for her. He writes the message on "blue-lined paper."

Night Swan is a mysterious and powerful woman. We know that she is associated with Ts'eh by her circumstances and the colors with which she surrounds herself. Many signs indicate that she is associated with the ceremony of which Tayo was an integral (though unknowing) part: the color of her eyes, her implication in the matter of the spotted (half-breed) cattle, Auntie's dislike of her, and her mysterious words to Tayo when he leaves her. Additionally her room is filled with blue: a blue armchair, curtains "feeling colored by the blue flowers painted in a border around the walls," blue sheets, a cup made of blue pottery painted with yellow flowers. She is dressed in a blue kimono when Tayo enters her room, and she wears blue slippers. Most important, she is associated with a mysterious power that Tayo associates with whatever is behind the white curtain:

> He could feel something back there, something of her life which he could not explain. The room pulsed with feeling, the feeling flowing with the music and the breeze from the curtains, feeling colored by the blue flowers painted in a border around the walls. He could feel it everywhere, even in the blue sheets that were stretched tightly across the bed.

This woman, who appeared out of the southeast one day and took up residence in Cubero, on the southern slope of the mountain, and who disappears as mysteriously after Josiah is buried, is surrounded with emblems of the mountain rain. She takes Tayo to bed. This is not an ordinary coupling, for nothing about Tayo's life is ordinary while the counter ceremony moves toward resolution:

She moved under him, her rhythm merging into the sound of the rain in the tree. And he was lost somewhere, deep beneath the surface of his own body and consciousness, swimming away from all his life before that hour.

The encounter with Night Swan sets the seal of Tayo's destiny in those moments. Through her body the love that Ts'eh bears for him is transmitted. Night Swan is aware of the significance of her act and tells Tayo, "You don't have to understand what is happening. But remember this day. You will recognize it later. You are part of it now."

These passages tell of the ceremonial nature of man and woman; they embody the meaning of the action of the relation between the characters and Thought Woman that is the basis of Laguna life:

> In the beginning Tse che nako, Thought Woman, finished everything, thoughts, and the names of all things. . . . And then our mothers, Uretsete and Naotsete, said they would make names and they would make thoughts. Thus they said, Thus they did.
> (Laguna Thought Woman Story)

From the foregoing it is clear that the Lagunas regard the land as feminine. What is not so clear is how this might be so. For it is not in the mind of the Laguna simply to equate, in primitive modes, earth-bearing-grain with woman-bearing-child. To paraphrase grandma, it isn't that easy. If the simplistic interpretation was accurate to their concept, the Lagunas would not associate the essential nature of femininity with the creative power of thought. The equation is more like earth-bearing-grain, goddess-bearing-thought, woman-bearing-child. Nor is ordinary thinking referred to here: that sort of "brain noise" that passes for thinking among moderns. The thought for which Grandmother Spider is known is the kind that results in physical manifestation of phenomena: mountains, lakes, creatures, or philosophical-sociological systems. Our mothers, Uretsete and Naotsete, are aspects of Grandmother Spider. They are certain kinds of thought forces if you will. The same can be said of Ts'eh, indeed, must be said of her if the tale that Silko tells, that Spider Woman *thinks* all into being is to have its proper significance. Psychoanalytically, we might say that Tayo's illness is a result of the repression of his anima and that through his love of Ts'eh he becomes conscious of the female side of his own nature and accepts and integrates feminine behavior into his life. This Jungian interpretation of the process of Tayo's healing is accurate enough, though it misses an essential point of the story: Tayo's illness is connected to the larger world. The drought-stricken land is also ill, perhaps because the land has also repressed its anima.

Silko illustrates this nexus with the metaphor of the witchery and the ceremony used to contravene its effects. Through the vehicle of the story, Ts'its'tsi'nako's thought, Silko explains how the witchery could be responsible for sickness in individuals, societies, and landscapes simultaneously:

> Thought-Woman, the spider
> named things and

> as she named them
> they appeared.

> She is sitting in her room
> Thinking of a story now.
> I'm telling you the story
> she is thinking.

After Tayo completes the first steps of the ceremony, he is ready to enter into the central rituals connected with a ceremony of cosmic significance, for only a cosmic ceremony can simultaneously heal a wounded man, a stricken landscape, and a disorganized, discouraged society.

He becomes a warrior, thus dissociating himself from the people. A warrior in a peace-centered culture must experience total separation from the tribe. He has been prepared for his role by the circumstances of his birth and upbringing: Auntie was especially forceful in propelling him away from the heart of what he was. By virtue of his status as an outcast who, at the same time, is one of the Laguna people in his heart, he is able to suffer the ritual of war and dissolution. Only total annihilation of the mundane self could produce a magic man of sufficient power to carry off the ceremony that Tayo is embroiled in.

At the opening of the story, Tayo is still experiencing this stage of the ceremony. He is formless, for his being is as yet unshaped, undistinguished from the mass it sprang from. Like rainless clouds, he seeks fulfillment—a ceremony, a story about his life that will make him whole. He has the idea that if he had died instead of Rocky or Josiah, the land would be full of rain. This "story" of his is inappropriate. Perhaps because of his status as an outcast, he does not understand the nature of death, nor does he know that it is not in the deaths of two individuals that the prosperity or the suffering of the people rests. Perhaps no one has told him that the departed souls are always within and part of the people on earth, that they are still obligated to those living on earth and come back in the form of rain regularly (when all is well), so that death is a blessing on the people, not their destruction. What Tayo and the people need is a story that will take the entire situation into account, that will bless life with a certain kind of integrity where spirit, creatures, and land can occupy a unified whole. That kind of story is, of course, a ceremony such as Betonie performs with Tayo as the active participant, the manifester of the thought.

After Tayo walks through Betonie's ceremony, finds the cattle, and puts them in a safe pasture, after he has confronted the witchery and abandoned all thought of retaliating against it, after he has been transformed by these efforts and his meeting with Ts'eh from isolated warrior to spiritually integrated person, after he has taken on the aspect of unity termed *naiya* (mother) in Laguna, he is free to understand the whole thing:

> He would go back there now, where she had shown him the plant. He would gather the seeds for her and plant them with great care in places near sandy hills. . . . The plants would grow there like the story, strong and translucent as stars.

"But you know, grandson, this world is fragile," old

Ku'oosh had told Tayo, and having entered the ways of unification of a fragmented persona, Tayo is free to experience that fragility directly:

> He dreamed with his eyes open that he was wrapped in a blanket in the back of Josiah's wagon, crossing the sandy flat below Paguate Hill. . . . the rumps of the two gray mules were twin moons in front of him. Josiah was driving the wagon, old Grandma was holding him, and Rocky whispered "my brother." They were taking him home.

The fragility of the world is a result of its nature as thought. Both land and human being participate in the same kind of being, for both are thoughts in the mind of Grandmother Spider. Tayo's illness is a function of disordered thinking—his own, that of those around him, and that of the forces that propelled them all into the tragic circumstances of World War II. The witchery put this disordered thinking into motion long ago and distorted human beings' perceptions so that they believed that other creatures—insects and beasts and half-breeds and whites and Indians and Japanese—were enemies rather than part of the one being we all share, and thus should be destroyed. The cure for that misunderstanding, for Tayo, was a reorientation of perception so that he could know directly that the true nature of being is magical and that the proper duty of the creatures, the land, and human beings is to live in harmony with what is. For Tayo, wholeness consists of sowing plants and nurturing them, caring for the spotted cattle, and especially knowing that he belongs exactly where he is, that he is and always has been home. The story that is capable of healing his mind is the story that the land has always signified:

> The transition was completed. In the west and in the south too, the clouds with round heavy bellies had gathered for the dawn. It was not necessary, but it was right, even if the sky had been cloudless the end was the same. The ear for the story and the eye for the pattern were theirs; the feeling was theirs; we came out of this land and we are hers. . . . They had always been loved. He thought of her then; she had always loved him, she had never left him; she had always been there. He crossed the river at sunrise.

So Tayo's initiation into motherhood is complete, and the witchery is countered for a time, at least for one human being and his beloved land. Tayo has bridged the distance between his isolated consciousness and the universe of being, because he has loved the spirit woman who brings all things into being and because he is at last conscious that she has always loved them, his people, and himself. He is able at last to take his normal place in the life of the Laguna, a place that is to be characterized by nurturing, caring for life, behaving like a good mother. Auntie can now treat him as she treats the other men, not as a stranger, but as a friend whom it is safe to complain about, to nag, and to care for. Even Grandmother knows that he is no longer special after he returns from the Paguate hills, where he became simply a part of the pattern of Laguna life and the enduring story within the land, and she comments that "these goings-on around Laguna don't get me excited any more." Perhaps she is also implying that ordi-

nariness can replace the extraordinary nature of life while the ceremony is being played out. Tayo has come home, ordinary in his being, and they can get on with serious business, the day-to-day life of a village, which is what the land, the ceremony, the story and time immemorial are all about. (pp. 127-33)

> *Paula Gunn Allen, "The Feminine Landscape of Leslie Marmon Silko's 'Ceremony',"* in Studies in American Indian Literature: Critical Essays and Course Designs, *edited by Paula Gunn Allen, Modern Language Association of America, 1983, pp. 127-33.*

Leslie Marmon Silko and Kim Barnes (interview date Winter 1986)

[In the following interview, Silko discusses her ideas on storytelling, the Laguna oral tradition, and the role of women in tribal culture.]

[Barnes]: The first question I want to ask you is, who do you consider to be your audience? Who are you writing for?

[Silko]: I've never thought too much about an audience per se. When I first started writing, I wasn't sure that anyone would want to read or listen to the work that I did. I didn't think about it at first. In a way, it's good not to think about an audience. If you start thinking about the audience, it can inhibit what you do. When I was younger, there was concern about what will Grandma think, or what will Mama say or something like this, and that in a sense is being concerned about audience and can really inhibit a writer. Initially, I guess I assumed that I wouldn't have to worry about an audience because there would not be an audience. I didn't think about it, and I didn't even worry too much about what Mama would think or what Grandma would think or what Uncle So-and-So would think or what the people would think because at first I didn't think that I would ever have to worry that they would see what I had written. Now, I'm working on this new novel which is long and complex to the point of being foolhardy. Who knows, a polite way would be to call it an ambitious project. But I'm so caught up in trying to see if I can make it happen. It's sort of a personal challenge, and again I'm not thinking about an audience. I've been quoted in other interviews as saying that I want this novel to be a novel that, when you shop at a Safeway store, it will be in the little wire racks at the check-out station and that I don't want to write something that the MLA will want. I want something that will horrify the people at the MLA. Mostly, I'm teasing, but in another way I'm not. I'm sad to see that so little serious fiction gets out into the world. I was amazed that Umberto Eco's *The Name of the Rose* and Mark Helprin's book *Winter's Tale* made it to the wire racks at the check-out stands in the United States. So I'm probably only part-way serious when I say that I don't think about an audience.

So you didn't write a book like Storyteller *for a particularly white or Indian audience.*

I don't think about Indian and white. What I wanted to do was clarify the interrelationship between the stories I had heard and my sense of storytelling and language that had been given to me by the old folks, the people back home. I gave examples of what I heard as best I could remember, and how I developed these elements into prose, into fiction and into poetry, moving from what was basically an oral tradition into a written tradition. The way I figured it, there would be some Native American people who would be interested in it and some Laguna Pueblo people who would be interested in it. There might be other people who are working out of a different cultural tradition but still working with oral material and working in their own art to bring the two together who would be interested. The book is for people who are interested in that relationship between the spoken and the written.

Do you consider yourself a storyteller in a traditional sense?

No, not at all. My friend Mei-mei Berssenbrugge, the poet, spent some time at Laguna Pueblo a few years ago, and she sat in on a kind of a session. I hesitate to call it a storytelling session because they're real spontaneous. It was at my uncle's house, and my uncle's wife Anita and her two sisters were there and some other people. It was in the evening and everyone was feeling jolly and talking. We might have started out with some kind of notorious incident that had happened recently, and pretty soon Mei-mei was sitting there listening to the way people would relate something that happened, and we'd all laugh and then one of Anita's sister's would say, "Well, you remember the time," then the other sister would take over. When the whole session was over, we all went back over to my grandma's house where Mei-mei and I were staying, and Mei-mei said, "They really have a way of telling these stories and incidents and kind of playing off one another." She was really impressed, and I said, "See, I'm not in that class at all." I suppose if I didn't have the outlook of the writer, I might get better at storytelling, but I always say that I'm not good at giving off-the-cuff presentations. Oh, sometimes I have a fine moment. If you really want to hear people who can get rolling in telling, you have to do down to Laguna and kind of fall into the right situation, right feelings and right time.

Was a storyteller a spiritual leader? Was he or she someone who was born into or inherited that role?

It's not like that at all. There is a period of time at the winter solstice when people get together for four days and four nights, and they re-tell all the stories connected with the emergence and the migration of the People. There are people who have to learn and remember those stories and people who have to participate in that telling and re-telling once a year. Those people would probably be designated persons, but they would not be specially designated in any kind of ceremonial or religious way. They wouldn't be called storytellers; they would be called ceremonial religious leaders. The key to understanding storytellers and storytelling at Laguna Pueblo is to realize that you grow up not just being aware of narrative and making a story or seeing a story in what happens to you and what goes on around you all the time, but just being appreciative and delighted in narrative exchanges. When you meet somebody at a post office, he or she says, "How are you, how are you doing?" At Laguna, people will stand there and

they'll tell you how they are doing. At Laguna, it's a way of interacting. It isn't like there's only one storyteller designated. That's not it at all. It's a whole way of being. When I say "storytelling," I don't just mean sitting down and telling a once-upon-a-time kind of story. I mean a whole way of seeing yourself, the people around you, your life, the place of your life in the bigger context, not just in terms of nature and location, but in terms of what has gone on before, what's happened to other people. So it's a whole way of being, but there are some people who are willing to be funnier or better storytellers than others, and some people because they are older or they remember better, have a larger repertoire of the *humma-hah* stories. It's not at all like the Irish idea of the bard or the chosen one.

Why are you writing these stories? Are you trying to put the oral tradition in a more stable or lasting form? Do you think anything is lost in the writing down of these stories?

Well, no, I'm not trying to save them, I'm not trying to put them in a stable or lasting form. I write them down because I like seeing how I can translate this sort of feeling or flavor or sense of a story that's told and heard onto the page. Obviously, some things will be lost because you're going from one medium to another. And I use *translate* in the broadest sense. I don't mean translate from the Laguna Pueblo language to English, I mean the feeling or the sense that language is being used orally. So I play with the page and things that you could do on the page, and repetitions. When you have an audience, when you're telling a story and people are listening, there's repetition of crucial points. That's something that on the printed page looks really crummy and is redundant and useless, but in the actual telling is necessary. So I play around with the page by using different kinds of spacing or indentations or even italics so that the reader can sense, say, that the tone of the voice has changed. If you were hearing a story, the speed would increase at certain points. I want to see how much I can make the page communicate those nuances and shifts to the reader. I'm intrigued with that. I recognize the inherent problem; there's no way that hearing a story and reading a story are the same thing; but that doesn't mean that everyone should throw up his hands and say it can't be done or say that what's done on the page isn't catching some of those senses. When I read off the page and read some of the *humma-hah* stories that I wrote down or go through some of the Aunt Susie material, then of course, I think it's more persuasive. In a way, that's not fair; because I'm reading it out loud, I've gone back again. But I think there are some instances where I've been successful so that the reader has a sense of how it might sound if I were reading it to him or her.

In a work like **Storyteller,** *are you actually creating something, or are you simply re-telling a myth?*

Every time a story is told, and this is one of the beauties of the oral tradition, each telling is a new and unique story, even if it's repeated word for word by the same teller sitting in the same chair. I work to try to help the reader have the sense of how it would sound if the reader could be hearing it. That's original. And no matter how carefully I remember, memory gets all mixed together with imagination. It does for everybody. But I don't change the spirit or the mood or the tone of the story. For some stories, I could just hear Aunt Susie's voice reverberating. The challenge was to get it down so you could have a sense of my Aunt Susie's sound and what it was like. Earlier you said something about writing the stories down in some way that they would be saved. Nobody saves stories. Writing down a story, even tape recording stories, doesn't save them in the sense of saving their life within a community. Stories stay alive within the community like the Laguna Pueblo community because the stories have a life of their own. The life of the story is not something that any individual person can save and certainly not someone writing it down or recording it on tape or video. That's a nice little idea, and in some places where they've had these kind of archival materials, younger people can go and see or listen to certain stories. But if for whatever reasons the community no longer has a place for a story or a story no longer has a life within that particular period, that doesn't mean that the story no longer has a life; that's something that no single person can decide. The old folks at Laguna would say, "If it's important, you'll remember it." If it's really important, if it really has a kind of substance that reaches to the heart of the community life and what's gone before and what's gone later, it will be remembered. And if it's not remembered, the people no longer wanted it, or it no longer had its place in the community.

People outside the community are often horrified to hear some old timer say, "No, I won't tell my stories to the tape recorder. No, I won't put them on video tape. If these younger folks don't listen and remember from me, then maybe these stories are meant to end with me." It's very tough-minded. It flies in the face of all the anthropologists and people who get moist-eyed over what a good turn they're doing for the Native American communities by getting down these stories. I tend to align myself with the tougher-minded people. The folks at home will say, "If it's important, if it has relevance, it will stay regardless of whether it's on video tape, taped, or written down." It's only the western Europeans who have this inflated pompous notion that every word, everything that's said or done is real important, and it's got to live on and on forever. And only Americans think that America, which has barely been around 200 years, which is a joke, what a short period of time, only Americans think that we'll just continue on. It takes a tremendous amount of stupid blind self-love to think that your civilization or your culture will continue on, when all you have to do is look at history and see that civilizations and people a lot better than people building the MX have disappeared. . . . It's like Momaday when he writes about the Kiowa, how the horse came and they became masters of the Plains. He says their great heyday lasted one or two hundred years. It passes and it's gone, you know? You could feel sad about it, but that's the way it is.

In your article, "An Old-Time Indian Attack," you say that the notion that the writer has the power to inhabit any soul, any consciousness, is an idea restricted to the white man. In "Humaweepi," the warrior priest believes that human beings are special, which means they can do anything. If we see the artist as a kind of priest, and this may once again be a white notion, why can't the artist, like Hu-

maweepi, transcend his own experience? Does a person necessarily have to experience something to write about it?

I think that it's possible that the most deeply felt emotions, like the deepest kind of fear or loss or bereavement or ecstasy or joy, those kinds of deep, deep, deep level feelings and emotions, are common in all human beings. But to have a sense of what sorts of things, what sorts of outside stimuli, if you will, or situations or occurrences, will trigger what in whom, then that becomes trickier. That essay was written at a time when there were all of these writers, white male writers, who wanted to be the white shaman. There was a whole white shaman movement, and it was so bogus, it was such a complete joke and a kind of con game. These were like followers of Snyder. They weren't even working; they couldn't have gotten to a deep level of fear, love, hate. They didn't have the artistic capacity to ever reach that level, even if they'd been writing about themselves and out of their own cultural experience. Again, it was that kind of superficiality, that materialistic notion that if you take the person's line break, or if you take the kind of scanning pattern of the reoccurrences of the bear image or something like that, then you have written something that's equivalent to the healing ceremony of the Chippewas. My friend Geary Hobson, who's a writer—he's a Cherokee—had been savaged by one of these nitwit white shaman, and so the essay was written under those circumstances. The main notion was that those people who were calling themselves white shaman no more had a sense of the deeper level of feeling or what is commonly shared between human beings; they had no more idea than a dog or a cat has an idea of deep levels of human feeling, and yet they were prancing around thinking that they could appropriate that level of experience. The essay was a reaction to that superficiality, and the fact of the matter is that a lot of these so-called white shaman who were kicking around at that time weren't even able to write about themselves or from their particular cultural perspective.

In **Ceremony,** *you write about a man's experience. Do you feel like you were going outside of your experience in doing this? Is the Native American male's experience much different from the female's?*

Well, I don't know if it is or not since I never was a Native American male, you know. But what I do believe is that again, on that deep, deep level, that deep level where we're moved to fear, sorrow, loss, joy, camaraderie, on that deep level, men and women are the same, just like all human beings are. The way the heart pushes in the chest feels the same, whether a woman or a man is experiencing terror. What would trigger it will differ. A woman walking alone at night can be terrified by the sound of other footsteps; it wouldn't necessarily terrify a man, unless an hour before some guys had said, "Look buddy, we're going to get you." Then I think the same physiological response would be there. In *Ceremony,* the male character was dealing with grief and loss and rage and a kind of sickness at heart and loneliness; I have great faith that my consciousness and experience on that level of feeling is true for him.

People have noticed that I write about men and what they

did and how they hung out together and so on. That's more complex. In Laguna Pueblo, little girls aren't kept with the women, and little boys aren't kept with the men. Children sort of range freely, and men and women range freely. The division of labor at Laguna Pueblo, especially when I was growing up, was much more flexible. Whoever was strong enough and ready to do a certain task would do it. (pp. 83-92)

I had this omnivorous appetite for watching people do things. And I watched how my great-grandmother got down on her knees even when she was old and feeble, but I also watched how men built things. Nobody shooed me away, no one told me girls couldn't watch men build a shed. In the Pueblo, men don't go off as much. It's not like your middle-America, white middle-class man who goes off to work, and work is far away from where the women and children are. In the Pueblo, the men are around. There's all kinds of stuff going on, and people are very busy. I spent a lot of time listening and watching men from the time I was a little girl. And I think that more people, women and men, could write about one another if there wasn't this kind of segregation of the sexes that we have in America. Men can handle writing about women only insofar as they are getting them into or out of bed. But, you know, that isn't because it can't be done, that isn't because only men know what men do, that's because in this particular stupid, great middle-America society, men and women really don't know very much about one another. But that doesn't mean that it is inherent and that it has to be. That's just this one particular place in time. (pp. 92-3)

I find the yellow woman, Kochininako, particularly interesting. Do you see the myths concerning her as having arisen from the need for escape on the part of the women from a kind of social and sexual domination?

No, not at all. The need for that kind of escape is the need of a woman in middle-America, a white Anglo, the WASP woman. In the Pueblo, the lineage of the child is traced through the mother, so it's a matrilineal system. The houses are the property of the woman, not the man. The land is generally passed down through the female side because the houses belong to the women. One of my early memories was when our house needed to be replastered with the traditional adobe and mud plaster. It was a crew of women who came and plastered the house. Why? The women own the houses so the women maintain what they own. The kinds of things that cause white upper-middle-class women to flee the home for awhile to escape or get away from domination and powerlessness and inferior status, *vis-a-vis* the husband, and the male, those kinds of forces are not operating, they're not operating at all. What's operating in those stories of Kochininako is this attraction, this passion, this connection between the human world and the animal and spirit worlds. Buffalo Man is a buffalo, and he can be in the form of a buffalo, but there is this link, and the link is sealed with sexual intimacy, which is emblematic of that joining of two worlds. At the end of the story, the people have been starving, and the buffalo says, "We will give up our spirits, we will come and die for these people because we are related to them. Kochininako is our

sister-in-law." She's a. . . . what do you call it in anthropology or sociology, one who shatters the cultural paradigms or steps through or steps out. She does that because there's a real overpowering sexual attraction that's felt. The attraction is symbolized by or typified by the kind of sexual power that draws her to the buffalo man, but the power which draws her to Buffalo Man is actually the human, the link, the animal and human world, those two being drawn together. It's that power that's really operating, and the sexual nature of it is just a metaphor for that power. So that's what's going on there. It doesn't have anything to do with, "Things are really bad at home, so I think I'll run off for awhile." That's not what it's about.

I wanted to ask you a question about the mother figures in some of your work. I was trying to look for a word to describe them. I couldn't quite come up with it. Ambivalent is the wrong word, but you never know quite how to feel about them. For instance, in the very first story in **Storyteller,** *the little girl wants corn to eat, and she drowns herself in the lake because her mother won't give it to her. And there's the mother in* **Ceremony** *. . .*

And then the aunt and the mother's sister. I know what you're talking about. People, women especially, ask me about that and men too. It's a real tough one. The story about the little girl who ran away, that's a story which is very clear in *Storyteller.* It's a story that Aunt Susie liked to tell. In a matrilineal society, in a matriarchy, and especially in this particular matriarchy, the women, as I've already said, control the houses, the lineage of the children, and a lot of the decisions about marriages and so forth. In a sense, the women have called the shots pretty much in the world of relationships and the everyday world. While the Pueblo women were kind of running the show, buying and selling sheep, and of course the Navajos are the same way too, the women making many of the business decisions, the Pueblo men would be taking care of ceremonial matters or maybe out hunting. Although there have been a few Laguna women who were great hunters also. So the female, the mother, is a real powerful person, and she's much more the authority figure. It's a kind of reversal. Your dad is the one who's the soft-touch, and it's the mother's brother who reprimands you. If you're really out of hand and she can't deal with you, it will be your mother's brother, not your father, she goes to. When a man marries, he goes to his wife's house or household or whatever, and his position is one you can feel more of an alliance with . . . more of an alliance with the father because he, in some ways, has less power in that household. So when you have a story like that one, that explains it. But then, how do you explain Tao's mother who is kind of a lost and unfortunate figure, or how do we explain Auntie? And people have talked about how my male characters have vulnerability and all kinds of complexities and the women . . . they're not as vulnerable. You have to have some vulnerability in a character for readers to be able to establish some kind of link with them. So why don't we see that in my female characters? We have to go back, I suppose, to the women I grew up with. I grew up with women who were really strong, women with a great deal of power, let us say, within the family. And I think about that, and I try to think about my mother: is there something about the way she and I have gotten along, or how we related to one another? But, just remember what the position of the father and the mother would be in Pueblo society. If someone was going to thwart you or frighten you, it would tend to be a woman; you see it coming from your mother, or sent by your mother.

I want to ask you a little bit about the form of your writing. Joseph Bruchac in his interview with Momaday notes the blurring of boundaries between prose and verse in **Ceremony.** *Do you write what you think to be prose poems? You seem to be bucking traditional form, and we've already talked about how you want it to look on a page to give the sense of storytellers. Are you working with anything new or unique in doing this type of writing? I mean, this blurring between verse and prose. And why, as in* **Ceremony,** *where it will break in?*

Well, in **Ceremony** the breaks would be the parts that ideally you would hear rather than read. As far as what I'm doing with the blurring of the two, Virgil and the old dudes, the old cats back in the old days, or the Greeks, they didn't worry so much it seems to me, although I'm sure some of the genre definitions and stuff came out of that period of time. In some ways, I feel that it's more valid to have a checklist or a discussion of what constitutes tragedy or comedy than what constitutes poetry or prose. I don't decide I'll take a stance. For my purposes, it's just useless, it's stupid, it doesn't interest me at all. What I'm interested in is getting a feeling or an idea that's part of the story. Getting the story across. And I'm really not particular how it's done. The important thing is that it goes across in a way that I want it to go. I don't waste my time on it. But if other people want to worry over whether what they've just written is a poem or a prose poem, if they want to worry about that or if literary critics want to worry about that, I don't like to tell people what they should spend their time on. I don't spend my time on that.

Have you ever had people say that to you that your poetry isn't poetry at all?

Well, certainly not to my face, but in 1973 I sent five of the Chimney poems to the *Chicago Review,* and that year they gave a prize for all poetry published in all the volumes for the year, and in 1973 I got *Chicago Review*'s prize for poetry, which I was really astonished to receive. Then I got the Pushcart prize for poetry, which is even better than the *Chicago Review*'s little poetry award. I must say, it gave me more confidence in what I was doing. The way the Pushcart prize works is all the small magazines nominate one writer's poem that has appeared in their small magazine, and then the Pushcart judges select one piece. I won that over all other poems published, or at least nominated and published, that year. Because of that, if someone says it's not poetry at all, then all I can say is don't argue with me, go fight with people who hand out prizes for poetry.

One of my favorite poems of yours is **"Deer Song."** *There's this line which I really like, "the struggle is the ritual." It seems to me that this line somehow takes in the essence of cooperative existence in the culture. Could you explain that line a little bit more?*

Well, on a literal level, there's some intimations that the wolves get the deer. The western European attitude towards things like this is, "Oh, I don't want to see an animal have to die, I don't want to see the blood. Oh, I can eat it, but oh, no, I couldn't kill it!" Well, I've always said if you couldn't kill it, then you better damn well not be eating it. It's sort of puritanical abhorrence of blood and a tremendous fear of death that western European people have; Americans especially. That's why everyone is out jogging and not eating salt because he's so scared of death; those are like amulets to keep death away. So on the literal level, it's not something nasty or awful or horrible or something to avert one's eyes from: *look* at it. It's actually almost like a sacred or ritualistic kind of thing, that giving up of the life. Of course, I also mean for it to transcend that and for people to be able to see that in a struggle to survive, it is again that you will be able to look and see things that are a part of a kind of ritual. Not ritual in a sense of following a set pattern, a form that can never vary, but ritual in a lighter sense that expands our senses. One should be able to see one's own life and lives of other beings as a part of something very sacred and special. Just because it isn't codified or put in a psalm book or a prayer book or just because it isn't a part of a ceremonial chant or something doesn't mean that it isn't valuable, moving, special. (pp. 95-100)

I know that you have said in the past that the greatest influence on your writing has been your surroundings. Has there been a single novelist or poet whose work you find particularly inspirational or informational?

You mean working right now?

Not necessarily. I know you have talked about Milton and Shakespeare.

Well, lately, the one person that's meant a lot to me is Wittgenstein. I think his remarks on color turn into some of the most beautiful poetry I've ever read. People call Wittgenstein a philosopher and I call him a poet. I really like reading Wittgenstein right now.

How about influences on your style?

That is for style. You can see the clarity of his remarks on color in one of the last pieces he wrote before he died. With style, I'm like a sponge. I don't consciously look towards anyone. The poetry of my friend Mei-mei Berssenbrugge, I think, influences me. Her writing influences me, my ideas, and some of the things I write about influences her. And I think in terms of my prose style something of what she does with her poetry filters into me and has influenced me, but I couldn't say how exactly. What she does is real important, and so are some of her ideas about her connection with the so-called avant-garde in New York, and so forth. And the kinds of musicians, a lot of her interests have kind of filtered through to me, and I in turn have picked up and taken off with that in my own directions. My friend Larry McMurtry is a rare book dealer, and he comes across wonderful books in looking for rare expensive books. He's been breaking me out of the mold of just reading fiction or poetry. For example, H. D.'s tribute to Freud is wonderful. I like H.D.'s tribute to Freud about a million times more than I like any of her damn poems.

I would really not mind if some of H.D.'s magical prose rubbed off on mine; I would not mind that at all.

Paula Gunn Allen has said that reading Momaday's House Made of Dawn *was a turning point in her life. Has Momaday had the same effect on you as a writer?*

I'm trying to think. Turning point? Where was Paula headed before? I don't quite understand. No. I like *The Way to Rainy Mountain* very much, but I would have been doing what I was doing regardless of what Scott had done or not, written or not written.

You've mentioned your novel in progress, **The Almanac of the Dead.** *Could you tell us a little bit about that?*

It's a very long complex novel, so it's hard to even tell about it. It's got five or six distinct narrative lines, sort of intertwined through it. The "Almanac" in the title refers to the Mayan almanacs or Mayan codices. There are four manuscripts that survived the on-going inquisition and persecution of the Mayan Indian people and all Indian peoples once the Spaniards and the Portuguese arrived. Apparently what happened is early on the priests chose, recruited, captured, whatever, promising young Mayan men, and taught them how to read and write Spanish. This happened very early after the Spaniards went into that area, and these anonymous Mayan people or men used their new knowledge to try to write down what had always been in more an oral state or what had been kept with the glyphs, the Mayan glyphs that were carved into stone. Although memory in passing down from person to person had worked before to hold these things, I think they realized that with the cataclysm of the coming of the Europeans, they could no longer count on human memory if humans themselves were being destroyed. So anyway, they wrote down what had, up until then, been kind of the knowledge of the various priests.

The almanacs were literally like a farmer's almanac. They told you the identity of the days, but not only what days were good to plant on, but some days that were extremely dangerous. There were some years that were extremely unfortunate with famine and war. There were other years, even epochs, that would come that would be extremely glorious and fertile. The Mayan people were obsessed with time and knowing each day. They believed that a day was a kind of being and it had a . . . we would maybe say a personality, but that it would return. It might not return again for five thousand or eight thousand years, but they believed that a day exactly as it had appeared before would appear again. It's a view that basically denies a lot of western European notions about linear time, death, simultaneous planes of experience, and so on. Anyway, the Mayan Almanacs or the Mayan codices exist. There's one in Dresden, one in Madrid, one in Paris, and one in Mexico City. I've seen what the fragments were like, and decided that I would like to use the structure of an almanac; it would free me to indulge in different narrative lines. Most of the action takes place in the present day. You get a few glimpses of the remaining fragments. You see, my characters in my novel have a fifth manuscript. There are in fact only four that are known to exist in the world now, but for my purposes, I say there's a fifth fragmentary manu-

script, and my characters have it. Every now and then, the reader gets to see a bit of the fragment. The novel centers in Tucson and encompasses Mexico and kind of the edge of Central America. It not only runs through the days when the Spaniards and the Portuguese were taking slaves from the Mayan area and dragging them up to northern Sonora to work in the silver mines until they died, but also, because the Mayan Almanacs were believed to be able to foretell the future, my novel will go a bit into the future. It goes to a time when the struggle which the indigenous peoples are having now in Guatemala and Honduras and Nicaragua spreads north into Mexico. The United States, of course, intervenes and sends troops and tanks and so on into Mexico. And that's as far forward in time as it goes.

You're thinking 1600 pages?

I was thinking 1600. It could be longer. I've got 800 right now. (pp. 102-05)

> *Leslie Marmon Silko and Kim Barnes, in an interview in* The Journal of Ethnic Studies, *Vol. 13, No. 4, Winter, 1986, pp. 83-105.*

Bernard A. Hirsch   (essay date Winter 1988)

[*In the following excerpt, Hirsch focuses on "Yellow Woman" and other pieces in* Storyteller *as he examines how Native American oral traditions shape the structure and themes of this collection.*]

Comprised of personal reminiscences and narratives, retellings of traditional Laguna stories, photographs, and a generous portion of her previously published short fiction and poetry, this multigeneric work [entitled ***Storyteller***] lovingly maps the fertile storytelling ground from which her art evolves and to which it is here returned—an offering to the oral tradition which nurtured it.

Silko has acknowledged often and eloquently the importance of the oral tradition to her work and tries to embody its characteristics in her writing. This effort, as she well knows, is immensely difficult and potentially dangerous, and this awareness surfaces at several points in ***Storyteller.*** She recalls, for instance, talking with Nora, whose "grandchildren had brought home / a . . . book that had my 'Laguna coyote' poem in it".

> "We all enjoyed it so much [says Nora] but I was telling the children the way my grandpa used to tell it is longer."
>
> "Yes, that's the trouble with writing," I said. You can't go on and on the way we do when we tell stories around here.

"The trouble with writing," in the context Silko here establishes for it is twofold: first, it is static; it freezes words in space and time. It does not allow the living story to change and grow, as does the old tradition. Second, though it potentially widens a story's audience, writing removes the story from its immediate context, from the place and people who nourished it in the telling, and thus robs it of much of its meaning. This absence of the story's dynamic context is why in writing "You can't go on the way we do / when we tell stories around.

But Nora does a wonderful thing. She uses Silko's poem to create a storytelling event of her own. In this sense Silko's poem itself becomes a part of the oral tradition and, through Nora's recollection of her grandfather's telling, a means of advancing it as well. The conversation with Nora is important in *Storyteller* because it reminds us of the flexibility and inclusiveness of the oral tradition. Even writing can be made to serve its ends.

Storyteller helps keep the oral tradition strong through Silko's masterful use of the written word, and the photographs, to recall and reestablish its essential contexts. The photographs are important because they reveal something of the particular landscape and community out of which Laguna oral tradition is born, and of specific individuals—of Aunt Susie, Grandma A'mooh, Grandpa Hank, and all those storytellers who have accepted responsibility for "remembering a portion . . . [of] the long story of the people." The photographs, however, as Silko uses them, do more than provide a survival record. As we shall see, they involve the reader more fully in the storytelling process itself and, "because they are part of many of the stories / and because many of the stories can be traced in the photographs," they expand the reader's understanding of individual works and also suggest structural and thematic links between them.

The photographs also are arranged to suggest the circular design of *Storyteller,* a design characteristic of oral tradition. The merging of past and present are manifest in the book's design, as is the union of personal, historical, and cultural levels of being and experience, and through such harmonies—and their periodic sundering—the ongoing flux of life expresses itself. . . . Though there is clearly an autobiographical dimension to *Storyteller,* Silko's arrangement of photographs at the beginning and end of the book subordinates the individual to the communal and cultural. Her life and art compels us, as does the literature itself, to acknowledge the ongoing power of Laguna oral tradition in her writing.

This cyclic design, of course, is not merely a function of the arrangement of photographs. It derives primarily from the episodic structure of *Storyteller* and the accretive process of teaching inherent in it. Each individual item is a narrative episode in itself which relates to other such episodes in various ways. Oral storytelling, Walter J. Ong tells us, "normally and naturally operated in episodic patterning . . . episodic structure was the natural way to talk out a lengthy story line if only because the experience of real life is more like a string of episodes than it is like a Freytag pyramid"; and it is real life, "the long story of the people," that is Silko's concern. Moreover, the telling of her portion of the story, and of the individual stories which comprise it, involves, like all oral storytelling, a teaching process, one in which the varieties of genre and voice Silko uses are essential.

In *Storyteller,* the reader learns by accretion. Successive narrative episodes cast long shadows both forward and back, lending different or complementary shades of mean-

ing to those preceding them and offering perspectives from which to consider those that follow. Such perspectives are then themselves often expanded or in some way altered as the new material reflects back upon them. This kind of learning process is part of the dynamic of oral tradition. Silko uses it in *Storyteller* to foster the kind of intimacy with the reader that the oral storyteller does with the listener. Such a relationship is born of both the powerful claims of the story, in whole and in part, on the reader's attention and the active engagement by the accretive process of the reader's imagination. This process in effect makes the reader's responses to the various narrative episodes a part of the larger, ongoing story these episodes comprise while simultaneously allowing the episodes to create the contexts which direct and refine these responses. In this way the stories continue; in this way both the story and the reader are renewed. (pp. 1-3)

· · · · ·

A photograph in what I will call the "Yellow Woman" section of *Storyteller* is of the Anaconda company's open-pit uranium mine. "This photograph," Silko tells us, "was made in the early 1960s. The mesas and hills that appear in the background and foreground are gone now, swallowed by the mine". This photograph deepens our understanding of many things in *Storyteller:* of the importance of the photographs to the stories, for one thing, and of Silko's father's love of photography for another. "He is still most at home in the canyons and sandrock," she says, "and most of his life regular jobs / have been a confinement he has avoided." Some might think less of him for this, but Silko stifles this tendency—first by the story of Reed Woman and Corn Woman that precedes the reminiscence about her father and second by his photographs themselves, one of which is that of the now vanished mesas and hills. Moreover, his photography intensified his love of the land and enabled him to relate to it in new and fulfilling ways. We learn, for instance, that

> His landscapes could not be done
> without certain kinds of clouds—
>   some white and scattered like river rock
>   and others
>   mountains rolling into themselves
>   swollen lavender before rainstorms

Clouds, as we know, are a source of life itself to the land, and for Lee H. Marmon they bring to it a profound and varied beauty as well. Essential to the continuity of physical life, the clouds are no less essential to his spirit in that they help him express through his art his particular vision of the land and by so doing, to define himself in terms of it. Equally important, in these times, is that his artistry can help others, be they Indians removed from the land or people who have never known it, to develop a richer, more meaningful sense of the land than is held by such as those who run Anaconda. It is precisely the development of such a relationship—to the land, to the spirits that pervade it, and to the stories that derive from it—that occupies the "Yellow Woman" section of *Storyteller.*

The "Yellow Woman" section, comprising the short story **"Yellow Woman,"** 4 poems, poetic retellings of two traditional stories, 4 reminiscences, 4 photographs, and 2 "gossip stories," is framed by **"Yellow Woman"** and **"Story-telling,"** a poem consisting of six brief vignettes based on the abduction motif of the traditional Yellow Woman stories. As does **"Storyteller"** in the [earlier] "Survival" section, **"Yellow Woman,"** and the traditional stories from which Silko's version evolves, establish the primary structural and thematic concerns of this section.

Based on the traditional stories in which Yellow Woman, on her way to draw water, is abducted by a mountain kachina, Silko's **"Yellow Woman"** concerns the development of the visionary character. This is hinted at in the story's epigram, **"What Whirlwind Man Told Kochininako, Yellow Woman"**:

> I myself belong to the wind
> and so it is we will travel swiftly
> this whole world
> with dust and with windstorms.

Whirlwind Man will take her on a journey beyond the boundaries of time and place, a journey alive with sensation and danger which promises a perspective from which she can see the world new and entire. This in effect is what happens in the story. Like the prophets and visionaries of many cultures, Indian and non-Indian, the narrator travels to the mountain where she learns to see beyond the range of mundane experience. She recalls that, at Silva's mountain cabin.

> I was standing in the sky with nothing around
>   me
> but the wind that came down from the blue
> mountain peak behind me. I could see faint
> mountain images in the distance miles across the
> vast spread of mesas and valleys and plains. I
> wondered who was over there to feel the moun-
>   tain
> wind on those sheer blue edges—who walks on
>   the
> pine needles in those blue mountains.
> "Can you see the pueblo?" Silva was standing
> behind me.
> I shook my head, "We're too far away."
> "From here I can see the world."

The pueblo, which comprised her whole world before, is, from the perspective of the mountain, but a barely discernible part of a much larger whole. With Silva, on the mountain, she has entered the more expansive and truer realm of imagination and myth.

When we can see imaginatively, William Blake has said, when we can see not merely with but through the eye, "the whole creation will appear infinite and holy whereas it now appears finite and corrupt. This will come to pass by an improvement of sensual enjoyment" (*The Marriage of Heaven and Hell*). This is the narrator's experience. She follows a strong impulse in running off with Silva; desire moves her to leave the familiar, secure world of the pueblo and her family to walk a new and daring road. She opens her story in the morning, after she and Silva first made love:

> My thigh clung to his with dampness, and I
> watched the sun rising up through the tama-
> racks and willows . . . I could hear the water,

almost at our feet where the narrow fast channel bubbled and washed green ragged moss and fearn leaves. I looked at him beside me, rolled in the red blanket on the white river sand.

She does not awaken to the proverbial harsh light of morning awash in guilt, but to a newly, more vibrantly alive world of sensation within and around her. But this is a world which, like Silva himself, is as frightening in its strength and intensity as it is seductive, and when Silva awakens she tells him she is leaving:

> He smiled now, eyes still closed. "You are
> coming with me, remember?" He sat up now
>   with
> his bare dark chest and belly in the sun.
> "Where?"
> "To my place."
> "And will I come back?"
> He pulled his pants on. I walked away from
> him, feeling him behind me and smelling the
> willows.
> "Yellow Woman," he said.
> I turned to face him, "Who are you?" I asked.

Last night, he reminds her, "you guessed my name, and you knew why I had come." Their lovemaking made her intuitively aware of another, more vital level of being, one which had been within her all along, nurtured since childhood by her grandfather's Yellow Woman stories—and she knew she was Yellow Woman and her lover the dangerous mountain ka'tsina who carries her off.

But imaginative seeing on this morning after is threatening to the narrator, for seeing oneself whole demands eradication of those perceptual boundaries which offer the security of a readily discernible, if severely limited, sense of self. The narrator clings to that historical, time-bound sense of self like a child to her mother's skirts on the first day of school. "I'm not really her," she maintains, not really Yellow Woman. "I have my own name and I come from the pueblo on the other side of the mesa." It is not so much "confusion about what is dream and what is fact" that besets her here as it is the fear of losing that reality which has heretofore defined her—and him. As they walk she thinks to herself:

> I will see someone, eventually I will see
> someone, and then I will be certain that he
> [Silva] is only a man—some man from nearby—
>   and
> I will be sure that I am not Yellow Woman.
> Because she is from out of time past and I live
> now and I've been to school and there are
> highways and pickup trucks that Yellow
>   Woman
> never saw.

Jim Ruppert is right, I think, when he says that the narrator "struggles to . . . establish time boundaries and boundaries between objective reality and myths," and that struggle is part of the learning process she undergoes in the story. Newly awakened to her own imaginative potential, she has yet to discern the proper relationship between experiential reality and the timeless, all-inclusive mythic reality of her grandfather's stories.

Her desire, however, is stronger than her fear. After they

reach his cabin, eat, and she looks out over the world from the mountain, Silva unrolls the bedroll and spreads the blankets. She hesitates, and he slowly undresses her. There is compulsion, this time, on his part, and fear on hers, but she is held to him more by her own passion than by his force. When she does leave, during their confrontation with a rancher who, rightly, accuses Silva of stealing cattle, it is at his command. "I felt sad at leaving him," she recalls, and considers going back, "but the mountains were too far away now. And I told myself, because I believe it, that he will come back sometime and be waiting again by the river."

She returns home. Yellow Woman stories usually end that way. And as she approaches her house, A. Lavonne Ruoff tells us, "she is brought back to the realities of her own life by the smell of supper cooking and the sight of her mother instructing her grandmother in the Anglo art of making Jell-O." The details here suggest a world governed more by routine than by passion, a world somewhat at odds with itself, as mother instructing grandmother suggests, and a world no longer receptive to the wonder and wisdom of the old stories. Having sensed this, she "decided to tell them that some Navajo had kidnapped me." But the unnamed narrator here, like the unnamed Eskimo girl in **"Storyteller,"** keeps the oral tradition alive by going on her own journey of self-discovery—a journey born of acknowledging the rightful demands of passion and imagination—and by intuitively accepting the guidance of her grandfather's stories. Her life itself has become part of a visionary drama to be completed by Silva's return, and within that context it has gained fullness and meaning. Her recognition, in the story's final sentence, that hers is a Yellow Woman story—and that she is Yellow Woman—reveals as much. She has come to see herself, in Momaday's words, "whole and eternal" and like Momaday when, on his journey, he came out upon the northern plains, she will "never again . . . see things as [she] saw them yesterday or the day before."

Cottonwood, which follows **"Yellow Woman,"** is in two parts, each a poetic rendering of a Laguna Yellow Woman story; taken together, these poems and Silko's story provide a richer, more inclusive perspective than they do separately on both the relationship between oral tradition and the written word and Silko's use of the Yellow Woman character.

The focus in **"Yellow Woman"** is on the unnamed woman narrator. She tells her own story, which concerns her evolving consciousness of who she is, and though that story has definite communal implications, its focus is interior and personal. *Cottonwood,* however, though undeniably Silko's creation, derives directly from the oral tradition and retains that tradition's communal perspective. Neither **"Story of Sun House"** nor **"Buffalo Story,"** the poems that comprise *Cottonwood,* deal with character development or internal conflict any more than do the stories on which they are based. Rather each poem underscores the communal consequences of Yellow Woman's action, and in each case those consequences are positive. Given the narrator's references within **"Yellow Woman"** to the grandfather's Yellow Woman stories—indeed, Silko's

story ends with such a reference—the *Cottonwood* poems, placed where they are, suggest that however offensive her actions may be to conventional morality, the narrator brings from her journey with Silva a boon for her people.

"Story of Sun House" ends as follows: "Cottonwood / cottonwood / So much depends / upon one in the great canyon." It is this tree, "among all the others" where Yellow Woman came to wait for the sun. Like the lone cottonwood, Yellow Woman too has been singled out, and much depends upon her as well. She is called by the Sun to journey to Sun House, and this involves the loss of what is familiar and secure and dear:

> She left precise stone rooms
> that hold the heart silently
> She walked past white corn
> hung in long rows from roof beams
> the dry husks rattled in a thin autumn wind.
>
> She left her home
> her clan
> and the people
> (three small children
> the youngest just weaned
> her husband away cutting firewood).

The sacrifice is great, and in the spare yet powerfully evocative images of these lines Silko conveys the intense pain of separation. Her versification here, with "home," "clan," and "people" isolated in separate lines and children and husband further isolated in parentheses to the right, makes such pain almost palpable, as does the southeastward movement of the verse as it mirrors her journey toward the sun. Such "drastic things," however, "must be done / for the world / to continue." Harmony between the people and the spirit powers of the universe is necessary to existence and, through her marriage to the Sun, Yellow Woman perpetuates this harmony. The "people may not understand" her going; the visionary is invariably misunderstood. But that does not deter her, for she goes "out of love for this earth."

The narrator in **"Yellow Woman,"** too, restores an essential harmony through her going—a going which is also likely to be misunderstood. Her experience in living the reality revealed in her grandfather's stories has shown her the oneness of past and present, of historical and mythic time, and of the stories and the people. More, she has given the people another story and that, too, "must be done / for the world / to continue."

Yellow Woman brings about good in **"Buffalo Story"** as well, and in a sense its link with Silko's short story is even stronger than that of **"Story of Sun House."** Like **"Sun House,"** it enriches the short story by locating it for the reader within the necessary cultural and communal context, but **"Buffalo Story"** is itself enriched by the individualistic perspective cast forward upon it by **"Yellow Woman."** **"Buffalo Story"** follows the abduction storyline somewhat more closely than does **"Story of Sun House"** and evokes the sexual aspects of the traditional Yellow Woman stories more insistently. During a time of drought, when game is scarce and crops cannot grow, Yellow Woman, looking for water for her family, comes to a churning, muddy pool. At first she fears that a great animal had fouled the water. Then

> she saw him.
> She saw him tying his leggings
> drops of water were still shining on his chest.
> He was very good to look at
> and she kept looking at him
> because she had never seen anyone like him.
> It was Buffalo Man who was very beautiful.

She has ventured far from her village, as has the narrator in **"Yellow Woman,"** and the intense sexual pull Buffalo Man has on her here recalls that of Silva on the narrator. When Arrowboy, her husband, finds her asleep and calls to her to run to him so that they might escape the Buffalo People, to whose country Buffalo Man had abducted her, "She seemed to / get up a little slowly / but he didn't think much of it then." Her slowness here, he later learns, is not due to fatigue. After he kills all the Buffalo People, he tells Yellow Woman to go tell the people that there is meat, but she refuses to come down from the cottonwood which they had climbed to escape the Buffalo People's pursuit. Arrowboy sees that she is crying and asks her why:

> "Because you killed them,"
>   she said.
> "I suppose you love them,"
>   Estoy-eh-muut [Arrowboy] said,
> "and you want to stay with them."
> And Kochininako nodded her head
> and then he killed her too.

Paula Gunn Allen, while acknowledging the underlying centrality of oral tradition in the lives of tribal people, nonetheless maintains that "the oral tradition is often deceptive in what it makes of the lives of women." She says that

> so cleverly disguised are the tales of matricide, abduction and humiliation that the Indian woman is likely to perceive consciously only the surface message of the beauty, fragility, and self-sacrificing strength of her sisters though she cannot help but get the more destructive message that is the point of many tribal tales.

Such a "destructive message" is at least potentially present in the "Buffalo Man" story in Boas' *Keresan Texts,* but Silko casts the killing of Yellow Woman in **"Buffalo Story"** in a much different light. In Boas' version, when Arrowboy explains to Yellow Woman's father why he killed her, the Chief says, "Indeed? . . . " "All right," said he, "never mind." His response seems to justify the killing. In **"Buffalo Story"** her father, though implicitly accepting the justice of what was done, cries and mourns. Moreover, in Silko's rendering we are told that "It was all because / one time long ago / our daughter, our sister Kochininako / went away with them" that the people were fed and buffalo hunting began. Yellow Woman here is not an adultress who deserted her people but rather remains "our daughter, our sister" whose journey, like her journey in **"Story of Sun House,"** brought good to her people.

The context here established by the written word—Silko's short story—is essential in helping us to see Yellow Woman more completely than do the traditional stories alone, just as those stories in turn provide the necessary cultural context for **"Yellow Woman."** Through the narrator's telling in Silko's story, the individual dimension predominates and personal longings are shown to be as powerful and worthwhile as communal needs. Silko well knows, as the *Cottonwood* poems make clear, that individual sacrifice is at times crucial to community survival. But, as **"Yellow Woman"** reveals, individual fulfillment can be equally important to a tribal community, especially in the modern world where acculturation pressures are perhaps greater than ever before. Silko shows us, in this opening sequence of the "Yellow Woman" section, that personal and communal fulfillment need not be mutually exclusive—that they in fact enhance each other. And, by extension, the same is true of oral tradition and the written word as ways of knowing and of expression. To attain this harmony requires a powerful and inclusive vision, one receptive both to internal and external demands and the diverse languages which give them meaning. The development of such a vision, and of the network of relationships to the land, the people, the stories, and oneself it fosters, is, as I have said, the controlling idea of what I have called the **"Yellow Woman"** section of *Storyteller,* and it is expressed in various ways in the narrative episodes that follow.

The five short pieces that follow **"Yellow Woman"** and the *Cottonwood* poems focus on learning to see the land rightly and developing the proper relationship to it. This learning process is implicit in the narrator's experience in **"Yellow Woman,"** both in her journey with Silva up the mountain and in the precise, evocative detail in which she describes particular aspects of the landscape; it becomes refined and expanded in these brief narratives. In the first one, a poem entitled **"The Time We Climbed Snake Mountain,"** the narrator is a teacher who knows the mountain intimately and knows that "Somewhere around here / yellow spotted snake is sleeping": "So / please, I tell them watch out / don't step on the spotted yellow snake / he lives here. / The mountain is his." "Them" are never identified, but that is unimportant because this kind of teaching has been going on for thousands of years. It is a simple lesson in perspective and respect.

What follows is a personal reminiscence which in a different way reinforces this lesson. It is of Silko's girlhood when she first learned to hunt, and through her telling we learn something of how she began to acquire the wisdom she hands down in **"The Time We Climbed Snake Mountain."** Hunting alone one day Silko saw, or thought she saw, a "giant brown bear lying in the sun below the hilltop. Dead or just sleeping, I couldn't tell." She "knew there were no bears that large on Mt. Taylor; I was pretty sure there were no bears that large anywhere," and she also knew "what hours of searching for motion, for the outline of a deer, for the color of a deer's hide can do to the imagination." Almost paralyzed with caution and curiosity, eager to examine the bear up close but unsure if it is dead or is just sleeping or is at all, she walks, "as quietly and as carefully as I probably will ever move," away from it. As she goes she looks back, still unsure of what she has seen, and "the big dark bear remained there. . . . " "I never told anyone what I had seen," Silko laughingly recalls, "because I knew they don't let people who see such things carry .30-30s or hunt deer with them."

That the bear impressed itself deeply on her imagination, however, is apparent as she recalls another hunting trip which took place two years after the first one. Her uncle had killed a big mule deer, and, as Silko went to help him, she realized that it was the same time of day as when she saw, or thought she saw, the bear:

> I walked past the place deliberately.
> I found no bones, but when a wind moved
>   through the
> light yellow grass that afternoon I hurried
>   around the
> hill to find my uncle.
> Sleeping, not dead, I decided.

At this point, there is no longer any doubt in her mind that the bear was real; and her use of poetic from further suggests that this place where she saw the great bear has become part of an inner as well as an outer landscape. Through an act of imagination she has learned a profound truth from the land which intensifies her bond to it.

The photograph which separates these two reminiscences reinforces this idea. In it, laid out on the porch of the old cabin in which Silko and her hunting party stayed on Mt. Taylor, are five mule deer bucks, prayer feathers tied to their antlers, Silko herself, and her Uncle Polly. She and her uncle had just finished "arranging the bucks . . . so they can have their pictures taken." Given the "special significance" of photographs to her family and to the people of Laguna, the careful arrangement of the deer, and the prayer feathers, we are prepared for the subtle revelation in her second reminiscence. Her vision of the bear, like the deer, was a gift to help the people survive. It was the intimate expression of the land to her imagination of its own spiritual integrity and that of its creatures. Through the mystery and wonder of her seeing, the land, impressed itself indelibly upon her memory.

Two photographs follow the second bear reminiscence. The first, discussed earlier, is of hills and means that no longer exist and, placed where it is in *Storyteller,* the photograph movingly conveys the need, more important now than ever before, for all people to know the land as the place that gives us being and the source of our profoundest wisdom. It reminds us, as does *Storyteller* as a whole, about the oral tradition—of the fragility of what was once thought whole and eternal and of how much all life ultimately depends on imagination and memory. The second photo, taken from the east edge of Laguna looking toward the west, enhances this idea by showing us the place from which the stories in *Storyteller,* old and contemporary, arise. What follows is a series of such stories and reminiscences unified not by subject or theme but by the shared landscape that nurtured them. They express the richness, diversity, playfulness and humor of Laguna oral tradition. Like the first of these two photographs, they also express its fragility.

The first story which follows these photographs is a poetic retelling of a hunting story Silko, when a child of seven, heard from her Aunt Alice. It flows smoothly out of the photograph of Laguna in that it endows a particular portion of the land with mystery and wonder, and by so doing makes it a gift of and to the imagination. Though she heard this story six years before she saw the great bear on a hunting trip, the story flows out of her recollection of this experience as well; and by using cyclic rather than chronological structure, she more strikingly evokes, as with the "Yellow Woman" and *Cottonwood* sequence, the timeless significance of the oral tradition to the understanding of human experience. Told, as are other such stories in the book, in the conversational accents and occasional expository digressions of the traditional storyteller, the story is again of Yellow Woman, here a young girl and a fine hunter who, having gotten seven big rabbits in a morning's hunting, comes upon "a great big animal" who asks for one of her rabbits, which he immediately devours. The animal's demands escalate with his appetite and they are rendered by Silko in a compellingly dramatic sequence as the animal, having demanded and received all the girl's rabbits and weapons, insists upon her clothes as well. Rightly fearful that she herself will be next, little Yellow Woman fools the animal into letting her remove her clothes in a cave too small for him to enter. Knowing, however, that her escape is at best temporary, she calls upon the twin Brothers, Ma'see'wi and Ou'yu'ye'wi, who kill the animal with their flint knives. They then cut the animal open, pull out his heart, and throw it. At this point in the telling the legend melds with contemporary reality, myth enters experience, as we are told that the heart landed "right over here / near the river / between Laguna and Paguate / where the road turns to go / by the railroad tracks / right around / from John Paisano's place— / that big rock there / looks just like a heart, / . . . and that's why / it is called / Yash'ka / which means 'heart'."

By telling this story to her seven year-old niece, who is disappointed at not having been allowed to join her parents on a hunting trip, Aunt Alice both entertains and teaches. She raises the child's self-esteem by showing her that young girls can be skillful and clever hunters, alerts the prospective young hunter to the unexpected dangers that at times confront a hunter, reassures her that such obstacles, however dangerous, may be overcome, and perhaps most importantly, helps her niece to see the land with the same sense of wonder and joy with which she heard the story. A part of the landscape heretofore ordinary and unremarked has by means of the story been made precious to the child. Six years later, when she sees the giant bear, Silko will have her own hunting story to tell—and Aunt Alice's story will be recalled anew, recreated as it is here, richer and truer than ever.

The story told by a loving aunt of a special place engenders a reminiscence of another place which is special because of the woman who may, or may not, be buried there. With this reminiscence Silko shifts her focus from the land per se to the people—more precisely, to how people get remembered. This reminiscence concerns two women. Silko's great-grandmother, Helen, was born of an old traditional family, and Silko recalls that "even as a very young child / I sensed she did not like children much and so I remember her / from a distance. . . . " Much dearer to memory is a woman Silko never knew, old Juana, of whom Silko learned from the stories of Grandma Lillie, one of Helen's daughters. Juana, who "raised Grandma Lillie and her sisters / and brothers," was not born into a "genteel tradition" as was Grandma Helen. A Navajo, "Juana had been kidnapped by slavehunters / who attacked her family . . . " Stripped of her family, of whom no trace remained, her language, and her heritage, Juana "continued with the work she knew" and was eventually hired by Silko's Grandpa Stagner to care for his family. Silko recalls going on Memorial Day with Grandma Lillie to take flowers to Juana's grave. The graveyard where she was buried was old and the "small flat sandstones" which served as grave markers were mostly broken or covered over; as a result Grandma Lillie could never be certain if they found her grave—"but we left the jar of roses and lilacs we had cut anyway." Juana's actual presence, like the giant bear's in the earlier hunting story, is ultimately irrelevant. As the bear lives in Silko's imagination, so Juana lives in her, and in Grandma Lillie's heart, where they have more perfect being. Though orphaned young, Juana is restored through the stories to a family, language, and heritage.

Juana is remembered for her loving kindness, but that is not the only way people get remembered. The tone shifts rather suddenly from the reminiscence about Juana to two "gossip" stories, both of them rich in humor and irony. The first story, of a man caught on flagrante in a cornfield by his wife and her two sisters, and Silko's telling of it—in which she uses the storyteller's conversational tone and shifts the point of view from the two lovers to the wife and sisters and then to the man alone—express a delicious comic blend of conspiracy, anticipation, antagonism and resignation. She dramatically sets the scene: "His wife had caught them together before / and probably she had been hearing rumors again / the way people talk." The lovers planned to meet in the afternoon, when it was so hot that "everyone just rested" until evening, when it was cool enough to return to work. "This man's wife was always / watching him real close at night / so afternoon was / the only chance they had." When they were caught the woman left, and the man had to take the inevitable chastisement alone. His "wife would cry a little," her sisters would comfort her, "and then they would start talking again / about how good their family had treated him / and how lucky he was. / He couldn't look at them / so he looked at the sky / and then over at the hills behind the village." Though the man's inability to look at the women may suggest guilt, his wandering gaze has something of boredom in it, as if he were merely playing a role in an ancient and rather tiresome domestic ritual. His manhood is not spared, as the women are quick to remind him that his lover "had a younger boyfriend / and it was only afternoons that she had any use / for an old man":

> So pretty soon he started hoeing weeds again
> because they were ignoring him
> like he didn't matter anyway
> now that
> that woman was gone.

The irony here is rich. The man, it seems, is important to

his wife and relatives, and perhaps to the community as a whole, only by virtue of his infidelity. It is this by which he lives in a communal memory, enriches the storytelling life of the people, and gains mythic dimension. Apart from that context he "didn't matter."

"Then there was the night," Silko gleefully continues, whetting our appetite for the story of old man George who, on a trip to the outhouse, "heard strange sounds / coming from one of the old barns / below." Checking, "just in case some poor animal / was trapped inside," the old man is shocked to discover Frank,

> so respectable and hard-working
> and hardly ever drunk—
> well there he was
> naked with that Garcia girl—
> you know,
> the big fat one.
> And here it was
> the middle of winter
> without their clothes on!

Silko's tone here expresses two points of view simultaneously. George, to say the least, is surprised to find a man like Frank in this situation and Silko, as storyteller, relishes the irony. Further, she creates the proper context here by giving us, through her "you know" aside, a sense of her immediate audience—another young person, perhaps, to whom Frank would be cited by conventional morality as an example to follow. "Poor old man George / he didn't know what to say," and his befuddlement is comically rendered in the story's closing lines: "so he just closed the door again / and walked back home— / he even forgot where he was going / in the first place." But he'll remember Frank and the Garcia girl.

It may at first glance seem strange that these stories are followed by a brief recollection of Grandma A'mooh and the way she read the children's book *Brownie the Bear* to her great-granddaughters, especially since **"Storytelling,"** which follows, consists of six vignettes largely in the same vein as the "gossip" stories. This reminiscence, however, mentioned earlier in another context, is wonderfully appropriate here. Taken in conjunction with the "gossip" stories that surround it, it reminds us again of the variety and inclusiveness of the oral tradition. It also underscores Silko's intent throughout **Storyteller** to convey the dynamic relationship between the oral tradition and the life it expresses. The life of a community, or of an individual, does not arrange itself into precise categories, literary or otherwise, nor does it follow neat, unbroken lines of development; and Silko, by juxtaposing different kinds of narratives and subjects, helps us to see vital, rewarding connections that might otherwise go unnoticed. Remember, too, that her emphasis in the "Grandma A'mooh" reminiscence is on how a story is told. A good story cannot exist apart from a good storyteller. Much of the fun of the "gossip" stories, as we have seen, is in Silko's manner of telling them. Grandma A'mooh

> always read the story with such animation and
>   expression
> changing her tone of voice and inflection
> each time one of the bears spoke—
> the way a storyteller would have told it.

Her telling makes the story live, recreates it in effect with each repetition. This is what Silko, in the "gossip" stories as well as in others, tries to do, to give a sense of the flux and immediacy of life lived. Too, it is her telling which links Grandma A'mooh to past generations of storytellers—as it does Silko.

The six vignettes in "Storytelling," all variations on the Yellow Woman abduction stories, bring what I have called the "Yellow Woman" section of *Storyteller* full circle. The first of these is Silko's abbreviated rendering of the opening of the **"Buffalo Story,"** when Yellow Woman goes for water:

> "Are you here already?"
> "Yes," he said.
> He was smiling.
> "Because I came for you."
> She looked into the
> shallow clear water.
> "But where shall I put my water jar?"

In this version Yellow Woman is apparently expecting Buffalo Man, and though coercion might be implied when he says he came for her, her response is willing, even coy and playful. The tone of the fifth vignette is quite similar:

> Seems like
> its always happening to me.
> Outside the dance hall door
> late Friday night
> in the summertime.
> and those
> brown-eyed men from Cubero,
> smiling.
> The usually ask me
> "Have you seen the way the stars shine
> up there in the sand hills?"
> And I usually say "No. Will you show me?"

Silko alerts us as **"Storytelling"** begins that we "should understand / the way it was / back then, / because it is the same / even now." The traditional stories, Silko is saying, both here and throughout *Storyteller,* offer profound and necessary insights into contemporary experiences. Specifically, the "Yellow Woman" stories, especially Silko's renderings of them, are among other things open, unqualified expressions of woman's sexuality. This is not to say that, because the traditional stories are abduction stories, Silko is dealing in rape fantasies. Quite the contrary. In her versions the coercive element, though present, is not the controlling one. Yellow Woman is at all times in charge of her own destiny. She understands and accepts her sexuality, expresses it honestly, and is guided by her own strong desire. We see this in Silko's short story, **"Yellow Woman,"** in the *Cottonwood* stories, and again in these two "Storytelling" vignettes. By focusing in these little narratives not on the lovemaking but on the prelude to it, Silko establishes the sexual integrity of both the mythic and contemporary Yellow Woman, and conveys with playful subtlety the charged eroticism between them and Buffalo Man and "those / brown-eyed men from Cubero" respectively.

Yellow Woman's sexual integrity gets a broadly comic touch in the fourth vignette, where Silko inverts the traditional abduction motif. The F.B.I. and state police in the summer of 1967 pursued a red '56 Ford with four Laguna women and three Navajo men inside. A kidnapping was involved, and the police followed a trail "of wine bottles and / size 42 panties / hanging in bushes and trees / all along the road." When they were caught, one of the men explained: " 'We couldn't escape them' . . . / 'We tried, but there were four of them and / only three of us'."

But sexual honesty, especially a woman's, is, as we have seen, likely to be misunderstood. In the first *Cottonwood* poem, **"Story of Sun House,"** the Sun tells Yellow Woman that even though their union is necessary for the world to continue, "the people may not understand"; and the narrator in **"Yellow Woman"** must make up a story for her family about being kidnapped by a Navajo. In fact, the abduction motif of the Yellow Woman stories proves useful, or almost so, in a number of situations. "No! that gossip isn't true," says a distraught mother in the third "Storytelling" vignette: "She didn't elope / She was *kidnapped* by / that Mexican / at Seama Feast. / You know / my daughter / isn't / *that* kind of girl." As was stated earlier, however, there cannot be a good story without a good storyteller, as the contemporary Yellow Woman of the sixth vignette learns, "It was / that Navajo / from Alamo, / you know, / the tall / good-looking / one," she tells her husband. "He told me / he'd kill me / if I didn't / go with him." That, rain, and muddy roads, she said, are why "it took me / so long / to get back home." When her husband leaves her, she blames herself: "I could have told / the story / better than I did."

In a *Sun-Tracks* interview, Silko said of "these gossip stories": "I don't look upon them as gossip. The connotation is all wrong. These stories about goings-on, about what people are up to, give identity to a place." What she argues for here is in effect what the "Yellow Woman" section is all about: a new way of seeing. Seen rightly, such stories are neither idle rumor nor trivial chatter, but are rather another mode of expression, a way in which people define themselves and declare who they are. Thus it is fitting that the "Yellow Woman" section, and this essay, conclude with a photograph taken of some of the houses in Laguna. Here, after all, is where the people live their lives and it is this sense of life being lived, of life timeless and ongoing, changing and evolving, contradictory and continuous, that Silko expresses with grace and power through her melding of oral tradition and the written word in *Storyteller.* (pp. 10-25)

Bernard A. Hirsch, " 'The Telling Which Continues': Oral Tradition and the Written Word in Leslie Marmon Silko's 'Storyteller'," in American Indian Quarterly, *Vol. 12, No. 1, Winter, 1988, pp. 1-28.*

James Ruppert   (essay date Spring 1988)

[*In the essay below, Ruppert discusses how* Ceremony *"fuses story and reality to define an identity for its protagonist and the reader."*]

When Leslie Marmon Silko published *Ceremony* in 1977, the critical reaction was good. The book was praised in the *New York Review of Books* and in other established critical publications. But, something of even greater significance happened for those interested in Southwestern literature and American Indian literature. A novel came into existence that challenged readers, Indian and White, to expand and merge their cultural frameworks. The novel was, at once, grounded in Indian tradition and informed by contemporary American fiction. While remaining a popular novel taught in many classes, it continues to open up fresh insights into fiction and culture, for it is not only a novel that presents a philosophical and cultural viewpoint, but a novel that teaches us how to read it and how to understand its special narrative structures. Through its formal and stylistic elements, it fuses story and reality to define an identity for its protagonist and the reader.

Perhaps the most immediate way the reader sees its uniqueness is in its form. *Ceremony* merges what we would call poetry and prose. Silko says that ideally these sections should be heard, not read, so that they approximate the position of a listener before the storyteller. The stories or myths told in the poems are broken up and placed periodically throughout the text, so that the completion of the poem stories and the prose narrative converge at the end. It would seem that Silko wants us to hear a different voice in the poetry, while still forcing the reader to acknowledge a unity of purpose underneath this apparent formal diversity. This discourse strategy is mirrored variously throughout the novel and is ultimately a reflection of the epistemological unity of Laguna narrative esthetic and world view.

When Thought-Woman thinks, whatever she is thinking about appears. "I'm telling you the story she is thinking," says Silko at the start. The story—the myth—is reality (a complete ontological system), and the novel leads the reader to an insight into that unity between myth and reality. Reality is a story, Silko explains. The mythic material presented in poetic form paces the reality of the prose, leading us to the climax of the novel, but it also comments on the action of the story and gives order. Only when we see the reality of the novel in terms of the mythic poem, do we see the order of the story. The loss of power and vision, or, as Tayo says, "how the world had come undone," the struggle to return the world to its proper order, the ultimate successful conclusion of the crisis, and the identity and harmony created by this successful conclusion of the story are all predicted, ordered, and directed by the myth/poem. The myth/poem expresses the reality of the prose meaning. It creates that meaning. It is not just an allegory or a quaint piece of local color. The drought, the Whites, the breakdown of tribal identity and integrity, World War II, and even nuclear power are given meaning through the interaction of the poetry and the prose; or, on another level, through the interface of story and reality.

When the speaker begins by saying that the stories are the only way to fight off illness, evil, and death, she is being quite literal, for it is the stories that grant order and form to the flow of events, and these stories codify meaning in such a way that the listener or reader can understand events in the world around him. Only when the reader understands the meaning of events can he act in an effective

manner. But to do so, it is essential that the reader understands that the stories and reality in the novel are one.

Stylistically, the form of the prose aids this realization in a number of ways. First, Silko uses no chapter breaks. As the prose flows continuously from beginning to end, the reader is encouraged to perceive the novel as one unified experience. Any breaks in the flow are short, temporary, and tend to lead the reader to the poetic or mythic plane. The artificial structures of numerical separation or of dramatic scenes are eliminated in favor of structures inherent in the rhythm of the narrative and the movements of the mythic story. Events and interactions are not isolated into chapters but are superimposed until they build a structure that continues throughout the novel. They grow out of a developing narrative context and are to be understood on multiple levels of significance in the same way that events in Laguna culture can be understood on mythic, religious, cultural, sociological, and individual levels simultaneously.

This lack of expected breaking of the flow of the prose also discourages the reader from imposing a strict chronological order on the narrative, thus reinforcing the perception that the novel is a simultaneous, unified moment that circles out like the waves around a rock dropped in a quiet pond, rather than a linear progression of moments. The thematic center point of the novel is when Tayo and the reader realize this, and Silko writes, "He took a deep breath of cold mountain air: there were no boundaries; the world below and the sand paintings inside became the same that night." As the false boundaries of time, distance, truth, and individuality fall away, Tayo and the reader are left with the fused story/reality unifying all experience, defining time, event, and identity. Western distinctions which slice reality are put aside by the structure of the novel.

When the pattern of the narrative is analyzed, this concern with the unity of experience and the fusion of story and reality is seen reflected in the way that Silko uses a fragmented story structure which does not make clear distinction between past and present. Events seem to be happening on various planes of existence at the same time. One obvious explanation is that the form of the narrative mirrors the psychological state of the protagonist, Tayo. At the beginning of the novel, he is a shattered war veteran. As he goes through Betonie's ceremony, he reintegrated himself into psychic health and Laguna culture. The swirl of memory and reality which paralyzes his broken mental state is healed and the narrative proceeds in a more standard, linear fashion because Tayo's mental state is improving, becoming more normal, more standard, more Western.

Perhaps the story becomes clearer and more patterned for the reader later in the novel for another more reader-centered reason. At the beginning of the novel, the reader is unsure of the relationship between the prose and poetry, agitated with the fragmented vision of the narrative, and uncertain who is speaking and why, but those confusions seem to be clarified by the end of the novel so that the reader tends not to ask such questions when approaching the resolution at the end. Not only has the novel taught us to disregard those artificial Western distinctions such as time and space, it has approximated a holistic vision close to the Laguna experience of the world and oral tradition. Silko assures us that in the story, time and distance are overcome and anything is possible if one knows the right story. But even more deeply, the reader has learned to trust the fusion of the story and reality; he has enriched his epistemological conditioning so that the story makes better sense. The reader has grown; he perceives the events in the story with greater insight, perhaps even a cross-cultural insight. It could be said that the reader's story perception has improved, somewhat like the way one's depth perception or pattern-recognition skills can be enhanced.

The formal structure is, of course, an expression of the thematic content. Tayo's return to individual and cultural identity and health (or harmony) through ceremonial integration with a unified story/reality is central to the novel. Tayo's act of cursing the rain parallels the loss of rain in the mythic story. His personal breakdown reflects the breakdown of Laguna cultural integrity. His personal dryness of emotion, spirit, and communal identity find physical manifestation in the drought suffered by the people of Laguna. Betonie's ceremony is Tayo's path to reintegration back to identity on the personal, cultural, and mythic level. But it is also the Laguna path back to reintegration, and ultimately, the world's.

Tayo's recovery is contingent upon his realization that mythic and real worlds are one, just as the success of the novel is contingent upon the reader realizing the same thing. As Tayo finally understands, "His sickness was only part of something larger, and his cure would be found only in something great and inclusive of everything." He realizes that the world is in danger and that his cure and the world's cure require his action. He cannot remain passive. When Tayo enters the story, or as Night Swan, says, "you are now part of it," he is given an identity; he might be called the-one-who-brings-back-the-rain. He felt after the war that he had become white smoke, that he had no identity, but in the unified story that the reader comes to understand as containing the underlying pattern of significance, he did have an identity. He was the blasphemer, the-one-who-drove-the-rain-away.

The trip that Tayo makes to the mountain helps convince him of the fusion of story and reality. He realizes in the mountain that "Betonie's vision was a story that he could feel happening." As Tayo moves deeper into that fusion, he meets Mountain Lion and falls in love with Elk Woman. His understanding of story/reality increases and emotion comes back into his life. He realizes that he and the world around him have come under the influence of the destroyers, the witches. Ts'eh tells him, "Their highest ambition is to gut human beings while they are still breathing, to hold the heart still beating so the victim will never feel anything again. When they finish, you watch yourself from a distance and you can't even cry—not even for yourself." Tayo's emerging understanding of epistemological unity and the destruction of time and space boundaries are complete on the mountain when he realizes:

> The silence was inside, in his belly; there was no

longer any hurry. The ride into the mountains had branched into all directions of time. He knew then why the oldtimers could only speak of yesterday and tomorrow in terms of the present moment: the only certainty; and this present sense of being was qualified with bare hints of yesterday or tomorrow, by saying, "I go up to the mountains tomorrow." The ck'o'yo Kaup'a'ta somewhere is stacking his gambling sticks and waiting for a visitor; Rocky and I are walking across the ridge in moonlight; Josiah and Robert are waiting for us. This night is a single night; and there has never been any other.

When Tayo returns to the pueblo, the old men of the tribe take him into the Kiva. As he tells them of his experiences, they realize that he has seen A'moo'ooh, the Elk Woman. The pueblo's shattered connection with the spirit world is now reestablished and they know the drought will end. The old men give Tayo the social identity he had always lacked as they take him in to become one of them, but they also acknowledge his mythic identity as the bringer of blessings, the gatherer of seeds, the lover of the Elk Woman.

Tayo's final realizations come only when he is able to end the story correctly. He understands enough about the witchery now to act on his own. He must not let the witchery encircle "slowly to choke the life away." He must draw strength from his vision, and then end the story in a way that completes the personal, social, and mythic story of the human beings and the destroyers. He gathers strength at this point from a unified vision of the interweaving of all life.

> Yet at that moment in the sunrise, it was all so beautiful, everything, from all directions, evenly, perfectly, balancing day with night, summer months with winter. The valley was enclosing this totality, like the mind holding all thoughts together in a single moment.
>
> The strength came from here, from this feeling. It had always been there.

Tayo is at that moment beginning to realize that the source of strength for him, Laguna, and those who would fight the destroyers is in a unified vision of experience, and he begins to act on it. Tayo looks out and sees the world as a giant sand painting and all humans as one clan—narrative and experience become one. "He cried the relief he felt at finally seeing the pattern, the way all the stories fit together—the old stories, the war stories, their stories—to become the story that was still being told. He was not crazy; he had never been crazy. He had only seen and heard the world as it always was: no boundaries, only transitions through all distances and time." This realization gives Tayo what he calls the "ear for the story, the eye for the pattern." His understanding of the story/reality creates meaning and identity.

As mentioned earlier, this fusion of story/reality is exactly the effect that the form and style of the novel encourage the reader to experience. As Tayo's confusion and lack of identity clear, the reader's confusion about the form and content of the narrative clears too. If the reader follows and understands the fusion of the story and reality, he too sees how all the stories merge into the story that is being told. He has effectively been educated into the unity that strengthens Tayo and brings back the rain and its blessings. Also, he has been introduced into the experience of the oral tradition. The perceptive reader, too, has the ear for the story, the eye for the pattern, and is encouraged to see the world as one large swirling sand painting.

But this realization brings obligations with it. He must understand the story and see the work of the destroyers in the world around him. Night Swan, Betonie, Ts'eh, or Tayo could also say to each of us, "you are part of it now." So the reader too must act. Great responsibility is placed on the shoulders of those who understand. They must see to it that the story ends properly. Consequently, the readers are also given an identity in the mythic story. They are members of a group of people who must tell the story correctly, who must defeat the destroyers. They are part of the story now. Others will speak of them when they learn the story.

Out of this new identity and these new understandings will come a new harmony with all that is. The reader knows that his presence is needed at the new ceremonies designed to defeat the destroyers. The new ceremonies are being made every day, for Silko explains the ceremonies and the stories must grow to meet the new conditions of evil and disharmony. The novel begins and ends with the word "Sunrise" because the Dawn people's ceremonial prayers do so. The novel itself is a prayer or a ceremony which continues in the world after the book is closed. The title *Ceremony* refers not only to the ceremony that Tayo experiences, but also to the harmony, healing, and increased awareness that the reader acquires through the reading and understanding of the novel itself. It has produced meaning, identity, and understanding in the reader. It has brought the reader into the story, brought him in touch with the unity of all that is, placed him at the center of the swirling sand painting of the world. It has brought him into harmony.

Silko's novel has amazingly fused contemporary American fiction with Native American story telling. Her novel uses narrative in a way unique to the Western literary tradition. But as she does so, she structures the reader's experience so that he will be forced to understand and participate in the cultural and epistemological framework of the people of Laguna. In a similar manner, a Native American reader is encouraged to utilize his understandings as a base for viewing White society, but he is also forced to use something of the Western psychological and social way of seeing. The cross-cultural racial tensions that surround the novel are ultimately dismantled and re-formed as the distinction between the destroyers and those who would stop the destroyers. Whites and Indians can unite through participation in the story/reality.

Silko's story brings all humanity together in a struggle to defeat the destroyers who "are working for the end of this world." The last page of the novel is not the finish of the fused story/reality. The ceremony continues and it is now the responsibility of the reader to act. (pp. 78-85)

James Ruppert, "The Reader's Lessons in

'Ceremony'," in Arizona Quarterly, *Vol. 44, No. 1, Spring, 1988, pp. 78-85.*

Linda L. Danielson (essay date Autumn 1988)

[*In the essay excerpted below, Danielson likens the thematic structure of* Storyteller *to the "radiating spokes" of a spider's web as she discusses how Silko reclaims the Laguna Pueblo's woman-centered traditions through storytelling.*]

Over the last twenty years, the general development of scholarship about women's lives and art parallels an unprecedented flowering of creative writing by American Indian women. But in view of these parallel developments, American Indian women have shown little interest in the feminist movement, and conversely mainstream feminist scholarship has paid strikingly little attention to the writing of American Indian women.

Leslie Silko's *Storyteller* (1981), a product of this literary florescence, has remained virtually undiscussed as a whole by critics of any stamp. With its emphasis on women tradition bearers, female deities, and its woman author's personal perspective, *Storyteller* seems to ask for a feminist critical treatment. (p. 325)

But feminism is not all one thing, and an Anglocentric feminism will not get us far with *Storyteller* or any other text by an American Indian woman writer. Rather . . . a tribal cultural awareness joined with a feminist sensitivity to the non-linear, harmonious, achronological, and inclusive field modes of perception will engender a tribally informed feminist critical perspective that can correct a skew introduced by both male and Anglocentric bias in the study of American Indian life and literature. What is more, such a perspective may provide what no other critical approach has—a unified and coherent interpretation of *Storyteller.*

Certainly, some mainstream feminist social concerns link Indian women with white women and with other women of color. In her essay, "Honoring the Vision of 'Changing Woman'" (1984), Rayna Green outlines some of these universal women's issues: wages, social services, reproductive rights, and large questions of peace, equality, and political power. But, as Kate Shanley Vangen points out [in *A Gathering of Spirit*], despite Indian women's concern with key issues of the majority women's movement, "equality *per se* may have a different meaning for Indian women and Indian people. That difference begins with personal and tribal sovereignty—the right to be legally recognized as peoples empowered to determine our own destiny."

A tribally informed feminism pays attention to cultural differences as well as to similarities of world view. Such a feminism, for example, acknowledges that roles and stereotypes of women within Laguna society are not those of white society. The power relations between Indian men and women are not the same as power relations between white women and men; white male-dominated institutions oppress both tribal men and women. Furthermore, both Indian men and women writers express in their work perceptual patterns and cultural values that stand in marked contrast to much of what is valorized by the white male schools of critical thought. The work of both Indian and white feminist editors and literary critics is essential to this understanding. In addition, feminist cultural scholars' responses to oral tradition, to Indian culture, and to men's cultural scholarship provide a fresh background against which to understand the literary works.

Several lines of inquiry among mainstream feminist literary critics can be usefully applied to the work of Indian women writers. For example, feminist scholars have challenged the institutional bases of literature within the critical establishment to demonstrate how our concept of "literature" has excluded and misread women's work.

Particularly applicable to Silko's *Storyteller* are feminist critical strategies to reclaim as legitimate literary subjects, women's experience and female mythic power. Sandra M. Gilbert sees this strategy as a matter of *re-vision,* seeing anew: "When I say we must redo our history, therefore, I mean we must review, reimagine, rethink, rewrite, revise, and reinterpret the events and documents that constitute it" [*Feminist Criticism*].

Silko's *Storyteller* represents just such a re-vision of the world from her vantage point as a Laguna Indian woman. In fact, understanding her re-vision and reinterpretation of personal and tribal memory leads us past the easy impulse to call *Storyteller* a collage, a family album, or pastiche, on into a conception of its unity and significance as a literary work. In seeing anew, Silko expresses a deeply unified view of the world, reclaiming as central to her craft the tribe, the significance of ordinary women's and men's lives, and the set of values arising from the female power of the primary Keresan deities.

> **Silko presents a highly personal view of tribal ways and at the same time a tribal slant on her personal memories, richly fed by the foremothers and forefathers whose words inspire *Storyteller*. Through the book she reclaims both personal and tribal traditions about men and women, animals and holy people, community and creativity.**
>
> **—Linda L. Danielson**

Clearly Silko's first loyalty is to family and tribe rather than to woman-ness. But we need to understand that, for a tribal woman, concern with the lives and dignity of the men of her tribe may well constitute a feminist stance. Much more than tribal men, the male-dominated Euro-American world view and its institutions have been the oppressive forces that Silko must resist. Sometimes white women participate in the racism of that Euro-American world. Equally, sometimes tribal men absorb and embody the colonizers' posture of male superiority, perhaps in an

unconscious effort to ameliorate the pain of their own oppression. But both men and women are victims of oppression by male-dominated institutions. *Storyteller,* like most writing by American Indian women, creatively resists that oppression.

Silko presents a highly personal view of tribal ways and at the same time a tribal slant on her personal memories, richly fed by the foremothers and forefathers whose words inspire *Storyteller.* Through the book she reclaims both personal and tribal traditions about men and women, animals and holy people, community and creativity. Silko is concerned with how humans fit into the cosmos, and the relationship between Creators and Destroyers engages her to the exclusion of any battle between the sexes. She pays constant attention to fair credit and representation for both men and women as active and responsible beings. While Silko maintains solidarity with tribal men (and deer and bears and Coyotes), she insists on the priority of female creator-gods, an idea that had been subverted through the tribe's colonial experience. In so doing, Silko insists on both a woman-centered traditionality and a personal independence of vision that constitutes such a reimagining as Gilbert recommends in order to know one's self and culture uncolonized.

Reclaiming identity, be it personal, sexual, or cultural, says Alicia Ostriker [in *Stealing the Language*], involves "a vigorous and varied invasion of the sanctuaries of existing language," one of which is certainly literature and its established forms. Ostriker continues, "Where women write strongly as women, it is clear that their intention is to subvert and transform the life and literature they inherit." As a product of Bureau of Indian Affairs (B.I.A.) schools and mainstream American university education, Silko has inherited Euro-American traditions about what constitutes a book and conventions about how one speaks as an author. But like many other contemporary women and tribal men writers, Silko subverts and transforms these inherited traditions, appropriating the making of books to her own purposes. *Storyteller* as physical object generally follows the conventions: the front cover, title page, and back cover blurb contain all the usual communications between publisher and book buyer. Silko's name appears as author. But past the title page she reclaims the interior of the book for her own purposes. There are no numbered divisions or chapters within *Storyteller.* The book is not a novel, not an autobiography. Lee Marmon's photo may stand next to Silko's poetic retelling of a traditional myth; nearby may be a letter to poet James Wright.

Inside the book Silko simply denies individual authorship. Self-effacement is not the usual author's stance in mainstream Euro-American literary practice. Taking such a stance, Silko reclaims authority as a storyteller who speaks for the community. It is the same authority expressed in the prefatory poem of her novel *Ceremony* when Thought-Woman, the Spider, "is sitting in her room / thinking of a story now / I'm telling you the story / she is thinking." The myths and stories have come to Silko through specific others, whom she credits: Aunt Susie Marmon, Great-Grandmother Maria Anaya Marmon, Aunt Alice Little, Grandma Lillie, Grandpa Hank Marmon, her father Lee Marmon, her friend and fellow writer Simon Ortiz. Among these, incidentally, the grandmothers are the primary sources instead of the unconsulted, as in so much anthropological fieldwork. At some points, Silko credits the "they say" of common oral tradition. "Traditionally," she says, "everyone from the youngest child to the oldest person, was expected to listen and to be able to recall or tell a portion, if only a small detail, from a narrative account or story. Thus the remembering and retelling were a communal process" [*Antaeus,* 1986] Silko's self-effacement in her writing suggests the traditional artist's lack of self-focus and declares her grounding in the values of Pueblo culture, at the same time that it expresses her faith in the creativity of the community.

This creative community, moreover, consists of listeners as well as artists or tellers. Silko says, "A great deal of the story is believed to be inside the listener, and the storyteller's role is to draw the story out of the listeners." But Silko is, after all, not a simple village artisan free of influence from the outside world. In adopting the written English literary tradition as her expressive vehicle, she moves into an artistic world that is shaped largely by white men and is not prepared to deal sympathetically with Indians of either sex nor with women of any color. So in effacing her own authorship, crediting the community, mixing once-sacrosanct genres, and abjuring linear structure—in short, by denying the standards and customs of white male-dominated literary criticism—Silko reclaims the making of books from the white male critical establishment.

Furthermore, Silko defies the usual white notions of the proper literary Indian. Jarold Ramsey warns that the ethnographic perspective in literary scholarship tends tacitly "to deny the imaginative freedom of the writer" by imposing "a kind of *classicism* on 'authentic' Indian literary materials and relegating everything else (assimilations, adaptations, and so on) to the status of impure curiosities unworthy of serious attention" [*College English* 41, October 1979]. Silko insists on a community (primarily of modern women as tradition bearers), on forms such as village gossip, and on an idea of individuality that does not fit most literary or cultural scholars' expectations. The title story of the work is set not in her own Laguna pueblo, but among the Inuit of Alaska. Silko preserves Aunt Susie's language, an educated English including words like *precipitous* and *accessible.* Besides the right to their own language, she emphasizes the storytellers' right to say, "The way I heard it was . . . ," and she extends these rights to herself as she both adapts traditional stories to her own ends and recreates specific tellers' versions. (pp. 325-31)

While Silko reclaims her individual and tribal identity from white male-dominated American scholarship, she has also reclaimed the centrality of female power and female artistic expression within Keresan culture. [In *The Sacred Hoop*] Paula Gunn Allen points to Keresan culture, with its female creator-figures, as "the last extreme mother-right people on earth," in which male leaders hold temporal power within the village through the agency of I'atyik'u or Corn Mother; these caciques are therefore referred to as *Mother.* But the fact remains that these are men exercising temporal power, and that women have generally been subservient to male authority, even though mythic power does reside in the female. . . .

Though Silko has apparently had no encounters with tribal authority over *Storyteller,* she and her grandmothers before her, judging from the work of Parsons and Franz Boas at least, were either subverting male control of tribal discourse or subverting portrayals of women in white anthropological documents. (p. 331)

Having in the very making of *Storyteller* asserted independence of both post-colonial tribal politics and white scholarly traditions, Silko uses structural, thematic, imagistic, and metacommunicative tools to reclaim a whole and woman-centered cosmos. In this nurturant and balanced community, both men and women can live and understand their relationship to relatives, storytelling, witchery, rain, deer, coyotes, and other inhabitants of the world.

The non-linear structure of the book provides the reader with the principal subtext. This structure, which may appear baffling and haphazard at first glance, makes sense when one looks hard at it, as one sometimes has to do in morning light to recognize a spider web. Silko's description of one of her essays applies equally well to *Storyteller:*

> For those of you accustomed to a structure that moves from point A to point B to point C, this presentation may be somewhat difficult to follow because the structure of Pueblo expression resembles something like a spider's web—with many little threads radiating from a center, criss-crossing each other. As with the web, the structure will emerge as it is made, and you must simply listen and trust, as the Pueblo people do, that meaning will be made.

The same patterning device, it could be argued, structures Silko's novel *Ceremony.* If we read *Storyteller* with a consciousness of this structure, we are reminded constantly of Grandmother Spider at the center of the web, and by extension of other aspects of female creative power in Keres cosmology: Thought-Woman, the sisters, Corn Mother. Through parallels between the holy people and modern people we are reminded of those values which Paula Gunn Allen sees as shared among women: nurturance and harmony.

Thematic clusters constitute the radiating spokes of the web. The first part of the book focuses on survival through storytelling. Near the beginning of this filament are the literal and literary grandmothers. By placing them first, Silko suggests that their voices matter, that the personal stories, gossip, oral history, and the "humma-hah" stories from a remote time when humans could communicate with other creatures, all are as important as myths to personal and tribal survival.

Throughout this sequence Silko's metanarrative strategies draw our attention to the identity and importance of the grandmother-tellers and to the process of communication. Metanarration, explains Barbara Babcock [in *Verbal Art as Performance*], deals with the personal and interactional elements of *how* a story is told. This attention to tellers and process reclaims the tellers' cultural, sexual, and individual identities from the all-too-often-standard anthropological procedure of recording texts with little or no data about context or teller, and of rarely talking to women in the first place.

Beginning, "This is the way Aunt Susie told the story," Silko tells a story about the story. Through metanarration we are aware of an audience of little girls; Aunt Susie's asides recognize the needs of these modern grandchildren as she comments on Laguna customs or explains, " 'Yashtoah' is the hardened crust on corn meal mush / that curls up." At the end of the narrative Silko, completing the contextual frame she has introduced, focuses on the qualities of Aunt Susie's voice and the way the sound of her voice affected listeners. Silko's story, finally, is about a storyteller, the living embodiment of Thought-Woman, as is the writer herself, thinking personal and tribal memory into existence.

Radial filaments of the spider web connect not only at the center, but also at points outward. Sometimes the connections are close and convenient; sometimes the spider finds it a long way from the corner of the steps up to the eaves. The book's title story, set far from Laguna country, nonetheless raises the same themes and issues we find in other early selections in the book: the old people as source of survival information, and storytelling as a way of being, of creating oneself and the world.

The central character in **"Storyteller"** uses narrative to maintain the integrity of self and culture in opposition to the pressures of white culture. She experiments with white culture, satisfying her curiosity about both school and sex. But when she leaves school to return to the village, "English was of no concern to her anymore, and neither was anything the Christians in the village might say about her or the old man."

The old man is not, as the local Catholic priest supposes, her grandfather. And the interpersonal politics of her sexual relationship with the old man are disturbing, especially at the moment when he screams at her and shakes her violently for having engaged in sex with the white man. But she always seems to choose freely in her relationship with the old man. Besides, the real significance of her sexuality with the old man may be to suggest her absorption into her culture. This, for Silko, overrides the implied oppressiveness of the relationship. Indeed, a similar putting on of old ways is suggested when she wears her grandmother's clothing: "She zipped the wolfskin parka. Her grandmother had worn it for many years, but the old man said that before she died, she had instructed him to bury her in an old black sweater and to give the parka to the girl." But the principal induction into the tradition comes as she learns the manner and reason for storytelling from the old man, and the subject of her own story, beginning with the death of her parents, from her grandmother.

Taking on the bodies and the stories of the old people, she comes to understand what the old man means: "It will take a long time, but the stories must be told. There must not be any lies." She insists on the integrity of her own story; in revenge for her parents' death after an opportunistic storekeeper had apparently sold them canned heat as drinking alcohol, she had lured the present storekeeper onto the weak river ice, where he had chased her and fallen through to his death. In her jail cell her liberal white attorney makes excuses for her. She couldn't possibly have planned it; her mind was confused. She insists, "I intended that he die. The story must be told as it is."

Through the contrast between the Anglo interpretation of the story and the girl's version, Silko is warning non-Indian readers to beware of the limits of their cultural system. Kate Shanley Vangen [in *Coyote Was Here*] cautions that readers often take delight in exoticism and fail to own up to the politics operative in the way we derive meaning from reading. In *Storyteller,* the white discursive system, suggests Vangen, does not allow people to think certain thoughts. The white characters—whether oil field workers, priests, educators, or functionaries of the Law—are all unable to accept who the protagonist is or what she says. Her curious, active sexuality causes them to try either to use or reform her. The lawyer cannot accept that she may have with justification actively planned the death of the storekeeper. Vangen suggests that if some legal functionary finally does believe her, the system will want to punish her for murder or have her hospitalized. The story teaches readers something about their part in the transaction. Grandmother Spider sometimes teaches through her bite. The lessons are disturbing but no less necessary.

While Silko reclaims her individual and tribal identity from white male-dominated American scholarship, she has also reclaimed the centrality of female power and female artistic expression within Keresan culture.

—*Linda L. Danielson*

Web imagery reinforces the structural statement in the story **"Lullaby"** as the old Navaho woman, Ayah, spins the narrative of the end of her and her husband's lives. One could see her as a victim. Her children have been taken by white people who "know best." Her husband's loyalty to an employer has been rewarded by callous dismissal and eviction. The husband, Chato, is evidently drinking himself into discouraged oblivion. But the structural context of the spider web, combined with the story's imagery, associates Ayah with Spider Woman, and thus with control over the making of her life.

Throughout the story Ayah is literally wrapped in the web of a foreign weaver—a faded, ravelled U.S. Army blanket sent to her by a son who died while in the service. But she remembers from her childhood the women who wove: "And while she combed the wool, her grandma sat beside her, spinning the silvery strand of yarn around the smooth cedar spindle. Her mother worked at the loom with yarns dyed bright yellow and red and gold." At the end of a long day's reminiscence, Ayah walks to Cebolleta to hunt for Chato at Azzie's bar. She stays long enough to shake the snow off her blanket and dry herself. "In past years," Silko writes, "they would have told her to get out. But her hair was white now and her face was wrinkled. They looked at her like she was a spider crawling slowly across the room." This is not a lowly or contemptible spider. What the bar customers fear is mythic power.

When Ayah finds Chato, he is in pitiful condition, wandering in mind and body. She looks at him with the objectivity and compassion of Grandmother Spider, and as they settle down for the night in an old adobe barn, she sings a lullaby that she knows from her own mother and grandmother:

> The earth is your mother,
> she holds you.
> The sky is your father,
> he protects you.

When she puts the Army blanket around Chato, knowing that he will freeze to death—and most likely she will too—she becomes like Grandmother Spider, appropriating the foreign web, using it as the mythic Spider so often does to carry someone away from a bad situation and to protect one who needs it. Both Ayah as memory maker and Silko as image maker create this protective web.

Another radiating filament involves stories of Kochininako, or Yellow Woman. In this sequence, Silko reclaims the creative and instrumental power of this Everywoman figure of Keresan mythology from the colonialized and trivialized figure we often see in modern anthropological documents. Yellow Woman is, Paula Gunn Allen observes [in *The Sacred Hoop*], marginal and atypical. She is also a role model, for possessing

> some behaviors that are not likely to occur in many of the women who hear her stories. . . . The stories do not necessarily imply that difference is punishable; on the contrary, it is often her very difference that makes her special adventures possible, and these adventures often have happy outcomes for Kochinnenako and her people.

This is one possible sense to be extracted from these stories, and clearly the one Silko emphasizes. However, it may not reflect the reality of masculine theocratic authority influenced by Catholicism and white culture. Barbara Babcock observes that in the Keres pueblo of Cochiti

> Wage labor, increased prosperity, and government housing have virtually abolished matrilineal residence. . . . And, with Catholicism in the Rio Grande pueblos, came absolute monogamy, greatly increasing male status in the household and power over his wife. At the same time, the two kiva organizations . . . are larger and more powerful than ever, and they are patrilineal ["'At Home No Womens Are Storytellers': Identity, Role, and Creativity in Cochiti Pueblo," *Journal of the Southwest* 30, Autumn 1988].

The Yellow Woman whom Allen describes would hardly fit into the modern situation outlined by Babcock. Several of the Yellow Woman stories recorded by Boas reflect this modern social order in which women, embodied in Yellow Woman, specifically lack power. Silko's versions, though,

seem to reclaim Yellow Woman for the world of Thought Woman, a world in which Grandmother Spider's power is reflected in the ways of other mythic and ordinary women.

Boas's version of the Buffalo Man story, for example, is clearly a man's story. Yellow Woman's actions are mentioned only briefly. Much is made of a scene in which Big Star tells his friend Arrow Youth (Estoy-eh-muut) that Buffalo Man has stolen Arrow Youth's wife, and therefore he cannot kill any deer. Here the causal connection is explicit: Yellow Woman's adventure threatens the people's food supply. With help from Grandmother Spider, Yellow Woman's return proceeds generally as in Silko's version. But in the Boas version, Arrow Youth kills her explicitly because she answers "yes" when he asks, "Did you love [Buffalo Man] very much?" No other meaning than simple revenge on a misbehaving woman could be ascribed to her death. The people go to get the buffalo meat that Arrow Youth has killed. Nothing is said about the tribe's future relationship to the buffalo.

Such a version denies Kochininako's ceremonial agency. It is this role that Silko reclaims, and thus the complementarity and equality of the male and female holy people. Silko's is not merely the story of a justifiably jealous husband in a society newly converted to male-dominant monogamy. Arrow Youth and Yellow Woman are both important because of what their actions portend for the people. As the story opens, the people are suffering for lack of food and water. Kochininako's actions, like Arrow Youth's, are fully narrated. On one hand, Arrow Youth suffers loss and is helped by Grandmother Spider, but on the other, Yellow Woman is neither bad, wrong, nor trivial. Their adventure will assure the people a food supply. Hunting as a ritual act requires both union with and killing of the game. Both actions occur in the story as Kochininako becomes one with the buffalo through sexual union, and in killing her, Estoy-eh-muut is confirming that union. Estoy-eh-muut explains Kochininako's death thus:

> I killed her
> because she wanted to stay with the Buffalo People
> she wanted to go with them
> and now she is with them.

Her father laments not her death, but simply her absence:

> A'moo-ooh, my daughter.
> You have gone away with them!

Through her symbolic union with the buffalo the people can depend upon the buffalo for food:

> It was all because
> one time long ago
> our daughter, our sister Kochininako
> went away with them.

In the narrative poem **"Cottonwood: Part Two Buffalo Man,"** Silko has already introduced the next filament's theme of hunting and survival through cooperation and respect for the animals. She sets the tone for the whole filament of hunting stories with the lyric, **"The Time We Climbed Snake Mountain,"** which concludes:

don't step on the spotted yellow snake
          he lives here.
The mountain is his.

Silko's personal hunting stories follow, along with a story of Kochininako and Estrucuyu, which reinforces the image of woman as hunter. (Here we need to bear in mind that spiders make lateral connections when they weave; thus the theme of hunting appears in a Kochininako story, while Kochininako appears in a hunting story.) Boas records versions of this story that, predictably, undercut Kochininako's power and significance. In one version Arrow Youth, the wise husband, warns Yellow Woman about the giant. She ignores the warning and gets caught by the giant. Arrow Youth comes to her rescue; then he hunts rabbits for her and presents her with a deer. In another version she kills one rabbit before she has to be rescued by the hero twins, who then kill ten rabbits for her; in an apparent fit of dishonesty and egoism she claims these as her kill when she arrives home. In a Cochiti version she makes excuses for hunting: her brother had not gone hunting, so she must. Once again the hero twins kill game for her.

It is possible that both Silko and Aunt Alice Marmon appropriated the story to express their own ideas about community and complementarity, but it is perhaps more likely that both are reclaiming a pre-colonialized version. Either way, the product is a reading that will satisfy both the ardent feminist and the traditional purist. As portrayed by Silko, Aunt Alice states at once that Kochininako is a fine hunter—no apology, no qualifications—and that she brought deer and rabbits to her mother and sisters. Aunt Alice adds, with personal significance for her little-girl listeners, "You know there have been Laguna women / who were good hunters / who could hunt as well as any man." Kochininako's escape from the giant into the cave is canny avoidance, no matter of mere chance: she calls out to the hero twins; she does not just weep. After the twins kill Estrucuyu, they do not offer to hunt rabbits for Kochininako. It is clear she can take care of that matter herself. Instead, they cut out the monster's heart and throw it away. Turning into a rock, the heart lands along a roadside where the little girls can see it on the way to a neighbor's ranch. The listeners are not cautioned about girls overreaching themselves as hunters. Rather, every time they travel that road they are reminded that Laguna girls can be good hunters.

With the next strand of Grandmother Spider's web, Silko moves away from her examination of the roles of men and women in society and toward the relations of all living beings within a harmonious universe, an interest Paula Gunn Allen declares is shared by tribal people and many non-tribal women. In the first of these sections Silko examines how individual destructiveness (witchcraft) affects the community. Then she focuses upon individual creative power, symbolized in water, which sustains the natural world. Here Silko's acts of reclamation are less obvious than in the earlier sections of the book where she is reclaiming stories and lives that had been shunted aside under the influence of white culture. But she is in fact reclaiming nothing less than the solid ground upon which the community must finally depend for its survival—the

practical and spiritual creativity of human beings working with the deities to assure the continuation of a stable and fruitful world. These are the concerns lost in such insensitive and often uncomprehending fieldwork as Silko complains of earlier in *Storyteller.* And they are indeed community concerns. Neither witchcraft nor the water cycle affects just one person. When problems arise, everyone is involved—plant, animal, human, and spirit beings.

The witchcraft section, at the physical center of the book, leads into the heart of the web, to the dark side of existence where Grandmother Spider lives because that is where people need her help. Two of the three narratives in which Grandmother Spider appears are in the witchcraft section of *Storyteller.*

Here both traditional and modern narratives portray sickness in the natural world resulting from someone's selfish manipulations. The story of the Ck'o'yo magician Pa'caya'ni and **"Tony's Story"** both emphasize aspects of community. As the creator-sister Nau'ts'ity'i says at the end of the magician story, it isn't easy to fix things up again once the people have been seduced by Ck'o'yo magic into believing that they don't have to care for the earth—for the Corn Mother altar. But the people do restore order, with considerable luck, labor, cooperation, and good will from the Mother.

Instead of seductive magic, the narrator of **"Tony's Story"** faces ordinary and contemporary violence. He immediately connects the suffering of the drought-stricken earth with the motiveless malignancy of the police officer's attack on Leon at the festival. Both, he concludes, are the work of witchery. But by contrast with the community of creatures in the Pa'caya'ni story, Tony is isolated in his belief and fear. He does not want to discuss his fear with his family because "even to speak about it risked bringing it closer." He cannot talk to Leon, whose experience in the military service has taught him to cope with the police officer's violence by going through channels and demanding his rights from government agencies.

Finally Tony has only the arrowhead necklace, old Teofilo's stories about witchery, and a gun. When Tony shoots the officer he breaks his isolation; Leon is necessarily implicated. A LaVonne Ruoff suggests that when Tony shoots the witch, he becomes a self-appointed old-time Pueblo war captain, and appoints Leon to the same role, derived from the mythic hero twins, Ma'sewi and Uyuyewi. Tony, as narrator, interprets his action as restoring natural balance. The rain clouds appearing on the horizon immediately after he shoots the officer seem to confirm his interpretation. But as with the Inuit girl in **"Storyteller,"** we are left to wonder what life will be like for him in a community now lacking a governmental and ritual structure for dealing with witches, a community encapsulated in a larger society that has power over, but is not part of, the Indian community. Here, of course, is another one of the spider web's lateral connections.

Culturally insensitive interpretations of witchcraft are, as much as anything, what Silko must reclaim in this section. Whereas Euro-American witchcraft traditions focus upon the evil power of an individual, Keres traditions, and

Silko's stories, emphasize what happens to the community when a selfish individualist abuses a basically neutral power. Only at first glance may **"Estoy-eh-muut and the Kunideeyahs"** appear to be a story of an evil witch-woman and her wronged husband. There are grounds for reading the Boas version of the story thus, with its focus on personal interaction and on Estoy-eh-muut's immediate suspicion of his wife. But Boas's colonialized male informant's story is not the one that Silko tells.

Besides, by this late in *Storyteller,* even the cultural outsider knows that Kochininako is not inherently evil; her adventures usually do the world good. The story is not about an evil woman, but about restoration of balance, something living beings must constantly work at. Silko, discussing her novel *Ceremony* in an interview [in *Persona,* 1980], says that at any time "the balance could come undone and any character could change." The problem is larger than the individual characters. As in the earlier witchery stories, the natural world is troubled: "the corn plants had been sickly that year / and the worms devoured all the bean plants." In the Keres tradition, trouble in nature is a sign that power is being selfishly used. But the power itself can be used for good as well as ill, as we see from Kochininako's other functions throughout the book. It is this view of power as well as the image of Kochininako herself that Silko reclaims from the white-influenced version of tribal tradition recorded by Boas.

Developing themes of water and fertility, the next strand of the web opens with an irony: benevolent, creative Corn Woman makes a critical error in judgment. She had scolded Reed Woman for bathing all day while Corn Woman herself worked hard in the field. Reed Woman had gone back to the lower world and there was no more rain. So, Silko reminds us, a creative being can cause just as much disharmony by acting self-righteous and forgetting that each being has her own nature as a bad-hearted witch can do by deliberate selfishness.

Much of this section deals with water as the artist's source of nourishment: the clouds that lured Silko's father away for entire afternoons to photograph them, the ways of water on the earth in **"How to Write a Poem About the Sky," "In Cold Storm Light," "Prayer to the Pacific,"** and **"Horses at Valley Store."** All these help her tell her world into being. In the midst of this section Silko credits the story **"Tony's Goat"** to friend and fellow writer Simon Ortiz. Its placement imparts some of its meaning, as stories given by friends nourish and water the life of a storyteller.

The last story in the group, **"The Man to Send Rainclouds,"** returns to themes of creativity and community. In accordance with Keres tradition, Old Teofilo, even in death, is still a valued member of the community, for the people are looking to him to send them big thunderclouds. There is seriousness and ceremony, but no sorrow at his death. He is not lost, just redefined within the community as a Kat'sina spirit associated with the cloud beings who bring rain.

Ruoff observes that the strength of Indian tradition for Silko is not in rigid adherence to old ways, but in creative incorporation of new elements. In **"The Man to Send Rainclouds,"** modern Indian people not only create new ritual, but offer community to an outsider. The gift of water for the old man's spirit comes from the Catholic priest whom Leon induces to participate in the funeral, on Indian terms. But the priest remains an outsider, suspicious of "some perverse Indian trick—something they did in March to insure a good harvest." Nonetheless, his action brings him to the edge of the community: "He sprinkled the grave and the water disappeared almost before it touched the dim, cold sand; it reminded him of something—he tried to remember what it was, because he thought if he could remember he might understand this." The flexibility that can find needed ritual power and extend the hand of community to the outsider assures the continuance of life, like water and thunderclouds.

These themes in **"The Man to Send Rainclouds"** connect the web laterally to the next strand, which develops the idea of community as lived in the modern world of people and animals, going out and returning, loving, taking, and giving. From the still place where the existence and use of power for creation and destruction define the grounds of permanence, we move back into a world of love, loss and change. Balance is not static; it is lived in the flux of daily existence, recreated constantly. Only in such change is there any permanence on the level of ordinary life.

Silko's family members and loved ones reappear. Animals are seen as part of the humans' community, and people join animal communities. In this cycle of daily lives and memories, Silko speaks of how the Navahos would return to the same Laguna homes year after year at feast time, of how the deer dance is performed each year to thank the deer spirits who have come home with the hunters. In **"Deer Dance/For Your Return,"** the speaker wishes for the return of a loved person. But the poem is also what the title says, a deer dance. The loved one may not return. The deer may not return, but one does one's best to insure that they will, through the dance. However, "Losses are certain/in the pattern of this dance." In an earlier section we were reminded that hunting is a ritual of community. Now we see the obverse, that the deer dance is part of the practical act of hunting.

Silko's beloved Grandpa Hank appears in **"A Hunting Story."** The person addressed combines qualities of grandfather, lover, and deer, whose returns are all desired. (pp. 332-44)

[In the] ordinary world the deer give themselves to other creatures for food. According to Grandma A'mooh's story when the Navahos stole some Laguna sheep, the Lagunas told them to ask for food instead of stealing, save them some sheep, and let them go. The crows pick clean the bones of a dead sheep in the poem **"Preparation."** Living beings go out and return, dying and living in memory or ceremony. These are the ways one lives a harmonious life in a changing but nurturant world, the circle of Spider Woman's web.

Coyote, like Grandmother Spider, is a maker figure, albeit a spirit of disorder, appetite, play, and potential. Coyote's disorder becomes part of Grandmother Spider's orderly world in the last section of *Storyteller.* But then, the Coyote spirit always was part of the larger scheme of things. According to the emergence story told by W. G. Marmon's widow,

> *Ivetik* said to her sisters, "I wish we had something to make us laugh. We sit around here so quiet without anything to make us laugh." *Ivetik* rubbed her skin. Rubbing both hands she got a ball like dough. She put it aside and covered it with a cloth. Out of the rubbings came the *kashare.*

Coyote, like the koshare, both subverts and transcends the rules and the ceremonies. As much as Grandmother Spider, Coyote assures the continuance of life. Whereas the preceding section of *Storyteller* looked to love and ceremonial interchange to reveal a wholeness and balance, the Coyote section suggests that out of chaos, exaggeration, the improper and the silly, the unlovely and the diverse come creativity and the possibility of a new synthesis, a new balance. As a Navajo informant said to folklorist J. Barre Toelken "If [Coyote] did not do all those things, then those things would not be possible in the world."

The Coyote section of *Storyteller* produces in the reader a sense of "we are all in this together"—holy people, ordinary people, everyday rooster-stealing coyotes, all riding for a fall through our own appetites and uncontrol, but all participants in the realm of creative possibility.

Making a world through stories is just such a creative act, requiring the spirit both of order and of disorder to succeed. Thought Woman, unmentioned but implicit in *Storyteller,* spoke the world into being. Her children continue to do so. A grandmother's stories shape a granddaughter's view of herself and how she relates to her culture. But whatever is subversive, playful, and re-visionary in those stories, that is the Coyote spirit working with Thought Woman. And in the microcosm of *Storyteller,* Silko herself, as writer, is both Thought Woman and Coyote. As we see the face of the author behind the Thought Woman mask of *Ceremony's* prefatory poem or behind the myths and Coyote tricks of *Storyteller,* we realize that of course there is a Thought Woman and a Coyote behind the Author mask.

As well as being a freewheeling experimenter and mistake maker, Coyote is a mediator and teacher. Like Pueblo ritual clowns' performances, Silko's Coyote carnival teaches and mediates between the holy people and everyday humanness. Coyotes and clowns teach people not to be bamboozled by sleight of hand or the appearance of power. Indian traditions satirizing white people are lessons of just this sort. (pp. 345-46)

Coyote's other major teaching is, don't be sucked in by impulsive appetites, but if it happens, see what comes of the event and grab the main chance. Silko embodies this lesson in the cultural comedy and creativity of the halfbreed, identifying her own family with Coyote:

> Some white men came to Acoma and Laguna a
>   hundred years ago
> and they fought over Acoma land and Laguna
>   women, and even now

> some of their descendants are howling in
>   the hills southeast of Laguna.

Coyotes are the ones who play tricks and also the ones who fall for the tricks. There is Coyote in all people.

Mediators though they be, neither Coyote nor Silko is a simple ambassador between ordinary and holy people. Still less is either a mediator bringing Indian humor to a white audience. As Mary V. Dearborn points out [in *Pocahonta's Daughters*], the role of mediator is frequently thrust upon ethnic women by the dominant society: "Her mission is peaceable, and the dominant culture can understand ethnic female identity in a way that is not threatening if it is presented in a work written with a mediating purpose". When the mediator is a translator of culture for outsiders, Dearborn suggests, she risks reinventing an inauthentic version of the native culture in the minds of readers. "In such a context, the ethnic woman's voice and identity are ultimately compromised . . . her writing is more interesting when it struggles against the concept of mediation than when it succumbs." Coyote enables Silko to short-circuit the sentimentality with which white readers might all too easily approach an Indian woman writer or female creator gods. Silko in no sense succumbs to the inauthentic or the sentimental. She resists throughout the work white notions about classic literary Indianness with its cliches about Noble Savagery, Dying Cultures, Helpless Victims, and Official Versions of traditional stories. Instead her Coyote self and stories mediate between kinds of creative energy.

Yet Coyote makes us uncomfortable. Something in all Coyote's efforts to satisfy various appetites borders upon the manipulation of witchery. While Coyote endows the community with the possibilities of change, his power "also carries the threat and possibility of chaos. His beneficence, though central, results from the breaking of rules and the violating of taboos" [Babcock, *Essays on Native American Literature*]. Furthermore, his beneficial actions do not necessarily result from altruism. Coyote will try anything once, and if it feels good he'll do it again, and whatever his motives, from his readiness to fulfill appetites comes the creative and adaptive energy that empowers people to survive.

In the Coyote section, the circling of *Storyteller's* spider-web pattern returns to themes, motifs, and narrative techniques familiar from earlier in the book. There are well-known names: Grandpa Hank, Grandma Lillie, Simon Ortiz. As Silko again employs some of the metanarrative devices described earlier, the reader's attention returns to the storyteller and the communicative process, with the story-maker as player. In **"Coyote and the Stro'ro'ka Dancers,"** the narrator comments on the story to explain about the traditional foods Coyote is lusting after, interrupts herself to translate Coyote language, and asks, "Do you see the picture?" The coyotes, of course, act just as Coyotes should, minds on food during a ceremony, no awareness of their own limits. But the Stro'ro'ka dancers, the human embodiments of holy people, act a bit like Coyotes themselves, grabbing and claiming the dead coyotes for neck pieces, much as the clowns possessively grab at the Kat'sinas, the Beautiful Beings, during a plaza dance. Anybody, it seems, can be a coyote at some point.

Silko in no sense succumbs to the inauthentic or the sentimental. She resists throughout [Storyteller] white notions about classic literary Indianness with its cliches about Noble Savagery, Dying Cultures, Helpless Victims, and Official Versions of traditional stories.

—Linda L. Danielson

The theme of hunting returns in **"A Geronimo Story,"** as a manhunt, inherently inharmonious, dissolves into a deer hunt, an expression of community. Here Coyote trickery serves the cause of peace and harmony. The Laguna Regulars have been pressed into service to track down Geronimo. But it is clear from the beginning of the story that this is no real man-hunt. Siteye, with his broken foot, has protested, "Shit, these Lagunas can't track Geronimo without me." When Captain Pratt agrees, Siteye continues, "I think I'll bring my nephew along. To saddle my horse for me."

The trip is leisurely under the command of Captain Pratt, a squaw-man who likes his lunchtime cup of Indian tea. Over a bag of gumdrops and licorice, Siteye explains to his narrator-nephew that Geronimo is not where they are going to look for him—"So we're going down." To the puzzled boy he continues, "It will be a beautiful journey for you." Pratt and the regulars take on a role familiar from many post-contact stories in which Coyote becomes a defender of Indianness by fooling the white people. These tricksters oppose white authority by doing exactly what the white cavalry officers—foolishly—want, telling them what they want to hear up to the last moment, collecting some pay for their trouble, and going off to hunt deer. This time the Coyote spirit serves appetites, the welfare of the people, and the ritual cycle of the hunt.

Several of the stories in this section invert themes and actions from earlier stories. **"Storyteller's Escape,"** like the book's title story, involves pursuit. But this time the ending is not constrained by inevitability. Rather, grasping luck and the main chance, the storyteller makes a Coyote-style escape, rescuing herself with a fresh, direct, comic perception of the situation. She is not trying to trick anybody, but her comic sense overcomes the entrapping old assumptions. Police officers at a feast echo **"Tony's Story,"** but this time the police resemble coyotes, not witches. Politicians, gas company officials, Marmon ancestors, and Mrs. Sekakaku's opportunistic admirer are all cast as coyotes. This complex of threads connecting elsewhere in *Storyteller* reminds the reader that this is Grandmother Spider's web. Thought Woman, Nau'ts'ity'i, Ik'tc'ts'ity'i, and Grandmother Spider are the ground of human nurturance and continuation in the world. On that

ground the basic pattern is created. But that pattern is constantly revised by the survivors, the foolers, and the fooled, all of the people who, like Coyote in some story traditions, are "going along." (pp. 347-49)

Silko's claim to the writer's dual role as creator and trickster, her rejection of the polite ambassadorial role, her rejection of sentimentality, and her recognition of the role of creative foolishness and luck in human survival may all help explain what at first seems like a strange ending to the book—the story **"Coyote Holds a Full House in His Hand."** The central character, the unnamed suitor of one Mrs. Sekakaku of Second Mesa, is the perfect Coyote type, lazy and self-justifying, driven by appetites, fixated on sexuality and genitalia. In a classic Coyote-gambler trick he manages to satisfy his appetites through a "ceremony" that involves feeling the thighs of every woman in Mrs. Sekakaku's clan in order to "cure" Aunt Mamie of her dizzy spells. He reinvents himself as medicine man, just as he has earlier reinvented himself as the dapper suitor in self-aggrandizing stories and carefully posed snapshots. Finally, he gets something close to what he wants. But that is not the whole of the story. Mrs. Sekakaku is something of a Coyote too. She has sent him perfumed letters and then treated him with disregard when he comes to visit. We have only the central character's assessment of the situation, but it rings true: "She had lured his letters and snapshots and the big poinsetta plant to show off for her sisters and aunts, and now his visit so she could pretend he had come uninvited, overcome with desire for her." Each of these Coyote characters in the course of the story fools the other, getting something he or she wants.

Most important, though, the ceremony works. Out of all that self-seeking, appetite-driven comedy, Aunt Mamie gets well. After caressing numerous women's thighs with juniper ash,

> he was out of breath and he knew he could not stand up to get to Aunt Mamie's bed so he bowed his head and pretended he was praying. "I feel better already. I'm not dizzy," the old woman said, not letting anyone help her out of bed or walk with her to the fireplace. He rubbed her thighs as carefully as he'd rubbed the others, and he could tell by the feel she'd live a long time.

Who knows what part the power of suggestion played or how much Aunt Mamie and the other women colluded in the trick? Who cares? The point is, the new ceremony works. It comes out of that ferment of uncontrolled creativity that supports survival. Babcock says that such tricksters "belong to the comic modality or marginality where violation is generally the precondition for laughter and communitas."

So while **"Coyote Holds a Full House in His Hand"** at first looks like a quit rather than an ending, we must remember that we have been reading a spider web, circular and whole. A spider web does not shoot off into space. It connects back to the beginning—the ongoing life of the people. Spider Woman may enlarge the web. The story is not over; it is just at a resting place. The people's lives will continue, as much because of laughter as because of ceremony, as much out of appetite as out of love. Balance, community, and creativity are all. Silko claims from her tribal woman's traditions, her nurturant woman-centered mythology, and her woman's experience that this is so.

A feminist reading of *Storyteller* does not give us a gynocratic manifesto. Here female strength does not imply liberation from the men of one's own tribe. Men's traditions dealing with transitoriness, change, and extinction complement women's nurturant traditions of continuance; the relationship is not adversarial as in the white feminist view of Euro-American culture. What we find in *Storyteller* is a woman's vision of her life and the traditions that nourish her. Silko reinvents those traditions so as to reclaim women's power that has been lost or reduced through colonialism: power over her body and her life, over a language not designed to carry her messages, over mythic stories adapted to serve male and colonial authority, even over the nature of authorship itself. *Storyteller* speaks into being the creative community of Thought Woman and Grandmother Spider. (pp. 350-52)

> Linda L. Danielson, "Storyteller: 'Grandmother Spider's Web'," in Journal of the Southwest, Vol. 30, No. 3, Autumn, 1988, pp. 325-55.

Alan Cheuse (review date 1 December 1991)

[*Cheuse is an American short story writer and novelist. In his review of* Almanac of the Dead *excerpted below, he applauds Silko's scathing indictment of European-American society and her radical vision of a North America reclaimed by its native peoples.*]

D. H. Lawrence once forthrightly declared that the novel was "the one bright book of life." If he were alive to read Leslie Marmon Silko's monumental new novel, the first full-length narrative in over a decade from this gifted Native American fiction writer, Lawrence might want to change his phrase to "the one bright book of death."

Almanac of the Dead is one of the great American naysaying creations, a novel that takes us on an odyssey through the lower depths of Southwest American and Mexican society in which scarcely an Anglo-American character (and in the Mexican sections, not a mestizo or mixed-blood character) is depicted with any socially redeeming qualities whatsoever. European-American society is portrayed in these pages as an endless skein of pornography, drug addiction, heinous racist criminality, bestial perversion, white-collar crime, Mafia assassinations and the fouling of the earth and air and water.

Take, for example, the white woman named Seese, one of the main characters in this 763-page extravaganza in which, it sometimes seems, a new and putatively important new character is introduced in every chapter.

Seese, a former topless dancer from Tucson with a cocaine habit, has a boyfriend David, a bisexual photographer, who fathers a child with her. Beaufrey, a moral monster who traffics in operating room pornography (films of sex-change operations, surgical torture and abortions), fears that the child may keep David, his lover, in Seese's sway.

He has the baby kidnapped and later dismembered on camera so he can show the film to the father.

As for Beaufrey's asexual companion, Serio, he is a member of an aristocratic Latin American-European conspiracy that fosters genocide by means of the AIDS virus and is working on luxury space stations for the rich that will feed off what remains of the polluted Earth's natural resources. And so on, from one obscene Anglo perversion to another.

Seese's quest for her missing child binds together a number of disparate scenes and locations and multitudes of characters, major and minor. Beaufrey has set things up so that Seese believes that David has engineered the kidnapping. She sees a Native American psychic on cable television and goes off to find her, hoping for a clue to the whereabouts of David and the baby. This leads her to the household of the psychic, Lecha, and her sister, Zeta, who are now nearing old age and whose ancient grandmother, old Yoeme, put in charge of an antique tribal scroll of prophecy, the "almanac" of the book's title.

"One day a story will arrive at your town," they read in the scroll's decoded pages. "It will come from far away, from the southwest or southeast—people won't agree. The story may arrive with a stranger or perhaps with the parrot trader. But when you hear this story, you will know it is the signal for you and the others to prepare. . . ."

The "others" include Lecha and Zeta's Laguana Pueblo Indian caretaker, Sterling, most of the embattled Native American and homeless and black and Mexican Indian characters and, toward the end of the novel, even some Anglo holistic healers and spiritualists. And what they are preparing for is the first major offensive against the North American European political hegemony—the goal being to repossess all of the tribal lands taken from them by the conquistadors, the settlers in covered wagons and the cavalry alongside them.

That accounts for the book's Jeremiad-like presentation of gringo culture and the association of the Native American resistance with the elemental forces of myth, such as the large stone snake that mysteriously appears and disappears and appears again on the Laguna Pueblo land where Sterling once made his home.

Like the ancient almanac itself, Silko's novel is a book with a vision, a vision of the possibility of the retaking of the old lands and the re-establishment of the old way of seeing and living. "We don't believe in boundaries," says the old Arizona Indian gunrunner named Calabazas.

> We are here thousands of years before the first whites. We are here before maps or quit claims. We know where we belong on this earth. We have always moved freely. . . . We never pay no attention to what isn't real. Imaginary lines. Imaginary minutes and hours. Written law. We recognize none of that. And we carry a great many things back and forth. We don't see any border we cross. We have been here and this goes on since the world was our world. . . .

Even the most sympathetic reader of Silko's novel will wish at times that the author herself believed a little bit more in boundaries and time constraints. During the inevitable march toward the declaration of war against Anglo culture, some of the sections seem a little extraneous.

But for the devoted fan of contemporary fiction, the book is well worth the trek through the jungles of Mexico and under the bridges of Tucson and across the face of an American Southwest that is beset with misery, dispossession and moral decay and marked by a new visionary zeal on the part of Native Americans who are struggling to come home again to old values and old lands.

Because Silko's production in the past has been slender—the novel *Ceremony* and *Story-Teller,* a collection of stories, legends and photographs—*Almanac of the Dead* seems like a sudden flood. Flawed, massive, scarred and visionary, it is book that must be dealt with.

> Alan Cheuse, "Dead Reckoning," in Chicago
> Tribune—Books, *December 1, 1991, p. 3.*

Elizabeth Tallent   (review date 22 December 1991)

[*An American novelist and critic, Tallent is best known for her fictional work* Museum Pieces *(1985), which is set in her native New Mexico. In the following review, she praises the apocalyptic vision and narrative force of* The Almanac of the Dead.]

One great possibility for the novel form is meditation upon the crucial death of a single character—think of Mrs. Ramsay in *To the Lighthouse,* the father in *A Death in the Family,* the mother in *Sons and Lovers.* But what if an entire culture reeks of cruelty and death, if the individual imagination confronts not a specific loss but fathomless brutality, if despair is no longer a matter of private experience but pervades an epoch?

Almanac of the Dead brilliantly grapples with just such questions, spinning tale after sanguinary tale with a vengeance. This wild, jarring, graphic, mordant, prodigious book embodies the bold wish to encompass in a novel the cruelty of contemporary America, a nation founded on the murder and deracination of the continent's native peoples.

Leslie Marmon Silko, who is of Laguna Pueblo, Mexican and Anglo descent, is the author of the novel *Ceremony* and the collection *Storyteller,* both works that honored the moral force of Native American tradition in conflict with intrusive, impoverishing Western European culture. Her new novel again treats the Native American ethos, reverence for the earth and especially one's ancestral land, as touchstone. It is not only scathing in its portrait of an ecologically catastrophic United States but sweeping in its chronology. The plot follows a far-flung conspiracy of displaced tribal people to retake North America toward the millennium's end.

There are sometimes ferocious, sometimes clinical accounts of savagery ranging from clitorectomy to serial murders. A Mexican revolutionary reflects that "the white man didn't seem to understand he had no future here because he had no past, no spirits of ancestors here." "No future" is literal: most whites must vanish, through massacre or migration, for the continent to be redeemed. The indigenous dead troubled even Cortez's soldiers, who talismanically dressed their wounds "in the fat of slain Indians." Now Native American ghosts direct "mothers from country club neighborhoods to pack the children in the car and drive off hundred-foot cliffs. . . . The spirits whisper in the brains of loners, the crazed young white men with automatic rifles who slaughter crowds in shopping malls or school yards." Still another character muses that "within 'history' reside relentless forces, powerful spirits, vengeful, relentlessly seeking justice." That ghosts urging slaughter in schoolyards could be as brutal as conquistadors is not an issue *Almanac of the Dead* illumines, and the novel's occasional blurred equation of "justice" with random violence is its shakiest imaginative leap.

As in Ms. Silko's previous work, one aspect of human experience is unequivocally celebrated: storytelling. Yoeme, a Yaqui woman who escaped a death sentence for sedition in 1918, "believed power resides within certain stories . . . and with each retelling a slight but permanent shift took place." Yoeme's gift to her twin granddaughters, Zeta and Lecha, is the ancient, fragmentary almanac of tribal narratives: "Yoeme and others believed the almanac had living power within it, a power that would bring all the tribal people of the Americas together to retake the land."

There is genius in the sheer, tireless variousness of the novel's interconnecting tales. Settings include an Alaskan village with one communal television and a stark postmodern mansion set within a numinous rain forest. In addition to outlining the economy of the black market in human organs, the book includes a kidnapping, a hanging, a cocaine bust and an assassination franchise. There are scenes of politics in Tucson, Ariz., the country-club lunching of powerful men's wives and the organization of a ragged troop of homeless Vietnam veterans.

How does a subversive Mexican Indian group persuade foreign governments to send aid? They request uniforms and dynamite "for clearing land for new baseball diamonds." How does a computer whiz "safecrack" vast computer networks from his desert trailer? "His prospective clients were asked to supply entry codes. Ninety-nine percent of his clients had been former employees motivated by revenge."

Ms. Silko seems scarcely able to *name* a character without that character's beginning instantly to brood, to remember, to plot vengeance. The most minor figure in *Almanac of the Dead* possesses formidable id, and in a cast of more than 70 (my count), their individual obsessions are as unique as fingerprints.

Some repetitions could have used deft editorial excision, but for the most part the pace is fast. In Pueblo cosmology, duality, particularly twinship, is very powerful. The plot is set off as much by the 60th birthday shared by Zeta, matriarch of an isolated Arizona ranch and a paranoid connoisseur of security systems, and Lecha, a "TV talk show psychic," as by their decoding of the almanac. Lecha's eyes "know many things never meant to be seen. The contents of shallow graves. The thrust of a knife."

Earlier, in California, blond, cocaine-addicted Seese—her very name a cry—had discovered her baby missing from his crib and sought out the psychic Lecha in Tucson. In Mexico, torture, riots and carnage proliferate; twin brothers are told by sacred macaws to lead their barefoot tribal army north across the border into North America.

Lecha and Zeta, who have seen so much violence, now prepare, along with the other native prophets and revolutionaries, for a great deal more. While the novel stops short of the ultimate crisis, the signs point one way, implacably. Appearing on the eve of the quincentennial of Columbus's arrival in the Americas, *Almanac of the Dead* burns at an apocalyptic pitch—passionate indictment, defiant augury, bravura storytelling.

> Elizabeth Tallent, "Storytelling with a Vengeance," in The New York Times Book Review, December 22, 1991, p. 6.

M. Annette Jaimes (review date April-May 1992)

[*In the review below, Jaimes ranks* The Almanac of the Dead *as "the masterpiece that will emerge from the crucible of polemic and propaganda attending commemoration of the 'Columbian Encounter'."*]

After a long publishing hiatus, lasting since the landmark efforts she offered during the 1970s with *Ceremony* and *Storyteller* Leslie Marmon Silko has released a massive tome of a novel entitled *Almanac of the Dead.* Thankfully, this 700-page opus is marred by none of the tedious pretension, rambling prose, or other forms of flabby self-congratulatory indulgence evidenced in . . . other recent volumes of comparable scale. Instead, from first page to last, what we encounter in *Almanac* is vintage Silko, albeit one who has become well matured as a writer over the past decade, casting her critico-philosophical nets ever so widely, and then delivering her message(s) in a tightly plotted and sustained flow. The author presents a near-perfect structural duality, an extended sequence of deftly constructed scenarios virtually crackling with surface tension, riveting the reader to her text in moment-to-moment fashion while longer-range and more subsurface thematics—rich in irony, nuance, and ambiguity—are allowed to unfold at a far more leisurely pace. The result is a veritable literary tour de force.

Set primarily in Tucson, and laden with historical snippets recounting moments in the evolution of how that city came to be the way it is (while simultaneously using it as a lens through which to examine the broader sociocultural reality in which it is embedded), *Almanac* explores the boundaries of that peculiarly perverse and all-pervasive form of contemporary insanity known variously as "progress," "rational order," or "Eurocentrism." Hence, the book abounds with the ludicrous, the paradoxical, the macabre, and the sublime, all of it based directly in observably topical circumstances: the City of Phoenix steals Tucson's water, arguing such action is justified because its more interesting neighbor to the south enjoys an average temperature 10 degrees cooler than the thieves' 117-degree summer days; a local Euroamerican elite claiming preoccupation with "the principles of pure science" (while in actuality obsessed with archaic myths of "sangre pura") ushers in an age where biotechnically created "superior"

human tissue can be refrigerated and sold from storage bins located next door to novelty sex malls; burgeoning "law enforcement" entities impose outright fascism on communities of color, ostensibly as a means of quelling the "national drug epidemic" and incipient Third World revolution, even while drug- and gun-running become governmentally sponsored fund-raising enterprises; a thriving black market in pornographic baby butchering lays the financial groundwork for a new round of entrepreneurial success stories.

If *Almanac*'s subject matter is not for the squeamish or faint-hearted, neither are its cast of characters. Included in the splendid array of weirdos, zanies, and politico-economic scum—a stunningly lifelike assortment of folks bearing nicknames like Ferro, Seese, Lecha ("Milk"), Zeta, and La Escapia, alias "The Meat Hook"—are psychic brujas and corpse finders, soothsayers and ghosts, eco-warriors and sleazy pin-up cops, vampire capitalists and soulless politicians, ruthless border mobsters and coyotes lurking through the shadows, wheelchair wonders and homeless vets, a poet-lawyer named Wilson Weasel Tail and a barefoot Hopi prophet, Communists and assassins for both the government and its opposition, Indian hustlers and Red-Black Mestizos and bisexual rivals caught up in violently jealous trysts. Throughout the book, this entire wondrous and seedy spectrum of humanity parades itself endlessly across the knotted tightrope of a world gone hopelessly, splendidly, and quite believably mad.

In *Almanac*'s jacket blurbs, writer Larry McMurtry contends that if "Karl Marx had chosen to make *Das Kapital* a novel set in the Americas, he might have come out with a book something like this." McMurtry radically misinterprets the situation. Silko has penned nothing so droll as a recapitulation of the Marxian catechism. Her vision has far more to do with anarchism and chaos theory, a set of insights leading her to create a powerful stew of spiritual black magic conveying menacing portents of the convergence of diverse but immutable cosmic forces destined to correct the conditions of imbalance and disharmony with which the planet is presently afflicted. One can hardly complete a reading of *Almanac of the Dead* without experiencing an intense desire to join the author's "spirit macaws" and their dispossessed/disenfranchised, indigenous vanguard swarming northward to dispense a long-overdue measure of justice to the haughty current minions of that malignant Euroamerican order that was first washed up on the shores of America in October 1492. This is what ultimately makes the novel, for all its harshness and the sheer discomfort induced by many of its passages, a work of life and liberation rather than of death and despair.

As a book to mark the quincentennial of Christopher Columbus' arrival in this hemisphere, *Almanac* must be ranked as a masterpiece, probably *the* masterpiece that will emerge from the crucible of polemic and propaganda attending commemoration of the "Columbian Encounter." As a work that would stand the test of critical scrutiny in any other time or context, it would inevitably fare equally well. If there is any justice at all remaining within our current intellectual environment, Silko's prose will in this instance come to be seen as a transcendent literary effort, helping immeasurably in the project of forging a popular consciousness capable of insuring that the next five hundred years are much different—and far, far better for all concerned—than the last. For this there should be universal applause, although there will undoubtedly be ample grousing from those whose inflated perceptions of their "natural" personal privileges and prerogatives are punctured in the process. In the end, all we can say to Leslie Marmon Silko is, "More! More!" And please make it soon.

M. Annette Jaimes, "The Disharmonic Convergence," in The Bloomsbury Review, *Vol. 12, No. 3, April-May, 1992, p. 5.*

FURTHER READING

Blumenthal, Susan. "Spotted Cattle and Deer: Spirit Guides and Symbols of Endurance and Healing in *Ceremony*." *The American Indian Quarterly* XIV, No. 4 (Fall 1990): 367-77.
 Regards the spotted cattle and deer in *Ceremony* as "messengers of ancient wisdoms vital to Tayo's quest for healing and identity."

Clements, Williams M. "Folk Historical Sense in Two Native American Authors." *Melus* 12, No. 1 (Spring 1985): 65-78.
 Examines how Silko and fellow writer N. Scott Momaday perceive Native American oral tradition, asserting that for Silko "Native American culture can survive if it is flexible enough to accommodate change."

Copeland, Marion W. "*Black Elk Speaks* and Leslie Silko's *Ceremony*: Two Visions of Horses." *Critique* XXIV, No. 3 (Spring 1983): 158-72.
 Compares the spiritual journey of Tayo in *Ceremony* to that of Black Elk, an Oglala Sioux who survived the massacre of Wounded Knee and later became the focus of John G. Neihardt's study *Black Elk Speaks*.

Dasenbrock, Reed Way. "Forms of Biculturalism in Southwestern Literature: The Work of Rudolfo Anaya and Leslie Marmon Silko." *Genre* XXI, No. 3 (Fall 1988): 307-19.
 Uses the works of Silko and Anaya to demonstrate how Chicano, Native American, and Anglo-American literary traditions have combined to form Southwestern literature.

Evasdaughter, Elizabeth. "Leslie Marmon Silko's *Ceremony*: Healing Ethnic Hatred by Mixed-Breed Laughter." *Melus* 15, No. 1 (Spring 1988): 83-95.
 Contends that Silko "plays off affectionate Pueblo humor against the black humor so prominent in 20th-Century white culture. This comic strategy has the end-result of opening our eyes to our general foolishness, and

also to the possibility of combining the merits of all races."

García, Reyes. "Senses of Place in *Ceremony*." *Melus* 10, No. 4 (Winter 1983): 37-48.
 Examines how Silko communicates the spiritual and cultural importance of place in *Ceremony*.

Herzog, Kristin. "Thinking Woman and Feeling Man: Gender in Silko's *Ceremony*." *Melus* 12, No. 1 (Spring 1985): 25-36.
 Discusses Silko's unstereotypical portrayal of men and women in *Ceremony*.

Manley, Kathleen. "Leslie Marmon Silko's Use of Color in *Ceremony*." *Southern Folklore* 46, No. 2 (1989): 133-46.
 Examines Silko's use of certain ceremonial colors and their contribution to the novel's theme and structure.

Nelson, Robert M. "Place and Vision: The Function of Landscape in *Ceremony*." *Journal of the Southwest* 30, No. 3 (Autumn 1988): 281-316.
 Explores the significance of the natural world in *Ceremony*.

Rabinowitz, Paula. "Naming, Magic and Documentary: The Subversion of the Narrative in *Song of Solomon, Ceremony*, and *China Men*." In *Feminist Re-Visions: What Has Been and Might Be*, edited by Vivian Patraka and Louise A. Tilly, pp. 26-42. Ann Arbor: The University of Michigan, 1983.
 Compares and contrasts Silko's treatment of race and gender in *Ceremony* to that of Toni Morrison's in *Song of Solomon* and Maxine Hong Kingston's in *China Men*.

St. Andrews, B. A. "Healing the Witchery: Medicine in Silko's *Ceremony*." *Arizona Quarterly* 44, No. 1 (Spring 1988): 86-94.
 Applies Native American principals of spiritual healing to *Ceremony*.

Swan, Edith. "Healing Via the Sunwise Cycle in Silko's *Ceremony*." *American Indian Quarterly* XII, No. 4 (Fall 1988): 313-28.
 Follows Tayo's journey through the Laguna symbolic universe in *Ceremony*.

Vangen, Kate Shanley. "The Devil's Domain: Leslie Silko's 'Storyteller'." In *Coyote Was Here: Essays on Contemporary Native American Literary and Political Mobilization*, edited by Bo Schöler, pp. 116-23. The Dolphin, No. 9. Aarhus, Denmark: Seklos, 1984.
 Contends that in "Storyteller" Silko undermines Native American stereotypes through her presentation of an authentic Indian perspective.

Wilson, Norma. "Outlook for Survival." *Denver Quarterly* 14, No. 4 (Winter 1980): 22-30.
 Contrasts Silko's ideas concerning Native American oral tradition with those of white ethnologists.

Additional coverage of Silko's life and career is contained in the following sources published by Gale Research: *Contemporary Authors,* Vols. 115, 122, and *Contemporary Literary Criticism,* Vol. 23.

Richard Wright

Black Boy

(Full name Richard Nathaniel Wright) Wright was an American novelist, autobiographer, short story writer, essayist, nonfiction writer, and playwright who lived from 1908 to 1960.

The following entry presents criticism on Wright's autobiography *Black Boy: A Record of Childhood and Youth* (1945). For further information on his life and career, see *CLC*, Volumes 1, 3, 4, 9, 14, 21, and 48.

INTRODUCTION

A seminal figure in American literature, Wright was one of the foremost writers of his generation to confront readers with the dehumanizing effects of racism. In his autobiography *Black Boy: A Record of Childhood and Youth*, Wright described in detail the physical and emotional hardships he and other African-Americans faced growing up in the American South during the 1920s and 1930s, when racial segregation was strictly enforced. As an examination of oppression, rebellion, and emancipation, *Black Boy* is a modern version of the slave narrative that continues to elicit popular and critical discussion, both as a major work of American literature and as an invaluable sociological document of race relations in the United States before the advent of the civil rights movement.

Wright initially garnered national acclaim in 1940 for his novel *Native Son,* a protest novel in which he candidly exposed the oppressed black American's capacity for hatred and violence in a racist society. He began writing *Black Boy* in 1943. Originally titled "American Hunger," the work covered Wright's early life in the South as well as his adulthood in the North. Due to the book's length, however, Wright's editors decided to publish the work in two parts: *Black Boy* examines Wright's childhood and youth growing up in and around the region of the Mississippi River where the borders of Tennessee, Mississippi, and Arkansas converge, while *American Hunger,* which remained unpublished until 1977, recounts Wright's migration North and early years as a writer in Chicago. Although Wright's publishers initially suggested such titles as "Black Hunger," "Raw Hunger," "The First Chapter," "Valley of Fear," and "Land of Liberty," Wright decided on "Black Boy," explaining to his editor Edward Aswell: "Now, this is not very original, but I think it covers the book. It is honest. Straight. And many people say it to themselves when they see a Negro and wonder how he lives. . . . 'Black Boy' seems to me to be not only a title, but also a kind of heading of the whole general theme."

Growing up in the American South, Wright experienced an unsettled and often lonely childhood. When he was six years old, his father deserted his mother, who subsequent-

ly suffered a series of paralytic strokes that "set the emotional tone" of poverty for Wright and his younger brother. After being briefly placed in an orphanage, Wright was sent to live with relatives who physically and emotionally abused him for resisting religious conversion. In *Black Boy* Wright describes his upbringing and, in graphic and often violent terms, the debasement that he felt characterized black existence in the South. In one episode, for example, he relates how, as an adolescent, he encountered a black man who begged white men to kick him for a quarter. When Wright asked him why he permitted such degradation, the man replied, "Listen, nigger, my ass is tough and quarters is scarce." Although Wright emerged from this and other experiences with a sense of self-disgust and loathing toward his race, he refused to believe that he was inferior to white men. He began to write stories and to read voraciously, particularly the works of H. L. Mencken, whose trenchant language and outspoken critical opinions awakened him to the possibility of social protest through writing. With a growing awareness of racial injustice and the universality of human suffering, Wright left the South at the age of nineteen: "With ever watchful eyes and bearing scars, visible and invisible, I headed North, full of a hazy notion that life could be lived with dignity, that the personalities of others should not be violated, that men would be able to confront other men without fear or shame, and that if men were lucky in their living on earth they might win some redeeming meaning for their having struggled and suffered here beneath the stars."

Black Boy became an instant best-seller upon its publication in 1945. While most initial reviewers applauded the work's realism and emotional validity, others, particularly W. E. Burghardt Du Bois, objected to the work's graphic language, violence, and bleak portrayal of southern life. Others, including some of Wright's friends, considered *Black Boy* more a work of fiction than autobiography, citing apparent contradictions and invented episodes within the work. Wright's supporters, however, have been quick to defend the authenticity of *Black Boy*. Claudia C. Tate wrote: "Although it is probably true that *Black Boy* contains many exaggerated and even fictitious incidents, the emotions that they excite within Richard truthfully adhere to Wright's emotional existence. . . . This subjective but very real dimension of Wright's existence exceeds the limitations of factual descriptions and rational explanations."

While interest in *Black Boy* ebbed during the 1950s as the works of younger black writers gained in popularity, a resurgence of interest in Wright's work occurred in the 1960s with the advent of the militant black consciousness movement. In the judgment of most modern critics, *Black Boy* remains a vital work of historical, sociological, and literary significance whose seminal portrayal of one black man's search for self-actualization in a racist society made possible the works of such successive writers as James Baldwin and Ralph Ellison. As early as 1945 Ellison himself acknowledged *Black Boy*'s ability to effect a positive change on American society; he argued that with *Black Boy* Wright "has converted the American Negro impulse toward self-annihilation and 'going-under-ground' into a will to confront the world, to evaluate his experience honestly and throw his findings unashamedly into the guilty conscience of America."

PRINCIPAL WORKS

Uncle Tom's Children: Four Novellas (short stories) 1938; also published as *Uncle Tom's Children: Five Long Stories* [enlarged edition], 1940
"How Bigger Was Born" (essay) 1940; published in periodical *The Saturday Review of Literature*
Native Son (novel) 1940
12 Million Black Voices: A Folk History of the Negro in the United States (nonfiction) 1941
Black Boy: A Record of Childhood and Youth (autobiography) 1945
The Outsider (novel) 1953
Black Power: A Record of Reactions in a Land of Pathos (nonfiction) 1954
Savage Holiday (novel) 1954
The Color Curtain: A Report on the Bandung Conference (nonfiction) 1956

Pagan Spain (nonfiction) 1957
White Man, Listen! (lectures) 1957
The Long Dream (novel) 1958
Eight Men (short stories) 1961
Lawd Today (novel) 1963
Daddy Goodness [with Louis Sapin] (drama) 1968
American Hunger (autobiography) 1977
The Richard Wright Reader (essays, novel excerpts, letters, and poetry) 1978
*Richard Wright: Works. 2 vols. [edited by Arnold Rampersad] (novels, essays, and autobiography) 1991

*Vols. 55 and 56 of "Library of America." Includes restored texts of *Native Son, Lawd Today,* and *Black Boy,* incorporating passages deleted or altered at time of first publication.

CRITICISM

Howard Mumford Jones   (review date 3 March 1945)

[*In the following review of* Black Boy, *Jones maintains that despite Wright's failure to delineate the development of his personality, his autobiography is important both as a work of literature and as a "deeply disturbing document in race relations."*]

The reception of this disturbing book is bound to be emotional and confused, nor can I pretend to avoid these weaknesses. But inasmuch as *Black Boy* has a dual purpose, it may keep discussion clear if one comments on the volume with reference to its two main aspects. It is at once a literary work and a document in race relationships.

As a literary work *Black Boy* belongs to the category of unashamed autobiography and suggests in method Jack London's *John Barleycorn* or Rousseau's *Confessions.* The writer purports to tell the whole truth, to conceal nothing, to expose his emotional weaknesses, the indignities he endured, the sins and errors into which he fell. The world of Mississippi was a world in which everybody, white and black, pushed him around; and the story of these cruelties is the story of his life. There are, of course, random instances of kindly treatment but these are rare, and the total effect of the volume is an effect of passive suffering, punctuated by outbursts of blind emotional rebellion. Only at the end does the central figure take positive action and escape to Chicago.

Mr. Wright has chosen this method to illustrate the wrongs of his race, but the effect of his procedure is to weaken his book as a literary work. He emphasizes an endless array of wrongs, but he minimizes the development of his own personality. The "I" of the book is, in London's phrase, only a bit of the protoplasm. Even the desire to "write stories" which, at one stage of this sad history, seems to promise relief is not so much an act of the will as a kind of emotional outpouring. When the author attempts to re-create the child he was, he once or twice catalogues the sense impressions of boyhood, but aside from the fact that the rhetoric of these passages is unconvincing, they only increase the grey helplessness of the central figure, who is defined principally in terms of tension and bewilderment.

In contrast to the passivity of virtue in these pages, the acts of the boy's persecutors, white and black, are presented in dramatic scenes of vivid and even violent writing and in dialogue of great vigor and a vocabulary that spares the chaste ears of Boston nothing whatsoever. In some degree this verbal violence may conceal the central failure of the story, which is the failure to chronicle the growth of a personality under suffering as a Dostoievsky would have done. But the failure is there; and it is the more awkward because this reduction of a Negro autobiography to a jerky succession of outraged reactions is going to be misinterpreted in some quarters and cited as proof that Negro human nature is like that. This, of course, is precisely what Mr. Wright does not say.

This either-or formula of passive virtue (or at least potential virtue) and active evil is the formula of melodrama; and just as an easy recourse to melodrama was the structural weakness of *Native Son,* so it is the structural weakness of *Black Boy.* Mr. Wright has therefore twice fallen into this trap, but he has done so for honorable reasons. He is so outraged by man's inhumanity to man that he is prepared to sacrifice artistic values for hortatory ones. He does not care whether you read *Black Boy* as a novel, an autobiography, or a case study, provided you read him. And read him you must. For *Black Boy* is a deeply disturbing document in race relations. Whatever its weaknesses as art, you cannot ignore its strength as indictment.

What Mr. Wright indicts is the whole Jim Crow system. His wretched persecutors were black as well as white, but let no white man comfort himself with this racial distinction. The cruelty, the violence, the neglect, the brutality with which the growing boy was treated by members of his own race are, as Mr. Wright is at some pains to show, not racial characteristics, they are the inevitable function, the inevitable product of a system of life that not merely dooms the Negro to second-class citizenship, but also begrudges him the sorry privileges of that ill-defined and deceitful status. His family and his friends do not treat him wisely because they do not know any better, and they do not know any better because they are forever cut off from graciousness, from culture, from universalisms. They therefore take refuge in two patterns of emotional response equally stultifying: a religion which, contrary to white belief, is as narrow as any form of decayed Calvinism could possibly be; and a "Sklavenmoral" which, if it serves as a shield against the white man, induces lying, dishonesty, irresponsibility, and a host of similar moral evils in those compelled to practise it. This is the simple and effective indictment made by Mr. Wright.

It is sometimes said we would have no racial trouble in this country if the cultivated leaders on both sides of the partition got together. This is a statement at once profoundly true and profoundly false. If it is true, the obligation of the white man is to afford the Negro every conceivable opportunity to secure cultivation. As a factual interpretation, it is, however, profoundly false, for the reason that it is with the mass of half-educated whites that the mass of half-educated Negroes come chiefly into contact. *Black Boy* is the chronicle of this sort of contact. It is a scornful history of one man's experience of the bitter truth that at the average level of contact the Negro has no rights the white man is bound to respect, if the white man thinks he can get away with it. A policeman once defended the little boy. A white man from Illinois once cautiously tried to befriend him. There may be another instance or two in the volume of something other than insult and hatred, but as I think over its bitter pages I do not recall any others, and I must suppose that in the main this is a truthful chronicle, however distorted one may find it as a literary work.

There are some surprising omissions. It seems odd that the boy had never heard a whisper of Fisk or Atlanta University or Tuskegee or Hampton. It seems odd that no trace of the work of any interracial commission should be found in the Mississippi of his childhood. It seems odd that, aside from a single excursion into the editor's office, he should have found no comfort in any Negro newspaper or magazine. And the sheer law of probability ought to have thrown into his way a larger number of decent white people than he seems to have known—or has the memory of undoubted wrong obliterated the recollection of goodness, as it often does?

It will be said by many concerned for race relations in the years ahead that a book as violent in tone as *Black Boy* does more harm than good, and there is truth in this assertion. But the book exists. A state of mind exists. A race exists, and that race regards itself as suffering grievous wrongs. The Jim Crow system is doomed. It will not end tomorrow or next week or next year, but it cannot maintain itself. The problem is no longer a Negro problem, it is a white problem, and the problem is whether the white race will continue a bitter, grudging, snarling rear guard action that can only induce verbal and physical violence, or whether it can give graciously, if by slow and wise degrees, that which it is bound to yield in the end.

> Unless above himself he can
> Arise, how poor a work is man.

(pp. 9-10)

Howard Mumford Jones, "Up from Slavery: Richard Wright's Story," in The Saturday Review of Literature, *Vol. XXVIII, No. 9, March 3, 1945, pp. 9-10.*

W. E. Burghardt Du Bois   (review date 4 March 1945)

[*Du Bois was an American educator, poet, novelist, historian, and sociologist who helped spark interest in black writers and black writing during the early twentieth century. His best-known work,* The Souls of Black Folk *(1903), is considered a landmark in the history of black self-awareness. In the following review, he criticizes Wright's "misjudgment of black folk" and asserts that* Black Boy *is more convincing as a work of fiction than autobiography.*]

[*Black Boy*] tells a harsh and forbidding story and makes one wonder just exactly what its relation to truth is. The [subtitle], "A Record of Childhood and Youth," makes one at first think that the story is autobiographical. It probably is, at least in part. But mainly it is probably intended to be fiction or fictionalized biography. At any rate the reader must regard it as creative writing rather than simply a record of life.

The hero whom Wright draws, and may be it is himself, is in his childhood a loathsome brat, foul-mouthed and "a drunkard." The family which he paints is a distressing aggregation. Even toward his mother he never expresses love or affection. Sometimes he comes almost to sympathy. He wonders why this poor woman, deserted by her husband, toiling and baffled, broken by paralysis and disappointment, should suffer as she does. But his wonder is intellectual inability to explain the suffering. It doesn't seem for a moment to be personal sorrow at this poor, bowed figure of pain and ignorance.

The father is painted as gross and bestial with little of human sensibility. The grandmother is a religious fanatic, apparently sincere but brutal. The boy fights with his aunt. And here again the artist in Richard Wright seems to fail. He repeats an incident of fighting his aunt with a knife to keep her from beating him. He tells the tale of his grandfather, a disappointed veteran of the Civil War, but tells it without sympathy. The Negroes whom he paints have almost no redeeming qualities. Some work hard, some are sly, many are resentful; but there is none who is ambitious, successful or really intelligent.

After this sordid, shadowy picture we gradually come upon the solution. The hero is interested in himself, is self-centered to the exclusion of everybody and everything else. The suffering of others is put down simply as a measure of his own suffering and resentment. There is scarcely a ray of light in his childhood: he is hungry, he is beaten, he is cold and unsheltered. Above all, a naturally shy and introverted personality is forced back upon itself until he becomes almost pathological. The world is himself and his suffering. He hates and distrusts it. He says "I was rapidly learning to distrust everything and everybody."

He writes of a mother who wanted him to marry her daughter. "The main value in their lives was simple, clean, good living, and when they thought they had found those same qualities in one of their race they instinctively embraced him, liked him and asked no questions. But such simple unaffected trust flabbergasted me. It was impossible!"

He tells of his own pitiful confusion, when as an imaginative, eager child he could not speak his thought: "I knew how to write as well as any pupil in the classroom, and no doubt I could read better than any of them, and I could talk fluently and expressively when I was sure of myself. Then why did strange faces make me freeze? I sat with my ears and neck burning, hearing the pupils whisper about me, hating myself, hating them."

Then here and there for a moment he forgets his role as artist and becomes commentator and prophet. Born on a plantation, living in Elaine, Ark., and the slums of Memphis, he knows the whole Negro race! "After I had outlived the shocks of childhood, after the habit of reflection had been born in me, I used to mull over the strange absence of real kindness in Negroes, how unstable was our tenderness, how lacking in genuine passion we were, how void of great hope, how timid our joy, how bare our traditions, how hollow our memories, how lacking we were in those intangible sentiments that bind man to man, and how shallow was even our despair."

Not only is there this misjudgment of black folk and the difficult repulsive characters among them that he is thrown with, but the same thing takes place with white folk. There is not a single broad-minded, open-hearted white person in his book. One or two start out seemingly willing to be decent, but as he says of one white family for whom he worked, "They cursed each other in an amazingly offhand manner and nobody seemed to mind. As they hurled invectives they barely looked at each other. I was tense each moment, trying to anticipate their wishes and avoid a curse, and I did not suspect that the tension I had begun to feel that morning would lift itself into the passion of my life."

From the world of whites and the world of blacks he grows up curiously segregated. "I knew of no Negroes who read the books I liked, and I wondered if any Negroes ever thought of them. I knew that there were Negro doctors, lawyers, newspaper men, but I never saw any of them."

One rises from the reading of such a book with mixed thoughts. Richard Wright uses vigorous and straightforward English; often there is real beauty in his words even when they are mingled with sadism:

> There was the disdain that filled me as I tortured a delicate, blue-pink crawfish that huddled fearfully in the mudsill of a rusty tin can. There was the aching glory in masses of clouds burning gold and purple from an invisible sun. There was the liquid alarm I saw in the blood-red glare of the sun's afterglow mirrored in the squared planes of whitewashed frame houses. There was the languor I felt when I heard green leaves rustling with a rainlike sound.

Yet at the result one is baffled. Evidently if this is an actual record, bad as the world is, such concentrated memories, filth and despair never completely filled it or any particular part of it. But if the book is meant to be a creative picture and a warning, even then, it misses its possible effectiveness because it is as a work of art so patently and terribly overdrawn.

Nothing that Richard Wright says is in itself unbelievable or impossible; it is the total picture that is not convincing.

> *W. E. Burghardt Du Bois, "Richard Wright Looks Back," in* New York Herald Tribune Weekly Book Review, *March 4, 1945, p. 2.*

Ralph Ellison   (essay date June 1945)

[*One of the most highly praised black American authors of the latter half of the twentieth century, Ellison is best known for* Invisible Man (1952). *In the following essay, a small portion of which was published in* Contemporary Literary Criticism, *Volume 9, he refutes the typical charge that Wright had exaggerated the extent of black violence in* Black Boy.]

As a writer, Richard Wright has outlined for himself a dual role: To discover and depict the meaning of Negro experience; and to reveal to both Negroes and whites those problems of a psychological and emotional nature which arise between them when they strive for mutual understanding.

Now in *Black Boy,* he has used his own life to probe what qualities of will, imagination, and intellect are required of a Southern Negro in order to possess the meaning of his life in the United States. Wright is an important writer, perhaps the most articulate Negro American, and what he has to say is highly perceptive. Imagine Bigger Thomas projecting his own life in lucid prose, guided, say, by the insights of Marx and Freud, and you have an idea of this autobiography.

Published at a time when any sharply critical approach to Negro life has been dropped as a wartime expendable, it should do much to redefine the problem of the Negro and American Democracy. Its power can be observed in the shrill manner with which some professional "friends of the Negro people" have attempted to strangle the work in a noose of newsprint.

What in the tradition of literary autobiography is it like, this work described as a "great American autobiography"? As a nonwhite intellectual's statement of his relationship to western culture, *Black Boy* recalls the conflicting pattern of identification and rejection found in Nehru's *Toward Freedom.* In its use of fictional techniques, its concern with criminality (sin) and the artistic sensibility, and in its author's judgment and rejection of the narrow world of his origin, it recalls Joyce's rejection of Dublin in *A Portrait of the Artist.* And as a psychological document of life under oppressive conditions, it recalls *The House of the Dead,* Dostoivski's profound study of the humanity of Russian criminals.

Such works were perhaps Wright's literary guides, aiding him to endow his life's incidents with communicable significance; providing him with ways of seeing, feeling, and describing his environment. These influences, however, were encountered only after these first years of Wright's life were past and were not part of the immediate folk culture into which he was born. In that culture the specific folk-art form which helped shape the writer's attitude toward his life and which embodied the impulse that contributes much to the quality and tone of his autobiography was the Negro Blues. This would bear a word of explanation:

The Blues is an impulse to keep the painful details and episodes of a brutal experience alive in one's aching consciousness, to finger its jagged grain, and to transcend it, not by the consolation of philosophy, but by squeezing from it a near-tragic, near-comic lyricism. As a form, the Blues is an autobiographical chronicle of personal catastrophe expressed lyrically. And certainly Wright's early childhood was crammed with catastrophic incidents. In a few short years his father deserted his mother, he knew intense hunger, he became a drunkard begging drinks from black stevedores in Memphis saloons; he had to flee Arkansas where an uncle was lynched; he was forced to live with a fanatically religious grandmother in an atmosphere of constant bickering; he was lodged in an orphan asylum; he observed the suffering of his mother who became a permanent invalid, while fighting off the blows of the poverty-stricken relatives with whom he had to live; he was cheated, beaten, and kicked off jobs by white employees who disliked his eagerness to learn a trade; and to these objective circumstances must be added the subjective fact that Wright, with his sensitivity, extreme shyness and intelligence was a problem child who rejected his family and was by them rejected.

Thus along with the themes, equivalent descriptions of milieu and the perspectives to be found in Joyce, Nehru, Dostoievski, George Moore and Rousseau, *Black Boy* is filled with blues-tempered echoes of railroad trains, the names of Southern towns and cities, estrangements, fights and flights, deaths and disappointments, charged with physical and spiritual hungers and pain. And like a blues sung by such an artist as Bessie Smith, its lyrical prose evokes the paradoxical, almost surreal image of a black boy singing lustily as he probes his own grievous wound.

In *Black Boy,* two worlds have fused, two cultures merged, two impulses of western man become coalesced. By discussing some of its cultural sources I hope to answer those critics who would make of the book a miracle and of its author a mystery. And while making no attempt to probe the mystery of the artist (who Hemingway says is "forged in injustice as a sword is forged") I do hold that basically the prerequisites to the writing of *Black Boy* were, on the one hand, the microscopic degree of cultural freedom which Wright found in the South's stony injustice, and, on the other, the existence of a personality agitated to a state of almost manic restlessness. There were, of course, other factors, chiefly ideological; but these came later.

Wright speaks of his journey north as,

> . . . taking a part of the South to transplant in alien soil, to see if it could grow differently, if it could drink of new and cool rains, bend in strange winds, respond to the warmth of other suns, and perhaps, to bloom. . . .

And just as Wright, the man, represents the blooming of the delinquent child of the autobiography, just so does *Black Boy* represent the flowering—cross-fertilized by pollen blown by the winds of strange cultures—of the humble blues lyric. There is, as in all acts of creation, a world of mystery in this, but there is also enough that is comprehensible for Americans to create the social atmosphere in which other black boys might freely bloom.

For certainly, in the historical sense, Wright is no exception. Born on a Mississippi plantation, he was subjected to all those blasting pressures which, in a scant eighty years, have sent the Negro people hurtling, without clearly defined trajectory, from slavery to emancipation, from log cabin to city tenement, from the white folks' fields and kitchens to factory assembly lines; and which, between two wars, have shattered the wholeness of its folk consciousness into a thousand writhing pieces.

Black Boy describes this process in the personal terms of *one* Negro childhood. Nevertheless, several critics have complained that it does not "explain" Richard Wright. Which, aside from the notion of art involved, serves to remind us that the prevailing mood of American criticism has so thoroughly excluded the Negro that it fails to recognize some of the most basic tenets of western democratic thought when encountering them in a black skin. They forget that human life possesses an innate dignity and mankind an innate sense of nobility; that all men possess the tendency to dream and the compulsion to make their dreams reality; that the need to be ever dissatisfied and the urge ever to seek satisfaction is implicit in the human organism; and that all men are the victims and the beneficiaries of the goading, tormenting, commanding, and informing activity of that imperious process known as the Mind—the Mind, as Valéry describes it, "armed with its inexhaustible questions."

Perhaps all this (in which lies the very essence of the human, and which Wright takes for granted) has been forgotten because the critics recognize neither Negro humanity nor the full extent to which the Southern community renders the fulfilment of human destiny impossible. And while it is true that *Black Boy* presents an almost unrelieved picture of a personality corrupted by brutal environment, it also presents those fresh, human responses brought to its world by the sensitive child:

> There was the *wonder* I felt when I first saw a brace of mountainlike, spotted, black-and-white horses clopping down a dusty road . . . the *delight* I caught in seeing long straight rows of red and green vegetables stretching away in the sun . . . the faint, cool kiss of *sensuality* when dew came on to my cheeks . . . the vague *sense of the infinite* as I looked down upon the yellow, dreaming waters of the Mississippi . . . the echoes of *nostalgia* I heard in the crying strings of wild geese . . . the *love* I had for the mute regality of tall, moss-clad oaks . . . the hint of *cosmic cruelty* that I *felt* when I saw the curved timbers of a wooden shack that had been warped in the summer sun . . . and there was the *quiet terror* that suffused my senses when vast hazes of gold washed earthward from star-heavy skies on silent nights. . . .

And a bit later, his reactions to religion:

> Many of the religious symbols appealed to my sensibilities and I responded to the dramatic vision of life held by the church, feeling that to live day by day with death as one's sole thought was to be so compassionately sensitive toward all life as to view all men as slowly dying, and the trembling sense of fate that welled up, sweet and melancholy, from the hymns blended with the sense of fate that I had already caught from life.

There was also the influence of his mother—so closely linked to his hysteria and sense of suffering—who (though he only implies it here) taught him, in the words of the dedication prefacing *Native Son*, "to revere the fanciful

and the imaginative." There were also those white men—the one who allowed Wright to use his library privileges and the other who advised him to leave the South, and still others whose offers of friendship he was too frightened to accept.

Wright assumed that the nucleus of plastic sensibility is a human heritage—the right and the opportunity to dilate, deepen, and enrich sensibility—democracy. Thus the drama of *Black Boy* lies in its depiction of what occurs when Negro sensibility attempts to fulfill itself in the undemocratic South. Here it is not the individual that is the immediate focus, as in Joyce's *Stephen Hero,* but that upon which his sensibility was nourished.

Those critics who complain that Wright has omitted the development of his own sensibility hold that the work thus fails as art. Others, because it presents too little of what they consider attractive in Negro life, charge that it distorts reality. Both groups miss a very obvious point: That whatever else the environment contained, it had as little chance of prevailing against the overwhelming weight of the child's unpleasant experiences as Beethoven's Quartets would have of destroying the stench of a Nazi prison.

We come, then, to the question of art. The function, the psychology, of artistic selectivity is to eliminate from art form all those elements of experience which contain no compelling significance. Life is as the sea, art a ship in which man conquers life's crushing formlessness, reducing it to a course, a series of swells, tides, and wind currents inscribed on a chart. Though drawn from the world, "the organized significance of art," writes Malraux, "is stronger than all the multiplicity of the world; . . . that significance alone enables man to conquer chaos and to master destiny."

Wright saw his destiny—that combination of forces before which man feels powerless—in terms of a quick and casual violence inflicted upon him by both family and community. His response was likewise violent, and it has been his need to give that violence significance which has shaped his writings.

What were the ways by which other Negroes confronted their destiny?

In the South of Wright's childhood there were three general ways: They could accept the role created for them by the whites and perpetually resolve the resulting conflicts through the hope and emotional cartharsis of Negro religion; they could repress their dislike of Jimcrow social relations while striving for a middle way of respectability, becoming—consciously or unconsciously—the accomplices of the whites in oppressing their brothers; or they could reject the situation, adopt a criminal attitude, and carry on an unceasing psychological scrimmage with the whites, which often flared forth into physical violence.

Wright's attitude was nearest the last. Yet, in it there was an all-important qualitative difference: it represented a groping for *individual* values, in a black community whose values were what the young Negro critic, Edward Bland, has defined as "pre-individual." And herein lay the setting for the extreme conflict set off, both within his family and in the community, by Wright's assertion of individuality. The clash was sharpest on the psychological level, for, to quote Bland:

> In the pre-individualistic thinking of the Negro the stress is on the group. Instead of seeing in terms of the individual, the Negro sees in terms of "races," masses of peoples separated from other masses according to color. Hence, an act rarely bears intent against him as a Negro individual. He is singled out not as a person but as a specimen of an ostracized group. He knows that he never exists in his own right but only to the extent that others hope to make the race suffer vicariously through him.

This pre-individual state is induced artifically—like the regression to primitive states noted among cultured inmates of Nazi prisons. The primary technique in its enforcement is to impress the Negro child with the omniscience and omnipotence of the whites to the point that whites appear as ahuman as Jehovah, and as relentless as a Mississippi flood. Socially it is effected through an elaborate scheme of taboos supported by a ruthless physical violence, which strikes not only the offender, but the entire black community. To wander from the paths of behavior laid down for the group is to become the agent of communal disaster.

In such a society the development of individuality depends upon a series of accidents; which often arise, as in Wright's case, from conditions within the Negro family. In Wright's life there was the accident that as a small child he could not distinguish between his fair-skinned grandmother and the white women of the town, thus developing skepticism as to their special status. To this was linked the accident of his having no close contacts with whites until after the child's normal formative period.

But these objective accidents not only link forward to those qualities of rebellion, criminality, and intellectual questioning expressed in Wright's work today. They also link backward into the shadow of infancy where environment and consciousness are so darkly intertwined as to require the skill of a psychoanalyst to define their point of juncture. Nevertheless, at the age of four, Wright set the house afire and was beaten near to death by his frightened mother. This beating, followed soon by his father's desertion of the family, seems to be the initial psychological motivation of his quest for a new identification. While delirious from this beating Wright was haunted "by huge wobbly white bags like the full udders of a cow, suspended from the ceiling above me [and] I was gripped by the fear that they were going to fall and drench me with some horrible liquid. . . ."

It was as though the mother's milk had turned acid, and with it the whole pattern of life that had produced the ignorance, cruelty, and fear that had fused with mother-love and exploded in the beating. It is significant that the bags were of the hostile color white, and the female symbol that of the cow, the most stupid (and, to the small child, the most frightening) of domestic animals. Here in dream symbolism is expressed an attitude worthy of an Orestes. And the significance of the crisis is increased by virtue of the historical fact that the lower-class Negro family is ma-

triarchal; the child turns not to the father to compensate if he feels mother-rejection, but to the grandmother, or to an aunt—and Wright rejected both of these. Such rejection leaves the child open to psychological insecurity, distrust, and all of those hostile environmental forces from which the family functions to protect it.

One of the Southern Negro family's methods of protecting the child is the severe beating—a homeopathic dose of the violence generated by black and white relationships. Such beatings as Wright's were administered for the child's own good; a good which the child resisted, thus giving family relationship an undercurrent of fear and hostility, which differs qualitatively from that found in patriarchal middle-class families, because here the severe beating is administered by the mother, leaving the child no parental sanctuary. He must ever embrace violence along with maternal tenderness, or else reject, in his helpless way, the mother.

The division between the Negro parents of Wright's mother's generation, whose sensibilities were often bound by their proximity to the slave experience, and their children, who historically and through the rapidity of American change, stand emotionally and psychologically much farther away, is quite deep. Indeed, sometimes as deep as the cultural distance between Yeats' *Autobiographies* and a Bessie Smith blues. This is the historical background to those incidents of family strife in **Black Boy** which have caused reviewers to question Wright's judgment of Negro emotional relationships.

We have here a problem in the sociology of sensibility that is obscured by certain psychological attitudes brought to Negro life by whites.

In [*Black Boy*] thousands of Negroes will for the first time see their destiny in public print. . . . And in this lies Wright's most important achievement: He has converted the American Negro impulse toward self-annihilation and "going-under-ground" into a will to confront the world, to evaluate his experience honestly and throw his findings unashamedly into the guilty conscience of America.

—Ralph Ellison

The first is the attitude which compels whites to impute to Negroes sentiments, attitudes, and insights which, as a group living under certain definite social conditions, Negroes could not humanly possess. It is the identical mechanism which William Empson identifies in literature as "pastoral." It implies that since Negroes possess the richly human virtues credited to them, then their social position is advantageous and should not be bettered; and, continuing syllogistically, the white individual need feel no guilt over his participation in Negro oppression.

The second attitude is that which leads whites to misjudge Negro passion, looking upon it as they do, out of the turgidity of their own frustrated yearning for emotional warmth, their capacity for sensation having been constricted by the impersonal mechanized relationships typical of bourgeois society. The Negro is idealized into a symbol of sensation, of unhampered social and sexual relationships. And when *Black Boy* questions their illusion they are thwarted much in the manner of the occidental who, after observing the erotic character of a primitive dance, "shacks up" with a native woman—only to discover that far from possessing the hair-trigger sexual responses of a Stork Club "babe," she is relatively phlegmatic.

The point is not that American Negroes are primitives, but that as a group, their social situation does not provide for the type of emotional relationships attributed them. For how could the South, recognized as a major part of the backward third of the nation, flower in the black, most brutalized section of its population, those forms of human relationships achievable only in the most highly developed areas of civilization?

Champions of this "Aren't-Negroes-Wonderful?" school of thinking often bring Paul Robeson and Marian Anderson forward as examples of highly developed sensibility, but actually they are only its *promise*. Both received their development from an extensive personal contact with European culture, free from the influences which shape Southern Negro personality. In the United States, Wright, who is the only Negro literary artist of equal caliber, had to wait years and escape to another environment before discovering the moral and ideological equivalents of his childhood attitudes.

Man cannot express that which does not exist—either in the form of dreams, ideas, or realities—in his environment. Neither his thoughts nor his feelings, his sensibility nor his intellect are fixed, innate qualities. They are processes which arise out of the interpenetration of human instinct with environment, through the process called experience; each changing and being changed by the other. Negroes cannot possess many of the sentiments attributed to them because the same changes in environment which, through experience, enlarge man's intellect (and thus his capacity for still greater change) also modify his feelings; which in turn increase his sensibility, i.e., his sensitivity to refinements of impression and subtleties of emotion. The extent of these changes depends upon the quality of political and cultural freedom in the environment.

Intelligence tests have measured the quick rise in intellect which takes place in Southern Negroes after moving north, but little attention has been paid to the mutations effected in their sensibilities. However, the two go hand in hand. Intellectual complexity is accompanied by emotional complexity; refinement of thought, by refinement of feeling. The movement north affects more than the Negro's wage scale, it affects his entire psychosomatic structure.

The rapidity of Negro intellectual growth in the North is due partially to objective factors present in the environment, to influences of the industrial city, and to a greater

political freedom. But there are also changes within the "inner world." In the North energies are released and given *intellectual* channelization—energies which in most Negroes in the South have been forced to take either a *physical* form or, as with potentially intellectual types like Wright, to be expressed as nervous tension, anxiety, and hysteria. Which is nothing mysterious. The human organism responds to environmental stimuli by converting them into either physical and/or intellectual energy. And what is called hysteria is suppressed intellectual energy expressed physically.

The "physical" character of their expression makes for much of the difficulty in understanding American Negroes. Negro music and dances are frenziedly erotic; Negro religious ceremonies violently ecstatic; Negro speech strongly rhythmical and weighted with image and gesture. But there is more in this sensuousness than the unrestraint and insensitivity found in primitive cultures; nor is it simply the relatively spontaneous and undifferentiated responses of a people living in close contact with the soil. For despite Jimcrow, Negro life does not exist in a vacuum, but in the seething vortex of those tensions generated by the most highly industrialized of western nations. The welfare of the most humble black Mississippi sharecropper is affected less by the flow of the seasons and the rhythm of natural events than by the fluctuations of the stock market; even though, as Wright states of his father, the sharecropper's memories, actions, and emotions are shaped by his immediate contact with nature and the crude social relations of the South.

All of this makes the American Negro far different from the "simple" specimen for which he is taken. And the "physical" quality offered as evidence of his primitive simplicity is actually the form of his complexity. The American Negro is a western type whose social condition creates a state which is almost the reverse of the cataleptic trance: Instead of his consciousness being lucid to the reality around it while the body is rigid, here it is the body which is alert, reacting to pressures which the constricting forces of Jimcrow block off from the transforming, concept-creating activity of the brain. The "eroticism" of Negro expression springs from much the same conflict as that displayed in the violent gesturing of a man who attempts to express a complicated concept with a limited vocabulary; thwarted ideational energy is converted into unsatisfactory pantomime, and his words are burdened with meanings they cannot convey. Here lies the source of the basic ambiguity of *Native Son,* wherein in order to translate Bigger's complicated feelings into universal ideas, Wright had to force into Bigger's consciousness concepts and ideas which his intellect could not formulate. Between Wright's skill and knowledge and the potentials of Bigger's mute feelings lay a thousand years of conscious culture.

In the South the sensibilities of both blacks and whites are inhibited by the rigidly defined environment. For the Negro there is relative safety as long as the impulse toward individuality is suppressed. (Lynchings have occurred because Negroes painted their homes.) And it is the task of the Negro family to adjust the child to the Southern milieu; through it the currents, tensions, and impulses generated within the human organism by the flux and flow of events are given their distribution. This also gives the group its distinctive character. Which, because of Negroes' suppressed minority position, is very much in the nature of an elaborate but limited defense mechanism. Its function is dual: to protect the Negro from whirling away from the undifferentiated mass of his people into the unknown, symbolized in its most abstract form by insanity, and most concretely by lynching; and to protect him from those unknown forces *within himself* which might urge him to reach out for that social and human equality which the white South says he cannot have. Rather than throw himself against the charged wires of his prison he annihilates the impulses within him.

The pre-individualistic black community discourages individuality out of self-defense. Having learned through experience that the whole group is punished for the actions of the single member, it has worked out efficient techniques of behavior control. For in many Southern communities everyone knows everyone else and is vulnerable to his opinions. In some communities everyone is "related" regardless of blood-ties. The regard shown by the group for its members, its general communal character and its cohesion are often mentioned. For by comparison with the coldly impersonal relationships of the urban industrial community, its relationships are personal and warm.

Black Boy, however, illustrates that this personal quality, shaped by outer violence and inner fear, is ambivalent. Personal warmth is accompanied by an equally personal coldness, kindliness by cruelty, regard by malice. And these opposites are as quickly set off against the member who gestures toward individuality as a lynch mob forms at the cry of rape. Negro leaders have often been exasperated by this phenomenon, and Booker T. Washington (who demanded far less of Negro humanity than Richard Wright) described the Negro community as a basket of crabs, wherein should one attempt to climb out, the others immediately pull him back.

The member who breaks away is apt to be more impressed by its negative than by its positive character. He becomes a stranger even to his relatives and he interprets gestures of protection as blows of oppression—from which there is no hiding place, because every area of Negro life is affected. Even parental love is given a qualitative balance akin to "sadism." And the extent of beatings and psychological maimings meted out by Southern Negro parents rivals those described by the nineteenth-century Russian writers as characteristic of peasant life under the Czars. The horrible thing is that the cruelty is also an expression of concern, of love.

In discussing the inadequacies for democratic living typical of the education provided Negroes by the South, a Negro educator has coined the term *mis-education.* Within the ambit of the black family this takes the form of training the child away from curiosity and adventure, against reaching out for those activities lying beyond the borders of the black community. And when the child resists, the parent discourages him; first with the formula,

"That there's for white folks. Colored can't have it," and finally with a beating.

It is not, then, the family and communal violence described by *Black Boy* that is unusual, but that Wright *recognized* and made no peace with its essential cruelty—even when, like a babe freshly emerged from the womb, he could not discern where his own personality ended and it began. Ordinarily, both parent and child are protected against this cruelty—seeing it as love and finding subjective sanction for it in the spiritual authority of the Fifth Commandment, and on the secular level in the legal and extralegal structure of the Jimcrow system. The child who did not rebel, or who was unsuccessful in his rebellion, learned a masochistic submissiveness and a denial of the impulse toward western culture when it stirred within him.

Why then have Southern whites, who claim to "know" the Negro missed all this? Simply because they too are armored against the horror and the cruelty. Either they deny the Negro's humanity and feel no cause to measure his actions against civilized norms; or they protect themselves from their guilt in the Negro's condition and from their fear that their cooks might poison them, or that their nursemaids might strangle their infant charges, or that their field hands might do them violence, by attributing to them a superhuman capacity for love, kindliness, and forgiveness. Nor does this in any way contradict their stereotyped conviction that all Negros (meaning those with whom they have no contact) are given to the most animal behavior.

It is only when the individual, whether white or black, *rejects* the pattern that he awakens to the nightmare of his life. Perhaps much of the South's regressive character springs from the fact that many, jarred by some casual crisis into wakefulness, flee hysterically into the sleep of violence or the coma of apathy again. For the penalty of wakefulness is to encounter ever more violence and horror than the sensibilities can sustain unless translated into some form of social action. Perhaps the impassioned character so noticeable among those white Southern liberals so active in the Negro's cause is due to their sense of accumulated horror; their passion—like the violence in Faulkner's novels—is evidence of a profound spiritual vomiting.

This compulsion is even more active in Wright and the increasing number of Negroes who have said an irrevocable "no" to the Southern pattern. Wright learned that it is not enough merely to reject the white South, but that he had also to reject that part of the South which lay within. As a rebel he formulated that rejection negatively, because it was the negative face of the Negro community upon which he looked most often as a child. It is this he is contemplating when he writes:

> Whenever I thought of the essential bleakness of black life in America, I knew that Negroes had never been allowed to catch the full spirit of Western civilization, that they lived somehow in it but not of it. And when I brooded upon the cultural barrenness of black life, I wondered if clean, positive tenderness, love, honor, loyalty, and the capacity to remember were native to

man. I asked myself if these human qualities were not fostered, won, struggled and suffered for, preserved in ritual from one generation to another.

But far from implying that Negroes have no capacity for culture, as one critic interprets it, this is the strongest affirmation that they have. Wright is pointing out what should be obvious (especially to his Marxist critics) that Negro sensibility is socially and historically conditioned; that western culture must be won, confronted like the animal in a Spanish bullfight, dominated by the red shawl of codified experience, and brought heaving to its knees.

Wright knows perfectly well that Negro life is a by-product of western civilization, and that in it, if only one possesses the humanity and humility to see, are to be discovered all those impulses, tendencies, life and cultural forms, to be found elsewhere in western society.

The problem arises because the special condition of Negroes in the United States, including the defensive character of Negro life itself (the "will toward organization" noted in the western capitalist appears in the Negro as a will to camouflage, to dissimulate) so distorts these forms as to render their recognition as difficult as finding a wounded quail against the brown and yellow leaves of a Mississippi thicket—even the spilled blood blends with the background. Having himself been in the position of the quail—to expand the metaphor—Wright's wounds have told him both the question and the answer which every successful hunter must discover for himself: "Where would I hide if *I* were a wounded quail?" But perhaps that requires more sympathy with one's quarry than most hunters possess. Certainly it requires such a sensitivity to the shifting guises of humanity under pressure as to allow them to identify themselves with the human content, whatever its outer form; and even with those Southern Negroes to whom Paul Robeson's name is only a rolling sound in the fear-charged air.

Let us close with one final word about the Blues: Their attraction lies in this, that they at once express both the agony of life and the possibility of conquering it through sheer toughness of spirit. They fall short of tragedy only in that they provide no solution, offer no scapegoat but the self. Nowhere in America today is there social or political action based upon the solid realities of Negro life depicted in **Black Boy;** perhaps that is why, with its refusal to offer solutions, it is like the Blues. Yet, in it thousands of Negroes will for the first time see their destiny in public print. Freed here of fear and the threat of violence, their lives have at last been organized, scaled down to possessable proportions. And in this lies Wright's most important achievement: He has converted the American Negro impulse toward self-annihilation and "going-under-ground" into a will to confront the world, to evaluate his experience honestly and throw his findings unashamedly into the guilty conscience of America. (pp. 198-211)

Ralph Ellison, "Richard Wright's Blues," in The Antioch Review, Vol. V, No. 2, June, 1945, pp. 198-211.

Arthur P. Davis (review date Fall 1945)

[*An American scholar of black literature, Davis is the author of* From the Dark Tower: Afro-American Writers, 1900-1960 *(1974). In the following essay, he examines the theme of violence in* Black Boy, *calling the work "one of the most important contributions to the literature of the race question made in our time."*]

One of the strongest works yet written by an American Negro, **Black Boy** almost repels one with its savage intensity. A brilliant and powerful piece of writing, it has angered and shocked many readers—particularly Negro readers. Many of the latter have felt that the book is unnecessarily bitter, that the picture of Negro life given in it is unnatural and distorted, that this picture is too unrelievedly dark, that there are several analyses and episodes in the book which do not ring true, that it is not real autobiography, and that the whole work is overdrawn in its violence.

Admitting that each of these criticisms has some validity, one also senses in them a bit of rationalizing. In many cases they are merely the surface explanation of a far deeper reaction on the part of the Negro reader. The real rub is that **Black Boy** jolts and disturbs us deeply. In probing to the core and laying bare the whole stark tragedy of Southern living, Wright has told us a truth which we have long known subconsciously but have tried not to face. He has painted the picture of Southern living so black, he has left us no hope.

With typical American optimism, we have fooled ourselves that conditions are not really as bad as they seem; and this ostrich-attitude has bred in us a measure of optimism. **Black Boy** rudely kicks this frail prop from under us, dumping us unceremoniously on the ground of ugly reality. And we do not like it.

Omitting practically all of the light and pleasant incidents of his boyhood and youth (and, of course, there were many no matter what he says to the contrary), Wright has concentrated upon and strongly exaggerated the dark side of his experience. Not for a moment does he let up; not for a moment does he allow the reader to forget the book's theme. With sledge hammer blows he beats into our consciousness the single message that Southern living is distorting and brutalizing, that no Negro boy in the South can grow up a normal human being.

The message hurts because we recognize its essential truth. Though our several experiences may differ radically from his, Wright has typified (and dramatized) the basic ugliness of the Southern pattern. One-sided as his delineation may be, it has enough elemental and poetic truth in it to convince us. One rises from the reading of **Black Boy** with something of the feeling he receives from a Greek tragedy. Indeed, in its relentless concern with the morbid and the violent, and in its classic compression and starkness, **Black Boy** strongly resembles a Greek tragedy.

Speaking of violence—all of Wright's major works have been based on that theme: **Uncle Tom's Children** and **Native Son** as well as **Black Boy.** It may be that Richard Wright sees in violence the most revealing symbol of Negro living in America; or to be more cynical, it may be that he has discovered that literary violence brings in more royalties than gentler approaches. In any case, as a portrayer of that characteristic, Wright has few equals among American writers.

From the curtain-burning episode and its cruel aftermath in the first chapter down to the fight between Richard and another porter—a fight promoted and enjoyed by some sadistic whites—the book never changes its sombre mood. The unconscious brutality of his mother who whips him for fighting white boys, the bestiality of the bar flies who made him a drunkard at six, the morbid religious fanaticism of his grandmother, the frustrated harshness of his aunt, the filthy conversation of the white family for whom he worked, the hatred of the white employees in the optician's shop, and the unbelievable degradation of the Negro elevator boy who allowed whites to kick him for a quarter—all of these scenes, presented with consummate skill, build for us an unforgettable mosaic of violence.

Wright tells us that his main desire in *Black Boy* "was to render a judgment" on his environment. A spiritual part of that environment which he heartily dislikes is the myth of Negro kindliness and sympathy. The following iconoclastic paragraphs, injected parenthetically in Chapter II, give one of the most cynical pictures of the Negro found in our literature:

> . . . I used to mull over the strange absence of real kindness in Negroes, how unstable was our tenderness, how lacking in genuine passion we were, how void of great hope, how timid our joy, how bare our traditions, how hollow our memories, how lacking we were in those intangible sentiments that bind man to man, and how shallow was even our despair. After I had learned other ways of life I used to brood upon the unconscious irony of those who felt that Negroes led so passional an existence! I saw that what had been taken for our emotional strength was our negative confusions, our flights, our fears, our frenzy under pressure.
>
> Whenever I thought of the essential bleakness of black life in America, I knew that Negroes had never been allowed to catch the full spirit of Western civilization, that they lived somehow in it but not of it. . . .

Impartial in his condemnation, Wright has not sentimentalized the shortcomings of blacks.

Though *Black Boy* may not be as some critics have already called it, the modern *Uncle Tom's Cabin,* it will probably do more than any other recent book to make America conscious of its most serious and most neglected problem. In all likelihood, *Black Boy* is one of the most important contributions to the literature of the race question made in our time.

With its brilliant style, its highly effective handling of narrative and dramatic material, and its penetrating analysis of emotional states, *Black Boy* as a work of art is a notable contribution to American letters.

Richard Wright has grown steadily since his first publica-
tion. Measured by any standards, he is now a significant American writer. (pp. 589-90)

> *Arthur P. Davis, in a review of "Black Boy,"*
> *in* The Journal of Negro Education, *Vol. XIV,*
> *No. 4, Fall, 1945, pp. 589-90.*

Rebecca Chalmers Barton   (essay date 1948)

[*In the following essay, Barton briefly compares* Black Boy *to the autobiographies of Frederick Douglass, W. E. B. Du Bois, and James Weldon Johnson and praises the work as intimate and appealing.*]

On the strength of his experience, Richard Wright belongs closer to Frederick Douglass than any of our autobiographers. A slave in deed, if not in name, trapped by a thousand cruelties and taboos, he pushes against the dead weight of his environment by virtue of the same untutored brilliance. He, too, knows the near-death of flogging, the humiliation of random blows, and the flaring resentment against an irrational violence. Born many decades after Douglass and the Abolitionists had fought the good fight, Wright is a child of the deepest South where the mores of new race relations are slow to penetrate, and where a dark skin still permits of no misstep in a white-dominated world without fear of reprisal. The fact that the boy's worst punishments were administered by his own relatives only proved the completeness of that dominance. His family, segregated from the whites, conformed to their dictates and tried to mold him into piety and subserviency. Why he rebelled and asserted his humanity while his brother, his cousins, his schoolmates fell into line remains one of the perennial miracles of personality development.

Since portions of *Black Boy* were published as early as 1937, when the author was still in his twenties, appropriately it intended to be only "a record of childhood and youth." But, in relation to the brief span of years it covers, compared to the autobiographies of Douglass, Du Bois, and James Weldon Johnson, it gives ample measure. Every facet of early experience is exposed with such clarity that the effect is startling in its illusion of reality. While a section of the general public, which has heard of *Black Boy* if of no other Negro-American autobiography, may like to explain its phenomenal sales and its many editions in terms of its "sensationalism," most literate Americans recognize that they stand in the presence of a masterpiece, that the bitterness and defeat of youth have come alive into the immortality of art. Even distortion of fact may be forgiven when it serves as handmaiden for the larger truth.

The youngest and the most famed of our autobiographers, Richard Wright is also the most generous. He approximates complete self-analysis and self-revelation. He leaves nothing to chance. The would-be discerning reader is allowed no surmises about the springs of his conduct or the state of his feelings from year to year. He even wonders why and how, under the existing conditions, the germs of higher aspiration could multiply in him; why, seething with hates and fears, he never succumbed to suggestions of inferiority. His own psychoanalyst, this brilliant writer wields the surgeon's scalpel ruthlessly and folds back layer after layer of motivation to reach the quivering reality beneath.

Yet Richard Wright never makes his diagnosis calmly. He does not utilize the detachment of a Du Bois or a Johnson in the midst of turmoil. They, too, feel the race problem at the heart of their lives, but they often approach it through tortuous intellectual channels, like scientists at work, observing even their own emotions of resentment. But Wright has a strange capacity of immediacy. He is direct, specific, personal, and of the earth. He flings himself into his analysis with an abandon which cannot be explained merely by his comparative youthfulness. He knows only what he knows and works from the bottom up, not the top down. Of our whole group, he is the most genuine representative of lower-class life and in the best position to portray its hunger, its misery, and its despair.

In an important way Wright touches the lives and writing of Langston Hughes and Saunders Redding. Each of them reacts with such acute sensitivity to people and situations that he is often on the verge of both physical and mental illness, and each is interested in explaining the process in psychological terms. But Wright goes a step further into subjectivity. We are taken into the darkest recesses of a consciousness which is cradled in conflict. Though tortured his mind is implacable in conviction, though warped his personality seeks its law of growth. The author reviews his development through the concepts of "rejection, rebellion, aggression," and relates it intimately to the "anxiety and compulsive cruelty" in the prejudice of the white South. His readiness to adopt up-to-date psychological concepts is due to the fact that they proffer the magic key to depths of maladjustment even greater than that experienced by Hughes and Redding. These two never felt the stifling grip of caste within the boundaries of the Deep South and never endured an involuntary lower-class status. By comparison, Richard Wright's heavier burdens sink him further into the morass of pain from which only prolonged psychological awareness can save him.

At first glance it might seem that Angelo Herndon offers the closest parallel to Richard Wright. He shares the fate of the low-class status within the caste restrictions of the Deep South. Poverty and hunger are his familiars also. Both Herndon and Wright were deprived of the high school education which Hughes and Redding received, and which they were equally capable of absorbing to the best advantage. Both knew the anger and frustration of job discrimination because of race. But Herndon, far apart as he drew in his ideology from his family, never was subjected to the final, crushing blow of family antagonisms. His father believed in him, his mother tended him through his illnesses. As his starting point he had that stability of family loyalty which was entirely lacking in the experience of his contemporary. Child of a broken home, Richard Wright had only unpleasant memories of the father who deserted and of the mother who was too harassed or too ill to cope with his problems adequately. Prematurely, the small child sensed that he was one against the odds. While Herndon, in adolescence, was finding the outlet of cooperation with others in vigorous action, Wright was still beating against the bars of solitary confinement.

The outer events of Wright's childhood formed a crazy quilt of experience. Growing up in the region through which the lower Mississippi flows, where Tennessee, Mississippi, and Arkansas converge, he shuttled between all three states, with Memphis his northernmost point and Natchez on the River his southernmost point. After his father's desertion and his mother's failure to support her two boys in the big city he was placed in an orphanage. Then he was taken within the circumference of his maternal relatives. His maternal grandmother had had nine children who felt called upon to take a hand when misfortune fell upon one of their number. When he was eight Richard Wright lived with an aunt, when he was nearing twelve with an uncle, but his grandmother's home in Jackson, Mississippi, where his invalid mother stayed, proved to be the center of the circle to which he constantly returned, and from which the seventeen-year-old finally ran away to Memphis.

His schooling was equally erratic. Up to the time he was twelve he had never completed a single year. In Memphis he had started school later than usual because his mother could not afford to buy him the necessary clothes. Instead he roamed the streets during the day, while she worked as a cook, and frequented saloons where the men took crude delight in giving him beer or whisky and watching its effect. His first days at school taught him little more than the "four letter words" he had already picked up without understanding as a five-year-old in tenement and saloon. The orphanage added nothing to his formal education. The various schools he attended were memorable only for the progressive fights they entailed to establish the newcomer's right on the playgrounds. At twelve he had the dubious privilege of a year in a private religious school under the stern aegis of his schoolteacher aunt. After taunts and physical abuse, she left her recalcitrant pupil strictly alone so that he merely occupied a seat for the remainder of the year.

Only at thirteen did the young boy have his opportunity to gain some of the knowledge he had longed for secretly since a coal deliverer had taught him to count to a hundred. By this time his personality was not only "lopsided," but his "knowledge of feeling" was far greater than his "knowledge of fact." Transferred to a public school and put into the fifth grade only because his age seemed to require it, he studied day and night for two weeks, won promotion to the sixth grade, and continued until his graduation from the ninth grade. This marked the end of his formal schooling, at sixteen years of age.

As with many boys from low-income homes, he was forced to work at odd jobs at an early age. Before he was twelve he had swept and delivered for a pressing shop, and carried food trays to trains, wood to cafes, and lunches to workers in the roundhouse. Because his grandmother was a Seventh Day Adventist who did not believe in work on Saturday he was cut off from opportunities for awhile. But by seventh grade his clothes were so ragged that he insisted he would leave home if he couldn't earn some money and began the usual routine of doing chores for white people. After eighth grade, when he weighed less than a hundred pounds, he worked as a water boy in a brickyard, after ninth grade as a porter in a cheap clothing store. The petty jobs which followed did not satisfy him. His one good opening to learn the optical trade under a "Yankee" employer was thwarted by the white workers who would not teach him the mechanics of grinding and polishing lenses and bullied him into leaving.

It was only in desperation that he entered into his single dishonest transaction in order to acquire the money to leave Jackson and make a fresh start in Memphis. Mopping at night in a hotel, and bootlegging liquor to white prostitutes depressed him. The alternative was to join the racket with the cashier of reselling movie tickets. The success of the plan enabled him to leave his old environment for good, to find a decent place to live and a steady job as errand boy of an optical company in Memphis. It was only a matter of months before he had saved enough money to send for his mother and brother and had laid definite plans toward their migrating northward to Chicago. On the verge of manhood, Richard Wright was in a position at last to shed the limitations of the Deep South and move in the direction of the creative life and work his cramped circumstances had only let him imagine faintly.

How much he had suffered under the insecurities and deprivations of his life can not be gauged by a mere summary of the events which caused them. What makes **Black Boy** distinctive as an autobiography is its running commentary of emotional response to every situation. It is only by participation in each nuance of mood and feeling that we can sense that elusive totality of personality.

To begin with, the small boy was attuned to sensation as "the moments of living slowly revealed their colored meaning." He felt wonder when he first saw "spotted black-and-white horses clopping down a dusty road through clouds of powdered clay"; delight when he looked at "long straight rows of red and green vegetables stretching away in the sun to the bright horizon"; melancholy when he caught "the tingling scent of burning hickory wood," languor when he heard "green leaves rustling with a rainlike sound." As the four-year-old gazed down on "the yellow, dreaming waters of the Mississippi River" from the bluffs above, a "vague sense of the infinite" flowed softly into his consciousness. He noticed immediately, when he was taken to Memphis, that "the absence of green, growing things made the city seem dead."

Later, in Arkansas, he welcomed again "the aura of limitless freedom distilled from the rolling sweep of tall green grass swaying and glinting in the wind and sun." Every morning he would get up early to walk barefooted in the dust, "reveling in the strange mixture of the cold dew-wet crust on the top of the road and the warm, sun-baked dust beneath." He loved to play and shout in wide, green fields or watch in silence "star-heavy skies." Like a thirsty plant he absorbed all natural beauty around him.

But his starved childhood held only a small quota of such experience. The very sensitivities which made him aware of the best also made him cringe before the worst in his environment. During a moment of boredom from enforced idleness, the four-year-old experimented with burning the curtains and accidentally set the house on fire.

When he was beaten into unconsciousness by his mother he was "lost in a fog of fear" and of illness for days. His imagination was no longer his friend. Exhausted, he was terrified of sleep for then he would see "huge wobbly white bags, like the full udders of cows, suspended from the ceiling," waiting to drench him with liquid.

Later, when he ran away from the orphanage, the streets seemed dangerous with buildings and trees which loomed ominously. Superstitions and fears fed his nature until he went through a period of nightmares and sleep-walking. At one time, when he learned that a boy had died in the bed he was using at his uncle's, his imagination "began to weave ghosts." Strange faces in new schools froze him into self-consciousness so that he could not recite and sat with burning neck and ears, "hating myself, hating them." His mother's sudden stroke of paralysis robbed him of any desire to play. "Within an hour the half-friendly world that I had known had turned cold and hostile." He brooded morosely, trying not to think of a "tomorrow that was neither real nor wanted," for all tomorrows held questions without answers.

Always there had been an undercurrent of hunger which sometimes swirled up around him and baffled him. It was as if a "hostile stranger" no longer waited at his elbow but stood beside his bed at night, watching gauntly, "nudging my ribs, twisting my empty guts until they ached." Often at the orphanage he would grow dizzy while working in the yard, and recover to stare "in bleak astonishment" at the grass. At his aunt's he hoarded his biscuits, afraid that "if I ate enough there would not be anything left for another time." During his grade school days he ate mush in the mornings and greens at night. At lunchtime he pretended to his schoolmates that he was never hungry at noon. "And I would swallow my saliva as I saw them split open loaves of bread and line them with juicy sardines." He knew what it was to "sway while walking," to feel his heart give "a sudden wild spurt of beating" which would leave him breathless.

By the time he was twelve, Richard Wright had already endured enough misfortune to fix his attitudes toward life. His mother's illness "grew into a symbol," and "set the emotional tone." It signified all the poverty, hunger, and dislocation he had known and cast over him "a somberness of spirit" that never left him. His innate sensitiveness had received such bruises that the dreamer had turned realist, the seeker skeptic. Circumstances demanded the cruel and violent rather than the tender, peaceful, and sympathetic side of his nature. His early sense of wonder lay buried under an accumulation of scorn and rebellion. At the start of adolescence, this boy faced more than the normal number of unresolved conflicts.

Adding to his burden of misery were some serious maladjustments in his family relationships. Worse than the shock of tenement life on his imagination or the pangs of hunger on his will to live was the fact that he seemed to be a misfit everywhere he went. He had a diabolic capacity for being misunderstood. From infancy his parents had treated him as a nuisance and a problem, to be dealt with severely. Automatically, he was the one always in the wrong.

His father assumed the role of lawgiver and became like a despised stranger, "alien and remote," in whose huge presence the small boy never ventured to laugh. The opportunity to express his resentment of this dominance came one day when he chose to take literally his father's injunction to kill the kitten disturbing his sleep. This was his first and only triumph over his father. "He could not punish me now without risking his authority . . . I had made him know that I felt he was cruel and I had done it without his punishing me." The boy's perverted happiness indicated the general unhealthiness of this father-son relationship. The image of his living with another woman and of refusing help to his wife and sons burned in the older son's memory so that in the hungry days ahead he thought of his father with "deep biological bitterness." It wasn't until years later that Richard Wright realized no basis of understanding could ever exist between them. Though tied by blood, they would always speak a different language, live "on vastly distant planes of reality."

Living with maternal relatives carried on the precedent. They regarded him as a lost soul when he unwittingly used the language picked up in his slum environment. He was beaten for trifles and blamed for his grandmother's fall when he dodged her blow one day. "I was already so conditioned toward my relatives that when I passed them I actually had a nervous tic in my muscles." Driven at last to self-defence, he threatened to use a knife or razor blade if he were touched and consequently drew down on his head the stigma of criminal. Often he asked himself what was the matter with him: "I never seemed to do things as people expected them to be done. Every word and gesture I made seemed to provoke hostility." By the time he was in ninth grade, he was treated like a pariah in the family circle: "My loneliness became organic. I felt walled in and I grew irritable."

Undoubtedly a large factor in the family antagonism was his resistance to their attempts at religious conversion. His grandmother's fanaticism connected up with her struggle from lower- to middle-class status. Her emphasis on respectability corresponded closely with her emphasis on finding God. Believing in the Second Coming of Christ, she had no intention of bringing down the wrath of God on her household because of one recalcitrant member. As a minor, an unwelcome dependent, the grandson at first "was compelled to make a pretense of worshiping her God" in return for his keep. But the imagery of burning lakes, vanishing seas, valleys of dry bones, blood red moons, fantastic beasts, and amazing miracles lost its emotional appeal whenever he stepped out of the church into the bright sunshine and world of people. He knew "that none of it was true and that nothing would happen."

Certainly his relatives did not make religion seem very attractive to him by their example. The quarreling and the violence in his grandmother's household convinced him that "the naked will to power seemed always to walk in the wake of a hymn." But an even more important inhibition lay in the power of his own reasoning. His personality had already been stamped into realism "by uncharterd conditions"; his sense of living was "as deep as that which the church was trying to give." He could discover no belief in original sin. What faith he had was rooted in the "common realities of life."

The existence or non-existence of God never worried him. An all-wise, all-powerful God would laugh at his foolish denial. If no God, "then why all the commotion?" When the community joined his grandmother in pressing him towards conversion before he encountered the sins of the public school, the twelve-year-old formulated a statement which expressed his feeling about God and about his own experience of fear, hunger, and loneliness; "If laying down my life could stop the suffering in the world, I'd do it. But I don't believe anything can stop it." After this, he became "dead" to his grandmother.

During his public school days he went through a meaningless rite of baptism. Improving slightly, his mother joined the Methodist church and pleaded with him not to disgrace his "old, crippled mother." Although disgusted with the emotionalism of the revival, and adamant that he had no religious feeling or conviction, this time public opinion was too strong for him. But he recognized that he and the other boys were being "shamelessly exploited," that "this business of saving souls had no ethics." It was a tribal matter, a way of enforcing community standards by which those who would not conform changed into "moral monsters." On the whole it seemed wiser to swallow his anger and shame, to share the lot of other boys, and to agree together later that they were bored with religion, that conversion was a fraud and that playing hooky from church offered the logical solution. His backsliding from grace made his daily sins appear more scarlet to his relatives.

Against such a background the facts of race loomed all the more terribly before the eyes of the growing boy. As the vague curiosity of childhood was replaced by sharp, direct experience, he learned to hate and fear white men. By the time he stood poised in flight northward the white South aroused an almost psychopathic response.

Strangely enough, he had no early aversion to whites. Many of his relatives were as white-looking as white people. His father had Indian, white, and Negro ancestry. Although his maternal grandfather was "a tall, skinny, silent, grim, black man" who had run away from slavery to fight on the Union side, his maternal grandmother, also a former slave, came from Irish, Scotch, and French stock and bore no trace of color. In Memphis, when the small boy first heard about the beating of a "black boy" by a "white man," it was natural for him to assume a father-son relationship. White people who were not relatives existed somewhere in the background of the city but carried no emotional validity.

It was a different matter, however, when he sometimes sat in the kitchens where his mother worked, and peered at the white people eating. He grew "vaguely angry," and tried to figure out why they had enough while he went hungry. As white people became real to him, he stared at them, "wondering what they were really like," wondering about the increasing tales of violence he heard. He plied his mother with questions. Did his grandmother who seemed white become colored when she married his grandfather? Why didn't she marry a white man? But his mother turned a deaf ear or silenced him angrily. "She was not concealing facts, but feelings, attitudes, convictions which she did not want me to know." By the time the small boy left Memphis to begin the round of living with relatives, he felt a vague uneasiness but no active fear of whites.

Almost immediately disaster struck home. White men who coveted the flourishing saloon business of Richard Wright's uncle in Arkansas and who warned him to leave, shot him down in cold blood when he ignored the threat. The relatives fled for their lives. "This was as close as white terror had ever come to me and my mind reeled. Why had we not fought back, I asked my mother, and the fear that was in her made her slap me into silence." Shortly after, he saw his first chain gang, with Negro convicts watched by white guards. And this time his mother answered his questions: White men don't wear stripes because they are harder on black men than on each other. Yet all the black men don't join together and fight back for the simple reason that they have no guns.

Increasingly the child identified himself with a mistreated group. World War I contained no real meaning for him intrinsically, but the rumors of racial conflicts disturbed him deeply. Although he had not yet been directly abused by whites, the mere mention of them set off "a vast complex of emotions," involving the whole of his personality. He was as conditioned to their existence as if he had been "the victim of a thousand lynchings." By adolescence he subscribed to the racial sentiments of other boys whose "touchstone of fraternity" was how much hostility they held towards white people. Large enough now to inspire fear, these boys began to play their "traditional racial roles" with the white boys in the community as though it was in their blood.

Yet there remained a crucial difference between him and his schoolmates. He worried about the problem of race relations, trying to fathom the causes of friction. But, when he posed the larger issues to them, they were nonplussed and either met him with silence or turned the matter into a joke. "They were vocal about the petty individual wrongs they suffered, but they possessed no desire for a knowledge of the picture as a whole." They gave his restless mind as little satisfaction as his mother in childhood. Without mental companionship, he was thrown back on the need to thrash out questions for himself.

In one way affairs ran along more smoothly for the other boys. In spite of their grievances, they worked out techniques of adjustment to the white community. They observed the code of behavior with their white employers with mechanical efficiency, and sloughed it off easily after work hours. But Richard Wright operated under tension each moment he spent in the presence of whites. Because his religious grandmother, with her work prohibition on Saturdays, had postponed the age when he started doing odd jobs for white people, the process of accommodation was apparently all the more painful and labored. According to the author, with earlier experience perhaps "the tension would have become an habitual condition, contained and controlled by reflex." As it was, he "overreacted to

each event" with a rush of emotion. Exhausted by conflict, he would go to bed tired and get up unrefreshed.

As he grew older, he realized that his attitude placed him in danger. He could not "grin" and seem affable and contented, he could not be subservient. He would dissemble for short periods, only to forget and "act straight and human again." When he was sixteen, a friend chided him for acting around white people as if he didn't know they were white and for letting them see it. The friend was concerned that he would forfeit his chances to eat, whereas Richard Wright was more interested in the psychology of these whites. Because he stole nothing and wanted to look them straight in the face as man to man, he seemed to make them uncomfortable. Evidently they encouraged deceit and irresponsibility in Negroes as a means of perpetuating their own "safe and superior" role. The Negro like himself who didn't conform to type was therefore an "uppity" Negro who required surveillance and might expect violence.

He was always complicating his life by this type of analysis. An inner compulsion drove him "to feel and think out each tiny item of racial experience in the light of the whole race problem." It was a much simpler matter to the whites. While he grew "conscious of the entirety" of his relations to them, they remained "conscious only of what was happening at a given moment." He could even gain a perspective on the very men who reviled and abused him, who refused him jobs or made him the butt of cruel jokes. They did not stand in his mind as individual men so much as a "part of a huge, implacable, elemental design toward which hate was futile." He longed to strike back, to assert his rights, but how, where, and at whom?

With no outlet for his aggression, his personality was shattered by each act of discrimination. Sometimes he seemed "numb," "reduced to a lumpish, loose, dissolved state," a "non-man, something that knew vaguely that it was human but felt that it was not." He was swayed by desperation, terror, and anxiety as well as by hate. At other times his reason took control. Then he would weigh his chances for continued life in the South, and conclude that he could never accept his "place" because he did not believe that he was inferior or belonged to an inferior race. This conviction gradually counteracted the negative emotional conditioning and helped him towards the decision of leaving the South.

As he studied his situation, he knew that he could not count on any "outright black rebellion" since whites outnumbered Negroes. Certainly he could never accede to the solution of transferring his hatred to other Negroes, a course of action which would be self-defeating and thus highly acceptable to whites. Neither sex nor alcohol appealed to him as escapes—a reaction which may be explainable in terms of his father's unwelcome behavior. He lacked the training and the inclination to strive towards success as a professional man. Wealthy Negroes were as alien to him as white people. Although white society had forced him outside any respect for their laws so that he no longer felt bound by them, crime held its own punishment for him. In some strange way he had acquired higher standards for himself than any of these responses to his environment implied. He still hoped that somehow, somewhere, "life could be different, could be lived in a fuller and richer manner." His star, like that of Douglass, pointed northward.

The writer can well ask himself, "From where in this southern darkness had I caught a sense of freedom?" Or again, "How dare I consider my feelings superior to the gross environment that sought to claim me?" To these we might add a question about his early childhood for which the same answer might suffice. Why did the pre-school boy thumb through the pages of stray books and burn to understand "the baffling black print?" What made him plead with his mother to tell him the meaning of every strange word he saw? In explaining that these words held no value for him in themselves but formed "the gateway to a forbidden and enchanting land," the author provides us with the clue to his survival and his hope.

Undoubtedly we have here an instance of a child who was gifted with a superior intelligence which reached out thirstily for understanding. In proportion to the thwarting effect of the real world developed the riches of the imaginative world. Family and race troubles soon deprived him of the pristine happiness in nature. But he could still endow his "bare and bleak" surroundings with "unlimited potentialities." No disciplining relatives or hostile white people could encroach. "Because I had no power to make things happen outside of me in the objective world, I made things happen within." While he always enjoyed exploring his environment and preferred going without meals at home to losing his chance to wander, his strongest curiosity was intellectual. Books thus served both as emotional outlet and mental stimulus.

In the beginning any kind of book sufficed, the more melodramatic the better. His first novel of intrigue and murder, relayed to him by an older person, filled him with sharp excitement and elicited from him his first "total emotional response." This was followed by the cheap pulp stories in a newspaper he peddled. He would lock his door at night and "revel in outlandish exploits of outlandish men in faraway, outlandish cities." But by now the appeal was more than an opportunity for vicarious violence. "For the first time in my life I became aware of the life of the modern world, of vast cities, and I was claimed by it; I loved it." He accepted these stories as true because he "hungered for a different life, for something new." His civics and English and geography books now took on fresh importance. At the beginning of each term in public school he read through them all at once and pondered over them, "weaving fantasies about cities."

But this eager mind could not content itself with mere receptivity. It had to create, in turn. Responding warmly to words and ideas, he needed to return something of himself. Even as early as twelve, during the time when his grandmother was trying to save his soul, he started to write. Closeted in his room, ostensibly for prayer, he composed a story. It had no plot or action, "nothing save atmosphere and longing and death," but it was all his own. "I had made something, no matter how bad it was; and it was mine."

Perhaps it was the community reaction to the newspaper publication of an eighth grade story which first made Richard Wright sense the full measure of his apartness from others. The Negroes who were shocked by his wasting his time and by his use of the word, *hell,* in the lurid title, as well as the whites who mocked his ambition to be a writer, forced upon him the thought of his "strange and separate road." His total environment was alien to the very notion of a Negro's desiring to express himself in writing. "I was building up in me a dream which the entire educational system of the South had been rigged to stifle." The type of consciousness such dreams presaged carried "the penalty of death."

But Richard Wright had reached the turning point where fear could no longer smother the flame within him. He realized the network of disadvantages which would entangle his efforts to write. In his "Jim Crow station in life," he would even have difficulty learning about people and places intimately enough to write truly of them. But this sobering thought quickened rather than deadened him. "I now knew what being a Negro meant. I could endure the hunger. I had learned to live with hate. But to feel that there were feelings denied me, that the very breath of life itself was beyond my reach, that more than anything else hurt, wounded me. I had a new hunger." Stubbornly, he planned to overcome his handicaps one by one. In the stirring of his own creativity lay the assurance of his rebellion as a man.

As he assumed adulthood in Memphis the reading of good books and magazines served as a means to his purpose. Reading became a drug, a dope, a sense of life itself. Although he was not allowed as a Negro to obtain books from the public library for himself, an Irish-Catholic in the optical firm secretly gave him the use of his library card. He not only ran through copies of *Harper's* and the *Atlantic Monthly,* but he read all the works he could find of modern American writers like H. L. Mencken, Theodore Dreiser, Sherwood Anderson, and Sinclair Lewis. Interested in the point of view rather than the plots, he found "new ways of looking and seeing." It was a revelation to him to discover that these men were also "defensively critical to the straitened American environment." And they had the courage to use words as weapons.

For the first time the young Negro felt an identity of mind with men whom society classified as white. "All my life had shaped me for the realism, the naturalism of the modern novel, and I could not read enough of them." He had experienced the cruelty and sordidness and stupidity these novelists portrayed at the core of American culture. Yet, because they seemed to think "that America could be shaped nearer to the hearts of those who lived in it," they held out a faint promise to readers like Richard Wright: "I felt touching my face a tinge of warmth from an unseen light." Possibly there existed, then, some "redeeming meaning" for all men who "struggled and suffered here beneath the stars."

At the end of this "record of childhood and youth" we can surmise that the north-bound traveller is awakening to a notion of collectivism. His own problems are losing their uniqueness. There must be other "black boys" who have been stunted in their development. There must be "white boys," too, young people not only in America but everywhere, at odds with their environments. Such a realization must have assuaged his loneliness and, at the same time, have laid on him the responsibility of playing spokesman for all those thousands of less articulate ones. Precipitated into manhood prematurely, the future author of *Uncle*

An excerpt from *Black Boy*

"Richard, I want to ask you something," Pease began pleasantly not looking up from his work.

"Yes, sir."

Reynolds came over and stood blocking the narrow passage between the benches; he folded his arms and stared at me solemnly. I looked from one to the other, sensing trouble. Pease looked up and spoke slowly, so there would be no possibility of my not understanding.

"Richard, Reynolds here tells me that you called me Pease," he said.

I stiffened. A void opened up in me. I knew that this was the showdown.

He meant that I had failed to call him Mr. Pease. I looked at Reynolds; he was gripping a steel bar in his hand. I opened my mouth to speak, to protest, to assure Pease that I had never called him simply *Pease,* and that I had never had any intention of doing so, when Reynolds grabbed me by the collar, ramming my head against a wall.

"Now, be careful, nigger," snarled Reynolds, baring his teeth. "I heard you call 'im *Pease.* And if you say you didn't, you're calling me a liar, see?" He waved the steel bar threateningly.

If I had said: No, sir, Mr. Pease, I never called you *Pease,* I would by inference have been calling Reynolds a liar; and if I had said: Yes, sir, Mr. Pease, I called you *Pease,* I would have been pleading guilty to the worst insult that a Negro can offer to a southern white man. I stood trying to think of a neutral course that would resolve this quickly risen nightmare, but my tongue would not move.

"Richard, I asked you a question!" Pease said. Anger was creeping into his voice.

"I don't remembering calling you *Pease,* Mr. Pease," I said cautiously. "And if I did, I sure didn't mean . . . "

"You black sonofabitch! You called me *Pease,* then!" he spat, rising and slapping me till I bent sideways over a bench.

Reynolds was up on top of me demanding:

"Didn't you call him *Pease?* If you say you didn't, I'll rip your gut string loose with this f–k–g bar, you black granny dodger! You can't call a white man a liar and get away with it!"

Richard Wright, in his Black Boy, *Harper & Row, 1945.*

Tom's Children and *Native Son* must have sensed at the start of his career as a writer that his work could assume symbolic importance. No one knew better than he the tale of exploitation. No one felt more strongly than he the need to exonerate its victims from moral blame.

All his life he had known what it was to suffer under false charges. Like a snowball gathering volume, his "crimes" had collected attitudes of expectation in those about him. In reality, however, as the autobiographer wishes to show, he was more sinned against than sinning, whereas society in its entity—white-instigated, white-controlled—was the master criminal. While an unfriendly milieu was forcing his personality into the mold of rebellion and rank individualism, his mind was grappling with factors in understanding. A stubborn weed, he persisted and survived until his reading and his knowledge of the wider world of men and affairs enlarged his consciousness to the point where he could pull himself out of the barrenness of his subjectivity. This process he describes minutely. The most intimate, the most emotional of all our autobiographies, *Black Boy* contains a solid nugget of social realism which weighs down its flights of feeling until they take on the importance of sober fact and interpretation for a whole culture to heed. (pp. 254-68)

Rebecca Chalmers Barton, "Protesters for a New Freedom," in her Witnesses for Freedom: Negro Americans in Autobiography, *Harper & Brothers Publishers, 1948, pp. 167-273.*

Sidonie Ann Smith (essay date Fall 1972)

[*In the following essay, Smith discusses* Black Boy *as a twentieth-century version of the slave narrative, echoing its themes of oppression, rebellion, and emancipation.*]

Prior to the recognition of such late nineteenth century black American writers as Paul Laurence Dunbar and Charles Chesnutt, the most widely known black literary form was the personal narrative of the escaped slave or freedman known as the slave narrative. Stripped brutally of traditional means through which to derive a sense of identity, denied access to the study of letters, alienated from American society, the black slave had only himself to rely on for self-discovery and self-fulfillment. His own life story became a natural medium of such an expression. The controlling theme of these narratives, under which all other themes are subsumed, is the "freeing" of an authentic and fully human identity from the chains of the less-than-human identity forced upon the slave by American society. The slave narrator was the rebel who refused to choose either of two other responses which he witnessed all around him: the acceptance of the fate of oppression and the apparent acquiescence to it through the conscious masking of true feelings.

With the Civil War the slave narrative as such disappeared. But the slave system had merely been replaced by the caste system which perpetuated the imprisonment of the black American in the stereotypes of white America and thus his condemnation to invisibility. As a result, the literature of the black American by and large continues to be a personal literature, indeed, a modern version of the slave narrative, describing the quest of the black self for the "promised land" of a free identity.

In his autobiography, **Black Boy,** Richard Wright captured one of the most powerfully moving personal narratives of this very journey. Young Wright, living in the South in the first decades of the twentieth century where disenfranchisement, segregation, and racial subordination comprised the terms of existence, comes to recognize fully his imprisonment within Southern society. His impulse is to rebel openly, but to do so is to risk death. Yet Richard recognizes an even greater risk than death. [The critic adds in a footnote: "To distinguish between Wright, the autobiographer, and Wright, the young protagonist, I refer to the former as Wright, the latter as Richard."] To accept—or even appear to accept—the servility the South demands of him is to invite psychological suicide. Richard, who finds it impossible to accept or to mask the rebellion against this fate, ultimately chooses open rebellion. Thus, for Wright, the autobiographer, warfare—between his essential self and his environment—becomes the basic metaphor for depicting his struggle from childhood innocence to self-awareness.

The autobiography opens with a vivid scene from Wright's childhood which dramatizes the complex nature of Richard's struggle with his environment.

> One winter morning in the long-ago, four-year-old days of my life I found myself standing before a fireplace, warming my hands over a mound of glowing coals, listening to the wind whistle past the house outside. All morning my mother had been scolding me, telling me to keep still, warning me that I must make no noise. And I was angry, fretful, and impatient. In the next room Granny lay ill and under the day and night care of a doctor and I knew that I would be punished if I did not obey. I crossed restlessly to the window and pushed back the long fluffy white curtains—which I had been forbidden to touch—and looked yearningly out into the empty street. I was dreaming of running and playing and shouting, but the vivid image of Granny's old, white, wrinkled, grim face, framed by a halo of tumbling black hair, lying upon a huge feather pillow, made me afraid.

His domestic environment oppressively denies Richard natural means for self-fulfillment. That the source of this deprivation should be the "old, white, wrinkled, grim face" of his grandmother is doubly significant: first, the feelings of repression and fear are symbolically linked to "whiteness"; second, literally and metaphorically, "black" becomes "white," rendering both "colors" potentially oppressive.

Richard, deprived of the normal outlets for his creative energies—running, playing, shouting, seeks an alternate form of self-affirmation:

> My idea was growing, blooming. Now I was wondering just how the long fluffy white curtains would look if I lit a bunch of straws and held it under them. Would I try it? Sure I pulled several straws from the broom and held them to the fire until they blazed; I rushed to the window

and brought the flame in touch with the hems of the curtains.

His imaginative curiosity combines with his childhood frustration to find another outlet, the destructive act of burning the curtains which he has been forbidden to touch. Putting the torch to them is a means of acting out his rebellion against his oppressive domestic environment. This act of domestic rebellion is the symbolic precursor of his larger social rebellion, for the curtains are "fluffy white." In addition, they cover the windows, thereby keeping out the sun, and, in this way, symbolize the restrictions of white society which he is forbidden to "touch," to challenge. Herein lies the beginning of Richard's quest for self-actualization through rebellion. The curiosity and unfocused energy which propel this primal event, when informed by knowledge and sharpened by later suffering, become the creativity of the writer, ultimately the most powerful "weapon" in his arsenal of self-defense.

Richard's act of rebellion ends in total destruction of his domestic environment as his later rebellion is to threaten the status quo of the larger Southern environment. And from this destruction he now must and later will have to flee. Afraid of being punished, he escapes beneath the burning house only to be dragged out to suffer the punitive wrath of his mother:

> "You almost scared us to death," my mother muttered as she stripped the leaves from a tree limb to prepare it for my back.

> I was lashed so hard and long that I lost consciousness. I was beaten out of my senses and later I found myself in bed, screaming, determined to run away, tussling with my mother and father who were trying to keep me still. I was lost in a fog of fear. A doctor was called—I was afterwards told—and he ordered that I be kept abed, that I be kept quiet, that my very life depended upon it. My body seemed on fire and I could not sleep. Packs of ice were put on my forehead to keep down the fever. Whenever I tried to sleep I would see huge wobbly white bags, like the full udders of cows, suspended from the ceiling above me. Later, as I grew worse, I could see the bags in the daytime with my eyes open and I was gripped by the fear that they were going to fall and drench me with some horrible liquid. Day and night I begged my mother and father to take the bags away, pointing to them, shaking with terror because no one saw them but me. Exhaustion would make me drift toward sleep and then I would scream until I was wide awake again; I was afraid to sleep. Time finally bore me away from the dangerous bags and I got well. But for a long time I was chastened whenever I remembered that my mother had come close to killing me.

Richard's delirious vision incorporates all these significances in its symbolism. The "huge wobbly white bags" (or breasts) represent his mother who has just beaten him mercilessly. They contain a horrible liquid which he fears will drench him: his mother's milk (symbolic of the family) has, so to speak, gone sour in the sense that it threatens to drown out his individuality.

Ralph Ellison describes this form of behavior in his essay on **Black Boy,** "Richard Wright's Blues." According to Ellison, the black family's impulse to suppress and even destroy self-assertion in the child is an impulse of distorted love. The family knows unconsciously that in order for the young boy to survive physically and psychologically in society he must be kept from questioning it too closely and from challenging it too overtly. The family's function is dual: it is

> to protect the Negro from whirling away from the undifferentiated mass of his people into the unknown, symbolized in its most abstract form by insanity, and most concretely by lynching; and to protect him from those unknown forces within himself which might urge him to reach out for that social and human equality which the white South says he cannot have. Rather than throw himself against the charged wires of his prison, he annihilates the impulses within him.

All throughout childhood, the family's protective instincts continue to terrify the youth who nevertheless challenges them repeatedly. In response the family resorts to beatings which Richard then refuses to suffer silently because he knows them to be unjustified. They are, rather, beatings that reflect the frustrations of the system. They are an act of love, but a distorted act of love: its intent is protection, its manner violence, its result destruction of personality. As Ellison observes:

> **Black Boy** . . . illustrates that this personal quality, shaped by outer violence and inner fear, is ambivalent. Personal warmth is accompanied by an equally personal coldness, kindliness by cruelty, regard by malice. And these opposites are as quickly set off against the member who gestures toward individuality as a lynch mob forms at the cry of rape.

These violent encounters with his family are microcosmic reflections of his violent encounters with society at large. For the white bags simultaneously symbolize white society which, in response to his act of rebellion, seeks to drown him in the terrible liquid of nonentity and thereby wash away his imagination and individuality. Later, after his uncle is killed by a white mob, Richard, his mother, and aunt must flee secretly at night. Wright explains:

> Uncle Hoskins had simply been plucked from our midst and we, figuratively, had fallen on our faces to avoid looking into that white-hot face of terror that we knew loomed somewhere above us. This was as close as white terror had ever come to me and my mind reeled. Why had we not fought back, I asked my mother, and the fear that was in her made her slap me into silence.

The "white-hot face" echoes the "white bags." His reaction to both is terror and fear and a subsequent need to rebel against both white and black society. Significantly his mother slaps him out of fear when he asks, "Why had we not fought back." Fear—violence—counter-violence is an established pattern of behavior in Richard's life. His world becomes a cosmos of violence and repressive "love"

as the black and white communities combine to demand a denial of self to which he cannot submit, against which he must rebel.

Richard, like the slave narrator, is imprisoned by the exigencies of survival in Southern society. Moreover, like the slave narrator, he is alone, a virtual orphan who must discover his own way to the "promised land" of self-actualization, for first his father and eventually his mother desert him. Early memories of his father, like the other early memories, abound in repression and violence:

> He became important and forbidding to me only when I learned that I could not make noise when he was asleep in the daytime. He was the lawgiver in our family and I never laughed in his presence. . . . He was always a stranger to me, always somehow alien and remote.

As a lawgiver Richard's father becomes an oppressor who controls rather than guides, an oppressor against whom he must rebel. When Richard and his brother bring home a stray cat, his father's response is emotionally violent: " 'Kill that damn thing! . . . Do anything, but get it away from here!' " Richard does precisely this. When his mother reports this to his father, Richard taunts him: " 'You told me to kill im.' " In this way, Richard defies his father's power and authority and thus triumphs over him. When soon after, his father leaves and hunger becomes a way of life, Richard's concepts of "father" and "hunger" merge: "As the days slid past the image of my father became associated with my pangs of hunger, and whenever I felt hunger I thought of him with a deep biological bitterness."

Paradoxically, it is Richard's mother who temporarily becomes his guide, teaching him the necessary lesson of self-defense when she refuses to protect him from a gang of youths who, having once succeeded in stealing his grocery money, await him again:

> She slammed the door and I heard the key turn in the lock. I shook with fright. I was alone upon the dark, hostile streets and gangs were after me. I had the choice of being beaten at home or away from home. I clutched the stick, crying, trying to reason. If I were beaten at home, there was absolutely nothing that I could do about it; but if I were beaten in the streets, I had a chance to fight and defend myself. I walked slowly down the sidewalk, coming closer to the gang of boys, holding the stick tightly. I was so full of fear that I could scarcely breathe. I was almost upon them now.
>
> "There he is again!" the cry went up.
>
> They surrounded me quickly and began to grab for my hand.
>
> "I'll kill you!" I threatened.

Superficially this act seems to contradict her earlier violent response to his self-assertion. In the earlier instance, she, as a representative of the community, punishes him for this violent self-assertiveness: in the latter instance, she forces him to respond violently towards others. But actually both these lessons are lessons in self-defense: the first is a lesson that is necessary for survival in white society; the second, a lesson necessary for survival in black. Richard is, at this time, forced literally to fight in order to survive the life of the streets. As he matures, the value of self-assertion through physical warfare will find new avenues of expression in psychological and verbal warfare.

When his mother finally succumbs to permanent illness and disability, Richard is deprived of his last familial source of strength. Her illness was to affect him profoundly:

> My mother's suffering grew into a symbol in my mind, gathering to itself all the poverty, the ignorance, the helplessness; the painful, baffling, hunger-ridden days and hours; the restless moving, the futile seeking, the uncertainty, the fear, the dread; the meaningless pain and the endless suffering. Her life set the emotional tone of my life, colored the men and women I was to meet in the future, conditioned my relation to events that had not yet happened, determined my attitude to situations and circumstances I had yet to face. A somberness of spirit that I was never to lose settled over me during the slow years of my mother's unrelieved suffering, a somberness that was to make me stand apart and look upon excessive joy with suspicion, that was to make me self-conscious, that was to make me keep forever on the move, as though to escape a nameless fate seeking to overtake me.

The older autobiographer looks back upon this loss, assigning to it in retrospect the meaning that it came to hold for his later life. For the more modern slave narrator, the dogs of the overseer still pursue, though they have assumed the qualities of a more general "fate"—one that has its origin in the bitter experience of childhood.

As a result of this bitter experience the twelve-year-old boy forms a "conception of life": "the meaning of living came only when one was struggling to wring a meaning out of meaningless suffering." This struggle is the struggle of the rebel who refuses to acquiesce in the conspiracy of this black family community, a microcosm of the community at large, to force him to deny his individuality and is, therefore, alienated completely from anything but his own self-consciousness. Richard recognizes that the separation he feels is deadly when he says of himself at the age of fifteen:

> In me was shaping a yearning for a kind of consciousness, a mode of being that the way of life around me had said could not be, must not be, and upon which the penalty of death had been placed.

His longing to be an authentic self struggles against society's demand that he be a "nigger." The struggle sharpens his anger towards a hostile world as it taxes his inner resolve to overcome that world.

Richard shrinks from the two frequently travelled roads to survival for a black in Southern society. There is the rigid, stifling religion of his grandmother, Aunt Aggie, and his mother, which encourages resignation to the world by preaching that there will be revenge enough in inheriting the next. Or, there is the masking of Griggs and Shorty which provides the limited psychological revenge of conscious deception. When Griggs warns Richard of the gravity of reacting honestly to whites, he explains and demonstrates the nature of masking:

> "You know, Dick, you may think I'm an Uncle Tom, but I'm not. I hate these white people, hate 'em with all my heart. But I can't show it; if I did, they'd kill me." He paused and looked around to see if there were any white people within hearing distance. "Once I heard an old drunk nigger say:
>
> All these white folks dressed so fine
> Their ass-holes smell just like mine. . . ."
>
> I laughed uneasily, looking at the white faces that passed me. But Griggs, when he laughed, covered his mouth with his hand and bent at the knees, a gesture which was unconsciously meant to conceal his excessive joy in the presence of whites.

The Christian tenet of long-suffering and Grigg's tactic of masking true feelings repel Richard, however much they insure survival. Religion, since it denies the self, applauds the selfless and promises heavenly fulfillment, devalues the needs of oppressed blacks in the here-and-now and counsels them to be content with their social position. Masking also denies legitimate self-assertion, since the real responses of the self must consciously be sacrificed to the mask. Sometimes it even demands self-degradation, as when Shorty allows a white man to kick him in order to get twenty-five cents for lunch. Both options spell mere survival. In the one instance, a wall of other-worldliness and, in the other, a wall of disguise protect the individual from destruction but keep him from attacking the sources of his oppression. So imprisoned, the individual is condemned to invisibility.

The curse of invisibility is to be treated as an object, a state of being symbolized by two names—"nigger" and "boy." The former is symbolic of the denial of individuality, the latter the denial of manhood. These two names function, as do the methods of survival, to keep Richard physically and psychologically in his invisible "place." They are used by white society, but, in a more immediate way, they are used by black society so that he will survive in a white society. (When his family chastises him for some breach of social action, they call him "nigger.")

Against his will, Richard temporarily succumbs to these social identities in order to survive: he lies, steals, wears the mask of fawning ingratiation. The price, of course, is a half-life. As he puts it:

> I had been what my surroundings had demanded, what my family—conforming to the dictates of the whites above them—had exacted of me, and what the whites had said that I must be. Never being fully able to be myself, I had slowly learned that the South could recognize but a part of a man.

But, ultimately, he chooses to reject this social mask of inferiority and invisibility and, in doing so, becomes a full-fledged rebel. Until this point his only weapon against this stigmatizing invisibility has been violence against his immediate family rather than society at large. But it is the "word" which will ultimately become the weapon, the sword, with which he attacks society and liberates his own essential self.

At an early age Richard perceives the power of words; his early experiences with them are violently punitive. There are the words he learns at school and scrawls on neighborhood walls, which his mother threateningly makes him wash off completely. Later, after the story of *Bluebeard and His Seven Wives* elicits a "total emotional response" from him, he tries to read by himself.

> Usually I could not decipher enough words to make the story have meaning. I burned to learn to read novels and I tortured my mother into telling me the meaning of every strange word I saw, not because the word itself had any value, but because it was the gateway to a forbidden and enchanting land.

Without understanding the meaning of words, Richard responds to their evocative power. Then one evening, as his grandmother washes him, "words—words whose meaning I did not fully know—had slipped out of my mouth." He had asked his grandmother to kiss him "back there," and for this he suffers the wrath of the entire family. Feeling no guilt, unable to comprehend why he should be punished, Richard only recognizes the effect of those words upon others, a power which fascinates him:

> The tremendous upheaval that my words had caused made me know that there lay back of them much more than I could figure out, and I resolved that in the future I would learn the meaning of why they had beat and denounced me.

The courtship with words extends throughout his youth: he reads everything he can find and even tries his hand at short-story writing. The successful publication of one story, however, does not gain him the praise he desires, but rather chastisement and misunderstanding. Later he idealistically decides upon a career in writing and shares his dream with a new employer, whose reaction is significantly described as an "assault" on his ego. She asks him why he is continuing his education beyond the seventh grade: he answers that he wants to become a writer.

> "A what" she demanded.
>
> "A writer," I mumbled.
>
> "For what?"
>
> "To write stories," I mumbled defensively.
>
> "You'll never be a writer," she said. "Who on earth put such ideas into your nigger head?"
>
> "Nobody," I said.
>
> "I didn't think anybody ever would," she declared indignantly.
>
> As I walked around her house to the street, I knew that I would not go back. The woman had assaulted my ego; she had assumed that she knew my place in life, what I felt, what I ought

to be, and I resented it with all my heart. Perhaps she was right; perhaps I would never be a writer; but I did not want her to say so.

Writing, for a black, lay beyond the structure of socially acceptable possibilities in the South and thus is linked with self-assertion, individuality, manhood, and, by association, with rebellion. His family's negative response to his successful attempt at short-story writing and the white woman's incredulous response both show a recognition of the rebellion inherent in such a dream.

Richard comes to appreciate this association fully when he reads Mencken, a decisive step in his development: he comes to recognize the militancy and potential violence of words, a violence he has already experienced emotionally but not intellectually.

> That night in my rented room, while letting the hot water run over my can of pork and beans in the sink, I opened *A Book of Prefaces* and began to read. I was jarred and shocked by the style, the clear, clean, sweeping sentences. Why did he write like that? And how did one write like that? I pictured the man as a raging demon, slashing with his pen, consumed with hate, denouncing everything American, extolling everything European or German, laughing at the weaknesses of people, mocking God, authority. What was this? I stood up, trying to realize what reality lay behind the meaning of the words. . . . Yes, this man was fighting, fighting with words. He was using words as a weapon, using them as one would use a club. Could words be weapons? Well, yes, for here they were. Then, maybe, perhaps, I could use them as a weapon?

Wright's portrait of Mencken is significant: "I pictured the man as a raging demon, slashing with his pen." The pen becomes the most effective weapon of warfare and, for the imagination, becomes the equivalent of physical violence. This initiation into the weaponry of words leads him on to more and more writers who awaken him to the reality of the world outside the South. He finds in writers the attitudes towards life he has harbored alone within himself.

Wright will imitate Mencken when, in his later writing, he uses the pen as weapon, the word as ammunition for protesting the life of the black American. *Native Son* itself is a powerful weapon Wright wields against American society. And the theme of violent self-expression is central to structural design and meaning in this novel as it is in the autobiography. Imprisoned in social invisibility, Bigger senses that his acts of murder are the only free creative actions of his life because they involve the power to determine a fate for himself and thus, at least momentarily, make him visible.

Since society does not sanction murder, at least theoretically, Bigger's act of violent self-assertion makes him a social outcast. In expressing his own individuality he is forced to violate societal norms as the slave narrator had been forced to do. And, like the slave narrator, his sense of freedom and, thus, his sense of identity emanate from these very acts of criminality. Bigger mirrors the experience of his creator: violence becomes the only way through which Richard can assert his individuality. Bigger is, of course, a real murderer and must flee from the police. But Richard too has to flee, for his attitudes are murderous to the way of life in the South and subject, therefore, to prosecution.

Richard cannot find self-fulfillment in the South:

> What, then, was there? I held my life in my mind, in my consciousness each day, feeling at times that I would stumble and drop it, spill it forever. My reading had created a vast sense of distance between me and the world in which I lived and tried to make a living, and that sense of distance was increasing each day.

The "vast sense of distance" is the distance, finally unbearable, between his authentic self and his social identity. So he chooses to leave the South, as the slave had chosen to escape one hundred years earlier, in hopes of finding a "place" of legitimate self-expression denied him in the South. His departure is a willed act of self-defense,

> a conviction that if I did not leave I would perish, either because of possible violence of others against me, or because of my possible violence against them.

Wright's autobiography is essentially a twentieth-century version of the earlier slave narrative, explicitly and implicitly echoing its themes. Emancipation has not brought freedom to the South even half a century after its inception: the South remains a slave plantation where Richard is still imprisoned in an oppressive, less-than-human social identity. There, he is—and will ever remain—a "nigger" and a "boy." Thus, like the slave narrator's story, Wright's autobiography is the story of a self willing to rebel to the point of annihilation in order to remain inviolate. Richard's longing for visible selfhood rather than deceptive invisibility makes subservience to the racial norms of the South impossible for him. He must flee to escape emasculation. His running is a positive act for it is potentially redemptive. And it has direction: the North beckons with possibility. The last pages of **Black Boy** testify to his hope, like that of the slave narrator before him, that a "home" and a "better day" await him in the North.

His journey, however, is not informed by unqualified hope. He realizes that he will always carry the South with him, for he is its child. But he envisions himself as a hopeful "experiment":

> So in leaving, I was taking a part of the South to transplant in alien soil, to see if it could grow differently, if it could drink of new and cool rains, bend in strange winds, respond to the warmth of other suns, and, perhaps, to bloom. . . . And if that miracle ever happened, then I would know that there was yet hope in that southern swamp of despair and violence, that light could emerge even out of the blackest of the southern night. I would know that the South too could overcome its fear, its hate, its cowardice, its heritage of guilt and blood, its burden of anxiety and compulsive cruelty.

Moreover, he knows that he is running *away* from the South as much as he is running *to* the North. The autobiography does not conclude with Wright's having achieved a new identity, but rather with his breaking away from his past and hoping for a rebirth, a blooming, into a new, more legitimate self. That the hope ultimately shatters and the new identity eludes him in the North is another story, the story narrated in the parts of **Black Boy** that have remained unpublished, the story implicit in Wright's eventual expatriation to France. (pp. 123-36)

> *Sidonie Ann Smith, "Richard Wright's 'Black Boy': The Creative Impulse as Rebellion," in* The Southern Literary Journal, *Vol. V, No. 1, Fall, 1972, pp. 123-36.*

Claudia C. Tate (essay date Winter 1976)

[*Tate is an American author and educator who specializes in the works of black women writers. In the following essay, she maintains that while* Black Boy *contains "many exaggerated and even fictitious incidents," the work accurately conveys "the slow and painstaking development of Wright's consciousness."*]

Richard Wright's friends and critics alike persistently remark that Wright actually did not experience a childhood like that depicted in his autobiography, **Black Boy.** They contend that his childhood was not characterized by the incessant hunger, the beatings and the suffering, and the general bleakness of life that he ascribed to young Richard. Nor did Richard's childhood characterize a quality of life experienced by the majority of Wright's Black contemporaries. His implying that it did incited controversy, especially in reference to one particular passage from the text:

> After I had outlived the shocks of childhood, after the habit of reflection had been born in me, I used to mull over the strange absence of real kindness in Negroes, how unstable was our tenderness, how lacking in genuine passion we were, how hollow our memories, how lacking we were in those intangible sentiments that bind man to man, and how shallow was even our despair. After I had learned other ways of life I used to brood upon the unconscious irony of those who felt that Negroes led so passional an existence! I saw that what had been taken for our emotional strength was our negative confusion, our flight, our fears, our frenzy under pressure.

> Whenever I thought of the essential bleakness of black life in America, I knew that Negroes had never been allowed to catch the full spirit of Western civilization, that they lived somehow in it but not of it. And when I brooded upon the cultural barrenness of black life, I wondered if clean, positive tenderness, love, honor, loyalty, and the capacity to remember were native with man. I asked myself if these human qualities were not fostered, won, struggled and suffered for, preserved in ritual from one generation to another.

It would be presumptuous of me to assume that I could account for the bleakness that Wright imposed upon the record of his childhood and youth. No one has this privilege, perhaps not even the author himself; however, in pondering about the discrepancy between the facts of Wright's life and its written account in **Black Boy,** which was in manuscript in 1943, one does well to note that in 1937 Wright read *The Tragic Sense of Life* by Miguel de Unamuno. The influence of this work on Wright's thinking may bear some responsibility for the tragic tone, vision and attitude with which Wright invested his autobiography in an attempt to describe and explain the growth of his consciousness.

In *The Tragic Sense of Life* Unamuno postulates that all human existence is tragic in its essential and fundamental nature, that " . . . there is something for lack of a better name, we will call the tragic sense of life, which carries with it a whole conception of life and of the universe, a whole philosophy more or less conscious." Unamuno's survey of human existence reveals the ubiquity of suffering from which he concludes that life is a perpetual struggle without even a hope for victory, and that the anguish which results from this struggle is the condition of all men. Accordingly, man's plight is that he should bear without relief the burden of physical and emotional distress, a struggle which is not without significant consequence. Suffering engenders consciousness, an acute awareness of both one's personal character and external reality:

> Suffering is the path of consciousness, and by it living beings arrive at the possession of self-consciousness. For to possess consciousness of oneself, to possess personality, is to know oneself and to feel oneself distinct from other beings, and this feeling of distinction is only reached through an act of collison, through suffering more or less severe, through the sense of one's own limits. Consciousness of oneself is simply consciousness of one's own limitations.

Consciousness is not inherent in the essential character of man; on the contrary, it is a psychological state which must be determined by experiencing distress and subsequently reflecting upon it. Particularly important to this thesis is Unamuno's insistence that life must not be subject to rational reflection and evaluation alone in order to assess its meaningfulness. He subscribes to the belief "that the real, the really real, is irrational, that reason builds upon irrationalities." Therefore, " . . . it is not enough to think about our destiny: it must be felt." Man must feel his life with his entire being (his heart, his mind, his senses) in order to reveal and evaluate the fundamental meaning of his existence. In this respect, Unamuno posits a qualitative distinction between the integrity of reason (rational truths) and the integrity of feelings (irrational truths) with the implication that rational analysis and facts have severe limitations, especially when one is probing metaphysical questions. His appreciation for irrational truthfulness in conjunction with his principal proposition that suffering engenders consciousness is precisely what appears to have had some influence on the substantive quality of Wright's portrayal of his childhood and youth.

Black Boy depicts the boy Richard's attempts to establish himself as a distinct and fully conscious individual and, as such, is more a portrait of Wright's developing personality and growth of consciousness than it is an accurate record of his childhood experiences. The book recalls in episodic fashion incidents which take the boy deeper into his quest for self-discovery. The raging brutality of racism and the deprivation of his home life, as depicted in **Black Boy,** are interwoven into an emblem of spiritual conflict which is metaphoric, rather than factual, of man's daily struggle to endure the pressures of existence. According to Unamuno, life at best is a struggle, tragic in nature, and Wright appears to have dramatized this struggle with the substance of his own life. In recalling the events of his childhood, Wright seems to have relied on the integrity of his feelings in order to describe the essence of his existence, its fundamental character and meaning, rather than rendering the events with factual detail alone. As a result, he altered incidents, invested them with exaggerated bleakness, brutality, and a sense of immense and tragic conflict, so as to depict the difficulty of his day to day struggle to survive with a vestige of humanity. In addition, he wove an intricate design of narrative patterns, motifs of silence, hunger and suffering, into the autobiography in order to create an added tragic dimension which enhances the brilliancy of his portrait of a small boy nurturing his budding personality.

The motif of silence conceptualizes the difficulty that Richard had in establishing himself as a distinct and fully conscious individual. Keeping silent had a special significance within the Black community; it indicated acceptance, submission to the conditions of life, especially those caused by racial practices. Throughout **Black Boy,** Richard is repeatedly told to be silent, but he finds that it is against his fundamental nature to withhold his expressed opinions. In his daily dealings with people, he reveals, often without thinking, the presence of his consciousness—and as a result disturbs every facet of the Southern social framework. He emphatically defies those who would silence him, and even blatantly declares his ambition to be a writer. Severe punishishment does not thwart his precocious self-consciousness, but reaffirms his determination to refuse to accept his "place" in either his household or society.

At the age of six, as Wright recalls, Richard's father deserted his family leaving Richard to face many a hungry day during his childhood. In addition to describing literally his deprivation, hunger serves as a symbolic motif for depicting Richard's compelling need to nurture his growing consciousness. Insatiable hunger defines the breadth of his childhood longings for imaginative adventure and his unfulfilled need to expand his awareness of himself and his environment. His physical craving for food and his emotional yearnings often coincide, and this fusion gives added emphasis to the very real nature of his compelling desire to nourish his developing personality:

> I now saw a world leap to life before my eyes because I could explore it, and that meant not going home when school was out, but wandering, watching, asking, talking. Had I gone home to eat my plate of greens, Granny would not have allowed me out again, so the penalty I paid for roaming was to forfeit my food for twelve hours. I would eat mush at eight in the morning and greens at seven or later at night. To starve

in order to learn about my environment was irrational, but so were my hungers.

Physical hunger isolates his personal needs from those of others and, as a consequence, makes him aware that he is a distinct and conscious individual. Emotional and spiritual hunger motivate his ceaseless questions and maintain his awareness of mental distress:

> Hunger stole upon me so slowly that at first I was not aware of what hunger really meant. Hunger had always been more or less at my elbow when I played, but now I began to wake up at night to find hunger standing at my bedside, staring at me gauntly. The hunger I had known before this had been no grim, hostile stranger; it had been a normal hunger that had made me beg constantly for bread, and when I ate a crust or two I was satisfied. But this new hunger baffled me, scared me, made me angry and insistent.

In this respect, virtual starvation engenders his consciousness and forces upon him the daily burden of struggling in order to survive. Food satiates his physical hunger, while knowledge of himself and the world nourishes his mind. Most significant of all the references to hunger is Wright's usage of this motif to stress Richard's growing awareness of his confined spiritual existence which longs to exceed the boundaries of social conventions: "I now knew what being a Negro meant. I could endure the [physical] hunger. I had learned to live with hate. But to feel that there were feelings denied me, that the very breath of life itself was beyond my reach, that more than anything else hurt, wounded me. I had a new hunger." He realizes that the possibility for a meaningful life is obstructed by his environment, and this knowledge awakens in him a new desire, a new and insatiable hunger. He yearns to satisfy this hunger and trains his sensibilities to reach beyond the confines of his environment to grasp as much of this life as possible. He says that "not only had the southern whites not known [him], but, more important still, as [he] had lived in the South [he] had not had the chance to learn who [he] was." Richard feels with alarming urgency that he has to know who he is and who he can be, and this compulsion, this hunger, ultimately forces him to leave the South in order that he might face the possibility of discovering his own identity: "The pressure of southern living kept me from being the kind of person that I might have been. I had been what my surroundings had demanded, what my family—conforming to the dictates of the whites above them—had exacted of me, and what the whites had said that I must be." *Black Boy* concludes with Wright mapping out Richard's journey north, which appears to be yet another quest within the microcosm of Richard's consciousness. Having developed sufficient self-awareness to know that he possesses a distinct and possibly meaningful existence, Richard feels an unwavering obligation to hold his destiny within his grasp and to design his future. His self-conscious desire to determine the fundamental quality of his existence is characteristic of man's inherent and essential nature and, as such, is Wright's expression of a legitimate existential imperative.

So ubiquitous is suffering that Wright made its expression not only the most overwhelming narrative element in *Black Boy,* but also the principal source of his tragic vision. He measured and defined the quality of his existence by degrees of personal and racial suffering, and dramatized them through the fabric of Richard's life. The mental anguish that Richard felt while witnessing his mother's excruciating pain, which resulted from several paralytic strokes, is not only a somewhat accurate account of an event in Wright's childhood but is also metaphoric for the human condition of inherent suffering, "the tragic sense of life." Richard observes:

> My mother's suffering grew into a symbol in my mind, gathering to itself all the poverty, the ignorance, the helplessness; the painful, baffling, hunger-ridden days and hours; the restless moving, the futile seeking, the uncertainty, the fear, the dread; the meaningless pain and the suffering. Her life set the emotional tone of my life, colored the men and women I was to meet in the future, conditioned my relation to events that had not yet happened, determined my attitude to situations and circumstances I had yet to face. A somberness of spirit that I was never to lose settled over me during the slow years of my mother's unrelieved suffering, a somberness that was to make me stand apart and look upon excessive joy with suspicion, that was to make me self-conscious, that was to make me keep forever on the move, as though to escape a nameless fate seeking to overtake me.

> At the age of twelve, before I had had one full year of formal schooling, I had a conception of life that no experience would ever erase, a predilection for what was real that no argument could ever gainsay, a sense of the world that was mine and mine alone, a conviction that the meaning of living came only when one was struggling to wring a meaning out of senseless suffering.

Senseless suffering, perpetual hunger and raging brutality characterize the quality of Richard's existence and temper his personal struggle to define and qualify for himself a meaningful life. These painful experiences convince him that meaningfulness can not be an individual assertion alone, but a quality of life that must be "fostered, won, struggled and suffered for, preserved [each and every day] in ritual from one generation to another." Life's inherent suffering teaches him to measure all of his future experiences against his "predilection for what [is] real." This predilection which Wright undoubtedly felt during his own youth qualified the very real and fundamental nature of his future life—and determined the substantive quality of his autobiography. Although it is probably true that *Black Boy* contains many exaggerated and even fictitious incidents, the emotions that they excite within Richard truthfully adhere to Wright's emotional existence. The work describes with a great degree of accuracy Wright's psychological reality, the emotional and intellectual determinants of his visible life. This subjective but very real dimension of Wright's existence exceeds the limitations of factual descriptions and rational explanations. Richard, the youth in *Black Boy,* is Wright's acknowledgment of these limitations; he is the psychological self-portraiture of the slow and painstaking development of Wright's consciousness. (pp. 117-19)

Claudia C. Tate, "'Black Boy': Richard Wright's 'Tragic Sense of Life'," in Black American Literature Forum, *Vol. 10, No. 4, Winter, 1976, pp. 117-19.*

Janice Thaddeus (essay date May 1985)

[In the following essay, Thaddeus discusses significant details concerning the origins and publication history of Black Boy.*]*

There are two kinds of autobiography—defined and open. In a defined autobiography, the writer presents his life as a finished product. He is likely to have reached a plateau, a moment of resolution which allows him to recollect emotion in tranquility. This feeling enables him to create a firm setting for his reliable self, to see this self in relief against society or history. Frederick Douglass's *Narrative of the Life of Frederick Douglass,* for instance, is a defined autobiography, a public document, moving undeviatingly from self-denial to self-discovery. It rests on the fulcrum of: "You have seen how a man was made a slave; you shall see how a slave was made a man." The writer of an open autobiography differs from Douglass and others like him in that he is searching, not telling, so that like Boswell or Rousseau he offers questions instead of answers. He does not wish to supply a fulcrum, does not proffer conclusions and solutions, and consequently he refrains from shaping his life neatly in a teleological plot. The tone and purpose of an open autobiography are entirely different from a defined autobiography. Therefore, if an author needs to write an open autobiography, it must not be changed into the defined variety. But Richard Wright's *Black Boy* experienced such a metamorphosis.

The publishing history of *Black Boy* is most fully told in Michel Fabre's "Afterword" to Wright's other autobiographical work, *American Hunger,* which was released in 1977. However, even in Fabre's account, some of the important details are hazy. It is the purpose of this essay to clarify the entire incident and to document the metamorphosis of *Black Boy.*

Wright's *Black Boy,* published in 1945, is—so far as plot goes—molded and shapely, beginning in speechlessness and anger, and ending in articulateness and hope. The boy who at the age of four set fire to his own house, became a drunkard at the age of six, and was so frightened of a new school that he could not write his name on the board, by the final pages has fought and lied his way out of the racist South. The book fits into the familiar plot of the slave narrative. And it ends twenty years before its publication, a long swath of time during which the author has become a famous novelist, writer of *Native Son.* To a degree which has puzzled many readers, however, *Black Boy* also introduces oppositions—both imagistic and thematic—which it never resolves.

Black Boy's epigraph sets its theme, but that theme is paradoxical. Wright initiates his book with an unsettling quotation from Job: "They meet with darkness in the daytime / And they grope at noonday as in the night. . . ." Darkness and daytime, black and white, are insistent images throughout. Given the subject matter, this is an obvious choice, but Wright presents his oppositions with puzzling complexity. He mentions in passing in the opening paragraph that his grandmother is white, but it is not until fifty pages later that we discover that Granny was a slave, that she bears the name as well as the color of her white owner, that she does not know—or does not care to know—who her father was. If Granny is white, why is she black? The question is simple, but the answer is not, and Wright emphasizes this indefiniteness. In many scenes, as Gayle Gaskill has shown [in "The Effect of Black/White Imagery in Richard Wright's *Black Boy,*" *Negro-American Literature Forum,* Vol. 7, 1973], Wright deliberately reverses the usual connotations Western tradition has assigned to black and white—that black is always bad and white is good. For instance, when Wright's mother beats him nearly to death for setting their house on fire, he has a feverish dream. "Huge wobbly white bags, like the full udders of cows," hang menacingly over him, and their whiteness is terrifying. Further, although they look like udders and therefore must represent mothers' milk, they threaten to engulf the four-year-old Wright in "some horrible liquid." His mother has become his potential destroyer, and although she is black, her milk is white, and whiteness is evil. In the earlier version of this dream published in *Uncle Tom's Children,* the nightmare is attached to an incident where in a fight with a white gang a flung bottle cuts Wright behind the ear. Here, the apparitions are menacing white faces, a simpler and less psychologically determined image. In *Black Boy,* Wright's mother, like his grandmother, is a mixture of black and white. Although it is true that in *Black Boy* white images are often repressive and black images are often positive, Wright does not entirely deny the traditional meanings of the words. Wright's poodle Betsy is white, and he loves her whiteness, but he will not sell her to white people. If he has to use a blackboard, he emphasizes that the chalk is white. The chalk represents education—and terror. Throughout *Black Boy* Wright's imagery of black and white resists simple formulations. He has not shaped and tailored it to a simple, clear purpose.

The imagery of light and dark is similarly mutable. The South is dark, so dark that Wright frequently wonders over the fact that the sun is still shining. When he hears that an acquaintance has been lynched for presumably consorting with a white prostitute, it seems uncanny that life can continue: "I stood looking down the quiet, sun-filled street. Bob had been caught by the white death." Here, although the light is beautiful, whiteness means death. As readers, we recognize the reference to the black death, and are forced to the analogy that the animals carrying this plague are human. When Pease and Reynolds force Wright out of the optical shop where he had hoped to learn a trade, to help people literally to improve their vision, he recounts: "I went into the sunshine and walked home like a blind man." The sun shines, but not for him. In ironic and various ways, then, aesthetically and thematically, the book fulfills its epigraph. The result, however, is anxiety, not resolution.

Black Boy is a violent book, but it has not been sufficiently noted that violence is always linked with its opposite, in a poised opposition resembling the metaphorical tension just discussed. Wright's experiences have made him "strangely tender and cruel, violent and peaceful." Besides the imagery mentioned above, Wright's chief word for this indefinable yearning is hunger. The word and the fact of hunger recur like drumbeats throughout the book, an insistent refrain. Wright never has enough to eat: he steals food even when there is plenty; he receives an orange for Christmas and eats it with preternatural care; he fills his aching stomach with water; he is too thin to pass the postal examination. The hunger is both "bodily and spiritual," and the spiritual hunger is as insistent as its bodily counterpart. The entire book is strung between hunger and satisfaction, as well as light and dark and black and white, and similarly opposing, irreconcilable forces. The word tension appears so many times that Wright had to cut out thirty instances of it in the final draft.

Among these oppositions the narrator becomes an immensely powerful but undefined force. Wright himself said, "One of the things that made me write is that I realize that I'm a very average Negro . . . maybe that's what makes me extraordinary" [*The Unfinished Quest of Richard Wright*]. This recognition of the self as typical is frequent in black autobiography, where beleaguering social forces chain the writer to his race. On the other hand, Wright also said, "I'm merely using a familiar literary form to unload many of the memories that have piled up in me, and now are coming out" [*Richard Wright: The Critical Reception*]. These views are quite incompatible, since an average person would not have to unload memories, and their rendering as competing forces in *Black Boy* is one of its greatest sources of interest—and tension.

But in spite of *Black Boy*'s insistent refusal to resolve the oppositions upon which it rests, the final six pages nonetheless attempt to summarize the preceding experiences, to explain them, give them a defined significance. Wright asks, "From where in this southern darkness had I caught a sense of freedom?" And he proceeds to answer his question. He argues that books alone had kept him "alive in a negatively vital way," and especially books by "Dreiser, Masters, Mencken, Anderson, and Lewis" which:

> seemed defensively critical of the straitened American environment. These writers seemed to feel that America could be shaped nearer to the hearts of those who lived in it. And it was out of these novels and stories and articles, out of the emotional impact of imaginative constructions of heroic or tragic deeds, that I felt touching my face a tinge of warmth from an unseen light; and in my leaving I was groping toward that invisible light, always trying to keep my face so set and turned that I would not lose the hope of its faint promise, using it as my justification for action.

These final words counteract the paradoxes of the epigraph. The black boy who was heading North was still blind at noonday, but he felt "warmth from an unseen light," and that warmth was hope. He was groping, but groping toward something. The ultimate paragraph states that Wright's search was for the essential significance of life. "With ever watchful eyes and bearing scars, visible and invisible, I headed North, full of a hazy notion that life could be lived with dignity, that the personalities of others should not be violated, that men should be able to confront other men without fear or shame, and that if men were lucky in their living on earth they might win some redeeming meaning for their having struggled and suffered here beneath the stars." Even though this last paragraph is presented conditionally, it is strong and eloquent. The promise, even the faint promise, of "redeeming meaning" seems adequate to the dignity of "having struggled and suffered here beneath the stars." We feel that hunger has at last changed to hope.

But this final statement, wrapping up and rounding out the book, is not what Wright had originally planned to publish when he finished *Black Boy* in December of 1943. As is now well known, the book was half again as long and its title was *American Hunger*. It reached page proofs and its jacket was designed. The full autobiography ends in 1937, ten years later than *Black Boy,* only six years before the actual writing of the book. Therefore, Wright had not achieved the sort of distance from his material which the shortened *Black Boy* implied. Partly for this reason, the full *American Hunger*—as distinct from the published *Black Boy*—retains that tentativeness which is the hallmark of the open autobiography.

In addition, the omitted second section of the autobiography expresses the tensions, the unresolved conflicts, of the first. *American Hunger* is the story, chiefly, of Wright's unsatisfying relationship with the Communist Party. Here, the themes of black and white are more subdued, but the theme of hunger persists and becomes more elaborate and universal. Of course, the question of black and white as a simple issue of race continues, but as Wright notes [in *American Hunger*], he now feels "a different sort of tension," a different kind of "insecurity." The distinction now is likely to be animal and human, dirty and clean. A re-consideration of *Black Boy*'s epigraph will best illustrate the qualities of the omitted section and its relationship to the whole.

The epigraph from Job which prefaced *Black Boy* was originally meant to summarize the entire *American Hunger.* The first line, "They meet with darkness in the daytime," as shown above, summarizes the action of *Black Boy.* The second line, "And they grope at noonday as in the night, . . ." although not denying the content of *Black Boy,* more properly applies to the second section of the book. When Wright first enters a John Reed Club, it seems that neither he nor the members of the club need to grope; they ignore his blackness, and he feels for the first time totally human. But soon they begin to reduce his humanity in other ways. The Communists thwart his attempts to write biographies of their black members. "I had embraced their aims with the freest impulse I had ever known. I, the chary cynic, the man who had felt that no idea on earth was worthy of self-sacrifice, had publicly identified myself with them, and now their suspicion of me hit me with a terrific impact, froze me within. I groped in the noon sun." The isolation Wright feels is different from what he experienced in the South, but it is in some ways more terrible. He is still blind, groping even in the sunshine.

Wright had also picked separate epigraphs and titles for each of the subdivisions of the original *American Hunger,* and when these are properly replaced, they reassert the anxiety, hunger, and searching. In its original form, *Black Boy-American Hunger* had specific titles for each book, and each book carried a separate epigraph. *Black Boy* was to be called "Southern Night," and its epigraph was also from Job: "His strength shall be hunger-bitten, / And destruction shall be ready at his side." The dark imagery of the "Southern Night" fulfilled its title, as did its violence and hunger. The second part was to be called "The Horror and the Glory," and its epigraph came from a Negro Folk Song:

> Sometimes I wonder, huh,
> Wonder if other people wonder, huh,
> Sometimes I wonder, huh,
> Wonder if other people wonder, huh,
> Just like I do, oh my Lord, just like I do!

This brief verse indicates tentativeness, indecision, and a total lack of communication. In company with this resistance to conclusiveness, Wright emphasizes throughout his sense of wonder, his innocence: "how wide and innocent were my eyes, as round and open and dew-wet as morning-glories." Besides elaborating on its epigraph, the section called "The Horror and the Glory" explicitly defines its subtitle. In a climactic scene toward the end of the book, Wright's friend Ross confesses in an open trial that he has fought the policies of his fellow Communists. The glory of this moment is that Ross "had shared and accepted the vision that had crushed him," the vision that all men are equal and sharing in a communal world. But the horror is that this vision has been oversimplified by its followers, that they have allowed the Party to truncate their abilities to think. Wright says, "This, to me, was a spectacle of glory; and yet, because it had condemned me, because it was blind and ignorant, I felt that it was a spectacle of horror." Wright is a writer, and as such it is his business to search deep into the human heart, to name blindness when he sees it. This is of necessity a lonely search, and a complex one. Like the protagonist of **"The Man Who Lived Underground,"** which Wright was working on during the years when he was finishing *American Hunger,* a writer may find himself separate from the rest, observing, innocent, condemned.

The final pages of the full *American Hunger,* unlike those of the revised *Black Boy,* do not in fact explain how Wright managed to separate himself from his black confrères in the south, how he became a writer. They do not even hint at his future successes, but rather at his sense of quest, and as Michel Fabre has put it, his feeling that the quest was unfinished and perhaps unfinishable. Wright did not plan to create in his readers nor to accept in himself a feeling of satisfaction, but of hunger, "a sense of the hunger for life that gnaws in us all." Here, too, Wright returns to his imagery of darkness and light: "Perhaps, I thought, out of my tortured feelings I could fling a spark into this darkness." The terminology is similar to [Joseph] Conrad's at the end of *Heart of Darkness,* with reference to the

continent before him and its immensity. Wright no longer believes in the Communist vision, no longer yearns for what Fishbelly's father in *The Long Dream* calls "the dream that can't come true," asserts that he is working "Humbly now, with no vaulting dream of achieving a vast unity." Wright knows that his effort is tentative and minimal, but also that he must try to write on the "white paper": "I would hurl words into this darkness and wait for an echo, and if an echo sounded, no matter how faintly, I would send other words to tell, to march, to fight, to create a sense of the hunger for life that gnaws in us all, to keep alive in our hearts a sense of the inexpressibly human." This statement is an admission that Wright cannot produce a work that is neat and conclusive, and as a result the content and effect of these final pages clash with the revised ending of *Black Boy.*

To understand why Wright's conclusion to *Black Boy* is so mismatched with the deliberate inconclusiveness of his full autobiography, one must consider in detail the events surrounding its writing. After the extraordinary success of *Native Son* in 1940, Wright turned to a novel about women, servants, and the problem of those who attempt to pass for white. This novel was never to be finished, but he was working at it consistently until 9 April 1943, when he gave a talk at Fisk University in Nashville. He had not prepared his remarks in advance, and he decided at the last minute to talk about his own life, to be honest with his audience. After the publication of *Black Boy,* he recounted this experience [in "Richard Wright Describes the Birth of *Black Boy,*" in the *New York Post,* 30 November 1944]:

> I gave a clumsy, conversational kind of speech to the folks, white and black, reciting what I felt and thought about the world; what I remembered about my life, about being a Negro. There was but little applause. Indeed, the audience was terribly still, and it was not until I was halfway through my speech that it crashed upon me that I was saying things that Negroes were not supposed to say publicly, things that whites had forbidden Negroes to say. What made me realize this was a hysterical, half-repressed, tense kind of laughter that went up now and then from the white and black faces

This experience convinced him that he ought to finish the book about his own life which he had long been writing in pieces. **"The Ethics of Living Jim Crow,"** for instance, written in 1937, he would eventually transport bodily into his autobiography. The book which he now set out to write, although revised, shaped, and ordered, was primarily an effort to tell the truth, not to convince a particular audience, black or white. Indeed, Wright wrote to his editor at Harper's, Edward Aswell, about a juvenile edition of *Black Boy* that "I'm just too self-conscious when I write for a special audience." He could not finish the juvenile edition.

The search for truth, for as much truth as one can possibly set down, is the primary motive of a writer of an open as opposed to a defined autobiography. He is not trying primarily to please an audience, to create an aesthetically satisfying whole, but to look into his heart. This attempt is perhaps the most difficult a writer can undertake, requiring as Wright put it in his Fisk speech "real hard terror."

> If you try it, you will find at times sweat will break out upon you. You will find that even if you succeed in discounting the attitudes of others to you and your life, you must wrestle with yourself most of all, fight with yourself; for there will surge up in you a strong desire to alter facts, to dress up your feelings. You'll find that there are many things that you don't want to admit about yourself or others. As your record shapes itself up, an awed wonder haunts you. And yet there is no more exciting an adventure than trying to be honest in this way. The clean, strong feeling that sweeps you when you've done it, makes you know that. . . . Well, it's quite inexplicable.

When Wright had at last, through a multitude of drafts, faced and finished these truths and these terrors, he forwarded his manuscript to his agent, Paul Reynolds. Reynolds sent the manuscript, which was at that moment called *Black Hunger,* to Harper's, where Aswell was expecting the novel about the problems of attempting to "pass." Aswell instantly recognized the autobiography's worth, however, and within three days had sent an advance. By this time the title was *American Hunger.* The unsigned reader's notes (presumably Aswell's) preserved in the Harper papers suggest, among other things, that Wright cut out some of the John Reed section. The reader adds, "I may be wrong but I personally would like to see some of this cut and the story carried on to the years of Wright's success—perhaps to the writing of *Native Son.* His own feeling of hope, his own preservation through adversity would somehow be justified as it is not here." It is an editor's business to ask that even lives be given justification, that order be imposed, that readers be given a sense of wholeness and completion. The suggestion that the autobiography be brought up to *Native Son* was somehow dropped, but Wright cut the John Reed section as much as he could. He rewrote the ending, but it resisted closure: "I tried and tried to strengthen the ending. One thing is certain, I cannot step outside of the mood rendered there and say anything without its sounding false. So, what I've done is this: I've expanded the end to deepen the mood, to hint at some kind of emotional resolution." The book moved toward its final stages. Wright objected to the phrase "courageous Negro" in the jacket copy and asked that it be changed to "Negro American," which "keeps the book related to the American scene and emphasizes the oneness of impulse, the singleness of aim of both black and white Americans." Wright's emphasis, once again, is on a general audience. He is trying to tell the truth, avoiding the need to mask, modify, change, which had characterized his life in white America. He is deviating from the model of the black slave narrative, which moved teleologically from slavery into freedom, from dehumanization to fulfillment. The pressure to round out the book was strong, but Wright successfully resisted.

The further metamorphosis, the addition of the final six pages to *Black Boy,* took place in the Spring of 1944, after *American Hunger* in its entirety had been forwarded to the Book-of-the-Month Club. There, the judges said that they would accept the book on condition that the second section be cut off and the first section be provided with more complete resolution. On 26 June, Aswell forwarded a draft of the new conclusion in which Wright had "tried to carry out a suggestion made by Mr. Fadiman to the effect that he summarize briefly, and make explicit, the meaning that is now implicit in the preceding pages."

Dorothy Canfield Fisher, who had written the introduction for *Native Son,* urged Wright to expand somewhat on his first draft, and to seek out the American sources for his feelings of hope. "From what other source than from the basic tradition of our country could the soul of an American have been filled with that 'hazy notion' that life could be lived with dignity? Could it be that even from inside the prison of injustice, through the barred windows of that Bastille of racial oppression, Richard Wright had caught a glimpse of the American flag?" With America at war, this spirit of patriotism was the general mood, and elsewhere Fisher contrasts American freedom with Nazi repression. Reflecting similar fervor, Aswell's list of possible titles for the truncated first half of *American Hunger* includes besides fifteen evocations of darkness such as *Raw Hunger* and *The Valley of Fear,* these familiar complacencies: *Land of the Free* and *Land of Liberty.* Wright replied that the Negro environment was such that very few could intuit the American way. Even these could desire nothing specific; they could feel only a hope, a hunger. He emphasized that accident, not fate or choice, had more often than not governed his own life. However, Fisher had suggested that Wright consider which American books might have influenced him, given him a vision of America which had inspired him. In response to this request, Wright added two more paragraphs. One defined his hope—or more precisely refused to define his hope, showing that he was simply running away from violence and darkness, not toward anything he could formulate. The second paragraph had to do with his reading. Although Wright was careful to emphasize that his reading had been accidental, that the books were alien, that Dreiser, Masters, Mencken, Anderson, and Lewis were critical of the American environment, he did give his hope a nearer reality. Even so, as mentioned above, he called it "a warmth from an unseen light," a phrase which Fisher praised with special emphasis. Wright had actually transported this phrase from *American Hunger,* where it appeared in a much more nebulous context: "Even so, I floundered, staggered; but somehow I always groped my way back to that path where I felt a tinge of warmth from an unseen light." Here there is blindness, the groping of the epigraph, and a tiny waft of hope. The *Black Boy* context, too, mentions groping, but the rhetoric is more assured, the feeling more triumphant.

Indeed, Wright realized that *American Hunger* was no longer an appropriate title for this transformed autobiography. The Book-of-the-Month Club suggested *The First Chapter,* which would have emphasized the initiation theme and implied a sequel, but this choice seemed jejune. Wright himself eventually suggested *Black Boy;* and his accompanying comment [in *The Unfinished Quest of Richard Wright*] emphasizes the unity he had attained by truncating his book: "Now, this is not very original, but I think it covers the book. It is honest. Straight. And many people say it to themselves when they see a Negro and wonder how he lives. . . . *Black Boy* seems to me to be not only a title, but also a kind of heading of the whole general theme. His suggested subtitles, however, retained the sense of process. Nearly all of them contained the word "anxiety." Eventually, however, the subtitle too reflected the pose of completeness. *Black Boy* became *A Record of Childhood and Youth.*

No one will ever know how the original *American Hunger* would have fared after publication, but *Black Boy* became an instant best-seller. In 1945 it ranked fourth among non-fiction sales. The content was new and shocking, but even so, many readers noted the hopeful ending. Responses ranged from outrage through misunderstanding and bi-ased readings to unalleviated praise. Senator Bilbo at-tacked the book from the right and Ben Burns hacked away at it from the left. Black opinion was divided over Wright's frequently sharp comments about members of his own race. [In the *New York Times,* 28 February 1945], Orville Prescott recognized and disliked some of the ele-ments of open autobiography and downgraded the book for its inclusiveness, criticizing Wright's "excessive deter-mination to omit nothing, to emphasize mere filth." Al-though we have seen that this inclusiveness was a deliber-ate and necessary choice, Prescott decided that it sprang "from a lack of artistic discrimination and selectivity." Milton Mayer made a similar criticism [in *Progressive,* 9 April 1945], defining the book's genre as "history." Lewis Gannett, claiming that "*Black Boy* may be one of the great American autobiographies" [in the *New York Her-ald Tribune* 28 February 1945], saw a double America in the book much like Dorothy Canfield Fisher's: "This, too is America: both the mud and scum in which Richard Wright grew up, and the something that sang within him, that ever since has been singing with an ever clearer, pain-fully sweeter, voice." Many others used Wright's subse-quent career as a defining measure, seeing in his earlier ex-periences the seeds of his genius. One typical review [in *Crisis,* Vol. 52, 1945] ended: "Soon after this discovery of the great world of books, we find our black boy born of the Mississippi plantation, now nineteen, packing up his bags for new worlds and horizons in the North. The rest of the story is well-known. Readers of *Black Boy,* no mat-ter what their race or persuasion, often made the easy leap from the trip North to best-sellerdom and success.

But for Wright himself this leap was not easy, as readers of *American Hunger* know. Although pieces of the end of the original *American Hunger* were published in the *At-lantic Monthly* and *Mademoiselle* before *Black Boy* itself actually appeared, it obviously could not reach as large an audience as *Black Boy* itself. Constance Webb produced a photo-offset version of the whole manuscript, but this was only privately circulated. Even readers who later read most of this material in *The God that Failed* or in *Eight Men* could not intuit the negative strength of the omitted pages which immediately followed Wright's escape to the North in *American Hunger.* Nothing short of Wright's opening words can convey the desolation he felt on arriv-ing in his hoped-for paradise: "My first glimpse of the flat black stretches of Chicago depressed and dismayed me,

mocked all my fantasies." Wright did at last find a place where he was comfortable, but it was not Chicago or any other place in the United States. In spite of Mencken, An-derson, Dreiser, Masters, and Lewis, the American dream which Wright could not honestly elicit in the last pages of his *Black Boy* simply did not exist for him. When Wright arrived in Paris on 15 May 1946, he wrote to his editor at Harper's: "Ed, Paris is all I ever hoped to think it was, with a clear sky, buildings so beautiful with age that one wonders how they happen to be, and with people so as-sured and friendly and confident that one knows that it took many centuries of living to give them such poise. There is such an absence of race hate that it seems a little unreal. Above all, Paris strikes me as being truly a gentle city, with gentle manners." Here he could live and work as a human being, released from the ungentleness he could never escape in the United States.

In spite of the tentativeness of Wright's ending for *Black Boy,* in spite of his ultimate emigration, subsequent read-ers have continued to misread those final pages. Arthur P. Davis, for instance, in *From the Dark Tower* says, "The book ends . . . on a note of triumph. Near the close of the work Wright describes his moment of truth." But there was no moment of truth. Similarly, although Stephen But-terfield [in his *Black Autobiography in America*] describes black autobiography in general as reflecting "a kind of cul-tural schizophrenia, where the author must somehow dis-cover roots in a country which does not accept him as a human being," he defines *Black Boy* as one of the modern survivals of the pattern of the slave narrative. In support of this argument, he writes, "The slave narrative's basic pattern, it will be remembered, was an escape from South to North as well as a movement up the social scale from the status of slave to that of respected, educated citizen and vanguard of black politics and culture." Without the *American Hunger* ending, *Black Boy* is indeed modeled on the slave-narrative pattern, but Wright intended the ending to remain ambiguous, groping, hungry. Unfortu-nately the pattern absorbs the deviating elements, and only an unusually careful reader will notice the hesitancy in the final pages, the conditional verbs, the haltered rhet-oric, the mention of luck.

In 1977, seventeen years after Wright's death, Harper and Row published *American Hunger* as a separate volume, with an afterword by Michel Fabre giving a brief outline of its publishing history. Fabre objected to the disjoining of the two parts of the original autobiography, observing, "*Black Boy* is commonly construed as a typical success story, and thus it has been used by the American liberal to justify his own optimism regading his country." The rhetoric is strong, but the point is valid, and indeed it is more generally true than Fabre implies. Davis and Butter-field also misread *Black Boy,* and they cannot easily be grouped with "American liberals." Reviewers of the 1977 *American Hunger,* those of both races and all political persuasions, generally agreed that reading it changes one's perceptions of *Black Boy.* Alden Whitman went one step further, arguing [in *Chicago Tribune Book World,* 22 May 1977] that *American Hunger* did not make sense alone, and suggesting: "It would have been more useful, in my opinion, to have issued *Black Boy* complete at last, so that the reader could get the full flavor of the autobiography as Wright initially wrote it."

Many books, through the influence of an editor, have been drastically changed before publication, and the published work is accepted as definitive. What we read is *The Waste Land,* not "He Do the Police in Three Voices." It is true that Wright concurred entirely in the division of *American Hunger* into *Black Boy* and its sequel, even supplying the new title. But, as I have tried to show here, the change was more drastic than Wright meant it to be; the ultimate significance of the book shifted further than Wright had intended. *Black Boy* became a more definitive statement than its themes of hope and hunger could support. Therefore, *American Hunger* needs to be reissued in its entirety, with the final six pages of the present *Black Boy* given as an appendix. Failing this, every reader of *Black Boy* should buy both books and read them together, recognizing that the last six pages of *Black Boy* were added in a final revision in part as a response to wartime patriotism. When combined, both of these books emphasize the lack of conviction, the isolation, and finally the lack of order in Wright's world as he saw it, a sadness and disarray which his truncated autobiography *Black Boy,* as published, seems at the end to deny. (pp. 199-214)

> *Janice Thaddeus, "The Metamorphosis of Richard Wright's 'Black Boy',"* in American Literature, *Vol. 57, No. 2, May, 1985, pp. 199-214.*

On Wright's perception of race relations in the South:

In *Black Boy* Wright is continually at pains to show that white people have a preconceived notion of a Negro's place in the South: He serves them, he is likely to steal, and he cannot read or write. The tabooed subjects that Southerners refused to discuss with black men included "American white women; the Ku Klux Klan; France, and how Negro soldiers fared while there; Frenchwomen; Jack Johnson; the entire northern part of the United States; the Civil War; Abraham Lincoln; U. S. Grant; General Sherman; Catholics; the Pope; Jews; the Republican Party; slavery; social equality; Communism; Socialism; the 13th, 14th, and 15th Amendments of the Constitution." Sex and religion were the most accepted subjects, for they were the topics that did not require positive knowledge or self-assertion on the part of the black man. White men did not mind black men's talking about sex as long as it was not interracial. Sex was considered purely biological, and like religion it would not call for the will power of an individual. Although blacks were physically free, the South had replaced traditional slavery with a system by which their freedom of speech and movement was closely monitored and restricted. The culprit was not any individual white man; it was the complicity of white society that had allowed the design of slavery to renew itself in the twentieth-century South.

> *Yoshinobu Hakutani, in "Creation of the Self in Richard Wright's* Black Boy," *Black American Literature Forum, Summer, 1985.*

John O. Hodges   (essay date June 1985)

[In the following essay, Hodges studies features of the bildungsroman in Black Boy.*]*

The early years of the twentieth century were marked by race riots, lynchings, and the revival of the Ku Klux Klan. The Klan was energetically gathering "qualified persons" under its banner of "Native, Protestant, Supreme," and by 1924 this organization could claim a membership exceeding four million individuals. The South, of course, with its rather large black population, became the center of the nation's unrest and disharmony.

In a statement before the Southern Conference for Education in 1904, Bishop Charles Betts Galloway presented the case for this region: "In the South there will never be any social mingling of the races. Whether it be prejudice or pride of race, there is a middle wall of partition which will not be broken down." Clearly marked signs of "White Only" and "For Colored" were strategically located to make sure that all knew their proper place, for the South was prepared to take stern measures against those who, for whatever reason, attempted to traverse the racial line.

This is a South to which few now, perhaps, would cling. But it is the South in which Richard Wright (b. September 4, 1908) spent his boyhood, and it is this image of the South, with its brutality, fear, and deprivation that haunts almost all of his fiction, whether the setting be the deep South or Chicago's South Side. So deeply wounded was he by the injustices of his youth that by 1945, when *Black Boy* appeared, he could still render those days of fear, hunger, and violence with remarkable vividness. And throughout his various writings, whether in fiction or in the polemical essay, he attempted to give voice to those, who, like himself, had suffered under the extreme pressures of injustice and racism. "Being a Negro," Wright once said [in *White Man, Listen*], "has to do with the American scene, with race hate, rejection, ignorance, segregation, slavery, murder, fiery crosses, and fear." These are the evils which mark the bleak landscape of Wright's *Black Boy* and of several of his other works, most notably *Uncle Tom's Children* and *Native Son.* Wright certainly had, in these two earlier works, achieved a measure of success in calling attention to the inimical effects of racial injustice and prejudice on the human personality. But in *Black Boy* he achieves even greater success. For here the themes of fear, hunger, and deprivation are related to his own development and therefore attain an immediacy and poignancy unlike that found in either *Uncle Tom's Children* or *Native Son.*

As the story of a boy's journey from ignorance to experience, *Black Boy* possesses significant features of the classical *Bildungsroman,* a work which recounts a young man's education or character formation. According to Roy Pascal in his book *The German Novel,* the *Bildungsroman* is the "story of the formation of a character up to the moment when he ceases to be self-centered and becomes society-centered, thus beginning to form his true Self." And *Black Boy* is the story of a boy whose selfhood must be forged in the crucible of a hostile society which is determined to suppress any positive assertion of personhood.

Since Richard is interested in pursuing a literary career, the restrictions which his society places upon him become all the more serious. *Black Boy,* then, like other exemplary works in the genre (such as Goethe's *Wilhelm Meister,* Keller's *Grüne Heinrich,* and Joyce's *Portrait of the Artist*), depicts the arduous pilgrimage of the embattled artist in a restrictive environment.

Like Keller's Heinrich Lee, young Richard "hungers"—both physically and spiritually—for the opportunity to release his creative potential. For Heinrich Lee the urge is to become a great painter, and during the long days of his apprenticeship he encounters problems similar to those which beset Richard. Parallels are also to be found in Goethe's *Lehrjahre* (that volume of *Wilhelm Meister* which treats Wilhelm's apprenticeship to the German theatre) and in Joyce's *Portrait of the Artist,* a work which Wright knew quite well.

But while *Black Boy* adheres to the structural design of the *Bildungsroman,* the book goes significantly beyond the genre's usual theme of a boy's awakening self-consciousness as he apprehends the mysteries of the world about him. In *Black Boy,* Richard must win self-knowledge in a society that is not only repressive and restrictive but profoundly antagonistic as well. And this antagonism is experienced not only in his effort to become a writer but at every level, even at the fundamental level of human survival itself. There is also, in *Black Boy,* a fraternal dimension unlike anything we find in the typical *Bildungsroman.* For Wright attempts to call attention not only to his own difficult journey but to that of other black youths who attempted to take hold of the meaning of their lives in the hostile atmosphere of the deep American South of a few generations ago.

In the course of a radio interview in the spring of 1945 [published in "How Richard Wright Looks at *Black Boy,*" *P M Magazine,* 14 April 1945], Wright set forth very candidly what had been his basic intention in *Black Boy*:

> I wrote the book to tell a series of incidents strung through my childhood, but the main desire was to render a judgment on my environment because I felt the necessity to. That judgment was this: the environment the South creates is too small to nourish human beings. . . . I wanted to lend, give my tongue to the voiceless Negro boys. . . .

Indeed, the self-portrait which emerges is of one whose experience embraced the worst hardships suffered by blacks under the Southern caste system. And, inevitably, his purpose required him to suppress certain details of his life and to exaggerate others, in order that the narrative design might stress the ordeals experienced by a typical Southern black. His account, though autobiographical, "would be more than that; he would use himself as a symbol of all the brutality wreaked upon the black man by the Southern environment . . . " [Constance Webb in *Richard Wright: A Biography*].

The writing of *Black Boy,* therefore, was meant to serve at least two purposes: that of enabling Wright to retrace his steps in order to understand himself and to understand where he stood in relationship to the black community;

and that of creating a platform from which a judgment might be pronounced on the Southern white society which blighted the hopes and aspirations of its black youth. My intention here is to demonstrate how Wright, by carefully designing and narrating the story of his life, attempts to accomplish simultaneously these distinct objectives within the narrative structure of his autobiography.

Wright's two-fold objective of reporting on his own experience and of exposing the brutality and insensitivity of the South required him to adopt a rather elaborate narrative strategy. He had to present the story from the perspective of an average black boy victimized and brutalized by his experiences in the South, while at the same time accounting for the fact that those very experiences, though daunting for so many, had actually goaded him toward significant achievement. Furthermore, he had to devise a method whereby he could criticize what he considered to be shortcomings in his own people, while also holding the white South responsible for those shortcomings. Wright's intention required him to exploit fully the tension between past and present, between the boy who experiences and the mature author who interprets.

Therefore, although the account appears to be presented from the perspective of a first-person narrator, we detect two distinct voices, two "I's." On the one hand, we have the "I" of the narrative present where the account is presented from the point of view of the boy's own developing consciousness as he confronts each new experience. On the other hand, we have the "I" of the writer as he imposes his present state of consciousness on the events of the narrative. This latter type of "telling" narration (in Wayne Booth's sense [as established in his *The Rhetoric of Fiction*]) makes it possible for the writer to interpret and even to criticize the protagonist's actions from the standpoint of his (the writer's) present knowledge of the outcome of those events. Furthermore, the "intrusive" narrator attempts to convince his audience of the soundness or unsoundness of the boy's actions.

Indeed, even when the narration is filtered through the consciousness of the boy, we recognize the author's hand, for young Richard is made to speak words and to handle metaphors and symbols which he, because of his immaturity, could not possibly have understood. So in this sense, too, the protagonist is made to speak for the author. Yet this type of narration succeeds in ways that the intrusive narration does not, because once the author has prepared the script for the ensuing action, he appears to withdraw from the scene and allows the hero to occupy the center of the stage. From this point of view the audience is able to judge firsthand not only the conduct of the protagonist who speaks the language and attempts to manipulate the symbols of the author, but also the attitude of the author toward his protagonist. And since the protagonist speaks for the author, we are actually determining the author's *present* attitude toward his past.

Perhaps one of the most effective means of charting Richard's growth of consciousness is through the author's use of a "naive" hero, a technique which is commonly associated with the *Bildungsroman* convention. It is only through incessant probing and at the expense of great pain and suffering that the boy begins to unlock the various secrets and mysteries of the adult world. After Granny gives him his bath, he tells her to "kiss back there," and his parents give him a stern beating. Concerning this he writes: "[I]n the future I would learn the meaning of why they had beat and denounced me." And, in general, he notices that his mother becomes extremely irritated whenever he inquires about the relationship between blacks and whites. When he asks her why the family chose not to fight back when Uncle Hoskins was killed, she immediately slaps him. Or again, when he sees a black chain gang being driven by white guards (which he at first takes to be a herd of elephants), he asks his mother whether the white men ever wore stripes, to which she reluctantly replies, "sometimes," though she herself never saw any. Thus, for young Richard, "[t]he days and hours began to speak with a clearer tongue. Each new experience had a sharp meaning of its own."

The primary role of the "naive" hero, however, is to call into question those injustices which blacks and whites, because of habit and custom, dismiss all too perfunctorily. In short, the boy, in wearing the mask of the author, forces those about him—and Wright's readers as well—to examine the deeper implications of their actions. The boy, perhaps because he is ignorant of the customs of Jim Crow, is free of the bigotry and prejudice that hinder blacks and whites from achieving any stable relationships in the South. He exhibits, furthermore, a higher moral sense and a greater sensitivity than do the more mature individuals about him, and he thus becomes an adequate "voice" for revealing the hypocrisy and ruthlessness of the South during Wright's youth.

Dialogue is yet another form of narration which enables us to observe the drama of selfhood as it unfolds in the autobiography. As the youth converses with others, both blacks and whites, who are more mature and sophisticated than he, we learn much about his personality and developing consciousness, especially about how he sees himself in relation to these individuals. Here again, however, as with the other forms of narration, the portrait that we have is one which is determined more by the author's present attitudes and experiences than by any actual events in his past. Since he cannot possibly recall with absolute exactness the various exchanges he has had with others, he must search his present storehouse of words, images, and symbols for suitable metaphors of those past experiences. The author, therefore, is "free" to recreate the dialogues in a manner which best accords with his own general purpose and intention. And it is by way of Wright's effort to give his narrative a true structure—that is, to make it stand for more than a mere chronology of the major events of his life—that the various modes of narration come to play such an important role.

The whole narrative design of the book functions in conjunction with elements of structure and theme in order to produce the total effect of a boy's difficult journey from innocence to experience. It is to a closer examination of the process of this boy's education that we must now turn.

Wright recounts the crucial experiences of his youth with extraordinary poignancy, and one feels that it is his hope to make his readers at once conscious of and also in some sense prepared to take responsibility for the anguish which he and other black boys experienced in the South of his day. The boy's awakening self-consciousness evolves in stages which correspond to the three sectors of society through which he successively moves: his own household, the black community, and the larger white world. Richard's understanding of himself and of the world he inhabits increases with each new *rite de passage,* so that once he has encountered the whole of Southern life, he has a clearer knowledge of who he is and of the future course his life must take.

The narrator begins the story of his life not with its beginning but with those "four-year-old days," the time when he first becomes conscious of the fear, hunger, and violence that are to plague him throughout his childhood. Wright's decision not to recount the circumstances of his birth betrays his intention to thrust young Richard's developing selfhood immediately into the center of the design.

The opening lines establish the tone of fear and despair which pervades the entire narrative. While the atmosphere of anxiety and dread stems at this point from within Richard's own household, we get the impression that it only presages the larger insecurities which he is to encounter in the outside world. Richard seems to fear his grandmother, for instance, not so much because she is a stern taskmaster, but because she is, for all intents and purposes, white: "I was dreaming of running and playing and shouting but the vivid image of Granny's old, white, wrinkled, grim face framed by a halo of tumbling black hair, lying upon a huge feather pillow, made me afraid." Later on in his recital the narrator confides to us that, indeed, his "grandmother was as nearly white as a Negro can get without being white, which means that she was white." The color white, then, already begins to take on a decidedly sinister aspect, and, though Richard appears unaware of the fact at this point, it seems to have been a color which in his experience was regularly associated with restrictiveness. He is forbidden, for example, to touch the fluffy white curtains in his room. And when he finally musters enough courage to strike out against this symbol, he accidentally sets the whole house on fire, an act for which, as he says, "[I was] lashed so hard and long that I lost consciousness. . . . I was lost in a fog of fear." Moreover, while recovering from this beating, he sees above him "wobbly white bags, like the full udders of cows, suspended from the ceiling. . . ." "Later on," he continues, "as I grew worse, I could see the bags in the daytime with my eyes open and I was grasped by the fear that they were going to fall and drench me in some horrible liquid." In using white as a symbol of fear and restriction, Wright was only further developing a theme which had earlier been a part of **Native Son** and of several of the stories in **Uncle Tom's Children.** For whether it is the white cat which attempts to corner a black rat or the white walls of Bigger's jail cell, white always seems to be a symbol of repression which threatens to imprison the Self.

The whippings this boy receives, though no doubt excessive, are meant to curb that natural curiosity which, outside the home, could result in his death. Furthermore, he is warned against asking too many questions regarding the nature of the relationship between blacks and whites. When he learns of a white man having beaten a black boy, Richard does not understand, for, as he reasons, "a paternal right is the only right that a man has to beat a child." And though his mother refuses to answer forthrightly all of the boy's queries—as he must be spared the bitter realities of his existence—the questions he raises are penetrating ones that are meant to disturb our consciences.

Richard's father is also a source of fear and anxiety. The narrator recalls: "He was the lawgiver in our family and I never laughed in his presence." Though his father's disappearance early on in his life means that he can enjoy a relatively greater degree of freedom, unfortunately it also means greater hardship for the family. There is, for example, never enough food in the house. Indeed, he recalls: "Hunger was with us always. . . . As the days slid past the image of my father became associated with my pangs of hunger, and whenever I felt hunger I thought of him with a deep biological bitterness."

Although the narrator insists that he has since forgiven his father, they were "forever strangers, speaking a different language, living on vastly different planes of reality. . . . " While he himself had gone on to achieve some measure of success, his father remained "imprisoned by the slow flow of the seasons, by wind and rain and sun." Wright's judgment is indeed a harsh one, as he seems to attack his father for a lack of resourcefulness and courage because he permitted himself to be defeated by the pressures of the Southern experience. Moreover, having by the end of the opening chapter been accounted a failure, the elder Wright from this point on plays no part in the narrative, as though the son had chosen simply to expel him from the circle of his attention.

Without the spiritual support of a father, Richard frequents bars where he learns to speak obscenities even before he can read. And worse, he declares, "I was a drunkard in my sixth year before I had begun school." His mother now not only has to provide the economic support for the family, but she has the added responsibility of teaching the boy those methods of survival on which his life depends. It is she, for example, who teaches him to fight back when he is attacked by a gang of boys in Memphis who threaten to take the money he has been given to purchase groceries.

Besides learning how to survive in the streets and taverns of Memphis, Richard has also to learn how to deal with the bitter friction which exists between the two races. While he had witnessed the beating of a black boy by a white policeman and had heard stories of violent encounters between blacks and whites, it is not until he visits Granny in Jackson that he begins to understand the seriousness of the hostility which exists between "the two races who lived side by side but never touched, it seemed, except in violence." Significantly, his first real experience of violence (apart from the harsh punishment he receives at the hands of his parents) is a vicarious one which he receives as Ella, a school teacher who rents a room in Gran-

ny's house, reads him one of her stories entitled "Bluebeard and His Seven Wives." He recalls:

> The tale made the world around me be, throb, live. As she spoke, reality changed, the look of things altered, and the world became peopled with magical presences. My sense of life deepened and the feel of things was different somehow. . . . My imagination blazed. The sensations the story aroused in me were never to leave me.

This is a most crucial passage in the narrative, for it gives us the first real indication of the boy's interest in imaginative literature. Moreover, the violence which lay at the heart of the story mirrored the violence in his own life and gave it a deeper meaning:

> I hungered for the sharp, frightening, breathtaking, almost painful excitement that the story had given me, and I vowed that as soon as I was old enough I would buy all the novels there were and read them to feed that thirst for violence that was in me, for intrigue, for plotting, for secrecy, for bloody murders. . . . They could not have known that Ella's whispered story of deception and murder had been the first experience in my life that had elicited from me a total emotional response.

He soon was to see the bloody drama of Bluebeard acted out in real life. While visiting his Aunt Maggie, Richard learns that Uncle Hoskins has been killed by whites who had long coveted his flourishing liquor business. On another occasion Matthews, Aunt Maggie's new husband, bludgeons the white girl who witnessed him stealing some money from her house and then sets the house on fire, leaving the girl to perish in the flames. There is also the violence which resulted at the close of the First World War when racial conflict permeated the South. The narrator recalls, "Though I did not witness any of it, I could not have been more thoroughly affected by it if I had participated directly in the clash."

The violence, the fear, the hunger—the basic realities of this boy's childhood—seemed to be symbolized in his mother's suffering, to the extent that, as he says, "her life set the emotional tone of my life." The suffering he experienced in his youth, he suggests, brought him to a deeper sense of communal responsibility:

> The spirit I had caught gave me insight into the sufferings of others, made me gravitate toward those whose feelings were like my own, made me sit for hours while others told me of their lives, made me strangely tender and cruel, violent and peaceful.

The entire passage here is clearly informed by a wider knowledge and consciousness than that of a twelve-year-old boy. The mature writer temporarily enters his narrative in order to interpret the experiences thus far recorded and to show their relevance to his general growth and development. By reflecting on his past in such a manner, he discovers himself in the present and justifies his present conduct and ideology in those past experiences.

When his mother's deteriorating health makes it necessary

that he find some kind of employment, he has to confront that hatred and fear which he has seen debase and even destroy other blacks. So as the narrator moves from the relatively safe confines of his home and the black community into the white world, he appears as apprehensive about this venture as a Bigger Thomas entering the household of the Daltons: Bigger wonders, "Would they expect him to come in the front way or the back?" And, similarly, Richard wonders if his experiences at home and in his community have adequately prepared him for the hazards of the white world: "What would happen now that I would be among white people for hours at a stretch? Would they hit me? Curse me?"

At his first job where he was to earn just two dollars a week, the white woman engages him in a significant dialogue:

> "Now, boy, I want to ask you one question and I want you to tell me the truth," she said.
>
> "Yes, ma'am." I said, all attention.
>
> "Do you steal?" she asked seriously.
>
> I bust into a laugh, then checked myself.
>
> "What's so damn funny about that?" she asked.
>
> "Lady, if I was a thief, I'd never tell anybody."
>
> "What do you mean?" she blazed with a red face.
>
> I had made a mistake during my first five minutes in the white world. I hung my head.

The two characters here are acting out a typical scene between blacks and whites in the South. But it is clearly a little drama in which the two parties are both to be viewed as victims of the Southern caste system—the one because she has been trained only to echo conventional clichés about blacks, the other because, while conscious of the woman's ignorance, he must learn to disguise his true feelings, to dissemble and deny his own worth and dignity. For Richard, however, this feigning in the presence of whites proves to be an art most difficult to master. Even the counsel of his friend Griggs is of little help: "When you're in front of white people, think before you act, think before you speak. Your way of doing things is all right among our people, but not for white people. They won't stand for it." Griggs explains his own situation thus: "You know, Dick, you may think I'm an Uncle Tom, but I'm not. I hate these white people, hate 'em with all my heart. But I can't show it; if I did, they'd kill me." And though Richard can never be as submissive as the other black boys, he too would soon learn that, in the South, "acting" is often the only weapon of survival. "The safety of my life," he tells us later on in his account, "depended on how well I concealed from all whites what I felt."

As he moves about from one job to the next, he slowly learns how a black boy is required to reckon with Jim Crow. At one job the woman is surprised that he, a black boy from Mississippi, does not know how to milk a cow; at another he is bitten by a dog only to be told by the foreman that he has "never seen a dog yet that could hurt a nigger"; at still another, he has what is nearly a violent confrontation with two white employees who are infuriated by his eagerness to learn a "white man's trade." Perhaps his most galling experience occurs while working as a hallboy in the Jackson hotel where, earlier, Ned's brother had been killed. While walking toward his home with one of the black maids headed in the same general direction, he becomes spellbound at seeing a white night watchman playfully slap her on the buttocks, but becomes even more astonished at the casualness with which the girl herself seems to treat the matter. He learns later that his brief moment of shock over such a routine act had almost cost him his life. And later, as a bellboy in the same hotel, he has to learn to avert his eyes from the white prostitutes who regularly lie nude across their beds. Reflecting on this, he writes: "Our presence awoke in them no sense of shame whatever, for we blacks were not considered human anyway."

In all these experiences, Richard notes a concerted effort on the part of whites—and given tacit approval by the blacks themselves—to consign him to a subservient role and to deny him that freedom of the will apart from which the creative mind cannot develop and flourish. In this context, the exchange with his first white employer takes on added significance. When the woman asks Richard why he is in school, the boy promptly responds that he wants to be a writer:

> "A what?" she demanded.
>
> "A writer," I mumbled.
>
> "For what?"
>
> "To write stories," I mumbled defensively.
>
> "You'll never be a writer," she said. "Who on earth put such ideas in your nigger head?"

Richard declares here what we have suspected all along, that he is interested in a literary career. The disclosure itself is not surprising, but the manner and circumstance under which it is made have significant implications. The woman was merely voicing a sentiment held by the majority of whites in the South: that there were certain areas of human endeavor beyond the range of possibility for any blacks. More tragic still, his own family and members of the black community seemed to have conspired with the white world in its effort to smother any capacity he might have for a literary career. Granny did not want Ella to read him her stories because they were "the devil's works." His own story, **"The Voodoo of Hell's Half-Acre,"** only served further to alienate him from his schoolmates and family: "From no quarter, with the exception of the Negro newspaper editor, had there come a single encouraging word."

From this point on in the narrative the restrictions which Richard faces are those associated with his quest to become a writer. He dreams of going to the North, which is for him a place of freedom where he might, in his words, "do something to redeem my being alive." In so thinking, the narrator tells us,

> I was building up in me a dream which the entire educational system of the South had been rigged to stifle. I was feeling the very thing the state of

Mississippi had spent millions of dollars to make sure I would never feel. . . . I was in my fifteenth year; in terms of schooling I was far behind the average youth of the nation, but I did not know that. In me was shaping a yearning for a kind of consciousness, a mode of being that the way of life about me had said could not be, must not be, and upon which the penalty of death had been placed.

By way of stealing goods and reselling them—an act which, where any black person was concerned, was morally acceptable to the South—he finally acquires enough money to leave for Memphis. Although his experience in Memphis is no happier, at least here he is able to satisfy his childhood hunger for reading by devising a scheme for getting books from the public library—which is generally off-limits to any blacks. Whites had often sent him to the library to get books for themselves. So he wonders how he might get books on his own. Having persuaded one of the more liberal whites to lend him his card, he forges the note: "Let this nigger boy have some books by H. L. Mencken." In this manner, he is able to read a body of literature ranging all the way from Anatole France to Sinclair Lewis. What interests Richard most about the writers he encounters in this way is their ability to use language as a weapon for striking out against the ills plaguing society. These writers were, in the boy's mind, "fighting with words." "I derived from these novels," he says, "nothing less than a sense of life itself. All my life had shaped me for the realism, the naturalism of the modern novel, and I could not read enough of them." He says further: "It had been my accidental reading of fiction and literary criticism that had evoked in me a glimpse of life's possibilities."

The language of this entire concluding section of *Black Boy* is not that of the boy but that of the mature man, not that of the aspiring writer but that of the accomplished author. As the narrative ends before Richard's nineteenth year, the author, for the sake of his readers, has to furnish such information as will enable us to see the relationship between the experiences of the boy and the writer he finally became. But it is, in fact, a difficult connection for us to make, since Wright himself at the time had no clear conception of his future lifework. His random reading, impressive in its range as it was for a boy in his circumstances, afforded him no clear vision of the possibility of his electing a literary vocation. Indeed, it was only after he had become sufficiently removed from the galling experiences of his boyhood and had gained some understanding of the writer's craft that he could impose some pattern on the raw experiences of his past and transmute them into literary art. In this respect, then, *Black Boy* clearly points to *American Hunger,* which details his struggles to become a writer in Chicago. The book, which appeared in 1977, was originally designed to be published along with *Black Boy* as a single work. But at the behest of his publisher, Wright agreed to have the section treating his experiences in the North issued later as a separate volume, for both men realized that though this work offered important insights into Wright's later years, it had neither the scope nor the intensity of the volume which chronicled his years in the South.

So *Black Boy* stands as Wright's major achievement in the mode of autobiographical literature, and it presents the important events comprising his apprenticeship to life and to art. The violence, the fear, the hunger, and all such negative experiences would in time provide him with rich resources for his art, for "wringing meaning out of meaningless suffering."

Wright knew well that the way of the literary imagination—by which he was able eventually to deliver himself from the horrid experiences of his youth—was not an avenue open to the majority of blacks in the South. And though he failed to propose any concrete solutions to the dilemmas facing his people, his own story is an attempt to achieve a closer identification with those Southern blacks who, like himself, had suffered under the heavy weight of racism but who, unlike Wright, lacked the talent to express in language the agony of their daily existence. In *American Hunger,* Wright observes: "I sensed that Negro life was a sprawling land of unconscious suffering and there were but a few Negroes who knew the meaning of their lives, who could tell their own stories." His autobiography, then, is meant to be a "voice" for those "voiceless" blacks of his generation. The narrative strategy of the book functions at once to detail Wright's own effort to transcend the "bleakness" of black life in the South and to provide inspiration to the numerous other native sons and daughters who "had never been allowed to catch the full spirit of Western civilization." Ralph Ellison is correct in pointing out that Wright, in *Black Boy,* "has used his own life to probe what qualities of will, imagination and intellect are required of a Southern Negro to possess the meaning of his life in the United States."

But, just as importantly, Wright wants to force the stewards of the Southern caste system to take full responsibility for the many violations of human rights that blacks experienced. So he presents his case through the consciousness of a boy who does not understand why things are as they are. However, in his bewilderment and naiveté, the boy forces both blacks and whites to examine long-held practices and customs that retard relations in the South.

This autobiography, which takes the form of the *Bildungsroman,* does depict a boy's growth in consciousness, but, in so doing, seeks to arouse the reader's consciousness as well. Wright knew well, of course, that those responsible for inflicting crimes upon blacks in the South were not likely to be moved to correct their abuses unless they could somehow be forced to see themselves not only as the perpetrators of those crimes but as their victims as well. In *Black Boy* and in Wright's other works, blacks commit acts of violence against whites, not necessarily out of any sense of vengeance but, rather, out of desperation and fear. Thus, Wright launches what amounts to a double-barrelled attack upon racial brutality in the South. Those white Southerners who would not be aroused by his portrayal of a boy's difficult journey would surely be stirred when their own safety appeared to be at stake.

Wright's sense of community, however, did not make him blind to the shortcomings of his own people. In *Black Boy* he is critical of those blacks who passively accept the inferior roles assigned to them by the stewards of the Southern caste system. He is keenly aware that "wearing the mask," even when such action appears expedient, means a sacrifice of one's dignity and self-respect. He laments, moreover, the fact that the blacks about him seem to be cut off from the spirit of Western culture, that they live in the "area of No Man's Land." But at the moment when Wright seems to be most convinced of the "barrenness of black life," one recognizes his own indebtedness to his folk tradition for his most essential subject matter and for the tones, images, and rhythms that constitute his style. For though he recognized the provinciality of Southern black life, he also realized that here, in the very heart of the Southern darkness, must be the starting point of his own quest for selfhood. (pp. 415-33)

> *John O. Hodges, "An Apprenticeship to Life and Art: Narrative Design in Wright's 'Black Boy'," in CLA Journal, Vol. XXVIII, No. 4, June, 1985, pp. 415-33.*

Timothy Dow Adams   (essay date September 1985)

[*In the following essay, Adams addresses the problem of authenticity in* Black Boy, *focusing on Wright's presumed "pattern of misrepresentation."*]

Since the publication of **Black Boy** in 1945, reactions to its authenticity have been curiously contradictory, often mutually exclusive. For many readers the book is particularly honest, sincere, open, convincing and accurate. But for others **Black Boy** leaves a feeling of inauthenticity, a sense that the story or its author is not to be trusted. These conflicting reactions are best illustrated by the following representative observations by Ralph White and W.E.B. DuBois. White, a psychologist, identified "ruthless honesty" as "the outstanding quality which made the book not only moving but also intellectually satisfying" [in "*Black Boy:* A Value Analysis," *Journal of Abnormal and Social Psychology*, Vol. 42, 1947]. But DuBois noted that while "nothing that Richard Wright says is in itself unbelievable or impossible; it is the total picture that is not convincing." Attempting to reconcile these opposing views, I wish to argue that both sides are correct, that the book is one of the most truthful accounts of the black experience in America, even though the protagonist's story often does not ring true, and that this inability to tell the truth is Wright's major metaphor of self. A repeated pattern of misrepresentation becomes the author's way of making us believe that his personality, his family, his race—his whole childhood and youth—conspired to prevent him from hearing the truth, speaking the truth, or even being believed unless he lied.

In terms of truth, we expect from an autobiography obedience to the conventions of the genre which hold that the story being presented is a significant part of a person's life, written in retrospect by the subject of the story, who purports to believe that he or she is telling a truthful version of the past. The reader expects, even enjoys, detecting misrepresentations, odd emphasis, telling omissions, and over and under determination, and will willingly overlook factual errors, but for most readers an autobiography is dishonest if the author does not seem to be trying to tell the

overall truth. I agree with A.O.J. Cockshut's assertion [in *The Art of Autobiography in 19th and 20th Century England*] that "the simple truth of accurate record of facts is clearly important; but as a rule this is overshadowed by other kinds. At the same time we are judging the autobiographer's central idea" which must have "its own momentous dignity" and must be "truly felt as working through the contingent and everyday." For most contemporary readers worries about **Black Boy**'s trustworthiness stemmed from questions of genre: although the book was clearly not called "The Autobiography of Richard Wright," its subtitle—"A Record of Childhood and Youth"—did suggest autobiography. The following descriptions of **Black Boy** reflect the confusion of readers: biography, autobiographical story, fictionalized biography, a masterpiece of romanced facts, a sort-of-autobiography, pseudo-autobiography, part fiction/part truth, autobiography with the quality of fiction, and case history.

Some of these generic confusions were generated by Wright's statements about his creation; he meant the work to be collective autobiography, a personalized record of countless black Americans growing up with a personal history of hunger, deprivation, and constant racism. He also remarked that he decided to write his life story after giving an autobiographical talk to a racially mixed audience at Fisk University in Nashville in 1943. After the talk, he noted that he "had accidentally blundered into the secret black, hidden core of race relations in the United States. That core is this: nobody is ever expected to speak honestly about the problem. . . . And I learned that when the truth was plowed up in their faces, they shook and trembled and didn't know what to do." A year later [in *The Unfinished Quest of Richard Wright*], Wright used the same metaphor when he wrote "the hardest truth to me to plow up was in my own life." But speaking honestly about a racism endemic throughout America was more complicated, both for author and for reader, than Wright could have known, and, for many, a more delicate instrument than a plow was needed for harvesting the past. Using truthfulness as his watchword, Wright began **Black Boy** as an attempt to set the record straight, including his personal one, which already consisted of a number of "biographies of the author" or "notes on contributors" written by himself in the third person, sometimes with exaggerated accounts of his youth. In several interviews, as well as in **"The Ethics of Living Jim Crow,"** an autobiographical sketch published originally in *American Stuff: WPA Writers' Anthology* in 1937, Wright had already given an incorrect birth date, and begun to establish a history overemphasizing the negative aspects of his early life.

Most revelatory about the conflict between his intentions and the actual writing of his personal narrative is the following observation from a newspaper article called **"The Birth of Black Boy"** [quoted in the "Afterword" to *American Hunger*]:

> The real hard terror of writing like this came when I found that writing of one's life was vastly different from speaking of it. I was rendering a close and emotionally connected account of my experience and the ease I had had in speaking

from notes at Fisk would not come again. I found that to tell the truth is the hardest thing on earth, harder than fighting in a war, harder than taking part in a revolution. If you try it, you will find that at times sweat will break upon you. You will find that even if you succeed in discounting the attitudes of others to you and your life, you must wrestle with yourself most of all, fight with yourself; for there will surge up in you a strong desire to alter facts, to dress up your feelings. You'll find that there are many things that you don't want to admit about yourself and others. As your record shapes itself an awed wonder haunts you. And yet there is no more exciting an adventure than trying to be honest in this way. The clean, strong feeling that sweeps you when you've done it makes you know that.

Although Wright seemed unsure of his book's generic identity, he never referred to *Black Boy* as an autobiography. His original title, *American Hunger,* later used for his life story after leaving Memphis for Chicago, came after he had rejected *The Empty Box, Days of Famine, The Empty Houses, The Assassin, Bread and Water,* and *Black Confession,* all of which sound like titles for novels. When his literary agent suggested the subtitle "The Biography of a Courageous Negro," Wright responded with "The Biography of An American Negro," then with eight other possibilities including "Coming of Age in the Black South," "A Record in Anguish," "A Study in Anguish," and "A Chronicle of Anxiety," which indicate his feeling that the book he had written was less personal, more documentary—a study, a record, a chronicle or even a biography—than autobiography. Constance Webb [in her *Richard Wright: A Biography*] reports that Wright was uneasy with the word *autobiography,* both because of "an inner distaste for revealing in first person instead of through a fictitious character the dread and fear and anguished self-questioning of his life" and because he realized he would write his story using "portions of his own childhood, stories told him by friends, things he had observed happening to others" and fictional techniques.

Although some readers see Wright as unsuccessful in his struggle neither "to alter facts" nor to "dress up feelings," the book's tendency to intermix fiction and fact is clearly part of both Wright's personal literary history and the Afro-American literary tradition in which he was writing. The form of *Black Boy* partly imitates the traditional slave narrative, a literary type which allowed for a high degree of fictionality in the cause of abolition. A number of major works of literature by black Americans, such as DuBois' *The Souls of Black Folks,* Toomer's *Cane,* and Johnson's *The Autobiography of an Ex-Coloured Man,* featured mixtures of genres, and Wright, simultaneously a poet, novelist, essayist, journalist, playwright, and actor, often used the same material in different genres. For example, **"The Ethics of Living Jim Crow,"** first an essay, later appeared attached to the stories of *Uncle Tom's Children,* one of which, **"Bright and Morning Star,"** is told in *Black Boy* as a tale which held the protagonist in thrall, even though he "did not know if the story was factually true or not." When "black boy" says that the story is emotionally true, he reflects exactly the kind of truth he wants his readers to respond to in *Black Boy.* Several episodes re-

counted in **"The Ethics of Living Jim Crow"** are told in significantly different ways in *Black Boy,* and portions of *Eight Men* were once planned as part of that book. Some of the characters in *Black Boy* have been given fictional names, while Bigger Thomas, the central character in *Native Son,* was the real name of one of Wright's acquaintances. That he used real names in fiction and fictional names in non-fiction is typical of Richard Wright who further confounded the usual distinctions between author and persona by playing the role of Bigger Thomas in the film version of *Native Son.*

Richard Wright makes clear that *Black Boy* is not meant as a traditional autobiography by presenting much of the story in the form of dialogue marked with quotation marks, which suggests the unusual degree of fiction within his factual story. Although critics often point to Wright's first novel, *Native Son* (1940), as the other half of *Black Boy,* another model for this autobiographical work was his just-completed *Twelve Million Black Voices: A Folk History of the American Negro in The United States* (1941). Writing *Black Boy* in the spirit of folk history seemed a reasonable thing to do, and Wright apparently saw no hypocrisy in omitting personal details which did not contribute to what he was simultaneously thinking of as his own story and the story of millions of others. Wright's claim to be composing the autobiography of a generic black child is reinforced by the narrator's particular reaction to racism: "The things that influenced my conduct as a Negro did not have to happen to me directly; I needed but to hear of them to feel their full effects in the deepest layers of my consciousness."

Roy Pascal is correct in asserting that "where a lie is the result of a calculated intention to appear right or important, danger is done to autobiographical truth" and that "the most frequent cause of failure in autobiography is an untruthfulness which arises from the desire to appear admirable" [*Design and Truth in Autobiography*]. However, most of the omission in *Black Boy* is designed not to make the persona appear admirable, but to make Richard Wright into "black boy," to underplay his own family's middle-class ways and more positive values. He does not mention that his mother was a successful school teacher and that many of his friends were children of college faculty members; he omits most of his father's family background, and his own sexual experiences. Reactions from sensitive Southern whites are mainly left out, including those of the Wall family to whom, we learn from Michel Fabre's biography [*The Unfinished Quest of Richard Wright*] "he sometimes submitted his problems and plans . . . and soon considered their house a second home where he met with more understanding than from his own family."

In addition to omissions, name changes, poetic interludes, and extensive dialogue, *Black Boy* is replete with questionable events that biographical research has revealed to be exaggerated, inaccurate, mistaken, or invented. Fabre's section dealing with the *Black Boy* years is characterized by constant disclaimers about the factuality of the story. Some omissions can be explained because the urbane ex-Communist who began *Black Boy* "wanted to see himself as a child of the proletariat" though "in reality he attached greater importance to the honorable position of his grandparents in their town than he did to his peasant background." While these distortions are acceptable to many, especially in light of Wright's intention of using his life to show the effects of racism, there are numerous other manipulations less acceptable because more self-serving.

Most of these incidents are relatively minor, and so doubts seem unimportant; however, the misrepresentations in two of the book's most important episodes—the high school graduation speech and the story of Uncle Hoskins and the Mississippi River—might be less acceptable. "Black boy's" refusal to deliver the principal's graduation speech rather than his own is apparently based on truth, but the version in *Black Boy* leaves out the important fact that Wright rewrote his speech, cutting out more volatile passages as a compromise. The story of Uncle Hoskins does not ring true, for how could a boy whose life had been to that point so violent, be scared of his uncle's relatively harmless trick? One reason the tale feels false is that the story, complete with revelations about Uncle Hoskins such as "I never trusted him after that. Whenever I saw his face the memory of my terror upon the river would come back, vivid and strong, and it stood as a barrier between us," actually happened to Ralph Ellison who told it to Wright.

For many critics, including Edward Margolies [in *The Art of Richard Wright*], these deliberate manipulations reduce *Black Boy*'s authenticity as autobiography because they set up doubts about everything, the same doubts that resonate through the remarks of black writers from DuBois to Baldwin to David Bradley, all of whom have persisted in taking *Black Boy*'s protagonist to be Richard Wright. But "Richard Wright is not the same person as the hero of that book, not the same as 'I' or 'Richard' or the 'Black boy', not by several light years," argues James Olney, who refers to the book's chief character as "black boy" [in his *Autobiography: Essays Theoretical and Critical*], explaining that "by means of an encompassing and creative memory, Richard Wright imagines it all, and he is as much the creator of the figure that he calls 'Richard' as he is of the figure that, in *Native Son*, he calls 'Bigger.'" Olney's idea that the central figure be treated as a single person referred to as "black boy," a literary character representing both the actual author as a child and the adult author—the famous writer imagining himself as representative of inarticulate black children—is finally convincing. That seems to be what Richard Wright meant to do, said he had done, and what he did.

Of course he was working in what we now see as dangerous areas, as recent literary history has shown. Black journalist Janet Cooke was labelled a liar, fired from the *Washington Post*, and relieved of her Pulitzer Prize for inventing a black boy in a series of articles on drug use; Clifford Irving was imprisoned for writing what he presented as Howard Hughes's autobiography; and Alastair Reid has recently been castigated for "cleaning up quotations," condensing, inventing personae and locations, and in general using new journalistic techniques in the *New Yorker*. But Wright's accomplishment in *Black Boy* is different,

first because he announces his intentions—in authorial statements external to the text, and by title, quotation marks, use of symbolic and imagistic description, and well-organized plot—and second because he is manipulating his own story, not someone else's. Ellison's review-essay on *Black Boy*, "Richard Wright's Blues," begins with the refrain, "If anybody ask you/ who sing this song,/ Say it was ole [Black Boy]/ done been here and gone," a blues singer's signature formula that clarifies two important facts about the book. First, the protagonist is a literary character named "Black Boy" who bears the same similarity to Richard Wright as the character Leadbelly, for example, does to the blues singer Huddie Ledbetter who sang about himself so often. Second, Ellison's refrain forewarned that the identity of the protagonist would be called into question by critics who would wonder who the elusive hero was and where he went. Unlike Ellison, who sees *Black Boy* as a talking blues, it is for me a be-bop jazz performance in which Wright uses his life as the melody on which he could improvise.

Part of the complication about lying in *Black Boy*—who is lying and to whom—derives from the interplay between audiences, the resonances between the actual audience, the authorial audience, and the narrative audience, to use Peter Rabinowitz's terms. The actual audience is the group of real humans holding *Black Boy* in their hands as they read. The authorial audience is the group Wright imagined himself addressing. The narrative audience, which Gerald Prince calls the narratee (*narrataire*), is the group of people to whom the narrator is speaking. Sorting out these audiences is particularly confusing but interesting in *Black Boy* because the book is autobiographical and therefore the relation between author and narrator is more complicated than in much fiction, and because both author and narrator are black. The important questions about the race, sex, and assumptions of the reader in the text are difficult to answer absolutely, but it seems clear that Richard Wright relates to the authorial audience as "black boy" does to the narrative audience. Because Wright's actual audience at Fisk University was racially mixed, and because he cited his speaking there as the specific impetus for writing the book, it is logical to assume that the authorial audience is composed of both black and white members. Because the book is dedicated to "ELLEN and JULIA," Wright's white wife and interracial daughter, it seems reasonable to assume that he thought of his authorial audience as being both male and female, black girls as well as black boys.

The question of the narrative audience is more complex, but I believe that the readers inscribed in and by the text, the audience to whom "black boy" is speaking, is also racially mixed. This audience is in one sense made up of all of the people described in the book, black and white, who failed to understand the narrator during his lifetime. At other times the narrator is addressing himself only to a white audience, as in the following presentation of school-boy boasting, glossed for the white reader:

> "Man, you reckon these white folks is ever gonna change?" Timid, questioning hope.

"Hell, no! They just born that way." Rejecting hope for fear that it could never come true.

"Shucks, man. I'm going north when I get grown." Rebelling against futile hope and embracing flight.

"A colored man's all right up north." Justifying flight.

Although the authorial audience includes males and females, the narrative audience seems limited to males, as the narrator makes plain in such statements as "It was degrading to play with girls and in our talk we relegated them to a remote island of life."

These distinctions between audiences are important because the actual reader's attempt to react to the book properly, that is in the right spirit, is somewhat like the narrator's attempts to react properly to the different values in the black and white worlds. Lying to white people is one thing, lying to blacks another. And, as Wright discovered after his speech in Nashville, telling the truth to a mixed audience is more dangerous than separating the truth into white and black versions. When *Black Boy*'s authorial and narrative audiences converge, the reader is the least likely to question the authenticity of the story. As the two audiences move apart, the reader begins to feel uneasy, partly because of trying to decide which audience to join.

Many critical objections to *Black Boy*'s methods of getting at the truth come from those who instinctly feel something strange about the work, not so much in its generic confusions, as in its tone and in what Albert Stone senses when he writes [in *Autobiographical Occasions and Original Acts*] that "a proud and secret self presides over the text, covertly revealing itself through event, style, and metaphor." When confronted with *Black Boy*'s deviations from absolute biographical truth, less sophisticated readers, such as students, are seldom bothered. They sense that discrepancies uncovered by reading other texts have little bearing on the truth of the text at hand. Nevertheless, the same students often respond unfavourably to what they perceive as inauthenticity arising from within *Black Boy*. And part of their dislike of and distrust for "black boy" grows from the sense of the times that "narrative past . . . has lost its authenticating power," as Lionel Trilling observes [in *Sincerity and Authenticity*]. "Far from being an authenticating agent, indeed, it has become the very type of inauthenticity." Caring little about the crossing of generic boundaries, students are disturbed by the idea that "life is susceptible of comprehension and thus of management," as Trilling further remarks. In short, they are uncomfortable with *Black Boy*, not because it is not true, but because for them it does not ring true. They experience what Barrett Mandel calls "dis-ease with the autobiography. It seems as if the author is lying (not, please, writing fiction), although readers cannot always easily put their finger on the lie" [in Olney's *Autobiography*].

The lying they sense centres on these three concerns: "black boy" is never wrong, is falsely naive, and is melodramatic, three characteristics of what Mandel refers to as autobiography in which "the ratification is negative—

the light of now shines on the illusion the ego puts forth and reveals it as false." Mandel believes that most autobiographers are basically honest, but those who are not give themselves away through tone: "Since the ego is in conflict with the truth, the reader very often gets that message. The author has created an illusion of an illusion. . . . The tone is forever slipping away from the content, giving itself away." While Mandel does not include *Black Boy* in the category of dishonest autobiographies, instead citing it as a typical reworking of the past, many critics have echoed my students' concerns. For example, Robert Stepto finds fault with two early incidents in which "black boy" insists on the literal meaning of words: when he pretends to believe his father's injunction to kill a noisy kitten, and when he refuses ninety-seven cents for his dog because he wants a dollar. "The fact remains that *Black Boy* requires its readers to admire Wright's persona's remarkable and unassailable innocence in certain major episodes, and to condone his exploitation of that innocence in others," writes Stepto [in his *From Behind the Veil*]. "This, I think, is a poorly tailored seam, if not precisely a flaw, in *Black Boy*'s narrative strategy." Rather than seeing these episodes, and others like them, as examples of bad faith or as rough edges in the narrative fabric, I see them as deliberate renderings of the terrible dilemma of black boys, and their need to dissemble about everything, especially about the nature of their naiveté. Wright's persona is confessing, not boasting. His family life and his difficulty with hypocrisy made lying at once a constant requirement for survival, and a nearly impossible performance, especially for a poor liar whose tone gives him away.

The inability to lie properly, exhibited in countless scenes, is "black boy's" major problem in adjusting to black/white relations in his youth. Asked by a potential white employer if he steals, "black boy" is incredulous: "Lady, if I was a thief, I'd never tell anybody," he replies. *Black Boy* is filled with episodes in which its hero is unable to lie, forced to lie, caught between conflicting lies, not believed unless he lies. Poorly constructed lies are appropriate metaphors to portray a boy whose efforts to set the record straight are as frustrated as his grandfather's attempts to claim a Navy pension, which is thwarted by bureaucratic error for his whole life. Falsehoods are an apt metaphor for the speech of a boy who distrusts everyone, himself included.

Black Boy's opening, in which Wright describes how his four-year old self burnt his grandmother's house out of boredom and experimentation, is cited by virtually every commentator as an allegory for the fear, rebellion, anxiety, and need for freedom of the hero, as well as for the motifs of fire, hunger, and underground retreat. After the fire, which destroys more than half of the house, the child delivers this recollection:

> I was lashed so hard and long that I lost consciousness. I was beaten out of my senses and later I found myself in bed, screaming, determined to run away. . . . I was lost in a fog of fear. A doctor was called—I was afterward told—and he ordered that I be kept abed, that I be kept quiet, that my very life depended upon it. . . . Whenever I tried to sleep I would see

huge wobbly white bags, like the full udders of cows, suspended from the ceiling above me. Later, as I grew worse, I could see the bags in the daytime with my eyes open and I was gripped by the fear that they were going to fall and drench me with some horrible liquid. . . . Time finally bore me away from the dangerous bags and I got well. But for a long time I was chastened whenever I remembered that my mother had come close to killing me.

Albert Stone perceptively notes that the last line of this passage represents "a striking reversal." "Where the reader expects a confession that the boy has tried (although inadvertently or unconsciously) to attack his own family, one finds the opposite. Such heavy rationalization clearly demands examination." The adult autobiographer is not justifying setting houses on fire; rather he is trying to show graphically and suddenly how distrustful a child of four had already become. The episode does not ring true because it is not necessarily literally true. In fact Wright used a contradictory description in **"The Ethics of Living Jim Crow,"** written eight years earlier. Describing a cinder fight between white and black children, he claims he was cut by a broken milk bottle, rushed to the hospital by a kind neighbour, and later beaten by his mother until he "had a fever of one hundred and two. . . . All that night I was delirious and could not sleep. Each time I closed my eyes I saw monstrous white faces suspended from the ceiling, leering at me." The cinder fight is retold in a later section of **Black Boy,** though in this version the hero's mother takes him to the doctor, and beats him less severely.

Like Nate Shaw in Theodore Rosengarten's National Book Award winning *All God's Dangers,* who distinguishes between stories "told for truth" and those "told to entertain," or the old time musician, Lily May Ledford, in Ellesa Clay High's *Past Titan Rock: Journeys Into An Appalachian Valley,* who says "I never tell a story the same way twice, but I tell the truth," Richard Wright has borrowed the rhetoric of the oral historian in consciously fictionalizing the story of the burning house and his subsequent punishment, while sending the reader signals that he has done so. He wants the reader to feel that there is something not quite right about the whole scene. That the three-year old brother can see the folly of playing with fire when the four-year old "black boy" cannot, that the reasons for setting the fire are as spurious as the explanation—"I had just wanted to see how the curtains would look when they burned"—that the nightmarish description of white bags filled with foul liquid are obviously meant to be symbolic, and finally that the boy is chastened, not by his actions, but by the thought that his mother had come close to killing him—all these signals are meant to paint a truthful picture of a boy who later came to hold "a conviction that the meaning of living came only when one was struggling to wring a meaning out of meaningless suffering." The opening scene suggests the whole atmosphere of the book, a desperate fear of meaningless visitations of violence without context, a life of deliberate misrepresentations of the truth and complete distrust of all people, a world in which "each event spoke with a cryptic tongue." Throughout **Black Boy** Wright presents a lonely figure whose life does not ring true because "that's

the way things were between whites and blacks in the South; many of the most important things were never openly said; they were understated and left to seep through to one," so that all actions are tempered by a subtext, though obvious to everyone, a strategy which the author claimed to have discovered when he delivered his Fisk University oration.

Whenever the narrator questions his mother about racial relationships, she is defensive and evasive. "I knew there was something my mother was holding back," he notes. "She was not concealing facts, but feelings, attitudes, convictions which she did not want me to know," a misrepresentation which disturbs "black boy" who later says "my personality was lopsided; my knowledge of feeling was far greater than my knowledge of fact." While he holds back or conceals facts, he is usually straightforward about emotional feelings, even though he can say "the safety of my life in the South depended upon how well I concealed from all whites what I felt." Worrying less about factual truth, Wright was determined to stress the emotional truth of Southern life to counteract the stereotypical myths shown in the song which prefaced *Uncle Tom's Children*: "Is it true what they say about Dixie? Does the sun really shine all the time?"

One of the particular ironies of **Black Boy** is that the narrator's constant lying is emblematic of the truth that all black boys were required not only to lie, but to lie about their lying. In the boxing match between "black boy" and a co-worker, this pattern is played out almost mathematically. The two black boys are coerced into a fight they both know is false, based on lies that are obvious to all. Much of the shamefulness of the whole situation is that they are forced to pretend that they are neither aware that the situation is false, nor that they know the whites know they know. These paradoxes are clearly analyzed in Roger Rosenblatt's essay "Black Autobiography: Life as the Death Weapon" [published in Olney's *Autobiography*]:

> They had been goaded into a false and illogical act that somehow became logical and true. At the end of their fight, Wright and Harrison *did* hold a grudge against each other, just as their white supervisors had initially contended. The madness of the situation did not reside in the hysteria of the onlookers, nor even in the confusion of defeat and victory or of power and impotency on the parts of the boxers. It resided in the fact that a lie became the truth and that two people who had thought they had known what the truth was wound up living the lie.

Although personal and institutional racism was everywhere evident, Southern whites generally maintained that they treated blacks more humanely than did Northern whites, that they understood blacks and knew how to deal with them, and that they were friendly with blacks (as evidenced by their calling them by their first names), all of which blacks were supposed to pretend they believed. Whites deliberately set up situations where blacks were forced to steal, and not only did they like to be stolen from, they forced blacks to lie by repeatedly asking them if they were thieves. "Whites placed a premium upon black deceit; they encouraged irresponsibility; and their rewards were bestowed upon us blacks in the degree that we could make them feel safe and superior," notes the narrator. When "black boy" forgets to call a white co-worker named Pease "Mister," he is caught in a trap from which the usual escape is "a nervous cryptic smile." The boy's attempt to lie his way out of the situation fails, despite his ingenuity in turning the false accusation into an ambiguous apology:

> If I had said: No, sir, Mr. Pease, I never called you *Pease,* I would by inference have been calling Reynolds a liar; and if I had said: Yes, sir, Mr. Pease, I called you *Pease,* I would have been pleading guilty to the worst insult that a Negro can offer to a southern white man. I stood trying to think of a neutral course that would resolve this quickly risen nightmare. . . .
>
> "I don't remember calling you *Pease,* Mr. Pease," I said cautiously, "And if I did, I sure didn't mean . . ."
>
> "You black sonofabitch! You called me *Pease,* then!" he spat, rising and slapping me till I bent sideways over a bench.

Episodes like this make clear that inability to tell the truth does not make black boys into liars. Instead the frequent descriptions of the protagonist as a prevaricator reveal to white readers the way blacks used lies to express truths, used, for example, the word "nigger" to mean one thing to white listeners, another to black. The elaborate system of signifying, of using words exactly the opposite of white usage (bad for good / cool for hot), of wearing the mask to cover emotions, of the lies behind black children's game of dozens—all of these are behind the motif of lying in *Black Boy.* Wright's metaphoric use of lying is made more complex by his awareness that a history of misrepresentation of true feelings made it difficult for black people to be certain when they were merely dissembling for protection, when they were lying to each other, or to themselves. "There are some elusive, profound, recondite things that men find hard to say to other men," muses "black boy," "but with the Negro it is the little things of life that become hard to say, for these tiny items shape his destiny." What sets him apart from his contemporaries is his difficulty with the lying they find so easy: "In my dealing with whites I was conscious of the entirety of my relations with them, and they were conscious only of what was happening at a given moment. I had to keep remembering what others took for granted; I had to think out what others felt."

The actual audience must narrow the gap between the narrative and authorial audience; the reader of *Black Boy* must strive to be like the narrator of *Black Boy,* must keep what is happening at a particular moment and the entire history of black/white relations—the content and the context—together in his or her mind. Wright's context includes the need to speak simultaneously as an adult and as a child, to remove everything from his story that, even if it happened to be true, would allow white readers to maintain their distorted stereotype of Southern blacks. He was searching for a way to confess his personal history of lying, forced on him by his childhood, while still demon-

strating that he could be trusted by both black and white. His solution is what Maya Angelou calls "African-bush secretiveness":

> "If you ask a Negro where he's been, he'll tell you where he's going." To understand this important information, it is necessary to know who uses this tactic and on whom it works. If an unaware person is told a part of the truth (it is imperative that the answer embody truth), he is satisfied that his query has been answered. If an aware person (one who himself uses the strategem) is given an answer which is truthful but bears only slightly if at all on the question, he knows that the information he seeks is of a private nature and will not be handed to him willingly [*I Know Why the Caged Bird Sings*].

What makes *Black Boy* compelling is its ability to remain autobiography despite its obvious subordination of historicity. Although a reader may not be aware of the complexities of "black boy's" "African-bush" slanting of truth, or know about the book's fictionalizing, there is, nevertheless, something unmistakably autobiographical about *Black Boy* that convinces even the unaware. What makes this true is the way the author signifies his lying through rhetoric, appeals in writing to both black and white, as he was unable to do in his speech at Nashville. One of the patterns of the book's lies involves just such a distinction between speaking and writing.

Wright's claim to be speaking for the millions of inarticulate children of the South is in an ironic way reinforced by the constant difficulty the narrator has with the spoken as opposed to the printed word. Although it is a love of literature that saves "black boy," he is constantly threatened by speaking. Often out of synchronization, he speaks when he should be quiet, or is unable to utter a word when questioned; his words slip unaware from his mouth, flow out against his will. But just as often he is totally paralyzed, unable to produce a phrase. In answer to his early questioning—"What on earth was the matter with me . . . every word and gesture I made seemed to provoke hostility?"—the narrator answers, toward the end of the book, "I knew what was wrong with me, but I could not correct it. The words and actions of white people were baffling signs to me."

The problem with the spoken word begins with the narrator's killing the kitten because of the pretence of not reading his father's command as figurative, and continues with the melodramatic description of himself begging drinks as a six-year-old child, memorizing obscenities taught to him in a bar. Later he learns "all the four-letter words describing physiological and sex functions," and yet claims to be astonished, while being bathed by his grandmother, at her reaction to his command: " 'When you get through, kiss back there,' I said, the words rolling softly but unpremeditatedly." Wishing to recall those words, though only vaguely understanding why he is once again being punished so severely, "black boy" says "none of the obscene words I had learned at school in Memphis had dealt with perversions of any sort, although I might have learned the words while loitering drunkenly in saloons." This explanation is weak and unconvincing, given his earlier description of himself and other children stationing themselves for hours at the bottom of a series of outdoor toilets, observing the anatomies of their neighbours.

Forced to declare his belief in God by his family of Seventh Day Adventists, "black boy" mis-speaks again and again. " 'I don't want to hurt God's feelings either,' I said, the words slipping irreverently from my lips before I was aware of their full meaning." Trying to keep his grandmother from questioning him about religion, he hits upon the strategy of likening himself to Jacob, arguing that he would believe in God if he ever saw an angel. Although this plan was imagined with the purpose of "salving . . . Granny's frustrated feelings toward him," the result is that his words are misconstrued. His grandmother thinks he *has* seen an angel, and "black boy" once again has "unwittingly committed an obscene act." His explanation is another example of his difficulty in speaking as others did: "I must have spoken more loudly and harshly than was called for."

Called before a teacher to explain a schoolyard fight with two bullies, the protagonist says, "You're lying!," which causes the teacher to reply, "Don't use that language in here," even though he is right. Once again daydreaming, the narrator interrupts his family's "arguing some obscure point of religious doctrine" with a remark which he says "must have sounded reekingly blasphemous." This time his grandmother is in bed for six weeks, her back wrenched in attempting to slap her grandson for his statements. Again "black boy" is an innocent victim, beaten for not allowing his grandmother to slap him—his physical, like his verbal skills, out of rhythm with his family. He is slapped for asking his grandmother, on a later occasion, what his dying grandfather's last words were, and for replying to the question "What time have you?" with "If it's a little slow or fast, it's not far wrong." "Black boy's" poor sense of timing makes him feel unreal, as if he "had been slapped out of the human race," makes him resemble Ellison's invisible man who believes that his condition "gives one a slightly different sense of time, you're never quite on the beat. Sometimes you're ahead and sometimes behind. Instead of the swift and imperceptible flowing of time, you are aware of its nodes, those points where time stands still or from which it leaps ahead." Ellison's words, which are also suggestive of the sense of time essential to jazz, describe the narrator who is out of phase with everyone until he can control the timing of his life through the syncopated rhythms of *Black Boy.*

In light of the repeated pattern—swift physical reprisal delivered to the totally astonished narrator for speaking out of turn—it is surprising to read the following justification for his resorting to threatening his Aunt with a knife: "I had often been painfully beaten, but almost always I had felt that the beatings were somehow right and sensible, that I was in the wrong." This confession sounds false because "black boy" never seems to admit that he is blameworthy for anything. "Nowhere in the book are Wright's actions and thoughts reprehensible," objects Edward Margolies [in *The Art of Richard Wright*], echoing a number of others. Robert Felgar makes a similar point when he remarks that "the reader does tire of his persis-

tent self-pity and self-aggrandizement." [Patsy Graves in *Opportunity,* July 1945] argues that "the simple law of averages would prevent any one boy from getting into as many situations as we have related in this story, and one senses with regret, that it is hard to know where biography leaves off and fiction begins." What these critics see as foolish self-pity is most apparent in the heavily melodramatic description of the familiar playground game of crack-the-whip, which the narrator describes in life or death terms: "They played a wildcat game called popping-the-whip, a seemingly innocent diversion whose excitement came only in spurts, but spurts that could hurl one to the edge of death itself. . . . The whip grew taut as human flesh and bone could bear and I felt that my arm was being torn from its socket."

Here the author is depicting a children's game using the kind of rhetoric usually reserved for a slave narrative—a cruel overseer whipping a runaway slave "to the edge of death." Wright's words are not self-pitying; instead he is presenting a naive youth who was never good at lying or exaggerating. The misrepresentation is so obvious that only a particularly inept liar would attempt it, a child who did not want to be good at lying. Only an outsider such as "black boy" to the established systems of lying by both races, a representative of the many black adolescents then coming of age—what Wright hoped would be a new generation of the children of Uncle Tom, no longer willing to accept the old lie that the best way to fight racism was to lie through both omission and commission—could fail to distinguish between melodrama and genuine oppression, and to be surprised at the power of his words.

Black Boy should not be read as historical truth which strives to report those incontrovertible facts that can be somehow corroborated, but as narrative truth, which psychiatrist Donald Spence defines [in *Narrative Truth and Historical Truth*] as "the criterion we use to decide when a certain experience has been captured to our satisfaction; it depends on continuity and closure and the extent to which the fit of the pieces takes on an aesthetic finality." The story that Richard Wright creates in *Black Boy,* whatever its value as an exact historical record, is important both in telling us how the author remembers life in the pre-Depression South and in showing us what kind of person the author was to have written his story as he did. Although he is often deliberately false to historical truth, he seldom deviates from narrative truth. "Consistent misrepresentation of oneself is not easy," writes Roy Pascal, and in *Black Boy* Wright has made both the horrifying dramatic and the ordinary events of his life fit into a pattern, shaped by a consistent, metaphoric use of lying. "Interpretations are persuasive," argues Donald Spence, "not because of their evidential value but because of their rhetorical appeal; conviction emerges because the fit is good, not because we have necessarily made contact with the past."

In *Black Boy* Wright creates a version of himself whose metaphor for survival and for sustenance is falsehood. But the multiple lies of the narrator, like the fibs of children trying to avoid what they see as irrational punishment, are palpably obvious. They are not meant to deceive; they are deliberately embarrassing in their transparency. For the protagonist, whose home life was so warped that only when he lied could he be believed, Alfred Kazin's dictum—"One writes to make a home for oneself, on paper"—is particularly true. The author's manipulations of genre and his metaphoric lies produced a book about which DuBois's assessment was, in my judgment, exactly backward: although much of what Wright wrote is not literally true, the total picture is ultimately convincing, taken in context. For all his lying, "black boy's" essential drive is for truth, and his constant revelation of how often he was forced to lie should be judged according to the standard set forth by Marcel Eck in *Lies and Truth:* "We will be judged not on whether we possess or do not possess the truth but on whether or not we sought and loved it." (pp. 172-87)

> *Timothy Dow Adams, "I Do Believe Him Though I Know He Lies: Lying as Genre and Metaphor in Richard Wright's 'Black Boy',"* in Prose Studies, *Vol. 8, No. 2, September, 1985, pp. 172-87.*

FURTHER READING

Biography

Brignano, Russell Carl. *Richard Wright: An Introduction to the Man and His Works.* Pittsburgh: University of Pittsburgh Press, 1970, 202 p.
> Biographical and critical study examining the ideological basis of Wright's works.

Fabre, Michel. *The Unfinished Quest of Richard Wright.* Translated by Isabel Barzun. New York: William Morrow, 1973, 652 p.
> Definitive biography.

Criticism

Butler, Robert J. "The Quest for Pure Motion in Richard Wright's *Black Boy.*" *MELUS* 10, No. 3 (Fall 1983): 5-17.
> Discusses the oppositional themes of motion and stasis in *Black Boy.*

Butterfield, Stephen. "Richard Wright." In his *Black Autobiography in America,* pp. 115-79. Amherst: University of Massachusetts Press, 1974.
> Demonstrates that *Black Boy* is a more accomplished work than earlier slave narratives because "it encompasses history and politics *through* the individual experience of the boy Richard, without ever leaving his personal story."

Cobb, Nina Kressner. "Richard Wright: Individualism Reconsidered." *CLA Journal* XXI, No. 3 (March 1978): 335-54.

Studies Wright's search for individuality and ultimate disillusionment as reflected in *Black Boy.*

Delbanco, Andrew. "An American Hunger." *The New Republic* 206, No. 13 (30 March 1992): 28-30, 32-3.
> Discusses the recent discovery of galley proofs containing passages originally deleted from *Black Boy* and other works by Wright.

Gaskill, Gayle. "The Effect of Black/White Imagery in Richard Wright's *Black Boy.*" *Negro American Literature Forum* 7, No. 2 (Summer 1973): 46-8.
> Examines Wright's use of color symbolism in *Black Boy.*

Hakutani, Yoshinobu. "Creations of the Self in Richard Wright's *Black Boy.*" *Black American Literature Forum* 19, No. 2 (Summer 1985): 70-5.
> Asserts that while *Black Boy* is chiefly autobiographical, the work is also a sociological study on the living conditions of blacks in the South.

Mackethan, Lucinda H. "*Black Boy* and *Ex-Coloured Man:* Version and Inversion of the Slave Narrator's Quest for Voice." *CLA Journal* XXXII, No. 2 (December 1988): 123-47.
> Explores the influence of the slave narrative on *Black Boy* and James Weldon Johnson's *Autobiography of an Ex-Coloured Man.*

McCarthy, Mary. "Portrait of a Typical Negro?" *The New Leader* XXVIII, No. 25 (23 June 1945): 10.
> Questions whether Wright's narrator in *Black Boy* represents the typical black experience.

Mechling, Jay. "The Failure of Folklore in Richard Wright's *Black Boy.*" *The Journal of American Folklore* 104, No. 413 (Summer 1991): 275-94.
> Examines the limitations of African-American folklore as a viable literary tradition in *Black Boy.*

Reilly, John M. "Self-Portraits by Richard Wright." *The Colorado Quarterly* XX, No. 1 (Summer 1971): 31-45.
> Discusses Wright's self-portrayal in *Black Boy* and in his short story "The Man Who Lived Underground."

Stepto, Robert B. "Literacy and Ascent: Richard Wright's *Black Boy.*" In his *From behind the Veil: A Study of Afro-American Narrative,* pp. 128-62. Urbana: University of Illinois Press, 1979.
> Asserts that *Black Boy* is a valuable contribution to the African-American narrative tradition.

Streator, George. Review of *Black Boy,* by Richard Wright. *The Commonweal* XLI, No. 23 (23 March 1945): 568-69.
> Characterizes *Black Boy* as "another milestone in the road to emancipation."

Trilling, Lionel. "A Tragic Situation." *The Nation* 160, No. 14 (7 April 1945): 390, 392.
> Praises Wright's realistic and objective depiction of black life in *Black Boy.*

Additional coverage of Wright's life and career is contained in the following sources published by Gale Research: *Authors and Artists for Young Adults,* Vol. 5; *Black Literature Criticism; Black Writers; Concise Dictionary of American Literary Biography, 1929-1941; Contemporary Authors,* Vol. 108; *Contemporary Literary Criticism,* Vols. 1, 3, 4, 9, 14, 21, 48; *Dictionary of Literary Biography,* Vols. 76, 102; *Dictionary of Literary Biography Documentary Series,* Vol. 2; *Major 20th-Century Writers;* and *Short Story Criticism,* Vol. 2.

☐ Contemporary Literary Criticism

Indexes

Literary Criticism Series
Cumulative Author Index
Cumulative Nationality Index

This Index Includes References to Entries in These Gale Series

Black Literature Criticism provides excerpts from criticism of the most significant works of black authors of all nationalities over the past 200 years. Complete in three volumes.

Children's Literature Review includes excerpts from reviews, criticism, and commentary on works of authors and illustrators who create books for children.

Classical and Medieval Literature Criticism offers excerpts of criticism on the works of world authors from classical antiquity through the fourteenth century.

Contemporary Authors series encompasses five related series. **Contemporary Authors** provides biographical and bibliographical information on more than 100,000 writers of fiction, nonfiction, poetry, journalism, drama, and film. **Contemporary Authors New Revision Series** provides completely updated information on active authors covered in previously published volumes of *CA*. **Contemporary Authors Permanent Series** consists of updated listings for deceased and inactive authors removed from the original volumes 9-36 when those volumes were revised. **Contemporary Authors Autobiography Series** presents specially commissioned autobiographies by leading contemporary writers. **Contemporary Authors Bibliographical Series** contains primary and secondary bibliographies as well as analytical bibliographical essays by authorities on major modern authors.

Contemporary Literary Criticism presents excerpts of criticism on the works of novelists, poets, dramatists, short story writers, scriptwriters, and other creative writers who are now living or who have died since 1960.

Dictionary of Literary Biography comprises four related series. **Dictionary of Literary Biography** furnishes illustrated overviews of authors' lives and works and places them in the larger perspective of literary history. **Dictionary of Literary Biography Documentary Series** illuminates the careers of major figures through a selection of literary documents, including letters, interviews, and photographs. **Dictionary of Literary Biography Yearbook** summarizes the past year's literary activity and includes updated and new entries on individual authors. A cumulative index to authors and articles is included in each new volume. **Concise Dictionary of**

American Literary Biography, a six-volume series, collects revised and updated sketches on major American authors that were originally presented in *Dictionary of Literary Biography*.

Drama Criticism provides excerpts of criticism on the works of playwrights of all nationalities and periods of literary history.

Literature Criticism from 1400 to 1800 compiles significant passages from the most noteworthy criticism on authors of the fifteenth through the eighteenth centuries.

Nineteenth-Century Literature Criticism offers significant passages from criticism on authors who died between 1800 and 1899.

Poetry Criticism presents excerpts of criticism on the works of poets from all eras, movements, and nationalities.

Short Story Criticism combines excerpts of criticism on short fiction by writers of all eras and nationalities.

Something about the Author series encompasses three related series. **Something about the Author** contains well-illustrated biographical sketches on authors and illustrators of juvenile and young adult literature from all eras. **Something about the Author Autobiography Series** presents specially commissioned autobiographies by prominent authors and illustrators of books for children and young adults. **Authors & Artists for Young Adults** provides high school and junior high school students with profiles of their favorite creative artists.

Twentieth-Century Literary Criticism contains critical excerpts by the most significant commentators on poets, novelists, short story writers, dramatists, and philosophers who died between 1900 and 1960.

World Literature Criticism, 1500 to the Present provides excerpts from criticism on 225 authors from the Renaissance to the present. Complete in six volumes.

Yesterday's Authors of Books for Children contains heavily illustrated entries on children's writers who died before 1961. Complete in two volumes.

Literary Criticism Series
Cumulative Author Index

A. E. . . . . TCLC 3, 10
See also Russell, George William
See also DLB 19

A. M.
See Megged, Aharon

Abasiyanik, Sait Faik 1906-1954
See Sait Faik
See also CA 123

Abbey, Edward 1927-1989 . . . . . . CLC 36, 59
See also CA 45-48; 128; CANR 2

Abbott, Lee K(ittredge) 1947- . . . . . . CLC 48
See also CA 124

Abe Kobo 1924- . . . . CLC 8, 22, 53
See also CA 65-68; CANR 24; MTCW

Abell, Kjeld 1901-1961 . . . . CLC 15
See also CA 111

Abish, Walter 1931- . . . . CLC 22
See also CA 101; CANR 37

Abrahams, Peter (Henry) 1919- . . . . . CLC 4
See also BW; CA 57-60; CANR 26;
DLB 117; MTCW

Abrams, M(eyer) H(oward) 1912- . . . CLC 24
See also CA 57-60; CANR 13, 33; DLB 67

Abse, Dannie 1923- . . . . CLC 7, 29
See also CA 53-56; CAAS 1; CANR 4;
DLB 27

Achebe, (Albert) Chinua(lumogu)
1930- . . . . CLC 1, 3, 5, 7, 11, 26, 51
See also BLC 1; BW; CA 1-4R; CANR 6,
26; CLR 20; DLB 117; MAICYA;
MTCW; SATA 38, 40; WLC

Acker, Kathy 1948- . . . . CLC 45
See also CA 117; 122

Ackroyd, Peter 1949- . . . . CLC 34, 52
See also CA 123; 127

Acorn, Milton 1923- . . . . CLC 15
See also CA 103; DLB 53

Adamov, Arthur 1908-1970 . . . . . . CLC 4, 25
See also CA 17-18; 25-28R; CAP 2; MTCW

Adams, Alice (Boyd) 1926- . . . CLC 6, 13, 46
See also CA 81-84; CANR 26; DLBY 86;
MTCW

Adams, Douglas (Noel) 1952- . . . CLC 27, 60
See also AAYA 4; BEST 89:3; CA 106;
CANR 34; DLBY 83

Adams, Francis 1862-1893 . . . . NCLC 33

Adams, Henry (Brooks)
1838-1918 . . . . TCLC 4
See also CA 104; 133; DLB 12, 47

Adams, Richard (George)
1920- . . . . CLC 4, 5, 18
See also AITN 1, 2; CA 49-52; CANR 3,
35; CLR 20; MAICYA; MTCW;
SATA 7, 69

Adamson, Joy(-Friederike Victoria)
1910-1980 . . . . CLC 17
See also CA 69-72; 93-96; CANR 22;
MTCW; SATA 11, 22

Adcock, Fleur 1934- . . . . CLC 41
See also CA 25-28R; CANR 11, 34;
DLB 40

Addams, Charles (Samuel)
1912-1988 . . . . CLC 30
See also CA 61-64; 126; CANR 12

Addison, Joseph 1672-1719 . . . . LC 18
See also CDBLB 1660-1789; DLB 101

Adler, C(arole) S(chwerdtfeger)
1932- . . . . CLC 35
See also AAYA 4; CA 89-92; CANR 19;
MAICYA; SATA 26, 63

Adler, Renata 1938- . . . . CLC 8, 31
See also CA 49-52; CANR 5, 22; MTCW

Ady, Endre 1877-1919 . . . . TCLC 11
See also CA 107

Afton, Effie
See Harper, Frances Ellen Watkins

Agapida, Fray Antonio
See Irving, Washington

Agee, James (Rufus)
1909-1955 . . . . TCLC 1, 19
See also AITN 1; CA 108;
CDALB 1941-1968; DLB 2, 26

Aghill, Gordon
See Silverberg, Robert

Agnon, S(hmuel) Y(osef Halevi)
1888-1970 . . . . CLC 4, 8, 14
See also CA 17-18; 25-28R; CAP 2; MTCW

Aherne, Owen
See Cassill, R(onald) V(erlin)

Ai 1947- . . . . CLC 4, 14, 69
See also CA 85-88; CAAS 13; DLB 120

Aickman, Robert (Fordyce)
1914-1981 . . . . CLC 57
See also CA 5-8R; CANR 3

Aiken, Conrad (Potter)
1889-1973 . . . CLC 1, 3, 5, 10, 52; SSC 9
See also CA 5-8R; 45-48; CANR 4;
CDALB 1929-1941; DLB 9, 45, 102;
MTCW; SATA 3, 30

Aiken, Joan (Delano) 1924- . . . . CLC 35
See also AAYA 1; CA 9-12R; CANR 4, 23,
34; CLR 1, 19; MAICYA; MTCW;
SAAS 1; SATA 2, 30

Ainsworth, William Harrison
1805-1882 . . . . NCLC 13
See also DLB 21; SATA 24

Aitmatov, Chingiz (Torekulovich)
1928- . . . . CLC 71
See also CA 103; CANR 38; MTCW;
SATA 56

Akers, Floyd
See Baum, L(yman) Frank

Akhmadulina, Bella Akhatovna
1937- . . . . CLC 53
See also CA 65-68

Akhmatova, Anna
1888-1966 . . . . CLC 11, 25, 64; PC 2
See also CA 19-20; 25-28R; CANR 35;
CAP 1; MTCW

Aksakov, Sergei Timofeyvich
1791-1859 . . . . NCLC 2

Aksenov, Vassily . . . . CLC 22
See also Aksyonov, Vassily (Pavlovich)

Aksyonov, Vassily (Pavlovich)
1932- . . . . CLC 37
See also Aksenov, Vassily
See also CA 53-56; CANR 12

Akutagawa Ryunosuke
1892-1927 . . . . TCLC 16
See also CA 117

Alain 1868-1951 . . . . TCLC 41

Alain-Fournier . . . . TCLC 6
See also Fournier, Henri Alban
See also DLB 65

Alarcon, Pedro Antonio de
1833-1891 . . . . NCLC 1

Alas (y Urena), Leopoldo (Enrique Garcia)
1852-1901 . . . . TCLC 29
See also CA 113; 131; HW

Albee, Edward (Franklin III)
1928- . . . CLC 1, 2, 3, 5, 9, 11, 13, 25, 53
See also AITN 1; CA 5-8R; CABS 3;
CANR 8; CDALB 1941-1968; DLB 7;
MTCW; WLC

Alberti, Rafael 1902- . . . . CLC 7
See also CA 85-88; DLB 108

Alcala-Galiano, Juan Valera y
See Valera y Alcala-Galiano, Juan

Alcott, Amos Bronson 1799-1888 . . NCLC 1
See also DLB 1

Alcott, Louisa May 1832-1888 . . . . NCLC 6
See also CDALB 1865-1917; CLR 1;
DLB 1, 42, 79; MAICYA; WLC;
YABC 1

Aldanov, M. A.
See Aldanov, Mark (Alexandrovich)

Aldanov, Mark (Alexandrovich)
1886(?)-1957 . . . . TCLC 23
See also CA 118

Aldington, Richard 1892-1962 . . . . . . CLC 49
See also CA 85-88; DLB 20, 36, 100

Aldiss, Brian W(ilson)
1925- . . . . CLC 5, 14, 40
See also CA 5-8R; CAAS 2; CANR 5, 28;
DLB 14; MTCW; SATA 34

Alegria, Fernando 1918- . . . . CLC 57
See also CA 9-12R; CANR 5, 32; HW

Aleichem, Sholom . . . . TCLC 1, 35
See also Rabinovitch, Sholem

Apuleius, (Lucius Madaurensis)
125(?)-175(?) .... **CMLC 1**

Aquin, Hubert 1929-1977......... **CLC 15**
See also CA 105; DLB 53

Aragon, Louis 1897-1982........ **CLC 3, 22**
See also CA 69-72; 108; CANR 28;
DLB 72; MTCW

Arany, Janos 1817-1882........ **NCLC 34**

Arbuthnot, John 1667-1735.......... **LC 1**
See also DLB 101

Archer, Herbert Winslow
See Mencken, H(enry) L(ouis)

Archer, Jeffrey (Howard) 1940- .... **CLC 28**
See also BEST 89:3; CA 77-80; CANR 22

Archer, Jules 1915- .... **CLC 12**
See also CA 9-12R; CANR 6; SAAS 5;
SATA 4

Archer, Lee
See Ellison, Harlan

Arden, John 1930- .... **CLC 6, 13, 15**
See also CA 13-16R; CAAS 4; CANR 31;
DLB 13; MTCW

Arenas, Reinaldo 1943-1990 .... **CLC 41**
See also CA 124; 128; 133; HW

Arendt, Hannah 1906-1975 .... **CLC 66**
See also CA 17-20R; 61-64; CANR 26;
MTCW

Aretino, Pietro 1492-1556 .... **LC 12**

Arguedas, Jose Maria
1911-1969 .... **CLC 10, 18**
See also CA 89-92; DLB 113; HW

Argueta, Manlio 1936-............ **CLC 31**
See also CA 131; HW

Ariosto, Ludovico 1474-1533......... **LC 6**

Aristides
See Epstein, Joseph

Aristophanes
450B.C.-385B.C....... **CMLC 4; DC 2**

Arlt, Roberto (Godofredo Christophersen)
1900-1942 .... **TCLC 29**
See also CA 123; 131; HW

Armah, Ayi Kwei 1939-......... **CLC 5, 33**
See also BLC 1; BW; CA 61-64; CANR 21;
DLB 117; MTCW

Armatrading, Joan 1950-.......... **CLC 17**
See also CA 114

Arnette, Robert
See Silverberg, Robert

Arnim, Achim von (Ludwig Joachim von Arnim) 1781-1831 .... **NCLC 5**
See also DLB 90

Arnim, Bettina von 1785-1859.... **NCLC 38**
See also DLB 90

Arnold, Matthew
1822-1888 .... **NCLC 6, 29; PC 5**
See also CDBLB 1832-1890; DLB 32, 57;
WLC

Arnold, Thomas 1795-1842 ...... **NCLC 18**
See also DLB 55

Arnow, Harriette (Louisa) Simpson
1908-1986 .... **CLC 2, 7, 18**
See also CA 9-12R; 118; CANR 14; DLB 6;
MTCW; SATA 42, 47

Arp, Hans
See Arp, Jean

Arp, Jean 1887-1966............... **CLC 5**
See also CA 81-84; 25-28R

Arrabal................... **CLC 2, 9, 18**
See also Arrabal, Fernando

Arrabal, Fernando 1932- .... **CLC 58**
See also Arrabal
See also CA 9-12R; CANR 15

Arrick, Fran.................... **CLC 30**

Artaud, Antonin 1896-1948 ..... **TCLC 3, 36**
See also CA 104

Arthur, Ruth M(abel) 1905-1979.... **CLC 12**
See also CA 9-12R; 85-88; CANR 4;
SATA 7, 26

Artsybashev, Mikhail (Petrovich)
1878-1927 .... **TCLC 31**

Arundel, Honor (Morfydd)
1919-1973 .... **CLC 17**
See also CA 21-22; 41-44R; CAP 2;
SATA 4, 24

Asch, Sholem 1880-1957 .... **TCLC 3**
See also CA 105

Ash, Shalom
See Asch, Sholem

Ashbery, John (Lawrence)
1927- ... **CLC 2, 3, 4, 6, 9, 13, 15, 25, 41**
See also CA 5-8R; CANR 9, 37; DLB 5;
DLBY 81; MTCW

Ashdown, Clifford
See Freeman, R(ichard) Austin

Ashe, Gordon
See Creasey, John

Ashton-Warner, Sylvia (Constance)
1908-1984 .... **CLC 19**
See also CA 69-72; 112; CANR 29; MTCW

Asimov, Isaac
1920-1992 .... **CLC 1, 3, 9, 19, 26**
See also BEST 90:2; CA 1-4R; 137;
CANR 2, 19, 36; CLR 12; DLB 8;
MAICYA; MTCW; SATA 1, 26

Astley, Thea (Beatrice May)
1925- .... **CLC 41**
See also CA 65-68; CANR 11

Aston, James
See White, T(erence) H(anbury)

Asturias, Miguel Angel
1899-1974 .... **CLC 3, 8, 13**
See also CA 25-28; 49-52; CANR 32;
CAP 2; DLB 113; HW; MTCW

Atares, Carlos Saura
See Saura (Atares), Carlos

Atheling, William
See Pound, Ezra (Weston Loomis)

Atheling, William Jr.
See Blish, James (Benjamin)

Atherton, Gertrude (Franklin Horn)
1857-1948 .... **TCLC 2**
See also CA 104; DLB 9, 78

Atherton, Lucius
See Masters, Edgar Lee

Atkins, Jack
See Harris, Mark

Atticus
See Fleming, Ian (Lancaster)

Atwood, Margaret (Eleanor)
1939- .... **CLC 2, 3, 4, 8, 13, 15, 25, 44;
SSC 2**
See also BEST 89:2; CA 49-52; CANR 3,
24, 33; DLB 53; MTCW; SATA 50; WLC

Aubigny, Pierre d'
See Mencken, H(enry) L(ouis)

Aubin, Penelope 1685-1731(?)........ **LC 9**
See also DLB 39

Auchincloss, Louis (Stanton)
1917- .... **CLC 4, 6, 9, 18, 45**
See also CA 1-4R; CANR 6, 29; DLB 2;
DLBY 80; MTCW

Auden, W(ystan) H(ugh)
1907-1973 ..... **CLC 1, 2, 3, 4, 6, 9, 11,
14, 43; PC 1**
See also CA 9-12R; 45-48; CANR 5;
CDBLB 1914-1945; DLB 10, 20; MTCW;
WLC

Audiberti, Jacques 1900-1965 ...... **CLC 38**
See also CA 25-28R

Auel, Jean M(arie) 1936-.......... **CLC 31**
See also AAYA 7; BEST 90:4; CA 103;
CANR 21

Auerbach, Erich 1892-1957 .... **TCLC 43**
See also CA 118

Augier, Emile 1820-1889 .... **NCLC 31**

August, John
See De Voto, Bernard (Augustine)

Augustine, St. 354-430.......... **CMLC 6**

Aurelius
See Bourne, Randolph S(illiman)

Aurelius
See Bourne, Randolph S(illiman)

Austen, Jane
1775-1817 .... **NCLC 1, 13, 19, 33**
See also CDBLB 1789-1832; DLB 116;
WLC

Auster, Paul 1947-............... **CLC 47**
See also CA 69-72; CANR 23

Austin, Mary (Hunter)
1868-1934 .... **TCLC 25**
See also CA 109; DLB 9, 78

Autran Dourado, Waldomiro
See Dourado, (Waldomiro Freitas) Autran

Averroes 1126-1198 .... **CMLC 7**
See also DLB 115

Avison, Margaret 1918-.......... **CLC 2, 4**
See also CA 17-20R; DLB 53; MTCW

Ayckbourn, Alan
1939- .... **CLC 5, 8, 18, 33, 74**
See also CA 21-24R; CANR 31; DLB 13;
MTCW

Aydy, Catherine
See Tennant, Emma (Christina)

Ayme, Marcel (Andre) 1902-1967... **CLC 11**
See also CA 89-92; CLR 25; DLB 72

Ayrton, Michael 1921-1975......... **CLC 7**
See also CA 5-8R; 61-64; CANR 9, 21

Azorin........................ **CLC 11**
See also Martinez Ruiz, Jose

Azuela, Mariano 1873-1952....... **TCLC 3**
See also CA 104; 131; HW; MTCW

Baastad, Babbis Friis
See Friis-Baastad, Babbis Ellinor

Bab
See Gilbert, W(illiam) S(chwenck)

Babbis, Eleanor
See Friis-Baastad, Babbis Ellinor

Babel, Isaac (Emanuilovich)........ TCLC **13**
See also Babel, Isaak (Emmanuilovich)

Babel, Isaak (Emmanuilovich)
1894-1941(?) .... TCLC **2**
See also Babel, Isaac (Emanuilovich)
See also CA 104

Babits, Mihaly 1883-1941 .... TCLC **14**
See also CA 114

Babur 1483-1530................... LC **18**

Bacchelli, Riccardo 1891-1985 ..... CLC **19**
See also CA 29-32R; 117

Bach, Richard (David) 1936-....... CLC **14**
See also AITN 1; BEST 89:2; CA 9-12R;
CANR 18; MTCW; SATA 13

Bachman, Richard
See King, Stephen (Edwin)

Bachmann, Ingeborg 1926-1973..... CLC **69**
See also CA 93-96; 45-48; DLB 85

Bacon, Francis 1561-1626 .... LC **18**
See also CDBLB Before 1660

Bacovia, George................... TCLC **24**
See also Vasiliu, Gheorghe

Badanes, Jerome 1937-............ CLC **59**

Bagehot, Walter 1826-1877 ...... NCLC **10**
See also DLB 55

Bagnold, Enid 1889-1981.......... CLC **25**
See also CA 5-8R; 103; CANR 5; DLB 13;
MAICYA; SATA 1, 25

Bagrjana, Elisaveta
See Belcheva, Elisaveta

Bagryana, Elisaveta
See Belcheva, Elisaveta

Bailey, Paul 1937- .... CLC **45**
See also CA 21-24R; CANR 16; DLB 14

Baillie, Joanna 1762-1851 .... NCLC **2**
See also DLB 93

Bainbridge, Beryl (Margaret)
1933- ... CLC **4, 5, 8, 10, 14, 18, 22, 62**
See also CA 21-24R; CANR 24; DLB 14;
MTCW

Baker, Elliott 1922- .... CLC **8**
See also CA 45-48; CANR 2

Baker, Nicholson 1957- .... CLC **61**
See also CA 135

Baker, Ray Stannard 1870-1946 ... TCLC **47**
See also CA 118

Baker, Russell (Wayne) 1925-...... CLC **31**
See also BEST 89:4; CA 57-60; CANR 11;
MTCW

Bakshi, Ralph 1938(?)-............ CLC **26**
See also CA 112; 138

Bakunin, Mikhail (Alexandrovich)
1814-1876 .... NCLC **25**

Baldwin, James (Arthur)
1924-1987 ..... CLC **1, 2, 3, 4, 5, 8, 13,**
15, 17, 42, 50, 67; DC 1; SSC 10
See also AAYA 4; BLC 1; BW; CA 1-4R;
124; CABS 1; CANR 3, 24;
CDALB 1941-1968; DLB 2, 7, 33;
DLBY 87; MTCW; SATA 9, 54; WLC

Ballard, J(ames) G(raham)
1930- .... CLC **3, 6, 14, 36; SSC 1**
See also AAYA 3; CA 5-8R; CANR 15, 39;
DLB 14; MTCW

Balmont, Konstantin (Dmitriyevich)
1867-1943 .... TCLC **11**
See also CA 109

Balzac, Honore de
1799-1850 .... NCLC **5, 35; SSC 5**
See also DLB 119; WLC

Bambara, Toni Cade 1939- .... CLC **19**
See also AAYA 5; BLC 1; BW; CA 29-32R;
CANR 24; DLB 38; MTCW

Bamdad, A.
See Shamlu, Ahmad

Banat, D. R.
See Bradbury, Ray (Douglas)

Bancroft, Laura
See Baum, L(yman) Frank

Banim, John 1798-1842 .... NCLC **13**
See also DLB 116

Banim, Michael 1796-1874 ...... NCLC **13**

Banks, Iain
See Banks, Iain M(enzies)

Banks, Iain M(enzies) 1954- .... CLC **34**
See also CA 123; 128

Banks, Lynne Reid .... CLC **23**
See also Reid Banks, Lynne
See also AAYA 6

Banks, Russell 1940- .... CLC **37, 72**
See also CA 65-68; CAAS 15; CANR 19

Banville, John 1945-.............. CLC **46**
See also CA 117; 128; DLB 14

Banville, Theodore (Faullain) de
1832-1891 .... NCLC **9**

Baraka, Amiri
1934- ... CLC **1, 2, 3, 5, 10, 14, 33; PC 4**
See also Jones, LeRoi
See also BLC 1; BW; CA 21-24R; CABS 3;
CANR 27, 38; CDALB 1941-1968;
DLB 5, 7, 16, 38; DLBD 8; MTCW

Barbellion, W. N. P............... TCLC **24**
See also Cummings, Bruce F(rederick)

Barbera, Jack 1945-.............. CLC **44**
See also CA 110

Barbey d'Aurevilly, Jules Amedee
1808-1889 .... NCLC **1**
See also DLB 119

Barbusse, Henri 1873-1935 .... TCLC **5**
See also CA 105; DLB 65

Barclay, Bill
See Moorcock, Michael (John)

Barclay, William Ewert
See Moorcock, Michael (John)

Barea, Arturo 1897-1957 .... TCLC **14**
See also CA 111

Barfoot, Joan 1946- .... CLC **18**
See also CA 105

Baring, Maurice 1874-1945 .... TCLC **8**
See also CA 105; DLB 34

Barker, Clive 1952- .... CLC **52**
See also BEST 90:3; CA 121; 129; MTCW

Barker, George Granville
1913-1991 .... CLC **8, 48**
See also CA 9-12R; 135; CANR 7, 38;
DLB 20; MTCW

Barker, Harley Granville
See Granville-Barker, Harley
See also DLB 10

Barker, Howard 1946- .... CLC **37**
See also CA 102; DLB 13

Barker, Pat 1943-................. CLC **32**
See also CA 117; 122

Barlow, Joel 1754-1812 .... NCLC **23**
See also DLB 37

Barnard, Mary (Ethel) 1909-....... CLC **48**
See also CA 21-22; CAP 2

Barnes, Djuna
1892-1982 ... CLC **3, 4, 8, 11, 29; SSC 3**
See also CA 9-12R; 107; CANR 16; DLB 4,
9, 45; MTCW

Barnes, Julian 1946-.............. CLC **42**
See also CA 102; CANR 19

Barnes, Peter 1931- .... CLC **5, 56**
See also CA 65-68; CAAS 12; CANR 33,
34; DLB 13; MTCW

Baroja (y Nessi), Pio 1872-1956 .... TCLC **8**
See also CA 104

Baron, David
See Pinter, Harold

Baron Corvo
See Rolfe, Frederick (William Serafino
Austin Lewis Mary)

Barondess, Sue K(aufman)
1926-1977 .... CLC **8**
See also Kaufman, Sue
See also CA 1-4R; 69-72; CANR 1

Baron de Teive
See Pessoa, Fernando (Antonio Nogueira)

Barres, Maurice 1862-1923 .... TCLC **47**

Barreto, Afonso Henrique de Lima
See Lima Barreto, Afonso Henrique de

Barrett, (Roger) Syd 1946- .... CLC **35**
See also Pink Floyd

Barrett, William (Christopher)
1913- .... CLC **27**
See also CA 13-16R; CANR 11

Barrie, J(ames) M(atthew)
1860-1937 .... TCLC **2**
See also CA 104; 136; CDBLB 1890-1914;
CLR 16; DLB 10; MAICYA; YABC 1

Barrington, Michael
See Moorcock, Michael (John)

Barrol, Grady
See Bograd, Larry

Barry, Mike
See Malzberg, Barry N(athaniel)

Barry, Philip 1896-1949.......... TCLC **11**
See also CA 109; DLB 7

Bart, Andre Schwarz
See Schwarz-Bart, Andre

Barth, John (Simmons)
1930- ...... **CLC 1, 2, 3, 5, 7, 9, 10, 14, 27, 51; SSC 10**
See also AITN 1, 2; CA 1-4R; CABS 1; CANR 5, 23; DLB 2; MTCW

Barthelme, Donald
1931-1989 ..... **CLC 1, 2, 3, 5, 6, 8, 13, 23, 46, 59; SSC 2**
See also CA 21-24R; 129; CANR 20; DLB 2; DLBY 80, 89; MTCW; SATA 7, 62

Barthelme, Frederick 1943- .... **CLC 36**
See also CA 114; 122; DLBY 85

Barthes, Roland (Gerard)
1915-1980 .... **CLC 24**
See also CA 130; 97-100; MTCW

Barzun, Jacques (Martin) 1907- .... **CLC 51**
See also CA 61-64; CANR 22

Bashevis, Isaac
See Singer, Isaac Bashevis

Bashkirtseff, Marie 1859-1884 ... **NCLC 27**

Basho
See Matsuo Basho

Bass, Kingsley B. Jr.
See Bullins, Ed

Bassani, Giorgio 1916- .... **CLC 9**
See also CA 65-68; CANR 33; MTCW

Bastos, Augusto (Antonio) Roa
See Roa Bastos, Augusto (Antonio)

Bataille, Georges 1897-1962 .... **CLC 29**
See also CA 101; 89-92

Bates, H(erbert) E(rnest)
1905-1974 .... **CLC 46; SSC 10**
See also CA 93-96; 45-48; CANR 34; MTCW

Bauchart
See Camus, Albert

Baudelaire, Charles
1821-1867 .... **NCLC 6, 29; PC 1**
See also WLC

Baudrillard, Jean 1929- .... **CLC 60**

Baum, L(yman) Frank 1856-1919 ... **TCLC 7**
See also CA 108; 133; CLR 15; DLB 22; MAICYA; MTCW; SATA 18

Baum, Louis F.
See Baum, L(yman) Frank

Baumbach, Jonathan 1933- ...... **CLC 6, 23**
See also CA 13-16R; CAAS 5; CANR 12; DLBY 80; MTCW

Bausch, Richard (Carl) 1945- ...... **CLC 51**
See also CA 101; CAAS 14

Baxter, Charles 1947- .... **CLC 45**
See also CA 57-60

Baxter, James K(eir) 1926-1972 .... **CLC 14**
See also CA 77-80

Baxter, John
See Hunt, E(verette) Howard Jr.

Bayer, Sylvia
See Glassco, John

Beagle, Peter S(oyer) 1939- .... **CLC 7**
See also CA 9-12R; CANR 4; DLBY 80; SATA 60

Bean, Normal
See Burroughs, Edgar Rice

Beard, Charles A(ustin)
1874-1948 .... **TCLC 15**
See also CA 115; DLB 17; SATA 18

Beardsley, Aubrey 1872-1898 ..... **NCLC 6**

Beattie, Ann
1947- .... **CLC 8, 13, 18, 40, 63; SSC 11**
See also BEST 90:2; CA 81-84; DLBY 82; MTCW

Beattie, James 1735-1803 .... **NCLC 25**
See also DLB 109

Beauchamp, Kathleen Mansfield 1888-1923
See Mansfield, Katherine
See also CA 104; 134

Beauvoir, Simone (Lucie Ernestine Marie Bertrand) de
1908-1986 ... **CLC 1, 2, 4, 8, 14, 31, 44, 50, 71**
See also CA 9-12R; 118; CANR 28; DLB 72; DLBY 86; MTCW; WLC

Becker, Jurek 1937- .... **CLC 7, 19**
See also CA 85-88; DLB 75

Becker, Walter 1950- .... **CLC 26**

Beckett, Samuel (Barclay)
1906-1989 ..... **CLC 1, 2, 3, 4, 6, 9, 10, 11, 14, 18, 29, 57, 59**
See also CA 5-8R; 130; CANR 33; CDBLB 1945-1960; DLB 13, 15; DLBY 90; MTCW; WLC

Beckford, William 1760-1844 .... **NCLC 16**
See also DLB 39

Beckman, Gunnel 1910- .... **CLC 26**
See also CA 33-36R; CANR 15; CLR 25; MAICYA; SAAS 9; SATA 6

Becque, Henri 1837-1899......... **NCLC 3**

Beddoes, Thomas Lovell
1803-1849 .... **NCLC 3**
See also DLB 96

Bedford, Donald F.
See Fearing, Kenneth (Flexner)

Beecher, Catharine Esther
1800-1878 .... **NCLC 30**
See also DLB 1

Beecher, John 1904-1980........... **CLC 6**
See also AITN 1; CA 5-8R; 105; CANR 8

Beer, Johann 1655-1700............ **LC 5**

Beer, Patricia 1924- .... **CLC 58**
See also CA 61-64; CANR 13; DLB 40

Beerbohm, Henry Maximilian
1872-1956 .... **TCLC 1, 24**
See also CA 104; DLB 34, 100

Begiebing, Robert J(ohn) 1946-..... **CLC 70**
See also CA 122

Behan, Brendan
1923-1964 .... **CLC 1, 8, 11, 15**
See also CA 73-76; CANR 33; CDBLB 1945-1960; DLB 13; MTCW

Behn, Aphra 1640(?)-1689 .... **LC 1**
See also DLB 39, 80; WLC

Behrman, S(amuel) N(athaniel)
1893-1973 .... **CLC 40**
See also CA 13-16; 45-48; CAP 1; DLB 7, 44

Belasco, David 1853-1931 .... **TCLC 3**
See also CA 104; DLB 7

Belcheva, Elisaveta 1893- .... **CLC 10**

Beldone, Phil "Cheech"
See Ellison, Harlan

Beleno
See Azuela, Mariano

Belinski, Vissarion Grigoryevich
1811-1848 .... **NCLC 5**

Belitt, Ben 1911-................. **CLC 22**
See also CA 13-16R; CAAS 4; CANR 7; DLB 5

Bell, James Madison 1826-1902 ... **TCLC 43**
See also BLC 1; BW; CA 122; 124; DLB 50

Bell, Madison (Smartt) 1957- ...... **CLC 41**
See also CA 111; CANR 28

Bell, Marvin (Hartley) 1937-..... **CLC 8, 31**
See also CA 21-24R; CAAS 14; DLB 5; MTCW

Bell, W. L. D.
See Mencken, H(enry) L(ouis)

Bellamy, Atwood C.
See Mencken, H(enry) L(ouis)

Bellamy, Edward 1850-1898 ...... **NCLC 4**
See also DLB 12

Bellin, Edward J.
See Kuttner, Henry

Belloc, (Joseph) Hilaire (Pierre)
1870-1953 .... **TCLC 7, 18**
See also CA 106; DLB 19, 100; YABC 1

Belloc, Joseph Peter Rene Hilaire
See Belloc, (Joseph) Hilaire (Pierre)

Belloc, Joseph Pierre Hilaire
See Belloc, (Joseph) Hilaire (Pierre)

Belloc, M. A.
See Lowndes, Marie Adelaide (Belloc)

Bellow, Saul
1915- ..... **CLC 1, 2, 3, 6, 8, 10, 13, 15, 25, 33, 34, 63**
See also AITN 2; BEST 89:3; CA 5-8R; CABS 1; CANR 29; CDALB 1941-1968; DLB 2, 28; DLBD 3; DLBY 82; MTCW; WLC

Belser, Reimond Karel Maria de
1929 .... **CLC 14**

Bely, Andrey .... TCLC 7
See also Bugayev, Boris Nikolayevich

Benary, Margot
See Benary-Isbert, Margot

Benary-Isbert, Margot 1889-1979... **CLC 12**
See also CA 5-8R; 89-92; CANR 4; CLR 12; MAICYA; SATA 2, 21

Benavente (y Martinez), Jacinto
1866-1954 .... **TCLC 3**
See also CA 106; 131; HW; MTCW

Benchley, Peter (Bradford)
1940- .... **CLC 4, 8**
See also AITN 2; CA 17-20R; CANR 12, 35; MTCW; SATA 3

Benchley, Robert (Charles)
1889-1945 .... **TCLC 1**
See also CA 105; DLB 11

Benedikt, Michael 1935- .... **CLC 4, 14**
See also CA 13-16R; CANR 7; DLB 5

Brooke-Rose, Christine   1926- ...... **CLC 40**
See also CA 13-16R; DLB 14

Brookner, Anita   1928- ...... **CLC 32, 34, 51**
See also CA 114; 120; CANR 37; DLBY 87;
MTCW

Brooks, Cleanth   1906- .... **CLC 24**
See also CA 17-20R; CANR 33, 35;
DLB 63; MTCW

Brooks, George
See Baum, L(yman) Frank

Brooks, Gwendolyn
1917- .... **CLC 1, 2, 4, 5, 15, 49**
See also AITN 1; BLC 1; BW; CA 1-4R;
CANR 1, 27; CDALB 1941-1968;
CLR 27; DLB 5, 76; MTCW; SATA 6;
WLC

Brooks, Mel.................... **CLC 12**
See also Kaminsky, Melvin
See also DLB 26

Brooks, Peter   1938- .... **CLC 34**
See also CA 45-48; CANR 1

Brooks, Van Wyck   1886-1963...... **CLC 29**
See also CA 1-4R; CANR 6; DLB 45, 63,
103

Brophy, Brigid (Antonia)
1929- .... **CLC 6, 11, 29**
See also CA 5-8R; CAAS 4; CANR 25;
DLB 14; MTCW

Brosman, Catharine Savage   1934-.... **CLC 9**
See also CA 61-64; CANR 21

Brother Antoninus
See Everson, William (Oliver)

Broughton, T(homas) Alan   1936- ... **CLC 19**
See also CA 45-48; CANR 2, 23

Broumas, Olga   1949- .... **CLC 10**
See also CA 85-88; CANR 20

Brown, Charles Brockden
1771-1810 .... **NCLC 22**
See also CDALB 1640-1865; DLB 37, 59,
73

Brown, Christy   1932-1981 .... **CLC 63**
See also CA 105; 104; DLB 14

Brown, Claude   1937- .... **CLC 30**
See also AAYA 7; BLC 1; BW; CA 73-76

Brown, Dee (Alexander)   1908- ... **CLC 18, 47**
See also CA 13-16R; CAAS 6; CANR 11;
DLBY 80; MTCW; SATA 5

Brown, George
See Wertmueller, Lina

Brown, George Douglas
1869-1902 .... **TCLC 28**

Brown, George Mackay   1921-.... **CLC 5, 48**
See also CA 21-24R; CAAS 6; CANR 12,
37; DLB 14, 27; MTCW; SATA 35

Brown, Moses
See Barrett, William (Christopher)

Brown, Rita Mae   1944- .... **CLC 18, 43**
See also CA 45-48; CANR 2, 11, 35;
MTCW

Brown, Roderick (Langmere) Haig-
See Haig-Brown, Roderick (Langmere)

Brown, Rosellen   1939-............ **CLC 32**
See also CA 77-80; CAAS 10; CANR 14

Brown, Sterling Allen
1901-1989 .... **CLC 1, 23, 59**
See also BLC 1; BW; CA 85-88; 127;
CANR 26; DLB 48, 51, 63; MTCW

Brown, Will
See Ainsworth, William Harrison

Brown, William Wells
1813-1884 .... **NCLC 2; DC 1**
See also BLC 1; DLB 3, 50

Browne, (Clyde) Jackson   1948(?)-... **CLC 21**
See also CA 120

Browning, Elizabeth Barrett
1806-1861 .... **NCLC 1, 16**
See also CDBLB 1832-1890; DLB 32; WLC

Browning, Robert
1812-1889 .... **NCLC 19; PC 2**
See also CDBLB 1832-1890; DLB 32;
YABC 1

Browning, Tod   1882-1962 .... **CLC 16**
See also CA 117

Bruccoli, Matthew J(oseph)   1931-.. **CLC 34**
See also CA 9-12R; CANR 7; DLB 103

Bruce, Lenny..................... **CLC 21**
See also Schneider, Leonard Alfred

Bruin, John
See Brutus, Dennis

Brulls, Christian
See Simenon, Georges (Jacques Christian)

Brunner, John (Kilian Houston)
1934- .... **CLC 8, 10**
See also CA 1-4R; CAAS 8; CANR 2, 37;
MTCW

Brutus, Dennis   1924- .... **CLC 43**
See also BLC 1; BW; CA 49-52; CAAS 14;
CANR 2, 27; DLB 117

Bryan, C(ourtlandt) D(ixon) B(arnes)
1936- .... **CLC 29**
See also CA 73-76; CANR 13

Bryan, Michael
See Moore, Brian

Bryant, William Cullen
1794-1878 .... **NCLC 6**
See also CDALB 1640-1865; DLB 3, 43, 59

Bryusov, Valery Yakovlevich
1873-1924 .... **TCLC 10**
See also CA 107

Buchan, John   1875-1940 .... **TCLC 41**
See also CA 108; DLB 34, 70; YABC 2

Buchanan, George   1506-1582 .... **LC 4**

Buchheim, Lothar-Guenther   1918- ... **CLC 6**
See also CA 85-88

Buchner, (Karl) Georg
1813-1837 .... **NCLC 26**

Buchwald, Art(hur)   1925-.......... **CLC 33**
See also AITN 1; CA 5-8R; CANR 21;
MTCW; SATA 10

Buck, Pearl S(ydenstricker)
1892-1973 .... **CLC 7, 11, 18**
See also AITN 1; CA 1-4R; 41-44R;
CANR 1, 34; DLB 9, 102; MTCW;
SATA 1, 25

Buckler, Ernest   1908-1984......... **CLC 13**
See also CA 11-12; 114; CAP 1; DLB 68;
SATA 47

Buckley, Vincent (Thomas)
1925-1988 .... **CLC 57**
See also CA 101

Buckley, William F(rank) Jr.
1925- .... **CLC 7, 18, 37**
See also AITN 1; CA 1-4R; CANR 1, 24;
DLBY 80; MTCW

Buechner, (Carl) Frederick
1926- ....**CLC 2, 4, 6, 9**
See also CA 13-16R; CANR 11, 39;
DLBY 80; MTCW

Buell, John (Edward)   1927-........ **CLC 10**
See also CA 1-4R; DLB 53

Buero Vallejo, Antonio   1916- ... **CLC 15, 46**
See also CA 106; CANR 24; HW; MTCW

Bufalino, Gesualdo   1920-.......... **CLC 74**

Bugayev, Boris Nikolayevich   1880-1934
See Bely, Andrey
See also CA 104

Bukowski, Charles   1920-.... **CLC 2, 5, 9, 41**
See also CA 17-20R; DLB 5; MTCW

Bulgakov, Mikhail (Afanas'evich)
1891-1940 .... **TCLC 2, 16**
See also CA 105

Bullins, Ed   1935- .... **CLC 1, 5, 7**
See also BLC 1; BW; CA 49-52; CAAS 16;
CANR 24; DLB 7, 38; MTCW

Bulwer-Lytton, Edward (George Earle Lytton)
1803-1873 .... **NCLC 1**
See also DLB 21

Bunin, Ivan Alexeyevich
1870-1953 .... **TCLC 6; SSC 5**
See also CA 104

Bunting, Basil   1900-1985.... **CLC 10, 39, 47**
See also CA 53-56; 115; CANR 7; DLB 20

Bunuel, Luis   1900-1983 .... **CLC 16**
See also CA 101; 110; CANR 32; HW

Bunyan, John   1628-1688 .... **LC 4**
See also CDBLB 1660-1789; DLB 39; WLC

Burford, Eleanor
See Hibbert, Eleanor Burford

Burgess, Anthony
.. **CLC 1, 2, 4, 5, 8, 10, 13, 15, 22, 40, 62**
See also Wilson, John (Anthony) Burgess
See also AITN 1; CDBLB 1960 to Present;
DLB 14

Burke, Edmund   1729(?)-1797........ **LC 7**
See also DLB 104; WLC

Burke, Kenneth (Duva)   1897- .... **CLC 2, 24**
See also CA 5-8R; CANR 39; DLB 45, 63;
MTCW

Burke, Leda
See Garnett, David

Burke, Ralph
See Silverberg, Robert

Burney, Fanny   1752-1840 .... **NCLC 12**
See also DLB 39

Burns, Robert   1759-1796............ **LC 3**
See also CDBLB 1789-1832; DLB 109;
WLC

Burns, Tex
See L'Amour, Louis (Dearborn)

Burnshaw, Stanley   1906-..... **CLC 3, 13, 44**
See also CA 9-12R; DLB 48

Burr, Anne 1937- . . . . CLC 6
See also CA 25-28R

Burroughs, Edgar Rice
1875-1950 . . . . TCLC 2, 32
See also CA 104; 132; DLB 8; MTCW;
SATA 41

Burroughs, William S(eward)
1914- . . . . CLC 1, 2, 5, 15, 22, 42
See also AITN 2; CA 9-12R; CANR 20;
DLB 2, 8, 16; DLBY 81; MTCW; WLC

Busch, Frederick 1941- . . . CLC 7, 10, 18, 47
See also CA 33-36R; CAAS 1; DLB 6

Bush, Ronald 1946- . . . . CLC 34
See also CA 136

Bustos, F(rancisco)
See Borges, Jorge Luis

Bustos Domecq, H(onorio)
See Bioy Casares, Adolfo; Borges, Jorge
Luis

Bustos Domecq, H(onrio)
See Borges, Jorge Luis

Butler, Octavia E(stelle) 1947- . . . . . CLC 38
See also BW; CA 73-76; CANR 12, 24, 38;
DLB 33; MTCW

Butler, Samuel 1612-1680 . . . . LC 16
See also DLB 101

Butler, Samuel 1835-1902 . . . . . . TCLC 1, 33
See also CA 104; CDBLB 1890-1914;
DLB 18, 57; WLC

Butor, Michel (Marie Francois)
1926- . . . . CLC 1, 3, 8, 11, 15
See also CA 9-12R; CANR 33; DLB 83;
MTCW

Buzo, Alexander (John) 1944- . . . . . . CLC 61
See also CA 97-100; CANR 17, 39

Buzzati, Dino 1906-1972 . . . . CLC 36
See also CA 33-36R

Byars, Betsy (Cromer) 1928- . . . . CLC 35
See also CA 33-36R; CANR 18, 36; CLR 1,
16; DLB 52; MAICYA; MTCW; SAAS 1;
SATA 4, 46

Byatt, A(ntonia) S(usan Drabble)
1936- . . . . CLC 19, 65
See also CA 13-16R; CANR 13, 33;
DLB 14; MTCW

Byrne, David 1952- . . . . CLC 26
See also CA 127

Byrne, John Keyes 1926- . . . . CLC 19
See also Leonard, Hugh
See also CA 102

Byron, George Gordon (Noel)
1788-1824 . . . . NCLC 2, 12
See also CDBLB 1789-1832; DLB 96, 110;
WLC

C.3.3.
See Wilde, Oscar (Fingal O'Flahertie Wills)

Caballero, Fernan 1796-1877 . . . . . NCLC 10

Cabell, James Branch 1879-1958 . . . TCLC 6
See also CA 105; DLB 9, 78

Cable, George Washington
1844-1925 . . . . TCLC 4; SSC 4
See also CA 104; DLB 12, 74

Cabrera Infante, G(uillermo)
1929- . . . . CLC 5, 25, 45
See also CA 85-88; CANR 29; DLB 113;
HW; MTCW

Cade, Toni
See Bambara, Toni Cade

Cadmus
See Buchan, John

Caedmon fl. 658-680 . . . . CMLC 7

Caeiro, Alberto
See Pessoa, Fernando (Antonio Nogueira)

Cage, John (Milton Jr.) 1912- . . . . . . CLC 41
See also CA 13-16R; CANR 9

Cain, G.
See Cabrera Infante, G(uillermo)

Cain, Guillermo
See Cabrera Infante, G(uillermo)

Cain, James M(allahan)
1892-1977 . . . . CLC 3, 11, 28
See also AITN 1; CA 17-20R; 73-76;
CANR 8, 34; MTCW

Caine, Mark
See Raphael, Frederic (Michael)

Caldwell, Erskine (Preston)
1903-1987 . . . . CLC 1, 8, 14, 50, 60
See also AITN 1; CA 1-4R; 121; CAAS 1;
CANR 2, 33; DLB 9, 86; MTCW

Caldwell, (Janet Miriam) Taylor (Holland)
1900-1985 . . . . CLC 2, 28, 39
See also CA 5-8R; 116; CANR 5

Calhoun, John Caldwell
1782-1850 . . . . NCLC 15
See also DLB 3

Calisher, Hortense 1911- . . . . CLC 2, 4, 8, 38
See also CA 1-4R; CANR 1, 22; DLB 2;
MTCW

Callaghan, Morley Edward
1903-1990 . . . . CLC 3, 14, 41, 65
See also CA 9-12R; 132; CANR 33;
DLB 68; MTCW

Calvino, Italo
1923-1985 . . . . CLC 5, 8, 11, 22, 33, 39;
SSC 3
See also CA 85-88; 116; CANR 23; MTCW

Cameron, Carey 1952- . . . . CLC 59
See also CA 135

Cameron, Peter 1959- . . . . CLC 44
See also CA 125

Campana, Dino 1885-1932 . . . . TCLC 20
See also CA 117; DLB 114

Campbell, John W(ood Jr.)
1910-1971 . . . . CLC 32
See also CA 21-22; 29-32R; CANR 34;
CAP 2; DLB 8; MTCW

Campbell, Joseph 1904-1987 . . . . CLC 69
See also AAYA 3; BEST 89:2; CA 1-4R;
124; CANR 3, 28; MTCW

Campbell, (John) Ramsey 1946- . . . . CLC 42
See also CA 57-60; CANR 7

Campbell, (Ignatius) Roy (Dunnachie)
1901-1957 . . . . TCLC 5
See also CA 104; DLB 20

Campbell, Thomas 1777-1844 . . . . NCLC 19
See also DLB 93

Campbell, Wilfred . . . . TCLC 9
See also Campbell, William

Campbell, William 1858(?)-1918
See Campbell, Wilfred
See also CA 106; DLB 92

Campos, Alvaro de
See Pessoa, Fernando (Antonio Nogueira)

Camus, Albert
1913-1960 . . . CLC 1, 2, 4, 9, 11, 14, 32,
63, 69; DC 2; SSC 9
See also CA 89-92; DLB 72; MTCW; WLC

Canby, Vincent 1924- . . . . CLC 13
See also CA 81-84

Cancale
See Desnos, Robert

Canetti, Elias 1905- . . . . CLC 3, 14, 25
See also CA 21-24R; CANR 23; DLB 85;
MTCW

Canin, Ethan 1960- . . . . CLC 55
See also CA 131; 135

Cannon, Curt
See Hunter, Evan

Cape, Judith
See Page, P(atricia) K(athleen)

Capek, Karel
1890-1938 . . . . TCLC 6, 37; DC 1
See also CA 104; WLC

Capote, Truman
1924-1984 . . . . . CLC 1, 3, 8, 13, 19, 34,
38, 58; SSC 2
See also CA 5-8R; 113; CANR 18;
CDALB 1941-1968; DLB 2; DLBY 80,
84; MTCW; WLC

Capra, Frank 1897-1991 . . . . CLC 16
See also CA 61-64; 135

Caputo, Philip 1941- . . . . CLC 32
See also CA 73-76

Card, Orson Scott 1951- . . . . CLC 44, 47, 50
See also CA 102; CANR 27; MTCW

Cardenal (Martinez), Ernesto
1925- . . . . CLC 31
See also CA 49-52; CANR 2, 32; HW;
MTCW

Carducci, Giosue 1835-1907 . . . . TCLC 32

Carew, Thomas 1595(?)-1640 . . . . LC 13

Carey, Ernestine Gilbreth 1908- . . . . CLC 17
See also CA 5-8R; SATA 2

Carey, Peter 1943- . . . . CLC 40, 55
See also CA 123; 127; MTCW

Carleton, William 1794-1869 . . . . . . NCLC 3

Carlisle, Henry (Coffin) 1926- . . . . . . CLC 33
See also CA 13-16R; CANR 15

Carlsen, Chris
See Holdstock, Robert P.

Carlson, Ron(ald F.) 1947- . . . . CLC 54
See also CA 105; CANR 27

Carlyle, Thomas 1795-1881 . . . . . . NCLC 22
See also CDBLB 1789-1832; DLB 55

Carman, (William) Bliss
1861-1929 . . . . TCLC 7
See also CA 104; DLB 92

Carpenter, Don(ald Richard)
1931- . . . . CLC 41
See also CA 45-48; CANR 1

Carpentier (y Valmont), Alejo
1904-1980 .... **CLC 8, 11, 38**
See also CA 65-68; 97-100; CANR 11;
DLB 113; HW

Carr, Emily 1871-1945 .... **TCLC 32**
See also DLB 68

Carr, John Dickson 1906-1977 ...... **CLC 3**
See also CA 49-52; 69-72; CANR 3, 33;
MTCW

Carr, Philippa
See Hibbert, Eleanor Burford

Carr, Virginia Spencer 1929-....... **CLC 34**
See also CA 61-64; DLB 111

Carrier, Roch 1937- .... **CLC 13**
See also CA 130; DLB 53

Carroll, James P. 1943(?)-......... **CLC 38**
See also CA 81-84

Carroll, Jim 1951- .... **CLC 35**
See also CA 45-48

Carroll, Lewis .... **NCLC 2**
See also Dodgson, Charles Lutwidge
See also CDBLB 1832-1890; CLR 2, 18;
DLB 18; WLC

Carroll, Paul Vincent 1900-1968.... **CLC 10**
See also CA 9-12R; 25-28R; DLB 10

Carruth, Hayden 1921- .... **CLC 4, 7, 10, 18**
See also CA 9-12R; CANR 4, 38; DLB 5;
MTCW; SATA 47

Carson, Rachel Louise 1907-1964... **CLC 71**
See also CA 77-80; CANR 35; MTCW;
SATA 23

Carter, Angela (Olive)
1940-1991 .... **CLC 5, 41**
See also CA 53-56; 136; CANR 12, 36;
DLB 14; MTCW; SATA 66; SATO 70

Carter, Nick
See Smith, Martin Cruz

Carver, Raymond
1938-1988 ... **CLC 22, 36, 53, 55; SSC 8**
See also CA 33-36R; 126; CANR 17, 34;
DLBY 84, 88; MTCW

Cary, (Arthur) Joyce (Lunel)
1888-1957 .... **TCLC 1, 29**
See also CA 104; CDBLB 1914-1945;
DLB 15, 100

Casanova de Seingalt, Giovanni Jacopo
1725-1798 .... **LC 13**

Casares, Adolfo Bioy
See Bioy Casares, Adolfo

Cascly-Hayford, J(oseph) E(phraim)
1866-1930 .... **TCLC 24**
See also BLC 1; CA 123

Casey, John (Dudley) 1939-........ **CLC 59**
See also BEST 90:2; CA 69-72; CANR 23

Casey, Michael 1947-.............. **CLC 2**
See also CA 65-68; DLB 5

Casey, Patrick
See Thurman, Wallace (Henry)

Casey, Warren (Peter) 1935-1988 ... **CLC 12**
See also CA 101; 127

Casona, Alejandro................. **CLC 49**
See also Alvarez, Alejandro Rodriguez

Cassavetes, John 1929-1989........ **CLC 20**
See also CA 85-88; 127

Cassill, R(onald) V(erlin) 1919-... **CLC 4, 23**
See also CA 9-12R; CAAS 1; CANR 7;
DLB 6

Cassity, (Allen) Turner 1929- .... **CLC 6, 42**
See also CA 17-20R; CAAS 8; CANR 11;
DLB 105

Castaneda, Carlos 1931(?)-......... **CLC 12**
See also CA 25-28R; CANR 32; HW;
MTCW

Castedo, Elena 1937- .... **CLC 65**
See also CA 132

Castedo-Ellerman, Elena
See Castedo, Elena

Castellanos, Rosario 1925-1974..... **CLC 66**
See also CA 131; 53-56; DLB 113; HW

Castelvetro, Lodovico 1505-1571..... **LC 12**

Castiglione, Baldassare 1478-1529 ... **LC 12**

Castle, Robert
See Hamilton, Edmond

Castro, Guillen de 1569-1631........ **LC 19**

Castro, Rosalia de 1837-1885 ..... **NCLC 3**

Cather, Willa
See Cather, Willa Sibert

Cather, Willa Sibert
1873-1947 ...... **TCLC 1, 11, 31; SSC 2**
See also CA 104; 128; CDALB 1865-1917;
DLB 9, 54, 78; DLBD 1; MTCW;
SATA 30; WLC

Catton, (Charles) Bruce
1899-1978 .... **CLC 35**
See also AITN 1; CA 5-8R; 81-84;
CANR 7; DLB 17; SATA 2, 24

Cauldwell, Frank
See King, Francis (Henry)

Caunitz, William J. 1933-......... **CLC 34**
See also BEST 89:3; CA 125; 130

Causley, Charles (Stanley) 1917-..... **CLC 7**
See also CA 9-12R; CANR 5, 35; DLB 27;
MTCW; SATA 3, 66

Caute, David 1936-............... **CLC 29**
See also CA 1-4R; CAAS 4; CANR 1, 33;
DLB 14

Cavafy, C(onstantine) P(eter)...... **TCLC 2, 7**
See also Kavafis, Konstantinos Petrou

Cavallo, Evelyn
See Spark, Muriel (Sarah)

Cavanna, Betty .... **CLC 12**
See also Harrison, Elizabeth Cavanna
See also MAICYA; SAAS 4; SATA 1, 30

Caxton, William 1421(?)-1491(?)..... **LC 17**

Cayrol, Jean 1911-............... **CLC 11**
See also CA 89-92; DLB 83

Cela, Camilo Jose 1916-...... **CLC 4, 13, 59**
See also BEST 90:2; CA 21-24R; CAAS 10;
CANR 21, 32; DLBY 89; HW; MTCW

Celan, Paul .... **CLC 53**
See also Antschel, Paul
See also DLB 69

Celine, Louis-Ferdinand
.... **CLC 1, 3, 4, 7, 9, 15, 47**
See also Destouches, Louis-Ferdinand
See also DLB 72

Cellini, Benvenuto 1500-1571 .... **LC 7**

Cendrars, Blaise
See Sauser-Hall, Frederic

Cernuda (y Bidon), Luis
1902-1963 .... **CLC 54**
See also CA 131; 89-92; HW

Cervantes (Saavedra), Miguel de
1547-1616 .... **LC 6**
See also WLC

Cesaire, Aime (Fernand) 1913- .. **CLC 19, 32**
See also BLC 1; BW; CA 65-68; CANR 24;
MTCW

Chabon, Michael 1965(?)- .... **CLC 55**

Chabrol, Claude 1930- .... **CLC 16**
See also CA 110

Challans, Mary 1905-1983
See Renault, Mary
See also CA 81-84; 111; SATA 23, 36

Chambers, Aidan 1934- .... **CLC 35**
See also CA 25-28R; CANR 12, 31;
MAICYA; SAAS 12; SATA 1, 69

Chambers, James 1948-
See Cliff, Jimmy
See also CA 124

Chambers, Jessie
See Lawrence, D(avid) H(erbert Richards)

Chambers, Robert W. 1865-1933... **TCLC 41**

Chandler, Raymond (Thornton)
1888-1959 .... **TCLC 1, 7**
See also CA 104; 129; CDALB 1929-1941;
DLBD 6; MTCW

Chang, Jung 1952-............... **CLC 71**

Channing, William Ellery
1780-1842 .... **NCLC 17**
See also DLB 1, 59

Chaplin, Charles Spencer
1889-1977 .... **CLC 16**
See also Chaplin, Charlie
See also CA 81-84; 73-76

Chaplin, Charlie
See Chaplin, Charles Spencer
See also DLB 44

Chapman, Graham 1941-1989 ...... **CLC 21**
See also Monty Python
See also CA 116; 129; CANR 35

Chapman, John Jay 1862-1933 ..... **TCLC 7**
See also CA 104

Chapman, Walker
See Silverberg, Robert

Chappell, Fred (Davis) 1936-....... **CLC 40**
See also CA 5-8R; CAAS 4; CANR 8, 33;
DLB 6, 105

Char, Rene(-Emile)
1907-1988 .... **CLC 9, 11, 14, 55**
See also CA 13-16R; 124; CANR 32;
MTCW

Charby, Jay
See Ellison, Harlan

Chardin, Pierre Teilhard de
See Teilhard de Chardin, (Marie Joseph)
Pierre

Charles I 1600-1649 .... **LC 13**

Charyn, Jerome 1937- .... **CLC 5, 8, 18**
See also CA 5-8R; CAAS 1; CANR 7;
DLBY 83; MTCW

Chase, Mary (Coyle) 1907-1981 . . . . . . **DC 1**
See also CA 77-80; 105; SATA 17, 29

Chase, Mary Ellen 1887-1973 . . . . **CLC 2**
See also CA 13-16; 41-44R; CAP 1;
SATA 10

Chase, Nicholas
See Hyde, Anthony

Chateaubriand, Francois Rene de
1768-1848 . . . . **NCLC 3**
See also DLB 119

Chatterje, Sarat Chandra 1876-1936(?)
See Chatterji, Saratchandra
See also CA 109

Chatterji, Bankim Chandra
1838-1894 . . . . **NCLC 19**

Chatterji, Saratchandra . . . . **TCLC 13**
See also Chatterje, Sarat Chandra

Chatterton, Thomas 1752-1770 . . . . . . **LC 3**
See also DLB 109

Chatwin, (Charles) Bruce
1940-1989 . . . . **CLC 28, 57, 59**
See also AAYA 4; BEST 90:1; CA 85-88;
127

Chaucer, Daniel
See Ford, Ford Madox

Chaucer, Geoffrey 1340(?)-1400 . . . . . **LC 17**
See also CDBLB Before 1660

Chaviaras, Strates 1935-
See Haviaras, Stratis
See also CA 105

Chayefsky, Paddy . . . . **CLC 23**
See also Chayefsky, Sidney
See also DLB 7, 44; DLBY 81

Chayefsky, Sidney 1923-1981
See Chayefsky, Paddy
See also CA 9-12R; 104; CANR 18

Chedid, Andree 1920- . . . . **CLC 47**

Cheever, John
1912-1982 . . . . . **CLC 3, 7, 8, 11, 15, 25, 64; SSC 1**
See also CA 5-8R; 106; CABS 1; CANR 5,
27; CDALB 1941-1968; DLB 2, 102;
DLBY 80, 82; MTCW; WLC

Cheever, Susan 1943- . . . . **CLC 18, 48**
See also CA 103; CANR 27; DLBY 82

Chekhonte, Antosha
See Chekhov, Anton (Pavlovich)

Chekhov, Anton (Pavlovich)
1860-1904 . . . . . . **TCLC 3, 10, 31; SSC 2**
See also CA 104; 124; WLC

Chernyshevsky, Nikolay Gavrilovich
1828-1889 . . . . **NCLC 1**

Cherry, Carolyn Janice 1942-
See Cherryh, C. J.
See also CA 65-68; CANR 10

Cherryh, C. J. . . . . **CLC 35**
See also Cherry, Carolyn Janice
See also DLBY 80

Chesnutt, Charles W(addell)
1858-1932 . . . . **TCLC 5, 39; SSC 7**
See also BLC 1; BW; CA 106; 125; DLB 12,
50, 78; MTCW

Chester, Alfred 1929(?)-1971 . . . . **CLC 49**
See also CA 33-36R

Chesterton, G(ilbert) K(eith)
1874-1936 . . . . **TCLC 1, 6; SSC 1**
See also CA 104; 132; CDBLB 1914-1945;
DLB 10, 19, 34, 70, 98; MTCW;
SATA 27

Chiang Pin-chin 1904-1986
See Ding Ling
See also CA 118

Ch'ien Chung-shu 1910- . . . . **CLC 22**
See also CA 130; MTCW

Child, L. Maria
See Child, Lydia Maria

Child, Lydia Maria 1802-1880 . . . . **NCLC 6**
See also DLB 1, 74; SATA 67

Child, Mrs.
See Child, Lydia Maria

Child, Philip 1898-1978 . . . . **CLC 19, 68**
See also CA 13-14; CAP 1; SATA 47

Childress, Alice 1920- . . . . **CLC 12, 15**
See also AAYA 8; BLC 1; BW; CA 45-48;
CANR 3, 27; CLR 14; DLB 7, 38;
MAICYA; MTCW; SATA 7, 48

Chislett, (Margaret) Anne 1943- . . . . . **CLC 34**

Chitty, Thomas Willes 1926- . . . . **CLC 11**
See also Hinde, Thomas
See also CA 5-8R

Chomette, Rene Lucien 1898-1981 . . **CLC 20**
See also Clair, Rene
See also CA 103

Chopin, Kate . . . . **TCLC 5, 14; SSC 8**
See also Chopin, Katherine
See also CDALB 1865-1917; DLB 12, 78

Chopin, Katherine 1851-1904
See Chopin, Kate
See also CA 104; 122

Chretien de Troyes
c. 12th cent. - . . . . **CMLC 10**

Christie
See Ichikawa, Kon

Christie, Agatha (Mary Clarissa)
1890-1976 . . . . . . **CLC 1, 6, 8, 12, 39, 48**
See also AAYA 9; AITN 1, 2; CA 17-20R;
61-64; CANR 10, 37; CDBLB 1914-1945;
DLB 13, 77; MTCW; SATA 36

Christie, (Ann) Philippa
See Pearce, Philippa
See also CA 5-8R; CANR 4

Christine de Pizan 1365(?)-1431(?) . . . . **LC 9**

Chubb, Elmer
See Masters, Edgar Lee

Chulkov, Mikhail Dmitrievich
1743-1792 . . . . **LC 2**

Churchill, Caryl 1938- . . . . **CLC 31, 55**
See also CA 102; CANR 22; DLB 13;
MTCW

Churchill, Charles 1731-1764 . . . . **LC 3**
See also DLB 109

Chute, Carolyn 1947- . . . . **CLC 39**
See also CA 123

Ciardi, John (Anthony)
1916-1986 . . . . **CLC 10, 40, 44**
See also CA 5-8R; 118; CAAS 2; CANR 5,
33; CLR 19; DLB 5; DLBY 86;
MAICYA; MTCW; SATA 1, 46, 65

Cicero, Marcus Tullius
106B.C.-43B.C. . . . . **CMLC 3**

Cimino, Michael 1943- . . . . **CLC 16**
See also CA 105

Cioran, E(mil) M. 1911- . . . . **CLC 64**
See also CA 25-28R

Cisneros, Sandra 1954- . . . . **CLC 69**
See also AAYA 9; CA 131; HW

Clair, Rene . . . . **CLC 20**
See also Chomette, Rene Lucien

Clampitt, Amy 1920- . . . . **CLC 32**
See also CA 110; CANR 29; DLB 105

Clancy, Thomas L. Jr. 1947-
See Clancy, Tom
See also CA 125; 131; MTCW

Clancy, Tom . . . . **CLC 45**
See also Clancy, Thomas L. Jr.
See also AAYA 9; BEST 89:1, 90:1

Clare, John 1793-1864 . . . . **NCLC 9**
See also DLB 55, 96

Clarin
See Alas (y Urena), Leopoldo (Enrique
Garcia)

Clark, (Robert) Brian 1932- . . . . **CLC 29**
See also CA 41-44R

Clark, Eleanor 1913- . . . . **CLC 5, 19**
See also CA 9-12R; DLB 6

Clark, J. P.
See Clark, John Pepper
See also DLB 117

Clark, John Pepper 1935- . . . . **CLC 38**
See also Clark, J. P.
See also BLC 1; BW; CA 65-68; CANR 16

Clark, M. R.
See Clark, Mavis Thorpe

Clark, Mavis Thorpe 1909- . . . . **CLC 12**
See also CA 57-60; CANR 8, 37; MAICYA;
SAAS 5; SATA 8

Clark, Walter Van Tilburg
1909-1971 . . . . **CLC 28**
See also CA 9-12R; 33-36R; DLB 9;
SATA 8

Clarke, Arthur C(harles)
1917- . . . . . . **CLC 1, 4, 13, 18, 35; SSC 3**
See also AAYA 4; CA 1-4R; CANR 2, 28;
MAICYA; MTCW; SATA 13, 70

Clarke, Austin C(hesterfield)
1934- . . . . **CLC 8, 53**
See also BLC 1; BW; CA 25-28R;
CAAS 16; CANR 14, 32; DLB 53

Clarke, Austin 1896-1974 . . . . **CLC 6, 9**
See also CA 29-32; 49-52; CAP 2; DLB 10,
20

Clarke, Gillian 1937- . . . . **CLC 61**
See also CA 106; DLB 40

Clarke, Marcus (Andrew Hislop)
1846-1881 . . . . **NCLC 19**

Clarke, Shirley 1925- . . . . **CLC 16**

. . . . **CLC 30**
See also Headon, (Nicky) Topper; Jones,
Mick; Simonon, Paul; Strummer, Joe

Claudel, Paul (Louis Charles Marie)
1868-1955 . . . . **TCLC 2, 10**
See also CA 104

Clavell, James (duMaresq)
1925- .... **CLC 6, 25**
See also CA 25-28R; CANR 26; MTCW

Cleaver, (Leroy) Eldridge 1935- .... **CLC 30**
See also BLC 1; BW; CA 21-24R;
CANR 16

Cleese, John (Marwood) 1939- ..... **CLC 21**
See also Monty Python
See also CA 112; 116; CANR 35; MTCW

Cleishbotham, Jebediah
See Scott, Walter

Cleland, John 1710-1789 .... **LC 2**
See also DLB 39

Clemens, Samuel Langhorne 1835-1910
See Twain, Mark
See also CA 104; 135; CDALB 1865-1917;
DLB 11, 12, 23, 64, 74; MAICYA;
YABC 2

Clerihew, E.
See Bentley, E(dmund) C(lerihew)

Clerk, N. W.
See Lewis, C(live) S(taples)

Cliff, Jimmy .... **CLC 21**
See also Chambers, James

Clifton, (Thelma) Lucille
1936- .... **CLC 19, 66**
See also BLC 1; BW; CA 49-52; CANR 2,
24; CLR 5; DLB 5, 41; MAICYA;
MTCW; SATA 20, 69

Clinton, Dirk
See Silverberg, Robert

Clough, Arthur Hugh 1819-1861.. **NCLC 27**
See also DLB 32

Clutha, Janet Paterson Frame 1924-
See Frame, Janet
See also CA 1-4R; CANR 2, 36; MTCW

Clyne, Terence
See Blatty, William Peter

Cobalt, Martin
See Mayne, William (James Carter)

Coburn, D(onald) L(ee) 1938- ...... **CLC 10**
See also CA 89-92

Cocteau, Jean (Maurice Eugene Clement)
1889-1963 .... **CLC 1, 8, 15, 16, 43**
See also CA 25-28; CAP 2; DLB 65;
MTCW; WLC

Codrescu, Andrei 1946- .... **CLC 46**
See also CA 33-36R; CANR 13, 34

Coe, Max
See Bourne, Randolph S(illiman)

Coe, Tucker
See Westlake, Donald E(dwin)

Coetzee, J(ohn) M(ichael)
1940- .... **CLC 23, 33, 66**
See also CA 77-80; MTCW

Cohen, Arthur A(llen)
1928-1986 .... **CLC 7, 31**
See also CA 1-4R; 120; CANR 1, 17;
DLB 28

Cohen, Leonard (Norman)
1934- .... **CLC 3, 38**
See also CA 21-24R; CANR 14; DLB 53;
MTCW

Cohen, Matt 1942- .... **CLC 19**
See also CA 61-64; DLB 53

Cohen-Solal, Annie 19(?)- .... **CLC 50**

Colegate, Isabel 1931- .... **CLC 36**
See also CA 17-20R; CANR 8, 22; DLB 14;
MTCW

Coleman, Emmett
See Reed, Ishmael

Coleridge, Samuel Taylor
1772-1834 .... **NCLC 9**
See also CDBLB 1789-1832; DLB 93, 107;
WLC

Coleridge, Sara 1802-1852 ...... **NCLC 31**

Coles, Don 1928- .... **CLC 46**
See also CA 115; CANR 38

Colette, (Sidonie-Gabrielle)
1873-1954 ...... **TCLC 1, 5, 16; SSC 10**
See also CA 104; 131; DLB 65; MTCW

Collett, (Jacobine) Camilla (Wergeland)
1813-1895 .... **NCLC 22**

Collier, Christopher 1930- .... **CLC 30**
See also CA 33-36R; CANR 13, 33;
MAICYA; SATA 16, 70

Collier, James L(incoln) 1928- ..... **CLC 30**
See also CA 9-12R; CANR 4, 33;
MAICYA; SATA 8, 70

Collier, Jeremy 1650-1726.......... **LC 6**

Collins, Hunt
See Hunter, Evan

Collins, Linda 1931- .... **CLC 44**
See also CA 125

Collins, (William) Wilkie
1824-1889 .... **NCLC 1, 18**
See also CDBLB 1832-1890; DLB 18, 70

Collins, William 1721-1759 .... **LC 4**
See also DLB 109

Colman, George
See Glassco, John

Colt, Winchester Remington
See Hubbard, L(afayette) Ron(ald)

Colter, Cyrus 1910- .... **CLC 58**
See also BW; CA 65-68; CANR 10; DLB 33

Colton, James
See Hansen, Joseph

Colum, Padraic 1881-1972......... **CLC 28**
See also CA 73-76; 33-36R; CANR 35;
MAICYA; MTCW; SATA 15

Colvin, James
See Moorcock, Michael (John)

Colwin, Laurie 1944- .... **CLC 5, 13, 23**
See also CA 89-92; CANR 20; DLBY 80;
MTCW

Comfort, Alex(ander) 1920-......... **CLC 7**
See also CA 1-4R; CANR 1

Comfort, Montgomery
See Campbell, (John) Ramsey

Compton-Burnett, I(vy)
1884(?)-1969 ...... **CLC 1, 3, 10, 15, 34**
See also CA 1-4R; 25-28R; CANR 4;
DLB 36; MTCW

Comstock, Anthony 1844-1915 .... **TCLC 13**
See also CA 110

Conan Doyle, Arthur
See Doyle, Arthur Conan

Conde, Maryse .... **CLC 52**
See also Boucolon, Maryse

Condon, Richard (Thomas)
1915- .... **CLC 4, 6, 8, 10, 45**
See also BEST 90:3; CA 1-4R; CAAS 1;
CANR 2, 23; MTCW

Congreve, William
1670-1729 .... **LC 5, 21; DC 2**
See also CDBLB 1660-1789; DLB 39, 84;
WLC

Connell, Evan S(helby) Jr.
1924- .... **CLC 4, 6, 45**
See also AAYA 7; CA 1-4R; CAAS 2;
CANR 2, 39; DLB 2; DLBY 81; MTCW

Connelly, Marc(us Cook)
1890-1980 .... **CLC 7**
See also CA 85-88; 102; CANR 30; DLB 7;
DLBY 80; SATA 25

Connor, Ralph .... **TCLC 31**
See also Gordon, Charles William
See also DLB 92

Conrad, Joseph
1857-1924 ...... **TCLC 1, 6, 13, 25, 43;
SSC 9**
See also CA 104; 131; CDBLB 1890-1914;
DLB 10, 34, 98; MTCW; SATA 27; WLC

Conrad, Robert Arnold
See Hart, Moss

Conroy, Pat 1945-............. **CLC 30, 74**
See also AAYA 8; AITN 1; CA 85-88;
CANR 24; DLB 6; MTCW

Constant (de Rebecque), (Henri) Benjamin
1767-1830 .... **NCLC 6**
See also DLB 119

Conybeare, Charles Augustus
See Eliot, T(homas) S(tearns)

Cook, Michael 1933- .... **CLC 58**
See also CA 93-96; DLB 53

Cook, Robin 1940- .... **CLC 14**
See also BEST 90:2; CA 108; 111

Cook, Roy
See Silverberg, Robert

Cooke, Elizabeth 1948- .... **CLC 55**
See also CA 129

Cooke, John Esten 1830-1886..... **NCLC 5**
See also DLB 3

Cooke, John Estes
See Baum, L(yman) Frank

Cooke, M. E.
See Creasey, John

Cooke, Margaret
See Creasey, John

Cooney, Ray .... **CLC 62**

Cooper, Henry St. John
See Creasey, John

Cooper, J. California............. **CLC 56**
See also BW; CA 125

Cooper, James Fenimore
1789-1851 .... **NCLC 1, 27**
See also CDALB 1640-1865; DLB 3;
SATA 19

Coover, Robert (Lowell)
1932- .... **CLC 3, 7, 15, 32, 46**
See also CA 45-48; CANR 3, 37; DLB 2;
DLBY 81; MTCW

Copeland, Stewart (Armstrong)
    1952- .... CLC 26
    See also The Police

Coppard, A(lfred) E(dgar)
    1878-1957 .... TCLC 5
    See also CA 114; YABC 1

Coppee, Francois 1842-1908 ...... TCLC 25

Coppola, Francis Ford 1939- ... CLC 16
    See also CA 77-80; DLB 44

Corcoran, Barbara 1911- .... CLC 17
    See also CA 21-24R; CAAS 2; CANR 11,
    28; DLB 52; SATA 3

Cordelier, Maurice
    See Giraudoux, (Hippolyte) Jean

Corman, Cid...................... CLC 9
    See also Corman, Sidney
    See also CAAS 2; DLB 5

Corman, Sidney 1924-
    See Corman, Cid
    See also CA 85-88

Cormier, Robert (Edmund)
    1925- .... CLC 12, 30
    See also AAYA 3; CA 1-4R; CANR 5, 23;
    CDALB 1968-1988; CLR 12; DLB 52;
    MAICYA; MTCW; SATA 10, 45

Corn, Alfred 1943- .... CLC 33
    See also CA 104; DLB 120; DLBY 80

Cornwell, David (John Moore)
    1931- .... CLC 9, 15
    See also le Carre, John
    See also CA 5-8R; CANR 13, 33; MTCW

Corrigan, Kevin................... CLC 55

Corso, (Nunzio) Gregory 1930-... CLC 1, 11
    See also CA 5-8R; DLB 5,16; MTCW

Cortazar, Julio
    1914-1984 ..... CLC 2, 3, 5, 10, 13, 15,
                    33, 34; SSC 7
    See also CA 21-24R; CANR 12, 32;
    DLB 113; HW; MTCW

Corwin, Cecil
    See Kornbluth, C(yril) M.

Cosic, Dobrica 1921- .... CLC 14
    See also CA 122; 138

Costain, Thomas B(ertram)
    1885-1965 .... CLC 30
    See also CA 5-8R; 25-28R; DLB 9

Costantini, Humberto
    1924(?)-1987 .... CLC 49
    See also CA 131; 122; HW

Costello, Elvis 1955-............. CLC 21

Cotter, Joseph S. Sr.
    See Cotter, Joseph Seamon Sr.

Cotter, Joseph Seamon Sr.
    1861-1949 .... TCLC 28
    See also BLC 1; BW; CA 124; DLB 50

Coulton, James
    See Hansen, Joseph

Couperus, Louis (Marie Anne)
    1863-1923 .... TCLC 15
    See also CA 115

Court, Wesli
    See Turco, Lewis (Putnam)

Courtenay, Bryce 1933-........... CLC 59
    See also CA 138

Courtney, Robert
    See Ellison, Harlan

Cousteau, Jacques-Yves 1910-...... CLC 30
    See also CA 65-68; CANR 15; MTCW;
    SATA 38

Coward, Noel (Peirce)
    1899-1973 .... CLC 1, 9, 29, 51
    See also AITN 1; CA 17-18; 41-44R;
    CANR 35; CAP 2; CDBLB 1914-1945;
    DLB 10; MTCW

Cowley, Malcolm 1898-1989 .... CLC 39
    See also CA 5-8R; 128; CANR 3; DLB 4,
    48; DLBY 81, 89; MTCW

Cowper, William 1731-1800...... NCLC 8
    See also DLB 104, 109

Cox, William Trevor 1928- ... CLC 9, 14, 71
    See also Trevor, William
    See also CA 9-12R; CANR 4, 37; DLB 14;
    MTCW

Cozzens, James Gould
    1903-1978 .... CLC 1, 4, 11
    See also CA 9-12R; 81-84; CANR 19;
    CDALB 1941-1968; DLB 9; DLBD 2;
    DLBY 84; MTCW

Crabbe, George 1754-1832....... NCLC 26
    See also DLB 93

Craig, A. A.
    See Anderson, Poul (William)

Craik, Dinah Maria (Mulock)
    1826-1887 .... NCLC 38
    See also DLB 35; MAICYA; SATA 34

Cram, Ralph Adams 1863-1942.... TCLC 45

Crane, (Harold) Hart
    1899-1932 .... TCLC 2, 5; PC 3
    See also CA 104; 127; CDALB 1917-1929;
    DLB 4, 48; MTCW; WLC

Crane, R(onald) S(almon)
    1886-1967 .... CLC 27
    See also CA 85-88; DLB 63

Crane, Stephen (Townley)
    1871-1900 ..... TCLC 11, 17, 32; SSC 7
    See also CA 109; CDALB 1865-1917;
    DLB 12, 54, 78; WLC; YABC 2

Crase, Douglas 1944- .... CLC 58
    See also CA 106

Craven, Margaret 1901-1980....... CLC 17
    See also CA 103

Crawford, F(rancis) Marion
    1854-1909 .... TCLC 10
    See also CA 107; DLB 71

Crawford, Isabella Valancy
    1850-1887 .... NCLC 12
    See also DLB 92

Crayon, Geoffrey
    See Irving, Washington

Creasey, John 1908-1973.......... CLC 11
    See also CA 5-8R; 41-44R; CANR 8;
    DLB 77; MTCW

Crebillon, Claude Prosper Jolyot de (fils)
    1707-1777 .... LC 1

Credo
    See Creasey, John

Creeley, Robert (White)
    1926- .... CLC 1, 2, 4, 8, 11, 15, 36
    See also CA 1-4R; CAAS 10; CANR 23;
    DLB 5, 16; MTCW

Crews, Harry (Eugene)
    1935- .... CLC 6, 23, 49
    See also AITN 1; CA 25-28R; CANR 20;
    DLB 6; MTCW

Crichton, (John) Michael
    1942- .... CLC 2, 6, 54
    See also AITN 2; CA 25-28R; CANR 13;
    DLBY 81; MTCW; SATA 9

Crispin, Edmund .... CLC 22
    See also Montgomery, (Robert) Bruce
    See also DLB 87

Cristofer, Michael 1945(?)- .... CLC 28
    See also CA 110; DLB 7

Croce, Benedetto 1866-1952 ...... TCLC 37
    See also CA 120

Crockett, David 1786-1836 ...... NCLC 8
    See also DLB 3, 11

Crockett, Davy
    See Crockett, David

Croker, John Wilson 1780-1857 .. NCLC 10
    See also DLB 110

Cronin, A(rchibald) J(oseph)
    1896-1981 .... CLC 32
    See also CA 1-4R; 102; CANR 5; SATA 25,
    47

Cross, Amanda
    See Heilbrun, Carolyn G(old)

Crothers, Rachel 1878(?)-1958..... TCLC 19
    See also CA 113; DLB 7

Croves, Hal
    See Traven, B.

Crowfield, Christopher
    See Stowe, Harriet (Elizabeth) Beecher

Crowley, Aleister.................. TCLC 7
    See also Crowley, Edward Alexander

Crowley, Edward Alexander 1875-1947
    See Crowley, Aleister
    See also CA 104

Crowley, John 1942-.............. CLC 57
    See also CA 61-64; DLBY 82; SATA 65

Crud
    See Crumb, R(obert)

Crumarums
    See Crumb, R(obert)

Crumb, R(obert) 1943-............ CLC 17
    See also CA 106

Crumbum
    See Crumb, R(obert)

Crumski
    See Crumb, R(obert)

Crum the Bum
    See Crumb, R(obert)

Crunk
    See Crumb, R(obert)

Crustt
    See Crumb, R(obert)

Cryer, Gretchen (Kiger) 1935-...... CLC 21
    See also CA 114; 123

Csath, Geza 1887-1919.......... TCLC 13
    See also CA 111

Cudlip, David 1933- . . . . **CLC 34**

Cullen, Countee 1903-1946 . . . . . **TCLC 4, 37**
See also BLC 1; BW; CA 108; 124;
CDALB 1917-1929; DLB 4, 48, 51;
MTCW; SATA 18

Cum, R.
See Crumb, R(obert)

Cummings, Bruce F(rederick) 1889-1919
See Barbellion, W. N. P.
See also CA 123

Cummings, E(dward) E(stlin)
1894-1962 . . . . . **CLC 1, 3, 8, 12, 15, 68;**
PC 5
See also CA 73-76; CANR 31;
CDALB 1929-1941; DLB 4, 48; MTCW;
WLC 2

Cunha, Euclides (Rodrigues Pimenta) da
1866-1909 . . . . **TCLC 24**
See also CA 123

Cunningham, E. V.
See Fast, Howard (Melvin)

Cunningham, J(ames) V(incent)
1911-1985 . . . . **CLC 3, 31**
See also CA 1-4R; 115; CANR 1; DLB 5

Cunningham, Julia (Woolfolk)
1916- . . . . **CLC 12**
See also CA 9-12R; CANR 4, 19, 36;
MAICYA; SAAS 2; SATA 1, 26

Cunningham, Michael 1952- . . . . **CLC 34**
See also CA 136

Cunninghame Graham, R(obert) B(ontine)
1852-1936 . . . . **TCLC 19**
See also Graham, R(obert) B(ontine)
Cunninghame
See also CA 119; DLB 98

Currie, Ellen 19(?)- . . . . **CLC 44**

Curtin, Philip
See Lowndes, Marie Adelaide (Belloc)

Curtis, Price
See Ellison, Harlan

Czaczkes, Shmuel Yosef
See Agnon, S(hmuel) Y(osef Halevi)

D. P.
See Wells, H(erbert) G(eorge)

Dabrowska, Maria (Szumska)
1889-1965 . . . . **CLC 15**
See also CA 106

Dabydeen, David 1955- . . . . **CLC 34**
See also BW; CA 125

Dacey, Philip 1939- . . . . **CLC 51**
See also CA 37-40R; CANR 14, 32;
DLB 105

Dagerman, Stig (Halvard)
1923-1954 . . . . **TCLC 17**
See also CA 117

Dahl, Roald 1916-1990 . . . . **CLC 1, 6, 18**
See also CA 1-4R; 133; CANR 6, 32, 37;
CLR 1, 7; MAICYA; MTCW; SATA 1,
26; SATO 65

Dahlberg, Edward 1900-1977 . . . **CLC 1, 7, 14**
See also CA 9-12R; 69-72; CANR 31;
DLB 48; MTCW

Dale, Colin . . . . **TCLC 18**
See also Lawrence, T(homas) E(dward)

Dale, George E.
See Asimov, Isaac

Daly, Elizabeth 1878-1967 . . . . **CLC 52**
See also CA 23-24; 25-28R; CAP 2

Daly, Maureen 1921- . . . . **CLC 17**
See also AAYA 5; CANR 37; MAICYA;
SAAS 1; SATA 2

Daniels, Brett
See Adler, Renata

Dannay, Frederic 1905-1982 . . . . **CLC 11**
See also Queen, Ellery
See also CA 1-4R; 107; CANR 1, 39;
MTCW

D'Annunzio, Gabriele
1863-1938 . . . . **TCLC 6, 40**
See also CA 104

d'Antibes, Germain
See Simenon, Georges (Jacques Christian)

Danvers, Dennis 1947- . . . . **CLC 70**

Danziger, Paula 1944- . . . . **CLC 21**
See also AAYA 4; CA 112; 115; CANR 37;
CLR 20; MAICYA; SATA 30, 36, 63

Dario, Ruben . . . . **TCLC 4**
See also Sarmiento, Felix Ruben Garcia

Darley, George 1795-1846 . . . . **NCLC 2**
See also DLB 96

Daryush, Elizabeth 1887-1977 . . . . **CLC 6, 19**
See also CA 49-52; CANR 3; DLB 20

Daudet, (Louis Marie) Alphonse
1840-1897 . . . . **NCLC 1**

Daumal, Rene 1908-1944 . . . . **TCLC 14**
See also CA 114

Davenport, Guy (Mattison Jr.)
1927- . . . . **CLC 6, 14, 38**
See also CA 33-36R; CANR 23

Davidson, Avram 1923-
See Queen, Ellery
See also CA 101; CANR 26; DLB 8

Davidson, Donald (Grady)
1893-1968 . . . . **CLC 2, 13, 19**
See also CA 5-8R; 25-28R; CANR 4;
DLB 45

Davidson, Hugh
See Hamilton, Edmond

Davidson, John 1857-1909 . . . . **TCLC 24**
See also CA 118; DLB 19

Davidson, Sara 1943- . . . . **CLC 9**
See also CA 81-84

Davie, Donald (Alfred)
1922- . . . . **CLC 5, 8, 10, 31**
See also CA 1-4R; CAAS 3; CANR 1;
DLB 27; MTCW

Davies, Ray(mond Douglas) 1944- . . **CLC 21**
See also CA 116

Davies, Rhys 1903-1978 . . . . **CLC 23**
See also CA 9-12R; 81-84; CANR 4

Davies, (William) Robertson
1913- . . . . **CLC 2, 7, 13, 25, 42**
See also BEST 89:2; CA 33-36R; CANR 17;
DLB 68; MTCW; WLC

Davies, W(illiam) H(enry)
1871-1940 . . . . **TCLC 5**
See also CA 104; DLB 19

Davies, Walter C.
See Kornbluth, C(yril) M.

Davis, B. Lynch
See Bioy Casares, Adolfo; Borges, Jorge
Luis

Davis, Gordon
See Hunt, E(verette) Howard Jr.

Davis, Harold Lenoir 1896-1960 . . . . **CLC 49**
See also CA 89-92; DLB 9

Davis, Rebecca (Blaine) Harding
1831-1910 . . . . **TCLC 6**
See also CA 104; DLB 74

Davis, Richard Harding
1864-1916 . . . . **TCLC 24**
See also CA 114; DLB 12, 23, 78, 79

Davison, Frank Dalby 1893-1970 . . . **CLC 15**
See also CA 116

Davison, Lawrence H.
See Lawrence, D(avid) H(erbert Richards)

Davison, Peter 1928- . . . . **CLC 28**
See also CA 9-12R; CAAS 4; CANR 3;
DLB 5

Davys, Mary 1674-1732 . . . . **LC 1**
See also DLB 39

Dawson, Fielding 1930- . . . . **CLC 6**
See also CA 85-88

Day, Clarence (Shepard Jr.)
1874-1935 . . . . **TCLC 25**
See also CA 108; DLB 11

Day, Thomas 1748-1789 . . . . **LC 1**
See also DLB 39; YABC 1

Day Lewis, C(ecil)
1904-1972 . . . . **CLC 1, 6, 10**
See also Blake, Nicholas
See also CA 13-16; 33-36R; CANR 34;
CAP 1; DLB 15, 20; MTCW

Dazai, Osamu . . . . **TCLC 11**
See also Tsushima, Shuji

de Andrade, Carlos Drummond
See Drummond de Andrade, Carlos

Deane, Norman
See Creasey, John

de Beauvoir, Simone (Lucie Ernestine Marie
Bertrand)
See Beauvoir, Simone (Lucie Ernestine
Marie Bertrand) de

de Brissac, Malcolm
See Dickinson, Peter (Malcolm)

de Chardin, Pierre Teilhard
See Teilhard de Chardin, (Marie Joseph)
Pierre

Dee, John 1527-1608 . . . . **LC 20**

Deer, Sandra 1940- . . . . **CLC 45**

De Ferrari, Gabriella . . . . **CLC 65**

Defoe, Daniel 1660(?)-1731 . . . . **LC 1**
See also CDBLB 1660-1789; DLB 39, 95,
101; MAICYA; SATA 22; WLC

de Gourmont, Remy
See Gourmont, Remy de

de Hartog, Jan 1914- . . . . **CLC 19**
See also CA 1-4R; CANR 1

de Hostos, E. M.
See Hostos (y Bonilla), Eugenio Maria de

Eiseley, Loren Corey 1907-1977 . . . . . **CLC 7**
See also AAYA 5; CA 1-4R; 73-76;
CANR 6

Eisenstadt, Jill 1963- . . . . **CLC 50**

Eisner, Simon
See Kornbluth, C(yril) M.

Ekeloef, (Bengt) Gunnar
1907-1968 . . . . **CLC 27**
See also Ekelof, (Bengt) Gunnar
See also CA 123; 25-28R

Ekelof, (Bengt) Gunnar . . . . **CLC 27**
See also Ekeloef, (Bengt) Gunnar

Ekwensi, C. O. D.
See Ekwensi, Cyprian (Odiatu Duaka)

Ekwensi, Cyprian (Odiatu Duaka)
1921- . . . . **CLC 4**
See also BLC 1; BW; CA 29-32R;
CANR 18; DLB 117; MTCW; SATA 66

Elaine . . . . **TCLC 18**
See also Leverson, Ada

El Crummo
See Crumb, R(obert)

Elia
See Lamb, Charles

Eliade, Mircea 1907-1986 . . . . **CLC 19**
See also CA 65-68; 119; CANR 30; MTCW

Eliot, A. D.
See Jewett, (Theodora) Sarah Orne

Eliot, Alice
See Jewett, (Theodora) Sarah Orne

Eliot, Dan
See Silverberg, Robert

Eliot, George 1819-1880 . . . . **NCLC 4, 13, 23**
See also CDBLB 1832-1890; DLB 21, 35,
55; WLC

Eliot, John 1604-1690 . . . . **LC 5**
See also DLB 24

Eliot, T(homas) S(tearns)
1888-1965 . . . . **CLC 1, 2, 3, 6, 9, 10, 13,
15, 24, 34, 41, 55, 57; PC 5**
See also CA 5-8R; 25-28R;
CDALB 1929-1941; DLB 7, 10, 45, 63;
MTCW; WLC 2

Elizabeth 1866-1941 . . . . **TCLC 41**

Elkin, Stanley L(awrence)
1930- . . . . **CLC 4, 6, 9, 14, 27, 51**
See also CA 9-12R; CANR 8; DLB 2, 28;
DLBY 80; MTCW

Elledge, Scott . . . . **CLC 34**

Elliott, Don
See Silverberg, Robert

Elliott, George P(aul) 1918-1980 . . . . . **CLC 2**
See also CA 1-4R; 97-100; CANR 2

Elliott, Janice 1931- . . . . **CLC 47**
See also CA 13-16R; CANR 8, 29; DLB 14

Elliott, Sumner Locke 1917-1991 . . . **CLC 38**
See also CA 5-8R; 134; CANR 2, 21

Elliott, William
See Bradbury, Ray (Douglas)

Ellis, A. E. . . . . **CLC 7**

Ellis, Alice Thomas . . . . **CLC 40**
See also Haycraft, Anna

Ellis, Bret Easton 1964- . . . . **CLC 39, 71**
See also AAYA 2; CA 118; 123

Ellis, (Henry) Havelock
1859-1939 . . . . **TCLC 14**
See also CA 109

Ellis, Landon
See Ellison, Harlan

Ellis, Trey 1962- . . . . **CLC 55**

Ellison, Harlan 1934- . . . . **CLC 1, 13, 42**
See also CA 5-8R; CANR 5; DLB 8;
MTCW

Ellison, Ralph (Waldo)
1914- . . . . **CLC 1, 3, 11, 54**
See also BLC 1; BW; CA 9-12R; CANR 24;
CDALB 1941-1968; DLB 2, 76; MTCW;
WLC

Ellmann, Lucy (Elizabeth) 1956- . . . . **CLC 61**
See also CA 128

Ellmann, Richard (David)
1918-1987 . . . . **CLC 50**
See also BEST 89:2; CA 1-4R; 122;
CANR 2, 28; DLB 103; DLBY 87;
MTCW

Elman, Richard 1934- . . . . **CLC 19**
See also CA 17-20R; CAAS 3

Elron
See Hubbard, L(afayette) Ron(ald)

Eluard, Paul . . . . **TCLC 7, 41**
See also Grindel, Eugene

Elyot, Sir Thomas 1490(?)-1546 . . . . . **LC 11**

Elytis, Odysseus 1911- . . . . **CLC 15, 49**
See also CA 102; MTCW

Emecheta, (Florence Onye) Buchi
1944- . . . . **CLC 14, 48**
See also BLC 2; BW; CA 81-84; CANR 27;
DLB 117; MTCW; SATA 66

Emerson, Ralph Waldo
1803-1882 . . . . **NCLC 1, 38**
See also CDALB 1640-1865; DLB 1, 59, 73;
WLC

Eminescu, Mihail 1850-1889 . . . . . **NCLC 33**

Empson, William
1906-1984 . . . . **CLC 3, 8, 19, 33, 34**
See also CA 17-20R; 112; CANR 31;
DLB 20; MTCW

Enchi Fumiko (Ueda) 1905-1986 . . . . **CLC 31**
See also CA 129; 121

Ende, Michael (Andreas Helmuth)
1929- . . . . **CLC 31**
See also CA 118; 124; CANR 36; CLR 14;
DLB 75; MAICYA; SATA 42, 61

Endo, Shusaku 1923- . . . . . **CLC 7, 14, 19, 54**
See also CA 29-32R; CANR 21; MTCW

Engel, Marian 1933-1985 . . . . **CLC 36**
See also CA 25-28R; CANR 12; DLB 53

Engelhardt, Frederick
See Hubbard, L(afayette) Ron(ald)

Enright, D(ennis) J(oseph)
1920- . . . . **CLC 4, 8, 31**
See also CA 1-4R; CANR 1; DLB 27;
SATA 25

Enzensberger, Hans Magnus
1929- . . . . **CLC 43**
See also CA 116; 119

Ephron, Nora 1941- . . . . **CLC 17, 31**
See also AITN 2; CA 65-68; CANR 12, 39

Epsilon
See Betjeman, John

Epstein, Daniel Mark 1948- . . . . **CLC 7**
See also CA 49-52; CANR 2

Epstein, Jacob 1956- . . . . **CLC 19**
See also CA 114

Epstein, Joseph 1937- . . . . **CLC 39**
See also CA 112; 119

Epstein, Leslie 1938- . . . . **CLC 27**
See also CA 73-76; CAAS 12; CANR 23

Equiano, Olaudah 1745(?)-1797 . . . . . . **LC 16**
See also BLC 2; DLB 37, 50

Erasmus, Desiderius 1469(?)-1536 . . . . **LC 16**

Erdman, Paul E(mil) 1932- . . . . **CLC 25**
See also AITN 1; CA 61-64; CANR 13

Erdrich, Louise 1954- . . . . **CLC 39, 54**
See also BEST 89:1; CA 114; MTCW

Erenburg, Ilya (Grigoryevich)
See Ehrenburg, Ilya (Grigoryevich)

Erickson, Stephen Michael 1950-
See Erickson, Steve
See also CA 129

Erickson, Steve . . . . **CLC 64**
See also Erickson, Stephen Michael

Ericson, Walter
See Fast, Howard (Melvin)

Eriksson, Buntel
See Bergman, (Ernst) Ingmar

Eschenbach, Wolfram von
See Wolfram von Eschenbach

Eseki, Bruno
See Mphahlele, Ezekiel

Esenin, Sergei (Alexandrovich)
1895-1925 . . . . **TCLC 4**
See also CA 104

Eshleman, Clayton 1935- . . . . **CLC 7**
See also CA 33-36R; CAAS 6; DLB 5

Espriella, Don Manuel Alvarez
See Southey, Robert

Espriu, Salvador 1913-1985 . . . . **CLC 9**
See also CA 115

Esse, James
See Stephens, James

Esterbrook, Tom
See Hubbard, L(afayette) Ron(ald)

Estleman, Loren D. 1952- . . . . **CLC 48**
See also CA 85-88; CANR 27; MTCW

Evans, Mary Ann
See Eliot, George

Evarts, Esther
See Benson, Sally

Everett, Percival
See Everett, Percival L.

Everett, Percival L. 1956- . . . . **CLC 57**
See also CA 129

Everson, R(onald) G(ilmour)
1903- . . . . **CLC 27**
See also CA 17-20R; DLB 88

Everson, William (Oliver)
    1912- . . . . CLC 1, 5, 14
    See also CA 9-12R; CANR 20; DLB 5, 16;
    MTCW

Evtushenko, Evgenii Aleksandrovich
    See Yevtushenko, Yevgeny (Alexandrovich)

Ewart, Gavin (Buchanan)
    1916- . . . . CLC 13, 46
    See also CA 89-92; CANR 17; DLB 40;
    MTCW

Ewers, Hanns Heinz   1871-1943 . . . TCLC 12
    See also CA 109

Ewing, Frederick R.
    See Sturgeon, Theodore (Hamilton)

Exley, Frederick (Earl)   1929- . . . . CLC 6, 11
    See also AITN 2; CA 81-84; 138; DLBY 81

Eynhardt, Guillermo
    See Quiroga, Horacio (Sylvestre)

Ezekiel, Nissim   1924- . . . . CLC 61
    See also CA 61-64

Ezekiel, Tish O'Dowd   1943- . . . . CLC 34
    See also CA 129

Fagen, Donald   1948- . . . . CLC 26

Fainzilberg, Ilya Arnoldovich   1897-1937
    See Ilf, Ilya
    See also CA 120

Fair, Ronald L.   1932- . . . . CLC 18
    See also BW; CA 69-72; CANR 25; DLB 33

Fairbairns, Zoe (Ann)   1948- . . . . CLC 32
    See also CA 103; CANR 21

Falco, Gian
    See Papini, Giovanni

Falconer, James
    See Kirkup, James

Falconer, Kenneth
    See Kornbluth, C(yril) M.

Falkland, Samuel
    See Heijermans, Herman

Fallaci, Oriana   1930- . . . . CLC 11
    See also CA 77-80; CANR 15; MTCW

Faludy, George   1913- . . . . CLC 42
    See also CA 21-24R

Faludy, Gyoergy
    See Faludy, George

Fanon, Frantz   1925-1961 . . . . CLC 74
    See also BLC 2; BW; CA 116; 89-92

Fanshawe, Ann   . . . . LC 11

Fante, John (Thomas)   1911-1983 . . . CLC 60
    See also CA 69-72; 109; CANR 23;
    DLBY 83

Farah, Nuruddin   1945- . . . . CLC 53
    See also BLC 2; CA 106

Fargue, Leon-Paul   1876(?)-1947 . . . TCLC 11
    See also CA 109

Farigoule, Louis
    See Romains, Jules

Farina, Richard   1936(?)-1966 . . . . CLC 9
    See also CA 81-84; 25-28R

Farley, Walter (Lorimer)
    1915-1989 . . . . CLC 17
    See also CA 17-20R; CANR 8, 29; DLB 22;
    MAICYA; SATA 2, 43

Farmer, Philip Jose   1918- . . . . CLC 1, 19
    See also CA 1-4R; CANR 4, 35; DLB 8;
    MTCW

Farquhar, George   1677-1707 . . . . LC 21
    See also DLB 84

Farrell, J(ames) G(ordon)
    1935-1979 . . . . CLC 6
    See also CA 73-76; 89-92; CANR 36;
    DLB 14; MTCW

Farrell, James T(homas)
    1904-1979 . . . . CLC 1, 4, 8, 11, 66
    See also CA 5-8R; 89-92; CANR 9; DLB 4,
    9, 86; DLBD 2; MTCW

Farren, Richard J.
    See Betjeman, John

Farren, Richard M.
    See Betjeman, John

Fassbinder, Rainer Werner
    1946-1982 . . . . CLC 20
    See also CA 93-96; 106; CANR 31

Fast, Howard (Melvin)   1914- . . . . . . CLC 23
    See also CA 1-4R; CANR 1, 33; DLB 9;
    SATA 7

Faulcon, Robert
    See Holdstock, Robert P.

Faulkner, William (Cuthbert)
    1897-1962 . . . . CLC 1, 3, 6, 8, 9, 11, 14,
                         18, 28, 52, 68; SSC 1
    See also AAYA 7; CA 81-84; CANR 33;
    CDALB 1929-1941; DLB 9, 11, 44, 102;
    DLBD 2; DLBY 86; MTCW; WLC

Fauset, Jessie Redmon
    1884(?)-1961 . . . . CLC 19, 54
    See also BLC 2; BW; CA 109; DLB 51

Faust, Irvin   1924- . . . . CLC 8
    See also CA 33-36R; CANR 28; DLB 2, 28;
    DLBY 80

Fawkes, Guy
    See Benchley, Robert (Charles)

Fearing, Kenneth (Flexner)
    1902-1961 . . . . CLC 51
    See also CA 93-96; DLB 9

Fecamps, Elise
    See Creasey, John

Federman, Raymond   1928- . . . . . . CLC 6, 47
    See also CA 17-20R; CAAS 8; CANR 10;
    DLBY 80

Federspiel, J(uerg) F.   1931- . . . . CLC 42

Feiffer, Jules (Ralph)   1929- . . . . CLC 2, 8, 64
    See also AAYA 3; CA 17-20R; CANR 30;
    DLB 7, 44; MTCW; SATA 8, 61

Feige, Hermann Albert Otto Maximilian
    See Traven, B.

Fei-Kan, Li
    See Li Fei-kan

Feinberg, David B.   1956- . . . . CLC 59
    See also CA 135

Feinstein, Elaine   1930- . . . . CLC 36
    See also CA 69-72; CAAS 1; CANR 31;
    DLB 14, 40; MTCW

Feldman, Irving (Mordecai)   1928- . . . . CLC 7
    See also CA 1-4R; CANR 1

Fellini, Federico   1920- . . . . CLC 16
    See also CA 65-68; CANR 33

Felsen, Henry Gregor   1916- . . . . CLC 17
    See also CA 1-4R; CANR 1; SAAS 2;
    SATA 1

Fenton, James Martin   1949- . . . . CLC 32
    See also CA 102; DLB 40

Ferber, Edna   1887-1968 . . . . CLC 18
    See also AITN 1; CA 5-8R; 25-28R; DLB 9,
    28, 86; MTCW; SATA 7

Ferguson, Helen
    See Kavan, Anna

Ferguson, Samuel   1810-1886 . . . . . NCLC 33
    See also DLB 32

Ferling, Lawrence
    See Ferlinghetti, Lawrence (Monsanto)

Ferlinghetti, Lawrence (Monsanto)
    1919(?)- . . . . CLC 2, 6, 10, 27; PC 1
    See also CA 5-8R; CANR 3;
    CDALB 1941-1968; DLB 5, 16; MTCW

Fernandez, Vicente Garcia Huidobro
    See Huidobro Fernandez, Vicente Garcia

Ferrer, Gabriel (Francisco Victor) Miro
    See Miro (Ferrer), Gabriel (Francisco
    Victor)

Ferrier, Susan (Edmonstone)
    1782-1854 . . . . NCLC 8
    See also DLB 116

Ferrigno, Robert . . . . CLC 65

Feuchtwanger, Lion   1884-1958 . . . . . TCLC 3
    See also CA 104; DLB 66

Feydeau, Georges (Leon Jules Marie)
    1862-1921 . . . . TCLC 22
    See also CA 113

Ficino, Marsilio   1433-1499 . . . . LC 12

Fiedler, Leslie A(aron)
    1917- . . . . CLC 4, 13, 24
    See also CA 9-12R; CANR 7; DLB 28, 67;
    MTCW

Field, Andrew   1938- . . . . CLC 44
    See also CA 97-100; CANR 25

Field, Eugene   1850-1895 . . . . NCLC 3
    See also DLB 23, 42; MAICYA; SATA 16

Field, Gans T.
    See Wellman, Manly Wade

Field, Michael . . . . TCLC 43

Field, Peter
    See Hobson, Laura Z(ametkin)

Fielding, Henry   1707-1754 . . . . LC 1
    See also CDBLB 1660-1789; DLB 39, 84,
    101; WLC

Fielding, Sarah   1710-1768 . . . . LC 1
    See also DLB 39

Fierstein, Harvey (Forbes)   1954- . . . CLC 33
    See also CA 123; 129

Figes, Eva   1932- . . . . CLC 31
    See also CA 53-56; CANR 4; DLB 14

Finch, Robert (Duer Claydon)
    1900- . . . . CLC 18
    See also CA 57-60; CANR 9, 24; DLB 88

Findley, Timothy   1930- . . . . CLC 27
    See also CA 25-28R; CANR 12; DLB 53

Fink, William
    See Mencken, H(enry) L(ouis)

Firbank, Louis 1942-
See Reed, Lou
See also CA 117

Firbank, (Arthur Annesley) Ronald
1886-1926 .... TCLC 1
See also CA 104; DLB 36

Fisher, Roy 1930-................ CLC 25
See also CA 81-84; CAAS 10; CANR 16;
DLB 40

Fisher, Rudolph 1897-1934 .... TCLC 11
See also BLC 2; BW; CA 107; 124; DLB 51,
102

Fisher, Vardis (Alvero) 1895-1968.... CLC 7
See also CA 5-8R; 25-28R; DLB 9

Fiske, Tarleton
See Bloch, Robert (Albert)

Fitch, Clarke
See Sinclair, Upton (Beall)

Fitch, John IV
See Cormier, Robert (Edmund)

Fitgerald, Penelope 1916- .... CLC 61

Fitzgerald, Captain Hugh
See Baum, L(yman) Frank

FitzGerald, Edward 1809-1883 .... NCLC 9
See also DLB 32

Fitzgerald, F(rancis) Scott (Key)
1896-1940 .... TCLC 1, 6, 14, 28; SSC 6
See also AITN 1; CA 110; 123;
CDALB 1917-1929; DLB 4, 9, 86;
DLBD 1; DLBY 81; MTCW; WLC

Fitzgerald, Penelope 1916-...... CLC 19, 51
See also CA 85-88; CAAS 10; DLB 14

FitzGerald, Robert D(avid)
1902-1987 .... CLC 19
See also CA 17-20R

Fitzgerald, Robert (Stuart)
1910-1985 .... CLC 39
See also CA 1-4R; 114; CANR 1; DLBY 80

Flanagan, Thomas (James Bonner)
1923- .... CLC 25, 52
See also CA 108; DLBY 80; MTCW

Flaubert, Gustave
1821-1880 ..... NCLC 2, 10, 19; SSC 11
See also DLB 119; WLC

Flecker, (Herman) James Elroy
1884-1915 .... TCLC 43
See also CA 109; DLB 10, 19

Fleming, Ian (Lancaster)
1908-1964 .... CLC 3, 30
See also CA 5-8R; CDBLB 1945-1960;
DLB 87; MTCW; SATA 9

Fleming, Thomas (James) 1927- .... CLC 37
See also CA 5-8R; CANR 10; SATA 8

Fletcher, John Gould 1886-1950... TCLC 35
See also CA 107; DLB 4, 45

Fleur, Paul
See Pohl, Frederik

Flying Officer X
See Bates, H(erbert) E(rnest)

Fo, Dario 1926-.................. CLC 32
See also CA 116; 128; MTCW

Fogarty, Jonathan Titulescu Esq.
See Farrell, James T(homas)

Folke, Will
See Bloch, Robert (Albert)

Follett, Ken(neth Martin) 1949- .... CLC 18
See also AAYA 6; BEST 89:4; CA 81-84;
CANR 13, 33; DLB 87; DLBY 81;
MTCW

Fontane, Theodor 1819-1898 ..... NCLC 26

Foote, Horton 1916-.............. CLC 51
See also CA 73-76; CANR 34; DLB 26

Forbes, Esther 1891-1967......... CLC 12
See also CA 13-14; 25-28R; CAP 1;
CLR 27; DLB 22; MAICYA; SATA 2

Forche, Carolyn (Louise) 1950-..... CLC 25
See also CA 109; 117; DLB 5

Ford, Elbur
See Hibbert, Eleanor Burford

Ford, Ford Madox
1873-1939 .... TCLC 1, 15, 39
See also CA 104; 132; CDBLB 1914-1945;
DLB 34, 98; MTCW

Ford, John 1895-1973............. CLC 16
See also CA 45-48

Ford, Richard 1944-.............. CLC 46
See also CA 69-72; CANR 11

Ford, Webster
See Masters, Edgar Lee

Foreman, Richard 1937-.......... CLC 50
See also CA 65-68; CANR 32

Forester, C(ecil) S(cott)
1899-1966 .... CLC 35
See also CA 73-76; 25-28R; SATA 13

Forez
See Mauriac, Francois (Charles)

Forman, James Douglas 1932-...... CLC 21
See also CA 9-12R; CANR 4, 19;
MAICYA; SATA 8, 70

Fornes, Maria Irene 1930-...... CLC 39, 61
See also CA 25-28R; CANR 28; DLB 7;
HW; MTCW

Forrest, Leon 1937- .... CLC 4
See also BW; CA 89-92; CAAS 7;
CANR 25; DLB 33

Forster, E(dward) M(organ)
1879-1970 .... CLC 1, 2, 3, 4, 9, 10, 13,
15, 22, 45
See also AAYA 2; CA 13-14; 25-28R;
CAP 1; CDBLB 1914-1945; DLB 34, 98;
MTCW; SATA 57; WLC

Forster, John 1812-1876 .... NCLC 11

Forsyth, Frederick 1938-...... CLC 2, 5, 36
See also BEST 89:4; CA 85-88; CANR 38;
DLB 87; MTCW

Forten, Charlotte L. .... TCLC 16
See also Grimke, Charlotte L(ottie) Forten
See also BLC 2; DLB 50

Foscolo, Ugo 1778-1827.......... NCLC 8

Fosse, Bob .... CLC 20
See also Fosse, Robert Louis

Fosse, Robert Louis 1927-1987
See Fosse, Bob
See also CA 110; 123

Foster, Stephen Collins
1826-1864 .... NCLC 26

Foucault, Michel
1926-1984 .... CLC 31, 34, 69
See also CA 105; 113; CANR 34; MTCW

Fouque, Friedrich Heinrich Karl) de la Motte
1777-1843 .... NCLC 2
See also DLB 90

Fournier, Henri Alban 1886-1914
See Alain-Fournier
See also CA 104

Fournier, Pierre 1916-............ CLC 11
See also Gascar, Pierre
See also CA 89-92; CANR 16

Fowles, John
1926- .... CLC 1, 2, 3, 4, 6, 9, 10, 15, 33
See also CA 5-8R; CANR 25; CDBLB 1960
to Present; DLB 14; MTCW; SATA 22

Fox, Paula 1923-................. CLC 2, 8
See also AAYA 3; CA 73-76; CANR 20,
36; CLR 1; DLB 52; MAICYA; MTCW;
SATA 17, 60

Fox, William Price (Jr.) 1926- ..... CLC 22
See also CA 17-20R; CANR 11; DLB 2;
DLBY 81

Foxe, John 1516(?)-1587 .... LC 14

Frame, Janet .... CLC 2, 3, 6, 22, 66
See also Clutha, Janet Paterson Frame

France, Anatole................... TCLC 9
See also Thibault, Jacques Anatole Francois

Francis, Claude 19(?)- .... CLC 50

Francis, Dick 1920- .... CLC 2, 22, 42
See also AAYA 5; BEST 89:3; CA 5-8R;
CANR 9; CDBLB 1960 to Present;
DLB 87; MTCW

Francis, Robert (Churchill)
1901-1987 .... CLC 15
See also CA 1-4R; 123; CANR 1

Frank, Anne(lies Marie)
1929-1945 .... TCLC 17
See also CA 113; 133; MTCW; SATA 42;
WLC

Frank, Elizabeth 1945-............ CLC 39
See also CA 121; 126

Franklin, Benjamin
See Hasek, Jaroslav (Matej Frantisek)

Franklin, (Stella Maraia Sarah) Miles
1879-1954 .... TCLC 7
See also CA 104

Fraser, Antonia (Pakenham)
1932- .... CLC 32
See also CA 85-88; MTCW; SATA 32

Fraser, George MacDonald 1925-.... CLC 7
See also CA 45-48; CANR 2

Fraser, Sylvia 1935-.............. CLC 64
See also CA 45-48; CANR 1, 16

Frayn, Michael 1933-...... CLC 3, 7, 31, 47
See also CA 5-8R; CANR 30; DLB 13, 14;
MTCW

Fraze, Candida (Merrill) 1945-..... CLC 50
See also CA 126

Frazer, J(ames) G(eorge)
1854-1941 .... TCLC 32
See also CA 118

Frazer, Robert Caine
See Creasey, John

Frazer, Sir James George
See Frazer, J(ames) G(eorge)

Frazier, Ian 1951- .... CLC 46
See also CA 130

Frederic, Harold 1856-1898...... NCLC 10
See also DLB 12, 23

Frederick the Great 1712-1786 ...... LC 14

Fredro, Aleksander 1793-1876..... NCLC 8

Freeling, Nicolas 1927- .... CLC 38
See also CA 49-52; CAAS 12; CANR 1, 17;
DLB 87

Freeman, Douglas Southall
1886-1953 .... TCLC 11
See also CA 109; DLB 17

Freeman, Judith 1946- .... CLC 55

Freeman, Mary Eleanor Wilkins
1852-1930 .... TCLC 9; SSC 1
See also CA 106; DLB 12, 78

Freeman, R(ichard) Austin
1862-1943 .... TCLC 21
See also CA 113; DLB 70

French, Marilyn 1929- ...... CLC 10, 18, 60
See also CA 69-72; CANR 3, 31; MTCW

French, Paul
See Asimov, Isaac

Freneau, Philip Morin 1752-1832 .. NCLC 1
See also DLB 37, 43

Friedan, Betty (Naomi) 1921- ...... CLC 74
See also CA 65-68; CANR 18; MTCW

Friedman, B(ernard) H(arper)
1926- .... CLC 7
See also CA 1-4R; CANR 3

Friedman, Bruce Jay 1930- .... CLC 3, 5, 56
See also CA 9-12R; CANR 25; DLB 2, 28

Friel, Brian 1929- .... CLC 5, 42, 59
See also CA 21-24R; CANR 33; DLB 13;
MTCW

Friis-Baastad, Babbis Ellinor
1921-1970 .... CLC 12
See also CA 17-20R; 134; SATA 7

Frisch, Max (Rudolf)
1911-1991 ..... CLC 3, 9, 14, 18, 32, 44
See also CA 85-88; 134; CANR 32;
DLB 69; MTCW

Fromentin, Eugene (Samuel Auguste)
1820-1876 .... NCLC 10

Frost, Robert (Lee)
1874-1963 ... CLC 1, 3, 4, 9, 10, 13, 15,
26, 34, 44; PC 1
See also CA 89-92; CANR 33;
CDALB 1917-1929; DLB 54; DLBD 7;
MTCW; SATA 14; WLC

Froy, Herald
See Waterhouse, Keith (Spencer)

Fry, Christopher 1907- .... CLC 2, 10, 14
See also CA 17-20R; CANR 9, 30; DLB 13;
MTCW; SATA 66

Frye, (Herman) Northrop
1912-1991 .... CLC 24, 70
See also CA 5-8R; 133; CANR 8, 37;
DLB 67, 68; MTCW

Fuchs, Daniel 1909- .... CLC 8, 22
See also CA 81-84; CAAS 5; DLB 9, 26, 28

Fuchs, Daniel 1934- .... CLC 34
See also CA 37-40R; CANR 14

Fuentes, Carlos
1928- ...... CLC 3, 8, 10, 13, 22, 41, 60
See also AAYA 4; AITN 2; CA 69-72;
CANR 10, 32; DLB 113; HW; MTCW;
WLC

Fuentes, Gregorio Lopez y
See Lopez y Fuentes, Gregorio

Fugard, (Harold) Athol
1932- .... CLC 5, 9, 14, 25, 40
See also CA 85-88; CANR 32; MTCW

Fugard, Sheila 1932- .... CLC 48
See also CA 125

Fuller, Charles (H. Jr.)
1939- .... CLC 25; DC 1
See also BLC 2; BW; CA 108; 112; DLB 38;
MTCW

Fuller, John (Leopold) 1937- .... CLC 62
See also CA 21-24R; CANR 9; DLB 40

Fuller, Margaret .... NCLC 5
See also Ossoli, Sarah Margaret (Fuller
marchesa d')

Fuller, Roy (Broadbent)
1912-1991 .... CLC 4, 28
See also CA 5-8R; 135; CAAS 10; DLB 15,
20

Fulton, Alice 1952- .... CLC 52
See also CA 116

Furphy, Joseph 1843-1912 .... TCLC 25

Fussell, Paul 1924- .... CLC 74
See also BEST 90:1; CA 17-20R; CANR 8,
21, 35; MTCW

Futabatei, Shimei 1864-1909 ..... TCLC 44

Futrelle, Jacques 1875-1912 ...... TCLC 19
See also CA 113

G. B. S.
See Shaw, George Bernard

Gaboriau, Emile 1835-1873 ...... NCLC 14

Gadda, Carlo Emilio 1893-1973 .... CLC 11
See also CA 89-92

Gaddis, William
1922- .... CLC 1, 3, 6, 8, 10, 19, 43
See also CA 17-20R; CANR 21; DLB 2;
MTCW

Gaines, Ernest J(ames)
1933- .... CLC 3, 11, 18
See also AITN 1; BLC 2; BW; CA 9-12R;
CANR 6, 24; CDALB 1968-1988; DLB 2,
33; DLBY 80; MTCW

Gaitskill, Mary 1954- .... CLC 69
See also CA 128

Galdos, Benito Perez
See Perez Galdos, Benito

Gale, Zona 1874-1938 .... TCLC 7
See also CA 105; DLB 9, 78

Galeano, Eduardo (Hughes) 1940-... CLC 72
See also CA 29-32R; CANR 13, 32; HW

Galiano, Juan Valera y Alcala
See Valera y Alcala-Galiano, Juan

Gallagher, Tess 1943- .... CLC 18, 63
See also CA 106; DLB 120

Gallant, Mavis
1922- .... CLC 7, 18, 38; SSC 5
See also CA 69-72; CANR 29; DLB 53;
MTCW

Gallant, Roy A(rthur) 1924- .... CLC 17
See also CA 5-8R; CANR 4, 29; MAICYA;
SATA 4, 68

Gallico, Paul (William) 1897-1976 ... CLC 2
See also AITN 1; CA 5-8R; 69-72;
CANR 23; DLB 9; MAICYA; SATA 13

Gallup, Ralph
See Whitemore, Hugh (John)

Galsworthy, John 1867-1933.... TCLC 1, 45
See also CA 104; CDBLB 1890-1914;
DLB 10, 34, 98; WLC 2

Galt, John 1779-1839 .... NCLC 1
See also DLB 99, 116

Galvin, James 1951- .... CLC 38
See also CA 108; CANR 26

Gamboa, Federico 1864-1939...... TCLC 36

Gann, Ernest Kellogg 1910-1991.... CLC 23
See also AITN 1; CA 1-4R; 136; CANR 1

Garcia Lorca, Federico
1898-1936 ..... TCLC 1, 7; DC 2; PC 3
See also CA 104; 131; DLB 108; HW;
MTCW; WLC

Garcia Marquez, Gabriel (Jose)
1928- ... CLC 2, 3, 8, 10, 15, 27, 47, 55;
SSC 8
See also Marquez, Gabriel (Jose) Garcia
See also AAYA 3; BEST 89:1, 90:4;
CA 33-36R; CANR 10, 28; DLB 113;
HW; MTCW; WLC

Gard, Janice
See Latham, Jean Lee

Gard, Roger Martin du
See Martin du Gard, Roger

Gardam, Jane 1928- .... CLC 43
See also CA 49-52; CANR 2, 18, 33;
CLR 12; DLB 14; MAICYA; MTCW;
SAAS 9; SATA 28, 39

Gardner, Herb.................... CLC 44

Gardner, John (Champlin) Jr.
1933-1982 .... CLC 2, 3, 5, 7, 8, 10, 18,
28, 34; SSC 7
See also AITN 1; CA 65-68; 107;
CANR 33; DLB 2; DLBY 82; MTCW;
SATA 31, 40

Gardner, John (Edmund) 1926-..... CLC 30
See also CA 103; CANR 15; MTCW

Gardner, Noel
See Kuttner, Henry

Gardons, S. S.
See Snodgrass, William D(e Witt)

Garfield, Leon 1921-.............. CLC 12
See also AAYA 8; CA 17-20R; CANR 38;
CLR 21; MAICYA; SATA 1, 32

Garland, (Hannibal) Hamlin
1860-1940 .... TCLC 3
See also CA 104; DLB 12, 71, 78

Garneau, (Hector de) Saint-Denys
1912-1943 .... TCLC 13
See also CA 111; DLB 88

Garner, Alan 1934-. . . . . CLC 17
See also CA 73-76; CANR 15; CLR 20;
MAICYA; MTCW; SATA 18, 69

Garner, Hugh 1913-1979 . . . . CLC 13
See also CA 69-72; CANR 31; DLB 68

Garnett, David 1892-1981 . . . . CLC 3
See also CA 5-8R; 103; CANR 17; DLB 34

Garos, Stephanie
See Katz, Steve

Garrett, George (Palmer)
1929- . . . . CLC 3, 11, 51
See also CA 1-4R; CAAS 5; CANR 1;
DLB 2, 5; DLBY 83

Garrick, David 1717-1779 . . . . LC 15
See also DLB 84

Garrigue, Jean 1914-1972 . . . . CLC 2, 8
See also CA 5-8R; 37-40R; CANR 20

Garrison, Frederick
See Sinclair, Upton (Beall)

Garth, Will
See Hamilton, Edmond; Kuttner, Henry

Garvey, Marcus (Moziah Jr.)
1887-1940 . . . . TCLC 41
See also BLC 2; BW; CA 120; 124

Gary, Romain . . . . CLC 25
See also Kacew, Romain
See also DLB 83

Gascar, Pierre . . . . CLC 11
See also Fournier, Pierre

Gascoyne, David (Emery) 1916- . . . . CLC 45
See also CA 65-68; CANR 10, 28; DLB 20;
MTCW

Gaskell, Elizabeth Cleghorn
1810-1865 . . . . NCLC 5
See also CDBLB 1832-1890; DLB 21

Gass, William H(oward)
1924- . . . . CLC 1, 2, 8, 11, 15, 39
See also CA 17-20R; CANR 30; DLB 2;
MTCW

Gasset, Jose Ortega y
See Ortega y Gasset, Jose

Gautier, Theophile 1811-1872 . . . . . NCLC 1
See also DLB 119

Gawsworth, John
See Bates, H(erbert) E(rnest)

Gaye, Marvin (Penze) 1939-1984 . . . CLC 26
See also CA 112

Gebler, Carlo (Ernest) 1954- . . . . CLC 39
See also CA 119; 133

Gee, Maggie (Mary) 1948-. . . . . CLC 57
See also CA 130

Gee, Maurice (Gough) 1931- . . . . CLC 29
See also CA 97-100; SATA 46

Gelbart, Larry (Simon) 1923- . . . CLC 21, 61
See also CA 73-76

Gelber, Jack 1932-. . . . . CLC 1, 6, 14
See also CA 1-4R; CANR 2; DLB 7

Gellhorn, Martha Ellis 1908- . . . CLC 14, 60
See also CA 77-80; DLBY 82

Genet, Jean
1910-1986 . . . CLC 1, 2, 5, 10, 14, 44, 46
See also CA 13-16R; CANR 18; DLB 72;
DLBY 86; MTCW

Gent, Peter 1942-. . . . . CLC 29
See also AITN 1; CA 89-92; DLBY 82

George, Jean Craighead 1919-. . . . . . CLC 35
See also AAYA 8; CA 5-8R; CANR 25;
CLR 1; DLB 52; MAICYA; SATA 2, 68

George, Stefan (Anton)
1868-1933 . . . . TCLC 2, 14
See also CA 104

Georges, Georges Martin
See Simenon, Georges (Jacques Christian)

Gerhardi, William Alexander
See Gerhardie, William Alexander

Gerhardie, William Alexander
1895-1977 . . . . CLC 5
See also CA 25-28R; 73-76; CANR 18;
DLB 36

Gerstler, Amy 1956-. . . . . CLC 70

Gertler, T. . . . . CLC 34
See also CA 116; 121

Ghelderode, Michel de
1898-1962 . . . . CLC 6, 11
See also CA 85-88

Ghiselin, Brewster 1903- . . . . CLC 23
See also CA 13-16R; CAAS 10; CANR 13

Ghose, Zulfikar 1935-. . . . . CLC 42
See also CA 65-68

Ghosh, Amitav 1956- . . . . CLC 44

Giacosa, Giuseppe 1847-1906 . . . . . . TCLC 7
See also CA 104

Gibb, Lee
See Waterhouse, Keith (Spencer)

Gibbon, Lewis Grassic . . . . TCLC 4
See also Mitchell, James Leslie

Gibbons, Kaye 1960- . . . . CLC 50

Gibran, Kahlil 1883-1931. . . . . . . TCLC 1, 9
See also CA 104

Gibson, William (Ford) 1948- . . . CLC 39, 63
See also CA 126; 133

Gibson, William 1914- . . . . CLC 23
See also CA 9-12R; CANR 9; DLB 7;
SATA 66

Gide, Andre (Paul Guillaume)
1869-1951 . . . . TCLC 5, 12, 36
See also CA 104; 124; DLB 65; MTCW;
WLC

Gifford, Barry (Colby) 1946-. . . . . . . CLC 34
See also CA 65-68; CANR 9, 30

Gilbert, W(illiam) S(chwenck)
1836-1911 . . . . TCLC 3
See also CA 104; SATA 36

Gilbreth, Frank B. Jr. 1911- . . . . CLC 17
See also CA 9-12R; SATA 2

Gilchrist, Ellen 1935-. . . . . CLC 34, 48
See also CA 113; 116; MTCW

Giles, Molly 1942- . . . . CLC 39
See also CA 126

Gill, Patrick
See Creasey, John

Gilliam, Terry (Vance) 1940-. . . . . . . CLC 21
See also Monty Python
See also CA 108; 113; CANR 35

Gillian, Jerry
See Gilliam, Terry (Vance)

Gilliatt, Penelope (Ann Douglass)
1932- . . . . CLC 2, 10, 13, 53
See also AITN 2; CA 13-16R; DLB 14

Gilman, Charlotte (Anna) Perkins (Stetson)
1860-1935 . . . . TCLC 9, 37
See also CA 106

Gilmour, David 1944-. . . . . CLC 35
See also Pink Floyd
See also CA 138

Gilpin, William 1724-1804. . . . . . . NCLC 30

Gilray, J. D.
See Mencken, H(enry) L(ouis)

Gilroy, Frank D(aniel) 1925-. . . . . CLC 2
See also CA 81-84; CANR 32; DLB 7

Ginsberg, Allen
1926- . . . . . CLC 1, 2, 3, 4, 6, 13, 36, 69;
PC 4
See also AITN 1; CA 1-4R; CANR 2;
CDALB 1941-1968; DLB 5, 16; MTCW;
WLC 3

Ginzburg, Natalia
1916-1991 . . . . CLC 5, 11, 54, 70
See also CA 85-88; 135; CANR 33; MTCW

Giono, Jean 1895-1970. . . . . CLC 4, 11
See also CA 45-48; 29-32R; CANR 2, 35;
DLB 72; MTCW

Giovanni, Nikki 1943- . . . . . CLC 2, 4, 19, 64
See also AITN 1; BLC 2; BW; CA 29-32R;
CAAS 6; CANR 18; CLR 6; DLB 5, 41;
MAICYA; MTCW; SATA 24

Giovene, Andrea 1904-. . . . . CLC 7
See also CA 85-88

Gippius, Zinaida (Nikolayevna) 1869-1945
See Hippius, Zinaida
See also CA 106

Giraudoux, (Hippolyte) Jean
1882-1944 . . . . TCLC 2, 7
See also CA 104; DLB 65

Gironella, Jose Maria 1917- . . . . CLC 11
See also CA 101

Gissing, George (Robert)
1857-1903 . . . . TCLC 3, 24, 47
See also CA 105; DLB 18

Giurlani, Aldo
See Palazzeschi, Aldo

Gladkov, Fyodor (Vasilyevich)
1883-1958 . . . . TCLC 27

Glanville, Brian (Lester) 1931- . . . . . . CLC 6
See also CA 5-8R; CAAS 9; CANR 3;
DLB 15; SATA 42

Glasgow, Ellen (Anderson Gholson)
1873(?)-1945 . . . . TCLC 2, 7
See also CA 104; DLB 9, 12

Glassco, John 1909-1981 . . . . CLC 9
See also CA 13-16R; 102; CANR 15;
DLB 68

Glasscock, Amnesia
See Steinbeck, John (Ernst)

Glasser, Ronald J. 1940(?)-. . . . . CLC 37

Glassman, Joyce
See Johnson, Joyce

Glendinning, Victoria 1937-. . . . . CLC 50
See also CA 120; 127

Glissant, Edouard 1928-. . . . . CLC 10, 68

Gloag, Julian 1930- .... CLC 40
See also AITN 1; CA 65-68; CANR 10

Gluck, Louise 1943- .... CLC 7, 22, 44
See also Glueck, Louise
See also CA 33-36R; DLB 5

Glueck, Louise.................. CLC 7, 22
See also Gluck, Louise
See also DLB 5

Gobineau, Joseph Arthur (Comte) de
1816-1882 .... NCLC 17

Godard, Jean-Luc 1930-........... CLC 20
See also CA 93-96

Godden, (Margaret) Rumer 1907-... CLC 53
See also AAYA 6; CA 5-8R; CANR 4, 27,
36; CLR 20; MAICYA; SAAS 12;
SATA 3, 36

Godoy Alcayaga, Lucila 1889-1957
See Mistral, Gabriela
See also CA 104; 131; HW; MTCW

Godwin, Gail (Kathleen)
1937- .... CLC 5, 8, 22, 31, 69
See also CA 29-32R; CANR 15; DLB 6;
MTCW

Godwin, William 1756-1836...... NCLC 14
See also CDBLB 1789-1832; DLB 39, 104

Goethe, Johann Wolfgang von
1749-1832 .... NCLC 4, 22, 34; PC 5
See also DLB 94; WLC 3

Gogarty, Oliver St. John
1878-1957 .... TCLC 15
See also CA 109; DLB 15, 19

Gogol, Nikolai (Vasilyevich)
1809-1852 ..... NCLC 5, 15, 31; DC 1;
SSC 4
See also WLC

Gold, Herbert 1924-....... CLC 4, 7, 14, 42
See also CA 9-12R; CANR 17; DLB 2;
DLBY 81

Goldbarth, Albert 1948-........ CLC 5, 38
See also CA 53-56; CANR 6; DLB 120

Goldberg, Anatol 1910-1982 .... CLC 34
See also CA 131; 117

Goldemberg, Isaac 1945- .... CLC 52
See also CA 69-72; CAAS 12; CANR 11,
32; HW

Golden Silver
See Storm, Hyemeyohsts

Golding, William (Gerald)
1911- ..... CLC 1, 2, 3, 8, 10, 17, 27, 58
See also AAYA 5; CA 5-8R; CANR 13, 33;
CDBLB 1945-1960; DLB 15, 100;
MTCW; WLC

Goldman, Emma 1869-1940...... TCLC 13
See also CA 110

Goldman, William (W.) 1931-.... CLC 1, 48
See also CA 9-12R; CANR 29; DLB 44

Goldmann, Lucien 1913-1970 ...... CLC 24
See also CA 25-28; CAP 2

Goldoni, Carlo 1707-1793 .... LC 4

Goldsberry, Steven 1949-.......... CLC 34
See also CA 131

Goldsmith, Oliver 1728(?)-1774...... LC 2

Goldsmith, Peter
See Priestley, J(ohn) B(oynton)

Gombrowicz, Witold
1904-1969 .... CLC 4, 7, 11, 49
See also CA 19-20; 25-28R; CAP 2

Gomez de la Serna, Ramon
1888-1963 .... CLC 9
See also CA 116; HW

Goncharov, Ivan Alexandrovich
1812-1891 .... NCLC 1

Goncourt, Edmond (Louis Antoine Huot) de
1822-1896 .... NCLC 7

Goncourt, Jules (Alfred Huot) de
1830-1870 .... NCLC 7

Gontier, Fernande 19(?)- .... CLC 50

Goodman, Paul 1911-1972.... CLC 1, 2, 4, 7
See also CA 19-20; 37-40R; CANR 34;
CAP 2; MTCW

Gordimer, Nadine
1923- .... CLC 3, 5, 7, 10, 18, 33, 51, 70
See also CA 5-8R; CANR 3, 28; MTCW

Gordon, Adam Lindsay
1833-1870 .... NCLC 21

Gordon, Caroline
1895-1981 .... CLC 6, 13, 29
See also CA 11-12; 103; CANR 36; CAP 1;
DLB 4, 9, 102; DLBY 81; MTCW

Gordon, Charles William 1860-1937
See Connor, Ralph
See also CA 109

Gordon, Mary (Catherine)
1949- .... CLC 13, 22
See also CA 102; DLB 6; DLBY 81;
MTCW

Gordon, Sol 1923-................ CLC 26
See also CA 53-56; CANR 4; SATA 11

Gordone, Charles 1925-.......... CLC 1, 4
See also BW; CA 93-96; DLB 7; MTCW

Gorenko, Anna Andreevna
See Akhmatova, Anna

Gorky, Maxim................... TCLC 8
See also Peshkov, Alexei Maximovich
See also WLC

Goryan, Sirak
See Saroyan, William

Gosse, Edmund (William)
1849-1928 .... TCLC 28
See also CA 117; DLB 57

Gotlieb, Phyllis Fay (Bloom)
1926- .... CLC 18
See also CA 13-16R; CANR 7; DLB 88

Gottesman, S. D.
See Kornbluth, C(yril) M.; Pohl, Frederik

Gottfried von Strassburg
fl. c. 1210-................ CMLC 10

Gottschalk, Laura Riding
See Jackson, Laura (Riding)

Gould, Lois .... CLC 4, 10
See also CA 77-80; CANR 29; MTCW

Gourmont, Remy de 1858-1915.... TCLC 17
See also CA 109

Govier, Katherine 1948-.......... CLC 51
See also CA 101; CANR 18

Goyen, (Charles) William
1915-1983 .... CLC 5, 8, 14, 40
See also AITN 2; CA 5-8R; 110; CANR 6;
DLB 2; DLBY 83

Goytisolo, Juan 1931- .... CLC 5, 10, 23
See also CA 85-88; CANR 32; HW; MTCW

Gozzi, (Conte) Carlo 1720-1806 .. NCLC 23

Grabbe, Christian Dietrich
1801-1836 .... NCLC 2

Grace, Patricia 1937-............. CLC 56

Gracian y Morales, Baltasar
1601-1658 .... LC 15

Gracq, Julien................... CLC 11, 48
See also Poirier, Louis
See also DLB 83

Grade, Chaim 1910-1982 .... CLC 10
See also CA 93-96; 107

Graduate of Oxford, A
See Ruskin, John

Graham, John
See Phillips, David Graham

Graham, Jorie 1951-.............. CLC 48
See also CA 111; DLB 120

Graham, R(obert) B(ontine) Cunninghame
See Cunninghame Graham, R(obert)
B(ontine)
See also DLB 98

Graham, Robert
See Haldeman, Joe (William)

Graham, Tom
See Lewis, (Harry) Sinclair

Graham, W(illiam) S(ydney)
1918-1986 .... CLC 29
See also CA 73-76; 118; DLB 20

Graham, Winston (Mawdsley)
1910- .... CLC 23
See also CA 49-52; CANR 2, 22; DLB 77

Granville-Barker, Harley
1877-1946 .... TCLC 2
See also Barker, Harley Granville
See also CA 104

Grass, Guenter (Wilhelm)
1927- .. CLC 1, 2, 4, 6, 11, 15, 22, 32, 49
See also CA 13-16R; CANR 20; DLB 75;
MTCW; WLC

Gratton, Thomas
See Hulme, T(homas) E(rnest)

Grau, Shirley Ann 1929-........ CLC 4, 9
See also CA 89-92; CANR 22; DLB 2;
MTCW

Gravel, Fern
See Hall, James Norman

Graver, Elizabeth 1964-........... CLC 70
See also CA 135

Graves, Richard Perceval 1945- .... CLC 44
See also CA 65-68; CANR 9, 26

Graves, Robert (von Ranke)
1895-1985 ... CLC 1, 2, 6, 11, 39, 44, 45
See also CA 5-8R; 117; CANR 5, 36;
CDBLB 1914-1945; DLB 20, 100;
DLBY 85; MTCW; SATA 45

Gray, Alasdair (James) 1934- ...... CLC 41
See also CA 126; MTCW

Gray, Amlin 1946- . . . . CLC 29
See also CA 138

Gray, Francine du Plessix 1930- . . . . CLC 22
See also BEST 90:3; CA 61-64; CAAS 2;
CANR 11, 33; MTCW

Gray, John (Henry) 1866-1934 . . . . TCLC 19
See also CA 119

Gray, Simon (James Holliday)
1936- . . . . CLC 9, 14, 36
See also AITN 1; CA 21-24R; CAAS 3;
CANR 32; DLB 13; MTCW

Gray, Spalding 1941- . . . . CLC 49
See also CA 128

Gray, Thomas 1716-1771 . . . . LC 4; PC 2
See also CDBLB 1660-1789; DLB 109;
WLC

Grayson, David
See Baker, Ray Stannard

Grayson, Richard (A.) 1951- . . . . CLC 38
See also CA 85-88; CANR 14, 31

Greeley, Andrew M(oran) 1928- . . . . CLC 28
See also CA 5-8R; CAAS 7; CANR 7;
MTCW

Green, Brian
See Card, Orson Scott

Green, Hannah . . . . CLC 3
See also CA 73-76

Green, Hannah
See Greenberg, Joanne (Goldenberg)

Green, Henry. . . . . CLC 2, 13
See also Yorke, Henry Vincent
See also DLB 15

Green, Julian (Hartridge)
1900- . . . . CLC 3, 11
See also CA 21-24R; CANR 33; DLB 4, 72;
MTCW

Green, Julien
See Green, Julian (Hartridge)

Green, Paul (Eliot) 1894-1981 . . . . . . CLC 25
See also AITN 1; CA 5-8R; 103; CANR 3;
DLB 7, 9; DLBY 81

Greenberg, Ivan 1908-1973
See Rahv, Philip
See also CA 85-88

Greenberg, Joanne (Goldenberg)
1932- . . . . CLC 7, 30
See also CA 5-8R; CANR 14, 32; SATA 25

Greenberg, Richard 1959(?)- . . . . CLC 57
See also CA 138

Greene, Bette 1934- . . . . CLC 30
See also AAYA 7; CA 53-56; CANR 4;
CLR 2; MAICYA; SATA 8

Greene, Gael . . . . CLC 8
See also CA 13-16R; CANR 10

Greene, Graham (Henry)
1904-1991 . . . CLC 1, 3, 6, 9, 14, 18, 27,
                                    37, 70, 72
See also AITN 2; CA 13-16R; 133;
CANR 35; CDBLB 1945-1960; DLB 13,
15, 77, 100; DLBY 91; MTCW;
SATA 20; WLC

Greer, Richard
See Silverberg, Robert

Greer, Richard
See Silverberg, Robert

Gregor, Arthur 1923- . . . . CLC 9
See also CA 25-28R; CAAS 10; CANR 11;
SATA 36

Gregor, Lee
See Pohl, Frederik

Gregory, Isabella Augusta (Persse)
1852-1932 . . . . TCLC 1
See also CA 104; DLB 10

Gregory, J. Dennis
See Williams, John A(lfred)

Grendon, Stephen
See Derleth, August (William)

Grenville, Kate 1950- . . . . CLC 61
See also CA 118

Grenville, Pelham
See Wodehouse, P(elham) G(renville)

Greve, Felix Paul (Berthold Friedrich)
1879-1948
See Grove, Frederick Philip
See also CA 104

Grey, Zane 1872-1939 . . . . TCLC 6
See also CA 104; 132; DLB 9; MTCW

Grieg, (Johan) Nordahl (Brun)
1902-1943 . . . . TCLC 10
See also CA 107

Grieve, C(hristopher) M(urray)
1892-1978 . . . . CLC 11, 19
See also MacDiarmid, Hugh
See also CA 5-8R; 85-88; CANR 33;
MTCW

Griffin, Gerald 1803-1840 . . . . NCLC 7

Griffin, John Howard 1920-1980 . . . . CLC 68
See also AITN 1; CA 1-4R; 101; CANR 2

Griffin, Peter . . . . CLC 39

Griffiths, Trevor 1935- . . . . CLC 13, 52
See also CA 97-100; DLB 13

Grigson, Geoffrey (Edward Harvey)
1905-1985 . . . . CLC 7, 39
See also CA 25-28R; 118; CANR 20, 33;
DLB 27; MTCW

Grillparzer, Franz 1791-1872 . . . . . . NCLC 1

Grimble, Reverend Charles James
See Eliot, T(homas) S(tearns)

Grimke, Charlotte L(ottie) Forten
1837(?)-1914
See Forten, Charlotte L.
See also BW; CA 117; 124

Grimm, Jacob Ludwig Karl
1785-1863 . . . . NCLC 3
See also DLB 90; MAICYA; SATA 22

Grimm, Wilhelm Karl 1786-1859 . . NCLC 3
See also DLB 90; MAICYA; SATA 22

Grimmelshausen, Johann Jakob Christoffel
von 1621-1676 . . . . LC 6

Grindel, Eugene 1895-1952
See Eluard, Paul
See also CA 104

Grossman, David . . . . CLC 67
See also CA 138

Grossman, Vasily (Semenovich)
1905-1964 . . . . CLC 41
See also CA 124; 130; MTCW

Grove, Frederick Philip . . . . TCLC 4
See also Greve, Felix Paul (Berthold
Friedrich)
See also DLB 92

Grubb
See Crumb, R(obert)

Grumbach, Doris (Isaac)
1918- . . . . CLC 13, 22, 64
See also CA 5-8R; CAAS 2; CANR 9

Grundtvig, Nicolai Frederik Severin
1783-1872 . . . . NCLC 1

Grunge
See Crumb, R(obert)

Grunwald, Lisa 1959- . . . . CLC 44
See also CA 120

Guare, John 1938- . . . . CLC 8, 14, 29, 67
See also CA 73-76; CANR 21; DLB 7;
MTCW

Gudjonsson, Halldor Kiljan 1902-
See Laxness, Halldor
See also CA 103

Guenter, Erich
See Eich, Guenter

Guest, Barbara 1920- . . . . CLC 34
See also CA 25-28R; CANR 11; DLB 5

Guest, Judith (Ann) 1936- . . . . CLC 8, 30
See also AAYA 7; CA 77-80; CANR 15;
MTCW

Guild, Nicholas M. 1944- . . . . CLC 33
See also CA 93-96

Guillemin, Jacques
See Sartre, Jean-Paul

Guillen, Jorge 1893-1984 . . . . CLC 11
See also CA 89-92; 112; DLB 108; HW

Guillen (y Batista), Nicolas (Cristobal)
1902-1989 . . . . CLC 48
See also BLC 2; BW; CA 116; 125; 129;
HW

Guillevic, (Eugene) 1907- . . . . CLC 33
See also CA 93-96

Guillois
See Desnos, Robert

Guiney, Louise Imogen
1861-1920 . . . . TCLC 41
See also DLB 54

Guiraldes, Ricardo (Guillermo)
1886-1927 . . . . TCLC 39
See also CA 131; HW; MTCW

Gunn, Bill . . . . CLC 5
See also Gunn, William Harrison
See also DLB 38

Gunn, Thom(son William)
1929- . . . . CLC 3, 6, 18, 32
See also CA 17-20R; CANR 9, 33;
CDBLB 1960 to Present; DLB 27;
MTCW

Gunn, William Harrison 1934(?)-1989
See Gunn, Bill
See also AITN 1; BW; CA 13-16R; 128;
CANR 12, 25

Gunnars, Kristjana 1948- . . . . CLC 69
See also CA 113; DLB 60

Gurganus, Allan 1947- . . . . CLC 70
See also BEST 90:1; CA 135

Henderson, F. C.
See Mencken, H(enry) L(ouis)

Henderson, Sylvia
See Ashton-Warner, Sylvia (Constance)

Henley, Beth .... CLC 23
See also Henley, Elizabeth Becker
See also CABS 3; DLBY 86

Henley, Elizabeth Becker 1952-
See Henley, Beth
See also CA 107; CANR 32; MTCW

Henley, William Ernest
1849-1903 ....TCLC 8
See also CA 105; DLB 19

Hennissart, Martha
See Lathen, Emma
See also CA 85-88

Henry, O............... TCLC 1, 19; SSC 5
See also Porter, William Sydney
See also WLC

Henryson, Robert 1430(?)-1506(?).... LC 20

Henry VIII 1491-1547............. LC 10

Henschke, Alfred
See Klabund

Hentoff, Nat(han Irving) 1925-..... CLC 26
See also AAYA 4; CA 1-4R; CAAS 6;
CANR 5, 25; CLR 1; MAICYA;
SATA 27, 42, 69

Heppenstall, (John) Rayner
1911-1981 .... CLC 10
See also CA 1-4R; 103; CANR 29

Herbert, Frank (Patrick)
1920-1986 ....CLC 12, 23, 35, 44
See also CA 53-56; 118; CANR 5; DLB 8;
MTCW; SATA 9, 37, 47

Herbert, George 1593-1633.......... PC 4
See also CDBLB Before 1660

Herbert, Zbigniew 1924-........ CLC 9, 43
See also CA 89-92; CANR 36; MTCW

Herbst, Josephine (Frey)
1897-1969 .... CLC 34
See also CA 5-8R; 25-28R; DLB 9

Hergesheimer, Joseph
1880-1954 .... TCLC 11
See also CA 109; DLB 102, 9

Herlihy, James Leo 1927-.......... CLC 6
See also CA 1-4R; CANR 2

Hermogenes fl. c. 175-.......... CMLC 6

Hernandez, Jose 1834-1886...... NCLC 17

Herrick, Robert 1591-1674 .... LC 13

Herriot, James.................. CLC 12
See also Wight, James Alfred
See also AAYA 1

Herrmann, Dorothy 1941-......... CLC 44
See also CA 107

Herrmann, Taffy
See Herrmann, Dorothy

Hersey, John (Richard)
1914-...........CLC 1, 2, 7, 9, 40
See also CA 17-20R; CANR 33; DLB 6;
MTCW; SATA 25

Herzen, Aleksandr Ivanovich
1812-1870 .... NCLC 10

Herzl, Theodor 1860-1904....... TCLC 36

Herzog, Werner 1942-............ CLC 16
See also CA 89-92

Hesiod c. 8th cent. B.C.-......... CMLC 5

Hesse, Hermann
1877-1962 ... CLC 1, 2, 3, 6, 11, 17, 25,
69; SSC 9
See also CA 17-18; CAP 2; DLB 66;
MTCW; SATA 50; WLC

Hewes, Cady
See De Voto, Bernard (Augustine)

Heyen, William 1940- .... CLC 13, 18
See also CA 33-36R; CAAS 9; DLB 5

Heyerdahl, Thor 1914-............. CLC 26
See also CA 5-8R; CANR 5, 22; MTCW;
SATA 2, 52

Heym, Georg (Theodor Franz Arthur)
1887-1912 .... TCLC 9
See also CA 106

Heym, Stefan 1913-.............. CLC 41
See also CA 9-12R; CANR 4; DLB 69

Heyse, Paul (Johann Ludwig von)
1830-1914 ....TCLC 8
See also CA 104

Hibbert, Eleanor Burford 1906-..... CLC 7
See also BEST 90:4; CA 17-20R; CANR 9,
28; SATA 2

Higgins, George V(incent)
1939-................. CLC 4, 7, 10, 18
See also CA 77-80; CAAS 5; CANR 17;
DLB 2; DLBY 81; MTCW

Higginson, Thomas Wentworth
1823-1911 .... TCLC 36
See also DLB 1, 64

Highet, Helen
See MacInnes, Helen (Clark)

Highsmith, (Mary) Patricia
1921-................ CLC 2, 4, 14, 42
See also CA 1-4R; CANR 1, 20; MTCW

Highwater, Jamake (Mamake)
1942(?)- .... CLC 12
See also AAYA 7; CA 65-68; CAAS 7;
CANR 10, 34; CLR 17; DLB 52;
DLBY 85; MAICYA; SATA 30, 32, 69

Hijuelos, Oscar 1951- .... CLC 65
See also BEST 90:1; CA 123; HW

Hikmet, Nazim 1902-1963......... CLC 40
See also CA 93-96

Hildesheimer, Wolfgang
1916-1991 .... CLC 49
See also CA 101; 135; DLB 69

Hill, Geoffrey (William)
1932-................ CLC 5, 8, 18, 45
See also CA 81-84; CANR 21;
CDBLB 1960 to Present; DLB 40;
MTCW

Hill, George Roy 1921-........... CLC 26
See also CA 110; 122

Hill, Susan (Elizabeth) 1942- .... CLC 4
See also CA 33-36R; CANR 29; DLB 14;
MTCW

Hillerman, Tony 1925-............ CLC 62
See also AAYA 6; BEST 89:1; CA 29-32R;
CANR 21; SATA 6

Hilliard, Noel (Harvey) 1929-...... CLC 15
See also CA 9-12R; CANR 7

Hillis, Rick 1956-................ CLC 66
See also CA 134

Hilton, James 1900-1954........ TCLC 21
See also CA 108; DLB 34, 77; SATA 34

Himes, Chester (Bomar)
1909-1984 .... CLC 2, 4, 7, 18, 58
See also BLC 2; BW; CA 25-28R; 114;
CANR 22; DLB 2, 76; MTCW

Hinde, Thomas .... CLC 6, 11
See also Chitty, Thomas Willes

Hindin, Nathan
See Bloch, Robert (Albert)

Hine, (William) Daryl 1936-....... CLC 15
See also CA 1-4R; CAAS 15; CANR 1, 20;
DLB 60

Hinkson, Katharine Tynan
See Tynan, Katharine

Hinton, S(usan) E(loise) 1950- ..... CLC 30
See also AAYA 2; CA 81-84; CANR 32;
CLR 3, 23; MAICYA; MTCW;
SATA 19, 58

Hippius, Zinaida .... TCLC 9
See also Gippius, Zinaida (Nikolayevna)

Hiraoka, Kimitake 1925-1970
See Mishima, Yukio
See also CA 97-100; 29-32R; MTCW

Hirsch, Edward 1950- .... CLC 31, 50
See also CA 104; CANR 20; DLB 120

Hitchcock, Alfred (Joseph)
1899-1980 .... CLC 16
See also CA 97-100; SATA 24, 27

Hoagland, Edward 1932-.......... CLC 28
See also CA 1-4R; CANR 2, 31; DLB 6;
SATA 51

Hoban, Russell (Conwell) 1925- .. CLC 7, 25
See also CA 5-8R; CANR 23, 37; CLR 3;
DLB 52; MAICYA; MTCW; SATA 1, 40

Hobbs, Perry
See Blackmur, R(ichard) P(almer)

Hobson, Laura Z(ametkin)
1900-1986 .... CLC 7, 25
See also CA 17-20R; 118; DLB 28;
SATA 52

Hochhuth, Rolf 1931-........ CLC 4, 11, 18
See also CA 5-8R; CANR 33; MTCW

Hochman, Sandra 1936-.......... CLC 3, 8
See also CA 5-8R; DLB 5

Hochwaelder, Fritz 1911-1986...... CLC 36
See also Hochwalder, Fritz
See also CA 29-32R; 120; MTCW

Hochwalder, Fritz................. CLC 36
See also Hochwaelder, Fritz

Hocking, Mary (Eunice) 1921-..... CLC 13
See also CA 101; CANR 18

Hodgins, Jack 1938-.............. CLC 23
See also CA 93-96; DLB 60

Hodgson, William Hope
1877(?)-1918 .... TCLC 13
See also CA 111; DLB 70

Hoffman, Alice 1952-............. CLC 51
See also CA 77-80; CANR 34; MTCW

Hoffman, Daniel (Gerard)
1923-................... CLC 6, 13, 23
See also CA 1-4R; CANR 4; DLB 5

Hoffman, Stanley 1944-. . . . . CLC 5
See also CA 77-80

Hoffman, William M(oses) 1939- . . . CLC 40
See also CA 57-60; CANR 11

Hoffmann, E(rnst) T(heodor) A(madeus)
1776-1822 . . . . NCLC 2
See also DLB 90; SATA 27

Hofmann, Gert 1931-. . . . . CLC 54
See also CA 128

Hofmannsthal, Hugo von
1874-1929 . . . . TCLC 11
See also CA 106; DLB 81, 118

Hogarth, Charles
See Creasey, John

Hogg, James 1770-1835. . . . . NCLC 4
See also DLB 93, 116

Holbach, Paul Henri Thiry Baron
1723-1789 . . . . LC 14

Holberg, Ludvig 1684-1754 . . . . LC 6

Holden, Ursula 1921-. . . . . CLC 18
See also CA 101; CAAS 8; CANR 22

Holderlin, (Johann Christian) Friedrich
1770-1843 . . . . NCLC 16; PC 4

Holdstock, Robert
See Holdstock, Robert P.

Holdstock, Robert P. 1948-. . . . . CLC 39
See also CA 131

Holland, Isabelle 1920- . . . . CLC 21
See also CA 21-24R; CANR 10, 25;
MAICYA; SATA 8, 70

Holland, Marcus
See Caldwell, (Janet Miriam) Taylor
(Holland)

Hollander, John 1929-. . . . . . CLC 2, 5, 8, 14
See also CA 1-4R; CANR 1; DLB 5;
SATA 13

Hollander, Paul
See Silverberg, Robert

Holleran, Andrew 1943(?)-. . . . . CLC 38

Hollinghurst, Alan 1954-. . . . . CLC 55
See also CA 114

Hollis, Jim
See Summers, Hollis (Spurgeon Jr.)

Holmes, John
See Souster, (Holmes) Raymond

Holmes, John Clellon 1926-1988. . . . CLC 56
See also CA 9-12R; 125; CANR 4; DLB 16

Holmes, Oliver Wendell
1809-1894 . . . . NCLC 14
See also CDALB 1640-1865; DLB 1;
SATA 34

Holmes, Raymond
See Souster, (Holmes) Raymond

Holt, Victoria
See Hibbert, Eleanor Burford

Holub, Miroslav 1923-. . . . . CLC 4
See also CA 21-24R; CANR 10

Homer c. 8th cent. B.C.-. . . . . CMLC 1

Honig, Edwin 1919-. . . . . CLC 33
See also CA 5-8R; CAAS 8; CANR 4;
DLB 5

Hood, Hugh (John Blagdon)
1928-. . . . . CLC 15, 28
See also CA 49-52; CANR 1, 33; DLB 53

Hood, Thomas 1799-1845. . . . . NCLC 16
See also DLB 96

Hooker, (Peter) Jeremy 1941-. . . . . . CLC 43
See also CA 77-80; CANR 22; DLB 40

Hope, A(lec) D(erwent) 1907-. . . . CLC 3, 51
See also CA 21-24R; CANR 33; MTCW

Hope, Brian
See Creasey, John

Hope, Christopher (David Tully)
1944-. . . . . CLC 52
See also CA 106; SATA 62

Hopkins, Gerard Manley
1844-1889 . . . . NCLC 17
See also CDBLB 1890-1914; DLB 35, 57;
WLC

Hopkins, John (Richard) 1931-. . . . . . CLC 4
See also CA 85-88

Hopkins, Pauline Elizabeth
1859-1930 . . . . TCLC 28
See also BLC 2; DLB 50

Horatio
See Proust,
(Valentin-Louis-George-Eugene-)Marcel

Horgan, Paul 1903-. . . . . CLC 9, 53
See also CA 13-16R; CANR 9, 35;
DLB 102; DLBY 85; MTCW; SATA 13

Horn, Peter
See Kuttner, Henry

Horovitz, Israel 1939-. . . . . CLC 56
See also CA 33-36R; DLB 7

Horvath, Odon von
See Horvath, Oedoen von
See also DLB 85

Horvath, Oedoen von 1901-1938. . . TCLC 45
See also Horvath, Odon von
See also CA 118

Horwitz, Julius 1920-1986. . . . . CLC 14
See also CA 9-12R; 119; CANR 12

Hospital, Janette Turner 1942-. . . . . CLC 42
See also CA 108

Hostos, E. M. de
See Hostos (y Bonilla), Eugenio Maria de

Hostos, Eugenio M. de
See Hostos (y Bonilla), Eugenio Maria de

Hostos, Eugenio Maria
See Hostos (y Bonilla), Eugenio Maria de

Hostos (y Bonilla), Eugenio Maria de
1839-1903 . . . . TCLC 24
See also CA 123; 131; HW

Houdini
See Lovecraft, H(oward) P(hillips)

Hougan, Carolyn 19(?)-. . . . . CLC 34

Household, Geoffrey (Edward West)
1900-1988 . . . . CLC 11
See also CA 77-80; 126; DLB 87; SATA 14,
59

Housman, A(lfred) E(dward)
1859-1936 . . . . TCLC 1, 10; PC 2
See also CA 104; 125; DLB 19; MTCW

Housman, Laurence 1865-1959 . . . . . TCLC 7
See also CA 106; DLB 10; SATA 25

Howard, Elizabeth Jane 1923- . . . CLC 7, 29
See also CA 5-8R; CANR 8

Howard, Maureen 1930- . . . . . CLC 5, 14, 46
See also CA 53-56; CANR 31; DLBY 83;
MTCW

Howard, Richard 1929- . . . . . . CLC 7, 10, 47
See also AITN 1; CA 85-88; CANR 25;
DLB 5

Howard, Robert Ervin 1906-1936. . . TCLC 8
See also CA 105

Howard, Warren F.
See Pohl, Frederik

Howe, Fanny 1940- . . . . CLC 47
See also CA 117; SATA 52

Howe, Julia Ward 1819-1910 . . . . . TCLC 21
See also CA 117; DLB 1

Howe, Susan 1937-. . . . . CLC 72
See also DLB 120

Howe, Tina 1937-. . . . . CLC 48
See also CA 109

Howell, James 1594(?)-1666 . . . . LC 13

Howells, W. D.
See Howells, William Dean

Howells, William D.
See Howells, William Dean

Howells, William Dean
1837-1920 . . . . TCLC 41, 7, 17
See also CA 104; 134; CDALB 1865-1917;
DLB 12, 64, 74, 79

Howes, Barbara 1914-. . . . . CLC 15
See also CA 9-12R; CAAS 3; SATA 5

Hrabal, Bohumil 1914-. . . . . CLC 13, 67
See also CA 106; CAAS 12

Hsun, Lu . . . . TCLC 3
See also Shu-Jen, Chou

Hubbard, L(afayette) Ron(ald)
1911-1986 . . . . CLC 43
See also CA 77-80; 118; CANR 22

Huch, Ricarda (Octavia)
1864-1947 . . . . TCLC 13
See also CA 111; DLB 66

Huddle, David 1942- . . . . CLC 49
See also CA 57-60

Hudson, Jeffery
See Crichton, (John) Michael

Hudson, W(illiam) H(enry)
1841-1922 . . . . TCLC 29
See also CA 115; DLB 98; SATA 35

Hueffer, Ford Madox
See Ford, Ford Madox

Hughart, Barry . . . . CLC 39
See also CA 137

Hughes, Colin
See Creasey, John

Hughes, David (John) 1930- . . . . CLC 48
See also CA 116; 129; DLB 14

Hughes, (James) Langston
1902-1967 . . . . CLC 1, 5, 10, 15, 35, 44;
PC 1; SSC 6
See also BLC 2; BW; CA 1-4R; 25-28R;
CANR 1, 34; CDALB 1929-1941;
CLR 17; DLB 4, 7, 48, 51, 86; MAICYA;
MTCW; SATA 4, 33; WLC

Jacobson, Dan 1929- . . . . CLC 4, 14
See also CA 1-4R; CANR 2, 25; DLB 14;
MTCW

Jacqueline
See Carpentier (y Valmont), Alejo

Jagger, Mick 1944-. . . . . CLC 17

Jakes, John (William) 1932- . . . . CLC 29
See also BEST 89:4; CA 57-60; CANR 10;
DLBY 83; MTCW; SATA 62

James, Andrew
See Kirkup, James

James, C(yril) L(ionel) R(obert)
1901-1989 . . . . CLC 33
See also BW; CA 117; 125; 128; MTCW

James, Daniel (Lewis) 1911-1988
See Santiago, Danny
See also CA 125

James, Dynely
See Mayne, William (James Carter)

James, Henry
1843-1916 . . . . . TCLC 2, 11, 24, 40, 47;
SSC 8
See also CA 104; 132; CDALB 1865-1917;
DLB 12, 71, 74; MTCW; WLC

James, Montague (Rhodes)
1862-1936 . . . . TCLC 6
See also CA 104

James, P. D. . . . . CLC 18, 46
See also White, Phyllis Dorothy James
See also BEST 90:2; CDBLB 1960 to
Present; DLB 87

James, Philip
See Moorcock, Michael (John)

James, William 1842-1910. . . . . TCLC 15, 32
See also CA 109

James I 1394-1437 . . . . LC 20

Jami, Nur al-Din 'Abd al-Rahman
1414-1492 . . . . LC 9

Jandl, Ernst 1925- . . . . CLC 34

Janowitz, Tama 1957- . . . . CLC 43
See also CA 106

Jarrell, Randall
1914-1965 . . . . CLC 1, 2, 6, 9, 13, 49
See also CA 5-8R; 25-28R; CABS 2;
CANR 6, 34; CDALB 1941-1968; CLR 6;
DLB 48, 52; MAICYA; MTCW; SATA 7

Jarry, Alfred 1873-1907. . . . . . . TCLC 2, 14
See also CA 104

Jarvis, E. K.
See Bloch, Robert (Albert); Ellison, Harlan;
Silverberg, Robert

Jeake, Samuel Jr.
See Aiken, Conrad (Potter)

Jean Paul 1763-1825 . . . . NCLC 7

Jeffers, (John) Robinson
1887-1962 . . . . CLC 2, 3, 11, 15, 54
See also CA 85-88; CANR 35;
CDALB 1917-1929; DLB 45; MTCW;
WLC

Jefferson, Janet
See Mencken, H(enry) L(ouis)

Jefferson, Thomas 1743-1826 . . . . NCLC 11
See also CDALB 1640-1865; DLB 31

Jeffrey, Francis 1773-1850. . . . . . NCLC 33
See also DLB 107

Jelakowitch, Ivan
See Heijermans, Herman

Jellicoe, (Patricia) Ann 1927- . . . . . . CLC 27
See also CA 85-88; DLB 13

Jen, Gish . . . . CLC 70
See also Jen, Lillian

Jen, Lillian 1956(?)-
See Jen, Gish
See also CA 135

Jenkins, (John) Robin 1912- . . . . CLC 52
See also CA 1-4R; CANR 1; DLB 14

Jennings, Elizabeth (Joan)
1926- . . . . CLC 5, 14
See also CA 61-64; CAAS 5; CANR 8, 39;
DLB 27; MTCW; SATA 66

Jennings, Waylon 1937-. . . . . CLC 21

Jensen, Johannes V. 1873-1950. . . . TCLC 41

Jensen, Laura (Linnea) 1948- . . . . . . CLC 37
See also CA 103

Jerome, Jerome K(lapka)
1859-1927 . . . . TCLC 23
See also CA 119; DLB 10, 34

Jerrold, Douglas William
1803-1857 . . . . NCLC 2

Jewett, (Theodora) Sarah Orne
1849-1909 . . . . TCLC 1, 22; SSC 6
See also CA 108; 127; DLB 12, 74;
SATA 15

Jewsbury, Geraldine (Endsor)
1812-1880 . . . . NCLC 22
See also DLB 21

Jhabvala, Ruth Prawer
1927- . . . . CLC 4, 8, 29
See also CA 1-4R; CANR 2, 29; MTCW

Jiles, Paulette 1943-. . . . . CLC 13, 58
See also CA 101

Jimenez (Mantecon), Juan Ramon
1881-1958 . . . . TCLC 4
See also CA 104; 131; HW; MTCW

Jimenez, Ramon
See Jimenez (Mantecon), Juan Ramon

Jimenez Mantecon, Juan
See Jimenez (Mantecon), Juan Ramon

Joel, Billy . . . . CLC 26
See also Joel, William Martin

Joel, William Martin 1949-
See Joel, Billy
See also CA 108

John of the Cross, St. 1542-1591 . . . . LC 18

Johnson, B(ryan) S(tanley William)
1933-1973 . . . . CLC 6, 9
See also CA 9-12R; 53-56; CANR 9;
DLB 14, 40

Johnson, Charles (Richard)
1948- . . . . CLC 7, 51, 65
See also BLC 2; BW; CA 116; DLB 33

Johnson, Denis 1949-. . . . . CLC 52
See also CA 117; 121; DLB 120

Johnson, Diane (Lain)
1934- . . . . CLC 5, 13, 48
See also CA 41-44R; CANR 17; DLBY 80;
MTCW

Johnson, Eyvind (Olof Verner)
1900-1976 . . . . CLC 14
See also CA 73-76; 69-72; CANR 34

Johnson, J. R.
See James, C(yril) L(ionel) R(obert)

Johnson, James Weldon
1871-1938 . . . . TCLC 3, 19
See also BLC 2; BW; CA 104; 125;
CDALB 1917-1929; DLB 51; MTCW;
SATA 31

Johnson, Joyce 1935-. . . . . CLC 58
See also CA 125; 129

Johnson, Lionel (Pigot)
1867-1902 . . . . TCLC 19
See also CA 117; DLB 19

Johnson, Mel
See Malzberg, Barry N(athaniel)

Johnson, Pamela Hansford
1912-1981 . . . . CLC 1, 7, 27
See also CA 1-4R; 104; CANR 2, 28;
DLB 15; MTCW

Johnson, Samuel 1709-1784. . . . . LC 15
See also CDBLB 1660-1789; DLB 39, 95,
104; WLC

Johnson, Uwe
1934-1984 . . . . CLC 5, 10, 15, 40
See also CA 1-4R; 112; CANR 1, 39;
DLB 75; MTCW

Johnston, George (Benson) 1913-. . . CLC 51
See also CA 1-4R; CANR 5, 20; DLB 88

Johnston, Jennifer 1930- . . . . CLC 7
See also CA 85-88; DLB 14

Jolley, (Monica) Elizabeth 1923- . . . CLC 46
See also CA 127; CAAS 13

Jones, Arthur Llewellyn 1863-1947
See Machen, Arthur
See also CA 104

Jones, D(ouglas) G(ordon) 1929-. . . . CLC 10
See also CA 29-32R; CANR 13; DLB 53

Jones, David (Michael)
1895-1974 . . . . CLC 2, 4, 7, 13, 42
See also CA 9-12R; 53-56; CANR 28;
CDBLB 1945-1960; DLB 20, 100; MTCW

Jones, David Robert 1947-
See Bowie, David
See also CA 103

Jones, Diana Wynne 1934- . . . . CLC 26
See also CA 49-52; CANR 4, 26; CLR 23;
MAICYA; SAAS 7; SATA 9, 70

Jones, Gayl 1949-. . . . . CLC 6, 9
See also BLC 2; BW; CA 77-80; CANR 27;
DLB 33; MTCW

Jones, James 1921-1977. . . . CLC 1, 3, 10, 39
See also AITN 1, 2; CA 1-4R; 69-72;
CANR 6; DLB 2; MTCW

Jones, John J.
See Lovecraft, H(oward) P(hillips)

Jones, LeRoi . . . . CLC 1, 2, 3, 5, 10, 14
See also Baraka, Amiri

Jones, Louis B. . . . . CLC 65

Jones, Madison (Percy Jr.) 1925-. . . . CLC 4
See also CA 13-16R; CAAS 11; CANR 7

Jones, Mervyn 1922- . . . . CLC 10, 52
See also CA 45-48; CAAS 5; CANR 1;
MTCW

Lamartine, Alphonse (Marie Louis Prat) de
  1790-1869 .... **NCLC 11**

Lamb, Charles 1775-1834........ **NCLC 10**
  See also CDBLB 1789-1832; DLB 93, 107;
  SATA 17; WLC

Lamb, Lady Caroline 1785-1828.. **NCLC 38**
  See also DLB 116

Lamming, George (William)
  1927- .... **CLC 2, 4, 66**
  See also BLC 2; BW; CA 85-88; CANR 26;
  MTCW

L'Amour, Louis (Dearborn)
  1908-1988 .... **CLC 25, 55**
  See also AITN 2; BEST 89:2; CA 1-4R;
  125; CANR 3, 25; DLBY 80; MTCW

Lampedusa, Giuseppe (Tomasi) di ... **TCLC 13**
  See also Tomasi di Lampedusa, Giuseppe

Lampman, Archibald 1861-1899 .. **NCLC 25**
  See also DLB 92

Lancaster, Bruce 1896-1963........ **CLC 36**
  See also CA 9-10; CAP 1; SATA 9

Landau, Mark Alexandrovich
  See Aldanov, Mark (Alexandrovich)

Landau-Aldanov, Mark Alexandrovich
  See Aldanov, Mark (Alexandrovich)

Landis, John 1950- .... **CLC 26**
  See also CA 112; 122

Landolfi, Tommaso 1908-1979... **CLC 11, 49**
  See also CA 127; 117

Landon, Letitia Elizabeth
  1802-1838 .... **NCLC 15**
  See also DLB 96

Landor, Walter Savage
  1775-1864 .... **NCLC 14**
  See also DLB 93, 107

Landwirth, Heinz 1927-
  See Lind, Jakov
  See also CA 9-12R; CANR 7

Lane, Patrick 1939- .... **CLC 25**
  See also CA 97-100; DLB 53

Lang, Andrew 1844-1912........ **TCLC 16**
  See also CA 114; 137; DLB 98; MAICYA;
  SATA 16

Lang, Fritz 1890-1976 .... **CLC 20**
  See also CA 77-80; 69-72; CANR 30

Lange, John
  See Crichton, (John) Michael

Langer, Elinor 1939- .... **CLC 34**
  See also CA 121

Langland, William 1330(?)-1400(?) ... **LC 19**

Langstaff, Launcelot
  See Irving, Washington

Lanier, Sidney 1842-1881 .... **NCLC 6**
  See also DLB 64; MAICYA; SATA 18

Lanyer, Aemilia 1569-1645 .... **LC 10**

Lao Tzu .... **CMLC 7**

Lapine, James (Elliot) 1949- .... **CLC 39**
  See also CA 123; 130

Larbaud, Valery (Nicolas)
  1881-1957 .... **TCLC 9**
  See also CA 106

Lardner, Ring
  See Lardner, Ring(gold) W(ilmer)

Lardner, Ring W. Jr.
  See Lardner, Ring(gold) W(ilmer)

Lardner, Ring(gold) W(ilmer)
  1885-1933 .... **TCLC 2, 14**
  See also CA 104; 131; CDALB 1917-1929;
  DLB 11, 25, 86; MTCW

Laredo, Betty
  See Codrescu, Andrei

Larkin, Maia
  See Wojciechowska, Maia (Teresa)

Larkin, Philip (Arthur)
  1922-1985 ... **CLC 3, 5, 8, 9, 13, 18, 33,
                                      39, 64**
  See also CA 5-8R; 117; CANR 24;
  CDBLB 1960 to Present; DLB 27;
  MTCW

Larra (y Sanchez de Castro), Mariano Jose de
  1809-1837 .... **NCLC 17**

Larsen, Eric 1941- .... **CLC 55**
  See also CA 132

Larsen, Nella 1891-1964 .... **CLC 37**
  See also BLC 2; BW; CA 125; DLB 51

Larson, Charles R(aymond) 1938-... **CLC 31**
  See also CA 53-56; CANR 4

Latham, Jean Lee 1902-.......... **CLC 12**
  See also AITN 1; CA 5-8R; CANR 7;
  MAICYA; SATA 2, 68

Latham, Mavis
  See Clark, Mavis Thorpe

Lathen, Emma.................... **CLC 2**
  See also Hennissart, Martha; Latsis, Mary
  J(ane)

Lathrop, Francis
  See Leiber, Fritz (Reuter Jr.)

Latsis, Mary J(ane)
  See Lathen, Emma
  See also CA 85-88

Lattimore, Richmond (Alexander)
  1906-1984 .... **CLC 3**
  See also CA 1-4R; 112; CANR 1

Laughlin, James 1914-........... **CLC 49**
  See also CA 21-24R; CANR 9; DLB 48

Laurence, (Jean) Margaret (Wemyss)
  1926-1987 .. **CLC 3, 6, 13, 50, 62; SSC 7**
  See also CA 5-8R; 121; CANR 33; DLB 53;
  MTCW; SATA 50

Laurent, Antoine 1952- .... **CLC 50**

Lauscher, Hermann
  See Hesse, Hermann

Lautreamont, Comte de
  1846-1870 .... **NCLC 12**

Laverty, Donald
  See Blish, James (Benjamin)

Lavin, Mary 1912- ...... **CLC 4, 18; SSC 4**
  See also CA 9-12R; CANR 33; DLB 15;
  MTCW

Lavond, Paul Dennis
  See Kornbluth, C(yril) M.; Pohl, Frederik

Lawler, Raymond Evenor 1922- .... **CLC 58**
  See also CA 103

Lawrence, D(avid) H(erbert Richards)
  1885-1930 .... **TCLC 2, 9, 16, 33; SSC 4**
  See also CA 104; 121; CDBLB 1914-1945;
  DLB 10, 19, 36, 98; MTCW; WLC

Lawrence, T(homas) E(dward)
  1888-1935 .... **TCLC 18**
  See also Dale, Colin
  See also CA 115

Lawrence Of Arabia
  See Lawrence, T(homas) E(dward)

Lawson, Henry (Archibald Hertzberg)
  1867-1922 .... **TCLC 27**
  See also CA 120

Laxness, Halldor.................. **CLC 25**
  See also Gudjonsson, Halldor Kiljan

Layamon fl. c. 1200-............ **CMLC 10**

Laye, Camara 1928-1980 .... **CLC 4, 38**
  See also BLC 2; BW; CA 85-88; 97-100;
  CANR 25; MTCW

Layton, Irving (Peter) 1912-..... **CLC 2, 15**
  See also CA 1-4R; CANR 2, 33; DLB 88;
  MTCW

Lazarus, Emma 1849-1887........ **NCLC 8**

Lazarus, Felix
  See Cable, George Washington

Lea, Joan
  See Neufeld, John (Arthur)

Leacock, Stephen (Butler)
  1869-1944 .... **TCLC 2**
  See also CA 104; DLB 92

Lear, Edward 1812-1888 .... **NCLC 3**
  See also CLR 1; DLB 32; MAICYA;
  SATA 18

Lear, Norman (Milton) 1922- ...... **CLC 12**
  See also CA 73-76

Leavis, F(rank) R(aymond)
  1895-1978 .... **CLC 24**
  See also CA 21-24R; 77-80; MTCW

Leavitt, David 1961-.............. **CLC 34**
  See also CA 116; 122

Lebowitz, Fran(ces Ann)
  1951(?)-.................. **CLC 11, 36**
  See also CA 81-84; CANR 14; MTCW

le Carre, John .... **CLC 3, 5, 9, 15, 28**
  See also Cornwell, David (John Moore)
  See also BEST 89:4; CDBLB 1960 to
  Present; DLB 87

Le Clezio, J(ean) M(arie) G(ustave)
  1940- .... **CLC 31**
  See also CA 116; 128; DLB 83

Leconte de Lisle, Charles-Marie-Rene
  1818-1894 .... **NCLC 29**

Le Coq, Monsieur
  See Simenon, Georges (Jacques Christian)

Leduc, Violette 1907-1972........ **CLC 22**
  See also CA 13-14; 33-36R; CAP 1

Ledwidge, Francis 1887(?)-1917 ... **TCLC 23**
  See also CA 123; DLB 20

Lee, Andrea 1953- .... **CLC 36**
  See also BLC 2; BW; CA 125

Lee, Andrew
  See Auchincloss, Louis (Stanton)

Lee, Don L....................... **CLC 2**
  See also Madhubuti, Haki R.

Lee, George W(ashington)
  1894-1976 .... **CLC 52**
  See also BLC 2; BW; CA 125; DLB 51

McCrae, John 1872-1918 . . . . TCLC **12**
See also CA 109; DLB 92

McCreigh, James
See Pohl, Frederik

McCullers, (Lula) Carson (Smith)
1917-1967 . . CLC **1, 4, 10, 12, 48;** SSC **9**
See also CA 5-8R; 25-28R; CABS 1, 3;
CANR 18; CDALB 1941-1968; DLB 2, 7;
MTCW; SATA 27; WLC

McCulloch, John Tyler
See Burroughs, Edgar Rice

McCullough, Colleen 1938(?)- . . . . . . CLC **27**
See also CA 81-84; CANR 17; MTCW

McElroy, Joseph 1930- . . . . CLC **5, 47**
See also CA 17-20R

McEwan, Ian (Russell) 1948- . . . CLC **13, 66**
See also BEST 90:4; CA 61-64; CANR 14;
DLB 14; MTCW

McFadden, David 1940- . . . . CLC **48**
See also CA 104; DLB 60

McFarland, Dennis 1950- . . . . CLC **65**

McGahern, John 1934- . . . . CLC **5, 9, 48**
See also CA 17-20R; CANR 29; DLB 14;
MTCW

McGinley, Patrick (Anthony)
1937- . . . . CLC **41**
See also CA 120; 127

McGinley, Phyllis 1905-1978 . . . . . . CLC **14**
See also CA 9-12R; 77-80; CANR 19;
DLB 11, 48; SATA 2, 24, 44

McGinniss, Joe 1942- . . . . CLC **32**
See also AITN 2; BEST 89:2; CA 25-28R;
CANR 26

McGivern, Maureen Daly
See Daly, Maureen

McGrath, Patrick 1950- . . . . CLC **55**
See also CA 136

McGrath, Thomas (Matthew)
1916-1990 . . . . CLC **28, 59**
See also CA 9-12R; 132; CANR 6, 33;
MTCW; SATA 41; SATO 66

McGuane, Thomas (Francis III)
1939- . . . . CLC **3, 7, 18, 45**
See also AITN 2; CA 49-52; CANR 5, 24;
DLB 2; DLBY 80; MTCW

McGuckian, Medbh 1950- . . . . CLC **48**
See also DLB 40

McHale, Tom 1942(?)-1982 . . . . . . CLC **3, 5**
See also AITN 1; CA 77-80; 106

McIlvanney, William 1936- . . . . CLC **42**
See also CA 25-28R; DLB 14

McIlwraith, Maureen Mollie Hunter
See Hunter, Mollie
See also SATA 2

McInerney, Jay 1955- . . . . CLC **34**
See also CA 116; 123

McIntyre, Vonda N(eel) 1948- . . . . . CLC **18**
See also CA 81-84; CANR 17, 34; MTCW

McKay, Claude . . . . TCLC **7, 41;** PC **2**
See also McKay, Festus Claudius
See also BLC 3; DLB 4, 45, 51, 117

McKay, Festus Claudius 1889-1948
See McKay, Claude
See also BW; CA 104; 124; MTCW; WLC

McKuen, Rod 1933- . . . . CLC **1, 3**
See also AITN 1; CA 41-44R

McLoughlin, R. B.
See Mencken, H(enry) L(ouis)

McLuhan, (Herbert) Marshall
1911-1980 . . . . CLC **37**
See also CA 9-12R; 102; CANR 12, 34;
DLB 88; MTCW

McMillan, Terry 1951- . . . . CLC **50, 61**

McMurtry, Larry (Jeff)
1936- . . . . CLC **2, 3, 7, 11, 27, 44**
See also AITN 2; BEST 89:2; CA 5-8R;
CANR 19; CDALB 1968-1988; DLB 2;
DLBY 80, 87; MTCW

McNally, Terrence 1939- . . . . . . CLC **4, 7, 41**
See also CA 45-48; CANR 2; DLB 7

McNamer, Deirdre 1950- . . . . CLC **70**

McNeile, Herman Cyril 1888-1937
See Sapper
See also DLB 77

McPhee, John (Angus) 1931- . . . . . . CLC **36**
See also BEST 90:1; CA 65-68; CANR 20;
MTCW

McPherson, James Alan 1943- . . . . . CLC **19**
See also BW; CA 25-28R; CANR 24;
DLB 38; MTCW

McPherson, William (Alexander)
1933- . . . . CLC **34**
See also CA 69-72; CANR 28

McSweeney, Kerry . . . . CLC **34**

Mead, Margaret 1901-1978 . . . . CLC **37**
See also AITN 1; CA 1-4R; 81-84;
CANR 4; MTCW; SATA 20

Meaker, Marijane (Agnes) 1927-
See Kerr, M. E.
See also CA 107; CANR 37; MAICYA;
MTCW; SATA 20, 61

Medoff, Mark (Howard) 1940- . . . CLC **6, 23**
See also AITN 1; CA 53-56; CANR 5;
DLB 7

Meged, Aharon
See Megged, Aharon

Meged, Aron
See Megged, Aharon

Megged, Aharon 1920- . . . . CLC **9**
See also CA 49-52; CAAS 13; CANR 1

Mehta, Ved (Parkash) 1934- . . . . CLC **37**
See also CA 1-4R; CANR 2, 23; MTCW

Melanter
See Blackmore, R(ichard) D(oddridge)

Melikow, Loris
See Hofmannsthal, Hugo von

Melmoth, Sebastian
See Wilde, Oscar (Fingal O'Flahertie Wills)

Meltzer, Milton 1915- . . . . CLC **26**
See also AAYA 8; CA 13-16R; CANR 38;
CLR 13; DLB 61; MAICYA; SAAS 1;
SATA 1, 50

Melville, Herman
1819-1891 . . . . . . NCLC **3, 12, 29;** SSC **1**
See also CDALB 1640-1865; DLB 3, 74;
SATA 59; WLC

Menander c. 342B.C.-c. 292B.C. . . . . CMLC **9**

Mencken, H(enry) L(ouis)
1880-1956 . . . . TCLC **13**
See also CA 105; 125; CDALB 1917-1929;
DLB 11, 29, 63; MTCW

Mercer, David 1928-1980 . . . . CLC **5**
See also CA 9-12R; 102; CANR 23;
DLB 13; MTCW

Merchant, Paul
See Ellison, Harlan

Meredith, George 1828-1909 . . . TCLC **17, 43**
See also CA 117; CDBLB 1832-1890;
DLB 18, 35, 57

Meredith, William (Morris)
1919- . . . . CLC **4, 13, 22, 55**
See also CA 9-12R; CAAS 14; CANR 6;
DLB 5

Merezhkovsky, Dmitry Sergeyevich
1865-1941 . . . . TCLC **29**

Merimee, Prosper
1803-1870 . . . . NCLC **6;** SSC **7**
See also DLB 119

Merkin, Daphne 1954- . . . . CLC **44**
See also CA 123

Merlin, Arthur
See Blish, James (Benjamin)

Merrill, James (Ingram)
1926- . . . . CLC **2, 3, 6, 8, 13, 18, 34**
See also CA 13-16R; CANR 10; DLB 5;
DLBY 85; MTCW

Merriman, Alex
See Silverberg, Robert

Merritt, E. B.
See Waddington, Miriam

Merton, Thomas
1915-1968 . . . . CLC **1, 3, 11, 34**
See also CA 5-8R; 25-28R; CANR 22;
DLB 48; DLBY 81; MTCW

Merwin, W(illiam) S(tanley)
1927- . . . . CLC **1, 2, 3, 5, 8, 13, 18, 45**
See also CA 13-16R; CANR 15; DLB 5;
MTCW

Metcalf, John 1938- . . . . CLC **37**
See also CA 113; DLB 60

Metcalf, Suzanne
See Baum, L(yman) Frank

Mew, Charlotte (Mary)
1870-1928 . . . . TCLC **8**
See also CA 105; DLB 19

Mewshaw, Michael 1943- . . . . CLC **9**
See also CA 53-56; CANR 7; DLBY 80

Meyer, June
See Jordan, June

Meyer-Meyrink, Gustav 1868-1932
See Meyrink, Gustav
See also CA 117

Meyers, Jeffrey 1939- . . . . CLC **39**
See also CA 73-76; DLB 111

Meynell, Alice (Christina Gertrude Thompson)
1847-1922 . . . . TCLC **6**
See also CA 104; DLB 19, 98

Meyrink, Gustav . . . . TCLC **21**
See also Meyer-Meyrink, Gustav
See also DLB 81

Michaels, Leonard 1933- . . . . CLC **6, 25**
See also CA 61-64; CANR 21; MTCW

Michaux, Henri 1899-1984 . . . . . . CLC 8, 19
See also CA 85-88; 114

Michelangelo 1475-1564. . . . . LC 12

Michelet, Jules 1798-1874 . . . . . . NCLC 31

Michener, James A(lbert)
1907(?)- . . . . CLC 1, 5, 11, 29, 60
See also AITN 1; BEST 90:1; CA 5-8R;
CANR 21; DLB 6; MTCW

Mickiewicz, Adam 1798-1855 . . . . . NCLC 3

Middleton, Christopher 1926- . . . . . . CLC 13
See also CA 13-16R; CANR 29; DLB 40

Middleton, Stanley 1919-. . . . . CLC 7, 38
See also CA 25-28R; CANR 21; DLB 14

Migueis, Jose Rodrigues 1901- . . . . . CLC 10

Mikszath, Kalman 1847-1910 . . . . . TCLC 31

Miles, Josephine
1911-1985 . . . . CLC 1, 2, 14, 34, 39
See also CA 1-4R; 116; CANR 2; DLB 48

Militant
See Sandburg, Carl (August)

Mill, John Stuart 1806-1873 . . . . . NCLC 11
See also CDBLB 1832-1890; DLB 55

Millar, Kenneth 1915-1983 . . . . CLC 14
See also Macdonald, Ross
See also CA 9-12R; 110; CANR 16; DLB 2;
DLBD 6; DLBY 83; MTCW

Millay, E. Vincent
See Millay, Edna St. Vincent

Millay, Edna St. Vincent
1892-1950 . . . . TCLC 4
See also CA 104; 130; CDALB 1917-1929;
DLB 45; MTCW

Miller, Arthur
1915- . . . . . . CLC 1, 2, 6, 10, 15, 26, 47;
DC 1
See also AITN 1; CA 1-4R; CABS 3;
CANR 2, 30; CDALB 1941-1968; DLB 7;
MTCW; WLC

Miller, Henry (Valentine)
1891-1980 . . . . CLC 1, 2, 4, 9, 14, 43
See also CA 9-12R; 97-100; CANR 33;
CDALB 1929-1941; DLB 4, 9; DLBY 80;
MTCW; WLC

Miller, Jason 1939(?)- . . . . CLC 2
See also AITN 1; CA 73-76; DLB 7

Miller, Sue 19(?)- . . . . CLC 44
See also BEST 90:3

Miller, Walter M(ichael Jr.)
1923- . . . . CLC 4, 30
See also CA 85-88; DLB 8

Millett, Kate 1934- . . . . CLC 67
See also AITN 1; CA 73-76; CANR 32;
MTCW

Millhauser, Steven 1943- . . . . CLC 21, 54
See also CA 110; 111; DLB 2

Millin, Sarah Gertrude 1889-1968 . . CLC 49
See also CA 102; 93-96

Milne, A(lan) A(lexander)
1882-1956 . . . . TCLC 6
See also CA 104; 133; CLR 1, 26; DLB 10,
77, 100; MAICYA; MTCW; YABC 1

Milner, Ron(ald) 1938- . . . . CLC 56
See also AITN 1; BLC 3; BW; CA 73-76;
CANR 24; DLB 38; MTCW

Milosz, Czeslaw
1911- . . . . CLC 5, 11, 22, 31, 56
See also CA 81-84; CANR 23; MTCW

Milton, John 1608-1674 . . . . LC 9
See also CDBLB 1660-1789; WLC

Minehaha, Cornelius
See Wedekind, (Benjamin) Frank(lin)

Miner, Valerie 1947- . . . . CLC 40
See also CA 97-100

Minimo, Duca
See D'Annunzio, Gabriele

Minot, Susan 1956- . . . . CLC 44
See also CA 134

Minus, Ed 1938- . . . . CLC 39

Miranda, Javier
See Bioy Casares, Adolfo

Miro (Ferrer), Gabriel (Francisco Victor)
1879-1930 . . . . TCLC 5
See also CA 104

Mishima, Yukio
. . . . CLC 2, 4, 6, 9, 27; DC 1; SSC 4
See also Hiraoka, Kimitake

Mistral, Gabriela . . . . TCLC 2
See also Godoy Alcayaga, Lucila

Mistry, Rohinton 1952- . . . . CLC 71

Mitchell, Clyde
See Ellison, Harlan; Silverberg, Robert

Mitchell, James Leslie 1901-1935
See Gibbon, Lewis Grassic
See also CA 104; DLB 15

Mitchell, Joni 1943- . . . . CLC 12
See also CA 112

Mitchell, Margaret (Munnerlyn)
1900-1949 . . . . TCLC 11
See also CA 109; 125; DLB 9; MTCW

Mitchell, Peggy
See Mitchell, Margaret (Munnerlyn)

Mitchell, S(ilas) Weir 1829-1914 . . TCLC 36

Mitchell, W(illiam) O(rmond)
1914- . . . . CLC 25
See also CA 77-80; CANR 15; DLB 88

Mitford, Mary Russell 1787-1855 . . NCLC 4
See also DLB 110, 116

Mitford, Nancy 1904-1973 . . . . CLC 44
See also CA 9-12R

Miyamoto, Yuriko 1899-1951 . . . . . TCLC 37

Mo, Timothy (Peter) 1950(?)- . . . . . . CLC 46
See also CA 117; MTCW

Modarressi, Taghi (M.) 1931- . . . . . . CLC 44
See also CA 121; 134

Modiano, Patrick (Jean) 1945- . . . . . CLC 18
See also CA 85-88; CANR 17; DLB 83

Moerck, Paal
See Roelvaag, O(le) E(dvart)

Mofolo, Thomas (Mokopu)
1875(?)-1948 . . . . TCLC 22
See also BLC 3; CA 121

Mohr, Nicholasa 1935- . . . . CLC 12
See also AAYA 8; CA 49-52; CANR 1, 32;
CLR 22; HW; SAAS 8; SATA 8

Mojtabai, A(nn) G(race)
1938- . . . . CLC 5, 9, 15, 29
See also CA 85-88

Moliere 1622-1673 . . . . LC 10
See also WLC

Molin, Charles
See Mayne, William (James Carter)

Molnar, Ferenc 1878-1952 . . . . TCLC 20
See also CA 109

Momaday, N(avarre) Scott
1934- . . . . CLC 2, 19
See also CA 25-28R; CANR 14, 34;
MTCW; SATA 30, 48

Monroe, Harriet 1860-1936 . . . . TCLC 12
See also CA 109; DLB 54, 91

Monroe, Lyle
See Heinlein, Robert A(nson)

Montagu, Elizabeth 1917- . . . . NCLC 7
See also CA 9-12R

Montagu, Mary (Pierrepont) Wortley
1689-1762 . . . . LC 9
See also DLB 95, 101

Montague, John (Patrick)
1929- . . . . CLC 13, 46
See also CA 9-12R; CANR 9; DLB 40;
MTCW

Montaigne, Michel (Eyquem) de
1533-1592 . . . . LC 8
See also WLC

Montale, Eugenio 1896-1981 . . . CLC 7, 9, 18
See also CA 17-20R; 104; CANR 30;
DLB 114; MTCW

Montesquieu, Charles-Louis de Secondat
1689-1755 . . . . LC 7

Montgomery, (Robert) Bruce 1921-1978
See Crispin, Edmund
See also CA 104

Montgomery, Marion H. Jr. 1925- . . . CLC 7
See also AITN 1; CA 1-4R; CANR 3;
DLB 6

Montgomery, Max
See Davenport, Guy (Mattison Jr.)

Montherlant, Henry (Milon) de
1896-1972 . . . . CLC 8, 19
See also CA 85-88; 37-40R; DLB 72;
MTCW

Monty Python . . . . CLC 21
See also Chapman, Graham; Cleese, John
(Marwood); Gilliam, Terry (Vance); Idle,
Eric; Jones, Terence Graham Parry; Palin,
Michael (Edward)
See also AAYA 7

Moodie, Susanna (Strickland)
1803-1885 . . . . NCLC 14
See also DLB 99

Mooney, Edward 1951- . . . . CLC 25
See also CA 130

Mooney, Ted
See Mooney, Edward

Moorcock, Michael (John)
1939- . . . . CLC 5, 27, 58
See also CA 45-48; CAAS 5; CANR 2, 17,
38; DLB 14; MTCW

Moore, Brian
1921- . . . . CLC 1, 3, 5, 7, 8, 19, 32
See also CA 1-4R; CANR 1, 25; MTCW

Moore, Edward
See Muir, Edwin

Moore, George Augustus
1852-1933 .... **TCLC 7**
See also CA 104; DLB 10, 18, 57

Moore, Lorrie .... **CLC 39, 45, 68**
See also Moore, Marie Lorena

Moore, Marianne (Craig)
1887-1972 ... **CLC 1, 2, 4, 8, 10, 13, 19,**
47; PC 4
See also CA 1-4R; 33-36R; CANR 3;
CDALB 1929-1941; DLB 45; DLBD 7;
MTCW; SATA 20

Moore, Marie Lorena 1957-
See Moore, Lorrie
See also CA 116; CANR 39

Moore, Thomas 1779-1852........ **NCLC 6**
See also DLB 96

Morand, Paul 1888-1976 .... **CLC 41**
See also CA 69-72; DLB 65

Morante, Elsa 1918-1985........ **CLC 8, 47**
See also CA 85-88; 117; CANR 35; MTCW

Moravia, Alberto...... **CLC 2, 7, 11, 27, 46**
See also Pincherle, Alberto

More, Hannah 1745-1833 .... **NCLC 27**
See also DLB 107, 109, 116

More, Henry 1614-1687............. **LC 9**

More, Sir Thomas 1478-1535 ...... **LC 10**

Moreas, Jean.................... **TCLC 18**
See also Papadiamantopoulos, Johannes

Morgan, Berry 1919-............. **CLC 6**
See also CA 49-52; DLB 6

Morgan, Claire
See Highsmith, (Mary) Patricia

Morgan, Edwin (George) 1920-..... **CLC 31**
See also CA 5-8R; CANR 3; DLB 27

Morgan, (George) Frederick
1922-...................... **CLC 23**
See also CA 17-20R; CANR 21

Morgan, Harriet
See Mencken, H(enry) L(ouis)

Morgan, Jane
See Cooper, James Fenimore

Morgan, Janet 1945- .... **CLC 39**
See also CA 65-68

Morgan, Lady 1776(?)-1859...... **NCLC 29**
See also DLB 116

Morgan, Robin 1941-.............. **CLC 2**
See also CA 69-72; CANR 29; MTCW

Morgan, Scott
See Kuttner, Henry

Morgan, Seth 1949(?)-1990 .... **CLC 65**
See also CA 132

Morgenstern, Christian
1871-1914 .... **TCLC 8**
See also CA 105

Morgenstern, S.
See Goldman, William (W.)

Moricz, Zsigmond 1879-1942 ..... **TCLC 33**

Morike, Eduard (Friedrich)
1804-1875 .... **NCLC 10**

Mori Ogai .... **TCLC 14**
See also Mori Rintaro

Mori Rintaro 1862-1922
See Mori Ogai
See also CA 110

Moritz, Karl Philipp 1756-1793 ...... **LC 2**
See also DLB 94

Morren, Theophil
See Hofmannsthal, Hugo von

Morris, Julian
See West, Morris L(anglo)

Morris, Steveland Judkins 1950(?)-
See Wonder, Stevie
See also CA 111

Morris, William 1834-1896 .... **NCLC 4**
See also CDBLB 1832-1890; DLB 18, 35, 57

Morris, Wright 1910-... **CLC 1, 3, 7, 18, 37**
See also CA 9-12R; CANR 21; DLB 2;
DLBY 81; MTCW

Morrison, Chloe Anthony Wofford
See Morrison, Toni

Morrison, James Douglas 1943-1971
See Morrison, Jim
See also CA 73-76

Morrison, Jim .... **CLC 17**
See also Morrison, James Douglas

Morrison, Toni 1931-..... **CLC 4, 10, 22, 55**
See also AAYA 1; BLC 3; BW; CA 29-32R;
CANR 27; CDALB 1968-1988; DLB 6,
33; DLBY 81; MTCW; SATA 57

Morrison, Van 1945- .... **CLC 21**
See also CA 116

Mortimer, John (Clifford)
1923-.................... **CLC 28, 43**
See also CA 13-16R; CANR 21;
CDBLB 1960 to Present; DLB 13;
MTCW

Mortimer, Penelope (Ruth) 1918-.... **CLC 5**
See also CA 57-60

Morton, Anthony
See Creasey, John

Mosher, Howard Frank .... **CLC 62**

Mosley, Nicholas 1923-........ **CLC 43, 70**
See also CA 69-72; DLB 14

Moss, Howard
1922-1987 .... **CLC 7, 14, 45, 50**
See also CA 1-4R; 123; CANR 1; DLB 5

Motion, Andrew 1952-............. **CLC 47**
See also DLB 40

Motley, Willard (Francis)
1912-1965 .... **CLC 18**
See also BW; CA 117; 106; DLB 76

Mott, Michael (Charles Alston)
1930-................... **CLC 15, 34**
See also CA 5-8R; CAAS 7; CANR 7, 29

Mowat, Farley (McGill) 1921- ..... **CLC 26**
See also AAYA 1; CA 1-4R; CANR 4, 24;
CLR 20; DLB 68; MAICYA; MTCW;
SATA 3, 55

Moyers, Bill 1934-............... **CLC 74**
See also AITN 2; CA 61-64; CANR 31

Mphahlele, Es'kia
See Mphahlele, Ezekiel

Mphahlele, Ezekiel 1919-........ **CLC 25**
See also BLC 3; BW; CA 81-84; CANR 26

Mqhayi, S(amuel) E(dward) K(rune Loliwe)
1875-1945 .... **TCLC 25**
See also BLC 3

Mr. Martin
See Burroughs, William S(eward)

Mrozek, Slawomir 1930-........ **CLC 3, 13**
See also CA 13-16R; CAAS 10; CANR 29;
MTCW

Mrs. Belloc-Lowndes
See Lowndes, Marie Adelaide (Belloc)

Mtwa, Percy (?)-................. **CLC 47**

Mueller, Lisel 1924-........... **CLC 13, 51**
See also CA 93-96; DLB 105

Muir, Edwin 1887-1959 .... **TCLC 2**
See also CA 104; DLB 20, 100

Muir, John 1838-1914 .... **TCLC 28**

Mujica Lainez, Manuel
1910-1984 .... **CLC 31**
See also Lainez, Manuel Mujica
See also CA 81-84; 112; CANR 32; HW

Mukherjee, Bharati 1940-......... **CLC 53**
See also BEST 89:2; CA 107; DLB 60;
MTCW

Muldoon, Paul 1951-.......... **CLC 32, 72**
See also CA 113; 129; DLB 40

Mulisch, Harry 1927-............. **CLC 42**
See also CA 9-12R; CANR 6, 26

Mull, Martin 1943-.............. **CLC 17**
See also CA 105

Mulock, Dinah Maria
See Craik, Dinah Maria (Mulock)

Munford, Robert 1737(?)-1783 .... **LC 5**
See also DLB 31

Mungo, Raymond 1946-........... **CLC 72**
See also CA 49-52; CANR 2

Munro, Alice
1931-........ **CLC 6, 10, 19, 50; SSC 3**
See also AITN 2; CA 33-36R; CANR 33;
DLB 53; MTCW; SATA 29

Munro, H(ector) H(ugh) 1870-1916
See Saki
See also CA 104; 130; CDBLB 1890-1914;
DLB 34; MTCW; WLC

Murasaki, Lady.................. **CMLC 1**

Murdoch, (Jean) Iris
1919-...... **CLC 1, 2, 3, 4, 6, 8, 11, 15,**
22, 31, 51
See also CA 13-16R; CANR 8;
CDBLB 1960 to Present; DLB 14;
MTCW

Murphy, Richard 1927-........... **CLC 41**
See also CA 29-32R; DLB 40

Murphy, Sylvia 1937-............. **CLC 34**
See also CA 121

Murphy, Thomas (Bernard) 1935-... **CLC 51**
See also CA 101

Murray, Les(lie) A(llan) 1938- ..... **CLC 40**
See also CA 21-24R; CANR 11, 27

Murry, J. Middleton
See Murry, John Middleton

Murry, John Middleton
1889-1957 .... **TCLC 16**
See also CA 118

Musgrave, Susan 1951- . . . . CLC 13, 54
See also CA 69-72

Musil, Robert (Edler von)
1880-1942 . . . . TCLC 12
See also CA 109; DLB 81

Musset, (Louis Charles) Alfred de
1810-1857 . . . . NCLC 7

My Brother's Brother
See Chekhov, Anton (Pavlovich)

Myers, Walter Dean 1937- . . . . CLC 35
See also AAYA 4; BLC 3; BW; CA 33-36R;
CANR 20; CLR 4, 16; DLB 33;
MAICYA; SAAS 2; SATA 27, 41, 70, 71

Myers, Walter M.
See Myers, Walter Dean

Myles, Symon
See Follett, Ken(neth Martin)

Nabokov, Vladimir (Vladimirovich)
1899-1977 . . . . CLC 1, 2, 3, 6, 8, 11, 15,
23, 44, 46, 64; SSC 11
See also CA 5-8R; 69-72; CANR 20;
CDALB 1941-1968; DLB 2; DLBD 3;
DLBY 80, 91; MTCW; WLC

Nagy, Laszlo 1925-1978. . . . . CLC 7
See also CA 129; 112

Naipaul, Shiva(dhar Srinivasa)
1945-1985 . . . . CLC 32, 39
See also CA 110; 112; 116; CANR 33;
DLBY 85; MTCW

Naipaul, V(idiadhar) S(urajprasad)
1932- . . . . CLC 4, 7, 9, 13, 18, 37
See also CA 1-4R; CANR 1, 33;
CDBLB 1960 to Present; DLBY 85;
MTCW

Nakos, Lilika 1899(?)- . . . . CLC 29

Narayan, R(asipuram) K(rishnaswami)
1906- . . . . CLC 7, 28, 47
See also CA 81-84; CANR 33; MTCW;
SATA 62

Nash, (Frediric) Ogden 1902-1971 . . CLC 23
See also CA 13-14; 29-32R; CANR 34;
CAP 1; DLB 11; MAICYA; MTCW;
SATA 2, 46

Nathan, Daniel
See Dannay, Frederic

Nathan, George Jean 1882-1958 . . . TCLC 18
See also Hatteras, Owen
See also CA 114

Natsume, Kinnosuke 1867-1916
See Natsume, Soseki
See also CA 104

Natsume, Soseki . . . . TCLC 2, 10
See also Natsume, Kinnosuke

Natti, (Mary) Lee 1919-
See Kingman, Lee
See also CA 5-8R; CANR 2

Naylor, Gloria 1950- . . . . CLC 28, 52
See also AAYA 6; BLC 3; BW; CA 107;
CANR 27; MTCW

Neihardt, John Gneisenau
1881-1973 . . . . CLC 32
See also CA 13-14; CAP 1; DLB 9, 54

Nekrasov, Nikolai Alekseevich
1821-1878 . . . . NCLC 11

Nelligan, Emile 1879-1941. . . . . . . TCLC 14
See also CA 114; DLB 92

Nelson, Willie 1933-. . . . . CLC 17
See also CA 107

Nemerov, Howard (Stanley)
1920-1991 . . . . CLC 2, 6, 9, 36
See also CA 1-4R; 134; CABS 2; CANR 1,
27; DLB 6; DLBY 83; MTCW

Neruda, Pablo
1904-1973 . . . . CLC 1, 2, 5, 7, 9, 28, 62;
PC 4
See also CA 19-20; 45-48; CAP 2; HW;
MTCW; WLC

Nerval, Gerard de 1808-1855. . . . . . NCLC 1

Nervo, (Jose) Amado (Ruiz de)
1870-1919 . . . . TCLC 11
See also CA 109; 131; HW

Nessi, Pio Baroja y
See Baroja (y Nessi), Pio

Neufeld, John (Arthur) 1938- . . . . . . CLC 17
See also CA 25-28R; CANR 11, 37;
MAICYA; SAAS 3; SATA 6

Neville, Emily Cheney 1919-. . . . . . . CLC 12
See also CA 5-8R; CANR 3, 37; MAICYA;
SAAS 2; SATA 1

Newbound, Bernard Slade 1930-
See Slade, Bernard
See also CA 81-84

Newby, P(ercy) H(oward)
1918- . . . . CLC 2, 13
See also CA 5-8R; CANR 32; DLB 15;
MTCW

Newlove, Donald 1928- . . . . CLC 6
See also CA 29-32R; CANR 25

Newlove, John (Herbert) 1938-. . . . . CLC 14
See also CA 21-24R; CANR 9, 25

Newman, Charles 1938-. . . . . CLC 2, 8
See also CA 21-24R

Newman, Edwin (Harold) 1919- . . . . CLC 14
See also AITN 1; CA 69-72; CANR 5

Newman, John Henry
1801-1890 . . . . NCLC 38
See also DLB 18, 32, 55

Newton, Suzanne 1936- . . . . CLC 35
See also CA 41-44R; CANR 14; SATA 5

Nexo, Martin Andersen
1869-1954 . . . . TCLC 43

Nezval, Vitezslav 1900-1958 . . . . . . TCLC 44
See also CA 123

Ngema, Mbongeni 1955- . . . . CLC 57

Ngugi, James T(hiong'o). . . . . CLC 3, 7, 13
See also Ngugi wa Thiong'o

Ngugi wa Thiong'o 1938-. . . . . CLC 36
See also Ngugi, James T(hiong'o)
See also BLC 3; BW; CA 81-84; CANR 27;
MTCW

Nichol, B(arrie) P(hillip)
1944-1988 . . . . CLC 18
See also CA 53-56; DLB 53; SATA 66

Nichols, John (Treadwell) 1940-. . . . CLC 38
See also CA 9-12R; CAAS 2; CANR 6;
DLBY 82

Nichols, Peter (Richard)
1927- . . . . CLC 5, 36, 65
See also CA 104; CANR 33; DLB 13;
MTCW

Nicolas, F. R. E.
See Freeling, Nicolas

Niedecker, Lorine 1903-1970. . . . CLC 10, 42
See also CA 25-28; CAP 2; DLB 48

Nietzsche, Friedrich (Wilhelm)
1844-1900 . . . . TCLC 10, 18
See also CA 107; 121

Nievo, Ippolito 1831-1861 . . . . NCLC 22

Nightingale, Anne Redmon 1943-
See Redmon, Anne
See also CA 103

Nik.T.O.
See Annensky, Innokenty Fyodorovich

Nin, Anais
1903-1977 . . . . . CLC 1, 4, 8, 11, 14, 60;
SSC 10
See also AITN 2; CA 13-16R; 69-72;
CANR 22; DLB 2, 4; MTCW

Nissenson, Hugh 1933-. . . . . CLC 4, 9
See also CA 17-20R; CANR 27; DLB 28

Niven, Larry . . . . CLC 8
See also Niven, Laurence Van Cott
See also DLB 8

Niven, Laurence Van Cott 1938-
See Niven, Larry
See also CA 21-24R; CAAS 12; CANR 14;
MTCW

Nixon, Agnes Eckhardt 1927-. . . . . . CLC 21
See also CA 110

Nizan, Paul 1905-1940. . . . . TCLC 40
See also DLB 72

Nkosi, Lewis 1936-. . . . . CLC 45
See also BLC 3; BW; CA 65-68; CANR 27

Nodier, (Jean) Charles (Emmanuel)
1780-1844 . . . . NCLC 19
See also DLB 119

Nolan, Christopher 1965-. . . . . CLC 58
See also CA 111

Norden, Charles
See Durrell, Lawrence (George)

Nordhoff, Charles (Bernard)
1887-1947 . . . . TCLC 23
See also CA 108; DLB 9; SATA 23

Norman, Marsha 1947- . . . . CLC 28
See also CA 105; CABS 3; DLBY 84

Norris, Benjamin Franklin Jr.
1870-1902 . . . . TCLC 24
See also Norris, Frank
See also CA 110

Norris, Frank
See Norris, Benjamin Franklin Jr.
See also CDALB 1865-1917; DLB 12, 71

Norris, Leslie 1921-. . . . . CLC 14
See also CA 11-12; CANR 14; CAP 1;
DLB 27

North, Andrew
See Norton, Andre

North, Captain George
See Stevenson, Robert Louis (Balfour)

Author Index

Orton, John Kingsley 1933-1967
See Orton, Joe
See also CA 85-88; CANR 35; MTCW

Orwell, George .... TCLC 2, 6, 15, 31
See also Blair, Eric (Arthur)
See also CDBLB 1945-1960; DLB 15, 98;
WLC

Osborne, David
See Silverberg, Robert

Osborne, George
See Silverberg, Robert

Osborne, John (James)
1929- .... CLC 1, 2, 5, 11, 45
See also CA 13-16R; CANR 21;
CDBLB 1945-1960; DLB 13; MTCW;
WLC

Osborne, Lawrence 1958- .... CLC 50

Oshima, Nagisa 1932- .... CLC 20
See also CA 116; 121

Oskison, John M(ilton)
1874-1947 .... TCLC 35

Ossoli, Sarah Margaret (Fuller marchesa d')
1810-1850
See Fuller, Margaret
See also SATA 25

Ostrovsky, Alexander
1823-1886 .... NCLC 30

Otero, Blas de 1916- .... CLC 11
See also CA 89-92

Otto, Whitney 1955-.............. CLC 70

Ouida .... TCLC 43
See also De La Ramee, (Marie) Louise
See also DLB 18

Ousmane, Sembene 1923- .... CLC 66
See also BLC 3; BW; CA 117; 125; MTCW

Ovid 43B.C.-18th cent. (?)... CMLC 7; PC 2

Owen, Wilfred 1893-1918 ...... TCLC 5, 27
See also CA 104; CDBLB 1914-1945;
DLB 20; WLC

Owens, Rochelle 1936-............. CLC 8
See also CA 17-20R; CAAS 2; CANR 39

Oz, Amos 1939- ... CLC 5, 8, 11, 27, 33, 54
See also CA 53-56; CANR 27; MTCW

Ozick, Cynthia 1928-...... CLC 3, 7, 28, 62
See also BEST 90:1; CA 17-20R; CANR 23;
DLB 28; DLBY 82; MTCW

Ozu, Yasujiro 1903-1963 .... CLC 16
See also CA 112

Pacheco, C.
See Pessoa, Fernando (Antonio Nogueira)

Pa Chin
See Li Fei-kan

Pack, Robert 1929-............... CLC 13
See also CA 1-4R; CANR 3; DLB 5

Padgett, Lewis
See Kuttner, Henry

Padilla (Lorenzo), Heberto 1932-... CLC 38
See also AITN 1; CA 123; 131; HW

Page, Jimmy 1944-............... CLC 12

Page, Louise 1955-.............. CLC 40

Page, P(atricia) K(athleen)
1916- .... CLC 7, 18
See also CA 53-56; CANR 4, 22; DLB 68;
MTCW

Paget, Violet 1856-1935
See Lee, Vernon
See also CA 104

Paget-Lowe, Henry
See Lovecraft, H(oward) P(hillips)

Paglia, Camille 1947-............. CLC 68

Pakenham, Antonia
See Fraser, Antonia (Pakenham)

Palamas, Kostes 1859-1943 .... TCLC 5
See also CA 105

Palazzeschi, Aldo 1885-1974 ...... CLC 11
See also CA 89-92; 53-56; DLB 114

Paley, Grace 1922-.... CLC 4, 6, 37; SSC 8
See also CA 25-28R; CANR 13; DLB 28;
MTCW

Palin, Michael (Edward) 1943-..... CLC 21
See also Monty Python
See also CA 107; CANR 35; SATA 67

Palliser, Charles 1947-............ CLC 65
See also CA 136

Palma, Ricardo 1833-1919........ TCLC 29

Pancake, Breece Dexter 1952-1979
See Pancake, Breece D'J
See also CA 123; 109

Pancake, Breece D'J............... CLC 29
See also Pancake, Breece Dexter

Papadiamantis, Alexandros
1851-1911 .... TCLC 29

Papadiamantopoulos, Johannes 1856-1910
See Moreas, Jean
See also CA 117

Papini, Giovanni 1881-1956....... TCLC 22
See also CA 121

Paracelsus 1493-1541............. LC 14

Parasol, Peter
See Stevens, Wallace

Parfenie, Maria
See Codrescu, Andrei

Parini, Jay (Lee) 1948- .... CLC 54
See also CA 97-100; CAAS 16; CANR 32

Park, Jordan
See Kornbluth, C(yril) M.; Pohl, Frederik

Parker, Bert
See Ellison, Harlan

Parker, Dorothy (Rothschild)
1893-1967 .... CLC 15, 68; SSC 2
See also CA 19-20; 25-28R; CAP 2;
DLB 11, 45, 86; MTCW

Parker, Robert B(rown) 1932-...... CLC 27
See also BEST 89:4; CA 49-52; CANR 1,
26; MTCW

Parkes, Lucas
See Harris, John (Wyndham Parkes Lucas)
Beynon

Parkin, Frank 1940-.............. CLC 43

Parkman, Francis Jr. 1823-1893.. NCLC 12
See also DLB 1, 30

Parks, Gordon (Alexander Buchanan)
1912- .... CLC 1, 16
See also AITN 2; BLC 3; BW; CA 41-44R;
CANR 26; DLB 33; SATA 8

Parnell, Thomas 1679-1718 .... LC 3
See also DLB 94

Parra, Nicanor 1914-.............. CLC 2
See also CA 85-88; CANR 32; HW; MTCW

Parson Lot
See Kingsley, Charles

Partridge, Anthony
See Oppenheim, E(dward) Phillips

Pascoli, Giovanni 1855-1912 ..... TCLC 45

Pasolini, Pier Paolo
1922-1975 .... CLC 20, 37
See also CA 93-96; 61-64; MTCW

Pasquini
See Silone, Ignazio

Pastan, Linda (Olenik) 1932- ...... CLC 27
See also CA 61-64; CANR 18; DLB 5

Pasternak, Boris (Leonidovich)
1890-1960 .... CLC 7, 10, 18, 63
See also CA 127; 116; MTCW; WLC

Patchen, Kenneth 1911-1972... CLC 1, 2, 18
See also CA 1-4R; 33-36R; CANR 3, 35;
DLB 16, 48; MTCW

Pater, Walter (Horatio)
1839-1894 .... NCLC 7
See also CDBLB 1832-1890; DLB 57

Paterson, A(ndrew) B(arton)
1864-1941 .... TCLC 32

Paterson, Katherine (Womeldorf)
1932- .... CLC 12, 30
See also AAYA 1; CA 21-24R; CANR 28;
CLR 7; DLB 52; MAICYA; MTCW;
SATA 13, 53

Patmore, Coventry Kersey Dighton
1823-1896 .... NCLC 9
See also DLB 35, 98

Paton, Alan (Stewart)
1903-1988 .... CLC 4, 10, 25, 55
See also CA 13-16; 125; CANR 22; CAP 1;
MTCW; SATA 11, 56; WLC

Paton Walsh, Gillian 1939-
See Walsh, Jill Paton
See also CANR 38; MAICYA; SAAS 3;
SATA 4

Paulding, James Kirke 1778-1860.. NCLC 2
See also DLB 3, 59, 74

Paulin, Thomas Neilson 1949-
See Paulin, Tom
See also CA 123; 128

Paulin, Tom...................... CLC 37
See also Paulin, Thomas Neilson
See also DLB 40

Paustovsky, Konstantin (Georgievich)
1892-1968 .... CLC 40
See also CA 93-96; 25-28R

Pavese, Cesare 1908-1950 .... TCLC 3
See also CA 104

Pavic, Milorad 1929-............. CLC 60
See also CA 136

Payne, Alan
See Jakes, John (William)

Paz, Gil
See Lugones, Leopoldo

Paz, Octavio
1914- ...... **CLC 3, 4, 6, 10, 19, 51, 65;**
PC 1
See also CA 73-76; CANR 32; DLBY 90;
HW; MTCW; WLC

Peacock, Molly 1947-........... **CLC 60**
See also CA 103; DLB 120

Peacock, Thomas Love
1785-1866 .... **NCLC 22**
See also DLB 96, 116

Peake, Mervyn 1911-1968....... **CLC 7, 54**
See also CA 5-8R; 25-28R; CANR 3;
DLB 15; MTCW; SATA 23

Pearce, Philippa .... **CLC 21**
See also Christie, (Ann) Philippa
See also CLR 9; MAICYA; SATA 1, 67

Pearl, Eric
See Elman, Richard

Pearson, T(homas) R(eid) 1956- .... **CLC 39**
See also CA 120; 130

Peck, John 1941- .... **CLC 3**
See also CA 49-52; CANR 3

Peck, Richard (Wayne) 1934- ...... **CLC 21**
See also AAYA 1; CA 85-88; CANR 19,
38; MAICYA; SAAS 2; SATA 18, 55

Peck, Robert Newton 1928-........ **CLC 17**
See also AAYA 3; CA 81-84; CANR 31;
MAICYA; SAAS 1; SATA 21, 62

Peckinpah, (David) Sam(uel)
1925-1984 .... **CLC 20**
See also CA 109; 114

Pedersen, Knut 1859-1952
See Hamsun, Knut
See also CA 104; 119; MTCW

Peeslake, Gaffer
See Durrell, Lawrence (George)

Peguy, Charles Pierre
1873-1914 .... **TCLC 10**
See also CA 107

Pena, Ramon del Valle y
See Valle-Inclan, Ramon (Maria) del

Pendennis, Arthur Esquir
See Thackeray, William Makepeace

Pepys, Samuel 1633-1703........... **LC 11**
See also CDBLB 1660-1789; DLB 101;
WLC

Percy, Walker
1916-1990 ... **CLC 2, 3, 6, 8, 14, 18, 47,**
65
See also CA 1-4R; 131; CANR 1, 23;
DLB 2; DLBY 80, 90; MTCW

Perec, Georges 1936-1982 .... **CLC 56**
See also DLB 83

Pereda (y Sanchez de Porrua), Jose Maria de
1833-1906 .... **TCLC 16**
See also CA 117

Pereda y Porrua, Jose Maria de
See Pereda (y Sanchez de Porrua), Jose
Maria de

Peregoy, George Weems
See Mencken, H(enry) L(ouis)

Perelman, S(idney) J(oseph)
1904-1979 ... **CLC 3, 5, 9, 15, 23, 44, 49**
See also AITN 1, 2; CA 73-76; 89-92;
CANR 18; DLB 11, 44; MTCW

Peret, Benjamin 1899-1959 .... **TCLC 20**
See also CA 117

Peretz, Isaac Loeb 1851(?)-1915... **TCLC 16**
See also CA 109

Peretz, Yitzkhok Leibush
See Peretz, Isaac Loeb

Perez Galdos, Benito 1843-1920... **TCLC 27**
See also CA 125; HW

Perrault, Charles 1628-1703 .... **LC 2**
See also MAICYA; SATA 25

Perry, Brighton
See Sherwood, Robert E(mmet)

Perse, St.-John .... **CLC 4, 11, 46**
See also Leger, (Marie-Rene) Alexis
Saint-Leger

Perse, Saint-John
See Leger, (Marie-Rene) Alexis Saint-Leger

Peseenz, Tulio F.
See Lopez y Fuentes, Gregorio

Pesetsky, Bette 1932-............. **CLC 28**
See also CA 133

Peshkov, Alexei Maximovich 1868-1936
See Gorky, Maxim
See also CA 105

Pessoa, Fernando (Antonio Nogueira)
1888-1935 .... **TCLC 27**
See also CA 125

Peterkin, Julia Mood 1880-1961.... **CLC 31**
See also CA 102; DLB 9

Peters, Joan K. 1945-............. **CLC 39**

Peters, Robert L(ouis) 1924-........ **CLC 7**
See also CA 13-16R; CAAS 8; DLB 105

Petofi, Sandor 1823-1849........ **NCLC 21**

Petrakis, Harry Mark 1923-........ **CLC 3**
See also CA 9-12R; CANR 4, 30

Petrov, Evgeny .... **TCLC 21**
See also Kataev, Evgeny Petrovich

Petry, Ann (Lane) 1908- ...... **CLC 1, 7, 18**
See also BW; CA 5-8R; CAAS 6; CANR 4;
CLR 12; DLB 76; MAICYA; MTCW;
SATA 5

Petursson, Halligrimur 1614-1674 .... **LC 8**

Philipson, Morris H. 1926-........ **CLC 53**
See also CA 1-4R; CANR 4

Phillips, David Graham
1867-1911 .... **TCLC 44**
See also CA 108; DLB 9, 12

Phillips, Jack
See Sandburg, Carl (August)

Phillips, Jayne Anne 1952- ..... **CLC 15, 33**
See also CA 101; CANR 24; DLBY 80;
MTCW

Phillips, Richard
See Dick, Philip K(indred)

Phillips, Robert (Schaeffer) 1938-... **CLC 28**
See also CA 17-20R; CAAS 13; CANR 8;
DLB 105

Phillips, Ward
See Lovecraft, H(oward) P(hillips)

Piccolo, Lucio 1901-1969......... **CLC 13**
See also CA 97-100; DLB 114

Pickthall, Marjorie L(owry) C(hristie)
1883-1922 .... **TCLC 21**
See also CA 107; DLB 92

Pico della Mirandola, Giovanni
1463-1494 .... **LC 15**

Piercy, Marge
1936- .... **CLC 3, 6, 14, 18, 27, 62**
See also CA 21-24R; CAAS 1; CANR 13;
DLB 120; MTCW

Piers, Robert
See Anthony, Piers

Pieyre de Mandiargues, Andre 1909-1991
See Mandiargues, Andre Pieyre de
See also CA 103; 136; CANR 22

Pilnyak, Boris .... **TCLC 23**
See also Vogau, Boris Andreyevich

Pincherle, Alberto 1907-1990 ... **CLC 11, 18**
See also Moravia, Alberto
See also CA 25-28R; 132; CANR 33;
MTCW

Pineda, Cecile 1942-............. **CLC 39**
See also CA 118

Pinero, Arthur Wing 1855-1934 ... **TCLC 32**
See also CA 110; DLB 10

Pinero, Miguel (Antonio Gomez)
1946-1988 .... **CLC 4, 55**
See also CA 61-64; 125; CANR 29; HW

Pinget, Robert 1919- .... **CLC 7, 13, 37**
See also CA 85-88; DLB 83

Pink Floyd .... **CLC 35**
See also Barrett, (Roger) Syd; Gilmour,
David; Mason, Nick; Waters, Roger;
Wright, Rick

Pinkney, Edward 1802-1828 ..... **NCLC 31**

Pinkwater, Daniel Manus 1941-.... **CLC 35**
See also Pinkwater, Manus
See also AAYA 1; CA 29-32R; CANR 12,
38; CLR 4; MAICYA; SAAS 3; SATA 46

Pinkwater, Manus
See Pinkwater, Daniel Manus
See also SATA 8

Pinsky, Robert 1940-........ **CLC 9, 19, 38**
See also CA 29-32R; CAAS 4; DLBY 82

Pinta, Harold
See Pinter, Harold

Pinter, Harold
1930- ..... **CLC 1, 3, 6, 9, 11, 15, 27, 58**
See also CA 5-8R; CANR 33; CDBLB 1960
to Present; DLB 13; MTCW; WLC

Pirandello, Luigi 1867-1936..... **TCLC 4, 29**
See also CA 104; WLC

Pirsig, Robert M(aynard) 1928- ... **CLC 4, 6**
See also CA 53-56; MTCW; SATA 39

Pisarev, Dmitry Ivanovich
1840-1868 .... **NCLC 25**

Pix, Mary (Griffith) 1666-1709....... **LC 8**
See also DLB 80

Plaidy, Jean
See Hibbert, Eleanor Burford

Plant, Robert 1948- .... **CLC 12**

Prowler, Harley
See Masters, Edgar Lee

Pryor, Richard (Franklin Lenox Thomas)
1940- .... **CLC 26**
See also CA 122

Przybyszewski, Stanislaw
1868-1927 .... **TCLC 36**
See also DLB 66

Pteleon
See Grieve, C(hristopher) M(urray)

Puckett, Lute
See Masters, Edgar Lee

Puig, Manuel
1932-1990 .... **CLC 3, 5, 10, 28, 65**
See also CA 45-48; CANR 2, 32; DLB 113;
HW; MTCW

Purdy, A(lfred) W(ellington)
1918- .... **CLC 3, 6, 14, 50**
See also Purdy, Al
See also CA 81-84

Purdy, Al
See Purdy, A(lfred) W(ellington)
See also DLB 88

Purdy, James (Amos)
1923- .... **CLC 2, 4, 10, 28, 52**
See also CA 33-36R; CAAS 1; CANR 19;
DLB 2; MTCW

Pure, Simon
See Swinnerton, Frank Arthur

Pushkin, Alexander (Sergeyevich)
1799-1837 .... **NCLC 3, 27**
See also SATA 61; WLC

P'u Sung-ling 1640-1715 .... **LC 3**

Putnam, Arthur Lee
See Alger, Horatio Jr.

Puzo, Mario 1920- .... **CLC 1, 2, 6, 36**
See also CA 65-68; CANR 4; DLB 6;
MTCW

Pym, Barbara (Mary Crampton)
1913-1980 .... **CLC 13, 19, 37**
See also CA 13-14; 97-100; CANR 13, 34;
CAP 1; DLB 14; DLBY 87; MTCW

Pynchon, Thomas (Ruggles Jr.)
1937-.. **CLC 2, 3, 6, 9, 11, 18, 33, 62, 72**
See also BEST 90:2; CA 17-20R; CANR 22;
DLB 2; MTCW; WLC

Qian Zhongshu
See Ch'ien Chung-shu

Qroll
See Dagerman, Stig (Halvard)

Quarrington, Paul (Lewis) 1953-.... **CLC 65**
See also CA 129

Quasimodo, Salvatore 1901-1968 ... **CLC 10**
See also CA 13-16; 25-28R; CAP 1;
DLB 114; MTCW

Queen, Ellery .... **CLC 3, 11**
See also Dannay, Frederic; Davidson,
Avram; Lee, Manfred B(ennington);
Sturgeon, Theodore (Hamilton); Vance,
John Holbrook

Queen, Ellery Jr.
See Dannay, Frederic; Lee, Manfred
B(ennington)

Queneau, Raymond
1903-1976 .... **CLC 2, 5, 10, 42**
See also CA 77-80; 69-72; CANR 32;
DLB 72; MTCW

Quin, Ann (Marie) 1936-1973 .... **CLC 6**
See also CA 9-12R; 45-48; DLB 14

Quinn, Martin
See Smith, Martin Cruz

Quinn, Simon
See Smith, Martin Cruz

Quiroga, Horacio (Sylvestre)
1878-1937 .... **TCLC 20**
See also CA 117; 131; HW; MTCW

Quoirez, Francoise 1935-........... **CLC 9**
See also Sagan, Francoise
See also CA 49-52; CANR 6, 39; MTCW

Raabe, Wilhelm 1831-1910 .... **TCLC 45**

Rabe, David (William) 1940-... **CLC 4, 8, 33**
See also CA 85-88; CABS 3; DLB 7

Rabelais, Francois 1483-1553 .... **LC 5**
See also WLC

Rabinovitch, Sholem 1859-1916
See Aleichem, Sholom
See also CA 104

Radcliffe, Ann (Ward) 1764-1823 .. **NCLC 6**
See also DLB 39

Radiguet, Raymond 1903-1923 .... **TCLC 29**
See also DLB 65

Radnoti, Miklos 1909-1944 .... **TCLC 16**
See also CA 118

Rado, James 1939- .... **CLC 17**
See also CA 105

Radvanyi, Netty 1900-1983
See Seghers, Anna
See also CA 85-88; 110

Raeburn, John (Hay) 1941-........ **CLC 34**
See also CA 57-60

Ragni, Gerome 1942-1991 .... **CLC 17**
See also CA 105; 134

Rahv, Philip .... **CLC 24**
See also Greenberg, Ivan

Raine, Craig 1944- .... **CLC 32**
See also CA 108; CANR 29; DLB 40

Raine, Kathleen (Jessie) 1908- ... **CLC 7, 45**
See also CA 85-88; DLB 20; MTCW

Rainis, Janis 1865-1929 .... **TCLC 29**

Rakosi, Carl .... **CLC 47**
See also Rawley, Callman
See also CAAS 5

Raleigh, Richard
See Lovecraft, H(oward) P(hillips)

Rallentando, H. P.
See Sayers, Dorothy L(eigh)

Ramal, Walter
See de la Mare, Walter (John)

Ramon, Juan
See Jimenez (Mantecon), Juan Ramon

Ramos, Graciliano 1892-1953 ..... **TCLC 32**

Rampersad, Arnold 1941-......... **CLC 44**
See also CA 127; 133; DLB 111

Rampling, Anne
See Rice, Anne

Ramuz, Charles-Ferdinand
1878-1947 .... **TCLC 33**

Rand, Ayn 1905-1982........ **CLC 3, 30, 44**
See also CA 13-16R; 105; CANR 27;
MTCW; WLC

Randall, Dudley (Felker) 1914-...... **CLC 1**
See also BLC 3; BW; CA 25-28R;
CANR 23; DLB 41

Randall, Robert
See Silverberg, Robert

Ranger, Ken
See Creasey, John

Ransom, John Crowe
1888-1974 .... **CLC 2, 4, 5, 11, 24**
See also CA 5-8R; 49-52; CANR 6, 34;
DLB 45, 63; MTCW

Rao, Raja 1909- .... **CLC 25, 56**
See also CA 73-76; MTCW

Raphael, Frederic (Michael)
1931- .... **CLC 2, 14**
See also CA 1-4R; CANR 1; DLB 14

Ratcliffe, James P.
See Mencken, H(enry) L(ouis)

Rathbone, Julian 1935- .... **CLC 41**
See also CA 101; CANR 34

Rattigan, Terence (Mervyn)
1911-1977 .... **CLC 7**
See also CA 85-88; 73-76;
CDBLB 1945-1960; DLB 13; MTCW

Ratushinskaya, Irina 1954- .... **CLC 54**
See also CA 129

Raven, Simon (Arthur Noel)
1927- .... **CLC 14**
See also CA 81-84

Rawley, Callman 1903-
See Rakosi, Carl
See also CA 21-24R; CANR 12, 32

Rawlings, Marjorie Kinnan
1896-1953 .... **TCLC 4**
See also CA 104; 137; DLB 9, 22, 102;
MAICYA; YABC 1

Ray, Satyajit 1921-.............. **CLC 16**
See also CA 114; 137

Read, Herbert Edward 1893-1968.... **CLC 4**
See also CA 85-88; 25-28R; DLB 20

Read, Piers Paul 1941- ...... **CLC 4, 10, 25**
See also CA 21-24R; CANR 38; DLB 14;
SATA 21

Reade, Charles 1814-1884 .... **NCLC 2**
See also DLB 21

Reade, Hamish
See Gray, Simon (James Holliday)

Reading, Peter 1946- .... **CLC 47**
See also CA 103; DLB 40

Reaney, James 1926- .... **CLC 13**
See also CA 41-44R; CAAS 15; DLB 68;
SATA 43

Rebreanu, Liviu 1885-1944 .... **TCLC 28**

Rechy, John (Francisco)
1934- .... **CLC 1, 7, 14, 18**
See also CA 5-8R; CAAS 4; CANR 6, 32;
DLBY 82; HW

Redcam, Tom 1870-1933 .... **TCLC 25**

Reddin, Keith.................... **CLC 67**

Redgrove, Peter (William)
1932- .... **CLC 6, 41**
See also CA 1-4R; CANR 3, 39; DLB 40

Redmon, Anne .... **CLC 22**
See also Nightingale, Anne Redmon
See also DLBY 86

Reed, Eliot
See Ambler, Eric

Reed, Ishmael
1938- .... **CLC 2, 3, 5, 6, 13, 32, 60**
See also BLC 3; BW; CA 21-24R;
CANR 25; DLB 2, 5, 33; DLBD 8;
MTCW

Reed, John (Silas) 1887-1920 ..... **TCLC 9**
See also CA 106

Reed, Lou. .... **CLC 21**
See also Firbank, Louis

Reeve, Clara 1729-1807 .... **NCLC 19**
See also DLB 39

Reid, Christopher 1949- .... **CLC 33**
See also DLB 40

Reid, Desmond
See Moorcock, Michael (John)

Reid Banks, Lynne 1929-
See Banks, Lynne Reid
See also CA 1-4R; CANR 6, 22, 38;
CLR 24; MAICYA; SATA 22

Reilly, William K.
See Creasey, John

Reiner, Max
See Caldwell, (Janet Miriam) Taylor
(Holland)

Reis, Ricardo
See Pessoa, Fernando (Antonio Nogueira)

Remarque, Erich Maria
1898-1970 .... **CLC 21**
See also CA 77-80; 29-32R; DLB 56;
MTCW

Remizov, A.
See Remizov, Aleksei (Mikhailovich)

Remizov, A. M.
See Remizov, Aleksei (Mikhailovich)

Remizov, Aleksei (Mikhailovich)
1877-1957 .... **TCLC 27**
See also CA 125; 133

Renan, Joseph Ernest
1823-1892 .... **NCLC 26**

Renard, Jules 1864-1910 .... **TCLC 17**
See also CA 117

Renault, Mary .... **CLC 3, 11, 17**
See also Challans, Mary
See also DLBY 83

Rendell, Ruth (Barbara) 1930- .. **CLC 28, 48**
See also Vine, Barbara
See also CA 109; CANR 32; DLB 87;
MTCW

Renoir, Jean 1894-1979 .... **CLC 20**
See also CA 129; 85-88

Resnais, Alain 1922- .... **CLC 16**

Reverdy, Pierre 1889-1960 .... **CLC 53**
See also CA 97-100; 89-92

Rexroth, Kenneth
1905-1982 ..... **CLC 1, 2, 6, 11, 22, 49**
See also CA 5-8R; 107; CANR 14, 34;
CDALB 1941-1968; DLB 16, 48;
DLBY 82; MTCW

Reyes, Alfonso 1889-1959 .... **TCLC 33**
See also CA 131; HW

Reyes y Basoalto, Ricardo Eliecer Neftali
See Neruda, Pablo

Reymont, Wladyslaw (Stanislaw)
1868(?)-1925 .... **TCLC 5**
See also CA 104

Reynolds, Jonathan 1942- .... **CLC 6, 38**
See also CA 65-68; CANR 28

Reynolds, Joshua 1723-1792 .... **LC 15**
See also DLB 104

Reynolds, Michael Shane 1937- .... **CLC 44**
See also CA 65-68; CANR 9

Reznikoff, Charles 1894-1976 .... **CLC 9**
See also CA 33-36; 61-64; CAP 2; DLB 28,
45

Rezzori (d'Arezzo), Gregor von
1914- .... **CLC 25**
See also CA 122; 136

Rhine, Richard
See Silverstein, Alvin

Rhys, Jean
1890(?)-1979 .... **CLC 2, 4, 6, 14, 19, 51**
See also CA 25-28R; 85-88; CANR 35;
CDBLB 1945-1960; DLB 36, 117; MTCW

Ribeiro, Darcy 1922- .... **CLC 34**
See also CA 33-36R

Ribeiro, Joao Ubaldo (Osorio Pimentel)
1941- .... **CLC 10, 67**
See also CA 81-84

Ribman, Ronald (Burt) 1932- .... **CLC 7**
See also CA 21-24R

Ricci, Nino 1959- .... **CLC 70**
See also CA 137

Rice, Anne 1941- .... **CLC 41**
See also AAYA 9; BEST 89:2; CA 65-68;
CANR 12, 36

Rice, Elmer (Leopold)
1892-1967 .... **CLC 7, 49**
See also CA 21-22; 25-28R; CAP 2; DLB 4,
7; MTCW

Rice, Tim 1944- .... **CLC 21**
See also CA 103

Rich, Adrienne (Cecile)
1929- ..... **CLC 3, 6, 7, 11, 18, 36; PC 5**
See also CA 9-12R; CANR 20; DLB 5, 67;
MTCW

Rich, Barbara
See Graves, Robert (von Ranke)

Rich, Robert
See Trumbo, Dalton

Richards, David Adams 1950- ...... **CLC 59**
See also CA 93-96; DLB 53

Richards, I(vor) A(rmstrong)
1893-1979 .... **CLC 14, 24**
See also CA 41-44R; 89-92; CANR 34;
DLB 27

Richardson, Anne
See Roiphe, Anne Richardson

Richardson, Dorothy Miller
1873-1957 .... **TCLC 3**
See also CA 104; DLB 36

Richardson, Ethel Florence (Lindesay)
1870-1946
See Richardson, Henry Handel
See also CA 105

Richardson, Henry Handel. .... **TCLC 4**
See also Richardson, Ethel Florence
(Lindesay)

Richardson, Samuel 1689-1761 .... **LC 1**
See also CDBLB 1660-1789; DLB 39; WLC

Richler, Mordecai
1931- .... **CLC 3, 5, 9, 13, 18, 46, 70**
See also AITN 1; CA 65-68; CANR 31;
CLR 17; DLB 53; MAICYA; MTCW;
SATA 27, 44

Richter, Conrad (Michael)
1890-1968 .... **CLC 30**
See also CA 5-8R; 25-28R; CANR 23;
DLB 9; MTCW; SATA 3

Riddell, J. H. 1832-1906 .... **TCLC 40**

Riding, Laura. .... **CLC 3, 7**
See also Jackson, Laura (Riding)

Riefenstahl, Berta Helene Amalia 1902-
See Riefenstahl, Leni
See also CA 108

Riefenstahl, Leni. .... **CLC 16**
See also Riefenstahl, Berta Helene Amalia

Riffe, Ernest
See Bergman, (Ernst) Ingmar

Riley, Tex
See Creasey, John

Rilke, Rainer Maria
1875-1926 .... **TCLC 1, 6, 19; PC 2**
See also CA 104; 132; DLB 81; MTCW

Rimbaud, (Jean Nicolas) Arthur
1854-1891 .... **NCLC 4, 35; PC 3**
See also WLC

Ringmaster, The
See Mencken, H(enry) L(ouis)

Ringwood, Gwen(dolyn Margaret) Pharis
1910-1984 .... **CLC 48**
See also CA 112; DLB 88

Rio, Michel 19(?)- .... **CLC 43**

Ritsos, Giannes
See Ritsos, Yannis

Ritsos, Yannis 1909-1990 ..... **CLC 6, 13, 31**
See also CA 77-80; 133; CANR 39; MTCW

Ritter, Erika 1948(?)- .... **CLC 52**

Rivera, Jose Eustasio 1889-1928... **TCLC 35**
See also HW

Rivers, Conrad Kent 1933-1968...... **CLC 1**
See also BW; CA 85-88; DLB 41

Rivers, Elfrida
See Bradley, Marion Zimmer

Riverside, John
See Heinlein, Robert A(nson)

Rizal, Jose 1861-1896 .... **NCLC 27**

Roa Bastos, Augusto (Antonio)
1917- .... **CLC 45**
See also CA 131; DLB 113; HW

Robbe-Grillet, Alain
1922- ...... **CLC 1, 2, 4, 6, 8, 10, 14, 43**
See also CA 9-12R; CANR 33; DLB 83;
MTCW

Robbins, Harold 1916- .... **CLC 5**
See also CA 73-76; CANR 26; MTCW

Robbins, Thomas Eugene 1936-
See Robbins, Tom
See also CA 81-84; CANR 29; MTCW

Robbins, Tom. .... **CLC 9, 32, 64**
See also Robbins, Thomas Eugene
See also BEST 90:3; DLBY 80

Robbins, Trina 1938- .... **CLC 21**
See also CA 128

Roberts, Charles G(eorge) D(ouglas)
1860-1943 .... **TCLC 8**
See also CA 105; DLB 92; SATA 29

Roberts, Kate 1891-1985 .... **CLC 15**
See also CA 107; 116

Roberts, Keith (John Kingston)
1935- .... **CLC 14**
See also CA 25-28R

Roberts, Kenneth (Lewis)
1885-1957 .... **TCLC 23**
See also CA 109; DLB 9

Roberts, Michele (B.) 1949- .... **CLC 48**
See also CA 115

Robertson, Ellis
See Ellison, Harlan; Silverberg, Robert

Robertson, Thomas William
1829-1871 .... **NCLC 35**

Robinson, Edwin Arlington
1869-1935 .... **TCLC 5; PC 1**
See also CA 104; 133; CDALB 1865-1917;
DLB 54; MTCW

Robinson, Henry Crabb
1775-1867 .... **NCLC 15**
See also DLB 107

Robinson, Jill 1936- .... **CLC 10**
See also CA 102

Robinson, Kim Stanley 1952- ...... **CLC 34**
See also CA 126

Robinson, Lloyd
See Silverberg, Robert

Robinson, Marilynne 1944- .... **CLC 25**
See also CA 116

Robinson, Smokey. .... **CLC 21**
See also Robinson, William Jr.

Robinson, William Jr. 1940-
See Robinson, Smokey
See also CA 116

Robison, Mary 1949- .... **CLC 42**
See also CA 113; 116

Roddenberry, Eugene Wesley 1921-1991
See Roddenberry, Gene
See also CA 110; 135; CANR 37; SATA 45

Roddenberry, Gene .... **CLC 17**
See also Roddenberry, Eugene Wesley
See also AAYA 5; SATO 69

Rodgers, Mary 1931- .... **CLC 12**
See also CA 49-52; CANR 8; CLR 20;
MAICYA; SATA 8

Rodgers, W(illiam) R(obert)
1909-1969 .... **CLC 7**
See also CA 85-88; DLB 20

Rodman, Eric
See Silverberg, Robert

Rodman, Howard 1920(?)-1985 ..... **CLC 65**
See also CA 118

Rodman, Maia
See Wojciechowska, Maia (Teresa)

Rodriguez, Claudio 1934- .... **CLC 10**

Roelvaag, O(le) E(dvart)
1876-1931 .... **TCLC 17**
See also CA 117; DLB 9

Roethke, Theodore (Huebner)
1908-1963 ...... **CLC 1, 3, 8, 11, 19, 46**
See also CA 81-84; CABS 2;
CDALB 1941-1968; DLB 5; MTCW

Rogers, Thomas Hunton 1927- ..... **CLC 57**
See also CA 89-92

Rogers, Will(iam Penn Adair)
1879-1935 .... **TCLC 8**
See also CA 105; DLB 11

Rogin, Gilbert 1929- .... **CLC 18**
See also CA 65-68; CANR 15

Rohan, Koda .... **TCLC 22**
See also Koda Shigeyuki

Rohmer, Eric. .... **CLC 16**
See also Scherer, Jean-Marie Maurice

Rohmer, Sax .... **TCLC 28**
See also Ward, Arthur Henry Sarsfield
See also DLB 70

Roiphe, Anne Richardson 1935- ... **CLC 3, 9**
See also CA 89-92; DLBY 80

Rolfe, Frederick (William Serafino Austin
Lewis Mary) 1860-1913 ..... **TCLC 12**
See also CA 107; DLB 34

Rolland, Romain 1866-1944 ...... **TCLC 23**
See also CA 118; DLB 65

Rolvaag, O(le) E(dvart)
See Roelvaag, O(le) E(dvart)

Romain Arnaud, Saint
See Aragon, Louis

Romains, Jules 1885-1972 .... **CLC 7**
See also CA 85-88; CANR 34; DLB 65;
MTCW

Romero, Jose Ruben 1890-1952 ... **TCLC 14**
See also CA 114; 131; HW

Ronsard, Pierre de 1524-1585 .... **LC 6**

Rooke, Leon 1934- .... **CLC 25, 34**
See also CA 25-28R; CANR 23

Roper, William 1498-1578 .... **LC 10**

Roquelaure, A. N.
See Rice, Anne

Rosa, Joao Guimaraes 1908-1967 ... **CLC 23**
See also CA 89-92; DLB 113

Rosen, Richard (Dean) 1949- .... **CLC 39**
See also CA 77-80

Rosenberg, Isaac 1890-1918 ...... **TCLC 12**
See also CA 107; DLB 20

Rosenblatt, Joe .... **CLC 15**
See also Rosenblatt, Joseph

Rosenblatt, Joseph 1933-
See Rosenblatt, Joe
See also CA 89-92

Rosenfeld, Samuel 1896-1963
See Tzara, Tristan
See also CA 89-92

Rosenthal, M(acha) L(ouis) 1917-... **CLC 28**
See also CA 1-4R; CAAS 6; CANR 4;
DLB 5; SATA 59

Ross, Barnaby
See Dannay, Frederic

Ross, Bernard L.
See Follett, Ken(neth Martin)

Ross, J. H.
See Lawrence, T(homas) E(dward)

Ross, (James) Sinclair 1908- .... **CLC 13**
See also CA 73-76; DLB 88

Rossetti, Christina (Georgina)
1830-1894 .... **NCLC 2**
See also DLB 35; MAICYA; SATA 20;
WLC

Rossetti, Dante Gabriel
1828-1882 .... **NCLC 4**
See also CDBLB 1832-1890; DLB 35; WLC

Rossner, Judith (Perelman)
1935- .... **CLC 6, 9, 29**
See also AITN 2; BEST 90:3; CA 17-20R;
CANR 18; DLB 6; MTCW

Rostand, Edmond (Eugene Alexis)
1868-1918 .... **TCLC 6, 37**
See also CA 104; 126; MTCW

Roth, Henry 1906- .... **CLC 2, 6, 11**
See also CA 11-12; CANR 38; CAP 1;
DLB 28; MTCW

Roth, Joseph 1894-1939 .... **TCLC 33**
See also DLB 85

Roth, Philip (Milton)
1933- ...... **CLC 1, 2, 3, 4, 6, 9, 15, 22,**
31, 47, 66
See also BEST 90:3; CA 1-4R; CANR 1, 22,
36; CDALB 1968-1988; DLB 2, 28;
DLBY 82; MTCW; WLC

Rothenberg, Jerome 1931- .... **CLC 6, 57**
See also CA 45-48; CANR 1; DLB 5

Roumain, Jacques (Jean Baptiste)
1907-1944 .... **TCLC 19**
See also BLC 3; BW; CA 117; 125

Rourke, Constance (Mayfield)
1885-1941 .... **TCLC 12**
See also CA 107; YABC 1

Rousseau, Jean-Baptiste 1671-1741 ... **LC 9**

Rousseau, Jean-Jacques 1712-1778... **LC 14**
See also WLC

Roussel, Raymond 1877-1933 ..... **TCLC 20**
See also CA 117

Rovit, Earl (Herbert) 1927- .... **CLC 7**
See also CA 5-8R; CANR 12

Rowe, Nicholas 1674-1718 .... **LC 8**
See also DLB 84

Rowley, Ames Dorrance
See Lovecraft, H(oward) P(hillips)

Rowson, Susanna Haswell
1762(?)-1824 .... **NCLC 5**
See also DLB 37

Roy, Gabrielle 1909-1983....... **CLC 10, 14**
See also CA 53-56; 110; CANR 5; DLB 68;
MTCW

Rozewicz, Tadeusz 1921-........ **CLC 9, 23**
See also CA 108; CANR 36; MTCW

Ruark, Gibbons 1941- .... **CLC 3**
See also CA 33-36R; CANR 14, 31;
DLB 120

Rubens, Bernice (Ruth) 1923-... **CLC 19, 31**
See also CA 25-28R; CANR 33; DLB 14;
MTCW

Rudkin, (James) David 1936- ...... **CLC 14**
See also CA 89-92; DLB 13

Rudnik, Raphael 1933-............. **CLC 7**
See also CA 29-32R

Ruffian, M.
See Hasek, Jaroslav (Matej Frantisek)

Ruiz, Jose Martinez .... **CLC 11**
See also Martinez Ruiz, Jose

Rukeyser, Muriel
1913-1980 .... **CLC 6, 10, 15, 27**
See also CA 5-8R; 93-96; CANR 26;
DLB 48; MTCW; SATA 22

Rule, Jane (Vance) 1931-........ **CLC 27**
See also CA 25-28R; CANR 12; DLB 60

Rulfo, Juan 1918-1986............. **CLC 8**
See also CA 85-88; 118; CANR 26;
DLB 113; HW; MTCW

Runyon, (Alfred) Damon
1884(?)-1946................ **TCLC 10**
See also CA 107; DLB 11, 86

Rush, Norman 1933-.............. **CLC 44**
See also CA 121; 126

Rushdie, (Ahmed) Salman
1947- .... **CLC 23, 31, 55**
See also BEST 89:3; CA 108; 111;
CANR 33; MTCW

Rushforth, Peter (Scott) 1945- ..... **CLC 19**
See also CA 101

Ruskin, John 1819-1900.......... **TCLC 20**
See also CA 114; 129; CDBLB 1832-1890;
DLB 55; SATA 24

Russ, Joanna 1937-.............. **CLC 15**
See also CA 25-28R; CANR 11, 31; DLB 8;
MTCW

Russell, George William 1867-1935
See A. E.
See also CA 104; CDBLB 1890-1914

Russell, (Henry) Ken(neth Alfred)
1927- .... **CLC 16**
See also CA 105

Russell, Willy 1947-.............. **CLC 60**

Rutherford, Mark .... **TCLC 25**
See also White, William Hale
See also DLB 18

Ruyslinck, Ward
See Belser, Reimond Karel Maria de

Ryan, Cornelius (John) 1920-1974 ... **CLC 7**
See also CA 69-72; 53-56; CANR 38

Ryan, Michael 1946- .... **CLC 65**
See also CA 49-52; DLBY 82

Rybakov, Anatoli (Naumovich)
1911- .... **CLC 23, 53**
See also CA 126; 135

Ryder, Jonathan
See Ludlum, Robert

Ryga, George 1932-1987 .... **CLC 14**
See also CA 101; 124; DLB 60

S. S.
See Sassoon, Siegfried (Lorraine)

Saba, Umberto 1883-1957 .... **TCLC 33**
See also DLB 114

Sabatini, Rafael 1875-1950 .... **TCLC 47**

Sabato, Ernesto (R.) 1911-...... **CLC 10, 23**
See also CA 97-100; CANR 32; HW;
MTCW

Sacastru, Martin
See Bioy Casares, Adolfo

Sacher-Masoch, Leopold von
1836(?)-1895 .... **NCLC 31**

Sachs, Marilyn (Stickle) 1927- ..... **CLC 35**
See also AAYA 2; CA 17-20R; CANR 13;
CLR 2; MAICYA; SAAS 2; SATA 3, 68

Sachs, Nelly 1891-1970 .... **CLC 14**
See also CA 17-18; 25-28R; CAP 2

Sackler, Howard (Oliver)
1929-1982 .... **CLC 14**
See also CA 61-64; 108; CANR 30; DLB 7

Sacks, Oliver (Wolf) 1933- .... **CLC 67**
See also CA 53-56; CANR 28; MTCW

Sade, Donatien Alphonse Francois Comte
1740-1814 .... **NCLC 3**

Sadoff, Ira 1945-.................. **CLC 9**
See also CA 53-56; CANR 5, 21; DLB 120

Saetone
See Camus, Albert

Safire, William 1929-............. **CLC 10**
See also CA 17-20R; CANR 31

Sagan, Carl (Edward) 1934-........ **CLC 30**
See also AAYA 2; CA 25-28R; CANR 11,
36; MTCW; SATA 58

Sagan, Francoise .... **CLC 3, 6, 9, 17, 36**
See also Quoirez, Francoise
See also DLB 83

Sahgal, Nayantara (Pandit) 1927-... **CLC 41**
See also CA 9-12R; CANR 11

Saint, H(arry) F. 1941- .... **CLC 50**
See also CA 127

St. Aubin de Teran, Lisa 1953-
See Teran, Lisa St. Aubin de
See also CA 118; 126

Sainte-Beuve, Charles Augustin
1804-1869 .... **NCLC 5**

**Saint-Exupery, Antoine (Jean Baptiste Marie
Roger) de** 1900-1944 .... **TCLC 2**
See also CA 108; 132; CLR 10; DLB 72;
MAICYA; MTCW; SATA 20; WLC

St. John, David
See Hunt, E(verette) Howard Jr.

Saint-John Perse
See Leger, (Marie-Rene) Alexis Saint-Leger

Saintsbury, George (Edward Bateman)
1845-1933 .... **TCLC 31**
See also DLB 57

Sait Faik .... **TCLC 23**
See also Abasiyanik, Sait Faik

Saki .... **TCLC 3**
See also Munro, H(ector) H(ugh)

Salama, Hannu 1936-............. **CLC 18**

Salamanca, J(ack) R(ichard)
1922- .... **CLC 4, 15**
See also CA 25-28R

Sale, J. Kirkpatrick
See Sale, Kirkpatrick

Sale, Kirkpatrick 1937-........... **CLC 68**
See also CA 13-16R; CANR 10

Salinas (y Serrano), Pedro
1891(?)-1951 .... **TCLC 17**
See also CA 117

Salinger, J(erome) D(avid)
1919- .... **CLC 1, 3, 8, 12, 55, 56; SSC 2**
See also AAYA 2; CA 5-8R; CANR 39;
CDALB 1941-1968; CLR 18; DLB 2, 102;
MAICYA; MTCW; SATA 67; WLC

Salisbury, John
See Caute, David

Salter, James 1925- .... **CLC 7, 52, 59**
See also CA 73-76

Saltus, Edgar (Everton)
1855-1921 .... **TCLC 8**
See also CA 105

Saltykov, Mikhail Evgrafovich
1826-1889 .... **NCLC 16**

Samarakis, Antonis 1919- .... **CLC 5**
See also CA 25-28R; CAAS 16; CANR 36

Sanchez, Florencio 1875-1910..... **TCLC 37**
See also HW

Sanchez, Luis Rafael 1936-........ **CLC 23**
See also CA 128; HW

Sanchez, Sonia 1934-.............. **CLC 5**
See also BLC 3; BW; CA 33-36R;
CANR 24; CLR 18; DLB 41; DLBD 8;
MAICYA; MTCW; SATA 22

Sand, George 1804-1876.......... **NCLC 2**
See also DLB 119; WLC

Sandburg, Carl (August)
1878-1967 ... **CLC 1, 4, 10, 15, 35; PC 2**
See also CA 5-8R; 25-28R; CANR 35;
CDALB 1865-1917; DLB 17, 54;
MAICYA; MTCW; SATA 8; WLC

Sandburg, Charles
See Sandburg, Carl (August)

Sandburg, Charles A.
See Sandburg, Carl (August)

Sanders, (James) Ed(ward) 1939- ... **CLC 53**
See also CA 13-16R; CANR 13; DLB 16

Sanders, Lawrence 1920-.......... **CLC 41**
See also BEST 89:4; CA 81-84; CANR 33;
MTCW

Sanders, Noah
See Blount, Roy (Alton) Jr.

Sanders, Winston P.
See Anderson, Poul (William)

Sandoz, Mari(e Susette)
1896-1966 .... **CLC 28**
See also CA 1-4R; 25-28R; CANR 17;
DLB 9; MTCW; SATA 5

Saner, Reg(inald Anthony) 1931- .... **CLC 9**
See also CA 65-68

Sannazaro, Jacopo 1456(?)-1530...... **LC 8**

Spengler, Oswald (Arnold Gottfried)
1880-1936 .... **TCLC 25**
See also CA 118

Spenser, Edmund 1552(?)-1599 .... **LC 5**
See also CDBLB Before 1660; WLC

Spicer, Jack 1925-1965 ...... **CLC 8, 18, 72**
See also CA 85-88; DLB 5, 16

Spielberg, Peter 1929- .... **CLC 6**
See also CA 5-8R; CANR 4; DLBY 81

Spielberg, Steven 1947- .... **CLC 20**
See also AAYA 8; CA 77-80; CANR 32;
SATA 32

Spillane, Frank Morrison 1918-
See Spillane, Mickey
See also CA 25-28R; CANR 28; MTCW;
SATA 66

Spillane, Mickey .... **CLC 3, 13**
See also Spillane, Frank Morrison

Spinoza, Benedictus de 1632-1677 .... **LC 9**

Spinrad, Norman (Richard) 1940-... **CLC 46**
See also CA 37-40R; CANR 20; DLB 8

Spitteler, Carl (Friedrich Georg)
1845-1924 .... **TCLC 12**
See also CA 109

Spivack, Kathleen (Romola Drucker)
1938- .... **CLC 6**
See also CA 49-52

Spoto, Donald 1941- .... **CLC 39**
See also CA 65-68; CANR 11

Springsteen, Bruce (F.) 1949- ...... **CLC 17**
See also CA 111

Spurling, Hilary 1940- .... **CLC 34**
See also CA 104; CANR 25

Squires, Radcliffe 1917- .... **CLC 51**
See also CA 1-4R; CANR 6, 21

Srivastava, Dhanpat Rai 1880(?)-1936
See Premchand
See also CA 118

Stacy, Donald
See Pohl, Frederik

Stael, Germaine de
See Stael-Holstein, Anne Louise Germaine
Necker Baronn
See also DLB 119

Stael-Holstein, Anne Louise Germaine Necker
Baronn 1766-1817 .... **NCLC 3**
See also Stael, Germaine de

Stafford, Jean 1915-1979... **CLC 4, 7, 19, 68**
See also CA 1-4R; 85-88; CANR 3; DLB 2;
MTCW; SATA 22

Stafford, William (Edgar)
1914- .... **CLC 4, 7, 29**
See also CA 5-8R; CAAS 3; CANR 5, 22;
DLB 5

Staines, Trevor
See Brunner, John (Kilian Houston)

Stairs, Gordon
See Austin, Mary (Hunter)

Stannard, Martin .... **CLC 44**

Stanton, Maura 1946- .... **CLC 9**
See also CA 89-92; CANR 15; DLB 120

Stanton, Schuyler
See Baum, L(yman) Frank

Stapledon, (William) Olaf
1886-1950 .... **TCLC 22**
See also CA 111; DLB 15

Starbuck, George (Edwin) 1931-.... **CLC 53**
See also CA 21-24R; CANR 23

Stark, Richard
See Westlake, Donald E(dwin)

Staunton, Schuyler
See Baum, L(yman) Frank

Stead, Christina (Ellen)
1902-1983 .... **CLC 2, 5, 8, 32**
See also CA 13-16R; 109; CANR 33;
MTCW

Steele, Richard 1672-1729 .... **LC 18**
See also CDBLB 1660-1789; DLB 84, 101

Steele, Timothy (Reid) 1948-....... **CLC 45**
See also CA 93-96; CANR 16; DLB 120

Steffens, (Joseph) Lincoln
1866-1936 .... **TCLC 20**
See also CA 117

Stegner, Wallace (Earle) 1909-... **CLC 9, 49**
See also AITN 1; BEST 90:3; CA 1-4R;
CAAS 9; CANR 1, 21; DLB 9; MTCW

Stein, Gertrude 1874-1946... **TCLC 1, 6, 28**
See also CA 104; 132; CDALB 1917-1929;
DLB 4, 54, 86; MTCW; WLC

Steinbeck, John (Ernst)
1902-1968 ..... **CLC 1, 5, 9, 13, 21, 34,
45; SSC 11**
See also CA 1-4R; 25-28R; CANR 1, 35;
CDALB 1929-1941; DLB 7, 9; DLBD 2;
MTCW; SATA 9; WLC

Steinem, Gloria 1934- .... **CLC 63**
See also CA 53-56; CANR 28; MTCW

Steiner, George 1929- .... **CLC 24**
See also CA 73-76; CANR 31; DLB 67;
MTCW; SATA 62

Steiner, Rudolf 1861-1925 .... **TCLC 13**
See also CA 107

Stendhal 1783-1842............. **NCLC 23**
See also DLB 119; WLC

Stephen, Leslie 1832-1904 .... **TCLC 23**
See also CA 123; DLB 57

Stephen, Sir Leslie
See Stephen, Leslie

Stephen, Virginia
See Woolf, (Adeline) Virginia

Stephens, James 1882(?)-1950...... **TCLC 4**
See also CA 104; DLB 19

Stephens, Reed
See Donaldson, Stephen R.

Steptoe, Lydia
See Barnes, Djuna

Sterchi, Beat 1949-.............. **CLC 65**

Sterling, Brett
See Bradbury, Ray (Douglas); Hamilton,
Edmond

Sterling, Bruce 1954-............. **CLC 72**
See also CA 119

Sterling, George 1869-1926 .... **TCLC 20**
See also CA 117; DLB 54

Stern, Gerald 1925- .... **CLC 40**
See also CA 81-84; CANR 28; DLB 105

Stern, Richard (Gustave) 1928-... **CLC 4, 39**
See also CA 1-4R; CANR 1, 25; DLBY 87

Sternberg, Josef von 1894-1969..... **CLC 20**
See also CA 81-84

Sterne, Laurence 1713-1768.......... **LC 2**
See also CDBLB 1660-1789; DLB 39; WLC

Sternheim, (William Adolf) Carl
1878-1942 .... **TCLC 8**
See also CA 105; DLB 56, 118

Stevens, Mark 1951- .... **CLC 34**
See also CA 122

Stevens, Wallace
1879-1955 .... **TCLC 3, 12, 45**
See also CA 104; 124; CDALB 1929-1941;
DLB 54; MTCW; WLC

Stevenson, Anne (Katharine)
1933- .... **CLC 7, 33**
See also CA 17-20R; CAAS 9; CANR 9, 33;
DLB 40; MTCW

Stevenson, Robert Louis (Balfour)
1850-1894 .... **NCLC 5, 14; SSC 11**
See also CDBLB 1890-1914; CLR 10, 11;
DLB 18, 57; MAICYA; WLC; YABC 2

Stewart, J(ohn) I(nnes) M(ackintosh)
1906- .... **CLC 7, 14, 32**
See also CA 85-88; CAAS 3; MTCW

Stewart, Mary (Florence Elinor)
1916- .... **CLC 7, 35**
See also CA 1-4R; CANR 1; SATA 12

Stewart, Mary Rainbow
See Stewart, Mary (Florence Elinor)

Still, James 1906-................ **CLC 49**
See also CA 65-68; CANR 10, 26; DLB 9;
SATA 29

Sting
See Sumner, Gordon Matthew

Stirling, Arthur
See Sinclair, Upton (Beall)

Stitt, Milan 1941-................ **CLC 29**
See also CA 69-72

Stockton, Francis Richard 1834-1902
See Stockton, Frank R.
See also CA 108; 137; MAICYA; SATA 44

Stockton, Frank R. .... **TCLC 47**
See also Stockton, Francis Richard
See also DLB 42, 74; SATA 32

Stoddard, Charles
See Kuttner, Henry

Stoker, Abraham 1847-1912
See Stoker, Bram
See also CA 105; SATA 29

Stoker, Bram .... **TCLC 8**
See also Stoker, Abraham
See also CDBLB 1890-1914; DLB 36, 70;
WLC

Stolz, Mary (Slattery) 1920-....... **CLC 12**
See also AAYA 8; AITN 1; CA 5-8R;
CANR 13; MAICYA; SAAS 3;
SATA 10, 70, 71

Stone, Irving 1903-1989............ **CLC 7**
See also AITN 1; CA 1-4R; 129; CAAS 3;
CANR 1, 23; MTCW; SATA 3; SATO 64

Stone, Robert (Anthony)
1937- .... **CLC 5, 23, 42**
See also CA 85-88; CANR 23; MTCW

Thurber, James (Grover)
1894-1961 . . . . . . **CLC 5, 11, 25; SSC 1**
See also CA 73-76; CANR 17, 39;
CDALB 1929-1941; DLB 4, 11, 22, 102;
MAICYA; MTCW; SATA 13

Thurman, Wallace (Henry)
1902-1934 . . . . **TCLC 6**
See also BLC 3; BW; CA 104; 124; DLB 51

Ticheburn, Cheviot
See Ainsworth, William Harrison

Tieck, (Johann) Ludwig
1773-1853 . . . . **NCLC 5**
See also DLB 90

Tiger, Derry
See Ellison, Harlan

Tilghman, Christopher   1948(?)- . . . . . **CLC 65**

Tillinghast, Richard (Williford)
1940- . . . . **CLC 29**
See also CA 29-32R; CANR 26

Timrod, Henry   1828-1867 . . . . **NCLC 25**
See also DLB 3

Tindall, Gillian   1938- . . . . **CLC 7**
See also CA 21-24R; CANR 11

Tiptree, James Jr. . . . . **CLC 48, 50**
See also Sheldon, Alice Hastings Bradley
See also DLB 8

Titmarsh, Michael Angelo
See Thackeray, William Makepeace

Tocqueville, Alexis (Charles Henri Maurice
Clerel Comte)   1805-1859 . . . . . **NCLC 7**

Tolkien, J(ohn) R(onald) R(euel)
1892-1973 . . . . **CLC 1, 2, 3, 8, 12, 38**
See also AITN 1; CA 17-18; 45-48;
CANR 36; CAP 2; CDBLB 1914-1945;
DLB 15; MAICYA; MTCW; SATA 2,
24, 32; WLC

Toller, Ernst   1893-1939 . . . . **TCLC 10**
See also CA 107

Tolson, M. B.
See Tolson, Melvin B(eaunorus)

Tolson, Melvin B(eaunorus)
1898(?)-1966 . . . . **CLC 36**
See also BLC 3; BW; CA 124; 89-92;
DLB 48, 76

Tolstoi, Aleksei Nikolaevich
See Tolstoy, Alexey Nikolaevich

Tolstoy, Alexey Nikolaevich
1882-1945 . . . . **TCLC 18**
See also CA 107

Tolstoy, Count Leo
See Tolstoy, Leo (Nikolaevich)

Tolstoy, Leo (Nikolaevich)
1828-1910 . . . . . **TCLC 4, 11, 17, 28, 44;
SSC 9**
See also CA 104; 123; SATA 26; WLC

Tomasi di Lampedusa, Giuseppe   1896-1957
See Lampedusa, Giuseppe (Tomasi) di
See also CA 111

Tomlin, Lily . . . . **CLC 17**
See also Tomlin, Mary Jean

Tomlin, Mary Jean   1939(?)-
See Tomlin, Lily
See also CA 117

Tomlinson, (Alfred) Charles
1927- . . . . **CLC 2, 4, 6, 13, 45**
See also CA 5-8R; CANR 33; DLB 40

Tonson, Jacob
See Bennett, (Enoch) Arnold

Toole, John Kennedy
1937-1969 . . . . **CLC 19, 64**
See also CA 104; DLBY 81

Toomer, Jean
1894-1967 . . . . . **CLC 1, 4, 13, 22; SSC 1**
See also BLC 3; BW; CA 85-88;
CDALB 1917-1929; DLB 45, 51; MTCW

Torley, Luke
See Blish, James (Benjamin)

Tornimparte, Alessandra
See Ginzburg, Natalia

Torre, Raoul della
See Mencken, H(enry) L(ouis)

Torrey, E(dwin) Fuller   1937- . . . . **CLC 34**
See also CA 119

Torsvan, Ben Traven
See Traven, B.

Torsvan, Benno Traven
See Traven, B.

Torsvan, Berick Traven
See Traven, B.

Torsvan, Berwick Traven
See Traven, B.

Torsvan, Bruno Traven
See Traven, B.

Torsvan, Traven
See Traven, B.

Tournier, Michel (Edouard)
1924- . . . . **CLC 6, 23, 36**
See also CA 49-52; CANR 3, 36; DLB 83;
MTCW; SATA 23

Tournimparte, Alessandra
See Ginzburg, Natalia

Towers, Ivar
See Kornbluth, C(yril) M.

Townsend, Sue   1946- . . . . **CLC 61**
See also CA 119; 127; MTCW; SATA 48,
55

Townshend, Peter (Dennis Blandford)
1945- . . . . **CLC 17, 42**
See also CA 107

Tozzi, Federigo   1883-1920 . . . . **TCLC 31**

Traill, Catharine Parr
1802-1899 . . . . **NCLC 31**
See also DLB 99

Trakl, Georg   1887-1914 . . . . **TCLC 5**
See also CA 104

Transtroemer, Tomas (Goesta)
1931- . . . . **CLC 52, 65**
See also CA 117; 129

Transtromer, Tomas Gosta
See Transtroemer, Tomas (Goesta)

Traven, B.   (?)-1969 . . . . **CLC 8, 11**
See also CA 19-20; 25-28R; CAP 2; DLB 9,
56; MTCW

Treitel, Jonathan   1959- . . . . **CLC 70**

Tremain, Rose   1943- . . . . **CLC 42**
See also CA 97-100; DLB 14

Tremblay, Michel   1942- . . . . **CLC 29**
See also CA 116; 128; DLB 60; MTCW

Trevanian (a pseudonym)   1930(?)- . . . **CLC 29**
See also CA 108

Trevor, Glen
See Hilton, James

Trevor, William
1928- . . . . **CLC 7, 9, 14, 25, 71**
See also Cox, William Trevor
See also DLB 14

Trifonov, Yuri (Valentinovich)
1925-1981 . . . . **CLC 45**
See also CA 126; 103; MTCW

Trilling, Lionel   1905-1975 . . . . **CLC 9, 11, 24**
See also CA 9-12R; 61-64; CANR 10;
DLB 28, 63; MTCW

Trimball, W. H.
See Mencken, H(enry) L(ouis)

Tristan
See Gomez de la Serna, Ramon

Tristram
See Housman, A(lfred) E(dward)

Trogdon, William (Lewis)   1939-
See Heat-Moon, William Least
See also CA 115; 119

Trollope, Anthony   1815-1882 . . **NCLC 6, 33**
See also CDBLB 1832-1890; DLB 21, 57;
SATA 22; WLC

Trollope, Frances   1779-1863 . . . . . **NCLC 30**
See also DLB 21

Trotsky, Leon   1879-1940 . . . . **TCLC 22**
See also CA 118

Trotter (Cockburn), Catharine
1679-1749 . . . . **LC 8**
See also DLB 84

Trout, Kilgore
See Farmer, Philip Jose

Trow, George W. S.   1943- . . . . **CLC 52**
See also CA 126

Troyat, Henri   1911- . . . . **CLC 23**
See also CA 45-48; CANR 2, 33; MTCW

Trudeau, G(arretson) B(eekman)   1948-
See Trudeau, Garry B.
See also CA 81-84; CANR 31; SATA 35

Trudeau, Garry B. . . . . **CLC 12**
See also Trudeau, G(arretson) B(eekman)
See also AITN 2

Truffaut, Francois   1932-1984 . . . . . . **CLC 20**
See also CA 81-84; 113; CANR 34

Trumbo, Dalton   1905-1976 . . . . **CLC 19**
See also CA 21-24R; 69-72; CANR 10;
DLB 26

Trumbull, John   1750-1831 . . . . **NCLC 30**
See also DLB 31

Trundlett, Helen B.
See Eliot, T(homas) S(tearns)

Tryon, Thomas   1926-1991 . . . . **CLC 3, 11**
See also AITN 1; CA 29-32R; 135;
CANR 32; MTCW

Tryon, Tom
See Tryon, Thomas

Ts'ao Hsueh-ch'in   1715(?)-1763 . . . . . . **LC 1**

Tsushima, Shuji 1909-1948
See Dazai, Osamu
See also CA 107

Tsvetaeva (Efron), Marina (Ivanovna)
1892-1941 .... TCLC 7, 35
See also CA 104; 128; MTCW

Tuck, Lily 1938- .... CLC 70

Tunis, John R(oberts) 1889-1975 ... CLC 12
See also CA 61-64; DLB 22; MAICYA;
SATA 30, 37

Tuohy, Frank .... CLC 37
See also Tuohy, John Francis
See also DLB 14

Tuohy, John Francis 1925-
See Tuohy, Frank
See also CA 5-8R; CANR 3

Turco, Lewis (Putnam) 1934- ... CLC 11, 63
See also CA 13-16R; CANR 24; DLBY 84

Turgenev, Ivan
1818-1883 .... NCLC 21; SSC 7
See also WLC

Turner, Frederick 1943- .... CLC 48
See also CA 73-76; CAAS 10; CANR 12,
30; DLB 40

Tusan, Stan 1936- .... CLC 22
See also CA 105

Tutuola, Amos 1920- .... CLC 5, 14, 29
See also BLC 3; BW; CA 9-12R; CANR 27;
MTCW

Twain, Mark ..... TCLC 6, 12, 19, 36; SSC 6
See also Clemens, Samuel Langhorne
See also DLB 11, 12, 23, 64, 74; WLC

Tyler, Anne
1941- .... CLC 7, 11, 18, 28, 44, 59
See also BEST 89:1; CA 9-12R; CANR 11,
33; DLB 6; DLBY 82; MTCW; SATA 7

Tyler, Royall 1757-1826 .... NCLC 3
See also DLB 37

Tynan, Katharine 1861-1931 ...... TCLC 3
See also CA 104

Tytell, John 1939- .... CLC 50
See also CA 29-32R

Tyutchev, Fyodor 1803-1873 ..... NCLC 34

Tzara, Tristan .... CLC 47
See also Rosenfeld, Samuel

Uhry, Alfred 1936- .... CLC 55
See also CA 127; 133

Ulf, Haerved
See Strindberg, (Johan) August

Ulf, Harved
See Strindberg, (Johan) August

Unamuno (y Jugo), Miguel de
1864-1936 .... TCLC 2, 9; SSC 11
See also CA 104; 131; DLB 108; HW;
MTCW

Undercliffe, Errol
See Campbell, (John) Ramsey

Underwood, Miles
See Glassco, John

Undset, Sigrid 1882-1949 .... TCLC 3
See also CA 104; 129; MTCW; WLC

Ungaretti, Giuseppe
1888-1970 .... CLC 7, 11, 15
See also CA 19-20; 25-28R; CAP 2;
DLB 114

Unger, Douglas 1952- .... CLC 34
See also CA 130

Updike, John (Hoyer)
1932- ...... CLC 1, 2, 3, 5, 7, 9, 13, 15,
23, 34, 43, 70
See also CA 1-4R; CABS 1; CANR 4, 33;
CDALB 1968-1988; DLB 2, 5; DLBD 3;
DLBY 80, 82; MTCW; WLC

Upshaw, Margaret Mitchell
See Mitchell, Margaret (Munnerlyn)

Upton, Mark
See Sanders, Lawrence

Urdang, Constance (Henriette)
1922- .... CLC 47
See also CA 21-24R; CANR 9, 24

Uris, Leon (Marcus) 1924- ...... CLC 7, 32
See also AITN 1, 2; BEST 89:2; CA 1-4R;
CANR 1; MTCW; SATA 49

Urmuz
See Codrescu, Andrei

Ustinov, Peter (Alexander) 1921- .... CLC 1
See also AITN 1; CA 13-16R; CANR 25;
DLB 13

V
See Chekhov, Anton (Pavlovich)

Vaculik, Ludvik 1926- .... CLC 7
See also CA 53-56

Valenzuela, Luisa 1938- .... CLC 31
See also CA 101; CANR 32; DLB 113; HW

Valera y Alcala-Galiano, Juan
1824-1905 .... TCLC 10
See also CA 106

Valery, (Ambroise) Paul (Toussaint Jules)
1871-1945 .... TCLC 4, 15
See also CA 104; 122; MTCW

Valle-Inclan, Ramon (Maria) del
1866-1936 .... TCLC 5
See also CA 106

Vallejo, Antonio Buero
See Buero Vallejo, Antonio

Vallejo, Cesar (Abraham)
1892-1938 .... TCLC 3
See also CA 105; HW

Valle Y Pena, Ramon del
See Valle-Inclan, Ramon (Maria) del

Van Ash, Cay 1918- .... CLC 34

Vanbrugh, Sir John 1664-1726 ...... LC 21
See also DLB 80

Van Campen, Karl
See Campbell, John W(ood Jr.)

Vance, Gerald
See Silverberg, Robert

Vance, Jack .... CLC 35
See also Vance, John Holbrook
See also DLB 8

Vance, John Holbrook 1916-
See Queen, Ellery; Vance, Jack
See also CA 29-32R; CANR 17; MTCW

**Van Den Bogarde, Derek Jules Gaspard Ulric
Niven** 1921-
See Bogarde, Dirk
See also CA 77-80

Vandenburgh, Jane .... CLC 59

Vanderhaeghe, Guy 1951- .... CLC 41
See also CA 113

van der Post, Laurens (Jan) 1906- ... CLC 5
See also CA 5-8R; CANR 35

van de Wetering, Janwillem 1931- .. CLC 47
See also CA 49-52; CANR 4

Van Dine, S. S. .... TCLC 23
See also Wright, Willard Huntington

Van Doren, Carl (Clinton)
1885-1950 .... TCLC 18
See also CA 111

Van Doren, Mark 1894-1972 ..... CLC 6, 10
See also CA 1-4R; 37-40R; CANR 3;
DLB 45; MTCW

Van Druten, John (William)
1901-1957 .... TCLC 2
See also CA 104; DLB 10

Van Duyn, Mona (Jane)
1921- .... CLC 3, 7, 63
See also CA 9-12R; CANR 7, 38; DLB 5

Van Dyne, Edith
See Baum, L(yman) Frank

van Itallie, Jean-Claude 1936- .... CLC 3
See also CA 45-48; CAAS 2; CANR 1;
DLB 7

van Ostaijen, Paul 1896-1928 ..... TCLC 33

Van Peebles, Melvin 1932- ...... CLC 2, 20
See also BW; CA 85-88; CANR 27

Vansittart, Peter 1920- .... CLC 42
See also CA 1-4R; CANR 3

Van Vechten, Carl 1880-1964 ...... CLC 33
See also CA 89-92; DLB 4, 9, 51

Van Vogt, A(lfred) E(lton) 1912- ..... CLC 1
See also CA 21-24R; CANR 28; DLB 8;
SATA 14

Vara, Madeleine
See Jackson, Laura (Riding)

Varda, Agnes 1928- .... CLC 16
See also CA 116; 122

Vargas Llosa, (Jorge) Mario (Pedro)
1936- .... CLC 3, 6, 9, 10, 15, 31, 42
See also CA 73-76; CANR 18, 32; HW;
MTCW

Vasiliu, Gheorghe 1881-1957
See Bacovia, George
See also CA 123

Vassa, Gustavus
See Equiano, Olaudah

Vassilikos, Vassilis 1933- .... CLC 4, 8
See also CA 81-84

Vaughn, Stephanie .... CLC 62

Vazov, Ivan (Minchov)
1850-1921 .... TCLC 25
See also CA 121

Veblen, Thorstein (Bunde)
1857-1929 .... TCLC 31
See also CA 115

Venison, Alfred
See Pound, Ezra (Weston Loomis)

Wallace, Irving 1916-1990....... **CLC 7, 13**
See also AITN 1; CA 1-4R; 132; CAAS 1;
CANR 1, 27; MTCW

Wallant, Edward Lewis
1926-1962 .... **CLC 5, 10**
See also CA 1-4R; CANR 22; DLB 2, 28;
MTCW

Walpole, Horace 1717-1797......... **LC 2**
See also DLB 39, 104

Walpole, Hugh (Seymour)
1884-1941 .... **TCLC 5**
See also CA 104; DLB 34

Walser, Martin 1927-............. **CLC 27**
See also CA 57-60; CANR 8; DLB 75

Walser, Robert 1878-1956........ **TCLC 18**
See also CA 118; DLB 66

Walsh, Jill Paton................. **CLC 35**
See also Paton Walsh, Gillian
See also CLR 2; SAAS 3

Walter, Villiam Christian
See Andersen, Hans Christian

Wambaugh, Joseph (Aloysius Jr.)
1937- .... **CLC 3, 18**
See also AITN 1; BEST 89:3; CA 33-36R;
DLB 6; DLBY 83; MTCW

Ward, Arthur Henry Sarsfield 1883-1959
See Rohmer, Sax
See also CA 108

Ward, Douglas Turner 1930-....... **CLC 19**
See also BW; CA 81-84; CANR 27; DLB 7,
38

Warhol, Andy 1928(?)-1987........ **CLC 20**
See also BEST 89:4; CA 89-92; 121;
CANR 34

Warner, Francis (Robert le Plastrier)
1937- .... **CLC 14**
See also CA 53-56; CANR 11

Warner, Marina 1946-............. **CLC 59**
See also CA 65-68; CANR 21

Warner, Rex (Ernest) 1905-1986.... **CLC 45**
See also CA 89-92; 119; DLB 15

Warner, Susan (Bogert)
1819-1885 .... **NCLC 31**
See also DLB 3, 42

Warner, Sylvia (Constance) Ashton
See Ashton-Warner, Sylvia (Constance)

Warner, Sylvia Townsend
1893-1978 .... **CLC 7, 19**
See also CA 61-64; 77-80; CANR 16;
DLB 34; MTCW

Warren, Mercy Otis 1728-1814... **NCLC 13**
See also DLB 31

Warren, Robert Penn
1905-1989 ... **CLC 1, 4, 6, 8, 10, 13, 18,**
              39, 53, 59; SSC 4
See also AITN 1; CA 13-16R; 129;
CANR 10; CDALB 1968-1988; DLB 2,
48; DLBY 80, 89; MTCW; SATA 46, 63;
WLC

Warshofsky, Isaac
See Singer, Isaac Bashevis

Warton, Thomas 1728-1790........ **LC 15**
See also DLB 104, 109

Waruk, Kona
See Harris, (Theodore) Wilson

Warung, Price 1855-1911........ **TCLC 45**

Warwick, Jarvis
See Garner, Hugh

Washington, Alex
See Harris, Mark

Washington, Booker T(aliaferro)
1856-1915 .... **TCLC 10**
See also BLC 3; BW; CA 114; 125;
SATA 28

Wassermann, (Karl) Jakob
1873-1934 .... **TCLC 6**
See also CA 104; DLB 66

Wasserstein, Wendy 1950-...... **CLC 32, 59**
See also CA 121; 129; CABS 3

Waterhouse, Keith (Spencer)
1929- .... **CLC 47**
See also CA 5-8R; CANR 38; DLB 13, 15;
MTCW

Waters, Roger 1944-............. **CLC 35**
See also Pink Floyd

Watkins, Frances Ellen
See Harper, Frances Ellen Watkins

Watkins, Gerrold
See Malzberg, Barry N(athaniel)

Watkins, Paul 1964-............. **CLC 55**
See also CA 132

Watkins, Vernon Phillips
1906-1967 .... **CLC 43**
See also CA 9-10; 25-28R; CAP 1; DLB 20

Watson, Irving S.
See Mencken, H(enry) L(ouis)

Watson, John H.
See Farmer, Philip Jose

Watson, Richard F.
See Silverberg, Robert

Waugh, Auberon (Alexander) 1939-.. **CLC 7**
See also CA 45-48; CANR 6, 22; DLB 14

Waugh, Evelyn (Arthur St. John)
1903-1966 ... **CLC 1, 3, 8, 13, 19, 27, 44**
See also CA 85-88; 25-28R; CANR 22;
CDBLB 1914-1945; DLB 15; MTCW;
WLC

Waugh, Harriet 1944- .... **CLC 6**
See also CA 85-88; CANR 22

Ways, C. R.
See Blount, Roy (Alton) Jr.

Waystaff, Simon
See Swift, Jonathan

Webb, (Martha) Beatrice (Potter)
1858-1943 .... **TCLC 22**
See also Potter, Beatrice
See also CA 117

Webb, Charles (Richard) 1939-...... **CLC 7**
See also CA 25-28R

Webb, James H(enry) Jr. 1946- .... **CLC 22**
See also CA 81-84

Webb, Mary (Gladys Meredith)
1881-1927 .... **TCLC 24**
See also CA 123; DLB 34

Webb, Mrs. Sidney
See Webb, (Martha) Beatrice (Potter)

Webb, Phyllis 1927-............. **CLC 18**
See also CA 104; CANR 23; DLB 53

Webb, Sidney (James)
1859-1947 .... **TCLC 22**
See also CA 117

Webber, Andrew Lloyd............. **CLC 21**
See also Lloyd Webber, Andrew

Weber, Lenora Mattingly
1895-1971 .... **CLC 12**
See also CA 19-20; 29-32R; CAP 1;
SATA 2, 26

Webster, John 1579(?)-1634(?) .... **DC 2**
See also CDBLB Before 1660; DLB 58;
WLC

Webster, Noah 1758-1843 .... **NCLC 30**

Wedekind, (Benjamin) Frank(lin)
1864-1918 .... **TCLC 7**
See also CA 104; DLB 118

Weidman, Jerome 1913-............ **CLC 7**
See also AITN 2; CA 1-4R; CANR 1;
DLB 28

Weil, Simone (Adolphine)
1909-1943 .... **TCLC 23**
See also CA 117

Weinstein, Nathan
See West, Nathanael

Weinstein, Nathan von Wallenstein
See West, Nathanael

Weir, Peter (Lindsay) 1944- .... **CLC 20**
See also CA 113; 123

Weiss, Peter (Ulrich)
1916-1982 .... **CLC 3, 15, 51**
See also CA 45-48; 106; CANR 3; DLB 69

Weiss, Theodore (Russell)
1916- .... **CLC 3, 8, 14**
See also CA 9-12R; CAAS 2; DLB 5

Welch, (Maurice) Denton
1915-1948 .... **TCLC 22**
See also CA 121

Welch, James 1940-......... **CLC 6, 14, 52**
See also CA 85-88

Weldon, Fay
1933(?)- .... **CLC 6, 9, 11, 19, 36, 59**
See also CA 21-24R; CANR 16;
CDBLB 1960 to Present; DLB 14;
MTCW

Wellek, Rene 1903- .... **CLC 28**
See also CA 5-8R; CAAS 7; CANR 8;
DLB 63

Weller, Michael 1942-......... **CLC 10, 53**
See also CA 85-88

Weller, Paul 1958-............... **CLC 26**

Wellershoff, Dieter 1925-.......... **CLC 46**
See also CA 89-92; CANR 16, 37

Welles, (George) Orson
1915-1985 .... **CLC 20**
See also CA 93-96; 117

Wellman, Mac 1945- .... **CLC 65**

Wellman, Manly Wade 1903-1986 .. **CLC 49**
See also CA 1-4R; 118; CANR 6, 16;
SATA 6, 47

Wells, Carolyn 1869(?)-1942 ...... **TCLC 35**
See also CA 113; DLB 11

Wilhelm, Kate .... CLC 7
See also Wilhelm, Katie Gertrude
See also CAAS 5; DLB 8

Wilhelm, Katie Gertrude 1928-
See Wilhelm, Kate
See also CA 37-40R; CANR 17, 36; MTCW

Wilkins, Mary
See Freeman, Mary Eleanor Wilkins

Willard, Nancy 1936-........... CLC 7, 37
See also CA 89-92; CANR 10, 39; CLR 5;
DLB 5, 52; MAICYA; MTCW;
SATA 30, 37, 71

Williams, C(harles) K(enneth)
1936-.................... CLC 33, 56
See also CA 37-40R; DLB 5

Williams, Charles
See Collier, James L(incoln)

Williams, Charles (Walter Stansby)
1886-1945 .... TCLC 1, 11
See also CA 104; DLB 100

Williams, (George) Emlyn
1905-1987 .... CLC 15
See also CA 104; 123; CANR 36; DLB 10,
77; MTCW

Williams, Hugo 1942-............. CLC 42
See also CA 17-20R; DLB 40

Williams, J. Walker
See Wodehouse, P(elham) G(renville)

Williams, John A(lfred) 1925-.... CLC 5, 13
See also BLC 3; BW; CA 53-56; CAAS 3;
CANR 6, 26; DLB 2, 33

Williams, Jonathan (Chamberlain)
1929-...................... CLC 13
See also CA 9-12R; CAAS 12; CANR 8;
DLB 5

Williams, Joy 1944-.............. CLC 31
See also CA 41-44R; CANR 22

Williams, Norman 1952- .... CLC 39
See also CA 118

Williams, Tennessee
1911-1983 .... CLC 1, 2, 5, 7, 8, 11, 15,
19, 30, 39, 45, 71
See also AITN 1, 2; CA 5-8R; 108;
CABS 3; CANR 31; CDALB 1941-1968;
DLB 7; DLBD 4; DLBY 83; MTCW;
WLC

Williams, Thomas (Alonzo)
1926-1990 .... CLC 14
See also CA 1-4R; 132; CANR 2

Williams, William C.
See Williams, William Carlos

Williams, William Carlos
1883-1963 ... CLC 1, 2, 5, 9, 13, 22, 42,
67
See also CA 89-92; CANR 34;
CDALB 1917-1929; DLB 4, 16, 54, 86;
MTCW

Williamson, David Keith 1942-..... CLC 56
See also CA 103

Williamson, Jack................. CLC 29
See also Williamson, John Stewart
See also CAAS 8; DLB 8

Williamson, John Stewart 1908-
See Williamson, Jack
See also CA 17-20R; CANR 23

Willie, Frederick
See Lovecraft, H(oward) P(hillips)

Willingham, Calder (Baynard Jr.)
1922-..................... CLC 5, 51
See also CA 5-8R; CANR 3; DLB 2, 44;
MTCW

Willis, Charles
See Clarke, Arthur C(harles)

Willy
See Colette, (Sidonie-Gabrielle)

Willy, Colette
See Colette, (Sidonie-Gabrielle)

Wilson, A(ndrew) N(orman) 1950- .. CLC 33
See also CA 112; 122; DLB 14

Wilson, Angus (Frank Johnstone)
1913-1991 .... CLC 2, 3, 5, 25, 34
See also CA 5-8R; 134; CANR 21; DLB 15;
MTCW

Wilson, August
1945- .... CLC 39, 50, 63; DC 2
See also BLC 3; BW; CA 115; 122; MTCW

Wilson, Brian 1942-.............. CLC 12

Wilson, Colin 1931-............. CLC 3, 14
See also CA 1-4R; CAAS 5; CANR 1, 22,
33; DLB 14; MTCW

Wilson, Dirk
See Pohl, Frederik

Wilson, Edmund
1895-1972 .... CLC 1, 2, 3, 8, 24
See also CA 1-4R; 37-40R; CANR 1;
DLB 63; MTCW

Wilson, Ethel Davis (Bryant)
1888(?)-1980 .... CLC 13
See also CA 102; DLB 68; MTCW

Wilson, John (Anthony) Burgess
1917-.................. CLC 8, 10, 13
See also Burgess, Anthony
See also CA 1-4R; CANR 2; MTCW

Wilson, John 1785-1854.......... NCLC 5

Wilson, Lanford 1937-....... CLC 7, 14, 36
See also CA 17-20R; CABS 3; DLB 7

Wilson, Robert M. 1944-......... CLC 7, 9
See also CA 49-52; CANR 2; MTCW

Wilson, Robert McLiam 1964- ..... CLC 59
See also CA 132

Wilson, Sloan 1920-.............. CLC 32
See also CA 1-4R; CANR 1

Wilson, Snoo 1948-.............. CLC 33
See also CA 69-72

Wilson, William S(mith) 1932- ..... CLC 49
See also CA 81-84

Winchilsea, Anne (Kingsmill) Finch Counte
1661-1720 .... LC 3

Windham, Basil
See Wodehouse, P(elham) G(renville)

Wingrove, David (John) 1954-...... CLC 68
See also CA 133

Winters, Janet Lewis .... CLC 41
See also Lewis, Janet
See also DLBY 87

Winters, (Arthur) Yvor
1900-1968 .... CLC 4, 8, 32
See also CA 11-12; 25-28R; CAP 1;
DLB 48; MTCW

Winterson, Jeanette 1959-........ CLC 64
See also CA 136

Wiseman, Frederick 1930-......... CLC 20

Wister, Owen 1860-1938 .... TCLC 21
See also CA 108; DLB 9, 78; SATA 62

Witkacy
See Witkiewicz, Stanislaw Ignacy

Witkiewicz, Stanislaw Ignacy
1885-1939 .... TCLC 8
See also CA 105

Wittig, Monique 1935(?)-.......... CLC 22
See also CA 116; 135; DLB 83

Wittlin, Jozef 1896-1976 .... CLC 25
See also CA 49-52; 65-68; CANR 3

Wodehouse, P(elham) G(renville)
1881-1975 ... CLC 1, 2, 5, 10, 22; SSC 2
See also AITN 2; CA 45-48; 57-60;
CANR 3, 33; CDBLB 1914-1945;
DLB 34; MTCW; SATA 22

Woiwode, L.
See Woiwode, Larry (Alfred)

Woiwode, Larry (Alfred) 1941-... CLC 6, 10
See also CA 73-76; CANR 16; DLB 6

Wojciechowska, Maia (Teresa)
1927-...................... CLC 26
See also AAYA 8; CA 9-12R; CANR 4;
CLR 1; MAICYA; SAAS 1; SATA 1, 28

Wolf, Christa 1929- .... CLC 14, 29, 58
See also CA 85-88; DLB 75; MTCW

Wolfe, Gene (Rodman) 1931-....... CLC 25
See also CA 57-60; CAAS 9; CANR 6, 32;
DLB 8

Wolfe, George C. 1954-........... CLC 49

Wolfe, Thomas (Clayton)
1900-1938 .... TCLC 4, 13, 29
See also CA 104; 132; CDALB 1929-1941;
DLB 9, 102; DLBD 2; DLBY 85;
MTCW; WLC

Wolfe, Thomas Kennerly Jr. 1930-
See Wolfe, Tom
See also CA 13-16R; CANR 9, 33; MTCW

Wolfe, Tom .... CLC 1, 2, 9, 15, 35, 51
See also Wolfe, Thomas Kennerly Jr.
See also AAYA 8; AITN 2; BEST 89:1

Wolff, Geoffrey (Ansell) 1937- ..... CLC 41
See also CA 29-32R; CANR 29

Wolff, Sonia
See Levitin, Sonia (Wolff)

Wolff, Tobias (Jonathan Ansell)
1945- .... CLC 39, 64
See also BEST 90:2; CA 114; 117

Wolfram von Eschenbach
c. 1170-c. 1220 .... CMLC 5

Wolitzer, Hilma 1930-............ CLC 17
See also CA 65-68; CANR 18; SATA 31

Wollstonecraft, Mary 1759-1797...... LC 5
See also CDBLB 1789-1832; DLB 39, 104

Wonder, Stevie .... CLC 12
See also Morris, Steveland Judkins

Wong, Jade Snow 1922-........... CLC 17
See also CA 109

Woodcott, Keith
See Brunner, John (Kilian Houston)

Zweig, Stefan   1881-1942 . . . . **TCLC 17**
  See also CA 112; DLB 81, 118

CLC Cumulative Nationality Index

Nationality Index

ISBN 0-8103-4978-7